Second Edition

POLITICAL THEORY

Classic and Contemporary Readings

VOLUME II
Machiavelli to Rawls

Joseph Losco
Ball State University

Leonard Williams
Manchester College

D1432171

OXFORD
UNIVERSITY PRESS

Oxford University Press, Inc., publishes works that further Oxford University's
objective of excellence in research, scholarship, and education.

Oxford   New York
Auckland   Cape Town   Dar es Salaam   Hong Kong   Karachi
Kuala Lumpur   Madrid   Melbourne   Mexico City   Nairobi
New Delhi   Shanghai   Taipei   Toronto

With offices in
Argentina   Austria   Brazil   Chile   Czech Republic   France   Greece
Guatemala   Hungary   Italy   Japan   Poland   Portugal   Singapore
South Korea   Switzerland   Thailand   Turkey   Ukraine   Vietnam

Copyright © 2006 by Oxford University Press, Inc.

Published by Oxford University Press, Inc.
198 Madison Avenue, New York, New York 10016
http://www.oup.com

Oxford is a registered trademark of Oxford University Press

ISBN 978-0-19-533023-6

Dedication

For Marcia and Michael for their continued love and support, and for my Uncle Sam, who first introduced me to the wisdom of the ages. (J.L.)

For my sons, Christopher and Jason, whom I cherish deeply, and for Robert Pettit, a dear friend through joys and trials alike. (L.W.)

Acknowledgments

At Roxbury: Thanks to Claude Teweles for his confidence in our approach to these volumes, Sacha Howells for meticulous care of the manuscript, and Stephanie Villavicencio for help in securing reprint permissions.

At Ball State University: Thanks to Stephanie Painter for her long, hard hours in manuscript preparation and to Jim Huffman and Patrick Breen for help in tracking down research materials.

At Manchester College: Thanks to Alicia Brant for research and secretarial assistance, to the College for a research grant that aided the completion of this project, and to numerous colleagues for their support and friendship. ✦

Contents

Part I: Enter Modernity

Chapter 1: Excerpts from *The Prince* 16
Niccolò Machiavelli

Chapter 2: Excerpts from the *Discourses* 23
Niccolò Machiavelli

Chapter 3: Introduction to *The Prince 31
Harvey C. Mansfield, Jr.

Mansfield summarizes the argument of *The Prince* to show that Machiavelli deserves his bad reputation because he separated the conduct of politics from justice and morality.

**Chapter 4: Public Versus Private Claims:
Machiavellianism from Another Perspective** 40
John Leonard

Leonard's examination of the concepts of *virtù* and *bontà* demonstrates that Machiavelli's chief concern was to preserve the public sphere from the corrupting influence of private interests.

Chapter 5: Excerpts from *Leviathan* 52
Thomas Hobbes

***Chapter 6: Intending (Political) Obligation:
Hobbes and the Voluntary Basis of Society** 67
Gordon J. Schochet

Schochet explores the voluntary basis of consent that is a cornerstone of Hobbes's theory of obligation.

---

*New to the Second Edition

---

*New to the Second Edition

Part II: The 19th Century and Beyond

---

*New to the Second Edition

---

*New to the Second Edition

---

*New to the Second Edition

*New to the Second Edition

---

*New to the Second Edition

Introduction

Consider the following questions: What do we mean by *freedom, human rights, equality,* and *justice*? Is there a *best* form of government? Why, and under what conditions, should citizens obey the state? How can a society's institutions and political life be changed for the better? [1] It does not take long to recognize that these questions raise some of our most enduring issues. Nor should it surprise anyone that courses in political theory address just such questions and concerns. Indeed, political theory courses have always met students' need for guidance as they face the extraordinary changes the world has witnessed in recent years. As a result, interest in political theory has increased greatly among college and university students in political science, philosophy, and many other disciplines.

This volume and its companion are intended to introduce undergraduate students to the history of Western political thought and the enterprise of political theory. For most students, this will be their only class in political theory; for all, it will likely be a new experience. Political science majors, for instance, will have studied the structures and processes of American politics, those of other nations, and the complexities of the international political arena. Their education will have focused on the debates surrounding a host of policy issues or on the empirical regularities of political behavior. Philosophy majors, on the other hand, will have had access to the history of Western thought about aesthetics, epistemology, logic, and metaphysics. For most undergraduate students, regardless of their disciplinary background, the study of political theory will no doubt be little more than a sideshow in a busy educational carnival. Nevertheless, it is our hope that by presenting the works of some of the West's most prominent political thinkers, as well as commentaries engaging in the debates these thinkers continue to generate, another generation of students will come to see political theory as a rich storehouse of ideas for addressing our enduring social and political concerns.

The Nature of Political Theory

What is political theory? What is it that political philosophers do? [2] Significant answers to these questions have been given by two prominent scholars, Leo Strauss and Sheldon Wolin. [3] Strauss, the originator of a widely influential approach to studying theory, believed that the task of political philosophy is to gain wisdom about the nature of human beings and politics. "Doing" political theory thus involves learning to read the classics so that one may effectively distinguish between mere opinion and authentic knowledge. Wolin, on the other hand, argued that the study of political theory is best understood as a reflective discourse on the meaning of the political. As a dialogue among philosophers, political theory seeks to highlight the relation between continuity and change in political life.

Two more recent conceptions of political theory simultaneously echo and refine the ideas advanced by Strauss and Wolin. Robert Fowler and Jeffrey Orenstein, for instance, suggest that political theory involves reflection on basic political concepts, the analysis of alternative views about human beings and politics, and the pursuit of normative truth about the nature of the best regime. [4] Dante Germino points to the ongoing nature of the theoretical enterprise when he characterizes political philosophy as a "conversation of many voices"—that is, a dialogue "between different orientations toward political reality as a whole." [5] Viewed in this way, political philosophy is both a criti-

1

cal and creative activity in which each generation participates in a continuous tradition that unites present and past.

Regardless of what one believes theory to be, it is all too clear that there are many different approaches to studying the history of political thought.[6] For instance, one may choose to study the theorist as a person with unique concerns and motivations (a biographical approach); or, one could study the theories themselves—locating them in their cultural contexts, accounting for their conceptual development and change, and tracing complex patterns of their influence and impact (an historical approach). Still other approaches have focused on great problems or eternal questions presumed to face all political thinkers without regard to time, place, or circumstance (a perennial-issues approach).

In the face of these diverse approaches, we believe that the undergraduate student's best option is to adopt a problem-solving orientation to the study of political theory. We therefore tend to define political theory as the systematic effort to understand the meaning and significance of political life. Motivated by a given political or philosophical problem, one turns to the history of political theory (or even contemporary political thought and political science), and then shows its relevance to that problem. That done, the task becomes one of reflecting on the ideas offered by theorists in order to solve the problem, or at least, to clarify it in some important way. In sum, the student of political theory regards "interpretations as alternative solutions to some puzzle or problem, and then goes on to assess their adequacy *vis-à-vis* each other and in relation to one's own proposed solution."[7] Studying political theory, then, is not simply about reading a body of authoritative texts (though it includes such authority); it is also about reflecting on the meaning of political life itself.

In a similar vein, John Nelson presented a useful list of goals for the practice of political theory.[8] He argued that political theory's aims can be summarized in terms of three Cs: *comprehend*, *conserve*, and *criticize*. *Comprehend* here refers to the twin objectives of explanation and understanding. Theories provide a conceptual vocabulary for describing and accounting for the most important features of political life and their interrelations, as well as for accounting for the forms and behaviors typically found in political practice. Simply put, political theory explores political phenomena by placing them in the context of human experience. The second aim, to *conserve*, connotes that the historical study of political thought helps preserve a cultural heritage. Lastly, to identify *criticize* as an aim for students of political theory underscores the fact that theory analyzes and evaluates both theoretical arguments and political phenomena.

To Nelson's list, we would add a fourth C: *create*. Theory shapes the way we view politics and gives insight into the problems and opportunities presented by political life. It can either restrict our vision or broaden our horizons. At all times, theorists must be aware that they are not engaging in pure philosophy, not living in a rarefied atmosphere of complete abstraction. As Benjamin Barber has observed,

> politics remains something human beings *do*, not something they possess or use or watch or talk or think about. Those who would do something about it must do more than philosophize, and philosophy that is politically intelligible must take full political measure of politics as conduct.[9]

Thus, theorists must be attuned to the political world, the world of praxis and action.[10] They should pay heed to the specific practices, behaviors, or orders recommended or implied by the political theories under investigation.

In the end, consensus on the essential definition of concepts such as politics, or of practices such as political theory, will likely elude our grasp. This does not mean, however, that conceptual definitions or political judgments are wholly subjective matters of whim or taste. Far from it. There are certain criteria good theories ought to meet, standards by which we can evaluate the political theories you will encounter in this book. We have in mind such criteria as logical consistency, breadth or comprehensiveness, clarity of thought and argument, and degree of insight, as well as acceptable implications for political practice. No matter which criterion you choose, though, take the time to argue with the theorists in this book, with your classmates and your instructor, or even with yourself.

About This Book

Like most books, the second edition of *Political Theory: Classic and Contemporary Readings* was inspired by a perceived need. Until recently, political theory instructors had a number of unsatisfactory options in selecting readings for their students. They could, for example, exclusively use primary works by the classic political theorists. Doing so usually meant, however, that students had to purchase as many as a dozen books in order to cover the major theorists in the traditional canon. Nor has the option of using a volume containing abridged selections from those works offered a solution to the problem. All too many students simply lack the background or context for making sense of the selections or for seeing their relevance to political life today.

Another option for the teacher of political theory has been to use a textbook of summary and commentary by a contemporary scholar. Such works certainly treat a large number of theorists in a short span of time, and they may provide students with insights into the classic writings. Yet, many instructors believe that students who read commentaries without encountering the texts themselves have not really learned political theory. Students should develop firsthand evaluations of the works of political philosophers, no matter how useful a scholar's commentary may be in placing those works in social and historical contexts.

We believe that *Political Theory: Classic and Contemporary Readings* brings together the best features of each of the above approaches, while minimizing their liabilities. For loyal users of the first edition, we believe you will be pleased with the enhancements in the present set of volumes. We have increased the number of entries of both canonical figures and nontraditional authors. We have updated a substantial number of commentaries to reflect more recent scholarship. There are new section introductions that provide an overview of the historic and intellectual currents giving rise to each generation of thinkers. Finally, we have improved the pedagogical section by adding web sites, class discussion and activity items, and annotated bibliographies. We believe all of these features make the second edition more comprehensive and easier to use.

For newcomers, let us review the basic features that distinguish this anthology from others. For one thing, this collection provides significant excerpts from classic writings for students to confront directly. The thinkers presented extend from Thucydides to Rawls, allowing instructors to pick and choose from a significant range of political theorists. Further, we have chosen commentaries that present multiple viewpoints from which to evaluate the tradition of Western political thought. These commentaries, representing a high degree of both scholarship and accessibility, raise important issues concerning the relevance of the classics to today's political problems.

By combining primary texts with scholarly commentaries, then, we allow students to study both the content and the practice of political theory. They should therefore be able to understand not only what classic theorists have had to say about politics, but they can also learn how contemporary theorists have approached the study of classic works.

Finally, because some classes in political theory are divided along traditional timelines of "ancient" and "modern," we have chosen to present this work in two volumes. We believe this will best accommodate the needs of students without sacrificing coverage. Students taking a class in only one time period can avoid the expense of a longer volume, while those involved in a two-semester sequence will find that most major political theorists have been covered by both volumes.

Where to split the volumes was initially a problem. Traditionalists and Straussians usually anoint Machiavelli or Hobbes as the initiator of the "modern era." On the other hand, theorists who are more historically inclined often speak of the modern period as properly beginning in the 18th century with the American and French Revolutions. While contemporary theorists are themselves divided over the proper interpretation of modernity, other works on the history of political thought have provided a solution to this problem. Many popular books divide the history of political thought around the work of Machiavelli, with some of them placing his work at the end of a volume on ancient political theory and others placing it at the beginning of a "modern" volume. Because his work is transitional in many respects, we have chosen to cover Machiavelli in both volumes. Purists may object, but again, we believe this provides flexibility for both professors and students.

Each unit in *Political Theory: Classic and Contemporary Readings* contains an introduction to a philosopher (his or her life and major theoretical contributions), selected readings from his or her work, and commentaries illuminating critical aspects of his or her thought. Though our selections are consistent with the type and extent of difficulty encountered in most undergraduate theory courses, some of the readings will undoubtedly require students to stretch themselves intellectually. We have sought to help students by summarizing the key arguments in our introductory essays and presenting brief annotated bibliographies. Further assistance for both the student and the instructor can be found in the discussion questions and World Wide Web addresses that we have included in each unit.

One important issue remaining to be addressed concerns how we selected the readings presented here. In selecting both philosophers and representative texts, our goal has been to provide a fairly comprehensive introduction to political theory, not a compendium of the world's political thought. We chose selections that represent the broad scope of the classics of Western political thought from Thucydides to the present day. These works are the subject of most of the teaching and commentary done by political theorists and philosophers today. They are works which have made singular contributions to our collective understanding of poli-

tics, works to which we often return when seeking answers to questions about political life.

As such, this book of readings follows a well-established pattern for textbooks in the history of Western political thought. Though we reject the idea that each theorist plays a specific role in a grand drama, we do believe that each has made a distinctive and indispensable contribution to understanding politics. Certainly, we could not include the writings of everyone who has had anything of interest to say about politics. Many works of classic or near-classic status simply had to be left aside. For instance, we have not felt competent enough to include material expressing the unique insights of Asian, African, or Middle Eastern political thought. Our own philosophical tastes and relative levels of ignorance may result in some taking us to task.

However, a more difficult problem with selection emerges from the limitations of political theory as a scholarly community and an intellectual enterprise.[11] Like much other historical writing, and like a good bit of political practice, political theory has derived its language and outlook from a largely masculine experience. The writers that traditionally have been accorded classic status have all been male; they have all emerged from the conventionally masculine preserve of politics; and they have all employed non-inclusive language to talk about political life. Thus, many works of political theory either said nothing about women, or if they did, what they had to say was dismissive, derogatory, and sexist. We do not share such sentiments, and have been pleased that the writings taught in political theory courses have been expanded to include works by women. We have reflected that enlarged canon in this volume and its companion.

We selected the commentaries for each of the chosen philosophers by basing our decisions on the following considerations: (1) We wanted commentaries that reflected important ideas or controversies associated with the philosopher under study, especially where the concepts advanced are rather murky. (2) We sought commentaries that represented significant recent scholarship in political theory. In this way, students may get a sense of the current state of the field. However, when we felt that earlier commentaries were superior in illuminating key ideas or controversies, currency took a back seat. (3) Finally, we included commentaries that would be within the grasp of the average student approaching political theory for the first time.

Thus, the readings we have selected for this volume are a mix of classic writings and contemporary views. We believe this mix will acquaint students with the writings of a representative set of political theorists; provide them with contemporary analyses and interpretations of those works; and raise the major issues or questions associated with a particular theorist's contributions to understanding political life. We hope to stimulate students' interest so that they will read in and about the theorists we do present, as well as the many thinkers we have been forced (through limits imposed by convention, space, and time) to omit from this collection.

A Note to the Student on Reading *Political Theory*

As you begin your study of political theory, keep in mind that this book is not a road atlas providing detailed directions to every theoretical city of consequence. Instead, it is a guidebook offering some useful perspectives on places of potential interest to you. Of course, no guidebook can ever substitute for the experience of going to those places yourself. You must use the book merely as an aid in finding your own destinations in the world of political thought.

Still, as you read this book, you will find that some of the material will appear rather complex or dense; it may even seem to be phrased in an alien tongue. To help you cope with the welter of words that you will find in political philosophy readings, let us present a few hints on how to read actively and critically.[12] In general, critical reading involves both identifying and evaluating the argument an author makes in a text. An argument consists of a thesis or conclusion and the evidence or reasons given that warrant or sup-

port the thesis. Any argument will thus show a chain of reasoning:[13]

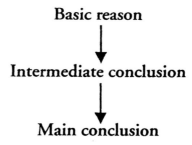

Basic reason

↓

Intermediate conclusion

↓

Main conclusion

Thus, the first step in reading complex texts is to locate the author's central argument or to read for his or her main point. Once you identify that primary conclusion, you should then think backward, as it were, to identify the evidence or reasons necessary to support that conclusion.

Specifically, for each text, ask yourself the following sets of questions:

1. What is the author's focus? What issue is being addressed? What problem is to be resolved?

2. What body of literature or belief does the author rely upon? What theoretical tradition has shaped the author's outlook or approach?

3. What is the author's primary conclusion? What evidence or reasons are given to support that conclusion?

4. Does the author's argument make sense? Is it logical and well-reasoned? Does it solve the problem the author initially raised?

5. What evidence or considerations has the author overlooked or neglected? What value assumptions has the author made that may or may not bear scrutiny?

6. What are the practical, theoretical, and ethical implications of the author's argument? Are those implications desirable? Why or why not?

In addition to these procedural guidelines, it might be helpful as you read to focus upon the answers to a set of key substantive questions. According to Dante Germino, political philosophers must grapple with at least three major concerns:[14] 1) What is the nature of human beings such that they engage in politics to coordinate their social dealings with others? While some political theorists are explicit regarding human nature, others (even those who discard the concept) often adopt implicit assumptions about human nature that inform their perspective. 2) What is the best regime for structuring human political relations? Here political theorists propose a wide range of options, as you will see; however, these options must conform to assumptions about human nature in order to be consistent and constructive. Some proposals are meant to broaden our perspective about the realm of human possibilities, but not all ideas about the "best" regime are meant to be realistic. Some ideas are meant only as goals more to be wished for than realized; others are intended to show inherent limits to what is humanly possible. 3) What role do historic forces play in the evolution and shaping of political solutions? Some have proposed that great individuals make history by force of their ideas, virtue, or skills; others assert that long-term social and economic developments play the major role in shaping not only political solutions but the ideas that inform them.

To this list of questions, we might add one more: How do the authors conceptualize the relationship between the individual good and the common good? Some theories assert that the innate sociality of the human animal mitigates potential conflicts along this dimension. By serving the common good, I am serving my own as well. An example might be contributing to a social insurance policy in which my contributions will combine with those of others to produce benefits for all those who need them, including myself. Other theorists focus on the difficulties involved in accommodating the individual and common good. During warfare, some individuals might be called upon to die so that others can live. Over the course of the history of political thought, there have been periods in which the place of one or the other type of good has assumed prominence. This question is no less important in the current era in which libertarian and communitarian ideals come into conflict.

This is the "stuff" of political theory. These are among the central ideas good political theorists explore. As you read each philosopher, try to discover the answers he or she provides to these questions. This will provide a basis for understanding the scope and breadth of ideas that have informed the Western tradition of political thought.

Notes

1. For similar queries, see Glenn Tinder, *Political Thinking: The Perennial Questions*, 6th ed. (New York: Longman, 1996); and Larry Arnhart, *Political Questions: Political Philosophy from Plato to Rawls*, 2nd ed. (Prospect Heights, IL: Waveland Press 1993).

2. Though the term *theory* frequently has been applied to both normative and empirical studies, some political scientists reserve the term *philosophy* for studies of the former sort (e.g., what is the best regime?) and apply *theory* to the latter sort (e.g., what models best explain voter turnout?). Nonetheless, empirical theorists must make normative assumptions in generating explanatory models, and normative philosophers clearly must take empirical data into account in formulating defensible views. Therefore, for our purposes, we treat the terms *political theory* and *political philosophy* as more or less interchangeable.

3. Leo Strauss, *What is Political Philosophy?* (Glencoe, IL: Free Press, 1959), 10–12; and Sheldon Wolin, *Politics and Vision* (Boston: Little Brown, 1960), 2–5.

4. Robert B. Fowler and Jeffrey R. Orenstein, *Contemporary Issues in Political Theory*, rev. ed. (New York: Praeger, 1985), 2.

5. Dante Germino, "The Contemporary Relevance of the Classics of Political Philosophy." In Fred Greenstein and Nelson Polsby, eds., *Handbook of Political Science*, vol. 1 (Reading, MA: Addison-Wesley, 1975), 229–281.

6. Daniel Sabia, "Political Education and the History of Political Thought," *American Political Science Review* 78 (December 1984): 985–999.

7. Terence Ball, *Reappraising Political Theory* (Oxford: Oxford University Press, 1995), 29.

8. John Nelson, "Natures and Futures for Political Theory," in Nelson, ed., *What Should Polit-*

ical Theory Be Now? (Albany: State University of New York Press, 1983), 3–24.

9. Benjamin Barber, *The Conquest of Politics: Liberal Philosophy in Democratic Times* (Princeton, NJ: Princeton University Press, 1988), 11, emphasis in the original.

10. Of course, political theorists have not always lived up to this charge. For a recent critique of the alienation of political theory from political practice, see Jeffrey C. Isaac, "The Strange Silence of Political Theory," *Political Theory* 23 (November 1995): 636–652.

11. For a discussion of the limits of political theory, see Judith Evans, Jill Hills, Karen Hunt, Elizabeth Meehan, Tessa ten Tusscher, Ursula Vogel, and Georgina Waylen, *Feminism and Political Theory* (London: Sage, 1986).

12. These hints are drawn from our teaching experiences and Anthony Daley, "On Reading," *PS: Politics and Political Science* 28 (March 1995): 89–100; Alec Fisher, *The Logic of Real Arguments* (Cambridge: Cambridge University Press, 1988); and Diane Schmidt, *Expository Writing in Political Science* (New York: HarperCollins, 1993).

13. Fisher, op. cit., 10.

14. Adapted from Dante Germino, "The Contemporary Relevance of the Classics of Political Philosophy," in Fred Greenstein and Nelson Polsby, eds., *Handbook of Political Science,* vol. 1 (Reading, Mass.: Addison-Wesley, 1975), 229–281.

Further Reading

Fowler, Robert Booth, and Jeffrey R. Orenstein. 1993. *An Introduction to Political Theory.* New York: HarperCollins.

Frank, Jason A., and John Tambornino, eds. 2000. *Vocations of Political Theory.* Minneapolis: University of Minnesota Press.

Galston, William. 1993. "Political Theory in the 1980s: Perplexity Amidst Diversity." In *Political Science: The State of the Discipline II*, ed. Ada Finifter, pp. 27–53. Washington, D.C.: American Political Science Association.

Gunnell, John. 1983. "Political Theory." In *Political Science: The State of the Discipline*, ed. Ada Finifter, pp. 3–45. Washington, D.C.: American Political Science Association.

Klosko, George. 1994. *History of Political Theory: An Introduction*, 2 vols. Fort Worth, TX: Harcourt Brace.

Morrow, John. 1998. *A History of Political Thought: A Thematic Introduction.* New York: New York University Press.

Nelson, John, ed. 1983. *What Should Political Theory Be Now?* Albany: State University of New York Press.

Okin, Susan Moller. 1979. *Women in Western Political Thought.* Princeton, NJ: Princeton University Press.

Portis, Edward. 1998. *Reconstructing the Classics: Political Theory from Plato to Marx*, 2nd ed. Chatham, NJ: Chatham House.

Shanley, Mary Lyndon, and Carole Pateman, eds. 1991. *Feminist Interpretations and Political Theory.* University Park, PA: Penn State University Press.

Skinner, Quentin, ed. 1985. *The Return of Grand Theory in the Human Sciences.* Cambridge: Cambridge University Press.

Spragens, Thomas. 1976. *Understanding Political Theory.* New York: St. Martin's Press.

Thiele, Leslie Paul. 1997. *Thinking Politics: Perspectives in Ancient, Modern and Postmodern Political Theory.* Chatham, NJ: Chatham House. ✦

Part I

Enter Modernity

Although the envious nature of men, so prompt to blame and so slow to praise, makes the discovery and introduction of any new principles and systems as dangerous almost as the exploration of unknown seas and continents, yet, animated by the desire which impels me to do what may prove for the common benefit of all, I have resolved to open a new route, which has not yet been followed by anyone, and may prove difficult and troublesome, but may also bring me some reward in the approbation of those who will kindly appreciate my efforts.

—Niccolò Machiavelli, The *Discourses*

Machiavelli's words capture the spirit of the coming age. He could see the world was about to change dramatically. The new era would usher in renewed exploration, new ways of understanding ourselves, and a politics more firmly based on man's ability to control events. The change was already enveloping the Renaissance world Machiavelli inhabited.

If the medieval outlook was shaped by Christian and classical ideas, the Renaissance (usually dated from the middle of the 14th century) both accepted and challenged them. For humanist scholars such as Petrarch (1304–1374) and Desiderius Erasmus (1469–1536), the classical world supplied the basic learning that one should acquire, but in many respects, that world was clearly relegated to the past. As such, the humanist approach favored by scholars in the provincial capitals of Italy and elsewhere came to be marked by a philosophical flexibility that allowed it to reevaluate the contributions of ancient thought and culture.

Without a doubt, the Renaissance was a time of scientific advance and artistic experimentation. It was also a time of political contrasts and philosophical change. Politically, in large states such as France and England, the sort of monarchy limited by feudal obligations and the claims of natural law gave way to a more or less absolute one. In Italy, by contrast, there were so many competing states that no overarching authority developed.

Even the Church began to lose whatever special claim to authority it once had as a series of popes behaved in ways that were no different from secular rulers. The challenge to religious authority instigated by papal mischief was perhaps most startlingly exhibited by the poet Dante Alighieri (1265–1321), who included Pope Boniface as one of the residents of the eighth circle of hell in his famous *Divine Comedy*. In *De Monarchia*, Dante insisted on severing the power of the state from the papacy. Challenges to the power of the Roman Church continued with Martin Luther (1483–1546) who disputed the authoritative role the clergy played in interpreting the Bible to believers and the secular authority of the pope over local bishops.

Economically, medieval feudalism was collapsing as a new landless commercial class exploited opportunities opened by expanding trade. In turn, commerce necessitated more centralized political power with the authority to "enforce uniform standards of weights and measures . . . , permanent institutions to oversee financial and judicial affairs, . . . and general systems of taxation."[1] As a result, the dispersion of economic and political power characteristic of the feudal state gave way to the centrifugal tendencies of the nation-state.

Philosophically, especially among writers on politics, the prevailing approach was to redirect thinking. An individualistic stress on making one's way in the world soon came to replace medieval Christianity's emphasis on community and interdependence. Renaissance thinkers had little use for the *vita contemplativa*, the monastic ideal of isolation and spiritual contemplation. For them, the life of action was where one should devote one's energies. Parallel to this advocacy of action was "the proliferation of independent areas of inquiry, each intent on staking out its autonomy, each concerned to develop a language of explanation suited to a particular set of phenomena, and each proceeding without benefit of clergy."[2]

As we noted in the Introduction, the political theory of Niccolò Machiavelli can be seen as marking the transition from the ancient world to the modern. An enthusiast of ancient republics, Machiavelli nonetheless realized that he confronted a quite different political world than had the classical thinkers. Where Plato had imagined an ideal community, Machiavelli turned his attention to actually existing ones. Where Aristotle theorized about ensuring the good life and Augustine contemplated the nature of sin, Machiavelli asserted that the mundane realities of statecraft were the proper subject of political theory. And where thinkers such as Aquinas and de Pizan encouraged rulers to abide by Christian principles and duties, Machiavelli pointedly observed that all too many people act in accordance with other, more secular values.

One could already see in the novelty of Machiavelli's method and findings the genesis of a new perspective that was to dominate the modern world. The findings of Copernicus (1473–1543) were especially breathtaking, even though the scientist was prudently circumspect about the impact of his celestial investigations in his own writings. The very possibility that the sun—not the earth—was the center of the universe challenged essential Church doctrine. It raised doubt about the Christian creation myth and called into question the central place of the Church (and of the pope) in the "great chain of being." Later, Galileo (1564–1642) was to feel the wrath of the Church for making similar claims. Common among the characteristics of these new-era thinkers was the spirit of discovery, faith in the capacity of reason, and the search for a verifiable method of inquiry.

The Age of Reason and the Advent of Liberalism

The same intellectual curiosity that drove Galileo inspired Thomas Hobbes (1588–1679), the English philosopher generally acknowledged to have brought political philosophy fully into the modern age. Hobbes, like Machiavelli, spoke of a "new method"; but whereas Machiavelli based his method on historical analysis, Hobbes relied upon geometry and the science of "motion." When an event or phenomenon was properly dissected, Hobbes believed, an analysis of its properties of space and movement would provide a fully satisfying and comprehensible explanation. Using these building blocks, one could produce a science of earthly things building from the simple motions of physics to the complex motions of the mind and ultimately to a rigorous science of morals and politics. While Hobbes did not deny the claims of revelation, earthly discoveries did not require their addition to complete one's understanding.

Hobbes's contemporaries equally displayed this new spirit of discovery at the dawn of the Age of Reason. René Descartes (1596–1650) confirmed a belief in the efficacy of reason and gave birth to its language, mathematics. Francis Bacon (1561–1626) expounded on the goals of the new age, insisting that the intellectual tools of modernity were designed as much to help individuals control the world that confronted them as they were to provide an understanding of it. Sir Isaac Newton (1642–1727) raised the bar for scientific inquiry even further, advancing the possibility that reason alone was capable of fathoming the universe on the basis of simple laws of motion and physics. Mechanism replaced teleology. The search for truth by use of a method open to all replaced revelation reserved for the few. The potential for understanding and control made progress possible. By the 17th century, the project of enlightenment thinkers was clear: to completely understand the cosmos by the use of reason and to bring it under rational human control.

If the Enlightenment raised the possibility that human beings could comprehend and control their own destinies as far as the physical universe was concerned, then it appeared even more certain that humans could exercise decisive control over their political destinies. Hobbes surmised from these premises that the absence of a natural hierarchy required agreement among relatively equal individuals to prevent degeneration into chaos. The idea that free and equal individuals could voluntarily enter into agreement for mutual advantage lies at the heart of the liberal ideal.

Of course, it wasn't Hobbes who perfected the ideal. For Hobbes, an all-powerful sovereign was needed to keep the peace once equal individuals voluntarily consigned their rights in the interest of peace. It was up to John Locke to complete the liberal creed by insisting that consent remained the glue that bound free individuals one to another

and that rational creatures would not likely consent to rule by an all-powerful monarch. Instead, the rights that defined and protected native individual freedom and equality could only be secured if the authority of government were limited, if government guaranteed natural human rights including property, and if the individual retained the ability to dissolve the bonds of social unity and begin again if government became hostile to the ends for which it was constructed. It is under the banner of these ideals that liberal political theory was born.

The Development of Revolutionary Thought

The themes developed by Enlightenment British thinkers in the 17th century—faith in reason and the scientific method, natural rights, progress, and limited secular political authority—found fertile terrain in France for explosive growth in the 18th century. A group of popular philosophers known as the *philosophes* sought to systematize knowledge and make it available for popular consumption. Denis Diderot (1713–1784) and Jean D'Alembert (1717–1783) commissioned pieces for and edited the great French *Encyclopédie*. François Voltaire (1694–1778), inspired by Locke, criticized established authority and invoked the message of natural rights against the *ancien régime*. Transplanted to France, however, Locke's work took on a radical flair. In the hands of some French theorists, Locke's challenge to traditional monarchical authority became a challenge to the authority of all men of power and substance and a source of inspiration for the masses. Events in America fueled the sparks of revolution smoldering in Paris. Liberal political thought was becoming radicalized.

Rightly or wrongly, the words of Jean-Jacques Rousseau (1712–1778) were to become associated with the French Revolution. Rousseau, like Locke, believed in natural rights and the importance of consent in the formation and maintenance of government. Unlike Locke, however, Rousseau attacked property as potentially injurious to natural rights. Curiously, he also attacked the basis for Lockean liberalism—a faith in the liberating potential of reason—contrasting the exaggerated appetites of civilized man with the simple pleasures of the presocial noble savage. Nevertheless, since man was forever removed from the simple life of his forebears, he could at least recapture some of his autonomy by helping to determine the "general will" as a blueprint for social policy in conjunction with his fellow man.

The suspicions Rousseau raised between the propertied and propertyless were bound to exasperate suspicions by other disaffected and powerless classes. Back in England, Mary Wollstonecraft (1759–1797) gave voice to women who were systematically excluded from political power and from the control over their destinies promised by the liberal project. She argued for education for women and their inclusion in the currents of social progress that had been limited thus far to men. Wollstonecraft was not simply building on the revolutionary ideology gaining momentum in America and France, however. She was also responding to the growing reaction to revolution already gaining strength in the works of theorists like Edmund Burke (1729–1797). Burke ushered in an era less hopeful about the human ability to escape the constraints of human nature and our ability to design our own futures.

Notes

1. James Wiser, *Political Philosophy: A History of the Search for Order* (Englewood Cliffs, N.J.: Prentice Hall, 1983), 132.
2. Sheldon Wolin, *Politics and Vision: Continuity and Innovation in Western Political Thought* (Boston: Little, Brown, 1960), 199.

References

Best, Judith A. 1980. *The Mainstream of Western Political Thought*. New York: Human Sciences Press.

Germino, Dante. 1972. *Modern Western Political Thought: Machiavelli to Marx*. Chicago: Rand McNally.

Tannenbaum, Donald and David Schultz. 1998. *Inventors of Ideas: An Introduction to Western Political Philosophers*. New York: St. Martin's Press.

Wiser, James. 1983. *Political Philosophy: A History of the Search for Order*. Englewood Cliffs, N.J.: Prentice Hall.

Wolin, Sheldon. 1960. *Politics and Vision: Continuity and Innovation in Western Political Thought*. Boston: Little, Brown. ✦

Niccolò Machiavelli

No name is more synonymous with politics, especially as politics is popularly conceived, than that of Niccolò Machiavelli. Machiavelli's reputation is based largely on the amoral, if not immoral, advice he gave in *The Prince*, written in 1513. Indeed, the book became so readily despised that at one time the name "Old Nick" was a synonym for the Devil. Although his works have been somewhat more charitably interpreted in recent years, the view persists that Machiavelli was little more than a "teacher of evil" who urged political rulers to disregard conventional norms and values. Beyond the appeal of tasting forbidden fruit, however, scholars have found other significant contributions in Machiavelli's work. Offering a rational, empirical analysis of the modern state and politics, his writings (although appearing in the form of practical maxims) are considered a key forerunner of contemporary political science. Moreover, he also advocated a politics of civic republicanism and freedom that continues to shape a number of currents in democratic thought.

The diverse, contradictory character of Machiavelli's writings is, to some extent, mirrored in his life. Born in 1469, Machiavelli spent his early career as a diplomat and administrator for his native city of Florence. Though he never attained the rank of ambassador, he conducted several diplomatic missions and became something of an expert in military affairs. When the Florentine republic fell and was replaced by the rule of the Medici family in 1512, Machiavelli was forced out of office and began a lifetime of study in the fields of history and politics. After years of seeking favors from the Medici, Machiavelli returned to public service in 1525, only to be removed with the Medici themselves a year later. Machiavelli died soon afterward, unable to win the trust of Florence's new republican leaders.

Machiavelli believed regimes fall into two types, principalities and republics. In *The Prince*, he offers advice on how to acquire and maintain a principality. To do so, a wise ruler would follow the path set forth by necessity, glory, and the good of the state. Only by combining machismo, martial spirit and political sagacity can a ruler fulfill one's duty to the state and achieve historical immortality. By contrast, Machiavelli turns his attention in the *Discourses* (a commentary on a history of Rome written by Titus Livius, also known as Livy) to the creation, maintenance, and renovation of a republican government. His chief concern is to show how republican governments can promote stability and freedom while avoiding the debilitating effects of corruption. For Machiavelli, glory (whether princely or republican) is the definitive political ambition—one pursued within limits set by reason, prudence, fortune, and necessity.

The Prince

Machiavelli's *The Prince* is an intriguing little book of advice to any ruler interested in conquering or reforming a state. Though of humble origin, Machiavelli feels he can give such advice not only because of his lengthy study of public affairs, but also because "one needs to be a ruler to understand properly the character of the people, and to be a man of the people to understand properly the character of rulers."[1] From this realistic standpoint, not one based in utopian conceptions of politics, Machiavelli examines the traits for which rulers are praised or blamed. In the selections reprinted below, he argues that the wise ruler should possess the following: (1) an ability to be both good and bad, both loved and feared; (2) such character traits as boldness, ruthlessness, independence, discipline, and self-control; and (3) a reputation for generosity, mercy, trustworthiness, and piety. He advises the prince to do whatever is necessary, no matter how apparently vicious, since people are ultimately concerned only with outcomes—that is, with the good of the state. Of course, even a vicious prince must nevertheless contend with the fickle nature of changing circumstances, the capriciousness of fortune.

The *Discourses*

In the *Discourses* (1519), Machiavelli suggests that, while the founder or reformer of a state should act alone or even ruthlessly, maintaining a state over the long haul requires a virtuous, democratic rule by the many. Here it should be noted that maintenance does not mean simple persistence; it also connotes the promotion of freedom and political stability, the avoidance of corruption and decadence. The selections from Book One thus illustrate both Machiavelli's classical scholarship and his disillusionment with princely rule. Machiavelli begins by outlining a typology of forms of government and the cycle through which governments pass from virtuous to corrupt forms. This leads quite naturally to a general discussion of corrupt peoples and institutions, and the means to renovate and reconstitute political life. Once that reconstitution occurs, Machiavelli (upon comparing the respective virtues and vices of masses and princes) recommends popular rule as the path to political stability, security, and glory.

Commentaries

In the introduction to his translation of *The Prince*, Harvey C. Mansfield, Jr. summarizes the essential argument of the book. His primary focus is on the qualities that the "new prince" should exhibit in order to secure his rule. In order to be an effective ruler, then, the prince should owe nothing to anyone, rely upon his own arms, ally himself with the people rather than the nobles, and most importantly, learn how not to be good. Mansfield leaves no doubt that, in this most famous of works on politics, Machiavelli himself was definitively Machiavellian. In other words, because he separated the conduct of politics from all connection to justice and morality, Machiavelli deserves the bad reputation that he has long since acquired.

One long-standing dispute among Machiavelli scholars has concerned the extent to which *The Prince* can be reconciled with the *Discourses*. In this context, John Leonard examines the vocabulary that Machiavelli employs in his defense of the extraordinary actions necessary to remedy political and social decadence. Leonard makes the case that the concepts of *virtù* and *bontà* have little to do with Christian virtue or goodness; instead, they respectively refer to such pursuits as glory and patriotism. Whether he is advising princes or peoples, Machiavelli's chief concern is to preserve the public sphere from the corrupting influences of private interests.

Note

1. Niccolò Machiavelli, *The Prince*, ed. Quentin Skinner and Russell Price (Cambridge: Cambridge University Press, 1988), 4.

Web Sources

http://www.utm.edu/research/iep/m/machiave.htm
The Internet Encyclopedia of Philosophy. A biographical profile and a summary of *The Prince*.

http://www.historyguide.org/intellect/machiavelli.html
Niccolò Machiavelli, 1469–1527. A brief profile with links to texts by Machiavelli.

Class Activities and Discussion Items

1. Have the class read and report on some of the works that have been modeled (more or less) after *The Prince*—for example, Gary Hart's *The Patriot*, Dick Morris's *The New Prince*, L.F. Gunlick's *The Machiavellian Manager's Handbook for Success*, or even Claudia Hart's *A Child's Machiavelli*. Discuss to what extent these works reflect either the letter or the spirit of Machiavelli's views.

2. What qualities does Machiavelli think a prince should have? Compare his views with those of de Pizan.

3. Is Machiavelli merely an advocate of violence, wickedness, and power-seeking? Why or why not?

4. What does Machiavelli mean by *virtù*? What import does the concept have for both princely and republican rule?

5. What is the relationship between Machiavelli's views expressed in *The Prince* and those expressed in the *Discourses?* Are they consistent or inconsistent? Why?

Further Reading

De Grazia, Sebastian. 1989. *Machiavelli in Hell.* Princeton, NJ: Princeton University Press. An engaging and rewarding intellectual biography that won a Pulitzer Prize.

Dietz, Mary. 1986. "Trapping the Prince: Machiavelli and the Politics of Deception." *American Political Science Review* 80 (September): 777–799. Captivating article which suggests that the scheming Machiavelli, even while advising princes, was an advocate of civic republicanism.

Hulliung, Mark. 1983. *Citizen Machiavelli.* Princeton, NJ: Princeton University Press. Regards Machiavelli's emphasis on the pursuit of glory as subversive of the humanist or republican tradition.

Pitkin, Hannah. 1984. *Fortune is a Woman: Gender and Politics in the Thought of Niccolò Machiavelli.* Berkeley: University of California Press. Identifies Machiavelli's ambivalence toward manhood and autonomy as the source of his fear of and contempt for feminine power.

Pocock, J.G.A. 1975. *The Machiavellian Moment: Florentine Political Thought and the Atlantic Republican Tradition.* Princeton, NJ: Princeton University Press. Noteworthy study of the nature and impact Machiavelli's republican ideas.

Skinner, Quentin. 1981. *Machiavelli.* New York: Hill and Wang. Brief but excellent introduction to Machiavelli's life and thought.

Strauss, Leo. 1958. *Thoughts on Machiavelli.* Glencoe, IL: Free Press. The classic case for regarding Machiavelli as a teacher of evil. ✦

1
Excerpts from *The Prince*

Niccolò Machiavelli

Chapter XV: The Things for Which Men, and Especially Rulers, Are Praised or Blamed

It remains now to consider in what ways a ruler should act with regard to his subjects and allies.[1] And since I am well aware that many people have written about this subject I fear that I may be thought presumptuous, for what I have to say differs from the precepts offered by others, especially on this matter. But because I want to write what will be useful to anyone who understands, it seems to me better to concentrate on what really happens rather than on theories or speculations. For many have imagined republics and principalities that have never been seen or known to exist.[2] However, how men live is so different from how they should live that a ruler who does not do what is generally done, but persists in doing what ought to be done, will undermine his power rather than maintain it. If a ruler who wants always to act honourably is surrounded by many unscrupulous men his downfall is inevitable. Therefore, a ruler who wishes to maintain his power must be prepared to act immorally when this becomes necessary.

I shall set aside fantasies about rulers, then, and consider what happens in fact. I say that whenever men are discussed, and especially rulers (because they occupy more exalted positions), they are praised or blamed for possessing some of the following qualities. Thus, one man is considered generous, another miserly (I use this Tuscan term because *avaro* in our tongue also signifies someone who is rapacious, whereas we call *misero* someone who is very reluctant to use his own possessions); one is considered a free giver, another rapacious; one cruel, another merciful; one treacherous, another loyal; one effeminate and weak, another indomitable and spirited; one affable, another haughty; one lascivious, another moderate; one upright, another cunning; one inflexible, another easy-going; one serious, another frivolous; one devout, another unbelieving, and so on.

I know that everyone will acknowledge that it would be most praiseworthy for a ruler to have all the above-mentioned qualities that are held to be good. But because it is not possible to have all of them, and because circumstances do not permit living a completely virtuous life, one must be sufficiently prudent to know how to avoid becoming notorious for those vices that would destroy one's power and seek to avoid those vices that are not politically dangerous; but if one cannot bring oneself to do this, they can be indulged in with fewer misgivings. Yet one should not be troubled about becoming notorious for those vices without which it is difficult to preserve one's power, because if one considers everything carefully, doing some things that seem virtuous may result in one's ruin, whereas doing other things that seem vicious may strengthen one's position and cause one to flourish.

Chapter XVI: Generosity and Meanness

To begin, then, with the first of the above-mentioned qualities, I maintain that it would be desirable to be considered generous; nevertheless, if generosity is practised in such a way that you will be considered generous, it will harm you. If it is practised virtuously, and as it should be, it will not be known about, and you will not avoid acquiring a bad reputation for the opposite vice. Therefore, if one wants to keep up a reputation for being generous, one must spend lavishly and ostentatiously. The inevitable outcome of acting in such ways is that the ruler will consume all his resources in sumptuous display; and if he wants to continue to be thought generous, he will eventually be compelled to become rapacious, to tax the people very heavily, and raise money by all possible means. Thus, he will begin to be hated by his subjects and, because he is impoverished, he will be held in little regard. Since this generosity of his has harmed many people and benefited few, he will feel the effects of any discontent, and the first real threat to his power will involve him in grave difficulties. When he realises this, and changes his ways, he will very soon acquire a bad reputation for being miserly.

Therefore, since a ruler cannot both practise this virtue of generosity and be known to do so without harming himself, he would do well not to worry about being called miserly. For eventually he will come to be considered more generous, when it is realised that, because of his parsimony, his revenues are sufficient to defend himself against any enemies that attack him, and to undertake campaigns without imposing special taxes on the people. Thus he will be acting generously towards the vast majority, whose property he does not touch, and will be acting meanly towards the few to whom he gives nothing.

Those rulers who have achieved great things in our own times have all been considered mean; all the others have failed. Although Pope Julius cultivated a reputation for generosity in order to become pope,[3] he did not seek to maintain it afterwards, because he wanted to be able to wage war. The present King of France[4] has fought many wars without imposing any special taxes on his subjects, because his parsimonious habits have always enabled him to meet the extra expenses. If the present King of Spain[5] had a reputation for generosity, he would not have successfully undertaken so many campaigns.

Therefore, a ruler should worry little about being thought miserly: he will not have to rob his subjects; he will be able to defend himself; he will avoid being poor and despised and will not be forced to become rapacious. For meanness is one of those vices that enable him to rule. It may be objected that Caesar obtained power through his open-handedness, and that many others have risen to very high office because they were open-handed and were considered to be so. I would reply that either you are already an established ruler or you are trying to become a ruler. In the first case, open-handedness is harmful; in the second, it is certainly necessary to be thought open-handed. Caesar was one of those who sought power in Rome; but if after gaining power he had survived, and had not moderated his expenditure, he would have undermined his power. And if it should be objected that many rulers who have been considered very generous have had remarkable military successes, I would reply: a ruler spends either what belongs to him or his subjects, or what belongs to others. In the former case, he should be parsimonious; in the latter, he should be as open-handed as possible. A ruler who accompanies his army, supporting it by looting, sacking and extortions, disposes of what belongs to others; he must be open-handed, for if he is not, his soldiers will desert. You can be much more generous with what does not belong to you or to your subjects, as Cyrus, Caesar and Alexander were. This is because giving away what belongs to others in no way damages your reputation; rather, it enhances it. It is only giving away what belongs to yourself that harms you.

There is nothing that is so self-consuming as generosity: the more you practise it, the less you will be able to continue to practise it. You will either become poor and despised or your efforts to avoid poverty will make you rapacious and hated. A ruler must above all guard against being despised and hated; and being generous will lead to both. Therefore, it is shrewder to cultivate a reputation for meanness, which will lead to notoriety but not to hatred. This is better than being forced, through wanting to be considered generous, to incur a reputation for rapacity, which will lead to notoriety and to hatred as well.

Chapter XVII: Cruelty and Mercifulness; And Whether It Is Better to Be Loved or Feared

Turning to the other previously mentioned qualities, I maintain that every ruler should want to be thought merciful, not cruel; nevertheless, one should take care not to be merciful in an inappropriate way. Cesare Borgia was considered cruel, yet his harsh measures restored order to the Romagna, unifying it and rendering it peaceful and loyal. If his conduct is properly considered, he will be judged to have been much more merciful than the Florentine people, who let Pistoia be torn apart, in order to avoid acquiring a reputation for cruelty. Therefore, if a ruler can keep his subjects united and loyal, he should not worry about incurring a reputation for cruelty; for by punishing a very few he will really be more merciful than those who over-indulgently permit disorders to develop, with resultant killings and plunderings. For the latter usually harm a whole community, whereas the executions ordered by a ruler harm only specific individuals. And a new ruler, in particular, cannot avoid being considered harsh, since new states are full of dangers. Virgil makes Dido say:

Res dura, et regni novitas me talia cogunt
moliri, et late fines custode tueri.[6]

Nevertheless, he should be slow to believe accusations and to act against individuals, and should not be afraid of his own shadow. He should act with due prudence and humanity so that being over-confident will not make him incautious, and being too suspicious will not render him insupportable.

A controversy has arisen about this: whether it is better to be loved than feared, or vice versa. My view is that it is desirable to be both loved and feared; but it is difficult to achieve both and, if one of them has to be lacking, it is much safer to be feared than loved.

For this may be said of men generally: they are ungrateful, fickle, feigners and dissemblers, avoiders of danger, eager for gain. While you benefit them they are all devoted to you: they would shed their blood for you; they offer their possessions, their lives, and their sons, as I said before, when the need to do so is far off. But when you are hard pressed, they turn away. A ruler who has relied completely on their promises, and has neglected to prepare other defences, will be ruined, because friendships that are acquired with money, and not through greatness and nobility of character, are paid for but not secured, and prove unreliable just when they are needed.

Men are less hesitant about offending or harming a ruler who makes himself loved than one who inspires fear. For love is sustained by a bond of gratitude which, because men are excessively self-interested, is broken whenever they see a chance to benefit themselves. But fear is sustained by a dread of punishment that is always effective. Nevertheless, a ruler must make himself feared in such a way that, even if he does not become loved, he does not become hated. For it is perfectly possible to be feared without incurring hatred. And this can always be achieved if he refrains from laying hands on the property of his citizens and subjects, and on their womenfolk. If it is necessary to execute anyone, this should be done only if there is a proper justification and obvious reason. But, above all, he must not touch the property of others, because men forget sooner the killing of a father than the loss of their patrimony. Moreover, there will always be pretexts for seizing property; and someone who begins to live rapaciously will always find pretexts for taking the property of others. On the other hand, reasons or pretexts for taking life are rarer and more fleeting.

However, when a ruler is with his army, and commands a large force, he must not worry about being considered harsh, because armies are never kept united and prepared for military action unless their leader is thought to be harsh. Among the remarkable things recounted about Hannibal is that, although he had a very large army, composed of men from many countries, and fighting in foreign lands, there never arose any dissension, either among themselves or against their leader, whether things were going well or badly. This could be accounted for only by his inhuman cruelty which, together with his many good qualities, made him always respected and greatly feared by his troops. And if he had not been so cruel, his other qualities would not have been sufficient to achieve that effect. Thoughtless writers admire this achievement of his, yet condemn the main reason for it.

That his other qualities would not have sufficed is proved by what happened to Scipio, considered a most remarkable man not only in his own times but in all others, whose armies rebelled against him in Spain. The only reason for this was that he was over-indulgent, and permitted his soldiers more freedom than was consistent with maintaining proper military discipline. Fabius Maximus rebuked him for this in the senate, and called him a corrupter of the Roman army. And when Locri was ravaged by one of Scipio's legates, the inhabitants were not avenged by him, and the legate was not punished for his arrogance, all because Scipio was too easy-going. Indeed, a speaker in the senate who wished to excuse him said that there were many men who were better at not committing misdeeds themselves than punishing the misdeeds of others. This character of his would eventually have tarnished his fame and glory, if he had continued his military command unchecked; but since he was controlled by the senate, this harmful quality was not only concealed but contributed to his glory.

Returning to the matter of being feared and loved, then, I conclude that whether men bear affection depends on themselves, but whether they are afraid will depend on what the ruler does. A wise ruler should rely on what is under his own control, not on what is under the control of others; he should contrive only to avoid incurring hatred, as I have said.

Chapter XVIII: How Rulers Should Keep Their Promises

Everyone knows how praiseworthy it is for a ruler to keep his promises, and live uprightly and not by trickery. Nevertheless, experience shows that in our times the rulers who have done great things are those who have set little store by keeping their word, being skilful rather in cunningly confusing men; they have got the better of those who have relied on being trustworthy.

You should know, then, that there are two ways of contending: one by using laws, the other, force. The first is appropriate for men, the second for animals; but because the former is often ineffective, one must have recourse to the latter. Therefore, a ruler must know well how to imitate beasts as well as employing properly human means. This policy was taught to rulers allegorically by ancient writers: they tell how Achilles and many other ancient rulers were entrusted to Chiron the centaur, to be raised carefully by him. Having a mentor who was half-beast and half-man signifies that a ruler needs to use both natures, and that one without the other is not effective.

Since a ruler, then, must know how to act like a beast, he should imitate both the fox and the lion, for the lion is liable to be trapped, whereas the fox cannot ward off wolves. One needs, then, to be a fox to recognise traps, and a lion to frighten away wolves. Those who rely merely upon a lion's strength do not understand matters.

Therefore, a prudent ruler cannot keep his word, nor should he, when such fidelity would damage him, and when the reasons that made him promise are no longer relevant. This advice would not be sound if all men were upright; but because they are treacherous and would not keep their promises to you, you should not consider yourself bound to keep your promises to them.

Moreover, plausible reasons can always be found for such failure to keep promises. One could give countless modern examples of this, and show how many peace treaties and promises have been rendered null and void by the faithlessness of rulers; and those best able to imitate the fox have succeeded best. But foxiness should be well concealed: one must be a great feigner and dissembler. And men are so naive, and so much dominated by immediate needs, that a skilful deceiver always finds plenty of people who will let themselves be deceived.

I must mention one recent case: Alexander VI was concerned only with deceiving men, and he always found them gullible. No man ever affirmed anything more forcefully or with stronger oaths but kept his word less. Nevertheless, his deceptions were always effective, because he well understood the naivety of men.

A ruler, then, need not actually possess all the above-mentioned qualities, but he must certainly seem to. Indeed, I shall be so bold as to say that having and always cultivating them is harmful, whereas seeming to have them is useful; for instance, to seem merciful, trustworthy, humane, upright and devout, and also to be so. But if it becomes necessary to refrain, you must be prepared to act in the opposite way, and be capable of doing it. And it must be understood that a ruler, and especially a new ruler, cannot always act in ways that are considered good because, in order to maintain his power, he is often forced to act treacherously, ruthlessly or inhumanely, and disregard the precepts of religion. Hence, he must be prepared to vary his conduct as the winds of fortune and changing circumstances constrain him and, as I said before, not deviate from right conduct if possible, but be capable of entering upon the path of wrongdoing when this becomes necessary.

A ruler, then, should be very careful that everything he says is replete with the five above-named qualities: to those who see and hear him, he should seem to be exceptionally merciful, trustworthy, upright, humane and devout. And it is most necessary of all to seem devout. In these matters, most men judge more by their eyes than by their hands. For everyone is capable of seeing you, but few can touch you. Everyone can see what you appear to be, whereas few have direct experience of what you really are, and those few will not dare to challenge the popular view, sustained as it is by the majesty of the ruler's position. With regard to all human actions, and especially those of rulers, who cannot be called to account, men pay attention to the outcome. If a ruler, then, contrives to conquer, and to preserve the state, the means will always be judged to be honourable and be praised by everyone. For the common people are impressed by appearances and results. Everywhere the common people are the vast majority, and the few are isolated when the majority and the government are at one. One present-day ruler, whom it is well to leave unnamed, is always preaching peace and trust, although he is really very hostile to both; and if he had practised them he would have lost either reputation or power several times over. . . .

Chapter XXV: How Much Power Fortune Has over Human Affairs, and How It Should Be Resisted

I am not unaware that many have thought, and many still think, that the affairs of the world are so ruled by fortune and by God that the ability of men cannot control them. Rather, they think that we have no remedy at all; and therefore it could be concluded that it is useless to sweat much over things, but let them be governed by fate. This opinion has been more popular in our own times because of the great changes that have taken place and are still to be seen even now, which could hardly have been predicted. When I think about this, I am sometimes inclined, to some extent, to share this opinion. Nevertheless, so as not to eliminate human freedom, I am disposed to hold that fortune is the arbiter of half our actions, but that it lets us control roughly the other half.

I compare fortune to one of those dangerous rivers that, when they become enraged, flood the plains, destroy trees and buildings, move earth from one place and deposit it in another. Everyone flees before it, everyone gives way to its thrust, without being able to halt it in any way. But this does not mean that, when the river is not in flood, men are unable to take precautions, by means of dykes and dams, so that when it rises next time, it will either not overflow its banks or, if it does, its force will not be so uncontrolled or damaging.

The same happens with fortune, which shows its powers where no force has been organised to resist it, and therefore strikes in the places where it knows that no dykes or dams have been built to restrain it. And if you consider Italy, which has been the seat of these changes, and which has given rise to them, you will see a countryside devoid of any embankments or defences. If it had been protected by proper defences, like Germany, Spain and France, the flood would not have caused such great changes or it would not have occurred at all. But I have said enough in general terms about resisting fortune.

Considering the matter in more detail, I would observe that one sees a ruler flourishing today and ruined tomorrow, without his having changed at all in character or qualities. I believe this is attributable, first, to the cause previously discussed at length, namely, that a ruler who trusts entirely to luck comes to grief when his luck runs out. Moreover, I believe that we are successful when our ways are suited to the times and circumstances, and unsuccessful when they are not. For one sees that, in the things that lead to the end which everyone aims at, that is, glory and riches, men proceed in different ways: one man cautiously, another impetuously; one man forcefully, another cunningly; one man patiently, another impatiently, and each of these different ways of acting can be effective. On the other hand, of two cautious men, one may achieve his aims and the other fail. Again, two men may both succeed, although they have different characters, one acting cautiously and the other impetuously. The reason for these different outcomes is whether their ways of acting conform with the conditions in which they operate. Consequently, as I have said, two men, acting differently, may achieve the same results; and if two men act in the same way, one may succeed and the other fail. From this, again, arise changes in prosperity; because if a man acts cautiously and patiently, and the times and circumstances change in ways for which his methods are appropriate, he will be successful. But if the times and circumstances change again, he will come to grief, because he does not change his methods. And one does not find men who are so prudent that they are capable of being sufficiently flexible: either because our natural inclinations are too strong to permit us to change, or because, having always fared well by acting in a certain way, we do not think it a good idea to change our methods. Therefore, if it is necessary for a cautious man to act expeditiously, he does not know how to do it; this leads to his failure. But if it were possible to change one's character to suit the times and circumstances, one would always be successful.

Pope Julius II always acted impetuously, and found the times and circumstances so suited to his ways that he was always successful. Consider the first expedition he made to Bologna, while messer Giovanni Bentivoglio was still alive. The Venetians were opposed to it, and so was the King of Spain; there were also discussions with the King of France about such an enterprise. Nevertheless, acting with his usual indomitable spirit and impetuosity, he led the expedition personally. This initiative caught the King of Spain and the Venetians off guard and constrained them to be passive spectators, the latter through fear and the former because of his desire to recover the whole of the Kingdom of Naples. On the other hand, Julius involved the King of France: for that King saw the Pope moving and, because he wanted to cultivate the Pope's friendship with a view to reducing the power of Venice, he decided that he could not refuse him troops without offending him very openly. With this swift initiative, then, Julius achieved what no other pope, acting with consummate prudence, could have attained. If he had not left Rome until everything had been agreed and settled, as any other pope would have done, he would never have succeeded. For the King of France would have contrived to find countless excuses, and the others would have produced countless reasons why the Pope should hesitate. I shall not discuss his other actions, which were similar in character, and all turned out well for him. The shortness of his pontificate did not permit him to taste of failure. But if circumstances had changed so that it was imperative to act cautiously, he would have been undone; for he would never have deviated from the methods that were natural to him.

I conclude, then, that since circumstances vary and men when acting lack flexibility, they are successful if their methods match the circumstances and unsuccessful if they do not. I certainly think that it is better to be impetuous than cautious, because fortune is a woman and if you want to control her, it is necessary to treat her roughly. And it is clear that she is more inclined to yield to men who are impetuous than to those who are calculating. Since fortune is a woman, she is always well disposed towards young men, because they are less cautious and more aggressive, and treat her more boldly. . . .

Notes

1. A ruler's conduct towards subjects is treated in Chs. XV–XVII, towards allies (*amici*) in Ch. XVIII.
2. M. apparently refers both to some ancient writers (e.g., Plato, in his *Republic*) and to more recent ones who emphasised ideals and the duties of rulers.
3. I.e., by bribes.
4. Louis XII.
5. Ferdinand the Catholic.
6. Virgil, *Aeneid*, 563–4: 'Harsh necessity and the newness of my kingdom force me to do such things, and to guard all the frontiers.'

Adapted from: Niccolò Machiavelli, *The Prince*, translated by Quentin Skinner and Russell Price, pp. 54–63, 84–87. Copyright © 1988. Reprinted by permission of Cambridge University Press. ✦

2
Excerpts from the *Discourses*

Niccolò Machiavelli

2. How Many Kinds of State There Are and of What Kind Was That of Rome

I propose to dispense with a discussion of cities which from the outset have been subject to another power, and shall speak only of those which have from the outset been far removed from any kind of external servitude, but, instead, have from the start been governed in accordance with their wishes, whether as republics or principalities. As such cities have had diverse origins, so too they have had diverse laws and institutions. For either at the outset, or before very long, to some of them laws have been given by some one person at some one time, as laws were given to the Spartans by Lycurgus; whereas others have acquired them by chance and at different times as occasion arose. This was the case in Rome.

Happy indeed should we call that state which produces a man so prudent that men can live securely under the laws which he prescribes without having to emend them. Sparta, for instance, observed its laws for more than eight hundred years without corrupting them and without any dangerous disturbance. Unhappy, on the other hand, in some degree is that city to be deemed which, not having chanced to meet with a prudent organizer, has to reorganize itself. And, of such, that is the more unhappy which is the more remote from order; and that is the more remote from order whose institutions have missed altogether the straight road which leads it to its perfect and true destiny. For it is almost impossible that states of this type should by any eventuality be set on the right road again; whereas those which, if their order is not perfect, have made a good beginning and are capable of improvement, may become perfect should something happen which provides the opportunity. It should, however, be noted that they will never introduce order without incurring danger, because few men ever welcome new laws setting up a new order in the state unless necessity makes it clear to them that there is need for such laws; and since such a necessity cannot arise without danger, the state may easily be ruined before the new order has been brought to completion. The republic of Florence bears this out, for owing to what happened at Arezzo in '02 it was reconstituted, and owing to what happened at Prato in '12 its constitution was destroyed.

It being now my intention to discuss what were the institutions of the city of Rome and what events conduced to its perfection, I would remark that those who have written about states say that there are to be found in them one of three forms of government, called by them *Principality, Aristocracy* and *Democracy*, and that those who set up a government in any particular state must adopt one of them, as best suits their purpose.[1]

Others—and with better judgement many think—say that there are six types of government of which three are very bad, and three are good in themselves but easily become corrupt, so that they too must be classed as pernicious. Those that are good are the three above mentioned. Those that are bad are the other three, which depend on them, and each of them is so like the one associated with it that it easily passes from one form to the other. For *Principality* easily becomes *Tyranny*. From *Aristocracy* the transition to *Oligarchy* is an easy one. *Democracy* is without difficulty converted into *Anarchy*. So that if anyone who is organizing a commonwealth sets up one of the three first forms of government, he sets up what will last but for a while, since there are no means whereby to prevent it passing into its contrary, on account of the likeness which in such a case virtue has to vice.

These variations of government among men are due to chance. For in the beginning of the world, when its inhabitants were few, they lived for a time scattered like the beasts. Then, with the multiplication of their off-spring, they drew together and, in order the better to be able to defend themselves, began to look about for a man stronger and more courageous than the rest, made him their head, and obeyed him.

It was thus that men learned how to distinguish what is honest and good from what is pernicious and wicked, for the sight of someone injuring his benefactor evoked in them hatred and sympathy and they blamed the ungrateful and respected those who showed gratitude, well aware that the same injuries might have been done to themselves. Hence to prevent evil of this kind they took to making laws and to assigning punishments to those who contravened them. The notion of justice thus came into being.

In this way it came about that, when later on they had to choose a prince, they did not have recourse to the boldest as formerly, but to one who excelled in prudence and justice.

But when at a yet later stage they began to make the prince hereditary instead of electing him, his heirs soon began to degenerate as compared with their ancestors, and, forsaking virtuous deeds, considered that princes have nought else to do but to surpass other men in extravagance, lasciviousness, and every other form of licentiousness. With the result that the prince came to be hated, and, since he was hated, came to be afraid, and from fear soon passed to offensive action, which quickly brought about a tyranny.

From which, before long, was begotten the source of their downfall; for tyranny gave rise to conspiracies and plots against princes, organized not by timid and weak men, but by men conspicuous for their liberality, magnanimity, wealth and ability, for such men could not stand the dishonourable life the prince was leading. The masses, therefore, at the instigation of these powerful leaders, took up arms against the prince, and, when he had been liquidated, submitted to the authority of those whom they looked upon as their liberators. Hence the latter, to whom the very term 'sole head' had become odious, formed themselves into a government. Moreover, in the beginning,

mindful of what they had suffered under a tyranny, they ruled in accordance with the laws which they had made, subordinated their own convenience to the common advantage, and, both in private matters and public affairs, governed and preserved order with the utmost diligence.

But when the administration passed to their descendants who had no experience of the changeability of fortune, had not been through bad times, and instead of remaining content with the civic equality then prevailing, reverted to avarice, ambition and to seizing other men's womenfolk, they caused government by an aristocracy to become government by an oligarchy in which civic rights were entirely disregarded; so that in a short time there came to pass in their case the same thing as happened to the tyrant, for the masses, sick of their government, were ready to help anyone who had any sort of plan for attacking their rulers; and so there soon arose someone who with the aid of the masses liquidated them.

Then, since the memory of the prince and of the injuries inflicted by him was still fresh, and since, having got rid of government by the few, they had no desire to return to that of a prince, they turned to a democratic form of government, which they organized in such a way that no sort of authority was vested either in a few powerful men or in a prince.

And, since all forms of government are to some extent respected at the outset, this democratic form of government maintained itself for a while but not for long, especially when the generation that had organized it had passed away. For anarchy quickly supervened, in which no respect was shown either for the individual or for the official, and which was such that, as everyone did what he liked, all sorts of outrages were constantly committed. The outcome was inevitable. Either at the suggestion of some good man or because this anarchy had to be got rid of somehow, principality was once again restored. And from this there was, stage by stage, a return to anarchy, by way of the transitions and for the reasons assigned.

This, then, is the cycle through which all commonwealths pass, whether they govern themselves or are governed. But rarely do they return to the same form of government, for there can scarce be a state of such vitality that it can undergo often such changes and yet remain in being. What usually happens is that, while in a state of commotion in which it lacks both counsel and strength, a state becomes subject to a neighbouring and better organized state. Were it not so, a commonwealth might go on for ever passing through these governmental transitions.

I maintain then, that all the forms of government mentioned above are far from satisfactory, the three good ones because their life is so short, the three bad ones because of their inherent malignity. Hence prudent legislators, aware of their defects, refrained from adopting as such any one of these forms, and chose instead one that shared in them all, since they thought such a government would be stronger and more stable, for if in one and the same state there was principality, aristocracy and democracy each would keep watch over the other. . . .

18. How in Corrupt Cities a Free Government Can Be Maintained Where It Exists, or Be Established Where It Does Not Exist

It will not, I think, be foreign to my purpose nor contrary to the plan of my previous discourse to consider whether in a corrupt city it is possible to maintain a free government where it exists, and whether, when there has been none, it can be set up. In regard to this question I maintain that in either case it will be a very difficult thing to do. It is, moreover, almost impossible to lay down rules, for the method to be adopted will of necessity depend upon the degree of corruption. None the less, since it is well to take account of all cases, I do not propose to shelve the question. I suppose then an exceedingly corrupt state, whereby the difficulty will clearly be intensified, since in it there will be found neither laws nor institutions which will suffice to check widespread corruption. Because, just as for the maintenance of good customs laws are required, so if laws are to be observed, there is need of good customs. Furthermore, institutions and laws made in

the early days of a republic when men were good, no longer serve their purpose when men have become bad. And, if by any chance the laws of the state are changed, there will never, or but rarely, be a change in its institutions. The result is that new laws are ineffectual, because the institutions, which remain constant, corrupt them.

In order to make this point more clear I would point out that in Rome there was a constitution regulating its government, or rather its form of government, and then laws enabling the magistrates to keep the citizens in order. To the constitution determining its form of government pertained the authority vested in the people, the senate, the tribunes, and in the consuls, the method of applying for and of appointing to magisterial posts, and its legislative procedure. These institutions underwent little or no change in the course of events, whereas there were changes in the laws which kept the citizens in order. There was, for instance, the law concerning adultery, the sumptuary law, a law concerning ambition, and many others. These laws were introduced step by step as the citizens became corrupt. But since the institutions determining its form of government remained unchanged and, when corruption had set in, were no longer good, these modifications of the laws did not suffice to keep men good, though they might have helped had the introduction of new laws been accompanied by a modification of the institutions.

That it is true to say that such institutions would not be good in a corrupted state is clearly seen in two important cases, in the appointing of magistrates and in the making of laws. The Roman people had never given the consulate or any other important office in the city except to such as had applied for the post. This institution was at the outset good, because only such citizens applied for posts as judged themselves worthy to fill them, and to be rejected was looked upon as ignominious; so that everybody behaved well in order to be judged worthy. This procedure, when the city became corrupt, was extremely harmful; because not those who had more virtue, but those who had more power, applied for magistracies, and the powerless, though virtuous, refrained from applying through fear. This inconvenience did not come about all at once, but by stages, as is the case with all inconveniences. For when the Romans had conquered Africa and Asia, and had reduced the greater part of Greece to subjection, they had become secure as to their liberty nor had they any more enemies whom there was ground to fear. This sense of security and this weakness on the part of their enemies caused the Roman people in appointing to the consulate to consider not a man's virtue, but his popularity. This drew to that office men who knew better how to get round men, not those who knew better how to conquer enemies. They then turned from those who had more popularity and gave it to those who had more power. Thus owing to the defectiveness of this institution it came about that good men were wholly excluded from consular rank.

Again, a tribune or any other citizen could propose to the people a law, in regard to which every citizen was entitled to speak either in favour of it or against, prior to a decision being reached. This institution was good so long as the citizens were good, because it is always a good thing that anyone anxious to serve the public should be able to propose his plan. It is also a good thing that everyone should be at liberty to express his opinion on it, so that when the people have heard what each has to say they may choose the best plan. But when the citizens had become perverse, this institution became a nuisance; because only the powerful proposed laws, and this for the sake, not of their common liberties, but to augment their own power. And against such projects no one durst speak for fear of such folk; with the result that the people were induced, either by deceit or by force, to adopt measures which spelt their own ruin.

In order to maintain Rome's liberty, therefore, when corruption had set in, it was necessary in the course of its development to introduce new institutions just as there had been made new laws; for different institutions and a different procedure should be prescribed for the governed according as they are good or bad, since similar forms cannot subsist in matter which is disposed in a contrary manner. Now defective institutions must either be renovated all at once as soon as the decline from goodness is noticed, or little by little before they become known to everybody. Neither of which courses is possible, I maintain. For if the renovation is to take place little by little, there is need of someone who shall see the inconvenience coming while yet it is far off and in its infancy. But it may quite easily happen in a state that no such person will ever arise, or, should he arise in point of fact, that he will never be able to persuade others to see things as he does himself; for men accustomed to a certain mode of life are reluctant to change it, especially when they have not themselves noticed the evil in question, but have had their attention called to it by conjectures. While with regard to modifying institutions all at once when everybody realizes that they are no good, I would point out that, though it is easy to recognize their futility, it is not easy to correct it; for, to do this, normal methods will not suffice now that normal methods are bad. Hence it is necessary to resort to extraordinary methods, such as the use of force and an appeal to arms, and, before doing anything, to become a prince in the state, so that one can dispose it as one thinks fit.

But, to reconstitute political life in a state presupposes a good man, whereas to have recourse to violence in order to make oneself prince in a republic supposes a bad man. Hence very rarely will there be found a good man ready to use bad methods in order to make himself prince, though with a good end in view, nor yet a bad man who, having become a prince, is ready to do the right thing and to whose mind it will occur to use well that authority which he has acquired by bad means.

It is on account of all this that it is difficult, or rather impossible, either to maintain a republican form of government in states which have become corrupt or to create such a form afresh. Should a republic simply have to be created or to be maintained, it would be necessary to introduce into it a form of government akin rather to a monarchy than to a democracy, so that those men whose arrogance is such that they cannot be corrected by legal processes, may yet be restrained to some extent by a quasi-regal power.[2] To try to make them become good in any other way would be either a most brutal or an impossible undertaking—the kind of thing that Cleomenes did, as I said above; for that he might rule alone, he killed the ephors, and for the same reasons Romulus killed his brother and Titus Tatius killed the Sabine, and afterwards both of them made good use of their authority. It should, however, be noted that neither the one nor the other had subjects steeped in corruption, which in this chapter we have taken as the basis of our argument; so that both were able to resolve on such steps, and, having done so, to camouflage their plan. . . .

58. The Masses Are More Knowing and More Constant Than Is a Prince

Nothing is more futile and more inconstant than are the masses. So says our author, Titus Livy, and so say all other historians. For in the records of the actions men have performed one often finds the masses condemning someone to death, and then lamenting him and ardently wishing he were alive. The Roman people did this in Manlius Capitolinus's case: first they condemned him to death, then urgently wished him back. Of this our author says that 'soon after he had ceased to be a danger, the desire for him took hold of the people'. And again, when describing the events which happened in Syracuse after the death of Hieronymus, the nephew of Hiero, he says: 'It is of the nature of the masses either servilely to obey or arrogantly to domineer'.

I know not whether the view I am about to adopt will prove so hard to uphold and so full of difficulties that I shall have either shamefully to abandon it or laboriously to maintain it; for I propose to defend a position which all writers attack, as I have said. But, however that may be, I think, and always shall think there can be no harm in defending an opinion by arguments so long as one has no intention of appealing either to authority or force.

I claim, then, that for the failing for which writers blame the masses, any body of men one cares to select may be blamed, and especially princes; for anyone who does not regulate his conduct by laws will make the same mistakes as the masses are guilty of. This is easily seen, for there are and have been any number of princes, but of good and wise ones there have been but few. I am speaking of princes who have succeeded in breaking the bonds which might have held them in check; among which I do not include those kings who were born in Egypt when that most ancient of ancient realms was governed in accordance with the law, nor those born in Sparta, nor those born in France in our own times, for the kingdom of France is better regulated by laws than is any other of which at present we have knowledge. Kings who are born under such conditions are not to be classed among those whose nature we have to consider in each individual case to see whether it resembles that of the masses; for, should there be masses regulated by laws in the same way as they are, there will be found in them the same goodness as we find in kings, and it will be seen that they neither 'arrogantly dominate nor servilely obey'. Such was the Roman populace which, so long as the republic remained uncorrupt, was never servilely obsequious, nor yet did it ever dominate with arrogance: on the contrary, it had its own institutions and magistrates and honourably kept its own place. But when it was necessary to take action against some powerful person, it did so, as is seen in the case of Manlius, of the Ten, and in the case of others who sought to oppress it. Also, when it had to obey dictators or consuls in the public interest, it did so. Nor is it any wonder that the Roman populace wanted Manlius Capitolinus back when he was dead, for what they wanted was his virtues, which had been such that his memory evoked everyone's sympathy, and would have had power to produce the same effect in a prince, for all writers are of opinion that virtue is praised and admired even in one's enemies. Again, had Manlius, in response to this desire, been raised from the dead, the Roman populace would have passed on him the same sentence as it did, have had him arrested and, shortly after, have condemned him to death: though, for that matter, one also finds that reputedly wise princes have put people to death and then wished them alive again; Alexander, for instance, in the case of Cleitus and other of his friends, and Herod in the case of Mariamne. But the truth is that what our historian says of the nature of the masses is not said of the masses when disciplined by laws, as were the Romans, but of undisciplined masses, like those of Syracuse, which made the same kind of mistakes as do men when infuriated and undisciplined, just as did Alexander the Great and Herod in the cases cited.[3]

The nature of the masses, then, is no more reprehensible than is the nature of princes, for all do wrong and to the same extent when there is nothing to prevent them doing wrong. Of this there are plenty of examples besides those given, both among the Roman emperors and among other tyrants and princes; and in them we find a degree of inconstancy and changeability in behaviour such as is never found in the masses.

I arrive, then, at a conclusion contrary to the common opinion which asserts that populaces, when in power, are variable, fickle and ungrateful; and affirm that in them these faults are in no wise different from those to be found in certain princes. Were the accusation made against both the masses and princes, it would be true; but, if princes be excepted, it is false. For when the populace is in power and is well-ordered, it will be stable, prudent and grateful, in much the same way, or in a better way, than is a prince, however wise he be thought. And, on the other hand, a prince who contemns the laws, will be more ungrateful, fickle and imprudent than is the populace. Nor is inconstancy of behaviour due to a difference in nature, for they are pretty much the same, or, if one be better than the other, it is the populace: it is due to the greater or less respect which they have for the laws under which both alike are living.

If we consider the Roman populace it will be found that for four hundred years they were enemies to the very name of king and lovers of glory and of the common good of their country. Of both characteristics the Roman populace affords numerous and striking examples. And, should anyone bring up against me the ingratitude the populace displayed towards Scipio, my answer is that I have already discussed this question at length and have there shown the ingratitude of the populace to be less than that of princes. While in the matter of prudence and stability I claim that the populace is more prudent, more stable, and of sounder judgement than the prince. Not without good reason is the voice of the populace likened to that of God; for public opinion is remarkably accurate in its prognostications, so much so that it seems as if the populace by some hidden power discerned the evil and the good that was to befall it. With regard to its judgement, when two speakers of equal skill are heard advocating different alternatives, very rarely does one find the populace failing to adopt the better view or incapable of appreciating the truth of what it hears. While, if in bold actions and such as appear advantageous it errs, as I have said above, so does a prince often err where his passions are involved, and these are much stronger than those of the populace.

It is found, too, that in the election of magistrates the populace makes a far better choice than does the prince; nor can the populace ever be persuaded that it is good to appoint to such an office a man of infamous life or corrupt habits, whereas a prince may easily and in a vast variety of ways be persuaded to do this. Again, one finds that when the populace begins to have a horror of something it remains of the same mind for many centuries; a thing that is never observed in the case of a prince. For both these characteristics I shall content myself with the evidence afforded by the Roman populace, which in the course of so many hundreds of years and so many elections of consuls and tribunes did not make four elections of which it had to repent. So much, too, as I have said, was the title of king hated that no service rendered by one of its citizens who ambitioned it, could render him immune from the penalties prescribed. Besides this, one finds that cities in which the populace is the prince, in a very short time extend vastly their dominions much more than do those which have always been under a prince; as Rome did after the expulsion of the kings, and Athens after it was free of Pisistratus.

This can only be due to one thing: government by the populace is better than government by princes. Nor do I care whether to this opinion of mine all that our historian has said in the aforesaid passage or what others have said, be objected; because if account be taken of all the disorders due to populaces and of all those due to princes, and of all the glories won by populaces and all those won by princes, it will be found that alike in goodness and in glory the populace is far superior. And if princes are superior to populaces in drawing up laws, codes of civic life, statutes and new institutions, the populace is so superior in sustaining what has been instituted, that it indubitably adds to the glory of those who have instituted them.

In short, to bring this topic to a conclusion, I say that, just as princely forms of government have endured for a very long time, so, too, have republican forms of government; and that in both cases it has been essential for them to be regulated by laws. For a prince who does what he likes is a lunatic, and a populace which does what it likes is unwise. If, therefore, it be a question of a prince subservient to the laws and of a populace chained up by laws, more virtue will be found in the populace than in the prince; and if it be a question of either of them loosed from control by the law, there will be found fewer errors in the populace than in the prince, and these of less moment and much easier to put right. For a licentious and turbulent populace, when a good man can obtain a hearing, can easily be brought to behave itself; but there is no one to talk to a bad prince, nor is there any remedy except the sword. From which an inference may be drawn in regard to the importance of their respective maladies; for, if to cure the malady of the populace a word suffices and the sword is needed to cure that of a prince, no one will fail to see that the greater the cure, the greater the fault.

When the populace has thrown off all restraint, it is not the mad things it does that are terrifying, nor is it of present evils that one is afraid, but of what may come of them, for amidst such confusion there may come to be a tyrant. In the case of bad princes it is just the opposite: it is present evils that are terrifying, but for the future there is hope, since men are convinced that the evil ways of a bad prince may make for freedom in the end. Thus one sees the difference between the two cases amounts to the same thing as the difference between what is and what must come to be. The brutalities of the masses are directed against those whom they suspect of conspiring against the common good; the brutalities of a prince against those whom he suspects of conspiring against his own good.[4] The reason why people are prejudiced against the populace is because of the populace anyone may speak ill without fear and openly, even when the populace is ruling. But of princes people speak with the utmost trepidation and the utmost reserve.

Nor does it seem to me foreign to my purpose, since I find the topic attractive, to discuss in the next chapter on which more reliance can be placed, on confederations made by a republic or on confederations formed by a prince. . . .

Notes

1. Here Machiavelli follows Polybius very closely, and in so doing virtually repeats Aristotle's classification of Book III of the *Politics* (see Walker, Vol. II, pp. 7–8).

2. *Discourses* I.16, 17 and 18 all show how Machiavelli would handle the transition from servitude to freedom and republican institutions according to the basic principle, set out most clearly in *Discourses* III.9, of conformity with 'the times' or circumstances. The difficulties are great, as he says in *Discourses* I.17 and 18 and in I.49, so great that 'quasi-regal' power may be needed to contain dissident elements during the transition (see also *Discourses* I.55). But this is fully consistent both with what he says about the need for dictatorship in times of emergency and his general view that a '*potestà regia*' is one of the '*qualità*' in the mixture of elements that go to make up even (or particularly) a flourishing republic.

3. His optimistic view of '*il popolo*' . . . is not contradicted even in *The Prince*, although there their fickleness and unpredictability—from the point of view of a prince—is naturally stressed. (See *Prince* 6, 9 and 17.)

4. Machiavelli does not in fact explain why the masses should ruthlessly defend the common good while a prince is more likely to fight back for his own good. But, of course, there never is any philosophical discussion of the meaning of 'common good'; it never seems to occur to Machiavelli that the phrase could have any meaning apart from, in some sense, the aggregation of the interests of the actual inhabitants. His philosophical simplicity saved him from a lot of irrelevant nonsense.

In this discourse, however, both his thesis about the most appropriate circumstance for which type of government gets stated at its most general, and we see him introducing the dimension of *time* as the solvent of apparent contradictions: 'If princes are superior to populaces in drawing up laws, codes of civic life, statutes and new institutions, the populace is . . . superior in sustaining what has been instituted.' Amid all the 'political development' literature of today, I will suspect that there are general grounds for thinking this proposition (albeit at a high level of abstraction) is true.

Adapted from: Niccolò Machiavelli, *Discourses*, translated by Leslie J. Walker, pp. 104–109, 160–164, 252–257. Copyright © 1970. Reprinted by permission of Taylor & Francis Books Ltd. ✦

3
Introduction to
The Prince

Harvey C. Mansfield, Jr.

Anyone who picks up Machiavelli's *The Prince* holds in his hands the most famous book on politics ever written. Its closest rival might be Plato's *Republic*, but that book discusses politics in the context of things above politics, and politics turns out to have a limited and subordinate place. In *The Prince* Machiavelli also discusses politics in relation to things outside politics, as we shall see, but his conclusion is very different. Politics according to him is not limited by things above it, and things normally taken to be outside politics—the "givens" in any political situation—turn out to be much more under the control of politics than politicians, peoples, and philosophers have hitherto assumed. Machiavelli's *The Prince*, then, is the most famous book on politics when politics is thought to be carried on for its own sake, unlimited by anything above it. The renown of *The Prince* is precisely to have been the first and the best book to argue that politics has and should have its own rules and should not accept rules of any kind or from any source where the object is not to win or prevail over others. *The Prince* is briefer and pithier than Machiavelli's other major work, *Discourses on Livy*, for *The Prince* is addressed to Lorenzo de' Medici, a prince like the busy executive of our day who has little time for reading. So *The Prince* with its political advice to an active politician that politics should not be limited by anything not political, is by far more famous than the *Discourses on Livy*.

We cannot, however, agree that *The Prince* is the most famous book on politics without immediately correcting this to say that it is the most infamous. It is famous for its in-

famy, for recommending the kind of politics that ever since has been called Machiavellian. The essence of this politics is that "you can get away with murder": that no divine sanction, or degradation of soul, or twinge of conscience will come to punish you. If you succeed, you will not even have to face the infamy of murder, because when "men acquire who can acquire, they will be praised or not blamed" (Chapter 3). Those criminals who are infamous have merely been on the losing side. Machiavelli and Machiavellian politics are famous or infamous for their willingness to brave infamy.

Yet it must be reported that the prevailing view among scholars of Machiavelli is that he was not an evil man who taught evil doctrines, and that he does not deserve his infamy. With a view to his preference for republics over principalities (more evident in the *Discourses on Livy* than in *The Prince*, but not absent in the latter), they cannot believe he was an apologist for tyranny; or, impressed by the sudden burst of Italian patriotism in the last chapter of *The Prince*, they forgive him for the sardonic observations which are not fully consistent with this generous feeling but are thought to give it a certain piquancy (this is the opinion of an earlier generation of scholars); or, on the basis of Machiavelli's saying in Chapter 15 that we should take our bearings from "what is done" rather than from "what should be done," they conclude that he was a forerunner of modern political science, which is not an evil thing because it merely tells us what happens without passing judgment. In sum, the prevailing view of the scholars offers excuses for Machiavelli: he was a republican, a patriot, or a scientist, and therefore, in explicit contradiction to the reaction of most people to Machiavelli as soon as they hear of his doctrines, Machiavelli was not "Machiavellian."

The reader can form his own judgment of these excuses for Machiavelli. I do not recommend them, chiefly because they make Machiavelli less interesting. They transform him into a herald of the future who had the luck to sound the tunes we hear so often today—democracy, nationalism or self-determination, and science. Instead of challenging our favorite beliefs and forcing us to think, Machiavelli is enlisted into a chorus of self-congratulation. There is, of course, evidence for the excuses supplied on behalf of Machiavelli, and that evidence consists of the excuses offered by Machiavelli himself. If someone were to accuse him of being an apologist for tyranny, he can indeed point to a passage in the *Discourses on Livy* (II 2) where he says (rather carefully) that the common good is not observed unless in republics; but if someone else were to accuse him of supporting republicanism, he could point to the same chapter, where he says that the hardest slavery of all is to be conquered by a republic. And, while he shows his Italian patriotism in Chapter 26 of *The Prince* by exhorting someone to seize Italy in order to free it from the barbarians, he also shows his fairmindedness by advising a French king in Chapter 3 how he might better invade Italy the next time. Lastly, it is true that he sometimes merely reports the evil that he sees, while (unnecessarily) deploring it; but at other times he urges us to share in that evil and he virtuously condemns half-hearted immoralists. Although he was an exceedingly bold writer who seems to have deliberately courted an evil reputation, he was nonetheless not so bold as to fail to provide excuses, or prudent reservations, for his boldest statements. Since I have spoken at length on this point in another place, and will not hesitate to mention the work of Leo Strauss, it is not necessary to explain it further here.

What is at issue in the question of whether Machiavelli was "Machiavellian"? To see that a matter of the highest importance is involved we must not rest satisfied with either scholarly excuses or moral frowns. For the matter at issue is the character of the rules by which we reward human beings with fame or condemn them with infamy, the very status of morality. Machiavelli does not make it clear at first that this grave question is his subject. In the Dedicatory Letter he approaches Lorenzo de' Medici with hat in one hand and *The Prince* in the other. Since, he says, one must be a prince to know the nature of peoples and a man of the people to know the nature of princes, he seems to offer Lorenzo the knowledge of princes he does not have but needs. In accordance with this half-serious promise, Machiavelli speaks about the kinds of principalities in the first part of *The Prince* (Chapters 1–11) and, as we learn of the necessity of conquest, about the kinds of armies in the second part (Chapters 12–14). But at the same time (to make a long story short), we learn that the prince must or may lay his foundations on the people (Chapter 9) and that while his only object should be the art of war, he must in time of peace pay attention to moral qualities in such manner as to be able to use them in time of war (Chapter 14, end).

Thus are we prepared for Machiavelli's clarion call in Chapter 15, where he proclaims that he "departs from the orders of others" and says why. For moral qualities are qualities "held good" by the people; so, if the prince must conquer, and wants, like the Medici, to lay his foundation on the people, who are the keepers of morality, then a new morality consistent with the necessity of conquest must be found, and the prince has to be taught anew about the nature of peoples by Machiavelli. In departing from the orders of others, it appears more fitting to Machiavelli "to go directly to the effectual truth of the thing than to the imagination of it." Many have imagined republics and principalities, but one cannot "let go of what is done for what should be done," because a man who "makes a profession of good in all regards" comes to ruin among so many who are not good. The prince must learn to be able not to be good, and use this ability or not according to necessity.

This concise statement is most efficacious. It contains a fundamental assault on all morality and political science, both Christian and classical, as understood in Machiavelli's time. Morality had meant not only doing the right action, but also doing it for the right reason or for the love of God. Thus, to be good was thought to require "a profession of good" in which the motive for doing good was explained; otherwise, morality would go no deeper than outward conformity to law, or even to superior force, and could not be distinguished from it. But professions of good could not accompany moral actions in isolation from each other; they would have to be elaborated so that moral actions would be consistent with each other and the life of a moral person would form a whole. Such elaboration requires an effort of imagination, since the consistency we see tells us only of the presence of outward conformity, and the elaboration extends over a society, because it is difficult to live a moral life by oneself; hence morality requires the construction of an imagined republic or principality, such as Plato's *Republic* or St. Augustine's *City of God.*

When Machiavelli denies that imagined republics and principalities "exist in truth," and declares that the truth in these or all matters is the effectual truth, he says that no moral rules exist, not made by men, which men must abide by. The rules or laws that exist are those made by governments or other powers acting under necessity, and they must be obeyed out of the same necessity. Whatever is necessary may be called just and reasonable, but justice is no more reasonable than what a person's prudence tells him he must acquire for himself, or must submit to, because men cannot afford justice in any sense that transcends their own preservation. Machiavelli did not attempt (as did Hobbes) to formulate a new definition of justice based on self-preservation. Instead, he showed what he meant by not including justice among the eleven pairs of moral qualities that he lists in Chapter 15. He does mention justice in Chapter 21 as a calculation of what a weaker party might expect from a prince whom it has supported in war, but even this little is contradicted by what Machiavelli says about keeping faith in Chapter 18 and about betraying one's old supporters in Chapter 20. He also brings up justice as something identical with necessity in Chapter 26. But, what is most striking, he never mentions—not in *The Prince,* or in any of his works—natural justice or natural law, the two conceptions of justice in the classical and medieval tradition that had been handed down to his time and that could be found in the writings on this subject of all his contemporaries. The grave issue raised by the dispute whether Machiavelli was truly "Machiavellian" is this: does justice exist by nature or by God, or is it the convenience of the prince (government)? "So let a prince win and maintain a state: the means will always be judged honorable, and will be praised by everyone" (Chapter 18). Reputation, then, is outward conformity to successful human force and has no reference to moral rules that the government might find inconvenient.

If there is no natural justice, perhaps Machiavelli can teach the prince how to rule in its absence—but with a view to the fact that men "profess" it. It does not follow of necessity that because no natural justice exists, princes can rule successfully without it. Governments might be as unsuccessful in making and keeping conquests as in living up to natural justice; indeed, the traditional proponents of natural justice, when less confident of their own cause, had pointed to the uncertainty of gain, to the happy inconstancy of fortune, as an argument against determined wickedness. But Machiavelli thinks it possible to "learn" to be able not to be good. For each of the difficulties of gaining and keeping, even and especially for the fickleness of fortune, he has a "remedy," to use his frequent expression. Since nature or God does not support human justice, men are in need of a remedy; and the remedy is the prince, especially the new prince. Why must the new prince be preferred?

In the heading to the first chapter of *The Prince* we see that the kinds of principalities are to be discussed together with the ways in which they are acquired, and then in the chapter itself we find more than this, that principalities are classified into kinds by the ways in which they are acquired. "Acquisition," an economic term, is Machiavelli's word for "conquest"; and acquisition determines the classifications of governments, not their ends or structures, as Plato and Aristotle had thought. How is acquisition related to the problem of justice?

Justice requires a modest complement of external goods, the equipment of virtue in Aristotle's phrase, to keep the wolf from the door and to provide for moral persons a certain decent distance from necessities in the face of which morality might falter or even fail. For how can one distribute justly without something to distribute? But, then, where is one to get this modest complement? The easy way is by inheritance. In Chapter 2, Machiavelli considers hereditary principalities, in which a person falls heir to everything he needs, especially the political power to protect what he has. The hereditary prince, the man who has everything, is called the "natural prince," as if to suggest that our grandest and most comprehensive inheritance is what we get from nature. But when the hereditary prince looks upon his inheritance—and when we, generalizing from his case, add up everything we inherit—is it adequate?

The difficulty with hereditary principalities is indicated at the end of Chapter 2, where Machiavelli admits that hereditary princes will have to change but claims that change will not be disruptive because it can be gradual and continuous. He compares each prince's own construction to building a house that is added on to a row of houses: you may not inherit all you need, but you inherit a firm support and an easy start in what you must acquire. But clearly a row of houses so built over generations presupposes that the first house was built without existing support and without an easy start. Inheritance presupposes an original acquisition made without a previous inheritance. And in the original acquisition, full attention to the niceties of justice may unfortunately not be possible. One may congratulate an American citizen for all the advantages to which he is born; but what of the nasty necessities that prepared this inheritance—the British expelled, Indians defrauded, blacks enslaved?

Machiavelli informs us in the third chapter, accordingly, that "truly it is a very natural and ordinary thing to desire to acquire." In the space of a few pages, "natural" has shifted in meaning from hereditary to acquisitive. Or can we be consoled by reference to Machiavelli's republicanism, not so prominent in *The Prince*, with the thought that acquisitiveness may be natural to princes but is not natural to republics? But in Chapter 3 Machiavelli praises the successful acquisitiveness of the "Romans," that is, the Roman republic, by comparison to the imprudence

of the king of France. At the time Machiavelli is referring to, the Romans were not weak and vulnerable as they were at their inception; they had grown powerful and were still expanding. Even when they had enough empire to provide an inheritance for their citizens, they went on acquiring. Was this reasonable? It was, because the haves of this world cannot quietly inherit what is coming to them; lest they be treated now as they once treated others, they must keep an eye on the have-nots. To keep a step ahead of the have-nots the haves must think and behave like have-nots. They certainly cannot afford justice to the have-nots, nor can they waste time or money on sympathy.

In the Dedicatory Letter Machiavelli presents himself to Lorenzo as a have-not, "from a low and mean state"; and one thing he lacks besides honorable employment, we learn, is a unified fatherland. Italy is weak and divided. Then should we say that acquisitiveness is justified for Italians of Machiavelli's time, including him? As we have noted, Machiavelli does not seem to accept this justification because, still in Chapter 3, he advises a French king how to correct the errors he had made in his invasion of Italy. Besides, was Machiavelli's fatherland Italy or was it Florence? In Chapter 15 he refers to "our language," meaning Tuscan, and in Chapter 20 to "our ancients," meaning Florentines. But does it matter whether Machiavelli was essentially an Italian or a Florentine patriot? Anyone's fatherland is defined by an original acquisition, a conquest, and hence is always subject to redefinition of the same kind. To be devoted to one's native country at the expense of foreigners is no more justified than to be devoted to one's city at the expense of fellow countrymen, or to one's family at the expense of fellow city-dwellers, or, to adapt a Machiavellian remark in Chapter 17, to one's patrimony at the expense of one's father. So to "unify" one's fatherland means to treat it as a conquered territory—conquered by a king or republic from within; and Machiavelli's advice to the French king on how to hold his conquests in Italy was also advice to Lorenzo on how to unify Italy. It appears that, in acquiring, the new prince acquires for himself.

What are the qualities of the new prince? What must he do? First, as we have seen, he should rise from private or unprivileged status; he should not have an inheritance, or if he has, he should not rely on it. He should owe nothing to anyone or anything, for having debts of gratitude would make him dependent on others, in the widest sense dependent on fortune. It might seem that the new prince depends at least on the character of the country he conquers, and Machiavelli says at the end of Chapter 4 that Alexander had no trouble in holding Asia because it had been accustomed to the government of one lord. But then in Chapter 5 he shows how this limitation can be overcome. A prince who conquers a city used to living in freedom need not respect its inherited liberties; he can and should destroy such cities or else rule them personally. Fortune supplies the prince with nothing more than opportunity, as when Moses found the people of Israel enslaved by the Egyptians, Romulus found himself exposed at birth, Cyrus found the Persians discontented with the empire of the Medes, and Theseus found the Athenians dispersed (Chapter 6). These famous founders had the virtue to recognize the opportunity that fortune offered to them—opportunity for them, harsh necessity to their peoples. Instead of dispersing the inhabitants of a free city (Chapter 5), the prince is lucky enough to find them dispersed (Chapter 6). This suggests that the prince could go so far as to make his own opportunity by creating a situation of necessity in which no one's inherited goods remain to him and everything is owed to you, the new prince. When a new prince comes to power, should he be grateful to those who helped him get power and rely on them? Indeed not. A new prince has "lukewarm defenders" in his friends and allies, because they expect benefits from him; as we have seen, it is much better to conciliate his former enemies who feared losing everything (compare Chapters 6 and 20).

Thus, the new prince has virtue that enables him to overcome his dependence on inheritance in the widest sense, including custom, nature, and fortune, and that shows him how to arrange it that others depend on him and his virtue (Chapters 9, 24). But if virtue is to do all this, it must have a new meaning. Instead of cooperating with nature or God, as in the various classical and Christian conceptions, virtue must be taught to be acquisitive on its own. Machiavelli teaches the new meaning of virtue by showing us both the new and the old meanings. In a famous passage on the successful criminal Agathocles in Chapter 8, he says "one cannot call it virtue to kill one's fellow citizens, betray one's friends, to be without faith, without mercy, without religion." Yet in the very next sentence Machiavelli proceeds to speak of "the virtue of Agathocles."

The prince, we have seen in Chapter 15, must "learn to be able not to be good, and to use this and not use it according to necessity." Machiavelli supplies this knowledge in Chapters 16 to 18. First, with superb calm, he delivers home-truths concerning the moral virtue of liberality. It is no use being liberal (or generous) unless it is noticed, so that you are "held liberal" or get a name for liberality. But a prince cannot be held liberal by being liberal, because he would have to be liberal to a few by burdening the many with taxes; the many would be offended, the prince would have to retrench, and he would soon get a name for stinginess. The right way to get a reputation for liberality is to begin by not caring about having a reputation for stinginess. When the people see that the prince gets the job done without burdening them, they will in time consider him liberal to them and stingy only to the few to whom he gives nothing. In the event, "liberality" comes to mean taking little rather than giving much.

As regards cruelty and mercy, in Chapter 8 Machiavelli made a distinction between cruelties well used and badly used; well-used cruelties are done once, for self-defense, and not continued but turned to the benefit of one's subjects, and badly used ones continue and increase. In Chapter 17, however, he does not mention this distinction but rather speaks only of using mercy badly. Mercy is badly used when, like the Florentine people in a certain instance, one seeks to avoid a reputation for cruelty and thus allows disorders to continue which might be stopped with a very few examples of cruelty. Disorders harm everybody; executions harm only the few or the one who is executed. As the prince may gain a name for liberality by taking little, so he may be held merciful by not being cruel too often.

Machiavelli's new prince arranges the obligation of his subjects to himself in a manner rather like that of the Christian God, in the eye of whom all are guilty by original sin; hence God's mercy appears less as the granting of benefits than as the remission of punishment. With this thought in mind, the reader will not be surprised that Machiavelli goes on to discuss whether it is better for the prince to be loved or feared. It would be best to be both loved and feared, but, when necessity forces a choice, it is better to be feared, because men love at their convenience but they fear at the convenience of the prince. Friends may fail you, but the dread of punishment will never forsake you. If the prince avoids making himself hated, which he can do by abstaining from the property of others, "because men forget the death of a father more quickly than the loss of a patrimony," he will again have subjects obligated to him for what he does not do to them rather than for benefits he provides.

It is laudable for a prince to keep faith, Machiavelli says in Chapter 18, but princes who have done great things have done them by deceit and betrayal. The prince must learn how to use the beast in man, or rather the beasts; for man is an animal who can be many animals, and he must know how to be a fox as well as a lion. Men will not keep faith with you; how can you keep it with them? Politics, Machiavelli seems to say, as much as consists in breaking promises, for circumstances change and new necessities arise that make it impossible to hold to one's word. The only question is, can one get away with breaking one's promises? Machiavelli's answer is a confident yes. He broadens the discussion, speaking of five moral qualities, especially religion; he says that men judge by appearances and that when one judges by appearances, "one looks to the end." The end is the outcome or the effect, and if a prince wins and maintains a state, the means will always be judged honorable. Since

Machiavelli has just emphasized the prince's need to appear religious, we may compare the people's attitude toward a successful prince with their belief in divine providence. As people assume that the outcome of events in the world is determined by God's providence, so they conclude that the means chosen by God cannot have been unworthy. Machiavelli's thought here is both a subtle attack on the notion of divine providence and a subtle appreciation of it, insofar as the prince can appropriate it to his own use.

It is not easy to state exactly what virtue is, according to Machiavelli. Clearly he does not leave virtue as it was in the classical or Christian tradition, nor does he imitate any other writer of his time. Virtue in his new meaning seems to be a prudent or well-taught combination of vice and virtue in the old meaning. Virtue for him is not a mean between two extremes of vice, as is moral virtue for Aristotle. As we have seen, in Chapter 15 eleven virtues (the same number as Aristotle's, though not all of them the same virtues) are paired with eleven vices. From this we might conclude that virtue does not shine of itself, as when it is done for its own sake. Rather, virtue is as it takes effect, its truth is its effectual truth; and it is effectual only when it is seen in contrast to its opposite. Liberality, mercy, and love are impressive only when one expects stinginess (or rapacity), cruelty, and fear. This contrast makes virtue apparent and enables the prince to gain a reputation for virtue. If this is so, then the new meaning Machiavelli gives to virtue, a meaning which makes use of vice, must not entirely replace but somehow continue to coexist with the old meaning, according to which virtue is shocked by vice.

A third quality of the new prince is that he must make his own foundations. Although to be acquisitive means to be acquisitive for oneself, the prince cannot do everything with his own hands: he needs help from others. But in seeking help he must take account of the "two diverse humors" to be found in every city—the people, who desire not to be commanded or oppressed by the great, and the great, who desire to command and oppress the people (Chapter 9). Of these two humors, the prince should choose the people. The people are easier to satisfy, too inert to move against him, and too numerous to kill, whereas the great regard themselves as his equals, are ready and able to conspire against him, and are replaceable.

The prince, then, should ally with the people against the aristocracy; but how should he get their support? Machiavelli gives an example in the conduct of Cesare Borgia, whom he praises for the foundations he laid (Chapter 7). When Cesare had conquered the province of Romagna, he installed "Remirro de Orco" (actually a Spaniard, Don Remiro de Lorqua) to carry out a purge of the unruly lords there. Then, because Cesare thought Remirro's authority might be excessive, and his exercise of it might become hateful—in short, because Remirro had served his purpose—he purged the purger and one day had Remirro displayed in the piazza at Cesena in two pieces. This spectacle left the people "at the same time satisfied and stupefied"; and Cesare set up a more constitutional government in Romagna. The lesson: constitutional government is possible but only after an unconstitutional beginning.

In Chapter 9 Machiavelli discusses the "civil principality," which is gained through the favor of the people, and gives as example Nabis, "prince" of the Spartans, whom he calls a tyrant in the *Discourses on Livy* because of the crimes Nabis committed against his rivals. In Chapter 8 Machiavelli considers the principality that is attained through crimes, and cites Agathocles and Oliverotto, both of whom were very popular despite their crimes. As one ponders these two chapters, it becomes more and more difficult to find a difference between gaining a principality through crimes and through the favor of the people. Surely Cesare Borgia, Agathocles, and Nabis seemed to have followed the same policy of pleasing the people by cutting up the great. Finally, in Chapter 19, Machiavelli reveals that the prince need not have the support of the people after all. Even if he is hated by the people (since in fact he cannot fail to be hated by someone), he can, like the Roman emperor Severus, make his foundation with his soldiers (see also Chapter 20). Severus had such virtue, Machiavelli says, with an unobstrusive com-

parison to Cesare Borgia in Chapter 7, that he "stupefied" the people and "satisfied" the soldiers.

Fourth, the new prince has his own arms, and does not rely on mercenary or auxiliary armies. Machiavelli omits a discussion of the laws a prince should establish, in contrast to the tradition of political science, because, he says, "there cannot be good laws where there are not good arms, and where there are good arms there must be good laws" (Chapter 12). He speaks of the prince's arms in Chapters 12 to 14, and in Chapter 14 he proclaims that the prince should have no other object or thought but the art of war. He must be armed, since it is quite unreasonable for one who is armed to obey one who is disarmed. With this short remark Machiavelli seems to dismiss the fundamental principle of classical political science, the rule of the wise, not to mention the Christian promise that the meek shall inherit the earth.

Machiavelli does not mean that those with the most bodily force always win, for he broadens the art of war to include the acquisition as well as the use of arms. A prince who has no army but has the art of war will prevail over one with an army but without the art. Thus, to be armed means to know the art of war, to exercise it in time of peace, and to have read histories about great captains of the past. In this regard Machiavelli mentions Xenophon's "Life of Cyrus," as he calls it (actually "The Education of Cyrus"), the first and best work in the literature of "mirrors of princes" to which *The Prince* belongs. But he calls it a history, not a mirror of princes, and says that it inspired the Roman general Scipio, whom he criticizes in Chapter 17 for excessive mercy. Not books of imaginary republics and principalities, or treatises on law, but histories of war, are recommended reading for the prince.

Last, the new prince with his own arms is his own master. The deeper meaning of Machiavelli's slogan, "one's own arms," is religious, or rather, antireligious. If man is obligated to God as his creature, then man's own necessities are subordinate or even irrelevant to his most pressing duties. It would not matter if he could not afford justice: God commands it! Thus Machiavelli must look at the new prince who is also a prophet, above all at Moses. Moses was a "mere executor of things that had been ordered by God" (Chapter 6); hence he should be admired for the grace that made him worthy of speaking with God. Or should it be said, as Machiavelli says in Chapter 26, that Moses had "virtue," the virtue that makes a prince dependent on no one but himself? In Chapter 13 Machiavelli retells the biblical story of David and Goliath to illustrate the necessity of one's own arms. When Saul offered his arms to David, David refused them, saying, according to Machiavelli, that with them he could not give a good account of himself, and according to the Bible, that the Lord "will deliver me out of the hand of this Philistine." Machiavelli also gives David a knife to go with his sling, the knife which according to the Bible he took from the fallen Goliath and used to cut off his head.

Must the new prince—the truly new prince—then be his own prophet and make a new religion so as to be his own master? The great power of religion can be seen in what Moses and David founded, and in what Savonarola nearly accomplished in Machiavelli's own time and city. The unarmed prince whom he disparages in Chapter 6 actually disposes of formidable weapons necessary to the art of war. The unarmed prophet becomes armed if he uses religion for his own purposes rather than God's; and because the prince cannot acquire glory for himself without bringing order to his principality, using religion for himself is using it to answer human necessities generally.

The last three chapters of *The Prince* take up the question of how far man can make his own world. What are the limits set on Machiavelli's political science (or the "art of war") by fortune? At the end of Chapter 24 he blames "these princes of ours" who accuse fortune for their troubles and not their own indolence. In quiet times they do not take account of the storm to come, but they should—they can. They believe that the people will be disgusted by the arrogance of the foreign conquerors and will call them back. But "one should never fall in the belief you can find someone to pick you up." Whether successful or not, such a defense is base, because it does not depend on you and your virtue.

With this high promise of human capability, Machiavelli introduces his famous Chapter 25 on fortune. He begins it by asking how much of the world is governed by fortune and God, and how much by man. He then supposes that half is governed by fortune (forgetting God) and half by man, and he compares fortune to a violent river that can be contained with dikes and dams. Turning to particular men, he shows that the difficulty in containing fortune lies in the inability of one who is impetuous to succeed in quiet times or of one who is cautious to succeed in stormy times. Men, with their fixed natures and habits, do not vary as the times vary, and so they fall under the control of the times, of fortune. Men's fixed natures are the special problem, Machiavelli indicates; so the problem of overcoming the influence of fortune reduces to the problem of overcoming the fixity of different human natures. Having a fixed nature is what makes one liable to changes of fortune. Pope Julius II succeeded because the times were in accord with his impetuous nature; if he had lived longer, he would have come to grief. Machiavelli blames him for his inflexibility, and so implies that neither he nor the rest of us need respect the natures or natural inclinations we have been given.

What is the new meaning of virtue that Machiavelli has developed but flexibility according to the times or situation? Yet, though one should learn to be both impetuous and cautious (these stand for all the other contrary qualities), on the whole one should be impetuous. Fortune is a woman who "lets herself be won more by the impetuous than by those who proceed coldly"; hence she is a friend of the young. He makes the politics of the new prince appear in the image of rape; impetuous himself, Machiavelli forces us to see the question he has raised about the status of morality. Whether he says what he appears to say about the status of women may be doubted, however. The young men who master Lady Fortune come with audacity and leave exhausted, but she remains ageless, waiting for the next ones. One might go so far as to wonder who is raping whom, cautiously as it were, and whether Machiavelli, who has personified fortune, can impersonate her in the world of modern politics he attempted to create.

Reprinted from: Harvey C. Mansfield, Jr., "Introduction" to *The Prince*, by Niccolò Machiavelli, pp. vii–xxiv. Copyright © 1985. Reprinted by permission of The University of Chicago Press. ✦

4

Public Versus Private Claims

Machiavellianism from Another Perspective

John Leonard

Machiavellianism is frequently conceived of as a derivative of the term Machiavellian. The Oxford English Dictionary, beginning with its definition of Machiavellian, reads:

> Of, pertaining to, or characteristic of Machiavelli, or his alleged principles; following the methods recommended by Machiavelli in preferring expediency to morality; practicing duplicity in statecraft or in general conduct; an instance of this.

This derivation of Machiavellianism from Machiavellian has the effect of shifting attention from the foundations of Machiavelli's theory, which are reduced to the principle that expediency should always be placed ahead of morality, and focusing it on various methods and practices consistent with this principle.

The aim of this article is to present a broader interpretation of Machiavelli's theoretical concerns, one which seeks neither to support nor refute the common understanding of Machiavellianism but to go beyond it. To this end the problem of Machiavelli's attitude toward virtue is examined in the context of crucial terms in his conceptual vocabulary, and this examination is used in turn to shed light on other aspects of Machiavelli's thought.

1. Why *Virtù* Is Never Virtue

The first task in assessing the place of virtue in Machiavelli's political thought is to see if we can locate something that resembles virtue in his writings. The first word to consider, both because Machiavelli uses it frequently and because in appearance it resembles virtue, is *virtù*. *Virtù* is, in fact, a standard equivalent of the English word virtue in contemporary Italian, and because it can be translated as virtue without apparent damage in some of the places Machiavelli uses it, *virtù* is often rendered as virtue in English translations of Machiavelli. This way of finding virtue in Machiavelli's writings is a false trail, but at the same time a promising one.

Virtue involves adherence to some set of moral principles. *Virtù* as Machiavelli uses the term is closer to the Latin *virtus* in its connotation of manly valor and signifies an excellence that manifests itself most clearly in military and political affairs, perhaps because it is associated most prominently with the capacity to act boldly at critical moments. Evidently *virtù* is not the same thing as virtue. A translator sensitive to the diverse contexts in which Machiavelli uses *virtù*, Allan Gilbert, recognizes that there is a problem with translating *virtù* as virtue when he translates *virtù* as ability in contexts in which virtue, with its moral connotations, is obviously out of place, such as Machiavelli's reference in Chapter 17 of *The Prince* to Hannibal's "inhuman cruelty . . . together with his infinite *virtù*." But this method of sometimes translating *virtù* as virtue and sometimes as something else according to context is more misleading than the clumsiness involved in consistently translating *virtù* as virtue, for such clumsiness at least reveals the incompatibility of the terms despite contexts in which they seem compatible at first sight.[1]

Chapter 8 of *The Prince* provides an interesting example of a context in which *virtù* at first sight appears equivalent to virtue. Machiavelli writes,

> Neither can one call it *virtù* to kill one's citizens, to betray one's friends, to be faithless, without pity, without religion; by these means rule may be acquired, but not glory.

Virtue seems a perfectly acceptable substitute for *virtù* in this passage because one certainly cannot call it virtue to kill one's citizens, betray one's friends, etc. But a moment's reflection leads to the realization that this is too obvious to require statement. Either Machiavelli is making an obvious point about what is inconsistent with morality, a proceeding which in the context of *The Prince* as a whole would be distinctly anomalous, or he is making a less obvious but important point about what is inconsistent with *virtù*. It will be necessary to return to this point later. Here it is enough to note that *virtù* turns out not to be equivalent to virtue even in contexts that at first glance suggest such equivalence.

The Prince contains no word equivalent to virtue but it does include a list of moral qualities and a phrase that indicates Machiavelli's view of what it would mean to live in accordance with these qualities. The list appears in Chapter 18 of *The Prince*, in which Machiavelli says a prince should seem to be compassionate, faithful, humane, sincere, and religious. The phrase, which occurs in Chapter 15, is "to make a profession of goodness in all things."[2] To make such a profession would presumably mean to live a life dedicated to the exemplification of the moral qualities listed in Chapter 18. Thus *The Prince* reveals Machiavelli's awareness of what would constitute a high standard of virtue. But Machiavelli does not want the prince to comply with this standard, only to seem to do so. His reasoning on this point helps clarify the incompatibility of virtue and *virtù*.

It is in Chapter 15 of *The Prince* that Machiavelli states his intention of writing for "he who understands" and contrasts this method with that of those who imagine states that have "never been seen nor known to exist in reality." He then proceeds to justify his choice on the grounds that there is such a difference between how men live and how they ought to live that he who departs from what is done for the sake of what should be done will learn his ruin rather than his preservation. The phrase "to make a profession of goodness in all things" occurs in this connection; he who wants to make a profession of goodness in all things, says Machiavelli, must bring about his ruin among the many who are not good.

Machiavelli deduces from this the proposition that a prince must learn how not to be good. He repeats this principle in Chapter 18, in which he advises that the prince should not part from the good without need, but should be able to enter into the bad when to do so is necessary for the maintenance of his position. The words good and bad here take on a moral emphasis deriving from the preceding list of moral qualities, and Machiavelli makes clear what he means by entering into the bad when, referring to these qualities, he says the prince must be able to act, "contrary to faith, contrary to charity, contrary to humanity, contrary to religion." This ability, evidently contrary to virtue, is consistent with *virtù*, as Machiavelli indicates in his treatment of Hannibal's "inhuman cruelty." This cruelty, says Machiavelli, was necessary to maintain order among Hannibal's mixed force of mercenary troops and thus was an essential aspect of Hannibal's excellence as a general, and for this reason Machiavelli includes it among Hannibal's "infinite *virtù*."

That such a quality could be included within *virtù* reveals its difference from virtue. It also raises the question whether *virtù* is defined solely in terms of success in the pursuit of military or political power.

Machiavelli's discussion of what is not *virtù* assumes special significance in this connection. It has been noted that in Chapter 8 of *The Prince* Machiavelli either makes an implausible argument for what is not virtue or some sort of argument for what is not *virtù*. Machiavelli says that it cannot be called *virtù* to kill one's citizens, betray one's friends, and be without honor, piety, and religion because although such methods can lead to rule they cannot lead to the acquisition of glory. If virtue is substituted for *virtù* Machiavelli is doing something very curious, for instead of making the obvious point that such acts and qualities cannot be called virtue because they are directly opposed to it, he is saying that they cannot be called virtue because they cannot lead to glory. Using glory to define virtue in this context makes little sense. But if we read *virtù* as *virtù* the attempt to set a boundary on it through the use of glory makes considerable sense. By limiting the ascription of *virtù* to actions that are consistent with the acquisition of glory Machiavelli can deny *virtù* to actions that involve "entering into the bad" out of choice rather than necessity. At the same time, and unlike virtue, glory is compatible with entering into the bad out of necessity. Thus glory is useful to Machiavelli because it is compatible with the necessities of public life while providing a standard for rejecting its worst excesses.

By employing glory as a critical standard Machiavelli reveals his awareness of the problem posed for political action by the incompatibility of virtue and *virtù*. At its core Machiavellian *virtù* represents pure efficacy unconstrained by any imperative except that of attaining one's end. For *virtù* to play a constructive role in politics such efficacy must be constrained to serve the needs of the public sphere. This is the basis of Machiavelli's appeal to glory. The effectiveness of this appeal will be considered later. At this point it is time to enter the world of the *Discourses* and consider another incompatibility, that of virtue and *bontà*.

2. Why *Bontà* Is Never Virtue

Machiavelli's *Discourses* differs from *The Prince* alike in its subject matter and its method. *The Prince* is concerned with the exigencies of princely government in the harsh political climate of Machiavelli's Italy. Thus, for example, Machiavelli's reference to states that have never been known to exist is designed to throw into relief the necessities imposed by the political realities of his day. This contrast serves Machiavelli's purposes in *The Prince*, but it also reflects *The Prince* as a whole in leaving no room between the harshness of the reality it describes and the fatuity of utopian thinking for consideration of what a well-ordered state that could exist in reality would look like.

In the *Discourses* Machiavelli opens the way to such consideration by taking as his model a state that actually did exist in an earlier period. This state is the Roman republic as Livy depicts it, and Machiavelli's method is to present the *Discourses* as a commentary on the first ten books of Livy's *History of Rome*. Because Machiavelli represents the Roman republic as a model state in the *Discourses* the role of virtue in public life should reveal itself in this work if it has a place anywhere in Machiavelli's thought.

A careful examination of Machiavelli's comments in the *Discourses* concerning the role of the popular element in Roman society reveals an emphasis on the concept of *bontà*. *Bontà* is worthy of consideration on several grounds. First, it represents Machiavelli's nearest approach to a workable concept of virtue. Second, this little discussed concept is of great importance to Machiavelli, being as important to his well-ordered state as *virtù*.

Chapter 55, Book 1 of the *Discourses* opens with an example of the Roman people's *bontà*. A similar example occurs in Chapter 13 of Book 1, though the word itself does not appear in Chapter 13.[3] Both examples concern oaths that are interpreted by the nobility in a way that threatens the people with the loss of something they desire. In both cases the people have a plausible excuse for evading the obligation created by the oath, and it is their decision not to break the oath outright that makes it possible to come to a workable compromise with the nobility.

In Chapter 13 Machiavelli recounts Livy's story of a feud between the nobles and the people that was interrupted by a slave revolt that succeeded in occupying the Capitol. The nobles called on the people to help put down the revolt whereas the Tribunes argued that no aid should be rendered until the nobles agreed to a proposed law for a committee to devise ways of limiting the power of the Consuls. The people decided to aid in the recapture of the Capitol and swore an oath to obey the Consul's orders. The attack was a success but the Consul was killed. His replacement, seeking to keep the people from renewing their consideration of the disputed law, ordered them out of the city to do battle against a neighboring state. The Tribunes protested that because the oath was made to the previous Consul it was no longer binding, but because the oath did not specify this the people were afraid of breaking it. Thus the Tribunes were forced to compromise with the nobility by promising to drop consideration of the law for a year in exchange for the Consul's promise not to order the people to war during that period.

In Chapter 55 Machiavelli relates how trouble flared up between the people and the nobles when the commander of a victorious Roman army decided to offer a tenth of the spoils of combat to Apollo. The Senate accordingly directed each member of the army to turn over a tenth of his spoils. The common soldiers protested, understandably enough, because they had not participated in the vow and the spoils were their only remuneration for the hardships and dangers of military service. But instead of evading the order individually by cheating, as they could easily have done, and thus invalidating the vow, they chose to protest openly and in a body. This open protest led to a compromise in which the people were released from their obligation and the vow was fulfilled by other means.

The *bontà* of the people in these examples is linked with their fear of breaking oaths. *Bontà* is normally translated as goodness, and inasmuch as the goodness in these examples seems to derive from a form of piety *bontà* appears to have something in common with Christian virtue. But the role of Roman religion with respect to *bontà* is very different from, though just as important as, the role of Christianity with respect to Christian virtue. For although Christianity reinforces admonitions to virtue with warnings of the punishments in store for sinners, it also establishes the principle that true virtue consists in obeying moral precepts out of an inner conviction of their rightness rather than out of fear. Roman religion reinforces *bontà* through fear of the gods, but its purpose in so doing is not to remind men of the wages of sin. The goal of Roman religion is rather to invest the concept of obedience to public authority with a sense of religious awe. It is this use of religious awe or piety to which Machiavelli refers in both his examples of *bontà*. *Bontà* does not lead to the creation of a moral sense in the individual, but it

does provide a peaceful means of controlling an armed populace.

That Machiavelli is concerned with *bontà* as an aid in maintaining the public sphere is confirmed by his description of the cause and effect of the loss of religious belief among a people. In Chapter 12, Book 1 of the *Discourses* he says that when religion begins to speak with the voice of the rich and powerful, and this is discovered by the people, "men become unbelievers and disposed to upset every good order." In other words, the loss of religious belief on the part of the people, caused by its shortsighted manipulation by the wealthy and powerful (a manipulation that proves they do not share this belief) leads to the loss of the *bontà* that helps control threats to public order.

Bontà is the closest Machiavelli comes to a workable concept of virtue, but it is a substitute for virtue rather than virtue by another name. In *The Prince* Machiavelli's rejection of virtue had to do with the practical requirements of survival in a disordered political environment. The reason virtue is also absent in Machiavelli's model state and the consequences of its absence remain to be considered.

Extraordinary Action and Its Enemy

Machiavelli's analysis of government begins with the institutional structure of political power. A well-ordered state, be it republic or princedom, is in the first instance one in which the structure of political power is well designed to meet the needs of that particular state. But he also shows great sensitivity to the fact that the usefulness of political institutions depends on their authority in the eyes of the citizenry and that a diminution of this authority can lessen the capacity of those institutions to meet the needs of the state.

Machiavelli's discussion of the Roman republic as a model state reveals two of his fundamental political premises. One is that a state that provides an institutional channel for popular participation in public affairs is potentially stronger than a state that makes no such provision. The other is that widespread participation in public affairs requires the highest possible esteem for public authority among all classes of citizens. Any lessening of this esteem signifies the onset of corruption, which manifests itself in inattention to, or self-serving uses of, the laws and religion. The prevention of such corruption requires sanctions against the misuse of the qualities associated with *virtù* as well as the reinforcement of the *bontà*, the almost religious awe with which public authority and its representatives were regarded at the time of the state's founding.

The importance of preventing corruption and various methods of combating it make up the subject matter of Chapter 1, Book 3 of the *Discourses*. The eradication of corruption is linked with a symbolic refounding of a state or religion through the revitalization of its orders. Machiavelli describes three ways by which such a refounding can occur. One is the appearance of danger in the form of a foreign threat so great that it seems capable of destroying the state. Such a threat may serve as a sort of shock therapy that brings the leaders and citizens back to the observance of the principles on which the state was founded. This method is clearly a dangerous one. A state content to rely on extrinsic accident to combat corruption would not be likely to have a long history.

Machiavelli next turns to a pair of methods that he lists under the category of intrinsic prudence. The first of these methods is legislative. The second is that of personal actions that set a good example for the citizens. Either the *virtù* of a new order created by legislation or the *virtù* exhibited by a citizen at a critical juncture can bring a state back to health. But of these two forms of *virtù* the one embodied in legislation suffers from the defect that it does not inspire men to obedience in itself. Thus Machiavelli concludes his discussion of rejuvenation by means of new orders with the comment: "Those orders need to be brought to life by the *virtù* of a citizen, who boldly agrees to execute them against the power of those who transgress them."

Machiavelli expands on this statement by providing a list of the kind of actions he has in mind. These actions are all taken from Roman history, and most of them are execu-tions. The list begins with the execution of Brutus's sons and continues with the execution of the Ten Citizens, Spurius Melius, Manlius Capitolinus and the son of Manlius Torquatus. It concludes with several prosecutions that did not result in executions. For Machiavelli the importance of all these actions resides in the fact that, "because they were extreme and noteworthy, whenever one of them occurred it made men retire to their place."

The connection between the extreme and noteworthy quality of these actions and their exemplary effect is revealed in Chapter 3, Book 1 of the *Discourses*. In this chapter Machiavelli notes that Brutus not only voted to condemn his sons to death for treason but actually attended their execution. He refers to this conduct as an example rare in all the records of historical events and claims that the severity exhibited by Brutus on this occasion was not merely useful but necessary to the maintenance of Roman liberty. What makes Brutus's action so extraordinary is the emphatic manner in which he resolved the conflict between the private affection of a father for his sons and the public duty of protecting the orders of the state. By not only condemning his sons to death but witnessing their execution Brutus made a public statement of the citizen's primary duty to maintain the state, a statement that renewed both the respect of the citizens for the state's laws and orders and their fear of transgressing those laws and orders.

A second look at the extraordinary actions listed in Chapter 3, Book 1 of the *Discourses* reveals that the offenses involved are ones that in every case pose threats to the authority of the public sphere. In every case this threat is also enhanced by the existence of a private bond between the transgressors and some or all of their judges that might conduce to leniency. It is in these circumstances that harsh punishments take on the character of extreme and noteworthy actions. This is so because in such circumstances these actions function, to borrow a phrase, by using punishment to make a memory.[4] Extraordinary actions are thus of particular importance in cases in which some obvious threat to public authority conceals the less evident threat of a conflict between personal feelings of affection or obligation and the good of the state.[5] That it is this latter threat to which Machiavelli is particularly sensitive is underscored by his treatment of two actions in which harsh punishment is thwarted by private pleadings.

One of Machiavelli's examples in Chapter 1, Book 3 of the *Discourses* is the prosecution of Papirius Cursor's master of cavalry. This prosecution was extreme and noteworthy because Papirius asked that his master of cavalry be condemned to death for having given battle contrary to orders even though the latter had been victorious. At the end of Chapter 31, Book 1 of the *Discourses* Machiavelli notes that the father of Papirius's master of cavalry argued against this punishment on the grounds that the Romans did not treat even their defeated commanders in such a fashion. But although earlier in the chapter Machiavelli approves the Roman practice of not punishing their generals for mistakes made in the course of military operations it would be a mistake to construe this as indicating support for the father's plea. For in Chapter 36, Book 3 of the *Discourses* he quotes with approval Livy's account of Papirius's speech in favor of the death penalty. The point of this speech is that an army cannot maintain good order unless discipline is strictly enforced. From this perspective the intervention of his father in the prosecution of the master of cavalry was clearly contrary to the interests of the state.

Another instance of a father interceding for his son is recounted in Chapter 22, Book 1 of the *Discourses*. Horatius, the sole survivor of a combat between three brothers from Rome and three brothers from the neighboring state of Alba, returned home in triumph, but shortly afterward killed his sister when he heard her lament the death of one of the Alban brothers, to whom she had been married. Horatius was put on trial for his life and was acquitted. According to Machiavelli this acquittal owed more to his father's prayers for the life of his last son than Horatius's recent services to the state. Two chapters later Machiavelli returns to this topic and states that although, superficially considered, it might have seemed an act of ingratitude had

the Roman people condemned Horatius to death after he had saved Rome, they were actually to blame for having acquitted him. Machiavelli's reasoning is that meritorious actions should never be allowed to mitigate punishment for crimes because examples of such mitigation might encourage men to whom the state owed a debt of gratitude to think they could plot against it with impunity.

Machiavelli's fears that private ties will be used to undermine the state center on leaders and potential leaders, for it is when men of prominence and ability seek the satisfaction of private ends at the expense of the state's laws and orders that the public sphere is most gravely threatened. It is with respect to such threats that the absence of virtue from Machiavelli's theory of politics is revealed as a major problem for what he seeks to accomplish.

Bontà, based as it is on religious credulity, is of considerable importance in controlling the populace but has much less bearing on the control of leaders. Yet the maintenance of *bontà* depends on a state's leaders, for when they become corrupt, religious disillusionment is sure to follow. Thus Machiavelli's fundamental problem is how to keep the most prominent and able members of the state on the path of *virtù* as he defines it: that is, as consistent with glory and, consequently, complementing the needs of the state. This problem is compounded by the ineffectiveness of the image of glory to keep men to the desired standard of conduct. In Chapter 10, Book 1 of the *Discourses* Machiavelli extols both the public and private advantages of actions that strengthen states and religions, including the advantage of a glorious reputation, and emphasizes the disadvantages of actions that harm public institutions. But though he says that given a choice between praiseworthy and blameworthy actions no one would mistake one for the other, he goes on to say that despite this, in practice most men, "deceived by a false good and a false glory," end up in the ranks of those who deserve more blame than praise.

The ineffectiveness of representations of glory to prevail over the urgings of private desire in any but a few cases explains

Machiavelli's necessary reliance on extraordinary action. Extraordinary action must fill the gap left by the absence of virtue because the majority of men are incapable of internalizing not only virtue but any code of conduct that requires them to define their own good in terms of a wider good. Thus Machiavelli feels he must rely on a purely external, public form of action that can cow the temptation to break laws and overthrow orders, but which has no roots in the private sphere and no connection with private values. Rather, extraordinary action is a response to a vision of private ties as posing a potential threat to public life. It is important to inquire why this vision should dominate Machiavelli's thinking even in the consideration of his model state. . . .

Conclusion

Machiavellianism is normally understood as the doctrine that no principle or moral scruple should be regarded as binding if it stands in the way of the acquisition or maintenance of political power. On examination, this interpretation stands revealed as a mixture of truth and inaccuracy.

The focus of Machiavelli's political thought is the good of the public sphere. He considers the pursuit of virtue to be incompatible with this good, yet his concern for public life and its fragility makes him highly critical of the means by which power is acquired and maintained. Thus in both *The Prince* and the *Discourses* Machiavelli judges the means by which power is acquired in terms of its effect on the maintenance of the public sphere over time. It is for the purpose of making this connection that Machiavelli attempts to link *virtù* and glory,[6] and the importance he attaches to maintaining *bontà* is likewise related to the needs of the public sphere.

What is troubling in Machiavelli's thought is not an uncritical admiration of power but his view that any conflict between the public and private spheres of life should be resolved in favor of the former. For Machiavelli there seems to be no possibility of mediation between these spheres. The threat posed to the public sphere by private claims and impulses is viewed as insidious, omnipresent, and, insofar as it has its roots in the family, ineradicable.[7]

The consequences of this viewpoint are twofold. First, not only the founding of the public sphere but its continuation must be made dependent on religious credulity and exemplary punishments in the form of extraordinary acts. Second, because the public sphere is represented as the only valid locus of self-assertion, the legitimate expression of private feelings of aggression and ambition is confined to this sphere. This channeling process, although it creates a tremendous dynamism in the public sphere, must also create an agonistic political life that poses a constant threat to the laws and orders established to contain it and give it expression, extraordinary acts notwithstanding.

The absence of virtue in Machiavelli's political thought is not the result of shallow and unprincipled cynicism but of a deeply rooted pessimism concerning the ability of most men to internalize a code of conduct that clashes with immediate self-interest combined with an exaltation of the public sphere as an arena of conflict in which the practice of Christian virtue would amount to self-martyrdom. A theory of politics based on such views is not without problems, but as portrayed by Machiavelli it offers insights and opportunities for thought that are lost to view when Machiavellianism is confused with a version of his thought that is little more than a stalking-horse for moral censure.

Notes

1. For a translation of *The Prince* in which *virtù* is rendered as virtue even in the unlikely context of Machiavelli's reference to Hannibal's cruelty, see the Luigi Ricci/E.R.P. Vincent translation of *The Prince* in the Modern Library College Editions' *The Prince and the Discourses* (Random House, 1950). Gilbert's translation is included in Volume 1 of *Machiavelli: The Chief Works and Others*, trs. Allan Gilbert (Duke University Press, 1965).

2. To "make a profession" of a quality can either mean to avow it in one's actions or to feign it. Here the term must be understood in the former sense and without any implication of

pretence. Otherwise Machiavelli's whole critique of this conduct and his argument in favor of making a false profession of goodness in Chapter 18 are unintelligible. Worth noting is the resemblance of making a profession of goodness in this context to making a profession of religious faith at the risk of martyrdom.

3. As explained below, the importance of religion and honesty in both chapters is the usefulness of these qualities in maintaining respect for public authority and the laws that uphold the public sphere and it is this respect that Machiavelli characterizes as *bontà* in Chapter 55. It is for this reason that he clinches the argument in Chapter 13 concerning the importance of religion with a quotation from Livy in which the latter connects the decline of religion with the interpretation of laws and oaths on the basis of self-interest.

4. The formulation is Nietzsche's and occurs in Section 13 of the second essay of *On the Genealogy of Morals.* The whole of this section and the last paragraph of Section 15 provide insights that can be fruitfully applied to Machiavelli's discussion of the function of extraordinary acts in Chapter 1, Book 3 of the *Discourses.*

5. This same potential conflict and the importance of dealing with it decisively also appear in Machiavelli's accounts of extraordinary acts in his own times. See, for example, his account of Cesare Borgia's execution of a trusted subordinate in Chapter 7 of *The Prince* (an action Machiavelli says is "worthy of notice and imitation by others") and that of Caterina Sforza's renunciation of her children in Chapter 6, Book 3 of the *Discourses.*

6. In Chapters 6 through 9 of *The Prince* Machiavelli discusses different ways of acquiring power in terms of their relation to its maintenance. A ruler who cannot maintain himself once he takes power is of no use to his state. At the same time, a ruler who destroys the public sphere to gain power when he could have achieved power without doing so is subject to censure, as Machiavelli implies in Chapter 8 of *The Prince* and states openly in Chapter 10, Book 1 of the *Discourses,* in which he defines glory and infamy in terms of what is beneficial and harmful to the establishment and maintenance of states and religions. Machiavelli's interest in power has to do not with the maintenance of the ruler per se but with the protection of the public sphere, though admittedly his conflation of ruler and public sphere in the concept of the state (*lo stato*) as he employs it in *The Prince* confuses the issue in that work.

7. Francesco Guicciardini, in his fragmentary but interesting commentary on Machiavelli's *Discourses,* reacts with displeasure to two aspects of the work. One is Machiavelli's foreshortening of the historical distance between the early Rome of Livy's description and the Italians of the early 16th century. The other is what Guicciardini perceives to be Machiavelli's excessive pleasure in the concept of extraordinary action. The first source of displeasure reveals Guicciardini's early sensitivity to the problem of anachronism. The second may spring from an equal sensitivity to the fact that Machiavelli's advocacy of extraordinary action to maintain a sharp division between the public and private spheres is fundamentally antagonistic to Guicciardini's aristocratic conception of politics.

Reprinted from: John Leonard, "Public versus Private Claims: Machiavellianism from Another Perspective." In *Political Theory,* Volume 12, Issue 4, pp. 491–501, 504–506. Copyright © 1984 by Sage Publications, Inc. Reprinted by permission of Sage Publications, Inc. ✦

Thomas Hobbes

John Aubrey tells a story of a clergyman who, upon seeing Thomas Hobbes give alms to a beggar, inquired of Hobbes if he were inspired by the commands of Jesus.[1] Hobbes reportedly replied that the commands of Jesus had nothing to do with his act; rather, he had given alms in order to relieve his own distress at the presence of the unsightly fellow. While the validity of the tale may be suspect, there is no mistaking the story's account of Hobbes's reputation as an ardent advocate of self-interest.

Hobbes was born at Malmesbury in Wiltshire, England in 1588. His premature birth as the Spanish Armada was approaching English shores prompted him to recollect that "fear and I were born twins," a phrase which many find typifies Hobbes's obsession with death. His father, a preacher, was forced to flee their home as a result of a brawl with a townsman when Thomas was young, leaving the boy to be raised by an uncle. He was educated at Magdalen Hall, Oxford where he developed a dislike for the classic philosophers and a distrust of academic life. After receiving his Bachelor's degree, he secured the position of tutor for William Cavendish, the future Earl of Devonshire. During this period he pursued his own liberal studies and wrote a translation of Thucydides. Hobbes developed an interest in geometry and in the new scientific method sweeping Europe. His tutoring posts allowed him the opportunity to travel, to correspond, and to meet with such Enlightenment notables as Galileo, René Descartes, and Francis Bacon.

Hobbes was particularly taken with the resoluto-compositive method which he appropriated from Galileo. According to this method, complex phenomena could be broken down into their simplest natural motions and components. Once these elements were understood, the workings of complex wholes could easily be derived. Hobbes's intent was to develop a systematic study in three parts, starting with simple motions in matter (*De Corpore*), moving on to the study of human nature (*De Homine*), and finally to politics (*De Cive*), each based on principles established at a "lower" level of analysis. Political upheavals at home caused him to attend to his political writings before the other volumes of his trilogy were completed. He circulated drafts of *The Elements of Law* in 1640 and a limited edition of *De Cive* (*On the Citizen*) in 1642. In these he developed the case for absolutism, which made him unpopular with many of his countrymen in civil-war England. He soon moved to France for fear of his life. There he served as mathematics tutor to the exiled Prince of Wales, the future King Charles II.

Leviathan appeared in 1651 during the tumultuous period between the execution of Charles I and the naming of Cromwell as Lord Protector. As a result of its bold assertions regarding sovereignty, monarchy, and religion, it received wide attention in political circles. Hobbes returned to England the following year and soon became embroiled in a number of controversies including one with John Wallis, professor of geometry at Oxford, over Hobbes's mathematical attempt to square the circle. In 1668, he finished a history of the period from 1640–1660, entitled *Behemouth*. Charles, his former charge now on the throne, sought to protect Hobbes from his critics by advising against its publication. It was only after Hobbes's death that it was allowed to surface. Hobbes died in 1679 at the age of 90, shortly after completing a translation of Homer's *Iliad* and *Odyssey*. The recent recovery of previously lost manuscripts has rekindled scholarly interest in Hobbes as a pivotal force in modern Western thought.

Leviathan

Leviathan is divided into four parts: Of Man, Of Commonwealth, Of a Christian Commonwealth, and Of the Kingdom of Darkness. While the first two parts are those most commonly read by students of politics today, the last two parts were probably of central importance in his own day when England was torn by religious strife. These parts focus on the power of the Church and the necessity for political control of religion.

The force of Hobbes's political teaching comes from his insistence that human morality and politics can be understood on the basis of simple units of motion. In the first several chapters of Book I, Hobbes builds a political psychology which advances a view of humans as driven by passions and appetites. Among those passions which create conflict is the desire for the good opinion of others. In a world where there exists no natural standard for the political superiority of any individual, a desire for good opinion leads to conflict and to the "restless desire of power after power that ceaseth only in death." But while there are passions that dispose us toward conflict, there also exist those which incline us toward peace, the most important of which is our fear of death. Working with these principles, Hobbes deduces 19 "laws of nature" which guide human action. Two principal laws include man's "right to everything" and the advisability of laying down this right in the interest of peace and safety so long as others do the same. These laws lead to the ultimate conclusion that men should unite under a contract for mutual safety and preservation. While those who contract are free to choose the type of enforcement (government) they like, Hobbes clearly favors monarchy as providing the most security with the least possibility of mischief brought by faction.

In the following selections, Hobbes reviews these principles and builds his case for monarchical rule. While Hobbes's absolutist tendencies may seem anachronistic in an era of democratic rule, his discussions of human nature, the roots of obligation, and the nature of contractarian justice continue to provide political scholars with much to ponder regarding the foundation of the nation-state.

Commentaries

In the first commentary, Gordon Schochet explores the voluntary basis of consent that is a cornerstone of Hobbes's theory of obligation. For Hobbes, obligation is the product of consent grounded in personal commitment, self-interest, and rationality. Schochet notes that while this solution works fairly well for commonwealths founded by institution, it works less well in the case of commonwealths originated by acquisition. Free will and intentionality must be supplemented as a basis for obligation in the latter case by a doctrine of gratitude, and gratitude transformed into a rational basis for consent. Schochet argues that his analysis demonstrates the futility of attempting to ground all duties and obligations in personal consent and shows the illiberal nature of Hobbes's project to use consent as the basis for an absolutist state.

If Schochet fears that Hobbes goes too far in ceding authority to a sovereign in the guise of contrived consent, Deborah Baumgold, by contrast, attempts to demonstrate how sovereign power is grounded and limited by reciprocal duties to the citizenry. Baumgold argues that traditional views portraying Hobbes as an authoritarian without regard for the typical citizen miss the point that Hobbes was a forceful advocate of good rule. Baumgold reminds us that Hobbes builds enticements for good rule and penalties against abuse into the role of sovereign while providing enough clout to limit the destabilizing effects of political rivalry. Contrary to popular visions of Hobbes, Baumgold sees in Hobbes the principle that only "lawful, fair rule enhances power."

Note

1. John Aubrey, *Brief Lives*, O. L. Dick, Ed. (Ann Arbor, MI: University of Michigan Press, 1957).

Web Sources

http://www.utm.edu/research/iep/h/hobbes.htm
The Internet Encyclopedia of Philosophy: Thomas Hobbes. Includes biographical information and exposition on Hobbes's basic ideas.

http://www.philosophypages.com/hy/3x.htm
Hobbes's Leviathan. Brief exploration of the basic ideas and themes in *Leviathan.*

http://jollyroger.com/zz/yphilo1d/Hobbes%2CThomashall/shakespeare1.html
Hobbes, Thomas Forum Frigate. Discussion forum on the philosophy of Hobbes. Visitors can ask and answer questions regarding the British philosopher.

http://hobbes.freeweb.supereva.it/english.htm?p
Hobbesiana.eng. Includes bibliographic entries, scholarly papers, and links to materials on Hobbes.

Class Activities and Discussion Items

1. To some, the world of Hobbes's *Leviathan* conjures up an all-powerful state in which citizens live in fear and enforced obedience. Compare this world with images presented in popular futuristic novels and films that stress centralized government authority (e.g., Orwell's *1984* or the science fiction classic *Blade Runner*). How is Hobbes's vision compatible with these? How is it different?

2. Hobbes presents a thorough-going egalitarian philosophy ("Men by nature equal," he proclaims in Chapter 13 of *Leviathan*). On what basis does Hobbes ground this equality? Is there a difference between the equality he grants and the vision of equality advanced by modern democratic institutions, or do they both ultimately draw upon the same grounds for justification?

3. Hobbes invents the notion of the "state of nature," a mind experiment in which we are asked to consider what humans might be like in a state totally divorced from social order and constraint. The portrait he draws is a cynical one, in which humans are pictured as passion-driven creatures with a "restless desire for power that ceases only with death." Do you agree with this portrait of humans in the state of nature? Can you arrive at a different portrait given the psychological premises with which Hobbes begins? Even if human nature does appear to be as Hobbes describes it, are less authoritarian solutions compatible with this view?

4. Machiavelli and Hobbes both portray individuals as self-interested and acknowledge that brute power must be wielded in order to bring stability and security to community life. Yet, Machiavelli comes to adopt a republican solution to the question of power in the political community, while Hobbes takes a monarchical stance. Explain the reasons why each theorist comes to a different resolution of the tensions between the individual and the community. Which account do you believe is most consistent? Why?

5. Hobbes presents a series of "Laws of Nature" that he believes emerge from his study of human nature. How does his approach compare to the *natural law* tradition of Aristotle and Aquinas? Compare the content of Hobbes's laws with the laws associated with classic natural law theorists.

Further Reading

Dietz, Mary G. (ed.). 1990. *Thomas Hobbes and Political Theory.* Lawrence, Kan.: University Press of Kansas. A collection of scholarly papers on a wide range of topics concerning Hobbes's political thought.

Hobbes, Thomas (M. Oakeshott, ed., with an Introduction by R. S. Peters). [1962.] *Leviathan.* London: Collier-Macmillan. The definitive edition of the classic text with extensive notes and an exceptional introduction.

Hobbes, Thomas (Noel Malcolm, ed.). 1998. *The Correspondence: Volume I: 1622–1659.* Cambridge: Cambridge University Press. The letters of Thomas Hobbes for the serious researcher.

Hobbes, Thomas (Noel B. Reynolds and Arlene W. Saxonhouse, eds.). [1995.] *Thomas Hobbes: Three Discourses: A Critical Modern Edition of Newly Identified Work of the Young Hobbes.* Chicago: University of Chicago Press.

A look at previously unavailable treatises with scholarly reference.

Strauss, Leo (Elsa Sinclair, trans.). 1963. *The Political Philosophy of Hobbes: Its Basis and Its Genesis.* Chicago: University of Chicago Press. Strauss looks at Hobbes's unique contributions to the modern era and the distinction between classic and modern natural right.

von Leyden, W. 1982. *Hobbes and Locke, the Politics of Freedom and Obligation.* New York: St. Martin's Press. A comparative analysis of the treatment of two important elements of political life in the works of the early contractarians. ✦

5
Excerpts from *Leviathan*

Thomas Hobbes

The First Part: Of Man

Chapter 11: Of the Difference of Manners

What is here meant by manners. By manners, I mean not here, decency of behaviour; as how one should salute another, or how a man should wash his mouth, or pick his teeth before company, and such other points of the *small morals;* but those qualities of mankind, that concern their living together in peace, and unity. To which end we are to consider, that the felicity of this life, consisteth not in the repose of a mind satisfied. For there is no such *finis ultimus,* utmost arm, nor *summum bonum,* greatest good, as is spoken of in the books of the old moral philosophers. Nor can a man any more live, whose desires are at an end, than he, whose senses and imaginations are at a stand. Felicity is a continual progress of the desire, from one object to another; the attaining of the former, being still but the way to the latter. The cause whereof is, that the object of man's desire, is not to enjoy once only, and for one instant of time; but to assure for ever, the way of his future desire. And therefore the voluntary actions, and inclinations of all men, tend, not only to the procuring, but also to the assuring of a contented life; and differ only in the way: which ariseth partly from the diversity of passions, in divers men; and partly from the difference of the knowledge, or opinion each one has of the causes, which produce the effect desired.

A restless desire of power in all men. So that in the first place, I put for a general inclination of all mankind, a perpetual and restless desire of power after power, that ceaseth only in death. And the cause of this, is not always that a man hopes for a more intensive delight, than he has already attained to; or that he cannot be content with a moderate power: but because he cannot assure the power and means to live well, which he hath present, without the acquisition of more. And from hence it is, that kings, whose power is greatest, turn their endeavors to the assuring it at home by laws, or abroad by wars: and when that is done, there succeedeth a new desire; in some, of fame from new conquest; in others, of ease and sensual pleasure; in others, of admiration, or being flattered for excellence in some art, or other ability of the mind.

Love of contention from competition. Competition of riches, honour, command, or other power, inclineth to contention, enmity, and war: because the way of one competitor, to the attaining of his desire, is to kill, subdue, supplant, or repel the other. Particularly, competition of praise, inclineth to a reverence of antiquity. For men contend with the living, not with the dead; to these ascribing more than due, that they may obscure the glory of the other.

Civil obedience from love of ease. From fear of death, or wounds. Desire of ease, and sensual delight, disposeth men to obey a common power: because by such desires, a man doth abandon the protection that might be hoped for from his own industry, and labour. Fear of death, and wounds disposeth to the same; and for the same reason. On the contrary, needy men and hardy, not contented with their present condition; as also, all men that are ambitious of military command, are inclined to continue the causes of war; and to stir up trouble and sedition: for there is no honour militarily but by war, nor any such hope to mend an ill game, as by causing a new shuffle.

And from love of arts. Desire of knowledge, and arts of peace, inclineth men to obey a common power: for such desire, containeth a desire of leisure; and consequently protection from some other power than their own.

Love of virtue from love of praise. Desire of praise, disposeth to laudable actions, such as please them whose judgment they value; for of those men whom we contemn, we contemn also the praises. Desire of fame after death does the same. And though after death, there be no sense of the praise given us on earth, as being joys, that are either swallowed up in the unspeakable joys of Heaven, or extinguished in the extreme torments of hell: yet is not such fame vain; because men have a present delight therein, from the foresight of it, and of the benefit that may redound thereby to their posterity; which though they now see not, yet they imagine; and any thing that is pleasure to the sense, the same also is pleasure in the imagination.

Hate, from difficulty of requiting great benefits. To have received from one, to whom we think ourselves equal, greater benefits than there is hope to requite, disposeth to counterfeit love; but really secret hatred; and puts a man into the estate of a desperate debtor, in that in declining the sight of his creditor, tacitly wishes him there, where he might never see him more. For benefits oblige, and obligation is thraldom; and unrequitable, obligation perpetual thraldom; which is to one's equal, hateful. But to have received benefits from one, whom we acknowledge far superior, inclines to love; because the obligation is no new depression: and cheerful acceptation, which men call *gratitude,* is such an honour done to the obliger, as is taken generally for retribution. Also to receive benefits, though from an equal, or inferior, as long as there is hope of requital, disposeth to love: for in the intention of the receiver, the obligation is of aid and service mutual; from whence proceedeth an emulation of who shall exceed in benefiting; the most noble and profitable contention possible; wherein the victor is pleased with his victory, and the other revenged by confessing it. . . .

Vain undertaking from vain-glory. Vainglorious men, such as without being conscious to themselves of great sufficiency, delight in supposing themselves gallant men, are inclined only to ostentation; but not to attempt: because when danger or difficulty appears, they look for nothing but to have their insufficiency discovered.

Vain-glorious men, such as estimate their sufficiency by the flattery of other men, or the fortune of some precedent action, without assured ground of hope from the true knowledge of themselves, are inclined to rash engaging; and in the approach of danger, or difficulty, to retire if they can: because not seeing the way of safety, they will rather hazard their honour, which may be salved with an excuse; than their lives, for which no salve is sufficient.

Ambition, from opinion of sufficiency. Men that have a strong opinion of their own wisdom in matter of government, are disposed to ambition. Because without public employment in council or magistracy, the honour of their wisdom is lost. And therefore eloquent speakers are inclined to ambition; for eloquence seemeth wisdom, both to themselves and others. . . .

Curiosity to know, from care of future time. Anxiety for the future time, disposeth men to inquire into the causes of things: because the knowledge of them, maketh men the better able to order the present to their best advantage.

Natural religion from the same. . . .

And they that make little, or no inquiry into the natural causes of things, yet from the fear that proceeds from the ignorance itself, of what it is that hath the power to do them much good or harm, are inclined to suppose, and feign themselves, several kinds of powers invisible; and to stand in awe of their own imaginations; and in time of distress to invoke them; as also in the time of an expected good success, to give them thanks; making the creatures of their own fancy, their gods. By which means it hath come to pass, that from the innumerable variety of fancy, men have created in the world innumerable sorts of gods. And this fear of things invisible, is the natural seed of that, which every one in himself calleth religion; and in them that worship, or fear that power otherwise than they do, superstition.

And this seed of religion, having been observed by many; some of those that have observed it, have been inclined thereby to nourish, dress, and form it into laws; and to add to it of their own invention, any opinion of the causes of future events, by which they thought they should be best able to govern others, and make unto themselves the greatest use of their powers.

Chapter 13: Of the Natural Condition of Mankind as Concerning Their Felicity and Misery

Men by nature equal. Nature hath made men so equal, in the faculties of the body, and mind; as that though there be found one man sometimes manifestly stronger in body, or of quicker mind than another; yet when all is reckoned together, the difference between man, and man, is not so considerable, as that one man can thereupon claim to himself any benefit, to which another may not pretend, as well as he. For as to the strength of body, the weakest has strength enough to kill the strongest, either by secret machination, or by confederacy with others, that are in the same danger with himself.

And as to the faculties of the mind, setting aside the arts grounded upon words, and especially that skill of proceeding upon general, and infallible rules, called science; which very few have, and but in few things; as being not a native faculty, born with us; nor attained, as prudence, while we look after somewhat else, I find yet a greater equality amongst men, than that of strength. For prudence, is but experience; which equal time, equally bestows on all men, in those things they equally apply themselves unto. That which may perhaps make such equality incredible, is but a vain conceit of one's own wisdom, which almost all men think they have in a greater degree, than the vulgar; that is, than all men but themselves, and a few others, whom by fame, or for concurring with themselves, they approve. For such is the nature of men, that howsoever they may acknowledge many others to be more witty, or more eloquent, or more learned; yet they will hardly believe there be many so wise as themselves; for they see their own wit at hand, and other men's at a distance. But this proveth rather that men are in that point equal, than unequal. For there is not ordinarily a greater sign of the equal distribution of any thing, than that every man is contented with his share.

From equality proceeds diffidence. From this equality of ability, ariseth equality of hope in the attaining of our ends. And therefore if any two men desire the same thing, which nevertheless they cannot both enjoy, they become enemies; and in the way to their end, which is principally their own conservation, and sometimes their delectation only, endeavour to destroy, or subdue one another. And from hence it comes to pass, that where an invader hath no more to fear, than another man's single power; if one plant, sow, build, or possess a convenient seat, others may probably be expected to come prepared with forces united, to dispossess, and deprive him, not only of the fruit of his labour, but also of his life, or liberty. And the invader again is in the like danger of another.

From diffidence war. And from this diffidence of one another, there is no way for any man to secure himself, so reasonable, as anticipation; that is, by force, or wiles, to master the persons of all men he can, so long, till he see no other power great enough to endanger him: and this is no more than his own conservation requireth, and is generally allowed. Also because there be some, that taking pleasure in contemplating their own power in the acts of conquest, which they pursue farther than their security requires; if others, that otherwise would be glad to be at ease within modest bounds, should not by invasion increase their power, they would not be able, long time, by standing only on their defence, to subsist. And by consequence, such augmentation of dominion over men being necessary to a man's conservation, it ought to be allowed him.

Again, men have no pleasure, but on the contrary a great deal of grief, in keeping company, where there is no power able to over-awe them all. For every man looketh that his companion should value him, at the same rate he sets upon himself: and upon all signs of contempt, or undervaluing, naturally endeavours, as far as he dares, (which amongst them that have no common power to keep them in quiet, is far enough to make them destroy each other), to extort a greater value from his contemners, by damage; and from others, by the example.

So that in the nature of man, we find three principal causes of quarrel. First, competition; secondly, diffidence; thirdly, glory.

The first, maketh men invade for gain; the second, for safety; and the third, for reputation. The first use violence, to make themselves masters of other men's persons, wives, children, and cattle; the second, to defend them; the third, for trifles, as a word, a smile, a different opinion, and any other sign of undervalue, either direct in their persons, or by reflection in their kindred, their friends, their nation, their profession, or their name.

Out of civil states, there is always war of every one against every one. Hereby it is manifest, that during the time men live without a common power to keep them all in awe, they are in that condition which is called war; and such a war, as is of every man, against every man. For WAR, consisteth not in battle only, or the act of fighting; but in a tract of time, wherein the will to contend by battle is sufficiently known: and therefore the notion of *time,* is to be considered in the nature of war; as it is in the nature of weather. For as the nature of foul weather, lieth not in a shower or two of rain; but in an inclination thereto of many days together: so the nature of war, consisteth not in actual fighting; but in the known disposition thereto, during all the time there is no assurance to the contrary. All other time is PEACE.

The incommodities of such a war. Whatsoever therefore is consequent to a time of war, where every man is enemy to every man; the same is consequent to the time, wherein men live without other security, than what their own strength, and their own invention shall furnish them withal. In such condition, there is no place for industry; because the fruit thereof is uncertain: and consequently no culture of the earth; no navigation, nor use of the commodities that may be imported by sea; no commodious building; no instruments of moving, and removing, such things as require much force; no knowledge of the face of the earth; no account of time; no arts; no letters; no society; and which is worst of all, continual fear, and danger of violent death; and the life of man, solitary, poor, nasty, brutish, and short.

It may seem strange to some man, that has not well weighed these things; that nature should thus dissociate, and render men apt to invade, and destroy one another: and he may therefore, not trusting to this inference, made from the passions, desire perhaps to have the same confirmed by experience. Let him therefore consider with himself, when taking a journey, he arms himself, and seeks to go well accompanied; when going to sleep, he locks his doors; when even in his house he locks his chests; and this when he knows there be laws, and public officers, armed, to revenge all injuries shall be done him; what opinion he has of his fellow-subjects, when he rides armed; of his fellow citizens, when he locks his doors; and of his children, and servants, when he locks his chests. Does he not there as much accuse mankind by his actions, as I do by my words? But neither of us accuse man's nature in it. The desires, and other passions of man, are in themselves no sin. No more are the actions, that proceed from those passions, till they know a law that forbids them: which till laws be made they cannot know: nor can any law be made, till they have agreed upon the person that shall make it.

It may peradventure be thought, there was never such a time, nor condition of war as this; and I believe it was never generally so, over all the world: but there are many places, where they live so now. For the savage people in many places of America, except the government of small families, the concord whereof dependeth on natural lust, have no government at all; and live at this day in that brutish manner, as I said before. Howsoever, it may be perceived what manner of life there would be, where there were no common power to fear, by the manner of life, which men that have formerly lived under a peaceful government, use to degenerate into, in a civil war.

But though there had never been any time, wherein particular men were in a condition of war one against another; yet in all times, kings, and persons of sovereign authority, because of their independency, are in continual jealousies, and in the state and posture of gladiators; having their weapons pointing, and their eyes fixed on one another; that is, their forts, garrisons, and guns upon the frontiers of their kingdoms; and continual spies upon their neighbours; which is a posture of war. But because they uphold thereby, the industry of their subjects; there does not follow from it, that misery, which accompanies the liberty of particular men.

In such a war nothing is unjust. To this war of every man, against every man, this also is consequent; that nothing can be unjust. The notions of right and wrong, justice and injustice have there no place. Where there is no common power, there is no law: where no law, no injustice. Force, and fraud, are in war the two cardinal virtues. Justice, and injustice are none of the faculties neither of the body, nor mind. If they were, they might be in a man that were alone in the world, as well as his senses, and passions. They are qualities, that relate to men in society, not in solitude. It is consequent also to the same condition, that there be no propriety, no dominion, no *mine* and *thine* distinct; but only that to be every man's, that he can get: and for so long, as he can keep it. And thus much for the ill condition, which man by mere nature is actually placed in; though with a possibility to come out of it, consisting partly in the passions, partly in his reason.

The passions that incline men to peace. The passions that incline men to peace, are fear of death; desire of such things as are necessary to commodious living; and a hope by their industry to obtain them. And reason suggesteth convenient articles of peace, upon which men may be drawn to agreement. These articles, are they, which otherwise are called the Laws of Nature: whereof I shall speak more particularly, in the two following chapters.

Chapter 14: Of the First and Second Natural Laws, and of Contracts

Right of nature what. THE RIGHT OF NATURE, which writers commonly call *jus naturale*, is the liberty each man hath, to use his own power, as he will himself, for the preservation of his own nature; that is to say, of his own life; and consequently, of doing any thing, which in his own judgment, and reason, he shall conceive to be the aptest means thereunto.

Liberty what. By LIBERTY, is understood, according to the proper signification of the word, the absence of external impediments: which impediments, may oft take away part of a man's power to do what he would; but cannot hinder him from using the power left him, according as his judgment, and reason shall dictate to him.

A law of nature what. Difference of right and law. A LAW OF NATURE, *lex naturalis*, is a precept or general rule, found out by reason, by which a man is forbidden to do that, which is destructive of his life, or taketh away the means of preserving the same; and to omit that, by which he thinketh it may be best preserved. For though they that speak of this subject, use to confound *jus*, and *lex*, right and law: yet they ought to be distinguished; because RIGHT, consisteth in liberty to do, or to forbear: whereas LAW, determineth, and bindeth to one of them: so that law, and right, differ as much, as obligation, and liberty; which in one and the same matter are inconsistent.

Naturally every man has right to every thing. The fundamental law of nature. And because the condition of man, as hath been declared in the precedent chapter, is a condition of war of every one against every one; in which case every one is governed by his own reason; and there is nothing he can make use of, that may not be a help unto him, in preserving his life against his enemies; it followeth, that in such a condition, every man has a right to every thing; even to one another's body. And therefore, as long as this natural right of every man to every thing endureth, there can be no security to any man, how strong or wise soever he be, of living out the time, which nature ordinarily alloweth men to live. And consequently it is a precept, or general rule of reason, *that every man, ought to endeavour peace, as far as he has hope of obtaining it, and when he cannot obtain it, that he may seek, and use, all helps, and advantages of war.* The first branch of which rule, containeth the first, and fundamental law of nature; which is, *to seek peace, and follow it.* The second, the sum of the right of nature; which is, *by all means we can, to defend ourselves.*

The second law of nature. From this fundamental law of nature, by which men are commanded to endeavour peace, is derived this second law; *that a man be willing, when others are so too, as far-forth, as for peace, and de-*

fence of himself he shall think it necessary, to lay down this right to all things; and be contented with so much liberty against other men, as he would allow other men against himself. For as long as every man holdeth this right, of doing any thing he liketh; so long are all men in the condition of war. But if other men will not lay down their right, as well as he; then there is no reason for any one, to divest himself of his: for that were to expose himself to prey, which no man is bound to, rather than to dispose himself to peace. This is that law of the Gospel; *whatsoever you require that others should do to you, that do ye to them.* And that law of all men, *quod tibi fieri non vis, alteri ne feceris.*

What it is to lay down a right. To *lay down* a man's *right* to any thing, is to *divest* himself of the *liberty,* of hindering another of the benefit of his own right to the same. For he that renounceth, or passeth away his right, giveth not to any other man a right which he had not before; because there is nothing to which every man had not right by nature: but only standeth out of his way, that he may enjoy his own original right, without hindrance from him; not without hindrance from another. So that the effect which redoundeth to one man, by another man's defect of right, is but so much diminution of impediments to the use of his own right original.

Renouncing a right, what it is. Transferring right what. Obligation. Duty. Injustice. Right is laid aside, either by simply renouncing it; or by transferring it to another. By *simply* RENOUNCING; when he cares not to whom the benefit thereof redoundeth. By TRANS-FERRING; when he intendeth the benefit thereof to some certain person, or persons. And when a man hath in either manner abandoned, or granted away his right; then he is said to be OBLIGED, or BOUND, not to hinder those, to whom such right is granted, or abandoned, from the benefit of it: and that he *ought,* and it is his DUTY, not to make void that voluntary act of his own: and that such hindrance is INJUSTICE, and INJURY, as being *sine jure;* the right being before renounced, or transferred. So that *injury,* or *injustice,* in the controversies of the world, is somewhat like to that, which in the disputa-

tions of scholars is called *absurdity.* For as it is there called an absurdity, to contradict what one maintained in the beginning: so in the world, it is called injustice, and injury, voluntarily to undo that, which from the beginning he had voluntarily done. The way by which a man either simply renounceth, or transferreth his right, is a declaration, or signification, by some voluntary and sufficient sign, or signs, that he doth so renounce, or transfer; or hath so renounced, or transferred the same, to him that accepteth it. And these signs are either words only, or actions only; or, as it happeneth most often, both words, and actions. And the same are the BONDS, by which men are bound, and obliged: bonds, that have their strength, not from their own nature, for nothing is more easily broken than a man's word, but from fear of some evil consequence upon the rupture.

Not all rights are alienable. Whensoever a man transferreth his right, or renounceth it; it is either in consideration of some right reciprocally transferred to himself; or for some other good he hopeth for thereby. For it is a voluntary act: and of the voluntary acts of every man, the object is some *good to himself.* And therefore there be some rights, which no man can be understood by any words, or other signs, to have abandoned, or transferred. As first a man cannot lay down the right of resisting them, that assault him by force, to take away his life; because he cannot be understood to aim thereby, at any good to himself. The same may be said of wounds, and chains, and imprisonment; both because there is no benefit consequent to such patience; as there is to the patience of suffering another to be wounded, or imprisoned: as also because a man cannot tell, when he seeth men proceed against him by violence, whether they intend his death or not. And lastly the motive, and end for which this renouncing, and transferring of right is introduced, is nothing else but the security of a man's person, in his life, and in the means of so preserving life, as not to be weary of it. And therefore if a man by words, or other signs, seem to despoil himself of the end, for which those signs were intended; he is not to be understood as if he meant it, or that it was his will; but that he was ignorant of how such words and actions were to be interpreted.

Contract what. The mutual transferring of right, is that which men call CONTRACT.

There is difference between transferring of right to the thing; and transferring, or tradition, that is delivery of the thing itself. For the thing may be delivered together with the translation of the right; as in buying and selling with ready-money; or exchange of goods, or lands: and it may be delivered some time after.

Covenant what. Again, one of the contractors, may deliver the thing contracted for on his part, and leave the other to perform his part at some determinate time after, and in the mean time be trusted; and then the contract on his part, is called PACT, or COVENANT: or both parts may contract now, to perform hereafter: in which cases, he that is to perform in time to come, being trusted, his performance is called *keeping of promise,* or faith; and the failing of performance, if it be voluntary, *violation of faith.* . . .

Covenants how made void. Men are freed of their covenants two ways; by performing; or by being forgiven. For performance, is the natural end of obligation; and forgiveness, the restitution of liberty; as being a retransferring of that right, in which the obligation consisted.

Covenants extorted by fear are valid. Covenants entered into by fear, in the condition of mere nature, are obligatory. For example, if I covenant to pay a ransom, or service for my life, to an enemy; I am bound by it: for it is a contract, wherein one receiveth the benefit of life; the other is to receive money, or service for it; and consequently, where no other law, as in the condition of mere nature, forbiddeth the performance, the covenant is valid. Therefore prisoners of war, if trusted with the payment of their ransom, are obliged to pay it: and if a weaker prince, make a disadvantageous peace with a stronger, for fear; he is bound to keep it; unless, as hath been said before, there ariseth some new, and just cause of fear, to renew the war. And even in commonwealths, if I be forced to redeem myself from a thief by promising him money, I am bound to pay it, till the civil law discharge me. For whatsoever I may lawfully do without obligation, the same I may lawfully covenant to do through fear: and what I lawfully covenant, I cannot lawfully break.

The former covenant to one, makes void the later to another. A former covenant, makes void a later. For a man that hath passed away his right to one man to-day, hath it not to pass to-morrow to another: and therefore the later promise passeth no right, but is null.

A man's covenant not to defend himself is void. A covenant not to defend myself from force, by force, is always void. For, as I have showed before, no man can transfer, or lay down his right to save himself from death, wounds, and imprisonment, the avoiding whereof is the only end of laying down any right; and therefore the promise of not resisting force, in no covenant transferreth any right; nor is obliging. For though a man may covenant thus, *unless I do so, or so, kill me;* he cannot covenant thus, *unless I do so, or so, I will not resist you, when you come to kill me.* For man by nature chooseth the lesser evil, which is danger of death in resisting; rather than the greater, which is certain and present death in not resisting. And this is granted to be true by all men, in that they lead criminals to execution, and prison, with armed men, notwithstanding that such criminals have consented to the law, by which they are condemned. . . .

Chapter 15: Of Other Laws of Nature

The third law of nature, justice. From that law of nature, by which we are obliged to transfer to another, such rights, as being retained, hinder the peace of mankind, there followeth a third; which is this, *that men perform their covenants made:* without which, covenants are in vain, and but empty words; and the right of all men to all things remaining, we are still in the condition of war.

Justice and injustice what. And in this law of nature, consisteth the fountain and original of JUSTICE. For where no covenant hath preceded, there hath no right been transferred, and every man has right to every thing; and consequently, no action can be unjust. But when a covenant is made, then to break it is *unjust:* and the definition of IN-JUSTICE, is no other than *the not performance of covenant.* And whatsoever is not unjust, is *just.*

Justice and propriety begin with the constitution of commonwealth. But because covenants of mutual trust, where there is a fear of not performance on either part, as hath been said in the former chapter, are invalid; though the original of justice be the making of covenants; yet injustice actually there can be none, till the cause of such fear be taken away; which while men are in the natural condition of war, cannot be done. Therefore before the names of just, and unjust can have place, there must be some coercive power, to compel men equally to the performance of their covenants, by the terror of some punishment, greater than the benefit they expect by the breach of their covenant; and to make good that propriety, which by mutual contract men acquire, in recompense of the universal right they abandon: and such power there is none before the erection of a commonwealth. And this is also to be gathered out of the ordinary definition of justice in the Schools: for they say, that *justice is the constant will of giving to every man his own.* And therefore where there is no *own,* that is no propriety, there is no injustice; and where there is no coercive power erected, that is, where there is no commonwealth, there is no propriety; all men having right to all things: therefore where there is no commonwealth, there nothing is unjust. So that the nature of justice, consisteth in keeping of valid covenants: but the validity of covenants begins not but with the constitution of a civil power, sufficient to compel men to keep them: and then it is also that propriety begins.

Justice not contrary to reason. . . .

For the question is not of promises mutual, where there is no security of performance on either side; as when there is no civil power erected over the parties promising; for such promises are no covenants: but either where one of the parties has performed already; or where there is a power to make him perform; there is the question whether it be against reason, that is, against the benefit of the other to perform, or not. And I say it is not against reason. For the

manifestation whereof, we are to consider; first, that when a man doth a thing, which notwithstanding any thing can be foreseen, and reckoned on, tendeth to his own destruction, howsoever some accident which he could not expect, arriving may turn it to his benefit; yet such events do not make it reasonably or wisely done. Secondly, that in a condition of war, wherein every man to every man, for want of a common power to keep them all in awe, is an enemy, there is no man who can hope by his own strength, or wit, to defend himself from destruction, without the help of confederates; where every one expects the same defence by the confederation, that any one else does: and therefore he which declares he thinks it reason to deceive those that help him, can in reason expect no other means of safety, than what can be had from his own single power. He therefore that breaketh his covenant, and consequently declareth that he thinks he may with reason do so, cannot be received into any society, that unite themselves for peace and defence, but by the error of them that receive him; nor when he is received, be retained in it, without seeing the danger of their error; which errors a man cannot reasonably reckon upon as the means of his security: and therefore if he be left, or cast out of society, he perisheth; and if he live in society, it is by the errors of other men, which he could not foresee, nor reckon upon; and consequently against the reason of his preservation; and so, as all men that contribute not to his destruction, forbear him only out of ignorance of what is good for themselves.

As for the instance of gaining the secure and perpetual felicity of heaven, by any way; it is frivolous: there being but one way imaginable; and that is not breaking, but keeping of covenant.

And for the other instance of attaining sovereignty by rebellion; it is manifest, that though the event follow, yet because it cannot reasonably be expected, but rather the contrary; and because by gaining it so, others are taught to gain the same in like manner, the attempt thereof is against reason. Justice therefore, that is to say, keeping of covenant, is a rule of reason, by which we are forbidden to do any thing destructive to our life; and consequently a law of nature. . . .

Justice commutative and distributive. Justice of actions, is by writers divided into *commutative*, and *distributive*: and the former they say consisteth in proportion arithmetical; the latter in proportion geometrical. Commutative therefore, they place in the equality of value of the things contracted for; and distributive, in the distribution of equal benefit, to men of equal merit. As if it were injustice to sell dearer than we buy; or to give more to a man than he merits. The value of all things contracted for, is measured by the appetite of the contractors: and therefore the just value, is that which they be contented to give. And merit (besides that which is by covenant, where the performance on one part, meriteth the performance on the other part, and falls under justice commutative, not distributive) is not due to justice; but is rewarded of grace only. And therefore this distinction, in the sense wherein it useth to be expounded, is not right. To speak properly, commutative justice, is the justice, of a contractor; that is, a performance of covenant, in buying, and selling; hiring, and letting to hire; lending, and borrowing; exchanging, bartering, and other acts of contract.

And distributive justice, the justice of an arbitrator; that is to say, the act of defining what is just. Wherein, being trusted by them that make him arbitrator, if he perform his trust, he is said to distribute to every man his own: and this is indeed just distribution, and may be called, though improperly, distributive justice; but more properly equity; which also is a law of nature, as shall be shown in due place. . . .

A rule, by which the laws of nature may easily be examined. And though this may seem too subtle a deduction of the laws of nature, to be taken notice of by all men; whereof the most part are too busy in getting food, and the rest too negligent to understand; yet to leave all men inexcusable, they have been contracted into one easy sum, intelligible even to the meanest capacity; and that is, *Do not that to another, which thou wouldest not have done to thyself;* which sheweth him, that he had no more to

do in learning the laws of nature, but, when weighing the actions of other men with his own, they seem too heavy, to put them into the other part of the balance, and his own into their place, that his own passions, and self-love, may add nothing to the weight; and then there is none of these laws of nature that will not appear unto him very reasonable.

The laws of nature oblige in conscience always, but in effect then only when there is security. The laws of nature oblige *in foro interno;* that is to say, they bind to a desire they should take place: but *in foro externo,* this is, to the putting them in act, not always. For he that should be modest, and tractable, and perform all he promises, in such time, and place, where no man else should do so, should but make himself a prey to others, and procure his own certain ruin, contrary to the ground of all laws of nature, which tend to nature's preservation. And again, he that having sufficient security, that others shall observe the same laws towards him, observes them not himself, seeketh not peace, but war; and consequently the destruction of his nature by violence.

And whatsoever laws bind *in foro interno,* may be broken, not only by a fact contrary to the law, but also by a fact according to it, in case a man think it contrary. For though his action in this case, be according to the law; yet his purpose was against the law; which, where the obligation is *in foro interno,* is a breach.

The laws of nature are eternal. The laws of nature are immutable and eternal; for injustice, ingratitude, arrogance, pride, iniquity, acception of persons, and the rest, can never be made lawful. For it can never be that war shall preserve life, and peace destroy it.

And yet easy. The same laws, because they oblige only to a desire, and endeavour, I mean an unfeigned and constant endeavour, are easy to be observed. For in that they require nothing but endeavour, he that endeavoureth their performance, fufilleth them; and he that fulfilleth the law, is just.

The science of these laws, is the true moral philosophy. And the science of them, is the true and only moral philosophy. For moral philosophy is nothing else but the science of what is *good,* and *evil,* in the conversation, and society of mankind. *Good,* and *evil,* are names that signify our appetites, and aversions; which in different tempers, customs, and doctrines of men, are different: and divers men, differ not only in their judgment, on the senses of what is pleasant, and unpleasant to the taste, smell, hearing, touch, and sight; but also of what is conformable, or disagreeable to reason, in the actions of common life. Nay, the same man, in divers times, differs from himself; and one time praiseth, that is, calleth good, what another time he dispraiseth, and calleth evil: from whence arise disputes, controversies, and at last war. And therefore so long as a man is in the condition of mere nature, which is a condition of war, as private appetite is the measure of good, and evil: and consequently all men agree on this, that peace is good, and therefore also the way, or means of peace, which, as I have shewed before, are *justice, gratitude, modesty, equity, mercy,* and the rest of the laws of nature, are good; that is to say; *moral virtues;* and their contrary *vices,* evil. Now the science of virtue and vice, is moral philosophy; and therefore the true doctrine of the laws of nature, is the true moral philosophy. But the writers of moral philosophy, though they acknowledge the same virtues and vices; yet not seeing wherein consisted their goodness; nor that they come to be praised, as the means of peaceable, sociable, and comfortable living, place them in a mediocrity of passions: as if not the cause, but the degree of daring, made fortitude; or not the cause, but the quantity of a gift, made liberality.

These dictates of reason, men used to call by the names of laws, but improperly: for they are but conclusions, or theorems concerning what conduceth to the conservation and defence of themselves; whereas law, properly, is the word of him, that by right hath command over others. But yet if we consider the same theorems, as delivered in the word of God, that by right commandeth all things; then are they properly called laws.

The Second Part: Of Commonwealth

Chapter 17: Of the Causes, Generation, and Definition of a Commonwealth

The end of commonwealth, particular security. The final cause, end, or design of men, who naturally love liberty, and dominion over others, in the introduction of that restraint upon themselves, in which we see them live in commonwealths, is the foresight of their own preservation, and of a more contented life thereby; that is to say, of getting themselves out from that miserable condition of war, which is necessarily consequent, as hath been shown (chapter 13), to the natural passions of men, when there is no visible power to keep them in awe, and tie them by fear of punishment to the performance of their covenants, and observation of those laws of nature set down in the fourteenth and fifteenth chapters.

Which is not to be had from the law of nature. For the laws of nature, as *justice, equity, modesty, mercy,* and, in sum, *doing to others, as we would be done to,* of themselves, without the terror of some power, to cause them to be observed, are contrary to our natural passions, that carry us to partiality, pride, revenge, and the like. And covenants, without the sword, are but words, and of no strength to secure a man at all. Therefore notwithstanding the laws of nature (which every one hath then kept, when he has the will to keep them, when he can do it safely) if there be no power erected, or not great enough for our security; every man will, and may lawfully rely on his own strength and art, for caution against all other men. And in all places, where men have lived by small families, to rob and spoil one another, has been a trade, and so far from being reputed against the law of nature, that the greater spoils they gained, the greater was their honour; and men observed no other laws therein, but the laws of honour; that is, to abstain from cruelty, leaving to men their lives, and instruments of husbandry. And as small families did then; so now do cities and kingdoms which are but greater families, for their own security, enlarge their dominions, upon all pretences of danger, and fear of invasion, or assistance that may be given to invaders, and endeavour as much as they can, to subdue, or weaken their neighbours, by open force, and secret arts, for want of other caution, justly; and are remembered for it in after ages with honour.

Nor from the conjunction of a few men or families. Nor is it the joining together of a small number of men, that gives them this security; because in small numbers, small additions on the one side or the other, make the advantage of strength so great, as is sufficient to carry the victory; and therefore gives encouragement to an invasion. The multitude sufficient to confide in for our security, is not determined by any certain number, but by comparison with the enemy we fear; and is then sufficient, when the odds of the enemy is not of so visible and conspicuous moment, to determine the event of war, as to move him to attempt.

Nor from a great multitude, unless directed by one judgment. And be there never so great a multitude; yet if their actions be directed according to their particular judgments, and particular appetites, they can expect thereby no defence, nor protection, neither against a common enemy, nor against the injuries of one another. For being distracted in opinions concerning the best use and application of their strength, they do not help but hinder one another; and reduce their strength by mutual opposition to nothing: whereby they are easily, not only subdued by a very few that agree together; but also when there is no common enemy, they make war upon each other, for their particular interests. For if we could suppose a great multitude of men to consent in the observation of justice, and other laws of nature, without a common power to keep them all in awe; we might as well suppose all mankind to do the same; and then there neither would be, nor need to be any civil government, or commonwealth at all; because there would be peace without subjection.

And that continually. Nor is it enough for the security, which men desire should last all the time of their life, that they be governed, and directed by one judgment, for a limited time; as in one battle, or one war. For though they obtain a victory by their unanimous endeavour against a foreign enemy; yet afterwards, when either they have no common enemy, or he that by one part is held for an enemy, is by another part held for a friend, they must needs by the difference of their interests dissolve, and fall again into a war amongst themselves.

Why certain creatures without reason, or speech, do nevertheless live in society, without any coercive power. It is true, that certain living creatures, as bees, and ants, live sociably one with another, which are therefore by Aristotle numbered amongst political creatures; and yet have no other direction, than their particular judgments and appetites; nor speech, whereby one of them can signify to another, what he thinks expedient for the common benefit: and therefore some man may perhaps desire to know, why mankind cannot do the same. To which I answer,

First, that men are continually in competition for honour and dignity, which these creatures are not; and consequently amongst men there ariseth on that ground, envy and hatred, and finally war; but amongst these not so.

Secondly, that amongst these creatures, the common good differeth not from the private; and being by nature inclined to their private, they procure thereby the common benefit. But man, whose joy consisteth in comparing himself with other men, can relish nothing but what is eminent.

Thirdly, that these creatures, having not, as man, the use of reason, do not see, nor think they see any fault, in the administration of their common business; whereas amongst men, there are very many, that think themselves wiser, and abler to govern the public, better than the rest; and these strive to reform and innovate, one this way, another that way; and thereby bring it into distraction and civil war.

Fourthly, that these creatures, though they have some use of voice, in making known to one another their desires, and other affections; yet they want that art of words, by which some men can represent to others, that which is good, in the likeness of evil; and evil, in the likeness of good; and augment, or diminish the apparent greatness of good and evil; discontenting men, and troubling their peace at their pleasure.

Fifthly, irrational creatures cannot distinguish between *injury*, and *damage;* and therefore as long as they be at ease, they are not offended with their fellows: whereas man is then most troublesome, when he is most at ease: for then it is that he loves to shew his wisdom, and control the actions of them that govern the commonwealth.

Lastly, the agreement of these creatures is natural; that of men, is by covenant only, which is artificial: and therefore it is no wonder if there be somewhat else required, besides covenant, to make their agreement constant and lasting; which is a common power, to keep them in awe, and to direct their actions to the common benefit.

The generation of a commonwealth. The definition of a commonwealth. The only way to erect such a common power, as may be able to defend them from the invasion of foreigners, and the injuries of one another, and thereby to secure them in such sort, as that by their own industry, and by the fruits of the earth, they may nourish themselves and live contentedly; is, to confer all their power and strength upon one man, or upon one assembly of men, that may reduce all their wills, by plurality of voices, unto one will: which is as much as to say, to appoint one man, or assembly of men, to bear their person; and every one to own, and acknowledge himself to be author of whatsoever he that so beareth their person, shall act, or cause to be acted, in those things which concern the common peace and safety; and therein to submit their wills, every one to his will, and their judgments, to his judgment. This is more than consent, or concord; it is a real unity of them all, in one and the same person, made by covenant of every man with every man, in such manner, as if every man should say to every man, *I authorize and give up my right of governing myself, to this man, or to this assembly of men, on this condition, that thou give up thy right to him, and authorize all his actions in like manner.* This done, the multitude so united in one person, is called a COMMONWEALTH, in Latin CIVITAS. This is the generation of that great LEVIATHAN, or rather, to speak more reverently, of that *mortal god,*

to which we owe under the *immortal God,* our peace and defence. For by this authority, given him by every particular man in the commonwealth, he hath the use of so much power and strength conferred on him, that by terror thereof, he is enabled to form the wills of them all, to peace at home, and mutual aid against their enemies abroad. And in him consisteth the essence of the commonwealth; which, to define it, is *one person, of whose acts a great multitude, by mutual covenants one with another, have made themselves every one the author, to the end he may use the strength and means of them all, as he shall think expedient, for their peace and common defence.*

Sovereign, and subject, what. And he that carrieth this person is called SOVEREIGN, and said to have *sovereign power;* and every one besides, his SUBJECT.

The attaining to this sovereign power, is by two ways. One by natural force; as when a man maketh his children, to submit themselves, and their children to his government, as being able to destroy them if they refuse; or by war subdueth his enemies to his will, giving them their lives on that condition. The other, is when men agree amongst themselves, to submit to some man, or assembly of men, voluntarily, on confidence to be protected by him against all others. This latter, may be called a political commonwealth, or commonwealth by *institution;* and the former, a commonwealth by *acquisition.* And first, I shall speak of a commonwealth by institution.

Chapter 18: Of the Rights of Sovereigns by Institution

The act of instituting a commonwealth, what. A *commonwealth* is said to be *instituted,* when a *multitude* of men do agree, and *covenant, every one, with every one,* that to whatsoever *man,* or *assembly of men,* shall be given by the major part, the *right to present* the person of them all, that is to say, to be their *representative;* every one, as well he that *voted for it,* as he that *voted against it,* shall *authorize* all the actions and judgments, of that man, or assembly of men, in the same manner, as if they were his own, to the end, to live peaceably amongst themselves, and be protected against other men.

The consequences to such institutions, are: From this institution of a commonwealth are derived all the *rights*, and *faculties* of him, or them, on whom the sovereign power is conferred by the consent of the people assembled.

1. *The subjects cannot change the form of government.* First, because they covenant, it is to be understood, they are not obliged by former covenant to any thing repugnant hereunto. And consequently they that have already instituted a commonwealth, being thereby bound by covenant, to own the actions, and judgments of one, cannot lawfully make a new covenant, amongst themselves, to be obedient to any other, in any thing whatsoever, without his permission. And therefore, they that are subjects to a monarch, cannot without his leave cast off monarchy, and return to the confusion of a disunited multitude; nor transfer their person from him that beareth it, to another man, or other assembly of men: for they are bound, every man to every man, to own, and be reputed author of all, that he that already is their sovereign, shall do and judge fit to be done: so that any one man dissenting, all the rest should break their covenant made to that man, which is injustice: and they have also every man given the sovereignty to him that beareth their person; and therefore if they depose him, they take from him that which is his own, and so again it is injustice. Besides, if he that attempteth to depose his sovereign, be killed, or punished by him for such attempt, he is author of his own punishment, as being by the institution, author of all his sovereign shall do: and because it is injustice for a man to do any thing, for which he may be punished by his own authority, he is also upon that title, unjust. And whereas some men have pretended for their disobedience to their sovereign, a new covenant, made, not with men, but with God; this also is unjust: for there is no covenant with God, but by mediation of somebody that representeth God's person; which none doth but God's lieutenant, who hath the sovereignty under God. But this pretence of covenant with God, is so evident a lie, even in the pretenders' own consciences, that it is not only an act of an unjust, but also of a vile, and unmanly disposition.

2. *Sovereign power cannot be forfeited.* Secondly, because the right of bearing the person of them all, is given to him they make sovereign, by covenant only of one to another, and not of him to any of them; there can happen no breach of covenant on the part of the sovereign; and consequently none of his subjects, by any pretence of forfeiture, can be freed from his subjection. That he which is made sovereign maketh no covenant with his subjects beforehand, is manifest; because either he must make it with the whole multitude, as one party to the covenant; or he must make a several covenant with every man. With the whole, as one party, it is impossible; because as yet they are not one person: and if he make so many several covenants as there be men, those covenants after he hath the sovereignty are void; because what act soever can be pretended by any one of them for breach thereof, is the act both of himself, and of all the rest, because done in the person, and by the right of every one of them in particular. Besides, if any one, or more of them, pretend a breach of the covenant made by the sovereign at his institution; and others, or one other of his subjects, or himself alone, pretend there was no such breach, there is in this case, no judge to decide the controversy; it returns therefore to the sword again; and every man recovereth the right of protecting himself by his own strength, contrary to the design they had in the institution. It is therefore in vain to grant sovereignty by way of precedent covenant. The opinion that any monarch receiveth his power by covenant, this is to say, on condition, proceedeth from want of understanding this easy truth, that covenants being but words and breath, have no force to oblige, contain, constrain, or protect any man, but what it has from the public sword; that is, from the untied hands of that man, or assembly of men that hath the sovereignty, and whose actions are avouched by them all, and performed by the strength of them all, in him united. But when an assembly of men is made sovereign; then no man imagineth any such covenant to have passed in the institu-

tion; for no man is so dull as to say, for example, the people of Rome made a covenant with the Romans, to hold the sovereignty on such or such conditions; which not performed, the Romans might lawfully depose the Roman people. That men see not the reason to be alike in a monarchy, and in a popular government, proceedeth from the ambition of some, that are kinder to the government of an assembly, whereof they may hope to participate, than of monarchy, which they despair to enjoy.

3. *No man can without injustice protest against the institution of the sovereign declared by the major part.* Thirdly, because the major part hath by consenting voices declared a sovereign; he that dissented must now consent with the rest; that is, be contented to avow all the actions he shall do, or else justly be destroyed by the rest. For if he voluntarily entered into the congregation of them that were assembled, he sufficiently declared thereby his will, and therefore tacitly covenanted, to stand to what the major part should ordain: and therefore if he refuse to stand thereto, or make protestation against any of their decrees, he does contrary to his covenant, and therefore unjustly. And whether he be of the congregation, or not; and whether his consent be asked, or not, he must either submit to their decrees, or be left in the condition of war he was in before; wherein he might without injustice be destroyed by any man whatsoever.

4. *The sovereign's actions cannot be justly accused by the subject.* Fourthly, because every subject is by this institution author of all the actions, and judgments of the sovereign instituted; it follows, that whatsoever he doth, it can be no injury to any of his subjects; nor ought he to be by any of them accused of injustice. For he that doth anything by authority from another, doth therein no injury to him by whose authority he acteth: but by this institution of a commonwealth, every particular man is author of all the sovereign doth: and consequently he that complaineth of injury from his sovereign, complaineth of that whereof he himself is author; and therefore ought not to accuse any man but himself; no nor himself of injury; because to do injury to one's self, is im-

possible. It is true that they that have sovereign power may commit iniquity; but not injustice, or injury in the proper signification.

5. *Whatsoever the sovereign doth is unpunishable by the subject.* Fifthly, and consequently to that which was said last, no man that hath sovereign power can justly be put to death, or otherwise in any manner by his subjects punished. For seeing every subject is author of the actions of his sovereign; he punisheth another for the actions committed by himself.

6. *The sovereign is judge of what is necessary for the peace and defence of his subjects.* And because the end of this institution, is the peace and defence of them all; and whosoever has right to the end, has right to the means; it belongeth of right, to whatsoever man, or assembly that hath the sovereignty, to be judge both of the means of peace and defence, and also of the hindrances, and disturbances of the same; and to do whatsoever he shall think necessary to be done, both beforehand, for the preserving of peace and security, by prevention of discord at home, and hostility from abroad; and, when peace and security are lost, for the recovery of the same. And therefore,

And judge of what doctrines are fit to be taught them. Sixthly, it is annexed to the sovereignty, to be judge of what opinions and doctrines are averse, and what conducing to peace; and consequently, on what occasions, how far, and what men are to be trusted withal, in speaking to multitudes of people; and who shall examine the doctrines of all books before they be published. For the actions of men proceed from their opinions; and in the well-governing of opinions, consisteth the well-governing of men's actions, in order to their peace, and concord. And though in matter of doctrine, nothing ought to be regarded but the truth; yet this is not repugnant to regulating the same by peace. For doctrine repugnant to peace, can no more be true, than peace and concord can be against the law of nature. It is true, that in a commonwealth, where by the negligence, or unskilfulness of governors, and teachers, false doctrines are by time generally received; the contrary truths may be generally offensive. Yet the most sudden, and rough busling in of a new truth, that can be, does never break the peace, but only sometimes awake the war. For those men that are so remissly governed, that they dare take up arms to defend, or introduce an opinion, are still in war; and their condition not peace, but only a cessation of arms for fear of one another; and they live, as it were, in the precincts of battle continually. It belongeth therefore to him that hath the sovereign power, to be judge, or constitute all judges of opinions and doctrines, as a thing necessary to peace; thereby to prevent discord and civil war. . . .

9. And of making war, and peace, as he shall think best. Ninthly, is annexed to the sovereignty, the right of making war and peace with other nations, and commonwealths; that is to say, of judging when it is for the public good, and how great forces are to be assembled, armed, and paid for that end; and to levy money upon the subjects, to defray the expenses thereof. For the power by which the people are to be defended, consisteth in their armies; and the strength of an army, in the union of their strength under one command; which command the sovereign instituted, therefore hath; because the command of the *militia*, without other institution, maketh him that hath it sovereign. And therefore whosoever is made general of an army, he that hath the sovereign power is always generalissimo. . . .

Sovereign power not so hurtful as the want of it, and the hurt proceeds for the greatest part from not submitting readily to a less. But a man may here object, that the condition of subjects is very miserable; as being obnoxious to the lusts, and other irregular passions of him, or them that have so unlimited a power in their hands. And commonly they that live under a monarch, think it the fault of monarchy; and they that live under the government of democracy, or other sovereign assembly, attribute all the inconvenience to that form of commonwealth; whereas the power in all forms, if they be perfect enough to protect them, is the same: not considering that the state of man can never be without some incommodity or other; and that the greatest, that in any form of government can possibly happen to the people in general, is scarce sensible in respect of the miseries, and horrible calamities, that accompany a civil war, or that dissolute condition of masterless men, without subjection to laws, and a coercive power to tie their hands from rapine and revenge: nor considering that the greatest pressure of sovereign governors, proceedeth not from any delight, or profit they can expect in the damage or weakening of their subjects, in whose vigour, consisteth their own strength and glory; but in the restiveness of themselves, that unwillingly contributing to their own defence, make it necessary for their governors to draw from them what they can in time of peace, that they may have means on any emergent occasion, or sudden need, to resist, or take advantage on their enemies. For all men are by nature provided of notable multiplying glasses, that is their passions and self-love, through which, every little payment appeareth a great grievance; but are destitute of those prospective glasses, namely moral and civil science, to see afar off the miseries that hang over them, and cannot without such payments be avoided.

Adapted from: Thomas Hobbes, *Leviathan*, pp. 80–83, 85–86, 98–102, 103–106, 109–110, 113–118, 122–124, 129–139, 141. Edited by Michael Oakeshott. Copyright © 1962 by Macmillan Publishing Company. Reprinted by permission of Scribner, a Division of Simon & Schuster, Inc. ✦

6

Intending (Political) Obligation

Hobbes and the Voluntary Basis of Society

Gordon J. Schochet

II

... For Hobbes, it was a foregone conclusion that any situation in which there was obligation or duty—indeed, any relationship between human beings—had to be the result of some prior "paction," "covenant," or act of consent. The only way a person could be subject to the power and authority of another was through the former's actual agreement or consent. Because there was no status in nature, all differentiations were conventional.

The "natural" and original human situation, as is well known, was one of utter equality and independence. This was no idyllic state of nature, but a desperate, insecure, and unstable isolation from which all the consequences, conventions, and conveniences of human sociability were absent. Self-interest and fear—the rawest and most basic of human emotions—reigned supreme, and people lived only by their wits and strengths. For beneath the equality and liberty of "meer nature" were the drive for self-preservation and the accompanying entitlement ("right" is the Hobbesian locution) to do anything that was conceived necessary to sustain one's life. This "right" included defensively attacking and even killing other humans, all of whom were regarded as enemies because they wanted the same things as the self, were driven by the same fears, and had the same entitlements. Such were the conditions that precipitated the bleak "war of all against all."[1] How, then, could it ever have been the case that people escaped this situation and found themselves in (long-term) relationships with others?

The same power and sheer, brute strength that characterized life in the state of nature provided the only route to a stable and secure existence. But the *imposition* of "authority" and the establishment of social ties by means of strength and might would destroy natural "freedom" and equality. Society, with its hierarchical structures—of which authority is preeminent—and the various behaviors it *requires* of people, appears to be in violation of the original provisions and guarantees of nature. What had happened to, and what was the point of, natural freedom and equality if they could *legitimately* be overcome simply by strength?

The point of freedom for Hobbes, seen in conjunction with his conception of natural rights, was that it made each person the sovereign lord over his—and pointedly *her*—own movements and activities. People had to be the authors of whatever statuses they occupied, which required the engagement, in some sense, of their wills. If the route from the state of nature to society was, paradoxically perhaps, by way of that very power whose absence made the natural condition so precarious, it was paved with the *intentional* surrender of equality and liberty. Anything short of strict intentionality deprived people of their rights in violation of the dictates of nature. But Hobbes found an effective way around what could have been a serious dilemma for his theory: he simply read consent back into the generation of all relationships, including that between parents and children.

III

Hobbes distinguished two sources of sovereign power: "acquisition" and "institution," the one based on the "Naturall force" of the sovereign-to-be, the other derived from people's "agreement amongst themselves, to submit to some Man, or Assembly of men, voluntarily."[2] In both cases, it was the "consent" of the individual that translated physical power into civil entitlement, thereby legitimating the existence of the sovereign. The general arguments are familiar enough, and we need not linger over their details.

Institution is the better known of the two processes and the one that seems more satisfactorily to comport with what is taken to be the primary structure of *Leviathan*. The awful state of nature, with its equality of natural rights and natural-law dictates that people *"endeavour Peace"* and *"be willing, when others are so too, . . . to lay down this right to all things,"*[3] would play little role in Hobbes's argument were there no account of sovereignty by institution. It is the general and collective or mutual fear of one's co-residents of the state of nature that leads to the renunciation in the so-called social contract, to which the emergent sovereign is not a party.

The rights of acquisition, on the other hand, have their roots in individual self-preservation, the fear of a *specific* person, and a direct relationship between subject and sovereign. Remarking that "the Rights and Consequences" of acquired sovereignty "are the very same as those of a Sovereign by Institution,"[4] Hobbes dropped the distinction after chapter 20 of *Leviathan*.[5]

It would be very difficult to put the two conceptions together, however, for there are important distinctions between the accounts of sovereign origins that Hobbes simply ignored. The rights of acquisition spring from the "gratitude" of subjects in response to the benevolence of the conquering sovereigns who spared their lives. Gratitude was the fourth law of nature and seems to have imposed a substantive rule of social behavior on the inhabitants of the state of nature apart from and prior to their agreement. In one of the most interesting but neglected passages in *Leviathan*, Hobbes wrote:

> As Justice dependeth on Antecedent Covenant; so does GRATITUDE depend on Antecedent Grace; that is to say, Antecedent Free-gift . . . [and] may be conceived in this Forme, *That a man which receiveth Benefit from another of meer Grace,*
> *Endeavour that he which giveth it, have no reasonable cause to repent him of his good will.* For no man giveth, but with intention of Good to himselfe; because Gift is Voluntary; and of all Voluntary Acts, the Object is to every man his own Good; of which if men see they shall be frustrated, there will be no beginning of benevolence, or trust; nor consequently of mutuall help; nor of reconciliation of one man to another; and therefore they are to remain still in the condition of *War;* which is contrary to the first and Fundamentall Law of Nature, which commandeth men to *Seek Peace.*[6]

When applied to conquest or the imposition of power by "Naturall Force," gratitude requires that people commit themselves to their new sovereigns *because* their lives have not been taken.

I shall argue below that sovereigns by acquisition, in effect, enter into reciprocal agreements with their subjects—to spare their lives in return for their obedience—and that the resultant obligation is directly conditional. These aspects of acquisition are related to the debt of gratitude and further distinguish it from institution. While it is true that subjects who collectively institute sovereign authority over themselves do so in the expectation that their lives will be rendered more secure, there is nothing in their agreement to impose that requirement upon the ruler. They and all subsequent members of civil society retain their rights to self-preservation because that is the one natural right that is not surrendered in the social compact.

Hobbes's reasons for this claim are logical rather than empirical or contractual: people cannot be supposed to have surrendered control over the very thing—security of life—for which they sought the safety and protection of civil society. Accordingly, their duties do not reach so far as to require that they cooperate in sovereign commands that jeopardize their lives, even if their prior actions would have justified the sovereign's attempt to take their lives.

This situation presents one of the most troublesome, but one of the clearest, dilemmas of *Leviathan*. The general principle—derived from Hobbes's notions of "personation" and "authorization"[7]—is that every subject is the author of every act of the sovereign and so cannot resist what he or she has already consented to. This principle is limited by each individual's retention of the right of self-preservation.[8] Nonetheless, the sovereign possesses the right of capital punishment, which is also a state of nature right carried over into civil society.[9] Any attempt to exercise it, however, places the sovereign in a state of nature relationship with the particular subject whose life is threatened.

True, no other subjects are entitled to join in the resistance to sovereign authority[10]—unless, of course, they perceive the threat to one subject's life as an attack on their own as well, in which case they too presumably have the right to resist[11]—so the entire fabric of the society is not destroyed. Also, subjects are not permitted to threaten one another's lives. Only the sovereign has that entitlement, but it is an entitlement that places no constraints on anyone else. It is a legitimate and proper right that is not matched by a corresponding duty on the part of whomever it is claimed against. Instead, the sovereign's right to take the lives of his or her subjects is actually challenged by an equally legitimate and proper right to resist the sovereign's power. This is precisely the theoretical impasse that characterized the state of nature and required the establishment of sovereignty for its resolution; but in this instance, it is the presence of sovereignty that creates the conflict. The negation of the sovereign's authority in cases such as this is a consequence of the private reservations unavoidably made by each party to the contract that created governance. It is a rare—if not unique and somewhat peculiar—circumstance in which Hobbes permitted the intrusion of private judgment into civil affairs.

Although Hobbesian sovereigns do not (ought not to?) wantonly or indifferently threaten the lives of their subjects, even though they have the right to do so, their grounds or reasons for refraining are strictly prudential.[12] Their actions are not based on a principled conception of the nature of sovereignty nor upon a necessary concern for the welfare of their subjects. Rulers do not (or should not) invade their subjects without

sufficient cause because they know that subjects who feel threatened are not so likely to obey as those who are contented. In short, the stable continuation of authority is a direct consequence of the subjects' continued obedience.

But this is hardly a limit on sovereign power, and certainly not a contractual one. Hobbes insisted that there could be no limits imposed on sovereignty without destroying it and the commonwealth as well.[13] Even though it is the reason people in the state of nature agree to the institution of a commonwealth and, from their perspectives, constitutes the ground of their obedience to the sovereign's rule, guaranteeing the personal security of the life and interests of each subject (by the provision of public peace and freedom from external threats) is not the sovereign's *duty*. Sovereigns—at least those who are instituted—have no duties other than those imposed by God. Acquired sovereignty presents rather a different picture from all this, for the political relationship is a consequence of a bargain struck between the sovereign—typically represented by Hobbes as a conqueror of some sort—and each would-be subject: "Every subject in a Common-wealth, hath covenanted to obey the Civill Law, (either one with another, as when they assemble to make a common Representative, or *with the Representative it selfe one by one, when subdued by the Sword they promise obedience, that they may receive life;*)."[14]

The context is suggestive of a "gunman situation" in which one is faced with the choice of surrendering either "your money or your life." In this case, the choice is "your liberty or your life." So far as Hobbes was concerned, the alternatives were not at all difficult for the rational person, who would naturally prefer life. In return for sparing their lives, the conqueror is entitled to the obedience of the vanquished foes. The obligation to obey the sovereign is rooted in the subject's consent and is therefore no less complete than that which results from the state of nature compact: "It is not therefore the Victory, that giveth the right of Dominion over the Vanquished, but his own Covenant."[15] Furthermore, the covenant is no less valid because coerced, for "Covenants entred into by fear, in the condition of meer Nature, are obligatory."[16]

There is at least one major difference between institution and acquisition that Hobbes never addressed: the sovereign is a party to the agreement. That agreement is actually a contract imposing conditions on both sides.[17] When the sovereign either ceases to protect the subject's life or appears to threaten it, the duty to obey is at an end.[18] This reading has the advantage of being able to account for the sovereign's protection of the subjects' lives on grounds that are theoretically more plausible than the prudence that results from the social contract. But by giving the subject a theoretical or moral claim against the sovereign, it calls into question Hobbes's insistence that the sovereign was answerable to no one on earth.[19]

The other form of acquired sovereignty that Hobbes discussed was "Dominion Paternall," the power of parents over their children in the state of nature. Like the rights of conquest, paternal authority was said to be derived from consent rather than the circumstance that brought parent and child together: "The right of Dominion by Generation, is that, which the Parent hath over his Children; and is called PATERNALL. And is not so derived from the Generation, as if therefore the Parent had Dominion over his Child because he begat him; but from the Childs Consent, either expresse, or by other sufficient arguments declared."[20] The actual consent of the child had to be projected into the future, because along with "naturall fooles" and "mad-men," they "had never the power to make any covenant, or to understand the consequences thereof; and consequently never took upon them to authorise the actions of any Soveraign."[21]

This entire discussion is rather strange and strained. It is part of Hobbes's attempt to deny the existence of status relationships in the condition of "meer Nature." It makes sense, ultimately, on the ground that in the prepolitical world of the state of nature, parents were sovereigns: "A great Family if it be not part of some Commonwealth, is of it self, as to the Rights of Soveraignty, a little Monarchy; whether that Family consist of a man and his children; or of a man and his servants; or of a man, and his children, and servants together: wherein the Father or Master is the Sovereign."[22]

The argument reveals a kind of conceptual embarrassment. Mothers did give birth in the state of nature, but Hobbes insisted upon rooting the consequences of this undeniably natural phenomenon in convention. Appealing to the law of gratitude without calling it by name, he said that children owed their parents obedience because they had let them live: "Preservation of life being the end, for which one man becomes subject to another, every man is *supposed*[23] to promise obedience, to him, in whose power it is to save, or destroy him."[24]

IV

One further point is worth mentioning in this context. Hobbes divided the process of instituting civil society into two forms, which can conveniently be termed "surrender" and "transfer." In the one case, prospective subjects simply set aside or renounced their natural rights to all things without further qualification;[25] whereas in the other, those rights were explicitly and specifically transferred or conveyed to someone else.[26] This distinction is not usually recognized in the literature, but even where it is, the prevailing interpretation is that no significant differences follow from one or the other method of institution.

Generally speaking, this is a correct but incomplete interpretation. By standing outside the state of nature agreement, the sovereign surrenders nothing and retains the natural right to all things, which cannot be increased by any transfer from those who do take part. More to the point, those state of nature rights are sufficient to establish sovereign power and entitlement, which do not require the addition of the rights previously belonging to the members of the civil society:

> He that renounceth, or passeth away his Right, giveth not any other man a Right which he had not before; because there is nothing to which every man had not Right by Nature: but onely standeth out of his way, that he may enjoy his own

originall Right, without hindrance from him; not without hindrance from another. So that the effect which redoundeth to one man, by another mans defect of Right, is but so much diminution of impediments to the use of his own Right originall.[27]

This is but a part of the picture, however, and the starkest one at that, for it contains only the absolutist kernel of sovereignty and nothing of the richness of Hobbes's conceptions of representation, "personation," and authorization. Without that part of the theory and without some means of linking it to the voluntary and intentional movement from the state of nature to civil society, the larger argument of *Leviathan* must collapse. Only if they have actually *transferred* some part of their own power and authority to the sovereign who is to exercise it in their behalf can the members of a commonwealth be said to be the *authors* of as well as to have *willed*—and therefore in both senses to have *intended*—the sovereign's laws. All the acts of the sovereign are equally the acts of every member of the commonwealth:

A Multitude of men, are made *One* Person, when they are by one man, or one Person, Represented; so that it be done with the consent of every one of that Multitude in particular. For it is the *Unity* of the Representer, not the *Unity* of the Represented, that maketh the Person *One*. And it is the Representer that beareth the Person, and but one Person: And *Unity*, cannot otherwise be understood in a Multitude.

And because the Multitude naturally is not *One*, but *Many;* they cannot be understood for one; but many Authors, of every thing their Representative saith,[28] or doth in their name; Every man giving their common Representer, Authority from himselfe in particular; and owning all the Actions the Representer doth, in case they give him Authority without stint.[29]

Political obligation is thus direct and, as it were, organic—almost Rousseauian, for people are required merely to obey themselves when they are commanded by their sovereign (with the obvious difference, of course, that they are hardly "as free as they were before").

In the absence of this connection, there is no tie between subject and sovereign. The *Reason* for obeying remains the fact that the sovereign's might replaces the instability and generalized and "continuall feare"[30] of the state of nature—instead of fearing everyone, subjects need only fear the sovereign— and provides the security that is prerequisite to the commodious industries and arts of organized society. The *justification* of the duty to obey is simply the obligation of the oath of renunciation itself and its commitment "not to hinder those, to whom such Right is granted, or abandoned, from the benefit of it."[31]

V

Theories of political obligation represent attempts to reconcile the conflicts between *duty* and *interest*, for it is at the intersection of those radically different concepts that the most significant and troublesome questions arise. The history of these theories appears to resemble a game in which only two winning moves are possible: either interest must be reduced to duty, or duty must be derived from interest. Only by collapsing one of the categories into the other can the conflicts between them be overcome.

It is the burden of *Leviathan* to validate the second of those moves and to argue, in [a] rather complex but never convoluted way, that whatever is revealed as one's duty is so because it fulfills her or his interests. As the sole and independent guardians of their own interests, people must personally be the authors of all their duties; they must *will* them upon themselves.

It is here, incidentally, that Hobbes's solution to the problem of political obligation in the Engagement Oath controversy is at its most brilliant. He held that the confusions and upheavals of the Civil War resulted from the intrusion of private conscience and judgment into the public, political realm. It was certainly true in the state of nature "and also under Civill Government, in such cases as are not determined by the law," that "*every private man is Judge of Good and Evil ac-*

tions." But this was not the case where the sovereign's will had been declared, for "the Law is the publique Conscience" by which everyone living in a commonwealth "hath already undertaken to be guided."[32] Hobbes distinguished between obligation and commitment, which were matters of will, and belief, which was a matter of conscience and judgment.[33] Thus, one could safely take the Engagement no matter what his moral, religious, or political scruples. Interest and duty happily coincided—as they always did according to Hobbes if they were properly understood—and the sanctity of conscience was preserved.

At the same time, Hobbes's insistence upon basing obligation on the self-willed act of the individual subject has the makings of an astoundingly anarchistic doctrine, for it followed from this premise that any one who had not committed himself or herself to the commonwealth was not bound by its laws. Such a person, of course, was in the condition of "meer nature" and was an outlaw and enemy to the commonwealth, one of those "masterlesse men" about whom Hobbes was so concerned.[34] But that was not the end of the story, for Hobbes had a number of traps set for his readers, starting with his indifference to coercion.

VI

An obligation one is *forced* to acknowledge because the costs of refusal are greater than those of acceptance is no less valid, no less binding than one that is fully and happily accepted. An obligation of recompense that stems from some "benefit" bestowed where there was no opportunity to reject is equally binding—not because "one good turn deserves another," as the adage goes, but because by reaping the benefits, a person was presumed to have agreed to their costs. Even the content of a prospective obligation was of little moment for Hobbes, so long as it did not violate the laws of the commonwealth or threaten the subject's sole, remaining natural right, the right to life.

Another of the snares employed by Hobbes is his conception of rationality. He argued that a proper and rational under-

standing of one's interests would lead to the recognition that the political order imposed by an absolute sovereign was always to be preferred to a situation in which each person individually sought to maximize his or her advantages. Rejection of sovereign rule would be a prima facie sign of nonrationality and, therefore, of a failure to comprehend the nature of one's own interests. The duty to obey the sovereign—political obligation—was thus a consequence of rationality. By using the subject's intentional act to create the *mechanism* that tied him or her to the sovereign, rationality permitted a person to appreciate and efficiently to pursue the objects of interest.

In the end, the argument rested upon a circular account of the relationship of rationality to consent. It appears to support Hobbes's case for the intentional origins of political organization and certainly strengthens his implicit case for the derivation of duty from interest. On closer examination, however, it turns out that the cost is part of the plausibility of his position. A consent that definitionally one cannot help but give lest she or he be deemed nonrational and therefore incapable of consenting in the first place is hardly consent in any standard sense of the term and adds nothing to the theoretical claim.

The very point of consent and intention, as Hobbes well appreciated, is that one *could have* done otherwise but, for whatever reason, *chose* not to do so and committed herself or himself. In these terms, it is possible to understand without necessarily embracing Hobbes's indifference to the coercive force of the conqueror's offer to spare a person's life as the intentional source of the subject's obligation to accept his rule. Life is filled with difficult and painful choices, but they are choices nonetheless. The fact that we can conceive of circumstances in which people would choose death over servitude or gross immorality[35] underscores the role of intention. On the other hand, a situation in which one had no choice—in which failure to make the requisite selection would be taken as a sign of incapacity—by its nature cannot be one that is controlled by volition. So-called acts of consent given under such circumstances would be no more intentional than the breaths drawn by someone who is asleep.

Hobbes was certainly correct in his implicit presumption that self-assumed obligations are in general more legitimate than those that are imposed on someone against her or his will. To say this is to agree with him that the starting point of a theory of obligation is human liberty,[36] for an individual can only be *bound* to do that which before becoming so obliged he or she was free not to do. This is especially true of promise making and, correspondingly, of consenting, for in these cases it is the engagement of the will that legitimately circumscribes personal freedom.

What problems there are with Hobbes's theory are consequences of both his presumption of the conventional nature of all forms of status among human beings and his corresponding insistence upon their voluntary origins. The "conventional state" is one of the identifying features of modern politics, and at its most basic level, it numbers Hobbes among its primary architects. But it does not follow from the view of the state as a malleable contrivance that can be tailored to suit human needs that all its structures were *intentionally* erected. Hobbes's reductionist claims reveal the futility of attempting to root all duties and obligations in personal consent. Some of his arguments are conceptually flawed or require strange or absurd distortions, but others are simply outrageous. Interestingly enough, he had at hand a means of salvaging the most substantial of his claims—his fourth law of nature, the law of gratitude—but he chose to derive even that dictate from consent.

The difficulty with a doctrine of strict intentionality, as Hobbes apparently understood, is that the failure or absence of intention defeats any claim for the existence of obligation or duty. For Hobbes, intentionality was necessary to preserve original and natural human freedom and equality. Some modern theories, notably those of Robert Nozick and other individualist libertarians, make the same presuppositions as Hobbes but end with strikingly different conclusions. Whereas the objectives for Hobbes were the preservation of social and political duties and the *practical* denigration of human freedom, libertarians seek to preserve freedom at the expense of the political order. Accordingly, Hobbes deduced intention from obligation, and libertarianism denies obligation in the absence of individual intentions to be bound. Hobbes's polity is maximal; that of libertarianism is minimal. Although not necessarily politically more acceptable than the theory of *Leviathan*, libertarianism on its face is more coherent and less exaggerated. Both doctrines show the difficulties inherent in any attempt to extract the whole of political duty from consent and intention.

VII

A "liberal" theory of political obligation would have to be very different from that of Hobbes. The essence of liberalism is its opposition to the absolutist conception of the "conventional state," of which Hobbes was an early and exceptionally articulate champion. That opposition usually takes the form of some version or another of *constitutionalism*, the doctrine that there are substantive limits to political authority as well as specific procedures through which it should act; the violation of either of these restrictions renders state action illegal. Constitutionalist restrictions spring from and have as their chief goal the preservation and enhancement of the rights and liberties of the members of the civil society. The contrasts with Hobbes are virtually self-evident, and it is something of a mystery that critics of liberalism should be so blind to these differences.

Far from being a "liberal" himself, Hobbes represented what emergent liberal ideology would have to overcome in order to sustain its defense of constitutionalist politics. The goal was to defend a conventional account of the state that did not collapse into absolutism or ineffectually wither away, leaving its members undefended in either case. It is a goal that still motivates the liberal spirit.[37]

Notes

1. See, of course, Thomas Hobbes, *Leviathan*, ed. C. B. Macpherson (Baltimore: Penguin, 1968), ch. 13, esp. p. 186.
2. Ibid., ch. 17, p. 228.

3. Ibid., ch. 14, p. 190.

4. Ibid., ch. 20, p. 256. See also ch. 20, p. 252: "But the Rights, and Consequences of Sovereignty are the same in both."

5. In his earlier *The Elements of Law: Natural and Politic*, he wrote of "Monarchy by acquisition" and monarchy "made by political institution, . . . whatsoever rights be in the one, the same also be in the other. And therefore I shall no longer speak of them, as distinct, but of monarchy in general" (2d ed., ed. Ferdinand Tönnies with an introduction by M. M. Goldsmith [London: Frank Cass and Co., 1969], pt. 2, ch. 4, sec. 10, p. 135).

6. *Leviathan*, ch. 15, p. 209. See also ch. 11, p. 163, and ch. 30, p. 382; cf. ch. 6, p. 123.

7. See ibid., ch. 16, esp. pp. 217–18, 221; and ch. 21, p. 265 ("Every Subject is Author of every act the Sovereign doth"); cf. ch. 27, p. 346.

8. Ibid., ch. 21, pp. 268–69.

9. Why the sovereign retains this right of nature will be considered shortly.

10. *Leviathan*, ch. 21, p. 270: "To resist the Sword of the Common-wealth, in defence of another man, guilty, or innocent, no man hath Liberty."

11. This is not merely a moot or arcane point, for there are many situations in which it is already too late to act in self-defense by the time one perceives direct threats to her or his life. One must be not only cautious and careful but prudent as well.

12. That is, they are based on inferences drawn from experience—which is the standard Hobbesian meaning of "prudence"—and are not merely the results of rationally calculated self-interest—which is one of the modern meanings of "prudence" that is often incorrectly read back into Hobbes. In this case, it is easy to understand the source of this interpretation, for it is clearly in the interest of sovereigns to protect and preserve their subjects.

13. *Leviathan*, ch. 29, esp. pp. 367–68 and 372–73.

14. Ibid., ch. 26, p. 314; emphasis added. See also ch. 21, p. 268: Sovereignty "by Acquisition [is] by Covenants of the Vanquished to the Victor, or Child to the Parent."

15. Ibid., ch. 20, pp. 255–56.

16. Ibid., ch. 19, p. 198; see also ch. 21, p. 262.

17. Cf. ibid., ch. 18, p. 231: "The opinion that any Monarch receiveth his Power by Covenant, that is to say on Condition, proceedeth from want of understanding."

18. Immediately after the passage just quoted, Hobbes wrote, "Nor is the Victor obliged by an enemies rendering himselfe, (without promise of life,) to spare him for this his yeelding to discretion; which obliges not the Victor longer, than in his own discretion hee shall think fit" (*Leviathan*, ch. 20, p. 256). The parenthesis especially supports my contention that upon acceptance of the offer of life, a reciprocal relationship is established between sovereign and vanquished subject.

19. See, e.g., *Leviathan*, ch. 19, p. 246, and ch. 21, p. 265.

20. Ibid., ch. 20, p. 253. For a fuller account of "Dominion Paternall," see chapter 12 of my *The Authoritarian Family and Political Attitudes in 17th-Century England: Patriarchalism in Political Thought*, 2d ed. (New Brunswick, N.J.: Transaction Books, 1987), part of which is summarized here.

21. *Leviathan*, ch. 26, p. 317.

22. Ibid., ch. 20, p. 257

23. "Supposed" is used here by Hobbes in the sense of presumed, not in the modern sense of ought.

24. *Leviathan*, ch. 20, p. 254; emphasis added.

25. E.g., ibid., ch. 14, p. 190.

26. E.g., ibid, ch. 17, p. 227.

27. Ibid., ch. 14, p. 191.

28. I have silently corrected an apparent and amusing typographer's error in McPherson's text, which reads "faith," presumably due to the substitution of an *f* for the elongated seventeenth-century *s*.

29. *Leviathan*, ch. 16, pp. 220–21. See also ch. 21, p. 265: "Every Subject is Author of every act the Sovereign doth."

30. Ibid., ch. 13, p. 186.

31. Ibid., ch. 14, p. 191. Obviously, this argument applies to the transfer of natural rights as well. My contention is that when rights are specifically transferred to someone else, an additional and more overtly *intentional* tie on the subject is created.

32. Ibid., ch. 29, pp. 365–66. The same argument had been made in *De Cive*, ch. 12, and *The Elements of Law*, pt. 2, ch. 8, sec. 4, but with considerably less force than in *Leviathan*.

33. Considering the command or law of a sovereign who claimed to be enforcing God's will, Hobbes wrote that the subject is "bound I say to obey it, but not bound to believe it" (*Leviathan*, ch. 26, p. 332; see also ch. 29, p. 366).

34. *Leviathan*, chs. 17 and 21, pp. 238 and 266.

35. On Hobbes's account, of course, such people would not be rational, which raises again the issues I have just discussed. Although we may agree with such characterizations in some general sense, there are significant exceptions, and presumably, we would not definitionally consign those who opted for the "less desirable" alternative to some status beyond the reach of this theory.

36. H. L. A. Hart's classic article, "Are There Any Natural Rights?" *Philosophical Review* 64 (1955): 175–91, still seems persuasive on this issue and unsurpassed in the subsequent literature.

37. The original impetus for this paper was provided many years ago by the late Benjamin Evans Lippincott, then my adviser and subsequently a valued friend. Even before I enrolled as a graduate student at the University of Minnesota, Ben imposed Warrender's *Political Philosophy of Hobbes* on me, and I have been dazzled by the book's conceptual brilliance but troubled by its interpretative perversity ever since. This paper is something of a response to the general problem posed by Warrender in terms that I hope Ben would have appreciated.

The first draft was completed during my tenure as a Fellow of the Center for the History of Freedom at Washington University, St. Louis, Missouri, during the winter and spring of 1988; both the Fellowship and Research Divisions of the National Endowment for the Humanities have supported the research out of which this essay has grown. It is a pleasure to record my indebtedness to these institutions. I also wish to thank Molly Shanley, Sharon Lloyd, Robinson Grover, Sharon Achinstein, David Wootton, Mary Dietz, and especially Louise Haberman, all of whom made valuable suggestions that helped to bridge the gap between this version and the initial draft as presented to the Benjamin Evans Lippincott Symposium on the Political Philosophy of Hobbes, at the University of Minnesota (spring 1988).

7

The Art of Government

Deborah Baumgold

> As if when Men quitting the State of
> Nature entered into Society, they agreed
> that all of them but one, should be under
> the restraint of Laws, but that he should
> still retain all the Liberty of the State of
> Nature, increased with Power, and made
> licentious by Impunity. This is to think
> that Men are so foolish that they take care
> to avoid what Mischiefs may be done them
> by Pole-Cats, or Foxes, *but are content,
> nay think it* Safety, *to be devoured by*
> Lions.

—John Locke, *The Second
Treatise of Government,*
section 93

In popular imagination, Hobbism has come to be identified with arbitrary despotism, even with twentieth-century totalitarianism. To be sure, Hobbes denies in principle the distinction between good and bad government, describing "tyranny" as but the term for monarchy misliked.[1] His formal permission of arbitrary rule inspires images of political horror, like this picture of a mad king. "The citizen of Hobbes's leviathan state is . . . faced with the terrifying absurdity of finding himself totally obligated to obey an insane individual who will not listen to Parliament's advice or seek its assent, and who may be utterly incapable of protecting and governing himself, much less the commonwealth."[2] But more careful readers notice that Hobbes commends fair and lawful government, directed to the common interest. Chapter 30 of *Leviathan,* "Of the OFFICE of the Sovereign Representative," enjoins concern for the people's safety and prosperity, political education, promulgation of good laws, equal justice and taxation, fair execution of punishments and rewards, and the discriminating choice of counselors and military commanders.

Noticing Hobbes's preference for good government is one thing; it is another thing to account this counsel an integral and significant part of the larger theory. The latter view faces several objections. On the supposition that Hobbism is a theory of obligation, which locates the source of state power in a supportive citizenry, his advice regarding the exercise of sovereignty has to be seen as a secondary part of the theory, tangential to the main account of the generation of sovereign power. This first objection merely reflects the familiar bias of orthodox Hobbes studies. Second, there is a common inclination to juxtapose Hobbes's discussion of sovereigns' duties against his account of their rights, and to give the latter much more importance than the former. Mario Cattaneo, for instance, whose commentaries on Hobbes's juridical doctrine emphasize the "liberal" character of this part of the theory, nonetheless concedes there is a "contradiction between the absolute power of the prince and the principle of legality for the protection of the subject."[3] But this is erroneous. Hobbes intended his discussion of rulers' duties to complement the prescription of an absolutist constitution. The enumeration of sovereigns' duties in chapter 30 of *Leviathan* corresponds, as Table 1 shows, to the enumeration of sovereigns' rights in chapter 18.[4] The correspondence is illustrative of an appreciation for the bearing of the conduct of government, as well as its constitution, on the possibility of good political order.

The last and strongest objection to taking seriously Hobbes's recommendation of good government is simply that it seems implausible to expect a ruler possessing unconditional authority to heed the counsel. As the duty to govern well cannot be enforced by any human agency, it seems unlikely it would count for much in the calculations of a Hobbesian sovereign. Thus the counsel

---

Table 1
Sovereigns' Rights and Duties in *Leviathan*

Chapter 18 "Of the RIGHTS of Soveraignes by Institution"	Chapter 30 "Of the OFFICE of the Soveraign Representative"
1. Foundation of the rights of sovereignty; applications of the principle of unconditional sovereignty (pp.229–232)	1. Duty to maintain essential rights of sovereignty (pp. 376–77)
2. Right to "Judge of what Doctrines are fit to be taught them" (p. 233)	2. Duty to teach the people (pp. 377–85): "The Essentiall Rights of Soveraignty" "Not to affect change of Government" "Nor adhere (against the Soveraign) to Popular men" "Nor to Dispute the Soveraign Power" "And to Honour their Parents" "And to avoyd doing of injury" "And to do all this sincerely from the heart"
3. Right of legislating (p. 234)	3. Duty to make good, i.e., necessary and perspicuous, laws (pp. 387–89)
4. "Right of Judicature" (p. 234)	4. Duty to administer equal justice (p. 385)
5. "Right of making War, and Peace"; of levying money for armies; and of being chief commander (pp. 234–35)	5. Duty to tax equally (pp. 386–87); and to choose good—loyal and popular—army commanders (pp. 393–94)
6. Right of "choosing all Councellours, Ministers, Magistrates, and Officers" (p. 235)	6. Duty "to choose good Counsellours; I mean such" as cannot benefit from evil counsel, and are knowledgeable (pp.391–93)
7. Power of reward and punishment (p. 235)	7. Duty "to make a right application of Punishments and Rewards" (389–391)
8. Right of appointing "Lawes of Honour," e.g., titles (pp. 235-36)	8. Rulers should not show partiality toward "the great," as doing so "encourages rebellion" (pp. 385–86)

stands as no more than a pious supplement to a theory that truly licenses tyranny. This is Locke's objection, and Hobbes himself took it seriously. He states the objection in *De Cive*: "If any man had such a Right [of "Absolute Command"], the condition of the Citizens would be miserable: For thus they think, He will take all, spoil all, kill all; and every man counts it his only happinesse that he is not already spoil'd and kill'd."[5]

There are three Hobbesian replies, the first of which is a negative argument weighing the hazard of wicked rule against the calamity of civil war:

The Power in all formes [of government], *if they be perfect enough to protect them*, is the same; not considering that the estate of Man can never be without some incommodity or other; and that the greatest, that in any forme of Government can possibly happen to the people in generall, is scarce sensible, in respect of the miseries, and horrible calamities, that accompany a Civill Warre; or that dissolute condition of masterlesse men, without

subjection to Lawes, and a coërcive Power to tye their hands from rapine, and revenge.[6]

There is more here than the cynical observation that government per se is a necessary evil in virtue of man's antisocial nature. Hobbes is making a narrower observation about the benefit of an absolutist constitution (i.e., a constitution in which "the [sovereign's] Power . . . is perfect enough to protect them") as a deterrent to civil war. The benefit outweighs the attendant danger of bad government: "He that hath strength enough to protect all, wants not sufficiency to oppress all."[7] In the first instance, then, Hobbes grants that tyranny is a danger inherent to an absolutist constitution, but a risk to be accepted because the constitution deters the greater evil of civil war.

He also thinks, however, that rulers have moral and instrumental reasons for governing well. This is the root issue between Hobbes and constitutionalist thinkers. In the latter's view, legal restraint and popular accountability—the antitheses of unconditional sovereignty—are requisites of good rule. Absolutism is therefore rightly equated with arbitrary government. Hobbes, in this respect typical of royalists in the early Stuart period, distinguishes between the structure of sovereign authority and the conduct of government, "between the *Right*, and the *exercise* of supreme authority.[8] Ruling well is a natural-law duty for which rulers are accountable to God. "And therefore," according to *De Cive*, "there is some security for Subjects in the Oaths which Princes take."[9] But Hobbesian skepticism about the tenets of positive religion precludes attaching strong weight to this consideration. Whereas constitutionalist thinkers favor procedural mechanisms to promote good government, Hobbes counts on sovereigns' interest in ruling well. Duty coheres with interest: "For the duty of a sovereign consisteth in the good government of the people. . . . And as the art and duty of sovereigns consist in the same acts, so also doth their profit."[10]

The argument concerning interest attaches to the role or office of the sovereign, the "politique Person" as opposed to the natural man.[11] Hobbes is therefore only committed to showing that ruling well really is in sovereigns' interest, not to a strong assertion about the propensities of actual rulers. He draws the distinction as between reason and passion, attributing bad rule to "the affections and passions which reign in every one, as well monarch as subject; by which the monarch may be swayed to use that power amiss."[12] In context, which is the comparison of forms of government, this is less than the damaging admission that rationality is unlikely in rulers. Hobbes's immediate point is the greater likelihood of rational rule in a monarchy than in any other form of government. "Where the publique and private interest are most closely united;" *Leviathan* claims, "there is the publique most advanced. Now in Monarchy, the private interest is the same with the publique."[13] Why this should be so, regarding hereditary monarchies at least, is suggested in *De Cive*. When the state is rulers' patrimony, there is dynastic reason for identifying personal with state interest: "We cannot on better con-

dition be subject to any, than one whose interest depends upon our safety, and welfare; and this then comes to passe when we are the Inheritance of the Ruler; for every man of his own accord endeavours the preservation of his inheritance."[14]

It improves the motivational plausibility of the role argument that the operative interest is the ubiquitous human passion of desire for power.[15] The secular motive is expressly contrasted, in *A Dialogue . . . of the Common Laws of England*, with the less certain constraint of divine punishment:

> For if, say they, the King may notwithstanding the law do what he please, and nothing to restrain him but the fear of punishment in the world to come, then, in case there come a king that fears no such punishment, he may take away from us, not only our lands, goods, and liberties, but our lives also if he will. And they say true; but they have no reason to think he will, unless it be for his own profit; which cannot be, for he loves his own power; and what becomes of his power when his subjects are destroyed or weakened, by whose multitude and strength he enjoys his power, and every one of his subjects his fortune?[16]

The proposition that Hobbes must establish is that ruling in the public interest and according to law enhances sovereign power. Good government is also powerful government. Right makes might. Contrary to Cattaneo's view, the same desideratum governs Hobbes's consideration of the exercise of power as guides the argument for absolutism. Good rule, in the framework of unified, unconditional sovereign right, provides twin prescriptions for generating coercive authority. Hobbes's "art of government" is the antipode of Machiavellian statecraft. Both are preoccupied with the very real problems for early modern rulers of consolidating central authority and controlling ambitious rivals. Only Hobbes holds that lawful, fair rule enhances power, while it is Machiavelli who endorses arbitrariness (arguing that for princes it is better to be unpredictable and feared than to be known and loved).[17] They also conceive the problem of good rule differently, Machiavelli focusing on rulers' personal characteristics, their *virtù*, and Hobbes on the incentives of the role.

The Governmental Art

. . . Like the arguments for absolutism, those concerning the exercise of power treat the problem from two sides: on the one hand, the positive prerequisites of power and, on the other, measures deterring challenges to sitting authority. Specifically, Hobbes holds that rulers have a positive interest in their subjects' well-being, and second, that good rule deters elite conflict and rebellion.

"If you be rich I cannot be poor." James I's well-known statement to Parliament is a Hobbesian argument.[18] *Salus populi* is the supreme law and duty of political rule, "by which must be understood, not the mere preservation of their lives, but generally their benefit and good."[19] Caring for the common good, meaning specifically the common wealth, also profits rulers. Hobbes has in mind the dependence of the state, and therefore the sovereign, on social prosperity. "The riches, power, and honour of a Monarch," *Leviathan* observes, "arise onely from the riches, strength and reputation of his Subjects. For no King can be rich, nor glorious, nor secure; whose Subjects are either poore, or contemptible, or too weak through want, or dissention, to maintain a war against their enemies."[20] Taxation, the state's supply, is the pertinent issue. "If therefore," Hobbes explains in *The Elements of Law*,

> the sovereign provide not so as that particular men may have means, both to preserve themselves, and also to preserve the public; the common or sovereign treasure can be none. And on the other side, if it were not for a common and public treasure belonging to the sovereign power, men's private riches would sooner serve to put them into confusion and war, than to secure or maintain them."[21]

Second, there is much that rulers can do to strengthen their position, and provide for public order, by way of deterring rebellion and elite conflict. The list of rulers' duties, which in *Leviathan* is framed to correspond to the list of sovereigns' rights, appears in the earlier versions of the political theory as a series of remedies to the causes of rebellion, although Hobbes's counsel remains substantially the same throughout.[22] According to *De Cive*, "Many things are required to the conservation of inward Peace, because many things concur (as hath been shewed in the foregoing Chapter) to its perturbation."[23] Specifically, Hobbes lists these "concurring" causes of rebellion: popular discontent, ambitious elites, ideological justification, and political organization.[24] Correspondingly, he commends equal taxation, as an antidote to discontent.[25] Equal justice, or the "constant application of rewards, and punishments," deters the ambitious.[26] Rulers ought also to root out false opinions and attack subversive factions. . . .[27]

Juridical Rule and Coercive Authority

. . . Hobbes's political discussions of juridical rule have two themes, general conditions of social order and, more specifically, the art of deterring ambitious rivals. Under the former heading, he explains why government according to law is preferable to arbitrary rule, and offers standards of good lawmaking. It is in connection with the latter that Hobbes sanctions selective justice, meaning the discriminating—but not capricious—exercise of juridical authority.

"Arbitrary" rule usually refers, in Hobbesian usage, to personal rule and is the opposite of rule according to law (e.g., a punishment is "arbitrary" that has not been defined in law).[28] To start, Hobbes's critique of Coke implies a preference for rule by law. Because men naturally disagree and are therefore in conflict, "it was necessary there should be a common measure of all things that might fall in controversy."[29] For the sovereign's judgments to function as that common measure, a settled standard, they must take the form of codified law. *De Cive* justifies legislative authority as an essential sovereign right in these terms:

> Furthermore, since it no lesse, nay it much more conduceth to Peace to prevent brawles from arising, then to appease them being risen; and that all con-

troversies are bred from hence, that the opinions of men differ concerning Meum & Tuum, just and unjust, profitable and unprofitable, good and evil, honest and dishonest, and the like, which every man esteems according to his own judgement; it belongs to the same chiefe power to make some common Rules for all men, and to declare them publiquely, by which every man may know what may be called his, what anothers, what just, what unjust.... But those Rules and measures are usually called the civill Lawes, or the Lawes of the City, as being the Commands of him who hath the supreme power in the City.[30]

The explanation of the bearing of law on social order hinges on the deterrence proposition: "It much more conduceth to Peace to prevent brawles from arising, then to appease them being risen." Hobbes has in mind the idea that laws, with appointed punishments, are efficacious in and of themselves in controlling behavior. Action is governed, generally, by expectations and opinions ("the will of doing, or omitting ought, depends on the opinion of the *good* and *evill* of the *reward*, or *punishment*, which a man conceives he shall receive by the act, or omission; so as the actions of all men are ruled by the opinions of each").[31] Under this general psychological principle, juridical rule provides one way of manipulating opinion, and political education is another. Laws, *The Elements* explains, supply a reason for action, distinct from calculations about the utility of an act. Whereas the latter reasoning is appropriate to covenants ("in simple covenants the action to be done, or not done, is first limited and made known, and then followeth the promise to do or not do"),[32] in the case of laws, "the command [itself] is the reason we have of doing the action commanded."[33]

There are two motivations, by Hobbes's account, for obedience to law: the prior promise to obey the legislator (that is, the political covenant) and fear of punishment. The first is the formal ground of the obligation (according to *De Cive*, for example, "the Law holds the party obliged by vertue of the universall *Contract* of yeelding obedience");[34] the second supplies a prudential motive for obedience ("the Law ... compells

him to make good his promise, for fear of the punishment appointed by the Law").[35] Thus, unlike John Selden, another member of the Tew Circle, Hobbes does not conflate the obligatoriness of law with the sanction of punishment. In Selden's view, " 'The idea of a law carrying obligation irrespective of any punishment annexed to the violation of it ... is no more comprehensible to the human mind than the idea of a father without a child'—i.e. [Richard Tuck comments] it is a logical and not contingent connexion."[36]

Still, Hobbes's position is virtually the same as Selden's inasmuch as he holds that it is fear of punishment that makes laws effectual. "Of all Passions, that which enclineth men least to break the Lawes, is Fear. Nay, (excepting some generous natures,) it is the onely thing, (when there is apparence of profit, or pleasure by breaking the Lawes,) that makes men keep them."[37] "Vindicative"—penal—sanctions are therefore an essential part of law. "In vain therefore is the Law, unlesse it contain both parts, that which *forbids* injuries to be done, and that which *punisheth* the doers of them."[38] In addition, the punishments appointed by law must be sufficient to the purpose of deterring crime. "We must therefore provide for our security, not by *Compacts*, but by *Punishments*." According to *De Cive*:

> And there is then sufficient provision made, when there are so great punishments appointed for every injury, as apparently it prove a greater evill to have done it, then not to have done it: for all men, by a necessity of nature, chuse that which *to them appears to be the lesse evill.*[39]

However, the sanction is not always explicitly included in the law, and is then either "implicit," based on prior instances of punishment, or "arbitrary," dependent on the sovereign's will.[40]

"To the care of the Soveraign, belongeth the making of Good Lawes. But what is a good Law? By a Good Law, I mean not a Just Law: for no Law can be Unjust."[41] From the first proposition, the need for common rules of property and justice, nothing follows about the quality of law. But the accompanying psychological account of the bearing of laws and punishments on expectations, and therefore action, generates criteria for good law and the "right application" of punishment. "A good law is that, which is *Needfull*, for the *Good of the People*, and withall *Perspicuous*."[42] It encourages obedience to limit legislation, as subjects are apt to forget or ignore laws when they are overabundant or otherwise obscure.[43] According to *De Cive*, the policy also encourages private enterprise: "As water inclosed on all hands with banks, stands still and corrupts . . . so subjects, if they might doe nothing without the commands of the Law would grow dull, and unwildly."[44] Brevity is similarly a virtue of good law, aiding understanding and deterring unnecessary litigation.[45] The third criterion falls under the larger claim that rulers have a stake in their subjects' well-being. It cannot be, *Leviathan* explains, that a good law benefits a ruler but not the ruled, "for the good of the Soveraign and People, cannot be separated."[46]

It is further necessary that penal authority be properly exercised because "the fear whereby men are deterred from doing evill, ariseth not from hence, namely, because penalties are set, but because they are executed; for we esteeme the future by what is past, seldome expecting what seldome happens."[47] *Leviathan*'s definition of punishment . . . includes the stipulation that punishment should regard the future good(as opposed to the past evil, meaning punishment for revenge).[48] There follow a series of discriminations between acts of punishment and acts of "hostility." All "evil" inflicted without the intention or possibility of encouraging obedience is simply "hostility," including retribution in excess of penalties set by law. Inadequate penalties also fail to qualify, because then the penalty is rather the price for obtaining the benefit of the crime.[49] When a punishment is not specified in law, and is therefore "arbitrary," it should reflect the same policy of encouraging service to the state and deterring disobedience.[50]

Politic Justice

Hobbes's preoccupation with discouraging those ambitious of political power enters into his discussion of juridical rule. All three works [*Leviathan*, *De Cive*, *The Elements of*

Law] recommend the policy of "equal justice" as a means, specifically, "for the keeping under of those, that are disposed to rebellion by ambition."[51] The consistent execution of punishments helps control political ambition: "By constant application of rewards, and punishments, they may so order it, that men may know that the way to honour is, not by contempt of the present government, nor by factions, and the popular ayre, but by the contraries."[52] In reverse, Hobbes warns against rewarding popular and ambitious subjects, seeking to buy their adherence with money or flattery.[53] Partiality toward the "great" encourages insolence, which encourages hatred, which brings rebellion and the ruin of the state.[54]

Going along with this special emphasis on "constant severity in punishing" great and ambitious subjects, Hobbes recognizes and commends a series of politic discriminations in the administration of justice.[55] "Seeing the end of punishing is not revenge, and discharge of choler; but correction, either of the offender, or of others by his example; the severest Punishments are to be inflicted for those Crimes, that are of most Danger to the Publique."[56] The political criterion of punishment has wide-ranging application—to causes, persons, and crimes and their effects. Crimes that proceed from "malice to the Government established" and "contempt of justice" are worse than "Crimes of Infirmity; such as are those which proceed from great provocation, from great fear, great need, or from ignorance."[57] Prominent persons, who teach and serve as examples to others, bear responsibility for the crimes they encourage, and therefore should be more severely treated:

> The Punishment of the Leaders, and teachers in a Commotion; not the poore seduced People, when they are punished, can profit the Common-wealth by their example. To be severe to the People, is to punish that ignorance, which may in great part be imputed to the Soveraign, whose fault it was, they were no better instructed.[58]

More generally, crimes by the vainglorious great, those who assume that wit, blood, or riches exempt them from punishment, "are not extenuated, but aggravated by the greatnesse of their persons; because they have least need to commit them."[59] Political crimes, for example, assassination attempts and giving secrets to the enemy, are more serious than crimes against private persons; accepting a bribe to perjure oneself is more serious than simple stealing, as are also robbing the public treasury and counterfeiting.[60] In short, the utilitarian principle applies: "The same fact, when it redounds to the dammage of many, is greater, than when it redounds to the hurt of few."[61] These distinctions technically concern the degree of responsibility for crime, excuses from crime, and extenuating circumstances.[62] But they introduce into Hobbesian theory, under the heading of the administration of justice, a substantive legal policy, a policy with more content than the criteria of good law associated with the general deterrent psychology of juridical rule.

Whereas Hobbesian absolutism and jurisprudence, his formal doctrines of sovereign right, license arbitrary rule and iniquitous law,[63] Hobbes's art of government is a normative account of the exercise of coercive and legislative authority. Rule according to law is preferable to personal rule, however fair, because laws and legally appointed punishments deter disobedience. Substantive criteria for legal policy, absent from Hobbesian jurisprudence, follow from that deterrent psychology and from its extension into a policy of discriminating, politic justice. . . .

Conclusion

Something striking follows from Hobbes's prudential accounts of the bearing of the conduct of government on the reality of political power. He holds rulers responsible for their fate and for their societies' character:

> This same *supreme command,* and *absolute power,* seems so harsh to the greatest part of men, as they hate the very naming of them; which happens chiefly through want of knowledge, what *humane nature,* and the *civill Lawes* are, and *partly also through their default, who when they are invested with so great authority, abuse their power to their own lust.*[64]

Political responsibility, of course, is the topic, as opposed to the formal accountability denied by the absolutist constitution. Still, Hobbes describes rebellion as the "naturall punishment" of negligent governments.[65] Furthermore, the "poore seduced People" in a rebellion ought not to be punished severely inasmuch as the sovereign is also at fault for not better instructing them.[66] Short of rebellion, subjects' crimes are extenuated by inconsistent punishment or tacit approval (e.g., duels) on the sovereign's part. In such cases, too, the sovereign "is in part a cause of the transgression"; he "hath his part in the offence."[67] Last, if "the Legislator doth set a lesse penalty on a crime, then will make our feare more considerable with us, then our lust; that excesse of lust above the feare of punishment, whereby sinne is committed, is to be attributed to the Legislator (that is to say) to the supreme";[68] or, as *Leviathan* puts it, such law is an "invitement" to crime.[69]

Assigning responsibility to rulers—to government—is a classic political response to individualistic, moral and psychological, treatments of public goods. The view is articulated by the figure of the "Defaulter" in Colin Strang's dialogue on the principle of universalization (viz., the moral argument that individuals must ask themselves what would happen if everyone acted as they proposed to act):

> If anyone is to blame it is the person whose job it is to circumvent [e.g., tax] evasion. If too few people vote, then it should be made illegal not to vote. If too few people volunteer, then you must introduce conscription. If too many people evade taxes, then you must tighten up your system of enforcement. My answer to your "If everyone did that" is "Then someone had jolly well better see to it that they don't."[70]

Hobbes states the same proposition in *Leviathan*'s introductory, metaphorical description of the commonwealth: "*Reward* and *Punishment* (by which fastned to the seate of the Soveraignty, every joynt and member is moved to performe his duty) are the *Nerves,* that do the same in the Body Naturall."[71] From the introduction of conscription in *Leviathan* to furnish an army, through the recommendation of a tax policy that will "least . . . trouble the mind of them that pay," and the recommendation that juridical rule promotes obedience and order, Hobbes translates political and social problems into problems of governmental policy. This of course does not commit him to the strong negative proposition that rulers bear exclusive responsibility.[72] At issue are the relative significance of governmental versus civic virtue in Hobbes's political understanding and the way in which he thinks about subjects' duties. In this chapter . . . , I have argued that Hobbes reflects first on governmental policy—how civic performance can be structured and encouraged by the state—and only secondarily calculates in terms of citizens' virtue and self-interest.

Last, Hobbes supplies good reasons why rulers ought to govern well, and defines good rule, which is different from and lesser than a defense of the proposition that good rule is expectable. The stronger claim, about the benevolence of Hobbesian absolutism, depends on the plausibility of the identification of role and personal interests. Although an interest in coercive authority may be inherent to the office of the sovereign, this does not assure that actual rulers may not desire other goods more than power, or may not perceive some discrepancy between the pursuit of power for themselves and the requisites of a strong state. It is an objection that Hobbes both grants (e.g., "all the acts of *Nero* are not essentiall to Monarchie")[73] and discounts, especially with regard to this relatively best form of government. The problem of translating institutional roles into descriptions of role occupants' intentions is a characteristic problem of structural political analyses.[74] For all that, it is one thing to charge, with Locke, that a benevolent *Leviathan*-state is implausible, and another to dismiss Hobbes's art of government as a trivial part of the political theory.

Notes

1. Thomas Hobbes, *Leviathan*, ed. C. B. MacPherson (Harmondsworth: Penguin, 1968), chapter 19, pp. 239–40. . . .

2. Susan Moller Okin, " 'The Soveraign and his Counsellours': Hobbes's Reevaluation of Parliament," *Political Theory* 10 (1982), p. 72.

3. Mario A. Cattaneo, "Hobbes Théoricien de L'Absolutisme Eclairé," in Reinhart Kosselleck and Roman Schnur (eds.), *Hobbes-Forschungen* (Berlin: Duncker & Humblot, 1969), p. 209, translation mine. See also "Hobbes's Theory of Punishment," trans. J. M. Hatwell, in K. C. Brown (ed.), *Hobbes Studies* (Cambridge, Mass.: Harvard University Press, 1965), pp. 275–97, esp. p. 276.

4. Only two duties do not refer to previously specified rights of sovereignty: public charity and policies to deter idleness (*Leviathan* 30, p. 387). . . .

5. Thomas Hobbes, *De Cive: The English Version*, entitled in the first edition, *Philosophical Rudiments Concerning Government and Society*, ed. Howard Warrender (Oxford: Clarendon, 1983), chapter vi, section 13, p. 99 (emphasis omitted). . . .

6. *Leviathan* 18, p. 238 (emphasis mine).

7. *De Cive* vi, 13, p. 99 (emphasis omitted). . . .

8. *De Cive* xiii, 1, p. 156. . . .

9. *De Cive* vi, 13, p. 99 . . . (emphasis omitted).

10. Thomas Hobbes, *The Elements of Law: Natural and Politic*, ed. Ferdinand Tönnies (Cambridge: Cambridge University Press, 1928), Part II, chapter ix, section 1, p. 142. . . .

11. *Leviathan* 19, p. 241.

12. *The Elements of Law* II, v, 4, p. III. See also *De Cive* x, 4 and 7, pp. 132, 133; and *Leviathan* 19, p. 241.

13. *Leviathan* 19, p. 241.

14. *De Cive* x, 18, p. 140.

15. *Leviathan* 11, p. 161: "I put for a generall inclination of all mankind, a perpetuall and restlesse desire of Power after power, that ceaseth onely in Death."

16. Thomas Hobbes, "A Dialogue between a Philosopher and a Student of the Common Laws of England," in *The English Works of Thomas Hobbes*, vol. vi, ed. Sir William Molesworth (London: John Bohn, 1840), pp. 33–34.

17. Niccolo Machiavelli, *The Prince*, trans. George Bull (Harmondsworth: Penguin, 1961), chapter 17.

18. The statement is quoted, e.g., in J. A. W. Gunn, *Politics and the Public Interest in the Seventeenth Century* (London: Routledge & Kegan Paul, 1969), p. 68.

19. *The Elements of Law* II, ix, 1, p. 142. . . .

20. *Leviathan* 19, pp. 241–42. . . .

21. *The Elements of Law* II, v, 1, p. 108. . . .
22. Chapters viii and ix in Part II of *The Elements of Law* treat the causes of rebellion and the duties of rulers; they are chapters xii and xiii in *De Cive*.
23. *De Cive* xiii, 9, p. 160. . . .
24. Accurately, there are three Hobbesian categories. *The Elements of Law* (II, viii, 1, p. 133) lists: (1) discontent, encompassing popular fear of punishment and burdensome taxation, as well as political ambition (2–3, pp. 133–35); (2) pretense of right, referring to seditious opinions (4–10, pp. 135–38); and (3) hope of success (11–14, pp. 138–41). Cf. the more abstract categories in *De Cive* (xii, 1, pp. 145–46): (1) "internall disposition," meaning seditious opinions (1–8, pp. 146–52); (2) "externall Agent," or popular and elite discontent (9–10, pp. 152–53); and (3) the "action it selfe," i.e., the organization of a seditious "faction" (11–13, pp. 153–56).
25. *The Elements of Law* II, ix, 5, p. 144; *De Cive* xiii, 10–11, pp. 161–62.
26. *De Cive* xiii, 12, pp. 162–63. See *The Elements of Law* II, ix, 7, p. 145.
27. *The Elements of Law* II, ix, 8, pp. 145–46; *De Cive* xiii, 9 and 13, pp. 160–61, 163–64.
28. *Leviathan* 18, p. 235 (margin note), and 27, pp. 338–39; *De Cive* xiii, 16, p. 166. . . .
29. *The Elements of Law* II, x, 8, p. 150. . . .
30. *De Cive* vi, 9, p. 95 (emphasis omitted). . . .
31. *De Cive* vi, I 1, p. 95 (the topic of the paragraph is political education). . . .
32. *The Elements of Law* II, x, 2, p. 147.
33. Ibid. II, viii, 6, p. 136. . . .
34. *De Cive* xiv, 2, p. 169. . . .
35. *De Cive* xiv, 2, p. 170 . . . (emphasis omitted). . . .
36. Richard Tuck, *Natural Rights Theories: Their Origin and Development* (Cambridge: Cambridge University Press, 1979), p. 91, quoting John Selden, *Opera*, I, col. 106. . . .
37. *Leviathan* 27, p. 343.
38. *De Cive* xiv, 7, p. 172. . . .
39. *De Cive* vi, 4, p. 93. . . .
40. *De Cive* xiv, 7, pp. 172–73. . . .
41. *Leviathan* 30, pp. 387–88.
42. *Leviathan* 30, p. 388.
43. *De Cive* xiii, 15, pp. 165–66; *Leviathan* 30, p. 388.
44. *De Cive* xiii, 15, p. 165.
45. *Leviathan* 30, pp. 388–89.
46. Ibid., p. 388.
47. *De Cive* xiii, 17, p. 167. . . .
48. *Leviathan* 28, p. 353. . . .
49. *Leviathan* 28, p. 355. Other distinctions follow from the requirements that punishments be inflicted by public authorities, for the transgression of law. E.g., "private injuries, and revenges," "pain inflicted without publique hearing," or by "Usurped power" are acts of hostility because they are not public acts carried out by public authorities (pp. 354–55). See also *De Cive* xiii, 16, p. 166.
50. *Leviathan* 18, p. 235, and *De Cive* xiii, 16, p. 166.
51. *The Elements of Law* II, ix, 7, p. 145. See *De Cive* xiii, 12, pp. 162–63, and *Leviathan* 30, pp. 385–86.
52. *De Cive* xiii, 12, p. 163; see *Leviathan* 27, pp. 342–43.
53. *Leviathan* 30, pp. 390–91, and 28, pp. 361–62.
54. Ibid. 30, p. 386.
55. Ibid. 27, p. 342.
56. Ibid. 30, p. 389.
57. Ibid., pp. 389–90. Indeed, extreme destitution totally excuses stealing, as necessary for self-preservation (27, p. 346).
58. *Leviathan* 30, p. 390.
59. Ibid., pp. 385–86. See also 27, p. 347.
60. Ibid. 27, pp. 350–51.
61. Ibid., p. 350.
62. Ibid., pp. 344–45: "For though all Crimes doe equally deserve the name of Injustice . . . yet it does not follow that all Crimes are equally unjust, no more than that all crooked lines are equally crooked; which the Stoicks not observing, held it as great a Crime, to kill a Hen, against the Law, as to kill ones Father."
63. Ibid. Review and Conclusion, p. 721: "I have set down for one of the causes of the Dissolutions of Common-wealths, their Imperfect Generation, consisting in the want of an *Absolute and Arbitrary Legislative Power*"(emphasis mine).
64. *De Cive* vi, 17, p. 102 (the latter emphasis—from "partly" to "lust"—is mine).
65. *Leviathan* 31, pp. 406–7.
66. Ibid. 30 ,p. 390 (the passage is quoted earlier; see text pertaining to note 58).
67. Ibid. 27, pp. 348–49.
68. *De Cive* xiii, 16, p. 166.
69. *Leviathan* 27, p. 339.

70. Colin Strang, "What if Everyone Did That?" In Judith J. Thomson and Gerald Dworkin (eds.), *Ethics* (New York: Harper & Row, 1968), pp. 155–56. In the continuation of the passage, the "Defaulter" announces: The principle of universalization "doesn't impress me as a reason why I should [pay, etc.], however many people do or don't." See pp. 159–60 for the argument that responsibility for public goods is shared between ruler and ruled.

71. *Leviathan* Introduction, p. 81.

72. Cf., e.g., *De Cive* vi, 13, p. 99 (annotation to the 1647 edition, emphasis omitted): "Although they, who have the chief Command, doe not all those things they would, and what they know profitable to the City," it is also the case that "Citizens, who busied about their private interest, and carelesse of what tends to the publique, cannot sometimes be drawn to performe their duties without the hazard of the City."

73. *De Cive* x, 7, p. 133.

74. On the importance of the translation, see Maurice Mandelbaum, "Societal Facts," in Alan Ryan (ed.), *The Philosophy of Social Explanation* (Oxford: Oxford University Press, 1973), esp. p. 113.

John Locke

John Locke is often introduced to students of American government as the intellectual ancestor of the liberal democratic ideals that gave rise to the American form of government. He is sometimes referred to as "America's philosopher" and his writings tied to the words of Jefferson, Paine, and even Publius (the pseudonym chosen by the writers of the *Federalist Papers*). His views on the right to life, liberty, and property; the consent of the governed; and the right of resistance all inform the founding documents of our nation.

Recent scholarship has found, however, that Locke was profoundly more complex than originally thought. While it is clear that the founders of the U.S. political system owe a debt to Locke for adopting some of his precepts and rhetoric, it is less clear exactly what Locke *meant* to convey in his writings. Depending on whether one examines Locke's political writings on their own or in the context of the overall body of his work, Locke can be seen either as an advocate of the secular state or as a defender of the faith, either as a natural law theorist in the classic sense or a natural right follower of Hobbes. Depending on whether one considers Locke's work on its own merits or in the context of political events of the day with which he was associated, Locke can be seen as either a conservative apologist for the British status quo or as a revolutionary radical in search of extending democratic reform; as an advocate for the unfettered free market or as a communitarian bent on insuring good stewardship of community resources. Perhaps the tensions that continue to haunt liberal democracy today are simply the most dramatic legacy of the man whose work inspired it.

Locke was born in 1632 in Wrington in Somerset, England. His father was an attorney and law clerk who gave John a Puritan upbringing. John studied the classics as a youth at Westminster School and obtained a scholarship to continue his education at Christ Church at Oxford. There he became disenchanted with the Scholastic program of studies and set his sights on empirical approaches. For example, he collaborated for a time with the chemist Robert Boyle. He served briefly in the diplomatic corps at Brandenburg where he had the opportunity to study the works of Descartes and began to rethink his earlier views on religion, which denied toleration to Catholics and others seen as enemies of the state. Upon his father's death, the inheritance left to him allowed him to pursue a degree in medicine. For a time, he worked with the noted physician Thomas Sydenham.

Ironically, Locke's medical training led him into the political intrigues which gave rise to his political writings. Locke's successful operation on the liver of Lord Ashley, Earl of Shaftesbury, led to the Earl's lifelong gratitude and political tutelage. Shaftesbury was a leader in the parliamentary opposition to the Stuarts. His politics ended in his trial for treason and, though he was acquitted, he thought it best to flee to Holland. Locke, who was under suspicion due to his association with Shaftesbury, soon followed. During this period of self-exile, Locke penned several of his most important works, including *A Letter on Toleration*, which displayed his newfound toleration for religious practices, *An Essay Concerning Human Understanding*, in which Locke expressed his famous "white paper" theory of human nature, and drafts of his *Two Treatises on Government*. The latter work was written partly as a response to the royalist views of Sir Robert Filmore and partly in support of the opposition movement against Charles II. Locke prudently postponed its publication until 1689.

Events conspired to bring Locke back to England and to accept another political post. The death of Charles II, followed by the ascension of the Catholic James II, brought political turmoil which resulted in a successful plot to seat William of Orange. With the Glorious Revolution of 1688 complete, Locke returned to England where he published his *Two Treatises*, served on the Board of Trade and Plantations, and ended his days in semi-retirement at a country estate at Oates. In his final days, he began to write *The Conduct of the Understanding*, which he never completed.

The Second Treatise of Government

Like Hobbes, Locke utilized the convention of the "state of nature" to elucidate his views on human nature and politics. Like Hobbes, he adopted the contract as the instrument by which societies and governments are founded. Unlike Hobbes's, however, Locke's state of nature is relatively peaceful. In it, most humans respect the law of nature, reason, which teaches the folly of pursuing unbridled passions and appetites. Disputes over the ownership of property, however, result in conflict which puts participants in a state of war not unlike the Hobbesian state of nature. Because there is no impartial umpire to settle such disputes in the state of nature, political societies and the governments which regulate them are forged on the basis of consent. Unlike Hobbes, Locke opposed monarchical rule. To give all power to one sovereign in the name of protecting us from one another, as Hobbes suggested, would be like avoiding the mischief done by "Pole Cats or Foxes" only to be "devoured by Lions." There is little doubt that Locke was familiar with Hobbes's work. Yet he steadfastly denied the connection, perhaps for fear of being too closely associated with his predecessor's unsavory reputation.

Three major themes Locke emphasized in the *Second Treatise* were property, consent, and the right of resistance. Locke advanced a species of the labor theory of value in which property arises from the efforts of the individual to make the land and its resources useful. While he insisted that no one has the right to collect resources beyond the use to which they can be put, he recognized that the invention of money allowed for the accumulation of wealth beyond spoilage. With property—and its unequal distribution—came the likelihood of dispute. Civil society and the government which regulates it are created to provide peaceable solutions to disputes which arise primarily over property. Civil society comes into existence on the basis of the consent of all and the governmental form it takes reflects majority rule. Locke staunchly supported the right of members of the commonwealth to resist abuses of power by including a right to dissolve the government, although he did not believe such a remedy would often be employed. These themes were treated within a religious context that some scholars say cannot be ignored. The excerpts below from the *Second Treatise* illustrate Locke's treatment of these themes—property, consent, and resistance.

Commentaries

Locke's treatment of property has frequently been tied to the growth of capitalism by providing the justification for possessive individualism and unlimited acquisition. In the first commentary, Richard Ashcraft provides a richly nuanced account of Locke's theory of property based on both attention to the text and to Locke's own background and political goals that indicates Locke's views cannot so easily be characterized. Ashcraft focuses on three aspects of Locke's property theory: 1) the religious foundation from which it stems; 2) the social utility of labor that envisions benefits for the larger community; 3) Locke's political involvement with the Whigs, who needed a theory of property amenable to both gentry and urban commercial leaders in order to advance their interests in expanding trade policy.

Even though Locke attacks patriarchy in both of his *Treatises*, feminists have criticized him for a host of reasons. Some argue that he speaks exclusively to a male-centered world of rights and economic rationality; others fault him for his failure to take seriously the subservient position women have traditionally held in both the family and in the larger political society. Feminists widely complain that Locke depoliticizes the family and bifurcates the domains of private and public life in a manner that serves to keep women's concerns from being addressed in the political arena. Mary B. Walsh, in the second commentary, takes issue with these feminist critiques of Locke, arguing that his distinction between private family matters and public matters of policy actually serves as a protection against the type of tyranny that threatens men and women equally. What some feminists represent as a dichotomy between public and private is actually for Locke a multitude of interacting spheres. Within this conception, Walsh finds latent potential for addressing women's particular circumstances.

Web Sources

http://www.fordham.edu/halsall/mod/modsbook06.html
Internet Modern History Sourcebook. See especially "Philosophic Reflections on Constitutional Politics." Examines Locke's influence in relation to other Enlightenment thinkers and in relation to his influence on political developments in the United States.

http://www.ilt.columbia.edu/projects/digitexts/locke/second/locke2nd.txt
The Second Treatise of Government by John Locke. Full original text of Locke's *Second Treatise.*

http://blupete.com/Literature/Biographies/Philosophy/Locke.htm#TOC
John Locke, The Philosopher of Freedom. Overview of Locke's life and works.

http://www.utm.edu/research/iep/l/locke.htm
Internet Encyclopedia of Philosophy: John Locke. Reviews basic philosophic ideas of Locke.

Class Activities and Discussion Items

1. Compare and contrast the states of nature advanced by Hobbes and Locke. How are they similar? How are they different? What do their differences tell us about the views of their inventors regarding human nature?

2. Compare the Declaration of Independence with chapter XIX of Locke's *Second Treatise* ("On the Dissolution of Government"). How does the Declaration mirror the *Second Treatise* with regard to the reasons for government and the reasons that permit dissolution? Do the reasons for breaking relations with England listed in the Declaration mirror the categories of permissible dissolution outlined by Locke? How do the two documents differ, if at all? Is it reasonable to conclude that the auhtors of the Declaration followed the outline for dissolution provided by Locke in the *Second Treatise?*

3. What role does consent play in the formation and ongoing operation of government according to Hobbes and to Locke? Discuss how the notion and scope of consent differ in the philosophies of the two thinkers.

4. You are a member of the town council. A group of investors has approached you to change a local ordinance to permit the building of an assembly plant. Another group of townspeople has come before you opposed to the change. The investors claim that the plant will bring many jobs to the town and will produce additional opportunities for economic growth and prosperity. The townspeople point out that the plant will bring poisonous pollution, unwanted congestion, and disrupt family life in the area. How will you vote—in favor of the change that permits the plant or against it? Write a defense of your position grounded in Lockean principles of property as you understand them.

5. Some scholars believe that Locke's permissible grounds for dissolution of government are genuinely radical. Others believe they mask a genuine conservatism in that they are too narrowly tailored. Which view do you believe best reflects Locke's work? Why? Would Lockean principles genuinely legitimize the American Revolution? The French Revolution? The Russian Revo-

lution? The Chinese Revolution? The Cuban Revolution?

Further Reading

Arneil, Barbara. 1996. *John Locke and America: The Defence of English Colonialism.* New York: Oxford University Press. A conservative reading of Locke's political agenda.

Ashcraft, Richard. 1987. *Locke's Two Treatises on Government.* London: Allen & Unwin. A rich examination of the text in the context of historic events and personalities. Ashcraft emphasizes both the revolutionary and religious elements of Locke's work.

Coby, Patrick. 1987. "The Law of Nature in Locke's *Second Treatise:* Is Locke a Hobbesian?" *The Review of Politics* 49 (1): 3–28. Coby says that if you scratch Locke's "state of nature," you will discover a Hobbesian.

Dunn, John. 1984. *John Locke.* Oxford: Clarendon Press. Dunn reads Locke as a staunch Christian advancing a moral vision.

Harpham, Edward J. (ed.). 1992. *John Locke's Two Treatises of Government: New Interpretations.* Lawrence, Kan.: University Press of Kansas. Includes recent interpretations of Locke's views on religion, economics, and republicanism as well as an excellent introduction detailing recent scholarship.

Macpherson, C. B. 1962. *The Political Theory of Possessive Individualism: Hobbes to Locke.* London: Clarendon. Classic work placing Hobbes and Locke at the forefront of the movement to rationalize capitalist acquisition.

Pangle, Thomas. 1988. *The Spirit of Modern Republicanism.* Chicago: University of Chicago Press. A look at Locke's contribution to modern republicanism. See especially Part III.

Shrader-Frechette, Kristin. 1993. "Locke and Limits on Land Ownership." *Journal of the History of Ideas* 54 (2): 201–219. Although Locke has been hailed as a defender of unlimited property rights, his writings indicate that he supported at least some restrictions on property rights regarding natural resources like land.

Strauss, Leo. 1953. *Natural Right and History.* Chicago: University of Chicago Press. Places Locke along with Hobbes as a defender of "modern" natural right.

Tarcov, Nathan. 1984. *Locke's Education for Liberty.* Chicago: University of Chicago Press. Locke as a radical thinker.

Yolton, John (ed.). 1969. *John Locke: Problems and Perspectives.* Cambridge: Cambridge University Press. Useful reexamination of natural law and the state of nature. ✦

8

Excerpts from *The Second Treatise of Government*

John Locke

Book II

Chapter I

1. It having been shewn in the foregoing Discourse,

1°. That *Adam* had not either by natural Right of Fatherhood, or by positive Donation from God, any such Authority over his Children, or Dominion over the World as is pretended.

2°. That if he had, his Heirs, yet, had no Right to it.

3°. That if his Heirs had, there being no Law of Nature nor positive Law of God that determines, which is the Right Heir in all Cases that may arise, the Right of Succession, and consequently of bearing Rule, could not have been certainly determined.

4°. That if even that had been determined, yet the knowledge of which is the Eldest Line of *Adam's* Posterity, being so long since utterly lost, that in the Races of Mankind and Families of the World, there remains not to one above another, the least pretence to be the Eldest House, and to have the Right of Inheritance.

All these premises having, as I think, been clearly made out, it is impossible that the Rulers now on Earth, should make any benefit, or derive any the least shadow of Authority from that, which is held to be the Fountain of all Power, *Adam's Private Dominion and Paternal Jurisdiction*, so that, he that will not give just occasion, to think that all Government in the World is the product only of Force and Violence, and that Men live together by no other Rules but that of Beasts, where the strongest carries it, and so lay a Foundation for perpetual Disorder and Mischief, Tumult, Sedition and Rebellion, (things that the followers of that Hypothesis so loudly cry out against) must of necessity find out another rise of Government, another Original of Political Power, and another way of designing and knowing the Persons that have it, then what Sir *Robert F.* hath taught us.

2. To this purpose, I think it may not be amiss, to set down what I take to be Political Power. That the Power of a *Magistrate* over a Subject, may be distinguished from that of a *Father* over his Children, a *Master* over his Servant, a *Husband* over his Wife, and a *Lord* over his Slave. All which distinct Powers happening sometimes together in the same Man, if he be considered under these different Relations, it may help us to distinguish these Powers one from another, and shew the difference betwixt a Ruler of a Commonwealth, a Father of a Family, and a Captain of a Galley.

3. *Political Power* then I take to be *a Right* of making Laws with Penalties of Death, and consequently all less Penalties, for the Regulating and Preserving of Property, and of employing the force of the Community, in the Execution of such Laws, and in the defence of the Common-wealth from Foreign Injury, and all this only for the Publick Good.

Chapter II: Of the State of Nature

4. To understand Political Power right, and derive it from its Original, we must consider what State all Men are naturally in, and that is, a *State of perfect Freedom* to order their Actions, and dispose of their Possessions, and Persons as they think fit, within the bounds of the Law of Nature, without asking leave, or depending upon the Will of any other Man.

A *State* also of *Equality*, wherein all the Power and Jurisdiction is reciprocal, no one having more than another: there being nothing more evident, than that Creatures of the same species and rank promiscuously born to all the same advantages of Nature, and the use of the same faculties, should also be equal one amongst another without Subordination or subjection, unless the Lord and Master of them all, should by any manifest Declaration of his Will set one above another, and confer on him by an evident and clear appointment an undoubted Right to Dominion and Sovereignty. . . .

6. But though this be a *State of Liberty*, yet it is *not a State of Licence*, though Man in that State have an uncontroleable Liberty, to dispose of his Person or Possessions, yet he has not Liberty to destroy himself, or so much as any Creature in his Possession, but where some nobler use, than its bare Preservation calls for it. The *State of Nature* has a Law of Nature to govern it, which obliges every one: And Reason, which is that Law, teaches all Mankind, who will but consult it, that being all equal and independent, no one ought to harm another in his Life, Health, Liberty, or Possessions. For Men being all the Workmanship of one Omnipotent, and infinitely wise Maker; All the Servants of one Sovereign Master, sent into the World by his order and about his business, they are his Property, whose Workmanship they are, made to last during his, not one anothers Pleasure. And being furnished with like Faculties, sharing all in one Community of Nature, there cannot be supposed any such *Subordination* among us, that may Authorize us to destroy one another, as if we were made for one anothers uses, as the inferior ranks of Creatures are for ours. Every one as he is *bound to preserve himself*, and not to quit his Station willfully; so by the like reason when his own Preservation comes not in competition, ought he, as much as he can, *to preserve the rest of Mankind*, and may not unless it be to do Justice on an Offender, take away, or impair the life, or what tends to the Preservation of the Life, the Liberty, Health, Limb or Goods of another.

7. And that all Men may be restrained from invading others Rights, and from doing hurt to one another, and the Law of Nature be observed, which willeth the Peace and Preservation of all Mankind, the Execution of the Law of Nature is in that State, put into every Mans hands, whereby every one has a right to punish the transgressors of that Law to such a Degree, as may hinder its Violation.

For the *Law of Nature* would, as all other Laws that concern Men in this World, be in vain, if there were no body that in the State of Nature, had a *Power to Execute* that Law, and thereby preserve the innocent and restrain offenders, and if any one in the State of Nature may punish another, for any evil he has done, every one may do so. For in that *State of perfect Equality*, where naturally there is no superiority or jurisdiction of one, over another, what any may do in Prosecution of that Law, every one must needs have a Right to do.

8. And thus in the State of Nature, *one Man comes by a Power over another*; but yet no Absolute or Arbitrary Power, to use a Criminal when he has got him in his hands, according to the passionate heats, or boundless extravagancy of his own Will, but only to retribute to him, so far as calm reason and conscience dictates, what is proportionate to his Transgression, which is so much as may serve for *Reparation* and *Restraint*. For these two are the only reasons, why one Man may lawfully do harm to another, which is that we call *punishment*. In transgressing the Law of Nature, the Offender declares himself to live by another Rule, than that of *reason* and common Equity, which is that measure God has set to the actions of Men, for their mutual security: and so he becomes dangerous to Mankind, the tye, which is to secure them from injury and violence, being slighted and broken by him. Which being a trespass against the whole Species, and the Peace and Safety of it, provided for by the Law of Nature, every man upon this score, by the Right he hath to preserve Mankind in general, may restrain, or where it is necessary, destroy things noxious to them, and so may bring such evil on any one, who hath transgressed that Law, as may make him repent the doing of it, and thereby deter him, and by his Example others, from doing the like mischief. And in this case, and upon this ground, *every Man hath a Right to punish the Offender, and be Executioner of the Law of Nature.* . . .

11. From these *two distinct Rights*, the one of *Punishing* the Crime *for restraint*, and preventing the like Offence, which right of punishing is in every body; the other of taking *reparation*, which belongs only to the injured

party, comes it to pass that the Magistrate, who by being Magistrate, hath the common right of punishing put into his hands, can often, where the publick good demands not the execution of the Law, *remit* the punishment of Criminal Offences by his own Authority, but yet cannot *remit* the satisfaction to any private Man, for the damage he has received. That, he who has suffered the damage has a Right to demand in his own name, and he alone can *remit:* The damnified Person has this Power of appropriating to himself, the Goods or Service of the Offender, by *Right of Self-preservation,* as every Man has a Power to punish the Crime, to prevent its being committed again, *by the Right he has of Preserving all Mankind,* and doing all reasonable things he can in order to that end: And thus it is, that every Man in the State of Nature, has a Power to kill a Murderer, both to deter others from doing the like Injury, which no Reparation can compensate, by the Example of the punishment that attends it from everybody, and also *to secure* Men from the attempts of a Criminal, who have renounced Reason, the common Rule and Measure, God hath given to Mankind, hath by the unjust Violence and Slaughter he hath committed upon one, declared War against all Mankind, and therefore may be destroyed as a *Lyon* or a *Tyger,* one of those wild Savage Beasts, with whom Men can have no Society nor Security: And upon this is grounded the great Law of Nature, *Who so sheddeth Mans Blood, by Man shall his Blood be shed.* And *Cain* was so fully convinced, that every one had a Right to destroy such a Criminal, that after the Murther of his Brother, he cries out, *Every one that findeth me, shall slay me;* so plain was it writ in the Hearts of all Mankind.

12. By the same reason, may a Man in the State of Nature *punish the lesser breaches* of that Law. It will perhaps be demanded, with death? I answer, Each Transgression may be *punished* to that *degree,* and with so much *Severity* as will suffice to make it an ill bargain to the Offender, give him cause to repent, and terrifie others from doing the like. Every Offence that can be committed in the State of Nature, may in the State of Nature be also punished, equally, and as far forth as it may, in a Common-wealth; for though it would be besides my present purpose, to enter here into the particulars of the Law of Nature, or its *measures of punishment;* yet, it is certain there is such a Law, and that too, as intelligible and plain to a rational Creature, and a Studier of that Law, as the positive Laws of Common-wealths, nay possibly plainer; As much as Reason is easier to be understood, than the Phansies and intricate Contrivances of Men, following contrary and hidden interests put into Words; For so truly are a great part of the *Municipal Laws* of Countries, which are only so far right, as they are founded on the Law of Nature, by which they are to be regulated and interpreted.

13. To this strange Doctrine, *viz.* That *in the State of Nature, every one has the Executive Power* of the Law of Nature, I doubt not but it will be objected, That it is unreasonable for Men to be Judges in their own Cases, that Self-love will make Men partial to themselves and their Friends. And on the other side, that Ill Nature, Passion and Revenge will carry them too far in punishing others. And hence nothing but Confusion and Disorder will follow, and that therefore God hath certainly appointed Government to restrain the partiality and violence of Men. I easily grant, that *Civil Government* is the proper Remedy for the Inconveniences of the State of Nature, which must certainly be Great, where Men may be Judges in their own Case, since 'tis easily to be imagined, that he who was so unjust as to do his Brother an Injury, will scarce be so just as to condemn himself for it: But I shall desire those who make this Objection, to remember that *Absolute Monarchs* are but Men, and if Government is to be the Remedy of those Evils, which necessarily follow from Mens being Judges in their own Cases, and the State of Nature is therefore not to be endured, I desire to know what kind of Government that is, and how much better it is than the State of Nature, where one Man commanding a multitude, has the Liberty to be Judge in his own Case, and may do to all his Subjects whatever he pleases, without the least liberty to any one to question or controle those who Execute his Pleasure? And in whatsoever he doth, whether led by Reason, Mistake or Passion, must be submitted to? Much better it is in

the State of Nature wherein Men are not bound to submit to the unjust will of another: And if he that judges, judges amiss in his own, or any other Case, he is answerable for it to the rest of Mankind.

14. 'Tis often asked as a mighty Objection, *Where are,* or ever were, there any *Men in such a State of Nature?* To which it may suffice as an answer at present; That since all *Princes* and Rulers of *Independent* Governments all through the World, are in a State of Nature, 'tis plain the World never was, nor ever will be, without Numbers of Men in that State. I have named all Governors of *Independent* Communities, whether they are, or are not, in League with others: For 'tis not every Compact that puts an end to the State of Nature between Men, but only this one of agreeing together mutually to enter into one Community, and make one Body Politick; other Promises and Compacts, Men may make one with another, and yet still be in the State of Nature. The Promises and Bargains for Truck, *&c.* between the two Men in the Desert Island, mentioned by *Garcilasso De la vega,* in his History of *Peru,* or between a *Swiss* and an *Indian,* in the Woods of *America,* are binding to them, though they are perfectly in a State of Nature, in reference to one another. For Truth and keeping of Faith belongs to Men, as Men, and not as Members of Society. . . .

Chapter III: Of the State of War

16. The *State of War* is a State of Enmity and Destruction; And therefore declaring by Word or Action, not a passionate and hasty, but a sedate settled Design, upon another Mans Life, *puts him in a State of War* with him against whom he has declared such an Intention, and so has exposed his Life to the others Power to be taken away by him, or any one that joyns with him in his Defence, and espouses his Quarrel: it being reasonable and just I should have a Right to destroy that which threatens me with Destruction. For *by the Fundamental Law of Nature, Man being to be preserved,* as much as possible, when all cannot be preserv'd, the safety of the Innocent is to be preferred: And one may destroy a Man who makes War upon him, or has discovered an Enmity to his being, for the same

Reason, that he may kill a *Wolf* or a *Lyon;* because such Men are not under the ties of the Common Law of Reason, have no other Rule, but that of Force and Violence, and so may be treated as Beasts of Prey, those dangerous and noxious Creatures, that will be sure to destroy him, whenever he falls into their Power.

17. And hence it is, that he who attempts to get another Man into his Absolute Power, does thereby *put himself into a State of War* with him; It being to be understood as a Declaration of a Design upon his Life. For I have reason to conclude, that he who would get me into his Power without my consent, would use me as he pleased, when he had got me there, and destroy me too when he had a fancy to it: for no body can desire to *have me in his Absolute Power,* unless it be to compel me by force to that, which is against the Right of my Freedom, *i.e.* make me a Slave. To be free from such force is the only security of my Preservation: and reason bids me look on him, as an Enemy to my Preservation, who would take away that *Freedom,* which is the Fence to it: so that he who makes an *attempt to enslave* me, thereby puts himself into a State of War with me. He that in the State of Nature, *would take away the Freedom,* that belongs to any one in that State, must necessarily be supposed to have a design to take away every thing else, that *Freedom* being the Foundation of all the rest: As he that in the State of Society, would take away the *Freedom* belonging to those of that Society or Common-wealth, must be supposed to design to take away from them every thing else, and so be looked on as *in a State of War.*

18. This makes it Lawful for a Man to *kill a Thief,* who has not in the least hurt him, nor declared any design upon his Life, any farther then by the use of Force, so to get him in his Power, as to take away his Money, or what he pleases from him: because using force, where he has no Right, to get me into his Power, let his pretence be what it will, I have no reason to suppose, that he, who would *take away my Liberty,* would not when he had me in his Power, take away every thing else. And therefore it is Lawful for me to treat him, as one who has put *himself into a State*

of War with me, *i.e.* kill him if I can; for to that hazard does he justly expose himself, whoever introduces a State of War, and is *aggressor* in it.

19. And here we have the plain *difference between the State of Nature, and the State of War*, which however some Men have confounded, are as far distant, as a State of Peace, Good Will, Mutual Assistance, and Preservation, and a State of Enmity, Malice, Violence, and Mutual Destruction are one from another. Men living together according to reason, without a common Superior on Earth, with Authority to judge between them, is *properly the State of Nature*. But force, or a declared design of force upon the Person of another, where there is no common Superior on Earth to appeal to for relief, *is the State of War*: And 'tis the want of such an appeal gives a Man the Right of War even against an *aggressor*, though he be in Society and a fellow Subject. Thus a *Thief*, whom I cannot harm but by appeal to the Law, for having stolen all that I am worth, I may kill, when he sets on me to rob me, but of my Horse or Coat: because the Law, which was made for my Preservation, where it cannot interpose to secure my Life from present force, which if lost, is capable of no reparation, permits me my own Defence, and the Right of War, a liberty to kill the aggressor, because the aggressor allows not time to appeal to our common Judge, nor the decision of the Law, for remedy in a Case, where the mischief may be irreparable. *Want of a common Judge with Authority, puts all Men in a state of Nature: Force without Right, upon a Man's Person, makes a State of War*, both where there is, and is not, a common Judge.

20. But when the actual force is over, the *State of War ceases* between those that are in Society, and are equally on both sides Subjected to the fair determination of the Law; because then there lies open the remedy of appeal for the past injury, and to prevent future harm: but where no such appeal is, as in the State of Nature, for want of positive Laws, and Judges with Authority to appeal to, *the State of War once begun, continues*, with a right to the innocent Party, to destroy the other whenever he can, until the aggressor offers Peace, and desires reconciliation

on such Terms, as may repair any wrongs he has already done, and secure the innocent for the future: nay where an appeal to the Law, and constituted Judges lies open, but the remedy is deny'd by a manifest perverting of Justice, and a barefaced wresting of the Laws, to protect or indemnifie the violence or injuries of some Men, or Party of Men, *there* it *is* hard to imagine any thing but *a State of War*. For wherever violence is used, and injury done, though by hands appointed to administer Justice, it is still violence and injury, however colour'd with the Name, Pretences, or Forms of Law, the end whereof being to protect and redress the innocent, by an unbiassed application of it, to all who are under it; wherever that is not *bona fide* done, *War is made* upon the Sufferers, who having no appeal on Earth to right them, they are left to the only remedy in such Cases, an appeal to Heaven. . . .

Chapter V: Of Property

25. Whether we consider natural *Reason*, which tells us, that Men, being once born, have a right to their Preservation, and consequently to Meat and Drink, and such other things, as Nature affords for their Subsistence: Or *Revelation*, which gives us an account of those Grants God made of the World to Adam, and to *Noah*, and his Sons, 'tis very clear, that God, as King *David* says, *Psal* CXV. xvj. *has given the Earth to the Children of Men*, given it to Mankind in common. But this being supposed, it seems to some a very great difficulty, how any one should ever come to have a *Property* in any thing: I will not content my self to answer, That if it be difficult to make out *Property*, upon a supposition, that God gave the World to *Adam* and his Posterity in common; it is impossible that any Man, but one universal Monarch, should have any *Property*, upon a supposition, that God gave the World to *Adam*, and his Heirs in Succession, exclusive of all the rest of his Posterity. But I shall endeavour to shew, how Men might come to have a *property* in several parts of that which God gave to Mankind in common, and without any express Compact of all the Commoners.

26. God, who hath given the World to Men in common, hath also given them reason to make use of it to the best advantage of Life, and convenience. The Earth, and all that is therein, is given to Men for the Support and Comfort of their being. And though all the Fruits it naturally produces, and Beasts it feeds, belong to Mankind in common, as they are produced by the spontaneous hand of Nature; and no body has originally a private Dominion, exclusive of the rest of Mankind, in any of them, as they are thus in their natural state: yet being given for the use of Men, there must of necessity be a means *to appropriate* them some way or other before they can be of any use, or at all beneficial to any particular Man. The Fruit, or Venison, which nourishes the wild *Indian*, who knows no Inclosure, and is still a Tenant in common, must be his, and so his, *i.e.* a part of him, that another can no longer have any right to it, before it can do him any good for the support of his Life.

27. Though the Earth, and all inferior Creatures be common to all Men, yet every Man has a *Property* in his own *Person*. This no Body has any Right to but himself. The *Labour* of his Body, and the *Work* of his Hands, we may say, are properly his. Whatsoever then he removes out of the State that Nature hath provided, and left it in, he hath mixed his *Labour* with, and joyned to it something that is his own, and thereby makes it his *Property*. It being by him removed from the common state Nature placed it in, it hath by this *labour* something annexed to it, that excludes the common right of other Men. For this *Labour* being the unquestionable Property of the Labourer, no Man but he can have a right to what that is once joyned to, at least where there is enough, and as good left in common for others.

28. He that is nourished by the Acorns he pickt up under an Oak, or the Apples he gathered from the Trees in the Wood, has certainly appropriated them to himself. No Body can deny but the nourishment is his. I ask then, When did they begin to be his? When he digested? Or when he eat? Or when he boiled? Or when he brought them home? Or when he pickt them up? And 'tis plain, if

the first gathering made them not his, nothing else could. That *labour* put a distinction between them and common. That added something to them more than Nature, the common Mother of all, had done; and so they became his private right. And will any one say he had no right to those Acorns or Apples he thus appropriated, because he had not the consent of all Mankind to make them his? Was it a Robbery thus to assume to himself what belonged to all in Common? If such a consent as that was necessary, Man had starved, notwithstanding the Plenty God had given him. We see in *Commons*, which remain so by Compact, that 'tis the taking any part of what is common, and removing it out of the state Nature leaves it in, which *begins the Property*; without which the Common is of no use. And the taking of this or that part, does not depend on the express consent of all the Commoners. Thus the Grass my Horse has bit; the Turfs my Servant has cut; and the Ore I have digg'd in any place where I have a right to them in common with others, become my *Property*, without the assignation or consent of any body. The *labour* that was mine, removing them out of that common state they were in, hath *fixed* my *Property* in them. . . .

31. It will perhaps be objected to this, That if gathering the Acorns, or other Fruits of the Earth, &c. makes a right to them, then any one may *ingross* as much as he will. To which I Answer, Not so. The same Law of Nature, that does by this means give us Property, does also *bound* that *Property* too. *God has given us all things richly*, 1 Tim. vi. 17. is the Voice of Reason confirmed by Inspiration. But how far has he given it us? *To enjoy.* As much as any one can make use of to any advantage of life before it spoils; so much he may by his labour fix a Property in. Whatever is beyond this, is more than his share, and belongs to others. Nothing was made by God for Man to spoil or destroy. And thus considering the plenty of natural Provisions there was a long time in the World, and the few spenders, and to how small a part of that provision the industry of one Man could extend it self, and ingross it to the prejudice of others; especially keeping within the *bounds*, set by reason of what might serve for his *use*; there

could be then little room for Quarrels or Contentions about Property so establish'd. . . .

37. This is certain, That in the beginning, before the desire of having more than Men needed, had altered the intrinsick value of things, which depends only on their usefulness to the Life of Man; or [Men] had *agreed, that a little piece of yellow Metal*, which would keep without wasting or decay, should be worth a great piece of Flesh, or a whole heap of Corn; though Men had a Right to appropriate, by their Labour, each one to himself, as much of the things of Nature, as he could use: Yet this could not be much, nor to the Prejudice of others, where the same plenty was still left, to those who would use the same Industry. To which let me add, that he who appropriates land to himself by his labour, does not lessen but increase the common stock of mankind. For the provisions serving to the support of humane life, produced by one acre of inclosed and cultivated land, are (to speak much within compasse) ten times more, than those, which are yielded by an acre of Land, of an equal richnesse, lyeing wast in common. And therefor he, that incloses Land and has a greater plenty of the conveniencys of life from ten acres, than he could have from an hundred left to Nature, may truly be said, to give ninety acres to Mankind. For his labour now supplys him with provisions out of ten acres, which were but the product of an hundred lying in common. I have here rated the improved land very low in making its product but as ten to one, when it is much nearer an hundred to one. For I aske whether in the wild woods and uncultivated wast of America left to Nature, without any improvement, tillage or husbandry, a thousand acres will yield the needy and wretched inhabitants as many conveniencies of life as ten acres of equally fertile land doe in Devonshire where they are well cultivated? . . .

45. Thus *Labour*, in the Beginning, *gave a Right of Property*, where-ever any one was pleased to imploy it, upon what was common, which remained, a long while, the far greater part, and is yet more than Mankind makes use of. Men, at first, for the most part, contented themselves with what un-assisted Nature offered to their Necessities: and though afterwards, in some parts of the World, (where the Increase of People and Stock, with the *Use of Money*) had made Land scarce, and so of some Value, the several *Communities* settled the Bounds of their distinct Territories, and by Laws within themselves, regulated the Properties of the private Men of their Society, and so, *by Compact* and Agreement, *settled the Property* which Labour and Industry began; and the Leagues that have been made between several States and Kingdoms, either expressly or tacitly disowning all Claim and Right to the Land in the others Possession, have, by common Consent, given up their Pretences to their natural common Right, which originally they had to those Countries, and so have, by *positive agreement, settled a Property* amongst themselves, in distinct Parts and parcels of the Earth: yet there are still *great Tracts of Ground* to be found, which (the Inhabitants thereof not having joyned with the rest of Mankind, in the consent of the Use of their common Money) *lie waste*, and are more than the People, who dwell on it, do, or can make use of, and so still lie in common. Tho' this can scarce happen amongst that part of Mankind, that have consented to the Use of Money.

46. The greatest part of *things really useful* to the Life of Man, and such as the necessity of subsisting made the first Commoners of the World look after, as it doth the *Americans* now, *are* generally things *of short duration;* such as, if they are not consumed by use will decay and perish of themselves: Gold, Silver, and Diamonds are things, that Fancy or Agreement hath put the Value on, more then real Use, and the necessary Support of Life. Now of those good things which Nature hath provided in common, every one had a Right (as hath been said) to as much as he could use, and had a Property in all that he could affect with his Labour: all that his Industry could extend to, to alter from the State Nature had put it in, was his. He that *gathered* a Hundred Bushels of Acorns or Apples, had thereby a *Property* in them; they were his Goods as soon as gathered. He was only to look that he used them before they spoiled; else he took more then his share, and robb'd others. And indeed it was a foolish thing, as

well as dishonest, to hoard up more than he could make use of. If he gave away a part to any body else, so that it perished not uselesly in his Possession, these he also made use of. And if he also bartered away Plumbs that would have rotted in a Week, for Nuts that would last good for his eating a whole Year, he did no injury; he wasted not the common Stock; destroyed no part of the portion of Goods that belonged to others, so long as nothing perished uselesly in his hands. Again, if he would give his Nuts for a piece of Metal, pleased with its colour; or exchange his Sheep for Shells, or Wool for a sparkling Pebble or a Diamond, and keep those by him all his Life, he invaded not the Right of others, he might heap up as much of these durable things as he pleased; the *exceeding of the bounds of his* just *Property* not lying in the largeness of his Possession, but the perishing of any thing uselesly in it.

47. And thus *came in the use of Money*, some lasting thing that Men might keep without spoiling, and that by mutual consent Men would take in exchange for the truly useful, but perishable Supports of Life.

48. And as different degrees of Industry were apt to give Men Possessions in different Proportions, so this *Invention of Money* gave them the opportunity to continue and enlarge them. For supposing an Island, separate from all possible Commerce with the rest of the World, wherein there were but a hundred Families, but there were Sheep, Horses and Cows, with other useful Animals, wholsome Fruits, and Land enough for Corn for a hundred thousand times as many, but nothing in the Island, either because of its Commonness, or Perishableness, fit to supply the place of *Money:* What reason could any one have there to enlarge his Possessions beyond the use of his Family, and a plentiful supply to its Consumption, either in what their own Industry produced, or they could barter for like perishable, useful Commodities, with others? Where there is not something both lasting and scarce, and so valuable to be hoarded up, there Men will not be apt to enlarge their *Possessions of Land*, were it never so rich, never so free for them to take. For I ask, What would a Man value Ten Thousand, or an Hundred Thousand Acres

of excellent *Land*, ready cultivated, and well stocked too with Cattle, in the middle of the inland Parts of *America*, where he had no hopes of Commerce with other Parts of the World, to draw *Money* to him by the Sale of the Product? It would not be worth the inclosing, and we should see him give up again to the wild Common of Nature, whatever was more than would supply the Conveniencies of Life to be had there for him and his Family.

49. Thus in the beginning all the World was *America*, and more so than that is now; for no such thing as *Money* was any where known. Find out something that hath the *Use and Value* of Money amongst his Neighbours, you shall see the same Man will begin presently to *enlarge* his *Possessions*.

50. But since Gold and Silver, being little useful to the Life of Man in proportion to Food, Rayment, and Carriage, has its *value* only from the consent of Men, whereof Labour yet makes, in great part, *the measure*, it is plain, that Men have agreed to disproportionate and unequal Possession of the Earth, they having by a tacit and voluntary consent found out a way, how a man may fairly possess more land than he himself can use the product of, by receiving in exchange for the overplus, Gold and Silver, which may be hoarded up without injury to any one, these metalls not spoileing or decaying in the hands of the possessor. This partage of things, in an inequality of private possessions men have made practicable out of the bounds of Societie, and without compact, only by putting a value on gold and silver and tacitly agreeing in the use of Money. For in Governments the Laws regulate the right of property, and the possession of land is determined by positive constitutions. . . .

Chapter VII: Of Political or Civil Society

87. Man being born, as has been proved, with a Title to perfect Freedom, and an uncontrouled enjoyment of all the Rights and Priviledges of the Law of Nature, equally with any other Man, or Number of Men in the World, hath by Nature a Power, not only to preserve his Property, that is, his Life, Liberty and Estate, against the Injuries and Attempts of other Men; but to judge of, and

punish the breaches of that Law in others, as he is perswaded the Offence deserves, even with Death it self, in Crimes where the heinousness of the Fact, in his Opinion, requires it. But because no *Political Society* can be, nor subsist without having in it self the Power to preserve the Property, and in order thereunto punish the Offences of all those of that Society; there, and there only is *Political Society*, where every one of the Members hath quitted this natural Power, resign'd it up into the hands of the Community in all cases that exclude him not from appealing for Protection to the Law established by it. And thus all private judgement of every particular Member being excluded, the Community comes to be Umpire, by settled standing Rules, indifferent, and the same to all Parties; and by Men having Authority from the Community, for the execution of those Rules, decides all the differences that may happen between any Members of that Society, concerning any matter of right; and punishes those Offences, which any Member hath committed against the Society, with such Penalties as the Law has established: Whereby it is easie to discern who are, and who are not, in *Political Society* together. Those who are united into one Body, and have a common established Law and Judicature to appeal to, with Authority to decide Controversies between them, and punish Offenders, *are in Civil Society* one with another: but those who have no such common Appeal, I mean on Earth, are still in the state of Nature, each being, where there is no other, Judge for himself, and Executioner; which is, as I have before shew'd it, the perfect *state of Nature*.

88. And thus the Commonwealth comes by a Power to set down, what punishment shall belong to the several transgressions which they think worthy of it, committed amongst the Members of that Society, (which is the *power of making Laws*) as well as it has the power to punish any Injury done unto any of its Members, by any one that is not of it, (which is the *power of War and Peace;*) and all this for the preservation of the property of all the Members of that Society, as far as is possible. But though every Man who has enter'd into civil Society, and is be-

come a member of any Commonwealth, has thereby quitted his power to punish Offences against the Law of Nature, in prosecution of his own private Judgment; yet with the Judgment of Offences which he has given up to the Legislative in all Cases, where he can Appeal to the Magistrate, he has given a right to the Commonwealth to imploy his force, for the Execution of the Judgments of the Commonwealth, whenever he shall be called to it; which indeed are his own Judgments, they being made by himself, or his Representative. And herein we have the original of the *Legislative* and *Executive Power* of Civil Society, which is to judge by standing Laws how far Offences are to be punished, when committed within the Commonwealth; and also to determine by occasional Judgments founded on the present Circumstances of the Fact, how far Injuries from without are to be vindicated, and in both these to imploy all the force of all the Members when there shall be need.

89. Where-ever therefore any number of Men are so united into one Society, as to quit every one his Executive Power of the Law of Nature, and to resign it to the publick, there and there only is a *Political, or Civil Society*. And this is done where-ever any number of Men, in the state of Nature, enter into Society to make one People, one Body Politick under one Supreme Government, or else when any one joyns himself to, and incorporates with any Government already made. For hereby he authorizes the Society, or which is all one, the Legislative thereof to make Laws for him as the publick good of the Society shall require; to the Execution whereof, his own assistance (as to his own Decrees) is due. And this *puts Men* out of a State of Nature *into* that of a *Commonwealth*, by setting up a Judge on Earth, with Authority to determine all the Controversies, and redress the Injuries, that may happen to any Member of the Commonwealth; which Judge is the Legislative, or Magistrates appointed by it. And where-ever there are any number of Men, however associated, that have no such decisive power to appeal to, there they are still *in the state of Nature*.

90. Hence it is evident, that *Absolute Monarchy*, which by some Men is counted the

only Government in the world, is indeed *inconsistent with Civil Society*, and so can be no Form of Civil Government at all. For the *end of Civil Society*, being to avoid, and remedy those inconveniencies of the State of Nature, which necessarily follow from every Man's being Judge in his own Case, by setting up a known Authority, to which every one of that Society may Appeal upon any Injury received, or Controversie that may arise, and which every one of the Society ought to obey; where-ever any persons are, who have not such an Authority to Appeal to, for the decision of any difference between them, there those persons are still *in the state of Nature*. And so is every *Absolute Prince* in respect of those who are under his *Dominion*. . . .

93. *In Absolute Monarchies* indeed, as well as other Governments of the World, the Subjects have an Appeal to the Law, and Judges to decide any Controversies, and restrain any Violence that may happen betwixt the Subjects themselves, one amongst another. This every one thinks necessary, and believes he deserves to be thought a declared Enemy to Society and Mankind, who should go about to take it away. But whether this be from a true Love of Mankind and Society, and such a Charity as we owe all one to another, there is reason to doubt. For this is no more, than what every Man who loves his own Power, Profit, or Greatness, may, and naturally must do, keep those Animals from hurting or destroying one another who labour and drudge only for his Pleasure and Advantage, and so are taken care of, not out of any Love the Master has for them, but Love of himself, and the Profit they bring him. For if it be asked, what Security, *what Fence is there in such a State, against the Violence and Oppression of this Absolute Ruler*? The very Question can scarce be born. They are ready to tell you, that it deserves Death only to ask after Safety. Betwixt Subject and Subject, they will grant, there must be Measures, Laws, and Judges, for their mutual Peace and Security: But as for the *Ruler*, he ought to be *Absolute*, and is above all such Circumstances: because he has Power to do more hurt and wrong, 'tis right when he does it. To ask how you may be guarded from harm, or injury on that side where the strongest hand is to do it, is presently the Voice of Faction and Rebellion. As if when Men quitting the State of Nature entered into Society, they agreed that all of them but one, should be under the restraint of Laws, but that he should still retain all the Liberty of the State of Nature, increased with Power, and made licentious by Impunity. This is to think that Men are so foolish that they take care to avoid what Mischiefs may be done them by *Pole-Cats*, or *Foxes*, but are content, nay think it Safety, to be devoured by *Lions*. . . .

Chapter VII: Of the Beginning of Political Societies

95. Men being, as has been said, by Nature, all free, equal and independent, no one can be put out of this Estate, and subjected to the Political Power of another, without his own *Consent*. The only way whereby any one devests himself of his Natural Liberty, and *puts on the bonds of Civil Society* is by agreeing with other Men to joyn and unite into a Community, for their comfortable, safe, and peaceable living one amongst another, in a secure Enjoyment of their Properties, and a greater Security against any that are not of it. This any number of Men may do, because it injures not the Freedom of the rest; they are left as they were in the Liberty of the State of Nature. When any number of Men have so *consented to make one Community* or Government, they are thereby presently incorporated, and make *one Body Politick*, wherein the *Majority* have a Right to act and conclude the rest.

96. For when any number of Men have, by the consent of every individual, made a *Community*, they have thereby made that *Community* one Body, with a Power to Act as one Body, which is only by the will and determination of the *majority*. For that which acts any Community, being only the consent of the individuals of it, and it being necessary to that which is one body to move one way; it is necessary the Body should move that way whither the greater force carries it, which is the *consent of the majority:* or else it is impossible it should act or continue one Body, *one Community*, which the consent of every individual that united into it, agreed that it should, and so every one is bound by that

consent to be concluded by the *majority*. And therefore we see that in Assemblies empowered to act by positive Laws where no number is set by that positive Law which impowers them, the *act of the Majority* passes for the act of the whole, and of course determines, as having by the Law of Nature and Reason, the power of the whole.

97. And thus every Man, by consenting with others to make one Body Politick under one Government, puts himself under an Obligation to every one of that Society, to submit to the determination of the *majority*, and to be concluded by it; or else this *original Compact*, whereby he with others incorporates into *one Society*, would signifie nothing, and be no Compact, if he be left free, and under no other ties, than he was in before in the State of Nature. For what appearance would there be of any Compact? What new Engagement if he were no farther tied by any Decrees of the Society, than he himself thought fit, and did actually consent to? This would be still as great a liberty, as he himself had before his Compact, or any one else in the State of Nature hath, who may submit himself and consent to any acts of it if he thinks fit.

98. For if *the consent of the majority* shall not in reason, be received, as *the act of the whole*, and conclude every individual; nothing but the consent of every individual can make any thing to be the act of the whole: But such a consent is next impossible ever to be had, if we consider the Infirmities of Health, and Avocations of Business, which in a number, though much less than that of a Common-wealth, will necessarily keep many away from the publick Assembly. To which if we add the variety of Opinions, and contrariety of Interests, which unavoidably happen in all Collections of Men, the coming into Society upon such terms, would be only like *Cato's* coming into the Theatre, only to go out again. Such a Constitution as this would make the mighty *Leviathan* of a shorter duration, than the feeblest Creatures; and not let it outlast the day it was born in: which cannot be suppos'd, till we can think, that Rational Creatures should desire and constitute Societies only to be dissolved. For where the *majority* cannot conclude the rest, there they

cannot act as one Body, and consequently will be immediately dissolved again.

99. Whosoever therefore out of a state of Nature unite into a *Community*, must be understood to give up all the power, necessary to the ends for which they unite into Society, to the *majority* of the Community, unless they expressly agreed in any number greater than the majority. And this is done by barely agreeing to *unite into one Political Society*, which is *all the Compact* that is, or needs be, between the Individuals, that enter into, or make up a *Common-wealth*. And thus that, which begins and actually *constitutes any Political Society*, is nothing but the consent of any number of Freemen capable of a majority to unite and incorporate into such a Society. And this is that, and that only, which did, or could give *beginning* to any *lawful Government* in the World. . . .

119. *Every Man* being, as has been shewed, *naturally free*, and nothing being able to put him into subjection to any Earthly Power, but only his own Consent; it is to be considered, what shall be understood to be a *sufficient Declaration of* a Mans *Consent, to make him subject* to the Laws of any Government. There is a common distinction of an express and a tacit consent, which will concern our present Case. No body doubts but an *express Consent*, of any Man, entring into any Society, makes him a perfect Member of that Society, a Subject of that Government. The difficulty is, what ought to be look'd upon as a *tacit Consent*, and how far it binds, *i.e.* how far any one shall be looked on to have consented, and thereby submitted to any Government, where he has made no Expressions of it at all. And to this I say, that every Man, that hath any Possession, or Enjoyment, of any part of the Dominions of any Government, doth thereby give his *tacit Consent*, and is as far forth obliged to Obedience to the Laws of that Government, during such Enjoyment, as any one under it; whether this his Possession be of Land, to him and his Heirs for ever, or a Lodging only for a Week; or whether it be barely travelling freely on the Highway; and in Effect, it reaches as far as the very being of any one within the Territories of that Government. . . .

122. But submitting to the Laws of any Country, living quietly, and enjoying Priviledges and Protection under them, *makes not a Man a Member of that Society:* This is only a local Protection and Homage due to, and from all those, who, not being in a state of War, come within the Territories belonging to any Government, to all parts whereof the force of its Law extends. But this no more *makes a Man a Member of that Society,* a perpetual Subject of that Commonwealth, than it would make a Man a Subject to another in whose Family he found it convenient to abide for some time; though, whilst he continued in it, he were obliged to comply with the Laws, and submit to the Government he found there. And thus we see, that *Foreigners,* by living all their Lives under another Government, and enjoying the Priviledges and Protection of it, though they are bound, even in Conscience, to submit to its Administration, as far forth as any Denison; yet do not thereby come to be *Subjects or Members of that Commonwealth.* Nothing can make any Man so, but his actually entering into it by positive Engagement, and express Promise and Compact. This is that, which I think, concerning the beginning of Political Societies, and that *Consent which makes any one a Member* of any Commonwealth.

Chapter IX: Of the Ends of Political Society and Government

123. If Man in the State of Nature be so free, as has been said; If he be absolute Lord of his own Person and Possessions, equal to the greatest, and subject to no Body, why will he part with his Freedom? Why will he give up this Empire, and subject himself to the Dominion and Controul of any other Power? To which 'tis obvious to Answer, that though in the state of Nature he hath such a right, yet the Enjoyment of it is very uncertain, and constantly exposed to the Invasion of others. For all being Kings as much as he, every Man his Equal, and the greater part no strict Observers of Equity and Justice, the enjoyment of the property he has in this state is very unsafe, very unsecure. This makes him willing to quit this Condition, which however free, is full of fears and continual dangers: And 'tis not without reason, that he seeks out, and is

willing to joyn in Society with others who are already united, or have a mind to unite for the mutual *Preservation* of their Lives, Liberties and Estates, which I call by the general Name, *Property.*

124. The great and *chief end* therefore, of Mens uniting into Commonwealths, and putting themselves under Government, *is the Preservation of their Property.* To which in the state of Nature there are many things wanting.

First, There wants an *establish'd,* settled, known *Law,* received and allowed by common consent to be the Standard of Right and Wrong, and the common measure to decide all Controversies between them. For though the Law of Nature be plain and intelligible to all rational Creatures; yet Men being biassed by their Interest, as well as ignorant for want of study of it, are not apt to allow of it as a Law binding to them in the application of it to their particular Cases.

125. *Secondly,* In the State of Nature there wants a *known and indifferent Judge,* with Authority to determine all differences according to the established Law. For every one in that state being both Judge and Executioner of the Law of Nature, Men being partial to themselves, Passion and Revenge is very apt to carry them too far, and with too much heat, in their own Cases; as well as negligence, and unconcernedness, to make them too remiss, in other Mens.

126. *Thirdly,* In the state of Nature there often wants *Power* to back and support the Sentence when right, and to *give* it due *Execution.* They who by any injustice offended, will seldom fail, where they are able, by force to make good their Injustice: such resistance many times makes the punishment dangerous, and frequently destructive, to those who attempt it.

127. Thus Mankind, notwithstanding all the Priviledges of the state of Nature, being but in an ill condition, while they remain in it, are quickly driven into Society. Hence it comes to pass, that we seldom find any number of Men live any time together in this State. The inconveniencies, that they are therein exposed to, by the irregular and uncertain exercise of the Power every Man has of punishing the transgressions of others,

make them take Sanctuary under the established Laws of Government, and therein seek *the preservation of their Property.* 'Tis this makes them so willingly give up every one his single power of punishing to be exercised by such alone as shall be appointed to it amongst them; and by such Rules as the Community, or those authorised by them to that purpose, shall agree on. And in this we have the original *right and rise* of both *the Legislative and Executive Power,* as well as of the Governments and Societies themselves. . . .

131. But though Men when they enter into Society, give up the Equality, Liberty, and Executive Power they had in the State of Nature, into the hands of the Society, to be so far disposed of by the Legislative, as the good of the Society shall require; yet it being only with an intention in every one the better to preserve himself his Liberty and Property; (For no rational Creature can be supposed to change his condition with an intention to be worse) the power of the Society, or *Legislative* constituted by them, *can never be suppos'd to extend farther than the common good;* but is obliged to secure every ones Property by providing against those three defects above-mentioned, that made the State of Nature so unsafe and uneasie. And so whoever has the Legislative or Supream Power of any Common-wealth, is bound to govern by established *standing Laws,* promulgated and known to the People, and not by Extemporary Decrees; by *indifferent* and upright *Judges,* who are to decide Controversies by those Laws; And to imploy the force of the Community at home, *only in the Execution of such Laws,* or abroad to prevent or redress Foreign Injuries, and secure the Community from Inroads and Invasion. And all this to be directed to no other *end,* but the *Peace, Safety,* and *publick good* of the People. . . .

Chapter XIX: Of the Dissolution of Government

211. He that will with any clearness speak of the *Dissolution of Government,* ought, in the first place to distinguish between the *Dissolution of the Society,* and the *Dissolution of the Government.* That which makes the Community, and brings Men out of the loose State of Nature, into *one Politick Society,* is the Agreement which every one has with the rest to incorporate, and act as one Body, and so be one distinct Commonwealth. The usual, and almost only way whereby *this Union is dissolved,* is the Inroad of Foreign Force making a Conquest upon them. For in that Case, (not being able to maintain and support themselves, as *one intire* and *independent Body*) the Union belonging to that Body which consisted therein, must necessarily cease, and so every one return to the state he was in before, with a liberty to shift for himself, and provide for his own Safety as he thinks fit in some other Society. Whenever the *Society is dissolved,* 'tis certain the Government of that Society cannot remain. Thus Conquerours Swords often cut up Governments by the Roots, and mangle Societies to pieces, separating the subdued or scattered Multitude from the Protection of, and Dependence on that Society which ought to have preserved them from violence. The World is too well instructed in, and too forward to allow of this way of dissolving of Governments to need any more to be said of it: and there wants not much Argument to prove, that where the *Society is dissolved,* the Government cannot remain; that being as impossible, as for the Frame of an House to subsist when the Materials of it are scattered, and dissipated by a Whirl-wind, or jumbled into a confused heap by an Earthquake.

212. Besides this over-turning from without, *Governments are dissolved from within,*

First, When the *Legislative* is *altered.* Civil Society being a State of Peace, amongst those who are of it, from whom the State of War is excluded by the Umpirage, which they have provided in their Legislative, for the ending all Differences, that may arise amongst any of them, 'tis in their *Legislative,* that the Members of a Commonwealth are united, and combined together into one coherent living Body. This *is the Soul that gives Form, Life, and Unity* to the Commonwealth: From hence the several Members have their mutual Influence, Sympathy, and Connexion: And therefore when the *Legislative* is broken, or *dissolved,* Dissolution and

Death follows. For the *Essence and Union of the Society* consisting in having one Will, the Legislative, when once established by the Majority, has the declaring, and as it were keeping of that Will. The *Constitution of the Legislative* is the first and fundamental Act of Society, whereby provision is made for the *Continuation of their Union*, under the Direction of Persons, and Bonds of Laws made by persons authorized thereunto, by the Consent and Appointment of the People, without which no one Man, or number of Men, amongst them, can have Authority of making Laws, that shall be binding to the rest. When any one, or more, shall take upon them to make Laws, whom the People have not appointed so to do, they make Laws without Authority, which the People are not therefore bound to obey; by which means they come again to be out of subjection, and may constitute to themselves a *new Legislative*, as they think best, being in full liberty to resist the force of those, who without Authority would impose any thing upon them. Every one is at the disposure of his own Will, when those who had by the delegation of the Society, the declaring of the publick Will, are excluded from it, and others usurp the place who have no such Authority or Delegation.

213. This being usually brought about by such in the Commonwealth who misuse the Power they have: It is hard to consider it aright, and know at whose door to lay it, without knowing the Form of Government in which it happens. Let us suppose then the Legislative placed in the Concurrence of three distinct Persons.

1. A single hereditary Person having the constant, supream, executive Power, and with it the Power of Convoking and Dissolving the other two within certain Periods of Time.

2. An Assembly of Hereditary Nobility.

3. An Assembly of Representatives chosen *pro tempore*, by the People: Such a Form of Government supposed, it is evident.

214. *First,* That when such a single Person or Prince sets up his own Arbitrary Will in place of the Laws, which are the Will of the Society, declared by the Legislative, then the *Legislative is changed.* For that being in effect the Legislative whose Rules and Laws are put in execution, and required to be obeyed; when other Laws are set up, and other Rules pretended, and inforced, than what the Legislative, constituted by the Society, have enacted, 'tis plain, that the *Legislative is changed.* Whoever introduces new Laws, not being thereunto authorized by the fundamental Appointment of the Society, or subverts the old, disowns and overturns the Power by which they were made, and so sets up a *new Legislative.*

215. *Secondly,* When the Prince hinders the Legislative from assembling in its due time, or from acting freely, pursuant to those ends, for which it was Constituted, the *Legislative is altered.* For 'tis not a certain number of Men, no, nor their meeting, unless they have also Freedom of debating, and Leisure of perfecting, what is for the good of the Society wherein the Legislative consists: when these are taken away or altered, so as to deprive the Society of the due exercise of their Power, the *Legislative* is truly *altered.* For it is not Names that Constitute Governments, but the use and exercise of those Powers that were intended to accompany them; so that he who takes away the Freedom, or hinders the acting of the Legislative in its due seasons, in effect *takes away the Legislative,* and *puts an end to the Government.*

216. *Thirdly,* When by the Arbitrary Power of the Prince, the Electors, or ways of Election are altered, without the Consent, and contrary to the common Interest of the People, there also the *Legislative is altered.* For if others, than those whom the Society has authorized thereunto, do chuse, or in another way, than what the Society hath prescribed, those chosen are not the Legislative appointed by the People.

217. *Fourthly,* The delivery also of the People into the subjection of a Foreign Power, either by the Prince, or by the Legislative, is certainly a *change of the Legislative,* and so a *Dissolution of the Government.* For the end why People entered into Society, being to be preserved one intire, free, independent Society, to be governed by its own Laws; this is lost, whenever they are given up into the Power of another. . . .

219. There is one way more whereby such a Government may be dissolved, and that is,

when he who has the Supream Executive Power, neglects and abandons that charge, so that the Laws already made can no longer be put in execution. This is demonstratively to reduce all to Anarchy, and so effectually to *dissolve the Government.* For Laws not being made for themselves, but to be by their execution the Bonds of the Society, to keep every part of the Body Politick in its due place and function, when that totally ceases, the *Government* visibly *ceases,* and the People become a confused Multitude, without Order or Connexion. Where there is no longer the administration of Justice, for the securing of Mens Rights, nor any remaining Power within the Community to direct the Force, or provide for the Necessities for the publick, there certainly is *no Government left.* Where the Laws cannot be executed, it is all one as if there were no Laws, and a Government without Laws, is, I suppose, a Mystery in Politicks, unconceivable to humane Capacity, and inconsistent with humane Society.

220. In these and the like Cases, *when the Government is dissolved,* the People are at liberty to provide for themselves, by erecting a new Legislative, differing from the other, by the change of Persons, or Form, or both as they shall find fit most for their safety and good. For the *Society* can never, by the fault of another, lose the Native and Original Right it has to preserve it self, which can only be done by a settled Legislative, and a fair and impartial execution of the Laws made by it. But the state of Mankind is not so miserable that they are not capable of using this Remedy, till it be too late to look for any. To tell *People* they *may provide for themselves,* by erecting a new Legislative, when by Oppression, Artifice, or being delivered over to a Foreign Power, their old one is gone, is only to tell them they may expect Relief, when it is too late, and the evil is past Cure. This is in effect no more than to bid them first be Slaves, and then to take care of their Liberty; and when their Chains are on, tell them, they may act like Freemen. This, if barely so, is rather Mockery than Relief; and Men can never be secure from Tyranny, if there be no means to escape it, till they are perfectly under it: And therefore it is, that they have

not only a Right to get out of it but to prevent it. . . .

224. But 'twill be said, this *Hypothesis* lays a *ferment* for frequent *Rebellion.* To which I Answer,

First, No more than any other *Hypothesis.* For when the *People* are made *miserable,* and find themselves *exposed to the ill usage of Arbitrary Power,* cry up their Governours, as much as you will for Sons of *Jupiter,* let them be sacred and Divine, descended or authorized from Heaven; give them out for whom or what you please, the same will happen. *The People generally ill-treated,* and contrary to right, will be ready upon any occasion to ease themselves of a burden that sits heavy upon them. They will wish and seek for the opportunity, which, in the change, weakness, and accidents of humane affairs, seldom delays long to offer it self. He must have lived but a little while in the World, who has not seen Examples of this in his time; and he must have read very little, who cannot produce Examples of it in all sorts of Governments in the World.

225. Secondly, I Answer, such *Revolutions happen* not upon every little mismanagement in publick affairs. *Great mistakes* in the ruling part, many wrong and inconvenient Laws, and all the *slips* of humane frailty will be *born by the People,* without mutiny or murmur. But if a long train of Abuses, Prevarications, and Artifices, all tending the same way, make the design visible to the People, and they cannot but feel, what they lie under, and see, whither they are going; 'tis not to be wonder'd, that they should then rouze themselves, and endeavour to put the rule into such hands, which may secure to them the ends for which Government was at first erected; and without which, ancient Names, and specious Forms, are so far from being better, that they are much worse, than the state of Nature, or pure Anarchy; the inconveniencies being all as great and as near, but the remedy farther off and more difficult.

226. Thirdly, I Answer, That *this Doctrine* of a Power in the People of providing for their safety a-new by a new Legislative, when their Legislators have acted contrary to their trust, by invading their Property, is *the best*

fence against Rebellion, and the probablest means to hinder it. For Rebellion being an Opposition, not to Persons, but Authority, which is founded only in the Constitutions and Laws of the Government; those, whoever they be, who by force break through, and by force justifie their violation of them, are truly and properly *Rebels.* For when Men by entering into Society and Civil Government, have excluded force, and introduced Laws for the preservation of Property, Peace, and Unity amongst themselves; those who set up force again in opposition to the Laws, do *Rebellare,* that is, bring back again the state of War, and are properly Rebels: Which

they who are in Power (by the pretence they have to Authority, the temptation of force they have in their hands, and the Flattery of those about them) being likeliest to do; the properest way to prevent the evil, is to shew them the danger and injustice of it, who are under the greatest temptation to run into it. . . .

Adapted from: John Locke, *Two Treatises of Government,* pp. 267–282, 285–294, 299–302, 323–328, 330–333,347–353, 406–416. Edited by Peter Laslett. Copyright © 1988. Reprinted by permission of Cambridge University Press. ✦

9
Class and Politics

Richard Ashcraft

. . . Much could be said concerning the intellectual antecedents of Locke's treatment of property, but since there is an extensive body of literature that discusses that subject, I will not pursue that topic here.[1] Rather, I shall focus upon the political context within which Locke's arguments on property are advanced. In that regard, there are three aspects of his treatment of property to which I wish to draw particular attention. The first point, drawn from his attack upon Filmer in the *First Treatise*, emphasizes the theological origins of property rights; the second concerns Locke's attribution of a social and political significance to the meaning of "labor" as a "title" to property; and the third relates to Locke's integration of the political objectives of his discussion of property into the political objectives of the *Second Treatise* as a whole.

To consider Locke's position on the relationship of labor to property divorced from its theological underpinnings is not only a serious interpretive mistake in terms of the intentional structure of Locke's intellectual commitments in the *Two Treatises*, it also misrepresents through omission a crucial dimension of the political radicalism that work expresses. Far from endorsing a secular and conservative attitude toward property ownership, the *Two Treatises* incorporates many features of a critical attack upon the private appropriation of property formulated within the framework of traditional Christianity.[2]

In his lectures on the Law of Nature, Locke described the individual's relationship to God and the moral duties derivable from that relationship in terms that were subsequently restated in his later writings. We are subject to God's authority, he argued, by "the right of creation, as when all things are justly subject to that by which they have first been made and are also constantly preserved."[3] Hence, man's obligation to obey God's will derives not merely from the divine wisdom of the lawmaker, but also "from the right which the Creator has over His creation."[4] On this point, Locke never changed his mind, and the argument reappears in both the *Essay Concerning Human Understanding* and the *Two Treatises of Government*.[5] At the beginning of the *Second Treatise*, for example. Locke declares that:

> For men being all the workmanship of one omnipotent, and infinitely wise Maker; all the Servants of one Sovereign Master, sent into the world by his order and about his business, They are his property, whose workmanship they are, made to last during his, not one anothers pleasure.[6]

This is a clear statement of the theory of creationism. . . . Creationism is employed by Locke as the primary axis for his rejection of Filmer's definition of political authority. It also establishes the moral boundaries for his discussion of property rights.

Both of these points can be illustrated, I believe, from a consideration of the implications that follow from the statement of the theory of creationism, as formulated by Richard Baxter. God, Baxter wrote, is more than "our creator"; he is also "our *owner*." Thus, "our obligation is founded in our being His creatures, and so His *own*."[7] As another writer put it, God is the great proprietor of the earth and "man has only the use, and stewardship, and employment of these things which are committed to him, by the allowance of God's providence."[8] Creationism, therefore, not only sets forth the reasons for our obedience to the Law of Nature, it also describes the individual's relationship to God as part of a theory of property. To his description of individuals as the property of God, Locke adds a characterization of the latter as the "sole Lord and Proprietor of the whole world."[9] Since, for Locke, the Deity is the Great Property Owner, it is possible to construct a model of the appropriate uses of property in terms of God's intentions and His relations with man. This model can then be employed as a critical standard according to which all other proprietors are assessed in light of their uses of property.

From the standpoint of Locke's critique of Filmer's conception of political authority, the most relevant aspect of property ownership is the owner's right to use his property even to the point of "destroying" the object through its usage. Such a proposition may appear innocuous enough when applied to nuts and berries and other articles of consumption, but its religious significance restates the kernel of terror at the heart of Calvinist theology.[10] In the *Two Treatises*, however, this owner/object relationship functions as a prohibitive injunction against any humanly advanced claims to exercise a right of destruction over God's "property," at least in the absence of any direct divine order to do so. In putting the problem in this way, it becomes clear why Filmer's argument presented such a fundamental challenge to Locke's own viewpoint; for Filmer claimed precisely that God had delivered a definite, positive instruction to man (Adam) that conferred on him the absolute political authority necessary to treat other human beings as his property.[11] Moreover, Filmer was willing to generalize this grant of authority so that all fathers, as creators of their children, could rightfully exercise a (potentially) destructive power over them.[12] This Locke denies, and he suggests that in attributing to fathers such a creative role with respect to their children, Filmer is guilty of a form of blasphemy. Those who subscribe to such a view "are so dazzled with the thoughts of monarchy," that they have forgotten that it is not human beings, but God "who is the author and giver of life."

> To give life to that which has yet no being, is to frame and make a living creature, fashion the parts, and mold and suit them to their uses, and having proportioned and fitted them together, to put into them a living soul. He that could do this, might indeed have some pretence to destroy his own workmanship. But is there any one so bold, that dares thus far arrogate to himself the incomprehensible works of the Almighty? Who alone did at first, and continues still to make a living soul, He alone can breathe in the breath of life . . . he is indeed Maker of us all, which no

parents can pretend to be of their children.[13]

In this passage the political message of Locke's commitment to creationism is starkly clear: Neither monarchs nor fathers have a right to destroy God's workmanship, since such a right belongs to the maker of the property. In view of the social composition of the audience to whom Locke's political message in the *Two Treatises* was addressed, this artisanal image of the Deity is rather interesting.[14] In any event, it is the existential and moral framework provided by creationism that sanctions Locke's rejection of the belief that "men were made as so many herds of cattle, only for the service, use, and pleasure of their princes," the position he attributes to Filmer and to all defenders of political absolutism.[15] Locke argues that "there cannot be supposed any such *subordination* among us, that may *authorize us to destroy one another,* as if we were made for one another's uses, as the inferior ranks of creatures are for ours."[16] This, if we may put it this way, is the negative contribution to Locke's theory of property stipulated by his theological argument against Filmer. Our freedom and equality with respect to one another is a function of our being the servants and the property of a higher Being.

There is, however, also a positive side to Locke's religious approach to property. Early in the *First Treatise*, Locke informs the reader that he intends to show that God did not give Adam "private dominion over the inferior creatures," and that, as a consequence, property was given to mankind "in common."[17] This point is repeatedly asserted by Locke throughout the work, and it has received prominent attention in the secondary literature on the Lockean concept of property. Yet the failure of Filmer to establish a claim for a positive proprietary grant from God, and the consequent reversion of property to a communal status, does not exhaust Locke's discussion of property in the *First Treatise*. For as we have seen, his defense of our right to be treated as free and equal beings is framed in terms of our obligations to a higher authority. Before turning to the political implications of Locke's conjunction of labor and property, it is important to place the former concept within the same framework of higher moral obligations. The labor of individuals that vouchsafes for them a claim to property, in other words, represents the positive fulfillment of a divine command. For Locke, if God is the Lord Proprietor of the world, then we are his productive tenants.

God not only "furnished the world with things fit for food and rayment and other necessaries of life," he also "directed" individuals "to make use of those things that were necessary or useful to his being." Thus, "man had a right to a use of the creatures, by the will and grant of God."[18] This directive receives an even sharper phraseology in the *Second Treatise*. There Locke declares that God "commanded man also to labor," and that it was "in obedience to this command of God" that man "subdued, tilled and sowed any part" of the land, and "thereby annexed to it something that was his property, which another had no title to, nor could without injury take from him."[19] As Locke restates the point several paragraphs later,

> So that God, by commanding to subdue, gave authority so far to appropriate. And the condition of human life, which requires labor and materials to work on, necessarily introduces private possessions.[20]

In short, if labor serves as a title to property, it does so, according to Locke, within a juridical structure in which the authority to appropriate objects is received by human beings in the form of a command to labor. Through their laboring activity, individuals are fulfilling an obligation to obey God's commands. This should not appear surprising since the command to labor is simply a specific manifestation of God's designs that govern the relationships posited by the theory of creationism. "It does not seem to fit in with the wisdom of the Creator," Locke observes, "to form an animal that is most perfect and ever active, and to endow it abundantly above all others with mind, intellect, reason, and all the requisites for working, and yet not assign to it any work."[21] It is clear to Locke that "God intends man to do

something," to be active; in short, to labor.[22] The particular mandate to do so is exemplary of the fact that we are "sent into the world by his order and about his business," and are "subservient to his designs."[23] Hence, property, as envisioned by Locke is totally enshrouded in a network of moral obligations. Nor should the religious characterization of labor as a "calling" be overlooked, since from Locke's perspective, the question of what place within God's designs for man may be claimed by those who do not labor has, potentially, socially radical implications. It is, therefore, a mistake to proceed directly from human labor to property, disengaged from the theological structure that Locke employs in the *Two Treatises*. Not only does such a viewpoint neglect the political resonance of Locke's critique of Filmer, but it also fails to appreciate the stewardship limitations upon property rights when the latter are interpreted in light of a reading of God's intentions. This point is applicable both in a negative sense (that is, what individuals cannot do with their property) and in the positive sense of a recognition of productive labor as a sign of obedience to God's demands.[24] As we shall see, this religious perspective is quite capable of supporting a radical theory of the uses and ownership of property.

Quite apart from the neglect of the religious premises of Locke's discussion of property, interpreters of his thought have displayed an inordinate propensity to regard labor as a metaphysical concept.[25] The point Locke repeatedly emphasizes throughout his chapter on property, however, is that it is laboring activity that is important. It is "the labor of those who broke the oxen, who digged and wrought the iron and stones, who felled and framed the timber," and "the ploughman's pains, the reaper and thresher's toil, and the baker's sweat" that provides the "useful products" for "the benefit of mankind."[26] The social implications of Locke's stress upon the value of "human industry" to society (or individual labor seen in a social context) has not received the attention it deserves. Too often commentators have contented themselves with a consideration of Locke's resolution of an intellectually constituted problem of explaining the relationship between the individual and his property.[27] Certainly, this was a genuine theoretical problem, for Locke as well as for many other writers. That he set out with the intention to resolve it cannot be denied. Nevertheless, this problem arose during the exclusion crisis within the precincts of a political debate, and that debate demanded that property ownership be viewed as a constituent element of "the common good," at least so far as the Whigs were concerned. Whether laboring activity or human industry was necessary for the solution of the theoretical problem, this social view of labor was clearly essential to the political argument Locke wished to make regarding property ownership.

When Locke writes that "justice gives every man a title to the product of his honest industry," this appears to be a reasonable, if [a] trifle innocuous, statement.[28] Yet the encouragement of "honest industry" could, under certain circumstances, take on a polemical and more sharply political meaning than is evident from its definitional association with justice. The chapter on property in the *Second Treatise*, I shall argue, has precisely this intentional objective: to provide a defense of "the industrious" and trading part of the nation—the constituency to whom the Whigs addressed their appeals—against the idle, unproductive, and Court-dominated property owners. Locke's argument, in other words, has the ring of much of the Whig election propaganda in its appeal to the nation to support "the industrious" rather than the "court parasites" or "pensioners."[29] If the overall political objectives of the *Two Treatises* are considered, this can hardly appear surprising. But I believe that with respect to his treatment of property, Locke's political aims can be more specifically stated.

"As much land as a man tills, plants, improves, cultivates, and can use the product of," Locke declares, "so much is his property." As we noted, this commandment to till the earth was a divine injunction, but, Locke adds, introducing the critical component of his teleological reading of God's intentions, man was commanded "to subdue the earth" in order to "improve it for the benefit of life,

and therein lay out something upon it that was his own, his labor."[30] In Locke's view, God has a wider purpose in mind than simply providing for the individual's self-preservation; rather, individual labor is seen as a contributory action to the improvement and benefit of life, taken in a collective sense. Again, this should not surprise us, for Locke's view of natural law is that it is designed to provide for the common good, and the benefit of mankind, and that it is given as a standard to individuals who exist as part of a "natural community."[31] It is within this teleological framework, I am arguing, that the entire discussion of property in chapter 5 of the *Second Treatise* must be viewed. In the passage immediately following the one cited above, Locke restates the same point in negative terminology: "Nor was this appropriation of any parcel of land, by improving it, any prejudice to any other man."[32] The fulfillment of God's intentions not only contributes to the common good, but it does no particular injury to any other individual. Moreover, Locke's reading of God's purposes—that "nothing was made by God for man to spoil or destroy"—is specifically applicable to the use of land.[33] Thus,

> God gave the world to men in common, but since he gave it to them for their benefit . . . it cannot be supposed he meant it should always remain common and uncultivated. He gave it to the use of the industrious and rational . . . not to the fancy or covetousness of the quarrelsome and contentious.[34]

Not only are God's designs realized by the industrious, the practical social benefits are both immense and, in a general sense, shared in common.[35] The empirical dimensions of this position seem self-evident to Locke. As he observes,

> The provisions serving to the support of human life, produced by one acre of enclosed and cultivated land, are . . . ten times more, than those which are yielded by an acre of land, of an equal richness, lying waste in common. And therefore he that encloses land and has a greater plenty of the conveniences of life from ten acres, than he could have from a hundred

left to nature, may truly be said to give ninety acres to mankind.[36]

From our perspective on property rights as expressions of self-interest, this passage appears oddly phrased, if not downright disingenuous. That an individual would have the benefit of mankind in mind as the outcome of his enclosure and cultivation of land can, at best, be said to be a rather naive reading of human motivations. But Locke is plainly not interested in *individual motivations* for property development; rather, what concerns him are the moral and social uses to which property (and labor) can be put. It is quite true that, even under this view, particular individuals may be able to acquire considerable wealth as the outcome of their productive and beneficial actions, but to suggest that Locke ever sets men free from their natural law obligations such that wealth may be accumulated solely because individuals desire to do so and without any social constraints on its employment is to reverse completely the thrust of his argument in the *Second Treatise*, not to mention the political rationale of the Whigs' claim to represent the common good against the arbitrary self-interest of an individual (the king).

Since it would be a mistake to convey the impression that the critical edge of Locke's attitude toward property is merely a response to the contingencies of the exclusion crisis, I want to place the argument of the *Two Treatises* within a broader perspective, one subscribed to by Locke both before and after he wrote the chapter on property. I have already alluded to the importance of the theological framework as a specific response to Filmer's formulation of the problem. There is, however, another, socially rooted conception of labor and property that Locke, at least from the time of his association with Shaftesbury, incorporated into his understanding of political society. This view supplies a positive endorsement of laboring activity, productivity, and commercial expansion, and a corresponding critique of idleness and waste, however these attributes are expressed in any particular social context.[37] Seen from this vantage point, Locke's chapter on property simply expresses

through a specific formulation a general attitude characteristic of Locke's thought since the 1660s.

In his manuscript and subsequently in the published work on the lowering of interest, Locke defended "the sober and industrious" individuals who labor for the benefit of society.[38] These "industrious and thriving men" are identified with those who contribute to the manufacture of goods and to the expansion of trade.[39] He is especially concerned to identify the interests of artisans, manufacturers, and tradesmen with "the wheels of trade."[40] Locke's argument is directed, as we have seen, against the bankers who hold a disproportionate share of the kingdom's money in their hands, to the detriment of the public good.[41] Nevertheless, some of the blame must fall upon the foolish country gentleman or aristocrat who has "carried his money to London" and put it in the hands of the bankers.[42] This remark is part of a muted critique of landowners that runs as a leitmotif throughout the *Considerations*. For example, when Locke raises the question as to why land is sold on the market, he suggests two basic causal factors, neither of which reflect favorably upon landowners: The first, "general ill husbandry," is self-explanatory; the second is indebtedness. This condition, of course, might befall almost anyone, regardless of his personal virtues, but Locke is especially concerned with the relationship between "debauchery" or a "depraved education" and indebtedness. Both of these characteristics are associated with the belief, held by many landowners, that it is "fashionable for men to live beyond their estates."[43] This "costly itch after the materials of . . . luxury from abroad" is one cause for the scarcity of money and the consequent decay of trade.[44] The latter, in turn, leads to a decline in rents for the landowner, and thus to his indebtedness. So whether or not he realizes it, the country gentleman must take a much greater interest in trade—and a correspondingly diminishing interest in the conspicuous consumption of imported goods—not only to free himself from this cycle of indebtedness, but also in order for the country as a whole to prosper.[45] Locke's message, therefore, is that "if ill husbandry has wasted our riches," then only the practice of "general industry and frugality, joined to a well-ordered trade" will restore the wealth of the nation.[46] Locke is thus able to contrast the social values of "sobriety, frugality, and industry" associated with trade with the "debauchery" and "expensive vanity" of "lazy and indigent people" who "waste" their resources through extravagant living.[47]

This aspect of Locke's argument has been little noticed. Much more attention has been paid to Locke's recognition of the fact that the laboring class lives from hand to mouth, an observation that is often cited as though it represented a derogatory judgment on Locke's part.[48] But this is not Locke's view. On the contrary, these individuals, whatever the paucity of their temporal rewards, are at least fulfilling the divine injunction given to all individuals to labor—and to labor, moreover, for the common good. "We ought to look on it as a mark of goodness in god," Locke argues, "that he has put us in this life under a necessity of labor." For, it is the "ill men at leisure" who are likely to commit "the mischiefs" that distress others. Thus labor preserves us "from the ills of idleness."[49] "I think," Locke wrote to a friend, "everyone, according to what way providence has placed him in, is bound to labor for the public good, as far as he is able, or else he has no right to eat."[50] As Dunn observes, anyone who fulfilled his "calling" in these terms executed his obligations under the Law of Nature.[51]

We can appreciate the socially critical dimensions of this general admonition if we attend to Locke's application of it to various social groups within his society. Here again, great emphasis has been given to the harshness of his attitude toward "the idle poor." Certainly, they are a problem with respect to the injunction both to labor and to pursue the common good. But they are not the only social group that poses a problem, and it could be argued that, unless their numbers grow exceedingly large, the poor are not even the primary example of idleness in Locke's society. In notes on trade he made in 1674 for Shaftesbury, Locke divided society into two groups: "those that contribute in any way" to trade, and those who are "idle" or who do not advance the wealth of society. In the first group Locke placed those who worked in the mines, the clothing industry, as well as artisans and farmers. In the second group, are those "retainers" employed by landowners (and logically, the landowners themselves) who simply consume the commodities produced by others.[52] Here the laboring class is certainly included among those who "contribute in any way" to trade and the public good, while the idle gentry are negatively assessed by Locke. Later, in some journal notes, he suggests that "gentlemen" ought to spend at least three hours a day "in some honest labor," by which he means "manual labor." The consequence of this slightly utopian demand would be an improvement of the condition of "all mankind," and hence, a truer fulfillment of the precepts of natural law than presently exists in society.[53] These notes, it is true, are somewhat fanciful, but the underlying attitude that they express is not, and it reappears in Locke's correspondence with Clarke in the 1680s, and subsequently in *Some Thoughts Concerning Education*, which is based upon that correspondence. Thus, Locke will not allow "a gentleman's calling" to be defined except in a manner that includes his learning "a manual trade, nay two or three."[54] Moreover, he appeals to the "ancients" who "understood very well how to reconcile manual labor with affairs of state" and even "great men" did not regard laboring activity as a "lessening [of] their dignity."[55]

Locke contrasts the "honest labor in useful and mechanical arts" favorably with "the luxury of Courts," the "idle and useless employments" of "the rich and noble" whose "pride and vanity" have led them to regard such laboring activity as a "disgrace."[56] Those who inherit "a plentiful fortune" may be "excused from having a particular calling in order to their subsistence in this life," but they are not excused from being "under an obligation of doing something" in order to carry out the precepts of "the law of God" to labor for the benefit of mankind.[57] Laboring activity, in other words, is never detached from its conjunction with the advancement of the public good.[58] Political society is instituted for the latter purpose, and even if

Locke did not have a more than slightly suspicious attitude toward "the rich and noble" and the possession of wealth, there is no way in which he could be supposed to have conceptualized political society in a manner that, in effect, excluded "the laboring class," as Macpherson suggests.[59] On the contrary, Locke's general attitude toward manual labor, toward "the necessity of labor," and toward those who have worked in the mines or textile industries, as I have tried to demonstrate, was overwhelmingly positive. His attitude toward idle landowners, the "useless employments" of the "rich and noble," and those of inherited wealth who do nothing to advance the common good, on the other hand, is decidedly negative. This framework, I am arguing, through which Locke perceived the activities of various groups within his own society, is one he developed prior to (and retained following) his writing of the *Two Treatises*. It ought, therefore, to be kept in mind as the prism through which the activities described in the chapter on property in the *Second Treatise* are reflected and evaluated.

Returning to the argument of that chapter, we have seen that to this point, Locke's theoretical and political objectives in his treatment of property have jointly reinforced the importance and natural law endorsement of those who cultivate the land and so benefit mankind. At this juncture, however, the theoretical argument takes a crucial turning, with the invention of money, but (and this is the point I wish to emphasize) Locke's *political* attitude remains unchanged. Throughout the chapter on property, Locke insists that those who cultivate the land contribute to the common good, while those who do not do so are wasteful landowners and, from the standpoint of society, useless individuals. The invention of money, along with certain other demographic factors, changes the form of the society within which this contrast takes on a distinct social importance, but it does not at all mitigate the forcefulness of Locke's moral and political argument. The invention of money, and commerce with other parts of the world, in other words, may themselves be justifiable practices if they are viewed as

being consonant with the natural law command to provide for the common good—which is the way Locke views them—but they provide no justification whatsoever for the "wasteful" use of landed property.[60]

"A thousand acres . . . without any improvement, tillage, or husbandry," Locke argues, is not worth "ten acres" of "well-cultivated" land in Devonshire. The former is simply an "uncultivated waste" and contributes nothing to "increase the common stock of mankind."[61] The contrast here is presented with the "wilds" of America, but Locke displays the same attitude toward the thousands of acres of uncultivated land in seventeenth-century England. "Even amongst us," he maintains, "land that is left wholly to Nature, that hath no improvement of pasturage, tillage, or planting, is called, as indeed it is, waste; and we shall find the benefit of it amount to little more than nothing."[62] Locke's approval for the individual who "by his labor does . . . enclose [land] from the common," is a major theme throughout the chapter on property in the *Second Treatise*.[63] And conversely, he insists, "the extent of ground is of so little value without labor" that it qualifies only as "wasteland."[64] It is true that, within civil society, where "the laws regulate the right of property, and the possession of land is determined by positive constitutions," no one can enclose the commons "without the consent of all his fellow commoners." Hence, "the law of the land . . . is not to be violated" merely for the sake of enclosure.[65] Yet in those instances in which the law is doubtful (as in Spain) or is nonexistent (as in America), Locke endorses enclosure even to the point of arguing that if someone has already enclosed the land but allowed it to remain uncultivated, then the land, "notwithstanding his enclosure, was still to be looked on as waste, and might be the possession of any other."[66] It seems strange that this rather radical endorsement of the claims of labor over those of land ownership has been so little commented upon by those who are so eager to award Locke the honor of having formulated the modern defense of the private ownership of property.

Obviously, Locke was not advocating the return of the Diggers, though his attitude toward property is not so far removed from theirs as is generally assumed.[67] Nevertheless, except in cases of extreme necessity, covered by the divine command to practice charity, individuals could not appeal to the Law of Nature to override the legally established property limits within society.[68] Even so, by framing his argument in such a way as to knit together "labor," "cultivated land," and "the common good," Locke produced a powerful natural law critique of those individuals in society who neither labored nor contributed to the common good of society. Indeed, Locke's chapter on property is one of the most radical critiques of the landowning aristocracy produced during the last half of the seventeenth century. A qualification of this statement, as was suggested earlier, is needed in order to distinguish between the aristocracy as such and those who were merely the useless members of that class. Locke makes this point clear when he notes that it is not "the largeness of his possession" in land, but rather the allowing of it or its products to perish "uselessly" that is the critical standard to be applied to landlords and landownership. So long as a landowner "made use of" his land in such a way as to benefit others, "he did no injury" to mankind through the mere "largeness" of his possessions.[69] Still, Locke has no doubt that, in general, "numbers of men are to be preferred to largeness of dominions" as a standard for the economic and social development of society.[70] Labor has an infinitely higher social value than does land for Locke. That is why "the right employing" of land—through the application of labor to it—"is the great art of government." For unless government encourages the productive, useful employment of land, unless it supports the "honest industry" of its subjects, society as a whole will suffer the consequences.[71] Again and again, the point was made by various writers that it was only the "laborious and industrious people" of the kingdom, such as butchers, brewers, drapers, mercers, bricklayers. carpenters, and productive farmers, who contributed to the advancement of trade; these efforts at "improvement" were con-

trasted with the behavior of "the landed and lazy," as William Petty called them.[72]

Thus far, I have presented Locke's argument in its negative terms, as a critique of a certain type of landowner among the aristocracy. There is, of course, a positive site to the argument as well. Here Locke's point is to establish an alliance among all those engaged in activities that do contribute to the advancement of the common good, and that are therefore in conformity with natural law commands. We have already seen Locke's admiration for the socially productive labor of those who "digged and wrought the iron" or "who felled and framed the timber," along with those who cultivate the land. These laboring activities clearly fulfilled the commands of God and the Law of Nature to employ labor "for the benefit of life. " The case to be made for the use of money, however, is more problematic, and it rests directly upon "the tacit consent of men" rather than upon a divine injunction. Nevertheless, if the invention and use of money can be shown to be compatible with the advancement of the common good of mankind, then it, too, will fall under the authoritative endorsement of natural law. This is the point Locke sets out to prove midway through the chapter on property.

It is useful to recall from our earlier discussion of the Whigs' defense of the two stages of social existence (which Locke endorsed in the *Two Treatises*) the fact that a congeries of social and economic relationships constitute the developed form of society. Thus, in the chapter on property, Locke places the invention of money in the context of the creation of this developed society, which is itself being defended by the Whigs as a normative model for the realization of the common good. In other words, such justification as can be claimed for the invention of money must be made in terms of its *social* benefits. It decidedly cannot be morally defensible on the grounds of hoarding by an individual.

It is true that Locke begins his discussion by conceding that the invention of money allows men to "enlarge" their possessions.[73] His aim, however, is not to supply a justification for the enlargement of possessions as such, but to show how "the disproportionate and unequal possession of the earth" has come about without the "express consent" of men, and to demonstrate that this transition and its consequences are in accordance with the dictates of natural law. Locke first mentions the invention of money in paragraph 36 of the chapter on property, but promises that he will consider the subject "More at large . . . by and by."[74] And, except for a passing reference in the following paragraph, Locke does not again take up the subject until paragraph 45. Between these references, Locke describes the conditions that explain the necessity for "the invention of money." From a subjective standpoint, the latter is rooted in "the desire of having more than men needed," but this fact alone could never explain the use of money, and, even if it could, it could not supply the necessary moral grounds to justify its use.[75] In paragraph 38, Locke writes:

> But as families increased, and industry enlarged their stocks, their possessions enlarged with the need of them; but yet it was commonly without any fixed property in the ground they made use of, till they incorporated, settled themselves together, and built cities, and then, by consent, they came in time, to set out the bounds of their distinct territories, and agree on limits between them and their neighbors, and by laws within themselves, settled the properties of those of the same society.[76]

The enlargement of families, the establishment of cities, and leagues or treaties with neighboring cities, and so on, are associated with the "enlargement" of men's possessions. "Associated" is, I believe, the proper word, since I wish to avoid—as I believe Locke does—positing a causal relationship as to the invention of money. There is, rather, a convergence of the psychological and sociological conditions in Locke's account of the latter. Commentators have generally focused their attention on the psychological aspect of Locke's discussion of property. But that Locke means to stress the importance of sociological conditions is evident from his repetition in paragraph 45 of the point cited above when, as he had prom-

ised, he takes up the subject of money "more at large."

Now he once again observes that "the increase of people and stock," the fact that "several communities settled the bounds of their distinct territories, and by laws within themselves, regulated the properties of the private men of their society, and so, by compact and agreement, settled the property which labor and industry began," and the fact that "leagues . . . have been made between states and kingdoms," are all associated "with the use of money."[77] In short, there is clearly a type of society "where there is plenty of people under government, who have money and commerce" and in which property regulations are based upon consent and laws that emerges at some point in history and does so in the form of a complex of interrelated factors, of which the invention of money is one.[78]

I will return to this point in a moment, but there is another aspect to Locke's treatment of property that is discussed in the hiatus between his first mention of money and his subsequent consideration of the subject that merits our attention. Most of the paragraphs between 36 and 45 are concerned to demonstrate that well-cultivated land is capable of producing much more than any one person or family could possibly consume. Hence, "an acre of land that bears here twenty bushels of wheat" produces a thousand times more "profit" for its owner than does an acre of land in America produce for its user, an Indian. What is especially interesting about this comparison (which, like all the others Locke makes in the chapter, is designed to emphasize the value of labor) is that Locke never suggests that the Indian's acre is not sufficient to support his existence. Nor does he suggest that the English landowner consumes himself the twenty bushels of wheat he produces. Rather, the comparison is stated in monetary terms and with reference to its social benefits. Thus, "the benefit mankind receives" from the English acre "in one year, is worth £5 and from the other possibly not worth a penny, if all the profit an Indian received from it were to be valued, and sold here."[79] The "useful products" of this piece of well-cultivated land, in other words, are seen in terms of the "profit" that accrues to the landowner who sells them in exchange for other goods, and through him, "the benefit mankind receives" that this sale and exchange of commodities passes on to other members of society. This fact of social existence, arising from the technical application of labor to land and the consequent productive surplus of goods that flow from cultivated land is simply carried forward by Locke and incorporated into his discussion of money beginning with paragraph 45.

In fact, that discussion begins with the presupposition that productive labor generates a surplus of goods, for, Locke argues, one individual was entitled "to give away" part of this surplus to another individual, and that if he did so, it could not be denied that he had "made use" of his property within the definitional limits set by the Law of Nature. The same principle applies, Locke maintains, "if he also bartered away" part of his surplus in exchange for some other useful product. This action could not be viewed as a waste of "the common stock" of property.[80] Immediately following this point, Locke applies the same reasoning to the exchange of goods for money.

> And thus came in the use of money, some lasting thing . . . that by mutual consent men would take in exchange for the truly useful, but perishable supports of life.[81]

Money, as Locke elsewhere emphasizes, is a commodity of exchange, an instrument for the development of trade. Indeed, this is its primary and its most socially beneficial role.[82] It is in terms of this definition that Locke provides a justification for the invention of money in the *Second Treatise.* "For supposing an island, separate from all possible commerce with the rest of the world," he asks the reader, "what reason could anyone have there to enlarge his possessions beyond the use of his family, and a plentiful supply to its consumption?" Without money and "commerce with the rest of the world," Locke argues, an individual would have no reason "to enlarge his possessions."

> For I ask, what would a man value ten thousand, or an hundred thousand acres of excellent land, ready cultivated, and

well stocked too with cattle, in the middle of the in-land parts of America, where he had no hopes of commerce with other parts of the world, to draw money to him by the sale of the product?[83]

Interestingly, he also remarks that, in these circumstances, the land "would not be worth the enclosing," indicating how closely linked in Locke's mind the value of land itself, and especially cultivated land, was to the existence of commerce and a money exchange economy.[84] The view that "the encouraging of tillage" was "the surest and effectualest means of promoting and advancing any trade," especially with respect to the "great quantities of land within this kingdom . . . lying in a manner waste and yielding little" was surely one shared by Shaftesbury and Locke.[85]

The point Locke believes he has demonstrated is that "a man may fairly possess more land than he himself can use the product of" if he lives under those social conditions in which "by receiving in exchange for the overplus, gold and silver," he is able to "make use of" his land through engaging in "commerce with other parts of the world."[86] This exchange not only does no injury to anyone, it is positively beneficial to society, and it explains why land in England is so much more profitable than land in America. It should be noted that it is in this context of Locke's discussion of money as an exchange commodity that he states that "largeness of possession" of land does not, in itself, exceed "the bounds of . . . just property."[87] Largeness of landownership, in other words, is tied to an exchange of its "useful products," so that whatever its actual size, productive use (that is, cultivation and exchange) remains the critical factor in assessing its value. To put the point another way, it could be said that while Locke's evaluative criterion—productive labor—remains constant, its meaning changes according to the nature of the social context within which this activity finds expression. Hence, once productive labor applied to land has produced a surplus that exceeds the limits of familial consumption, that labor must, in order to retain its productive character, be viewed in relation to the extended world of commerce. Macpherson's statement that Locke's argument justifies "unlimited appropriation" of property is an ill-chosen phrase, since it is not land nor its appropriation that Locke wishes to justify, but rather the extension of trade. And although limitless commercial expansion cannot be simply equated with capitalist appropriation, nevertheless in terms of the political and economic attitude underlying Locke's general argument about property, as well as in terms of the historical relationship between commercial expansion and the development of capitalism, perhaps Locke's position is not so far removed from what Macpherson has in mind as some of the latter's critics have argued.[88]

In any event, Locke's examples, both hypothetical and real, are intended to illustrate the obvious (to the Whigs) point that trade does benefit society as a whole. And, incidentally, it also increases the value of land. Thus, the invention of money and the institution of commerce are practices that are within the compass of natural law commands to provide for the common good of mankind. To summarize, I have tried to show that, in its negative application, Locke's chapter on property in the *Second Treatise* constitutes a radical critique of a wasteful section of the landowning aristocracy, and that, in its positive formulation, Locke's argument attempts to prove that laboring activity, the cultivation of land, and commercial exchange are all beneficial activities for the development of English society. The political message of the chapter was clear enough: Artisans, small gentry, yeoman farmers, tradesmen, and merchants were all productive members of society and ought, therefore, to unite in the pursuit of their interests against an idle and wasteful landowning aristocracy in order to establish that kind of society in which all sections of the social structure could work together for the realization of the common good.

Prior to this extended discussion of Locke's treatment of property, I had suggested that the Whigs very much needed a theory of property rights that would appeal to the gentry, reassuring them as to the security of their property, without, at the same time, abandoning the language and defense of property rights in terms that appealed to the urban commercial classes of Whig supporters. If we place Locke's discussion of property within this political context, we can appreciate how admirably he fulfilled these requirements while also resolving the theoretical problem of property that had preoccupied Grotius and Pufendorf. Moreover, if we compare Locke's treatment of property with that of Tyrrell, we can see why, despite the numerous parallels and similarities that exist between the two arguments, Locke's is not only the superior theoretical formulation, it is also far more radical in its political implications.

Though Tyrrell gives prominence to the relationship of labor to property, he confuses the issue by also allowing "occupancy"—which was also the criterion of Pufendorf and Grotius—to supply a claim for property rights.[89] Occupancy, however, carries with it no necessary injunction to improve the land, and the concept could therefore be easily stretched to include a justification of the aristocratic landowner's occupancy of land that, in Locke's terminology, would be adjudged wasteland. This was probably not Tyrrell's intention; he was, after all, a "disaffected" Whig. Yet, some Royalists were willing to use occupancy in their accounts of the origins of property, and they were certainly not embarked upon a critique of aristocratic landownership.[90]

Second, Tyrrell is so terribly conscious of the necessity to refute the accusation of levelling imputed to the Whigs that much of the emphasis of his argument is defensive in tone. He is so eager to disassociate himself from any intention of advocating a "change" in "the course" of property as it is "already established" that his argument amounts to a wholesale endorsement of existing property relations, whatever their form or social utility. Without his advocating that any individual in civil society could actually be deprived of his property—and in fact reaffirming several times that this cannot happen within societies based on consent—Locke, nevertheless, is able to convey an altogether different tone in his discussion of property, one that is much more radical and hostile in its attitude toward a certain form of "established" property than anything to be found in *Patriarcha non Monarcha.*

Third, Locke's argument supporting the need for labor, cultivated land, and commerce—and their concomitant interests—to unite in defense of their common interests is much more clearly formulated and tightly knit together in its theoretical structure than is Tyrrell's effort to realize the same general objectives. This last point, to return to the discussion of Whig election propaganda, was one the Whigs wished to convey to the electorate, but in fact, only a few attempts were made to construct a bridge between the gentry's economic interests and those of "the trading part of the nation." Possibly more efforts were not undertaken owing to the difficulty in dealing with the theoretical problem of property, or perhaps many individuals genuinely did not see how the gentry's interests could be rendered compatible with those of the urban trading classes. There are, however, a few references in the exclusion literature that reveal, on a purely pragmatic level, the basis for this alliance between members of the various social classes. William Petyt, for example, spoke of "a concatenation and sympathy between the interest of land and trade," and he affirmed the proposition that the value of land increased as a consequence of the advancement of trade. The growth of trade, Petyt reasoned, would lead to a higher level of domestic consumption of agricultural products, and in order to accommodate this growth in demand, the land would have to "receive an inevitable improvement": that is, cultivation undertaken by the "industrious members" of the landowning classes.[91] As another writer put it,

> The more a country is enclosed, and the less waste grounds, commons, and forests there are, the more populous, wealthy, and full of trade it will be. And the smaller estates the land is divided into, the better for the nation.[92]

In this regard, Locke's attack upon primogeniture deserves mention, since the abolition of this practice would have undercut the rationale for many of the then existing large landed estates, and thus would have produced the consequences advocated in the citation above.[93] In this respect, too, as well as in some of the language he used, Locke's views on property are much closer to those of the Levellers than we have generally been led to believe.[94] It may not have been Locke's intention, or one in which the Whigs generally wanted to give prominent attention, but as the radical author of one Civil War tract had observed, the effect of this encouragement of industrious labor, enclosure of waste, and the elimination of primogeniture was that "the wealth of the land is more equally distributed amongst the natives."[95]

Other Whigs, following what I believe was Shaftesbury's view of the matter, argued that the encouragement of trade would not only bring material benefits to the nation as a whole, but it would also foster a general spirit of "industry" among the people. According to the author of one tract, this would, for example, help to discourage the "idleness" that characterized the social behavior of many landowners.[96] As more than one writer argued, "tradesmen are a very substantial and useful part" of the nation, and they exemplify "more industry" in "their way of living" than do gentlemen and the nobility.[97]

It is, of course, difficult to assess the efficacy of these Whig arguments, but judged purely in terms of the prevailing economic situation in the last quarter of the seventeenth century, they should have carried some force among the gentry. The latter were under considerable economic pressure exerted against them by large landowners who were attempting to increase the size of their estates through a consolidation of small parcels of land. Hence, throughout this period, the small landowner was being squeezed—economically and politically—out of the marketplace.[98] This situation did not automatically push him into the waiting arms of the urban bourgeoisie, nor did it necessarily make the Whig ideas of equality or resistance any less unpalatable than they had been during his most prosperous days. Nonetheless, there was a real economic basis for the political strategy of fomenting an ideological opposition between the small gentry and the large landowning aristocracy.

Without discounting the primary importance of the antipopery issue, it seems likely that some measure of the success as the Whigs did achieve in getting their message across to the gentry—which surprised even their opponents—was due to the ideological appeals the Whigs addressed to their "country neighbors" that were grounded in extolling the virtues of "honest industry."

On reflection, the electoral struggles of the exclusion crisis amounted to something of a high point in the success of the Whig political movement. The Whigs created an efficient party organization and mounted an effective propaganda campaign. They won each of the three elections, gaining increasingly larger majorities in the House of Commons. And that body passed the exclusion bill and steadfastly refused to grant Charles II any money until the bill had received the royal assent. From the standpoint of a purely electoral movement, and in relation to the political institutions of Restoration England open to their influence through electoral success, it is difficult to see what more the Whigs could have hoped to have accomplished. But, of course, the Whig political movement was not a purely electoral undertaking, and as the remaining obstacles to the achievement of their aims appeared to be oblivious to the effects of petitions, elections, and Commons' votes, a more treacherous and perilous path lay before Shaftesbury and his followers.

Notes

1. Schlatter, *Private Property*, pp. 1–150; James Tully, *A Discourse on Property: John Locke and His Adversaries*, Cambridge: Cambridge University Press, 1980. pp. 1–94; Paschal Larkin, *Property in the Eighteenth Century*, 1930; reprint ed., New York: Howard Fertig, 1969, pp. 1–53; Tuck, *Natural Rights;* Karl Olivecrona, "Locke's Theory of Appropriation," *Philosophical Quarterly* 24, no. 96 (July 1974):220–234; idem, "Appropriation in the State of Nature: Locke on the Origin of Property," *Journal of the History of Ideas* 35, no. 2 (April–June 1974):211–230.

2. For a brief discussion of the importance of various propositions concerning property by Christian writers and the similarity of their position to Locke's theory of property, see Schlatter, *Private Property*, pp. 33–76; A.J. Carlyle, "The Theory of Property in Medieval Theology," and H.G. Wood, "The Influence of the Reformation on Ideas Concerning Wealth and Property," in *Property: Its Duties and Rights*, 2d ed., ed. J.V. Bartlett, London: Macmillan, 1915, pp. 119–132 and 135–167, respectively. In general, it seems more accurate to say that the Christian paradigm of property is a radical/conservative one, unstable at its core. It justifies an original state of common property with individual use, and this standard can be invoked in cases of extreme individual necessity or a general economic crisis (and sometimes on religious grounds and for those who live closest to the dictates of natural law) in order to override the claims of private ownership. At the same time, the paradigm provides a defense for private property, not only as an integral part of an Aristotelian conception of the family or household, but also as a badge of that lost innocence which makes the institution of government necessary. The latter is especially useful as a defense against external interference as a means of restricting the claims of temporal power by the king or the pope over individuals, while the former relies upon the social bond of the community to unite individuals in the pursuit of the common good.

3. *Essays on the Law of Nature (ELN)*, p. 185; cf. ibid., pp. 155, 157.

4. *ELN*, pp. 183, 187; *An Essay Concerning Human Understanding (ECHU)*, 2:28, 8.

5. For a discussion of the importance of creationism to Locke's thought, see Tully, *Discourse on Property*, pp. 40–42, 58–59.

6. *Second Treatise (ST)*, par. 6: cf. *First Treatise (FT)*, par. 53; *ECHU*, 4:3.18.

7. Cited in Tully, *Discourse on Property*, p. 42; cf. *Life of Richard Baxter*, ed. Matthew Sylvester. 1696, p. 22; Richard Schlatter, *Richard Baxter and Puritan Politics*. New Brunswick, N.J.: Rutgers University Press, 1957, p. 154; H.G. Wood, "Influence of Reformation," pp. 154–156; Hunt, *Postscript*, p. 67.

8. M.S., *Submission to the Will of God in Times of Affliction*, 1683, pp. 13–14. This sermon was dedicated to Lady Russell, following the execution of her husband. In view of the argument's similarity to Baxter's own statements, M.S. is probably Baxter's close friend and editor, Matthew Sylvester. See also Schlatter, *Social Ideas*, pp. 125ff.

9. *FT*, par. 39. All property belongs to God (*ELN*, p. 203).

10. *FT*, pars. 39, 92. Locke's relationship to Calvinist theology is extremely elusive, but with respect to the obligation the individual owes to God by "the right of creation," this is an expression that occurs in Calvin's *Institutes*, as von Leyden notes (*ELN*, p. 185n.). For a discussion of the general importance of Calvinism to Locke's thought, see John Dunn, *The Political Thought of John Locke*, Cambridge: Cambridge University Press, 1969.

11. *FT*, pars. 8, 9.

12. *FT*, par. 52

13. *FT*, par. 53.

14. Tully, *Discourse on Property*, pp. 4, 9, 33–36, 40.

15. *FT*, par. 156: *ST*. par. 163.

16. *ST*, par. 6.

17. *FT*, par. 24

18. *FT*, pars. 85, 86.

19. *ST*, par. 32. It is within this theological framework that M.S., for example, endorses the proposition that "whosoever makes anything by his own proper art and labor . . . is counted to have a full right to it, and a full power to dispose of it" (*Submission to the Will of God*, p. 13).

20. *ST*, par. 35.

21. *ELN*, p. 117.

22. *ELN*, p. 157.

23. *ST*, par. 6.

24. Though it has received little attention from commentators, there is no question but that Locke did accept the "stewardship" conception of property. As he put it, we are all keepers of "the treasure of which God has made us the economists" (King, 2:58; see also *ELN*, p. 203; and Lady Masham's statement that Locke regarded individuals as "but stewards" of the property they possessed, cited in Fox-Bourne, 2:536). J. Dunn does not mention stewardship, but he does discuss the "calling" as a concept applicable to property ownership, which belongs to the same tradition (*Political Thought of Locke*, pp. 252ff.).

25. Olivecrona, for example, maintains that the individual's "spiritual ego was infused into the object," and that Locke's theory of property seems "to make sense only on this interpretation" ("Locke's Theory of Appropriation," p. 226). And for a methodologically metaphysical treatment of the philosophical problem of property, see J. P. Day, "Locke on Property," *Philosophical Quarterly* 16 (1966): 207–221.

26. *ST*, pars. 32, 42, 43.

27. Sabine's discussion is a classic example of the interpretation of Locke's theory of property in terms of the individual's egotistical interests (George Sabine, A *History of Political Theory*, 3d ed., New York: Holt, Rinehart and Winston, 1961, pp. 525ff.; see also Leo Strauss, *Natural Right and History*, Chicago: University of Chicago Press, 1953, p. 248).

28. *FT*, par. 42.

29. *Popery and Arbitrary Government*, pp. 6–7; Penn, *England's Great Interest*, pp.3–4; Bethel, *Interest of Princes and States*, p. 15. As framed by John Phillips, the contest was between "the industrious part of the nation" versus "the voluptuous" aristocracy and Court sycophants (*The Character of a Popish Successor . . . Part II*, 1681. p. 31 (LL #660); Thomas Hunt, *A Defence of Charter and Municipal Rights of the City of London*, 1683, p. 45). Owen's defense against Parker's criticisms of the "honest industry" of those associated with "the trading interest" of England should also be kept in mind (John Owen, *Truth and Innocency Vindicated: In a Survey of a Discourse Concerning Ecclesiastical Polity*, 1669, pp. 78–80).

30. *ST*, par. 32.

31. *ST*, pars. 7, 128, 134, 135, 182; cf. Tyrrell, *Patriarcha non Monarcha*, pp. 15, 17, 29. "If the preservation of all mankind . . . were everyone's persuasion, as indeed it is everyone's duty, and the true principle to regulate our religion, politics, and morality by," we should all be much better off than we are (*Some Thoughts Concerning Education* [*STCE*] #116).

32. *ST*, par. 33.

33. *ST*, par. 31. "No man in the state of nature, has a right to more land or territory than he can well manure for the necessities of himself and family" (Tyrrell, *Patriarcha non Monarcha*, p. 154).

34. *ST*, par. 34.

35. Locke applies the same reasoning, from the standpoint of the public good, to his argument for the institution of political society, wherein the individual "is to enjoy many conveniencies from the labor, assistance, and society of others in the same community" (*ST*, par. 130). This point is reaffirmed in the *Letter Concerning Toleration*, where Locke argues that the "honest industry" of every individual can be preserved through the "mutual assistance" of others to secure "the things that

contribute to the comfort and happiness of this life," which can only "be procured or preserved by pains and industry" of all the members of society (*Works*, 5:42).

36. *ST*, par. 37. These lines were added to a later edition of the *Two Treatises*, but the argument, with respect to the benefits to mankind of cultivated land versus "waste in common" was already present in the chapter (cf. ibid., pars. 36,42).

37. Locke's attitude toward "waste," for example, is not merely a convenient attribute of his characterization of the early stage of social existence. "Waste of anything," Lady Masham wrote, Locke "could not bear to see," and she especially associated this character trait with his attitude toward property. Thus, "he often found fault" with proprietors who thought they could do anything they pleased with their property (Fox-Bourne, 2:536). "People should be accustomed from their cradles," Locke argued, "to spoil or *waste* nothing at all." The "spoiling of anything to no purpose" is nothing less than "*doing of mischief*" (*STCE* #116; italics in original). Since this is the way in which Locke viewed goods and property in general, not only does the prohibition against waste not disappear in the course of his discussion of property, but it can hardly be branded an "irrelevant" part of that discussion, as Plamenatz, for example, labels it (John Plamenatz, *Man and Society*, 2 vols., New York: McGraw-Hill, 1963, 1:242).

38. *Works*, 4:20. "The industrious and frugal" (p. 72); cf. ibid., p. 75.

39. *Works*, 4:39.

40. *Works*, 4:8–9, 14–15, 28, 39. "All encouragement should be given to artifacers." Also, "manufacture deserves to be encouraged" (pp. 28–29).

41. *Works*, 4:8–9, 28.

42. *Works*, 4:9. "If money were more equally distributed . . . into a greater number of hands, according to the exigencies of trade," most of the problems addressed by Locke would be resolved (p. 64).

43. *Works*, 4:53. Locke's observation that the "industrious" individual who accumulates wealth through manufacturing is shrewd enough to invest in land near enough to his businesses that "the estate may be under his eye" might be regarded as a subtle critique of absentee landlordism (p. 39).

44. *Works*, 4:72.

45. *Works*, 4:54–55.

46. *Works*, 4:61, 55.

47. *Works*, 4:53–55, 72–75.

48. *Works*, 4:71. C. B. Macpherson, *The Political Theory of Possessive Individualism*, Oxford: Oxford University Press, 1962, pp. 224ff.; Strauss, *Natural Right*, pp. 242–243. The context of Locke's description, which is almost universally ignored, is the removal of the working class from "the usual struggle and contest" over economic goods, which "is between the landed man and the merchant." Locke, in other words, is noting that laborers as a "body of men" have no "time or opportunity to . . . struggle with the richer" classes in society, except when "some common and great distress" has the effect of "uniting them . . . as one common interest" and makes them de facto participants in the "struggle and contest" between classes. Not only is the meaning of Locke's observation generally distorted (with talk about rationality, which is not mentioned at all in the passage), but it is far from clear that the nonparticipation by the laborers in the class struggle is not, in Locke's view, a socially positive comment about their behavior.

49. Cited in J. Dunn, *Political Thought of Locke*, p. 232.

50. Locke to William Molyneux (January 19, 1694), *Works*, 8:332.

51. J. Dunn, *Political Thought of Locke*, p. 253.

52. MS c.30, fol. 18. I say that Locke wrote these notes for Shaftesbury because, like the *Essay on Toleration*, they are written with respect to "your" (Charles') kingdom.

53. Cited in J. Dunn, *Political Thought of Locke*, pp. 231–232.

54. *STCE* #201; *Correspondence*, 3:343–353.

55. *STCE* #205.

56. Cited in J. Dunn, *Political Thought of Locke*, pp. 232–233.

57. King, 1:181.

58. See Locke's discussion in his journal (1677) of the labor we expend "to procure new and beneficial productions . . . whereby our stock of riches . . . may be increased, or better preserved," which is written from the standpoint of our divinely constituted natures and the "concernment mankind hath" in our fulfillment of our capacities for labor (King, 1:162–166).

59. "Locke recognized . . . that the members of the laboring class . . . were unfit to participate in political life" (Macpherson, *Possessive Individualism*, p. 230). Apart from the fact that

Locke never said anything of the sort, this statement must be measured against the fact that Shaftesbury and the Whigs were busily engaged in organizing members of the laboring class (including apprentices) to sign petitions, engage in political demonstrations, and even vote, and hence they contributed more to the integration of laborers into participation in political life than any other force in the seventeenth century, except, perhaps, the Levellers.

60. Strauss's contention that "the natural law prohibition against waste is no longer valid in civil society" (*Natural Right*, p. 241) is mistaken not only in terms of the text (of *ST*, chap. 5), but also for the reasons given in note 37 above.

61. *ST*, par. 37.

62. *ST*, par. 42. This is the way such land is referred to in, for example, the Calendar of Treasury Books.

63. *ST*, pars. 30, 32, 37, 40, 43. There is no warrant for Tully's conclusion that Locke is attacking the enclosure of land. The passage he cites (par. 35) is simply a defense of the requirement of the consent of commoners before anyone can enclose *their* land; it is certainly not an attack upon the enclosure of "waste" land. Nor, in my view, is there any basis for his conclusion that "the only form of property in land which [Locke] endorses in the *Two Treatises* is the English Common" (Tully, *Discourse on Property*, pp. 153–154, 169). See note 85 below.

64. *ST*, pars. 36, 37, 38, 42, 45.

65. *ST*, par. 35.

66. *ST*, pars. 36, 38. Thomas Hunt also endorsed the natural right "to break the civil enclosure of property" if the choice were between productive subsistence and idle ownership (*Postscript*, preface). Hunt was a radical Whig lawyer who may or may not have been privy to the Rye House conspiracy; he did, however, leave England to become one of the exiles in Holland sometime after the discovery of that conspiracy. According to Winstanley, "God made the earth for the use and comfort of all mankind: and because "we have a right to the common ground" derived from both the Law of Nature and Scriptures, "the common and waste grounds belong to the poor" (cited in Lewis H. Berens, *The Digger Movement in the Days of the Commonwealth*, London: Holland Press and Merlin Press, 1961, pp. 150–151).

67. It should be recalled that the Diggers maintained that they did not intend "to meddle with any man's property nor to break down any . . . enclosures." Rather, they were merely claiming the right to cultivate "what was common and untilled" in order "to make it fruitful for the use of man." This argument presupposed that every individual had the natural right to produce his own subsistence (Berens, *Digger Movement*, p. 37; see also David W. Petegorsky, *Left-Wing Democracy in the English Civil War*, London: Victor Gollancz, 1940, pp. 163, 204–205). Whatever else may be said about the differences between the thought of Winstanley and that of Locke, the two men shared these fundamental assumptions. For other specific phrases and assumptions common to both thinkers, see *Left-Wing Democracy*, pp. 140–141, 147.

68. *FT*, par. 42. This does not mean, however, as Strauss and Macpherson maintain, that the duties of charity are abandoned within civil society, or that "individuals can pursue their productive–acquisitive activity without obstruction" (Strauss, *Natural Right*, pp. 246–248; Macpherson, *Possessive Individualism*, p. 221). Speaking of those within society, Locke declares that "common charity teaches that those should be most taken care of by the law, who are least capable of taking care of themselves" (*Works*, 4:11). Nor is this merely a pietistic endorsement of a system of poor relief. The harshness of the treatment accorded to the idle poor in Locke's draft proposal for the Board of Trade has been much remarked upon; what has received little notice, however, is the provision that makes it a crime for any parish to allow any individual to die of starvation within its precincts (Fox-Bourne, 2:390). Not only is every individual entitled by the claims of charity (and the natural right to subsistence) to meat, drink, clothes, shelter, and heat, whether he works or not (p. 382), but Locke presses the issue further: It is an offense "against the common rule of charity" for one individual to "enrich himself so as to make another perish." Indeed, to take advantage of another in the marketplace by accumulating goods in such a fashion that "by reason of extortion" or the exploitation of another's "necessity" the individual suffers is, at a minimum, a form of robbery and, in the extreme instance, it is "murder" ("Venditio," Locke's journal note, published in John Dunn, "Justice and the Interpretation of Locke's Political Theory," *Political Studies*, 16, no. 1 [1968]: 85–86; cf. Jean LeClerc, *An Account of the Life and Writings of John Locke*, 3d ed., 1714, p. 25).

69. *ST*, par. 46. Olivecrona thus misses the point altogether by taking "appropriation" rather than use as the standard of property. In reversing Locke's emphasis, he not only gives precedence to enclosure over the cultivation of land, but he also places Locke unproblematically within that part of natural law tradition which grants priority to occupation as a title to property rather than labor (Olivecrona, "Locke's Theory of Appropriation," p. 228). Similarly, Lamprecht's assertion that Locke's treatment of property is written from the standpoint of the aristocratic governing class represents a failure to understand the political context of the argument Locke is making in the *Two Treatises* (Lamprecht, *Moral Philosophy of Locke*, p. 125). It is certainly not based upon any evidence supplied by members of that class which indicates that this is the standpoint from which they read that work, nor, so far as I am aware, is there any such evidence to be found until well into the eighteenth century, when the political context for reading the *Two Treatises* had changed considerably.

70. *ST*, par. 42. It is "plenty of people and money in proportion to . . . land" that is the pathway to wealth (MS c.8, in William Letwin, *The Origins of Scientific Economics*, London: Methuen, 1963, p. 274: *Works*, 4:63). "Riches consist in plenty of moveables . . . but especially in plenty of gold and silver" and "power consists in numbers of men and ability to maintain them" (MS c.30, fol. 18). Thus, it is a large laboring force that is essential to "the riches of every country and that which makes it flourish" (MS f.3, fols. 198–199). For other contemporary opinions stressing the importance of industrious labor over land, see William Penn, *One Project for the Good of England*, [1680], p. 2; *Petty–Southwell Correspondence*, pp. 153–155; Reynell, *True English Interest*, p. 18; E. Lipson, *The Economic History of England*, 6th ed., 3 vols., London: Adam and Charles Black, 1961, 3:66; Joyce Oldham Appleby, *Economic Thought and Ideology in Seventeenth–Century England*, Princeton: Princeton University Press, 1978, pp. 133–134, 155. On the socioeconomic implications of this perspective, see D. C. Coleman, "Labor in the English Economy of the Seventeenth Century," in *Seventeenth–Century England*, ed. Paul S. Seaver, New York: New Viewpoints, 1976, pp. 112–138: T.E. Gregory, "The Economics of Employment in England, 1660–1713," *Economica* (January 1921), pp. 37–51.

71. *ST*, par. 42. It is the labor of the landlord's tenant that gives the land its value (MS e.8, fol. 21).

72. Appleby, *Economic Thought*, pp. 133–134, 155, 183.

73. *ST*, par. 48.

74. *ST*, par. 36.

75. *ST*, par. 37. "Covetousness, and the desire of having in our possession . . . more than we have need of, being the root of all evil" (*STCE*, #110: cf. ibid., #105; *ELN*, pp. 205–215).

76. *ST*, par. 38.

77. *ST*, par. 45.

78. *ST*, par. 35.

79. *ST*, par. 43. The other side of this comparison is drawn between "a king of a large and fruitful territory" in America who "is clad worse than a day laborer in England" (par. 41). In his clarification of this point in the following paragraph, Locke refers to the value of "human industry" that produces clothes, bread, and the other items that explain why the day laborer is better off (par. 42). In other words, the reference is not simply to the laboring activity of the individual(s)—even if the Indian chief worked harder than the day-laborer, his expenditure of effort would not affect the comparison—but between the social consequences of "labor and industry" within different types of societies.

80. *ST*, par. 46.

81. *ST*, par. 47. According to "the universal consent of mankind," individuals have agreed to accept money as a medium of exchange (*Works*, 4:22).

82. Money is "a universal commodity" and as "necessary to trade as food is to life" (*Works*, 4:7, 14). It is the "standing measure" of all other commodities because individuals have agreed to accept it as a medium of exchange for all commodities (p. 44; MS b.3). Locke says this so often that the point would hardly be worth noting, except for the fact that Macpherson blithely discounts this social function, arguing that "the characteristic purpose of money is to serve as capital. . . . Indeed its function as a medium of exchange was seen as subordinate to its function as capital" (*Possessive Individualism*, pp. 206–207). Macpherson derives this odd conclusion from the fact that Locke recognizes that, in addition to serving as a medium of exchange, money can yield income through interest (*Works*, 4:33). It is, one might have thought, a rather long historical step from in-

terest-bearing capital to a justification of "unlimited capitalist appropriation," such as Macpherson suggests Locke had in mind (p. 221). Locke had no particular objections to the interest function of money, but everything he ever wrote on that subject subordinated that function *entirely* to the advancement of trade, and hence to the importance of the function of money as a medium of exchange. He wrote of money "considered in its *proper* use as a commodity passing in exchange," and not in terms of Macpherson's conception of capitalist appropriation (*Works*, 4:42; italics added). After he has drawn the comparison between the "use" of money (which yields interest) and the use of land through labor (which yields rent), both of which are a consequence of unequal distribution, Locke argues that more "use" can be gained from employing money in trade—this is the whole point of his essay—than through any other means (Letwin, *Origins*, pp. 285–288). At best, one might say that Locke recognizes the need for circulating capital, but his is not an argument for the priority of "real" capital that Macpherson imputes to him. For a critique of Macpherson's argument along these lines, see Karen Ivarsen Vaughn, *John Locke: Economist and Social Scientist*, Chicago: University of Chicago Press, 1982, pp. 53–54, 102. Hence, if such a thing as capitalism were to arise from the ashes of Locke's argument, it would have to emerge from the accumulation of merchant's capital, and not by way of the circuitous route of interest, which Macpherson takes to be the basis for Locke's endorsement of capital accumulation.

83. *ST*, par. 48: cf. ibid., par. 26. Tyrell also makes this point (*Patriarcha non Monarha*, p. 153).

84. This point was stressed, for example, by Petyt, *Britannia Languens*, pp. 10–14; Reynell, *True English Interest*, pp. 18–20, 41.

85. The quotation is taken from a 1663 statute on the exportation of corn (Lipson, *Economic History*, 2:451). The subject of enclosures in seventeenth–century England is too complicated to be dealt with here. Suffice it to say that there was no simple pro or con position on enclosure because there were various types of enclosure, undertaken by different classes of landowners, with differing benefits to the public. As Lipson points out, enclosure "to promote better methods of tillage . . . enlisted general approval," especially among those social groups which comprised the political constituency of the Whigs, while the enclosure of arable land for pasture or for parks, which depopulated the countryside, was "generally condemned" (pp. 397, 406). Which of these two types of enclosure could provide the greater number of examples for the Restoration period is not easy to say, but the most spectacular example of land redevelopment was certainly the reclaiming of large expanses of wasteland in eastern England. (Barry Coward, *The Stuart Age: A History of England, 1603–1714*, London: Longman Group, 1980, p. 13; cf. W. H. R. Curtler, *The Enclosure and Redistribution of Our Land*, Oxford: Clarendon Press, 1920; E. C. K. Gonner, "The Progress of Inclosure during the Seventeenth Century," *English Historical Review* 91 [July 1908]:477–501). In the general process of reclamation of wasteland, it was the small and middle gentry, or yeomen, who played the leading role, not the aristocracy or larger landowners (John Clapham, *A Concise Economic History of Britain*, Cambridge: Cambridge University Press, 1963, p. 206; Charles Wilson, *England's Apprenticeship, 1603–1763*, London: Longman, 1965, pp. 151–153). In a memorial drafted in 1669 among the Shaftesbury papers, it is argued that the wealth of the kingdom depends chiefly upon a large industrious labor force and the "enclosing of wastes and manuring them to tillage." Though both Christie and Cranston assumed Shaftesbury to be the author of the memorial, Haley disagrees, on the basis of certain statements contained in the document (Haley, p. 258). Haley may be right, though in this case I find his arguments weak and I am inclined to agree with Christie. In any case, I would argue that the document certainly expresses Shaftesbury's views on the points I have cited. The work is printed as appendix 1 in W. D. Christie, *A Life of Anthony Ashley Cooper, First Earl of Shaftesbury*, 2 vols., 1871, 2: vi–ix.

86. *ST*, par. 50.

87. *ST*, pars. 49, 50, 51.

88. It is striking how many of Macpherson's critics have accepted the basic dimensions of his argument. Isaiah Berlin, for example, has no qualms in proclaiming that Macpherson has established "Locke's claims to be regarded as the spokesman of unlimited capitalist appropriation," and this point is seconded by Geriant Parry, and by Strauss (Isaiah Berlin, "Hobbes, Locke and Professor Macpherson," *Political Quarterly* 35, no. 4 [October–December 1964]:461; Geriant Parry, *John Locke*, London: George Allen and Unwin, 1978, p. 123). As Dunn, Tully, E. J. Hundert ("The

Making of Homo Faber: John Locke Between Ideology and History," *Journal of the History of Ideas* 33, no. 1 [January–March 1972]:3–22), and others have argued, not only did Locke not set out with the intention of providing such a justification, but Macpherson's inattention to what Locke was trying to do obscures the extent to which the chapter on property in the *Second Treatise* functions as a critique of existing property relationships. I trust it is clear that in this debate I have sided with Macpherson's critics, both on general methodological grounds and with respect to particular substantive suggestions. In the first category are the significance of the actor's intentions as a guide to the meaning of his actions, and the sociological evidence necessary to establish what type of social structure exists (both in reality and in his consciousness). In the second category are the theological assumptions about labor, property, and the calling, and Locke's critical attitude toward landownership and wealth. Having said this, I nevertheless think that some of Macpherson's critics, and Dunn especially, have implied that the very objective of providing a rationalization for the social structure as a whole represents a serious misconception on the part of the interpreter as to the kind of action a political theorist like Locke could have taken. I cannot accept this position, either in general with respect to political theorists as historical individuals or with respect to Locke in particular. More concretely, if Macpherson had not fastened so precipitously upon "capitalist appropriation" as the construct through which he views Locke, a pathway leading from "productive labor"—tying together artisans, merchants, laborers, and small farmers—might, in the end, have eventually led him, as it did Adam Smith and other eighteenth-century thinkers, to perceive that the seeds for a justification of a new order were indeed embedded in the ideological critique of an unproductive landowning aristocracy.

89. All property in the state of nature, Tyrrell argues, "being but occupancy or possession" (Tyrrell, *Patriarcha non Monacha*, pp. 49, 65, 139, 149–150). Richard Cumberland also argued for occupancy as the basis for the right to property in the state of nature. Tyrell subsequently published *A Brief Disquisition of the Law of Nature, According to the Principles and Method laid down in the Rev. D. Cumberland's Latin Treatise on that Subject*, 1692, which as the title suggests, indicates how closely he followed Cumberland's approach. Burnet also regarded occupancy as the source of a title to property (Burnet, 2:36, 38).

90. J. Turner, *Sermon before Ward*, epistle dedicatory.

91. Petyt, *Britiannia Languens*, preface, pp. 13–14.

92. Reynell, *True English Interest*, pp. 20, 41.

93. Locke makes a direct and sustained attack on primogeniture in the *First Treatise*. His argument is that all children of the father have "the same title" to his property as a consequence of their natural rights claim and his natural law obligation to provide for their nourishment. Moreover, Locke makes it clear that since this is "a right not only to a bare subsistence but to the conveniences and comforts of life, as far as the conditions of their parents can afford it," the rights claim of the children extends to all the property owned by the father (*FT*, pars. 87–98, 111, 112, 119; Tully, *Discourse on Property*, p. 169).

94. For the Levellers' attack on primogeniture, see Petegorsky, *Left-Wing Democracy*, p. 109; Margaret James, *Social Problems and Policy during the Puritan Revolution 1640–1660*, London: Routledge and Kegan Paul, 1966, pp. 26, 97–99. Tully emphasizes the extent to which Locke is willing to make the "community of goods . . . mutual assistance, and maintenance" of all its members an essential part of his definition of the family (*ST*, par. 83; Tully, *Discourse on Property*, pp. 133–134). Locke also endorsed the need for a national land registry of titles, another demand the Levellers had put forward (*Works*, 4:75; Haley, p. 245).

95. Appleby, *Economic Thought*, p. 113.

96. Bethel, *The Interest of Princes and States*, p. 3. Shaftesbury had frequently emphasized the importance of "the industrious part of the nation" to the social and economic welfare of England (Haley, p. 254).

97. Cited in Schlatter, *Social Ideas*, p. 161.

98. By the end of the seventeenth century, land was becoming "more and more concentrated in the hands of the larger farmers" (Joan Thirsk, "Seventeenth Century Agriculture and Social Change," in *Seventeenth Century England*, ed. Seaver, pp. 80–81; Lawrence Strone, "Social Mobility in England, 1500–1700," in ibid., p. 36; L. A. Clarkson, *The Pre-Industrial Economy in England, 1500–1750*, London: Batsford, 1971, pp. 63–64, 218; D.C. Coleman, *The Economy of England*, 1450–

1750, London: Oxford University Press, 1977, pp. 125, 128; G. E. Mingay, *English Landed Society in the Eighteenth Century*, London: Routledge and Kegan Paul, 1963, pp. 15, 50).

10
Locke and Feminism on Private and Public Realms of Activities

Mary B. Walsh

The Feminist Critique of Locke

Feminist critics of Locke perceive a conflict between his promises of political liberty and equality and women's individual and social circumstances. Two broad strains of antiliberal feminist criticism of Locke exist: a communitarian feminist critique and a radical feminist critique.[1] The former stresses women's particular biological and familial situations and concludes that the person Locke frees is biologically and socially male. The latter concentrates on women's unique familial and economic circumstances and concludes that the structure of society and politics which Locke defends leads inevitably to women's domination by men. Both the communitarian feminist and radical feminist analyses conclude that Locke's liberalism oppresses rather than liberates women. They agree that Locke's attack on patriarchy fails to undermine men's patriarchal rule over women.

The communitarian feminist reading of Locke argues that Locke's philosophy revolves around an exclusively male individual who concerns himself with self-preservation, maximizing rights and accumulating wealth. He is the center of his world; his own needs drive his actions.[2] Communitarian feminists assert that women's experience of themselves and the world differs significantly from male—and "liberal"—individuals. Liberalism tries to fit women into a mold which they cannot and should not accommodate. Some communitarian feminists trace a difference in men's and women's moral agendas—that is, their empathic capability—to their different reproductive capacities interacting within social context. Man's alienation from the product of his body at conception actualizes itself in his greater sense of separateness, in abstract moral reasoning, and in his historical and institutional attempts to mediate his alienation from the means of reproduction.[3] Women, in contrast, immediately and profoundly experience themselves as connected, both in their reproductive experience and their historical roles as nurturers. Women, who traditionally have centered their lives around the activities of the family, realize themselves as members of a group, members bound by the needs and desires of others, as well as the limits of that unique familial context.[4] In this way, communitarian feminists challenge not only liberal individualism but also liberal rights, liberal obligation and liberal rationality.[5] For women, rights are not primary, obligations are not conventional and rationality is not completely objective and abstract.

Jean Bethke Elshtain's analysis of Locke centers on this sexually differentiated understanding of self. "The presumption that human beings are rational, metaphysically free, prudential calculators of marginal utility . . . is used as a contrast model for the qualities and activities in a private world from which the public sphere is bifurcated theoretically."[6] According to Elshtain, the emphasis on rights and self-interest in Locke's politics eliminates the distinctly feminine voice from liberal political discourse. Women's moral sense of connectedness and compassion is relegated to extrapolitical institutions such as family. This works to the detriment of both women and liberalism by secluding women's compassionate natures in the private family and robbing politics of the compassion women can bring to political endeavors. The male perspective further fails politics, because government's purpose is to guide compassionate coexistence not hedonistic anarchy.

The radical feminist critique similarly emphasizes Locke's understanding of private and public, detailing how women's actual marital, familial and economic (i.e., private) positions mitigate against promises of political emancipation for women. Radical feminists point to an incongruence in Locke's thought between formal political rights and the substantive inequalities women experience in a variety of societal relationships. These feminists maintain that the elimination of male control over female demands an understanding of the political character of women's private, familial situations—an understanding which Locke's liberal political philosophy obscures. In this way, the radical feminist critique of Locke incorporates and extends the more general marxian critique of liberalism. Whereas Marx revealed the intricate relationship between the economy and politics, the pointing to the patterns of coercion operating in the economy, radical feminists unmask the patterns of coercion present in the family which are reflected in the economy and politics.[7] Locke's failure to recognize the patterns of coercion in marriage, family and the economy obliterates any hope for equal rights for women within his political system. In fact, radical feminists conclude that the private-public distinction in Locke merely serves as a tool for the continuation of patriarchy. Formal equality for women both masks and legitimates the actual inequality in marriage, family and economy.

According to the radical feminist approach, Locke's particular version of the marriage contract is patriarchal, demanding the subordination of women. Despite Locke's assertion that each person has "Property in his own Person" and that the "Labour of his Body and the Work of his Hands . . . are properly his" (II. 27), he determines that a wife's labor in a marriage produces community property (or offspring) which the husband controls as the "abler and the stronger" (II. 82). This communality of property in the family, and the husband's ultimate control over property produced

through his wife's labor, conflicts with the woman's right to the value of the property produced by her own labor.[8] The husband's control over community marital property ignores both women's productive and reproductive labor. Furthermore, Locke's claim that marriage provides for a "Right in one anothers Bodies" (II. 78) in effect translates into male control over the female body given the inequalities of the marriage contract and the cultural reality, where women have historically not owned their bodies but have been subject to both the control of their fathers and their husbands. In this way, the marriage contract legitimizes "masculine sex-right."[9]

Radical feminists conclude that for Locke the institution of marriage functions primarily as an insurance of legitimate heirs for the biologically alienated father. Lorenne Clark asks, in reference to Locke, "If Adam does not own Eve, how can he be sure who his descendants are, and hence, on whom his apples ought properly to devolve? And if Eve owns her own apples, why should she obey Adam?"[10] Along similar lines, O'Brien concludes that Locke's liberalism mediates male uncertainty about his biological offspring by maintaining patriarchal families. "The final solution of the problem of patriarchy is elaborated by John Locke in his first 'Treatise of Government,' while the legitimacy of property as a self-generating 'principle of continuity' is celebrated in his second."[11] That is, Locke's celebration of private property demands a system—patriarchal marriage— whereby the father can, with certainty, identify his rightful (biological) heir. Locke captures women in patriarchal marriage contracts in order to ensure the continuation and transfer of property to legitimate heirs.

Radical feminists offer an even more stinging critique of Locke's thought as applied to women's actual economic position.[12] In this view, Locke's rationality is inextricably tied to property; property expresses human rationality and individuality. Locke's optimism about the abundance of land and raw materials leads him to conclude that the rational and industrious can and will acquire private property. Furthermore, to the "degree that the right to private property excludes the working classes and women, they are excluded from the realm of free and rational activity."[13] Locke writes, "opportunities of knowledge and inquiry are commonly as narrow as their fortune and their understanding are but little instructed, when all their whole time and pain is laid out to still the croaking of their own bellies, or the cries of their children."[14] The distractions of the cries from their children and the husband's control of the wife's property indicate women's inferior rationality for Locke.

On the basis of this examination of Locke's notion of family, economy and politics, radical feminists oppose Locke's separation of family from politics, of private from public. Women's subordinate position in family and the economy profoundly affects their possibilities for autonomy and equality. Even if Locke's liberalism does grant women formal, abstract freedoms in the political realm, in separating family from politics, Locke leaves woman enslaved in family, society and the economy. In "reifying"[15] the distinction between family and politics, Locke "mystifies" women's subordination.[16] Locke's separation of public from private offers the vision of freedom and equality with one hand while pulling it back with the other.

Thus both the communitarian and radical feminist critiques revolve around Locke's attempt to depoliticize the family. The separation of private and public life renders Locke unacceptable and necessarily patriarchal to feminist critics. An elaboration of Locke's principles of liberty and equality as they operate in the private and public spheres, however, will demonstrate how Locke's understanding of the distinction between private and public is essential to attaining the feminist goals of liberty and equality.

Locke's Liberal Response

I argue that these anti-liberal feminists not only misinterpret Locke's distinction between private and public as dichotomous[17] and "reified"[18] but also they endanger the feminist project (women's emancipation) in abandoning it. The feminist claim that the "personal is political" may collapse human relationships into a single dimension. Patri-archy touches all human relationships, but not all human relationships are defined by patriarchy. Some feminists resurrect exactly that notion of politics which Locke finds most repugnant and dangerous in his protagonist, Sir Robert Filmer: the failure to recognize the difference between private and public pursuits.[19] Locke distinguishes private from public concerns as a protection against tyranny. Tyrants, according to Locke, extend their "Power beyond, what of Right belonged to the lawful Princes, or Governours of the Commonwealth" (II. 197).[20] In protesting Locke's separation of family from politics some feminists threaten individual freedom and choice. These feminists lose the protection this separation offers individuals—men and women.

Indeed many feminists do assert the need to distinguish private from public.[21] The crucial problem becomes one of identifying a model which articulates the differences between private and public while providing an avenue for the elimination of patriarchy. Properly understood, Locke provides the beginning of such a model. Feminists misread Locke when they describe his separation of private (family) and public (politics) as dichotomous and reified. Rather Locke explores the dynamics at work in a number of different spheres of human relationships. His attempt to balance demands of both individual liberty and equality in the political sphere carries profound emancipatory implications for the private, familial sphere.

For Locke, adults are rational, free and equal.[22] This rationality allows the individuals to discern an ordered reality which reveals certain laws of justice to humanity (natural law).[23] In moving from the pre-political state of nature to civil government, individuals consent to a common judge to interpret and to enforce natural law through civil law. Thus, natural law operates within civil arrangements as well as the state of nature. For this reason, the individual cannot sell him or herself into slavery in or out of the social contract. Natural law forbids the arbitrary destruction of one's own or another's life.[24] Furthermore, individuals are equal before natural law; nature neither assigns rulers nor subjects.[25] Among adults:

Power and Jurisdiction is reciprocal, no one having more than another: there being nothing more evident, than that Creatures of the same species and rank promiscuously born to all the same advantages of Nature, and use of the same faculties, should also be equal one amongst another without Subordination or Subjection. (II.4)[26]

Nature lends equal authority to each individual, although individuals vary in terms of strength, beauty or intelligence.

Locke illustrates these principles of freedom and equality at work in a variety of human relationships, specifically in his thoughts on family, politics and the relationships between them. Locke explicitly and systematically distinguishes political from familial relationships. He does so in response to Sir Robert Filmer, who confounds the two. Filmer's *Patriarcha*, the leading exposition and defense of patriarchy in Locke's time, grounded political authority in paternal right which, according to Filmer, reflected divine will. That is, Adam's dominion over Eve, their children and the world has been passed, father to son, to present day rulers. Indeed, occasionally God intervenes to ensure his will but the justification of political power remains the same: Adam's fatherhood passed to his heirs legitimizes political authority. For Filmer, politics is not like family; politics *is* family.[27] The king exerts both paternal and political power over his subjects because the king is literally both patriarch of this extended political family and head of the political institutions.

In response, Locke's *First Treatise* directs itself to demonstrating the differences between family and politics, between natural and conventional authority. Locke separates familial from political ends in an attempt to protect individual liberty, to free adults from patriarchal political rule. Locke's distinction between family and politics safeguards both adults and children. Children benefit because politics can never adequately replace a loving parent. Adults benefit because politics recognizes their status as mature, rational beings.

According to Locke, the family's purpose is procreation and the education of children.

Sexual and emotional affinity and the sharing of common goals guide its movement. "God hath made it their business to employ this Care of their Offspring, and hath placed in them suitable Inclinations of Tenderness and Concern to temper this power, to apply it as his Wisdom designed it, to the Children's good, as long as they should need be under it" (II.63). Parenting requires tenderness and a personal understanding of each unique child. Locke's *Some Thoughts Concerning Education* (*STCE*) demonstrates the need for flexible, loving parents. The ill-tempered child's discipline and upbringing should differ from that of a timid child. Each child enters a family with particular dispositions. A parent can appropriately and lovingly gear a child's education to his or her particular strengths and weaknesses.[28]

In contrast, protection of property directs political action; politics operates in terms of individual rights, each person's interest in securing body, liberty and estate from injury. "Political Power then I take to be a Right of making Laws . . . for the Regulating and Preserving of Property, and of employing the force of the Community, in the Execution of such Laws" (II.3).

Locke's distinction between politics and family is founded in the difference between adults and children. Adults are free; children require guidance until they reach an age of reason where they are presumed to perceive natural law for themselves. "And thus we see how natural Freedom and Subjection to Parents may consist together, and are both founded on the same principle" (II.61). Adulthood brings with it both reason and freedom. Feminists who misinterpret this distinction as resting ultimately on differences between man and woman not only misread Locke but also fail to grasp the liberating potential in Locke. Locke distinguishes adults from children, politics from family, so that adults will be treated as adults, not children.[29] Women can utilize Locke's distinction between family and politics to safeguard both adults and children. Locke's private-public distinction allows women to claim their adult status in politics and family without detracting from the unique parental relationship. Children remain under the authority of their parents. In principle, wives need not remain under the authority of their husbands.

Locke's distinction between family and politics is also founded in the difference between intimacy and citizenship. The former relies on personal, emotional ties; the latter relies on mutual respect for each person as a rational, free and equal individual. Actually two types of emotional relationships compose modern nuclear families: parent/child, and wife/husband. Locke's distinction between family and politics captures both features of modern families: the mutual, intimate, sexual support present in the spousal relationship and the nurturing, loving support present in the parental relationship. Neither spousal nor parental relationships can survive translation to the political sphere. One cannot love a stranger as one loves a spouse or a child.[30]

Locke's understanding of adult freedom and equality profoundly influences his understanding of marriage. While feminists correctly point out some disturbingly patriarchal features of Locke's thought, some also neglect its deeper potential for a radical transformation of patriarchal marriage. For example, although Locke does grant control of community property to the husband as the "abler and the stronger," he does so only after having already undermined the notion that strength gives authority.[31] Locke himself denies "that Men live together by no other Rules but that of Beasts" (II.1). Furthermore, not only is Locke tentative in granting marital authority to the husband— it "should be placed somewhere" (II.82)—he immediately opens the possibility of marriage without male domination and female submission. "But the ends of matrimony requiring no such Power in the Husband," that power "might be varied and regulated by that Contract, which unites Man and Wife in that Society, as far as may consist with Procreation and bringing up of Children till they could shift for themselves; nothing being necessary to any Society, that is not necessary to the ends for which it is already made" (II.83).[32]

This radical Locke also surfaces in an examination of his thought on family, as well as

marriage. Locke denies the husband's ultimate control over the children, as God, not the children's father, is the "Author and Giver of Life" (I.52) and "the Mother cannot be denied an equal share in begetting the Child, and so the Absolute Authority of the Father will not arise from hence" (I.55).[33] Mere paternity does not lend authority, at least no more than the mother herself shares by virtue of her maternity. In addition, although Locke tenuously grants control of joint property and the children to the husband, he explicitly excludes property belonging to the wife before the union (II.82). This is significant because every woman enters the contract with a fundamental property right in her own body, and therefore retains control of that property. This carries radical repercussions for the traditional institutions of marriage and family. On this basis, women can protect their bodies, and the product of their bodies from masculine domination. Neither nature nor God demands that the woman relinquish control of her body, or her labor, to her husband. Furthermore the wife's and the child's independent claim on familial property (II.83) suggests that paternal authority over property is one of trust rather than absolute control.[34] A violation of political trust allows revolution. Conceiving of paternal authority as a trust, not only indicates a move away from a patriarchal conception of the family but also implicitly recognizes the redress available in the case of a breach of that private trust-revolution.[35]

Locke not only undermines his own apparent support for an authoritarian patriarchal family structure, he also recognizes the historically and culturally fluctuating nature of this social unit. Although Locke describes an historically specific family, he leaves open the possibility of cultural and historical adaptations. As long as the family fulfills its purpose—educating young—Locke can accommodate it. Locke cites various circumstances where "the Children are all left to the Mother" and even where "one Woman hath more than one Husband at a time" (II.65). For Locke, the marriage contract could include polyandry.[36] Although Locke's familial illustrations reveal a bias toward a traditional nuclear family, the application of

Locke's principles are not limited by any one historical or cultural manifestation.

Locke's understanding of individuals as free and equal persons interacting in a variety of relationships informs his picture of marriage, family and politics and the possibilities inherent to those institutions. In addition, although politics and family are distinct spheres, Locke argues that the boundary between them is not impermeable. Locke opens doors through which politics can actively encourage the actualization of liberty and equality in the family. Politics can, on some bases, interfere in the family (as with the economy and religion, as will be indicated below). Family and politics are not separate, dichotomous and reified for Locke as some feminists claim. He not only discusses the interactive relationship between family and politics but also, more implicitly, the extent of political intrusion in the family.

The interactive relationship between family and politics becomes apparent when put in the context of natural law. The family's role is to educate children to assume roles as free and responsible adults. Appropriate familial education becomes almost a patriotic duty for Locke. In his introduction to *Some Thoughts Concerning Education*, Locke declares: "The well Educating of their Children is so much the Duty and Concern of Parents, and the Welfare and Prosperity of the Nation so much depends on it, that I would have everyone lay it seriously to Heart" (*STCE*, 80). The family educates for liberty while liberal politics allows the exercise of that liberty.[37] Specifically, Locke designs his education so as to subdue the child's desire for mastery over others and direct this desire to mastery over one's self and one's desires.[38] Children must not be allowed to master their parents, their maids, their rewards or their environments; rather, they should be taught to master their desires through reason (*STCE*, 33–36). Locke also tells us that example is the best teacher; surely a patriarchal master of the household would undermine any attempt to subdue the desire in children to master others.

Both the marriage contract and the political contract are bound by natural law.[39] These boundaries are most evident in the limits to the consent which forms each society. In neither case may one sell one's self into or consent to slavery.[40] Consent to slavery violates the natural law to preserve one's own, and another's life.[41] This indicates that mere efficiency is neither the standard of a good political or familial order. Locke denies the justice of an efficient, absolute monarchy,[42] and implicitly of the efficient absolute authority of the father. This demonstrates that both political and familial relationships appeal to a principle of justice which transcends each. In this way, Locke implicitly recognizes the steps civil government can take to discourage, even outlaw, authoritarian, patriarchal marriages. Liberal politics can actively attack patriarchal marriages which violate this principle of liberty, which violate natural law (the principle of justice in families). For example, feminists could use Locke's notion of liberty and consent to attack, and outlaw, all types of rape, including marital rape. Regardless of the marital contract a woman's body remains her own. Penetrating that woman's body without her consent violates natural law. Politics legitimately steps in to protect that woman and punish the perpetrator. In sum, although Locke distinguishes politics from family, both appeal to natural law as the standard of a just familial, or political order.

A comparison of marriage and political contracts yields evidence to suggest that politics can interfere with family.[43] Consent grounds both types of contracts according to Locke. Just as Locke argues that the social contract can legitimately support a number of political institutional arrangements, monarchy, aristocracy and democracy (although Locke does have preferences), so the marriage contract can support a number of familial arrangements. *But*, according to Locke, in politics we cannot consent to an absolute monarchy;[44] this would deny the freedom and equality which justifies consent in the first place and which is a necessary feature of societies bringing together rational individuals. Similarly, although Locke does not expressly make this argument, authoritarian, patriarchal marital contracts would violate the inalienable rights to life, liberty and property of those contracting (in this case, the wife) and be illegitimate.[45] Politics, in its legitimate role as a caretaker of these inalienable rights, can and should step into the family to support these rights and to subvert illegitimate marriage contracts. Politics protects the life, liberty and property of women as well as men and can step into the family to do so. Locke's principles of freedom and equality can be used to attack patriarchal families as well as patriarchal politics and allows politics to conduct such an attack on patriarchy in the family. Just as politics can interfere in the economy in the interest of life, liberty and property, so it can interfere in the family "the end of Government being the preservation of all" (II. 159).[46]

The political sphere provides an environment within which the marital union occurs and familial activities take place (II.83). Just as family relations can influence politics, liberal politics can influence family and marital relationships. Politics can support and encourage nonpatriarchal marriage contracts. In addition, Locke's defense of individual freedom and rationality encourages individual action in order to establish and protect liberty. Illegitimate rule allows, demands, revolution. The principles of justice constraining family and politics, and Locke's explicit assertion that individuals can ascertain those principles of justice for themselves,[47] logically support a right to revolution in both the familial or political spheres. Oppressors do not give up power, the oppressed seize it.[48]

> What is my Remedy against a Robber, that so broke into my House? Appeal to the Law for Justice. But perhaps Justice is denied, or I am crippled and cannot stir, robbed and have not the means to do it. If God has taken away all means of seeking remedy, there is nothing left but patience . . . then they may appeal . . . to Heaven, and repeat their Appeal till they have recovered the native Right. (II.176)

Mary O'Brien argues that the feminist revolution, unlike any revolution in the past, occurs in the private realm.[49] Locke's liberal principles open the door to such a private revolution. As Shanley says, "Women, like men, were free beings able to define their relationship to others by their own wills and

consent."[50] Locke's theory of revolution derives from Locke's conception of both men and women as free, rational beings.

A revolution in the private realm, in the family, is far from easy or certain, given the pervasiveness of patriarchy. Since those who benefit from patriarchy will not simply relinquish control, women must demand freedom and equality across the spectrum of familial, economic and political life. In addition, as we have seen, liberal politics encourages the enhancement of freedom and equality in the family. Freedom and equality in any realm reverberates into others. Locke provides for both an individual and political attack on patriarchal families.

Marriage, family and politics are only three spheres of human relationships which Locke explores in terms of rights and obligations. Throughout his writing Locke locates a number of different spheres of human activity which operate according to different principles, different centers of gravity. Locke's treatment of these other spheres echoes in his treatment of the relationship between family and politics. Politics can interfere in religion, or in the economy, to protect each person's right to life, liberty and property.

In religion charity grounds action. Love, as in love thy neighbor, defines religious relationships. Religion concerns itself with the "Interest of Mens Souls" (*Letter*, 26) whereas politics concerns itself with property, body and estate. Locke, in rebuttal to those who confound these two spheres, distinguishes faith from coercion. Once again, the interests of liberty and equality demand that politics not preach and preachers not coerce. The souls Locke protects from overarching political control are both male and female. In the religious sphere, Locke recognizes women as equal and rational moral creatures, capable of independent decisions regarding their own salvation. This combined with Locke's anti-clericism undermines patriarchal society.[51] Individual conscience, male or female, no longer questioningly submits to clerical (*i.e.*, male) authority. Locke's defense of toleration addresses itself to freeing the souls of men and women.[52]

While exploring the different laws of conduct guiding religion and politics, however, Locke implicitly recognizes the interactive nature of these spheres of action. In a *Letter Concerning Toleration* Locke "undertake[s] to represent how happy and how great would be the Fruit, both in Church and State, if the Pulpits everywhere founded with the Doctrine of Peace and Toleration" (*Letter,* 34). Furthermore, Locke demonstrates the necessity for mitigating, and eliminating, the prejudicial impact of religion on other spheres: "All . . . care is to be taken that the Sentence of Excommunication, and the Execution thereof, carry with it no rough usage, of Word or Action, whereby the ejected Person may any wise be damified in Body or Estate" (*Letter,* 30). Politics protects property and religion cares for souls. Politics cannot interfere in religion for the sake of souls (*i.e.,* faith) but it may for the sake of property. When religious rites threaten life, liberty or property, government legitimately intervenes.

> But those things that are prejudicial to the Commonweal of a People in their ordinary use, and are therefore forbidden by Laws, those things ought not to be permitted to Churches in their sacred Rites. Onely the Magistrate ought always be very careful that he do not misuse his Authority. (*Letter,* 42).

In the economic sphere utility guides action. Property originates in each person's drive for self-preservation and has as its end the comfortable life of the laborer, and by extension, those who benefit through his/her labor. Rational individuals best serve their own interests as well as those of the community. Free individuals exercise their liberty through labor and the procurement of property.[53] In this way, property manifests liberty, rather than sheer materialism.[54] By extension, an individual's right to property encompasses actually two rights: (1) the right to private property, to keep what one labors for or inherits, and (2) the right to acquire property in the first place.[55] The former generates inequalities while manifesting liberty; the latter demands a modicum of equality in order to ensure liberal expression through property. This becomes most apparent when one reads Locke's use of the word "property" in its broadest sense: "property" connotes one's liberty as well as one's estate.[56]

So, once again, Locke attempts to balance freedom and equality, this time structuring the interaction between politics and the economy. Class divisions can neither be so great that one class of people is permanently crippled in its attempts to acquire property,[57] nor so small that they inadequately reflect individual effort. In this way, politics protects property while setting the terms of economic relationships, establishing the limits of procurement, and enforcing taxation:

> In some parts of the World (where the Increase of People and Stock, with the Use of Money) had made Land scarce, and so of some Value, the several Communities settled the Bounds of their distinct Territories, and by Laws within themselves, regulated the Properties of the Private Men of their Society, and so, by Compact and Agreement settled the Property which Labour and Industry began. (II.45).

Over and above this, because "all the Members of the Society are to be preserved" (II.159): "he that hath, and to spare, must remit something of his full Satisfaction, and give away to the pressing and preferable Title of those, who are in danger to perish without it" (II.183). One may be coerced, presumably through political means, to provide for the needy. Furthermore, Locke's injunction to leave "enough and as good" (II.33) for others when procuring property, although considerably weakened with the introduction of money,[58] demands that neither disparity of wealth be so great, nor monopolies of goods be so extensive, as to bar the opportunities of others to an equal exercise of labor and enjoyment of goods. Locke protects each person's right to acquire, as well as own, property.[59]

Following this same line of argument, as politics can interfere in the economic realm it can intervene in the family for the sake of protecting each individual's right to property. In the case of the family, it may not, however, usurp the family's educational authority. It may not wholly equalize, or regulate the intimate marital relationship. It steps into these roles only to the extent that is necessary to ensure each person's right to protect and acquire property. Importantly, Locke understands property broadly as life, liberty and estate.

Understanding the underlying dimensions of liberty and equality at work in the interaction among private and public spheres sheds light on the potential within Locke's paradigm for addressing his communitarian and radical feminist critics. Putting Locke's individual within the context of these multiple spheres reveals an individual who is not the egotistical, self-preserving maximizer of rights and accumulator of goods that some communitarian feminists depict. A closer look at Locke himself reveals an emphasis on "person" as well as, and above, the individual. This person realizes himself or herself in a variety of social contexts. My religious obligation to my fellow person—love (charity)—which differs again from my political obligation—protecting property—differs again from my familial obligation. Even self-preservation, the motivation behind politics, manifests God's Will ("Workmanship") rather than desire (although the two do not conflict in this instance.) Self-preservation is an obligation before it is a right. "Every one as he is bound to preserve himself, and not to quit his station willfully; so by the like reason when his own Preservation comes not in competition, ought he, as much as he can, to preserve the rest of mankind" (II.6). The communitarian feminists' stress on Locke's individualism neglects the constellation of relationships which surround each person, relationships which, each in varying degrees, reflect both man's and woman's connectedness. Communitarian feminists' stress on Locke's natural rights fails to put those rights within the context of natural law and various human relationships. On this same basis, communitarian feminists who take Locke to task for removing "compassion" or "virtue" from politics have misread Locke's own intention. Locke removed considerations of virtue—for Locke, religion—from politics in the hope of promoting both peace and virtue. As Locke argues in a *Letter Concerning Toleration*, faith cannot be induced by force, but encouraged through love. For Locke, virtue is self-generating (or at least more likely to surface) given the appropriate tolerant political environment. "The care of Souls cannot belong to the Civil Magistrate, because his Power consists only in outward force; but true and saving Religion consists in the inward persuasion of the Mind" (*Letter*, 27) and the recognition of this distinction works to the "true interest of the Publick" (*Letter*, 21). Indeed, virtue in one sphere benefits another: religious individuals make good citizens; compassionate, reasonable familial education creates liberal citizens; removing direct and explicit concerns for virtue from politics promotes virtuous politics.

Locke illustrates what Nancy Rosenblum might call a "divine egotism." Locke's identification of political interests with "Life, Liberty, Health and Indolency of Body; and the Possession of outward things, such as Money, Lands" (*Letter*, 26) serves not only to protect each individual from political tyranny but also to provide a space for "inwardness" or in Locke's words "inward sincerity."[60] Removing virtue as a political concern allows virtue to surface in an atmosphere in individuality and plurality because virtue is not the product of force but of persuasion. Coercion promotes blind acceptance rather than thoughtful, ingrained understanding of rational virtue.

The radical feminist error in reading Locke also results from an oversimplification of Locke's distinction between private and public. As the preceding discussion of the spheres at work in Locke's thought indicates, Locke does depoliticize the family, but he does not isolate it. He demonstrates an understanding of both the adverse effect one sphere can have on another (*e.g.*, note the adverse effect politics can have on religion) and the welcome influence one sphere can have on another (*e.g.*, note the positive impact family can have on politics). Because Locke allows for an interaction between spheres, he can accommodate the dialogue between substantive and formal rights without degrading either the family or politics. Politics can encourage free, equal families while respecting the unique nature of that familial community. In this interpretation, Locke's political philosophy would allow for government-subsidized day care as a necessary, although clearly not sufficient, prerequisite to female equality. Politics enforces each individual's right to protect and acquire property. This demands some interference in the economic and familial sphere. This also allows politics to outlaw marital rape. Politics can step into the family, but it does so carefully, ever mindful of the liberty expressed in that marital, familial contract.

A correct understanding of the underlying dimensions of liberty and equality at work in the interaction between two particular spheres, economics and politics, contradicts the argument by some feminists that for Locke women were not considered rational by virtue of their unique historical relationship to property. Not only does circumstantial evidence indicate that Locke thought women to be rational, but understanding Locke's rationality in terms of the richness of human contexts and the principles of liberty and equality clearly reveals that Locke considered, in fact assumed, women to be rational beings. In *An Essay Concerning Human Understanding* Locke refers to "rational parents" (*Essay*, IV.4.16) suggesting that both parents are rational, despite the mother's tending to her child's call. Furthermore, in discussing political conquest Locke refers to both the wife's title in property *and* the wife's labor in producing goods (thereby confirming women's rationality even by Macpherson's standard): The Conqueror "cannot take the Goods of his Wife and Children; they too had a Title to the Goods he enjoy'd, and their shares in the Estate he possessed" (II.183). In addition, "whether her own Labour or Compact gave her a Title to it, 'tis plain, Her Husband could not forfeit what was hers" (II.183).

Over and above this circumstantial evidence, Ashcraft (1987) unveils a more radical interpretation of Locke which directly confronts both Macpherson's and, by extension, the radical feminists' reading of Locke. Ashcraft argues against Macpherson's narrow equation of Locke's rationality with property on three bases. First, Locke refers to all men as free in the state of nature, without any reference to socioeconomic conditions which underlie that freedom. Second, even if Locke did correlate property with rea-

son, every man (and woman) has property in his (or her) own body and Macpherson (and some feminists) mistakenly equate property solely with estate. Finally, and most importantly, Locke's indication that reason is presumed with maturity, where one "might be supposed capable of knowing the Law, and so living within the Rules of it" (II.60), demonstrates the more universal character of reason. *Some Thoughts Concerning Education* buttresses this meaning of Locke's rationality. Locke describes education as making the mind of a child "pliant to Reason" (*STCE*, 34) and providing habits so one may submit to his own Reason, when he is of an Age to make use of it (*STCE*, 36). Not estate, but "reason and property in one's person" is the criterion for legitimate political involvement and consent.[61] Macpherson, and some feminists, are misled by reading passages out of context; in a political context reason is not socially, economically or sexually differentiated for Locke.[62] Not property (as understood as goods) but self-guidance, the ability to render legitimate contracts and the perception of natural law all indicate rationality for Locke.

Clearly, the principles of freedom and equality inform the relationships (marital, familial, economic, religious and political) of all individuals, men and women. Locke's liberal political philosophy begins to illustrate the transformation which all human relationships undergo when individuals are considered rational, free and equal. In this way, the misinterpretation of Locke's distinction between private and public domains as reified yields mistaken conclusions about the possibilities of emancipation for women within Locke's liberal system. The oversimplification, by some feminists, of Locke's understanding of private and public leads them to err in concluding that Locke's liberal individual is artificially divorced from social particularities, that Locke's liberal family is necessarily patriarchal, that women are not rational and that politics does not and cannot influence family. More specifically, because feminists misread Locke's distinction between politics and family as one between male and female and not between adult and child, they discount his paradigm.

Instead of rejecting Locke's distinction, feminists can use it as both a protection of (male and female) adult liberty and as a principle with which they can press for equality and liberty in different social contexts. Locke's liberal political philosophy allows women, like men, to be treated as rational adults in family and politics. Politics should treat neither men nor women as children. Feminists should be activating Locke's principles of personhood and antipaternalism, of rationality, freedom and equality while criticizing specific instances of patriarchy in Locke's thought.

Locke supplies the beginning of a model, with all its rough edges, which captures the differences and overlap between private and public concerns. In doing this, Locke creates a paradigm which discourages tyranny and maximizes individual liberty. In establishing and protecting the family as private, Locke disarms political, tyrannical intrusions in that sphere. Locke's thought, in contrast to some feminist thought, provides a shelter for families from tyranny. This paradigm also distinguishes essential differences between different spheres while providing a basis for understanding the overlap among spheres. The organizing principle in one sphere differs from another, but actions in each reverberate in others. Locke's liberalism begins to reconcile the demands of freedom and equality within a variety of contexts. Although Locke never explicitly explores the impact of familial gender disadvantages as they influence political aspirations of freedom and autonomy, he plants the seeds for a deeper understanding of these influences, and even leaves open the possibility of tempering their impact among private and public positions. In so doing, he opens the possibility of enhancing freedom and autonomy in each sphere of activity. Liberalism needs to systematically and self-consciously work out the interacting and partially integrated relationship among spheres of human activities, to specifically address gender differences and formally incorporate those differences into its paradigm. This does not undercut as much as continue the liberal, or Lockean, project.

In addition, Locke's autonomous, rational individual, who nonetheless perceives the need for justice (natural law) to instruct his or her actions, offers a compelling vision of woman reflectively and reasonably directing her life, neither denying her victimization by social circumstances nor falling victim to those circumstances. Reflective action centers liberalism. Reflective action also provides the key to woman's control of her own destiny.

Notes

1. Mary Dietz identifies two feminist challenges to the liberal notion of citizenship which she labels maternalist feminism and marxist feminism in "Context Is All: Feminism and Theories of Citizenship" *Daedalus* 116 (Fall 1987): 1–24. The two critiques I discuss here are substantially the same. I have changed the names for two reasons. The former label, "maternalist feminism" neglects, I think, the debt of these feminists to more traditional communitarian thought. The latter, "marxist feminism" collapses, too readily, feminist thought on patriarchy with marxist thought on class.

2. These individuals tend "naturally toward egoism" according to Alison Jaggar, *Feminist Politics and Human Nature* (Sussex: Rowman and Allanheld, 1983), p. 31.

3. Mary O'Brien, *The Politics of Reproduction* (Boston: Routledge & Kegan Paul, 1981), p. 159.

4. See Carol Gilligan, *In a Different Voice* (Cambridge, MA: Harvard University Press, 1982), p. 100. Gilligan: "The moral imperative that emerges repeatedly in interviews with women is an injunction to care, a responsibility to discern and alleviate 'the real and recognizable trouble' of this world. For men, the moral imperative appears rather as an injunction to respect the rights to life and self-fulfillment."

5. See Jaggar, *Feminist Politics and Human Nature*; Nancy Hirschmann, "Freedom, Recognition and Obligation," *American Political Science Review* (December, 1989): 1227–44; Jean Bethke Elshtain, *Public Man, Public Woman* (New Jersey: Princeton University Press, 1981), p. 118.

6. Elshtain, *Public Man, Public Woman*, pp. 118–26.

7. Linda Nicholson, *Gender and History* (New York: Columbia University Press, 1986), p. 30.

8. *Ibid.*, p. 156.

9. Carol Pateman, *The Sexual Contract* (Stanford University Press, 1988), p. 168.

10. Lorene Clark, "Women and Locke: Who Owns the Apples in the Garden of Eden?" in *The Sexism of Social and Political Theory* (Toronto: University of Toronto Press, 1979), p. 38.

11. O'Brien, *Politics of Reproduction*, p. 159.

12. See B. Macpherson, *The Political Theory of Possessive Individualism* (Oxford: The Clarendon Press, 1962) for the origins of the argument.

13. Zillah Eisenstein, *The Radical Future of Liberal Feminism* (New York: Longman, 1981), p. 44; see also, Jaggar, *Feminist Politics and Human Nature;* and Diana Coole, *Women in Political Theory* (Sussex: Lynne Riener, 1988), p. 98.

14. Quoted in Jaggar, *Feminist Politics and Human Nature*, p. 32.

15. Nicholson, *Gender and History*, p. 137.

16. Eisenstein, *Radical Future of Liberal Feminism*, p. 49.

17. Pateman describes the liberal distinction between private and public as a dichotomy and argues that "Locke's theory . . . shows how the private and public spheres are grounded in opposing principles of association which are exemplified in the conflicting status of women and men; natural subordination stands opposed to free individualism." See Carole Pateman, "Feminist Critiques of the Public/ Private Dichotomy" in *Feminism and Equality*, ed. Anne Phillips (New York: New York University Press, 1987), p. 106. Eisenstein also identifies this dichotomy. In discussing the woman as mother she argues that "derived from this are the more subtle forms of patriarchal organization: . . . the division between public and private life, and the divorce of political and family life. The separation of male from female constructs a *dichotomous* world view that limits insight into the structure of patriarchal organization itself" (my emphasis). Eisenstein, *Radical Future of Liberal Feminism*, p. 16.

18. Feminists use the term "reified" to describe what they perceive as the liberal abstraction of public from private life, an abstraction founded on an inappropriate understanding of reality. Pateman states that in Locke, "a reified conception of the political is built upon what I shall call the fiction of citizenship." She continues "Liberal-democratic theory today . . . continues to present the political as something abstracted from, as autonomous or separate from, the social relationships of every-

day life." Carole Pateman, *The Disorder of Women* (Cambridge: Polity Press, 1989), pp. 91–92. Nicholson also describes Locke's distinction between private and public as "reified" and argues that modern feminism, in contrast, recognizes the "complex interconnections" between the family and other spheres of society. Nicholson, *Gender and History*, pp. 2–4, 137.

19. Elshtain, *Public Man, Private Woman*, pp. 212–20, points this out. Elshtain remarks that for radical feminists, "Nothing 'personal' is exempt, then, from political definition, direction, and manipulation—neither sexual intimacy, nor love, nor parenting" (*Public Man, Private Woman*, p. 217). Some feminists rightly identify patriarchy in the variety of spheres which it surfaces, but fail to clearly distinguish among these spheres.

20. Michael Walzer, *Spheres of Justice* (New York: Basic Books, 1983), p. 19, explains the relationship between private and public spheres and the protection against tyranny more explicitly. "The regime of complex equality is the opposite of tyranny. It establishes a set of relationships such that domination is impossible. In formal terms, complex equality means that no citizen's standing in one sphere . . . can be undercut by his standing in some other sphere."

21. For example, Mary O'Brien, *Reproducing the World* (Boulder: Westview Press, 1989), p. 79, distinguishes between "intimate" space and "public" space. Elshtain (1981) also criticizes radical feminists for forgetting about this important distinction. Pateman claims that the feminist critique of the liberal distinction between private and public does not "necessarily suggest that no distinction can or should be drawn between the personal and political aspects of social life." Rather "Feminism looks toward a differentiated social order within which the various dimensions are distinct but not separate or opposed." Pateman, "Feminist Critiques," pp. 119, 122.

22. See Richard Ashcraft, *Locke's Two Treatises of Government* (London: Unwin Hymen, 1987), pp. 47–48, 168. Locke explains, "Thus we are born Free, as we are born Rational; not that we have actually the Exercise of either: Age that brings one, brings with it the other too" (II. 61).

23. Raymond Polin, "John Locke's Conception of Freedom" in *John Locke—Problems and Perspectives*, ed. J.W. Yolton (Cambridge: Cam-

bridge University Press, 1969), pp. 3–6. See II.6.

24. Ruth Grant, *John Locke's Liberalism* (Chicago: University of Chicago Press, 1987), pp. 67–71.

25. Thomas Pangle, *The Spirit of Modern Republicanism* (Chicago: University of Chicago Press, 1988), p. 234.

26. Locke makes this same point many times. "The Equality, which all Men are in, in respect of Jurisdiction for Dominion one over another . . . being the equal Right that every Man hath, to his Natural Freedom, without being subjected to the Will or Authority of any other Man" (II.54).

27. Nicholson, *Gender and History*, p. 141.

28. Yolton and Yolton, *Some Thoughts Concerning Education*, pp. 14–15. Locke states, "He therefore, that is about Children, should well study their Nature and Aptitudes, and see, by often trials, what turn they easily take, and what becomes them, observe what their Native Stock is, how it may be improved . . . He should consider, what they want; whether they be capable of having it wrought into them . . . and whether it be worth while to endeavor it" (*STCE*, 122).

29. II.2 clearly distinguishes parental from political authority; II.54 identifies "that equal right every man hath, to his natural freedom, without being subjected to the will or authority of any other man." Children differ from adults in that they have not yet reached a state of full equality. "Children, I confess are not born in this full state of equality, though they are born to it. Their parents have a sort of rule and jurisdiction over them when they come into this world, and for some time after, but 'tis but a temporary one. The bonds of this subjection are like the swaddling cloths they are wrapt in, and supported by, in the weakness of their infancy. Age and reason as they grow up, loosen them till at length they drop quite off, and leave a man at his own free disposal" (II.55).

30. See Ashcraft, *Locke's Two Treatise's*, pp. 109–112, for a discussion of the role of intimacy in Locke's family.

31. Gordon Schochet, *Paternalism and Political Thought* (New York Basic Books, Inc., 1975), pp. 249–50.

32. Melissa Butler has shown that Locke often consciously departs from traditional views about women in the interest of individualism. Locke understood that his individualism required a consideration of women as well as men as individuals. Melissa Butler, "Early Liberal Roots of Feminism," *APSR* 72 (March,

1978): 135–50. Similarly, Mary Lyndon Shanley's study of seventeenth century marriage contract theory leads her to conclude that Locke revolutionized marriage, not in basing it in a voluntary contract, but in making the terms of the contract negotiable. "Locke's notion that contract might regulate property rights and maintenance obligations in marriage was an astonishing notion, and not for the seventeenth century alone." Mary Lyndon Shanley, "Marriage Contract and Social Contract in Seventeenth Century English Political Thought," *Western Political Quarterly* 32 (June 1979): 91. For Locke, a woman could control not only who her partner was to be, but also the terms of her relationship to that chosen partner.

33. See Nicholson's, *Gender and History*, p. 142. Also Ashcraft, *Locke's Two Treatises*, p. 72.

34. Supporting this Locke identifies the "Community of Goods, and the Power over them, mutual Assistance and Maintenance, and other things" as "belonging to Conjugal Society" (II.83).

35. An anonymous referee for *The Review of Politics* pointed this out.

36. Nathan Tarcov, *Locke's Education for Liberty* (Chicago: University of Chicago Press, 1984), p. 209.

37. *Ibid.*, p. 76.

38. *Ibid.*, pp. 89–90.

39. Locke explains, "Thus the Law of Nature stands as an Eternal Rule to all Men, Legislators as well as others. The Rules that they make for other Mens Actions, must, as well as their own and other Mens Actions, be conformable to the Law of Nature, i.e., to the Will of God, of which that is a Declaration, and the fundamental Law of Nature being the preservation of Mankind, no Humane Sanction can be good, or valid against it" (II.135).

40. Ramon Lemos, *Hobbes and Locke* (Athens, GA: University of Georgia Press, 1978).

41. Grant, *John Locke's Liberalism*, p. 71.

42. *Ibid.*, p. 92.

43. Butler, "Early Liberal Roots," p. 145.

44. More exactly, absolute monarchy is in principle legitimate. As Ashcraft points out, absolute monarchs exist and historically people have consented to them; but, in principle this consent, and those absolute monarchies, are illegitimate. People living under an absolute monarch remain, in fact, in a state of nature (Ashcraft, *Locke's Two Treatises*, pp. 118–20, 155–57).

45. Locke limits authority in various contexts. "For the exceeding the Bounds of Authority is no more a Right in a great, than a petty Officer, no more justified in a King, than a Constable" (II.202).

46. Later in this article I will provide a detailed discussion of the relationship between the economy and politics, and specific examples of the ability of the latter to interfere in the former.

47. Locke, throughout the *Second Treatise*, asserts this individual capability to discern natural law: "The State of Nature has a Law of Nature to govern it . . . which . . . teaches all Mankind, who will but consult it, that being all equal and independent, no one ought to harm another in his Life, Health, Liberty, or Possessions" (II.6). The people, the oppressed, serve as judge of the oppression: "If a long train of Abuses, Prevarications, and Artifices, all tending the same way, make the design visible to the People, and they cannot but feel, what they lie under, and see, whither they are going, it is not to be wonder'd, that they should then rouze themselves, and endeavor to put the rule into such hands, which may secure to them the ends for which Government was first erected" (II.225).

48. It should be noted that Locke is not inciting citizens to immediate or imprudent revolution. "And he that appeals to Heaven, must be sure he has Right on his side; and a Right too, that is worth the Trouble and the Cost of the Appeal, as he will answer at a Tribunal, that cannot be deceived, and will be sure to retribute to every one according to the Mischiefs he has created to his Fellow-Subjects" (II.176). Only a "long train of Abuses, Prevarications, and Artifaces, all tending the same way" (II.225) will incite a majority which is typically rather complacent (II.168). Locke is, however, emphatically defending a people's right to protect their own liberty when circumstances demand it.

49. O'Brien, *Reproducing the World*.

50. Shanley, "Marriage Contract," p. 70.

51. See Locke's preface to the *Two Treastises*. See also I.125; *Letter*, 29.

52. I am indebted to an anonymous referee at *The Review of Politics* for this preceding argument.

53. Polin, "John Locke's Conception of Freedom," p. 6.

54. Peter Myers, "John Locke on the Naturalness of Rights" (Ph.D. diss., Loyola University Chicago, December, 1991).

55. Lemos, *Hobbes and Locke*, pp. 140–41. Putting the individual's right to property within the context of each person's duty to preserve God's workmanship also supports this conclusion. In this interpretation, a right to property is based upon appropriate use, upon its promotion of human preservation. See James Tully, *A Discourse on Property* (Cambridge: Cambridge University Press, 1980), pp. 121–54. See also, Ashcraft, *Locke's Two Treatises*, pp. 123–47.

56. Myers, "John Locke," pp. 327–29.

57. "Man can no more justly make use of another's necessity, to force him to become his vassal, by withholding that relief, God acquires him to afford to the want of his Brother, than he that has more strength can seize upon a weaker, master him to his Obedience, and with a Daggar to his throat offer him Death or Slavery" (I.42). Quoted in Tully, *A Discourse on Property*, p. 138.

58. The introduction of money provides that "he who appropriates land to himself by his labor, does not lessen but increase the common stock of mankind" (II.37). With or without the presence of money, however, when procurement lessens the common stock of mankind, obstructs the rights of others to acquire property through labor, Locke would, in this interpretation, curtail appropriation.

59. Furthermore, Locke limits the right to property. "And thus Man's Property in the Creatures, was founded upon the right he had, to make use of those things, that were necessary or useful to his Being" (I.86).

60. Nancy Rosenblum, *Another Liberalism* (Cambridge, MA: Harvard University Press, 1987), p. 55.

61. Ashcraft, *Locke's Two Treatises*, p. 175.

62. *Ibid.*, pp. 167–73.

Adapted from: Mary B. Walsh, "Locke and Feminism on Private and Public Realms of Activities." In *The Review of Politics*, Volume 57, pp. 254–277. Copyright © 1995. Reprinted by permission of *The Review of Politics*. ✦

Jean-Jacques Rousseau

Paradox is a word often associated with Jean-Jacques Rousseau—and with good reason. Paradox abounds in his writings and in his personal life as well. The most famous line from his *Social Contract* illustrates this penchant: "Man was born free and everywhere he is in chains." Elsewhere in the same work he speaks of the relationship between individual will and the general will of the community, noting that in some cases men must be "forced to be free." His life and writings seem to some a web of inconsistency. Despite his admonition to parents in his treatise on education, *Emile*, to heed parental responsibilities—especially the duty of rearing one's own children—he abandoned his five children in a foundling home. Because Rousseau's prose and lifestyle are so deeply steeped in paradox, his work continues to inspire fierce debate and has led to diametrically opposed characterizations of him as both totalitarian and libertarian. The persistent student of his work will find, however, that Rousseau's use of paradox is intended not to obscure or mislead, but to provide insights that may not adequately be captured in any other manner.

Rousseau's life was both colorful and tragic. His mother died while giving birth to him in Geneva in 1712. His father, a watchmaker, exposed the boy to his own ribald lifestyle and abandoned Jean-Jacques when the boy was only 10. Thereafter, Rousseau drifted through Geneva and France taking odd jobs and making many acquaintances, including some influential friends who helped him through rough times. One of these, Mme de Warens, took Rousseau into her house in Chambéry. He used his time there to study the classics and developed an interest in music. A dispute involving one of his hostess's lovers sent him packing for Paris in 1742. There, he wrote about and composed music, including an opera.

When he was 31, one of his well-placed friends secured for him the post of Secretary to the French Ambassador in Venice. The job did not last long as Rousseau became bored and disenchanted with political life, especially as practiced in the city of canals. It was during this brief political exposure, however, that he became convinced of the centrality of politics to all aspects of life, a theme that informs all of his political writings. When Rousseau returned to Paris, he met Thérèse Levasseur and commenced a relationship, which ended in matrimony only after 25 years of companionship, during which he was involved in several affairs.

In 1749, Rousseau entered a contest sponsored by the Academy of Dijon with an essay on the topic: "Has the Restoration of the Sciences and Arts Tended to Purify Morals?" Arguing against the tide of Enlightenment thinking, Rousseau asserted that advances in these disciplines had a corrupting effect on the human personality. Exposure to them was harmful to morals and destructive of natural freedom. Ironically, the publication of the *First Discourse* won for Rousseau the attention of artistic and scientific luminaries in Parisian café society who sought him out for intellectual exchange. These were the same people Rousseau implicitly criticized for corrupting humankind. Rousseau took pleasure in rejecting their lifestyle and went so far as to abandon the typical dress of this circle in favor of peasant garb.

Rousseau submitted *On the Origin and Foundations of Inequality Among Men*, his *Second Discourse*, to the same academy in 1754. Although this discourse won no prize, its influence was substantial. In this work, Rousseau speculated about the origins of society, identifying humans as solitary yet peaceable creatures prior to the onset of society. With the development of speech, reason, and particularly with the advent of private property, the human race began its steady decline to the point where existing governments arose to protect property while subjugating citizens.

In 1756, Rousseau retreated to the country cottage of one of his admirers, Mme D'Épinay. He began working on a number of projects, including a romantic novel, *Julie, ou la Nouvelle Héloïse,* as well as his *Social Contract.* This period was marked by growing disputes between Rousseau and his former café society friends, some of whom he accused of conspiring against him.

In 1762 both the *Social Contract* and *Emile* were published. The latter, a treatise on education in which an unidentified tutor shapes the personality of his student by rejecting book learning in favor of a more "natural" experiential approach, drew wide attention and fire. The section on religion proved politically unpopular for Rousseau: among Enlightenment intellectuals for its reliance on faith, and among French churchgoers for its utilitarian treatment of religion. The Parliament of Paris ordered the volume burned and issued an arrest warrant for Rousseau. The *Social Contract,* an attempt to forge a theory of government upon the premises articulated in the *Second Discourse,* received little attention until after Rousseau's death, particularly by zealots of the French Revolution.

After 1762 Rousseau was a fugitive, darting from one town to another to avoid arrest. These years were marked by an increasing paranoia, reflected in his later writings, where he accused old friends like Diderot and Voltaire of conspiring with political opponents to ruin him. Rousseau returned to Paris incognito in 1770 where he composed his frank *Confessions,* as well as a series of recollections titled *Reveries of a Solitary Walker.* He and Thérèse retired to Ermonvoille, just outside Paris, where he died in 1778.

Second Discourse and *Social Contract*

In the *Second Discourse,* or the *Discourse on the Origin and Foundations of Inequality Among Men,* Rousseau speculates about the origin of society and the emergence of government. The first part is an anthropological sketch of life among early humans as Rousseau envisions it might have been (though no claim is made for historical accuracy). In this early state, humans are characterized as equal and free; differences in ability mattered little, and no individual had claim or title over the actions of another. In developing this portrait, Rousseau identifies two important characteristics of humans that set them apart from other animals: freedom and perfectibility. Together, these yield a nature that is malleable, as capable of vice as of virtue, and subject to direction by the type of political community one inhabited. Part Two reveals how natural man was corrupted by the liberation of reason and by claims to private property that, once institutionalized, led to the subservience of the many by the few. This view differs from both classic and modern political accounts. Unlike Aristotle, for example, Rousseau envisions humans as essentially solitary. Unlike Hobbes and other moderns, however, Rousseau paints natural man as innocent, with self-interest tempered by natural, though weak, sympathy for other living beings. Ultimately, Rousseau does not advocate the return to bestial simplicity. Rather, he insists that social man must reorganize political life in such a manner as to affirm his freedom and equality, as far as is practicable, in the context of the political community. The selections from the *Second Discourse* illustrate these themes.

Rousseau states clearly the purpose of the *Social Contract* at the outset: legitimizing the political state to which man has arrived and from which there is no return. What is also clear is the mechanism by which legitimate government is founded. All men must unite by contracting to put themselves and their power under the supreme control of the "general will," and to receive each contracting member as an indivisible part of the whole. By virtue of this contract, each member trades the natural freedom to do what he wishes for the moral freedom to do what the general will determines he must. What is not clear is the nature of some of the arrangements by which this contract is to be executed. For example, the general will is an elusive concept. It is more than a collection of individual wills and resembles what we might call today the common good. The general will becomes known under the skillful leadership of the legislator, who resembles a superhuman with the knowledge of human nature but suffering none of its deficiencies. How the general will is made known, and how the legislator leads without manipulating the governed, continue to be sources of debate among Rousseau scholars. While Rousseau is not wholly successful in explicating how his system of government will operate, he does identify the paradoxes faced by the modern nation-state as only he can.

Commentaries

One of the most important, yet opaque, concepts advanced by Rousseau is that of the general will. Somehow he envisions citizens submitting to the will of the community while being as free as before they had entered civil society. In the first commentary, an excerpt from a longer work, Patrick Riley attempts to deconstruct this troublesome concept. Riley believes that the terms "generality" and "will" represent two main strands that run throughout Rousseau's thought. Will, for Rousseau, stands for the conviction that civil association is the most voluntary act in the world. If one could "generalize" it so as to elect only the common good and to avoid willful self-love, one would achieve a type of moral freedom consonant with the public good. As Riley shows, this necessitates the education of one's will. Riley goes on to compare Rousseau's solution to that offered by Prussian philosopher Immanuel Kant (1724–1804), who attempted to find universal rules or "categorical imperatives" that are supposed to direct men's actions on the basis of reason alone. For Rousseau, unlike Kant, the most we can hope for is a blended education of reason and passion through character that attaches us to the citizens of a particular commonwealth.

In the second commentary, Penny Weiss and Anne Harper tackle Rousseau's treatment of the sexes. Though he has been variously attacked as a misogynist and biological determinist—particularly since he finds "natural" man without reason to mate for life with the same individual—the authors of this commentary find that Rousseau's advocacy of sexual differentiation is based on his understanding of its ability to bring individuals outside of themselves into interdependent communities. This counteracts human tendencies toward vanity and self-love.

Web Sources

www.wabash.edu/Rousseau
Rousseau Association Home Page. News about the association and its activities honoring the Swiss philosopher and links to his works, commentary, images, and music he composed along with links to related sites.

http://books.mirror.org/gb.rousseau.html
Great Books Rousseau Page. Links to complete text of many of the philosopher's works.

http://www.utm.edu/research/iep/r/rousseau.htm
The Internet Encyclopedia of Philosophy: Jean-Jacques Rousseau. Overview of Rousseau's life and work.

http://www.constitution.org/jjr/ineq.htm
Rousseau: On the Origin of Inequality. Full text of the *Second Discourse*.

http://www.constitution.org/jjr/socon.htm
Rousseau: Social Contract. Full text of *The Social Contract or Principles of Political Right*.

Class Activities and Discussion Items

1. Conduct your own thought experiment regarding the hypothetical "state of nature." Imagine human beings unencumbered by the constraints of social and political institutions. Create a portrait of human behavior under these conditions. What kind of political institutions are most compatible with this portrait—democratic, authoritarian, or somewhere in-between? Compare the portrait you have created with those of other students in your class. Identify elements of basic agreement and disagreement regarding human qualities.

2. Rousseau's portrait of human nature has been compared by some theorists to the portrait advanced by Charles Darwin. In what ways does Rousseau's an-

thropological account resemble Darwin's notion of descent by natural selection and adaptation? How does Rousseau's account of human nature compare to recent sociobiological theories?

3. One of the most opaque notions in Rousseau's philosophy is that of the "general will." How does this notion compare with traditional theories of representation? Can the general will be realized through representative government alone? In what ways does it necessitate direct involvement by all citizens?

4. While political scientists do not speak of a general will, they often speak of the public good. How does Rousseau's portrait of the general will compare with the idea of the public good? Do you believe some public good independent of the various interests of particular groups can be achieved politically? Does Rousseau offer a valid blueprint for arriving at this goal?

5. Consider the proposition that America should adopt a policy that restricts the amount of personal wealth one can accumulate to some considerably high level indexed to inflation with excess wealth siphoned off for community improvements. Do you believe Rousseau would support such a plan? Why? Why not? Take a poll in your class to discover how many students would support this proposition. Discuss reasons for support and opposition. How might Rousseau respond to opponents?

Further Reading

Cranston, Maurice William. 1991. *The Noble Savage: Jean-Jacques Rousseau, 1754—1762*. Chicago: University of Chicago Press. The author ties together the life and work of Rousseau.

Cullen, Daniel E. 1993. *Freedom in Rousseau's Political Philosophy*. DeKalb: Northern Illinois University Press. An examination of the pivotal and sometimes confusing role of freedom in Rousseau's thought.

Masters, R. D. 1968. *The Political Philosophy of Rousseau*. Princeton, N.J.: Princeton University Press. Analyzes Rousseau by emphasizing his integration of classic and modern ideas.

Orwin, Clifford and Nathan Tarcov (eds.). 1997. *The Legacy of Rousseau*. Chicago: University of Chicago Press. Fourteen essays considering, from the vantage point of the end of the 20th century, how current perceptions of various issues that face us derive from or are challenged by Rousseau's multifaceted and sophisticated diagnoses of modernity.

Rousseau, Jean-Jacques. [1979.] *Emile*, ed. Allan Bloom. New York: Basic Books. Rousseau's classic work on education.

—— (Roger D. Masters and Christopher Kelly, eds.). [1990]. *The Collected Writings of Rousseau*. Hanover, NH : University Press of New England. A well-translated anthology containing the essential classics including the *First* and *Second Discourses*, *Political Economy*, *Reveries*, *Letters to Malesherbes*, and others.

Schwartz, Joel. 1984. *The Sexual Politics of Jean-Jacques Rousseau*. Chicago: University of Chicago Press. A complex and thorough review of Rousseau's thoughts on sex, men, women, and family life.

Shklar, J. 1969. *Men and Citizens*. Cambridge: Cambridge University Press. The author tackles Rousseau's political views by examining his treatment of private and public realms of activity.

Starobinski, Jean (Arthur Goldhammer, trans.; with an introduction by Robert J. Morrissey). 1988. *Jean-Jacques Rousseau, Transparency and Obstruction*. Chicago: University of Chicago Press. Classic analysis of Rousseau's quest for "unmediated authenticity," or the true self in the face of social constructs.

Strong, Tracy. 1994. *The Politics of the Ordinary*. Thousand Oaks, CA: Sage Publications. The author contends that Rousseau's democratic individual is an ordinary self, paradoxically multiple and thoroughly modern.

Weiss, Penny A. 1993. *Gendered Community: Rousseau, Sex, and Politics*. New York: New York University Press. A feminist exploration of Rousseau's treatment of women and the family. ✦

11
Excerpts from *Discourse on the Origin and Foundations of Inequality Among Men*

Jean-Jacques Rousseau

First Part

I see nothing in any animal but an ingenious machine, to which nature hath given senses to wind itself up, and to guard itself, to a certain degree, against anything that might tend to disorder or destroy it. I perceive exactly the same things in the human machine, with this difference, that in the operations of the brute, nature is the sole agent, whereas man has some share in his own operations, in his character as a free agent. The one chooses and refuses by instinct, the other from an act of free-will: hence the brute cannot deviate from the rule prescribed to it, even when it would be advantageous for it to do so; and, on the contrary, man frequently deviates from such rules to his own prejudice. Thus a pigeon would be starved to death by the side of a dish of the choicest meats, and a cat on a heap of fruit or grain; though it is certain that either might find nourishment in the foods which it thus rejects with disdain, did it think of trying them. Hence it is that dissolute men run into excesses which bring on fevers and death; because the mind depraves the senses, and the will continues to speak when nature is silent.

Every animal has ideas, since it has senses; it even combines those ideas in a certain degree; and it is only in degree that man differs, in this respect, from the brute. Some philosophers have even maintained that there is a greater difference between one man and another than between some men and some beasts. It is not, therefore, so much the understanding that constitutes the specific difference between the man and the brute, as the human quality of free-agency. Nature lays her commands on every animal, and the brute obeys her voice. Man receives the same impulsion, but at the same time knows himself at liberty to acquiesce or resist: and it is particularly in his consciousness of this liberty that the spirituality of his soul is displayed. For physics may explain, in some measure, the mechanism of the senses and the formation of ideas; but in the power of willing or rather of choosing, and in the feeling of this power, nothing is to be found but acts which are purely spiritual and wholly inexplicable by the laws of mechanism.

However, even if the difficulties attending all these questions should still leave room for difference in this respect between men and brutes, there is another very specific quality which distinguishes them, and which will admit of no dispute. This is the faculty of self-improvement, which, by the help of circumstances, gradually develops all the rest of our faculties, and is inherent in the species as in the individual: whereas a brute is, at the end of a few months, all he will ever be during his whole life, and his species, at the end of a thousand years, exactly what it was the first year of that thousand. Why is man alone liable to grow into a dotard? Is it not because he returns, in this, to his primitive state; and that, while the brute, which has acquired nothing and has therefore nothing to lose, still retains the force of instinct, man, who loses, by age or accident, all that his perfectibility had enabled him to gain, falls by this means lower than the brutes themselves? It would be melancholy, were we forced to admit that this distinctive and almost unlimited faculty is the source of all human misfortunes; that it is this which, in time, draws man out of his original state, in which he would have spent his days insensibly in peace and innocence; that it is this faculty, which, successively producing in different ages his discoveries and his errors, his vices and his virtues, makes him at length a tyrant both over himself and over nature.[1] It would be shocking to be obliged to regard as a benefactor the man who first suggested to the Oroonoko Indians the use of the boards they apply to the temples of their children, which secure to them some part at least of their imbecility and original happiness.

Savage man, left by nature solely to the direction of instinct, or rather indemnified for what he may lack by faculties capable at first of supplying its place, and afterwards of raising him much above it, must accordingly begin with purely animal functions: thus seeing and feeling must be his first condition, which would be common to him and all other animals. To will, and not to will, to desire and to fear, must be the first, and almost the only operations of his soul, till new circumstances occasion new developments of his faculties.

Whatever moralists may hold, the human understanding is greatly indebted to the passions, which, it is universally allowed, are also much indebted to the understanding. It is by the activity of the passions that our reason is improved; for we desire knowledge only because we wish to enjoy; and it is impossible to conceive any reason why a person who has neither fears nor desires should give himself the trouble of reasoning. The passions, again, originate in our wants, and their progress depends on that of our knowledge; for we cannot desire or fear anything, except from the idea we have of it, or from the simple impulse of nature. Now savage man, being destitute of every species of intelligence, can have no passions save those of the latter kind: his desires never go beyond his physical wants. The only goods he recognises in the universe are food, a female, and sleep: the only evils he fears are pain and hunger. I say pain, and not death: for no animal can know what it is to die; the knowledge of death and its terrors being one of the first acquisitions made by man in departing from an animal state. . . .

It appears, at first view, that men in a state of nature, having no moral relations or determinate obligations one with another, could not be either good or bad, virtuous or vicious; unless we take these terms in a physical sense, and call, in an individual, those qualities vices which may be injurious to his preservation, and those virtues which contribute to it; in which case, he would have to be accounted most virtuous, who put least check on the pure impulses of nature. But without deviating from the ordinary sense of the words, it will be proper to suspend the judgment we might be led to form on such a state, and be on our guard against our prejudices, till we have weighed the matter in the scales of impartiality, and seen whether virtues or vices preponderate among civilised men; and whether their virtues do them more good than their vices do harm; till we have discovered, whether the progress of the sciences sufficiently indemnifies them for the mischiefs they do one another, in proportion as they are better informed of the good they ought to do; or whether they would not be, on the whole, in a much happier condition if they had nothing to fear or to hope from any one, than as they are, subjected to universal dependence, and obliged to take everything from those who engage to give them nothing in return.

Above all, let us not conclude, with Hobbes, that because man has no idea of goodness, he must be naturally wicked; that he is vicious because he does not know virtue; that he always refuses to do his fellow-creatures services which he does not think they have a right to demand; or that by virtue of the right he truly claims to everything he needs, he foolishly imagines himself the sole proprietor of the whole universe. Hobbes had seen clearly the defects of all the modern definitions of natural right: but the consequences which he deduces from his own show that he understands it in an equally false sense. In reasoning on the principles he lays down, he ought to have said that the state of nature, being that in which the care for our own preservation is the least prejudicial to that of others, was consequently the best calculated to promote peace, and the most suitable for mankind. He does say the exact opposite, in consequence of having improperly admitted, as a part of savage man's care for self-preservation, the gratification of a multitude of passions which are the work of society, and have made laws necessary. A bad man, he says, is a robust child. But it remains to be proved whether man in a state of nature is this robust child: and, should we grant that he is, what would he infer? Why truly, that if this man, when robust and strong, were dependent on others as he is when feeble, there is no extravagance he would not be guilty of; that he would beat his mother when she was too slow in giving him her breast; that he would strangle one of his younger brothers, if he should be troublesome to him, or bite the arm of another, if he put him to any inconvenience. But that man in the state of nature is both strong and dependent involves two contrary suppositions. Man is weak when he is dependent, and is his own master before he comes to be strong. Hobbes did not reflect that the same cause, which prevents a savage from making use of his reason, as our jurists hold, prevents him also from abusing his faculties, as Hobbes himself allows: so that it may be justly said that savages are not bad merely because they do not know what it is to be good: for it is neither the development of the understanding nor the restraint of law that hinders them from doing ill; but the peacefulness of their passions, and their ignorance of vice: *tanto plus in illis proficit vitiorum ignoratio, quam in his cognitio virtutis.*[2]

There is another principle which has escaped Hobbes; which, having been bestowed on mankind, to moderate, on certain occasions, the impetuosity of egoism, or, before its birth, the desire of self-preservation, tempers the ardour with which he pursues his own welfare, by an innate repugnance at seeing a fellow-creature suffer.[3] I think I need not fear contradiction in holding man to be possessed of the only natural virtue, which could not be denied him by the most violent detractor of human virtue. I am speaking of compassion, which is a disposition suitable to creatures so weak and subject to so many evils as we certainly are: by so much the more universal and useful to mankind, as it comes before any kind of reflection; and at the same time so natural, that the very brutes themselves sometimes give evident proofs of it. Not to mention the tenderness of mothers for their offspring and the perils they encounter to save them from danger, it is well known that horses show a reluctance to trample on living bodies. One animal never passes by the dead body of another of its species: there are even some which give their fellows a sort of burial; while the mournful lowings of the cattle when they enter the slaughter-house show the impressions made on them by the horrible spectacle which meets them. We find, with pleasure, the author of the *Fable of the Bees* obliged to own that man is a compassionate and sensible being, and laying aside his cold subtlety of style, in the example he gives, to present us with the pathetic description of a man who, from a place of confinement, is compelled to behold a wild beast tear a child from the arms of its mother, grinding its tender limbs with its murderous teeth, and tearing its palpitating entrails with its claws. What horrid agitation must not the eyewitness of such a scene experience, although he would not be personally concerned! What anxiety would he not suffer at not being able to give any assistance to the fainting mother and the dying infant!

Such is the pure emotion of nature, prior to all kinds of reflection! Such is the force of natural compassion, which the greatest depravity of morals has as yet hardly been able to destroy! For we daily find at our theatres men affected, nay shedding tears at the sufferings of a wretch who, were he in the tyrant's place, would probably even add to the torments of his enemies; like the bloodthirsty Sulla, who was so sensitive to ills he had not caused, or that Alexander of Pheros who did not dare to go and see any tragedy acted, for fear of being seen weeping with Andromache and Priam, though he could listen without emotion to the cries of all the citizens who were daily strangled at his command.

Mollissima corda
Humano generi dare se natura fatetur,
Quae lacrimas dedit.
——Juvenal, *Satires*, xv. 151[4]

Mandeville well knew that, in spite of all their morality, men would have never been better than monsters, had not nature bestowed on them a sense of compassion, to aid their reason: but he did not see that from this quality alone flow all those social virtues, of which he denied man the possession. But what is generosity, clemency or humanity but compassion applied to the weak, to the guilty, or to mankind in general? Even benevolence and friendship are, if we judge rightly, only the effects of compassion, constantly set upon a particular object: for how is it different to wish that another person may not suffer pain and uneasiness and to wish him happy? Were it even true that pity is no more than a feeling, which puts us in the place of the sufferer, a feeling, obscure yet lively in a savage, developed yet feeble in civilised man; this truth would have no other consequence than to confirm my argument. Compassion must, in fact, be the stronger, the more the animal beholding any kind of distress identifies himself with the animal that suffers. Now, it is plain that such identification must have been much more perfect in a state of nature than it is in a state of reason. It is reason that engenders self-respect, and reflection that confirms it: it is reason which turns man's mind back upon itself, and divides him from everything that could disturb or afflict him. It is philosophy that isolates him, and bids him say, at sight of the misfortunes of others: "Perish if you will, I am secure." Nothing but such general evils as threaten the whole community can disturb the tranquil sleep of the philosopher, or tear him from his bed. A murder may with impunity be committed under his window; he has only to put his hands to his ears and argue a little with himself, to prevent nature, which is shocked within him, from identifying itself with the unfortunate sufferer. Uncivilised man has not this admirable talent; and for want of reason and wisdom, is always foolishly ready to obey the first promptings of humanity. It is the populace that flocks together at riots and street-brawls, while the wise man prudently makes off. It is the mob and the market-women, who part the combatants, and hinder gentlefolks from cutting one another's throats.

It is then certain that compassion is a natural feeling, which, by moderating the violence of love of self in each individual, contributes to the preservation of the whole species. It is this compassion that hurries us without reflection to the relief of those who are in distress: it is this which in a state of nature supplies the place of laws, morals and virtues, with the advantage that none are tempted to disobey its gentle voice: it is this which will always prevent a sturdy savage from robbing a weak child or a feeble old man of the sustenance they may have with pain and difficulty acquired, if he sees a possibility of providing for himself by other means: it is this which, instead of inculcating that sublime maxim of rational justice, *Do to others as you would have them do unto you,* inspires all men with that other maxim of natural goodness, much less perfect indeed, but perhaps more useful; *Do good to yourself with as little evil as possible to others.* In a word, it is rather in this natural feeling than in any subtle arguments that we must look for the cause of that repugnance, which every man would experience in doing evil, even independently of the maxims of education. Although it might belong to Socrates and other minds of the like craft to acquire virtue by reason, the human race would long since have ceased to be, had its preservation depended only on the reasonings of the individuals composing it. . . .

Second Part

The first man who, having enclosed a piece of ground, bethought himself of saying *This is mine,* and found people simple enough to believe him, was the real founder of civil society. From how many crimes, wars and murders, from how many horrors and misfortunes might not any one have saved mankind, by pulling up the stakes, or filling up the ditch, and crying to his fellows, "Beware of listening to this impostor; you are undone if you once forget that the fruits of the earth belong to us all, and the earth itself to nobody." But there is great probability that things had then already come to such a pitch, that they could no longer continue as they were; for the idea of property depends on many prior ideas, which could only be acquired successively, and cannot have been formed all at once in the human mind. Mankind must have made very considerable progress, and acquired considerable knowledge and industry which they must also have transmitted and increased from age to age, before they arrived at this last point of the state of nature. Let us then go farther back, and endeavour to unify under a single point of view that slow succession of events and discoveries in the most natural order.

Man's first feeling was that of his own existence, and his first care that of self-preservation. The produce of the earth furnished him with all he needed, and instinct told him how to use it. Hunger and other appetites made him at various times experience various modes of existence; and among these was one which urged him to propagate his species—a blind propensity that, having nothing to do with the heart, produced a merely animal act. The want once gratified, the two sexes knew each other no more; and even the offspring was nothing to its mother, as soon as it could do without her.

Such was the condition of infant man; the life of an animal limited at first to mere sensations, and hardly profiting by the gifts nature bestowed on him, much less capable of entertaining a thought of forcing anything from her. But difficulties soon presented themselves, and it became necessary to learn how to surmount them: the height of the trees, which prevented him from gathering their fruits, the competition of other animals desirous of the same fruits, and the ferocity of those who needed them for their own preservation, all obliged him to apply himself to bodily exercises. He had to be active, swift of foot, and vigorous in fight. Natural weapons, stones and sticks, were easily found: he learnt to surmount the obstacles of nature, to contend in case of necessity with other animals, and to dispute for the means of subsistence even with other men, or to indemnify himself for what he was forced to give up to a stronger.

In proportion as the human race grew more numerous, men's cares increased. The difference of soils, climates and seasons, must have introduced some differences into their manner of living. Barren years, long and sharp winters, scorching summers which parched the fruits of the earth, must have demanded a new industry. On the seashore and the banks of rivers, they invented the hook and line, and became fishermen and eaters of fish. In the forests they made bows and arrows, and became huntsmen and warriors. In cold countries they clothed themselves with the skins of the beasts they had slain. The lightning, a volcano, or some lucky chance acquainted them with fire, a new resource against the rigours of winter: they next learned how to preserve this element, then how to reproduce it, and finally how to prepare with it the flesh of animals which before they had eaten raw. . . .

Everything now begins to change its aspect. Men, who have up to now been roving in the woods, by taking to a more settled manner of life, come gradually together, form separate bodies, and at length in every country arises a distinct nation, united in character and manners, not by regulations or laws, but by uniformity of life and food, and the common influence of climate. Permanent neighbourhood could not fail to produce, in time, some connection between different families. Among young people of opposite sexes, living in neighbouring huts, the transient commerce required by nature soon led, through mutual intercourse, to another kind not less agreeable, and more permanent. Men began now to take the difference between objects into account, and to make comparisons; they acquired imperceptibly the ideas of beauty and merit, which soon gave rise to feelings of preference. In consequence of seeing each other often, they could not do without seeing each other constantly. A tender and pleasant feeling insinuated itself into their souls, and the least opposition turned it into an impetuous fury: with love arose jealousy; discord triumphed, and human blood was sacrificed to the gentlest of all passions.

As ideas and feelings succeeded one another, and heart and head were brought into play, men continued to lay aside their original wildness; their private connections became every day more intimate as their limits extended. They accustomed themselves to assemble before their huts round a large tree; singing and dancing, the true offspring of love and leisure, became the amusement, or rather the occupation, of men and women thus assembled together with nothing else to do. Each one began to consider the rest, and to wish to be considered in turn; and thus a value came to be attached to public esteem. Whoever sang or danced best, whoever was the handsomest, the strongest, the most dexterous, or the most eloquent, came to be of most consideration; and this was the first step towards inequality, and at the same time towards vice. From these first distinctions arose on the one side vanity and contempt and on the other shame and envy: and the fermentation caused by these new leavens ended by producing combinations fatal to innocence and happiness. . . .

If the reader thus discovers and retraces the lost and forgotten road, by which man must have passed from the state of nature to the state of society; if he carefully restores, along with the intermediate situations which I have just described, those which want of time has compelled me to suppress, or my imagination has failed to suggest, he cannot fail to be struck by the vast distance which separates the two states. It is in tracing this slow succession that he will find the solution of a number of problems of politics and morals, which philosophers cannot settle. He will feel that, men being different in different ages, the reason why Diogenes could not find a man was that he sought among his contemporaries a man of an earlier period. He will see that Cato died with Rome and liberty, because he did not fit the age in which he lived; the greatest of men served only to astonish a world which he would certainly have ruled, had he lived five hundred years sooner. In a word, he will explain how the soul and the passions of men insensibly change their very nature; why our wants and pleasures in the end seek new objects; and why, the original man having vanished by degrees, society offers to us only an assembly of artificial men and factitious passions, which are the work of all these new relations, and without any real foundation in nature. . . .

Notes

1. A famous author, reckoning up the good and evil of human life, and comparing the aggregates, finds that our pains greatly exceed our pleasures: so that, all things considered, human life is not at all a valuable gift. This conclusion does not surprise me; for the writer drew all his arguments from man in civilisation. Had he gone back to the state of nature, his inquiries would clearly have had a different result, and man would have been seen to be subject to very few evils not of his own creation. It has indeed cost us not a little trouble to make ourselves as wretched as we are. When we consider, on the one hand, the immense labours of mankind, the many sciences brought to perfection, the arts invented, the powers employed, the deeps filled up, the mountains levelled, the rocks shattered, the rivers made navigable, the tracts of land cleared, the lakes emptied, the marshes drained, the enormous structures erected on land, and the teeming vessels that cover the sea; and, on the other hand, estimate with ever so little thought, the real advantages that have accrued from all these works to mankind, we cannot help being amazed at the vast disproportion there is between these things, and deploring the infatuation of man, which, to gratify his silly pride and vain self-admiration, induces him eagerly to pursue all the miseries he is capable of feeling, though beneficent nature had kindly placed them out of his way.

That men are actually wicked, a sad and continual experience of them proves beyond doubt: but, all the same, I think I have shown that man is naturally good. What then can have depraved him to such an extent, except the changes that have happened in his constitution, the advances he has made, and the knowledge he has acquired? We may admire human society as much as we please; it will be none the less true that it necessarily leads men to hate each other in proportion as their interests clash, and to do one another apparent services, while they are really doing every imaginable mischief. What can be thought of a relation, in which the interest of every individual dictates rules directly opposite to those the public reason dictates to the community in general—in which every man finds his profit in the misfortunes of his neighbour? There is not perhaps any man in a comfortable position who has not greedy heirs, and perhaps even children, secretly wishing for his death; not a ship at sea, of which the loss would not be good news to some merchant or other; not a house, which some debtor of bad faith would not be glad to see reduced to ashes with all the papers it contains; not a nation which does not rejoice at the disasters that befall its neighbours. Thus it is that we find our advantage in the misfortunes of our fellow-creatures, and that the loss of one man almost always constitutes the prosperity of another. But it is still more pernicious that public calamities are the objects of the hopes and expectations of innumerable individuals. Some desire sickness, some mortality, some war, and some famine. I have seen men wicked enough to weep for sorrow at the prospect of a plentiful season; and the great and fatal fire of London, which cost so many unhappy persons their lives or their fortunes, made the fortunes of perhaps ten thousand others. I know that Montaigne censures Demades the Athenian for having caused to be punished a workman who, by selling his coffins very dear, was a great gainer by the deaths of his fellow-citizens; but, the reason alleged by Montaigne being that everybody ought to be punished, my point is clearly confirmed by it. Let us penetrate, therefore, the superficial appearances of benevolence, and survey what passes in the inmost recesses of the heart. Let us reflect what must be the state of things, when men are forced to caress and destroy one another at the same time; when they are born enemies by duty, and knaves by interest. It will perhaps be said that society is so formed that every man gains by serving the rest. That would be all very well, if he did not gain still more by injuring them. There is no legitimate profit so great, that it cannot be greatly exceeded by what may be made illegitimately; we always gain more by hurting our neighbours than by doing them good. Nothing is required but to know how to act with impunity; and to this end the powerful employ all their strength, and the weak all their cunning.

Savage man, when he has dined, is at peace with all nature, and the friend of all his fellow-creatures. If a dispute arises about a meal, he rarely comes to blows, without having first compared the difficulty of conquering his antagonist with the trouble of finding subsistence elsewhere: and, as pride does not come in, it all ends in a few blows; the victor eats, and the vanquished seeks provision somewhere else, and all is at peace. The case is quite different with man in the state of society, for whom first necessaries have to be provided, and then superfluities; delicacies follow next, then immense wealth, then subjects, and then slaves. He enjoys not a moment's relaxation; and what is yet stranger, the less natural and pressing his wants, the more headstrong are his passions, and, still worse, the more he has

it in his power to gratify them; so that after a long course of prosperity, after having swallowed up treasures and ruined multitudes, the hero ends up by cutting every throat till he finds himself, at last, sole master of the world. Such is in miniature the moral picture, if not of human life, at least of the secret pretensions of the heart of civilised man.

2. Justin, *Hist.* ii. 2. So much more does the ignorance of vice profit the one sort than the knowledge of virtue the other.

3. Egoism must not be confused with self-respect: for they differ both in themselves and in their effects. Self-respect is a natural feeling which leads every animal to look to its own preservation, and which, guided in man by reason and modified by compassion, creates humanity and virtue. Egoism is a purely relative and factitious feeling, which arises in the state of society, leads each individual to make more of himself than of any other, causes all the mutual damage men inflict one on another, and is the real source of the "sense of honour." This being understood, I maintain that, in our primitive condition, in the true state of nature, egoism did not exist; for as each man regarded himself as the only observer of his actions, the only being in the universe who took any interest in him, and the sole judge of his deserts, no feeling arising from comparisons he could not be led to make could take root in his soul; and for the same reason, he could know neither hatred nor the desire for revenge, since these passions can spring only from a sense of injury: and as it is the contempt or the intention to hurt, and not the harm done, which constitutes the injury, men who neither valued nor compared themselves could do one another much violence, when it suited them, without feeling any sense of injury. In a word, each man, regarding his fellows almost as he regarded animals of different species, might seize the prey of a weaker or yield up his own to a stronger, and yet consider these acts of violence as mere natural occurrences, without the slightest emotion of insolence or despite, or any other feeling than the joy or grief of success or failure.

4. Nature avows she gave the human race the softest hearts, who gave them tears.

Adapted from: Jean-Jacques Rousseau, *On the Social Contract,* translated by G. D. H. Cole, pp. 184–186, 195–200, 207–208, 212–213, 236. Originally published by E. P. Dutton, 1913. ✦

12
Excerpts from *On the Social Contract*

Jean-Jacques Rousseau

Book I

Chapter I: Subject of This First Book

Man is born free; and everywhere he is in chains. One thinks himself the master of others, and still remains a greater slave than they. How did this change come about? I do not know. What can make it legitimate? That question I think I can answer.

If I took into account only force, and the effects derived from it, I should say: "As long as a people is compelled to obey, and obeys, it does well; as soon as it can shake off the yoke, and shakes it off, it does still better; for, regaining its liberty by the same right as took it away, either it is justified in resuming it, or there was no justification for those who took it away." But the social order is a sacred right which is the basis of all other rights. Nevertheless, this right does not come from nature, and must therefore be founded on conventions. Before coming to that, I have to prove what I have just asserted.

Chapter II: The First Societies

The most ancient of all societies, and the only one that is natural, is the family: and even so the children remain attached to the father only so long as they need him for their preservation. As soon as this need ceases, the natural bond is dissolved. The children, released from the obedience they owed to the father, and the father, released from the care he owed his children, return equally to independence. If they remain united, they continue so no longer naturally, but voluntarily; and the family itself is then maintained only by convention.

This common liberty results from the nature of man. His first law is to provide for his own preservation, his first cares are those which he owes to himself; and, as soon as he reaches years of discretion, he is the sole judge of the proper means of preserving himself, and consequently becomes his own master.

The family then may be called the first model of political societies: the ruler corresponds to the father, and the people to the children; and all, being born free and equal, alienate their liberty only for their own advantage. The whole difference is that, in the family, the love of the father for his children repays him for the care he takes of them, while, in the State, the pleasure of commanding takes the place of the love which the chief cannot have for the peoples under him. . . .

Chapter III: The Right of the Strongest

The strongest is never strong enough to be always the master, unless he transforms strength into right, and obedience into duty. Hence the right of the strongest, which, though to all seeming meant ironically, is really laid down as a fundamental principle. But are we never to have an explanation of this phrase? Force is a physical power, and I fail to see what moral effect it can have. To yield to force is an act of necessity, not of will—at the most, an act of prudence. In what sense can it be a duty?

Suppose for a moment that this so-called "right" exists. I maintain that the sole result is a mass of inexplicable nonsense. For, if force creates right, the effect changes with the cause: every force that is greater than the first succeeds to its right. As soon as it is possible to disobey with impunity, disobedience is legitimate; and, the strongest being always in the right, the only thing that matters is to act so as to become the strongest. But what kind of right is that which perishes when force fails? If we must obey perforce, there is no need to obey because we ought; and if we are not forced to obey, we are under no obligation to do so. Clearly, the word "right" adds nothing to force: in this connection, it means absolutely nothing.

Obey the powers that be. If this means yield to force, it is a good precept, but superfluous: I can answer for its never being violated. All power comes from God, I admit; but so does all sickness: does that mean that we are forbidden to call in the doctor? A brigand surprises me at the edge of a wood: must I not merely surrender my purse on compulsion; but, even if I could withhold it, am I in conscience bound to give it up? For certainly the pistol he holds is also a power.

Let us then admit that force does not create right, and that we are obliged to obey only legitimate powers. In that case, my original question recurs.

Chapter IV: Slavery

Since no man has a natural authority over his fellow, and force creates no right, we must conclude that conventions form the basis of all legitimate authority among men.

If an individual, says Grotius, can alienate his liberty and make himself the slave of a master, why could not a whole people do the same and make itself subject to a king? There are in this passage plenty of ambiguous words which would need explaining; but let us confine ourselves to the word *alienate*. To alienate is to give or to sell. Now, a man who becomes the slave of another does not give himself; he sells himself, at the least for his subsistence: but for what does a people sell itself? A king is so far from furnishing his subjects with their subsistence that he gets his own only from them; and, according to Rabelais, kings do not live on nothing. Do subjects then give their persons on condition that the king takes their goods also? I fail to see what they have left to preserve.

It will be said that the despot assures his subjects civil tranquillity. Granted; but what do they gain, if the wars his ambition brings down upon them, his insatiable avidity, and the vexatious conduct of his ministers press harder on them than their own dissensions would have done? What do they gain, if the very tranquillity they enjoy is one of their miseries? Tranquillity is found also in dungeons; but is that enough to make them desirable places to live in? The Greeks imprisoned in the cave of the Cyclops lived there very tranquilly, while they were awaiting their turn to be devoured.

To say that a man gives himself gratuitously, is to say what is absurd and inconceivable; such an act is null and illegitimate, from the mere fact that he who does it is out of his mind. To say the same of a whole people is to suppose a people of madmen; and madness creates no right.

Even if each man could alienate himself, he could not alienate his children: they are born men and free; their liberty belongs to them, and no one but they has the right to dispose of it. Before they come to years of discretion, the father can, in their name, lay down conditions for their preservation and well-being, but he cannot give them irrevocably and without conditions: such a gift is contrary to the ends of nature, and exceeds the rights of paternity. It would therefore be necessary, in order to legitimise an arbitrary government, that in every generation the people should be in a position to accept or reject it; but, were this so, the government would be no longer arbitrary.

To renounce liberty is to renounce being a man, to surrender the rights of humanity and even its duties. For him who renounces everything no indemnity is possible. Such a renunciation is incompatible with man's nature; to remove all liberty from his will is to remove all morality from his acts. Finally, it is an empty and contradictory convention that sets up, on the one side, absolute authority, and, on the other, unlimited obedience. Is it not clear that we can be under no obligation to a person from whom we have the right to exact everything? Does not this condition alone, in the absence of equivalence or exchange, in itself involve the nullity of the act? For what right can my slave have against me, when all that he has belongs to me, and, his right being mine, this right of mine against myself is a phrase devoid of meaning?

Grotius and the rest find in war another origin for the so-called right of slavery. The victor having, as they hold, the right of killing the vanquished, the latter can buy back his life at the price of his liberty; and this convention is the more legitimate because it is to the advantage of both parties.

But it is clear that this supposed right to kill the conquered is by no means deducible from the state of war. Men, from the mere fact that, while they are living in their primitive independence, they have no mutual relations stable enough to constitute either the state of peace or the state of war, cannot be naturally enemies. War is constituted by a relation between things, and not between persons; and, as the state of war cannot arise out of simple personal relations, but only out of real relations, private war, or war of man with man, can exist neither in the state of nature, where there is no constant property, nor in the social state, where everything is under the authority of the laws.

Individual combats, duels and encounters, are acts which cannot constitute a state; while the private wars, authorised by the Establishments of Louis IX, King of France, and suspended by the Peace of God, are abuses of feudalism, in itself an absurd system if ever there was one, and contrary to the principles of natural right and to all good polity.

War then is a relation, not between man and man, but between State and State, and individuals are enemies only accidentally, not as men, nor even as citizens,[1] but as soldiers; not as members of their country, but as its defenders. Finally, each State can have for enemies only other States, and not men; for between things disparate in nature there can be no real relation.

Furthermore, this principle is in conformity with the established rules of all times and the constant practice of all civilised peoples. Declarations of war are intimations less to powers than to their subjects. The foreigner, whether king, individual, or people, who robs, kills or detains the subjects, without declaring war on the prince, is not an enemy, but a brigand. Even in real war, a just prince, while laying hands, in the enemy's country, on all that belongs to the public, respects the lives and goods of individuals: he respects rights on which his own are founded. The object of the war being the destruction of the hostile State, the other side has a right to kill its defenders, while they are bearing arms; but as soon as they lay them down and surrender, they cease to be ene-mies or instruments of the enemy, and become once more merely men, whose life no one has any right to take. Sometimes it is possible to kill the State without killing a single one of its members; and war gives no right which is not necessary to the gaining of its object. These principles are not those of Grotius: they are not based on the authority of poets, but derived from the nature of reality and based on reason.

The right of conquest has no foundation other than the right of the strongest. If war does not give the conqueror the right to massacre the conquered peoples, the right to enslave them cannot be based upon a right which does not exist. No one has a right to kill an enemy except when he cannot make him a slave, and the right to enslave him cannot therefore be derived from the right to kill him. It is accordingly an unfair exchange to make him buy at the price of his liberty his life, over which the victor holds no right. Is it not clear that there is a vicious circle in founding the right of life and death on the right of slavery, and the right of slavery on the right of life and death?

Even if we assume this terrible right to kill everybody, I maintain that a slave made in war, or a conquered people, is under no obligation to a master, except to obey him as far as he is compelled to do so. By taking an equivalent for his life, the victor has not done him a favour; instead of killing him without profit, he has killed him usefully. So far then is he from acquiring over him any authority in addition to that of force, that the state of war continues to subsist between them: their mutual relation is the effect of it, and the usage of the right of war does not imply a treaty of peace. A convention has indeed been made; but this convention, so far from destroying the state of war, presupposes its continuance.

So, from whatever aspect we regard the question, the right of slavery is null and void, not only as being illegitimate, but also because it is absurd and meaningless. The words *slave* and *right* contradict each other, and are mutually exclusive. It will always be equally foolish for a man to say to a man or to a people: "I make with you a convention wholly at your expense and wholly to my advantage; I shall keep it as long as I like, and you will keep it as long as I like."

Chapter V: That We Must Always Go Back to a First Convention

Even if I granted all that I have been refuting, the friends of despotism would be no better off. There will always be a great difference between subduing a multitude and ruling a society. Even if scattered individuals were successively enslaved by one man, however numerous they might be, I still see no more than a master and his slaves, and certainly not a people and its ruler; I see what may be termed an aggregation, but not an association; there is as yet neither public good nor body politic. The man in question, even if he has enslaved half the world, is still only an individual; his interest, apart from that of others, is still a purely private interest. If this same man comes to die, his empire, after him, remains scattered and without unity, as an oak falls and dissolves into a heap of ashes when the fire has consumed it.

A people, says Grotius, can give itself to a king. Then, according to Grotius, a people is a people before it gives itself. The gift is itself a civil act, and implies public deliberation. It would be better, before examining the act by which a people gives itself to a king, to examine that by which it has become a people; for this act, being necessarily prior to the other, is the true foundation of society.

Indeed, if there were no prior convention, where, unless the election were unanimous, would be the obligation on the minority to submit to the choice of the majority? How have a hundred men who wish for a master the right to vote on behalf of ten who do not? The law of majority voting is itself something established by convention, and presupposes unanimity, on one occasion at least.

Chapter VI: The Social Compact

I suppose men to have reached the point at which the obstacles in the way of their preservation in the state of nature show their power of resistance to be greater than the resources at the disposal of each individual for his maintenance in that state. That primitive condition can then subsist no longer; and the human race would perish unless it changed its manner of existence.

But, as men cannot engender new forces, but only unite and direct existing ones, they have no other means of preserving themselves than the formation, by aggregation, of a sum of forces great enough to overcome the resistance. These they have to bring into play by means of a single motive power, and cause to act in concert.

This sum of forces can arise only where several persons come together: but, as the force and liberty of each man are the chief instruments of his self-preservation, how can he pledge them without harming his own interests, and neglecting the care he owes to himself? This difficulty, in its bearing on my present subject, may be stated in the following terms: "*The problem is to find a form of association which will defend and protect with the whole common force the person and goods of each associate, and in which each, while uniting himself with all, may still obey himself alone, and remain as free as before.*" This is the fundamental problem of which the *Social Contract* provides the solution.

The clauses of this contract are so determined by the nature of the act that the slightest modification would make them vain and ineffective; so that, although they have perhaps never been formally set forth, they are everywhere the same and everywhere tacitly admitted and recognised, until, on the violation of the social compact, each regains his original rights and resumes his natural liberty, while losing the conventional liberty in favour of which he renounced it.

These clauses, properly understood, may be reduced to one—the total alienation of each associate, together with all his rights, to the whole community; for, in the first place, as each gives himself absolutely, the conditions are the same for all; and, this being so, no one has any interest in making them burdensome to others.

Moreover, the alienation being without reserve, the union is as perfect as it can be, and no associate has anything more to demand: for, if the individuals retained certain rights, as there would be no common superior to decide between them and the public, each, being on one point his own judge, would ask to be so on all; the state of nature would thus continue, and the association would necessarily become inoperative or tyrannical.

Finally, each man, in giving himself to all, gives himself to nobody; and as there is no associate over whom he does not acquire the same right as he yields others over himself, he gains an equivalent for everything he loses, and an increase of force for the preservation of what he has.

If then we discard from the social compact what is not of its essence, we shall find that it reduces itself to the following terms: *"Each of us puts his person and all his power in common under the supreme direction of the general will, and, in our corporate capacity, we receive each member as an indivisible part of the whole."*

At once, in place of the individual personality of each contracting party, this act of association creates a moral and collective body, composed of as many members as the assembly contains votes, and receiving from this act its unity, its common identity, its life and its will. This public person, so formed by the union of all other persons formerly took the name of *city*,[2] and now takes that of *Republic* or *body politic*; it is called by its members *State* when passive, *Sovereign* when active, and *Power* when compared with others like itself. Those who are associated in it take collectively the name of *people*, and severally are called *citizens*, as sharing in the sovereign power, and *subjects*, as being under the laws of the State. But these terms are often confused and taken one for another: it is enough to know how to distinguish them when they are being used with precision.

Chapter VII: The Sovereign

This formula shows us that the act of association comprises a mutual undertaking between the public and the individuals, and that each individual, in making a contract, as we may say, with himself, is bound in a double capacity; as a member of the Sovereign he is bound to the individuals, and as a member of the State to the Sovereign. But the maxim of civil right, that no one is bound by undertakings made to himself, does not apply in this case; for there is a great difference between incurring an obligation to yourself and incurring one to a whole of which you form a part.

Attention must further be called to the fact that public deliberation, while competent to bind all the subjects to the Sovereign, because of the two different capacities in which each of them may be regarded, cannot, for the opposite reason, bind the Sovereign to itself; and that it is consequently against the nature of the body politic for the Sovereign to impose on itself a law which it cannot infringe. Being able to regard itself in only one capacity, it is in the position of an individual who makes a contract with himself; and this makes it clear that there neither is nor can be any kind of fundamental law binding on the body of the people—not even the social contract itself. This does not mean that the body politic cannot enter into undertakings with others, provided the contract is not infringed by them; for in relation to what is external to it, it becomes a simple being, an individual.

But the body politic or the Sovereign, drawing its being wholly from the sanctity of the contract, can never bind itself, even to an outsider, to do anything derogatory to the original act, for instance, to alienate any part of itself, or to submit to another Sovereign. Violation of the act by which it exists would be self-annihilation; and that which is itself nothing can create nothing.

As soon as this multitude is so united in one body, it is impossible to offend against one of the members without attacking the body, and still more to offend against the body without the members resenting it. Duty and interest therefore equally oblige the two contracting parties to give each other help; and the same men should seek to combine, in their double capacity, all the advantages dependent upon that capacity.

Again, the Sovereign, being formed wholly of the individuals who compose it, neither has nor can have any interest contrary to theirs; and consequently the sovereign power need give no guarantee to its subjects, because it is impossible for the body to wish to hurt all its members. We shall also see later on that it cannot hurt any in particular. The Sovereign, merely by virtue of what it is, is always what it should be.

This, however, is not the case with the relation of the subjects to the Sovereign, which, despite the common interest, would have no security that they would fulfill their undertakings, unless it found means to assure itself of their fidelity.

In fact, each individual, as a man, may have a particular will contrary or dissimilar to the general will which he has as a citizen. His particular interest may speak to him quite differently from the common interest: his absolute and naturally independent existence may make him look upon what he owes to the common cause as a gratuitous contribution, the loss of which will do less harm to others than the payment of it is burdensome to himself; and, regarding the moral person which constitutes the State as a *persona ficta*, because not a man, he may wish to enjoy the rights of citizenship without being ready to fulfil the duties of a subject. The continuance of such an injustice could not but prove the undoing of the body politic.

In order then that the social compact may not be an empty formula, it tacitly includes the undertaking, which alone can give force to the rest, that whoever refuses to obey the general will shall be compelled to do so by the whole body. This means nothing less than that he will be forced to be free; for this is the condition which, by giving each citizen to his country, secures him against all personal dependence. In this lies the key to the working of the political machine; this alone legitimises civil undertakings, which, without it, would be absurd, tyrannical, and liable to the most frightful abuses.

Chapter VIII: The Civil State

The passage from the state of nature to the civil state produces a very remarkable change in man, by substituting justice for instinct in his conduct, and giving his actions the morality they had formerly lacked. Then only, when the voice of duty takes the place of physical impulses and right of appetite, does man, who so far had considered only himself, find that he is forced to act on different principles, and to consult his reason before listening to his inclinations. Although, in this state, he deprives himself of some advantages which he got from nature, he gains in return others so great, his faculties are so stimulated and developed, his ideas so extended, his feelings so ennobled, and his whole soul so uplifted, that, did not the abuses of this new condition often degrade him below that which he left, he would be bound to bless continually the happy moment which took him from it for ever, and, instead of a stupid and unimaginative animal, made him an intelligent being and a man.

Let us draw up the whole account in terms easily commensurable. What man loses by the social contract is his natural liberty and an unlimited right to everything he tries to get and succeeds in getting; what he gains is civil liberty and the proprietorship of all he possesses. If we are to avoid mistake in weighing one against the other, we must clearly distinguish natural liberty, which is bounded only by the strength of the individual, from civil liberty, which is limited by the general will; and possession, which is merely the effect of force or the right of the first occupier, from property, which can be founded only on a positive title.

We might, over and above all this, add, to what man acquires in the civil state, moral liberty, which alone makes him truly master of himself; for the mere impulse of appetite is slavery, while obedience to a law which we prescribe to ourselves is liberty. But I have already said too much on this head, and the philosophical meaning of the word liberty does not now concern us.

Chapter IX: Real Property

Each member of the community gives himself to it, at the moment of its foundation, just as he is, with all the resources at his command, including the goods he possesses. This act does not make possession, in changing hands, change its nature, and become property in the hands of the Sovereign; but, as the forces of the city are incomparably greater than those of an individual, public possession is also, in fact, stronger and more irrevocable, without being any more legitimate, at any rate from the point of view of foreigners. For the State, in relation to its members, is master of all their goods by the social contract, which, within the State, is the basis of all rights; but, in relation to other powers, it is so only by the right of the first occupier, which it holds from its members.

The right of the first occupier, though more real than the right of the strongest, becomes a real right only when the right of property has already been established. Every man has naturally a right to everything he needs; but the positive act which makes him proprietor of one thing excludes him from everything else. Having his share, he ought to keep to it, and can have no further right against the community. This is why the right of the first occupier, which in the state of nature is so weak, claims the respect of every man in civil society. In this right we are respecting not so much what belongs to another as what does not belong to ourselves.

In general, to establish the right of the first occupier over a plot of ground, the following conditions are necessary: first, the land must not yet be inhabited; secondly, a man must occupy only the amount he needs for his subsistence; and, in the third place, possession must be taken, not by an empty ceremony, but by labour and cultivation, the only sign of proprietorship that should be respected by others, in default of a legal title.

In granting the right of first occupancy to necessity and labour, are we not really stretching it as far as it can go? Is it possible to leave such a right unlimited? Is it to be enough to set foot on a plot of common ground, in order to be able to call yourself at once the master of it? Is it to be enough that a man has the strength to expel others for a moment, in order to establish his right to prevent them from ever returning? How can a man or a people seize an immense territory and keep it from the rest of the world except by a punishable usurpation, since all others are being robbed, by such an act, of the place of habitation and the means of subsistence which nature gave them in common? When Nunez Balboa, standing on the sea-shore, took possession of the South Seas and the whole of South America in the name of the crown of Castile, was that enough to dispossess all their actual inhabitants, and to shut out from them all the princes of the world? On such a showing, these ceremonies are idly multiplied, and the Catholic King need only take possession all at once, from his apartment, of the whole universe, merely making a subsequent reservation about what was already in the possession of other princes.

We can imagine how the lands of individuals, where they were contiguous and came to be united, became the public territory, and how the right of Sovereignty, extending from the subjects over the lands they held, became at once real and personal. The possessors were thus made more dependent, and the forces at their command used to guarantee their fidelity. The advantage of this does not seem to have been felt by ancient monarchs, who called themselves Kings of the Persians, Scythians, or Macedonians, and seemed to regard themselves more as rulers of men than as masters of a country. Those of the present day more cleverly call themselves Kings of France, Spain, England, etc.: thus holding the land, they are quite confident of holding the inhabitants.

The peculiar fact about this alienation is that, in taking over the goods of individuals, the community, so far from despoiling them, only assures them legitimate possession, and changes usurpation into a true right and enjoyment into proprietorship. Thus the possessors, being regarded as depositaries of the public good, and having their rights respected by all the members of the State and maintained against foreign aggression by all its forces, have, by a cession which benefits both the public and still more themselves, acquired, so to speak, all that they gave up. This paradox may easily be explained by the distinction between the rights which the Sovereign and the proprietor have over the same estate, as we shall see later on.

It may also happen that men begin to unite one with another before they possess anything, and that, subsequently occupying a tract of country which is enough for all, they enjoy it in common, or share it out among themselves, either equally or according to a scale fixed by the Sovereign. However the acquisition be made, the right which each individual has to his own estate is always subordinate to the right which the community has over all: without this, there would be neither stability in the social tie, nor real force in the exercise of Sovereignty.

I shall end this chapter and this book by remarking on a fact on which the whole social system should rest: i.e., that, instead of destroying natural inequality, the fundamental compact substitutes, for such physical inequality as nature may have set up between men, an equality that is moral and legitimate, and that men, who may be unequal in strength or intelligence, become every one equal by convention and legal right.[3]

Book II

Chapter I: That Sovereignty is Inalienable

The first and most important deduction from the principles we have so far laid down is that the general will alone can direct the State according to the object for which it was instituted, i.e., the common good: for if the clashing of particular interests made the establishment of societies necessary, the agreement of these very interests made it possible. The common element in these different interests is what forms the social tie; and, were there no point of agreement between them all, no society could exist. It is solely on the basis of this common interest that every society should be governed.

I hold then that Sovereignty, being nothing less than the exercise of the general will, can never be alienated, and that the Sovereign, who is no less than a collective being, cannot be represented except by himself: the power indeed may be transmitted, but not the will.

In reality, if it is not impossible for a particular will to agree on some point with the general will, it is at least impossible for the agreement to be lasting and constant; for the particular will tends, by its very nature, to partiality, while the general will tends to equality. It is even more impossible to have any guarantee of this agreement; for even if it should always exist, it would be the effect not of art, but of chance. The Sovereign may indeed say: "I now will actually what this man wills, or at least what he says he wills"; but it cannot say: "What he wills tomorrow, I too shall will" because it is absurd for the will

to bind itself for the future, nor is it incumbent on any will to consent to anything that is not for the good of the being who wills. If then the people promises simply to obey, by that very act it dissolves itself and loses what makes it a people; the moment a master exists, there is no longer a Sovereign, and from that moment the body politic has ceased to exist.

This does not mean that the commands of the rulers cannot pass for general wills, so long as the Sovereign, being free to oppose them, offers no opposition. In such a case, universal silence is taken to imply the consent of the people. This will be explained later on.

Chapter II: That Sovereignty is Indivisible

Sovereignty, for the same reason as makes it inalienable, is indivisible; for will either is, or is not, general;[4] it is the will either of the body of the people, or only of a part of it. In the first case, the will, when declared, is an act of Sovereignty and constitutes law: in the second, it is merely a particular will, or act of magistracy—at the most a decree.

But our political theorists, unable to divide Sovereignty in principle, divide it according to its object: into force and will; into legislative power and executive power; into rights of taxation, justice and war; into internal administration and power of foreign treaty. Sometimes they confuse all these sections, and sometimes they distinguish them; they turn the Sovereign into a fantastic being composed of several connected pieces: it is as if they were making man of several bodies, one with eyes, one with arms, another with feet, and each with nothing besides. We are told that the jugglers of Japan dismember a child before the eyes of the spectators; then they throw all the members into the air one after another, and the child falls down alive and whole. The conjuring tricks of our political theorists are very like that; they first dismember the Body politic by an illusion worthy of a fair, and then join it together again we know not how.

This error is due to a lack of exact notions concerning the Sovereign authority, and to taking for parts of it what are only emanations from it. Thus, for example, the acts of declaring war and making peace have been regarded as acts of Sovereignty; but this is not the case, as these acts do not constitute law, but merely the application of a law, a particular act which decides how the law applies, as we shall see clearly when the idea attached to the word *law* has been defined.

If we examined the other divisions in the same manner, we should find that, whenever Sovereignty seems to be divided, there is an illusion: the rights which are taken as being part of Sovereignty are really all subordinate, and always imply supreme wills of which they only sanction the execution. . . .

Chapter III: Whether the General Will Is Fallible

It follows from what has gone before that the general will is always right and tends to the public advantage; but it does not follow that the deliberations of the people are always equally correct. Our will is always for our own good, but we do not always see what that is; the people is never corrupted, but it is often deceived, and on such occasions only does it seem to will what is bad.

There is often a great deal of difference between the will of all and the general will; the latter considers only the common interest, while the former takes private interest into account, and is no more than a sum of particular wills: but take away from these same wills the pluses and minuses that cancel one another,[5] and the general will remains as the sum of the differences.

If, when the people, being furnished with adequate information, held its deliberations, the citizens had no communication one with another, the grand total of the small differences would always give the general will, and the decision would always be good. But when factions arise, and partial associations are formed at the expense of the great association, the will of each of these associations becomes general in relation to its members, while it remains particular in relation to the State: it may then be said that there are no longer as many votes as there are men, but only as many as there are associations. The differences become less numerous and give a less general result. Lastly, when one of these associations is so great as to prevail over all

the rest, the result is no longer a sum of small differences, but a single difference; in this case there is no longer a general will, and the opinion which prevails is purely particular.

It is therefore essential, if the general will is to be able to express itself, that there should be no partial society within the State, and that each citizen should think only his own thoughts:[6] which was indeed the sublime and unique system established by the great Lycurgus. But if there are partial societies, it is best to have as many as possible and to prevent them from being unequal, as was done by Solon, Numa and Servius. These precautions are the only ones that can guarantee that the general will shall be always enlightened, and that the people shall in no way deceive itself.

Chapter IV: The Limits of the Sovereign Power

If the State is a moral person whose life is in the union of its members, and if the most important of its cares is the care for its own preservation, it must have a universal and compelling force, in order to move and dispose each part as may be most advantageous to the whole. As nature gives each man absolute power over all his members, the social compact gives the body politic absolute power over all its members also; and it is this power which, under the direction of the general will, bears, as I have said, the name of Sovereignty.

But, besides the public person, we have to consider the private persons composing it, whose life and liberty are naturally independent of it. We are bound then to distinguish clearly between the respective rights of the citizens and the Sovereign,[7] and between the duties the former have to fulfill as subjects, and the natural rights they should enjoy as men.

Each man alienates, I admit, by the social compact, only such part of his powers, goods and liberty as it is important for the community to control; but it must also be granted that the Sovereign is sole judge of what is important.

Every service a citizen can render the State he ought to render as soon as the Sovereign demands it; but the Sovereign, for its part, cannot impose upon its subjects any fetters that are useless to the community, nor can it even wish to do so; for no more by the law of reason than by the law of nature can anything occur without a cause.

The undertakings which bind us to the social body are obligatory only because they are mutual; and their nature is such that in fulfilling them we cannot work for others without working for ourselves. Why is it that the general will is always in the right, and that all continually will the happiness of each one, unless it is because there is not a man who does not think of "each" as meaning him, and consider himself in voting for all? This proves that equality of rights and the idea of justice which such equality creates originate in the preference each man gives to himself, and accordingly in the very nature of man. It proves that the general will, to be really such, must be general in its object as well as its essence; that it must both come from all and apply to all; and that it loses its natural rectitude when it is directed to some particular and determinate object, because in such a case we are judging of something foreign to us, and have no true principle of equity to guide us.

Indeed, as soon as a question of particular fact or right arises on a point not previously regulated by a general convention, the matter becomes contentious. It is a case in which the individuals concerned are one party, and the public the other, but in which I can see neither the law that ought to be followed nor the judge who ought to give the decision. In such a case, it would be absurd to propose to refer the question to an express decision of the general will, which can be only the conclusion reached by one of the parties and in consequence will be, for the other party, merely an external and particular will, inclined on this occasion to injustice and subject to error. Thus, just as a particular will cannot stand for the general will, the general will, in turn, changes its nature, when its object is particular, and, as general, cannot pronounce on a man or a fact. When, for instance, the people of Athens nominated or displaced its rulers, decreed honours to one, and imposed penalties on another, and, by a multitude of particular decrees, exercised all the functions of government indiscriminately, it had in such cases no longer a general will in the strict sense; it was acting no longer as Sovereign, but as magistrate. This will seem contrary to current views; but I must be given time to expound my own.

It should be seen from the foregoing that what makes the will general is less the number of voters than the common interest uniting them; for, under this system, each necessarily submits to the conditions he imposes on others: and this admirable agreement between interest and justice gives to the common deliberations an equitable character which at once vanishes when any particular question is discussed, in the absence of a common interest to unite and identify the ruling of the judge with that of the party.

From whatever side we approach our principle, we reach the same conclusion, that the social compact sets up among the citizens an equality of such a kind, that they all bind themselves to observe the same conditions and should therefore all enjoy the same rights. Thus, from the very nature of the compact, every act of Sovereignty, i.e., every authentic act of the general will, binds or favours all the citizens equally; so that the Sovereign recognises only the body of the nation, and draws no distinctions between those of whom it is made up. What, then, strictly speaking, is an act of Sovereignty? It is not a convention between a superior and an inferior, but a convention between the body and each of its members. It is legitimate, because based on the social contract, and equitable, because common to all; useful, because it can have no other object than the general good, and stable, because guaranteed by the public force and the supreme power. So long as the subjects have to submit only to conventions of this sort, they obey no-one but their own will; and to ask how far the respective rights of the Sovereign and the citizens extend, is to ask up to what point the latter can enter into undertakings with themselves, each with all, and all with each.

We can see from this that the sovereign power, absolute, sacred and inviolable as it is, does not and cannot exceed the limits of general conventions, and that every man may dispose at will of such goods and liberty as these conventions leave him; so that the Sovereign never has a right to lay more charges on one subject than on another, because, in that case, the question becomes particular, and ceases to be within its competency.

When these distinctions have once been admitted, it is seen to be so untrue that there is, in the social contract, any real renunciation on the part of the individuals, that the position in which they find themselves as a result of the contract is really preferable to that in which they were before. Instead of a renunciation, they have made an advantageous exchange: instead of an uncertain and precarious way of living they have got one that is better and more secure; instead of natural independence they have got liberty, instead of the power to harm others security for themselves, and instead of their strength, which others might overcome, a right which social union makes invincible. Their very life, which they have devoted to the State, is by it constantly protected; and when they risk it in the State's defence, what more are they doing than giving back what they have received from it? What are they doing that they would not do more often and with greater danger in the state of nature, in which they would inevitably have to fight battles at the peril of their lives in defence of that which is the means of their preservation? All have indeed to fight when their country needs them; but then no one has ever to fight for himself. Do we not gain something by running, on behalf of what gives us our security, only some of the risks we should have to run for ourselves, as soon as we lost it? . . .

Chapter VII: The Legislator

In order to discover the rules of society best suited to nations, a superior intelligence beholding all the passions of men without experiencing any of them would be needed. This intelligence would have to be wholly unrelated to our nature, while knowing it through and through; its happiness would have to be independent of us, and yet ready to occupy itself with ours; and lastly, it would have, in the march of time, to look forward to a distant glory, and, working in one century,

to be able to enjoy in the next.[8] It would take gods to give men laws.

What Caligula argued from the facts, Plato, in the dialogue called the *Politicus*, argued in defining the civil or kingly man, on the basis of right. But if great princes are rare, how much more so are great legislators? The former have only to follow the pattern which the latter have to lay down. The legislator is the engineer who invents the machine, the prince merely the mechanic who sets it up and makes it go. "At the birth of societies," says Montesquieu, "the rulers of Republics establish institutions, and afterwards the institutions mould the rulers."[9]

He who dares to undertake the making of a people's institutions ought to feel himself capable, so to speak, of changing human nature, of transforming each individual, who is by himself a complete and solitary whole, into part of a greater whole from which he in a manner receives his life and being; of altering man's constitution for the purpose of strengthening it; and of substituting a partial and moral existence for the physical and independent existence nature has conferred on us all. He must, in a word, take away from man his own resources and give him instead new ones alien to him, and incapable of being made use of without the help of other men. The more completely these natural resources are annihilated, the greater and the more lasting are those which he acquires, and the more stable and perfect the new institutions; so that if each citizen is nothing and can do nothing without the rest, and the resources acquired by the whole are equal or superior to the aggregate of the resources of all the individuals, it may be said that legislation is at the highest possible point of perfection.

The legislator occupies in every respect an extraordinary position in the State. If he should do so by reason of his genius, he does so no less by reason of his office, which is neither magistracy, nor Sovereignty. This office, which sets up the Republic, nowhere enters into its constitution; it is an individual and superior function, which has nothing in common with human empire; for if he who holds command over men ought not to have command over the laws, he who has command over the laws ought not any more to have it over men; or else his laws would be the ministers of his passions and would often merely serve to perpetuate his injustices: his private aims would inevitably mar the sanctity of his work.

When Lycurgus gave laws to his country, he began by resigning the throne. It was the custom of most Greek towns to entrust the establishment of their laws to foreigners. The Republics of modern Italy in many cases followed this example; Geneva did the same and profited by it.[10] Rome, when it was most prosperous, suffered a revival of all the crimes of tyranny, and was brought to the verge of destruction, because it put the legislative authority and the sovereign power into the same hands.

Nevertheless, the decemvirs themselves never claimed the right to pass any law merely on their own authority. "Nothing we propose to you," they said to the people, "can pass into law without your consent. Romans, be yourselves the authors of the laws which are to make you happy."

He, therefore, who draws up the laws has, or should have, no right of legislation, and the people cannot, even if it wishes, deprive itself of this incommunicable right, because, according to the fundamental compact, only the general will can bind the individuals, and there can be no assurance that a particular will is in conformity with the general will, until it has been put to the free vote of the people. This I have said already; but it is worth while to repeat it.

Thus in the task of legislation we find together two things which appear to be incompatible: an enterprise too difficult for human powers, and, for its execution, an authority that is no authority.

There is a further difficulty that deserves attention. Wise men, if they try to speak their language to the common herd instead of its own, cannot possibly make themselves understood. There are a thousand kinds of ideas which it is impossible to translate into popular language. Conceptions that are too general and objects that are too remote are equally out of its range: each individual, having no taste for any other plan of government than that which suits his particular interest, finds it difficult to realise the advantages he might hope to draw from the continual privations good laws impose. For a young people to be able to relish sound principles of political theory and follow the fundamental rules of statecraft, the effect would have to become the cause; the social spirit, which should be created by these institutions, would have to preside over their very foundation; and men would have to be before law what they should become by means of law. The legislator therefore, being unable to appeal to either force or reason, must have recourse to an authority of a different order, capable of constraining without violence and persuading without convincing.

This is what has, in all ages, compelled the fathers of nations to have recourse to divine intervention and credit the gods with their own wisdom, in order that the peoples, submitting to the laws of the State as to those of nature, and recognising the same power in the formation of the city as in that of man, might obey freely, and bear with docility the yoke of the public happiness.

This sublime reason, far above the range of the common herd, is that whose decisions the legislator puts into the mouth of the immortals, in order to constrain by divine authority those whom human prudence could not move.[11] But it is not anybody who can make the gods speak, or get himself believed when he proclaims himself their interpreter. The great soul of the legislator is the only miracle that can prove his mission. Any man may grave tablets of stone, or buy an oracle, or feign secret intercourse with some divinity, or train a bird to whisper in his ear, or find other vulgar ways of imposing on the people. He whose knowledge goes no further may perhaps gather round him a band of fools; but he will never found an empire, and his extravagances will quickly perish with him. Idle tricks form a passing tie; only wisdom can make it lasting. The Judaic law, which still subsists, and that of the child of Ishmael, which, for ten centuries, has ruled half the world, still proclaim the great men who laid them down; and, while the pride of philosophy or the blind spirit of faction sees in them no more than lucky impostures, the true political theorist admires, in the institutions they set up, the great and powerful genius which presides over things made to endure.

We should not, with Warburton, conclude from this that politics and religion have among us a common object, but that, in the first periods of nations, the one is used as an instrument for the other. . . .

Book III

Chapter I: Government in General

I warn the reader that this chapter requires careful reading, and that I am unable to make myself clear to those who refuse to be attentive. Every free action is produced by the concurrence of two causes; one moral, i.e., the will which determines the act; the other physical, i.e., the power which executes it. When I walk towards an object, it is necessary first that I should will to go there, and, in the second place, that my feet should carry me. If a paralytic wills to run and an active man wills not to, they will both stay where they are. The body politic has the same motive powers; here too force and will are distinguished, will under the name of legislative power and force under that of executive power. Without their concurrence, nothing is, or should be, done.

We have seen that the legislative power belongs to the people, and can belong to it alone. It may, on the other hand, readily be seen, from the principles laid down above, that the executive power cannot belong to the generality as legislature or Sovereign, because it consists wholly of particular acts which fall outside the competency of the law, and consequently of the Sovereign, whose acts must always be laws.

The public force therefore needs an agent of its own to bind it together and set it to work under the direction of the general will, to serve as a means of communication between the State and the Sovereign, and to do for the collective person more or less what the union of soul and body does for man. Here we have what is, in the State, the basis of government, often wrongly confused with the Sovereign, whose minister it is.

What then is government? An intermediate body set up between the subjects and the Sovereign, to secure their mutual correspondence, charged with the execution of the laws and the maintenance of liberty, both civil and political.

The members of this body are called magistrates or *kings*, that is to say *governors*, and the whole body bears the name *prince*.[12] Thus those who hold that the act, by which a people puts itself under a prince, is not a contract, are certainly right. It is simply and solely a commission, an employment, in which the rulers, mere officials of the Sovereign, exercise in their own name the power of which it makes them depositaries. This power it can limit, modify or recover at pleasure; for the alienation of such a right is incompatible with the nature of the social body, and contrary to the end of association.

I call then *government*, or supreme administration, the legitimate exercise of the executive power, and prince or magistrate the man or the body entrusted with that administration.

In government reside the intermediate forces whose relations make up that of the whole to the whole, or of the Sovereign to the State. This last relation may be represented as that between the extreme terms of a continuous proportion, which has government as its mean proportional. The government gets from the Sovereign the orders it gives the people, and, for the State to be properly balanced, there must, when everything is reckoned in, be equality between the product or power of the government taken in itself, and the product or power of the citizens, who are on the one hand sovereign and on the other subject.

Furthermore, none of these three terms can be altered without the equality being instantly destroyed. If the Sovereign desires to govern, or the magistrate to give laws, or if the subjects refuse to obey, disorder takes the place of regularity, force and will no longer act together, and the State is dissolved and falls into despotism or anarchy. Lastly, as there is only one mean proportional between each relation, there is also only one good government possible for a State. But, as countless events may change the relations of a people, not only may different governments be good for different peoples, but also for the same people at different times.

In attempting to give some idea of the various relations that may hold between these two extreme terms, I shall take as an example the number of a people, which is the most easily expressible.

Suppose the State is composed of ten thousand citizens. The Sovereign can only be considered collectively and as a body; but each member, as being a subject, is regarded as an individual: thus the Sovereign is to the subject as ten thousand to one, i.e., each member of the State has as his share only a ten-thousandth part of the sovereign authority, although he is wholly under its control. If the people numbers a hundred thousand, the condition of the subject undergoes no change, and each equally is under the whole authority of the laws, while his vote, being reduced to a hundred-thousandth part, has ten times less influence in drawing them up. The subject therefore remaining always a unit, the relation between him and the Sovereign increases with the number of the citizens. From this it follows that, the larger the State, the less the liberty.

When I say the relation increases, I mean that it grows more unequal. Thus the greater it is in the geometrical sense, the less relation there is in the ordinary sense of the word. In the former sense, the relation, considered according to quantity, is expressed by the quotient; in the latter, considered according to identity, it is reckoned by similarity.

Now, the less relation the particular wills have to the general will, that is, morals and manners to laws, the more should the repressive force be increased. The government, then, to be good, should be proportionately stronger as the people is more numerous.

On the other hand, as the growth of the State gives the depositaries of the public authority more temptations and chances of abusing their power, the greater the force with which the government ought to be endowed for keeping the people in hand, the greater too should be the force at the disposal of the Sovereign for keeping the government in hand. I am speaking, not of absolute force, but of the relative force of the different parts of the State.

It follows from this double relation that the continuous proportion between the Sovereign, the prince and the people, is by no means an arbitrary idea, but a necessary consequence of the nature of the body politic. It follows further that, one of the extreme terms, viz., the people, as subject, being fixed and represented by unity, whenever the duplicate ratio increases or diminishes, the simple ratio does the same, and is changed accordingly. From this we see that there is not a single unique and absolute form of government, but as many governments differing in nature as there are States differing in size.

If, ridiculing this system, any one were to say that, in order to find the mean proportional and give form to the body of the government, it is only necessary, according to me, to find the square root of the number of the people, I should answer that I am here taking this number only as an instance; that the relations of which I am speaking are not measured by the number of men alone, but generally by the amount of action, which is a combination of a multitude of causes; and that, further, if, to save words, I borrow for a moment the terms of geometry, I am none the less well aware that moral quantities do not allow of geometrical accuracy.

The government is on a small scale what the body politic which includes it is on a great one. It is a moral person endowed with certain faculties, active like the Sovereign and passive like the State, and capable of being resolved into other similar relations. This accordingly gives rise to a new proportion, within which there is yet another, according to the arrangement of the magistracies, till an indivisible middle term is reached, i.e., a single ruler or supreme magistrate, who may be represented, in the midst of this progression, as the unity between the fractional and the ordinal series.

Without encumbering ourselves with this multiplication of terms, let us rest content with regarding government as a new body within the State, distinct from the people and the Sovereign, and intermediate between them.

There is between these two bodies this essential difference, that the State exists by itself, and the government only through the

Sovereign. Thus the dominant will of the prince is, or should be, nothing but the general will or the law; his force is only the public force concentrated in his hands, and, as soon as he tries to base any absolute and independent act on his own authority, the tie that binds the whole together begins to be loosened. If finally the prince should come to have a particular will more active than the will of the Sovereign, and should employ the public force in his hands in obedience to this particular will, there would be, so to speak, two Sovereigns, one rightful and the other actual, the social union would evaporate instantly, and the body politic would be dissolved.

However, in order that the government may have a true existence and a real life distinguishing it from the body of the State, and in order that all its members may be able to act in concert and fulfill the end for which it was set up, it must have a particular personality, a sensibility common to its members, and a force and will of its own making for its preservation. This particular existence implies assemblies, councils, power and deliberation and decision, rights, titles, and privileges belonging exclusively to the prince and making the office of magistrate more honourable in proportion as it is more troublesome. The difficulties lie in the manner of so ordering this subordinate whole within the whole, that it in no way alters the general constitution by affirmation of its own, and always distinguishes the particular force it possesses, which is destined to aid in its preservation, from the public force, which is destined to the preservation of the State; and, in a word, is always ready to sacrifice the government to the people, and never to sacrifice the people to the government.

Furthermore, although the artificial body of the government is the work of another artificial body, and has, we may say, only a borrowed and subordinate life, this does not prevent it from being able to act with more or less vigour or promptitude, or from being, so to speak, in more or less robust health. Finally, without departing directly from the end for which it was instituted, it may deviate more or less from it, according to the manner of its constitution.

From all these differences arise the various relations which the government ought to bear to the body of the State, according to the accidental and particular relations by which the State itself is modified, for often the government that is best in itself will become the most pernicious, if the relations in which it stands have altered according to the defects of the body politic to which it belongs.

Chapter II: The Constituent Principle in the Various Forms of Government

To set forth the general cause of the above differences, we must here distinguish between government and its principle, as we did before between the State and the Sovereign.

The body of the magistrate may be composed of a greater or a less number of members. We said that the relation of the Sovereign to the subjects was greater in proportion as the people was more numerous, and, by a clear analogy, we may say the same of the relation of the government to the magistrates.

But the total force of the government, being always that of the State, is invariable; so that, the more of this force it expends on its own members, the less it has left to employ on the whole people.

The more numerous the magistrates, therefore, the weaker the government. This principle being fundamental, we must do our best to make it clear.

In the person of the magistrate we can distinguish three essentially different wills: first, the private will of the individual, tending only to his personal advantage; secondly, the common will of the magistrates, which is relative solely to the advantage of the prince, and may be called corporate will, being general in relation to the government, and particular in relation to the State, of which the government forms part; and, in the third place, the will of the people or the sovereign will, which is general both in relation to the State regarded as the whole, and to the government regarded as a part of the whole.

In a perfect act of legislation, the individual or particular will should be at zero; the corporate will belonging to the government should occupy a very subordinate position; and, consequently, the general or sovereign will should always predominate and should be the sole guide of all the rest.

According to the natural order, on the other hand, these different wills become more active in proportion as they are concentrated. Thus, the general will is always the weakest, the corporate will second, and the individual will strongest of all: so that, in the government, each member is first of all himself, then a magistrate, and then a citizen—in an order exactly the reverse of what the social system requires.

This granted, if the whole government is in the hands of one man, the particular and the corporate will are wholly united, and consequently the latter is at its highest possible degree of intensity. But, as the use to which the force is put depends on the degree reached by the will, and as the absolute force of the government is invariable, it follows that the most active government is that of one man.

Suppose, on the other hand, we unite the government with the legislative authority, and make the Sovereign prince also, and all the citizens so many magistrates: then the corporate will, being confounded with the general will, can possess no greater activity than that will, and must leave the particular will as strong as it can possibly be. Thus, the government, having always the same absolute force, will be at the lowest point of its relative force or activity.

These relations are incontestable, and there are other considerations which still further confirm them. We can see, for instance, that each magistrate is more active in the body to which he belongs than each citizen in that to which he belongs, and that consequently the particular will has much more influence on the acts of the government than on those of the Sovereign; for each magistrate is almost always charged with some governmental function, while each citizen, taken singly, exercises no function of Sovereignty. Furthermore, the bigger the State grows, the more its real force increases, though not in direct proportion to its growth; but, the State remaining the same, the number of magistrates may increase to any extent, without the government gaining any greater real force; for its force is that of the State, the dimension of which remains equal. Thus the relative force or activity of the government decreases, while its absolute or real force cannot increase.

Moreover, it is a certainty that promptitude in execution diminishes as more people are put in charge of it: where prudence is made too much of, not enough is made of fortune; opportunity is let slip, and deliberation results in the loss of its object.

I have just proved that the government grows remiss in proportion as the number of the magistrates increases; and I previously proved that, the more numerous the people, the greater should be the repressive force. From this it follows that the relation of the magistrates to the government should vary inversely to the relation of the subjects to the Sovereign; that is to say, the larger the State, the more should the government be tightened, so that the number of the rulers diminish in proportion to the increase of that of the people.

It should be added that I am here speaking of the relative strength of the government, and not of its rectitude: for, on the other hand, the more numerous the magistracy, the nearer the corporate will comes to the general will; while, under a single magistrate, the corporate will is, as I said, merely a particular will. Thus, what may be gained on one side is lost on the other, and the art of the legislator is to know how to fix the point at which the force and the will of the government, which are always in inverse proportion, meet in the relation that is most to the advantage of the State.

Chapter III: The Division of Governments

We saw in the last chapter what causes the various kinds or forms of government to be distinguished according to the number of the members composing them: it remains in this to discover how the division is made.

In the first place, the Sovereign may commit the charge of the government to the whole people or to the majority of the people, so that more citizens are magistrates than are mere private individuals. This form of government is called *democracy*.

Or it may restrict the government to a small number, so that there are more private citizens than magistrates; and this is named *aristocracy.*

Lastly, it may concentrate the whole government in the hands of a single magistrate from whom all others hold their power. This third form is the most usual, and is called *monarchy,* or royal government.

It should be remarked that all these forms, or at least the first two, admit of degree, and even of very wide differences; for democracy may include the whole people, or may be restricted to half. Aristocracy, in its turn, may be restricted indefinitely from half the people down to the smallest possible number. Even royalty is susceptible of a measure of distribution. Sparta always had two kings, as its constitution provided; and the Roman Empire saw as many as eight emperors at once, without it being possible to say that the Empire was split up. Thus there is a point at which each form of government passes into the next, and it becomes clear that, under three comprehensive denominations, government is really susceptible of as many diverse forms as the State has citizens.

There are even more: for, as the government may also, in certain aspects, be subdivided into other parts, one administered in one fashion and one in another, the combination of the three forms may result in a multitude of mixed forms, each of which admits of multiplication by all the simple forms.

There has been at all times much dispute concerning the best form of government, without consideration of the fact that each is in some cases the best, and in others the worst.

If, in the different States, the number of supreme magistrates should be in inverse ratio to the number of citizens, it follows that, generally, democratic government suits small States, aristocratic government those of middle size, and monarchy great ones. This rule is immediately deducible from the principle laid down. But it is impossible to count the innumerable circumstances which may furnish exceptions. . . .

Book IV

Chapter I: That the General Will Is Indestructible

As long as several men in assembly regard themselves as a single body, they have only a single will which is concerned with their common preservation and general well-being. In this case, all the springs of the State are vigorous and simple and its rules clear and luminous; there are no embroilments or conflicts of interests; the common good is everywhere clearly apparent, and only good sense is needed to perceive it. Peace, unity and equality are the enemies of political subtleties. Men who are upright and simple are difficult to deceive because of their simplicity; lures and ingenious pretexts fail to impose upon them, and they are not even subtle enough to be dupes. When, among the happiest people in the world, bands of peasants are seen regulating affairs of State under an oak, and always acting wisely, can we help scorning the ingenious methods of other nations, which make themselves illustrious and wretched with so much art and mystery?

A State so governed needs very few laws; and, as it becomes necessary to issue new ones, the necessity is universally seen. The first man to propose them merely says what all have already felt, and there is no question of factions or intrigues or eloquence in order to secure the passage into law of what every one has already decided to do, as soon as he is sure that the rest will act with him.

Theorists are led into error because, seeing only States that have been from the beginning wrongly constituted, they are struck by the impossibility of applying such a policy to them. They make great game of all the absurdities a clever rascal or an insinuating speaker might get the people of Paris or London to believe. They do not know that Cromwell would have been put to "the bells" by the people of Berne, and the Duc de Beaufort on the treadmill by the Genevese.

But when the social bond begins to be relaxed and the State to grow weak, when particular interests begin to make themselves felt and the smaller societies to exercise an influence over the larger, the common interest changes and finds opponents: opinion is no longer unanimous; the general will ceases to be the will of all; contradictory views and debates arise; and the best advice is not taken without question.

Finally, when the State, on the eve of ruin, maintains only a vain, illusory and formal existence, when in every heart the social bond is broken, and the meanest interest brazenly lays hold of the sacred name of "public good," the general will becomes mute: all men, guided by secret motives, no more give their views as citizens than if the State had never been; and iniquitous decrees directed solely to private interest get passed under the name of laws.

Does it follow from this that the general will is exterminated or corrupted? Not at all: it is always constant, unalterable and pure; but it is subordinated to other wills which encroach upon its sphere. Each man, in detaching his interest from the common interest, sees clearly that he cannot entirely separate them; but his share in the public mishaps seems to him negligible beside the exclusive good he aims at making his own. Apart from this particular good, he wills the general good in his own interest, as strongly as any one else. Even in selling his vote for money, he does not extinguish in himself the general will, but only eludes it. The fault he commits is that of changing the state of the question, and answering something different from what he is asked. Instead of saying, by his vote, "It is to the advantage of the State," he says, "It is of advantage to this or that man or party that this or that view should prevail." Thus the law of public order in assemblies is not so much to maintain in them the general will as to secure that the question be always put to it, and the answer always given by it.

I could here set down many reflections on the simple right of voting in every act of Sovereignty—a right which no one can take from the citizens—and also on the right of stating views, making proposals, dividing and discussing, which the government is always most careful to leave solely to its members, but this important subject would need a treatise to itself, and it is impossible to say everything in a single work.

Notes

1. The Romans, who understood and respected the right of war more than any other nation on earth, carried their scruples on this head so far that a citizen was not allowed to serve as a volunteer without engaging himself expressly against the enemy, and against such and such an enemy by name. A legion in which the younger Cato was seeing his first service under Popilius having been reconstructed, the elder Cato wrote to Popilius that, if he wished his son to continue serving under him, he must administer to him a new military oath, because, the first having been annulled, he was no longer able to bear arms against the enemy. The same Cato wrote to his son telling him to take great care not to go into battle before taking this new oath. I know that the siege of Clusium and other isolated events can be quoted against me; but I am citing laws and customs. The Romans are the people that least often transgressed its laws; and no other people has had such good ones.

2. The real meaning of this word has been almost wholly lost in modern times; most people mistake a town for a city, and a townsman for a citizen. They do not know that houses make a town, but citizens a city. The same mistake long ago cost the Carthaginians dear[ly]. I have never read of the title of citizens being given to the subjects of any prince, not even the ancient Macedonians or the English of to-day, though they are nearer liberty than any one else. The French alone everywhere familiarly adopt the name of citizens, because, as can be seen from their dictionaries, they have no idea of its meaning; otherwise they would be guilty in usurping it, of the crime of *lèse-majesté*: among them, the name expresses a virtue, and not a right. When Bodin spoke of our citizens and townsmen, he fell into a bad blunder in taking the one class for the other. M. d'Alembert has avoided the error, and, in his article on Geneva, has clearly distinguished the four orders of men (or even five, counting mere foreigners) who dwell in our town, of which two only compose the Republic. No other French writer, to my knowledge, has understood the real meaning of the word citizen.

3. Under bad governments, this equality is only apparent and illusory: it serves only to keep the pauper in his poverty and the rich man in the position he has usurped. In fact, laws are always of use to those who possess and harm-

ful to those who have nothing: from which it follows that the social state is advantageous to men only when all have something and none too much.

4. To be general, a will need not always be unanimous; but every vote must be counted: any exclusion is a breach of generality.

5. "Every interest," says the Marquis d'Argenson, "has different principles. The agreement of two particular interests is formed by opposition to a third." He might have added that the agreement of all interests is formed by opposition to that of each. If there were no different interests, the common interest would be barely felt, as it would encounter no obstacle; all would go on of its own accord, and politics would cease to be an art.

6. "In fact," says Machiavelli, "there are some divisions that are harmful to a Republic and some that are advantageous. Those which stir up sects and parties are harmful; those attended by neither are advantageous. Since, then, the founder of a Republic cannot help enmities arising, he ought at least to prevent them from growing into sects" (*History of Florence*, Book vii).

7. Attentive readers, do not, I pray, be in a hurry to charge me with contradicting myself. The terminology made it unavoidable, considering the poverty of the language; but wait and see.

8. A people becomes famous only when its legislation begins to decline. We do not know for how many centuries the system of Lycurgus made the Spartans happy before the rest of Greece took any notice of it.

9. Montesquieu, *The Greatness and Decadence of the Romans*, ch. i.

10. Those who know Calvin only as a theologian much under-estimate the extent of his genius. The codification of our wise edicts, in which he played a large part, does him no less honour than his *Institute*. Whatever revolution time may bring in our religion, so long as the spirit of patriotism and liberty still lives among us, the memory of this great man will be for ever blessed.

11. "In truth," says Machiavelli, "there has never been, in any country, an extraordinary legislator who has not had recourse to God; for otherwise his laws would not have been accepted: there are, in fact, many useful truths of which a wise man may have knowledge without their having in themselves such clear reasons for their being so as to be able to convince others" (*Discourses on Livy*, Bk. v, ch. xi).

12. Thus at Venice the College, even in the absence of the Doge, is called "Most Serene Prince."

Adapted from: Jean-Jacques Rousseau, *On the Social Contract*, translated by G. D. H. Cole, pp. 5–6, 8–24, 25–30, 35–38, 49–57, 90–92. Originally published by E. P. Dutton, 1913. ✦

13
Rousseau's General Will

Freedom of a Particular Kind

Patrick Riley

Rousseau's Reasons for Using 'the General Will'

Rousseau's reasons for using 'general will' as his central political concept were essentially philosophical, however ready-made for his purposes the seventeenth-century theological notion may have been. (Does not the Spartan mother have a *volonté générale* to 'save' the city, as God has a general will to save 'all men'?) After all, the two terms of *volonté générale*—'will' and 'generality'—represent two main strands in Rousseau's thought. Generality stands, *inter alia,* for the rule of law, for civic education that draws us out of ourselves and toward the general (or common) good, for the non-particularist citizen-virtues of Sparta and republican Rome.[1] Will stands for Rousseau's conviction that civil association is 'the most voluntary act in the world', that 'to deprive your will of all freedom is to deprive your actions of all morality'.[2] If one could generalize the will, so that it elects only law, citizenship and the common good, and avoids wilful self-love, then one would have a general will in Rousseau's particular sense. The originally divine *volonté générale* of Pascal, Malebranche, Fénelon and Leibniz corresponded closely to these moral aims; hence why not employ a term already rendered politically usable by Bayle?[3]

It is scarcely open to doubt, indeed, that the notions of *will* and *generality* are equally essential in Rousseau's moral and political philosophy. Without will there is no free-dom, no self-determination, no 'moral causality',[4] no obligation; without generality the will may be capricious, egoistic, self-obsessed, wilful.

Rousseau shared with modern individualist thinkers (notably Hobbes and Locke) the conviction that all political life is conventional, that it can be made obligatory only through voluntary, individual consent. Despite the fact that he sometimes treats moral ideas as if they simply 'arise' in a developmental process, in the course of socialization,[5] he often—particularly in his contractarian vein—falls back on the view that the wills of free men are the 'causes' of duties and of legitimate authority. Thus in an argument against slavery in *Du contrat social,* Rousseau urges that 'to deprive your will of all freedom' is to deprive your actions of 'all morality'. The reason one can derive no notion of right or morality from mere force is that 'to yield to force is an act of necessity, not of will'.[6] (This shows in advance how carefully one must interpret the *deliberately* paradoxical phrase, 'forced to be free'.) In a passage that almost prefigures Kant, he insists on the importance of free agency, arguing that while natural science might explain the 'mechanism of the senses', it could never make intelligible 'the power of willing or rather of choosing'—a power in which 'nothing is to be found but acts which are purely spiritual and wholly inexplicable by the laws of mechanism'.[7] It is this power of freely willing, rather than reason, which distinguishes men from beasts. He had even said that 'every free action has two causes which concur to produce it: the first a moral cause, namely the will which determines the act; the other physical, namely the power which executes it'.[8] Rousseau, then, not only requires the Kant-anticipating idea of will as moral causality, he actually uses that term.

All of this is confirmed by what Rousseau says about will in *Émile,* in which he argues that 'the motive power of all action is in the will of a free creature', that 'it is not the word freedom that is meaningless, but the word necessity'. The will is 'independent of my senses': I 'consent or resist, I yield or I win the victory, and I know very well in myself when I have done what I wanted and when I have merely given way to my passions'. Man, he concludes, is 'free to act', and he 'acts of his own accord'.[9] Moreover, human free will does not derogate from Providence but magnifies it, since God has 'made man of so excellent a nature, that he has endowed his actions with that morality by which they are enobled'. Rousseau cannot agree with those theologians (for example Hobbes) who argue that human freedom would diminish God by robbing him of his omnipotence.

> Providence has made man free that he may choose the good and refuse the evil . . . what more could divine power itself have done on our behalf? Could it have made our nature a contradiction and have given the prize of well-doing to one who was incapable of evil? To prevent a man from wickedness, should Providence have restricted him to instinct and made him a fool?[10]

To be sure, the pre-Kantian voluntarism of *Émile* and *Inégalité* is not the whole story. Even in the *Lettres morales* (1757), which were used as a quarry in writing *Émile*, the relation of free will to morality is complicated and problematical. The opening of the fifth *Lettre*—'the whole morality of human life is in the intention of man[11]—seems at first to be a voluntarist claim, almost prefiguring Kant's notion that a 'good will' is the only 'unqualifiedly' good thing on earth.[12] But this intention refers not to the 'will' of *Émile*, but rather to 'conscience'—which is a 'divine instinct' and an 'immortal and heavenly voice'. Rousseau, after a striking passage on moral feelings ('if one sees . . . some act of violence or injustice, a movement of anger and indignation arises at once in our heart'), goes on to speak of feelings of 'remorse' which 'punish hidden crimes in secret'; and this 'importunate voice' he calls an involuntary feeling which 'torments' us. That the phrase is not a mere slip of the pen or of the mind is proven by Rousseau's deliberate repetition of 'involuntary':

> Thus there is, at the bottom of all souls, an innate principle of justice and of moral truth [which is] prior to all national prejudices, to all maxims of education. This principle is the involuntary rule by which, despite our own maxims, we

judge our actions, and those of others, as good or bad; and it is to this principle that I give the name conscience.

Conscience, then, is an involuntary moral feeling—not surprisingly, given Rousseau's view that 'our feeling is incontestably prior to our reason itself'.[13] So, while the fifth *Lettre morale* opens with an apparent anticipation of *Émile*'s voluntarism, this is only an appearance which proves that it is not straightforwardly right to find in Rousseau a predecessor of Kant. Rousseau's *morale sensitive* is not easy to reconcile with rational self-determination, for if Rousseau says that 'to deprive your will of all freedom is to deprive your actions of all morality', he also says that conscience is a feeling which is involuntary.

The fact remains, however, that while *Émile* was published, the *Lettres morales* were held back. In *Émile*, Rousseau insists on the moral centrality of free will: so much for the supposed 'Calvinism' of one who was often closer to being a Pelagian—as Pascal would have pointed out.[14] Hence Rousseau can understand 'will' as an independent moral causality with the power to produce moral effects. He definitely thought that he had derived political obligation and rightful political authority from this power of willing: 'Civil association is the most voluntary act in the world, since every individual is born free and his own master, no one is able, on any pretext whatsoever, to subject him without his consent'. Indeed the first four chapters of *Du contrat social* are devoted to refutations of erroneous theories of obligation and right—paternal authority, the 'right of the strongest', and obligations derived from slavery. 'Since no man', Rousseau concludes, 'has natural authority over his fellow men, and since might in no sense makes right, [voluntary] convention remains as the basis of legitimate authority among men'.[15]

Even if 'will' is plainly a central moral, political and theological notion in Rousseau, this does not mean that he was willing to settle for just any will, such as a particular will or a wilful will. His constant aim, indeed, is to 'generalize' will[16]—either through civic education, as in the *Gouvernement de Pologne*, or through private education, as in

Émile. In his view, ancient societies such as Sparta and Rome had been particularly adept at generalizing human will: through their simplicity, their morality of the common good, their civic religion, their moral use of fine and military arts, and their lack of extreme individualism and private interest, the city-states of antiquity had been political societies in the proper sense. In them man had been part of a greater whole from which he 'in a sense receives his life and being';[17] on the other hand, modern 'prejudices', 'base philosophy' and 'passions of petty self-interest' assure that 'we moderns can no longer find in ourselves anything of that spiritual vigour which was inspired in the ancients by everything they did'.[18] And that 'spiritual vigour' may be taken to mean the avoidance—through identity with a greater whole—of 'that dangerous disposition which gives rise to all our vices', self-love. Political education in an extremely unified ('generalized') state will 'lead us out of ourselves' and provide us with a general will before the human ego 'has acquired that contemptible activity which absorbs all virtue and constitutes the life and being of little minds'.[19] It follows that the best social institutions are those best able to denature man, to take away his absolute existence and to give him a relative one, and to carry the *moi* into the common unity'.[20]

If these reflections on the pernicious character of self-love and particularism are reminiscent of Malebranche—who had urged that 'to act by *volontés particulières* shows a limited intelligence',[21] and whose love or divine *généralité* had led Rousseau to rank the great Oratorian Father with Plato and Locke[22]—it is in contrasting Rousseau with Malebranche that an important difficulty arises. In Malebranche, God's will is essentially and naturally general; in Rousseau, men's will must be *made* general—a problem which he likens (in the correspondence with Malesherbes) to that of squaring the circle.[23] But one can reasonably ask: is will still 'will' (*qua* independent 'moral cause') if it must be denatured, transformed? Do Rousseau's notions of education—private and civic—leave will as the autonomous producer of moral 'effects' that he seems to want? One is tempted to say that this is *the* question for

one who wants *volonté* and *généralité* to fuse—so that (at the end of time) a perfect '*union* of will and understanding' will synthesize (Lockean) 'voluntary agreement' and (Platonic) generalizing education, will blend antiquity ('Sparta') and modernity ('contract') in this 'modern who has an ancient soul'.[24]

To retain the moral attributes of free will while doing away with will's particularity and selfishness and 'wilfulness'—to generalize this, moral 'cause' without causing its destruction—is perhaps the central problem in Rousseau's political, moral and educational thought, and one which reflects the difficulty Rousseau found in making free will and rational, educative authority coexist in his practical thought. Freedom of the will is as important to the morality of actions for Rousseau as for any voluntarist coming after Augustine's insistence that *bona voluntas* alone is good;[25] but Rousseau was suspicious of the very 'faculty'—the only faculty—that could moralize. Thus he urges that 'the most absolute authority is that which penetrates into a man's inmost being, and concerns itself with his will no less than with his actions'.[26] Can the will be both an autonomous 'moral cause' and subject to the rationalizing, generalizing effect of educative authority? This is Rousseau's constant difficulty. Even Émile, the best-educated of men, chooses to continue to accept the guidance of his teacher: 'Advise and control us, we shall be easily led, as long as I live I shall need you'.[27] How much more, then, do ordinary men need the guidance of a 'great legislator'—the Numa or Moses or Lycurgus of whom Rousseau speaks so often[28]—when they embark on the setting up of a system which will not only aid and defend but also moralize them! The relation of will to authority, of autonomy to educative 'shaping', is one of the most difficult problems in Rousseau. The general will is dependent on 'a union of understanding and will within the social body'.[29] But that understanding, which is provided (at least initially) by educative authority—rather than by a Kantian 'fact of reason' giving 'objective ends'—is difficult to make perfectly congruent with 'will' as an autonomous 'moral cause'.

This notion of the relation of educative authority to will appears not just in Rousseau's theories of public or civic education,[30] but also in his theory of private education in *Émile*. In educating a child, Rousseau advises the tutor, 'let him think he is master while you are really master'. And then: 'there is no subjection so complete as that which preserves the forms of freedom; it is thus that the will itself is taken captive'.[31] One can hardly help asking what has become of 'will' when it has been 'taken captive', and whether it is enough to preserve the mere 'forms' of freedom. On this point Rousseau appears to have been of two minds: the poor who 'agree' to a social contract that merely legitimizes the holdings of the rich 'preserve the forms of freedom', but Rousseau dismisses this contract as a fraud.[32] Thus it cannot be straightforwardly the case—as John Charvet argues in his remarkable Rousseau study—that the *citoyen de Génève* simply was not 'worried by the gap which opens up between the appearance and the reality of freedom'.[33] Yet Charvet has something of a point, since will is 'taken captive' in *Émile* and 'penetrated' by authority in the *Économie politique;* and neither that captivity nor that penetration is criticized by Rousseau—despite his *dictum* about depriving one's actions of all morality if one deprives his will of freedom. So one sees again why a general will would appeal to him: capricious wilfulness would be 'cancelled', will rationalized by authority, 'preserved'.[34]

If will in Rousseau is generalized primarily through an educative authority, so that volition as 'moral cause' is not quite so free as he would sometimes prefer, it is at least arguable that any tension between will and the authority that 'generalizes' it is only a provisional problem. Rousseau seems to have hoped that at the end of political time (so to speak) men would finally be citizens and would will only the common good in virtue of what they had learned *over* time, at the end of civic time, they might actually be free, and not just 'forced to be free'.[35] At the end of its political education—no more 'denaturing' than any education—political society would finally be in a position to say what Émile says at the end of his 'domestic' educa-

tion: 'I have decided to be what you made me'.[36] At this point (of 'decision') there would be a 'union of understanding and will' in politics, but one in which 'understanding' is no longer the private possession of a Numa or a Lycurgus. At this point, too, 'agreement' and 'contract' would finally have real meanings: the 'general will', which is 'always right', would be enlightened as well, and contract would go beyond being the mere rich man's confidence-trick (legalizing unequal property) that it is in *Inégalité*. At the end of political time, the 'general will one has as a citizen' would have become a kind of second nature, approaching the true naturalness of *volonté générale* in Malebranche's version of the divine *modus operandi*. 'Approaching', however, is the strongest term one can use, and the relation of will to the educative authority that generalizes it remains a problem in Rousseau—the more so because he often denied (in his more Lockean moods) that there is any natural authority on earth.[37]

One can still ask: how can one reconcile Rousseau's insistence on an all-shaping educative authority with his equal insistence on free choice and personal autonomy ('civil association is the most voluntary act in the world')? A possible answer is: through his theory of education, which is the heart of his thought, the one thing which can make Rousseaueanism 'work'. At the end of civic time, when men have been denatured and transformed into citizens, they will finally have civic knowledge and a general will— just as adults finally have the moral knowledge and the independence that they (necessarily) lacked as children. For Rousseau there are unavoidable stages in all education, whether private or public: the child, he says in *Émile*, must first be taught necessity, then utility, and finally morality, in that inescapable order; and if one says 'ought' to an infant he simply reveals his own ignorance and folly. This notion of necessary educational time, of *becoming* what one was not— Aristotelian potentiality-becoming-actuality, transfered from *physis* to the *polis*—is revealed perfectly in Émile's utterance, 'I have decided to be what you made me'.[38] That is deliberately paradoxical (as many of Rousseau's central moral-political beliefs are cast in the form of paradoxes), but it shows that the capacity to 'decide' is indeed 'made'. (It is education that 'forces one to be free'—by slowly 'generalizing' the will.) Similarly. Rousseau's 'nations' are at first ignorant: 'There is with nations, as with men, a time of youth, or, if you prefer, of maturity, for which we must *wait* before subjecting them to laws'.[39] Waiting, however, requires time; autonomy arrives at the end of a process, and the general will is at last as enlightened as it was (always) right. On the most favourable reasonable reading, then, Rousseau does not, as some critics allege, vibrate incoherently between Platonic education and Lockean voluntariness;[40] if his notion of becoming-in-time works, 'then the *généralité* of antiquity and the *volonté* of modernity are truly fused by this 'modern who has an ancient soul.'

Will and Freedom in Rousseau and Kant

In the end, the 'generality' cherished by Pascal, Malebranche, Fénelon, Bayle and Rousseau turns out to occupy a place midway between *particularity* and *universality;* and that *recherche de la généralité* is something distinctively French. This becomes visible if one contrasts French moral-political *généralisme* with the thought of Kant, viewed as the perfect representative of German rationalistic universalism ('I am never to act otherwise than so that I could also will that my maxim should become a universal law ... reason extorts from me immediate respect for such [universal] legislation'[41]), and with that of William Blake, seen as a typical representative of English ethical 'empiricism':

> He who would do good to another
> must do it in Minute Particulars,
> General Good is the plea
> of the scoundrel, hypocrite and flatterer.[42]

The discovery of an *ethos* that rises above 'minute particulars', that moves toward universality but has its reasons for not building *on* reason, and for drawing up short at a more modest *généralité*—the advocacy of a kind of (free) willing that is more than egoistic and self-loving and *particulière* but less

than a Kantian, universal, 'higher' will[43]— that is the distinctively French contribution to practical thought worked out by Rousseau, who socialized the 'general will' bequeathed to him by his greatest French predecessors. The genesis of 'general will' is in God; the creation of the political concept— yielding a covenant and a law that is a mosaic of the Mosaic, the Spartan, the Roman, and Lockean—is the testament of Rousseau.

But why should Rousseau, unlike Kant, have drawn the dividing line between *généralité* and *universalité*, between the *polis* and the *cosmopolis*, between the 'citizen' and the 'person'? And why does this particular 'placing' of the line make it visibly easier for Kant to *reconcile* freedom with 'what men ought to be' than for Rousseau? Here a fuller Rousseau–Kant comparison will be helpful.

No one has ever doubted that Kant begins his moral philosophy with insistence on 'good will'[44]—that is, with the idea of a 'moral causality' (owed to Rousseau), itself independent of natural causality, which is the foundation man's freedom and responsibility. That good will is crucial to Kant's understanding of politics is quite clear. 'Public legal justice' is necessitated by the partial or total absence of a good will that would yield, if it could, a non-coercive, universal 'ethical commonwealth' (or 'kingdom of ends') under laws of virtue. Good will's absence necessitates politics' presence. The *idea* of an ethical commonwealth generated by good will serves as a kind of utopia that earthly politics can 'legally' approximate through eternal peacefulness, both internal and international.[45]

Kant was by no means the first moral philosopher to insist that a good will is the only unqualifiedly good thing on earth; on this point he simply reflects and repeats St Augustine, who argued that a *bona voluntas* is 'a will by which we seek to live a good and upright life' and that 'when anyone has a good will he really possesses something which ought to be esteemed far above all earthly kingdoms and all delights of the body'.[46] (This is remarkably 'pre-Kantian': indeed one can wonder whether Kant's kingdom of ends was not suggested by Augustine's denigration of earthly kingdoms.) But Kant, given his radical distinction between 'pathology' and morality, could not have accepted Augustine's further notion of moral 'delectation', could never have said, with Augustine, that the 'man of good will' will 'embrace' rightness as the 'object of his joy and delight'.[47] The Augustinian notion of opposing higher 'delectations' to lower ones, so that 'concupiscence' is replaced by the love of temperance, prudence, justice, ultimately *God*—by quasi-Platonic sublimated (made-sublime) erotism[48]—is alien to Kant (though not always to the Rousseau who could speak of *morale sensitive*). If, then, Kantian good will is not an Augustinian *delectio*, or 'higher' love, what is it? If it is not to be 'pathological', it must surely be the capacity to determine oneself to action through what ought to be, so that 'ought' is the complete and sufficient incentive. And if what ought to be is defined as respect for persons as members of a kingdom of ends, then Kantian good will will mean 'determining oneself to act from respect for persons'.[49] Surely this is a reasonable way to read Kant's moral philosophy; for at the outset one cannot know exactly what post-Augustinian *bona voluntas* actually involves.

If, however, good will begins in Augustinianism, Kant, in insisting on will as a kind of undetermined 'moral causality', is still more closely related to Rousseau—who, as was seen, had actually urged that '... every free action ... has a moral cause, namely the will which determines the act'.[50] And Rousseau had also insisted—in an already-examined passage from *Inégalité*—that while 'physics' might explain the senses and empirical ideas, it could never explain 'acts which are purely spiritual and wholly inexplicable by the laws of mechanism'; above all 'the power of willing or rather of choosing', and 'the feeling of this power'.[51] All of this—will as free 'moral cause', as something spiritual and not mechanically determined—Kant could and did applaud. But then Rousseau had gone on to say that one must draw a line between 'free agency' and 'understanding'; that 'if I am bound to do no injury to my fellow-creatures, this is less because they are rational than because they are sentient beings'.[52] This Kant could not accept at all. In

Kant's view, if the duty not to injure others rests on 'sentience', then one can have duties only if one feels (and sympathizes with) the pains and pleasures of sentient beings. For Kant this is a calamitous view of morality: it makes duty a mere reflection of psychological facts (feelings) that change from moment to moment.[53] Rousseau, in Kant's view, cannot have it both ways: it cannot be the case that 'will' is an independent 'moral cause' that freely determines moral acts, and the mere tip of an iceberg of feelings. For in the second case 'good will' would once again become a quasi-Augustinian *delectio;* it would not be self-determination through a rational concept (such as 'ought').

Indeed, had not Kant been so boundlessly devoted to the 'Newton of the moral world' as the moralist who had 'set him straight' and taught him to 'honour' mankind[54]—had Rousseau's thought been a mere *objet trouvé* that Kant stumbled across—he would have dealt more harshly with Rousseau. He might easily have said that Rousseau gets the concept of 'negative freedom'—not being determined by mechanism—right, but without knowing why. To use the arguments from the *Critique of Pure Reason*, negative freedom in Rousseau is not 'critically' established by showing that while *phenomena* must be understood as caused, *noumena* or 'things in themselves' are undetermined.[55] At best, from a Kantian perspective, Rousseau can offer an intuitive account of the *feeling* of freedom, as in: 'A reasoner proves to me in vain that I am not free, [for] inner feeling, stronger than all his arguments, refutes them ceaselessly.'[56] For Kant this anti-Spinozist feeling, however eloquently expressed, must yield to the 'Transcendental Deduction's' proof in *Pure Reason* that being an undetermined 'moral cause' is conceivable.[57]

But in the treatment of 'positive freedom', Rousseau is still more problematical from a Kantian point of view. For positive freedom in Kant means self-determination through an objective moral law ('ought') enjoining respect for persons-as-ends. But Rousseau (a strict Kant would say) is wholly sound neither on self-determination nor on 'ought'. He frequently undercuts real self-determination—true spontaneity or 'autonomy'—by reducing morality to a natural, 'pathological' feeling (such as sympathy), or by saying that 'conscience' is an involuntary feeling which precedes both reason and will.[58] As for 'ought', that shifts from work to work: in *Du contrat social* it is *généralité* and the avoidance of 'particularism' in one's willing;[59] in the *Profession de foi du Vicaire Savoyard* it is an 'order' that reflects the divine world order, making morality nature's 'analogue';[60] in the earlier books of *Émile* it is Stoicism or limiting one's desire's to match one's powers.[61] Only in the eighth of the *Lettres écrites de la montagne* (1764) does Rousseau get both negative and positive freedom nearly right from a Kantian perspective; there he speaks of not being determined and of not determining others.

> It is vain to confuse independence and liberty. These two things are so different that they even mutually exclude each other. When each does what pleases him, he often does something displeasing to others; and that cannot be called a free condition. Liberty consists less in doing one's will than in not being subject to that of another; it consists again in not submitting the will of another to our own. Whoever is master cannot be free, to rule is to obey.[62]

(This is one reason why the 'great legislator' does not *rule*, but only helps a people to 'find' the general will it is 'seeking'—or would seek, if it 'knew'. If the legislator were a 'master', he would not have to bend backwards to 'persuade without convincing'—so that freedom can *finally* arrive.)

One wonders whether Kant did not have this passage in mind when he said that 'Rousseau set me straight . . . I learned to honour mankind'. Rousseau's notion in *Montagne* that one should neither be subjected, nor subject others, comes closest to a Kantian 'negative' freedom which allows one 'positively' to respect persons as objective ends. But if this is Rousseau's closest approach to Kant, Kant still wanted to turn back Rousseau's claim that 'free agency' is separated from understanding or reason. Against that, Kant wanted to show that a truly free will—finally *good*, not merely *gen-*

eral—would be determined by 'practical reason' itself. That is why Kant insisted that

> Everything in nature works according to law. Rational beings alone have the faculty of acting according to the conception of laws, that is according to principles, i.e. have a will. Since the deduction of actions from principles requires reason, the will is nothing but practical reason. The will is a faculty to choose that only which reason independent of inclination recognizes as practically necessary, i.e. good.[63]

Had Rousseau (consistently) risen to this view of rational self-determination, in Kant's opinion, he would not (occasionally) have undermined his own distinction between 'physics' and free agency by reducing good will to non-rational sympathy for sentient beings. For Kant sympathy and sentience are, equally, 'pathological' feelings caused by nature;[64] that being so, one does not escape from the very 'laws of mechanism' which Rousseau himself rejected by placing a gulf (unreasonably) between reason and freedom. All of this suggests what Kant actually believed: that one cannot find a real duty in sympathy, feelings of pleasure and pain, or happiness, simply because the concept 'ought' cannot be extracted from these facts of pathology. The concept of moral necessity cannot be derived from the bare *data* of psychology.[65] Why Kant thought that 'ought' cannot be extracted from nature—even human 'nature' or psychology—he made especially clear in a quasi-Platonic passage from *Pure Reason* that is the foundation of his whole practical philosophy.

> That our reason has causality, or that we at least represent it to ourselves as having causality, is evident from the *imperatives* which in all matters of conduct we impose as rules upon our active powers. 'Ought' expresses a kind of necessity . . . which is found nowhere else in the whole of nature. The understanding can know in nature only what is, what has been, or what will be. . . . When we have the course of nature alone in view, 'ought' has no meaning whatsoever.[66]

Precisely here—and equally in *Practical Reason*'s insistence that the moral law is just there as a 'fact of reason', underivable from *anything* else (nature, custom, God)[67]—lies the gulf that separates Rousseau and Kant (anti-wilful voluntarists though they both are). If, for Rousseau, reason had 'causality', we would not stand in need of Moses' or Lycurgus' *educative* 'causality': the will would be generalized (or rather universalized) by a Kantian 'objective end' (respect for persons as members of a kingdom of ends) which is *unproblematical* for freedom because all rational beings simply 'see' that end (at the age of reason). The whole Kantian 'universalizing' operation is completely impersonal: there is no person (Lycurgus) bending backwards to be impersonal, nonauthoritarian, persuading without convincing. In Kant one is not made free (in time): one simply knows 'ought' and takes himself to be free (able to perform ought's commands) *ab initio*[68]—much as Meno's slave just 'has' astonishing geometrical knowledge.[69] Of course—and Rousseau would reasonably insist on this—Kantianism works only if there are universal reason-ordained 'objective ends' which we 'ought to have'.[70] Rousseau worried about every term in that sentence: whether we can know a *morale universalle* which is 'beyond' the *générale,* whether 'reason' ordains anything (morally), whether there are 'ends' that all rational beings 'see' (as facts of reason). Negatively, Kant and Rousseau are companions-in-flight from self-loving particular will; positively, they offer the still-viable *contrasting* possibilities once that flight is over—rational, universal, cosmopolitan morality valid for persons, versus educator-shaped, general, politan *civisme* valid for a citizen of Geneva or of Sparta. (Try to imagine Kant as citizen of Königsberg: that will measure very precisely the distance from Switzerland to Prussia.)

In advance, Rousseau treated 'Kantian' moral universalism and rationalism in his great attack on Diderot, the *Première version du contrat social*—a work in which Rousseau says, in effect: *of course* one can readily make freedom and 'what men ought to be' congruent if autonomous rational agents just 'see' the right and the good for themselves. But what if a moral or general standpoint has to be *attained* over time, through a denaturing

anti-egoism which will nonetheless finally use autonomy? That is the permanent 'Rousseau-question' which Kantians ought (suitably enough) to keep in mind—as Kant himself certainly did.

Rousseau's radical doubts about the real existence of any universal, reason-ordained morality come out most plainly and brilliantly in the *Première version*—that remarkable refutation of Diderot's *Encyclopédie* article, 'Droit naturel', arguing that there is a universal *volonté générale* of and for the entire *genre humain*, a rational *morale universelle.* Diderot had argued that 'if we deprive the individual of the right to decide about the nature of the just and the unjust', we must then 'take this great question . . . before the human race', for the 'good of all' is the 'sole passion' that this most-inclusive group has. Paralleling Rousseau (initially), Diderot goes on to say that '*volontés particulières* are suspect', for they can be indifferently good or wicked, but that 'the general will is always good', since it has never 'deceived' and never will. It is to this always-good, never-deceiving *volonté générale* 'that the individual must address himself', Diderot insists, 'in order to know how far he must be a citizen, a subject, a father, a child, and when it is suitable for him to live or to die'.[71]

So far, no great gap has opened up between Diderot and Rousseau, but when Diderot begins to indicate where the general will is *deposited*, he moves in the direction of a proto-Kantian universalism which is usually foreign to the citizen of Geneva. The general will can be 'consulted', he urges,

in the principles of the written law of all civilized nations; in the social actions of primitive and barbarous peoples; in the tacit conventions of the enemies of the human race between themselves, and even in indignation and resentment, those two passions that nature seems to have placed even in animals, to supply the defect of social laws and public vengeance.

Diderot's nominal *généralité* is in fact a *morale universelle* (to use his own term); it relates to the whole *genre humain*, and seems to extend even to 'honour among thieves'.[72]

Rousseau's *volonté générale*—of Rome, of Sparta, of Geneva—is a great deal more *particulière;* indeed in the *Gouvernement de Pologne* Rousseau insists on the importance of national peculiarities and particularities that should not be submerged in a cosmopolitan universalism.[73] For Diderot, then—as Robert Wokler has elegantly put it—the general will is to be found almost everywhere, whereas Rousseau doubts that it has ever been fully realized anywhere.[74]

In the next section of 'Droit naturel', Diderot goes on to urge—after repeating that 'the man who listens only to his *volonté particulière* is the enemy of the human race'[75]—that 'the general will is, in each individual, a pure act of the understanding which reasons in the silence of the passions about what a man can demand of his fellowman and about what his fellow-man has the right to demand of him'.[76] And it is at this very point that Diderot begins to be separated from Rousseau: the citizen of Geneva, as he styled himself, would have stressed precisely 'citizenship' and 'Geneva', and would never have urged that *volonté générale* is immediately dictated by understanding or reason (as distinguished from will-generalizing civic education). Had Rousseau thought that, the passions being 'silent' (a phrase Diderot borrows from Malebranche[77]), understanding and reason could alone dictate what is right, he would never have made his famous claim that 'the general will is always right' but 'the judgement which guides it is not always enlightened'. If reason alone dictated right (as in Kant it furnishes 'ought'), Rousseauean men would have no need of a Numa or a Moses to help effect 'a union of understanding and will'.[78]

Book 1, chapter 2 of Rousseau's *Première version* is a refutation of Diderot's rationalism and universalism; but it also provides more than a hint of what Rousseau *would* have said about Kant's distinctive way of combining 'ought' and freedom. At one time, to be sure, Rousseau had himself stressed a roughly comparable *morale universelle;* in an early, unpublished fragment called *Chronologie universelle* (c. 1737) he had appealed to Fénelon's notion of a universal Christian republic:

We are all brothers; our neighbours ought to be as dear to us as ourselves. 'I love the human race more than my country', said the illustrious M. de Fénelon, 'my country more than my family and my family more than myself'. Sentiments so full of humanity ought to be shared by all men. . . . The universe is a great family of which we are all members. . . . However extensive may be the power of an individual, he is always in a position to make himself useful . . . to the great body of which he is a part. If he can [do this], he indispensably ought to. . . .[79]

Later, of course—most clearly of all in the *Première version*—Rousseau would abandon the *universelle* in favour of the *générale* and exchange the *respublica christiana* for more modest republics: Sparta, Rome, Geneva. Indeed his great difference from Diderot—and, 'in advance', from Kant—rests precisely in the difference between the *universelle* (known to all by reason alone, in the 'silence of the passions') and the *générale* (known to citizens of a particular republic through a civic education supplied by Numa or Moses or Lycurgus). Hence Rousseau's problem with freedom: he must find an authoritative person who is neither authoritarian nor personal, who generalizes will while leaving it voluntary. Diderot and Kant, different as they are, do not have this difficulty.

That Rousseau is not going to argue for a reason-ordained *morale universelle* valid for the entire human race—whether in a late-Stoic, Diderotian, or Kantian shape—is evident in the opening sentence of the *Première version:* 'Let us begin by inquiring why the necessity for political institutions arises'.[80] If a passion-silencing reason spoke to and governed all men, no mere particular political institutions would arise at all (as Locke had already shown in section 128 of the *Second Treatise*, saying that only a 'corrupt' rejection of reason keeps a unitary, unified mankind from being perfectly governed by natural law[81]). Rousseau is struck by the beauty of Diderot's *morale universelle:* 'No one will *deny* that the general will in each individual is a pure act of the understanding, which reasons in the silence of the passions about what man can demand of his fellow-man and what his fellow-man has the right to demand of him'. But where, Rousseau immediately and characteristically asks,

> is the man who can be so objective about himself, and if concern for his self-preservation is nature's first precept, can he be forced to look in this manner at the species *en général* in order to impose on himself duties whose connection with his particular constitution is not evident to him?

If reason is not directly morally efficacious (as it cannot be, if great legislators are to have the important formative function that is assigned to them in *Du contrat social*), and if 'natural law' is scarcely natural (as *Inégalité* tries to prove), then the natural man who fails to find his particular good in the general good will instead become the enemy of the *genre humain*, allying himself with the strong and the unjust to despoil the weak. 'It is false', Rousseau insists, 'that in the state of independence, reason leads us to cooperate from the common good.'[82]

So strongly does this current of thought sweep Rousseau along that he mounts a brief assault on *généralité* that would be fatal not just to Diderot, but to his own political aims as well:

> If the general society [of the human race] did exist somewhere other than in the systems of philosophers, it would be . . . a moral being with qualities separate and distinct from those of the particular beings constituting it, somewhat like chemical compounds which have properties that do not belong to any of the elements composing them.

In such a *société générale* 'there would be a universal language which nature would teach all men and which would be their first means of communication'; there would also be a 'kind of central nervous system which would connect all the parts'. Finally,

> the public good or ill would not be merely the sum of private goods and ills as in a simple aggregation, but would lie in the liaison uniting them. It would be greater than this sum, and public felicity, far from being based on the happiness of private individuals, would itself be the source of this happiness.[83]

Plainly this argument goes too far, since Rousseau himself wants to argue for a general good that is more than a mere sum or aggregation of private goods and ills; it is no wonder that he suppressed the *Première version*. Nevertheless the dilemma remains that a general society cannot be produced by passion-silencing 'reason' alone.[84] The only way out of the dilemma, according to Rousseau, is through denatured, non-natural 'new associations' (Sparta, Rome, Geneva) that take the place of well-meant but imaginary reason-governed *sociétés générales* and which, through rigorous civic education, draw natural beings out of their (equally natural) egocentrism, bringing them to think of themselves finally as 'parts of a greater whole'—a whole less extensive, but more realizable, than a *respublica christiana* or a kingdom of ends. The particular social remedies designed to overcome *particularité* and self-preference at the end of the *Première version* are rather abstractly, even vaguely, characterized ('new associations,' 'new insights,' perfected art'[85]); but one knows from other works how Rousseau proposes to produce, through an educative shaping which finally yields 'enlightened' free choice, a civic *volonté générale* which is certainly no cosmopolitan *esprit universel*.[86]

In the end, for Rousseau, no *morale universelle*—not a Christian one based on universal charity, not a Diderotian one grounded in passion-silencing reason, not a Kantian one resting on reason-ordained 'objective ends'—can help in the transformation of natural men into denatured citizens. The *générale* must be (somewhat) *particulière*. This explains the weight which Rousseau gives to education. For him, men do not naturally think of themselves as parts of a greater whole[87] and must therefore be *brought* to a non-natural civic belief. At the end of civic time—if *volonté* is to be equal to *généralité*—they must finally see the force of Émile's 'I have decided to be what you made me.'

The Centrality of 'Will' in Rousseau's Thought

If Rousseau's 'generalism' can be illuminated by contrasting it with Kant's 'universalism'—and this makes it plain that for

Rousseau freedom must be made congruent with *shaping* and *becoming*, while for Kant ought is just 'there' and does not endanger autonomy—one can throw some further light on Rousseau's effort to find a generalized *volonté* which will be voluntary but not 'wilful' by looking finally at his notion of 'will' itself.

Rousseau not only wanted to 'secularize' the general will—to turn it (mainly) away from theology (and God's will to save 'all men'); he wanted to endow human beings with a will, a really efficacious 'power' of choosing, which can then be subjected to the generalizing influence of civic education—a republican education which Montesquieu eloquently described but took to have vanished from the modern (monarchical) world. First *real* will, then *general* will; that is what Rousseau would say to his great French predecessors. This is not to say that Rousseau thought he knew perfectly what will is: but in his most extensive and important treatment of volition Rousseau never allowed (unavoidably incomplete) knowledge of will to cast doubt on either the real existence or the moral necessity of this 'faculty'. And so he has the Savoyard Vicar ask:

> How does a will produce a physical and corporeal action? I know nothing about that, but I experience in myself [the fact] that it produces it. I will to act, and I act; I will to move my body, and it moves; but that an inanimate body at rest should begin to move itself by itself, or produce movement—that is incomprehensible and unexampled. The will is known to me by its acts, not by its nature. I know this will as motor cause, but to conceive matter as the producer of movement is clearly to conceive an effect without cause, which is to conceive absolutely nothing.[88]

This doctrine, Rousseau has the Vicar say, is admittedly 'obscure' but it 'makes sense' and contains nothing repugnant to either reason or observation. 'Can one say as much of materialism?' the Vicar finally asks.[89]

The answer is clearly 'no'. That answer remained constant, seven years after *Émile*, when Rousseau wrote urging M. de Franquières to abandon a materialism and a determinism which are fatal to freedom and morality:

> Why do you not appreciate that the same law of necessity which, according to you, rules the working of the world, and all events, also rules all the actions of men, every thought in their heads, all the feelings of their hearts, that nothing is free, that all is forced, necessary, inevitable, that all the movements of man which are directed by blind matter, depend on his will only because his will itself depends on necessity; that there are in consequence neither virtues, nor vices, nor merit, nor demerit, nor morality in human actions, and that the words 'honourable man' or 'villain' must be, for you, totally devoid of sense. . . . Your honest heart, despite your arguments, declaims against your sad philosophy. The feeling of liberty, the charm of virtue, are felt in you despite you.[90]

Here, more than anywhere else in Rousseau, *le coeur a ses raisons que la raison ne connaît point*. But this Pascalian 'heart' is used to defend a freedom of willing that Pascal himself would certainly have called 'Pelagian'. And if that will can be generalized by a non-authoritarian educative authority, the final product will be the realization of Rousseau's highest civic ideal: the *volonté générale* one has 'as a citizen'.

Conclusion

Had Rousseau not been centrally concerned with freedom—above all with the voluntariness of morally legitimate human actions—he would never have made 'the general will' the core idea of his political philosophy. But a comparison of the 'citizen of Geneva' with world-citizen Kant reveals a permanent question in political and moral philosophy: is freedom to be conceived as the final product of a 'denaturing' education in time, or is it timelessly just 'there' in all rational beings? Do politics and civic 'generalizing' ultimately cause adult autonomy or is that an intolerable paradox which Kant avoids? It is because there is no definitive answer to such questions that Rousseau and Kant will continue to be thought of as the most brilliant exponents of two kinds of freedom.

Notes

1. Jean-Jacques Rousseau, *Gouvernement de Pologne*, in *Political Writings*, edited by C. Vaughan (Oxford, Basil Blackwell, 1962), Vol. II, pp. 424 ff.

2. Rousseau, *Du contrat social*, in *Political Writings*, ed. by C. Vaughn (Oxford, Basil Blackwell, 1962), vol. II, pp. 105, 29.

3. Pierre Bayle, *Pensées diverses, Écrites à un Docteur de Sorbonne* (Rotterdam, Reinier Leers, 4th ed, 1704), Vol. 2, pp. 452 ff. (for praise of *généralité* as good).

4. Jean-Jacques Rousseau, *Première version du contrat social*, in *Political Writings*, edited by C. Vaughan (Oxford, Basil Blackwell, 1962), Vol. I. p. 499.

5. Jean-Jacques Rousseau, 'Lettre à M. de Beaumont', in *Oeuvres complètes* (Paris, Éditions du Seuil, 1971), Vol. 3, pp. 340 ff.

6. Rousseau, *Du contrat social*, p. 26.

7. Jean-Jacques Rousseau, *Discourse on Inequality*, in *The Social Contract and Discourses*, translated by G. D. H. Cole (New York, Everyman, 1950), p. 208.

8. Rousseau, *Première version*, p. 499.

9. Rousseau, *Émile*, translated by B. Foxley (London, Dent, 1910) pp. 242–4.

10. Rousseau, *Émile*, pp. 243–4.

11. Jean-Jacques Rousseau, *Lettres morales*, in *Oeuvres complètes* (Paris, Pleiade, 1961), Vol. 4, pp. 1106 ff. For the importance of the *Lettres*, see Shklar, *Men and Citizens* (Cambridge, Cambridge University Press, 1969) pp. 229–30.

12. Immanuel Kant, *Grundlegung*, translated by T.K. Abbott as *Fundamental Principles* (Indianapolis, Library of Liberal Arts, 1949). p. 11.

13. Rousseau, *Lettres morales*, pp. 1111, 1107–9.

14. Blaise Pascal, 'Ecrits sur la grâce', in *Oeuvres de Blaise Pascal*, edited by L. Brunschvicg (Paris, Hachette, 1914), Vol. 11, p. 134.

15. Rousseau, *Du contrat social*, pp. 105, 27.

16. Rousseau, *Première version*, pp. 472–3, in which he urges that every authentic 'act of sovereignty' involves 'an agreement between the body politic and each of its members' which is 'equitable because it is voluntary and general'. Here *volonté* and *généralité* are of equal weight.

17. Rousseau, *Du contrat social*, p. 52.

18. Rousseau, *Gouvernement de Pologne*, p. 130.

19. Rousseau, *Économie politique*, in *The Social Contract and Discourses*, translated by G. D. H. Cole (New York, Everyman, 1950), p. 308.

20. Jean-Jacques Rousseau, *Émile*, excerpt in *Political Writings*, edited by C. Vaughan (Oxford, Basil Blackwell, 1962), Vol. II, p. 145.

21. Malebranche, *Nature et grâce*, pp. 147–66.

22. Jean-Jacques Rousseau, 'Le Persifleur', in *Les Confessions* (Paris, Pleiade, 1959), p. 1111, where Rousseau urges that 'the most profound metaphysics' is that of 'Plato, Locke or Malebranche.'

23. Jean-Jacques Rousseau, letter to Malesherbes, in *Lettres philosophiques*, edited by Henri Gouhier (Paris, Vrin., 1974). p. 124.

24. Jean-Jacques Rousseau, 'Jugement sur la Polysynodie', in *Political Writings*, edited by C. Vaughan (Oxford, Basil Blackwell, 1962), Vol. I, p. 421.

25. St. Augustine, *De Libero Arbitrio*, Book I, Ch. 12.

26. Rousseau, *Économie politique*, p. 297.

27. Rousseau, *Émile* (Foxley edn), p. 444.

28. Rousseau, *Gouvernement de Pologne*, pp. 427–30.

29. Rousseau, *Du contrat social*, p. 51.

30. Rousseau, *Gouvernement de Pologne*, pp. 437–43.

31. Rousseau, *Émile*, p. 84.

32. Rousseau, *Discourse on Inequality*, pp. 180–2.

33. John Charvet, *The Social Problem in the Philosophy of Rousseau* (Cambridge, Cambridge University Press, 1974), p. 58.

34. F. Hegel, *Phenomenology of Mind*, translated by J. Batillie (New York, Harper & Row, 1967), p. 234.

35. Rousseau, *Du contrat social*, p. 36.

36. Rousseau, *Émile*, p. 435.

37. Rousseau, *Du contrat social*, p. 27.

38. Rousseau, *Émile*, p. 435.

39. Rousseau, *Du contrat social*, p. 56.

40. Particularly C. Vaughan, in his 'Introduction' to *Political Writings* (Oxford, Basil Blackwell, 1962). Vol. I, pp. 35 ff.

41. Kant, *Grundlegung*, pp. 19–21.

42. In A. J. Ayer, *Part of My Life* (New York, Oxford University Press, 1977), p. 176.

43. Judith N. Shklar, 'General Will', in P. Wiener (ed.), *Dictionary of the History of Ideas* (New York, Scribners, 1973), Vol. 2, pp. 275 ff.

44. Kant, *Grundlegung*, pp. 11–12.

45. The notion that the 'ethical commonwealth' of *Religion within the Limits* should be viewed as Kant's 'utopia' was suggested (*en passant*) by Judith Shklar.

46. St. Augustine, *De Libero Arbitrio*, translated by W. Russell (Washington, Catholic University America Press, 1968), pp. 95–6.

47. St. Augustine, *De Libero Arbitrio*, p. 97.

48. Plato, *Phaedrus*, 253b–257b.

49. Kant, *Grundlegung*, pp. 19–21.

50. Rousseau, *Première version*, p. 499.

51. Rousseau, *Discourse on Inequality*, p. 208.

52. Rousseau, *Discourse on Inequality*, pp. 208, 194.

53. Kant, *Grundlegung*, p. 29: '. . . all moral conceptions have their seat and origin completely *à priori* in the reason'.

54. Cited by Ernst Cassirer in *Rousseau, Kant and Goethe*, translated by H. Gutmann et al. (New York, Harper, 1963), pp. 1–2.

55. Immanuel Kant, *Critique of Pure Reason*, translated by N. K. Smith (London, Macmillan, 1962), pp. 464–5 (A533/B561).

56. Jean-Jacques Rousseau, *La Nouvelle Heloise*, edited by R. Pomeau (Paris, Garnier, 1960), p. 671.

57. Kant, *Critique of Pure Reason*, pp. 464–5 (A 533/B 561).

58. Rousseau, *Lettres morales*, p. 1107.

59. Rousseau, *Du contrat social*, pp. 42–50.

60. Jean-Jacques Rousseau, *Émile*, in *Oeuvres complètes* (Paris, Pleiade, 1961), Vol. 4, p. 588: 'Le mal général ne peut être que dans le désordre, et je vois dans le système du monde un ordre qui ne se dement jamais.'

61. Rousseau, *Émile* (Foxley edn), pp. 303–6.

62. Jean-Jacques Rousseau, *Lettres écrites de la montagne (Amsterdam, Rey, 1764), Vol. II, p. 57.*

63. Kant, *Grundlegung*, p. 30.

64. Kant, *Grundlegung*, pp. 17, 58–9.

65. Kant, *Grundlegung*, p. 29.

66. Kant, *Critique of Pure Reason*, A547/B575.

67. Kant, *Critique of Pure Reason*, p. 48.

68. Kant, *Critique of Pure Reason*, p. 29. For Kant we *think* freedom because we know 'ought'.

69. Plato, *Meno*, 82b ff.

70. Immanuel Kant, *Religion within the Limits of Reason Alone*, translated by T.M. Greene and Hoyt Hudson (New York, Harper and Row, 1960). p. 6n.

71. Denis Diderot, 'Droit naturel', in Jean-Jacques Rousseau, *Political Writings*, edited by C. Vaughan (Oxford, Basil Blackwell, 1962), Vol. I, p. 431.

72. Diderot, 'Droit naturel', pp. 431–2.

73. Rousseau, *Gouvernement de Pologne*, Chs 1–4.

74. Robert Wokler, 'The influence of Diderot on Rousseau', in R. A. Leigh, *Studies on Voltaire and the 18th Century* (Banbury, Voltaire Foundation, 1975), p. 132.

75. Diderot, 'Droit naturel', p. 432.

76. Diderot, 'Droit naturel', p. 432.

77. Nicolas de Malebranche, *Recherche de la Vérité*, in *Oeuvres complètes* (Paris, Vrin, 1958), Vol. II, p. 490.

78. Rousseau, *Du contrat social*, II, 6.

79. Jean-Jacques Rousseau, 'Chronologie universelle', in *Annales de la Société Jean-Jacques Rousseau* (Geneva, Jullien, 1905), Vol. 1, pp. 205 ff.

80. Jean-Jacques Rousseau, *Première version*, in *On the Social Contract*, translated by R. Masters (New York, St Martin's Press, 1973), p. 157.

81. John Locke, *Second Treatise of Government* (1690), s. 128.

82. Rousseau, *Première version* (Masters edn), pp. 159–60.

83. Rousseau, *Première version* (Masters edn), pp. 159–60.

84. Rousseau, *Du contrat social*, p. 48.

85. Rousseau, *Première version* (Masters edn), pp. 162–3.

86. Rousseau, *Gouvernement de Pologne*, p. 437: 'Every true republican . . . sees only the fatherland, and lives for it alone'.

87. Rousseau, *Du contrat social*, p. 52.

88. Rousseau, *Émile* (Pleiade edn), p. 576.

89. Rousseau, *Émile* (Pleiade edn), p. 576.

90. Rousseau, 'Lettre à M. de Franquières', pp. 180–1.

14
Rousseau's Political Defense of the Sex-Roled Family

Penny Weiss
Anne Harper

The task of returning to the major historical figures of philosophy in order to document the sexual inegalitarianism in their thought seems of limited usefulness for projects on the agenda of feminist theory and practice. It would appear that there are endless tasks for feminist scholars more pressing, constructive, and relevant to the attainment of sexual equality than reconstructing the arguments of someone such as Rousseau—an eighteenth-century, white, male, European writing in defense of enforced sexual differentiation.

It is necessary, however, for the cogency of feminist theory and the success of feminist politics to hear and answer the concerns and questions of the opposition, concerns and questions too often ignored or oversimplified. Rousseau, for example, was not simply a misogynist determined to interpret nature, history, or culture in such a way as to bless male supremacy with the stamp of inevitability or justifiability. In fact, the concerns that led him to support sexual differentiation, especially the concern with moving beyond self-interest to real community, are often laudable and shared by many feminists. We will argue that Rousseau's resistance to feminism, as expressed in his endorsement of the sex-roled family, is not based on the same morally offensive principles and logically flawed reasoning as are

many other anti-feminists. But because Rousseau's anti-feminism is as troubling in its implications as are the others, it is one that deserves to be heard and responded to.

Recent feminist critiques of Rousseau's sexual politics have generally been severe (Okin 1979, Lange 1979, Eisenstein 1981). Perhaps more was reasonably expected of someone with such high praise for liberty and equality, one actually familiar with feminist ideas, an individual with painful personal experience of second-class treatment, and a thinker utterly convinced of how fatal oppressive power is to the existence of true community. When, in spite of these experiences and principles, Rousseau sends women to the home and men to the assembly, there is some cause for thinking he was in a position to know better and want more.

There is, however, much disagreement in the secondary literature regarding both what Rousseau prescribes for the sexes, and why. We are left with often incompatible descriptions and explanations of his sexual politics that sometimes mirror more general disagreements about his politics and philosophy. It has been claimed, for example, that Rousseau limits women's activity because he is fearful of women's power (Wexler 1976), that he thinks women's inferior nature requires a circumscribed role (Christenson 1972, Okin 1979), that he endorses women's subservience as a necessary condition of men's freedom (Eisenstein 1981), and that he empowers the sexes differently from real concern with establishing sexual equality (Schwartz 1984, Bloom 1985). Consequently, Rousseau's treatment of the sexes has been held to be both a major breech of his principles and an integral part of his politics.

We hope to offer an interpretation of Rousseau's sex-roled family that can incorporate and surpass some of these incompatible interpretations of his work, and that can demonstrate what he might have been trying to accomplish in endorsing sexual differentiation. We argue that at least on the theoretical level he is internally consistent. Rousseau's advocacy of sexual roles is based on his understanding of their ability to bring individuals outside of themselves into interdependent communities, and thus to combat egoism, selfishness, indolence and narcissism—goals that consistently inform much of his politics. In order to demonstrate this, we show that Rousseau's rejections of both aristocratic and bourgeois families are founded upon their inability to accomplish politically what the sex-roled, affectionate family can accomplish.

Defenses of the "traditional" family are often thought to arise either from ignorance of its oppressiveness, disdain for women, or belief that its differentiated roles fulfill the distinct natures of women and men. While each of these explanations does capture a part of the reality, the picture they paint of defenses of the sex-roled family is seriously incomplete.

Rousseau's rationale for sexual differentiation in general, and within the family in particular, is not to be found in an appeal to the different natures of the sexes. By his own account no natural differences in strength, intellect, reproductive capacities or interests mandate a strict sexual division of roles and traits in society (Weiss 1987). But if Rousseau does not resort to claims about the different natures of the sexes, and if his scheme reflects more than the misogyny or blindness of its author, as we believe it does, then how is it possible to explain his system of sexual differentiation?

While frequently making rhetorical reference to the different natures of men and women in defending his proposals, Rousseau ultimately appeals to claims quite unrelated to sexual natures. For instance, in discussing female chastity he speaks of how the "Supreme Being . . . while abandoning woman to unlimited desires . . . joins modesty to these desires in order to constrain them" (Rousseau 1979, 359). However, despite the apparent reliance here on the (divine) given of woman's nature, his more consistent and convincing position emerges when he writes that "Even if it could be denied that a special sentiment of chasteness was natural to women . . . it is in society's interest that women acquire these qualities" (Rousseau 1960, 87). By referring to what traits women should *acquire* in "society's interest," Rousseau introduces a completely independent, and more internally consistent

justification for his rigidly sexually differentiated society. Instead of focusing on the supposed *causes* of sexual differentiation, as found in nature, we must turn instead to an examination of the *effects* of sexual differentiation on various social relations. Then we can discover why it is that Rousseau considers sexual differentiation to be "in society's interest."

Rousseau's strategy of evaluating and justifying sexual differentiation by its consequences, especially after comparing them to the effects of the alternatives, is not so surprising. It is not the question, "is X good in itself?" that preoccupies the citizen of Geneva but, instead, "is X beneficial and useful?" For example, the *Letter to d'Alembert* inquires into the effects on different peoples of establishing a theater. He writes in that letter that "To ask if the theater is good or bad in itself is to pose too vague a question. . . . The theater is made for the people, and it is only by its effects on the people that one can determine its absolute qualities" (Rousseau 1960, 17). Similarly, Rousseau's famous opposition to the Enlightenment stems not from a belief that the arts and sciences are unequivocally bad in themselves, but from reflection on the consequences of imperfect learning by the masses. Thus, the suggestion that Rousseau's sexual scheme is devised for its social consequences is not as idiosyncratic as it might at first appear.

Figuring out why Rousseau sees sexual differentiation as socially beneficial requires considering Rousseau's preferred family in two related contexts. The first context is his general thought, where sexual differentiation can be understood as a response to certain aspects of what he perceives as "the human condition." For example, according to Rousseau, the bonds created in the sex-roled family, and the interdependence fostered by sex roles in general, motivate and teach us how to be part of a political community, which he holds to be necessary for survival and morality. The second context is the historical forms of the family with which Rousseau was familiar. Rousseau witnessed the decline of the traditional, aristocratic family, and the emergence of the bourgeois family (both of which may be considered patriarchal), and found both politically unacceptable. A look at the families Rousseau rejects gives a sense of both what goods he is trying to attain by creating sexual differences, and what evils he is trying to skirt.

Rousseau's views on the sexes are thus strongly political, in at least two senses. First, Rousseau is certain that the private and public affect each other in numerous and central ways—that women, children, sexuality, families, etc. matter to politics as much as do the actions of men in the assembly. Because the private has political consequences, Rousseau to a great extent constructs the private with an eye to its political repercussions. The private becomes the parent and servant of the public: sex roles serve political ends and teach us lessons that give birth to certain desirable social possibilities. Rousseau's views on the sexes are also political in a second sense, in that they reflect assumptions and choices about what kinds of communities are possible, necessary, and desirable, and involve practical strategies for attaining them.

Rousseau might be considered anti-feminist at the outset because he evaluates the role of women in a light other than simply what women want to or can do. However, it is at least true that Rousseau does the same for men (Martin 1981, Weiss 1990), and that what women want or can do is not irrelevant. Indeed, some opposition to feminism, including Rousseau's, may arise from viewing feminists as evaluating the role of women abstracted from political considerations. Rousseau's argument is that certain necessary social benefits result from the establishment of sexual differentiation, far-reaching benefits that serve as a large part of its justification. Such a defense of the traditional family presents a different set of questions to feminists than do more familiar ones based on appeals to biological determinism, and needs more thorough understanding and critique by feminists.

The first two sections of this paper develop the two contexts in which the ends of Rousseau's sexual politics can be discerned. The succeeding two sections explore the negative personal and social consequences of the aristocratic and bourgeois families he rejects. These "case studies" offer a picture of what Rousseau thinks a family ought to provide for its members and to society and why he finds the sex-roled, affectionate family to be the most personally and politically beneficial. The conclusion will point out some of the questions Rousseau's defense of the sex-roled family raises for feminist theory and some of the questions feminist theory raises for Rousseau.

Rousseau and the Human Condition

Rousseau portrays people in the state of nature as free, happy, independent, amoral, innocent, and isolated. They are without need for the services or esteem of others and can generally satisfy their minimal desires independently. While self-absorbed, they do not desire to harm others. These asocial individuals possess numerous faculties in potentiality, but neither internal nor external forces naturally operate to motivate them to do any more than is necessary to survive. Rousseau's primitives are lazy, content, independent and generally harmless.

All relations in the state of nature are temporary and amoral, and provide no precedent or model for the sorts of relations needed between social beings. There may be some infrequent instances of cooperation in the search for food, but such liaisons are temporary and based entirely on self-interest. Sexual encounters are random and fleeting, motivated by the coincidence of desire and opportunity, and cause no lasting attachment between the partners.

Even the mother-child relation in the state of nature provides a poor model for the interdependent, moral, sustained relations modern social people need. As Rousseau portrays it, mother-child relations in the state of nature do not differ significantly from those of other animals. He sees the demands of children in the state of nature as simple, of short duration, and compatible with the satisfaction of the mother's meager needs and desires. A father's assistance is unnecessary, even were he able to grasp his relation to a child, which Rousseau thinks he is not. A mother cares for a child to relieve her own swollen breasts of milk out of compassion for a crying creature, and finally out of affection born of habit. But Rousseau imagines that in the state of nature children venture off on their own permanently at a very young age—as soon as they have learned to feed and defend themselves—and that this rather uneventfully marks the end of all relations between mother and child.[1]

However, accidental events and developments alter the easy balance between desires and powers in the state of nature, until interdependence finally becomes necessary for survival. The question now becomes how to teach and motivate asocial, lazy, independent individuals to work with and for each other as well as for themselves. Rousseau considers this change radical and difficult. The fact that people need each other does not automatically mean that they will cooperate for mutual advantage rather than attempt to exploit each other for personal gain. Self-love, once complicated by social relations, easily leads to selfishness and concern with advantage over others, bringing about the long train of personal and social evils so magnificently described in the first *Discourse*.

Rousseau does not like egoism, competitiveness or conflict to be endemic to the human condition. Nor does he assume, however, that by nature people are as concerned with others, including children, as with ourselves. Rousseau's quest is to establish a social framework that can provide us with the skills and desire both to end the isolation, self-absorption, and independence of natural people, and combat the egoism, competitiveness, and conflict among "civilized" people who have become interdependent.

The contrast between childhood in the state of nature and modern social childhood helps clarify Rousseau's "political problem." As society "advances," the period of childhood is extended, and being a parent becomes more demanding. In civil society children are dependent for much longer than in the state of nature, for they must learn to speak, to read, to earn a living, to behave properly—the list is virtually endless, and the specific skills needed can change rapidly.[2] Further, parents are now subject to judgments by others regarding the quality of

the care they bestow upon their children, making their task even more burdensome.

It is the case that the range of solutions considered by Rousseau is narrow. Or, perhaps more accurately, his very framing of the problems itself colors the solutions. Looking at Rousseau's thoughts on sexual differentiation and the family in the context of his general thought, the problems he addresses might include the following: "How can we help ensure that women, once sufficiently motivated by pity, full breasts, and modest requests to pay some minimal attention to a child for a relatively short period of time, will now invest so much more for so much longer? And what will turn a naturally lazy and asocial male, whose participation in child rearing was once largely unnecessary, into a father? What will turn both into citizens?"

What such questions indicate is that the possible range of child-rearing arrangements considered all generally appeal to some form of the nuclear, heterosexual family. The attempt to motivate parental, especially maternal, "sacrifice" presupposes both a particular model of public-private relations and a distinct conception of community that can fairly be said to beg as many questions as they answer. Nonetheless, such are the questions Rousseau considers and, as we will argue below, his position on sexual relations provides a large part of his answer to them. Rousseau's rejection of certain families arises from their inability to respond to fundamental crises of the human social condition, and their tendency to support corrupt political relations. His defense of the sex-roled, affectionate family is likewise based on its beneficial social consequences.

The Changing Family

In the traditional noble family of sixteenth, seventeenth, and early eighteenth century France, the male exerted powerful rule over both his children and wife. Arranged marriages were standard with economic and family advantage the criteria in mate selection. "Within these marriages, relations between husband and wife and between parents and children were cold, distant, and unloving. . . . Noble wives were poorly treated by their husbands," and remote from their children (Fairchilds 1984b, 97, 98).

> The marriage contract seemed to have little meaning in Paris, except in separating a man and a woman effectively, so that they were ashamed to seem to care for each other, and in most cases lived apart, slept in separate apartments, and had each other announced when they called. (Josephson 1931, 123–124)

Needless to say, this family was not a reliable source of emotional satisfaction for any of its members, and illicit relationships regularly filled the vacuum. Even here, it has been said that "The ceremony of taking a lover was momentous; position, family, social attainments, were all weighed" (Josephson 1931, 126). Children were cared for by wet nurses, nursemaids, and tutors, successively. This aristocratic family was thus seldom more than a reproductive and economic entity, with birthing legitimate heirs a primary function. Rousseau, we shall see, rejects this family on a number of grounds. It is to this family that his remarks about "unfaithful" wives, "brilliant" wives, and women turning to "entertainments of the city" (Rousseau 1979, 44, 409) are directed, as are comments about tyrannical and neglectful fathers (Rousseau 1979, 38n).

In addition to analyzing the defects of the family of the Ancien Regime, Rousseau focuses his attention on its likely successor: the bourgeois family. Actually, in Rousseau's view the self-absorbed bourgeois individual is incapable of really being a member of a family. This is because

> he is the man who, when dealing with others, thinks only of himself, and on the other hand, in his understanding of himself, thinks only of others. . . . The bourgeois distinguishes his own good from the common good. His good requires society, and hence he exploits others while depending on them. . . . The bourgeois comes into being when men no longer believe that there is common good. . . .[3]

These self-interested bourgeois "role-players" are not part of a greater whole, be it the family or community, in any sense but the limited and inadequate one based on self-interest. "I observe," writes Rousseau, "that in the modern age men no longer have a hold on each other except by force or by self-interest" (Rousseau 1979, 321). People are self-centered and view others as means to their ends. The bourgeois family, accordingly, is without a common interest or firm bond. Members of the family pursue their own interests, considering the others and fulfilling obligations when it is useful or convenient, or when they are forced to do so. Such relations are superficial and unreliable, and do nothing to teach us the important lessons Rousseau thinks we need to learn about interdependence, loyalty, and community. It is to this emerging family that Rousseau's remarks about families of strangers are directed, as are many of his comments about women seeking entry into previously male arenas—comments, that is, about liberal feminism.

The general framework of Rousseau's thought and his particular understanding of the propensities inherent in aristocratic and bourgeois families provide a basis for interpreting his views on sexual differentiation. Examining specific features of the families he condemns offers a picture of what Rousseau held to be their negative effects on parent-child and male-female relations and, consequently, on general social and political arrangements. These families are cast aside on political grounds—because of their inability to mitigate, or their propensity to encourage, undesirable human relations—and the sex-roled affectionate family is offered as a better alternative.

Parent-Child Relations

As discussed above, parent-child relations in the state of nature are of unlimited usefulness in helping establish the kinds of human bonds Rousseau asserts we now need. He also considers the families of his own time inadequate. The status quo to which Rousseau was responding was parental neglect of children, and the lowly status of the child is uninteresting, useless, or sinful (Charlton 1984). Until almost the very end of the Ancien Regime, child care in most noble and bourgeois households was handled primarily by servants. Even in the 1760's, '70's, and '80's, when a few notable women begin to breast-feed and supervise their own children, household servants played a major role in childrearing (Fairchilds 1984a).

The role of servants in the lives of children began at birth when the infant was immediately sent to a wet-nurse (*nourrice*). This custom was deeply rooted by Rousseau's time, having begun as early as the thirteenth century, when Paris had a bureau of *recommanderesses* that arranged hired nurses. In the eighteenth century the hiring of wet-nurses was prevalent among the bourgeoisie and the artisanate as well as the aristocracy. In artisanal families the motives for wet-nursing were primarily economic: the mother's labor was essential to the family economy, and she could not afford the interruption that nursing would entail (Fox-Genovese 1984). There were social reasons for wet-nursing as well: nursing was considered a degrading and vulgar activity which supposedly ruined one's figure and strained one's health. Another reason was sexual: there were folk taboos against resuming sexual intercourse during lactation. Thus wet-nursing was an economic necessity for some women and their families and a response to social pressures and taboos for others. Rousseau's opposition to wet-nursing in particular, and to parental neglect of children in general, is unwavering, and he is given much credit for persuading mothers to breast-feed their babies and for contributing to "what was almost a cult of the mother figure" (Jirmack 1979, 161).

Sounding like some twentieth century anti-feminists, Rousseau states that in certain childcare arrangements, greater risk of poor care exists because the caretakers generally have no long-term stake in the child's upbringing. Their primary concern is simply minimizing the amount of trouble a child causes them while under their charge, and no more. (It is interesting to note how often today infants are called "good" who are, more precisely, easy to care for, i.e., who sleep a lot and cry but a little.) Rousseau refers to wet-nurses as "mercenaries" (Rousseau 1979, 44), evoking the imagery of pro-

fessional soldiers who serve any country merely for wages. Rousseau's inference is that the nurse really takes no interest in the child him or herself, but is basically concerned with earning an income and saving herself trouble. This assumption explains the practice of swaddling infants, which Rousseau abhors, and which he uses as representative of the poor treatment of children under such arrangements. However, while there is no reason to doubt Rousseau's sincere concern with the physical health and welfare of children, and while the stories of neglect and abuse of children by nurses in his time were numerous (Fairchilds 1984b, 100; Sussman 1982, 73–97), such concern amounts for but the smallest part of his reconstruction of the family.

That Rousseau's concern is not primarily the quality of care given children outside the nuclear family is supported by his awareness of the need to strengthen family ties beyond what may "naturally" exist; he never takes their strength, safety, or reliability for granted. Rousseau does not believe that nature goes too far in ensuring that children will be cared for because, as discussed earlier, outside of pity, which motivates one to help a suffering child, and full breasts, which encourage women to nurse for their own comfort, nature is essentially silent. The point is that even if Rousseau could be shown that children are as well-tended by nurses or childcare workers as by parents, he would hesitate to endorse the former. By spelling out some of the numerous negative consequences of such arrangements, it is possible to understand that the basis of Rousseau's objection to them is essentially political.

Rousseau first notes the simple fact that with a child under the charge of one other than his or her parents, the family spends less time together. He finds the consequences of this worrisome, for habit is not then allowed the opportunity to strengthen the ties of blood (Rousseau 1979, 46). Given his assumption that such blood ties are fragile and require reinforcement, extra-familial childcare will not enhance the potential care and love between family members that Rousseau would want to develop. Spending so much time apart, and in different pursuits, family members do not even know each other well. Rousseau's concern is that in the end they will be like residents of a corrupt city, polite strangers (Rousseau 1979, 49) who really think for themselves.

The habit of caring for one another is vital to the strengthening of blood ties, which alone are easily broken. Rousseau's definition of nature is important here: he would like the word to be "limited to habits comfortable to nature" (Rousseau 1979, 39). Such habits would never be lost once learned, because they would conform to our dispositions as strengthened by our senses, but not yet corrupted by our opinions. Thus habit can strengthen nature, even though it can also stifle it. In this case, the habit of caring for one's own infant can strengthen the rather meager biological bond just as the habit of not caring can destroy it. In the family that does not spend ample time together, members may not be drawn to one another from affection born of habit, an arrangement that threatens to maintain original human separateness and fails to combat egoism.

From the child's point of view, as well, extra-familial childcare has drawbacks. A child spending long hours away from the family can easily come to love the care-giver rather than the parents (Rousseau 1979, 49) or become prone to making "secret comparisons which always tend to diminish his esteem for those who govern him and consequently have authority over him" (Rousseau 1979, 57). The "losing" party in such comparisons—whether parents, wet-nurses, or tutors—may consequently find it difficult to elicit affection and obedience from the child, making their already unnatural duties more distasteful and possibly leading to lack of concern for child-rearing responsibilities. Or they may attempt to win back the child's affection by educational practices which are of dubious merit. Even if parents are preferred, their children may resent them for having entrusted them to those whose care is inferior, rather than providing it themselves.

Rousseau also fears that a child cared for by "mercenaries" may "bring back the habit of having no attachments" (Rousseau 1979, 49). It is especially this politically dangerous possibility that arouses his concern. While not uninterested in nutrition and the high rate of infant mortality, the alienation of affection between mother and child was what most bothered Rousseau about a practice like wet-nursing. Once wet-nursing was finished, at about two years of age, the child was usually brought back into its family of origin and taught to regard its former nurse as a servant. Sometimes children were no longer allowed to see their nurses. Weaning is often traumatic for a child, no matter how well or poorly cared for, and some infants shed tears upon being separated from their nurses. Rousseau thinks this attempt to make children forget or disdain their first caretakers instills in them a general contempt and ingratitude (Rousseau 1979, 45). He fears the child will in the end despise both the biological parents, who do not offer much care during infancy, and the substitute parents, whose class or status now makes them an unacceptable object of affection. In addition, the failure of the mother to nurse her child robs her of an opportunity to learn to care for someone other than the self.

Thus, Rousseau's argument for breast-feeding is not a materialist one. His main concern is not infant health and the quality of milk—its vitamins, antibodies, or other nutritional aspects emphasized by some twentieth-century advocates—but the quality of human relationships formed from the beginning of life. If one allows a young child to be completely cared for by a servant for whom one then teaches the child contempt, one creates a monstrous person who does not know how to treat anyone else properly.[4]

Rousseau's arguments are not directed only to "neglectful mothers." His injunction to fathers to take responsibility for their children is less well-known than his pleas to mothers, but it is no less important and is based on similar considerations.

Rousseau first tries to counter the notions that fathers are either inept parents or rightly consumed with more "important" tasks than caring for their children.

> He will be better raised by a judicious and limited father than the cleverest master in the world; for zeal will make up for tal-

ent better than talent for zeal. . . . But business, offices, duties. . . . Ah, duties! Doubtless the least is that of father? (Rousseau 1979, 48–49)

It is possible and important that men be fathers, for Rousseau regards "surrogate fathers," or tutors, in the same light as wet-nurses—as mercenaries who corrupt the family just as mercenary soldiers do the state. Rich men who claim that they do not have time to care for their children purchase the time of others to perform their parental duties.[5] As Rousseau well knew, preceptors were often picked from among the male domestics in the household and were treated as family servants. He chastises fathers for subjecting their children to a master-servant relationship that ultimately produces a servile mentality.

> Venal soul! Do you believe that you are with money giving your son another father? Make no mistake about it; what you are giving him is not even a master but a valet. This first valet will soon make a second one out of your son. (Rousseau 1979, 49)

Hiring tutors may leave children and fathers unattached, and thereby also fail to develop a common interest between parents. Use of "mercenaries" teaches children that money buys servants and that people only "care" out of self-interest; further, it fails to allow any true attachment even between child and tutor to develop, for theirs is in fact a relationship based on money.

The family in the Ancien Regime was an institution primarily organized for the transmission of property and rank from one generation to the next. Rousseau's new definition of fatherhood is rooted in the anti-patriarchalism of Locke's political theory. He expands Locke's view of the father as friend of his children to include the notion of father as educator or governor of his sons (Locke 1968). Like Locke, Rousseau emphasizes that the legacy or "portion" that a father bestows on his children should be a personal involvement in their education. While Locke still places high value on the transmission of property along with the "good breeding" of a gentleman, Rousseau is occupied with the transmission of a set of values that will enable children to be independent of wealth and rank.

Rousseau wants fathers to give their children something of themselves, rather than only their money. He wants them to provide an example of citizenship that rests on love and benevolence for others rather than on wealth. At the outset of *Emile*, he complains about "Fathers' ambition, avarice, tyranny, and false foresight, their negligence, their harsh insensitivity" (Rousseau 1979, 38n). Fathers are rather like the laws, which Rousseau finds "always so occupied with property and so little with persons, because their object is peace, not virtue" (Rousseau 1979, 37n).

Another negative political consequence Rousseau cites of having two sets of care-givers is the risk of presenting conflicting guidelines to children. Rousseau writes,

> A child ought to know no other superiors than his father and his mother or, in default of them, his nurse and his governor; even one of the two is already too many. But this division is inevitable, and all that one can do to remedy it is to make sure that the persons of the two sexes who govern him are in such perfect agreement concerning him that the two are only one as far as he is concerned. (Rousseau 1979, 57)

Certainly, if Rousseau expresses doubts about two people sharing care of a child, he will be extremely hesitant to involve more parties, who might introduce additional principles into education. But why is this so problematic?

Rousseau's concern about the conflicting guidelines of multiple care-givers seems to involve the way children will come to regard the guidelines themselves well as their source. If different authorities espouse conflicting rules, children may conclude that the guidelines are merely reflections of individual wills, and/or may see authority as merely an obstacle, a set of arbitrary rules that one may be able to evade with sufficient study of them. Such perspectives, according to a Rousseauean framework, encourage rebellion and disrespect for rules, and maintain a picture of human relations that is essentially based on subjectivity and self-interest. Thus, multiple care-givers potentially undermine the rule of law, considered by Rousseau to be the basis of all legitimate states, and complete the already difficult project of moving self-absorbed individuals into a greater whole.

According to Rousseau, then, aristocratic and bourgeois families pose grave problems both for the bonds between parents and children and for general social relations. First, these families fail to reinforce natural ties with habitual ones, leaving people separate and self-absorbed. Second, these arrangements present children with torn loyalties, leading to any of three negative consequences: childcare, already "unnatural" and a sacrifice, is made more onerous by the weak bonds; education, essential for making us responsible social creatures, may be compromised for the sake of children's affection; or, most important, children cared for by "mercenaries" may learn that people only tend to others when it is in their interest or convenient for them to do so. The ultimate danger is that respect for persons and for law is not learned. Rousseau's firm belief in the insufficiency of self-interest as a basis for community, and in the necessity and difficulty of combatting natural human isolation and egoism, leads him to reject aristocratic and bourgeois families as personally and politically useless or dangerous. Similar problems are presented by the relationships between spouses in these families.

Male-Female Marital Relations

Rousseau advocates not only that women and men be good parents, but good spouses, as well. We next explore Rousseau's sense of the negative repercussions of an aristocratic or bourgeois family structure on relations between spouses, and the consequences of these "inadequate" male-female relations on general social arrangements.

Rousseau's words on sex education are often remarkable for the sense of danger they portray. "How many precautions must be taken!" (Rousseau 1979, 335), he exclaims. The relations one will have with other people in general will, Rousseau believes, be affected by how one deals with the need for a partner. Human sexuality has political implications.

In the contemporary discussions of marriage there was a debate about ill-matched marriages (*mesalliances*), which meant marriages between members of aristocracy and the bourgeoisie. Rousseau changes the meaning of the term: for him an ill-matched marriage is one where the characters of the partners, rather than their ranks, are not compatible. Rousseau draws a further inference:

> the farther we are removed from equality, the more our natural sentiments are corrupted; the more the gap between noble and commoner widens, the more the conjugal bond is relaxed; and the more there are rich and poor, the less there are fathers and husbands. Neither master nor slave any longer has a family; each of the two sees only his status. (Rousseau 1979, 405)

The message here is striking: Rousseau is saying that the greater the social and political inequality, the less husbands and wives are bound to each other. Apparently this is because people marry for reasons of social rank and not for compatibility of character; thus making it less likely that they will love each other and be sexually faithful. The "family" is destroyed, or is never truly established in the first place, by the inequality of the social structure. The quality of married life affects the morality of the citizens. Rousseau witnesses individuals who by and large seem incapable of establishing meaningful relationships as family members or as fellow citizens.

In contrast to eighteenth-century French law and practice, Rousseau emphasizes that a woman should have a voice determining whom she will marry, and that marriage is a social institution requiring mutual respect and fidelity from both partners. He opposes the authoritarian relations of parent and child whereby parents choose the husband for the daughter based on wealth and rank. Aristocratic families with arranged marriages based on economics did not establish an arena of love and affection between the spouses. Rousseau seems to see this as encouraging adultery. In fact, it can be said that adultery was institutionalized at the highest level of French society, for the married Louis XV had a publicly-acknowledged relationship with Madame de Pompadour, herself a married bourgeois who played a powerful role in France as advisor to the King and as patron of the arts.

Rousseau has the greatest wrath for the adulterer, who inevitably "destroys the family" (Rousseau 1979, 324). His argument here is quite different from many offered today, for Rousseau does not consider that only one model of male-female relations is somehow ordained and that any straying from it is sinful. One need only consider relations in his state of nature, where sexual encounters occurred when and with whom the desire arose, and established no moral bond.

Infidelity is condemned because of its undesirable personal and political effects, which may be several. First, there is the possibility of a woman bearing children which biologically are not her husband's. A man unsure of his biological relation to his wife's children may see less of himself in them, identify with them less strongly, and be less motivated to work and sacrifice for them; this injures both his relation with his children and his partnership with his wife. Given Rousseau's assumption that such motivation to sacrifice for others is already in short supply, the loss could be a significant one for the family unit. Second, an unfaithful partner, male or female, causes one to distrust others outside the family, who become potential competitors. This creates strained social relations in general, precisely what Rousseau wants to avoid. Third, with suspicions of infidelity in the air, spouses do not trust one another, and only feign love. "Under such circumstances the family is little more than a group of secret enemies" (Rousseau 1979, 325).

The worrisome political consequence here is that without love of one's nearest, it is difficult to develop love for the larger community. There appear to be two connections between familiar love and patriotism for Rousseau. First, the "unnatural" lessons of cooperation and obligation are more easily learned on the "micro" level of the family— where habit breeds affection, and others are known well—and then extended to larger groups. Second, one is motivated to sacrifice for the state in large part by the protection and other benefits the state offers one's family. In either case, Rousseau's opposition to aristocratic spousal relations is rooted in their failure to move people beyond the self, while responsible, reliable bonds within the family help establish the habits and motives for true political community.

Rousseau also rails against the aristocratic wife "seeking entertainment" in the city, and the bourgeois wife demanding entry into previously male educational and social institutions. In both cases, according to Rousseau, women are not fulfilling their domestic duties. This seems to be both symptom and cause of political problems for him.

Women engaged in activities outside the household may come to see motherhood as a burden. They are apt to try to avoid pregnancy through birth control (Rousseau 1979, 44), to which Rousseau objects vehemently. The basis of his objection is at least in part related to population increase, a familiar concern in eighteenth-century France, where one-quarter of the babies born died before their first birthday. But Rousseau also sees reproduction as a barometer of attitudes toward parental sacrifice and the level of self-interestedness;[6] in this sense, neglect of domestic duties is a symptom of political problems.

Rousseau in several places focuses on the negative consequences of women's refusal to dedicate themselves to their mates. He responds to women's demand for education in short shrift: "They have no colleges. What a great misfortune! Would God that there were none for boys; they would be more sensibly and decently raised!" (Rousseau 1979, 363). This may be taken as an example of Rousseau's general response to the desire of some women to engage in heretofore male activities, rather than devoting themselves to their families. That is, his response is to question the worth of the (male) enterprise.

All the evils of modern civil society, according to Rousseau, are derived ultimately from the fact that personal or particular interest is the dominant rationale for action. . . . Rousseau thought that the idea that the sexes might both operate on these principles and that women should not be denied the right to advance their particular interests as men do was one of the most absurd and lamentable consequences of this modern philosophy. (Lange 1981, 246–247)

To the extent that women's participation in certain arenas expands the mentality of self-interested individualism, it is a cause of continued political decline. In this light, Rousseau's opposition to liberal feminism, with which he was familiar, can be understood as rooted more in an opposition to liberalism than to women's equality. And, it must be noted, Rousseau does not desire men to be self-interested individuals either.

Rousseau also says that if women do not dedicate themselves to the home it will not be a refuge for men, who will then be less devoted to the family (Rousseau 1979, 46), will seek their pleasure elsewhere, and will not fulfill duties owed to their wives and children. Her concentration on her husband however, causes him to respect and support her—to be a good husband. Once again Rousseau's assumption is that these domestic relationships are not "natural" and that without certain "enticements" to draw people to them, isolation and egoism are likely to prevail. The arrangement he envisions is at least intended to "entice" both sexes and to involve a sharing of the burdens and benefits of social life.

In the bourgeois and aristocratic families Rousseau portrays, the family is of little importance to any of its members. The children are burdensome strangers to the parents, who find their principal pleasures separately outside of the family. None is firmly attached to the others, and each remains self-interested and essentially alone.

Rousseau's vision of the family, however sentimental, is an attempt to control the "civilized" Hobbesian individual. In a world in which the individual is posited as a self-interested actor whose only legitimate obligations are those she or he contracts, Rousseau proposes that the marriage contract should be akin to the social contract—an irrevoca-ble commitment freely undertaken, a set of legitimate chains that makes true community possible.

Conclusion

Rousseau's endorsement of a sex-roled, nuclear, sentimental family has been contrasted with the aristocratic and bourgeois families he rejects. His advocacy of sexual differentiation has been shown to be rooted in his understanding of the human condition. He is concerned with establishing a family that can lead people to be better social creatures, capable of attachments to others that go beyond limited and destructive self-interested liaisons. His argument is that natural independence, self-absorption and asociality, as well as social competitiveness and egoism, must be countered and that a politically effective means is found in the relations of the sexes.

Rousseau's political advocacy of the sex-roled family differs from much anti-feminist argument today. For example, contemporary opponents of extra-familial childcare tend to emphasize the "enormous care" demanded by children, "the nurture and support" only a mother can offer, or how "vitally important" to women mothering is.[7] Rousseau, as we have seen, does not think a natural nurturing ability or desire exists in either sex and does not assume that only parents can possibly tend to the health and welfare of a child. Rousseau's general defense of sexual differentiation thus also differs from more familiar ones, which frequently appeal to different sexual natures finding fulfillment in different social roles. In fact, Rousseau provides a potent critique of biological determinism that feminists can make use of.

Rousseau at least deserves some credit for not assuming, as do so many figures in the history of political thought, that a certain (usually patriarchal) form of the family is dictated by nature, for not assuming that sex roles are biological givens, for realizing the political centrality of the private, and for calling upon both sexes to transcend narrow individual interests and establish true community. He should also be distinguished from anti-feminists who make harmful or derogatory assumptions about women's potential or character; for example, he does not portray women as inherently more evil, sinful, ignorant, immoral, selfish or selfless than men. While simply condemning Rousseau for advocating sexual differentiation at all, for whatever reason, is tempting, it is worth at least pausing to consider his reasons, and the questions they raise for feminists.

Rousseau assumes that humans are originally asocial and self-interested, that survival requires the overcoming of both of these conditions, and that human malleability allows them to be overcome, though such a task is as difficult as it is important. It is these assumptions that lead Rousseau to endorse sexual differentiation. Its consequences are a major part of the solution to what he sees as the fundamental human dilemma. It is a solution that purports to bring parents together in a common enterprise and to bring each together with children in a situation in which they are bound by love and duty, not just self-interest. That each sex is made "incomplete" by sexual differentiation is usually held against such arrangements by feminists—yet this result is precisely what Rousseau wants, for it creates a reliable need for others, for interdependence, which nature did not take care of and which is essential to survival and non-exploitative relations. Rousseau is concerned that in the quest for equality, for each having the right to live as he or she chooses as an individual, liberals, including liberal feminists, fail to address the instrumental and inherent goods of interdependence and community. While women in his scheme are in a sense treated as means to greater ends, so are men, and the ends are held to be legitimate and advantageous to both. Each must play a part in the whole on which Rousseau's eyes are turned, a part which directs her or him toward certain things and away from others, developing some potentialities in each and leaving others dormant. And it is important to remember here that Rousseau often challenges the supposed superiority of such things as the public over the private realm, abstract over practical reason, and reason over affection. Thus, that both sexes are excluded from certain activities may not result in inequality according to his standards.

Rousseau sees the sentiment of attachment and the lessons of legitimate obligation as best learned in a loving family and as necessary developmental predecessors of unselfish dedication to the common good in the state.[8] He comes to endorse what feminism will not by his attention to questions that feminists need to show can be answered differently. What devices can we suggest to overcome exploitation and egoism, and develop community? Do the diverse forms of the family feminism supports nourish community? Can any supersede Rousseau's by both alleviating the tension between self-development and care for others, and constructively contributing to politics? It is not enough to say that competitiveness and conflict are not "natural"—indeed, Rousseau would agree! Instead, we need to work out educational, political, and familial institutional arrangements that combat the egoistic, privatistic status quo without the sexual differentiation Rousseau's remedy relies upon. Rousseau's sense of the dangers of forsaking the affectionate, sex-roled family needs to be addressed thoroughly, and showing that his means are unnecessary to and/or destructive of his own ends are avenues to pursue.

Feminist theory raises questions for Rousseau, as well. The motive behind Rousseau's advocacy of the sex-roled, affectionate family is its ability to develop communal bonds, an ability he finds other families lacking; thus, his family is a means to other ends, ends which are both necessary and desirable. Rousseau is not so crude, however, as to argue that the ends justify any means—a family which oppresses any of its members would be both unjustifiable and ineffective. That is, it would not teach us to treat others decently and to sacrifice for them. Thus, like the larger political community, in order to be legitimate the family must involve the members fairly sharing the benefits and burdens of social life, and must in fact establish the equality he deems essential to community.

Since Rousseau's family and society are based on sexual differentiation, the tasks of each sex are different. For feminists, Rousseau must show that these differences, in the family and in politics, really are compatible with equality, and thus with community. Too often anti-feminists simply claim the sexes are different but equal. In the first book devoted to the question of Rousseau's sexual politics, Joel Schwartz seems to follow this trend, for he tends to assume that the fact that women have some power is an argument that the sexes are *equally* empowered (Schwartz 1984). While he is right to assert that Rousseau's women are not powerless, the burden is on Rousseau to show that different kinds of empowerment really can be compatible with equality, with equal voice and respect for all. For example, is indirect authority, which is what women have most access to, as effectively heard and dignifying as the direct authority to which men have most access? Does Rousseau (or Schwartz) show that the personal and social costs, as well as the positive potential, of the sexually differentiated forms of empowerment in fact balance out?

While anti-feminists are too quick to assert that sexual differentiation poses no problem for equality, feminists should not be too quick to point to any difference as proof of inequality. The differences have to be evaluated in terms of their personal and political consequences. A closer analysis of Rousseau's "balance sheet" would not only help in resolving questions of consistency in his thought, but, in answering the question of when different can be equal, could be part of a truly feminist political theory.

Notes

1. Rousseau's discussion of mother-child relations in the state of nature is noteworthy for a number of reasons, including that it takes the fact that we are born independent as relevant, and that it assumes female independence from males in childrearing. It is certainly intriguing that mothers tending to children is not thought by him to necessarily entail lasting emotional attachment on either side, or to lead to any further desire for communal relations. Perhaps he understands the bond between mother and child to be superficial, like bonds between corrupt social people, which

also entail little attachment and fail to lead to community. It's debatable, however, whether this understanding does full justice to the reality of a nursing, teaching, protective mother, even in his state of nature.

2. The period called "childhood" is not stable. Even among lower-class families of late eighteenth century France childhood was remarkably short by our standards. "Children in poor families had to work instead of play. From the age of four, they were considered able to work; and they were set to gathering wood, feeding chickens, or helping to card wool. . . . Children left the family at very young ages—nine to twelve—to work as apprentices and servants" (Fairchilds 1984b, 106). Further, "Work constituted the very fabric of the lives of most French women during the eighteenth century. At least ninety percent of them, from the age of fourteen on, spent most of their waking hours engaged in one or another form of work . . ."(Fox-Genovese 1984, 111).

3. Allan Bloom, Introduction to *Emile:* 4–5. The sexist pronouns are Bloom's—Rousseau thought it was equally possible for both sexes to be bourgeois in this sense, and equally undesirable, as will be explained later.

4. See the play *Master Harold and the Boys*, where a white South African is disturbed by his relationship with the black servants who have cared for him as a child. Adrienne Rich has also written of this problem for whites in the South, brought up by black mammies whom they were later taught to despise as black people. Even without the aspect of racism, Rousseau sees the danger of allowing people for whom one has no respect be the primary caretakers of one's children.

5. Likewise, in the *Social Contract*, Book III, Chapter XV, Rousseau considers it a sign of social decay when we pay others to do our jobs, or pay taxes instead of doing the work ourselves.

6. This would explain why, in the *Social Contract*, Book III, Chapter IX, Rousseau considers the fertility rate a sign of the health of the state.

7. These quotes are taken from a roundtable discussion among contemporary conservatives in "Sex and God in American Politics," *Policy Review* (Summer 1984): 15–17. The first quote is from Phyllis Schlafly, the second from Rabbi Seymour Siegel, and the last from Midge Decter.

8. We thank one of *Hypatia's* anonymous readers for this wording of this issue.

References

Bloom, Allan. 1985. Rousseau on the equality of the sexes. *Justice and equality here and now.* Frank Lucash, ed. Ithaca, New York: Cornell University Press.

Charlton, D.G. 1984. *New images of the natural in France: A study in European cultural history 1750–1800.* Cambridge: Cambridge University Press.

Christenson, Ron. 1972. The political theory of male chauvinism: J.J. Rousseau's paradigm. *Midwest Quarterly* 13; 291–299.

Eisenstein, Zillah. 1981. *The radical future of radical feminism.* New York: Longan.

Fairchilds, Cissie. 1984a. *Domestic enemies: Servants and their masters in old regime France.* Baltimore: John Hopkins University Press.

Fairchilds, Cissie. 1984b. Women and family. *French women and the age of enlightenment.* Samia Spencer, ed. Bloomington, IN: Indiana University Press.

Fox-Genovese, Elizabeth. 1984. Women and work. *French women and the age of enlightenment.* Samia Spencer, ed. Bloomington, IN: Indiana University Press.

Jirmack, P.D. 1979. The paradox of Sophie and Julie: Contemporary response to Rousseau's ideal wife and ideal mother. *Women and society in eighteenth-century France.* Eva Jacobs, et. al., ed. London: The Athlone Press.

Josephson, Matthew. 1931. *Jean-Jacques Rousseau.* New York: Harcourt, Brace & Co.

Lange, Lynda. 1981. Rousseau and modern feminism. *Social Theory and Practice* 7: 245–277.

Lange, Lynda. 1979. Rousseau: Women and the general will. *The sexism of social and political theory.* Lorenne Clark and Lynda Lange, eds. Toronto: University of Toronto Press.

Locke, John. 1968. *The educational writings of John Locke.* James L. Axtell, ed. Cambridge: Cambridge University Press.

Martin, Jane Roland. 1981. Sophie and Emile: A case study of sex bias in the history of educational thought. *Harvard Educational Review* 51: 357–372.

Okin, Susan Moller. 1979. *Women in western political thought.* Princeton, N.J.: Princeton University Press.

Rousseau, Jean-Jacques. [1979.] *Emile, or an education.* New York: Basic Books.

Rousseau, Jean-Jacques. [1978.] *On the social contract.* Rogers Masters, ed. New York: St. Martin's Press.

Rousseau, Jean-Jacques. [1960.] *Politics and the arts.* Ithaca, New York: Cornell University Press.

Schwartz, Joel. 1984. *The sexual politics of Jean-Jacques Rousseau.* Chicago: University of Chicago Press.

Sussman, George. 1982. *Selling mother's milk: The wet-nursing business in France: 1715–1914.* Urbana: University of Illinois Press.

Weiss, Penny. 1987. Rousseau, anti-feminism, and woman's nature. *Political Theory* 15: 81–89.

Weiss, Penny. 1990. Sex, freedom, and equality in Rousseau's Emile. *Polity* (forthcoming).

Wexler, Victor. 1976. Made for man's delight: Rousseau as anti-feminist. *American Historical Review* 81: 266–291.

Reprinted from: Penny Weiss and Anne Harper, "Rousseau's Political Defense of the Sex-Roled Family." In *Hypatia* 5 (3), pp. 90–109. Copyright © 1990. Reprinted by permission of Indiana University Press. ✦

Edmund Burke

Edmund Burke is widely regarded as the founder and most articulate representative of conservative political ideology. Indeed, some discussions of what conservatives reputedly believe amount to little more than catalogues of Burke's chief ideas.[1] However, his work offers a version of conservatism largely unfamiliar to students in the United States. With such notable exceptions as George Will and Russell Kirk, most American "conservatives" are really classical liberals whose views have more in common with those of John Locke and Adam Smith than with those of Burke.

Burke was born in Dublin, Ireland, in 1729 and later studied at Dublin's Trinity College. He began his working life as a "man of letters," publishing two works (including *A Philosophical Enquiry into the Origin of Our Ideas of the Sublime and the Beautiful*) before he turned 30. Soon, he began writing for and editing literary and political journals, and serving as an adviser to politically prominent aristocrats such as the Marquis of Rockingham. As a member of the Whig party, Burke entered upon a parliamentary career (1774–1794) noteworthy for his defense of the American struggle for political rights and for a theory of representation outlined in his "Speech to the Electors of Bristol" (1780). By his death in 1797, Burke had left a body of writings and speeches addressing the major political issues of his day and expressing a political theory that advocated tradition and stability.

Burke's most famous writings, of course, were those in which he criticized the theory and practice of the French Revolution. Unlike the Glorious Revolution of 1688 or the American Revolution, the French Revolution did not defend "traditional liberties" nor did it produce a cautious, limited change in a constitutional government. Based on rationalist political theories and abstract conceptions of human rights, the revolution in France destroyed a long-established social order and led to elitist abuses of power (ending with the Reign of Terror). For Burke, the Enlightenment's influence in public affairs was nothing to celebrate, for it replaced the steady guidance of custom, tradition, and feeling with the cold calculations of reason and the pernicious ideas of "metaphysical scribblers."

As you might expect from someone who spent many years in Parliament, Burke tended not to trace his economic and political views directly to abstract philosophical principles. He believed that sound policy would more likely emerge from pragmatism and prudence than either dogmatism or doctrine. On the whole, what general principles he held can be summarized by the following terms: prescription, prejudice, and presumption. By prescription, Burke meant that political rights or privileges, duties or obligations, as well as property were truly acquired only through long, patient, and considerate use. By prejudice, he meant not bigotry, but the natural feelings people use to guide them through the complexities of life. It is largely a product of the distilled wisdom of the ages found in custom, habit, tradition, and ritual. Finally, by presumption, Burke invoked the idea that long-established practices or institutions are to be seen as beneficial until proven otherwise. They should not be changed, except for very good reasons, and even then, only in a cautious and gradual manner—that is, only when change will bring definite improvement.

This stance of prudence, of course, is the only acceptable course of action given Burke's conception of society. He viewed society as very much like a living organism, whose parts are shaped by the common life of the whole. Society is not a human artifact, as the model of social contract theory would suggest. It cannot be created at will by a band of radical reformers proclaiming a new, absolute theory of politics. A social order has to grow and develop over many generations, slowly adapt to changing circumstances over a long period of time. Thus, Burke believed that the institutions and ideas that have survived thus far have proved themselves in a historical trial by fire, have shown their adaptability, and, having endured, they are worthy of our belief, respect, and support.

Reflections on the Revolution in France

Burke's most celebrated work is the *Reflections on the Revolution in France*, which first appeared in 1790. It was originally intended to be a lengthy letter to a French friend, commenting upon recent political events and criticizing the Revolution's supporters in England. In the selections reprinted here, Burke attacks the Revolution's claims regarding the natural rights of individuals. He argues against the Lockean view that governments are formed to protect these rights and suggests, instead, that governments aim to provide for human wants largely by restraining our passions. Moreover, Burke asserts that whatever rights are worth protecting are the ancient liberties that form the core of our cultural inheritance.

In these excerpts, Burke also criticizes the radical's belief that the world can be remade with relative ease. He does so by asserting that statesmanship does not involve actions based on *a priori* principles. Rather, statesmanship is more a matter of prudential decision making, rooted in the particular circumstances of day-to-day experience. Burke is also critical of the rational individualism found in the social contract theory embraced by many of the Revolution's supporters. In his eyes, such a theory ultimately denies society's true foundation in religion. Rather than treating society like a business partnership in which people come and go at will, Burke regards it as a different sort of partnership—an invisible link across the generations, a sacred commonwealth of established customs and institutions.

Commentaries

Bruce Frohnen presents an excellent, nuanced summary of the principles underlying Burke's political thought. Although Burke was clearly opposed to "metaphysical" and speculative arguments, he nonetheless held positions that we could label a political theory. For example, he argued that, because of the fragile nature of the social order, human affairs should be guided by the lessons of historical experience and not by the claims of abstract reason. As Frohnen's work suggests, Burke believed that tradition, habit, and custom—in a word, prejudice—constitute the very bedrock of order in human society. Only by acknowledging the religious nature of life can we hope to retain the moral code, the good thoughts and dutiful actions, necessary for human progress.

In a selection from his study of Burke, James Conniff examines the particulars of Burke's reaction to the French Revolution. Though Burke took some time to move from concern to outright opposition to the events in France, his criticism of them was nonetheless consistent with his general views. At the time the Revolution occurred, Burke had seen the traditional government of France to be a generally good one. It faltered, however, for two reasons: (1) revolutionary activists mercilessly attacked its fundamental institutions and practices, and (2) governmental leaders did not have the foresight to enact useful reforms. Nevertheless, Burke believed that the Revolution had to be steadfastly opposed because of the political threats it posed—not just to France and its traditions, but to the whole of Europe as well.

Note

1. Samuel Huntington, "Conservatism as Ideology," *American Political Science Review* 52 (1958): 454–473; Russell Kirk, "Introduction," in *The Portable Conservative Reader* (New York: Penguin, 1982), xi–xl.

Web Sources

**http://www.blupete.com/Literature/Biographies/
Philosophy/Burke.htm#TOC**
The Political Philosopher, Edmund Burke. A
biographical sketch with quotations from
Burke's works.

**http://www.c18.rutgers.edu/biblio/burke.
html**
Selected Bibliography: Edmund Burke. An extensive bibliography of writings by and about
Burke.

**http://www.knuten.liu.se/~bjoch509/works/
burke/reflections/reflections.html**
Reflections on the Revolution in France. The
complete text.

**http://www.blupete.com/Literature/Speeches/
1780BurkeBristol.htm**
Burke's Speech at Bristol, Sept. 9, 1780.
Burke's famous theory of representation was
presented in this speech.

Class Activities and Discussion Items

1. Read the writings of some contemporary conservative thinkers. Compare
their views with those of Burke. In what
sense is Burke a conservative theorist?
In what sense are contemporary conservatives Burkean?

2. Describe Burke's general view of the
French Revolution. Compare his response to the Revolution with those
produced by other political theorists—

Joseph de Maistre, Thomas Paine, Mary
Wollstonecraft, and G. W. F. Hegel, for
example.

3. What are Burke's fundamental ideas
about the nature of human beings and
political life? To what extent are these
ideas valid?

Further Reading

Ayling, Stanley. 1988. *Edmund Burke: His Life
and Opinions.* New York: St. Martin's. An important biography.

Freeman, Michael. 1980. *Edmund Burke and the
Critique of Political Radicalism.* Chicago: University of Chicago Press. An argument that
Burke's lasting contribution lies in his critique of radicalism and his corresponding defense of pragmatic politics.

Harbour, William R. 1982. *The Foundations of
Conservative Thought: An Anglo-American Tradition in Retrospect.* Notre Dame, IN: University of Notre Dame Press. Burke's ideas are
discussed in the context of a broader treatment of conservative ideology.

Kramnick, Isaac. 1979. *The Rage of Edmund
Burke: The Conscience of an Ambivalent Conservative.* New York: Basic Books. A challenging interpretation of Burke's life and works.

White, Stephen K. 1994. *Edmund Burke: Modernity, Politics, and Aesthetics.* Thousand Oaks,
CA: Sage Publications. A study of the relationship between Burke's political thought and
his musings about the sublime and the beautiful. ✦

15
Excerpts from *Reflections on the Revolution in France*

Edmund Burke

You will observe that from Magna Charta to the Declaration of Right it has been the uniform policy of our constitution to claim and assert our liberties as an *entailed inheritance* derived to us from our forefathers, and to be transmitted to our posterity—as an estate specially belonging to the people of this kingdom, without any reference whatever to any other more general or prior right. By this means our constitution preserves a unity in so great a diversity of its parts. We have an inheritable crown, an inheritable peerage, and a House of Commons and a people inheriting privileges, franchises, and liberties from a long line of ancestors.

This policy appears to me to be the result of profound reflection, or rather the happy effect of following nature, which is wisdom without reflection, and above it. A spirit of innovation is generally the result of a selfish temper and confined views. People will not look forward to posterity, who never look backward to their ancestors. Besides, the people of England well know that the idea of inheritance furnishes a sure principle of conservation and a sure principle of transmission, without at all excluding a principle of improvement. It leaves acquisition free, but it secures what it acquires. Whatever advantages are obtained by a state proceeding on these maxims are locked fast as in a sort of family settlement, grasped as in a kind of mortmain forever. By a constitutional policy, working after the pattern of nature, we receive, we hold, we transmit our government and our privileges in the same manner in which we enjoy and transmit our property and our lives. The institutions of policy, the goods of fortune, the gifts of providence are handed down to us, and from us, in the same course and order. Our political system is placed in a just correspondence and symmetry with the order of the world and with the mode of existence decreed to a permanent body composed of transitory parts, wherein, by the disposition of a stupendous wisdom, molding together the great mysterious incorporation of the human race, the whole, at one time, is never old or middle-aged or young, but, in a condition of unchangeable constancy, moves on through the varied tenor of perpetual decay, fall, renovation, and progression. Thus, by preserving the method of nature in the conduct of the state, in what we improve we are never wholly new; in what we retain we are never wholly obsolete. By adhering in this manner and on those principles to our forefathers, we are guided not by the superstition of antiquarians, but by the spirit of philosophic analogy. In this choice of inheritance we have given to our frame of polity the image of a relation in blood, binding up the constitution of our country with our dearest domestic ties, adopting our fundamental laws into the bosom of our family affections, keeping inseparable and cherishing with the warmth of all their combined and mutually reflected charities our state, our hearths, our sepulchres, and our altars.

Through the same plan of a conformity to nature in our artificial institutions, and by calling in the aid of her unerring and powerful instincts to fortify the fallible and feeble contrivances of our reason, we have derived several other, and those no small, benefits from considering our liberties in the light of an inheritance. Always acting as if in the presence of canonized forefathers, the spirit of freedom, leading in itself to misrule and excess, is tempered with an awful gravity. This idea of a liberal descent inspires us with a sense of habitual native dignity which prevents that upstart insolence almost inevitably adhering to and disgracing those who are the first acquirers of any distinction. By this means our liberty becomes a noble freedom. It carries an imposing and majestic aspect. It has a pedigree and illustrating ancestors. It has its bearings and its ensigns armorial. It has its gallery of portraits, its monumental inscriptions, its records, evidences, and titles. We procure reverence to our civil institutions on the principle upon which nature teaches us to revere individual men: on account of their age and on account of those from whom they are descended. All your sophisters cannot produce anything better adapted to preserve a rational and manly freedom than the course that we have pursued, who have chosen our nature rather than our speculations, our breasts rather than our inventions, for the great conservatories and magazines of our rights and privileges.

You might, if you pleased, have profited of our example and have given to your recovered freedom a correspondent dignity. Your privileges, though discontinued, were not lost to memory. Your constitution, it is true, whilst you were out of possession, suffered waste and dilapidation; but you possessed in some parts the walls and in all the foundations of a noble and venerable castle. You might have repaired those walls; you might have built on those old foundations. Your constitution was suspended before it was perfected, but you had the elements of a constitution very nearly as good as could be wished. In your old states you possessed that variety of parts corresponding with the various descriptions of which your community was happily composed; you had all that combination and all that opposition of interests; you had that action and counteraction which, in the natural and in the political world, from the reciprocal struggle of discordant powers, draws out the harmony of the universe. These opposed and conflicting interests which you considered as so great a blemish in your old and in our present constitution interpose a salutary check to all precipitate resolutions. They render deliberation a matter, not of choice, but of necessity; they make all change a subject of *compromise*, which naturally begets moderation; they produce *temperaments* preventing the sore evil of harsh, crude, unqualified refor-

mations, and rendering all the headlong exertions of arbitrary power, in the few or in the many, for ever impracticable. Through that diversity of members and interests, general liberty had as many securities as there were separate views in the several orders, whilst, by pressing down the whole by the weight of a real monarchy, the separate parts would have been prevented from warping and starting from their allotted places.

You had all these advantages in your ancient states, but you chose to act as if you had never been molded into civil society and had everything to begin anew. You began ill, because you began by despising everything that belonged to you. You set up your trade without a capital. If the last generations of your country appeared without much luster in your eyes, you might have passed them by and derived your claims from a more early race of ancestors. Under a pious predilection for those ancestors, your imaginations would have realized in them a standard of virtue and wisdom beyond the vulgar practice of the hour; and you would have risen with the example to whose imitation you aspired. Respecting your forefathers, you would have been taught to respect yourselves. You would not have chosen to consider the French as a people of yesterday, as a nation of lowborn servile wretches until the emancipating year of 1789. In order to furnish, at the expense of your honor, an excuse to your apologists here for several enormities of yours, you would not have been content to be represented as a gang of Maroon slaves suddenly broke loose from the house of bondage, and therefore to be pardoned for your abuse of the liberty to which you were not accustomed and ill fitted. Would it not, my worthy friend, have been wiser to have you thought, what I, for one, always thought you, a generous and gallant nation, long misled to your disadvantage by your high and romantic sentiments of fidelity, honor, and loyalty; that events had been unfavorable to you, but that you were not enslaved through any illiberal or servile disposition; that in your most devoted submission you were actuated by a principle of public spirit, and that it was your country you worshiped in the person of your king? Had you made it to be understood that in the delusion of this amiable error you had gone further than your wise ancestors, that you were resolved to resume your ancient privileges, whilst you preserved the spirit of your ancient and your recent loyalty and honor; or if, diffident of yourselves and not clearly discerning the almost obliterated constitution of your ancestors, you had looked to your neighbors in this land who had kept alive the ancient principles and models of the old common law of Europe meliorated and adapted to its present state—by following wise examples you would have given new examples of wisdom to the world. You would have rendered the cause of liberty venerable in the eyes of every worthy mind in every nation. You would have shamed despotism from the earth by showing that freedom was not only reconcilable, but, as when well disciplined it is, auxiliary to law. You would have had an unoppressive but a productive revenue. You would have had a flourishing commerce to feed it. You would have had a free constitution, a potent monarchy, a disciplined army, a reformed and venerated clergy, a mitigated but spirited nobility to lead your virtue, not to overlay it; you would have had a liberal order of commons to emulate and to recruit that nobility; you would have had a protected, satisfied, laborious, and obedient people, taught to seek and to recognize the happiness that is to be found by virtue in all conditions; in which consists the true moral equality of mankind, and not in that monstrous fiction which, by inspiring false ideas and vain expectations into men destined to travel in the obscure walk of laborious life, serves only to aggravate and embitter that real inequality which it never can remove, and which the order of civil life establishes as much for the benefit of those whom it must leave in a humble state as those whom it is able to exalt to a condition more splendid, but not more happy. You had a smooth and easy career of felicity and glory laid open to you, beyond anything recorded in the history of the world, but you have shown that difficulty is good for man. . . .

It is no wonder, therefore, that with these ideas of everything in their constitution and government at home, either in church or state, as illegitimate and usurped, or at best as a vain mockery, they look abroad with an eager and passionate enthusiasm. Whilst they are possessed by these notions, it is vain to talk to them of the practice of their ancestors, the fundamental laws of their country, the fixed form of a constitution whose merits are confirmed by the solid test of long experience and an increasing public strength and national prosperity. They despise experience as the wisdom of unlettered men; and as for the rest, they have wrought underground a mine that will blow up, at one grand explosion, all examples of antiquity, all precedents, charters, and acts of parliament. They have "the rights of men". Against these there can be no prescription, against these no agreement is binding; these admit no temperament and no compromise; anything withheld from their full demand is so much of fraud and injustice. Against these their rights of men let no government look for security in the length of its continuance, or in the justice and lenity of its administration. The objections of these speculatists, if its forms do not quadrate with their theories, are as valid against such an old and beneficent government as against the most violent tyranny or the greenest usurpation. They are always at issue with governments, not on a question of abuse, but a question of competency and a question of title. I have nothing to say to the clumsy subtilty of their political metaphysics. Let them be their amusement in the schools.—"*Illa se jactet in aula Aeolus, et clauso ventorum carcere regnet*".[1]—But let them not break prison to burst like a *Levanter*, to sweep the earth with their hurricane and to break up the fountains of the great deep to overwhelm us.

Far am I from denying in theory, full as far is my heart from withholding in practice (if I were of power to give or to withhold) the *real* rights of men. In denying their false claims of right, I do not mean to injure those which are real, and are such as their pretended rights would totally destroy. If civil society be made for the advantage of man, all the advantages for which it is made become his right. It is an institution of beneficence; and law itself is only beneficence acting by a rule. Men have a right to live by that rule; they have a right to do justice, as between their fellows, whether their fellows are in public function or in ordinary occupation. They have a right to the fruits of their industry and to the means of making their industry fruitful. They have a right to the acquisitions of their parents, to the nourishment and improvement of their offspring, to instruction in life, and to consolation in death. Whatever each man can separately do, without trespassing upon others, he has a right to do for himself; and he has a right to a fair portion of all which society, with all its combinations of skill and force, can do in his favor. In this partnership all men have equal rights, but not to equal things. He that has but five shillings in the partnership has as good a right to it as he that has five hundred pounds has to his larger proportion. But he has not a right to an equal dividend in the product of the joint stock; and as to the share of power, authority, and direction which each individual ought to have in the management of the state, that I must deny to be amongst the direct original rights of man in civil society; for I have in my contemplation the civil social man, and no other. It is a thing to be settled by convention.

If civil society be the offspring of convention, that convention must be its law. That convention must limit and modify all the descriptions of constitution which are formed under it. Every sort of legislative, judicial, or executory power are its creatures. They can have no being in any other state of things; *and how can any man claim under the conventions of civil society rights which do not so much as suppose its existence—rights which are absolutely repugnant to it?* One of the first motives to civil society, and which becomes one of its fundamental rules, is *that no man should be judge in his own cause.* By this each person has at once divested himself of the first fundamental right of uncovenanted man, that is, to judge for himself and to assert his own cause. He abdicates all right to be his own governor. He inclusively, in a great measure, abandons the right of self-defense, the first law of nature. Men cannot enjoy the rights of an uncivil and of a civil

state together. That he may obtain justice, he gives up his right of determining what it is in points the most essential to him. That he may secure some liberty, he makes a surrender in trust of the whole of it.

Government is not made in virtue of natural rights, which may and do exist in total independence of it, and exist in much greater clearness and in a much greater degree of abstract perfection; but their abstract perfection is their practical defect. By having a right to everything they want everything. Government is a contrivance of human wisdom to provide for human *wants.* Men have a right that these wants should be provided for by this wisdom. Among these wants is to be reckoned the want, out of civil society, of a sufficient restraint upon their passions. Society requires not only that the passions of individuals should be subjected, but that even in the mass and body, as well as in the individuals, the inclinations of men should frequently be thwarted, their will controlled, and their passions brought into subjection. This can only be done *by a power out of themselves,* and not, in the exercise of its function, subject to that will and to those passions which it is its office to bridle and subdue. In this sense the restraints on men, as well as their liberties, are to be reckoned among their rights. But as the liberties and the restrictions vary with times and circumstances and admit to infinite modifications, they cannot be settled upon any abstract rule; and nothing is so foolish as to discuss them upon that principle.

The moment you abate anything from the full rights of men, each to govern himself, and suffer any artificial, positive limitation upon those rights, from that moment the whole organization of government becomes a consideration of convenience. This it is which makes the constitution of a state and the due distribution of its powers a matter of the most delicate and complicated skill. It requires a deep knowledge of human nature and human necessities, and of the things which facilitate or obstruct the various ends which are to be pursued by the mechanism of civil institutions. The state is to have recruits to its strength, and remedies to its distempers. What is the use of discussing a man's abstract right to food or medicine? The question is upon the method of procuring and administering them. In that deliberation I shall always advise to call in the aid of the farmer and the physician rather than the professor of metaphysics.

The science of constructing a commonwealth, or renovating it, or reforming it, is, like every other experimental science, not to be taught *a priori*. Nor is it a short experience that can instruct us in that practical science, because the real effects of moral causes are not always immediate; but that which in the first instance is prejudicial may be excellent in its remoter operation, and its excellence may arise even from the ill effects it produces in the beginning. The reverse also happens: and very plausible schemes, with very pleasing commencements, have often shameful and lamentable conclusions. In states there are often some obscure and almost latent causes, things which appear at first view of little moment, on which a very great part of its prosperity or adversity may most essentially depend. The science of government being therefore so practical in itself and intended for such practical purposes—a matter which requires experience, and even more experience than any person can gain in his whole life, however sagacious and observing he may be—it is with infinite caution that any man ought to venture upon pulling down an edifice which has answered in any tolerable degree for ages the common purposes of society, or on building it up again without having models and patterns of approved utility before his eyes.

These metaphysic rights entering into common life, like rays of light which pierce into a dense medium, are by the laws of nature refracted from their straight line. Indeed, in the gross and complicated mass of human passions and concerns the primitive rights of men undergo such a variety of refractions and reflections that it becomes absurd to talk of them as if they continued in the simplicity of their original direction. The nature of man is intricate; the objects of society are of the greatest possible complexity; and, therefore, no simple disposition or direction of power can be suitable either to man's nature or to the quality of his affairs. When I hear the simplicity of contrivance aimed at and boasted of in any new political constitutions, I am at no loss to decide that the artificers are grossly ignorant of their trade or totally negligent of their duty. The simple governments are fundamentally defective, to say no worse of them. If you were to contemplate society in but one point of view, all these simple modes of polity are infinitely captivating. In effect each would answer its single end much more perfectly than the more complex is able to attain all its complex purposes. But it is better that the whole should be imperfectly and anomalously answered than that, while some parts are provided for with great exactness, others might be totally neglected or perhaps materially injured by the over-care of a favorite member.

The pretended rights of these theorists are all extremes; and in proportion as they are metaphysically true, they are morally and politically false. The rights of men are in a sort of *middle*, incapable of definition, but not impossible to be discerned. The rights of men in governments are their advantages; and these are often in balances between differences of good, in compromises sometimes between good and evil, and sometimes between evil and evil. Political reason is a computing principle: adding, subtracting, multiplying, and dividing, morally and not metaphysically or mathematically, true moral denominations.

By these theorists the right of the people is almost always sophistically confounded with their power. The body of the community, whenever it can come to act, can meet with no effectual resistance; but till power and right are the same, the whole body of them has no right inconsistent with virtue, and the first of all virtues, prudence. Men have no right to what is not reasonable and to what is not for their benefit; for though a pleasant writer said, *liceat perire poetis*, when one of them, in cold blood, is said to have leaped into the flames of a volcanic revolution, *ardentem frigidus Aetnam insiluit*,[2] I consider such a frolic rather as an unjustifiable poetic license than as one of the franchises of Parnassus; and whether he was a poet, or divine, or politician that chose to exercise this kind of right, I think that more wise, because more charitable, thoughts would urge me rather to save the man than to preserve his brazen slippers as the monuments of his folly.

The kind of anniversary sermons to which a great part of what I write refers, if men are not shamed out of their present course in commemorating the fact, will cheat many out of the principles, and deprive them of the benefits, of the revolution they commemorate. I confess to you, Sir, I never liked this continual talk of resistance and revolution, or the practice of making the extreme medicine of the constitution its daily bread. It renders the habit of society dangerously valetudinary; it is taking periodical doses of mercury sublimate and swallowing down repeated provocatives of cantharides to our love of liberty.

This distemper of remedy, grown habitual, relaxes and wears out, by a vulgar and prostituted use, the spring of that spirit which is to be exerted on great occasions. It was in the most patient period of Roman servitude that themes of tyrannicide made the ordinary exercise of boys at school—*cum perimit saevos classis numerosa tyrannos.*[3] In the ordinary state of things, it produces in a country like ours the worst effects, even on the cause of that liberty which it abuses with the dissoluteness of an extravagant speculation. Almost all the high-bred republicans of my time have, after a short space, become the most decided, thorough-paced courtiers; they soon left the business of a tedious, moderate, but practical resistance to those of us whom, in the pride and intoxication of their theories, they have slighted as not much better than Tories. Hypocrisy, of course, delights in the most sublime speculations, for, never intending to go beyond speculation, it costs nothing to have it magnificent. But even in cases where rather levity than fraud was to be suspected in these ranting speculations, the issue has been much the same. These professors, finding their extreme principles not applicable to cases which call only for a qualified or, as I may say, civil and legal resistance, in such cases employ no resistance at all. It is with them a war or a revolu-

tion, or it is nothing. Finding their schemes of politics not adapted to the state of the world in which they live, they often come to think lightly of all public principle, and are ready, on their part, to abandon for a very trivial interest what they find of very trivial value. Some, indeed, are of more steady and persevering natures, but these are eager politicians out of parliament who have little to tempt them to abandon their favorite projects. They have some change in the church or state, or both, constantly in their view. When that is the case, they are always bad citizens and perfectly unsure connections. For, considering their speculative designs as of infinite value, and the actual arrangement of the state as of no estimation, they are at best indifferent about it. They see no merit in the good, and no fault in the vicious, management of public affairs; they rather rejoice in the latter, as more propitious to revolution. They see no merit or demerit in any man, or any action, or any political principle any further than as they may forward or retard their design of change; they therefore take up, one day, the most violent and stretched prerogative, and another time the wildest democratic ideas of freedom, and pass from one to the other without any sort of regard to cause, to person, or to party....

We know, and what is better, we feel inwardly, that religion is the basis of civil society and the source of all good and of all comfort. In England we are so convinced of this, that there is no rust of superstition with which the accumulated absurdity of the human mind might have crusted it over in the course of ages, that ninety-nine in a hundred of the people of England would not prefer to impiety. We shall never be such fools as to call in an enemy to the substance of any system to remove its corruptions, to supply its defects, or to perfect its construction. If our religious tenets should ever want a further elucidation, we shall not call on atheism to explain them. We shall not light up our temple from that unhallowed fire. It will be illuminated with other lights. It will be perfumed with other incense than the infectious stuff which is imported by the smugglers of adulterated metaphysics. If our ecclesiastical establishment should want a revision, it is not avarice or rapacity, public or private, that we shall employ for the audit, or receipt, or application of its consecrated revenue. Violently condemning neither the Greek nor the Armenian, nor, since heats are subsided, the Roman system of religion, we prefer the Protestant, not because we think it has less of the Christian religion in it, but because, in our judgment, it has more. We are Protestants, not from indifference, but from zeal.

We know, and it is our pride to know, that man is by his constitution a religious animal; that atheism is against, not only our reason, but our instincts; and that it cannot prevail long. But if, in the moment of riot and in a drunken delirium from the hot spirit drawn out of the alembic of hell, which in France is now so furiously boiling, we should uncover our nakedness by throwing off that Christian religion which has hitherto been our boast and comfort, and one great source of civilization amongst us and amongst many other nations, we are apprehensive (being well aware that the mind will not endure a void) that some uncouth, pernicious, and degrading superstition might take place of it.

For that reason, before we take from our establishment the natural, human means of estimation and give it up to contempt, as you have done, and in doing it have incurred the penalties you well deserve to suffer, we desire that some other may be presented to us in the place of it. We shall then form our judgment.

On these ideas, instead of quarrelling with establishments, as some do who have made a philosophy and a religion of their hostility to such institutions, we cleave closely to them. We are resolved to keep an established church, an established monarchy, an established aristocracy, and an established democracy, each in the degree it exists, and in no greater. I shall show you presently how much of each of these we possess.

It has been the misfortune (not, as these gentlemen think it, the glory) of this age that everything is to be discussed as if the constitution of our country were to be always a subject rather of altercation than enjoyment. For this reason, as well as for the satisfaction of those among you (if any such you have among you) who may wish to profit of examples, I venture to trouble you with a few thoughts upon each of these establishments. I do not think they were unwise in ancient Rome who, when they wished to new-model their laws; set commissioners to examine the best constituted republics within their reach.

First, I beg leave to speak of our church establishment, which is the first of our prejudices, not a prejudice destitute of reason, but involving in it profound and extensive wisdom. I speak of it first. It is first and last and midst in our minds. For, taking ground on that religious system of which we are now in possession, we continue to act on the early received and uniformly continued sense of mankind. That sense not only, like a wise architect, hath built up the august fabric of states, but, like a provident proprietor, to preserve the structure from profanation and ruin, as a sacred temple purged from all the impurities of fraud and violence and injustice and tyranny, hath solemnly and forever consecrated the commonwealth and all that officiate in it. This consecration is made that all who administer the government of men, in which they stand in the person of God himself, should have high and worthy notions of their function and destination, that their hope should be full of immortality, that they should not look to the paltry pelf of the moment nor to the temporary and transient praise of the vulgar, but to a solid, permanent existence in the permanent part of their nature, and to a permanent fame and glory in the example they leave as a rich inheritance to the world.

Such sublime principles ought to be infused into persons of exalted situations, and religious establishments provided that may continually revive and enforce them. Every sort of moral, every sort of civil, every sort of politic institution, aiding the rational and natural ties that connect the human understanding and affections to the divine, are not more than necessary in order to build up that wonderful structure Man, whose prerogative it is to be in a great degree a creature of his own making, and who, when made as he ought to be made, is destined to hold no trivial place in the creation. But whenever man is put over men, as the better nature ought ever to preside, in that case more particularly, he should as nearly as possible be approximated to his perfection.

The consecration of the state by a state religious establishment is necessary, also, to operate with a wholesome awe upon free citizens, because, in order to secure their freedom, they must enjoy some determinate portion of power. To them, therefore, a religion connected with the state, and with their duty toward it, becomes even more necessary than in such societies where the people, by the terms of their subjection, are confined to private sentiments and the management of their own family concerns. All persons possessing any portion of power ought to be strongly and awfully impressed with an idea that they act in trust, and that they are to account for their conduct in that trust to the one great Master, Author, and Founder of society. . . .

To avoid, therefore, the evils of inconstancy and versatility, ten thousand times worse than those of obstinacy and the blindest prejudice, we have consecrated the state, that no man should approach to look into its defects or corruptions but with due caution, that he should never dream of beginning its reformation by its subversion, that he should approach to the faults of the state as to the wounds of a father, with pious awe and trembling solicitude. By this wise prejudice we are taught to look with horror on those children of their country who are prompt rashly to hack that aged parent in pieces and put him into the kettle of magicians, in hopes that by their poisonous weeds and wild incantations they may regenerate the paternal constitution and renovate their father's life.

Society is indeed a contract. Subordinate contracts for objects of mere occasional interest may be dissolved at pleasure—but the state ought not to be considered as nothing better than a partnership agreement in a trade of pepper and coffee, calico, or tobacco, or some other such low concern, to be taken up for a little temporary interest, and to be dissolved by the fancy of the parties. It is to be looked on with other reverence, because it is not a partnership in things subservient only to the gross animal existence of a temporary and perishable nature. It is a partnership in all science; a partnership in all art; a partnership in every virtue and in all perfection. As the ends of such a partnership cannot be obtained in many generations, it becomes a partnership not only between those who are living, but between those who are living, those who are dead, and those who are to be born. Each contract of each particular state is but a clause in the great primeval contract of eternal society, linking the lower with the higher natures, connecting the visible and invisible world, according to a fixed compact sanctioned by the inviolable oath which holds all physical and all moral natures, each in their appointed place. This law is not subject to the will of those who by an obligation above them, and infinitely superior, are bound to submit their will to that law. The municipal corporations of that universal kingdom are not morally at liberty at their pleasure, and on their speculations of a contingent improvement, wholly to separate and tear asunder the bands of their subordinate community and to dissolve it into an unsocial, uncivil, unconnected chaos of elementary principles. It is the first and supreme necessity only, a necessity that is not chosen but chooses, a necessity paramount to deliberation, that admits no discussion and demands no evidence, which alone can justify a resort to anarchy. This necessity is no exception to the rule, because this necessity itself is a part, too, of that moral and physical disposition of things to which man must be obedient by consent or force; but if that which is only submission to necessity should be made the object of choice, the law is broken, nature is disobeyed, and the rebellious are outlawed, cast forth, and exiled from this world of reason, and order, and peace, and virtue, and fruitful penitence, into the antagonist world of madness, discord, vice, confusion, and unavailing sorrow.

These, my dear Sir, are, were, and, I think, long will be the sentiments of not the least learned and reflecting part of this kingdom.

They who are included in this description form their opinions on such grounds as such persons ought to form them. The less inquiring receive them from an authority which those whom Providence dooms to live on trust need not be ashamed to rely on. These two sorts of men move in the same direction, though in a different place. They both move with the order of the universe. They all know or feel this great ancient truth: *Quod illi principi et praepotenti Deo qui omnem hunc mundum regit, nihil eorum quae quidem faant in terris acceptius quam concilia et coetus hominum jure sociati quae civitates appellantur.*[4] They take this tenet of the head and heart, not from the great name which it immediately bears, nor from the greater from whence it is derived, but from that which alone can give true weight and sanction to any learned opinion, the common nature and common relation of men. Persuaded that all things ought to be done with reference, and referring all to the point of reference to which all should be directed, they think themselves bound, not only as individuals in the sanctuary of the heart or as congregated in that personal capacity, to renew the memory of their high origin and cast, but also in their corporate character to perform their national homage to the institutor and author and protector of civil society; without which civil society man could not by any possibility arrive at the perfection of which his nature is capable, nor even make a remote and faint approach to it. They conceive that He who gave our nature to be perfected by our virtue willed also the necessary means of its perfection. He willed therefore the state—He willed its connection with the source and original archetype of all perfection. They who are convinced of this His will, which is the law of laws and the sovereign of sovereigns, cannot think it reprehensible that this our corporate fealty and homage, that this our recognition of a seigniory paramount, I had almost said this oblation of the state itself as a worthy offering on the high altar of universal praise, should be performed as all public, solemn acts are performed, in buildings, in music, in decoration, in speech, in the dignity of persons, according to the customs of mankind taught by their nature; that is, with modest splendor and unassuming state, with mild majesty and sober pomp. For those purposes they think some part of the wealth of the country is as usefully employed as it can be in fomenting the luxury of individuals. It is the public ornament. It is the public consolation. It nourishes the public hope. The poorest man finds his own importance and dignity in it, whilst the wealth and pride of individuals at every moment makes the man of humble rank and fortune sensible of his inferiority and degrades and vilifies his condition. It is for the man in humble life, and to raise his nature and to put him in mind of a state in which the privileges of opulence will cease, when he will be equal by nature, and may be more than equal by virtue, that this portion of the general wealth of his country is employed and sanctified.

I assure you I do not aim at singularity. I give you opinions which have been accepted amongst us, from very early times to this moment, with a continued and general approbation, and which indeed are worked into my mind that I am unable to distinguish what I have learned from others from the results of my own meditation.

It is on some such principles that the majority of the people of England, far from thinking a religious national establishment unlawful, hardly think it lawful to be without one. In France you are wholly mistaken if you do not believe us above all other things attached to it, and beyond all other nations; and when this people has acted unwisely and unjustifiably in its favor (as in some instances they have done most certainly), in their very errors you will at least discover their zeal.

This principle runs through the whole system of their polity. They do not consider their church establishment as convenient, but as essential to their state, not as a thing heterogeneous and separable, something added for accommodation, what they may either keep or lay aside according to their temporary ideas of convenience. They consider it as the foundation of their whole constitution, with which, and with every part of which, it holds an indissoluble union. Church and state are ideas inseparable in their minds, and scarcely is the one ever mentioned without mentioning the other. . . .

Notes

1. Virgil, *Aeneid*, I, 140–41. "Let Aeolus bluster in that hall, and reign in the closed prison of the winds". Aeolus was a wind god, and the winds were imagined as shut up until released. A Levanter was a strong gale from the east.
2. Horace, *Ars poetica*, 465–66. "Poets are permitted to perish. . . . In cold blood he jumped into burning Etna"; a reference to the suicide of Empedocles, supposed to have thrown himself into a volcano, where his sandals alone survived.
3. Juvenal, *Satires*, VII, 151: "When numerous class destroys the cruel tyrants".
4. Cicero, *De Republica*, VI, 13: "That nothing indeed of the events which occur on earth is more pleasing to that supreme and prepotent God who rules this entire universe than those societies and associations of men, cemented by laws, which are called states".

Adapted from: Edmund Burke, *Reflections on the Revolution in France*, pp. 29–33, 50–56, 79–81, 84–87. Hackett Publishing Company, 1987. Originally published 1790. ✦

16
Philosophy, Man, and Society

Burkean Political Philosophy

Bruce Frohnen

We shall say the imitative poet produces a bad regime in the soul of each private man by making phantoms that are very far removed from the truth and by gratifying the soul's foolish part, which doesn't distinguish big from little, but believes the same things are at one time big and at another little.

—Plato, *The Republic*

Strepsiades: What are they doing over there who are so stooped over?
Student: They are delving into Erebus under Tartarus.
Strepsiades: Why then is the anus looking at the heaven?
Student: It itself by itself is being taught astronomy.

—Aristophanes, *The Clouds*

"There is an old quarrel between poetry and philosophy."[1] So Socrates asserted soon after banishing poets from his model city. Poets, according to Socrates, corrupt men's souls by teaching them that the apparent or, more precisely, the conventional, is true. They half-wittingly enslave men to their passions and to the partial and false perceptions embodied in traditional institutions, beliefs, and practices. Poets have returned the philosopher's compliments in kind. Socrates, founder of the Western philosophical tradition, was portrayed in his own time as little

more than an arrogant dimwit by the comic poet Aristophanes. For Aristophanes, Socrates's foolish search for an absolute, rational truth independent of human circumstance is dangerous, not because it may succeed and so transform the city, but because it teaches a prideful disregard for the traditions and even for the gods that make life in the city possible. For the poet, Socrates's search for a truth independent of the circumstances making up our social natures is not just dangerous, but also silly. By constantly searching for some independent, abstract truth the philosopher ends up with his head in the ground and his anus sticking up in the air, pathetically attempting to learn "by itself."

The philosopher believes that our concern with circumstances—with the things we believe are at one time big and at another little—corrupts our nature by distracting us from the unchanging truths revealed by philosophical reason. But if he disregards the varying circumstances of life, Aristophanes tells us, man is incapable of truly rational action. The "rational" philosopher is capable only of corruption, impiety, and foolishness. His rejection of circumstance entails rejection of our family, our God, and our community—those things that make us truly human.

Traditions of thought and action—our codes of conduct or manners and our accepted beliefs or prejudices—essentially are responses, developed and refined over time, to the circumstances of our communities. Circumstances—from the weather to the current state of our family or nation—and our often habituated responses to these circumstances make up a large part of our lives. Thus they also make up a large part of our natures. For Burke, who was confronted with a *movement* of impious "philosophy," namely French revolutionary Jacobinism, habituated responses to circumstances *are* human nature. "Art is man's nature" because mere rational thought is incapable of maintaining society.[2] Rational thought, disconnected from habit and circumstance, would destroy convention and thereby man himself.

Burke preferred the poet to the philosopher because the poet must apply himself to "the moral constitution of the heart" in his audience.[3] The heart, when not subverted by rationalistic philosophies, is less critical of society and accepted moral standards than is philosophical reason. Where philosophical reason may see only age, infirmity, and imperfection, the heart may see an old, familiar, and dear friend.

Philosophical (or speculative) reason is more dangerous than the passions themselves, for "there is a boundary to men's passions, when they act from feeling; none when they are under the influence of imagination. Remove a grievance, and, when men act from feeling, you go a great way towards quieting a commotion. But the good or bad conduct of a government, the protection men have enjoyed or the oppression they have suffered under it, are of no sort of moment, when a faction, proceeding upon speculative grounds, is thoroughly heated against its form. When a man is from system furious against monarchy or episcopacy, the good conduct of the monarch or the bishop has no other effect than further to irritate the adversary."[4]

Speculative reason is more dangerous than passion because it respects no limits save its own internal logic. Immoderate by nature, this reason may blind men to the good in their society and so destroy it and themselves. Only if one loves one's society (and love is, after all, a passion) may one see that its goodness transcends merely "rationalistic" criteria.

Abstraction and Idealization

Burke gave early warning of the dangers of Jacobinism. Before the French Terror had begun, Burke observed that French society, like all societies, was fragile. This fragile society was destroyed by the rational principles of the Jacobins. Their schemes to impose their notions of "liberty, equality, and fraternity" on their nation, without reference to its preexisting circumstances, left no room for traditional forms and practices, no room even for humanity or simple pity. The fruit of Jacobin rationalism was mass murder. And, Burke observed, the poison was spreading. English radicals now justified

their own monarchy on the grounds that it was, in fact, "elective." They thereby called into question the traditional foundations of the British Constitution, undermining the very bases of British society. But why is it so dangerous to legitimize a monarchy by recasting it in terms dictated by abstract democratic principles? What differentiates the use of bad, abstract philosophical criteria from the reason whose use Burke said "is not to revolt against authority"?[5] The answer seems to lie in the kind of questions that may be asked while still serving true reason. For Burke, reason "is a friend who makes an useful suggestion to the court, without questioning its jurisdiction. Whilst he acknowledges its competence, he promotes its efficiency."[6]

One uses reason properly when one seeks to improve the already existing structure of society, without calling its fundamental bases into question. The proper use of reason is based upon the acceptance of society as it stands. Proper reason takes into account, not its own coherence, but its probable effects on that which it is supposed to serve—the existing, virtuous way of life and the fundamental institutions, beliefs, and practices making that good life possible.

Whether they were used in the service of increased liberty or of increased governmental power, Burke abhorred metaphysical arguments of abstract, idealized right. For Burke, "Circumstances are what render every civil and political scheme beneficial or noxious to mankind."[7] Thus, in discussing the French revolutionaries, Burke asked, "Is it because liberty in the abstract may be classed amongst the blessings of mankind, that I am seriously to felicitate a madman who has escaped from the protecting restraint and wholesome darkness of his cell on his restoration to the enjoyment of light and liberty?"[8]

Liberty, for Burke, is not bad as an ideal. But when liberty is judged in practice, the nature of those who are to enjoy it and the uses to which it is to be put must be taken into account; and this account must take human nature as it is, not as one might wish it to be.

The effect of liberty to individuals is, that they may do what they please: we ought to see what it will please them to do, before we risk congratulations, which may be soon turned into complaints. Prudence would dictate this in the case of separate, insulated, private men. But liberty, when men act in bodies, is *power*. Considerate people, before they declare themselves, will observe the use which is made of *power*,—and particularly of so trying a thing as *new* power in *new* persons, of whose principles, tempers, and dispositions they have little or no experience, and in situations where those who appear the most stirring in the scene may possibly not be the real movers.[9]

The quality of its practitioners determines the quality (good *or bad*) of the liberty at their disposal. The only reasonable course, then, is to entrust men with only that liberty that their natures and circumstances fit them to exercise properly. "Men have no right to what is not reasonable, and to what is not for their benefit."[10]

Loathing philosophers, Burke had to refute them with necessarily philosophical argument. According to John MacCunn, Burke's hatred was aimed not so much at philosophy as at abstraction.[11] But a key distinction must be made between the kind of abstraction that cannot be avoided if philosophical, or even practical political, discussion is to take place and the kind of rationality that conservatives such as Burke find abhorrent.

Onora O'Neill points out that "abstraction, taken literally, is a matter of selective omission, of leaving out some predicates from descriptions and theories." Even in differentiating dog from cat we are engaging in abstraction. The categories "dog" and "cat" are themselves abstract—they are not fully determinate. When we want to refer to the category "dog" we say "dog," not "small brown dog with white paws" let alone "quadruped, standing so high, weighing so much" and so on. Such rigid criteria for differentiation would make categorization, and thus discourse, impossible.

To communicate without abstraction is impossible. What is more, to minimize abstraction beyond a certain point is undesirable. "The less abstract our reasoning the greater the likelihood that it hinges upon premises that others will dispute, and that its conclusions will seem irrelevant to those others."[12] Is a Great Dane a dog? According to some overly specific criteria, it may be too big to be a dog, yet we *know* that a Great Dane is a dog.

A reasonable man, Burke did not attack abstraction per se; to do so would have rendered his own arguments incomprehensible. Burke's attacks upon "metaphysical" arguments and "abstract" rights were actually attacks upon idealization. According to O'Neill, "an idealised account or theory not merely *omits* certain predicates that are true of the matter to be considered, but *adds* predicates that are false of the matter to be considered."[13] Such an account not only abstracts human nature from its particular circumstances, but posits hypothetical human actors with abilities, motives, and capacities not necessarily reflecting *any* reality. At the root of Burkean political philosophy lies the conviction that any attempt to study men without reference to their particular historical and cultural positions is idealized; it is to argue that universal truths may be found that do not rely upon and act themselves out through circumstance; it is to deny, not only that man is fallible, but that he is a creature of circumstance and convention.

Jacobin theories of the abstract rights of men ignore the role of circumstance in forming human nature and thus the variety of human characters and capacities.

Men are qualified for civil liberty in exact proportion to their disposition to put moral chains upon their own appetites,—in proportion as their love to justice is above their rapacity,—in proportion as their soundness and sobriety of understanding is above their vanity and presumption,—in proportion as they are more disposed to listen to the counsels of the wise and good, in preference to the flattery of knaves. Society cannot exist, unless a controlling power upon will and appetite be placed somewhere; and the less of it there is within, the more there must be without. It is ordained in the eternal constitution of things, that men of intemperate minds cannot be free. Their passions forge their fetters.[14]

The amount of liberty which a people should have is the amount which they may use without becoming licentious. The amount of liberty must fit the character of those who are to enjoy it. For Burke, circumstances determine what is a good and what is a bad policy. However, it is what makes for a circumstance which distinguishes Burke's view of man and society from the metaphysical philosophers he despised.

Just as idealized theories may be used to undermine existing authority, they also may be used to extend it to the point of tyranny. And the result may well be rebellion. Urging British moderation toward the American colonies, Burke argued against all uses of idealized theory. "I am not here going into the distinction of rights, nor attempting to mark their boundaries. I do not enter into these metaphysical distinctions; I hate the very sound of them. . . . But if, intemperately, unwisely, fatally, you sophisticate and poison the very source of government, by urging subtle deductions, and consequences odious to those you govern, from the unlimited and illimitable nature of supreme sovereignty, you will teach them by these means to call that sovereignty itself in question."[15]

Actions based upon idealized principles are extreme by their very nature. Based on "metaphysical distinctions" rather than reality, these principles lead their adherents to ignore circumstance and may lead to ruin by calling the existing order into question. Abstract doctrines contemn tradition, and because they contemn reality itself, their practical failures lead only to redoubled destructive efforts. The French revolutionaries had their doctrine of the rights of men. This doctrine made them supremely dangerous since against these rights "there can be no prescription; against these no argument is binding: these admit no temperament and no compromise: anything withheld from their full demand is so much of fraud and injustice."[16]

Particularly when cast in metaphysical terms, the act of questioning may itself cause destruction because "it may be truly said, that 'once to doubt is once to be decided.' "[17] To doubt the goodness of a particular institu-

tion or belief is to fail to support it and thus to let it fall. Doubt is, in a very real sense, opposition. "They who do not love religion hate it."[18] Thus the system set up by the French revolutionaries was not merely irreligious; it was a system of atheism. "Whilst everything prepares the body to debauch and the mind to crime, a regular *church of avowed atheism*, established by law, with a direct and sanguinary persecution of Christianity, is formed to prevent all amendment and remorse. Conscience is formally deposed from its dominion over the mind. What fills the measure of horror is, that schools of atheism are set up at the public charge in every part of the country."[19]

For Burke, "Man is by his constitution a religious animal."[20] By rejecting religion the French revolutionaries rejected a fundamental part of human nature. By establishing a state which was not religious, they set themselves up as the creators of a new human nature. Since there is no fundamental, uncorrupted nature of man that can exist completely divorced from institutions and circumstance (since art is man's nature), to reject one, in this case religious, institution is to advocate its replacement by another. By rejecting their established church, the French revolutionaries necessarily set up an official "church" of atheism. They established an institution that taught bad morals but that taught a certain set of morals, nonetheless.

The prudent thinker recognizes that human nature is malleable. His reason is a tool in the search for ways to benefit the community, in accordance with preexisting circumstances and conventions. After all, these gifts of history and Providence are the basis, not only of society, but of man himself.

Circumstance, Convention, and Fittingness

For Burke, the abstract rights of men are all-encompassing—and therefore useless. Everyone cannot enjoy everything in peace. What is more,

The moment you abate anything from the full rights of men each to govern himself, and suffer any artificial, positive limitation upon those rights, from that moment the whole organization of government becomes a consideration of convenience. This it is which makes the constitution of a state, and the due distribution of its powers, a matter of the most delicate and complicated skill. It requires a deep knowledge of human nature and human necessities, and of the things which facilitate or obstruct the various ends which are to be pursued by the mechanism of civil institutions. . . . What is the use of discussing a man's abstract right to food or medicine? The question is upon the method of procuring and administering them. In that deliberation I shall always advise to call in the aid of the farmer and the physician, rather than the professor of metaphysics.[21]

Society is the product of convention, and "if civil society be the offspring of convention, that convention must be its law."[22] The guiding force for society is and ought to be a combination of accepted opinion (existing conventions and prejudices) and a practical wisdom that uses preexisting tools to face new and continuing circumstances.

Because conservatism emphasizes the use of what already exists, scholars such as Mansfield have termed it uncreative. Unlike the republican, the conservative must make do with society as it is and with the tools it provides. The conservative may not create a particular society and particular kinds of citizens in order to fit his needs or desires. Republican, "creative" virtue is impossible and undesirable because so much already exists. Man may not and should not be reduced to a block of clay to be molded and remolded. Man already has a nature, the character of which is the result of preexisting institutions and experiences.

Burke viewed the role of the statesman, and even of the original legislator in those rare cases where he may exist, as that of seeing to it that social institutions fit the preexisting dispositions of the people to be governed. But these dispositions are themselves the results of preexisting institutions and arrangements, such as social status at birth, education, occupation, and religion—in short, circumstances over which the individual has, and should have, little or no control.[23] "Man is by nature reasonable; and he is never perfectly in his natural state, but when he is placed where reason may be best cultivated and most predominates."[24] True reason and the natural state that perfects it act, not through the creation of new institutions, but through habituation to old ones. Thus for Burke,

A true natural aristocracy is not a separate interest in the state, or separable from it. It is an essential integrant part of any large body rightly constituted. It is formed out of a class of legitimate presumptions, which, taken as generalities, must be admitted for actual truths. To be bred in a place of estimation; . . . to be habituated to the censorial inspection of the public eye; to look early to public opinion; to stand upon such elevated ground as to be enabled to take a large view of the wide-spread and infinitely diversified combinations of men and affairs in a large society; to have leisure to read, to reflect, to converse; to be enabled to draw the court and attention of the wise and learned, wherever they are to be found; to be habituated in armies to command and to obey; to be taught to despise danger in the pursuit of honor and duty; . . . to be led to a guarded and regulated conduct, from a sense that you are considered as an instructor of your fellow-citizens in their highest concerns, and that you act as a reconciler between God and man; to be employed as an administrator of law and justice, . . . to be a professor of high science, . . . to be amongst rich traders, . . . these are the circumstances of men that form what I should call a *natural* aristocracy, without which there is no nation.[25]

Nature dictates a hierarchical structure for society. But nature produces this necessary Chain of Being by operating "in the common modification of society." That is, nature produces the particulars of man's nature through convention. Natural law dictates that there be hierarchy, but the nature and makeup of particular classes is produced by a number of forces. Hierarchy is an "array of truth and Nature, as well as of habit and prejudice."[26]

Living in a particular way forms habits that in turn form a character appropriate to a given way of life. The aristocrat is brought up to respect himself and to pursue honor with the knowledge that he is by nature a public figure. He has the leisure and the means to cultivate his mind and character so that he may become that which his station dictates. And the same rules of character formation apply to the other, less august stations in life that complete the Great Chain of social Being.

Society is not a reflection of pure or, more properly for the conservative, mere reason. Reason is only one tool to be used in confronting circumstance. The rational faculties must be guided by prudence and affection so that man may aid his society to fit the nature of its people and the dictates of natural law in the face of changing circumstances.

The character of a people is determined, not by some metaphysical human nature, but by particular experiences. History produces a particular set of institutions and prejudices within a given society, and these institutions and prejudices determine, in large measure, the nature of the people of that society. They also largely determine the appropriate responses within that society to changed circumstances. In dealing with current problems, men must look to experience and seek to preserve society's inheritance from history.

History and the Limits of Reform

Burke argued that man is in large part that which society, over the course of history, has made him. This is not to say that man is somehow part of a "spirit" of history that has little to do with him and that has goals of its own, which man unknowingly carries out; the Burkean view of history is not so abstract. For Burke, divine will is worked out through circumstance and the ways in which men and societies choose to respond to it. History is a proving ground, testing institutions through circumstance and so producing the wisdom of the ages. Thus Burke praised

the uniform policy of our Constitution to claim and assert our liberties as an *entailed inheritance* derived to us from our forefathers, and to be transmitted to our posterity,—as an estate specially belonging to the people of this kingdom, without any reference whatever to any other more general or prior right. By this means our Constitution preserves an unity in so great a diversity of its parts. We have an inheritable crown, an inheritable peerage, and a House of Commons and a people inheriting privileges, franchises, and liberties from a long line of ancestors.

This policy appears to me to be the result of profound reflection,—or rather the happy effect of following Nature, which is wisdom without reflection, and above it.[27]

On the other hand, those, like the French revolutionaries, "whose principle it is to despise the ancient, permanent sense of mankind, and to set up a scheme of society on new principles, must naturally expect that such of us who think better of the judgment of the human race than of theirs would consider both them and their devices as men and schemes upon their trial."[28]

Burke argued that man's reason is limited, subject to his passions and the inevitable mistakes of idealization. Thus, rather than trusting independent wisdom, we should trust the wisdom of the ages: those institutions, practices, and beliefs that have grown up over time through interaction between nature ("wisdom without reflection"), the limited reason or prudence that reads the dictates of natural law, and circumstance. When faced with a crisis, those men who are in a position of authority should look to their ancestors for guidance, and should use the tools that history has placed in their hands, rather than their own weak reason.

Even kings may be accused of foolish hubris for failing to follow the wisdom of the ages. Addressing a member of the French National Assembly, Burke criticized the reforms made by the French king during the events leading up to the revolution, asserting that

I am constantly of opinion that your States, in three orders, on the footing on which they stood in 1614, were capable of being brought into a proper and harmonious combination with royal authority. This constitution by Estates was the natural and only just representation of France. It grew out of the habitual conditions, relations, and reciprocal claims of men. It grew out of the circumstances of the country, and out of the state of property. The wretched scheme of your present masters is not to fit the Constitution to the people, but wholly to destroy conditions, to dissolve relations, to change the state of the nation, and to subvert property, in order to fit their country to their theory of a Constitution.[29]

The French king had at his disposal the means of proper reform. This reform would have been based upon the historical arrangements of French society. The circumstances of French history had produced a particular hierarchy of French classes and a representational system predicated upon this hierarchy. By basing his new actions upon old institutions and old relations among Frenchmen, the king would have been acting according to French history and thus the French nature. By grounding his actions upon a false, metaphysical view of human nature the king contributed to the downfall of his nation—and of himself.

History provides the proper guide to action, even, and perhaps especially, in the face of severe crises. But it is important to note that for Burke history is not a collection of known facts and institutions that should be studied scientifically to find answers to all of society's problems. History's validity should not be questioned, and neither should the extent to which existing institutions and practices are in accordance with ancient practice. Such questioning would constitute reliance upon independent reason rather than on the collective wisdom of the ages.

Taking his political opponents in Britain to task for asserting the right of Englishmen to form their own government, Burke argued that their mistakes were the result of an improper view of history. Contrary to his opponents, who viewed the English Revolution of 1688 as the source of a number of rights belonging to the people, for Burke "the Revolution was made to preserve our *ancient* indisputable laws and liberties, and that *ancient* constitution of government which is our only security for law and liberty. If you are desirous of knowing the spirit of our Constitution, and the policy which predominated in that great period which has secured it to this hour, pray look for both in our histories, in our records, in our acts of Parliament and journals of Parliament, and not in the sermons of [radical dissenters], and the after-dinner toasts of the Revolution Society."[30]

Claims to the right of fabricating new governments are based on opinions directly contrary to those of the English people at large. It was Burke's feeling, and in his view the feeling of the English people, that the revolution was a *preserving* one, forced upon the nation by the actions of a bad king and aimed solely at protecting ancient rights. Indeed, for Burke the preserving impulse was the primary force behind all actions of the English people in relation to their governors.

> Our oldest reformation is that of Magna Charta. You will see that Sir Edward Coke, that great oracle of our law, and indeed all the great men who follow him, to Blackstone, are industrious to prove the pedigree of our liberties. They endeavor to prove that the ancient charter, the Magna Charta of King John, was connected with another positive charter from Henry the First, and that both the one and the other were nothing more than a reaffirmance of the still more ancient standing law of the kingdom. In the matter of fact, for the greater part, these authors appear to be in the right; perhaps not always; but if the lawyers mistake in some particulars, it proves my position still the more strongly; because it demonstrates the powerful prepossession towards antiquity with which the minds of all our lawyers and legislators, and of all the people whom they wish to influence, have been always filled, and the stationary policy of this kingdom in considering their most sacred rights and franchises as an *inheritance*.[31]

Burke emphasized, not the fact of historical continuity, but the impulse toward it in both historical action and in the interpretation of historical action. Burke praised the habituated desire of Englishmen to establish and to justify their rights. These rights were to be justified, not through appeals to abstract theories, but through appeals to the actual practice and history that, in their view, produced the specific rights of Englishmen.

The backward-looking, legal frame of mind cultivated by the English established the concrete bases of English society. A profession and a people that seek in their historical practices both the justifications for and the origins of their rights will not discard their inheritance in favor of abstract notions of absolute, ideal rights. As Pocock asserts, "What [Burke] is saying, then, is not a piece of antiquarian's lore, but an account of contemporary practice. This is how we conduct our politics, he is saying; how we have always conducted them. He is not calling upon his contemporaries to return to a seventeenth-century habit of mind, but assuming that it is still alive and meaningful among them."[32]

The purpose of reform, for Burke, must always be the preservation of ancient and established liberties. This does not mean, however, that reform itself is ruled out.

> A state without the means of some change is without the means of its conservation. Without such means it might even risk the loss of that part of the Constitution which it wished the most religiously to preserve. The two principles of conservation and correction operated strongly at the two critical periods of the Restoration and Revolution, when England found itself without a king. At both those periods the nation had lost the bond of union in their ancient edifice: they did not, however, dissolve the whole fabric. On the contrary, in both cases they regenerated the deficient part of the old Constitution through the parts which were not impaired. . . . At no time, perhaps, did the sovereign legislature manifest a more tender regard to that fundamental principle of British constitutional policy than at the time of the Revolution, when it deviated from the direct line of hereditary succession. The crown was carried somewhat out of the line in which it had before moved; but the new line was derived from the same stock. It was still a line of hereditary descent; still an hereditary descent in the same blood, though an hereditary descent qualified with Protestantism. When the legislature altered the direction, but kept the principle, they showed that they held it inviolable.[33]

Those men who are entrusted with governmental power in times of great national need have the duty to rejuvenate the old when facing new circumstances. They must resist the hubristic impulse to create a new government or, even worse, to create a new human nature or national character. Human reason is limited, and man is fallible; but history, collective wisdom, and the forms of the existing constitution provide the necessary guidance for prudent action. If followed, these guides will lead to the preservation of the existing, good society.

Prejudice

Burke emphasized the wisdom of man over the wisdom of men. He argued that men must enter into corporate societies and be treated as corporate beings if they are to live properly. "He who gave our nature to be perfected by our virtue willed also the necessary means of its perfection: He willed, therefor, the state."[34] Burke did not argue only that the state as an abstract entity is the necessary means to virtue. He insisted upon the maintenance of the *parts* of the British Constitution—including its *categories* of individuals. The Great Chain of Being dictates for every member of society a specific place, but this place is itself corporate, not individual. As one has the place of a man rather than of an angel or a beast, one also has the place of a peasant, a businessman, or a member of the landed gentry. Habits of both opinion and action are formed in the particular circumstances of each station in life; and the resulting characters are themselves integral parts of a society's constitution.

For Burke our views of the world are the results of our experiences, and these necessarily depend in great measure upon the place in society into which we are born. The nobleman is habituated into his proper role by his corporate experiences: Seeing nothing mean, he has no mean feelings. Feeling that society looks up to and depends upon him, the nobleman comes to recognize his importance and his responsibility. All that is required is that the nobleman be educated properly and protected from metaphysical teachings that disregard the importance of place and circumstance. These, then, are the bases of that great guiding force of proper human action Burke called prejudice.

According to Burke the French revolutionaries enslaved the people in the name of the rights of men, or, more properly, in the name of revolutionary "reason." British humility produced better results.

> We are afraid to put men to live and trade each on his own private stock of reason; because we suspect that the stock in each man is small, and that the individuals would do better to avail themselves of the general band and capital of nations and of ages. Many of our men of speculation, instead of exploding general prejudices, employ their sagacity to discover the latent wisdom which prevails in them. If they find what they seek, (and they seldom fail,) they think it more wise to continue the prejudice, with the reason involved, than to cast away the coat of prejudice, and to leave nothing but the naked reason; because prejudice, with its reason, has a motive to give action to that reason, and an affection which will give it permanence.[35]

Commonly painted as a great scourge today, prejudice or unexamined belief, according to Burke, embodies a wisdom superior to that of individual reason. If prudent thinkers find no reason behind the prejudice, they will doubt themselves rather than the wisdom of nations and of ages. Prejudice is a rich source of right thinking and a necessary basis for right action. "Prejudice is of ready application in the emergency; it previously engages the mind in a steady course of wisdom and virtue, and does not leave the man hesitating in the moment of decision, skeptical, puzzled, and unresolved. Prejudice renders a man's virtue his habit, and not a series of unconnected acts. Through just prejudice, his duty becomes a part of his nature."[36] Prejudice, then, is the proper guide to action because it is more reliable than individual reason. Based upon collective experience, it has an intimate connection, strengthened over time, with the object of its concern—be it society, class, or a more universal category. It is the proper educator of mankind because, as the product of the ages, it is ever ready for use in current circumstances.

But the idealized programs of would-be founders, by opposing all accepted beliefs, do not endanger a mere useful tool; they endanger man himself. "The moral sentiments, so nearly connected with early prejudice as to be almost one and the same thing, will assuredly not live long under a discipline which has for its basis the destruction of all prejudices, and the making the mind proof against all dread of consequences flowing from the pretended truths that are taught by their philosophy."[37]

Prejudices are the guardians of the moral sentiments. Bereft of accepted beliefs, men no longer can choose to act properly and are reduced to less than truly rational beings. If one sets up a system, such as that of the French revolutionaries, that is not based upon the people's natural prejudices, "everything depends upon the army in such a government as yours; for you have industriously destroyed all the opinions and prejudices, and, as far as in you lay, all the instincts which support government. Therefor the moment any difference arises between your National Assembly and any part of the nation, you must have recourse to force."[38] It is prejudice that allows men to deal with one another in a peaceful, mutually beneficial manner, that binds a society together, and that guards the moral sentiments and the public affections necessary if men are to live with one another on any basis other than fear and violence.

As prejudices must be protected as the guardians of morality and human society itself, so must the bases of prejudices also be protected. And the bases of these prejudices are to be found in the local arrangements that naturally induce affection in the individual. Local affection, "to love the little platoon we belong to in society,"[39] is a virtue in and of itself, but it is also good because it is necessary for the unquestioned ("prejudiced") attachments which hold together any stable society. For this reason, respect on the part of those in power for family, locality, class attachments, the idea of nation—and even the idea of a European commonwealth based upon common history and Christianity[40]—is necessary if society is to be maintained.

Aristotle constructed his polis as a hierarchy of attachments from the family to the household to the village and then to the polis itself. Burke also constructs the necessary attachments and affections of men from the more local to the more universal. Society itself depends upon the continued good health of the family. Thus, for Burke, liberal French revolutionary divorce laws were designed to produce "the total corruption of all morals, the total disconnection of social life."[41] Burke's own life and career were guided by his desire to achieve his concept of the proper, ultimate goal (and reward) of a life of virtuous public service: the founding of a great family of power, influence, and inheritable prestige. A great family, of course, is an institution built upon and held together by natural attachments.[42]

Human sociability, in all its forms, rests upon the affections, attachments, and prejudices that arise naturally from shared, local experience.

> Men are not tied to one another by papers and seals. They are led to associate by resemblances, by conformities, by sympathies. It is with nations as with individuals. Nothing is so strong a tie of amity between nation and nation as correspondence in laws, customs, manners, and habits of life. They have more than the force of treaties in themselves. They are obligations written in the heart. They approximate men to men without their knowledge, and sometimes against their intentions. The secret, unseen, but irrefragable bond of habitual intercourse holds them together, even when their perverse and litigious nature sets them to equivocate, scuffle, and fight about the terms of their written obligations.[43]

The old proverb "like to like," which Socrates ignored, was restated by Burke in describing the very nature of human affections. We like what is familiar, and familiarity grows from common experience, and this is as it should be.

In arguing against the repression of Catholicism in Ireland, Burke pointed out with regret that there existed in England and Ireland

a number of persons whose minds are so formed that they find the communion of religion to be a close and an endearing tie, and their country to be no bond at all,—to whom common altars are a better relation than common habitations and a common civil interest,—whose hearts are touched with the distresses of foreigners, and are abundantly awake to all the tenderness of human feeling on such an occasion, even at the moment that they are inflicting the very same distresses, or worse, upon their fellow-citizens, without the least sting of compassion or remorse. To commiserate the distresses of all men suffering innocently, perhaps meritoriously, is generous, and very agreeable to the better part of our nature,—a disposition that ought by all means to be cherished. But to transfer humanity from its natural basis, our legitimate and home-bred connections,—to lose all feeling for those who have grown up by our sides, in our eyes, the benefit of whose cares and labors we have partaken from our birth, and meretriciously to hunt abroad after foreign affections, is such a disarrangement of the whole system of our duties, that I do not know whether benevolence so displaced is not almost the same thing as destroyed, or what effect bigotry could have produced that is more fatal to society.[44]

Attachments—even religious attachments—that do not have their basis in habituated affection, in the daily interactions of men with a common background, are perverse if not kept in their proper place. And this place is less exalted than that of local attachments. Religious attachments, if bereft of closer ties, are too metaphysical, too divorced from daily life, to bind men to one another properly. Dogmatic religious attachments may destroy the natural, habituated attachments of common experience that are the bases of society and of moral life. Man is by nature a religious animal, but he is not necessarily an Anglican animal. The particulars of dogma and ritual must not be allowed to overshadow and destroy the local circumstances and attachments that bind together a society.

Prejudice is good because men, their reason, and their affections are limited. We are not capable of making attachments or of developing the proper affections on purely rational grounds. Instead, men's natural attachments grow from their locality, their occupation, and their station in life. Habituation is the rule in affection as well as in behavior, and since God's will has dictated the hierarchy of society as well as the nature of man, both must be accepted.

Government, Religion, and Manners

Society, history, and the human race possess great wisdom; men, for Burke, by and large do not. Burke also argued that government's capacity for wise action is easily overestimated. Society and government, according to Burke, are not the same thing—in many ways they are quite different. Government is the weaker entity, best confined to the tending of existing arrangements. The ability of a government to see to the needs of its people is quite limited; indeed, "A frost too long continued or too suddenly broken up with rain and tempest, the blight of the spring or the smut of the harvest will do more to cause the distress of the belly than all the contrivances of all statesmen can do to relieve it."[45]

The moderation that Burke demanded of the statesman he also demanded of the government itself. Severely limited in their ability to help those they govern, statesmen must see to it that government does not harm them. This is why Burke praised balanced government and justified his own career on the grounds that he had opposed "all the various partisans of destruction, let them begin where or when or how they will."[46] All attempts to destroy the proper power and role of one or another of the branches of England's balanced monarchy eventually would end by destroying the British Constitution and British society. The British Constitution was based upon balance and properly limited liberty—both for individuals and for branches of government. Because governors are no more omniscient or perfectly moral than are those whom they govern, those who govern are no more to be trusted with unlimited power or liberty than the governed. Power must counteract or, more properly,

limit power lest one branch grow beyond its proper bounds and cause the entire structure to topple.

As the proper power of each branch is limited, so is the power of government itself. "The coercive authority of the state is limited to what is necessary for its existence." Rather than pursuing some metaphysical ideal of human perfection, the good government "does bear, and must, with the vices and the follies of men, until they actually strike at the root of order. This it does in things actually moral. In all matters of speculative improvement the case is stronger, even where the matter is properly of human cognizance. But to consider an averseness to improvement, the not arriving at perfection, as a crime, is against all tolerably correct jurisprudence; for, if the resistance to improvement should be great and any way general, they would in effect give up the necessary and substantial part in favor of the perfection and the finishing."[47] Should man's government attempt to give him an ideal nature, his nature would be corrupted. The role of government is not to create a virtuous people; it does not possess the means to produce human perfection and will succeed only in destroying society if it makes the attempt.

Burke seems to advocate a government that does very little and that acts according to rather utilitarian rules. He insisted that "there are two, and only two, foundations of law; and they are both of them conditions without which nothing can give it any force: I mean equity and utility."[48] According to Burke, equity means that all men shall be treated equally according to the law, and utility means that all laws shall be in the general interest. Any idea of human interconnection, let alone virtue, seems to have no place within Burke's materialistic/utilitarian governmental structure. This makes all the more seemingly strange Burke's statement that, in the production of the great English people of "high mind and a constancy unconquerable" and in the establishment of English preeminence under the reign of King William, "government gave the impulse."[49]

Burke himself answered the question of whether improvement may be "brought into society? Undoubtedly; but not by compulsion,—but by encouragement,—but by countenance, favor, privileges, which are powerful, and are lawful instruments."[50] Government is, then, somehow concerned with social improvement and has some duty beyond the mere tending of arrangements. It seems clear, however, that the role of government in this area is purely secondary, that government is not the true teacher of virtue but the guardian of the true teachers: tradition, manners, and prejudice.

Limited in its ability to act in the public interest without endangering it, government acts best when it merely tends to arrangements. These arrangements, then, do most of society's work in perfecting man in the only way reasonable: by showing him the possibility of virtue and by habituating him to virtue's modes. This does not mean, however, that the government plays no role in the moral life of the nation. The institutions that inculcate virtue require governmental protection from atheists, experimenters, and those men who do not recognize the need for the maintenance, and supremacy, of existing traditions, manners, and prejudices.

Burke opposed atheism, not just because he believed that it is incorrect and wrong, but also because it corrupts all morals. For Burke, man's natural religiosity is of supreme importance. Religious beliefs or prejudices help shape human behavior, and religious institutions embody the traditions of a people while teaching a particular set of practices (manners) and beliefs. This is why religions, like governments, must be viewed as historical institutions, closely connected with the national life. Like governments, particular religions require historical justification and unquestioning acceptance, but they need at least one other support if they are to play their proper role in society: official recognition. As Burke related,

some years ago, I strenuously opposed the clergy who petitioned, to the number of about three hundred, to be freed from subscription to the Thirty-Nine Articles [of the Episcopal Church], without proposing to substitute any other in their place. There never has been a religion of the state (the few years of the Parliament only excepted) but that of *the Episcopal Church of England:* the Episcopal Church of England, before the Reformation, connected with the see of Rome; since then, disconnected, and protesting against some of her doctrines, and against the whole of her authority, as binding in our national church: nor did the fundamental laws of this kingdom (in Ireland it has been the same) ever know, at any period, any other church *as an object of establishment,*—or, in that light, any other Protestant religion. Nay, our Protestant *toleration* itself, at the Revolution, and until within a few years, required a signature of thirty-six, and a part of the thirty-seventh, out of the Thirty-Nine Articles. So little idea had they at the Revolution of *establishing* Protestantism indefinitely, that they did not indefinitely *tolerate* it under that name.[51]

Episcopalianism, like the mixed and limited monarchy, has been the established rule in Britain from time immemorial. Like the government, it must remain unquestioned. Episcopalianism is natural to England because it is an integral part of it, having gone through time and trial with it, guiding the nation through its troubles with its moral teachings.

Religion does not provide only a shared set of beliefs. Shared forms of worship and prescriptive religious conduct also form men's actions. For Burke, behavior is guided from the surface inward. That is, habituation acts upon the outward forms of behavior and thence inward affections and opinions. Affections and opinions in turn affect concrete behavior—and thence society. Proper thought and proper action are related intimately, and religion aids both.

Good government supports religion because religion is a primary support of proper government—and because both are integral elements of any good society. Religion supports good government by habituating the people, through manners, to act and to believe in such a way as to make governemnt stable. More important, religion promotes modes of thought and action that are intrinsically *good* in the society's given circumstances. In listing the French revolutionaries' crimes, Burke argued that when to these etablishments of Regicide, of Jacobinism, and of Atheism, you add the *correspondent system of manners*, no doubt can be left on the mind of a thinking man concerning their determined hostility to the human race. Manners are of more importance than laws. Upon them, in a great measure, the laws depend. The law touches us but here and there, and now and then. Manners are what vex or soothe, corrupt or purify, exalt or debase, barbarize or refine us, by a constant, steady, uniform, insensible operation, like that of the air we breathe in. They give their whole form and color to our lives. According to their quality, they aid morals, they supply them, or they totally destroy them.[52]

Manners are more important than laws because they have a greater effect on men's actions. Men always act in relation to the given set of manners. Thus they are habituated in accordance with a given set of rules and forms. Their behavior is directed by a given set of precepts that correspond to, but are not the same as, political and religious establishments. The "rationalistic" radicalism and atheism of the French revolutionaries produced a corrupt system of manners. The Jacobins destroyed the old system of proper manners and replaced it with an immoral one that habituated men into the wrong modes of activity.

The doctrines of Jacobinism and atheism are barbaric; they reject all notions of prescription and deference to established hierarchy. Supplemented by the uncouth egalitarianism of their corresponding system of manners, Jacobin and atheist doctrines produced a society in which the sanctity of rights, and even of life itself, was uncrecognized by the unchastened mob. This was to be expected, because a mob, undirected by a confining system of manners that support and are supported by an unquestioning belief in the goodness of existing hierarchical relations, is capable only of destruction.

The importance of convention in promoting proper behavior extends even to the realm of taste. For Burke, "Taste and elegance, though they are reckoned only among the smaller and secondary morals, yet are of no mean importance in the regulation of life. A moral taste is not of force to turn vice into virtue; but it recommends virtue with something like the blandishments of pleasure, and it infinitely abates the evils of vice."[53] Men require encouragements to right action. Standards of taste produce social and thence internal pressure to act according to their dictates, which properly correspond to society's religious, moral, and political norms. Elegance, by showing men the rewards of right action in secondary matters, inculcates proper habits and so helps men to act rightly in matters of greater importance.

Government, for Burke, should support the more capable guardians of human nature: tradition, manners, prejudice, and the greatest embodiment of all three—religion. Social institutions act upon man in his daily activities. They reward and punish the individual according to how well he acts in relation to the dictates of his particular religion, locality, and station in life. Social institutions teach men to accept unquestioningly the prescriptive role of preexisting modes of coduct. That is, they habituate men to proper conduct. And habituation is the only reasonable method by which to produce by right action because "prescriptions" not based on historical practice are not truly prescriptive.

Prescriptions based upon idealized models fail to take into account the fundamental natures of philosophy, man, and society. They fail to recognize that the natural function of philosophy is to discern the role of appropriate conventions in habituating men to right action. They do not recognize that man is by nature a creature of habit and circumstance. They ignore the fact that society is naturally fragile and that its natural role is to provide prescriptive, conventional criteria by which to judge the virtue of men's actions. Social institutions and conventions require unquestioning acceptance if they are to survive and function properly. Purely metaphysical prescriptions may destroy the social fabric and cannot possibly produce virtue.

Natural Law

Since convention rules most of our lives, our conventions must be proper or they will corrupt rather than perfect human nature. Burke's emphasis upon the need for fitting conventions brings into focus the basis of the Burkean reading of natural law in a particular view of divine will. Although philosophy must limit itself to recognizing man as a creature of particular circumstances—including history and convention—history is not philosophically self-justifying. The course of history may produce abomination as well as virtue, and there is a kernel of human nature that is not the mere product of convention.

Man is religious by nature. He is limited by nature—that is, he is incapable of ultimate perfection. He has only limited rationality and so must be guided by prejudice. He is best treated as the member of a corporate body, for this is where his nature may achieve its fulfillment. Divine will intends that man be in society—where his true perfection, or virtue, may be attained. The Great Chain of Being is an instrument of divine will, providing the possibility of human virtue by allowing men to come together and so rely on a greater stock of human reason than that afforded by any individual. Society also is the realm in which virtue may be practiced, for right action is action that accepts ·the natural hierarchy arising from the circumstances of society and that acts according to its basic dictates so as to further its interests (the common good) in accordance with divine will.

Both "creative" and "rationalistic" reason are dangerous since they lead to hubris and perhaps to the destruction of society itself. But there is a safe and proper reason: the reason (in truth the wisdom) of conservatism, based upon the unchanging wisdom of natural law. Conservative wisdom dictates the prudent tending of existing arrangements so that men will not be corrupted. It also dictates prudent defense of the moral institutions of society against idealized theories and against the circumstances that history inevitably produces. Most of all, conservative wisdom dictates faith in the goodness of God's will and in what He has given. Any proper defense of society must grow from a desire to serve that which is old, familiar, and accepted as the will of God. And virtue is acting in ways that promote and provide the means for this defense.

Notes

1. Plato, *The Republic*, trans. Allan Bloom (New York: Basic Books, 1968), 290, 607b.
2. Edmund Burke, *Appeal from the New to the Old Whigs*, in vol. 4 of *Works* (London: John C. Nimmo, 1889), 176.
3. Edmund Burke, *Reflections on the Revolution in France*, in vol. 3 of *Works*, 338.
4. Burke, *Appeal, Works*, 4: 192.
5. Edmund Burke, *Letters on a Regicide Peace, Letter 1*, in vol. 5 of *Works*, 341.
6. Ibid.
7. Burke, *Reflections*, 3: 240.
8. Ibid., 241.
9. Ibid., 242; emphasis in original.
10. Ibid., 313.
11. Ibid., 4–5.
12. Onora O'Neill, "Ethical Reasoning and Ideological Pluralism," *Ethics* 99 (July 1988): 9.
13. Ibid., 10; emphasis in original.
14. Edmund Burke, "Letter to a Member of the French National Assembly," *Works*, 4: 51–51.
15. Edmund Burke, "Speech on American Taxation," *Works*, 2: 72–73.
16. Burke, *Reflections*, 3:307–8.
17. Burke, *Regicide Peace, Letter 4*, in vol. 6 of *Works*, 28.
18. Burke, *Regicide Peace, Letter 2*, in vol. 5 of *Works*, 362.
19. Ibid., 106; emphasis added.
20. Burke, *Reflections*, 3: 350.
21. Ibid., 311.
22. Ibid., 309.
23. Ibid., 477.
24. Burke, *Appeal*, 4: 176.1
25. Ibid., 175; emphasis in original.
26. Ibid., 176.
27. Burke, *Reflections*, 3: 274; emphasis in original.
28. Ibid., 450.
29. Burke, "Letter to a Member of the French National Assembly," 4: 51.
30. Burke, *Reflections*, 3: 271–72; emphasis in original.
31. Ibid., 272–73; emphasis in original.
32. J. G. A. Pocock, "Burke and the Ancient Constitution," in *Politics, Language and Time: Es-*

says on Political Thought and History (New York: Atheneum, 1971), 208.

33. Burke, *Reflections*, 3: 259–60.
34. Ibid., 361.
35. Ibid., 346–47.
36. Ibid., 347.
37. Burke, *Appeal*, 4: 205.
38. Burke, *Reflections*, 3: 527.
39. Ibid., 559.
40. See especially *Regicide Peace, Letter 1* 5: 320, for a discussion of Jacobinism's inherent hostility to the "community of Europe."
41. Ibid., 314.
42. See Harvey J. Mansfield, Jr., *Statesmanship and Party Government: A Study of Burke and Bolingbroke* (Chicago: University of Chicago Press, 1965), 204–7, for a discussion of Burke's comments, particularly in his "Letter to a Noble Lord," concerning his own (unfulfilled) desire to found a family and his views on the necessary role of such families in providing "presumptive" virtue.
43. Burke, *Reflections*, 3: 317–318.
44. Edmund Burke, *Fragments of a Tract Relative to the Laws against Poopery in Ireland*, in vol. 6 of *Works*, 330.
45. Burke, *Regicide Peace, Letter 3*, in vol. 5 of *Works*, 466.
46. Burke, *Appeal*, 4: 115.
47. Burke, *Fragments of a Tract*, 6: 340.
48. Ibid., 323.
49. Burke, *Regicide Peace, Letter 1*, 5: 302.
50. Burke, *Fragments of a Tract*, 6: 339–40.
51. Edmund Burke, "Letter to Sir Hercules Langrishe," *Works*, 4: 257–58; emphasis in original.
52. Burke, *Regicide Peace, Letter 1*, 5: 310; emphasis in original.
53. Burke, "Letter to a Member of the French National Assembly," 4: 30.

Adapted from: Bruce Frohnen, *Virtue and the Promise of Conservatism: The Legacy of Burke and Tocqueville*, pp. 42–64, 222–223. Copyright © 1993. Reprinted by permission of the University Press of Kansas. ✦

17
The French Revolution and the Crisis of European Civilization

James Conniff

The discussion and analysis of Burke's position on the French Revolution is a central test for most studies of his thought. This is so not because of any intrinsic difficulty in the topic but because one's handling of the French Revolution reveals how effectively one's approach covers the entire reach of Burke's thought. Michael Freeman's *Edmund Burke and the Critique of Political Radicalism* is a good example.[1] Freeman opens with a claim that a "perennial issues" approach to political theory is valid. Thus, he believes that what Burke said about the radicalism of the 1790s is useful to us because we face similar issues today. As he puts it, "the main thesis of the present book is that Edmund Burke, in the face of a particular revolution which he detested and feared, proposed a general conservative theory of revolution and of political radicalism in order to combat and refute the general radical ideas he believed the revolutionaries to hold."[2] Freeman sees the foundation of Burke's theory to lie in Christian metaphysics, specifically in his adherence to traditional natural law, and argues that for Burke the chief error of the radicals was to challenge the morality inherent in the "nature of things."[3] After discussing Burke's views on revolution in general, Freeman turns to the French Revolution as a particular case. Un-

fortunately, what he unwittingly demonstrates is that Burke has no theory of revolution in general. Indeed, Freeman's own treatment of Burke's presumed general theory is so contaminated with arguments drawn from the French example that the two categories—general and French—collapse into one.[4] By the end of the book, Burke emerges as the one thing he always refused to be: the author of a universally applicable political theory. Ironically, Freeman is joined in his preoccupation with the counterrevolutionary Burke by some recent radical critics. C. B. Macpherson, for instance, sees the French Revolution as forcing a major reorientation on Burke.[5] Although he notes many of the more reformist themes in Burke's early writings, Macpherson insists that Burke reversed himself in the 1790s. Thus, he argues, "the impression of Burke as the archconservative seemed indelibly fixed: his crusade against the French Revolution had eclipsed all his other works" and goes on to interpret Burke as an apologist for early Capitalism.[6]

That the conservative and radical strategies for interpreting Burke lead to such similar conclusions ought to be a sign that they, in fact, rest on common assumptions. For example, Freeman and Macpherson both assume that the Revolution dwarfed Burke's other concerns. Yet, that was not the case. In the early days of the Revolution, Burke was probably more interested in the Regency Crisis, and, indeed, while the split in the Whig Party during the crisis did not precisely prefigure the later split over the Revolution, it certainly prepared the ground for that break.[7] Later, as the Revolution became more of an issue in English politics, Burke's interest was divided between it and the Hastings Impeachment. Finally, in his last years, after leaving Parliament, Burke's *Correspondence* shows as much concern with the deteriorating state of Irish affairs as with the French Revolution. During the so-called Treason Trials of the mid-1790s, Burke's letters seldom mention the trials but are full of pained discussions of Ireland. Nor were these various concerns separate isolated issues for Burke. He constantly sought to find common denominators. In a draft of a letter to Loughborough in 1796, Burke linked

Hastings and France thusly: "Our Government and our Laws are beset by two different Enemies, which are sapping its foundations, Indianism, and Jacobinism. In some Cases they act separately, in some they act in conjunction. But of this I am sure; that the first is the worst by far, and the hardest to deal with; and for this amongst other reasons, that it weakens, discredits, and ruins that force, which ought to be employd [*sic*] with the greatest Credit and Energy against the other; and that it furnishes Jacobinism with its strongest arms against all *formal* Governments."[8] Here we have it all: Burke combining India and France in a letter about Ireland—a letter in which he suggests that domestic reform is a prerequisite to a successful campaign against radicalism.

Thus, for the student of Burke's thought, the principal difficulty presented by the French Revolution is that it reveals elements of both continuity and change in his position. Burke saw the Revolution as a unique and novel event. In the *Reflections*, he wrote, "it appears to me as if I were in a great crisis, not of the affairs of France alone, but of all Europe, perhaps of more than Europe. All circumstances taken together, the French Revolution is the most astonishing that has hitherto happened in the world."[9] And in the *Thoughts on French Affairs*, he noted, "one must not judge of the state of France by what has been observed elsewhere. It does not in the least resemble any other country. Analogical reasoning from history or from recent experience in other places is wholly delusive."[10] At the same time, Burke approached the Revolution through the framework provided by his previous experience. In his eyes, the Revolution was the occasion of yet another opportunity for, and challenge to, Whiggish reform. As he watched the Revolution unfold, Burke became increasingly convinced that it was the perfectly predictable result of the French monarchy's failure to achieve timely and moderate reform. It grew, in a sense, out of a failure of trusteeship. This was the point of Burke's contrast in the *Reflections* of the English Revolution of 1688 with the French Revolution. In the first case, he argued, the political elite had responded to a threat quickly and effectively, and, therefore, had avoided disaster. In the latter case, no reform had been forthcoming, and the nation was destroyed accordingly. Burke's conclusion from this analysis was also familiar: that reform was the only true alternative to Revolution. The French Revolution, then, in my opinion, caused no change in Burke's fundamental orientation: he continued to promote progress, and, therefore, still defined himself as a reform politician, and he remained true to his Whig creed of aristocratic government. However, the Revolution did lead Burke to introduce new themes into his argument. What is new is, in part, a sense of a changed situation: Burke now believed that reform must be achieved in a revolutionary context. He no longer saw himself as debating the peaceful and rational improvement of the British system, but as involved in a multi-dimensional conflict to restore a stable regime in France, to purge Europe of radicalism, and to defend the advanced English constitution against those fanatics who would destroy it. As Burke's assessment of the political circumstances of France emphasized what was novel, so, he believed, should the response be based on a new strategy and employ new tactics. Therefore, in recognition of the ideological nature of the conflict, he waged a campaign to discredit radicalism at home, and he promoted a joint European crusade against the revolutionary government of France. In short, to understand Burke, I believe that one must see the Revolution as he saw it. While he believed that a new threat required new forms of countervailing action, he also maintained that his new approach was in support of values which were both tested by time and progressive in their own right.

I

I begin with Burke's analysis of the causes and course of the French Revolution. Burke's understanding of the Revolution developed slowly. At first, his comments were ambiguous and noncommittal. For instance, in a letter to Charlemont dated August 9, 1789, he wrote, "the spirit it is impossible not to admire; but the old Parisian ferocity has broken out in a shocking manner. . . . But if it should be character rather than accident, then that people are not fit for Liberty, and must have a Strong hand like that of their former master to coerce them."[11] Even such a landmark event as the Fall of the Bastille on July 14, 1789, was met only by a mild statement of surprise accompanied by an expression of concern for the future. As late as November 1789, after the Declaration of the Rights of Man and the October unrest, Burke was still reluctant to condemn the French reformers: he told Depont, "but it would ill become Me to be too ready in forming a positive opinion upon matters transacted in a Country, with the correct, political Map of which I must be very imperfectly acquainted. Things indeed have already happen'd so much beyond the scope of all speculation, that persons of infinitely more sagacity than I am ought to be ashamed of anything like confidence in their reasoning upon the operation of any principle or the effect of any measure."[12] Gradually, however, Burke began to formulate a position. I think that the development of his thought can be divided into five distinct stages: (1) an initial period of inattention and uncertainty combined with rather wary statements of disapproval on specific points; (2) sometime in the fall of 1789 this disapproval hardened into open opposition, but Burke continued to be courteous in his style and was nervous about the issue of his own consistency; (3) by the time of the publication of the *Reflections* in November of 1790, Burke's tentative concern had hardened into certainty, and he was becoming increasingly intolerant in his claim to be the voice of true Whiggism; (4) after the French Declaration of War in February 1793, Burke resigned from the Whig Club, thus breaking openly with his party, and became an outspoken advocate of a European crusade against Jacobinism; and (5) finally, by the fall of 1795, Burke recognized that the Revolution might succeed, and feared that the war against Jacobinism had a good chance of failure. Meanwhile, becoming concerned about the potential absolutism he perceived among the refugees, he declared a mere return to an unreformed Ancien Regime unacceptable. At the time of his death

in July 1797, Burke was pessimistic about the future; still opposed to the Revolution, he, nonetheless, had become increasingly alienated from its opponents. Moreover, Irish politics had largely superseded the Revolution as his major concern.

The centerpiece of Burke's anti-Revolutionary rhetoric actually developed slowly, and did not appear in his discussions of French politics until rather late. That centerpiece was the claim that the Revolution had so far followed, and was likely to continue to follow, an inevitable course of ever increasing violence and chaos. At the height of his anti-Revolutionary zeal, for example, Burke wrote to one correspondent, "Nothing has happen'd but what was the Natural and inevitable effect of that fatal Constitution, and its absurd and wicked principles. Nothing has been the effect of accident; Every successive Event was the direct result of that which preceded it; and the whole, the Effect of the false Bases on which that constitution was originally laid."[13] Similarly, he argued that the proposals of the English radicals, whatever their intent, could only lead to the same kind of disaster which had engulfed France: "their Revolution too will run exactly the same course, as it is founded on the same principles which that of their Brethren in France; it will be pursued in the same manner and all its proceedings will be executed by the same necessities."[14] As James T. Boulton has pointed out, there is here an intimate relationship between Burke's politics and his literary techniques.[15] His message was simple—like causes produce like results—but its presentation was not. Burke's argument was the very traditional claim that there exists a cosmic and divine natural order, which creates binding moral obligations on man. In the past, he continued, the English succeeded by adhering to that order, but the French are destined to fail because they violate it. However, the techniques Burke used to deliver that message were complex indeed. Especially in the *Reflections*, but throughout his writings on the Revolution, Burke used a wealth of images of order, drawn from the Bible, from nature, and from analogy to the family, and of disorder, like drunkenness and sickness, to reinforce his point. One simply cannot, Burke maintained, have radical reform without its being accompanied by anarchy, and that anarchy will necessarily be followed by tyranny and international conflict.

This concern with what one might call the pathology of the Revolution led Burke to focus a great deal of attention on its causes. He believed it obvious that, if unrest and radical reform inevitably lead to revolution, the best way to avoid revolution is not to permit unrest and radical reform to begin. Thus, Burke's analysis of the Revolution begins with his description of France prior to the agitation for reform. In his view, France was an important and stable part of the commonwealth of Europe. All of Europe, Burke declared, was "virtually one great state, having the same basis of general law, with some diversity of provincial customs and local establishments."[16] The same religion, with minor variations, prevailed in all states, and each drew its politics and its economy from the same Germanic or Gothic customs. While the individual nations varied in their political institutions, none was a despotism and all, even the republics, were imbued with the principles of mixed monarchy. Moreover, all Europe shared a common culture based on the same traditional moral values: "this mixed system of opinion and sentiment had its origin in the ancient chivalry; and the principle, though varied in its appearance by the varying state of human affairs, subsisted and influenced through a long succession of generations even to the time we live in."[17] However, like all great human attainments, the civilization of Europe was a fragile thing, requiring great respect and care, for, "if it should ever be totally extinguished, the loss I fear will be great."[18] For this reason, along with its obvious rhetorical purpose, the paean to Marie-Antoinette in the *Reflections* played an important symbolic role in Burke's argument, for, "the Queen symbolizes all that is finest in a whole civilization, and with her perish the benefits which society derived from that civilization: dignified obedience, exalted freedom, the unifying and ennobling power of human emotions."[19] Finally, Burke argued that France, like all of Europe, was improving before the Revolution. The

French king was well-meaning and concerned, if indeed a bit inept, and the governmental bureaucracy was both public-spirited and progressive.

How, then, could such a noble and beneficial system fail? Burke's many explanations can, I think, be grouped under two heads. First, he maintained that the old order had long been under attack by a revolutionary party. Burke usually stigmatized these revolutionaries with the label of "Jacobin," a term he seldom bothered to define. As he put it, "Jacobinism is the Vice of men of Parts; and in this age it is the Chanel [*sic*] in which all discontents will run."[20] That is, Burke saw the Jacobins as drawn from those elements of the middle and upper classes who believe that they had a natural right to power and privilege because of their intellectual or political merits. "Talents," Burke said, "naturally gravitate to Jacobinism," for "whatever tends to persuade the people that the *few*, called by whatever name you please, religious or political, are of opinion that their interest is not compatible with that of the *many*, is a great point gained to Jacobinism."[21] Such men come, according to Burke, in two varieties—the philosophers and the politicians.[22] The first group was composed of all those who attack religion and conventional morality, including, of course, those Burke listed as the "literary cabal" in the *Reflections*. In his words, "these atheistical fathers have a bigotry of their own, and they have learned to talk against monks with the spirit of a monk."[23] Among the philosophers, then, were writers like Collins, Toland, Tindal, and Bolingbroke. The second group, the politicians, were those who, without any real concern with the issues of religion and morality, realized that the philosophers had provided a means of weakening their enemies, and, therefore, employed those tools to further their own bid for power. As Burke saw it, "they do not commit crimes for their designs; but they form designs that they may commit crimes."[24] They sought to gain power, and to strengthen the state, so that they might give their desires free reign. According to Burke, their hero was Rousseau. He was "their canon of holy writ; in his life he is their canon of Polycletus; he is their standard figure of perfection."[25] What they admired most was his extremism and his hypocrisy: "he melts with tenderness for those only who touch him by the remotest relation . . . and sends his children to the hospital of foundlings."[26] In sum, Burke believed that, armed with the ideas of the philosophers, the politicians took dead aim at the French Crown and aristocracy. They did not miss their target, and the Revolution was their prize.

Second, Burke believed that the radicals had considerable help in undermining the pre-revolutionary French state from the government itself. In his view, the leaders of France encouraged revolution by repeatedly failing to make necessary reforms. Years earlier, in discussing the American Revolution, Burke had suggested a general rule: "we deplored, as your Majesty has done in your speech from the throne, the disorders which prevail in your empire; but we are convinced that the disorders of the people, in the present time and the present place, are owing to the usual and natural cause of such disorder . . . the misconduct of government. . . ."[27] He saw no reason to alter his position in the 1790s. Indeed, in both the *Reflections* and the *Appeal*, Burke admitted that, in an extreme case, misgovernment might even justify revolution. In the *Reflections*, he suggested that, during the English Revolution, "aided with the powers derived from force and opportunity, the nation was . . . in some sense, free to take what course it pleased for filling the throne. . . ."[28] However, Burke also insisted that such an extreme course was not often justified: before the people ought to resume power, he wrote, ". . . no occasion can justify such a resumption, which would not equally authorize a dispensation with any other moral duty, perhaps with all of them together."[29] Far better, then, he concluded, was reform: "I would not exclude alteration neither, but even when I changed it should be to preserve. I should be led to my remedy by a great grievance. In what I did, I should follow the example of our ancestors. I would make the reparation as nearly as possible in the style of the building."[30] So Burke recognized that reform might be slow, but it was sure, and, moreover, it left room for further

adjustment. In a letter to the King of Poland, Burke praised a series of Polish reforms both for what had been done and what had been left undone: "there is Room for a long succession of acts of Politick beneficence. Nothing is forced, or crude, or before its time. The circumstances which make the improvement gradual, will make it more sure, and will not make it the less rapid."[31] Burke was, in short, quite consistent on the issue of reform and revolution. From the 1760s to the 1790s, he always held that extreme oppression justified rebellion, but he also insisted that gradual and limited reform was better than either.

Unfortunately, in Burke's view, the French monarchy had made a botch of reform. Even in the *Reflections*, he conceded the need existed: "your government in France, though usually, and I think justly, reputed the best of the unqualified or ill-qualified monarchies, was still full of abuses. . . ."[32] In his private letters, he was even more emphatic. Burke told one correspondent, "if any one means that system of Court Intrigue miscalled a Government as it stood, at Versailles before the present confusions as the thing to be established, that I believe will be found absolutely impossible. . . . If it were even possible to lay things down exactly as they stood, before the series of experimental politicks began, I am quite sure that they could not long continue in that situation."[33] Many modern scholars place a significant share of the blame for the failure of reform in France on the vacillating policies of the king.[34] They argue that prerevolutionary France was less a true community or nation than a collection of various ranks, classes, and regions, each with its own highly structured body of rights and privileges. Thus, effective action was difficult, and, with so many focal points for resistance, change easy to block. Therefore, they argue that the only possible means of reform was a vigorous Crown. As J. M. Roberts puts it, the only sound tactic for the monarchy would have been "To capture the allegiance of reforming opinion, and mobilize it in the shape of a strong Third Estate which could over-ride the other two in support of a coherent strategy of reform."[35] A number of Burke's French contemporaries, including

Voltaire, perceived this and supported a series of reform-minded royal ministers.[36] Burke understood it as well, but he also realized that Louis XVI was just not up to the task. Of Louis, Burke said, "His conduct in its principles was not unwise; but, like most other of his well-meant designs, it failed in his hands. . . . The failure, perhaps, in part, was owing to his suffering his system to be vitiated and disturbed by those intrigues which it is, humanly speaking, impossible wholly to prevent in courts. . . ."[37] In private, Burke even acknowledged that the Queen was among the worst offenders: "that most unfortunate woman is not to be cured of the spirit of Court Intrigue even by a prison."[38] In fact, on occasion, he admitted that, if it came to a choice between the revolutionary government and the Ancien Regime, he would be hard put to decide.[39]

For Burke, the combination of the abstract and detached radicalism of the reformers and the indecisive and venial corruption of the Crown was a recipe for civic collapse. Ignoring the lessons of experience and prudence, the French "chose to act as if you had never been molded into civil society and had everything to begin anew. You began ill, because you began by despising everything that belonged to you. You set up your trade without a capital."[40] The result, he thought, was both forseeable and ironic: "they have found their punishment in their success: laws overturned; tribunals subverted; industry without vigor; commerce expiring; the revenues unpaid, yet the people impoverished; a church pillaged, and a state not relieved; civil and military anarchy made the constitution of the kingdom; everything human and divine sacrificed to the idol of public credit, and national bankruptcy the consequence; . . . ."[41] From foolishness, according to Burke, the Revolution had proceeded to the destruction of all social bonds and anarchy. Once freed from the discipline, and protection, of the laws, the people became the dupes of impostors and charlatans. They ran wild in their delusions: "but the deluded people of France are like other madmen, who, to a miracle, bear hunger, and thirst, and cold, and confinement, and the claims and lash of their keeper, whilst all the while they support themselves by the imagination that they are generals of armies, prophets, kings, and emperors."[42] The would-be animal tamers have become the animals, and the animals now direct the show. The National Assembly, Burke claimed, no longer governs, for it is controlled by the Paris mob, and, "under the terror of the bayonet and the lamppost and the torch to their houses, they are obliged to adopt all the crude and desperate measures suggested by clubs composed by a monstrous medley of all conditions, tongues, and nations."[43] Yet, Burke did not think that this was the end of the matter, for he predicted that anarchy could not long endure. It, in turn, could only lead to a seizure of power by some conspiratorial elite. Of the French people, Burke noted, "by their violent haste and their defiance of the process of nature, they are delivered over blindly to every projector and adventurer, to every alchemist and empiric."[44] Eventually one or a group of these adventurers will seize control of the state and use its power to discipline the mobs and restore order.

Still, the story would not be over, for despotism has a logic of its own. Burke asserted: "The design is wicked, immoral, impious, oppressive: but it is spirited and daring; it is systematic; it is simple in its principle; it has unity and consistency in perfection. In that country, entirely to cut off a branch of commerce, to extinguish a manufacture, to destroy the circulation of money, to violate credit, to suspend the course of agriculture, even to burn a city or to lay waste a province of their own, does not cost them a moment's anxiety. . . . The state is all in all."[45] Nor did he consider such a state to be unstable. While many leading English politicians supported the Revolution on the presumption that it would weaken France, Burke maintained, "it is not to be imagined, because a political system is, under certain aspects, very unwise in its contrivance, and very mischievous in its effects, that it therefore can have no long duration. Its very defects may tend to its stability, because they are agreeable to its nature."[46] Burke saw several forces as working to unify and strengthen France: the economic policy of the confiscation of property and the issuing of paper currency, the supremacy of Paris, the Army, and, most of all, a systematic policy of repression at home and expansion abroad. Indeed, he argued that there was a close connection between the internal and external sides of the Revolution. In Burke's opinion, the Revolution had to be exported or die on the vine. As he put it, "it is not an enemy of accident that we have to deal with. Enmity to us, and to all civilized nations, is wrought into the stamina of its Constitution."[47] By its very nature, he suggested, the French Revolution must be at war with all of civilized Europe, for, while Europe exists unreformed, the Revolution can never be secure, and, so long as France remains revolutionary, Europe is in danger. Yet, Burke saw the imperialism of the Revolution as a mixed benefit for its leaders. Eventually, he insisted, the militarization of the Revolution would be its downfall. Sooner or later, the government would become incapable of controlling or disciplining the army. When that occurred, "in the weakness of one kind of authority, and in the fluctuation of all, the officers of an army will remain for some time mutinous and full of faction until some popular general, who understands the art of conciliating the soldiery, and who possesses the true spirit of command, shall draw the eyes of all men upon him. Armies will obey him on his personal account. . . . But the moment in which that event shall happen, the person who really commands the army is your master. . . ."[48] Only then, Burke concluded, will the Revolution be over.

One final point concerning Burke's analysis of the pathology of the French Revolution remains to be considered. That is the question of whether Burke should be seen as some kind of genius of the Counterrevolution. Did he see further into the dynamics of the Revolution than other men? Some of Burke's protagonists seem to think so. Freeman, for example, claims that "Burke identified the classic conditions for revolution: a weak, highly centralized state presiding over a society divided between a decadent ruling class and an aspirant powerful new class. The chief cause of the French Revolution was not the conspiracy of intellectuals, but

the policy of the French monarchy."[49] Freeman further believes that Burke correctly determined the necessary course of all revolutions.[50] Similarly, J. M. Robert's description of the Terror invokes memories of Burke: "much of the Terror was mindless. It was not an ordered movement, sweeping France irresistibly towards a clear goal of political and social reform. . . . If it had a pervasive principle, it was one more often implicit than explicit and it lay in the fact that what all those involved in it were trying to do—save France—required the biggest attempt yet seen to nationalize the life of a whole State, to regulate it in all its aspects from a central source of impulse."[51] Burke's insistence on a link between French internal politics and the war holds up quite well under the test of modern scholarship.[52]

Yet, one wonders. Burke's view of the Revolution developed slowly and was never so clearcut as his defenders seem to think. Moreover, upon examination, much of what he said simply mirrors the classical sources on revolution. In the *Republic*, Plato held that despotism arises out of anarchy, noted the relationship between tyranny and foreign wars, and referred to its militarization of the state.[53] Similarly, Aristotle suggested that, "in democracies changes are chiefly due to the wanton licence of demagogues," that democracies are generally followed by oligarchies, that oligarchies often fall because of the abuse of the masses or dissension among oligarchs, and that military leaders often seize control of declining oligarchies.[54] Burke had other sources at hand as well. I would think, for example, that he could find inspiration in the writings on Oliver Cromwell. Cromwell's position as Lord Protector was, after all, Janus-faced: on the one hand, it looked back to the classical world, but, on the other, it evoked the more modern concept of the military as the "protector of the constitution." Indeed, Burke had only to look to David Hume's *Histories*. After the death of the king, Hume wrote, "the bands of society were everywhere loosened; and the irregular passions of men were encouraged by speculative principles still more unsocial and irregular."[55] Only Cromwell's personal strength and the discipline of the army kept things going, Hume argued, for, "illegal violence, with whatever pretences it may be covered, and whatever object it may pursue, must inevitably and at last end in the arbitrary and despotic government of a single person."[56] I do not mean to suggest that Burke grounded his account of the Revolution directly on Hume or on anyone else. I merely wish to maintain that, along with an impressive element of originality and a considerable talent for vivid expression, Burke drew on a traditional model of revolution which fit French circumstances rather well.

II

Burke's analysis of the causes and probable course of the French Revolution led him to see it as posing a multi-dimensional threat to European security. In his view, the Revolution, because of its ideological and imperialistic aspects, could not be contained within France, and would, by its very nature, spread until it was confronted by superior moral and political power. Thus, I believe that students of Burke's thought commit a serious error when they neglect one or another of the several facets of the crisis Burke felt was facing the international community of his day. Such a narrow focus seriously underestimates the magnitude of Burke's fears, and, moreover, distorts our understanding of his thought by making various aspects of his proposals for fighting the Revolution appear irrational or excessive. Before proceeding to consider Burke's strategy and tactics for opposing the Revolution, I will, therefore, first consider his interpretation of the threat it represented in more detail. First, Burke held that the Revolution promised to destroy the old order within France, and, with its elimination, remove one of the great centers of European civilization. He believed that it was not only an assault on the government of France, but an attack on the very culture of the most advanced section of the world. Second, Burke claimed that once France fell to the radicals, the remainder of Europe would be exposed to the danger of attack from that nation, and, consequently, the commonwealth of Europe would be exposed to the

threat of a kind of civil war. In more modern terms, Burke believed that a revolutionary government in France would become both militaristic and expansionistic. Finally, Burke also feared that revolutionary France would become a threat by example. In part, Burke was concerned that France would export revolutionary propaganda which would undermine the intellectual foundations of European government. However, his anxiety went further, for he also argued that the mere existence of France's radical government would serve as an inspiration to radicals elsewhere. Here, Burke saw the danger as twofold. On the one hand, successful revolutions in other countries would lead to further rupture of the European community. On the other hand, unsuccessful revolutions would precipitate reaction which, in turn, would endanger freedom and block reform.

I will begin with France, itself. As we have seen, Burke was a firm believer in both the unity and the progressiveness of the European community: "the states of the Christian world have grown up to their present magnitude in a great length of time and by a great variety of accidents. They have been improved to what we see them with greater or less degrees of felicity and skill. . . . The objects which they embrace are of the greatest possible variety, and have become in a manner infinite. . . . Every state has pursued not only every sort of social advantage, but it has cultivated the welfare of every individual."[57] Such traditionalism was not entirely, or even largely, a conservative doctrine, for at its core, as J. G. A. Pocock has pointed out, was the belief that commerce and progress "can flourish only under the protection of manners, and that manners require the pre-eminence of religion and nobility, the natural protectors of society. To overthrow religion and nobility, therefore, is to destroy the possibility of commerce itself."[58] In Burke's view, the French Revolution threatened to do just that: "there is the hand of God in this business, and there is an end of the system of Europe, taking in laws, manners, religion and politics, in which I delighted so much."[59] When Burke, in the *Reflections*, deplored the end of the age of chivalry, and claimed as a result, "that of sophisters, economists, and calculators has succeeded, and the glory of Europe is extinguished forever," he meant to be taken literally.[60] Burke believed that a successful revolution in France would, by destroying what was perhaps the most shining example of Enlightenment culture, signal the advent of a new age. The hard-won achievements of time, he insisted, would be destroyed and replaced by the false idols of a temporary aberration. As he insisted that a queen was more than a woman, and a woman was more than an animal, so he believed that a society was more than a collection of self-interested calculators. Burke believed that the French materialists would reduce man to a machine. He was equally sure that they were wrong to do so. Indeed, the very attempt, would, itself, he thought, destroy much of what he valued.

Moreover, from the very beginning, Burke insisted that the French radicals had something more in mind than just the conquest of power in France. They sought, he noted, not to limit the French state, but to capture and strengthen it. They attacked monarchy for it weakness, not its excessive and arbitrary power, and they advocated a republic because, like Machiavelli, Harrington, and Montesquieu, they believed that it was more suitable for expansion.[61] In short, Burke said, "those who acted in the Revolution *as statesmen* had the exterior aggrandizement of France as their ultimate end in the most minute part of the internal changes that were made."[62] Viewed in this light, Burke held that the Revolution displayed a character totally new in the world; it took on the aura of a kind of secular holy war: "*a Revolution of doctrine and theoretic dogma.*"[63] He maintained that, like the Reformation, the Revolution could leave no part of the world unchanged and had to become imperialistic by its very nature. The French, Burke continued, "made a schism with the whole universe, and that schism extended to almost everything, great and small."[64] In the realm of politics, "this violent breach of the community of Europe we must conclude to have been made (even if they had not expressly declared it over and over again) either to force mankind into an adoption of their system or to live in perpetual enmity with a community

the most potent we have ever known."[65] What was worse, according to Burke, like many of the other mutations of nature, the new French form of government possessed an amazing strength: "were France but half of what it is in population, in compactness, in applicability of its force, situated as it is, and being what it is, it would be too strong for most of the states of Europe, constituted as they are, and proceeding as they proceed."[66] In sum, Burke concluded, the Revolution must be destroyed or it will destroy everything in its path: "From all this what is my inference? It is, that this new system of robbery in France cannot be rendered safe by any art; that it *must* be destroyed, or that it will destroy all Europe. . . ."[67] Like a cancer, the Revolution, Burke said, must be annihilated before it kills its host.

Finally, as the English Revolution inspired the American, and the American inspired the French, so Burke feared that the French Revolution would encourage reformers in other nations to imitate its example. Burke recognized the irony of France's support for the American Revolution for Louis XVI: where he "meant to found but one republic, he set up two; when he meant to take away half the crown of his neighbor, he lost the whole of his own."[68] With such an example in mind, he asked, can the leaders of Europe really believe that a martial republic can be established in their own vicinity without posing a threat to them? This was, he thought, especially so, for the spirit of proselytism attended the fanaticism of the French: "they have societies to cabal and correspond at home and abroad for the propagation of their tenets."[69] Indeed, the entire first half of Burke's "Thoughts on French Affairs," more than thirty pages, was given over to a survey of the progress of revolutionary ideas throughout the countries of Europe.[70] For example, Burke argued, "that this doctrine has made an amazing progress in Germany there cannot be a shadow of doubt."[71] He, therefore, predicted that there would soon be a German revolution even greater than the one in France. For Burke, the problem was that everywhere he looked there was a French party, often led by the French ambassador, seeking converts. In England, for instance, he noted the Constitutional and Revolutionary Societies: "the National Assembly of France has given importance to these gentlemen by adopting them; and they return the favor by acting as a committee in England for extending the principles of the National Assembly."[72] According to Burke, when the principles and politics of the French Revolution are extended to other nations, their constitutions will be unable to cope. They are not made for such conflict. Burke maintained that, even with all its history of tyranny and rebellion, England "has never been debauched from its domestic relations. To this time it has been English liberty, and English liberty only."[73] To be sure, Burke felt that, "we cannot be too liberal in our general wishes for the happiness of our kind. But in all questions on the mode of procuring it for any particular community, we ought to be fearful of admitting those who have no interest in it, or who have, perhaps, an interest against it, into the consultation."[74] In the past, Burke insisted, all the parties to a given English conflict could, at least, be assumed to want the best for their country, even if they might have defined that best in different ways. With the advent of the French Revolution, however, he feared that there would always be a substantial pro-French party, intent on the realization of its alien creed regardless of the consequences.

As the preceding example indicates, Burke was particularly apprehensive about the effects of the French Revolution on England. His uneasiness was, in part, a product of natural prudence and caution. As he pointed out in the *Reflections*, "when our neighbor's house is on fire, it cannot be amiss for the engines to play a little on our own."[75] But it was also based on his judgment that England was particularly vulnerable to some of the propaganda coming out of France. Burke always insisted that the mass of English citizens, of all ranks and callings, were steadfast in their loyalty to the English Constitution. In the "Letters on a Regicide Peace," he claimed that, "the people have nowhere and in no way expressed their wish of throwing themselves and their sovereign at the feet of a wicked and ravenous foe. . . ."[76] Rather, what Burke was afraid of was the fel-

low-travelling minority, both within and without Parliament. These, he admitted, were not, strictly speaking, Jacobins themselves, but they were, nonetheless, not to be trusted, for they could already be found attacking the government, "in the same modes, and on the very same grounds, and nearly in the same terms, with the Directory."[77] Modern scholars agree that there was considerable correspondence between the French Revolutionaries and the English reformers, and some see a revolutionary potential in English politics. E. P Thompson, for instance, supports Burke's analysis, arguing that the politics of the 1790s "was not an agitation about France, although French events both inspired and bedevilled it. It was an English agitation, of impressive dimensions, for an English democracy."[78] Most writers, however, do not go so far.[79] They maintain that the English reformers, contrary to Burke's assessment, were moderate until near the end of the century. Veitch's comments on the Society for Constitutional Information is typical: "nothing could well be more harmless than the vague and high-flown sentiments exchanged during the period of French constitutionalism."[80] Burke, it seems, exaggerated.

At the center of Burke's concern stood the Protestant Dissenters. Early in his political career, Burke had been allied with the Dissenters, especially in the movements for broader religious toleration. For example, in 1773 he had vigorously supported a Methodist petition for toleration.[81] Gradually, however, his support diminished as he became increasingly convinced that the Dissenters were overly political and radical to boot. Thus, in May of 1789, Burke could be found agonizing over his vote on a relief bill, and attributing his reluctance to support relief to the enthusiasm among Dissenters for Pitt's constitutional coup of 1784. His indecision soon turned to opposition. The turning point seems to have come in early March 1790. About that time, the Dissenters made three moves: they adopted a strategy of provocation against their opponents; they attempted to pressure Parliament by exacting electoral pledges from candidates; and they openly committed to French revolutionary principles.[82] Burke was furious. In response to a Unitarian petition, he exclaimed: "let them disband as a faction, and let them act as individuals, and when I see them with no other views than to enjoy their own conscience in peace, I, for one, shall most cheerfully vote for their relief."[83] "Rather," he argued, "George the Third, or George the Fourth, than Dr. Priestly, or Dr. Keppis. . . ."[84] For a religious group to act as a political faction was offensive enough to Burke, but he also objected to the mode of argument the Dissenters employed. In a letter to John Noble, he complained that their arguments smacked of the natural law and abstract rights rhetoric of the French. He was offended, he said, by "the eager manner in which several dissenting Teachers shewed themselves disposed to connect themselves in Sentiment and by imitation (and perhaps by something more) with what was done and is doing in France. . . ."[85] Similarly, over a year and a half later, Burke wrote to Henry Dundas that he was not much concerned with the scattered pro-French individuals, but that he greatly feared the "Phalanx of Party" which the Dissenters had become.[86] I have argued that Burke was, in many respects, a disciple of John Locke. Like Locke, one of the few justifications he accepted for discrimination against a religious group was the political consequences of that group's ideas and actions.

Burke did not believe that the Dissenters, taken alone, constituted a serious threat to the English political system. However, he was convinced that they had like-minded allies among certain other groups and parties. In his "Thoughts on French Affairs," Burke maintained that, while the Dissenters constituted the core of the pro-French party, they were joined by "all who are Dissenters in character, temper, and disposition, though not belonging to any of their congregations: that is, all the restless people who resemble them, of all ranks and parties,—Whigs, and even Tories; the whole race of half-bred speculators; all the Atheists, Deists, and Socinians; all those who hate the clergy and envy the nobility; a good many among the moneyed people; the East Indians almost to a man. . . ."[87] He even asserted that the sick-

ness had spread even to his own party and among his own friends. In a letter to William Weddell, he described the Dissenters' seduction of Charles James Fox: "in their unprecedented compliment to Mr. Fox 'for Governing his conduct by the true principles of the Revolution,' they plainly alluded to a transaction not quite an hundred years old."[88] Yet more surprising, according to Burke, the radicals had made extensive inroads among the aristocracy itself. In his reply to the Duke of Bedford's criticism of his pension, Burke was quick to note the irony of Bedford's support of French ideas. The radicals, Burke said, "are the Duke of Bedford's natural hunters; and he is their natural game."[89] Still, Burke acknowledged that, in spite of their difference in objective interests, the support of a man like Bedford could be of great advantage to the radicals: "there is scope for seven philosophers to proceed in their analytical experiments upon Harrington's seven different forms of republics, in the acres of this one Duke."[90] Burke doubted that Bedford's lack of class interest would save him. He believed that, in the end, the radicals would turn on their sponsors, for, no matter what they were given, they would always "want new lands for new trials."[91] As sound as the English public might presently be, the example of men like Bedford demonstrated for Burke that no one was completely safe until the Revolution and its doctrine were both obliterated.

III

In considering Burke's strategy for opposing the French Revolution and its creed, several general points should be kept in mind. First, Burke was by no means a mere reactionary. He knew full well that the clock could not be turned back, and he would not have it so even if it could. The New Whigs, Burke insisted, were the extremists, not he, for, "they build their politics, not on convenience, but on truth. . . . With them there is no compromise."[92] He, on the other hand, was, in his own eyes, a moderate: "the opinions maintained in that book never can lead to an extreme, because their foundation is laid in an opposition to extremes."[93] Second, though a reformer, Burke was also yet a gradualist. As he put it, "the burden of proof lies heavily on those who tear to pieces the whole frame and contexture of their country, that they could find no other way of settling a government fit to obtain its rational ends, except that which they have pursue[d] by means unfavorable to all the present happiness of millions of people...."[94] Third, Burke always insisted that his response to the Revolution was consistent with his earlier stands on other issues. In the letter on his pension, he made a typical argument: citing his proposals for economic reform in the 1780–82 period as an example, he maintained that he had always been a practical-minded reformer.[95] The specific references changed, one time it was a comparison of his reactions to the American and French Revolutions and another it was his speech at the polls at Bristol, but Burke's theme never changed. He constantly claimed that not all change is reform—"the former alters the substance of the objects themselves, and gets rid of all their essential good as well as all the accidental evil annexed to them.... Reform is ... a direct application of a remedy to the grievance complained of.... It stops there; and if it fails, the substance ... is but where it was"—and that he favored only true reform and not mere change.[96] Fourth, Burke's tone and style were rarely hysterical or violent. Most often, he assumed the role of a man of affairs: he was knowledgeable, prudent, world[l]y and moderate. The "Fourth Letter on a Regicide Peace" is a good case in point. While it is often denounced by critics as excessively emotional, a close examination shows the letter to be a tightly controlled and very systematic work. Though over one hundred pages in length, it is a point-by-point refutation of the arguments which were being made by Burke's opponents in favor of the treaty at issue. Where there are flights of imagination and rhetoric, and there are several, they always serve some quite specific political purpose.[97]

Finally, while his analysis of French events was pretty well fixed by the time of the publication of the *Reflections*, Burke's strategy of opposition was quite complex and sophisticated, and, therefore, revealed itself fully only over time. At first, Burke claimed to have no solution to the crisis. He concluded the 1791 "Thoughts on French Affairs," on an open note: "the evil is stated, in my opinion, as it exists. The Remedy must be where power, wisdom, and information, I hope, are more united with good intentions than they can be with me."[98] Within a year, with the publication of the "Heads for Consideration on the Present State of Affairs," Burke offered a more detailed analysis, but one that was marred by a central inconsistency. In that work he tried to combine a balance of power argument with an insistence that the French Revolution presented a totally new threat to European civilization.[99] This ambiguity in approach, in turn, led Burke into confusion in his policy recommendations. In the balance of power portions of the tract, he held that France should be weakened but not totally defeated, but, in other sections, he treated the French ideology as an evil which must be exterminated. This was, then, one of the oddest of all Burke's works on the Revolution. His critique of government policy was powerful, but the remedy proposed did not seem adequate to the evil decried. As England was drawn into the War and the debate became more heated, Burke dropped the balance of power line and advanced to a more militant position. In his view, the central issue had become whether the War could be fought in the traditional way or whether a new, more rigorous, effort was necessary.[100] Some (Charles Fox, for example) even believed that trade with France could be continued as the war went on. Burke, for his part, was sure that a new form of warfare was required. He wrote, "you may as well think of opposing one of these old fortresses to the mass of artillery brought by a French irruption into the field as to think of resisting by your old laws and your old forms the new destruction which the corps of Jacobin engineers of today prepare for all such forms and all such laws."[101] At this point, Burke had finally reached his fully articulated position: the French Revolution, he maintained, was a new, and monstrous phenomenon which was so antagonistic to civilization that only total warfare to the death could exist between them.

The first step, Burke believed, was to promote an accurate understanding of the political situation. He argued that each allied state must be brought to recognize the unique nature of the challenge, encouraged to form the will to resist, and mobilized to deny the enemy a cheap victory. The truth is, he said: "we are in a war of a *peculiar* nature. It is not with an ordinary community.... We are at war with a system which by its essence is inimical to all other governments, and which makes peace or war as peace and war may best contribute to their subversion. It is with an *armed doctrine* that we are at war. It has, by its essence, a faction of opinion and of interest and of enthusiasm in every country."[102] Properly speaking, then, Burke maintained, France is not a state, but an organized faction within the community of Europe, and the French War is a form of civil war: "it is a war between the partisans of the ancient civil, moral, and political order of Europe against a sect of fanatical and ambitious atheists which means to change them all."[103] With its partisans in every state, one of the chief dangers of the French ideology is that it is ideally situated for subversion. To be sure, the French have arms aplenty, but their best weapon lies in the sapping of the strength of their opponents before the actual fighting begins. The example of the Ancien Regime of France was instructive for Burke: "if armies and fortresses were a defense against Jacobinism, Louis the Sixteenth would this day reign a powerful monarch over an happy people."[104] Even in England, he believed, the problem was acute, for, "public prosecutions are become little better than schools for treason,—of no use but to improve the dexterity of criminals in the mystery of evasion."[105] With subversion so rampant, the temptation to surrender could be overwhelming. Still, Burke held that the temptation must be resisted, for the struggle was not lost: "this seems the temper of the day. At first the French force was too much despised. Now it is too much dreaded."[106] As the defenders of traditional Europe ought not to resign the struggle prematurely, neither should they compromise. The French

system is a cancer which constantly attempts to expand; a temporary peace only permits it to advance by some other means. The fight must be to the end: "... more safety was to be found in the most arduous war than in the friendship of that kind of being."[107] In short, according to Burke, if peace is made with France, the revolutionaries will not keep it. The only security lies in unity and unrelenting struggle.

As the campaign against international radicalism progressed, Burke made clear that he did not think that a purely defensive alliance against French militarism could be successful. Rather, he demanded that the war be carried into France, itself, by a European community-based invasion. As early as January of 1791, he wrote to a friend: "I cannot persuade myself that any thing whatsoever can be effected without a great force from Abroad. The predominant Faction is the strongest as I conceive, without comparison."[108] When the Revolution spread beyond the borders of France, Burke also expanded his rationale, for, where he had previously justified his call for invasion in terms of internal French politics, he now did so on the basis of the French threat to the rest of Europe. In the "Heads for Consideration of French Affairs," he argued that an offensive alliance was preferable to a defensive one because offensive alliances are held together by their common efforts while defensive alliances fall apart while awaiting action. In addition, he continued, "this evil in the heart of Europe must be extirpated from that centre, or no part of the circumference can be free from the mischief which radiates from it, and which will spread, circle beyond circle, in spite of all the little defensive precautions which can be employed against it."[109] How was such an invasion to be justified? Burke's explanations varied, but generally he relied on two arguments. First, he asserted that there is a natural right to intervene where one perceives injustice. To a French correspondent, he wrote, "that fury which arises in the minds of men on being stripped of their goods, and turned out of their houses by acts of power, and our sympathy with them under Such wrongs, are feelings implanted in us by our creator.... They arise out of instinctive principles of self-defense and are executive powers under the legislation of nature, enforcing its first law."[110] Second, Burke appealed to international law. He maintained that, "the government of that kingdom is fundamentally monarchical. The public law of Europe has never recognized in it any other form of government. The potentates of Europe have, by that law, a right, an interest, and a duty to know with what government they are to treat, and what they are to admit into the federative society."[111] According to Burke, then, the community of Europe had a right to decide who was the legal government of France. Furthermore, in the event of a civil war within the boundaries of one of its member states, he felt that the community had an additional right to intervene in support of that party which it had determined to be the legitimate government.[112] Indeed, as an interesting corollary of this argument, Burke held that the proposed invasion of France should be conducted in league with representatives of the traditional French regime.

Once a successful invasion of France was accomplished, Burke saw yet one more task for the allied powers to perform: they would then have to establish some sort of interim government. This, Burke believed, would necessarily have to be a dictatorship of some form, for it must have power "equal at least in vigor, vigilance, promptitude, and decision, to a military government . . . no slow-paced . . . lawyer-like system, still less that of a showy, superficial, trifling, intriguing court. . . ."[113] For Burke, the role of this temporary government would be to protect the counter-revolution, and to restore the real French nation. Indeed, in his opinion, "the truth is, that France is out of itself,—the moral France is separated from the geographical. The master of the house is expelled, and the robbers are in possession."[114] Since, in Burke's view, the true corporate people of France were in exile in "Flanders and Germany, in Switzerland, Spain, Italy, and England," they must be returned to their homes before a proper government could be reconstructed.[115] Only when this reverse migration was completed, would it be safe to restore the monarchy. It, in turn, should then

"assist the dignity, the religion, and the property of France to repossess themselves of the means of their natural influence."[116] Finally, once reconstituted, the French elite could act to purify the remainder of society: "this will be compassed, when every gentleman, everywhere being restored to his landed estate, each on his patrimonial ground, may join the clergy in reanimating the loyalty, fidelity, and religion of the people . . . that they may arm the honest and well-affected, and disarm and disable the factious and ill-disposed."[117] Thus, Burke held that the French should be left to themselves to punish the defeated revolutionaries.[118] In this regard, though he disclaimed any right to speak, Burke recommended against a general indemnity, but also counseled moderation: no one should be punished on a broad charge of rebellion, or for anything done in the field of battle, and punishment should be reserved for those who engaged in what would be considered criminal conduct by ordinary society.[119] . . .

Notes

1. Michael Freeman, *Edmund Burke and the Critique of Political Radicalism*.
2. Ibid., p. 4.
3. Ibid., p. 38.
4. See the exchange in *Political Theory*, Vol. 6, No. 3 (August 1978), between Freeman, "Edmund Burke and the Theory of Revolution," pp. 227–297, and Ted Robert Gurr, "Burke and the Modern Theory of Revolution: A Reply to Freeman," pp. 299–311.
5. C. B. Macpherson, *Burke*, Hill and Wang, New York, 1980.
6. Ibid., p. 3.
7. See Frank O'Gorman, *The Whig Party and the French Revolution*, p. 33 ff.
8. Edmund Burke, *Correspondence*, Vol. VIII, To Lord Loughborough, Circa 17/March/1796, p. 432.
9. Edmund Burke, *Reflection on the Revolution in France*, p. 11.
10. Edmund Burke, "Thoughts on French Affairs," *Works*, Vol. IV, pp. 313–377, pp. 352–353.
11. Burke, *Correspondence*, Vol. VI, To Lord Charlemont, 9/Aug./1789, p. 9.

12. Burke, *Correspondence*, Vol. VI, To Charles-Jean-Francois DePont, Nov./1789, p. 41.

13. Burke, *Correspondence*, Vol. VII, To Chevalier de Grave, 24/Aug./1792, p. 183.

14. Burke, *Correspondence*, Vol. VII, To Mrs. Crewe, Post 11/Aug./1795, p. 300.

15. James T. Boulton, *The Language of Politics in the Age of Wilkes and Burke*, University of Toronto Press, Toronto, 1963, p. 98. Olivia Smith, *The Politics of Language 1791–1819*, Clarendon Press, Oxford, 1984, takes the discussion down through the Napoleonic Wars. Two more recent works on Burke's rhetoric are Christopher Reid, *Edmund Burke and the Practice of Political Writing*, St. Martin's Press, New York, 1985 and Steven Blakemore, *Burke and the Fall of Language*, University Press of New England, Hanover, 1988. Boulton's book, however, remains the indispensible source.

16. Burke, "Three Letters on a Regicide Peace," pp. 318–319.

17. Burke, *Reflections on the Revolution in France*, p. 86.

18. Ibid., pp. 86–87.

19. Boulton, *The Language of Politics in the Age of Wilkes and Burke*, p. 131.

20. Burke, *Correspondence*, Vol. VIII, To Lord Fitzwilliam, 15/May/1795, pp. 242–243.

21. Burke, *Correspondence*, Vol. VIII, To Sir Hercules Langrishe, 26/May/1795, p. 254.

22. Edmund Burke, "Three Letters on a Regicide Peace," pp. 361.

23. Burke, *Reflections on the Revolution in France*, p. 127.

24. Edmund Burke, "Letter to a Member of the National Assembly, in Answer to Some Objections to His Book on French Affairs," *Works*, Vol. IV, pp. 1–55, p. 23.

25. Ibid., p. 25.

26. Ibid., pp. 27–28.

27. Edmund Burke, "Address to the King," pp. 162–163.

28. Burke, *Reflections on the Revolution in France*, p. 22.

29. Edmund Burke, "An Appeal From the New to the Old Whigs," p. 169.

30. Burke, *Reflections on the Revolution in France*, p. 290.

31. Burke, *Correspondence*, Vol. VII, To the King of Poland, 28/Feb./1792, p. 77.

32. Burke, *Reflections on the Revolution in France*, p. 145.

33. Burke, *Correspondence*, Vol. VI, To Unknown, 1791, pp. 479–480.

34. See, for example, J. M. Roberts, *The French Revolution*, Oxford University Press, New York, 1978. The nature of French society before the Revolution, the possibilities for reform, and who was to blame for the failure of reform are matters of intense controversy. What might be styled a neo-conservative school argues that the Ancien Regime was reforming itself, and the Revolution was both unjustified and, indeed, a failure. For pre-Revolutionary France, see Willaim Doyle, *The Ancien Regime*, Macmillan Education Ltd., London, 1986, and especially the exhaustive Keith Michael Baker (ed.), *The Political Culture of the Old Regime*, Pergamon Press, New York, 1987. The latter is Volume I in a series, "The French Revolution and the Creation of Modern Political Culture." For the neo-conservative reinterpretation of the Revolution, see Doyle's *The Oxford History of the French Revolution*, Clarendon Press, Oxford, 1989 and Simon Schama, *Citizens: A Chronicle of the French Revolution*, Alfred A. Knopf, 1989. I must admit to being unconvinced.

35. Roberts, *The French Revolution*, p. 13.

36. For Voltaire as a reformer, see Peter Gay, *Voltaire's Politics*, Princeton University Press, Princeton, 1959. Two useful biographies are Jean Orieux, *Voltaire*, Doubleday and Co., Inc., Garden City, 1979 and Haydon Mason, *Voltaire*, Johns Hopkins University Press, Baltimore, 1981. On the intellectual background, see Peter Gay, *The Enlightenment: An Interpretation*, Two Volumes, Alfred A. Knopf, New York, 1969 and especially Nannerl O. Keohane, *Philosophy and the State in France*, Princeton University Press, Princeton, New Jersey, 1980. Burke rarely commented on Voltaire, but one notable, and amusing, mention is in *Correspondence*, Vol. VI, To Unknown, Jan./1790, p. 81: "Who ever dreamt of Voltaire and Rousseau as legislators? The First has the merit of writing agreeably; and nobody has ever united blasphemy and obscenity so happily together. . . ."

37. Burke, "Letters on a Regicide Peace," p. 378.

38. Burke, *Correspondence*, Vol. VI, To Richard Burke, Jr., 18/Aug./1791, p. 361.

39. Burke, *Correspondence*, Vol. VI, To Richard Burke, Jr., 26/Sept./1791, p. 414.

40. Burke, *Reflections on the Revolution in France*, p. 44.

41. Ibid., p. 31.

42. Burke, "Letter to a Member of the National Assembly," pp. 15–16.

43. Burke, *Reflections on the Revolution in France*, p. 77.

44. Ibid., p. 199.

45. Burke, "Letters on a Regicide Peace," p. 375.

46. Burke, "Thoughts on French Affairs," p. 353.

47. Burke, "Fourth Letter on a Regicide Peace," p. 91.

48. Burke, *Reflections on the Revolution in France*, p. 258.

49. Freeman, *Edmund Burke and Political Radicalism*, pp. 196–197.

50. Ibid., p. 204 ff.

51. Roberts, *The French Revolution*, p. 63.

52. For a discussion of the war, see Ibid., p. 45 ff.

53. Plato, *The Republic of Plato*, F. M. Cornford, (Trans.), Oxford University Press, New York, 1945, p. 286 (VII 562A–IX 576B).

54. Aristotle, *The Politics of Aristotle*, Ernest Baker (ed.), Oxford University Press, New York, 1946, p. 215 (1304B), p. 217 (1305A), and p. 219 (1306A).

55. David Hume, *A History of England*, Vol. V, pp. 280–281.

56. Ibid., p. 334.

57. Burke, "Letters on a Regicide Peace," p. 373.

58. J. G. A. Pocock, "Burke's Analysis of the French Revolution," in *Virtue, Commerce, and History*, pp. 194–212, p. 199.

59. Burke, *Correspondence*, Vol. IX, To French Laurence, 11/April/1797, p. 307.

60. Burke, *Reflections on the Revolution in France*, p. 86.

61. See Burke, "Letters on a Regicide Peace," p. 364 ff.

62. Ibid., p. 364.

63. Burke, "Thoughts on French Affairs," p. 319.

64. Burke, "Letters on a Regicide Peace," p. 320.

65. Ibid., p. 320.

66. Burke, "Letters on a Regicide Peace," p. 376.

67. Ibid., p. 377.

68. Ibid., pp. 380–381.

69. Burke, *Reflections on the Revolution in France*, p. 177.

70. See Burke, "Thoughts on French Affairs," p. 327 ff.

71. Ibid., p. 329.

72. Burke, *Reflections on the Revolution in France*, p. 6.

73. Burke, "Fourth Letter on a Regicide Peace," p. 99.

74. Ibid.

75. Burke, *Reflections on the Revolution in France*, p. 10.

76. Burke, "Letters on a Regicide Peace," p. 431.

77. Ibid., p. 426.

78. E. P. Thompson, *The Making of the English Working Class*, p. 102.

79. There is an extensive literature on the nature and extent of English radicalism in the era of the French Revolution. A good history of England during the years of the French Revolution may be found in Ian R. Christie, *Wars and Revolutions Britain, 1760–1815*, Harvard University Press, Cambridge, Mass., 1982. Also helpful are several of the papers in H. T. Dickinson (ed.), *Britain and the French Revolution, 1789–1815*, Macmillan Education Ltd., 1989. H. T. Dickinson, *British Radicalism and the French Revolution*, Basil Blackwell, Inc., New York, 1985 is a good brief introduction. George Stead Veitch, *The Genesis of Parliamentary Reform*, is the traditional standby. Other useful studies are Carl B. Cone, *The English Jacobins*, Charles Scribner's Sons, New York, 1968, Clive Emsley, *British Society and the French Wars, 1793–1815*, Rowman and Littlefield, Totwa, New Jersey, 1979, Albert Goodwin, *The Friends of Liberty*, Harvard University Press, Cambridge, Mass., 1979, and, of course, Thompson's *The Making of the English Working Class*. Ian R. Christie, *Stress and Stability in Late Eighteenth Century Britain*, Clarendon Press, Oxford, 1984, is a good counterpoint to Thompson and the others, for he sees little threat of revolution in the period. R. R. Fennessy, *Burke, Paine, and the Rights of Man*, Martinus Nijhoff, 1963, is more specialized but very good on the intellectual dimensions of the struggle. Finally, E. C. Black, *The Association*, Harvard University Press, Cambridge, Mass., 1963 and Robert R. Dozier, *For King, Constitution, and Country*, The University Press of Kentucky, Lexington, 1983, studies of the Loyalist movement, go a long way toward correcting the lack of balance which has resulted from the scholarly concentration on the radicals. A useful brief discussion of the conservatives may be found in H. T. Dickinson, "Popular Conservatism and Militant Loyalism 1789–1815," in H. T. Dickinson (ed.), *Britain and the French Revolution*, pp. 103–126.

80. Veitch, *The Genesis of Parliamentary Reform*, p. 159.

81. Edmund Burke, "Speech on a Bill for the Relief of Protestant Dissenters, *Works*, Vol. II, pp. 21–38.

82. Goodwin, *The Friends of Liberty*, p. 89.

83. Edmund Burke, "Speech on a Motion for Leave to Bring in a Bill to Repeal and Alter Certain Acts Respecting Religious Opinions, upon the Occasion of a Petition to the Unitarian Society," *Works*, Vol. VII, pp. 39–58, 54.

84. Ibid., p. 51.

85. Burke, *Correspondence*, Vol. VI, To John Noble, 14/March/1790, P. 103.

86. Burke, *Correspondence*, Vol. VI, To Henry Dundas, 30/Sept./1791, p. 419. Was he right? Opinions vary but see Isaac Kramnick, "Revolution and Radicalism: English Political Theory in the Age of Revolution," *Political Theory*, Vo. V, No. 4 (Nov. 1977), pp. 505–534, for a strongly argued supporting position—though one with a rather different value bias.

87. Burke, "Thoughts on French Affairs," p. 324.

88. Burke, *Correspondence*, Vol. VII, To William Weddell, 31/Jan./1792, p. 51.

89. Burke, "Letter to a Noble Lord on the Attacks Made Upon Mr. Burke and His Pension . . . ," p. 213.

90. Ibid., p. 217.

91. Ibid., p. 218.

92. Burke, "An Appeal From the New to the Old Whigs," p. 206.

93. Ibid.

94. Ibid., p. 80.

95. Burke, "Letter to a Noble Lord on the Attacks Made Upon Mr. Burke and His Pension . . . ," p. 184 ff.

96. Ibid., pp. 186–187.

97. For a good example, see Burke's "Fourth Letter on a Regicide Peace." Reid, *Edmund Burke and the Practice of Political Writing*, p. 12 ff., is a particularly good discussion of the various "voices" adopted by Burke in his polemical writings.

98. Burke, "Thoughts on the French Revolution," p. 377.

99. Edmund Burke, "Heads for Consideration on the Present State of Affairs," *Works*, Vol. IV, pp. 379–402.

100. Ermsely, *British Society and the French Revolution*, p. 20 ff.

101. Burke, "Fourth Letter on a Regicide Peace," pp. 100–101.

102. Burke, "Letters on a Regicide Peace," p. 250.

103. Ibid., p. 345.

104. Ibid., p. 347.

105. Ibid., p. 247.

106. Ibid., p. 238.

107. Ibid., p. 245.

108. Burke, *Correspondence*, Vol. VI, To John Trevor, Jan./1791, p. 217.

109. Burke, "Heads for Consideration on the Present State of Affairs," *Works*, Vol. IV, p. 401.

110. Burke, *Correspondence*, Vol. VI, To Claude-Francois De Rivarol, 1/June/1791, p. 266.

111. Edmund Burke, "Remarks on the Policy of the Allies with Respect to France," *Works*, Vol. IV, pp. 403–482, p. 433. Written in late 1793, this work deals with the proposal to issue an allied manifesto on war policy. Burke opposed the manifesto on the grounds that it was inappropriate in a time of calamity and defeat.

112. Ibid., p. 434. The work concludes with an appendix citing examples, precedents, and authorities (out of Vattel) in support of Burke's argument that the other European nations had a right to intervene in internal French affairs if those affairs threatened their own stability.

113. Ibid., pp. 459–460.

114. Ibid., p. 421.

115. Ibid.

116. Ibid., p. 425.

117. Ibid., p. 420. See p. 452 for Burke's proposal to restore the French clergy.

118. Ibid., p. 428.

119. Ibid., p. 462, ff.

Adapted from: James Conniff, *The Useful Cobbler: Edmund Burke and the Politics of Progress*, pp. 215–237, 324–330. Copyright © 1994. Reprinted by permission of the State University of New York Press, Albany. ✦

Mary Wollstonecraft

Born in London in 1759, Mary Wollstonecraft grew up in a poor family headed by an alcoholic, abusive father. Her early life consisted of many efforts to gain personal and financial independence. She tried to earn a living by doing everything from acting as a lady's companion to teaching school to serving as a governess. Self-taught, Wollstonecraft penned her first book, *Thoughts on the Education of Daughters*, in 1785 and thus embarked on a career as a woman of letters. During the next several years she would publish reviews, translate works, and write more books. She would eventually gain notoriety for her spirited advocacy of republican principles in *A Vindication of the Rights of Men* (1790), which was one of the many responses to Edmund Burke's criticism of the French Revolution. Her most famous work, *A Vindication of the Rights of Woman*, followed shortly thereafter. After an affair with an American writer, she gave birth to a daughter, Fanny, in 1794. Three years later, though, she married a fellow radical, William Godwin, author of the *Enquiry into Political Justice*. She died that same year, from complications resulting from the birth of their daughter Mary—who later married the poet Percy Bysshe Shelley and became noteworthy as the author of Frankenstein.

Among the first writers to take what we now regard as a feminist position, Wollstonecraft argued that men and women have an equal capacity for reason. She was firmly opposed to any form of arbitrary, coercive authority—whether aristocratic or paternalistic. For many readers, her essential argument is that the principles of liberal, egalitarian reform should be applied to improve the condition of women. Though she believed in the power of education to transform the nature of women's lives, she understood that other factors shape women's destinies.

A Vindication of the Rights of Woman

One of the most universal features of human society has been the subordination of women. Even today, despite the political and cultural advances made by women in many countries, their position in society remains subordinate to that of men. In some respects, this is because women themselves have bought into a very jaundiced view of their own talents and capacities—a view advanced by a host of misogynistic writers and thinkers. In *A Vindication of the Rights of Woman* (1792), Mary Wollstonecraft challenged the view of women presented by those writers and thinkers.

In the selections presented here, Wollstonecraft argues that men and women are equally capable of reason and self-improvement. Nonetheless, women's capacity for rational action, for true virtue, has been diminished by a variety of social institutions and cultural demands. Wollstonecraft's position is that their legal status and socialization have constrained the opportunities women have for using their natural abilities for the good of society. "Docile virtues" and "vain amusements" encourage women to focus on flattering and pleasing men, and thus, keep women from fully contributing to moral and political life.

Wollstonecraft was one of the first to observe that women had an inferior status partly because they somewhat willingly accepted this unflattering image of themselves. Told that their lives are for little more than ornament, and specifically trained to do little but soothe and entertain their husbands, the middle-class women of Wollstonecraft's era seemingly embraced their situation. Lacking an education that fully developed their rational capacities, many women took their place among the "feathered race"—devoting themselves to such idle pursuits as reading novels or flirting with men.

Given the opportunities presented by an education equivalent to that men received, though, women could claim their place as contributing members of society. The better their education, the better citizens, wives, and mothers women could be. In other words, educated women are both more rational and more virtuous persons.

Commentaries

The selection from Virginia Sapiro's study of Wollstonecraft's political theory focuses on the topic of gender distinctions. In considering whether the prevailing negative image of women was indeed justified, Wollstonecraft explored two areas of difference between men and women—physical strength and maternity. Wollstonecraft clearly saw women as weaker than men in a physical sense, but not necessarily in a moral sense. Moral weakness does occur, though, if only because women are taught both a sense of inferiority and a belief that women must be dependent upon men. With regard to motherhood, Sapiro argues that Wollstonecraft saw its performance as fundamentally shaped by social conditions, much like that of other duties. Women must have an education equal to that of men if they are to have the same possibilities for human improvement.

Susan Ferguson's essay ponders the extent to which Wollstonecraft can be seen as either a "liberal" or a "radical" thinker. The difference between the two labels centers on conceptions of the economy and the family—liberalism relegates both to a private sphere free of regulation, while radicalism asserts that relations of class and gender structure those areas in ways that benefit the powerful. Ferguson finds that Wollstonecraft largely accepts liberal assumptions: Although she was opposed to the excesses of the propertied aristocracy, she nevertheless believed in private property and inheritance; although she believed in equality, her picture of the domestic good life had a decidedly

middle-class character. For all her liberalism, though, Wollstonecraft was still considerably radical for her time. Education may be the key factor in improving the lives of women, but it would not do the job unless it was accompanied by substantial political reform.

Web Sources

http://womenshistory.about.com/cs/wollstonecraft/
About.com: Mary Wollstonecraft. A useful gateway to a number of resources on Wollstonecraft's life and work.

http://www.historyguide.org/intellect/wollstonecraft.html
The History Guide: Lectures on Modern European Intellectual History. A brief biographical sketch.

http://www.bartleby.com/144/
Bartleby.com: Great Books Online. The complete text of *A Vindication of the Rights of Woman.*

Class Activities and Discussion Items

1. Research the evaluations of Wollstonecraft made by contemporary feminists. How have they regarded Wollstonecraft? How should feminists today regard her?

2. In what sense is Wollstonecraft a liberal theorist? If she is a liberal, how does her liberalism shape her feminism?

3. Compare and contrast the views of Wollstonecraft and other political theorists on both the roles played by women in society and the ends of political life.

4. Does Wollstonecraft's work address the tensions between such concepts as reason and feeling, equality and difference? How might it help us resolve those tensions?

Further Reading

Bromwich, David. 1995. "Wollstonecraft as a Critic of Burke." *Political Theory* 23 (November): 617–635. Examines Wollstonecraft's response to Burke's views on morality, sensibility, and politics in *A Vindication of the Rights of Men.*

Falco, Maria J. (ed.). 1996. *Feminist Interpretations of Mary Wollstonecraft*. University Park: Pennsylvania State University Press. Collection of essays investigating Wollstonecraft's thought from the perspectives of gender and politics.

Gubar, Susan. 1994. "Feminist Misogyny: Mary Wollstonecraft and the Paradox of 'It Takes One to Know One.'" *Feminist Studies* 20 (Fall): 452–474. Explores the portrait of the feminine painted by Wollstonecraft in *A Vindication of the Rights of Woman*.

Todd, Janet. 2000. *Mary Wollstonecraft: A Revolutionary Life*. New York: Columbia University Press. Biography that draws heavily from Wollstonecraft's letters. ✦

18

Excerpts from *A Vindication of the Rights of Woman*

Mary Wollstonecraft

Chapter 4: Observations on the State of Degradation to which Woman is Reduced by Various Causes

That woman is naturally weak, or degraded by a concurrence of circumstances, is, I think, clear. But this position I shall simply contrast with a conclusion, which I have frequently heard fall from sensible men in favour of an aristocracy: that the mass of mankind cannot be anything, or the obsequious slaves, who patiently allow themselves to be driven forward, would feel their own consequence, and spurn their chains. Men, they further observe, submit everywhere to oppression, when they have only to lift up their heads to throw off the yoke; yet, instead of asserting their birthright, they quietly lick the dust, and say, 'Let us eat and drink, for tomorrow we die.' Women, I argue from analogy, are degraded by the same propensity to enjoy the present moment, and at last despise the freedom which they have not sufficient virtue to struggle to attain. But I must be more explicit.

With respect to the culture of the heart, it is unanimously allowed that sex is out of the question; but the line of subordination in the mental powers is never to be passed over.[1] Only 'absolute in loveliness', the portion of rationality granted to woman is, indeed, very scanty; for denying her genius and judgement, it is scarcely possible to divine what remains to characterize intellect.

The stamen of immortality, if I may be allowed the phrase, is the perfectibility of human reason; for, were man created perfect, or did a flood of knowledge break in upon him, when he arrived at maturity, that precluded error, I should doubt whether his existence would be continued after the dissolution of the body. But, in the present state of things, every difficulty in morals that escapes from human discussion, and equally baffles the investigation of profound thinking, and the lightning glance of genius, is an argument on which I build my belief of the immortality of the soul. Reason is, consequentially, the simple power of improvement; or, more properly speaking, of discerning truth. Every individual is in this respect a world in itself. More or less may be conspicuous in one being than another; but the nature of reason must be the same in all, if it be an emanation of divinity, the tie that connects the creature with the Creator; for, can that soul be stamped with the heavenly image, that is not perfected by the exercise of its own reason?[2] Yet outwardly ornamented with elaborate care, and so adorned to delight man, 'that with honour he may love',[3] the soul of woman is not allowed to have this distinction, and man, ever placed between her and reason, she is always represented as only created to see through a gross medium, and to take things on trust. But dismissing these fanciful theories, and considering woman as a whole, let it be what it will, instead of a part of man, the inquiry is whether she have reason or not. If she have, which, for a moment, I will take for granted, she was not created merely to be the solace of man, and the sexual should not destroy the human character.

Into this error men have, probably, been led by viewing education in a false light; not considering it as the first step to form a being advancing gradually towards perfection[4]; but only as a preparation for life. On this sensual error, for I must call it so, has the false system of female manners been reared, which robs the whole sex of its dignity, and classes the brown and fair with the smiling flowers that only adorn the land. This has ever been the language of men, and the fear of departing from a supposed sexual character, has made even women of superior sense adopt the same sentiments.[5] Thus understanding, strictly speaking, has been denied to woman; and instinct, sublimated into wit and cunning, for the purposes of life, has been substituted in its stead.

The power of generalizing ideas, of drawing comprehensive conclusions from individual observations, is the only acquirement, for an immortal being, that really deserves the name of knowledge. Merely to observe, without endeavouring to account for anything, may (in a very incomplete manner) serve as the common sense of life; but where is the store laid up that is to clothe the soul when it leaves the body?

This power has not only been denied to women; but writers have insisted that it is inconsistent, with a few exceptions, with their sexual character. Let men prove this, and I shall grant that woman only exists for man. I must, however, previously remark, that the power of generalizing ideas, to any great extent, is not very common amongst men or women. But this exercise is the true cultivation of the understanding; and everything conspires to render the cultivation of the understanding more difficult in the female than the male world.

I am naturally led by this assertion to the main subject of the present chapter, and shall now attempt to point out some of the causes that degrade the sex, and prevent women from generalizing their observations.

I shall not go back to the remote annals of antiquity to trace the history of woman; it is sufficient to allow that she has always been either a slave or a despot, and to remark that each of these situations equally retards the progress of reason. The grand source of female folly and vice has ever appeared to me to arise from narrowness of mind; and the very constitution of civil governments has put almost insuperable obstacles in the way to prevent the cultivation of the female understanding; yet virtue can be built on no other foundation. The same obstacles are thrown in the way of the rich, and the same consequences ensue.

Necessity has been proverbially termed the mother of invention; the aphorism may be extended to virtue. It is an acquirement, and an acquirement to which pleasure must be sacrificed; and who sacrifices pleasure when it is within the grasp, whose mind has not been opened and strengthened by adversity, or the pursuit of knowledge goaded on by necessity? Happy is it when people have the cares of life to struggle with, for these struggles prevent their becoming a prey to enervating vices, merely from idleness. But if from their birth men and women be placed in a torrid zone, with the meridian sun of pleasure darting directly upon them, how can they sufficiently brace their minds to discharge the duties of life, or even to relish the affections that carry them out of themselves?

Pleasure is the business of woman's life, according to the present modification of society; and while it continues to be so, little can be expected from such weak beings. Inheriting in a lineal descent from the first fair defect in nature—the sovereignty of beauty—they have, to maintain their power, resigned the natural rights which the exercise of reason might have procured them, and chosen rather to be short-lived queens than labour to obtain the sober pleasures that arise from equality. Exalted by their inferiority (this sounds like a contradiction), they constantly demand homage as women, though experience should teach them that the men who pride themselves upon paying this arbitrary insolent respect to the sex, with the most scrupulous exactness, are most inclined to tyrannize over, and despise the very weakness they cherish. Often do they repeat Mr Hume's sentiments, when, comparing the French and Athenian character, he alludes to women,—'But what is more singular in this whimsical nation, say I to the Athenians, is, that a frolic of yours during the saturnalia, when the slaves are served by their masters, is seriously continued by them through the whole year, and through the whole course of their lives, accompanied, too, with some circumstances, which still further augment the absurdity and ridicule. Your sport only elevates for a few days those whom fortune has thrown down, and whom she too, in sport, may really elevate for ever above you. But this nation gravely exalts those whom nature has subjected to them, and whose inferiority and infirmities are absolutely incurable. The women, though without virtue, are their masters and sovereigns.'

Ah! why do women—I write with affectionate solicitude—condescend to receive a degree of attention and respect from strangers different from that reciprocation of civility which the dictates of humanity and the politeness of civilization authorize between man and man? And why do they not discover, when 'in the noon of beauty's power', that they are treated like queens only to be deluded by hollow respect, till they are led to resign, or not assume, their natural prerogatives? Confined, then, in cages like the feathered race, they have nothing to do but to plume themselves, and stalk with mock majesty from perch to perch. It is true they are provided with food and raiment, for which they neither toil nor spin; but health, liberty, and virtue are given in exchange. But where, amongst mankind, has been found sufficient strength of mind to enable a being to resign these adventitious prerogatives—one who, rising with the calm dignity of reason above opinion, dared to be proud of the privileges inherent in man? And it is vain to expect it whilst hereditary power chokes the affections, and nips reason in the bud.

The passions of men have thus placed women on thrones, and till mankind become more reasonable, it is to be feared that women will avail themselves of the power which they attain with the least exertion, and which is the most indisputable. They will smile—yes, they will smile, though told that:

> In beauty's empire is no mean,
> And woman, either slave or queen,
> Is quickly scorned when not adored.

But the adoration comes first, and the scorn is not anticipated.

Louis XIV, in particular, spread factitious manners, and caught, in a specious way, the whole nation in his toils; for, establishing an artful chain of despotism, he made it the interest of the people at large individually to respect his station, and support his power. And women, whom he flattered by a puerile attention to the whole sex, obtained in his reign that prince-like distinction so fatal to reason and virtue.

A king is always a king, and a woman always a woman.[6] His authority and her sex ever stand between them and rational converse. With a lover, I grant, she should be so, and her sensibility will naturally lead her to endeavour to excite emotion, not to gratify her vanity, but her heart. This I do not allow to be coquetry; it is the artless impulse of nature. I only exclaim against the sexual desire of conquest when the heart is out of the question.

This desire is not confined to women. 'I have endeavoured,' says Lord Chesterfield, 'to gain the hearts of twenty women, whose persons I would not have given a fig for.' The libertine who, in a gust of passion, takes advantage of unsuspecting tenderness, is a saint when compared with this cold-hearted rascal—for I like to use significant words. Yet only taught to please, women are always on the watch to please, and with true heroic ardour endeavour to gain hearts merely to resign or spurn them when the victory is decided and conspicuous.

I must descend to the minutiae of the subject.

I lament that women are systematically degraded by receiving the trivial attentions which men think it manly to pay to the sex, when in fact, they are insultingly supporting their own superiority. It is not condescension to bow to an inferior. So ludicrous, in fact, do these ceremonies appear to me that I scarcely am able to govern my muscles when I see a man start with eager and serious solicitude to lift a handkerchief or shut a door, when the *lady* could have done it herself, had she only moved a pace or two.

A wild wish has just flown from my heart to my head, and I will not stifle it, though it may excite a horse-laugh. I do earnestly wish to see the distinction of sex confounded in society, unless where love animates the behaviour. For this distinction is, I am firmly persuaded, the foundation of the weakness of character ascribed to woman; is the cause why the understanding is neglected, whilst accomplishments are acquired with sedulous care; and the same cause accounts for their preferring the graceful before the heroic virtues.

Mankind, including every description, wish to be loved and respected by *something*, and the common herd will always take the nearest road to the completion of their wishes. The respect paid to wealth and beauty is the most certain and unequivocal, and, of course, will always attract the vulgar eye of common minds. Abilities and virtues are absolutely necessary to raise men from the middle rank of life into notice, and the natural consequence is notorious—the middle rank contains most virtue and abilities. Men have thus, in one station at least, an opportunity of exerting themselves with dignity, and of rising by the exertions which really improve a rational creature; but the whole female sex are, till their character is formed, in the same condition as the rich, for they are born—I now speak of a state of civilization—with certain sexual privileges; and whilst they are gratuitously granted them, few will ever think of works of supererogation to obtain the esteem of a small number of superior people.

When do we hear of women who, starting out of obscurity, boldly claim respect on account of their great abilities or daring virtues? Where are they to be found? 'To be observed, to be attended to, to be taken notice of with sympathy, complacency, and approbation, are all the advantages which they seek.' True! my male readers will probably exclaim; but let them, before they draw any conclusion, recollect that this was not written originally as descriptive of women, but of the rich. In Dr Smith's *Theory of Moral Sentiments*[7] I have found a general character of people of rank and fortune, that, in my opinion, might with the greatest propriety be applied to the female sex. I refer the sagacious reader to the whole comparison, but must be allowed to quote a passage to enforce an argument that I mean to insist on, as the one most conclusive against a sexual character. For if, excepting warriors, no great men of any denomination have ever appeared amongst the nobility, may it not be fairly inferred that their local situation swallowed up the man, and produced a character similar to that of women, who are *localized*—

if I may be allowed the word—by the rank they are placed in by *courtesy*? Women, commonly called ladies, are not to be contradicted, in company, are not allowed to exert any manual strength; and from them the negative virtues only are expected, when any virtues are expected—patience, docility, good humour, and flexibility—virtues incompatible with any vigorous exertion of intellect. Besides, by living more with each other, and being seldom absolutely alone, they are more under the influence of sentiments than passions. Solitude and reflection are necessary to give to wishes the force of passions, and to enable the imagination to enlarge the object, and make it the most desirable. The same may be said of the rich; they do not sufficiently deal in general ideas, collected by impassioned thinking or calm investigation, to acquire that strength of character on which great resolves are built. But hear what an acute observer says of the great:

'Do the great seem insensible of the easy price at which they may acquire the public admiration; or do they seem to imagine that to them, as to other men, it must be the purchase either of sweat or of blood? By what important accomplishments is the young nobleman instructed to support the dignity of his rank, and to render himself worthy of that superiority over his fellow-citizens, to which the virtue of his ancestors had raised them? Is it by knowledge, by industry, by patience, by self-denial, or by virtue of any kind. As all his words, as all his motions are attended to, he learns an habitual regard to every circumstance of ordinary behaviour, and studies to perform all those small duties with the most exact propriety. As he is conscious how much he is observed, and how much mankind are disposed to favour all his inclinations, he acts, upon the most indifferent occasions, with that freedom and elevation which the thought of this naturally inspires. His air, his manner, his deportment, all mark that elegant and graceful sense of his own superiority, which those who are born to inferior station can hardly ever arrive at. These are the arts by which he proposes to make mankind more easily submit to his authority, and to govern their inclinations according to his own pleasure; and in this he is seldom disappointed. These arts, supported by rank and pre-eminence, are, upon ordinary occasions, sufficient to govern the world. Louis XIV, during the greater part of his reign, was regarded, not only in France, but all over Europe, as the most perfect model of a great prince. But what were the talents and virtues by which he acquired this great reputation? Was it by the scrupulous and inflexible justice of all his undertakings, by the immense dangers and difficulties with which they were attended, or by the unwearied and unrelenting application with which he pursued them? Was it by his extensive knowledge, by his exquisite judgement, or by his heroic valour? It was by none of these qualities. But he was, first of all, the most powerful prince in Europe, and consequently held the highest rank among kings; and then, says his historian, "he surpassed all his courtiers in the gracefulness of his shape, and the majestic beauty of his features. The sound of his voice, noble and affecting, gained those hearts which his presence intimidated. He had a step and a deportment which could suit only him and his rank, and which would have been ridiculous in any other person. The embarrassment which he occasioned to those who spoke to him, flattered that secret satisfaction with which he felt his own superiority." These frivolous accomplishments, supported by his rank, and, no doubt too, by a degree of other talents and virtues, which seems, however, not to have been much above mediocrity, established this prince in the esteem of his own age, and have drawn, even from posterity, a good deal of respect for his memory. Compared with these, in his own times, and in his own presence, no other virtue, it seems, appeared to have any merit. Knowledge, industry, valour, and beneficence trembled, were abashed, and lost all dignity before them.'

Woman also thus 'in herself complete', by possessing all these *frivolous* accomplishments, so changes the nature of things:

That what she wills to do or say
Seems wisest, virtuousest, discreetest, best;
All higher knowledge in *her presence* falls
Degraded. Wisdom in discourse with her

Loses discountenanced, and, like folly shows;
Authority and reason on her wait.

And all this is built on her loveliness!

In the middle rank of life, to continue the comparison, men, in their youth, are prepared for professions, and marriage is not considered as the grand feature in their lives; whilst women, on the contrary, have no other scheme to sharpen their faculties. It is not business, extensive plans, or any of the excursive flights of ambition, that engross their attention; no, their thoughts are not employed in rearing such noble structures. To rise in the world, and have the liberty of running from pleasure to pleasure, they must marry advantageously, and to this object their time is sacrificed, and their persons often legally prostituted. A man when he enters any profession has his eye steadily fixed on some future advantage (and the mind gains great strength by having all its efforts directed to one point), and, full of his business, pleasure is considered as mere relaxation; whilst women seek for pleasure as the main purpose of existence. In fact, from the education, which they receive from society, the love of pleasure may be said to govern them all; but does this prove that there is a sex in souls? It would be just as rational to declare that the courtiers in France, when a destructive system of despotism had formed their character, were not men, because liberty, virtue, and humanity, were sacrificed to pleasure and vanity. Fatal passions, which have ever domineered over the *whole* race!

The same love of pleasure, fostered by the whole tendency of their education, gives a trifling turn to the conduct of women in most circumstances; for instance, they are ever anxious about secondary things; and on the watch for adventures instead of being occupied by duties.

A man, when he undertakes a journey, has, in general, the end in view; a woman thinks more of the incidental occurrences, the strange things that may possibly occur on the road; the impression that she may make on her fellow-travellers; and, above all, she is anxiously intent on the care of the finery that she carries with her, which is more than ever a part of herself, when going to figure on a new scene; when, to use an apt

French turn of expression, she is going to produce a sensation. Can dignity of mind exist with such trivial cares?

In short, women, in general, as well as the rich of both sexes, have acquired all the follies and vices of civilization, and missed the useful fruit. It is not necessary for me always to premise, that I speak of the condition of the whole sex, leaving exceptions out of the question. Their senses are inflamed, and their understandings neglected, consequently they become the prey of their senses, delicately termed sensibility, and are blown about by every momentary gust of feeling. 'Civilized women are, therefore, so weakened by false refinement, that, respecting morals, their condition is much below what it would be were they left in a state nearer to nature. Ever restless and anxious, their overexercised sensibility not only renders them uncomfortable themselves, but troublesome, to use a soft phrase, to others. All their thoughts turn on things calculated to excite emotion and feeling, when they should reason, their conduct is unstable, and their opinions are wavering—not the wavering produced by deliberation or progressive views, but by contradictory emotions. By fits and starts, they are warm in many pursuits; yet this warmth, never concentrated into perseverance, soon exhausts itself; exhaled by its own heat, or meeting with some other fleeting passion, to which reason has never given any specific gravity, neutrality ensues. Miserable, indeed, must be that being whose cultivation of mind has only tended to inflame its passions! A distinction should be made between inflaming and strengthening them. The passions thus pampered, whilst the judgement is left unformed, what can be expected to ensue? Undoubtedly, a mixture of madness and folly!

This observation should not be confined to the *fair* sex; however, at present, I only mean to apply it to them.

Novels, music, poetry, and gallantry, all tend to make women the creatures of sensation, and their character is thus formed in the mould of folly during the time they are acquiring accomplishments, the only improvement they are excited, by their station in society, to acquire. This overstretched sensibility naturally relaxes the other powers of the mind, and prevents intellect from attaining that sovereignty which it ought to attain to render a rational creature useful to others, and content with its own station; for the exercise of the understanding, as life advances, is the only method pointed out by nature to calm the passions.

Satiety has a very different effect, and I have often been forcibly struck by an emphatical description of damnation; when the spirit is represented as continually hovering with abortive eagerness round the defiled body, unable to enjoy anything without the organs of sense. Yet, to their senses, are women made slaves, because it is by their sensibility that they obtain present power.

And will moralists pretend to assert that this is the condition in which one-half of the human race should be encouraged to remain with listless inactivity and stupid acquiescence? Kind instructors! what were we created for? To remain, it may be said, innocent; they mean in a state of childhood. We might as well never have been born, unless it were necessary that we should be created to enable man to acquire the noble privilege of reason, the power of discerning good from evil, whilst we lie down in the dust from whence we were taken, never to rise again.

It would be an endless task to trace the variety of meannesses, cares, and sorrows, into which women are plunged by the prevailing opinion, that they were created rather to feel than reason, and that all the power they obtain must be obtained by their charms and weakness:

Fine by defect, and amiably weak!

And, made by this amiable weakness entirely dependent, excepting what they gain by illicit sway, on man, not only for protection, but advice, is it suprising that, neglecting the duties that reason alone points out, and shrinking from trials calculated to strengthen their minds, they only exert themselves to give their defects a graceful covering, which may serve to heighten their charms in the eye of the voluptuary, though it sink them below the scale of moral excellence.

Fragile in every sense of the word, they are obliged to look up to man for every comfort. In the most trifling danger they cling to their support, with parasitical tenacity, piteously demanding succour; and their *natural* protector extends his arm, or lifts up his voice, to guard the lovely trembler—from what? Perhaps the frown of an old cow, or the jump of a mouse; a rat would be a serious danger. In the name of reason, and even common sense, what can save such beings from contempt; even though they be soft and fair.

These fears, when not affected, may produce some pretty attitudes; but they show a degree of imbecility which degrades a rational creature in a way women are not aware of—for love and esteem are very distinct things.

I am fully persuaded that we should hear of none of these infantine airs, if girls were allowed to take sufficient exercise, and not confined in close rooms till their muscles are relaxed, and their powers of digestion destroyed. To carry the remark still further, if fear in girls, instead of being cherished, perhaps, created, were treated in the same manner as cowardice in boys, we should quickly see women with more dignified aspects. It is true, they could not then with equal propriety be termed the sweet flowers that smile in the walk of man; but they would be more respectable members of society, and discharge the important duties of life by the light of their own reason. 'Educate women like men,' says Rousseau, 'and the more they resemble our sex the less power they will have over us.' This is the very point I aim at. I do not wish them to have power over men; but over themselves.

In the same strain have I heard men argue against instructing the poor; for many are the forms that aristocracy assumes. 'Teach them to read and write,' say they, 'and you take them out of the station assigned them by nature.' An eloquent Frenchman has answered them, I will borrow his sentiments. 'But they know not, when they make man a brute, that they may expect every instant to see him transformed into a ferocious beast. Without knowledge there can be no morality.'

Ignorance is a frail base for virtue! Yet, that it is the condition for which woman was organized, has been insisted upon by the writers who have most vehemently argued in favour of the superiority of man; a superiority not in degree, but offence; though, to soften the argument, they have laboured to prove, with chivalrous generosity, that the sexes ought not to be compared; man was made to reason, woman to feel: and that together, flesh and spirit, they make the most perfect whole, by blending happily reason and sensibility into one character.

And what is sensibility? 'Quickness of sensation, quickness of perception, delicacy.' Thus is it defined by Dr Johnson; and the definition gives me no other idea than of the most exquisitely polished instinct. I discern not a trace of the image of God in either sensation or matter. Refined seventy times seven they are still material; intellect dwells not there; nor will fire ever make lead gold!

I come round to my old argument: if woman be allowed to have an immortal soul, she must have, as the employment of life, an understanding to improve. And when, to render the present state more complete, though everything proves it to be but a fraction of a mighty sum, she is incited by present gratification to forget her grand destination, nature is counteracted, or she was born only to procreate and rot. Or, granting brutes of every description a soul, though not a reasonable one, the exercise of instinct and sensibility may be the step which they are to take, in this life, towards the attainment of reason in the next; so that through all eternity they will lag behind man, who, why we cannot tell, had the power given him of attaining reason in his first mode of existence.

When I treat of the peculiar duties of women, as I should treat of the peculiar duties of a citizen or father, it will be found that I do not mean to insinuate that they should be taken out of their families, speaking of the majority. 'He that hath wife and children,' says Lord Bacon, 'hath given hostages to fortune; for they are impediments to great enterprises, either of virtue or mischief. Certainly the best works, and of greatest merit for the public, have proceeded from the unmarried or childless men.' I say the same of women. But the welfare of society is not built on extraordinary exertions; and were it more reasonably organized, there would be still less need of great abilities, or heroic virtues.

In the regulation of a family, in the education of children, understanding, in an unsophisticated sense, is particularly required—strength both of body and mind; yet the men who, by their writings, have most earnestly laboured to domesticate women, have endeavoured, by arguments dictated by a gross appetite, which satiety had rendered fastidious, to weaken their bodies and cramp their minds. But, if even by these sinister methods they really *persuaded* women, by working on their feelings, to stay at home, and fulfil the duties of a mother and mistress of a family, I should cautiously oppose opinions that led women to right conduct, by prevailing on them to make the discharge of such important duties the main business of life, though reason were insulted. Yet, and I appeal to experience, if by neglecting the understanding they be as much, nay, more detached from these domestic employments, than they could be by the most serious intellectual pursuit, though it may be observed, that the mass of mankind will never vigorously pursue an intellectual object,[8] I may be allowed to infer that reason is absolutely necessary to enable a woman to perform any duty properly, and I must again repeat, that sensibility is not reason.

The comparison with the rich still occurs to me; for, when men neglect the duties of humanity, women will follow their example; a common stream hurries them both along with thoughtless celerity. Riches and honours prevent a man from enlarging his understanding, and enervate all his powers by reversing the order of nature, which has ever made true pleasure the reward of labour. Pleasure—enervating pleasure—is, likewise, within women's reach without earning it. But, till hereditary possessions are spread abroad, how can we expect men to be proud of virtue? And, till they are, women will govern them by the most direct means, neglecting their dull domestic duties to catch the pleasure that sits lightly on the wing of time.

'The power of the woman,' says some author, 'is her sensibility'; and men, not aware of the consequence, do all they can to make this power swallow up every other. Those who constantly employ their sensibility will have most; for example, poets, painters, and composers.[9] Yet, when the sensibility is thus increased at the expense of reason, and even the imagination, why do philosophical men complain of their fickleness? The sexual attention of man particularly acts on female sensibility, and this sympathy has been exercised from their youth up. A husband cannot long pay those attentions with the passion necessary to excite lively emotions, and the heart, accustomed to lively emotions, turns to a new lover, or pines in secret, the prey of virtue or prudence. I mean when the heart has really been rendered susceptible, and the taste formed; for I am apt to conclude, from what I have seen in this fashionable life, that vanity is oftener fostered than sensibility by the mode of education, and the intercourse between the sexes, which I have reprobated; and that coquetry more frequently proceeds from vanity than from that inconstancy which overstrained sensibility naturally produces.

Another argument that has had great weight with me must, I think, have some force with every considerate benevolent heart. Girls who have been thus weakly educated are often cruelly left by their parents without any provision, and, of course, are dependent on not only the reason, but the bounty of their brothers. These brothers are, to view the fairest side of the question, good sort of men, and give as a favour what children of the same parents had an equal right to. In this equivocal humiliating situation a docile female may remain some time with a tolerable degree of comfort. But when the brother marries—a probable circumstance—from being considered as the mistress of the family, she is viewed with averted looks as an intruder, an unnecessary burden on the benevolence of the master of the house and his new partner.

Who can recount the misery which many unfortunate beings, whose minds and bodies are equally weak, suffer in such situations—unable to work, and ashamed to beg? The wife, a cold-hearted, narrow-minded woman—and this is not an unfair supposition, for the present mode of education does not tend to enlarge the heart any more than the understanding—is jealous of the little kindness which her husband shows to his relations; and her sensibility not rising to humanity, she is displeased at seeing the property of *her* children lavished on an helpless sister.

Chapter 9: Of the Pernicious Effects Which Arise from the Unnatural Distinctions Established in Society

From the respect paid to property flow, as from a poisoned fountain, most of the evils and vices which render this world such a dreary scene to the contemplative mind. For it is in the most polished society that noisome reptiles and venomous serpents lurk under the rank herbage; and there is voluptuousness pampered by the still sultry air, which relaxes every good disposition before it ripens into virtue.

One class presses on another, for all are aiming to procure respect on account of their property; and property once gained will procure the respect due only to talents and virtue. Men neglect the duties incumbent on man, yet are treated like demigods. Religion is also separated from morality by a ceremonial veil, yet men wonder that the world is almost, literally speaking, a den of sharpers or oppressors.

There is a homely proverb, which speaks a shrewd truth, that whoever the devil finds idle he will employ. And what but habitual idleness can hereditary wealth and titles produce? For man is so constituted that he can only attain a proper use of his faculties by exercising them, and will not exercise them unless necessity of some kind first set the wheels in motion. Virtue likewise can only be acquired by the discharge of relative duties; but the importance of these sacred duties will scarcely be felt by the being who is cajoled out of his humanity by the flattery of sycophants. There must be more equality established in society, or morality will never gain ground, and this virtuous equality will not rest firmly even when founded on a rock, if one-half of mankind be chained to its bottom by fate, for they will be continually undermining it through ignorance or pride.

It is vain to expect virtue from women till they are in some degree independent of men; nay, it is vain to expect that strength of natural affection which would make them good wives and mothers. Whilst they are absolutely dependent on their husbands they will be cunning, mean, and selfish; and the men who can be gratified by the fawning fondness of spaniel-like affection have not much delicacy, for love is not to be bought; in any sense of the words, its silken wings are instantly shrivelled up when anything beside a return in kind is sought. Yet whilst wealth enervates men, and women live, as it were, by their personal charms, how can we expect them to discharge those ennobling duties which equally require exertion and self-denial? Hereditary property sophisticates the mind, and the unfortunate victims to it—if I may so express myself—swathed from their birth, seldom exert the locomotive faculty or body of mind, and thus viewing everything through one medium, and that a false one, they are unable to discern in what true merit and happiness consist. False, indeed, must be the light when the drapery of situation hides the man, and makes him stalk in masquerade, dragging from one scene of dissipation to another the nerveless limbs that hang with stupid listlessness, and rolling round the vacant eye, which plainly tells us that there is no mind at home.

I mean therefore to infer that the society is not properly organized which does not compel men and women to discharge their respective duties by making it the only way to acquire that countenance from their fellow-creatures, which every human being wishes some way to attain. The respect consequently which is paid to wealth and mere personal charms is a true north-east blast that blights the tender blossoms of affection and virtue. Nature has wisely attached affections to duties to sweeten toil, and to give that vigour to the exertions of reason which only the heart can give. But the affections which is put on merely because it is the appropriated insignia of a certain character, when its duties are not fulfilled, is one of the empty compliments which vice and folly are obliged to pay to virtue and the real nature of things.

To illustrate my opinion, I need only observe that when a woman is admired for her beauty, and suffers herself to be so far intoxicated by the admiration she receives as to neglect to discharge the indispensable duty of a mother, she sins against herself by neglecting to cultivate an affection that would equally tend to make her useful and happy. True happiness—I mean all the contentment and virtuous satisfaction that can be snatched in this imperfect state—must arise from well-regulated affections, and an affection includes a duty. Men are not aware of the misery they cause, and the vicious weakness they cherish, by only inciting women to render themselves pleasing; they do not consider that they thus make natural and artificial duties clash by sacrificing the comfort and respectability of a woman's life to voluptuous notions of beauty when in nature they all harmonize.

Cold would be the heart of a husband, were he not rendered unnatural by early debauchery, who did not feel more delight at seeing his child suckled by its mother than the most artful wanton tricks could ever raise, yet this natural way of cementing the matrimonial tie, and twisting esteem with fonder recollections, wealth leads women to spurn. To preserve their beauty, and wear the flowery crown of the day, which gives them a kind of right to reign for a short time over the sex, they neglect to stamp impressions on their husbands' hearts that would be remembered with more tenderness when the snow on the head began to chill the bosom than even their virgin charms. The maternal solicitude of a reasonable affectionate woman is very interesting, and the chastened dignity with which a mother returns the caresses that she and her child receive from a father who has been fulfilling the serious duties of his station is not only a respectable, but a beautiful sight. So singular, indeed, are my feelings—and I have endeavoured not to catch factitious ones—that after having been fatigued with the sight of insipid grandeur and the slavish ceremonies that with cumbrous pomp supplied the place of domestic affections, I have turned to some other scene to relieve my eye by resting it on the refreshing green everywhere scattered by Nature. I have then viewed with pleasure a woman nursing her children, and discharging the duties of her station with perhaps merely a servant-maid to take off her hands the servile part of the household business. I have seen her prepare herself and children, with only the luxury of cleanliness, to receive her husband, who, returning weary home in the evening, found smiling babes and a clean hearth. My heart has loitered in the midst of the group, and has even throbbed with sympathetic emotion when the scraping of the well-known foot has raised a pleasing tumult.

Whilst my benevolence has been gratified by contemplating this artless picture, I have thought that a couple of this description, equally necessary and independent of each other, because each fulfilled the respective duties of their station, possessed all that life could give. Raised sufficiently above abject poverty not to be obliged to weigh the consequence of every farthing they spend, and having sufficient to prevent their attending to a frigid system of economy which narrows both heart and mind, I declare, so vulgar are my conceptions, that I know not what is wanted to render this the happiest as well as the most respectable situation in the world, but a taste for literature, to throw a little variety and interest into social converse, and some superfluous money to give to the needy and to buy books. For it is not pleasant when the heart is opened by compassion, and the head active in arranging plans of usefulness, to have a prim urchin continually twitching back the elbow to prevent the hand from drawing out an almost empty purse, whispering at the same time some prudential maxim about the priority of justice.

Destructive, however, as riches and inherited honours are to the human character, women are more debased and cramped, if possible, by them than men, because men may still in some degree unfold their faculties by becoming soldiers and statesmen.

As soldiers, I grant they can now only gather for the most part vain-glorious laurels, whilst they adjust to a hair the European balance, taking especial care that no bleak northern nook or sound incline the beam. But the days of true heroism are over, when a citizen fought for his country like a Fabricius or a Washington, and then returned to his farm to let his virtuous fervour run in a more placid, but not a less salutary, stream. No, our British heroes are oftener sent from the gaming-table than from the plough; and their passions have been rather inflamed by hanging with dumb suspense on the turn of a die, than sublimated by panting after the adventurous march of virtue in the historic page.

The statesman, it is true, might with more propriety quit the faro bank, or card-table, to guide the helm, for he has still but to shuffle and trick—the whole system of British politics, if system it may courteously be called, consisting in multiplying dependents and contriving taxes which grind the poor to pamper the rich. Thus a war, or any wild-goose chase, is, as the vulgar use the phrase, a lucky turn-up of patronage for the minister, whose chief merit is the art of keeping himself in place. It is not necessary then that he should have bowels for the poor, so he can secure for his family the odd trick. Or should some show of respect, for what is termed with ignorant ostentation an Englishman's birthright, be expedient to bubble the gruff mastiff that he has to lead by the nose, he can make an empty show, very safely, by giving his single voice, and suffering his light squadron to file off to the other side. And when a question of humanity is agitated, he may dip a sop in the milk of human kindness to silence Cerberus, and talk of the interest which his heart takes in an attempt to make the earth no longer cry for vengeance as it sucks in its children's blood, though his cold hand may at the very moment rivet their chains, by sanctioning the abominable traffic. A minister is no longer a minister, than while he can carry a point, which he is determined to carry. Yet it is not necessary that a minister should feel like a man, when a bold push might shake his seat.

But, to have done with these episodical observations, let me return to the more specious slavery which chains the very soul of woman, keeping her for ever under the bondage of ignorance.

The preposterous distinctions of rank, which render civilization a curse, by dividing the world between voluptuous tyrants and cunning envious dependents, corrupt, almost equally, every class of people, because respectability is not attached to the discharge of the relative duties of life, but to the station, and when the duties are not fulfilled the affections cannot gain sufficient strength to fortify the virtue of which they are the natural reward. Still there are some loop-holes out of which a man may creep, and dare to think and act for himself; but for a woman it is an herculean task, because she has difficulties peculiar to her sex to overcome, which require almost superhuman powers.

A truly benevolent legislator always endeavours to make it the interest of each individual to be virtuous; and thus private virtue becoming the cement of public happiness, an orderly whole is consolidated by the tendency of all the parts towards a common centre. But the private or public virtue of woman is very problematical, for Rousseau, and a numerous list of male writers, insist that she should all her life be subjected to a severe restraint, that of propriety. Why subject her to propriety—blind propriety—if she be capable of acting from a nobler spring, if she be an heir of immortality? Is sugar always to be produced by vital blood? Is one half of the human species, like the poor African slaves, to be subjected to prejudices that brutalize them, when principles would be a surer guard, only to sweeten the cup of man? Is not this indirectly to deny woman reason? for a gift is a mockery, if it be unfit for use.

Women are, in common with men, rendered weak and luxurious by the relaxing pleasures which wealth procures; but added to this they are made slaves to their persons, and must render them alluring that man may lend them his reason to guide their tottering steps aright. Or should they be ambitious, they must govern their tyrants by sinister tricks, for without rights there cannot be any incumbent duties. The laws respecting woman, which I mean to discuss in a future part, make an absurd unit of a man and his wife; and then, by the easy transition of only considering him as responsible, she is reduced to a mere cipher.

The being who discharges the duties of its station is independent; and, speaking of women at large, their first duty is to themselves as rational creatures, and the next, in point of importance, as citizens, is that, which includes so many, of a mother. The rank in life which dispenses with their fulfilling this duty, necessarily degrades them by making them mere dolls. Or should they turn to something more important than merely fitting drapery upon a smooth block, their minds are only occupied by some soft platonic attachment; or the actual management of an intrigue may keep their thoughts in motion; for when they neglect domestic duties, they have it not in their power to take the field and march and counter-march like soldiers, or wrangle in the senate to keep their faculties from rusting.

I know that, as a proof of the inferiority of the sex, Rousseau has exultingly exclaimed, How can they leave the nursery for the camp! And the camp has by some moralists been proved the school of the most heroic virtues; though I think it would puzzle a keen casuist to prove the reasonableness of the greater number of wars that have dubbed heroes. I do not mean to consider this question critically; because, having frequently viewed these freaks of ambition as the first natural mode of civilization, when the ground must be torn up, and the woods cleared by fire and sword, I do not choose to call them pests; but surely the present system of war has little connection with virtue of any denomination, being rather the school of *finesse* and effeminacy than of fortitude.

Yet, if defensive war, the only justifiable war, in the present advanced state of society, where virtue can show its face and ripen amidst the rigours which purify the air on the mountain's top, were alone to be adopted as just and glorious, the true heroism of antiquity might again animate female bosoms. But fair and softly, gentle reader, male or female, do not alarm thyself, for though I have compared the character of a modern soldier with that of a civilized woman, I am not going to advise them to turn their distaff into a musket, though I sincerely wish to see the bayonet converted into a pruning-hook. I only re-created an imagination, fatigued by contemplating the vices and follies which all proceed from a feculent stream of wealth that has muddied the pure rills of natural affection, by supposing that society will some time or other be so constituted, that man must necessarily fulfil the duties of a citizen, or be despised, and that while he was employed in any of the departments of civil life, his wife, also an active citizen, should be equally intent to manage her family, educate her children, and assist her neighbours.

But to render her really virtuous and useful, she must not, if she discharge her civil duties, want individually the protection of civil laws; she must not be dependent on her husband's bounty for her subsistence during his life, or support after his death; for how can a being be generous who has nothing of its own? or virtuous who is not free? The wife, in the present state of things, who is faithful to her husband, and neither suckles nor educates her children, scarcely deserves the name of a wife, and has no right to that of a citizen. But take away natural rights, and duties become null.

Women then must be considered as only the wanton solace of men, when they become so weak in mind and body that they cannot exert themselves unless to pursue some frothy pleasure, or to invent some frivolous fashion. What can be a more melancholy sight to a thinking mind, than to look into the numerous carriages that drive helter-skelter about this metropolis in a morning full of pale-faced creatures who are flying from themselves! I have often wished, with Dr Johnson, to place some of them in a little shop with half a dozen children looking up to their languid countenances for support. I am much mistaken, if some latent vigour would not soon give health and spirit to their eyes, and some lines drawn by the exercise of reason on the blank cheeks, which before were only undulated by dimples, might restore lost dignity to the character, or rather enable it to attain the true dignity of its nature. Virtue is not to be acquired even by speculation, much less by the negative supineness that wealth naturally generates.

Besides, when poverty is more disgraceful than even vice, is not morality cut to the quick? Still to avoid misconstruction, though I consider that women in the common walks of life are called to fulfil the duties of wives and mothers, by religion and reason, I cannot help lamenting that women of a superior cast have not a road open by which they can pursue more extensive plans of usefulness and independence. I may excite laughter, by dropping a hint, which I mean to pursue, some future time, for I really think that women ought to have representatives, instead of being arbitrarily governed without having any direct share allowed them in the deliberations of government.

But, as the whole system of representation is now, in this country, only a convenient handle for despotism, they need not complain, for they are as well represented as a numerous class of hard-working mechanics, who pay for the support of royalty when they can scarcely stop their children's mouths with bread. How are they represented whose very sweat supports the splendid stud of an heir-apparent, or varnishes the chariot of some female favourite who looks down on shame? Taxes on the very necessaries of life, enable an endless tribe of idle princes and princesses to pass with stupid pomp before a gaping crowd, who almost worship the very parade which costs them so dear. This is mere gothic grandeur, something like the barbarous useless parade of having sentinels on horseback at Whitehall, which I could never view without a mixture of contempt and indignation.

How strangely must the mind be sophisticated when this sort of state impresses it! But, till these monuments of folly are levelled by virtue, similar follies will leaven the whole mass. For the same character, in some degree, will prevail in the aggregate of society; and the refinements of luxury, or the vicious repinings of envious poverty, will equally banish virtue from society, considered as the characteristic of that society, or only allow it to appear as one of the stripes of the harlequin coat, worn by the civilized man.

In the superior ranks of life, every duty is done by deputies, as if duties could ever be waived, and the vain pleasures which consequent idleness forces the rich to pursue, appear so enticing to the next rank, that the numerous scramblers for wealth sacrifice everything to tread on their heels. The most sacred trusts are then considered as sinecures, because they were procured by interest, and only sought to enable a man to keep *good company.* Women, in particular, all want to be ladies. Which is simply to have nothing to do, but listlessly to go they scarcely care where, for they cannot tell what.

But what have women to do in society? I may be asked, but to loiter with easy grace; surely you would not condemn them all to suckle fools and chronicle small beer! No. Women might certainly study the art of healing and be physicians as well as nurses. And midwifery, decency seems to allot to them though I am afraid the word midwife, in our dictionaries, will soon give place to *accoucheur,* and one proof of the former delicacy of the sex be effaced from the language.

They might also study politics, and settle their benevolence on the broadest basis; for the reading of history will scarcely be more useful than the perusal of romances, if read as mere biography; if the character of the times, the political improvements, arts, etc., be not observed. In short, if it be not considered as the history of man; and not of particular men, who filled a niche in the temple of fame, and dropped into the black rolling stream of time, that silently sweeps all before it into the shapeless void called eternity.— For shape, can it be called, 'that shape hath none'?

Business of various kinds, they might likewise pursue, if they were educated in a more orderly manner, which might save many from common and legal prostitution. Women would not then marry for a support, as men accept of places under Government, and neglect the implied duties; nor would an attempt to earn their own subsistence, a most laudable one! sink them almost to the level of those poor abandoned creatures who live by prostitution. For are not milliners and mantua-makers reckoned the next class? The few employments open to women, so far, from being liberal, are menial; and when a superior education enables them to take charge of the education of children as governesses, they are not treated like the tutors of sons, though even clerical tutors are not always treated in a manner calculated to render them respectable in the eyes of their pupils, to say nothing of the private comfort of the individual. But as women educated like gentlewomen, are never designed for the humiliating situation which necessity sometimes forces them to fill; these situations are considered in the light of a degradation; and they know little of the human heart, who need to be told, that nothing so painfully sharpens sensibility as such a fall in life.

Some of these women might be restrained from marrying by a proper spirit of delicacy, and others may not have had it in their power to escape in this pitiful way from servitude; is not that Government then very defective, and very unmindful of the happiness of one-half of its members, that does not provide for honest, independent women, by encouraging them to fill respectable stations? But in order to render their private virtue a public benefit, they must have a civil existence in the State, married or single; else we shall continually see some worthy woman, whose sensibility has been rendered painfully acute by undeserved contempt, droop like 'the lily broken down by a plowshare'.

It is a melancholy truth; yet such is the blessed effect of civilization! the most respectable women are the most oppressed; and, unless they have understandings far superior to the common run of understandings, taking in both sexes, they must, from being treated like contemptible beings, become contemptible. How many women thus waste life away the prey of discontent, who might have practised as physicians, regulated a farm, managed a shop, and stood erect, supported by their own industry, instead of hanging their heads surcharged with the dew of sensibility, that consumes the beauty to which it at first gave lustre; nay, I doubt whether pity and love are so near akin as poets feign, for I have seldom seen much compassion excited by the helplessness of females, unless they were fair; then, perhaps, pity was the soft handmaid of love, or the harbinger of lust.

How much more respectable is the woman who earns her own bread by fulfilling any duty, than the most accomplished beauty!—beauty did I say!—so sensible am I of the beauty of moral loveliness, or the harmonious propriety that attunes the passions of a well-regulated mind, that I blush at making the comparison; yet I sigh to think how few women aim at attaining this respectability by withdrawing from the giddy whirl of pleasure, or the indolent calm that stupefies the good sort of women it sucks in.

Proud of their weakness, however, they must always be protected, guarded from care, and all the rough toils that dignify the mind. If this be the fiat of fate, if they will make themselves insignificant and contemptible, sweetly to waste 'life away', let them not expect to be valued when their beauty fades, for it is the fate of the fairest flowers to be admired and pulled to pieces by the careless hand that plucked them. In how many ways do I wish, from the purest benevolence, to impress this truth on my sex; yet I fear that they will not listen to a truth that dear bought experience has brought home to many an agitated bosom, nor willingly resign the privileges of rank and sex for the privileges of humanity, to which those have no claim who do not discharge its duties.

Those writers are particularly useful, in my opinion, who make man feel for man, independent of the station he fills, or the drapery of factitious sentiments. I then would fain convince reasonable men of the importance of some of my remarks; and prevail on them to weigh dispassionately the whole tenor of my observations. I appeal to their understandings; and, as a fellow-creature, claim, in the name of my sex, some interest in their hearts. I entreat them to assist to emancipate their companion, to make her a *helpmeet* for them.

Would men but generously snap our chains, and be content with rational fellowship instead of slavish obedience, they would find us more observant daughters, more affectionate sisters, more faithful wives, more reasonable mothers—in a word, better citizens. We should then love them with true affection, because we should learn to respect ourselves; and the peace of mind of a worthy man would not be interrupted by the idle vanity of his wife, nor the babes sent to nestle in a strange bosom, having never found a home in their mother's.

Notes

1. Into what inconsistencies do men fall when they argue without the compass of principles. Women, weak women, are compared with angels; yet, a superior order of beings should be supposed to possess more intellect than man; or, in what does their superiority consist? In the same strain, to drop the sneer, they are allowed to possess more goodness of heart; piety, and benevolence. I doubt the fact, though it be courteously brought forward, unless ignorance be allowed to be the mother of devotion; for I am firmly persuaded that, on an average, the proportion between virtue and knowledge, is more upon a par than is commonly granted.

2. 'The brutes,' says Lord Monboddo, 'remain in the state in which nature has placed them, except in so far as their natural instinct is improved by the culture *we* bestow upon them.' [Lord Monboddo: James Burnet (1714–99), Scottish judge, eminent man of letters, author of books on society and language—M.K.]

3. *Vide* Milton.

4. This word is not strictly just, but I cannot find a better.

5. 'Pleasure's the portion of th' *inferior* kind;
   But glory, virtue, Heaven for *man* designed.'

   After writing these lines, how could Mrs Barbauld write the following ignoble comparison?

   'TO A LADY WITH SOME
   PAINTED FLOWERS
   'Flowers to the fair: to you these flowers I bring,
   And strive to greet you with an earlier spring.
   Flowers, SWEET, and gay, and DELICATE LIKE YOU;
   Emblems of innocence, and beauty too.
   With flowers the Graces bind their yellow hair

And flowery wreaths consenting lovers wear.
Flowers the sole luxury which Nature knew,
In Eden's pure and guiltless garden grew.
To loftier forms are rougher tasks assign'd;
The sheltering oak resists the stormy wind,
The tougher yew repels invading foes,
And the tall pine for future navies grows;

But this soft family, to cares unknown,
Were born for pleasure and delights ALONE.
Gay without toil, and lovely without art,
They spring to CHEER the sense, and GLAD the heart.
Nor blush, my fair, to own you copy these;
Your BEST, your SWEETEST empire is— to PLEASE.'

So the men tell us; but virtue, says reason, must be acquired by *rough* toils, and useful struggles with worldly *cares.*

[Mrs Barbauld: Anna Letitia Barbauld (1743–1825), dissenting essayist, poet, bluestocking, writer of children's stories—M.K.].

6. And a wit always a wit, might be added, for the vain fooleries of wits and beauties to obtain attention, and make conquests, are much upon a par.

7. Adam Smith (1723–90), political economist and professor of moral philosophy, author of *Wealth of Nations* (1776) and *The Theory of Moral Sentiments* (1759)[—M. K.].

8. The mass of mankind are rather the slaves of their appetites than of their passions.

9. Men of these descriptions pour sensibility into the compositions, to amalgamate the gross materials; and, moulding them with passion, give to the inert body a soul; but, in woman's imagination, love alone concentrates these ethereal beams.

Adapted from: Mary Wollstonecraft, *A Vindication of the Rights of Woman*, pp. 141–157, 252–263. Penguin Books, 1975. Originally published 1792. ✦

19
The Same Subject Continued

Virginia Sapiro

You know that as a female I am particularly attached to her—I feel more than a mother's fondness and anxiety, when I reflect on the dependent and oppressed state of her sex. I dread lest she should be forced to sacrifice her heart to her principles, or principles to her heart. With trembling hand I shall cultivate sensibility, and cherish delicacy of sentiment, lest, whilst I lend fresh blushes to the rose, I sharpen the thorns that will wound the breast I would fain guard—I dread to unfold her mind, lest it should render her unfit for the world she is to inhabit—Hapless woman! what fate is thine!

(Scand. 269)

When Mary Wollstonecraft reflected on her infant daughter's future she retained the commitments voiced in the *Vindication of the Rights of Woman*. She wrote of them in *A Short Residence* and again, most forcefully of all, in *The Wrongs of Woman*. But she expressed the difficulties of basing practice on her principles especially poignantly here, where she feared for her child and felt the weight of the responsibility of cultivating that child's mind and sentiments. Even if she could help her daughter become a strong and virtuous person, was she at the same time dooming her by making her unfit to inhabit a world in which women must succeed through dependence and servility? Wollstonecraft was learning what it meant for an individual character, even an idealistic one, to be in conflict with the expectations embedded in the surrounding culture and so-

cial institutions, a lesson reinforced when even her "friends" reacted against the personal life-choices she made.

This passage in which she reflects about her daughter points more clearly to the significance of Wollstonecraft's writing on women than does the title of her most famous book, which seems to have misled many people into believing that her writing on women revolved primarily around rights, especially in a strict juridical sense. Even in the *Rights of Woman* most of her specific discussion of rights as such is located in the prefatory letter. The bulk of the book is on the mind and virtue, duties and social practices. Most of her argument concerns education broadly conceived: the unfolding of mind and development of sensibility through the whole of one's experiences.

Her central point should be familiar by now: In the historical and current state of society unnatural distinctions are created between women and men that necessarily corrupt social relationships and inhibit the development of virtue in all the involved parties. In her attack on gender distinctions, Wollstonecraft paralleled the more widely criticized (among radicals, in any case), inequalities based on rank, property, or position. In this chapter I begin by summarizing her argument on gender, then examine it in more detail.

Wollstonecraft believed that women and men displayed different characters and in the *Rights of Woman* acknowledged the "inferiority of woman, according to the present appearance of things" (103).[1] She attributed much of the difference, and all inferiority other than physical strength, to the impact of social conditions. As we shall see, she also had strong views about the inferiority of men in the current state of society. But these are only differences of appearance; her definition of natural inequality hinged on differences in the native ability to develop reason and, possibly, sensibility, the foundations of virtue. All other distinctions in the character of human beings could be perfectly real, but unnaturally developed and maintained.

Wollstonecraft was well aware of the relative lack of liberty for women compared with men. Men had formal authority over women in the state as a whole and in its component social institutions. Men's rights might be contingent on their property or position, but women could not even own property if they were married and they were barred from almost all positions of authority. As usual, her complaint against such enslavement (the term she often used) rested on its impact on the potential improvement of human beings and their path toward virtue:

Females, in fact, denied all political privileges, and not allowed, as married women, excepting in criminal cases, a civil existence, have their attention naturally drawn from the interest of the whole community to that of the minute parts, though the private duty of any member of society must be very imperfectly performed when not connected with the general good. The mighty business of female life is to please, and restrained from entering into more important concerns by political and civil oppression, sentiments become events, and reflection deepens what it should, and would have effaced, if the understanding had been allowed to take a wider range. (256)

She rarely discussed legal rights and privileges without drawing the focus to their impact on the development of virtue.

Wollstonecraft prefaced the *Vindication of the Rights of Woman* with a letter to Talleyrand in an apparent attempt to convince the French government to include women within the new framework of the rights of "citizens." Her vindication returned to the natural principles governing human thought and behavior which must undergird positive law. She asked Talleyrand to consider her question,

whether, when men contend for their freedom, and to be allowed to judge for themselves respecting their own happiness, it be not inconsistent and unjust to subjugate women, even though you firmly believe that you are acting in the manner best calculated to promote their happiness. Who made man the exclusive judge, if woman partake with him the gift of reason? (67)

She appealed to Talleyrand first in the political language and categories he was likely to

find familiar, then extended the analysis to her parallel case:

In this style, argue tyrants of every denomination, from the weak king to the weak father of a family; they are all eager to crush reason; yet always assert that they usurp its throne only to be useful. Do you not act a similar part, when you *force* all women, by denying them civil and political rights, to remain immured in their families groping in the dark? (67)

The French revolutionaries had employed Enlightenment arguments regarding reason, liberty, and protection of the rights of man in their efforts to reconstruct government, but the new French constitution at the same time denied all political rights to women.

But, if women are to be excluded, without having a voice, from a participation of the natural rights of mankind, prove first, to ward off the charge of injustice and inconsistency, that they want reason—else this flaw in your NEW CONSTITUTION will ever shew that man must, in some shape, act like a tyrant, and tyranny, in whatever part of society it rears its brazen front, will ever undermine morality. (68)[2]

No matter how different women and men might be in some respects, by the logic of enlightened thinkers no group of people could be denied full liberty and basic rights if it was endowed with the power of reason. She concluded her address to Talleyrand by arguing that "when your constitution is revised the Rights of Woman may be respected, if it be fully proved that reason calls for this respect, and loudly demands JUSTICE for one half of the human race" (69).

Her text turns on a critical question: Are women and men equally human beings capable of improvement, or is one sex not "a moral agent, or the link which unites man with brutes"? (104). In Wollstonecraft's judgment other authors on women's education had treated women "as a kind of subordinate beings, and not as a part of the human species, when improveable reason is allowed to be the dignified distinction which raises men above the brute creation" (73–74). Her treatise was designed to inquire whether these authors were just in their denigration of women. The first task, then, was to identify any natural distinctions between women and men bearing on their ability to develop virtue.

Wollstonecraft seems to have identified two natural physical differences that might affect the human capacity for moral agency, and she in fact left some ambiguity about their significance. The first is the natural sex difference in strength, the second is the distinction between motherhood and fatherhood. I will discuss them in turn.

Physical and Mental Strength

Wollstonecraft's acceptance of unity between mind and body and the centrality of strength as an element of virtue could point to a natural inequality between women and men. "I will allow that bodily strength seems to give man a natural superiority over woman; and this is the only solid basis on which the superiority of the sex can be built" (108). For Wollstonecraft, did sex differences in strength confirm sex differences in reasoning capacity and virtue?

In fact physical-strength differences as commonly understood did not collapse into natural inequality of mind for Wollstonecraft because she believed a different kind of strength conditioned the mind: "natural soundness of constitution,—not that robust tone of nerves and vigour of muscles, which arise from bodily labour, when the mind is quiescent, or only directs the hands" (107). A sound constitution provides a framework for the mind and allows the human body to be useful to people in performing their duties and pursuing virtue, rather than being a distraction.[3] Strength thus defined includes health and the ability to tolerate discomfort, rendering an individual more independent (*Stories* 437–38). Nowhere did Wollstonecraft clearly suggest that strength in the sense of an ability to marshall force is a natural support to virtue; most of her references to that type of physical strength are negative.[4] She certainly never indicated that force bore any natural relation to reason. She was more concerned with resilience or fitness than with force.

Although Wollstonecraft worried that the strongly constituted body had grown out of fashion for both men and women in the wealthier classes (107), she argued that women were much more likely to suffer from a weak constitution, and they were certainly less strong in other ways.

> In the government of the physical world it is observable that the female in point of strength is, in general, inferior to the male. This is the law of nature; and it does not appear to be suspended or abrogated in favor of woman. A degree of physical superiority cannot, therefore, be denied—and it is a noble prerogative! But not content with this natural pre-eminence, men endeavour to sink us still lower, merely to render us alluring objects for a moment; and women, intoxicated by the adoration which men, under the influence of their senses, pay to them, do not seek to obtain a durable interest in their hearts, or to become the friends of the fellow creatures who find amusement in their society. (74)

Unreasonable men subject only to the impulse of their senses, rather than their reason, encourage women to be weak because they find weakness in women pleasing. Women, also under the dominion of their unreasoning senses, become "intoxicated" enough to emphasize their own weakness. As in other cases of gross inequality, the need to act in a servile manner corrupts the character of the oppressed. Actions devoid of reasonable principles lead men and women to participate in a mutually corrupting system.

Wollstonecraft had discussed the exaggeration of women's weakness and the adverse impact this was likely to have on their development as early as the *Vindication of the Rights of Men*, where she argued against Burke's very gender-based contentions in his *Philosophical Enquiry into the Origins of Our Ideas of the Sublime and the Beautiful*. There he defines the sublime in terms of power, force, bigness, and terror, while beauty consists of the qualities that "cause love,"[5] presumably in males. "The beauty of women is considerably owing to their weakness, or delicacy, and is even enhanced by their timidity, a quality of mind analogous to it."[6] It is difficult to imagine a passage more calculated to make Wollstonecraft's prose rage.

Wollstonecraft taunted Burke with her version of "ladies" who had cultivated his notion of beautiful weakness rather than the strength of moral virtue. These are the ladies mentioned earlier, whom the slaves were cursing. "It is probable that some of them, after the sight of a flagellation, compose their ruffled spirits and exercise their tender feelings by the perusal of the last imported novel" (*VM* 45). She threw back at him his picture of female beauty which "almost always carries with it an idea of weakness and imperfection," embodied by women who "learn to lisp, to totter in their walk, to counterfeit weakness, and even sickness."[7] In that case, she wrote, "the Supreme Being, in giving women beauty in the most supereminent degree, seemed to command them, by the powerful voice of Nature, not to cultivate the moral virtues that might chance to excite respect . . ." (*VM* 45).[8] She would find such a suggestion impious.

Wollstonecraft repeatedly argued that weakness was as much a defect in women as in men. Physically weak women are not even capable of fulfilling the one clearly "natural" duty women have: suckling their children (251); and weak women produce weak children (*Mary* 10). But above all, strength bears the same relation to reason and virtue in women and in men. Many of the passages from Wollstonecraft's work I used earlier to present these ideas in the first place are actually drawn from her discussion of women.

Wollstonecraft believed women's education was designed primarily to nurture weakness. Women, of course, were encouraged to have a *feminine* character. She dissected the components of this character and concluded that most were simply other names for weakness. She scorned "those female weaknesses which we term delicacy" (*Revs* 1789:109), and thought women had been taught to "glory in their weakness, giving it the softened name of delicacy" (*Revs* 1789:174). As for Burke's attraction to female timidity, she retorted, "Weak minds are always timid" (*VM* 47).[9] Likewise prudence, a feminine virtue and even a popular Calvin-

ist female name, "is ever the resort of weakness" (*Scand.* 244). As for innocence, widely considered a requirement for women, she observed, "Children, I grant, should be innocent; but when the epithet is applied to men, or women, it is but a civil term for weakness" (89).

Wollstonecraft agreed that gentleness is the primary characteristic in "the portrait of an accomplished woman" (102), but the trait usually encouraged in women was not the "gentleness of manners, forbearance, and long-suffering, [which] are such amiable Godlike qualities (101–2)" as well as qualities that speak of "grandeur," but rather the "submissive demeanour of dependence, the support of weakness that loves, because it wants protection; and is forbearing, because it must silently endure injuries; smiling under the lash at which it dare not snarl" (102).

Weakness had been recast as feminine beauty. Women were degraded into stunted development by learning to be "proud of their weakness" (219). Therefore, "Civilized women are . . . so weakened by false refinement, that, respecting morals, their condition is much below what it would be were they left in a state nearer to nature" (129). She painted a portrait in which this "false education" leads women to become ridiculous creatures as they become increasingly dependent on men, so weak that they cling to their "*natural* protector"[10] from "the frown of an old cow, or the jump of a mouse; a rat, would be a serious danger" (131). She called this "imbecility which degrades a rational creature" (131).

Wollstonecraft expressed her disgust with the language of oppression bluntly, rejecting what she saw as the oxymoronic notions of "fair defects, amiable weaknesses, etc." (103). She pleaded with women to reject the influence of those who flatter weakness in them, which only keeps them in servitude:

My own sex, I hope, will excuse me, if I treat them like rational creatures, instead of flattering their *fascinating* graces, and viewing them as if they were in a state of perpetual childhood, unable to stand alone. I earnestly wish to point out in what true dignity and human happiness consists—I wish to persuade women to endeavor to acquire strength, both of mind and body, and to convince them that the soft phrases, susceptibility of heart, delicacy of sentiment, and refinement of taste, that are almost synonymous with epithets of weakness, and those beings who are only the objects of pity and that kind of love, which has been termed its sister, will soon become objects of contempt. (75)

Because dependence of mind is a mark of the child, whether male or female, the character assigned to women must be understood as "infantine." Women were unnaturally educated to remain children even as they aged. She wrote, "we should hear none of these infantine airs, if girls were allowed to take sufficient exercise, and not confined in close rooms till their muscles are relaxed, and their powers of digestion destroyed" (131). Fear should be treated the same way in girls as in boys (131).

Weakness could not be a source of strength of mind, but it could be a source of power. She wondered, if strength is generally regarded as the basis of men's superiority, "why are women so infatuated as to be proud of a defect?"

Rousseau has furnished them with a plausible excuse, which could only have occurred to a man, whose imagination had been allowed to run wild . . . ;—that they might, forsooth, have a pretext for yielding to a natural appetite without violating a romantic species of modesty, which gratifies the pride and libertinism of men.

Woman, deluded by these sentiments, sometimes boast of their weakness, cunningly obtaining power by playing on the *weakness* of men; and they may well glory in their illicit sway, for . . . they have more real power than their masters: but virtue is sacrificed to temporary gratifications, and the respectability of life to the triumph of an hour (109).

Here, once again, Wollstonecraft presented weakness and dependence not merely as an absolute characteristic of an individual, but as a part of a corrupt and complex social system, in this case relating to sexual con-quest. One could even have limited forms of power over others without having real power over the self.

In Wollstonecraft's writing, women's weakness is not a characteristic simply pressed on the *tabula rasa* of the mind by external forces. She did not imagine a process of passive socialization. Women are induced into acting in a "feminine" manner by a social system that puts it in their short-term self-interest to do so. Men, the more powerful agents in society,[11] had rigged the system to make strength an asset for them (but not for women) and weakness more valuable to women. Self degradation and weakness therefore become women's illusory rational choice because they are more likely to lead to "success" as defined by the participants in the system. In Wollstonecraft's moral and political theory, of course, self-degradation could not truly be rational because it is based on impulses of present gain or, as Wollstonecraft put it, "temporary gratifications,"[12] rather than on principles of virtue. Rational choice is defined by long-term interests of improvement. Only a rational person, one with independence or strength of mind, could transcend this short-term self-gratification.

Wollstonecraft discussed the power of weakness extensively. Weakness allows women to negotiate serving two masters at once, although at great cost. They could conform to culturally accepted notions of women's honor and modesty by never *choosing* to act on sexual passions. This sexual reluctance "gratifies the pride and libertinism of men." But sexuality is, as she wrote, "a natural appetite," and weakness provides a means to satisfy that appetite in an apparently passive way. At the same time Wollstonecraft was well aware of some of the costs of this condition.

She explored the power of female weakness further. "Women are . . . so much degraded by mistaken notions of female excellence, that I do not mean to add a paradox when I assert, that this artificial weakness produces a propensity to tyrannize, and gives birth to cunning, the natural opponent of strength, which leads them to play off those contemptible infantine airs that undermine esteem even whilst they excite desire" (77). We have seen this story before in Wollstonecraft's analysis. Those who occupy positions of dependence and servility or do not live in a condition of liberty become degraded and corrupted. Their condition does not allow them to move beyond acting on immediate selfish interest because this seems the means to survival. It is extremely difficult to develop the strength or independence of mind required for virtue when one is a dependent.

"Women, . . . obtaining power by unjust means, by practicing or fostering vice . . . become either abject slaves or capricious tyrants. They lose all simplicity, all dignity of mind, in acquiring power, and act as men are observed to act when they have been exalted by the same means" (114). Women are not different from other dependents or from others who gain power unjustly for whatever reason. They have learned to use beauty and outward appearances to gain some control over men. Wollstonecraft explained, "this exertion of cunning is only an instinct of nature to enable them to obtain indirectly a little of that power of which they are unjustly denied a share" (68).

Not only are women corrupted into exerting tyrannical power over men, but their resource for exerting tyranny is a form of inherited wealth: not money, but their bodies. Like those with inherited property who become indolent because they only pay attention to their wealth, women's beauty serves the same role in their lives:

Inheriting, in a lineal descent from the first fair defect in nature, the sovereignty of beauty, they have, to maintain their power, resigned the natural rights, which the exercise of reason might have procured them, and chosen rather to be short-lived queens than labour to obtain the sober pleasures that arise from equality. Exalted by their inferiority (this sounds like a contradiction), they constantly demand homage as women, though experience should teach them that the men who pride themselves upon paying this arbitrary insolent respect to the sex, with the most scrupulous exactness, are most inclined to tyrannize over,

and despise, the very weakness they cherish. (124)

She thereby placed women simultaneously in the position of king and courtier, slave and slaveholder. But she understood that women's power, like that of other subordinates, was so limited as to be largely illusory.

For Wollstonecraft neither women's minds nor men's are strong; and therefore they cannot see the truth. They cannot see where their "real interests" (173) lie.

Women are every where in this deplorable state; for, in order to preserve their innocence, as ignorance is courteously termed, truth is hidden from them, and they are made to assume an artificial character before their faculties have any strength. Taught from their infancy that beauty is woman's sceptre, the mind shapes itself to the body, and, roaming round its gilt cage, only seeks to adorn its prison. (113)

Here we have variation of the story of the emperor's new clothes. The clothes actually exist; it is the monarch who does not.

Wollstonecraft's analysis of the dynamics of inequality was sophisticated for someone who wrote before the development of widespread movements of psychological and sociological theory focusing on the dynamics of inequality. Indeed, most theorists of power and inequality tend to use more unidirectional analyses of the oppressed and oppressor. Contemporary feminist scholars are still struggling to comprehend the multiple positions an individual can hold within power relations. Wollstonecraft offered a sense of this complexity and, as she said, the paradoxes of power, in the late eighteenth century.[13]

Late twentieth-century radical thinkers are often critical of theories ascribing negative characteristics to victims of oppression, claiming these "blame the victim," even if only by implication. Wollstonecraft would certainly be regarded as suspicious on these grounds. She argued that women often became tyrants over men (and, indeed, over their own children), and that their tyranny was based in part on "hereditary honors," or their bodies. But she no more suggested that women and men were equally powerful or that women were ultimately the source of the problem than she claimed that king and courtier or slavemaster and slave were equal or equally responsible. Women's cunning, their tendency to tyrannize, and all the other negative characteristics Wollstonecraft said could be observed in women were created by stripping them of their liberty and placing them in a servile, dependent position in the first place. It was, after all, the degradation of human character that so angered her.

Women who tyrannized did so from a position of dependence and subordination. Using explicitly political vocabulary, Wollstonecraft wrote that women become like "viceregents," and "will act like men subjected by fear, and make their children and servants endure their tyrannical oppression. As they submit without reason, they will, having no fixed rules to square their conduct by, be kind, or cruel, just as the whim of the moment directs" (116–17).[14] Men are vulnerable to women's tyranny because they, too, have not developed sufficient strength of mind to govern themselves; they become slaves to their passions and therefore to the women who learn how to excite those passions (166). It was not just her specific problems with Imlay that led her to write to him, "You know my opinion of men in general; you know that I think them systematic tyrants, and that it is the rarest thing in the world, to meet with a man with sufficient delicacy of feeling to govern desire" (*Letters* 1795:273).[15]

Men, of course, were no more naturally bad than women. They were also creatures of their circumstances, in this case their own corrupting unnatural power and privilege. But Wollstonecraft insisted on laying the lion's share of responsibility for maintenance of this corrupt system at the feet of men. They were not merely slaves to their nervous systems leaving them helpless on account of lust. After all, even if women had taken what power they could, men had a near monopoly on public and private authority and considerably more governing power than women. Women's financial dependence on their husbands gives men a special power:

> The common run of men have such an ignoble way of thinking that, if they debauch their hearts, and prostitute their persons, following perhaps a gust of inebriation, they suppose the wife, slave rather, whom they maintain, has no right to complain, and ought to receive the sultan, whenever he deigns to return, with open arms, though his have been polluted by half an hundred promiscuous amours during his absence. (*Letters* 1794:273)[16]

She believed that "men are domestic tyrants, considering them as fathers, brothers, or husbands," although "there is a kind of interregnum between the reign of the father and husband, which is the only period of freedom and pleasure that the women enjoy" (*Scand.* 326).

Wollstonecraft used an explicitly political analogy to show where the ultimate power should be placed even in the midst of the mutual corruption of women and men:

> I have every where been struck by one characteristic difference in the conduct of the two sexes; women, in general, are seduced by their superiors, and men jilted by their inferiors; rank and manners awe the one, and cunning and wantonness subjugate the other; ambition creeping into the woman's passion, and tyranny giving force to the man's; for most men treat their mistresses as kings do their favourites: *ergo* is not man then the tyrant of the creation? (*Scand.* 325)

Wollstonecraft would not be deflected from her belief that men held the greater power and therefore greater blame in this social relation. "From the tyranny of man, I firmly believe, the greater number of female follies proceed; and the cunning, which I allow makes at present a part of their character, I likewise have repeatedly endeavoured to prove, is produced by oppression" (265). She did not blame the masses for the relationship between them and the king, or the poor for the relationship between them and the rich. She did not blame women for their relationship with men. She did, however, despise each of these relationships. . . .

Virtue, Duty, and Employment

A remaining argument conventionally used in support of gender difference and inequality regarded motherhood as a natural marker of the different character of women and men and of their different social employment. Wollstonecraft certainly believed that mind and character are shaped by occupation. What role, then, did reproduction play in her understanding of sex difference?

Wollstonecraft believed that motherhood was one of the most important duties of women, although as time went on she seemed more sure that domestic duties were not the sole responsibility of women: it was a responsibility shared with men, and women could not be confined only to domestic tasks. But she strongly maintained throughout her writing that the female character instilled by the current state of society was thoroughly inappropriate for virtuous fulfillment of motherhood. As one of the most important duties of life, childraising requires strength of body and mind thus far denied women.[17] Women could not be capable of producing good children and citizens if they themselves were not educated to be virtuous adults and citizens (66). Her arguments were very similar to the notions of republican motherhood Kerber found in her investigation of gender ideology in the early United States.[18] The duty of motherhood must be regarded in the same light as other duties and virtues. "Women, I allow, may have different duties to fulfil; but they are *human* duties, and the principles that should regulate the discharge of them, I sturdily maintain, must be the same" (*VW* 120).

Is motherhood the foremost and natural duty of women? It is and it isn't. Wollstonecraft in effect distinguished between reproduction and nurturing children. The first is a natural occurrence prompted by natural passions. There is no evidence that Wollstonecraft was aware of contraception (although she was aware of abortion),[19] so pregnancy was the probable outcome of any sexual relationship. It took no learning; it would inevitably happen to most women.

Nurturing children is another matter. It is a natural duty for those who have children, therefore a natural duty of most people. "As I conceive it to be the duty of every rational creature to attend to its offspring, I am sorry to observe, that reason and duty together have not so powerful an influence over human conduct, as instinct has in the brute creation" (*Thoughts* 7). Two points stand out. First, in humans it is not instinct but reason that creates nurturance; "maternal tenderness arises . . . as much from habit as instinct" (*Thoughts* 7). She abhorred the tendency for wealthy women to delegate childraising to servants, but regarded the prevalence of this practice as evidence that "Natural affection, as it is termed, I believe to be a very faint tie, affections must grow out of the habitual exercise of a mutual sympathy; and what sympathy does a mother exercise who sends her babe to a nurse, and only takes it from a nurse to send it to a school?" (*VW* 223). Women (especially wealthy women) have even learned not to breast-feed their own children, often because they looked on it as "immodest," which Wollstonecraft regarded as a remarkable contravention of the laws of nature.[20]

An assumption of a specifically maternal tie with a child does underlie her writing, but it plays a very interesting role. When she wrote of her fears for her daughter Fanny, she said, "You know that as a female I am particularly attached to her—I feel more than a mother's fondness and anxiety, when I reflect on the dependent and oppressed state of her sex" (*Scand.* 269). Although this passage suggests the importance of a mother-child bond, the link is forged in this case because of their common womanhood (for later in the passage Wollstonecraft uses this "adult" term for her female infant) which ensnares them in similar bonds of oppression. This commonality, drawn here between mother and daughter, later came to be called "sisterhood."

In the *Wrongs of Woman* Jemima is described as thoroughly hardened by her experience of oppression, but when told that Maria's infant had been taken away from her, "the woman awoke in a bosom long estranged from female emotions" and vowed to help Maria. Here again the "maternal instinct" merges into a fellow-feeling with another woman; it forges a moral bond. But elsewhere in the same novel, in describing Jemima's nurse, Wollstonecraft wrote that "the habit of seeing children die off her hands, had so hardened her heart, that the office of a mother did not awaken the tenderness of a woman" (107).

Maternal bonding, so often considered natural, is like other social feelings, shaped by the social conditions of the relationships. The relationship between a parent—male or female—and child will be shaped by the conditions of that relationship. Wollstonecraft showed an awareness that women's relationships with children tended to be not only more extensive than men's, but also to exist within a condition of gender oppression. In the *Wrongs of Woman* Maria writes to her infant daughter that she had special things to teach her, which "only a mother—a mother schooled in misery" could have. She did see a difference between mothers and fathers, but it seemed largely shaped by experience. "The tenderness of a father who knew the world, might be great; but could it equal that of a mother—of a mother, labouring under a portion of the misery, which the constitution of society seems to have entailed on all her kind?" (123). Wollstonecraft did not live in an era of mass movements of women engaged in what is now called feminism. But the sense of her writing on maternal bonding, including the attention to its social conditions, is very much like the thinking of the many women who turned their motherhood into political sisterhood not many years later.[21]

Due to ambiguities and contradictions in Wollstonecraft's writing it sometimes suggests that women should have the exclusive duty of caring for children, and sometimes that it should be a shared responsibility. She often discussed women as mothers, certainly more than she discussed men as fathers, but much of the time she was describing social conditions as they existed. She wrote vaguely of women's and men's "peculiar," "respective," or "different" duties.[22] Once she defined "peculiar duties" specifically: breastfeeding (251). Her references to "natural" maternal duties revolve around infancy. Once she wrote that "the care of chil-

dren in their infancy is one of the grand duties annexed to the female character by nature," and twice she argued that it is unnatural not to breast-feed (248, 251). She wrote that "whatever tends to incapacitate maternal character, takes woman out of her sphere" (247), but this passage appeared as part of her discussion advocating breast-feeding, and more specifically, criticizing men's discouragement of women from nursing their babies. I will shortly return to the question of the compatibility of maternal character with other activities.

Wollstonecraft noted that "Mankind seem to agree that the children should be left under the management of women during their childhood" (137). But she followed this sentence immediately with a discussion of women who were probably unsuitable for the task. Women "of sensibility" would probably be carried away by their feelings and spoil children, and "a person of genius" would have an unsuitable temperament. This leaves aside the masses of women, especially of the upper class, who are much too weak-minded. If women, for whatever reason, are more suitable than men to educate their children, their ability to do so is not natural but instilled through education.

Wollstonecraft very often used gender-neutral terminology to speak of the duties of parenthood and raising children and sometimes spoke specifically of the duty of fathers. Often her writing on fathers suggests that, whatever the specific division of labor might be, the point was for mothers and fathers to work together or they would mutually corrupt each other and both become bad parents. She accused men of discouraging women from breast-feeding their children because of their own "debauchery" (212), and predicted that "till men become attentive to the duty of father, it is vain to expect women to spend that time in the nursery which they . . . choose to spend at their glass" (68).

Above all she believed that the unnatural gender distinctions barring women from self-improvement and causing violence and corruption in the relationship between husbands and wives also hurt children. "[Children] will never be properly educated till friendship subsists between parents. Virtue flies from a house divided against itself" (265). Men have important responsibilities in the family. "The conclusion I wish to draw, is obvious: make women rational creatures, and free citizens, and they will quickly become good wives, and mothers; that is—if men do not neglect the duties of husbands and fathers" (250).

Regardless of the duties men could perform with regard to their children, they tended to have a self-regarding sense of their relationship to them. Wollstonecraft's own pregnancy provided a context for one of her very few reflections on "natural rights" and their relationship to obligations or responsibility:

> Considering the care and anxiety a woman must have about a child before it comes into the world, it seems to me, by a *natural right*, to belong to her. When men get immersed in the world, they seem to lose all sensations, excepting those necessary to continue or produce life!—Are those the privileges of reason? Amongst the feathered race, whilst the hen keeps the young warm, her mate stays by to cheer her; but it is sufficient for a man to condescend to get a child, in order to claim it.—A man is a tyrant!" (*Letters* 1794:242)

Wollstonecraft never appeared as Lockean in her view of property rights as she was here in her assertion that women's labor gave them, not men, the right to custody of their children. She deemed the accepted legal view of her day, that men have a natural or (through marriage) contractual right over women and their labor, tyrannical. She seemed to have the glimmering of an idea that women's labor—in this case reproductive labor—should be held as the basis of rights over their children.

Wollstonecraft certainly favored an education to make women good wives and mothers, but her writing suggests that such education should be roughly similar to men's; the part that is most important is strengthening the mind and body. She was adamantly opposed to another form of education for motherhood:

> [Yet] the men who, by their writings, have most earnestly laboured to domesticate women, have endeavoured, by arguments dictated by a gross appetite, which satiety had rendered fastidious, to weaken their bodies and cramp their minds. But, if even by these sinister methods, they really *persuaded* women, by working on their feelings, to stay at home, and fulfil the duties of a mother and mistress of a family, I should cautiously oppose opinions that led women to right conduct, by prevailing on them to make the discharge of such important duties the main business of life, though reason were insulted. (133)

Following this passage she suggested again that women will more likely be "detached from these domestic employments" by *neglecting* the development of their understanding, as compared with their sensibility, than they would be by pursuing "the most serious intellectual pursuit" (133). Elsewhere she condemned men for "forcing" women to remain in their families "by denying them civil and political rights" (*VM* 67).

If women's education is simply aimed at preparation for homemaking, as was that of the Scandinavian women she observed, women become "simply notable housewives; without accomplishments, or any of the charms that adorn more advanced social life. This total ignorance may enable them to save something in their kitchens; but it is far from rendering them better parents" (*Scand.* 321); they become drudges, which is also likely to send their husbands out of the house in search of more interesting company (*VW* 135).

Familial relationships, although important, do not constitute the ultimate purpose of female existence because they do not constitute the ultimate purpose of human existence. "Connected with man as daughters, wives, and mothers, their moral character may be estimated by their manner of fulfilling those simple duties; but the end, the grand end of their exertions should be to unfold their own faculties and acquire the dignity of conscious virtue" (95). She wanted women and men to be better human beings, which includes but is not limited to performing their specific tasks well. "The being who discharges the duties of its station is independent; and, speaking of women at large, their first duty is to themselves as rational creatures, and the next, in point of importance, as citizens, is that, which includes so many, of mother" (216).

One last question about motherhood and fatherhood concerns the relationship between caring for children and engaging in other activities. She did not want anything to "incapacitate maternal character (247)," but even the early Wollstonecraft wrote, "No employment of the mind is a sufficient excuse for neglecting domestic duties, and I cannot conceive that they are incompatible. A woman may fit herself to be the companion and friend of a man of sense, and yet know how to take care of his family" (*Thoughts* 21). Later she focused more on the need for women to be able to earn their own living, and even to do so while married. Wollstonecraft repeated that women should be prepared for the time when her husband will not be available to support her. She also considered the needs of women who never marry and would not survive if they were not self-sufficient. I have already addressed the question of women's independence within marriage. But she also argued,

> It is plain from the history of all nations, that women cannot be confined to merely domestic pursuits, for they will not fulfil family duties unless their minds take a wider range, and whilst they are kept in ignorance they become in the same proportion the slaves of pleasure as they are slaves of man. Nor can they be shut out of great enterprises. (245)

What, then, are the appropriate possibilities for women's employment?

Early in her career Wollstonecraft expressed great discontent about the few avenues available to women, and her anger that some of "women's" trades were being taken over by men (*Thoughts* 25–26). Teaching, domestic service, and textile work were available, but she saw many other possibilities; indeed, she could identify few natural limits on women. Women could be "physicians as well as nurses," and she thought decency required that only women be midwives

(218).[23] She argued women could be more involved in politics, and that

> business of various kinds . . . might save them from common and legal prostitution. Women would not then marry for a support, as men accept places under government, and neglect the implied duties; nor would an attempt to earn their own subsistence, a most laudable one! sink them almost to the level of those poor abandoned creatures who live by prostitution. (218)

She even teased her readers with the possibility of women turning "their distaff into a musket," but delicately passed over the subject by noting she would like to see the "bayonet converted into a pruninghook" (216).

Wollstonecraft abhorred the position of women forced into servitude—including marital servitude—by the lack of alternatives. The unnatural distinctions between women and men were not just matters of custom, but of law.

> [Is] not that government then very defective, and very unmindful of the happiness of one half of its members, that does not provide for honest, independent women, by encouraging them to fill respectable stations? But in order to render their private virtue a public benefit, they must have a civil existence in the state, married or single. . . .
>
> It is a melancholy truth; yet such is the blessed effect of civilization! the most respectable women are the most oppressed; and, unless they have understandings far superiour to the common run of understanding, taking in both sexes, they must, from being treated like contemptible beings, become contemptible. How many women thus waste life away the prey of discontent, who might have practiced as physicians, regulated a farm, managed a shop, and stood erect, supported by their own industry. (219)

Women are turned into slaves and prostitutes by their governors in family and state, then treated with contempt for being slaves and prostitutes by those same governors.

Wollstonecraft suggested that wealthy women and men had special obligations to find employment because, unlike those of other classes, their lives were likely to be idle and indolent. Their employment could save them from being tyrants and could make them useful. Like others in her intellectual and social circle, she feared the impact of idleness on people, and advocated staying busy, not just with one's domestic duties or paid work, but also with other forms of usefulness, particularly helping the poor if one was in a position to do so.

For some people employment might well mean not being able to take on family duties. She cited Francis Bacon's saying that men with wives and children were unlikely to be involved in great enterprises for good or evil, and that the greatest works have been done by single and childless men. "I say the same of women," Wollstonecraft wrote (132–33). But "the welfare of society is not built on extraordinary exertions; and were it more reasonably organized, there would be still less need of great abilities, or heroic virtues" (133). Therefore, despite her writing about various employments, generally speaking neither women nor men would be taken out of their families (132).

Wollstonecraft guessed that most women "in the common walks of life are called to fulfill the duties of wives and mothers, by religion and reason" (217). She also hoped that "society will some time or other be so constituted, that man must necessarily fulfil the duties of a citizen, or be despised, and that while he was employed in any of the departments of civil life, his wife, also an active citizen, should be equally intent to manage her family, educate her children, and assist her neighbours" (216). She argued that "the society is not properly organized which does not compel men and women to discharge their respective duties, by making it the only way to acquire [respect]. The respect . . . which is paid to wealth and mere personal charms, is a true north-east blast, that blights the tender blossoms of affection and virtue" (212). Virtue was not yet rewarded in society, which is why few people of either sex wanted to perform their duties virtuously. They would rather be wealthy or beautiful.

But even if the education of children could be more highly regarded, Wollstonecraft still believed that "to render her really virtuous and useful," woman must have full protection of the law and must avoid total dependence on her husband, "for how can a being be generous who has nothing of its own? or virtuous, who is not free?" (216–17). Family duties, including motherhood, do not constitute a reason for denying women liberty; they are, if anything, one of the primary reasons for granting women liberty.

In the end the question of family duty could not have meant to Wollstonecraft what it does to feminist writers today. Her conclusions are likely to appear limited. It seems that she was certain that virtue was the same for women and men because it consisted of the proper exercise of the mind and passions. But whether she believed that the specific virtues of women and men would be the same is likely contingent to an important degree on the material possibilities she could imagine in her time. Nevertheless, it is insupportable to argue that she had any clear sense of separate spheres.

Bugbears

Although she devoted considerably more attention to it, Wollstonecraft's analysis of unnatural distinctions based on gender is essentially the same as her analysis of the other distinctions. Humanity is defined as the "active exertions of virtue" (*VM* 53), or "virtue arising from reflection" (*Revs* 1789:150). The value and meaning of virtue, reason, and sensibility are not different for different categories of people; to be virtuous requires being strong and independent. Virtue is developed in social life and depends on the structure of society and its relationships. Gross inequality leads to the mutual corruption of all parties involved. The society Wollstonecraft observed was not yet enlightened; in gender relations as in others the definition of virtue had been shaped according to the personal utility of those in positions of power, in this case by men. But such social structures also teach the subalterns to pursue dangerous, false images of virtue.

Because of the existence of natural principles, liberty would make things right. "Let there be no coercion *established* in society, and the common law of gravity prevailing, the sexes will fall into their proper places" (68). If women are "really capable of acting like rational creatures, let them not be treated like slaves" (105). If, on the other hand, they were incapable of rationality, liberty would prove that too. "Nay, the order of society as it is at present regulated would not be inverted, for woman would then only have the rank that reason assigned her, and arts could not be practiced to bring the balance even, much less to turn it" (105).

Wollstonecraft's writing suggests she knew she would frighten her male readers (especially), and she took care to remind men they were, at least, physically stronger than women, and therefore might be able to handle a wider range of duties. "Let it not be concluded that I wish to invert the order of things; I have already granted, that, from the constitution of their bodies, men seem to be designed by Providence to attain a greater degree of virtue" on the average, but she also reasserted that the virtues of women and men were not different in kind (95, also 108).

She knew people would fear that if women were educated to be strong they would become too "masculine." But, she argued, "the word masculine is only a bugbear" (76). She had no intention of seeing women jostling men at the gaming table, but she favored the "imitation of manly virtues, or, more properly speaking, the attainment of those talents and virtues, the exercise of which ennobles the human character, and which raise females in the scale of animal being, when they are comprehensively termed mankind . . ." (74).

Wollstonecraft suggested we may call these qualities what we wish; what she wanted was for women and men to improve themselves as human beings. The fact that they were "not in a healthy state" may be attributed "to a false system of education, gathered from the books written on this subject by men who, *considering females rather as women than human creatures,* have been more anxious to make them alluring mistresses than affectionate wives and rational mothers" (73, emphasis added). She concluded that women "had been drawn out of their sphere by false refinement, and not by

an endeavour to acquire masculine qualities" (90, also 103, 241).

Wollstonecraft battled against the tyrannical power she saw exerted over women, but her political psychology of inequality was also based on the notion that tyranny and oppression were caused by the weakness and dependence of tyrants. Their power is supported by force, ceremonies, rituals, and blind faith; they are therefore dependent on the weakness and dependence of those they oppress. Wollstonecraft took her theoretical cue from one of the foremost theorists of sexual politics, Jean-Jacques Rousseau.

Rousseau expressed his commitment to the state of affairs that Wollstonecraft observed and attacked: "Thus the different constitution of the two sexes leads us to [conclude] that the stronger party seems to be master, but is as a matter of fact dependent on the weaker."[24] Here is where he explained the need for women to be subjugated by men and, indeed, to subjugate themselves. Then he offered one of his apparent paradoxes that so intrigued Wollstonecraft.[25] He scoffed at women's complaints that female education is inferior and leads to their subjugation.[26] "Well, then, educate them like men. The more women are like men, the less influence they will have over men, and then men will be masters indeed."[27] Wollstonecraft answered him thirty years later. "This is the very point I aim at. I do not wish them to have power over men; but over themselves" (*VW* 131).

Here is where Wollstonecraft's political psychology was more subtle and radical than that of many democratic theorists, and anticipates many later feminist and communitarian theorists. At least one major interpreter of Rousseau's sexual politics thoroughly misunderstood its relationship to feminist theory. Joel Schwartz, accepting Rousseau's argument that gender relations were structured as ultimately equal mutual dependencies because each sex had power over the other in different ways, argued that Rousseau's and Wollstonecraft's approaches were merely different strategies to equality,[28] and that Rousseau's understanding of mutual dependence makes him "a sort of ancestor" to contemporary feminists because he "celebrates the power of women."[29]

Wollstonecraft never labeled mutual subjugation—or any form of subjugation—as a condition of equality, and in this she is the ancestor of much of modern feminism, not just in its theories of gender politics, but in power politics more generally. "I love man as my fellow; but his scepter, real, or usurped, extends not to me, unless the reason of an individual demands my homage; and even then the submission is to reason, and not to man" (105). Wollstonecraft's critique was very much a part of the liberal tradition's search for a form of governance that does not depend on the caprices of fallible human beings.

A most interesting part of her critique of power and governance is found in her most persistent comparison: between monarchy and gender, the government of the state and the government of the family.[30] Sometimes men are compared with kings in their roles as masters, sometimes women are compared with kings because of their sovereignty of beauty. She took her cue from Burke's famous passage . . . in which he argued that without the ancient prejudices and ceremonies there would be nothing to stop brutality from reigning while "a king is but a man; a queen is but a woman; a woman is but an animal; and an animal not of the highest order."[31] For him, we must sink into a gross and inhuman world if we leave off our fancy dress.

Wollstonecraft posed the opposite vision. From the king to the mere woman all would do best to understand we are human, and press toward virtue and mutual respect, so that we do not corrupt ourselves with the self-protective intrigues that evolve out of mutual tyranny. She accepted Burke's charge about the radicals' construction of kings, queens, and women, although she accepted that a woman is "not of the highest order" only while society was structured unnaturally. Indeed, in the current construction of society she believed "A king is always a king—and a woman always a woman: his authority and her sex, ever stand between them and rational converse" (*VW* 125).[32]

"Contending for the rights of woman, my main argument is built on this simple principle, that if she be not prepared by education to become the companion of man, she will stop the progress of knowledge and virtue; for truth must be common to all, or it will be inefficacious with respect to its influence on general practice" (*VW* 66). If Wollstonecraft's text has any internal consistency this does not simply mean women must become good companions in the sense of wives, but of fellow travelers. She had the optimistic view that if women were freed, "they will quickly become wise and virtuous, as men become more so; for the improvement must be mutual, or the injustice which one half of the human race are obliged to submit to, retorting on their oppressors, the virtue of man will be worm-eaten by the insect whom he keeps under his feet" (247).

Liberty would free people to become strong of mind and to base their actions and the structure of their society on reasoned principles of virtue.

> And where then will be found the man who will simply say that a king can do no wrong; . . . that the priest, who takes advantage of the dying fears of a vicious man, to cheat his heirs, is not more despicable than a highwayman?—or that obedience to parents should go one jot beyond the deference due to reason, enforced by affection?—And who will coolly maintain, that it is just to deprive a woman, not to insist on her being treated as an outcast of society, of all the rights of a citizen, because her revolting heart turns from the man, whom, a husband only in name, and by the tyrannical power he has over her person and property, she can neither love nor respect, to find comfort in a more congenial or humane bosom? These are a few of the leading prejudices, in the present constitution of society, that blast the blossoms of hope, and render life wretched and useless. (*FrRev* 111)

Here, finally, is a theorist who struggled toward the possibility of the mutual improvement of all humanity, not just the male half, loyally served and accompanied by their wives.

Wollstonecraft's political texts moved among critiques of unnatural distinctions based on rank, property, occupations and professions, familial ties, and gender, as she subjected such distinctions to parallel and, to some degree, integrated analysis. Her extension of radicalism to incorporate gender rested on applying political language and analysis to "private" life and institutions, conventionally deemed outside politics. Because one of the cornerstones of liberalism is usually thought to be the careful distinction between public and private, it is important to turn directly to her treatment of the problem.

Notes

1. All quotations in this chapter are from the *Vindication of the Rights of Woman* unless otherwise noted.

2. It is interesting that in the second edition of the *Rights of Woman* she omitted an important phrase. The original read "your NEW CONSTITUTION, the first constitution founded on reason." It is unlikely that she decided the constitution was not founded on reason, at least as far as it went, but rather that in her second thoughts she joined the radicals who claimed that the new constitution of the United States was the first founded on reason. See, for example, *Revs* 1791: 375; *FrRev* 20.

3. This is one of many times Wollstonecraft used parallel analysis and language to understand individuals, societies, and governments. *Constitution* was in more common usage to refer to the human body (rather than the body politic) in Wollstonecraft's day, but the echoes were not coincidental.

4. Wollstonecraft unfortunately used *strength* in different ways in her writing without clearly marking the specific meaning she was using. My argument here, especially, depends on contextual clues. For a fascinating related discussion of the history of the body and of ideology concerning the body in Wollstonecraft's day, see Dorinda Outram, *The Body and the French Revolution: Sex, Class, and Political Culture* (Yale University Press, 1989).

5. Edmund Burke, *A Philosophic Enquiry into the Origin of Our Ideas of the Sublime and Beautiful*, edited by James T. Boulton (Basil Blackwell, 1987), p. 91.

6. Ibid., p. 116.

7. Ibid., p. 110.

8. Also *VW* 98.

9. Also *Thoughts* 23.

10. Here as elsewhere Wollstonecraft used emphasis to indicate a sarcastic tone and to make fun of the words of another writer.

11. We shall return to men and their role and character shortly.

12. Elsewhere I have written on this problem of rationality, considering the relationship between the now conventional notion of rationality and oppression. See Virginia Sapiro, "Sex and Games: On Oppression and Rationality," *British Journal of Political Science* 9 (October 1979): 318–24.

13. One of the best contemporary theorists on this problem is Bell Hooks. See Bell Hooks, *Talking Back, Thinking Feminist, Thinking Black* (South End Press, 1989).

14. Nearly two centuries later radical feminist theorist Mary Daly became well known for writing that women became not "viceregents" for men but the "token torturers." See Mary Daly, *Gyn/Ecology: The Metaethics of Radical Feminism* (Beacon, 1978).

15. Also *FrRev* 28.

16. Here she seemed to offer an implicit criticism of establishing relationships between women and men on a contract basis, which would have been consistent with her views on friendship (*VM* 39).

17. *VW* 118, 133, 222–23; *Scand.* 321.

18. Linda K. Kerber, *Women of the Republic: Intellect and Ideology in Revolutionary America* (W. W. Norton, 1986). Although some early writers on this theme may have gained insights about what we now label *republican motherhood* from Wollstonecraft, there is little evidence her work played a great role in developing the notion, largely because her views in fact seem less supportive of the separate-spheres argument that is often noted. It seems, rather, that there was a general shift toward reinterpreting women's roles as potentially serving the interests of the state or republic.

19. *Wrongs* 112.

20. *Revs* 1791: 386, *Elements* 11; *VW* 212.

21. I discuss this passage and its implication for the development of feminism in Virginia Sapiro, *A Vindication of Political Virtue: The Political Theory of Mary Wollstonecraft* (University of Chicago Press, 1992), chapter 8.

22. *VW* 70, 120, 132, 212, 237, 241.

23. When she was pregnant she demanded a midwife rather than a male doctor.
24. Rousseau, *Émile*, p. 323.
25. "I am now reading Rousseau's *Émile*, and love his paradoxes" (*Letters* 1787: 145).
26. It is noteworthy that he was aware of such complaints.
27. Rousseau, *Émile*, p. 327. In her text she quoted the first part of Rousseau's sentence but left out the part about men becoming masters.
28. Joel Schwartz, *The Sexual Politics of Jean-Jacques Rousseau* (University of Chicago Press, 1984), p. 85.
29. Ibid., p. 9.
30. *VW* 67, 90, 93, 105, 106, 109, 110, 111, 113, 114, 116, 124, 125, 226; *FrRev* 111; *Scand.* 330.
31. Edmund Burke, *Reflections on the Revolution in France* (Doubleday, 1961), p. 90.
32. This passage also responds to Rousseau's comment that "The male is only a male now and again, the female is always a female or at least all her youth; everything reminds her of her sex." See Rousseau, *Émile*, p. 324. The feminist would probably note that it is more likely that everything reminds *him* of her sex.

Abbreviations

References to Wollstonecraft's writing are noted in the text. With the exception of her personal letters, all page numbers refer to the *Works of Mary Wollstonecraft*, edited by Marilyn Butler and Janet Todd. Page numbers for her letters refer to *The Collected Letters of Mary Wollstonecraft*, edited by Ralph Wardle. In the case of letters I have included the date of writing and for book reviews the date of publication in the reference. Following is a list of abbreviations used.

Elements: Translation of Christian Salzmann, *Elements of Morality*, 1790.
FrRev: An Historical and Moral View of the Origin and Progress of the French Revolution, 1794.
Letters: Personal correspondence.
Mary: Mary: A Fiction, 1788.
Revs: Reviews published in the *Analytical Review*, 1788–1797.
Scand.: Letters Written during a Short Residence in Sweden, Norway, and Denmark, 1796.
Stories: Original Stories from Real Life, 1788.
Thoughts: Thoughts on the Education of Daughters, 1787.
VM: A Vindication of the Rights of Men, 1790.
VW: A Vindication of the Rights of Woman, 1792.
Wrongs: The Wrongs of Woman, or Maria, 1798.

20
The Radical Ideas of Mary Wollstonecraft

Susan Ferguson

Introduction

According to the standard narrative of feminist intellectual history, modern feminism in the English-speaking world begins with Mary Wollstonecraft's bold appeals for women's inclusion in a public life overwhelmingly dominated by men. Specific attention is drawn to her theories of character-formation and the importance of public education for women in nurturing the female faculty for reason.[1] More recent scholarship, however, suggests this portrait of Wollstonecraft is unduly narrow, since it inspires a somewhat facile categorization of the first modern feminist as a liberal reformer and thus fails to elucidate the breadth of her social vision and the extent to which her ideas threatened to destabilize the ruling elite in late-eighteenth-century Britain.

Rooting their analyses in a wide range of Wollstonecraft's writings, feminist scholars now maintain a greater sensitivity to the historical and biographical context informing her work. As a result, a richer, more nuanced portrait of this early feminist emerges, one that convincingly attributes to her ideas a spirit of radicalism—that is, a commitment to push beyond the limited legislative reforms traditionally associated with the label "liberal feminism."[2]

These revised accounts generally attribute Wollstonecraft's radical spirit to her recognition and condemnation of the pervading economic and social inequities of her day. In linking the project of women's emancipation to a broader socio-economic critique, they suggest, Wollstonecraft politicizes two institutions central to liberal theory: class and family. In the process, she not only distinguishes herself from others within the classical liberal tradition but also challenges the very separation of public and private spheres around which that tradition is constructed. For some, this feature of Wollstonecraft's thought is evidence of the radical potential that liberalism holds for feminism; for others it opens the door to subverting the liberal paradigm altogether. In fact, historian Barbara Taylor considers Wollstonecraft's treatment of class and family to be evidence of a socialist subtext, and credits her with paving the way for the emergence of the utopian brand of socialist feminism some 30 years later.[3]

Efforts to draw attention to Wollstonecraft's rebelliousness and the distance between her ideas and classical liberalism are long overdue, and prove a valuable point of departure for discussions of late-eighteenth-century feminism. But, in their enthusiasm to highlight the potential subversiveness of Wollstonecraft's feminism, many scholars have lapsed into an uncritical celebration of the possibilities of that feminism. As a result, some have attributed to Wollstonecraft political commitments she did not hold while obscuring the limits of the feminist ideals she did promote.

This article assesses Wollstonecraft's politicization of family and class through an exploration of her (incipient) critique of political economy. That critique, I suggest, rests squarely on what is, essentially, a liberal socio-economic model: the free-market activities of independent commodity producers (or, in Marxist terminology, a model of petty-bourgeois economic competition).[4] This model is predicated on the sanctity of private property and a concomitant naturalization of the distinction between private and public realms. While welcoming the general point that Wollstonecraft is no mere liberal in the classical sense, I propose two qualifications to the more recent interpretations of her radicalism. First, Wollstonecraft's critique of class and family—though trenchant and politically explosive in her day—stops short of challenging the centrality of these institutions to liberalism; second, the relationship between Wollstonecraft's feminism and the feminism of the utopian socialists 20 years after her death is marked as much by rupture as by continuity. To develop these points we need, first, to clarify a few essential terms.

Property, Family and Society: Liberal and Socialist Views[5]

Classical liberalism developed in response to the quintessentially capitalist era differentiation of economic power from political power. That is, economic power came increasingly to depend upon private property and its utilization in the market, not on public title and office.[6] Classical liberalism sought to explain and justify an economic sphere composed of (competitive) individual property owners who were also male heads of households. It begins by defining the economy and family as unchanging universal features of human life; these are, in other words, *natural* spheres. The activities each encompasses are treated as self-regulating, with the economy operating in accordance to the laws of competition based on private property and the family adhering to the moral-social code of patriarchal authority. Individual freedom is expressed in and through these economic and familial relations, or civil society. That freedom, however, needs to be protected—the task of a third institution, the state. Early liberal theory thus presents the state as the guarantor of rights and liberties appropriate to ownership and exchange. Whereas the state is a public authority, freedom can only be guaranteed, from the liberal point of view, if the essentially *private* nature of the economy and the family is respected.[7]

Two distinguishing features of classical liberal thought can be highlighted. First, liberalism is premised on the distinction between public and private realms of activities. In fact, the liberal project of emancipation depends entirely on maintaining the optimal balance between the two; whatever the nature of the interaction, without both sides of the equation there can be no freedom. The second defining feature of classical liberalism flows from the first: because the family and the economy are private and self-regulating, the social relations (of gender, class and race) that comprise these institutions are either ignored or are presumed to be manifestations of individual preference or ability. As such, they may be subject to a *moral* critique, but any challenge to inequality in the private sphere that fails to respect and preserve the private, self-regulating, nature of these relations is essentially illiberal.

On the other hand, classical socialism as it developed in the nineteenth century rejects both the privatization and naturalization of the family and the economy.[8] It points instead to the essentially historical nature of each set of social relations, and in so doing uncovers the inequality on which each is premised. That is, family and economy are conditioned by, and representative of, changing social relations which develop, in turn, according to the ongoing conflicts and compromises of class forces. Rather than expressions of natural laws, class, gender and race relations (and their inequalities) broadly express the socioeconomic interests of the dominant class of property owners. The state, far from being the neutral protector of freedom, works to reproduce the conditions of that domination. In historicizing the economy and family in this way, classical socialism challenges the liberal thesis of self-regulation,[9] thereby rejecting the notion that the private sphere is free, or even fully distinct, from the public sphere. The very dichotomy of state and civil society on which liberal thought is based must be transcended if the socialist definition of emancipation is to prevail. And this can only occur if the basis of that distinction in private property and class exploitation is transcended as well.

Where Does Wollstonecraft Fit In?

Situating Wollstonecraft within the movement for radical democracy at the end of the nineteenth century, Barbara Taylor, Virginia Muller and others point to the political economic critique that underwrote that movement. As with her contemporaries, they suggest, at the heart of Wollstonecraft's egalitarian social vision stands a hostility to the dominant forms of property. In fact, some contend, she pushes beyond the limits of her contemporaries' political radicalism by extending that critique to the family. Wollstonecraft is portrayed in these accounts either as a liberal who disrupts the public/private dichotomy (and thereby proves the elasticity and, some argue, the inherently subversive potential of the liberal paradigm); or, as a sort of proto-socialist—a post-liberal who incorporates aspects of socialism into her work and ultimately bridges the two paradigms.[10]

Neither of these characterizations, however, accurately captures the essence of Wollstonecraft's radicalism. While attributing the subversive quality of her work to her critique of political economy, current accounts offer surprisingly little detailed exploration of that critique. In taking a closer look at Wollstonecraft's economic views, I place particular emphasis on the ways in which she qualifies her hostility to property. Her target is not property in general but *aristocratic* forms of property. She in fact *endorses* moderately sized private holdings (along with the class divisions underwriting these). This advocacy of private property and class reflects the economic and social priorities of competitive independent commodity producers, the social class at the heart of the classical liberal economic model.

But Wollstonecraft's liberalism is not "merely" economic. The competitive, capitalist economy has historically rested on a particular configuration of domestic relations: a nuclear household headed by a male breadwinner and managed by a female caretaker in the dual roles of wife and mother.[11] It is precisely this domestic structure that informs Wollstonecraft's work. Rather than politicizing class and family in a way that challenges the separation of public and private spheres, her programme for female emancipation assumes these institutions are necessary, good and, indeed, natural. Her naturalization of the family leads her to argue, despite an openness to women's economic independence, that freedom is fundamentally about middle-class women fulfilling their duties as wives and mothers. And,

against those who claim she speaks for and to all women, I suggest that Wollstonecraft's feminism is in fact class-based; her naturalization of class leaves her no strategy for the emancipation of working-class women. Despite egalitarian sentiments, Wollstonecraft ends up advocating the very oppressive conditions working-class women must struggle against. The class limits of such an approach are most clearly grasped when her views are compared to those of a near-contemporary, the early-nineteenth-century utopian socialist, William Thompson. Thus, in economic and social relations, this early feminist remains firmly within the liberal tradition. Her radicalism is based neither in a peculiarly socialist critique of political economy nor in any disruption of the public/private dichotomy on which liberalism rests.[12]

While I position Wollstonecraft squarely within the liberal paradigm, I am not merely reasserting the standard account of her work. Indeed, I am challenging overly rigid readings of liberalism, though from a different perspective than those I criticize. Wollstonecraft does have strong ties to paradigmatically liberal views on the issues of family and political economy; but such positions can, and do, co-exist with a certain kind of radicalism. That radicalism is based neither in a peculiarly (proto-)socialist economic critique, nor in a potential to collapse the distinction between public and private spheres; it is based in what I will term a social radicalism—a radical politics that disrupts status quo notions of governance and authority. The political economic critique of aristocratic property forms is an important element of this radicalism as it pushes liberalism toward the logical limits of its premises. But it does so in a period politically unripe for such a logic—unripe because the liberal ruling class (the bourgeoisie), although economically powerful, has not yet gained political ascendancy over the old ruling class, the aristocracy. It *is* radical to call for equality of property and women's education in a period when these demands would, if granted, seriously upset the ruling classes' hold on power.[13] Far from seeing Wollstonecraft as a "mere liberal," I affirm the radical scope of her social critique, but argue that her radicalism is best understood historically, as part of a *liberal-democratic politics of resistance* in late-eighteenth-century Britain.

A Radical Democratic Feminism

The British radical reformers in the 1790s, with whom Wollstonecraft associated, were broadly grouped around the republican ideals articulated in Thomas Paine's *Rights of Man*. They blamed the arbitrary and disproportionate political power of the aristocratic few for the misery and poverty of the many. Men (and some included women in this designation) were rational and deserved to be ruled by reason rather than might. They were thus entitled by natural right to equal political representation. If only the corrupt institutions of aristocratic privilege could be swept away, human nature's potential for perfection could be realized.

Corresponding to this political analysis was an economic critique that shunned excessive wealth and the inheritance rules of primogeniture. Aristocratic privileges, Paine and others insisted, stood in the way of a family-based economy of artisans and farmers with relatively equal holdings of private property. In other words, they presumed an economic model of independent commodity producers which, despite its implied attack on the existing political and economic elite, was largely consistent with the premises of Adam Smith's *Wealth of Nations*.[14]

Because Wollstonecraft lived and worked alongside Paineite radicals, she was far removed from the respectable circles of bourgeois life—a fact used to advantage by her detractors. Published in the heated aftermath of the French Revolution, *A Vindication of the Rights of Woman* was identified by political and religious counter-revolutionaries as a Jacobin document, and Wollstonecraft's "degenerate" lifestyle (her first daughter was illegitimate and her second was born only a few months after she married William Godwin) was proclaimed proof of the dangerous implications of its arguments. "Viewed through the smoke of the Bastille," writes Barbara Taylor, "Wollstonecraft

loomed like a blood-stained Amazon, the high priestess of 'loose-tongued Liberty.' "[15]

Although its contents offended middle-class sensibility, it is precisely with the middle layer of society—those women in the "most natural of states"—that Wollstonecraft is concerned, depicting them in what, at first glance, appears to be a surprisingly harsh light.[16] In their current state, writes Wollstonecraft, women are weak and artificial: "Taught from their infancy that beauty is a woman's sceptre, the mind shapes itself to the body, and, roaming round its gilt cage, only seeks to adorn its prison."[17] They are ignorant of virtue and largely incapable of fulfilling their duties as mothers and wives with any degree of competence: they either neglect or spoil their children while frivolity causes husbands to look elsewhere for companionship. Although Wollstonecraft portrays the isolation of women's lives as oppressive, the dominant image she evokes speaks less of hardship and denial than it does of the (corrupting) privileges that result from the refined and pampered world women inhabit. Although women are in a state of "slavish dependence," she means only "in a political and civil sense; for, indirectly, they obtain too much power, and are debased by their exertions to obtain illicit sway."[18]

Yet, for Wollstonecraft, this scathing portrayal of women is not just moral patter. Her harsh words are not *simply* directed at women; they are meant more as a lever of social criticism and, in fact, indict a whole society. Like that of her radical contemporaries, Wollstonecraft's work is informed by a firm conviction that people are the products of their environment. Women are not predisposed to be petty and self-indulgent. These traits develop only because political and social forces deny them the expression and development of the defining feature of humanity: the capacity to reason.

Wollstonecraft's conviction that rationality is equally present in men and women is argued in part on theological grounds. Because all people owe their existence to a rational deity, they must share in the faculty of reason to an equal extent: "the nature of reason must be the same in all, if it be an emanation of divinity, the tie that connects the creature with the Creator."[19] Thus it follows that a just society is one based on reason. And the rational organization of relations on earth is nothing more than the unfolding of God's will:

> I love man as my fellow; but his scepter, real, or usurped, extends not to me, unless the reason of an individual demands my homage; and even then the submission is to reason, and not to man. In fact, the conduct of an accountable being must be regulated by the operations of its own reason; or on what foundation rests the throne of God?[20]

Herein lies the fundamental contradiction of the political organization of society: it extends the rational sceptre to middle-class men but not to women. Men's civil superiority is, Wollstonecraft argues, nothing but the residue of an era marked by inequality and force. It is a vestige of that "pestiferous purple which renders the progress of civilization a curse, and warps the understanding."[21] Insisting that it is entirely inconsistent for men to fight against aristocratic privilege amongst themselves while maintaining similar distinctions with respect to their wives and daughters, she suggests the task is to eliminate the hypocrisy which denies women are fully human (rational beings) and to raise men *and* women to a level at which they are able to relate to each other as equals.

Wollstonecraft's programme for reform clearly places the emphasis on the self-development of the individual woman: "It is time to effect a revolution in female manners— time to restore to them their lost dignity— and make them, as a part of the human species, labour *by reforming themselves* to reform the world."[22] This requires that women be permitted to participate in all areas of political, economic and cultural life. And, as so much of the scholarship on Wollstonecraft emphasizes, the key to "reforming themselves" is education. Lamenting that the "grand source of misery [is] the neglected education of my fellow-creatures," she offers a detailed discussion of what an appropriate education for girls (and boys) should entail.[23] These passages serve to reinforce the traditional view of Wollstonecraft as a bourgeois liberal campaigner for reform.

Any portrait of the first modern feminist that comes to rest here, however, is incomplete; for Wollstonecraft, issues of feminism do not simply revolve around the question of women's denied opportunity for education and their restricted access to civil society. Reform of the education system is impotent in face of the general lack of freedom which characterizes late-eighteenth-century Britain. "Till society be differently constituted," she insists, "much cannot be expected from education."[24] Specifically, Wollstonecraft attacks the system of representation which excludes most men (in addition to all women) from the franchise. But her criticism is not limited to the constitution. Rather, she indicts the system of unequal representation for upholding damaging socio-economic arrangements—arrangements which work to perpetuate the inequality between the sexes. The British system of representation, she notes, is nothing less than "a convenient handle for despotism" which keeps the majority of humanity in the bondage of ignorance.[25] It serves only to maintain the idle rich by taxing the poor. Without a total transformation of society in which people relate to each other as equal partners (in politics and in all else), women's emancipation is impossible.

The egalitarian thrust of Wollstonecraft's work is not a frivolous addition, but an integral element of her feminism. Women simply cannot be free and rational in an irrational world. Elissa Guralnick is thus correct to stress that for the eighteenth-century feminist: "all will *be* right [only when the whole of] society has undergone a radical reordering. In the promise of that reordering lies the extreme political radicalism that is at once the premise and the *sine qua non* of *A Vindication of the Rights of Woman*."[26]

The Radical Edge to Economic Liberalism

It is certain that Wollstonecraft's attack on the broader political order distinguishes her feminism as a radical social critique. The nature of the threat it represents to the social order, however, is not clearly established. Guralnick and Taylor point to the fact that Wollstonecraft's socio-economic critique revolves around an attack on private property. But they both slide too easily from this observation to the claim that Wollstonecraft opposes fundamental features of capitalist social relations—a claim they back with assertions about the inclusiveness of her emancipatory project. Guralnick, for instance, writes that Wollstonecraft "closely associates the betterment of woman's plight with the rise of the *classless* society." And, referring readers to Wollstonecraft's plea for equality, she contends that the eighteenth-century feminist's vision of a rational society translates into a "*total leveling* of distinction among men (and women)."[27]

Taylor, for her part, agrees with this assessment and applauds Wollstonecraft for beginning to overcome "the narrow class assumptions on which so much of the radical tradition was based." She, too, suggests Wollstonecraft's programme was directed to "the social and political liberation of 'the people' as a whole," locating in her egalitarianism "the ideological roots of Socialist feminism."[28] It is not, Taylor believes, that Wollstonecraft consciously articulates a socialist perspective. Rather, its presence in *A Vindication of the Rights of Men* is embryonic. Evidence for this kernel of socialist thought can be found not only in the threat to property represented by the demands of radical democracy, but also in Wollstonecraft's repudiation of commercial society and her condemnation of the inhumanity of industry's drive for profit. As well, Taylor highlights a passage from *A Vindication of the Rights of Men* in which, she claims, Wollstonecraft puts forward "a proposal for a *communalist* society of small peasant-producers which could be established . . . simply by expropriating all the large estates in Britain and redistributing the land *across the entire population.*"[29] For Guralnick and Taylor, Wollstonecraft's radicalism has its roots in an economic critique of property which, if pursued politically, would emancipate women and men from class exploitation. By this reading, Wollstonecraft is indeed a proto-socialist, at least in political economic terms.

The hostility Wollstonecraft expresses toward certain forms of property cannot be denied. In *A Vindication of the Rights of Men* (her reply to Edmund Burke's *Reflections on the Revolution in France*[30]), she castigates those moderns who claim to speak for the rights of all but "bow down to rank, and are careful to secure property." Liberty has yet to be realized anywhere on the globe, she writes, because "the demon of property has ever been at hand to encroach on the sacred rights of men, and to fence round with awful pomp laws that war with justice."[31] Two years later she compares it to a poisoned fountain from which flows "most of the evils and vices which render this world such a dreary scene to the contemplative mind."[32] These are undeniably powerful indictments of the British system of property ownership and, viewed in isolation, could foster the belief that Wollstonecraft's goal is the elimination of private property and the economic leveling of all wealth. But this conclusion is not warranted within the context of Wollstonecraft's work as a whole. Rather than attacking class distinction and possibly setting the stage for a socialist politics of feminism, Wollstonecraft remains wedded to the basic framework of a liberal critique of political economy. As with her radical democratic associates, her ire is directed at the very rich, those who comprise the old authoritative order.

The specific plea for a return to equality and nature which Guralnick cites goes out, not to property owners in general, but specifically to "kings and nobles," to whom Wollstonecraft appeals to "throw off their gaudy *hereditary* trappings." The navy and the clergy come under attack alongside "the sacred majesty of kings" because within these professions men, who are themselves trained to a blind submission to authority, wield power by virtue of the same irrational impulse. The main instrument of class distinction and social oppression is not property itself, but excessive wealth, perpetuated by the unequal system of inheritance. Thus Wollstonecraft's egalitarianism is not an argument for classlessness; rather, it is an indictment of precapitalist British social relations in which distinction is inherited rather than "earned."[33]

But the critique of inheritance is less radical than might be expected: Wollstonecraft does not call for an end to inherited wealth, but for a reform in its practice and an end only to inherited honours. Property passed down the generations is objectionable only if it is tied to rules of primogeniture. Further, contrary to Taylor's suggestion, Wollstonecraft does not advocate the *communalization* of large estates but calls instead for their *parcelization*. The text reads: "Why cannot large estates be divided into small farms? these dwellings would indeed grace our land."[34] Her vision here is of a certain form of private property—the moderate holdings of independent commodity producers. It is a form she also advocates in her discussion of enclosure; engaging in the essentially liberal discourse of improvement which originates with the agrarian concerns of seventeenth-century British liberalism, Wollstonecraft calls for the transformation of common land into individual private farms.[35] The above passage continues:

> Why are huge forests still allowed to stretch out with idle pomp and all the indolence of Eastern grandeur? Why does the brown waste meet the traveller's view, when men want work? But commons cannot be enclosed without *acts of parliament* to increase the property of the rich! Why might not the industrious peasant be allowed to steal a farm from the heath?

Unlike others in her day who responded to poverty and despair of the dispossessed by arguing for the *preservation* of common land, Wollstonecraft is more interested in establishing rights to private property. She argues for their consolidation in a particular, albeit relatively egalitarian, form. In other words, although she challenges the liberal rights claim to unlimited accumulation, Wollstonecraft does not advocate interference with the fundamental precondition of that claim—the right to private property. The proximity of her views to those of the classical liberal political economists is striking. While they did not go so far as to advocate an absolute equality of property, many (including Adam Smith) believed that the competitive system, by its own accord, would result in precisely the relative equality of condition Wollstonecraft endorses—that is, an economy of moderately prosperous independent producers.[36]

Moreover, Wollstonecraft supports this economic liberalism with corresponding social values. Her endorsement of improvement through enclosure has already been noted; she also embraces the quintessentially liberal notion of reward according to merit. Moira Ferguson and Janet Todd suggest Wollstonecraft's ideas are "potentially revolutionary," but they impute a peculiar meaning to this phrase—one that has little to do with a socialist critique of society. Rather, it refers to Wollstonecraft's desire to replace the current system not with classless or communal social relations, but with "a system based on individual talent and reason."[37] Wollstonecraft singles out royalty, the military and noblemen for criticism precisely on the basis that they hold no virtuous (rational) justification for their rank. Distinctions of rank corrupt, she holds, "because respectability is not attached to the discharge of the relative duties of life, but to the station."[38] That merit (measured in accordance with the performance of duties), rather than station, should be the basis of distinction is not a view that sits easily with the classical socialist concept of equality in which wealth is distributed according to need.

Thus, while it is indisputable that Wollstonecraft's criticism of the sacrosanctity of certain forms of property is sometimes bitter, she is not opposed to it in all its manifestations. Far from undermining rights to private property, like her radical contemporaries she assumes their presence and argues for their continuity on a relatively egalitarian basis—but an egalitarianism that is, in fact, limited to a certain class of people: property owners. The class basis of Wollstonecraft's economic model is confirmed and elaborated in her discussion of women's work, working-class women and freedom.

Women's Work, Working-Class Women and Freedom

Wollstonecraft describes the ideal situation as that in which the family is moderately wealthy, able to sustain itself in comfort (although not luxury) with some funds remaining for charitable allowances and the purchase of books. Women find fulfillment as wives and mothers and their education is primarily justified as a means to that fulfillment. Their husbands, who are also their best friends (passionate love is not, she believes, a stable basis for a relationship) and intellectual equals, arrive home from work to a clean and contented household. In fact, the scenario of domesticity Wollstonecraft paints is nothing short of idyllic. She reflects, "I have thought that a couple of this description, equally necessary and independent of each other, because each fulfilled the respective duties of their station, *possessed all that life could give*."[39]

This vision is not very far removed from the life to which the middle classes actually aspired (which, according to Wollstonecraft, was simply a more frivolous version of the same basic structures and relations). And, like the period's middle-class households, Wollstonecraft's ideal rests squarely on a given class relation. Sustaining a household in a moderate degree of comfort, she claims, necessitates the employment of a female servant. For a woman to discharge "the duties of her station" she requires "merely a servant maid to take off her hands the servile part of the household business."[40] Women's emancipation, then, is utterly dependent upon the prior existence of a class of women whose labour power is available to perform the more menial and mundane household chores of the middle classes. It is emancipation of the few at the expense of the many.

More often than not, however, feminist scholars ignore or explain away this assumption of class exploitation in an effort to claim for Wollstonecraft a radical legacy. Zillah Eisenstein, for example, agrees *Vindication* does not directly address the needs of working-class women. Still, she claims, Wollstonecraft's egalitarianism extends to all and thereby successfully provides the conditions of emancipation for poor women, although she fails to explain how Wollstonecraft's appeal for equality overrides her assumption of an economic class of labourers.[41]

Indeed, in a period when most young women worked as domestic servants, Wollstonecraft offers comparatively little discussion of their plight. An important exception is her novel, *The Wrongs of Woman, or Maria*.[42] Here she portrays Jemima, a young servant woman, as lacking the escapes available to the middle-class Maria. Commenting on this novel, Ferguson and Todd write "the tale from beginning to end indicts society, as women's social conditioning, their social (lack of) possibilities, and the inability to work for a decent living reappear in a reformulation of the laboring class."[43] Ferguson and Todd do not suggest that the author harbours anything more than sympathy for the poor, pointing out that "she eschewed concrete proposals for the amelioration of [servants'] condition."[44] Moreover, in Jemima's case, oppression is not resolved through economic independence, but through the heroism of individual strength of character. This, coupled with Wollstonecraft's attachment to the principle of reward for merit, suggests that Wollstonecraft may believe working-class women do not enjoy financial security because they have not earned it.

Her commitment to a class-divided society is reinforced in her comments on women's duties within the household and on education reform. On women's duties, Wollstonecraft writes, "To render the poor virtuous they must be employed, and women in the middle rank of life . . . might employ them, whilst they themselves managed their families, instructed their children, and exercised their own minds." She lists gardening, experimental philosophy and literature as pursuits appropriate to the middle-class woman.[45] And on education, although ahead of her day in advocating schooling for *all* members of society, her proposals are not free of class bias: children from all classes were to begin school at the age of five and pursue a common curriculum to age nine, at which point they are to be "streamed" according to class. Those from the middle class or, as Wollstonecraft calls them, "the young people of superior abilities, or fortune," would study academic subjects, while working-class children would learn the skills appropriate to their station.[46] Feminists often overlook this important qualification to the democratizing of education, and thus exaggerate the degree to which Wollstonecraft stretches a more conventional liberal approach to education. Virginia Miller, for instance, writes, "Progress and education are linked, as for all liberal thinkers, but Wollstonecraft broadens their scope to insist that all citizens be educated. It is significant that she does not exclude the lower classes from this argument either."[47]

I argue above that at the heart of Wollstonecraft's emancipatory project is the nuclear household. But how does she reconcile this commitment to the household with her insistence that women be allowed to use their education to gain economic independence? For Wollstonecraft, after all, it is essential to humanity and consistent with a rational society that women be permitted access to all the occupations. She advocates that they be allowed to work as physicians and nurses or midwives; to study politics and history; to enter into business relationships.[48] These two prescriptions are at odds with one another, for how can a woman be both responsible for the domestic sphere and economically independent?

To what degree Wollstonecraft's individualism contradicts her assumption of traditional sex roles is a question that could feasibly be asked of all liberal theorists who preceded her and many of those who followed. Carole Pateman explores this issue specifically in the work of social contract theorists in *The Sexual Contract*. For these thinkers, the confrontation of the autonomous individual who enjoys rights and freedoms beyond the household with the assumption of household labour and childrearing is resolved at the level of gender, where it becomes clear that the category "individual" is not intended for women at all.[49] For Wollstonecraft, this conflict resides within the individual woman.

The standard resolution to this conflict is to invoke the liberal concept of equality of opportunity. Wollstonecraft, it is claimed, actually intends women to have the option to search for satisfying employment outside the home. And while she fails to explain how this can co-exist with their household duties, "presumably women who wanted to work would do so, and their participation and contribution would necessarily improve the level of civilized society."[50] But the equal opportunity Wollstonecraft endorses is not that simple. First, a whole class of women have been cut off from exercising the right to economic independence: the schooling she proposes for working-class women falls well short of that required to practise medicine or business. Second, Wollstonecraft stresses that although women should be given access to careers, she wants to ensure that access is exercised only by the very few. Women who work outside the home are likely to be single or at least childless, and of "exceptional talent."[51]

Moreover, for the "equal opportunity" thesis to be convincing, the essence of female emancipation for Wollstonecraft would be found neither in motherhood nor careers, but in the *opportunity* for women to choose to live as they will. But this completely misses the moral thrust of *Vindication*. Wollstonecraft's understanding of liberty has little to do with the negative concept implied by the more modern liberal principle of equality of opportunity. Rather, she suggests, a free society must be a virtuous society. Freedom is a positive phenomenon corresponding with a specific code of ethics, which she believes emanates from a rational deity. The moral imperative to do one's duty is definitive of rationality and thus of freedom. Ralph Wardle observes that Wollstonecraft's feminism is informed by a strong sense of ethics: "to Mary politics was always subservient to religion. . . . Unlike most of her fellow radicals she was a devout believer, convinced that the perfection attainable in this world was not the ultimate toward which man should strive, but only a pale shadow of the perfection which God had reserved for him in heaven."[52]

Women, in her view, should be granted equal opportunity, but not in order to do as they will. Equal opportunity must serve a greater end: "the only method of *leading women to fulfill their peculiar duties*, is to free them from all restraint by allowing them to participate in the inherent rights of mankind."[53] That is, while women should be free to be individuals in the so-called public sphere, they are most truly free when they are fulfilling their rational natures. And for all but the exceptional women, that nature (or "their peculiar duties") is found in their roles as wives and mothers: "I consider that women in the common walks of life are called to fulfil the duties of wives and mothers, by religion and reason, I cannot help lamenting that women of a superiour cast have not a road open by which they can pursue more extensive plans of usefulness and independence."[54] For the vast majority of middle-class women, then, motherhood informed by reason is and must be the essence of emancipation. This is not simply the most rational arrangement, it is also the most virtuous.

The Public/Private Dichotomy in Wollstonecraft's Feminism

A number of studies of Wollstonecraft suggest that her critique of the family is in fact a challenge to the very structures which define it as a private, self-regulating, institution. Guralnick, for instance, argues that the connection Wollstonecraft draws between the public and private spheres is inherently radical. She cites Wollstonecraft's analogy of the family and the state ("A man has been termed a microcosm; and every family might also be called a state") as well as her contention that the virtue of the public domain is largely dictated by that of the private as evidence that Wollstonecraft challenges the distinction between the two spheres.[55] Dorothy McBride Stetson agrees: "Wollstonecraft had an *organic* view of the interdependence of all social institutions; separation of public and private spheres was *artificial* and the root of the sorry state of women in the aristocratic circles she observed."[56]

The claim that Wollstonecraft challenges the structural distinction between public and private realms, however, is difficult to accept. She clearly politicizes the family insofar as she mounts a moral critique of the unequal gender relations therein. And because she attributes that inequality to the "irrational" organization of society at large, drawing a link between private and public realms, her moral critique leads to advocacy of structural change: increase women's access to education and careers, and establish a relative equality amongst property holders.

But this manner of politicizing the private realm does not, in itself, *disrupt* the structural separation of public and private spheres that is at the heart of liberalism. First, although she suggests the two spheres do not exist in isolation from each other, in her mind the relationship between them is not particularly problematic. She simply proposes that they are mutually influential with one sphere mirroring the other. To be consistent, Guralnick, McBride Stetson and others would also have to argue that the sixteenth-century political theorist Jean Bodin, for one, shares this radical quality, since he posits exactly the same relation between household and state as Wollstonecraft.

Second, despite endorsing certain types of structural changes, Wollstonecraft sees no reason to blur the distinction between the household and civil society. In fact she argues for its consolidation by confirming a natural sexual division of labour.[57] In their reformed state, the household becomes the fundamental social unit, morally and economically, of the new society: the preservation of "private virtue" (by which she means a marriage between equals that accepts the traditional sexual division of labour) is "the only security of public freedom and universal happiness."[58] Her criticism of domestic arrangements, then, is limited to the effect marriage and the household have on women's character formation. As a result, the reforms she suggests are directed to improving the quality of the individuals within what is considered to be an essential and natural social unit. She would like women to be capable of moving more easily between the household and civil society, but without jeopardizing the sanctity of the former. It is, in fact, not at all clear that Wollstonecraft's ideal rational domestic sphere would be any more politicized or any less isolated from the economic realm, than the irrational sphere she wants it to replace.

In politicizing familial relations in this manner, Wollstonecraft undoubtedly pushes liberalism in a particular, arguably progressive, direction. And in drawing attention to the inequalities of gender, she highlights the fundamental contradiction of liberalism so aptly analyzed by Carole Pateman. But to suggest that she *resolves* (or points to a resolution of) that contradiction by challenging "the *structure* of the family and the *institution* of marriage" or that she "confronted and bridged" the public/private dichotomy is to misread her work and attribute to her a *more* radical position than she in fact held.[59] . . .

Conclusion

Although Wollstonecraft does politicize class and family by advocating radical social re-organization as a precondition of women's emancipation and drawing attention to unequal gender relations within the family, she neither harbours a proto-socialist feminist politics nor a propensity to disrupt the essential distinction between private and public spheres inherent to the liberal tradition. These claims, however, do not diminish the radical quality of her politics. Indeed, the viciousness with which the radical democratic movement was suppressed in the late 1790s (along with the fact that the repression was spearheaded by an economic liberal, William Pitt) is a telling indication of the extent to which such ideas posed, or were perceived to pose, a real threat to the existing order.[60]

Moreover, Wollstonecraft's radicalism *is* based in her politicization of class and family. But we have to be careful to explain the nature of that politicization. Wollstonecraft's economic and moral egalitarianism are radical insofar as they confront the sociohistoric limits of the ruling ideas of her day. It *was* radical to argue for women's essential rationality, their right to education and careers, and to tie those demands to an argument for a relative equality of property in a period when the dominant liberal ideas were heavily influenced by notions of aristocratic privilege and inherited honours. Such demands, like those of her fellow radical democrats, were beyond the historic possibilities imagined by a ruling class composed of those from bourgeois *and aristocratic* backgrounds.

But her radicalism did not threaten the very existence of class and family as institu-tions. The author of *Vindication* is unabashedly committed to the sanctity of private property, and it is this commitment that leads her to endorse the distinction between the private and public spheres as necessary and desirable. In other words, despite an inherent radicalism, Wollstonecraft's feminism is shaped by some of the most fundamental moral and economic principles of liberalism. One needs only to peruse the tracts of the Owenite socialists, written some 30 years later, to gain a sense of a feminist politics that develops out of a theoretical framework which rejects class, private property and a public/private dichotomy.

Notes

1. Between 1951 and the early 1970s, many of the commentaries on Wollstonecraft's life noted her participation in the movement for radical democracy but stressed her reformist aspirations, ignoring her radical socio-economic critique. See, for example, Ralph M. Wardle, *Mary Wollstonecraft: A Critical Biography* (Lawrence: University of Kansas Press, 1951); G. R. Stirling Taylor, *Mary Wollstonecraft: A Study in Economics and Romance* (1911; New York: Haskell House, 1969); H. R. James, *Mary Wollstonecraft: A Sketch* (New York: Haskell House, 1971); and Edna Nixon, *Mary Wollstonecraft: Her Life and Times* (London: Dent, 1971).

2. See, for example, Barbara Taylor, *Eve and the New Jerusalem* (London: Virago, 1983); Elissa Guralnick, "Radical Politics in Mary Wollstonecraft's *A Vindication of the Rights of Woman*," in Mary Wollstonecraft, *A Vindication of the Rights of Woman*, edited by Carol Poston (2d ed.; New York: W. W. Norton, 1988), 308–16; and Virginia Muller, "What Can Liberals Learn from Mary Wollstonecraft?" and Wendy Gunther-Canada, "Mary Wollstonecraft's 'Wild Wish': Confounding Sex in the Discourse on Political Rights," in Maria J. Falco, ed., *Feminist Interpretations of Mary Wollstonecraft* (University Park: The Pennsylvania State University Press, 1996) 47–60; 61–84, respectively.

3. Taylor, *Eve and the New Jerusalem*, 5–6. Admittedly, the proto-socialist position on Wollstonecraft represents a relatively thin current of feminist thought, but it is a current that has passed without challenge. Nor are its representatives insignificant: Barbara Taylor, for

example, is widely accepted as the authority on nineteenth-century socialist feminism. As well, it can be argued, casting Wollstonecraft's work in this light reinforces a more pervasive claim that the demand for women's equality is, in itself, always and everywhere destabilizing—a position articulated early on by Zillah Eisenstein (*The Radical Future of Liberal Feminism* [New York: Longman, 1981]) but evident in more recent scholarship. See, for example, Pamela Grande Jensen, ed., *Finding a New Feminism: Rethinking the Woman Question for Liberal Democracy* (Lanham: Rowman & Littlefield, 1996).

4. For a discussion of the "petty-bourgeois" model and its centrality for both Classical Political Economy and early critics of that tradition, see David McNally, *Against the Market* (London: Verso, 1993).

5. The discussion that follows is necessarily, if regrettably, brief. I have tried to elucidate the key distinctions between socialism and liberalism, as they apply to the issues I raise around Wollstonecraft's politics. For more in-depth analysis, see Stuart Hall, "The State in Question" and David Held, "Central Perspectives on the Modern State" in Gregor McLennan, David Held and Stuart Hall, eds., *The Idea of the Modern State* (Philadelphia: Open University Press, 1984) 1–28; 29–79, respectively.

6. See Ellen Meiksins Wood, "The Separation of the 'Economic' and the 'Political' in Capitalism," *New Left Review* 127 (1981), 66–95.

7. See C. B. MacPherson, *The Political Theory of Possessive Individualism: Hobbes to Locke* (London: Oxford University Press, 1962). As critics of liberalism have convincingly argued, the state is also instrumental in reinforcing the structure and relations of the family (see Carole Pateman, *The Sexual Contract* [Stanford: Stanford University Press, 1988]).

8. Classical socialism here refers to the nineteenth-century utopian and scientific socialists. See George Lichtheim, *The Origins of Socialism* (London: Weidenfeld and Nicolson, 1968).

9. Not all feminists agree that socialism offers a critical analysis of the family. Many reject it as inherently hostile to women's interests—more of an obstacle than an avenue to liberation. Others, however, criticize *socialists* for incorporating sexist assumptions and ignoring the issue of women's oppression, but remain convinced that the basic principles and methodology developed within *socialism* have a great deal to offer women. These feminists have done ground-breaking work on analyzing women's oppression from a socialist perspective in a nonreductionist manner, and have immeasurably enriched the socialist tradition. See, for example, the work of Dorothy Smith, Pat and Hugh Armstrong, Stephanie Coontz and Himani Bannerji.

10. Taylor, *Eve and the New Jerusalem*, 5–7, 17; Muller, "What Can Liberals Learn?" 49, 55–56; and Gunther-Canada, "The Same Subject Continued," 211–12.

11. The literature on the historical and theoretical relationship between nuclear households and capitalism is vast. While early articles were often marred by an uncritical functionalism, more recent work is better attuned to the contradictory nature of social processes. Still, the most convincing accounts of this relationship are historical; even if capitalism does not, strictly speaking, *require* a nuclear household and sexual division of labour, such domestic relations only developed with the beginning of capitalism. Many of the seminal articles on households and capitalism are reproduced in Rosemary Hennessy and Chrys Ingraham, eds., *Materialist Feminism: A Reader in Class, Difference, and Women's Lives* (New York: Routledge, 1997). For an excellent historical account see Bonnie J. Fox, "The Feminist Challenge: A Reconsideration of Social Inequality and Economic Development," in Robert J. Prym and Bonnie J. Fox, eds., *From Culture to Power: The Sociology of English Canada* (Toronto: Oxford University Press, 1989), 120–77.

12. I am not suggesting Wollstonecraft does not politicize both class and family, but simply that she politicizes them by way of a moral critique. However significant a development within liberalism, her critique does not challenge the structural division between public and private spheres on which liberalism depends.

13. Barbara Taylor hints at this meaning of radicalism in arguing that the utopian vision of a world free of all oppression runs up against the reformist limits of bourgeois democracy (*Eve and the New Jerusalem*, 95–96). For an informed discussion of the nature of ruling-class power in the 1790s, see E. P. Thompson, *The Making of the English Working Class* (London: Penguin, 1963); and Roger Wells, *Insurrection: The British Experience 1795–1803* (Gloucester: Alan Sutton, 1983).

14. E. P. Thompson provides a wonderful social history of radical politics in the 1790s in *Making of the English Working Class*. For an insightful account of the links between popular political economy and the tradition of bourgeois political economy, see McNally, *Against the Market*, 43–61.

15. Taylor, *Eve and the New Jerusalem*, 11. According to R. M. Janes, *A Vindication of the Rights of Woman* initially passed largely unnoticed. It was not until Wollstonecraft's lifestyle was made public (with the appearance of Godwin's *Memoirs* in 1798) and the reaction against the French Revolution was in full swing that the book and its author were subjected to such vehement denunciation (R. M. Janes, "On the Reception of Mary Wollstonecraft's *A Vindication of the Rights of Woman*," *Journal of the History of Ideas* 39 [1978], 293–302). For other accounts of *A Vindication of the Rights of Woman*'s reception see Wardle, *Mary Wollstonecraft*, 158–60; Hal Draper, "James Morrison and Working-Class Feminism," in Hal Draper, ed., *Socialism from Below* (Atlantic Highlands, N.J.: Humanities Press, 1992), 226–27.

16. Wollstonecraft, *Vindication*, 9. Hereafter, the word "women" will refer specifically to middle-class women. References to women from other social classes will be made explicit.

17. Ibid., 44.

18. Ibid., 167. She consistently draws an analogy between women and the very wealthy—an important reminder of just how far from her mind the plight of working-class and peasant women often was. See, for instance, 7, 60, 57.

19. Ibid., 53. Without reason, Wollstonecraft argues, women would be animals (rather than persons or moral beings) who live by the rule of brute force. But, she states, "surely there can be but one rule of right, if morality has an eternal foundation." And that one rule is reason. Mankind, she writes, is to be guided by "a rational will that bows only to God" (36).

20. Ibid., 37.

21. Ibid., 18.

22. Ibid., 45; emphasis added.

23. Ibid., 7. For the discussion of education reform see 157–78.

24. Ibid., 21.

25. Ibid., 147. Interestingly, she does not outrightly advocate female suffrage, but only hints that it might not be as preposterous a proposal as she assumes her readership believes.

26. Guralnick, "Radical Politics," 317.

27. Ibid., 314; emphasis added. Guralnick's source is questioned below.

28. Taylor, *Eve and the New Jerusalem*, 6, 5 and 1.

29. Ibid., 6–7; emphases added. The passage to which Taylor refers is found in Wollstonecraft, *A Vindication of the Rights of Men* . . . (2d ed.; London, 1790) reproduced in The Pickering Masters series, Janet Todd and Marilyn Butler, eds., *The Works of Mary Wollstonecraft*, Vol. 5 (London, 1989), 57, hereafter, *Men*. Taylor's interpretation is criticized below.

30. Edmund Burke, *Reflections on the Revolution in France*, edited and introduced by Conor Cruise O'Brien (Penguin: Harmondsworth, 1968).

31. Wollstonecraft, *Men*, 60, 9. To be clear, Wollstonecraft does not include Burke amongst the moderns she condemns. See also Moira Ferguson and Janet Todd, *Mary Wollstonecraft* (Boston: Twayne, 1984), 46.

32. Wollstonecraft, *Vindication*, 140.

33. Ibid., 22; emphasis added; 17–18, 44, 140–41. Guralnick gives two references: Poston, ed., *Vindication*, 22, 38 or pages 38 and 74 of an unspecified early edition, marked London, 1792, of which I found two publications (a 1929 Everyman's Library edition and a 1970 Gregg International edition). Searching the second reference yields nothing that substantiates Guralnick's thesis.

34. Wollstonecraft, *Men*, 57.

35. The centrality of the "improvement discourse" to early liberal theory is ably discussed by Neal Wood in *John Locke and Agrarian Capitalism* (Berkeley: University of California Press, 1984), 15–30.

36. This is the model Smith develops in the early chapters of Book I of *The Wealth of Nations*. Although this model was popularized in the political economy tradition, in later chapters Smith introduces a more complex model. On this point, see David McNally, *Political Economy and the Rise of Capitalism: A Reinterpretation* (Berkeley: University of California Press, 1988), 215–16.

37. Ferguson and Todd, *Mary Wollstonecraft*, 118.

38. Wollstonecraft, *Vindication*, 144.

39. Ibid., 143; emphasis added.

40. Ibid., 142. See also 66.

41. Eisenstein, *The Radical Future of Liberal Feminism*, 98.

42. Mary Wollstonecraft, *The Wrongs of Woman, or Maria*, in Gary Kelly, ed., *Mary, A Fiction & the Wrongs of Woman* (London: Oxford University Press, 1976).

43. Ferguson and Todd, *Mary Wollstonecraft*, 110.

44. Ibid., 122. They write: "In more general terms, Wollstonecraft seems to be saying that an individual, from whatever class, has an internal, events-motivated power that can bring about or at least allow for the possibility of personal, if not economic, autonomy" (111).

45. Wollstonecraft, *Vindication*, 75.

46. Ibid., 169. Wollstonecraft's willingness to advance those of superior abilities softens the naked class bias that underwrites her system to advance those of superior fortune regardless of ability—but only in a manner that is consistent with the liberal principles of merit.

47. Muller, "What Can Liberals Learn?" 53.

48. Wollstonecraft, *Vindication*, 147–49.

49. Neither is it intended for working-class men, although Pateman suggests (I think unconvincingly) that they ultimately are implicated through a fraternity of male power.

50. Ferguson and Todd, *Mary Wollstonecraft*, 122. See also Wardle, *Mary Wollstonecraft*, 154; Gary Kelly, *Revolutionary Feminism: The Mind and Career of Mary Wollstonecraft* (London: Macmillan, 1992), 130; and Syndy McMillen Conger, *Mary Wollstonecraft and the Language of Sensibility* (Toronto: Associated University Press, 1994) 123.

51. Wollstonecraft, *Vindication*, 64. The whole discussion linking work to economic independence is far removed from the reality of working-class women's lives. While plenty of women worked, female wages in the 1790s were not sufficient to provide women with a meaningful level of independence—an issue Wollstonecraft does not consider.

52. Wardle, *Mary Wollstonecraft*, 164. See also Carolyn W. Korsmeyer, "Reason and Morals in the Early Feminist Movement: Mary Wollstonecraft," in Poston, ed., *Vindication*, 285–97.

53. Wollstonecraft, *Vindication*, 175; emphasis added.

54. Ibid., 146–47. She is, on this point, unequivocal: "whatever tends to incapacitate the maternal character, takes woman out of her sphere" (177). Wollstonecraft's suggestion that career woman would be "exceptional" is indicative of an elitist predisposition. Although all persons may be equally capable of great achievements, only a few, those of a "superiour cast," can and should fulfill that potential. Beneath people's apparently equal natures, then, dwells a critical variation in abilities which possibly explains not only the division within the middle class between career women and mothers, but also the division between working- and middle-class women. For her explicit statements on human nature, see 9–10, 23, 42, 51–57. The same elitist predisposition can be traced in John Stuart Mill's work as well. See Paul Smart, *Mill and Marx: Individual Liberty and the Roads to Freedom* (Manchester: Manchester University Press, 1991).

55. Guralnick, "Radical Politics," 314. She cites Wollstonecraft, *Vindication*, 177, 192.

56. Dorothy McBride Stetson, "Women's Rights and Human Rights: Intersection and Conflict," in Falco, ed., *Feminist Interpretations*, 172; emphases added. Similarly, Virginia Muller contends that it is the *structure* of the family and the institution of marriage that Wollstonecraft identifies as the "linchpins of women's problems" ("What Can Liberals Learn?" 55; emphasis added).

57. Wollstonecraft, *Vindication*, 7, 150–52.

58. Ibid., 6.

59. Muller, "What Can Liberals Learn?" 55; emphases added; and McBride Stetson, "Women's Rights," 172.

60. This attack on the established order was predominantly posed in political, rather than economic, terms, with most of the radical democrats either ignoring questions of political economy or endorsing a "petty-bourgeois" model. This, however, in the context of aristocratic privilege and the aftermath of the French Revolution, was sufficient to unleash the full power of the state's repressive arm. That is, the radical democrats were vilified because the authorities feared political democracy would lead to economic leveling (see Wells, *Insurrection*).

Adapted from: Susan Ferguson, "The Radical Ideas of Mary Wollstonecraft." In *Canadian Journal of Political Science*, 23: 3, September 1999, pp. 427–446, 449–450. Copyright © 1999. Reprinted by permission of Susan Ferguson. ✦

Part II

The 19th Century and Beyond

Beginning in the 19th century, the nature of modernity underwent vast and sweeping changes. Old ways of looking at the world seemed less meaningful, less valid, as the French Revolution spread across Europe with the armies of Napoleon. New outlooks emerged as scientists and philosophers struggled to make sense of the world around them. In political theory, for example, the classical formulations of liberalism (found in the theories of John Locke and Adam Smith) had stressed such doctrines as natural rights, *laissez-faire,* and negative freedom. While those doctrines have not disappeared from liberalism, thinkers such as John Stuart Mill (1806–1873) and Thomas Hill Green (1836–1882) began to acknowledge new realities—the rise of mass society, the advent of a psychology of self-fulfillment, and the growing awareness of substantial obstacles to human happiness.

As a result, liberalism in the 19th century took on a more contemporary cast as it began to advocate the desirability of an interventionist government and a positive conception of freedom. Major historical forces such as industrialization, urbanization, and democratization not only transformed liberalism, but they also began to shape all social and political thought. Jeremy Bentham, for example, continued the individualist and ra-

tionalist traditions begun during the Enlightenment, but adapted them for an industrial and democratic society. Thinkers such Henri de Saint-Simon (1760–1825) and Auguste Comte (1798–1857), impressed by the astounding progress of science, embraced the possibility that society could one day be run on a purely rational basis. With aristocratic society showing signs of strain, Alexis de Tocqueville (1805–1859) analyzed the political culture of democracy in America and held that its foundational principle of equality was cause for both concern and celebration. Tensions between rights and responsibilities, between the individual and the community, frequently became the subject of critical thought. Nowhere were those tensions more at issue than in the political ideas emerging from G. W. F. Hegel's (1770–1831) grand synthesis of Western philosophy—the premier effort to transcend the oppositions found in both theory and practice.

Sometimes described as the age of ideologies, the 19th century saw both the extension of rights to the working class in some countries and the brutal exploitation of that same class in others. The presence of dramatic political, social, and economic contradictions (the very stuff of the novels of Charles Dickens and Fyodor Dostoevsky) gave birth to a new form of theory—theory as critique. With the work of theorists such as Karl Marx (1818–1883), Friedrich Nietzsche (1844–1900), and (at the turn of the century) Sigmund Freud (1856–1939), we see the emergence of what the philosopher Paul Ricoeur has called the "hermeneutics of suspicion." These theorists helped remind us that people act from base as well as noble motives, that we often misapprehend and misunderstand the phenomena we encounter, and that things are not always what they seem.

Political Theory in the 20th Century

In many ways, the 20th century began with all of the trends found in the 19th, but then accelerated, intensified, and altered them. World-historical conflicts between liberalism and its opponents, particularly fascism and communism, dramatically shaped the outlooks of political theorists and government officials alike. Industrialization and urbanization gave rise to a mass society, wherein pressures toward conformity and crowd behavior produced some of humanity's worst excesses. Theorists from José Ortega y Gassett (1883–1955) and Michael Oakeshott (1901–1990), on the conservative side, to Hannah Arendt (1906–1975) on the more progressive side all criticized the ideological pressures that permitted and justified totalitarian politics. Despite the challenges to democracy presented by two world wars, the goal of a rational society nonetheless remained front and center in several schools of thought—from the pragmatism of John Dewey (1859–1952) to the neo-Marxist critical theory of Jürgen Habermas (1929–). Suspicion of the motives of political actors and a sense of the pervasive character of power steadily grew as socialization processes, ideological orthodoxies, and the mass media all seemed to shape our outlooks on the world. Indeed, this suspicion grew throughout the last century until postmodern theorists such as Michel Foucault (1926–1984) and Jacques Derrida

(1930–) even began to cast doubt on the very notion of reason itself.

Further, as we entered the last half of the century, challenges to institutions and their ideologies continued to come from nearly every direction. Advocates of traditional values and established social orders, as well as their feminist critics, suggested that liberal democracies lacked a firm moral grounding. Theorists and activists alike rooted the good society in various locations—whether shared values (as in communitarianism), equal consideration and respect (as in contemporary liberalism), or radical individualism (as in a revived anarchism). While we have seen the possibility of firm, indisputable foundations for our beliefs recede, theorists continue to seek some valid standpoint for political theory and practice in everything from the absolutes of fundamentalism to the diversity embodied in multiculturalism.

In sum, political theory today draws on a past that is very much with us even as thinkers quarrel with it and aim to transcend it. As we re-examine the political challenges faced by the theorists to follow and as we confront the new challenges to come in the 21st century, know that political theory has never been a more vital nor a more valuable enterprise.

Further Reading

Bronner, Stephen Eric. 1999. *Ideas in Action: Political Tradition in the Twentieth Century.* Lanham, MD: Rowman & Littlefield.

Gaus, Gerald F. 2000. *Political Concepts and Political Theories.* Boulder, CO: Westview Press.

Kymlicka, Will. 1990. *Contempory Political Philosophy: An Introduction.* Oxford: Clarendon Press.

Portis, Edward Bryan. 1998. *Reconstructing the Classics: Political Theory from Plato to Marx,* 2nd edition. Chatham, NJ: Chatham House.

Tannenbaum, Donald G., and David Schultz. 1998. *Inventors of Ideas: An Introduction to Western Political Philosophy.* New York: St. Martin's. ✦

Georg Wilhelm Friedrich Hegel

In the last few decades, interest in the philosophy of G. W. F. Hegel has undergone a substantial revival. His ideas have been used to develop a less deterministic brand of Marxism, criticize liberalism for its excessive individualism, and even proclaim that history came to an end with the fall of Communist regimes in Eastern Europe. Though part of the Hegel revival can be attributed to intellectual fashion, Hegel's widespread influence on many significant philosophical and political traditions cannot be denied. Indeed, his rational syntheses of thought in philosophy, history, and politics provide an excellent starting point for understanding various intellectual trends from communitarianism to postmodernism.

However, Hegel's name sends shivers down the spine of almost any philosopher or political theorist. The complexity of Hegel's work frequently challenges even the most advanced student of political theory, and his verbose, ponderous writing style is difficult to comprehend because he uses a unique philosophical language. Often his verbal monsters hide very simple ideas, and once one deciphers the code in which Hegel speaks, his thoughts can be understood. In many respects, reading Hegel is like beginning an exercise program—the basic rule of thumb is "no pain, no gain."

Hegel was born in 1770 in Stuttgart in what is now Germany, though at the time it was part of the duchy of Württemberg. In 1788, he began his study of philosophy and theology at the seminary in Tübingen, and after graduation, became a private tutor in both Switzerland and Germany. Struggling to make a living as a man of letters and teacher, Hegel served initially as an unpaid lecturer in philosophy at the University of Jena in 1801. There, interacting with such philosophers as Fichte and Schelling, he began to develop his own system of thought—a system first articulated in the *Phenomenology of Spirit* (1807). After fathering an illegitimate child, and still struggling financially, Hegel served as rector of the *Gymnasium* in Nuremberg until he took a paid professorship at the university in Heidelberg. The peak of Hegel's philosophical career, and the completion of his system of thought, both occured after he earned a prestigious appointment at the University of Berlin, where he wrote and lectured from 1818 until his death in 1831.

Hegel's thought can be seen as a philosophical effort to overcome the tensions or oppositions between human beings and nature, between the individual and society, between human beings as they are and as they ought to be, or between finite and infinite spirit. These oppositions cannot be undone in any simple fashion, since we cannot return to an original state of unity. Instead, Hegel's "aspiration is to retain the fruits of separation, free rational consciousness, while reconciling this with unity, that is, society, God and fate."[1]

Hegel's tool of choice for reconciling these oppositions is the dialectic, often stereotyped as the sterile formula of Thesis-Antithesis-Synthesis. Yet the dialectic is better understood as (1) a dynamic unity of opposites, in which the world is a developmental unfolding of partial, yet essential natures, or (2) a method of probing ideas and phenomena for their internal contradictions in order to arrive at comprehensive knowledge of the whole. From this standpoint, Hegel sees the universe as an expression and an embodiment of *Geist* (Spirit). His view is that *Geist* creates (that is, "posits") the world in order to realize itself, to express and thereby understand the full range of its powers. Since this expression creates a world apart from

Geist, history becomes the story of efforts by human beings to fully understand both themselves and the material world as various forms of *Geist*. The unity of creation and creator can only be restored when the universe is finally seen as operating by rational necessity, when we understand that the world cannot be other than it is and still be rational. Of course, by then, the story itself will be at an end; Absolute Knowledge, for Hegel, is always retrospective.

The Philosophy of History

Hegel produced a remarkably consistent philosophical system, whose parts form a seamless web. For our purposes, though, we will have to treat his philosophy of history and politics apart from his epistemology and logic. The first selection comes from Hegel's introduction to the *Lectures on the Philosophy of History* (1837), edited notes taken by students from Hegel's lectures in Berlin. As he observes in the introduction, Hegel seeks to demonstrate that reason rules the world, that it directs the specific, concrete aspects of history (whether good or bad, positive or negative) toward an identifiable end. As such, Hegel believes that through various stages of development, one can see that the fundamental reality of world history is Spirit's progressive consciousness of freedom. Since *Geist* acts through humans, though, the "slaughter-bench" of world history is actually a rational process by which people come to realize universal freedom.

The Philosophy of Right

Hegel's political theory was most clearly detailed in his 1820 work, the *Philosophy of Right*. There, Hegel begins by outlining the philosopher's task of comprehending the concrete aspects of political life, of developing a theory of the rational state. After pursuing the idea of Right through the "moments" (dialectical stages of development) of morality and abstract right, Hegel seeks to outline a social order (labeled "ethical life" or *Sittlichkeit*) which would overcome the oppositions between individual and society, between particular and universal wills, and

between right and duty. Emerging out of the unreflective unity of the family, a person becomes an individual pursuing his or her unique needs in civil society—the realm of economic activity and private welfare, safeguarded by the structures of civil and criminal law. These structures themselves depend upon the state, ideally organized as a constitutional monarchy. For Hegel, that idealized state functions as a rational, overarching unity of our particular and universal interests.

Commentaries

The selections from Charles Taylor's interpretive survey analyze the general outlines of both Hegel's philosophy of history and his theory of the state. Taylor first discusses the dialectical unfolding of Spirit through various civilizations. He also shows how Hegel's philosophy of history yields important lessons for political theory, namely, the need for the modern state to consist of a constitutional monarch, a trained bureaucracy, and a people organized into estates or classes. Taylor then summarizes the opening parts of *The Philosophy of Right* and outlines Hegel's views on the family, civil society, and the state.

Kenneth Westphal's essay provides further in-depth discussion of the ideas expressed in *The Philosophy of Right*. He begins by noting Hegel's disagreements with several political theories—namely, conservatism, romanticism, and liberalism. Though Hegel could not accept any one of these points of view, he nonetheless saw enough merit in each to derive from them his central idea that freedom can only be realized in a community. Westphal then presents a summary of Hegel's arguments concerning "abstract right," "morality," and "ethical life." The structure and substance of *The Philosophy of Right* suggest that Hegel's chief concern is to combat the fragmentation of modern life (rooted in the pursuit of economic self-interest) by creating institutions that promote both autonomy and community.

Note

1. Charles Taylor, *Hegel* (Cambridge: Cambridge University Press, 1975), 79.

Web Sources

http://www.marxists.org/reference/archive/hegel/
Hegel Resource. Selected works by and about Hegel.

http://www.historyguide.org/intellect/hegel.html
The History Guide: Lectures on Modern European Intellectual History. Introduction to Hegel's life and thought.

http://www.susx.ac.uk/Units/philosophy/chitty/hegel.html#politics
A Hegel Bibliography. An extensive bibliography, organized by philosophical topics.

Class Activities and Discussion Items

1. Gather information about a world-historical event of your choosing. Discuss how the event appeared to people at the time, and then compare and contrast those understandings with ours. Frame this discussion in light of Hegel's thinking about the role of reason in history and his comment about the "owl of Minerva."

2. Read and discuss the core argument of Francis Fukuyama's *The End of History and the Last Man* (New York: Free Press, 1992). Did Fukuyama interpret Hegel correctly in identifying the fall of Communism and the triumph of liberalism as "the end of history?" Why or why not?

3. What role does the dialectic play in Hegel's thought? Give examples of its use in both *The Philosophy of History* and *The Philosophy of Right*.

4. What sort of political system did Hegel favor? For what reasons? Do his political ideas have any bearing on contemporary politics?

Further Reading

Marcuse, Herbert. 1960. *Reason and Revolution: Hegel and the Rise of Social Theory.* Boston: Beacon Press. Classic discussion of Hegel from a leading exponent of critical theory.

Mills, Patricia J., ed. 1996. *Feminist Interpretations of G. W. F. Hegel.* University Park: Pennsylvania State University Press. Considerations of gender and politics in Hegel's thought.

Pinkard, Terry. 2000. *Hegel: A Biography.* Cambridge: Cambridge University Press. Excellent, detailed discussion of Hegel's life and works.

Smith, Steven B. 1989. *Hegel's Critique of Liberalism: Rights in Context.* Chicago: University of Chicago Press. Argues that Hegel's concept of right is fundamentally a right of recognition, of equal concern and respect for persons.

Williams, Robert R. 1997. *Hegel's Ethics of Recognition.* Berkeley: University of California Press. Uses the concept of intersubjective recognition to explore the nature and contributions of Hegel's thought. ✦

21
Excerpts from *The Philosophy of History*

Georg Wilhelm Friedrich Hegel

Chapter Two: Reason in History

The only thought which philosophy brings with it, in regard to history, is the simple thought of Reason—the thought that Reason rules the world, and that world history has therefore been rational in its course. This conviction and insight is a *presuppostion* in regard to history as such, although it is not a presupposition in philosophy itself.

In philosophy, speculative reflection has shown that Reason is the *substance* as well as the *infinite power*; that Reason is for itself the *infinite material* of all natural and spiritual life, as well as the *infinite form*, and that its actualization of itself is its content. (And we can stand by the term "Reason" here, without examining its relation and connection with "God" more closely.)

Thus Reason is the *substance* [of our historic world] in the sense that it is that whereby and wherein all reality has its being and subsistence. It is the *infinite power*, since Reason is not so powerless as to arrive at nothing more than the ideal, the ought, and to remain outside reality—who knows where—as something peculiar in the heads of a few people. Reason is the *infinite content*, the very stuff of all essence and truth, which it gives to its own *activity* to be worked up. For, unlike finite activity, it does not need such conditions as an external material, or given means from which to get its nourishment and the objects of its activity. It lives on itself, and it is itself the material upon which it works. Just as Reason is its own presuppo-

sition and absolute goal, so it is the activation of that goal in world history—bringing it forth from the inner source to external manifestation, not only in the natural universe but also in the spiritual. That this Idea is the True, the Eternal, simply the Power—that it reveals itself in the world, and that nothing else is revealed in the world but that Idea itself, its glory and majesty—this, as we said, is what has been shown in philosophy, and it is here presupposed as already proven.

Those of you who are not yet acquainted with philosophy can at least be expected to come to these lectures on world history with the belief in Reason, with the desire, the thirst to know it. And indeed what must be presupposed as a subjective need in the study of the sciences is the desire for rational insight, for knowledge, not merely for a collection of facts. Thus, even if you do not bring to world history the thought and the knowledge of Reason, you ought at least to have the firm and unconquerable belief that there is Reason in history, together with the belief that the world of intelligence and self-conscious will is not subject to chance, but rather that it must demonstrate itself in the light of the self-conscious Idea.

But in fact I need not require this belief on your part in advance. What I have said so far, and will say again, is not just to be taken as a presupposition of our science, but as a summary of the totality—as the *result* of the discussion upon which we are embarking, a result that is known to *me* because I already know that totality. Thus it is the consideration of world history itself that must reveal its rational process—namely, that it has been the rational necessary course of the World Spirit, the Spirit whose nature is indeed always one and the same, but which reveals this one nature in the world's reality. As I said, this must be the outcome of the study of history.

Yet we must take history as it is, and proceed historically, i.e., empirically. Among other things, we must not be misled by the professional historians, particularly the Germans, who possess great authority, and do precisely what they accuse philosophers of doing, namely creating *a priori* fabrications in history. For example, there is a widespread fabrication that there existed an original, primeval people, taught directly by God and having complete insight and wisdom, with a penetrating knowledge of all the laws of nature and spiritual truth; or that there were such or such priestly peoples; or, to speak of something more specific, that there was a Roman epic from which the Roman historians drew their earliest history, and so on. Let us leave all such *a priori* constructions to the clever professionals, for whom (in Germany) such constructions are not uncommon.

As the first condition to be observed, we could therefore declare that we must apprehend the historical faithfully. But with such general terms as "apprehend" and "faithfully" there lies an ambiguity. Even the ordinary, average historian, who believes and says that he is merely receptive to his data, is not passive in his thinking; he brings his categories along with him, and sees his data through them. In every treatise that is to be scientific, Reason must not slumber, and reflection must be actively applied. To him who looks at the world rationally, the world looks rational in return. The relation is mutual. But the various kinds of reflection, of possible viewpoints, of judgment even in regard to the mere importance and unimportance of facts (the most basic category in historical judgment)—all this does not concern us here. . . .

In world history, however, we are concerned with "individuals" that are nations, with wholes that are states. Accordingly, we cannot stop at the (so to speak) "retail" version of the belief in providence—still less can we be content with the merely abstract, indefinite belief which goes only so far as the general view that there is a providence, and says nothing of its more definite acts. On the contrary, we must seriously try to recognize the ways of providence, and to connect its means and manifestations in history—relating these to that universal principle.

But in mentioning the possibility of our knowing the plan of divine providence in general, I have touched on a question that has become prominent in our own time: the question about the possibility of our knowing God—or, inasmuch as it has ceased to be a question, there is the doctrine (which has now become a prejudice) that it is impossible to know God. Holy Scripture commands it as our highest duty not only to love God but also to know God. But in direct opposition to this, there now prevails the denial of what is there written: that it is the Spirit that leads us to truth, that the Spirit knows all things and penetrates even to the depths of the Godhead.[1]

When the Divine Being is placed beyond the reach of our knowing and beyond human affairs altogether, we gain the convenience of indulging in our own imaginings. We are thereby excused from having to give our knowledge some relation to the Divine and the True. On the contrary, the vanity of human knowledge and subjective feeling receives a complete justification for itself. And when pious humility places the knowing of God at a distance, it knows full well what it has thereby gained for its arbitrariness and vain efforts.

I could not avoid mentioning the connection between our thesis (that Reason rules the world and has ruled it) and the question about the possibility of our knowing God, since I did not want to dodge the accusation that philosophy shuns (or must shun) all discussion of religious truths due to a bad conscience about them. On the contrary, in modern times we have come to the point where philosophy has to take up the defense of religious truths against many types of theological doctrine. In the Christian religion God has revealed Himself: that is to say, He has allowed human beings to understand what He is, so that He is no longer hidden and secret. With this possibility of our knowing God, the obligation to know Him is placed upon us. God wants no narrow-minded souls and empty heads for His children. Rather, He wants those who (however poor in spirit) are rich in the knowledge of Him, and who place the highest value in this knowledge of Him. The development of the thinking spirit, which began from this basis in the revelation of the Divine Being, must finally come to the point where what was originally present only to feeling and to the imagining spirit, can now be grasped by thought. And the time must finally come when we comprehend the rich product of creative Reason that is world history.

For some time, it was customary to admire God's wisdom at work in animals, in plants, and in the destinies of individuals. If we grant that providence reveals itself in such objects and materials, then why not also in world history? Here, the material seems too great. Yet the divine wisdom, i.e., Reason, is one and the same on the large scale and on the small, and we must not consider God to be too weak to apply His wisdom on a large scale. In our knowledge, we aim for the insight that whatever was intended by the Eternal Wisdom has come to fulfillment—as in the realm of nature, so in the realm of spirit that is active and actual in the world. To that extent our approach is a theodicy, a justification of the ways of God. Leibniz attempted a theodicy in metaphysical terms, using indefinite abstract categories—so that when once the evil in the world was comprehended in this way, the thinking mind was supposed to be reconciled to it. Nowhere, in fact, is there a greater challenge to such intellectual reconciliation than in world history. This reconciliation can be achieved only through the recognition of that positive aspect, in which the negative disappears as something subordinate and overcome. It is attained (on the one hand) through the awareness of the true end-goal of the world, and (on the other) through the awareness that this end has been actualized in the world and that the evil has not prevailed in it in any ultimate sense.

For this purpose, however, the mere belief in *nous* and providence is still quite inadequate. "Reason"—which is said to rule the world—is just as indefinite a term as "Providence." We hear Reason spoken of, without anyone being able to say just what its definition is, or its content (according to which we could judge whether something is rational or irrational). To grasp Reason in its definition—that is of primary importance. If we merely stick to the bare term, "Reason", throughout, the rest of what we say is just words. With these declarations behind us, we can go on to the second viewpoint we wish to consider in this Introduction.

Chapter Three: Freedom, the Individual, and the State

If we think of Reason in its relation to the world, then the question of the *definition* of Reason in itself coincides with the question about the *final goal* of the world. Implicit in that latter term is the suggestion that the goal is to be realized, made actual. There are two things to be considered here: the content of that goal (i.e., the definition itself, as such), and its actualization.

At the outset we must note that our object—*world history*—takes place in the realm of Spirit. The term "world" includes both physical and mental nature. Physical nature impinges on world history as well, and from the very beginning we shall have to draw attention to the fundamental relations [between the two natures] in the definition. But it is Spirit, and the process of its development, that is the substance of history. Nature in itself, which is likewise a rational system in its particular and characteristic element, is not our concern here, except as related to Spirit.

Spirit is to be observed in the theater of world history, where it has its most concrete reality. In spite of this, however (or rather in order for us to grasp the universal aspect in this mode of Spirit's concrete reality), we must set forth, before all else, some abstract definitions of the *nature of Spirit*. These can, of course, be no more than mere assertions here. This is not the place to go into the Idea of Spirit in a speculative fashion, for what can be said in an introduction is simply to be taken historically—as a presupposition which (as we said) has either been worked out and proven elsewhere, or else is to receive its verification only as the outcome of the science of history itself.

We have therefore to address the following topics:

 I. The abstract characteristics of the nature of Spirit

 II. The means Spirit uses in order to realize its Idea

 III. The shape taken on by Spirit in its complete realization in the world—the State.

I. THE NATURE OF SPIRIT. This can be seen by looking at its complete antithesis—matter. Just as the essence of matter is gravity [that is, in being determined by a force outside it], so the essence of Spirit is its freedom [that is, in its self-determination]. Everyone will immediately agree that Spirit is endowed with freedom, among other characteristics. Philosophy, however, teaches us that all the characteristics of Spirit subsist only by means of freedom; that all of them are only the means to freedom, and that they seek and produce only freedom. This is one of the truths of speculative philosophy: that freedom is the only truth of Spirit.

Matter has weight insofar as it strives toward a central point outside itself. It is essentially composed of parts which are separable. It seeks its unity, which would be its own negation, its opposite. If it were to achieve this, it would no longer be matter but would have perished. It strives toward the ideal, for in unity [i.e., in being self-determining, self-moving], matter is idealized.

Spirit, on the other hand, is that which has its center in itself. Its unity is not outside itself; rather, it has found it within its own self. It is in its own self and alone unto itself. While matter has its "substance" [i.e., its source of support] outside itself, Spirit is autonomous and self-sufficient, a Being-by-itself (*Bei-sich-selbst-sein*). But this, precisely, is freedom—for when I am dependent, I relate myself to something else, something which I am not; as dependent, I cannot be without something which is external. I am free when I exist independently, all by myself. This self-sufficient being is self-consciousness, the consciousness of self.

Two things must be distinguished in consciousness: first, the fact *that* I know; and second, *what* I know. In self-consciousness, the two—subject and object—coincide. Spirit knows itself: it is the judging of its own nature, and at the same time it is the activity of coming to itself, of producing itself, making itself actually what it is in itself potentially.

According to this abstract definition, we can say of world history that it is the exhibition of the Spirit, the working out of the explicit knowledge of what it is potentially. Just as the germ of the plant carries within itself the entire nature of the tree, even the taste and shape of its fruit, so the first traces of Spirit virtually contain all history.

In the world of the ancient Orient, people do not yet know that the Spirit—the human as such—is free. Because they do not know this, they are not free. They know only that *one* person is free; but for this very reason such freedom is mere arbitrariness, savagery, stupified passion; or even a softness or tameness of passion, which is itself a mere accident of nature and therefore quite arbitrary. This *one* person is therefore only a despot, not a free man.

·It was among the Greeks that the consciousness of freedom first arose, and thanks to that consciousness they were free. But they, and the Romans as well, knew only that *some* persons are free, not the human as such. Even Plato and Aristotle did not know this. Not only did the Greeks have slaves, therefore—and Greek life and their splendid freedom were bound up with this—but their freedom itself was partly a matter of mere chance, a transient and limited flowering, and partly a hard servitude of the human and the humane.

It was first the Germanic peoples, through Christianity, who came to the awareness that *every* human is free by virtue of being human, and that the freedom of spirit comprises our most human nature. This awareness arose first in religion, in the innermost region of Spirit. But to introduce this principle into worldly reality as well: that was a further task, requiring long effort and civilization to bring it into being. For example, slavery did not end immediately with the acceptance of the Christian religion; freedom did not suddenly prevail in Christian states; nor were governments and constitutions organized on a rational basis, or indeed upon the principle of freedom.

This application of the principle of freedom to worldly reality—the dissemination of this principle so that it permeates the worldly situation—this is the long process that makes up history itself. I have already drawn attention to the distinction between a principle as such and its application, its introduction and implementation in the actuality of spirit and life. This distinction is fundamental to our science, and it must be kept in mind. Just as this distinction was noted in a preliminary way with regard to the Christian principle of self-consciousness and freedom, so it has its essential place in regard to the principle of freedom in general. World history is the progress in the consciousness of freedom—a progress that we must come to know in its necessity.

Above, I made a general statement regarding the different levels in the awareness of freedom—namely, that the Orientals knew only that *one* person is free; the Greeks and Romans that *some* are free; while *we* know that *all* humans are implicitly free, *qua* human. At the same time, this statement gives us the division of world history and the basis for our consideration of it. But this is noted merely provisionally and in passing. We must first explain some other concepts.

The *final goal of the world*, we said, is Spirit's consciousness of its freedom, and hence also the actualization of that very freedom. This, then, is what characterizes the spiritual world—and this therefore is the substantially real world, to which the physical world is subordinate (or, to say this in speculative terms, the physical world has no truth as against the spiritual). But this "freedom," as so far described, is itself indefinite and infinitely ambiguous. As the highest of concepts it carries with it infinitely many misunderstandings, confusions and errors, and comprises all possible excesses within it. Never has all this been better known and felt than at the present time. For the time being, however, we must content ourselves with using it in that general sense.

We have also drawn attention to the importance of the infinite difference between the principle, which is as yet merely implicit, and that which is real. But at the same time it is freedom in itself that contains the infinite necessity of bringing itself to consciousness (for in its very concept it is knowledge of itself) and thereby to reality. Freedom is for itself the goal to be achieved, and the only goal of Spirit.

It is this final goal—freedom—toward which all the world's history has been working. It is this goal to which all the sacrifices have been brought upon the broad altar of the earth in the long flow of time. This is the one and only goal that accomplishes itself and fulfills itself—the only constant in the change of events and conditions, and the truly effective thing in them all. It is this goal that is God's will for the world. But God is the absolutely perfect Being, and He can therefore will nothing but Himself, His own will. The nature of His will, however—i.e., His own nature, that is what we are here calling the Idea of freedom (since we are translating the religious image into philosophic thought). The question that now follows immediately, then, can be this: What means does this Idea of freedom use for its realization? This is the second point to be considered.

II. THE MEANS OF SPIRIT. This question—as to the *means* whereby freedom develops itself into a world—leads us into the phenomenon of history itself. While freedom as such is primarily an internal concept, its means are external: namely, the phenomena which present themselves directly before our eyes in history. Our first look at history convinces us that the actions of human beings stem from their needs, their passions, their interests, their characters and talents. And it appears that the only springs of action in this theater of activity, and the mainsprings, are these needs, passions, and interests. Of course, the play also involves universal aims, benevolence, noble patriotism, and so on. But these virtues and their universality are insignificant in their relation to the world and its doings.

We might well see the ideal of Reason realized in these subjective individuals themselves and in their sphere of influence, but individuals are of slight importance compared to the mass of the human race; likewise, the scope of their virtues is relatively restricted in its range. Instead, it is the passions, the aims of particular interests, the satisfaction of selfish desire that are the most forceful things. They get their power from the fact that they observe none of the limits which the law and morality would seek to impose upon them—and from the fact that these forces of nature are closer and more immediate to human beings than the artificial and tedious discipline toward order and moderation, toward law and morality.

When we look at this drama of human passions, and observe the consequences of their violence and of the unreason that is linked not only to them but also (and especially) to good intentions and rightful aims; when we see arising from them all the evil, the wickedness, the decline of the most flourishing nations mankind has produced, we can only be filled with grief for all that has come to nothing. And since this decline and fall is not merely the work of nature but of the will of men, we might well end with moral outrage over such a drama, and with a revolt of our good spirit (if there is a spirit of goodness in us). Without rhetorical exaggeration, we could paint the most fearful picture of the misfortunes suffered by the noblest of nations and states as well as by private virtues—and with that picture we could arouse feelings of the deepest and most helpless sadness, not to be outweighed by any consoling outcome. We can strengthen ourselves against this, or escape it, only by thinking that, well, so it was at one time; it is fate; there is nothing to be done about it now. And finally—in order to cast off the tediousness that this reflection of sadness could produce in us and to return to involvement in our own life, to the present of our own aims and interests—we return to the selfishness of standing on a quiet shore where we can be secure in enjoying the distant sight of confusion and wreckage.

But as we contemplate history as this slaughter-bench, upon which the happiness of nations, the wisdom of states, and the virtues of individuals were sacrificed, the question necessarily comes to mind: What was the ultimate goal for which these monstrous sacrifices were made? And from this there usually follows the question which we made the starting-point of our consideration. And in this perspective the events that present such a grim picture for our troubled feeling and thoughtful reflection have to be seen as the *means* for what we claim is the substantial definition, the absolute end-goal or, equally, the true *result* of world history. . . .

Note

1. See I Corinthians 2:10. "God has revealed these things to us through the Spirit. For the Spirit searches all things, even the depths of God." [Translator's note.]

Adapted from: Georg Wilhelm Friedrich Hegel, *The Philosophy of History*, translated by Leo Rauch, pp. 12–14, 16–24. Hackett Publishing Company, Inc., 1988. ✦

22

Excerpts from *The Philosophy of Right*

Georg Wilhelm Friedrich Hegel

Preface

. . . It is therefore to be taken as a piece of *luck* for philosophic science—though in actual fact, as I have said, it is the *necessity* of the thing—that this philosophizing which like an exercise in scholasticism might have continued to spin its web in seclusion, has now been put into closer touch and so into open variance with actuality, in which the principles of rights and duties are a serious matter, and which lives in the light of its consciousness of these.

It is just this placing of philosophy in the actual world which meets with misunderstandings, and so I revert to what I have said before, namely that, since philosophy is the exploration of the rational, it is for that very reason the apprehension of the present and the actual, not the erection of a beyond, supposed to exist, God knows where, or rather which exists, and we can perfectly well say where, namely in the error of a one-sided, empty, ratiocination. In the course of this book, I have remarked that even Plato's *Republic*, which passes proverbially as an empty ideal, is in essence nothing but an interpretation of the nature of Greek ethical life. Plato was conscious that there was breaking into that life in his own time a deeper principle which could appear in it directly only as a longing still unsatisfied, and so only as something corruptive. To combat it, he needs must have sought aid from that very longing itself. But this aid had to come from on High and all that Plato could do was to seek it in the first place in a particular external form of that same Greek ethical life. By that means he thought to master this cor-

ruptive invader, and thereby he did fatal injury to the deeper impulse which underlay it, namely free infinite personality. Still, his genius is proved by the fact that the principle on which the distinctive character of his idea of the state turns is precisely the pivot on which the impending world revolution turned at that time.

What is rational is actual and what is actual is rational.[1] On this conviction the plain man like the philosopher takes his stand, and from it philosophy starts in its study of the universe of mind as well as the universe of nature. If reflection, feeling, or whatever form subjective consciousness may take, looks upon the present as something vacuous and looks beyond it with the eyes of superior wisdom, it finds itself in a vacuum, and because it is actual only in the present, it is itself mere vacuity. If on the other hand the Idea passes for 'only an Idea', for something represented in an opinion, philosophy rejects such a view and shows that nothing is actual except the Idea. Once that is granted, the great thing is to apprehend in the show of the temporal and transient the substance which is immanent and the eternal which is present. For since rationality (which is synonymous with the Idea) enters upon external existence simultaneously with its actualization,[2] it emerges with an infinite wealth of forms, shapes, and appearances. Around its heart it throws a motley covering with which consciousness is at home to begin with, a covering which the concept has first to penetrate before it can find the inward pulse and feel it still beating in the outward appearances. But the infinite variety of circumstance which is developed in this externality by the light of the essence glinting in it—this endless material and its organization—this is not the subject matter of philosophy. To touch this at all would be to meddle with things to which philosophy is unsuited; on such topics it may save itself the trouble of giving good advice. Plato might have omitted his recommendation to nurses to keep on the move with infants and to rock them continually in their arms. And Fichte too need not have carried what has been called the 'construction' of his passport regulations to such a pitch of perfection as to require suspects not merely to sign their passports but to have their likenesses painted on them. Along such tracks all trace of philosophy is lost, and such super-erudition it can the more readily disclaim since its attitude to this infinite multitude of topics should of course be most liberal. In adopting this attitude, philosophic science shows itself to be poles apart from the hatred with which the folly of superior wisdom regards a vast number of affairs and institutions, a hatred in which pettiness takes the greatest delight because only by venting it does it attain a feeling of its selfhood.

This book, then, containing as it does the science of the state, is to be nothing other than the endeavour to apprehend and portray the state as something inherently rational. As a work of philosophy, it must be poles apart from an attempt to construct a state as it ought to be. The instruction which it may contain cannot consist in teaching the state what it ought to be; it can only show how the state, the ethical universe, is to be understood.

ἰδοὺ Ῥόδος ἰδοὺ καὶ τὸ πήδημα

Hic Rhodus, *hic* saltus.[3]

To comprehend what is, this is the task of philosophy, because what is, is reason. Whatever happens, every individual is a child of his time; so philosophy too is its own time apprehended in thoughts. It is just as absurd to fancy that a philosophy can transcend its contemporary world as it is to fancy that an individual can overleap his own age, jump over Rhodes. If his theory really goes beyond the world as it is and builds an ideal one as it ought to be, that world exists indeed, but only in his opinions, an unsubstantial element where anything you please may, in fancy, be built.

With hardly an alteration, the proverb just quoted would run:

Here is the rose, dance thou here.[4]

What lies between reason as self-conscious mind and reason as an actual world before our eyes, what separates the former from the latter and prevents it from finding satisfaction in the latter, is the fetter of some abstraction or other which has not been liberated [and so transformed] into the concept. To recognize reason as the rose in the cross of the present[5] and thereby to enjoy the present, this is the rational insight which reconciles us to the actual, the reconciliation which philosophy affords to those in whom there has once arisen an inner voice bidding them to comprehend, not only to dwell in what is substantive while still retaining subjective freedom, but also to possess subjective freedom while standing not in anything particular and accidental but in what exists absolutely.[6]

It is this too which constitutes the more concrete meaning of what was described above rather abstractly as the unity of form and content; for form in its most concrete signification is reason as speculative knowing, and content is reason as the substantial essence of actuality, whether ethical or natural. The known identity of these two is the philosophical Idea. It is a sheer obstinacy, the obstinacy which does honour to mankind, to refuse to recognize in conviction anything not ratified by thought. This obstinacy is the characteristic of our epoch, besides being the principle peculiar to Protestantism. What Luther initiated as faith in feeling and in the witness of the spirit, is precisely what spirit, since become more mature, has striven to apprehend in the concept in order to free and so to find itself in the world as it exists to-day. The saying has become famous that 'a half-philosophy leads away from God'—and it is the same half-philosophy that locates knowledge in an 'approximation' to truth—'while true philosophy leads to God'; and the same is true of philosophy and the state. Just as reason is not content with an approximation which, as something 'neither cold nor hot', it will 'spue out of its mouth', so it is just as little content with the cold despair which submits to the view that in this earthly life things are truly bad or at best only tolerable, though here they cannot be improved and that this is the only reflection which can keep us at peace with the world: There is less chill in the peace with the world which knowledge supplies.

One word more about giving instruction as to what the world ought to be. Philosophy in any case always comes on the scene too late to give it. As the thought of the world, it appears only when actuality is already there cut and dried after its process of formation has been completed. The teaching of the concept, which is also history's inescapable lesson, is that it is only when actuality is mature that the ideal first appears over against the real and that the ideal apprehends this same real world in its substance and builds it up for itself into the shape of an intellectual realm. When philosophy paints its grey in grey, then has a shape of life grown old. By philosophy's grey in grey it cannot be rejuvenated but only understood. The owl of Minerva spreads its wings only with the falling of the dusk.

But it is time to close this preface. After all, as a preface, its only business has been to make some external and subjective remarks about the standpoint of the book it introduces. If a topic is to be discussed philosophically, it spurns any but a scientific and objective treatment, and so too if criticisms of the author take any form other than a scientific discussion of the thing itself, they can count only as a personal epilogue and as capricious assertion, and he must treat them with indifference.

Berlin, June 25th, 1820. . . .

Third Part: Ethical Life

142. Ethical life is the Idea of freedom in that on the one hand it is the good become alive—the good endowed in self-consciousness with knowing and willing and actualized by self-conscious action—while on the other hand self-consciousness has in the ethical realm its absolute foundation and the end which actuates its effort. Thus ethical life is the concept of freedom developed into the existing world and the nature of self-consciousness.

143. Since this unity of the concept of the will with its embodiment—i.e. the particular will—is knowing, consciousness of the distinction between these two moments of the Idea is present, but present in such a way that now each of these moments is in its own eyes the totality of the Idea and has that totality as its foundation and content.

144. (α) The objective ethical order, which comes on the scene in place of good in the abstract, is substance made concrete by subjectivity as infinite form.[7] Hence it posits within itself distinctions whose specific character is thereby determined by the concept, and which endow the ethical order with a stable content independently necessary and subsistent in exaltation above subjective opinion and caprice. These distinctions are absolutely valid laws and institutions.

145. It is the fact that the ethical order is the system of these specific determinations of the Idea which constitutes its rationality. Hence the ethical order is freedom or the absolute will as what is objective, a circle of necessity whose moments are the ethical powers which regulate the life of individuals. To these powers individuals are related as accidents to substance, and it is in individuals that these powers are represented, have the shape of appearance, and become actualized.

146. (β) The substantial order, in the self-consciousness which it has thus actually attained in individuals, knows itself and so is an object of knowledge. This ethical substance and its laws and powers are on the one hand an object over against the subject, and from his point of view they *are*—'are' in the highest sense of self-subsistent being. This is an absolute authority and power infinitely more firmly established than the being of nature.

The sun, the moon, mountains, rivers, and the natural objects of all kinds by which we are surrounded, *are*. For consciousness they have the authority not only of mere being but also of possessing a particular nature which it accepts and to which it adjusts itself in dealing with them, using them, or in being otherwise concerned with them. The authority of ethical laws is infinitely higher, because natural objects conceal rationality under the cloak of contingency and exhibit it only in their utterly external and disconnected way.

147. On the other hand, they are not something alien to the subject. On the contrary, his spirit bears witness to them as to its own essence, the essence in which he has a feeling of his selfhood, and in which he lives as in his

own element which is not distinguished from himself. The subject is thus directly linked to the ethical order by a relation which is more like an identity than even the relation of faith or trust.

Faith and trust emerge along with reflection; they presuppose the power of forming ideas and making distinctions. For example, it is one thing to be a pagan, a different thing to believe in a pagan religion. This relation or rather this absence of relation, this identity in which the ethical order is the actual living soul of self-consciousness, can no doubt pass over into a relation of faith and conviction and into a relation produced by means of further reflection, i.e. into an *insight* due to reasoning starting perhaps from some particular purposes, interests, and considerations, from fear or hope, or from historical conditions. But adequate *knowledge* of this identity depends on thinking in terms of the concept.

148. As substantive in character, these laws and institutions are duties binding on the will of the individual, because as subjective, as inherently undetermined, or determined as particular, he distinguishes himself from them and hence stands related to them as to the substance of his own being.

The 'doctrine of duties' in moral philosophy (I mean the objective doctrine, not that which is supposed to be contained in the empty principle of moral subjectivity, because that principle determines nothing—see Paragraph 134) is therefore comprised in the systematic development of the circle of ethical necessity which follows in this Third Part. The difference between the exposition in this book and the form of a 'doctrine of duties' lies solely in the fact that, in what follows, the specific types of ethical life turn up as necessary relationships; there the exposition ends, without being supplemented in each case by the addition that 'therefore men have a duty to conform to this institution'.

A 'doctrine of duties' which is other than a philosophical science takes its material from existing relationships and shows its connexion with the moralist's personal notions or with principles and thoughts, purposes, impulses, feelings, &c., that are forthcoming everywhere; and as reasons for accepting each duty in turn, it may tack on its further consequences in their bearing on the other ethical relationships or on welfare and opinion. But an immanent and logical 'doctrine of duties' can be nothing except the serial exposition of the relationships which are necessitated by the Idea of freedom and are therefore actual in their entirety, to wit in the state.

149. The bond of duty can appear as a restriction only on indeterminate subjectivity or abstract freedom, and on the impulses either of the natural will or of the moral will which determines its indeterminate good arbitrarily. The truth is, however, that in duty the individual finds his liberation; first, liberation from dependence on mere natural impulse and from the depression which as a particular subject he cannot escape in his moral reflections on what ought to be and what might be; secondly, liberation from the indeterminate subjectivity which, never reaching reality or the objective determinancy of action, remains self-enclosed and devoid of actuality. In duty the individual acquires his substantive freedom. . . .

155. Hence in this identity of the universal will with the particular will, right and duty coalesce, and by being in the ethical order a man has rights in so far as he has duties, and duties in so far as he has rights. In the sphere of abstract right, I have the right and another has the corresponding duty. In the moral sphere, the right of my private judgement and will, as well as of my happiness, has not, but only ought to have, coalesced with duties and become objective.

156. The ethical substance, as containing independent self-consciousness united with its concept, is the actual mind of a family and a nation.

157. The concept of this Idea has being only as mind, as something knowing itself and actual, because it is the objectification of itself, the movement running through the form of its moments. . . . It is therefore

(A) ethical mind in its natural or immediate phase—the *Family*. This substantiality loses its unity, passes over into division, and into the phase of relation, i.e. into

(B) *Civil Society*—an association of members as self-subsistent individuals in a universality which, because of their self-subsistence, is only abstract. Their association is brought about by their needs, by the legal system—the means to security of person and property—and by an external organization for attaining their particular and common interests. This external state

(C) is brought back to and welded into unity in the *Constitution of the State* which is the end and actuality of both the substantial universal order and the public life devoted thereto.

158. The family, as the immediate substantiality of mind, is specifically characterized by love, which is mind's feeling of its own unity. Hence in a family, one's frame of mind is to have self-consciousness of one's individuality within this unity as the absolute essence of oneself, with the result that one is in it not as an independent person but as a member. . . .

181. The family disintegrates (both essentially, through the working of the principle of personality, and also in the course of nature) into a plurality of families, each of which conducts itself as in principle a self-subsistent concrete person and therefore as externally related to its neighbours. In other words, the moments bound together in the unity of the family, since the family is the ethical Idea still in its concept, must be released from the concept to self-subsistent objective reality. This is the stage of difference. This gives us, to use abstract language in the first place, the determination of particularity which is related to universality but in such a way that universality is its basic principle, though still only an inward principle; for that reason, the universal merely shows in the particular as its form.[8] Hence this relation of reflection prima facie portrays the disappearance of ethical life or, since this life as the essence necessarily shows itself, this relation constitutes the world of ethical appearance—civil society. . . .

187. Individuals in their capacity as burghers in this state are private persons whose end is their own interest. This end is *mediated* through the universal which thus *appears* as a *means* to its realization. Consequently, individuals can attain their ends only in so far as they themselves determine their knowing, willing, and acting in a universal way and make themselves links in this chain of social connexions. In these circumstances, the interest of the Idea—an interest of which these members of civil society are as such unconscious—lies in the process whereby their singularity and their natural condition are raised, as a result of the necessities imposed by nature as well as of arbitrary needs, to formal freedom and formal universality of knowing and willing—the process whereby their particularity is educated up to subjectivity. . . .

255. As the family was the first, so the Corporation is the second ethical root of the state, the one planted in civil society. The former contains the moments of subjective particularity and objective universality in a substantial unity. But these moments are sundered in civil society to begin with; on the one side there is the particularity of need and satisfaction, reflected into itself, and on the other side the universality of abstract rights. In the Corporation these moments are united in an inward fashion, so that in this union particular welfare is present as a right and is actualized.

The sanctity of marriage and the dignity of Corporation membership are the two fixed points round which the unorganized atoms of civil society revolve.

256. The end of the Corporation is restricted and finite, while the public authority was an external organization involving a separation and a merely relative identity of controller and controlled. The end of the former and the externality and relative identity of the latter find their truth in the absolutely universal end and its absolute actuality. Hence the sphere of civil society passes over into the state.

The town is the seat of the civil life of business. There reflection arises, turns in upon itself, and pursues its atomizing task; each man maintains himself in and through his relation to others who, like himself, are persons possessed of rights. The country, on the other hand, is the seat of an ethical life resting on nature and the family. Town and country thus constitute the two moments, still ideal moments, whose true ground is the state, although it is from them that the state springs.

The philosophic proof of the concept of the state is this development of ethical life from its immediate phase through civil society, the phase of division, to the state, which then reveals itself as the true ground of these phases. A proof in philosophic science can only be a development of this kind.

Since the state appears as a result in the advance of the philosophic concept through displaying itself as the true ground [of the earlier phases], that show of mediation is now cancelled and the state has become directly present before us. Actually, therefore, the state as such is not so much the result as the beginning. It is within the state that the family is first developed into civil society, and it is the Idea of the state itself which disrupts itself into these two moments. Through the development of civil society, the substance of ethical life acquires its infinite form, which contains in itself these two moments: (1) infinite differentiation down to the inward experience of independent self-consciousness, and (2) the form of universality involved in education, the form of thought whereby mind is objective and actual to itself as an organic totality in laws and institutions which are its will in terms of thought. . . .

257. The state is the actuality of the ethical Idea. It is ethical mind *qua* the substantial will manifest and revealed to itself, knowing and thinking itself, accomplishing what it knows and in so far as it knows it. The state exists immediately in custom, mediately in individual self-consciousness, knowledge, and activity, while self-consciousness in virtue of its sentiment towards the state finds in the state, as its essence and the end and product of its activity, its substantive freedom.

The *Penates* are inward gods, gods of the underworld; the mind of a nation (Athene for instance) is the divine, knowing and willing itself. Family piety is feeling, ethical behaviour directed by feeling; political virtue is the willing of the absolute end in terms of thought.

258. The state is absolutely rational inasmuch as it is the actuality of the substantial will which it possesses in the particular self-consciousness once that consciousness has been raised to consciousness of its universality. This substantial unity is an absolute unmoved end in itself, in which freedom comes into its supreme right. On the other hand this final end has supreme right against the individual, whose supreme duty is to be a member of the state.

If the state is confused with civil society, and if its specific end is laid down as the security and protection of property and personal freedom, then the interest of the individuals as such becomes the ultimate end of their association, and it follows that membership of the state is something optional. But the state's relation to the individual is quite different from this. Since the state is mind objectified, it is only as one of its members that the individual himself has objectivity, genuine individuality, and an ethical life. Unification pure and simple is the true content and aim of the individual, and the individual's destiny is the living of a universal life. His further particular satisfaction, activity, and mode of conduct have this substantive and universally valid life as their starting point and their result.

Rationality, taken generally and in the abstract, consists in the thorough-going unity of the universal and the single. Rationality, concrete in the state, consists (*a*) so far as its content is concerned, in the unity of objective freedom (i.e. freedom of the universal or substantial will) and subjective freedom (i.e. freedom of everyone in his knowing and in his volition of particular ends); and consequently, (*b*) so far as its form is concerned, in self-determining action on laws and principles which are thoughts and so universal. This Idea is the absolutely eternal and necessary being of mind.[9]

But if we ask what is or has been the historical origin of the state in general, still more if we ask about the origin of any particular state, of its rights and institutions, or again if we inquire whether the state originally arose out of patriarchal conditions or out of fear or trust, or out of Corporations, &c., or finally if we ask in what light the basis of the state's rights has been conceived and consciously established, whether this basis has been supposed to be positive divine right, or contract, custom, &c.—all these questions are no concern of the Idea of the state. We are here dealing exclusively with the philosophic science of the state, and from that point of view all these things are mere appearance and therefore matters for history. So far as the authority of any existing state has anything to do with reasons, these reasons are culled from the forms of the law authoritative within it. . . .

260. The state is the actuality of concrete freedom. But concrete freedom consists in this, that personal individuality and its particular interests not only achieve their complete development and gain explicit recognition for their right (as they do in the sphere of the family and civil society) but, for one thing, they also pass over of their own accord into the interest of the universal, and, for another thing, they know and will the universal; they even recognize it as their own substantive mind; they take it as their end and aim and are active in its pursuit. The result is that the universal does not prevail or achieve completion except along with particular interests and through the co-operation of particular knowing and willing; and individuals likewise do not live as private persons for their own ends alone, but in the very act of willing these they will the universal in the light of the universal, and their activity is consciously aimed at none but the universal end. The principle of modern states has prodigious strength and depth because it allows the principle of subjectivity to progress to its culmination in the extreme of self-subsistent personal particularity, and yet at the same time brings it back to the substantive unity and so maintains this unity in the principle of subjectivity itself.

261. In contrast with the spheres of private rights and private welfare (the family and civil society), the state is from one point of view an external necessity and their higher authority; its nature is such that their laws and interests are subordinate to it and dependent on it. On the other hand, however, it is the end immanent within them, and its strength lies in the unity of its own universal

end and aim with the particular interest of individuals, in the fact that individuals have duties to the state in proportion as they have rights against it (see Paragraph 155). . . .

Translator's Notes

1. This statement is further explained and defended in *Enc.*, § 6. Note that Hegel is not saying that what exists or is 'real' is rational. By 'actuality' . . . he means the synthesis of essence and existence. If we say of a statesman who accomplishes nothing that he is not a 'real' statesman, then we mean by 'real' what Hegel calls 'actual'. The statesman exists as a man in office, but he lacks the essence constitutive of what statesmanship ought to be, say effectiveness. Conversely, and in Hegel's view no less important, if effectiveness were never the quality of an existing statesman, then it would not be the rational essence of statesmanship, but a mere ideal or dream. Hegel's philosophy as a whole might be regarded as an attempt to justify his identification of rationality with actuality and vice versa, but his doctrine depends ultimately on his faith in God's Providence, his conviction that history is the working out of His rational purpose. That purpose, as the purpose of the Almighty, is not so impotent as to remain a mere ideal or aspiration, and conversely, what is genuinely actual or effective in the world is simply the working of that purpose.—It follows that Hegel's identification of the actual and the rational is not a plea for conservatism in politics. The actualization of God's purpose is not yet complete. See the Addition to Paragraph 270 and the closing pages of the *Philosophy of History*.

2. Thought at any stage does not attain full actuality until it passes over into existence and embodies itself in something objective. E.g. religious convictions are not genuinely actual until they are objectified in institutions, churches, &c. Similarly, the state, as an objectification in the external world of man's rational will, is that in which alone his freedom, the essence of his will, is fully actualized.

3. The ultimate source of the Greek proverb ('here is Rhodes, here's your jump') is Michael Apostolius viii. 100 (Leutsch: *Paroemiographi Graeci*, Göttingen, 1851, vol. ii). But in its Latin form it is a commonplace of German elementary Latin text-books, and it may have reached them, and Hegel also, from Erasmus,

Adagia, III. iii. 28. Erasmus quotes the Greek, gives a Latin translation, and continues: 'The proverb will be apt when someone is asked to show on the spot that he can do what he boasts he has done elsewhere.' (Hegel's interpretation seems to have been slightly different.) Cf. Goethe: *Zahme Xenien*, III. ii.

4. Hegel is playing on words. Ῥόδος means not only the island of Rhodes, but also a rose. *Saltus* means a jump, but *salta* is the imperative of the verb 'to dance'. The rose is the symbol of joy, and the philosopher's task is to find joy in the present by discovering reason within it. In other words, philosophy may 'dance' for joy in this world; it need not postpone its 'dancing' until it builds an ideal world elsewhere.

5. If the actual is rational, then however tragic the actual may seem to be, reason will be able to find joy in it, because it will find itself in it as its essence. Hegel uses the same metaphor in *Philosophy of Religion*, i. 284–5. As he indicates in *Werke*, xvii. 227, the metaphor was suggested to him by the Rosicrucians. (See Lasson: *Beiträge zur Hegel-Forschung*, Part 2, Berlin, 1910, pp. 49–50.)

6. Cf. Hegel's criticism of Spinoza in, e.g., *Phenomenology*, p. 80, and *Enc.*, § 151. His point is that Spinoza's view of the universe as substance or necessity needs to be supplemented by the Christian doctrine of subjectivity and subjective freedom. God is substance, but is person or subject as well. Hegel applies this doctrine to the state and holds that although the state is a substance, in modern times it has come to consciousness of itself in its citizens and its monarch, and so has become not a mere external necessity but the embodiment of freedom. . . .

7. We have seen . . . that right and morality were both abstractions; the whole from which they are abstracted is therefore that on which they depend. This whole is a unity of universal and particular, of object and subject. Now 'a thing which has subsistence in itself, a thing that upholdeth that which else would fall' (a phrase of Hobbes, quoted here from Laird: *Hobbes*, London, 1943, pp. 92–3) is a substance. And throughout Hegel's account of ethical life, it is with substance that we are dealing; each type of this life—family, civil society, state—is a substantiality, but it is a substantiality of *mind*, and so one of a special sort. 'In my view', says Hegel (*Phenomenology*, p. 80), 'everything depends on grasping and expressing the ultimate truth not as sub-stance but as subject as well.' (*a*) The family is a substance (in Hegel's view a single mind—see Paragraph 156) of which its members are accidents, but the substantiality is not external or visible; it depends solely on the consciousness of its members. The family's bond of union, its substance, is love; and love, in Hegel's view, is reason in its immediacy, i.e. an immature form of reason. Here there is no explicit difference between substance and accident; unity is present and the family members are not conscious that their unity is a unity of differences. (*b*) At the next stage, civil society, difference becomes explicit; the substance (the mind of the nation), 'appears' in particulars and it is their essence even though they may not realize it. They have risen above love to intelligence, but this is concentrated on a private end. (*c*) The third stage is the synthesis of the first two. The substantial mind of the nation, objectified in the state, rises to consciousness of itself in the minds of the citizens; it particularizes itself into rational laws and institutions. It is concrete because, unlike the family, it is particularized consciously and because, unlike civil society, its particulars are not an 'appearance' of its substantial essence, but the differentiation of that essence. It is concrete again because these laws and institutions, like the state itself as the unity of these, are actual in the minds of the citizens who live under them. They regulate their willing deliberately in accordance with rational ends; the members of the family pursue an ethical end, but only under the influence of feeling; members of civil society are intelligent, but pursue the universal end only under the disguise of the particular. The state, then, has acquired the form of subjectivity, and subjectivity as we have seen, is infinite because self-related. Hegel contrasts his state with an oriental despotism, i.e. with a substance which is an absolute power over individual accidents and alien to them. The essence of his state is that it is not only a substance but one which incorporates individual freedom by means of the parliamentary and other institutions which he later describes.

8. The transition from family to civil society corresponds on a higher level to that from right to morality. In each case the transition is the emergence of the particular; in each case we leave behind an undifferentiated universality and arrive at a realm of appearance, i.e. what is visible and obvious is particularity, though universality is its underlying essence. . . . Uni-

versal and particular, form and content, appear in civil society to fall apart, the Idea appears to be divided, but none the less the pursuit of private ends here turns out to be conditioned by universal laws. These are implicit to start with (as the laws of economics), but they become explicit later as a system of laws and institutions for the protection of private property and as barriers against private selfishness. . . .

9. Hegel's theory of the state has his theory of syllogism for its background. 'The syllogism is the rational and everything rational' (*Enc.*, § 181) because it is a concrete unity of explicit differences, and these differences are the three moments of the concept, universality, particularity, and individuality. 'The state is a system of three syllogisms: (i) The individual or person, through his particularity or physical or mental needs . . . is coupled with the universal, i.e. with society, law, right, government. (ii) The will or action of individuals is the intermediating force which procures for these needs satisfaction in society, law, &c., and which gives to society, law, &c., their fulfilment and actualization. (iii) But the universal, i.e. the state, government, and law, is the permanent underlying mean in which the individuals and their satisfaction have and receive their fulfilled reality, intermediation, and persistence. Each of the moments of the concept, as it is brought by intermediation to coalesce with the other extreme, is brought into union with itself and produces itself. . . . It is only by this triad of syllogisms with the same terms that the whole is thoroughly understood in its organization' (*Enc.*, § 198). What essentially differentiates the state from civil society and makes it rational, is the parliamentary organization which mediates between particulars on the one hand and the individual monarch on the other (see Paragraphs 302–4). The state is the Idea because it is in this way the unity of universal and particular, form and content, and since in the state this is a conscious unity, it may be described as mind in being, since reason is 'essential and actual truth' and 'truth, aware of what it is, is mind' (*Enc.*, §§438–9).

Adapted from: G. W. F. Hegel, *The Philosophy of Right*, translated by T. M. Knox, pp. 9–13, 105–107, 109–110, 122, 124–125, 154–156, 160–161. Copyright © 1942. Reprinted by permission of Oxford University Press. ✦

23
History and Politics

Charles Taylor

Chapter XV: Reason and History

2

Let us now look at the main themes of the philosophy of history. The principal drama of the sweep of history is the one which builds towards the major crux of Hegel's philosophy of politics; how to reconcile the freedom of the individual who knows himself as universal rationality with a restored *Sittlichkeit*. The main drama of history is then opened by the breakdown of the perfect unity of *Sittlichkeit* in the Greek world, the birth of the individual with universal consciousness. It then follows the slow development through the succeeding centuries both of the individual (his *Bildung*) and of the institutions embodying *Sittlichkeit*, so that the two can eventually rendez-vous in the rational state.

The version of the history in compressed form which we have in Chapter VI of the *PhG* [*Phänomenologie des Geistes*] starts with the Greek world. But the major version contained in the lectures on the philosophy of history starts earlier, takes us through Chinese, Indian, Persian, Phoenician, Egyptian civilizations in the run up to Greek. It also deals with the Jews. There are also differences in the way Hegel cuts into even the areas common to the two versions; as there are between different cycles of the lectures. This reinforces what was said above about the detail of Hegel's philosophy of history.

My aim here will be simply to give the general line of the dialectic of history, as a background to the main political problem mentioned above. In dealing with the pre-Greek civilizations, Hegel discusses their religious consciousness, and there are many elements here which reappear in the philosophy of religion. Their political structures and public life are closely bound up with this religious consciousness. As ever with Hegel the different aspects of a people's life are bound together in its *Geist*. But the religious consciousness for these early peoples offers the most striking expression of the stage they were at, of the way in which they tried to realize the ontological reality, *Geist*, and its relation to the world and subject.

Spirit is struggling to achieve an understanding of itself as spirit, that is, as free subjectivity, and to see this as the absolute. But with the pre-Greek peoples—except for the Jews—the absolute is still less than subject; it is still bound up with external, hence impersonal reality, nature, or the total abstraction of the void (one aspect of Indian religion). The Persians achieve a high form of this in that they see the absolute symbolized in light, which is the most spiritual among natural forms, but they are still not yet at the breakthrough point.

This comes in one form with the Jews. Here we suddenly come to the realization that God is pure subject, spirit. But this realization can only be won at that stage by a radical separation of God as spirit from all contamination with natural, finite reality. The Jewish spirit, thinks Hegel, is therefore one of separation, radical transcendence. Abraham starts off by leaving his family and home in Ur of the Chaldees to become a wanderer. The Jewish people wage a constant fight against idolatry, which amounts to a mixing of the divine again with the finite. But this solution can only be a stage on the way, for it is radically imperfect. God is spirit, but at the cost of being beyond the world, and above all beyond, above and over finite subjectivity, that of man. Man is not reconciled with God, does not see himself as at one with the absolute, as its vehicle, but rather the absolute is over against him, he is its slave, totally submitted to it. Similarly, the natural world is totally emptied of the divine. It is 'entgöttert', as Hegel puts it; Jewish consciousness sees only a world of finite things, which are to be used by man, not the embodiment of Deity. The world is totally under spirit, at our disposal, even as we are totally under God. Hegel also speaks of this vision of God as of 'pure thought', which in Hegelian terms is closely linked with being pure subject. In this formulation he stresses again that the Jewish concept of the absolute is of something universal, totally without particularization.

The Greek solution is in a sense the opposite of the Jewish one. The Greeks, too, win through to a consciousness of God as subject. But it is not a subjectivity which is frighteningly beyond nature, which negates natural expression in the purity of thought. Rather the Greek gods are perfectly harmonized with their natural expression. But instead of this being something infra-personal, as with the earlier natural religions, the paradigm expression of these Gods is in the form of realized subjectivity, that is, in human form.

But the Greek God, unlike the Jewish, is parochial. And this same parochial nature is what we shall see reflected in the Greek polis, and will be the cause of its downfall. A similar advantage is won at similar cost. On one hand, the Greek concept of the divine is the charter of Greek freedom. It is the sense that the divine is not totally other, that finite subjectivity has its place in it. And this is the sense of freedom, that man is not the slave of the absolute, of something which is utterly foreign to his will. Hence the Greek polity will be the first home of freedom.

It was this which enabled the Greeks to build an embodiment of *Sittlichkeit* for which Hegel's day pined, one in which men were fully at home, in which their whole identity was bound up with the living public reality of their polis. The vision of God in human form was the foundation for a public life woven around this divinity, the God of the city, in which the citizens could fully recognize themselves. This public life was a reality which was fully theirs. Their activity kept it going, and yet it also represented what was of ultimate significance for them, an expression of the divine. Hence their realized public life was their 'substance', the basis of their identity. Their ethic was one of *Sittlichkeit*, where what ought to be also was.

But this was a limited freedom. Only those who were citizens, who were thus members of a certain polis and the servers of its God, were so reflected in public reality. Slaves, and in general outsiders, were not. Each state had its own God, own laws, with which its members were fully reconciled, but these were different from state to state. The reassuring form of the divine was reassuring only for some. It reflected only part of humanity. Hence the Greeks did not have the intuition that man as such is free. Freedom was the appanage of citizens; slaves and barbarians were outside its ban.[1]

Correspondingly, the identification with the city on the part of its citizens was not based on universal reflection, but was one of immediate unreflecting adherence. The laws must be obeyed because they are those of our city, *sans plus*.

In this world, democracy (direct democracy) is the most natural form of government. For all men are totally identified with the whole. They only want to live and die for it; they can thus be entrusted with running it. But it is a parochial democracy, it excludes slaves and metics; for the identification is parochial.

Hegel makes clear why in his view ancient democracy is inappropriate as a model for the modern world. Ancient, direct democracy was possible in part because societies were so small; all could really take part and be really present when decisions were taken. But this is not all. One of the essential conditions of Greek democracy was precisely its exclusiveness. All the menial economic tasks were taken over by non-citizens. This not only meant that citizens had in general more leisure than otherwise would be possible to attend the ecclesia and see to affairs of state. It also meant a homogeneity of the population which cannot be attained in a modern polity where all functions are fulfilled by citizens. But heterogeneity makes essential an articulation of the modern state which in Hegel's view excludes democracy.

But there is a third reason why ancient democracy is not an appropriate model for our time. The Greek state could work because men were immediately identified with it. Now while we hope to restore the integrity of

Sittlichkeit, we can never restore this immediate, unreflecting unity. Modern man will also remain a universal individual. And this individuality will be reflected in the structure of modern society, and we shall see—in the form of civil society. This necessary articulation of the polity to take account of the greater complexity of man requires a balance between institutions which Hegel thinks is incompatible with direct democracy. More of this below.

This beautiful unity of the Greek state is doomed. It is doomed because of its limitations, its parochialness. The world spirit has to march on. Hence once the polis is realized the cunning of reason calls world-historical individuals to look beyond. Such a figure in his own way is Socrates. Socrates turns his allegiance to universal reason. And although he wants to remain obedient to the laws of his polis, he would like to found them on reason. Thus while he maintains his allegiance to Athens to the death, nevertheless his teaching cannot but corrupt the youth, for it undermines that immediate identification with the public life on which the polis rests. Men turn to a universal reason, turn their back on the parochial state and its gods. But this universal reason is not embodied in public life, it is the beyond.

The dissolution of the polity is the birth of the individual with universal consciousness. This is an individual who defines himself as subject of universal reason. But he can find no identification with the public life of his city. He lives in a larger community, the city of men and Gods of the Stoics, but this is unrealized. Hence the new individual is an internal émigré.

But this has the necessary consequence that the life goes out of the public institutions of the polis. It cannot but go under and gives way to the universal empire, a form of dominance from on top which is predicated precisely on there being no such identification. This universal empire is no more than the polis a realization of the universal reason which has now come to consciousness. It is the correlative in the sense that the individual of universal reason must bring about the collapse of the city-state, but it is not at all expression in public life of this reason. On the contrary, it is the expression of the fact that this reason is now felt as beyond the world. Thus the individual is cast into an external world which is ruled not by reason but by the arbitrary will of emperors, powerful despots. Internally he defines himself as universal reason, but externally he is a bit of flotsam on the huge flood of events, entirely at the mercy of external power.

In this diremption he goes even more to an inward definition of himself. This is the age in which Stoicism flourishes. But for Hegel, this cannot be a solution, for it is a completely unrealized figure of reason and freedom. Hence the individual cannot but yearn to go beyond this, to find realization. The ground is laid for the unhappy consciousness.

This is the era of the Roman Empire. Thus Roman society is the place of origin of the idea of the Person, an individual defined as a subject of rights in abstraction from his relation to the substance of *Sittlichkeit*. The Person is the bearer of 'abstract' right, right unconnected to social and political role; he is the bearer of right as property. This will be one of the dimensions of the modern state. It has its origins here.

The stage is set for the birth of Christianity. Christianity comes to answer the yearning of the universal individual, who cannot be reconciled with the universal in this political world, that nevertheless the finite subject and the absolute be fully united. And so they become so united once, in the person of Christ. There is no question of this happening many times, as with the avatars of Hindu religion. The absolute is one, and the paradigmatic founding unity can only be realized once. But this unity, as we have seen, must also be overcome in its immediate form. Christ must die. And he must rise again, go to the Father, and return in spirit to animate the community.

But with the birth of Christianity this unity is only realized in principle. It is still not fully realized in the world. The Church which is the external realization of the new community is thus in inner exile at first as well, just like the universal individual. The task of history now is to make this reconciliation externally, politically real; to make the church community in a sense one with the society. And this means a slow transformation of institutions, and a slow making over of men—*Bildung*. This is the task of the next eighteen centuries, and it will be undertaken by a new world historical people, the Germanic nations.

The German nations Hegel means are the barbarians who swarmed over the Roman empire at its end and founded the new nations of Western Europe. There is no particular chauvinism in this use of the word German. Montesquieu and others also recognized that modern European politics had issued out of these Germanic barbarian kingdoms.

But these Germans were ideally suited to take history to the next stage—the *Weltgeist* always sees to such convergence of material and ends—because they were naturally very conscious of their individual independence from authority. They were only with difficulty, and then precariously, submitted to authority. Hegel pictures the early German as being loosely under leaders who, like Agamemnon, were barely primus inter pares. In this way, they were as it were pre-programmed to build a civilization which would be based on the freedom of the individual. But first this freedom has to be purified, it has to grow into and incorporate the rational inner freedom which was achieved by the ancient world and Christianity. The real, external independence of the German in the woods has to be united to this spiritual freedom, and this freedom given reality. But second, it is essential to this that the wild independent German must learn to accept rational authority, must accept to be integrated into a rational state.

The development of medieval and modern Europe is the working out of these two related processes. The feudal system in which the public realm is shot through with private relationships is the natural form in which these German tribes set up states. But then the process starts by which these loose skeins of private relations are united into the common overarching will which is inseparable from the state. In Europe this comes in the form of the growing power of the monar-

chy. Charlemagne represents a crucial phase in this process.

We have here the foundation of one of the essential features of a modern state for Hegel. It must be united at the top by a monarchy. Hegel seems to hold that this is essentially linked with the principle of modern individual freedom. The Greek city-state could be a republic since all gave themselves immediately to the state, they had no private will outside it. But the modern universal individual also has a private identity, he cannot be simply a member of the state. In order to be real as a common will, any state must however have this moment of immediate unity in it. At some moment, at some point, the will of the whole must be one with a real existent will. This not just in the sense that in order for the state to act, some men must act in its name. Rather Hegel is making the ontological point that there must be some place in which the immediate unity of concrete and general will is realized. The state cannot be for everybody just one dimension among many of their action and will.

What Hegel is presenting here, and later in the *PR* [*Philosophy of Right*], is a renewed variant of the medieval idea of the representative individual, that is, an individual who bodies forth a basic principle of the common life. This is 'representation' not in the modern sense of standing in for someone else or being delegated by him, but of bodying forth, of incarnating an underlying common reality to which all show allegiance. The notion of kingly majesty, that the king is the point at which the majesty of the whole is manifest, belongs to this idea. In the ontological dimension of his political thought, where he is concerned to derive the structures of the state from the 'Concept', that is, from the ontological structure of things, Hegel has recourse to an idea of this kind. Different features of the constitution 'represent' in this sense different aspects of ontological reality.

Alongside the powerful monarch, who draws together the unruly subjects, there grow up the institutions known as estates, which in England became Parliament. These are the necessary mediating elements between the sovereign will and the particulars. And hence we have here another essential institution of a modern state, thinks Hegel. It is by the estates that the people as a whole take part in the life of the state. Here again we shall see that Hegel's notion of the participation of the people is not founded on the modern notion of representation, as it is in theories of modern representative government. It is not a matter of legitimating decisions, by leading them back to popular choices, but of establishing some kind of identification.

At the same time the state develops more and more towards impersonality, the dependence on law, and what Weber was later to call rationality. The kingly power becomes less and less a private appanage, and is seen as the public power of government. Service by magnates is replaced over the centuries by a trained bureaucracy. The state becomes more and more founded on general principles, on legal rationality.

As these institutions are developing—to what final fruition we shall discuss further below—the parallel process of spiritualization is going on, purification of the raw, primitive human material, and its formation (*Bildung*). One of the key stages in this is the Reformation. The Christian Church took over a good part of the task of forming the raw barbarians. But in the process it had to sink to some degree to their level. The higher spiritual truths of Christianity were united with gross external realities. Men tried to find God by the actual physical conquest of the Holy Land, the presence of God was reified in the host, and so on. This is Hegel's notion of what underlay medieval Catholicism. In order for the spirit to progress, there had to be a recovery of purity, a rediscovery of the spiritual meaning of the presence of the spirit in the world, a setting aside of the gross sensuous meaning this had with Catholicism. This is essential to the development of the modern state; so much so that Catholic countries are incapable of realizing this state integrally.

With the Reformation, and the freeing of spirituality from its imprisonment in gross external things, with the recovery of a sense of the presence of God in the community which was purely spiritual, the way was free for the task of making this presence objec-tive and real in the external world, not in the gross and inadequate way of the external rites and hierarchy of Catholicism, but by building a real earthly community which would realize the universal, reason. The world was ready for a state founded on reason. In other words, the unity of God and man has to be externally realized. But we have to go beyond the primitive, purely external, and hence totally inadequate realization in host, sanctuary, relics, indulgences, etc.; we have to liberate the true spiritual dimension, if we are to achieve the adequate realization in a political community. Thus from the Reformed Europe comes the attempt to realize the rational state, to overcome the opposition of Church and state. The Protestant religion is at the foundation of this state.

The spiritualization process begun by the Reformation, however, carries on and brings about what we call the Enlightenment. More and more aware of themselves as at one with the universal, men come to recognize that they are inwardly free with the freedom of pure thought. The spiritualization brings them back to an understanding of their identity as resting in the freedom of universal thought. But this is not simply a return to the ancients. For these latter found themselves faced with a world which was totally refractory to reason; their sense of their identity as reason was a purely inner one, buffeted by the forces of the world; the world of reason was a beyond. But since then men have come to see that they are at one with the very foundation of things. Christian culture has wrought this. Consequently the modern Enlightenment does not just define man as thought, it is sure that the whole of external reality conforms to thought too. This is Hegel's reading of the new scientific consciousness which strives to understand the world as law-governed order.

In other words, thought and being are one. This is Hegel's rather idiosyncratic reading of the Cogito ergo sum of Descartes. The point is that man is reason, and he is as such one with the principle of things; so he will find reason in the external world if he only looks for it. . . .

Chapter XVI: The Realized State

1

PR explores what flows from the notion of rational will concerning human affairs. It goes beyond a simple political theory. It turns out to englobe also what Hegel calls civil society, and the family. But also it discusses the dimension of morality and private rights.[2]

Hegel intends to proceed from the most abstract to the most concrete. He will end with a picture of the state, because this is the highest embodiment of *Sittlichkeit*, which is implicit in the notion that man is the vehicle of rational will.

But we start off with the notion of private rights. Man is a bearer of private rights because he is essentially a vehicle of rational will. As such he commands respect. Man is a bodily existence who has to have commerce with the external world in order to live; he has to appropriate things and use them. But this fact becomes a value because man is the essential vehicle of the realization of reason or spirit, which is the same thing as saying that man is endowed with will. Hence man's appropriation is to be seen as in fulfilment of the ontologically grounded purpose. It is something infinitely worthy of respect. Thus the de facto process of appropriation becomes the de jure right to property. Man is a bearer of rights because as a will he is worthy of respect. An attack on his external bodily existence or his property is thus a crime, an attack against the very purpose underlying reality as a whole, including my own existence. The right of appropriation over things comes from the fact that these have no inherent ends; they are given to them by will. Will has the rights (*PR*, § 44).

Hegel thus justifies the right to property. He sees this as a right to private property. For this right falls to man in the abstract, as an individual rational will. This is because it is on this immediate, individual level that man is related to things, that he is in interchange with nature.[3] Man is also part of a community of *Sittlichkeit*, but this touches him at another, higher level than this commerce with things. It touches his identification, his

spiritual life, that for which he should be ready to give up life and property.

Hence in property we are dealing with the will of man as a single individual, as a person (*PR*, § 46). Of course, this very basic consideration of man as a person, bearer of abstract right, although the starting point for the Logic-derived exposition of the *PR*, is not the point of departure, historically speaking. A long development was necessary before man was actually first considered in history as a person, as we saw in our consideration of the philosophy of history above. This occurred in the Roman world.

Hegel then goes on to consider a number of other matters related to rights, particularly property rights; for instance, contract, and crime and punishment. Crime, says Hegel, taking up a theme we saw in the Logic is a negative infinite judgement. It is not just saying, as it were, this particular thing is not mine, which my rival in a civil suit says; it denies the whole category of 'mine' and 'thine'.

Crime is an attack on the very purpose underlying things, the purpose even of the criminal, his will *an sich* (*PR*, § 100). Punishment has as goal to undo this rebellion against the purpose of things. This attack has come from a will which has set itself against the very principle of will. The undoing must therefore be a counter-injury against the particular will of the criminal.

> The sole positive existence which the injury possesses is that it is the particular will of the criminal. Hence to injure (or penalize) this particular will as a will determinately existent is to annul the crime, which otherwise would have been held valid, and to restore the right. (*PR*, § 99)

Hegel is therefore quite out of sympathy with the various liberal theories of punishment as preventive, deterrent, reformative, etc. And he opposes the softening of the penal code which springs from this kind of philosophy. in particular, he is opposed to the abolition of capital punishment. In an important sense if the punishment is to undo the crime it has to 'fit the crime'. To let someone off on the grounds that punishment is reformative is not to treat man with the full dignity of a bearer of will, whose will can thus incarnate wrong, and hence cry for punishment. It is treating him 'as a harmful animal who has to be made harmless' (*PR*, § 100). Punishment is a *right* of the criminal. He calls for it with his will *an sich*.

The exploration of what is involved in man's being rational will has led us first to see him as the bearer of rights, as such, as a person, outside of specific political contexts. But now we go farther. As will he not only has rights, but he has the duty to determine himself. He determines himself by giving a content to his will; and this should be a rational, universal content. This is the sphere of morality.

Man is a moral agent because as a bearer of will he ought to conform his will to universal reason. Man as a willing being is first of all a natural being, seeking the fulfilment of his own inclinations, needs, passions. But he has to purify his will and make the rationally conceived good his goal.

But as the subject of morality man still figures as an individual. The demand of morality is that I come to recognize that I am under the obligation of willing universal reason, simply in virtue of being a man. And this means as well that I come to this realization myself, by my own reason. The subject of morality is the universal subjectivity which rose on the ruins of the ancient city.

The demands of morality in other words are inner as well as outer. It is not enough that I do the right thing. If the requirement is that I conform my will to universal reason, then I must not only do what is right, but will the right as the right. In other words I have to do the right because it is the right; and it follows from this that I have to understand the right myself. This is, of course, what Kant made central to morality, following a hint of Rousseau's: morality consists in the purity of the will, and this is considered by Hegel to be the highest expression of this category. Morality touches our intentions and not just our acts.

But this, of course, is radically incomplete for reasons which are now familiar to us. Morality needs a complement in the external world, a world of public life and practices where it is realized. For without this it remains a pure aspiration, a pure ought to be (Sollen) as Hegel puts it. It remains something purely inner. But there is more than that. The concept of rational will alone, as the will of an individual, is ultimately vacuous, as we saw in Chapter XIV. We cannot derive a content from the notion of duty for duty's sake (*PR*, § 135). It is only as ontological reason, which seeks its own embodiment in a community with a certain necessary structure, that rationality yields a criterion of the good. The content of the rational will is what this community requires of us. This then is our duty. It is not derived from formal reason but from the nature of the community which alone can embody reason.

Hence morality, the individual's search to conform his will to universal reason, refers us beyond itself both in order to complete its own attempt of deriving the right from reason, and in order to realize this right effectively. The demands on man as a bearer of rational will are thus that he live in a community which embodies reason, which is the fulfilled goal of reason. That is, what is implicit in the concept of man as a vehicle of rational will is only fully realized in such a community.

The two earlier stages thus refer us beyond to the concept of *Sittlichkeit* which is the third and major part of *PR*. Right is inadequate because it is simply the external expression of the fact that man is a bearer of will. It has no interiority. Besides it too requires to be defended by political power. By itself it is powerless. Morality shows a dimension of human life which answers one of the lacks of right; it shows human moral life as an inner purification of the will. But it cannot reach its goal of deriving the fullness of human moral duties from reason, nor realize these unless it is completed by a community in which morality is not simply an 'ought', but is realized in the public life. Thus right and morality find their place and are secured as parts of a larger whole.

But one essential feature of morality must be preserved in this community as it arises in its mature form in history. It must not as the earlier city-state have no place for moral man. On the contrary the basic freedom of moral man as man, the freedom to judge in conscience, must be preserved. This is an essential requirement of a *Sittlichkeit* which can incorporate modern man and with which he can identify himself. For the modern state, therefore, conscience is a sanctuary not to be violated (*PR*, § 137). Man retains this reflective dimension and this is why he cannot recapture the immediate unity and identity of the citizens with the state characteristic of the polis. But this is not to say that the modern or any state can allow men to decide by conscience alone whether to obey the laws. It means rather that freedom of conscience is an essential right in the modern state.

We thus come to *Sittlichkeit* which is substantial freedom in Hegel's terms. It is realized good. Men identify with it. It becomes their 'second nature' (*PR*, § 151), and they are its effective realization in subjectivity.

The *sittlich* is what has to do with a community in which the good is realized in a public or common life. Hence the category englobes more than the state. And Hegel will deal with three forms of common life in this section, which are also placed in an ascending order: the family, civil society and the state.

The first is an immediate unreflecting unity based on feeling. The second is society in so far as it conforms to the vision of the modern atomist theories of contract, a society of individuals who come together out of mutual need. Radically inadequate as a theory of the state, this vision is realized in Hegel's view in the modern bourgeois economy. Civil society is modern society seen as an economy of production and exchange between men considered as subjects of needs. This is at the antipodes of the family, for here there is no immediate unity but maximum consciousness of individuality in which men are bound together by external ties.

The state comes to complete this trio. For it offers once more a deeper unity, an inward unity, like the family. But it will not be just an immediate one based on feeling. Rather unity here is mediated by reason. The state is a community in which universal subjectivities can be bound together while being recognized as such.

First the family is a unity of feeling, of love. Men sense themselves as members

within a family, not as persons with rights vis-à-vis each other. When rights enter into it, the family is dissolving. In this section Hegel deals with marriage, family property and the education of children. The main point of the family as *sittlich* is this fact that within it men see themselves as members of something greater, as having identity by their part in a common life.

But of course the family is quite inadequate alone as *Sittlichkeit*, for within it man is not really an individual and the allegiance to the common life is not founded on reason but on feeling only. Hence beyond the family, man is in another community in which he operates purely as an individual. This is what Hegel calls civil society.

Civil society is the society considered as a set of economic relations between individuals. Hegel had read and carefully considered the writings of the British political economists, most notably James Steuart and Adam Smith, whose works had been translated into German. His model of civil society owes a lot to these writers.

Civil society is the level of relations into which men enter not as members of family, nor as members of some ethical community, such as a state or a church, but just as men. It is a sphere in which men are related to each other as persons in Hegel's sense, i.e., as bearers of rights. In this sphere 'a man counts as a man in virtue of his humanity alone, not because he is a Jew, Catholic, Protestant, German, Italian, etc.' (*PR*, § 209 E).

In the level of social relations called civil society, men are thus individuals on their own; their relations to each other are founded on the fact that in fulfilling their needs they require each other. In other words, in this sphere we look at men as the subjects of individual purposes; they become related through these individual purposes whose fulfilment requires social cooperation. . . .

But Hegel now goes on to develop traits of civil society (*PR*, § 201–7) which properly belong to his own ideas. He argues for the necessary articulation of civil society into classes or estates. The necessary division of labour gives rise to groups (allgemeinen Massen, *PR*, § 201) which have not just a different type of work, but also different life-styles and hence values. These are the Hegelian 'estates' (Stände). Hegel uses the older term, rather than class, and it is better to follow him here since these groups are not just differentiated by their relation to the means of production, but by their life-style.

Hegel singles out three: the substantial or agricultural class which lives close to nature and which is generally unreflective, living rather 'an ethical life which is immediate, resting on family relationship and trust' (_PR_, § 203); the reflecting or business class which really lives the life of individuality, that is which has the orientation to the fulfilment of individual needs through rationalized work. This is the class which is most saliently identified with civil society as a system of needs. Thirdly, there is the universal class; this is the class of civil servants which identifies itself with the interests of the community as a whole.

We see here Hegel's notion of the inescapable differentiation of society which underlay his critique of the French Revolutionaries and their attempt to abolish differences in a régime of total participation. Because men in order to fulfil their needs cannot but differentiate themselves in this way, a polity which tries to abstract from this is bound to come to grief. But the differentiation is not simply to be understood as a by-product of the division of labour; we can also see in it by anticipation the structures of rational necessity.

The three classes represent each a dimension which must be present in the modern state. There must be the sense of allegiance to a whole which is above and greater than oneself, the dependence on something bigger; this the substantial class has in an unreflecting way. There must be a sense of the individual as a universal subjectivity; this the business class has. There must finally be a reasoned identification with the universal in a will which embodies this universal; and this the class of civil servants has. These three classes can also be lined up against the three levels of _Sittlichkeit_: family, civil society and state.

One of the crucial points of Hegel's philosophy is his belief that these three cannot be brought to synthesis by being present in all citizens and harmonized in each of them. Rather the synthesis is achieved by a community in which the different dimensions are carried primarily by a specific group; but where these are bound together and live a common allegiance to the whole. A state in which everyone is immediately identified with the principle of common life in the same way, this was possible among the ancients, but not with the more complex moderns. Today, we unite individuality and identification with the state by an articulation into estates where these different dimensions respectively are preponderant, and yet where all have a sense of common life, and recognize that they are part of a larger whole. . . .

This of course sharply differentiates Hegel's 'estate' from those of traditional society. These usually defined a station into which men were born and to which they had to cleave throughout life. But Hegel rejects this immobile society, along with anything approaching a caste system. For this is incompatible with the principle of individual freedom, which is central to the fully realized state. This is generally overlooked by those who want to class Hegel simply as a conservative.[4]

Civil society as a system of needs is naturally forced to develop further beyond the simple set of relations of production and exchange. Since it is the sphere in which men are related as persons, it has to protect and maintain men's rights. Hence it is involved in the administration of justice. But beyond this, the operation of the economy for the good of its members is far from being entirely assured by automatic mechanisms, in spite of the good work of the invisible hand. Lots of things can go wrong; and in the name of the good of individuals public authority has to intervene.

Hegel thus takes us in the second and third sections of civil society beyond the level of economic relations to functions which are judicial and properly political. But we are not yet dealing with the state. The reason is that we are still dealing here with individual men, the subjects of needs, united together for their common interest. What we discover is that the exigency of this common interest takes us beyond relations of production and exchange; and requires as well the administration of justice and a certain amount of regulation of economic activity. But we are not yet at the stage where we are looking on the political community as the substance, that is as constituting itself the end. The goal of all the regulations spoken of in the third section of civil society is still the good of individuals.

Hegel sees the necessary regulation being done partly by public authority, partly by corporations which are representative of various groups and professions and which operate with a publically recognized status. But what is particularly interesting and worth pausing over for a moment is Hegel's insights into the problems of civil society. It is not just that many accidents of economic life, natural disasters, overproduction, etc., can reduce men to poverty and that society thus has to operate some kind of welfare state. It is also that there is an inherent drive in civil society towards dissolution.

If civil society expands in an unimpeded way, it grows indefinitely in GNP and population. This increases greatly the wealth of some. But it also leads to an intensification of the division of labour, the increasing subdivision of jobs, and the growth of a proletariat which is tied to work of this sort. This proletariat is both materially impoverished, and spiritually as well by the narrowness and monotony of its work. But once men are reduced in this way materially and spiritually they lose their sense of self-respect and their identification with the whole community, they cease really to be integrated into it and they become a 'rabble' (Pöbel). The creating of this rabble goes along with the concentration of wealth in a few hands (*PR*, § 244). . . .

For Hegel civil society is thus to be kept in balance by being incorporated in a deeper community. It cannot govern itself. Its members need allegiance to a higher community to turn them away from infinite self-enrichment as a goal and hence the self-destruction of civil society. Self-management through corporations can be seen as a stage on this road. It makes the individual member of a larger whole, and lifts him, as it were, toward

the state. In the corporation he has the respect and dignity which he would otherwise seek, left as a simple individual, in endless self-enrichment (*PR*, § 253 E).

2

We come now to the state which is the full realization of the Idea of *Sittlichkeit*, that is a community in which the good is realized in common life. The family and civil society were only partial, non-self subsistent realizations. With the state, we have a full and self-subsistent one. It is the manifestation of substantial will. It is the community in which the fullness of rational will is manifest in public life. The fully realized state reconciles the fully developed individual subjectivity and the universal. It is concrete freedom.

> Concrete freedom consists in this, that personal individuality and its particular interests not only achieve their complete development and gain explicit recognition for their right (as they do in the sphere of the family and civil society) but, for one thing, they also pass of their own accord into the interest of the universal, and, for another thing, they know and will the universal; they even recognize it as their own substantive mind; they take it as their end and aim and are active in its pursuit. (*PR*, § 260)

This is what is achieved in the modern state.

The state is to be seen as a realization of rational necessity, of the Idea. As such, its articulations are to be understood as self-articulations of the idea. Hegel speaks of the state as an 'organism'. But it is an organism which is thought of as producing its articulations according to a necessary plan. These articulations are fixed by the Concept (*PR*, § 269). They form the constitution of the state.

Hegel here has a note on the relations of Church and state. Religion contains the same truths as the state expresses in reality. True religion should thus support the state; it should cultivate the inner conviction that the state ought to be obeyed, supported, identified with. It is a deviation when religion either retreats into other-worldliness or turns around and sets itself up against the state. The state should afford help and protection to the Church, for religion is a form of spirit's knowledge of itself. But it cannot accept a claim by the Church to be higher, for this would imply that the state was simply an external authority, an association for utility, like civil society, and not itself an embodiment of reason (*PR*, § 270 E).

Because the constitution of the state is rational, that is, the state is articulated like an organism into its different members, we cannot think of the division of powers in a spirit of checks and balances. This assumes that the different powers are already self-subsistent and have either to strive against each other or reach a compromise. But this is contrary to the very principle of the state as an organic unity, a unity which articulates itself, and in which a common life flows through all the members. If we have got as far as to engage in the game of checks and balances 'the destruction of the state is forthwith a fait accompli' (*PR*, § 272 E).

There is an important general point here which is central to Hegel's philosophy of the state. The state as a community embodying reason has to be lived as an organic whole; it cannot be seen simply as an aggregation of its elements, be these groups or individuals. For in this case it could not be lived by its citizens as the locus of a larger life with which they identify. Hegel argues strenuously against the type of constitution or constitutional provision which is based on this atomistic or composite view of the state. This is the view of men in society as simply 'a heap', as against an articulated unity. If we start with men fractioned into individual atoms, no rational state or indeed common life will be possible. . . .

Notes

1. This is, of course, the background to the famous passage in which Hegel resumes the history of freedom (*VG*, 62): The oriental world knew only that one man was free—the king represented the absolute principle, e.g.,

the Persian despot (but of course in an important sense not even he was free, as a really rational subjectivity). The Greek world won through to an intuition of freedom, but saw only that some were free. Only with Christianity do we win through to the intuition that man as such is free.

2. This scope was not, of course, entirely original. Standard treatises on law or right had to discuss private right and law relating to the family, marriage, inheritance, etc. And Kant in his treatise dealing with law, *Metaphysik der Sitten*, had also dealt with morality or a theory of duties (Pflichtenlehre) as well. What is new is the distinction of civil society and the state, and of course, the whole 'architectonic' of Hegel's system in which these different parts are deduced from the Idea.

3. We can see the important differences from Marx. Although Hegel understood the importance of the division of labour, and was astonishingly prescient about the consequences of its extension in the industrial system, as we shall see, he did not see this necessary interdependence as an integral, conscious expression of ethical substance. The domain of interchange with nature, or civil society, remains that of individual action and goals. The substantial element, which brings men to unity here, is quite unconscious. It is the operation of an 'invisible hand'.

4. But by the same token one cannot but doubt the viability of this system. Is it possible to sustain estates with really different modes of life in a society where there is real mobility, and where men are free to choose their profession? Does not for instance the unreflecting loyalty of the agricultural class presuppose a way of life into which one is born? So that entry could only be free into the other two estates. Generalized mobility is a powerful solvent. It would end up destroying estates altogether. Which is, indeed, what has happened. Although, of course, we benefit from hindsight in second-guessing Hegel on this.

Adapted from: Charles Taylor, *Hegel*, pp. 393–400, 428–439. Copyright © 1975. Reprinted by permission of Cambridge University Press. ✦

24

The Basic Context and Structure of Hegel's *Philosophy of Right*

Kenneth Westphal

I

My aim in this essay is to sketch the political and philosophical context of Hegel's *Philosophy of Right* and to reconstruct the basic aim and structure of its main argument.[1] I argue that Hegel is a reform-minded liberal who based his political philosophy on the analysis and fulfillment of individual human freedom. Hegel gave this theme a profound twist through his social conception of human individuals. He argued that individual autonomy can be achieved only within a communal context.

II

To understand Hegel's political views, it is helpful to see how they stand with regard to conservatism, romanticism, and liberalism. Hegel has been accused of conservatism or worse. The most common basis for this charge is Hegel's claim that what is rational is actual and what is actual is rational (Preface 24/20). This claim has been taken as a blanket endorsement of the status quo, but in the paragraph headed by this statement, Hegel distinguished between phenomena that embody a rational structure and those that do not. The mere fact that a state exists, on Hegel's view, does not entail that it is either rational or, in Hegel's technical sense, "actual." Hegel's distinction between existence and actuality is tied to his metaphysics, according to which the universe's rational structure progressively actualizes itself. In the political sphere, this means that social institutions aspire and tend to achieve a fundamentally rational form. The basis of this view cannot be explored here. For present purposes it suffices to note that Hegel's slogan is not a blanket endorsement of extant institutions.[2] This does not, however, determine where Hegel's politics lie in the political spectrum. That requires determining what political institutions Hegel thought were rational and why.

Hegel has been branded a conservative by associating him with the historical school of jurisprudence, whose most prominent representative was Friedrich Karl von Savigny. In a phrase, the historical school of jurisprudence sought to justify (then) contemporary German law by tracing its roots back to Roman law. Hegel refuted this main principle of the historical school by charging it with the genetic fallacy—with a twist. Instead of justifying laws by determining their origins in specific historical circumstances, this effort *de*legitimizes laws because those circumstances no longer exist (§3R)![3] The historical school also opposed codification of civil law because they viewed law as an organic growth thoroughly rooted in a changing society. Codification appeared to them to be antithetical to an organic conception of law and society. Hegel opposed the historical school on this point, too, firmly insisting on the need for law codified and promulgated in the national language as a key element in achieving rational freedom (§§258R, 211R).

Hegel has also been styled the philosopher of the Prussian *Restauration*. This is incredible, in view of Hegel's merciless attack on the leading figure of the *Restauration*, Karl Ludwig von Haller, author of *Restauration der Staatswissenschaft* (1818). Haller appealed to a version of natural law and so is subject to Hegel's criticisms of natural law in general (see below). Haller's version of natural law equated natural law with divine law, and regarded the natural might of the stronger as the basis for their natural right to rule. Haller opposed any binding legal codification, regarding a code only as a way princes could choose to inform judges of their commands. Hegel condemned Haller's view that legal codes are optional and reiterated the irrelevance of historical origins for determining matters of legitimacy (§219R; *cf.* §258R). Hegel further condemned Haller's antirationalism and opposition to codification in a long paragraph and an even longer note appended to it (§258R & N). Hegel's tone in these passages is extremely sharp and makes plain his opposition to the main tenets of the *Restauration.*[4]

Hegel has also been taken as a conservative because he espouses an organic conception of individuals and society. Most organic theories at the time, such as Burke's, were conservative. Organicism opposes atomistic individualism by holding that people do not enter society fully formed in order to satisfy their pre- or non-social aims and interests. According to organic views, individuals are formed, together with their needs, aims, and ways of thinking, within the social group to which they belong. An organic view becomes specifically conservative if it additionally holds that individuals have no conception of themselves apart from their group, that individuals cannot escape their group because it has formed their identities and needs, that individuals thus are incapable of evaluating society by pre- or non-social standards, and that because individuals are formed by their society's cultural traditions and social and political institutions, their society also suits them.

Hegel did espouse an organic conception of individuals and society. However, it is crucial to understand how he recast the issue. Typically it is supposed that there are two positions on this issue. Either individuals are more fundamental than or are in principle independent of society, or vice versa: society is more basic than or "prior to" human individuals. Hegel realized that these two options form a false dichotomy. Briefly, Hegel held that individuals are fundamentally social practitioners. Everything one does, says, or thinks is formed in the context of social practices that provide material and conceptual resources, objects of desire, skills, procedures, and the like. No one acts on the general, merely biological needs for food, safety,

companionship, or sex; and no one seeks food, safety, companionship, or sex in general. Rather, one acts on much more specific needs for much more specific kinds of objects that fulfill those needs, and one acts to achieve one's aims in quite specific ways; one's society deeply conditions one's ends because it provides specific objects that meet those ends, and it specifies procedures for obtaining them. Even so, Hegel realized that this fact does not render individuals subservient to society. First, what individuals do depends on their own response to their social context. In addition, Hegel argued that there are no individuals, no social practitioners, without social practices, and vice versa, there are no social practices without social practitioners—without individuals who learn, participate in, perpetuate, *and who modify* those social practices as needed to meet their changing needs, aims, and circumstances. The issue of the ontological priority of individuals or society is bogus.[5] Hegel's views have been widely misunderstood and castigated by critics who were beholden to a false dichotomy.

Conservatives of a certain stripe recognize that social institutions and practices are subject to change in the face of changing circumstances; Hegel's stress on the corrigibility of social practices alone does not absolve him of conservatism. Reform conservatives, as they may be called, do not believe in progress, but will adapt the status quo piecemeal to accommodate ineluctable social, economic, and political changes. Like conservatives in general, reform conservatives are skeptical about our ability to comprehend society rationally, much less to reconstruct it rationally. They place much more trust in customs, traditions, or even prejudice than in human reason, and they regard the non-rational components of human nature as the foundation of society and as a bulwark against the aspirations of rationalist reformers.[6] Conservatives thus stress the importance of a society's molding of individual character and sentiment to inculcate allegiance to one's society. In conservative political thought, feelings of patriotism are fundamental to political allegiance.

Hegel acknowledged the force of Romantic criticisms of the Enlightenment's a-historical, a-social, individualist account of reason, but he held strong Enlightenment ideals concerning human rationality. For Hegel, as for Kant, human rationality is the key to autonomy, to self-determination, and Hegel stressed this point as Kant's great contribution to practical philosophy (§135R). Hegel regarded the demand for rational understanding and justification of norms and institutions as the hallmark of modern times,[7] and he sought an account of society and government that met that demand (Preface 26/21). He also held that, although important, patriotism is too weak and insufficiently rational a basis for a modern state (§273R). In this regard, Hegel was a rationalist in principle, not out of rear-guard action, and so in this crucial regard Hegel was not a conservative, not even a reform conservative. He firmly believed in historical progress as a rational process (§§342, 343, 345). Finally, Hegel's organicism is not inherently conservative because he stressed that a society's practices are subject to rational criticism and revision. This point has been overlooked due to the assumption that rational criticism must be based on non-social standards. Hegel denied this assumption and developed subtle accounts of internal criticism, of self-criticism, and of the social bases for evaluating norms and principles. These views cannot be explored here,[8] but they are crucial for understanding the fundamental role assigned to social practices in Hegel's political philosophy.

Hegel is also reputed to be the philosopher of the reactionary Prussian state. In fact, Hegel's political philosophy became prominent during a fortunate break in conservative dominance. Conservative forces in Germany were in retreat after the Battle of Jena in 1806. The Prussian Restoration began reversing this political trend in 1815 and achieved dominance only after Hegel's death in 1831. Hegel's political philosophy is rightly associated with the core of an energetic liberal reform movement led by Prime Minister Baron Karl von Stein, Prince Karl August von Hardenberg, Wilhelm von Humbolt, and Baron von Altenstein. The de-

tails of Stein's and Hegel's views converged significantly, and Altenstein and Hegel agreed on a number of fundamentals.[9] Among the reforms instituted by Stein were the abolition of trade barriers between provinces, the break-up of the ossified Guild system, and improvements of roads and canals for the sake of commerce. Hardenberg recognized the civil rights of Jews and championed the political interests of the middle class. Altenstein brought Hegel to Berlin in 1818 and fostered the Hegelian school at the University of Berlin, in part as a bulwark against Romantics and the Historical School. Hegel first published the *Philosophy of Right* while at Berlin in 1821.

There was a deep split between these ministers and both the conservative nobility and the superstitious and reactionary king, Friedrich Willhelm III. The king was suspicious and fearful of Stein, and the nobility regarded both Stein and Hardenberg as the worst of republicans. Although the king twice promised a constitution, he probably never intended to provide one. The king belonged to the Rosicrucians, an anti-scientific cabalistic Christian sect devoted to the occult,[10] and he was quite taken with Haller's *Restauration der Staatswissenschaft*. He showed his antipathy to sharing power with the middle class by suppressing Görres's newspaper and book, which advocated these policies, and by ordering his arrest.

Hegel distinguished between the old absolutist form of monarchy and the modern constitutional form, and he held that the constitutional form is the sole rational form worthy of the times (§273). Hegel thus took a decisive and progressive stand on a burning issue in Prussia at the time. Hegel also advocated a permanent representative assembly, although none was to exist in Prussia until 1848. In attacking Savigny and especially Haller, Hegel vociferously attacked views shared by the king. Moreover, his admonition near the end of the Preface to dance in the cross of the present was directed against other-worldliness, in particular, that of the Rosicrucians—including that of the king (Preface 26/22)![11]

Hegel's differences with the Prussian conservatives, the landed nobility or *Junkers*, deserve comment. The *Junkers* favored a monarchy that was independent of popular consent but was nevertheless limited by the nobility's positions in the military, in government, and as land owners. Haller was the political philosopher most closely associated with the *Junker* aspiration to reestablish a feudal state. Hegel opposed these conservative elements. He put the government bureaucracy in the hands of an educated middle class instead of the nobility (§297). He also placed the landed classes in the upper house of his representative assembly, where they would have to function under pressure from the crown above and from the commercial classes from below (§304; *cf.* §302 & R). This institutional arrangement would preclude a return to the feudal "dualistic state" (where power was shared between the king and landed nobility) and would thwart independent political action by the estates, including the landed nobility. In sum, Hegel opposed all the conservative forces of his day.

Hegel unquestionably shares some themes with Romanticism, for example, an organicism according to which things are essentially related by their contrasts, and a social conception of individuals. Romantics loved symbols and viewed the monarch as a symbol of political unity. Hegel's governmental arrangements vaguely resemble Novalis's proposal.[12] The Romantic Görres advocated a corporate constitution that shared political power with the provinces and the middle class. Even so, when one examines their respective treatments of these themes, the differences between Hegel and the Romantics strongly predominate.

In style, Romantics tended to be epigrammatic and intuitive or inspirational rather than rationally systematic or argumentative. They began as fanatic individualists, but they came to view individuals as lacking self-sufficiency, a defect to be corrected by membership in an organically organized society.[13] Romantics were suspicious of capitalism; they venerated the nobility and denigrated the bourgeois as an acquiescent philistine. They fled from their present dissatisfactions into an idealized feudal age. They held that individuals are related to the state through devotion and veneration. They based state authority on religion, and many Romantics reacted against rationalism by converting to Catholicism. Novalis even denounced Protestantism as an interruption of the organic development of humanity.

On all these counts, Hegel differed unequivocally with Romanticism. Hegel regarded the Reformation as an important contribution to the historical development of autonomous, morally reflective individuals who rightly require rational justification for acts and institutions (Preface 27/22).[14] He denied that religious authority is the basis of state authority (§270R), and in his lectures he castigated the Romantics' conversions to Catholicism as willful capitulation to intellectual servitude (§141Z).[15] When Hegel grandiloquently described the state as God standing in the world (§270R), his point was not to divinize the state. One main point of this remark is best understood against the backdrop of the Dialectic of Kant's *Second Critique*. According to Kant, happiness results from fulfilling one's inclinations. For moral agents, on Kant's view, happiness is a gift of divine grace, first, because it's luck that one's causally determined inclinations are morally permissible, and second, because God is required to ensure that one has the luck and ability to achieve one's morally permissible ends.[16] In ways indicated below, Hegel's state is designed to minister to both these allegedly divine tasks.

Although Hegel sought to incorporate many traditional elements, such as corporations, in his view of society, he did so because he thought that they could serve a current rational purpose. Hegel rejected any retreat to a prior age or circumstance. His detailed political studies of Württemberg taught him what the Romantics never realized, that reestablishing a feudal order could not provide a stable state.[17] He looked to the middle class as a crucial foundation of any modern state, both in commerce and in the civil service. Hegel qualified his approval of capitalism (§236), but he did not oppose it and indeed based his political philosophy on a careful rethinking of modern political economy.

Having distinguished Hegel's views from conservatism and Romanticism, I now turn to his stance toward liberalism, in particular to his views on political autonomy, natural law, the social contract tradition, and utilitarianism. Modern liberalism typically has upheld two important principles. One is the principle of individual autonomy, that each person is competent to and ought to participate in making law. The other principle is the rule of justice, the idea that there are standards any law must meet to be good or just. Providing for individual autonomy requires coordinating individual decisions in order to maintain a viable social unit, and conjoining these two principles requires explaining the relationship between autonomous individuals and objective standards of justice. There are three general strategies explaining this relationship. One strategy holds that the general will is an aggregate of individual wills. Another holds that correct policy is independent of individual wills and awaits their discovery. The third, collective strategy holds that there is a general or collective will that is not simply a function of individual wills and is not simply a reflection of some antecedent correct principle.[18] Hegel took a collective approach to reconciling the two liberal principles of individual autonomy and the rule of law. In his view, individuals do play a crucial role in determining the content of law, although it is not performed by plebiscite. Individuals play a role in forming the content of law by maintaining and modifying social practices as needed to secure their freedom and their individual ends. Those social practices necessary for achieving freedom are, in Hegel's view, the proper basis of and content for statutory law. (I return to this point below.)

Hegel's rejection of two standard liberal strategies for justifying normative principles may be considered together, since Hegel makes analogous criticisms of both. One strategy for justifying normative principles or claims, especially in morals, is to appeal to conscience. Another strategy, especially in politics, is to appeal to natural law or, analogously, to natural rights. In either case, one appeals to a kind of self-evidence to justify one's claim or principle. Hegel disputed such alleged "self-evidence" for two basic reasons. First, theories of self-evidence either conflate or fail properly to distinguish between being certain that something is true, and thus believing it, and something's being true, and thus being certain of it. Second, he knew that the claims allegedly justified by appeals to conscience or to natural law are diverse and even mutually incompatible. A main desideratum for any mode of justification is to sort justified from unjustified claims, in order to help sort true from false claims. This is especially important for the controversies in our collective moral and political life. Any mode of justification that can warrant a claim and its negation fails to meet this basic desideratum and is, as such, inadequate. Appeals to conscience or to natural law fail to meet this basic requirement.[19] Hegel also held that appeals to natural law or conscience tend to omit relevant principles or considerations. This produces incomplete accounts of an issue, what Hegel called one-sided or abstract accounts.[20] Although Hegel disagreed fundamentally with standard approaches to determining the *content* of natural law, he nevertheless upheld and revamped a basic principle of natural law, namely, that right is a function of freedom of the individual will. This principle is fundamental to his argument in the *Philosophy of Right*.

Hegel's objections to the social contract tradition are merely suggested in the *Philosophy of Right*. They may be summarized briefly. Hegel argued that the state of nature is arbitrarily contrived to obtain the theorist's desired outcomes, and that abstracting from any points that might be regarded as inessential, arbitrary, or controversial would empty the state of nature of all descriptive content.[21] The principles attributed to the state of nature often have the same sort of justification as natural laws and suffer the same deficiencies. Most important, the social contract misrepresents the nature of our membership in society. Our membership in society is inevitable, necessary, and constitutive of much of our character, whereas the social contract models our membership on an elective association of otherwise independent individuals (§§75R, 100R, 258R, 281R). Viewing membership in society in this way misrepresents ourselves as mutually independent parties to a fictitious contract whereby we agree to join society, or to form a government, in order to achieve some specified range of antecedent interests we independently choose to pursue. This thwarts recognizing and understanding the social dimensions of human life. On this basis, laws or principles of justice can only be seen as restricting individual freedom of action in return for security and peaceful coexistence (§29).[22] Hegel stressed instead the role of laws and principles of justice as enabling conditions for a wide range of aspects of character development and individual action. On this basis he claimed to sketch a far more detailed and accurate account of our social involvements and our political allegiance. Hegel agreed with the social contract tradition that membership in society and obedience to government are matters that require rational justification, but he sought this justification in rational insight into the nature of our involvement in actual institutions (Preface 24–26/20–22, §31R, *cf.* §189R). Taken together, Hegel's most-fundamental objection to the social contract tradition is that the abstractions used by social contract theories to describe the state of nature, and to describe persons in that state, evade a whole range of benefits and obligations we have as members of a politically organized society (including the obligation to defend the state [§§325, 326]). Consequently, social contract theory is implicitly skeptical about those benefits and obligations and is morally and politically irresponsible, since it precludes their proper recognition and analysis. Hegel's objections to the social contract tradition do not, however, preclude him from sharing many issues and points of doctrine with that tradition.

Hegel agreed with one of Kant's main criticisms of utilitarianism, that it cannot account or provide for human autonomy because it takes given desires as the basic locus of value and source of ends.[23] He believed that utilitarianism does not take proper account of the intellectual character of the will; that it involves too atomistic a view of individuals, too instrumental a view of the state and the government; and that it is incompatible with the proper basis of right, which

rests on freedom and autonomy. He regarded the concept of utility as an important component of an intelligent grasp of one's alternative courses of action and of the coherence of one's long-range plans (§§20, 63, 77). He also regarded utility writ large, welfare, as a fundamental component of the aims of individuals and organizations and a basic responsibility of a number of civil institutions (§§123, 125, 128–30). However, he viewed freedom as a more-fundamental value than utility—considerations of utility cannot justify sacrificing freedom or individual rights (§§125, 126)—and he regarded securing freedom as the most-basic obligation of governmental institutions. Indeed, Hegel regarded happiness as beyond the competence of political arrangements. A rational state and its government are obliged to secure the conditions for the success of individual actions; they are not obliged to secure success itself, and so not the happiness it brings. These are Hegel's basic reasons for rejecting utilitarianism.

Hegel thus opposed the main forms of liberal thought in his day and in our own. I nevertheless maintain that Hegel is a progressive liberal. One basis for this claim has already been suggested, namely, that Hegel upheld the liberal principles of individual autonomy and the rule of law. There is in fact a deep point of continuity between Hegel and the social contract tradition: both Hegel and the social contract tradition take the analysis of the individual will and its freedom as the starting point for justifying basic political principles and institutions. Indeed, Hegel expressly credits Rousseau with contributing the fundamental idea that the state must be based on the will (§258R). . . .

IV

Analyzing the structure of Hegel's argument in the *Philosophy of Right* shows that achieving political autonomy is fundamental to Hegel's analysis of the state and government. Hegel divides his exposition into several distinct parts. His introduction sketches an account of the will, freedom, and the nature of right. Part One, "Abstract Right," treats principles governing property, its transfer, and wrongs against property. Part Two, "Morality," treats the rights of moral subjects, responsibility for one's actions, and *a priori* theories of right. Part Three, "Ethical Life" (*Sittlichkeit*), analyzes the principles and institutions governing central aspects of rational social life, including the family, civil society, and the state as a whole, including the government.

The *Philosophy of Right* analyzes the concept of the will (§§4–7, 279R); the main issue is what is required for a will to achieve its freedom.[24] Hegel's introduction indicates two basic requirements for achieving freedom: achieving one's ends and engaging in actions voluntarily. Hegel's sense of "voluntary" combines Aristotle's sense of not regretting one's act after the fact in full view of the actual consequences (§7 & R) with Kant's sense of autonomy, of obeying only laws one legislates for oneself. Acting freely, on Hegel's view, requires both achieving one's ends and matching one's intentions with the consequences of one's acts (*cf.* §§10 & R, 22, 23, 28, 39). Unintended consequences may give grounds for *post facto* regret, or for the sense of being bound by circumstances one did not foresee and would not desire or approve.

The main question of Hegel's analysis is, What sort of action, in what sort of context, constitutes this kind of free action? Hegel's dialectical arguments rely on indirect proof, critically analyzing alternative views that purport to solve this problem. When analyzing alternative accounts of freedom, Hegel's main critical question is, To what extent does the kind of act or intention in question succeed at its aim? Hegel argued that the conditions for successful free action are enormously rich and ultimately involve membership in a well-ordered state. His argument rests on an unspoken principle much like Kant's principle of rational willing: Whoever rationally wills an end is rationally committed to willing the requisite means or conditions for achieving that end.[25] On Hegel's analysis, the most basic end of the human will is to act freely (§27). Hegel held that obligations are generated by commitment to the basic end of willing to be free, and by the consequent commitment to

the necessary legitimate means or conditions for achieving freedom (*cf.* §261R). Correlatively, rights are generated and justified by showing that a right secures some necessary legitimate means or condition for achieving freedom (§§4, 29, 30, 261R). Principles, practices, and institutions are justified by showing that they play a necessary and irreplaceable role in achieving freedom.

Hegel's discussion of "abstract right" concerns basic principles of property rights. It is abstract in three ways. First, actions and principles are (initially) abstracted from interpersonal relations; second, they are abstracted from moral reflection; third, they are abstracted from legal and political institutions. These abstractions are sequentially shed as Hegel's analysis develops. Hegel's argument begins by analyzing a standard liberal individualist proposal for the most basic free act, taking something into possession. He holds that thoroughly analyzing the presuppositions and the inadequacies of this alleged basic free act ultimately leads to justifying membership in a specific kind of modern state.

According to most modern social contract theories, taking something into possession is the most-elementary free act, at least as regards political philosophy. For example, according to Locke, the rights that make such an act intelligible and possible are natural. In opposition to this view, Hegel expands upon Hume's and Rousseau's lesson that property rights are not natural, but are founded on conventions.[26] Hegel aimed to show that possession and other rights of property exist only on the basis of mutually recognizing the principles that constitute those rights. He defended this point through the internal criticism of the opposed natural law or "possessive individualist" view.

Although Hegel came close to Hume's view that rights are a matter of conventions, Hegel disagreed with Hume about the nature and philosophical import of conventions. Hume held that reason is primarily analytic and deductive, that given motives and desires set the ends of human action, and that custom was the great guide of human life. He therefore stressed the affective and habitual components in the customary basis of conventions. Most significant, while Hume justified conventions in terms of utility, Hegel justified conventions by their contribution to actualizing freedom. This standard follows directly from the concept of a rational will. Hegel stressed that the will is an intellectual and rational faculty (§21R, 258R), and he denied that reason only analyzes and deduces. Reason legislates the fundamental end of human action, achieving freedom, and rationality involves recognizing principles, acting on their basis, and critically assessing or revising them. Consequently, Hegel stressed the rational aspects of social conventions, especially in his discussion of the abstract principles governing property and its exchange (§§13R, 21R, 211R). Hegel highlighted the necessary role of mutual agreement to principles in any system of property rights and the intellectual achievement reflected in such agreement. Such agreement involves a common "object" among individual wills, where that object is a set of principles and their maintenance, since these are required for any successful individual act that is constituted by those principles.

Simply grasping and holding an object is not an adequate example of freedom, because it does not achieve its aim, which includes stability of holding (§45). Mere seizure of things doesn't prohibit others from making off with one's holdings. Possession (or ownership) is distinguished from mere holding by others' recognition that one possesses something (§51). Such recognition involves recognizing a set of principles that govern possession (§71). While such mutual recognition may be implicit in simple possession, it is quite explicit in contractual relations, because contractual relations involve agreeing to the principles of contractual exchange as well as agreeing to the particular exchange governed by a specific contract (§§72–74).

Hegel argued that these property rights are abstract, and that they do not constitute a self-sufficient system of actions and principles because they generate several problems that cannot be resolved within such an abstract system of rights. Hegel analyzed these problems under the heading of "wrong"

(*Unrecht*). The first problem is that this system of principles enables agents to commit wrong acts in the form of theft, fraud, or extortion. Hegel noted that, within this system of rights as such, the agreement between contracting parties is merely contingent (§81); the express contractual agreement may be duplicitous (as in fraud) or the exchange may be forced (as in coercion or crime). This abstract system of rights cannot of itself train agents habitually and intentionally to uphold rather than to violate the system of rights. This problem, which is generated on principles internal to the abstract system of property rights (including the fact that people make contracts to advance their personal aims), cannot be solved within the abstract system of rights. It can be solved only within a system of education. This is one way in which an effective and stable system of property rights presupposes a social ethos as one of its conditions of success.

It is possible to define wrongs against property within this abstract system of property rights and to argue that wrong acts are incoherent expressions of freedom. Wrongs against property are defined as acts that violate specific rightful acts of others (§92; *cf.* §126). Wrongdoers, thieves, seek to own something that rightfully belongs to someone else. Successful theft thus presupposes a system of principles of ownership while also violating that system of principles of ownership. Therefore, thefts are incoherent expressions of freedom (§92).

It is not possible to distinguish between revenge and punishment within the abstract system of property rights. Revenge can be defined within the abstract system of property rights as the informal exchange of bads for (alleged) bads, instead of goods for goods. The principles that define violations are defined within the abstract system of property rights; they simply are the system of property rights. And in addition to principles that define violations, punishment requires impartial application of those principles, and it requires common recognition of the impartiality of judgment. The common recognition of impartial judges directly anticipates social institutions of courts. But courts without impartial judges are illegitimate. Impartial judgment requires individuals to ignore their individual circumstances and to judge according to universally valid and accepted norms (§103). This is much more stringent than can be defined within the abstract system of property rights. Within the abstract system of property rights, agents commit themselves to and act in accord with the system of property rights only insofar as doing so enables them to achieve their private wants and desires. This is an insufficient basis for impartiality, because impartiality may require judging to the disadvantage of one's personal interests. The concept of a particular agent who judges impartially thus transcends the realm of abstract property rights. Indeed, such an agent is fundamentally a moral agent (§104). This is the key to Hegel's transition from "Abstract Right" to "Morality." The abstract system of property rights is not self-sufficient because its maintenance and stability require impartial judges, but the capacity of impartial judgment cannot be defined or developed within the abstract system of property rights. For this reason, the abstract system of property rights must be augmented by moral agency and reflection.

The second part of Hegel's exposition, "Morality," has two basic aims. The first is to enumerate a set of rights that are fundamental to moral agency. The second is to argue that moral principles cannot be generated or justified *a priori*. I treat these in turn.

Hegel distinguished between mere proprietors and moral agents, referring to abstract proprietors as "persons" and moral agents as "subjects." Hegel identified a number of "rights of the subjective will." These rights are due to and required by moral subjects. These rights include the rights only to recognize something (such as a principle) insofar as one adopts it as one's own (§107), only to recognize as valid what one understands to be good (§132), only to be responsible for one's actions insofar as one anticipates their results (§117), and in general to be satisfied with one's acts (§121). These rights are due moral subjects because they are necessary to preserve and promote the autonomy of thought and action that are required to assess alternative courses of ac-

tion, to justify and accept responsibility for one's acts and their consequences, to evaluate behavior, and to form impartial, well-reasoned judgments. Although the rights of subjectivity are abstract (they are too general to determine any specific injunctions or directives), they are crucial to Hegel's enterprise, and Hegel regarded them as crucial to humanity. The recognition of these rights marks the divide between antiquity and modernity (§124R); freedom simply isn't actual, it doesn't exist, without the free voluntary action of moral subjects (§106).[27]

One responsibility involved in moral reflection is to reflect adequately on the principles, circumstances, and consequences of action. Hegel was aware that the rights due moral subjects just enumerated, as such, allow a radical subjectivism or backsliding due to ignorance or irresponsibility (§132R). He insisted that moral reflection must be based on correct principles (*cf.* §140R), and he insisted on a "right of objectivity" to the effect that agents are responsible for the actual consequences of their acts, even if they were unintended (§§118 & R, 120, 132R). Furthermore, important as the rights and capacities of moral subjectivity are, Hegel held that moral reflection alone can neither generate nor justify a set of substantive moral principles (§258R). Having criticized natural law theory and utilitarianism elsewhere, Hegel focused his critical attention in *The Philosophy of Right* on the two strongest remaining contenders, Kant's ethics and the ethics of conscience. I treat these in turn.

Hegel's criticisms of Kant's moral theory are as brief and obscure as they are crucial to his whole undertaking; only their basic import may be indicated here. One basic issue between Hegel and Kant concerns moral motivation. Hegel agreed with Kant that duties ought to be done because they are duties (§133), but he disagreed with Kant that duties ought to be done *solely* because they are duties. Kant distinguished sharply between motives and ends of action, and he held that the cause of action, the motive, determines the moral worth of an action. Acting from duty is the sole morally worthy motive. Any other motive is an inclination. While acting on inclination may lead one to do the right act, it cannot give an act unconditional moral worth, because inclinations only contingently motivate right acts.[28] Kant devised a special motive, "respect," just for this case. According to Kant, respect for law is the sole rationally generated motive. Consequently it is the sole motive that reflects our transcendental freedom, and it is the sole motive that is entirely self-determined.[29] Thus it contrasts with all other "heteronomous" motives that may be caused by our (phenomenal) psychology, upbringing, environment, or other circumstance not chosen by us. (Kant allowed us to perform duties out of mixed motives, as long as the motive of respect predominates and as long as we strive to act solely on the basis of respect.)[30]

Hegel held that there can be no such pure rational motive as Kant's "respect for law." One of his reasons is straightforward: He held that Kant's arguments for transcendental idealism, and in particular for the distinction between phenomena and noumena, are inadequate. Hence transcendental idealism provides no legitimate basis for distinguishing between the sole noumenally grounded motive of respect and all other phenomenally grounded motives (that is, inclinations) in the way Kant proposed. Furthermore, all else being equal, parsimony requires a uniform account of human motivation. This point underscores how Kant devised his account of "respect" to fit the narrow requirements of transcendental idealism.[31] Hegel also held that one cannot distinguish sharply between motives, as causes of action, and the ends of action. He held that humans act on the basis of the ends they seek to achieve, and that there are various ends sought in any action. In addition to any specific ends, Hegel believed that there is always a general end to any act, the end of enjoying one's abilities. This is reflected in successfully executing one's intended action, which results in what Hegel called "self-satisfaction" (§124 & R). If Hegel is right about this, then Kant's view that we must abstract from all ends, determine how to act solely on the formal requirement of the conformity of a maxim to universal lawfulness, and perform an act solely because it is a duty, is impossible (*cf.* §124). It is impossible because

such an abstraction would leave us with no reason to act, because reasons for acting always concern ends. If we did nevertheless act, our action could not be specified on the basis of pure dutifulness. Since Kant's requirement of doing one's duty solely because it is a duty abstracts from all ends, it cannot have any content at all, since (Hegel held) actions are always conceived, intended, and performed in view of ends (§135R).[32]

Hegel also charged that Kant's Categorical Imperative cannot determine duties unless some other principle is antecedently presupposed. Hegel's charge appears to rest on some crude mistakes about Kant's test of the categorical imperative. Kant insisted, after all, that the categorical imperative requires "anthropology" to apply it to human circumstances.[33] Kant's categorical imperative takes into account a wide range of logically contingent information about our abilities, ends, and circumstances by using a principle of rational willing, that "who wills the end, wills (so far as reason has decisive influence on his [or her] action) also the means which are indispensably necessary and in his power."[34] Hegel seems to ignore this crucial aspect of Kant's view.

This Kantian rejoinder does not meet Hegel's fundamental contention. Roughly put, on Kant's theory, inclinations propose and the categorical imperative, as a test on maxims, disposes. The main way in which the categorical imperative disposes of maxims is by ruling out selfish maxims, maxims that allow one to make demands on others without allowing them to make similar demands on oneself. Because maxims are formed in specific circumstances, in view of an agent's desires, abilities, and available resources, Kant's test on maxims does presuppose a rich context of wants, ends, circumstances, practices, and institutions. Hegel argued that the categorical imperative cannot be the *fundamental* normative principle, because what needs evaluation is the normative status of precisely those antecedent wants, ends, social circumstances, practices, and institutions. The idea that ends are permissible insofar as they do not violate the categorical imperative must itself be justified by a normative analysis of ends and their permissibility. Perhaps, for example, theft does involve treating others as a mere means, but why is property legitimate to begin with? Kant of course offered grounds to suppose, for instance, that human life must be respected and that there must be property. Human life is to be respected because humans are rational agents and as such have an incommensurable value called "dignity."[35] Property must be possible (roughly) because to regard any object as, in principle, ownerless involves contradicting the principle that the will can and must be able to make use of anything it needs.[36] Hegel's point is that this is where the fundamental normative principles and justifications lie, not in subsequent tests of the categorical imperative about whether our maxims are consistent with such norms and institutions (§135R). I must leave aside for now issues between Kant and Hegel about the nature and adequacy of Kant's reasoning about these more fundamental matters.

Hegel continued his argument to show that moral reflection is not sufficient, of itself, to generate a substantive set of moral norms by criticizing the ethics of conscience. He distinguished two forms of conscience. One holds that conscience, of itself, is sufficient to generate a substantive set of moral norms. The other holds that conscience is an important aspect of moral reflection that is properly rooted in an ongoing system of social practices. Hegel called this latter type "true conscience," and he indicated that this type was not the object of his criticism (§137 & R). He criticized only the stronger type of conscience that claims normative self-sufficiency. To repeat, Hegel's basic objection to this type of theory of conscience is that it cannot reliably and adequately distinguish between subjective certainty, being convinced of something and thus concluding that it is right, and objective certainty, where the correctness of a principle forms the basis on which one is certain of its rightness (§137 & R). Subjective certainty is no guarantee of the correctness of moral principles, yet reasoning with correct moral principles is essential (§140R).

To recapitulate, one aim of Hegel's analysis of "Morality" was to show that moral re-

flection is essential to the individual integrity required for impartial judgment and for the stability of the system of property conventions, and yet that moral reflection *alone* cannot establish any principles of right. If Hegel was right that objective principles cannot be justified on the basis of natural law, utility, Kant's categorical imperative, or conscience, then he had very strong grounds for concluding, by elimination, that the relevant standards must be social. If Hegel substantiated these conclusions, then he established an important pair of biconditionals: first, principles of right can exist if and only if there is personal integrity and moral reflection; second, there are principles of right on which to reflect if and only if there are social practices. (Social practices were presented abstractly in "Abstract Right" as mutually recognized principles.) Such a system of integrated principles, practices, and morally developed agents is what Hegel called *Sittlichkeit* ("ethics" or "ethical life").

Hegel explicitly stated that his argument for introducing "Ethical Life" is regressive, since the communal phenomena analyzed in this Part provide the ground for the possibility of the phenomena analyzed in "Abstract Right" and "Morality" (§141R). "Ethical Life" analyzes a wide range of social practices that form the basis of legitimate normative principles. Social practices, however, cannot occur without social practitioners, agents who behave in accordance with social practices and who understand themselves and others as engaging in those practices. Thus these practices also include subjective awareness on the part of agents of their own actions and the actions of others. In "Abstract Right" Hegel argued that property rights cannot be understood adequately or established in abstraction from subjective reflection on the principles of action. In "Morality" Hegel argued that moral reflection on principles of action cannot be understood adequately or be effective apart from some set of objectively valid norms. In "Ethical Life" he argued that rational social life accounts both for the validity of objective norms and for the conscious knowledge and acceptance of those norms. His justification of ethical life is that the conditions for the possibility of abstract right and of morality are not given within the accounts of abstract right or of morality. The conditions for their possibility—their grounds—are provided only by ethical life.

Hegel held that normative moral, social, and political theory should focus on rational social life because so doing solves the related problems of the possibility, the principles, and the motivation of moral action. Since rational social life couldn't exist unless it were practiced and supported by individuals, action in accordance with its norms must be possible (§151), and transcendental idealism is not required to explain the possibility of moral action. Second, since rational social life consists of recognizable norms that guide the action of particular people, there can be no problem in principle about its being abstract or empty of content (§150R). Third, since individuals inevitably develop their aims, desires, skills, and knowledge by maturing within their particular society, they naturally tend to develop characters and a self-understanding that value what their rational social life promotes. Hence, by doing what their rational social life requires, they fulfill aims essential to their own characters, and their motivation for behaving ethically is quite understandable (§§152–55).

Even so, justifying *Sittlichkeit* as the proper locus for analyzing human freedom and its conditions does not, of itself, solve much. Hegel addressed several problems in his analysis of *Sittlichkeit*. First, how does rationally ordered social life enable agents to achieve their aims successfully? Second, how can the principle that one is responsible only for the anticipated consequences of one's acts be reconciled with the principle that one is responsible for all the consequences of one's acts? Hegel proposed to reconcile these principles by regularizing and making known the social context of individual action, so that individuals could act knowingly and reliably succeed. A third problem then is, how can the social context of action be regularized and made known? Fourth, how are natural needs and desires customized to make them rational self-given ends? Fifth, how can political autonomy, the right to obey only those laws and principles that one legislates for oneself, be preserved within a social context? Finally, how do extant institutions perform the functions required by the points just indicated?

The usual objection to Hegel's emphasis on a community's practices and standards is that it simply endorses the status quo of any community. Two points should be made in advance. First, on Hegel's account, not just any communal structure will do; it must be a structure that in fact aids the achievement of individual freedom. This is central to his whole account of the justification of acts, norms, and institutions; they are justified only insofar as they make a definite and irreplaceable contribution to achieving individual freedom. Moreover, Hegel required that an adequate rational society make the civil, legal, and political structure of the community known to its members, along with how individual activities contribute to and benefit from this structure. This is crucial to preserving political autonomy within a social context. Ultimately, Hegel required that a society be so effective at providing this knowledge and at satisfying individual needs for objects, relations, culture, and for belonging, that once individuals understand all of these features of their community and their roles within it, individuals will affirm their community as fulfilling their aims, requirements, and needs. Only in this way can individuals freely engage in actions in their society. This requirement stems directly from Hegel's initial analysis of freedom (§7).

Because humans act collectively to promote their freedom, the primary question of modern political philosophy, on Hegel's view, is not *a priori* what institutions would fulfill these functions, but rather how and to what extent existing institutions do fulfill these functions. This is why Hegel analyzed the rationality of extant institutions.[37] Some of the institutions to which Hegel assigned basic functions are now long gone, while others never developed in the form he described. Although we may find neither merit nor likelihood in the specific institutions Hegel advocated, we may still learn much from his accounts of the functions he assigned to various institutions and how those institutions are supposed to fulfill those functions. I turn now to an overview of Hegel's interpretation of modern social and political life, of the roles he assigned to the family, civil society, and the government....

Among other things, the family provides an institutional context for customizing and rationalizing sexual desire, and it affords a way of fulfilling the duty to raise the next generation. This involves not simply reproducing human organisms but raising human beings by introducing the child to the ways and means available in one's society for meeting basic needs and by educating the child in the principles and practices established in one's society for achieving various purposes and upholding various rights. Customizing whatever needs are due solely to biological and psychological nature occurs here, through upbringing and socialization §§174, 175). Since in modern economies the vast majority of families do not produce for their own subsistence, the family must have dealings with the economic and civil life of society.

Civil society comprises the institutions and practices involved in the production, distribution, and consumption of products that meet a variety of needs and wants. Hegel called this the "system of needs" (§188). The system of needs transforms natural impulses, needs, and wants by providing socially specific goods that meet those needs and wants, by modifying and multiplying those needs and wants (§§185, 187R, 193, 194 & R), and by inculcating the social practices through which individuals can achieve their ends (§§182, 183, 187). Hegel saw what atomistic individualists overlook in the division of labor: specialization requires coordination, and coordination requires conformity to "the universal," to common practices (§§182, 198, 199). (Hegel indicated that the "universal" he analyzed just *are* those practices, since those practices are the relations among individuals in question [§182].) Furthermore, the collective development of social practices, based on the joint pursuit of individual aims, *is* the collective development of implicit principles of right (§187R; cf. §§260, 270). Hegel stressed the fact that these "universal" principles derive their con-

tent from the ends and activities of particular agents who determine for themselves what to do (§187R). This is the most-fundamental role individuals have in developing the content of principles of right, in Hegel's view. Legitimate law simply codifies those practices that require legal protection in order to remain effective (§§209–12). In this connection he refers back to his opening endorsement of Montesquieu's point that laws are justified on the basis of their systematic interconnection within present social circumstances (§§212, 3R).

Civil society and the economy must support the basic freedom of choosing one's vocation (§§206, 207). Everyone has equal civil (and later, political) rights, not on the basis of *recherché* grounds of the incommensurable value of rational agency (Kant's "dignity"), but because there is no legitimate reason to distinguish among persons to the disadvantage of some and the advantage of others (§§36, 38, 209R, 270N3). (Hegel explicitly repudiated the antisemitism of his conservative and liberal contemporaries [§209R; cf. §270N3].)

Civil society contains three distinct kinds of institution: the Administration of Justice, the Public Authority, and Corporations. The Administration of Justice codifies, promulgates, and administers statutory law. Codification makes explicit the normative principles implicit in social practices (§§209–12; cf. §§187R, 249). Promulgating codified law contributes to informing people about the structure of their social context of action (§§132R, 209, 211R, 215; cf. 228R). This is why law must be codified and promulgated in the national language (§216), and why judicial proceedings must be public (§§224, 228R). The enforcement of law regularizes the context of individual action and protects and preserves the social practices people have developed to exercise their freedom and achieve their individual aims (§§208, 210, 218, 219). Establishing recognized courts replaces revenge with punishment (§220).

The Public Authority is responsible for removing or remedying "accidental hindrances" to achieving individual ends; it minimizes and tends to the natural and social accidents that impair or disrupt successful free individual action (§§230–33, 235). Its responsibilities include crime prevention and penal justice (§233), price controls on basic commodities (§236), civil engineering, utilities, and public health (§236R), public education (§239), moderation of economic fluctuations (including unemployment) (§236), the eradication of the causes of poverty and poverty relief (§§240, 241, 242, 244),[38] and the authorization and regulation of corporations (§252). If these factors are not regulated, individuals cannot plan or conduct their lives reliably; their freedom is compromised.

The coordination among different economic agents, whether persons or businesses, entails that the economy consists of sectors or branches of industry or commerce (§201, 251). This results from the division of labor and the distribution of specialized manufacture across various regions of the country. In modern specialized production, individual jobs and businesses depend on a complex of far-flung economic factors (§183; *cf.* §§182, 187, 289R, 332). Hegel recognized this fact and sought to ensure that such factors would not hold uncomprehended sway over people's activities and lives. Such unknown influences limit freedom and autonomy. He addressed this need by advocating a certain kind of professional and commercial "corporation." These corporations are a kind of trade association, one for each significant branch of the economy, to which all people working in that sector belong. Membership in a corporation integrates one's gainful employment explicitly into a sector of the economy and provides information about how one's sector of the economy fits with and depends on the other sectors. Corporations also moderate the impact of business fluctuations on their members (§§252 & R, 253 & R). Corporations counteract the divisive tendencies of individual self-seeking in commerce by explicitly recognizing individual contributions to the corporate and social good and by bringing together people who would otherwise form two antagonistic groups, an underclass of rabble and a class of elite captains of industry who would wield inordinate social influence due to their disproportionate wealth (§§244, 253R).

The final institution in Hegel's state is a central goverment.[39] He distinguished between the government and the state as a whole. He called the government the "strictly political state" (§§273, 276) and reserved the term "state" for the whole of a civilly and politically well-organized society (§§257–71). He called civil society—*sans* representative government—"the state external" (§183). Civil society is an "external" state because it does not fulfill the requirements of political autonomy and because the state institutions in civil society, the Administration of Justice and the Public Authority, are viewed as mere instruments for achieving personal aims. The members of civil society are bourgeois but not (as such) citizens, since they must obey coercive laws without recognizing, and without having public and official recognition of, their role in constituting legitimate law. The Public Authority and the Administration of Justice act on their behalf, but not under their purview. Thus the political aspect of autonomy is not achieved within civil society (*cf.* §266). Achieving political autonomy and, with that, citizenship is the primary function of Hegel's government.

Hegel ascribed sovereignty to the state as a whole, and not simply to the monarch or even to "the princely power" (*die fürstliche Gewalt* or "crown") as a whole (§278). No element of the state holds sovereignty (although each has an institutionally defined role in sovereignty), and no office is a private, individual possession (§§277, 278R). Hegel treated the government under the general heading of the constitution. It is important to note that, although Hegel said that the constitution ought to be viewed as eternal (§273R), he recognized that the constitution is subject to change (§§273R, 298). What he said of law in general holds of constitutional law as well, namely, that to be executed, a law must be determinate. By being specific enough to be acted upon, a law must have what Hegel called an "empirical side," where this empirical side is subject to change in the process of implementing the law (§299R). Although this may seem to contravene the nature of law, it does not since, as

336 Part II ◆ *The 19th Century and Beyond*

Hegel stressed, following Montesquieu (§3R), a law is justified by the function it presently performs within an integrated society. As conditions change, so must laws change in order to remain legitimate and effective (§298). In this way, Hegel noted in his lectures, a country can gradually bring its constitution to a very different condition from where it began (§298z).[40] Hegel regarded this not as an inevitable concession to historical contingency, but as a rational process of gradual collective revision of the legal conditions required to achieve and preserve freedom. He held that the constitution ought to be regarded as eternal to ensure that change results gradually from detailed knowledge of genuine need, rather than from insufficiently informed ratiocination. He equally held that reform must be a deliberate ongoing process, so that it does not require revolution.

Hegel's government comprises the "princely power" or Crown, the Executive, and the Legislature (§273). The Crown consists of a hereditary monarch and chief ministers of state (§275). The ministers formulate laws that articulate and protect the basic social practices necessary for individual free action (§283). Cabinet ministers must meet objective qualifications (§§291, 292) and are strictly accountable for their actions (§284). At their recommendation laws are enacted by the monarch (§§275, 283, 284). The Crown protects the interests of one's state and one's interests in the state through foreign policy, either by diplomacy or war (§329). The Executive administers the laws necessary for knowledgeable individual free action (§287). The Legislature consists of an advisory body, drawn from high-level servants with direct ties to the Crown and the Executive (§300), and the bicameral Estates Assembly.

Hegel assigned a quite restricted but very important role to the Estates Assembly. The Estates Assembly provides crucial popular insight into affairs of state (§§287, 301). In particular, the Assembly affords popular insight into the fact that the laws enacted by the Crown and administered by the Executive are laws that codify and protect the social practices in which one participates and

through which one achieves one's ends (*cf.* §§314, 315). The Estates Assembly thus places the government under popular purview (§302). Corporate representatives to the lower house of the Estates Assembly are elected by their respective memberships (§§288, 311). Representatives from the agricultural sector, landed aristocrats (§306), inherit their right to enter the upper house (§307). Hegel based his system of representation on the Corporations and other branches of civil society, because doing otherwise would divide political from civil life and leave "political life hanging in the air" (§303R). It must be stressed again that citizens have a hand in developing and modifying social practices as needed, and the law, on Hegel's view, is to follow suit. The main function of Hegel's Estates Assembly is educative, to inform people systematically and thoroughly about the activities of their government and the principles, procedures, and resources for acting within their society, so that individuals can resolve to act in an informed and responsible manner, unencumbered insofar as possible by unexpected consequences. This education and information enables individuals to act voluntarily and autonomously within their society (§301 & R). Hegel expected that when people understood how their society meets their needs and facilitates their ends, they would affirm their membership in society and would act in it willingly. The fact that the institutions of government, especially the legislative assembly, are necessary for free, autonomous action is their primary political justification, according to Hegel.[41]

Hegel opposed rule by open democratic election. He held that democracy rests too much on political sentiment (§173R), that open elections encourage people to vote on the basis of their apparent particular interests at the expense of their interests in the community as a whole (§§281R, 301R), and that the tiny role each elector has in large general elections results in electoral indifference (§311R). Open elections also do not guarantee that each important economic and civil branch of society is represented (§§303R, 308R, 311R). Consequently, open elections threaten to allow what Hegel's corporate representative system was designed to avoid: the overbearing influence of factions, especially of monied interests, on the political process (§§253R, 303R). Hegel also recognized that legislation requires expert knowledge; he expected popular opinion to supply general ideas or feedback about matters of detail (§301R). Finally, Hegel was aware of the relative political inexperience of his contemporary Germans. His civil and political institutions were designed to provide regular, publicly acknowledged, institutionalized channels for political education so that people would not act in political ignorance. Hegel may have opposed standard democratic procedures, but he was a staunch republican, and he took the vital issue of an informed body politic and universal participation in political life much more seriously, and at a much deeper institutional level, than any modern democracy. . . .

Notes

1. I refer to Hegel's works, including *Grundlinien der Philosophie des Rechts*, in *Werke in Zwanzig Bänden* ed. Moldenhauer & Michel (Frankfurt: Suhrkamp, 1970; cited as *Werke*). I give my own translations. I cite *Elements of the Philosophy of Right* ed. A. W Wood, tr. H. B. Nisbet (Cambridge: Cambridge University Press, 1991). References to Hegel's Preface are indicated as "Preface," followed by the German page number/ and the page number of Nisbet's translation. With the exception of Hegel's Preface, all references to Hegel's *Philosophy of Right* are given by section number, which are shared by the original and the translations. The "Remarks" Hegel wrote and appended to these sections are designated with an "R" suffix: "§138R." If a section and its remark are cited, they are cited as "§138 & R." Notes are indicated similarly with an "N" suffix; if there is more than one note to a section, its number follows: N3. Citations from lecture notes appended to the *Philosophy of Right* are indicated by a "Z" suffix.

2. See *Enzyklopädie der philosophischen Wissenschaften im Grundrisse 1* (*Werke* 8; hereafter "*Enz.*"); *The Encyclopedia Logic* tr. T. F. Geraets, H. S. Harris, & W. A. Suchting (Indianapolis: Hackett, 1991), §6.

3. Reinhold Aris mistakenly attributes to Hegel the very principle of the historical school Hegel criticized (*History of Political Thought*

in Germany from 1789–1815 [rpt: New York: Kelly, 1968], 227). I have relied on Aris for historical details.

4. See Walter Jaeschke, "Die Vernünftigkeit des Gesetzes" in *Hegels Rechtsphilosophie im Zusammenhang der europäischen Verfassungsgeschichte*, ed. H.-C. Lucas & O. Pöggeler, (Stuttgart-Bad Cannstatt: Frommann-Holzboog, 1986), 221–56.

5. See my *Hegel's Epistemological Realism* (Dordrecht & Boston: Kluwer, 1989 [hereafter "HER"]), 166, 169–72. Hegel stated his view in easily misunderstood metaphysical terms. He stated that individuals are related to the ethical order and its powers "as accidents to substance" (§145). This certainly can sound like individuals are subservient to a social whole. Yet Hegel held that "substance is in essence the relation of accidents to itself" (§163R). This is to say that substance is essentially the relation among the "accidents" (properties or members) of something. More briefly, he stated that "substance is the totality of its accidents" (§67R). This doctrine is part of Hegel's holistic metaphysics, and it is stated in the section of the *Encyclopedia* to which Hegel refers in §163R, *Enz.* §150. On Hegel's holism, see *HER*, ch. 10.

6. This characterization of reform conservatism is adapted from Klaus Epstein, *The Genesis of German Conservatism* (Princeton: Princeton University Press, 1966), 13. I have relied much on this work for historical details.

7. This demand and its satisfaction are essential to what Hegel calls the modern "rights of subjectivity" (§§ 106, 107, 117, 121, 124R, 132) and to Hegel's effort in the *Philosophy of Right* to present and justify an integrated doctrine of rights and duties (§§148R, 149, 150)

8. See *HER*, chs. 1, 6–8.

9. Compare what is said below with Aris's account of Stein's views (*Political Thought*, ch. 13), and see Wood's editorial notes to §§271n2, 273n9, 277n1, 288, 289, 291, 303, and 312.

10. On Rosicrucianism, see John Passmore's entry on Robert Flood in *The Encyclopedia of Philosophy* ed. P. Edwards (New York & London: Macmillan, 1967), vol. 3, 207–8, and Epstein, *Genesis*, pp. 104–11.

11. See Adriaan Peperzak, *Philosophy and Politics: A Commentary on the Preface to Hegel's Philosophy of Right* (Dordrecht: Nijhoff, 1987), 108.

12. Compare Aris's citation from Novalis's 1798 *Athenäum* (*Political Thought* p. 279) with Hegel's account of the government, discussed below.

13. See Jacob Baxa's citation of Friedrich Schlegel in *Einführung in die romantische Staatswissenschaft*, 2nd ed. (Jena: Gustav Fischer, 1931), 68.

14. Also see *Vorlesungen über die Geschichte der Philosophie* III (*Werke* 20; hereafter "*VGP*"), p. 57; *Lectures on the History of Philosophy: The Lectures of 1825–1826* ed. & tr. R. F. Brown and tr. J. M. Stewart (Berkeley: University of California Press, 1990 hereafter "*LHP*") III, 102–3. Also see *Vorlesungen über die Philosophie der Geschichte* (*Werke* 12; hereafter "*VPG*"), 496–97; *The Philosophy of History* tr. J. Sibree (New York: Dover, 1956; hereafter "*LPH*"), 416–17.

15. Lectures of 1822–23. See *G. W. F. Hegel: Vorlesungen über Rechtsphilosophie 1818–1831. Edition and Kommentar in sechs Bänden* ed. K-H Ilting (Stuttgart-Bad Cannstatt: Frommann-Holzboog, 1974; hereafter "Ilting"), vol. III, 475.

16. See my "Hegel's Critique of Kant's Moral World View," *Philosophical Topics* 19, No. 2 (1991): 133–76, §IV.

17. "Die Verfassung Deutchlands" (*Werke* 1), pp. 461–581, and "Verhandlungen in der Versammlung der Landstände des Königreichs Württemberg im Jahr 1815 und 1816" (*Werke* 4), pp. 462–597; "The German Constitution" and "Proceedings of the Estates Assembly in the Kingdom of Württemberg, 1815–1816" in *Hegel's Political Writings*, ed. Z. A. Pelczynski, tr. T. M. Knox (Oxford: Clarendon Press, 1964), 143–242 and 246–94.

18. I have adapted the formulation of this issue from C. Dyke, "Collective Decision Making in Rousseau, Kant, Hegel, and Mill," *Ethics* 80, No. 1 (1969): 22. Dyke misunderstands Hegel's approach to this issue.

19. Hegel makes this point against Jacobi's doctrine of "immediate knowledge." See my "Hegel's Attitude Toward Jacobi in the 'Third Attitude of Thought Toward Objectivity,'" *The Southern Journal of Philosophy* 27, No.1 (1989): 135–56 §VII, 148–51.

20. "Wer Denkt Abstrakt?" (*Werke* 2, pp. 575–81); "Who Thinks Abstractly?" in *Hegel: Texts and Commentary* tr. W Kaufmann (Garden City: Anchor, 1966), 113–18.

21. "Über die wissenschaftlichen Behandlung des Naturrechts, seine Stelle in der praktischen Philosophie und sein Verhältnis zu den positiven Rechtswissenschaften" (*Werke* II, pp. 434–530), p. 445; *Natural Law* tr. T. M. Knox (Philadelphia: University of Pennsylvania Press, 1975), 63–64.

22. See Joyce Beck Hoy, "Hegel's Critique of Rawls," *Clio* 10, No. 4 (1981) 407–22.

23. *VGP* III, p. 334; *LHP* III, pp. 244–45.

24. Hegel often speaks simply of "the concept" (see §§19, 106). One must recall that "the concept" at issue is the concept of the will.

25. *Grundlegung der Metaphysik der Sitten* (*Gesammelte Schriften*, Königliche Preussische Akademie der Wissenschaft: Berlin and Leipzig: de Gruyter, 1904–; hereafter "Ak"); *Groundwork of the Metaphysic of Morals* tr. Paton (New York: Harper, 1964), vol. IV, 412, (cited hereafter as "*Groundwork*"). I cite only the Akademie pagination, which appears in all recent translations of Kant's writings.

26. Hume, *A Treatise of Human Nature*, ed. Selby-Bigge (Oxford: Clarendon Press, 1888, 1965), 488–91; Rousseau, *On the Social Contract*, tr. Masters & Masters (New York: St. Martin's, 1978), 47.

27. Hegel's view that "individuals" develop historically has raised controversy. What was Thrasymachus, if not an individual? Two points need to be noted. First, Thrasymachus was a product of the decline of Greek life, a decline brought on, according to Hegel, in part by the development of individualism. More important, the conception of "individual" of interest to Hegel is a conception of an individual who has the moral ability to reflect on and evaluate normative principles, the kind of individual who is capable of such acts as conscientious objection or civil disobedience. Hegel finds the first clear precedents of that development in Antigone, Socrates, and Jesus. This conception of the individual is not an historical constant; even less are examples of it an historical constant. (Socrates *may* have engaged in something approximating conscientious objection when he openly refused to obey the command of the thirty tyrants to arrest the general Leon in Salamis [*Apology* 32cd], but he nowhere considers civil disobedience; this is not a Greek notion.)

28. *Groundwork*, Ak IV, p. 398, *cf.* pp. 393–94.

29. Ibid., p. 401*n*.

30. *Kritik der praktischen Vernunft* (*Critique of Practical Reason*, tr. Beck [Indianapolis: Bobbs-Merrill, 1956]), Ak V, 155–56.

31. *Phänomenologie des Geistes* (*Werke* 3), p. 457; *Phenomenology of Spirit* tr. Miller (Oxford: Clarendon, 1977), 377.

32. See Allen Wood, "The Emptiness of the Moral Will," *The Monist* 72, No. 3 (1989): 454–83.

33. *Groundwork*, Ak IV, p. 412.

34. Ibid., p. 417.

35. Ibid., pp. 428, 434–35.

36. *Metaphysische Anfangsgründe der Rechtslehre* (*Metaphysical Principles of Justice*, tr. J. Ladd [Indianapolis: Bobbs-Merrill, 1965]), Ak VI, 246.

37. More properly, extant modern institutions (§299R). Hegel thought, *e.g.*, that the Roman and medieval epochs objectively lacked properly rational institutions and so were not amenable to such interpretation. Roughly, the Roman world lacked sufficient community; the Middle Ages lacked sufficient individuality. See *VPG*, pp. 340, 345–46, 349, 351, 358, 359, 441, 444–47, 455–60; *LPH*, pp. 279, 284, 287, 289, 295, 366, 369–72, 378–83.

38. Although the Public Authority is to deal with accidental events, and Hegel here listed poverty relief under its authority, he did not think that poverty was an accidental phenomenon. Rather, he recognized that it results from the workings of civil society (§245), and in his lectures he stated what his text clearly implies, that poverty is a wrong done by one class to another (§244Z; lectures of 1824–25, Ilting IV, p. 609). He held it to be an evil because it produces wretched living conditions and because it systematically excludes the poor from participation in society (§244). He was deeply concerned with this problem and was not satisfied with any solution to it he proposed.

39. Although Hegel advocated a centralized national government, he also held that regional and municipal concerns should be handled by regional or municipal government (§§288, 290).

40. Lectures of 1822–23 (Ilting III, pp. 788–90). *Cf.* Hegel's lectures of 1824–25 (Ilting IV, p. 698).

41. One might wonder about a situation like that described in *Brave New World*, or about a society that progressively reduced its needs and ends so that they were simpler to satisfy and required little political or social activity. Would either society meet Hegel's criteria of freedom by default? The "Brave New World" circumstance is ruled out by the fact that in it social harmony is produced by social engineering initiated and directed by the government. This directly contradicts the nature of legitimate law on Hegel's view, where the content and legitimacy of law flows from the free actions of individuals up through the legislative and executive apparatus. The prospect of social degeneracy is very real, on Hegel's view, but also fails his criteria for freedom. Hegel believed that part of the development of rationality and freedom through history involves an expansion of the understanding of the range of human possibilities, activities, and responsibilities, which, once achieved, serves as an historical benchmark for assessing how free a society is.

Reprinted from: Kenneth Westphal, "The Basic Context and Structure of Hegel's *Philosophy of Right*," in *The Cambridge Companion to Hegel*, edited by Frederick C. Beiser, pp. 234–244, 246–262, 264–268. Copyright © 1993. Reprinted by permission of Cambridge University of Press. ✦

Karl Marx

Karl Marx, widely known as the founder of communist ideology, was actually a great theorist of capitalism. Creating a brave new world out of the ashes of feudalism, capitalism was a revolutionary force in the modern world—totally transforming economics, technology, politics, and culture. Despite capitalism's achievements, though, brutal exploitation still characterized most people's lives. This glaring contradiction spurred Marx to begin a lifetime of study of the origins, development, and operations of capitalism. It also made him a lifelong political activist, working for organizations dedicated to creating a more rational and democratic society. As his colleague Friedrich Engels once observed, Marx's ideas had roots in three strains of thought—German philosophy, British political economy, and French socialist politics. The circumstances of Marx's life make it easy to see how such a theoretical synthesis might have been possible.

Born in Trier, Germany, in 1818, Marx's university years (in Bonn, Berlin, and Jena) were influenced by Hegel's thought and by reformist intellectuals known as the Young Hegelians. After completing his Ph.D. in philosophy in 1841, Marx began a career in journalism as editor of the liberal newspaper, *Rheinische Zeitung*. Expelled from Germany for his radical democratic views, he embarked on the life of an exile. With his wife and children, Marx stayed first in Paris (where he wrote critiques of Hegelian philosophy and began collaborating with Engels), then Brussels (where *The Communist Manifesto* was written), then back to Germany (where he participated in the 1848 revolution), finally settling in London. Gregarious but essentially a loner, frequently impoverished yet often extravagant, respected for his leadership abilities yet prone to quarrelling with others—Marx's life and intellect grappled with a maze of contradictions.[1] After devoting his life to the study of political economy and to working-class politics, Marx died in London in 1883.

True to the synthetic origins of his study of capitalism, Marx views society as a web of interpersonal relations, an organic whole that undergoes historical evolution, shapes human activities, and constitutes what we might call human nature. Though there are many places from which to begin a study of social relations (e.g., religion, politics, literature, or philosophy), production (or, more broadly, economics) is for Marx the most fruitful starting point, since it colors all other aspects of social life. Any specific mode of production (the structures and processes of material life) thus tends to be associated with a certain social or historical stage of development, with a particular way of life. Although the economic aspect is central, it does not always dominate or directly determine all features of society and culture.

Because its political conflicts and economic crises make it an obstacle to further progress, capitalism will inevitably fall and give rise to a new mode of production—called both socialism and communism by Marx. This social transformation will not occur without class conflict, without people's spontaneous, yet prepared revolutionary activity. Marx left no utopian blueprint for communist society, but he did describe its major features: an end to private property, the division of labor, and social classes; a radical democratic polity and economic planning; and a true community of authentic individuals.

Economic and Philosophic Manuscripts

In the selection from the *Economic and Philosophic Manuscripts* (1844), Marx begins with a Hegelian critique of political economy, centered about the contradictions spawned by private property and alienated labor. The remainder of the selection examines the fourfold nature of this alienation—namely, alienation from one's product, from the activity of production, from fellow human beings, and from one's "species being."

The German Ideology

In the first selection from *The German Ideology* (written between 1845 and 1847), Marx and Engels present an overview of the materialist interpretation of history. After outlining the primary stages of history, Marx and Engels then set forth the premises of their outlook. Their starting point is the production of material life, the process by which labor is simultaneously the means of satisfying needs, renewing life, and actualizing oneself. Unlike the work of animals, human labor is potentially a free and conscious activity; however, capitalism erects serious obstacles to fulfilling that potential. The final selection identifies the division of labor as the locus of the central contradictions in capitalist society. It concludes by discussing the nature of communist society and the struggles necessary to bring it about.

The Communist Manifesto

As Marx and Engels illustrate in *The Communist Manifesto* (1848), capitalism was a revolutionary force in the modern world. Its scientific discoveries and technological innovations created wonders far superior to Egyptian pyramids or Gothic cathedrals, and yielded riches far beyond the wildest dreams of past rulers and conquerors. It developed a social order marked by constant change in economics, technology, politics, and culture. Despite capitalism's achievements, however, brutal exploitation still characterized the life of most people. In the selections from the *Manifesto* below, Marx and Engels recount the history and nature of bourgeois society as well as the current condition and future aims of the proletariat.

Capital

The final selections—from Marx's last work, the first volume of *Capital* (1867)—set forth the labor theory of value, one of his most important economic concepts. Initially, Marx distinguishes between a commodity's use-value (the utility we get from a thing, its ability to satisfy a particular need we have) and its exchange-value (what we can get in exchange for it). He does so to show the extent to which bourgeois political economy has misread the nature of material life. Next, Marx develops the concept of surplus value as an indicator of the degree to which capitalists exploit workers. Here, he argues that workers are exploited not because individual capitalists are vicious or immoral, but because of the very nature of wage labor itself.

Commentaries

The selection from Steven Best explores Marx's general outlook in some detail. He starts by noting that, for Marx, Hegel's dialectic provided both a method of analysis and the means to envision a better future. Critical of any deterministic interpretation, Best argues that Marx actually presented a multifaceted theory of historical continuity and change. From time to time, he employed three basic models—humanist, productive forces, and class struggle—each emphasizing a different aspect of the complex nature of social relations. Vitally attuned to context, Marx developed his views on proletarian revolution and communist society by examining the possibilities found in contemporary political and economic life.

William James Booth analyzes Marx's vision of the end of alienation, a vision expressed in a famous passage from *The German Ideology*. Booth focuses on the themes of "activity, time, and community" in order to gain insight into Marx's particular sketch of communist society and his broader critique of political economy. Marx's vision of communism suggests that it would create a society where individuals themselves determine how to spend their time in the context of a cooperative, self-governing community.

That vision, says Booth, transformed political theory from a meditation on the nature of justice to a thoroughgoing critique of political economy.

Note

1. This portrait of Marx is drawn from Francis Wheen, *Karl Marx: A Life* (New York: Norton, 1999).

Web Sources

http://www.marxists.org/archive/marx/index.htm

Marx and Engels Internet Archive. Gateway to the works of and information about Marx and Engels.

http://www.knuten.liu.se/~bjoch509/philosophers/mar.html

Björn's Guide to Philosophy. Another helpful portal site for information about Marx and Engels.

http://www.historyguide.org/intellect/marx.html

The History Guide: Lectures on Modern European Intellectual History. Summary of Marx's life and thought.

Class Activities and Discussion Items

1. Outline the central elements of Marx's materialist interpretation of history. What strengths and weaknesses does this outlook have? Are its assumptions well-grounded?

2. Describe Marx's view of the condition of the proletariat under capitalism. How would workers alter their condition? In what ways would communism bring about a better life?

3. Compare and contrast the analysis of the modern condition presented by Marx and other theorists. What fundamental flaws can be found in modern society, according to each of these theorists? What suggested remedy to the problems of modernity does each theorist offer?

Further Reading

Avineri, Shlomo. 1968. *The Social and Political Thought of Karl Marx.* Cambridge: Cambridge University Press. Classic exposition of Marx's political theory.

Carver, Terrell, ed. 1991. *The Cambridge Companion to Marx.* Cambridge: Cambridge University Press. Important collection of essays on various aspects of Marx's thought.

Cohen, G.A. 2000. *Karl Marx's Theory of History: A Defence,* expanded edition. Princeton, NJ: Princeton University Press. Founding work of the school of thought now known as "analytical Marxism."

Milward, Bob. 2000. *Marxian Political Economy: Theory, History and Contemporary Relevance.* London: Macmillan. Contemporary appraisal of Marx's economic views.

Wheen, Francis. 1999. *Karl Marx: A Life.* New York: Norton. Engaging and revealing look at the personal side of Marx. ✦

25

Excerpts from *Economic and Philosophical Manuscripts*

Karl Marx

Alienated Labour

We started from the presuppositions of political economy. We accepted its vocabulary and its laws. We presupposed private property, the separation of labour, capital, and land, and likewise of wages, profit, and ground rent; also division of labour; competition; the concept of exchange value, etc. Using the very words of political economy we have demonstrated that the worker is degraded to the most miserable sort of commodity; that the misery of the worker is in inverse proportion to the power and size of his production; that the necessary result of competition is the accumulation of capital in a few hands, and thus a more terrible restoration of monopoly; and that finally the distinction between capitalist and landlord, and that between peasant and industrial worker disappears and the whole of society must fall apart into the two classes of the property owners and the propertyless workers.

Political economy starts with the fact of private property, it does not explain it to us. It conceives of the material process that private property goes through in reality in general abstract formulas which then have for it a value of laws. It does not understand these laws, i.e. it does not demonstrate how they arise from the nature of private property. Political economy does not afford us any explanation of the reason for the separation of la-

bour and capital, of capital and land. When, for example, political economy defines the relationship of wages to profit from capital, the interest of the capitalist is the ultimate court of appeal, that is, it presupposes what should be its result. In the same way competition enters the argument everywhere. It is explained by exterior circumstances. But political economy tells us nothing about how far these exterior, apparently fortuitous circumstances are merely the expression of a necessary development. We have seen how it regards exchange itself as something fortuitous. The only wheels that political economy sets in motion are greed and war among the greedy, competition.

It is just because political economy has not grasped the connections in the movement that new contradictions have arisen in its doctrines, for example, between that of monopoly and that of competition, freedom of craft and corporations, division of landed property and large estates. For competition, free trade, and the division of landed property were only seen as fortuitous circumstances created by will and force, not developed and comprehended as necessary, inevitable, and natural results of monopoly, corporations, and feudal property.

So what we have to understand now is the essential connection of private property, selfishness, the separation of labour, capital, and landed property, of exchange and competition, of the value and degradation of man, of monopoly and competition, etc.—the connection of all this alienation with the money system.

Let us not be like the political economist who, when he wishes to explain something, puts himself in an imaginary original state of affairs. Such an original stage of affairs explains nothing. He simply pushes the question back into a grey and nebulous distance. He presupposes as a fact and an event what he ought to be deducing, namely the necessary connection between the two things, for example, between the division of labour and exchange. Similarly, the theologian explains the origin of evil through the fall, i.e. he presupposes as an historical fact what he should be explaining. We start with a contemporary fact of political economy:

The worker becomes poorer the richer is his production, the more it increases in power and scope. The worker becomes a commodity that is all the cheaper the more commodities he creates. The depreciation of the human world progresses in direct proportion to the increase in value of the world of things. Labour does not only produce commodities; it produces itself and the labourer as a commodity and that to the extent to which it produces commodities in general.

What this fact expresses is merely this: the object that labour produces, its product, confronts it as an alien being, as a power independent of the producer. The product of labour is labour that has solidified itself into an object, made itself into a thing, the objectification of labour. The realization of labour is its objectification. In political economy this realization of labour appears as a loss of reality for the worker, objectification as a loss of the object or slavery to it, and appropriation as alienation, as externalization.

The realization of labour appears as a loss of reality to an extent that the worker loses his reality by dying of starvation. Objectification appears as a loss of the object to such an extent that the worker is robbed not only of the objects necessary for his life but also of the objects of his work. Indeed, labour itself becomes an object he can only have in his power with the greatest of efforts and at irregular intervals. The appropriation of the object appears as alienation to such an extent that the more objects the worker produces, the less he can possess and the more he falls under the domination of his product, capital.

All these consequences follow from the fact that the worker relates to the product of his labour as to an alien object. For it is evident from this presupposition that the more the worker externalizes himself in his work, the more powerful becomes the alien, objective world that he creates opposite himself, the poorer he becomes himself in his inner life and the less he can call his own. It is just the same in religion. The more man puts into God, the less he retains in himself. The worker puts his life into the object and this means that it no longer belongs to him but to the object. So the greater this activity, the more the worker is without an object. What the product of his labour is, that he is not. So the greater this product the less he is himself. The externalization of the worker in his product implies not only that his labour becomes an object, an exterior existence but also that it exists outside him, independent and alien, and becomes a self-sufficient power opposite him, that the life that he has lent to the object affronts him, hostile and alien.

Let us now deal in more detail with objectification, the production of the worker, and the alienation, the loss of the object, his product, which is involved in it.

The worker can create nothing without nature, the sensuous exterior world. It is the matter in which his labour realizes itself, in which it is active, out of which and through which it produces.

But as nature affords the means of life for labour in the sense that labour cannot live without objects on which it exercises itself, so it affords a means of life in the narrower sense, namely the means for the physical subsistence of the worker himself.

Thus the more the worker appropriates the exterior world of sensuous nature by his labour, the more he doubly deprives himself of the means of subsistence, firstly since the exterior sensuous world increasingly ceases to be an object belonging to his work, a means of subsistence for his labour; secondly, since it increasingly ceases to be a means of subsistence in the direct sense, a means for the physical subsistence of the worker.

Thus in these two ways the worker becomes a slave to his object: firstly he receives an object of labour, that is he receives labour, and secondly, he receives the means of subsistence. Thus it is his object that permits him to exist first as a worker and secondly as a physical subject. The climax of this slavery is that only as a worker can he maintain himself as a physical subject and it is only as a physical subject that he is a worker.

(According to the laws of political economy the alienation of the worker in his object is expressed as follows: the more the worker produces the less he has to consume, the more values he creates the more value-less and worthless he becomes, the more formed the product the more deformed the worker, the more civilized the product, the more barbaric the worker, the more powerful the work the more powerless becomes the worker, the more cultured the work the more philistine the worker becomes and more of a slave to nature.)

Political economy hides the alienation in the essence of labour by not considering the immediate relationship between the worker (labour) and production. Labour produces works of wonder for the rich, but nakedness for the worker. It produces palaces, but only hovels for the worker; it produces beauty, but cripples the worker; it replaces labour by machines but throws a part of the workers back to a barbaric labour and turns the other part into machines. It produces culture, but also imbecility and cretinism for the worker.

The immediate relationship of labour to its products is the relationship of the worker to the objects of his production. The relationship of the man of means to the objects of production and to production itself is only a consequence of this first relationship. And it confirms it. We shall examine this other aspect later.

So when we ask the question: what relationship is essential to labour, we are asking about the relationship of the worker to production.

Up to now we have considered only one aspect of the alienation or externalization of the worker, his relationship to the products of his labour. But alienation shows itself not only in the result, but also in the act of production, inside productive activity itself. How would the worker be able to affront the product of his work as an alien being if he did not alienate himself in the act of production itself? For the product is merely the summary of the activity of production. So if the product of labour is externalization, production itself must be active externalization, the externalization of activity, the activity of externalization. The alienation of the object of labour is only the résumé of the alienation, the externalization in the activity of labour itself.

What does the externalization of labour consist of then?

Firstly, that labour is exterior to the worker, that is, it does not belong to his essence. Therefore he does not confirm himself in his work, he denies himself, feels miserable instead of happy, deploys no free physical and intellectual energy, but mortifies his body and ruins his mind. Thus the worker only feels a stranger. He is at home when he is not working and when he works he is not at home. His labour is therefore not voluntary but compulsory, forced labour. It is therefore not the satisfaction of a need but only a means to satisfy needs outside itself. How alien it really is is very evident from the fact that when there is no physical or other compulsion, labour is avoided like the plague. External labour, labour in which man externalizes himself, is a labour of self-sacrifice and mortification. Finally, the external character of labour for the worker shows itself in the fact that it is not his own but someone else's, that it does not belong to him, that he does not belong to himself in his labour but to someone else. As in religion the human imagination's own activity, the activity of man's head and his heart, reacts independently on the individual as an alien activity of gods or devils, so the activity of the worker is not his own spontaneous activity. It belongs to another and is the loss of himself.

The result we arrive at then is that man (the worker) only feels himself freely active in his animal functions of eating, drinking, and procreating, at most also in his dwelling and dress, and feels himself an animal in his human functions.

Eating, drinking, procreating, etc. are indeed truly human functions. But in the abstraction that separates them from the other round of human activity and makes them into final and exclusive ends they become animal.

We have treated the act of alienation of practical human activity, labour, from two aspects. (1) The relationship of the worker to the product of his labour as an alien object that has power over him. This relationship is at the same time the relationship to the sensuous exterior world and to natural objects as to an alien and hostile world opposed to him. (2) The relationship of labour to the act of production inside labour. This relationship is the relationship of the worker to his own activity as something that is alien and does not belong to him; it is activity that is passivity, power that is weakness, procreation that is castration, the worker's own physical and intellectual energy, his personal life (for what is life except activity?) as an activity directed against himself, independent of him and not belonging to him. It is self-alienation, as above it was the alienation of the object.

We now have to draw a third characteristic of alienated labour from the two previous ones.

Man is a species-being not only in that practically and theoretically he makes both his own and other species into his objects, but also, and this is only another way of putting the same thing, he relates to himself as to the present, living species, in that he relates to himself as to a universal and therefore free being.

Both with man and with animals the species-life consists physically in the fact that man (like animals) lives from inorganic nature, and the more universal man is than animals the more universal is the area of inorganic nature from which he lives. From the theoretical point of view, plants, animals, stones, air, light, etc. form part of human consciousness, partly as objects of natural science, partly as objects of art; they are his intellectual inorganic nature, his intellectual means of subsistence, which he must first prepare before he can enjoy and assimilate them. From the practical point of view, too, they form a part of human life and activity. Physically man lives solely from these products of nature, whether they appear as food, heating, clothing, habitation, etc. The universality of man appears in practice precisely in the universality that makes the whole of nature into his inorganic body in that it is both (i) his immediate means of subsistence and also (ii) the material object and tool of his vital activity. Nature is the inorganic body of a man, that is, in so far as it is not itself a human body. That man lives from nature means that nature is his body with which he must maintain a constant interchange so as not to die. That man's physical and intellectual life depends on nature merely means that nature depends on itself, for man is a part of nature.

While alienated labour alienates (1) nature from man, and (2) man from himself, his own active function, his vital activity, it also alienates the species from man; it turns his species-life into a means towards his individual life. Firstly it alienates species-life and individual life, and secondly in its abstraction it makes the latter into the aim of the former which is also conceived of in its abstract and alien form. For firstly, work, vital activity, and productive life itself appear to man only as a means to the satisfaction of a need, the need to preserve his physical existence. But productive life is species-life. It is life producing life. The whole character of a species, its generic character, is contained in its manner of vital activity, and free conscious activity is the species-characteristic of man. Life itself appears merely as a means to life.

The animal is immediately one with its vital activity. It is not distinct from it. They are identical. Man makes his vital activity itself into an object of his will and consciousness. He has a conscious vital activity. He is not immediately identical to any of his characterizations. Conscious vital activity differentiates man immediately from animal vital activity. It is this and this alone that makes man a species-being. He is only a conscious being, that is, his own life is an object to him, precisely because he is a species-being. This is the only reason for his activity being free activity. Alienated labour reverses the relationship so that, just because he is a conscious being, man makes his vital activity and essence a mere means to his existence.

The practical creation of an objective world, the working-over of inorganic nature, is the confirmation of man as a conscious species-being, that is, as a being that relates to the species as to himself and to himself as to the species. It is true that the animal, too, produces. It builds itself a nest, a dwelling, like the bee, the beaver, the ant, etc. But it only produces what it needs immediately for itself or its offspring; it produces one-sidedly whereas man produces universally; it produces only under the pressure of immediate physical need, whereas man produces freely from physical need and only truly produces when he is thus free; it produces only itself whereas man reproduces the whole of nature. Its product belongs immediately to its physical body whereas man can freely separate himself from his product. The animal only fashions things according to the standards and needs of the species it belongs to, whereas man knows how to produce according to the measure of every species and knows everywhere how to apply its inherent standard to the object; thus man also fashions things according to the laws of beauty.

Thus it is in the working over of the objective world that man first really affirms himself as a species-being. This production is his active species-life. Through it nature appears as his work and his reality. The object of work is therefore the objectification of the species-life of man; for he duplicates himself not only intellectually, in his mind, but also actively in reality and thus can look at his image in a world he has created. Therefore when alienated labour tears from man the object of his production, it also tears from him his species-life, the real objectivity of his species and turns the advantage he has over animals into a disadvantage in that his inorganic body, nature, is torn from him.

Similarly, in that alienated labour degrades man's own free activity to a means, it turns the species-life of man into a means for his physical existence.

Thus consciousness, which man derives from his species, changes itself through alienation so that species-life becomes a means for him. Therefore alienated labour:

(3) makes the species-being of man, both nature and the intellectual faculties of his species, into a being that is alien to him, into a means for his individual existence. It alienates from man his own body, nature exterior to him, and his intellectual being, his human essence.

(4) An immediate consequence of man's alienation from the product of his work, his vital activity and his species-being, is the alienation of man from man. When man is opposed to himself, it is another man that is opposed to him. What is valid for the relationship of a man to his work, of the product of his work and himself, is also valid for the relationship of man to other men and of their labour and the objects of their labour.

In general, the statement that man is alienated from his species-being, means that one man is alienated from another as each of them is alienated from the human essence.

The alienation of man and in general of every relationship in which man stands to himself is first realized and expressed in the relationship with which man stands to other men.

Thus in the situation of alienated labour each man measures his relationship to other men by the relationship in which he finds himself placed as a worker.

We began with a fact of political economy, the alienation of the worker and his production. We have expressed this fact in conceptual terms: alienated, externalized labour. We have analysed this concept and thus analysed a purely economic fact. . . .

Adapted from: *Karl Marx: Selected Writings*, edited by David McLellan, pp. 77–83. Copyright © 1977. Reprinted by permission of Oxford University Press. ✦

26
Excerpts from *The German Ideology*

Karl Marx
Friedrich Engels

The Premisses of the Materialist Method

The premisses from which we begin are not arbitrary ones, not dogmas, but real premisses from which abstraction can only be made in the imagination. They are the real individuals, their activity and the material conditions under which they live, both those which they find already existing and those produced by their activity. These premisses can thus be verified in a purely empirical way.

The first premiss of all human history is, of course, the existence of living human individuals. Thus the first fact to be established is the physical organization of these individuals and their consequent relation to the rest of nature. Of course, we cannot here go either into the actual physical nature of man, or into the natural conditions in which man finds himself—geological, oro-hydrographical, climatic, and so on. The writing of history must always set out from these natural bases and their modification in the course of history through the action of men.

Men can be distinguished from animals by consciousness, by religion, or anything else you like. They themselves begin to distinguish themselves from animals as soon as they begin to produce their means of subsistence, a step which is conditioned by their physical organization. By producing their means of subsistence men are indirectly producing their actual material life.

The way in which men produce their means of subsistence depends first of all on the nature of the actual means of subsistence they find in existence and have to reproduce. This mode of production must not be considered simply as being the production of the physical existence of the individuals. Rather it is a definite form of activity of these individuals, a definite form of expressing their life, a definite mode of life on their part. As individuals express their life, so they are. What they are, therefore, coincides with their production, both with *what* they produce and with *how* they produce. The nature of individuals thus depends on the material conditions determining their production.

This production only makes its appearance with the increase of population. In its turn this presupposes the intercourse of individuals with one another. The form of this intercourse is again determined by production.

The relations of different nations among themselves depend upon the extent to which each has developed its productive forces, the division of labour, and internal intercourse. This statement is generally recognized. But not only the relation of one nation to others, but also the whole internal structure of the nation itself depends on the stage of development reached by its production and its internal and external intercourse. How far the productive forces of a nation are developed is shown most manifestly by the degree to which the division of labour has been carried. Each new productive force, in so far as it is not merely a quantitative extension of productive forces already known (for instance the bringing into cultivation of fresh land), causes a further development of the division of labour.

The division of labour inside a nation leads at first to the separation of industrial and commercial from agricultural labour, and hence to the separation of town and country and to the conflict of their interests. Its further development leads to the separation of commercial from industrial labour. At the same time, through the division of labour inside these various branches there develop various divisions among the individuals co-operating in definite kinds of labour. The relative position of these individual groups is determined by the methods employed in agriculture, industry, and commerce (patriarchalism, slavery, estates, classes). These same conditions are to be seen (given a more developed intercourse) in the relations of different nations to one another.

The various stages of development in the division of labour are just so many different forms of ownership, i.e. the existing stage in the division of labour determines also the relations of individuals to one another with reference to the material, instrument, and product of labour.

The first form of ownership is tribal ownership. It corresponds to the undeveloped stage of production, at which a people lives by hunting and fishing, by the rearing of beasts, or, in the highest stage, agriculture. In the latter case it presupposes a great mass of uncultivated stretches of land. The division of labour is at this stage still very elementary and is confined to a further extension of the natural division of labour existing in the family. The social structure is, therefore, limited to an extension of the family; patriarchal family chieftains, below them the members of the tribe, finally slaves. The slavery latent in the family only develops gradually with the increase of population, the growth of wants, and with the extension of external relations, both of war and of barter.

The second form is the ancient communal and State ownership which proceeds especially from the union of several tribes into a city by agreement or by conquest, and which is still accompanied by slavery. Beside communal ownership we already find movable, and later also immovable, private property developing, but as an abnormal form subordinate to communal ownership. The citizens hold power over their labouring slaves only in their community, and on this account alone, therefore, they are bound to the form of communal ownership. It is the communal private property which compels the active citizens to remain in this spontaneously derived form of association over against their slaves. For this reason the whole structure of society based on this communal ownership, and with it the power of the people, decays in the same measure as, in particular, immov-

able private property evolves. The division of labour is already more developed. We already find the antagonism of town and country; later the antagonism between those states which represent town interests and those which represent country interests, and inside the towns themselves the antagonism between industry and maritime commerce. The class relation between citizens and slaves is now completely developed.

With the development of private property, we find here for the first time the same conditions which we shall find again, only on a more extensive scale, with modern private property. On the one hand, the concentration of private property, which began very early in Rome (as the Licinian agrarian law proves) and proceeded very rapidly from the time of the civil wars and especially under the Emperors; on the other hand, coupled with this, the transformation of the plebeian small peasantry into a proletariat, which, however, owing to its intermediate position between propertied citizens and slaves, never achieved an independent development.

The third form of ownership is feudal or estate property. If antiquity started out from the town and its little territory, the Middle Ages started out from the country. This differing starting-point was determined by the sparseness of the population at that time, which was scattered over a large area and which received no large increase from the conquerors. In contrast to Greece and Rome, feudal development at the outset, therefore, extends over a much wider territory, prepared by the Roman conquests and the spread of agriculture at first associated with it. The last centuries of the declining Roman Empire and its conquest by the barbarians destroyed a number of productive forces; agriculture had declined, industry had decayed for want of a market, trade had died out or been violently suspended, the rural and urban population had decreased. From these conditions and the mode of organization of the conquest determined by them, feudal property developed under the influence of the Germanic military constitution. Like tribal and communal ownership, it is based again on a community; but the directly producing class standing over against it is not, as in the case of the ancient community, the slaves, but the enserfed small peasantry. As soon as feudalism is fully developed, there also arises antagonism towards the towns. The hierarchical structure of landownership, and the armed bodies of retainers associated with it, gave the nobility power over the serfs. This feudal organization was, just as much as the ancient communal ownership, an association against a subjected producing class; but the form of association and the relation to the direct producers were different because of the different conditions of production.

This feudal system of landownership had its counterpart in the towns in the shape of corporative property, the feudal organization of trades. Here property consisted chiefly in the labour of each individual person. The necessity for association against the organized robber barons, the need for communal covered markets in an age when the industrialist was at the same time a merchant, the growing competition of the escaped serfs swarming into the rising towns, the feudal structure of the whole country: these combined to bring about the guilds. The gradually accumulated small capital of individual craftsmen and their stable numbers, as against the growing population, evolved the relation of journeyman and apprentice, which brought into being in the towns a hierarchy similar to that in the country.

Thus the chief form of property during the feudal epoch consisted on the one hand of landed property with serf labour chained to it, and on the other of the labour of the individual with small capital commanding the labour of journeymen. The organization of both was determined by the restricted conditions of production—the small-scale and primitive cultivation of the land and the craft type of industry. There was little division of labour in the heyday of feudalism. Each country bore in itself the antithesis of town and country; the division into estates was certainly strongly marked; but apart from the differentiation of princes, nobility, clergy, and peasants in the country, and masters, journeymen, apprentices, and soon also the rabble of casual labourers in the towns, no division of importance took place. In agriculture it was rendered difficult by the strip-system, beside which the cottage industry of the peasants themselves emerged. In industry there was no division of labour at all in the individual trades themselves, and very little between them. The separation of industry and commerce was found already in existence in older towns; in the newer it only developed later, when the towns entered into mutual relations.

The grouping of larger territories into feudal kingdoms was a necessity for the landed nobility as for the towns. The organization of the ruling class, the nobility, had, therefore, everywhere a monarch at its head.

The fact is, therefore, that definite individuals who are productively active in a definite way enter into these definite social and political relations. Empirical observation must in each separate instance bring out empirically, and without any mystification and speculation, the connection of the social and political structure with production. The social structure and the State are continually evolving out of the life-process of definite individuals, but of individuals, not as they may appear in their own or other people's imagination, but as they really are, i.e. as they operate, produce materially, and hence as they work under definite material limits, presuppositions, and conditions independent of their will.

The production of ideas, of conceptions, of consciousness, is at first directly interwoven with the material activity and the material intercourse of men, the language of real life. Conceiving, thinking, the mental intercourse of men, appear at this stage as the direct efflux of their material behaviour. The same applies to mental production as expressed in the language of politics, laws, morality, religion, metaphysics, etc. of a people. Men are the producers of their conceptions, ideas, etc.—real, active men, as they are conditioned by a definite development of their productive forces and of the intercourse corresponding to these, up to its furthest forms. Consciousness can never be anything else than conscious existence, and the existence of men is their actual life-process. If in all ideology men and their circumstances appear upside-down as in a *camera obscura*, this phenomenon arises just as much from their historical life-process as the inversion of objects on the retina does from their physical life-process.

In direct contrast to German philosophy which descends from heaven to earth, here we ascend from earth to heaven. That is to say, we do not set out from what men say, imagine, conceive, nor from men as narrated, thought of, imagined, conceived, in order to arrive at men in the flesh. We set out from real, active men, and on the basis of their real life-process we demonstrate the development of the ideological reflexes and echoes of this life-process. The phantoms formed in the human brain are also, necessarily, sublimates of their material life-process, which is empirically verifiable and bound to material premises. Morality, religion, metaphysics, all the rest of ideology and their corresponding forms of consciousness, thus no longer retain the semblance of independence. They have no history, no development; but men, developing their material production and their material intercourse, alter, along with this their real existence, their thinking and the products of their thinking. Life is not determined by consciousness, but consciousness by life. In the first method of approach the starting-point is consciousness taken as the living individual; in the second method, which conforms to real life, it is the real living individuals themselves, and consciousness is considered solely as their consciousness.

This method of approach is not devoid of premises. It starts out from the real premises and does not abandon them for a moment. Its premises are men, not in any fantastic isolation and rigidity, but in their actual, empirically perceptible process of development under definite conditions. As soon as this active life-process is described, history ceases to be a collection of dead facts as it is with the empiricists (themselves still abstract), or an imagined activity of imagined subjects, as with the idealists.

Where speculation ends—in real life—there real, positive science begins: the representation of the practical activity, of the practical process of development of men. Empty talk about consciousness ceases, and real knowledge has to take its place. When reality is depicted, philosophy as an independent branch of knowledge loses its medium of existence. At the best its place can only be taken by a summing-up of the most general results, abstractions which arise from the observation of the historical development of men. Viewed apart from real history, these abstractions have in themselves no value whatsoever. They can only serve to facilitate the arrangement of historical material, to indicate the sequence of its separate strata. But they by no means afford a recipe or schema, as does philosophy, for neatly trimming the epochs of history. On the contrary, our difficulties begin only when we set about the observation and the arrangement—the real depiction—of our historical material, whether of a past epoch or of the present. The removal of these difficulties is governed by premises which it is quite impossible to state here, but which only the study of the actual life-process and the activity of the individuals of each epoch will make evident. We shall select here some of these abstractions, which we use in contradistinction to the ideologists, and shall illustrate them by historical examples.

Since we are dealing with the Germans, who are devoid of premises, we must begin by stating the first premiss of all human existence and, therefore, of all history, the premiss, namely, that men must be in a position to live in order to be able to 'make history'. But life involves before everything else eating and drinking, a habitation, clothing, and many other things. The first historical act is thus the production of the means to satisfy these needs, the production of material life itself. And indeed this is an historical act, a fundamental condition of all history, which today, as thousands of years ago, must daily and hourly be fulfilled merely in order to sustain human life. Even when the sensuous world is reduced to a minimum, to a stick as with Saint Bruno, it presupposes the action of producing the stick. Therefore in any interpretation of history one has first of all to observe this fundamental fact in all its significance and all its implications and to accord it its due importance. It is well known that the Germans have never done this, and they have never, therefore, had an earthly basis for history and consequently never an historian. The French and the English, even if they have conceived the relation of this fact with so-called history only in an extremely one-sided fashion, particularly as long as they remained in the toils of political ideology, have nevertheless made the first attempts to give the writing of history a materialistic basis by being the first to write histories of civil society, of commerce and industry.

The second point is that the satisfaction of the first need (the action of satisfying, and the instrument of satisfaction which has been acquired) leads to new needs; and this production of new needs is the first historical act. Here we recognize immediately the spiritual ancestry of the great historical wisdom of the Germans who, when they run out of positive material and when they can serve up neither theological nor political nor literary rubbish, assert that this is not history at all, but the 'prehistoric era'. They do not, however, enlighten us as to how we proceed from this nonsensical 'prehistory' to history proper; although, on the other hand, in their historical speculation they seize upon this 'prehistory' with especial eagerness because they imagine themselves safe there from interference on the part of 'crude facts', and, at the same time, because there they can give full rein to their speculative impulse and set up and knock down hypotheses by the thousand.

The third circumstance which, from the very outset, enters into historical development is that men, who daily remake their own life, begin to make other men, to propagate their kind: the relation between man and woman, parents and children, the family. The family, which to begin with is the only social relationship, becomes later, when increased needs create new social relations and the increased population new needs, a subordinate one (except in Germany), and must then be treated and analysed according to the existing empirical data, not according to 'the concept of the family', as is the custom in Germany. These three aspects of social activity are not of course to be taken as three different stages, but just as three aspects or, to make it clear to the Germans, three 'moments', which have existed simultaneously since the dawn of history and the first men, and which still assert themselves in history today.

The production of life, both of one's own in labour and of fresh life in procreation, now appears as a double relationship: on the one hand as a natural, on the other as a social, relationship. By social we understand the co-operation of several individuals, no matter under what conditions, in what manner, and to what end. It follows from this that a certain mode of production, or industrial stage, is always combined with a certain mode of co-operation, or social stage, and this mode of co-operation is itself a 'productive force'. Further, that the multitude of productive forces accessible to men determines the nature of society, hence, that the 'history of humanity' must always be studied and treated in relation to the history of industry and exchange. . . .

Private Property and Communism

With the division of labour, in which all these contradictions are implicit, and which in its turn is based on the natural division of labour in the family and the separation of society into individual families opposed to one another, is given simultaneously the distribution, and indeed the unequal distribution, both quantitative and qualitative, of labour and its products, hence property: the nucleus, the first form of which lies in the family, where wife and children are the slaves of the husband. This latent slavery in the family, though still very crude, is the first property, but even at this early stage it corresponds perfectly to the definition of modern economists who call it the power of disposing of the labour-power of others. Division of labour and private property are, moreover, identical expressions: in the one the same thing is affirmed with reference to activity as is affirmed in the other with reference to the product of the activity.

Further, the division of labour implies the contradiction between the interest of the separate individual or the individual family and the communal interest of all individuals who have intercourse with one another. And indeed, this communal interest does not exist merely in the imagination, as the 'general interest', but first of all in reality, as the mutual interdependence of the individuals among whom the labour is divided. And finally, the division of labour offers us the first example of how, as long as man remains in natural society, that is, as long as a cleavage exists between the particular and the common interest, as long, therefore, as activity is not voluntarily, but naturally, divided, man's own deed becomes an alien power opposed to him, which enslaves him instead of being controlled by him. For as soon as the distribution of labour comes into being, each man has a particular, exclusive sphere of activity, which is forced upon him and from which he cannot escape. He is a hunter, a fisherman, a shepherd, or a critical critic, and must remain so if he does not want to lose his means of livelihood; while in communist society, where nobody was one exclusive sphere of activity but each can become accomplished in any branch he wishes, society regulates the general production and thus makes it possible for me to do one thing today and another tomorrow, to hunt in the morning, fish in the afternoon, rear cattle in the evening, criticize after dinner, just as I have a mind, without ever becoming hunter, fisherman, cowherd, or critic. This fixation of social activity, this consolidation of what we ourselves produce into an objective power above us, growing out of our control, thwarting our expectations, bringing to naught our calculations, is one of the chief factors in historical development up till now.

And out of this very contradiction between the interest of the individual and that of the community the latter takes an independent form as the State, divorced from the real interests of individual and community, and at the same time as an illusory communal life, always based, however, on the real ties existing in every family and tribal conglomeration—such as flesh and blood, language, division of labour on a larger scale,

and other interests—and especially, as we shall enlarge upon later, on the classes, already determined by the division of labour, which in every such mass of men separate out, and of which one dominates all the others. It follows from this that all struggles within the State, the struggle between democracy, aristocracy, and monarchy, the struggle for the franchise, etc. etc. are merely the illusory forms in which the real struggles of the different classes are fought out among one another. Of this the German theoreticians have not the faintest inkling, although they have received a sufficient introduction to the subject in the *Deutsch–französische Jahrbücher* and *Die heilige Familie*. Further, it follows that every class which is struggling for mastery, even when its domination, as is the case with the proletariat, postulates the abolition of the old form of society in its entirety and of domination itself, must first conquer for itself political power in order to represent its interest in turn as the general interest, which immediately it is forced to do. Just because individuals seek only their particular interest, which for them does not coincide with their communal interest, the latter will be imposed on them as an interest 'alien' to them, and 'independent' of them, as in its turn a particular, peculiar 'general' interest; or they themselves must remain within this discord, as in democracy. On the other hand, too, the practical struggle of these particular interests, which constantly really run counter to the communal and illusory communal interests, makes practical intervention and control necessary through the illusory 'general' interest in the form of the State.

The social power, i.e. the multiplied productive force, which arises through the co-operation of different individuals as it is determined by the division of labour, appears to these individuals, since their co-operation is not voluntary but has come about naturally, not as their own united power, but as an alien force existing outside them, of the origin and goal of which they are ignorant, which they thus cannot control, which on the contrary passes through a peculiar series of phases and stages independent of the will and the action of man, nay even being the prime governor of these.

How otherwise could, for instance, property have had a history at all, have taken on different forms, and landed property, for example, according to the different premises given, have proceeded in France from parcellation to centralization in the hands of a few, in England from centralization in the hands of a few to parcellation, as is actually the case today? Or how does it happen that trade, which after all is nothing more than the exchange of products of various individuals and countries, rules the whole world through the relation of supply and demand—a relation which, as an English economist says, hovers over the earth like the Fates of the ancients, and with invisible hand allots fortune and misfortune to men, sets up empires and overthrows empires, causes nations to rise and to disappear—while with the abolition of the basis of private property, with the communistic regulation of production (and, implicit in this, the destruction of the alien relation between men and what they themselves produce), the power of the relation of supply and demand is dissolved into nothing, and men get exchange, production, the mode of their mutual relation, under their own control again?

This 'alienation' (to use a term which will be comprehensible to the philosophers) can, of course, only be abolished given two practical premises. For it to become an 'intolerable' power, i.e. a power against which men make a revolution, it must necessarily have rendered the great mass of humanity 'propertyless', and produced, at the same time, the contradiction of an existing world of wealth and culture, both of which conditions presuppose a great increase in productive power, a high degree of its development. And, on the other hand, this development of productive forces (which itself implies the actual empirical existence of men in their world historical, instead of local, being) is an absolutely necessary practical premiss because without it want is merely made general, and with destitution the struggle for necessities and all the old filthy business would

necessarily be reproduced; and furthermore, because only with this universal development of productive forces is a universal intercourse between men established, which produces in all nations simultaneously the phenomenon of the 'propertyless' mass (universal competition), makes each nation dependent on the revolutions of the others, and finally has put world-historical, empirically universal individuals in place of local ones. Without this, (1) communism could only exist as a local event; (2) the forces of intercourse themselves could not have developed as universal, hence intolerable powers: they would have remained home-bred conditions surrounded by superstition; and (3) each extension of intercourse would abolish local communism. Empirically, communism is only possible as the act of the dominant peoples 'all at once' and simultaneously, which presupposes the universal development of productive forces and the world intercourse bound up with communism. Moreover, the mass of propertyless workers—the utterly precarious position of labour-power on a mass scale cut off from capital or from even a limited satisfaction and, therefore, no longer merely temporarily deprived of work itself as a secure source of life—presupposes the world market through competition. The proletariat can thus only exist world-historically, just as communism, its activity, can only have a 'world-historical' existence. World-historical existence of individuals means existence of individuals which is directly linked up with world history.

Communism is for us not a state of affairs which is to be established, an ideal to which reality will have to adjust itself. We call communism the real movement which abolishes the present state of things. The conditions of this movement result from the premisses now in existence. . . .

Adapted from: Karl Marx and Friedrich Engels, *Karl Marx and Friedrich Engels: The German Ideology, A Student Edition*, C. J. Arthur, ed., pp. 270ff. Copyright © 1970 by Lawrence and Wishart. Reprinted by permission of Lawrence and Wishart (London). ◆

27

Excerpts from *The Communist Manifesto*

Karl Marx
Friedrich Engels

A spectre is haunting Europe—the spectre of Communism. All the Powers of old Europe have entered into a holy alliance to exorcise this spectre: Pope and Tsar, Metternich and Guizot, French Radicals and German police-spies.

Where is the party in opposition that has not been decried as Communistic by its opponents in power? Where the Opposition that has not hurled back the branding reproach of Communism, against the more advanced opposition parties, as well as against its reactionary adversaries? Two things result from this fact.

I. Communism is already acknowledged by all European Powers to be itself a Power.

II. It is high time that Communists should openly, in the face of the whole world, publish their views, their aims, their tendencies, and meet this nursery tale of the Spectre of Communism with a Manifesto of the party itself.

To this end, Communists of various nationalities have assembled in London, and sketched the following Manifesto, to be published in the English, French, German, Italian, Flemish, and Danish languages.

I

Bourgeois and Proletarians

The history of all hitherto existing society is the history of class struggles.

Freeman and slave, patrician and plebeian, lord and serf, guild-master and journeyman—in a word, oppressor and oppressed, stood in constant opposition to one another, carried on an uninterrupted, now hidden, now open fight, a fight that each time ended either in a revolutionary re-constitution of society at large or in the common ruin of the contending classes.

In the earlier epochs of history, we find almost everywhere a complicated arrangement of society into various orders, a manifold gradation of social rank. In ancient Rome we have patricians, knights, plebeians, slaves; in the Middle Ages, feudal lords, vassals, guild-masters, journeymen, apprentices, serfs; in almost all of these classes, again, subordinate gradations.

The modern bourgeois society that has sprouted from the ruins of feudal society has not done away with class antagonisms. It has but established new classes, new conditions of oppression, new forms of struggle in place of the old ones.

Our epoch, the epoch of the bourgeoisie, possesses, however, this distinctive feature: it has simplified the class antagonisms. Society as a whole is more and more splitting up into two great hostile camps, into two great classes directly facing each other: Bourgeoisie and Proletariat.

From the serfs of the Middle Ages sprang the chartered burghers of the earliest towns. From these burgesses the first elements of the bourgeoisie were developed.

The discovery of America, the rounding of the Cape, opened up fresh ground for the rising bourgeoisie. The East Indian and Chinese markets, the colonization of America, trade with the colonies, the increase in the means of exchange and in commodities generally, gave to commerce, to navigation, to industry, an impulse never before known, and thereby, to the revolutionary element in the tottering feudal society, a rapid development.

The feudal system of industry, under which industrial production was monopolized by closed guilds, now no longer sufficed for the growing wants of the new markets. The manufacturing system took its place. The guild-masters were pushed on one side by the manufacturing middle class; division of labour between the different corporate guilds vanished in the face of division of labour in each single workshop.

Meantime the markets kept ever growing, the demand ever rising. Even manufacture no longer sufficed. Thereupon, steam and machinery revolutionized industrial production. The place of manufacture was taken by the giant, Modern Industry, the place of the industrial middle class, by industrial millionaires, the leaders of whole industrial armies, the modern bourgeois.

Modern industry has established the world-market, for which the discovery of America paved the way. This market has given an immense development to commerce, to navigation, to communication by land. This development has, in its turn, reacted on the extension of industry; and in proportion as industry, commerce, navigation, railways extended, in the same proportion the bourgeoisie developed, increased its capital, and pushed into the background every class handed down from the Middle Ages.

We see, therefore, how the modern bourgeoisie is itself the product of a long course of development, of a series of revolutions in the modes of production and of exchange.

Each step in the development of the bourgeoisie was accompanied by a corresponding political advance of that class. An oppressed class under the sway of the feudal nobility, an armed and self-governing association in the medieval commune; here independent urban republic (as in Italy and Germany), there taxable 'third estate' of the monarchy (as in France), afterwards, in the period of manufacture proper, serving either the semi-feudal or the absolute monarchy as a counterpoise against the nobility, and, in fact, corner-stone of the great monarchies in general, the bourgeoisie has at last, since the establishment of Modern Industry and of the world-market, conquered for itself, in the modern representative State, exclusive political sway. The executive of the modern State is but a committee for managing the common affairs of the whole bourgeoisie.

The bourgeoisie, historically, has played a most revolutionary part.

The bourgeoisie, wherever it has got the upper hand, has put an end to all feudal, patriarchal, idyllic relations. It has pitilessly torn asunder the motley feudal ties that bound man to his 'natural superiors', and has left remaining no other nexus between man and man than naked self-interest, than callous 'cash payment'. It has drowned the most heavenly ecstasies of religious fervour, of chivalrous enthusiasm, of philistine sentimentalism, in the icy water of egotistical calculation. It has resolved personal worth into exchange value, and in place of the numberless indefeasible chartered freedoms, has set up that single, unconscionable freedom—Free Trade. In one word, for exploitation, veiled by religious and political illusions, it has substituted naked, shameless, direct, brutal exploitation.

The bourgeoisie has stripped of its halo every occupation hitherto honoured and looked up to with reverent awe. It has converted the physician, the lawyer, the priest, the poet, the man of science into its paid wage-labourers.

The bourgeoisie has torn away from the family its sentimental veil, and has reduced the family relation to a mere money relation.

The bourgeoisie has disclosed how it came to pass that the brutal display of vigour in the Middle Ages, which Reactionists so much admire, found its fitting complement in the most slothful indolence. It has been the first to show what man's activity can bring about. It has accomplished wonders far surpassing Egyptian pyramids, Roman aqueducts, and Gothic cathedrals; it has conducted expeditions that put in the shade all former Exoduses of nations and crusades.

The bourgeoisie cannot exist without constantly revolutionizing the instruments of production, and thereby the relations of production, and with them the whole relations of society. Conservation of the old modes of production in unaltered form, was, on the contrary, the first condition of existence for all earlier industrial classes. Constant revolutionizing of production, uninterrupted disturbance of all social conditions, everlasting uncertainty and agitation distinguish the bourgeois epoch from all earlier ones. All fixed, fast-frozen relations, with their train of ancient and venerable prejudices and opinions, are swept away, all new-formed ones become antiquated before they can ossify. All that is solid melts into air, all that is holy is profaned, and man is at last compelled to face with sober senses, his real conditions of life, and his relations with his kind.

The need of a constantly expanding market for its products chases the bourgeoisie over the whole surface of the globe. It must nestle everywhere, settle everywhere, establish connections everywhere.

The bourgeoisie has through its exploitation of the world-market given a cosmopolitan character to production and consumption in every country. To the great chagrin of Reactionists, it has drawn from under the feet of industry the national ground on which it stood. All old-established national industries have been destroyed or are daily being destroyed. They are dislodged by new industries, whose introduction becomes a life-and-death question for all civilized nations, by industries that no longer work up indigenous raw material, but raw material drawn from the remotest zones; industries whose products are consumed, not only at home, but in every quarter of the globe. In place of the old wants, satisfied by the productions of the country, we find new wants, requiring for their satisfaction the products of distant lands and climes. In place of the old local and national seclusion and self-sufficiency, we have intercourse in every direction, universal interdependence of nations. And as in material, so also in intellectual production. The intellectual creations of individual nations become common property. National one-sidedness and narrow-mindedness become more and more impossible, and from the numerous national and local literatures, there arises a world literature.

The bourgeoisie, by the rapid improvement of all instruments of production, by the immensely facilitated means of communication, draws all, even the most barbarian, nations into civilization. The cheap prices of its commodities are the heavy artillery with which it batters down all Chinese walls, with which it forces the barbarians' intensely obstinate hatred of foreigners to capitulate. It compels all nations, on pain of extinction, to adopt the bourgeois mode of production; it compels them to introduce what it calls civilization into their midst, i.e., to become bourgeois themselves. In one word, it creates a world after its own image.

The bourgeoisie has subjected the country to the rule of the towns. It has created enormous cities, has greatly increased the urban population as compared with the rural, and has thus rescued a considerable part of the population from the idiocy of rural life. Just as it has made the country dependent on the towns, so it has made barbarian and semi-barbarian countries dependent on the civilized ones, nations of peasants on nations of bourgeois, the East on the West.

The bourgeoisie keeps more and more doing away with the scattered state of the population, of the means of production, and of property. It has agglomerated population, centralized means of production, and has concentrated property in a few hands. The necessary consequence of this was political centralization. Independent or but loosely connected provinces, with separate interests, laws, governments, and systems of taxation, became lumped together into one nation, with one government, one code of laws, one national class-interest, one frontier, and one customs-tariff.

The bourgeoisie, during its rule of scarcely one hundred years, has created more massive and more colossal productive forces than have all preceding generations together. Subjection of Nature's forces to man, machinery, application of chemistry to industry and agriculture, steam-navigation, railways, electric telegraphs, clearing of whole continents for cultivation, canalization of rivers, whole populations conjured out of the ground—what earlier century had even a presentiment that such productive forces slumbered in the lap of social labour?

We see then that the means of production and of exchange, on whose foundation the bourgeoisie built itself up, were generated in feudal society. At a certain stage in the development of these means of production and of exchange, the conditions under which feudal society produced and exchanged, the feudal organization of agriculture and manufacturing industry, in one word, the feudal relations of property become no longer compatible with the already developed productive forces; they became so many fetters. They had to be burst asunder; they were burst asunder.

Into their place stepped free competition, accompanied by a social and political constitution adapted to it, and by the economical and political sway of the bourgeois class.

A similar movement is going on before our own eyes. Modern bourgeois society with its relations of production, of exchange and of property, a society that has conjured up such gigantic means of production and of exchange, is like the sorcerer, who is no longer able to control the powers of the nether world which he has called up by his spells. The history of industry and commerce for many a decade past is but the history of the revolt of modern productive forces against modern conditions of production, against the property relations that are the conditions for the existence of the bourgeoisie and of its rule. It is enough to mention the commercial crises that by their periodical return put on trial, each time more threateningly, the existence of the entire bourgeois society. In these crises a great part not only of the existing products, but also of the previously created productive forces, are periodically destroyed. In these crises there breaks out an epidemic that, in all earlier epochs, would have seemed an absurdity—the epidemic of overproduction. Society suddenly finds itself put back into a state of momentary barbarism; it appears as if a famine, a universal war of devastation, has cut off the supply of every means of subsistence; industry and commerce seem to be destroyed; and why? Because there is too much civilization, too much means of subsistence, too much industry, too much commerce. The productive forces at the disposal of society no longer tend to further the development of the conditions of bourgeois property; on the contrary, they have become too powerful for these conditions, by which they are fettered, and so soon as they overcome these fetters, they bring disorder into the whole of bourgeois society, endanger the existence of bourgeois property. The conditions of bourgeois society are too narrow to comprise the wealth created by them. And how does the bourgeoisie get over these crises? On the one hand by enforced destruction of a mass of productive forces; on the other, by the conquest of new markets, and by the more thorough exploitation of the old ones. That is to say, by paving the way for more extensive and more destructive crises, and by diminishing the means whereby crises are prevented.

The weapons with which the bourgeoisie felled feudalism to the ground are now turned against the bourgeoisie itself.

But not only has the bourgeoisie forged the weapons that bring death to itself; it has also called into existence the men who are to wield those weapons—the modern working class—the proletarians.

In proportion as the bourgeoisie, i.e., capital, is developed, in the same proportion is the proletariat, the modern working class, developed—a class of labourers, who live only so long as they find work, and who find work only so long as their labour increases capital. These labourers, who must sell themselves piecemeal, are a commodity, like every other article of commerce, and are consequently exposed to all the vicissitudes of competition, to all the fluctuations of the market.

Owing to the extensive use of machinery and to division of labour, the work of the proletarians has lost all individual character, and, consequently, all charm for the workman. He becomes an appendage of the machine, and it is only the most simple, most monotonous, and most easily acquired knack, that is required of him. Hence, the cost of production of a workman is restricted, almost entirely, to the means of subsistence that he requires for his maintenance, and for the propagation of his race. But the price of a commodity, and therefore also of labour, is equal to its cost of production. In proportion, therefore, as the repulsiveness of the work increases, the wage decreases. Nay more, in proportion as the use of machinery and division of labour increases, in the same proportion the burden of toil also increases, whether by prolongation of the working hours, by increase of the work exacted in a given time or by increased speed of the machinery, etc.

Modern industry has converted the little workshop of the patriarchal master into the great factory of the industrial capitalist. Masses of labourers, crowded into the factory, are organized like soldiers. As privates of the industrial army they are placed under the command of a perfect hierarchy of officers and sergeants. Not only are they slaves of the bourgeois class, and of the bourgeois State; they are daily and hourly enslaved by the machine, by the overlooker, and, above all, by the individual bourgeois manufacturer himself. The more openly this despotism proclaims gain to be its end and aim, the more petty, the more hateful, and the more embittering it is.

The less the skill and exertion of strength implied in manual labour, in other words, the more modern industry becomes developed, the more is the labour of men superseded by that of women. Differences of age and sex have no longer any distinctive social validity for the working class. All are instruments of labour, more or less expensive to use, according to their age and sex.

No sooner is the exploitation of the labourer by the manufacturer, so far, at an end, and he receives his wages in cash, than he is set upon by the other portions of the bourgeoisie, the landlord, the shopkeeper, the pawnbroker, etc.

The lower strata of the middle class—the small tradespeople, shopkeepers, and retired tradesmen generally, the handicraftsmen and peasants—all these sink gradually into the proletariat, partly because their diminutive capital does not suffice for the scale on which Modern Industry is carried on, and is swamped in the competition with the large capitalists, partly because their specialized skill is rendered worthless by new methods of production. Thus the proletariat is recruited from all classes of the population.

The proletariat goes through various stages of development. With its birth begins its struggle with the bourgeoisie. At first the contest is carried on by individual labourers, then by the workpeople of a factory, then by the operatives of one trade, in one locality, against the individual bourgeois who directly exploits them. They direct their attacks not against the bourgeois conditions of production, but against the instruments of production themselves; they destroy imported wares that compete with their labour, they smash to pieces machinery, they set factories ablaze, they seek to restore by force the vanished status of the workman of the Middle Ages.

At this stage the labourers still form an incoherent mass scattered over the whole country, and broken up by their mutual competition. If anywhere they unite to form more compact bodies, this is not yet the consequence of their own active union, but of the union of the bourgeoisie, which class, in order to attain its own political ends, is compelled to set the whole proletariat in motion, and is moreover yet, for a time, able to do so. At this stage, therefore, the proletarians do not fight their enemies, but the enemies of their enemies, the remnants of absolute monarchy, the landowners, the nonindustrial bourgeois, the petty bourgeoisie. Thus the whole historical movement is concentrated in the hands of the bourgeoisie; every victory so obtained is a victory for the bourgeoisie.

But with the development of industry the proletariat not only increases in number; it becomes concentrated in greater masses, its strength grows, and it feels that strength more. The various interests and conditions of life within the ranks of the proletariat are more and more equalized, in proportion as machinery obliterates all distinctions of labour, and nearly everywhere reduces wages to the same low level. The growing competition among the bourgeois, and the resulting commercial crises, make the wages of the workers ever more fluctuating. The unceasing improvement of machinery, ever more rapidly developing, makes their livelihood more and more precarious; the collisions between individual workmen and individual bourgeois take more and more the character of collisions between two classes. Thereupon the workers begin to form combinations (Trades' Unions) against the bourgeois; they club together in order to keep up the rate of wages; they found permanent associations in order to make provision beforehand for these occasional revolts. Here and there the contest breaks out into riots.

Now and then the workers are victorious, but only for a time. The real fruit of their battles lies, not in the immediate result, but in the everexpanding union of the workers. This union is helped on by the improved means of communication that are created by modern industry and that place the workers of different localities in contact with one another. It was just this contact that was needed to centralize the numerous local struggles, all of the same character, into one national struggle between classes. But every class struggle is a political struggle. And that union, to attain which the burghers of the Middle Ages, with their miserable highways, required centuries, the modern proletarians, thanks to railways, achieve in a few years.

This organization of the proletarians into a class, and consequently into a political party, is continually being upset again by the competition between the workers themselves. But it ever rises up again, stronger, firmer, mightier. It compels legislative recognition of particular interests of the workers, by taking advantage of the divisions among the bourgeoisie itself. Thus the ten-hours' bill in England was carried.

Altogether, collisions between the classes of the old society further in many ways the course of development of the proletariat. The bourgeoisie finds itself involved in a constant battle. At first with the aristocracy; later on, with those portions of the bourgeoisie itself whose interests have become antagonistic to the progress of industry; at all times, with the bourgeoisie of foreign countries. In all these battles it sees itself compelled to appeal to the proletariat, to ask for its help, and thus to drag it into the political arena. The bourgeoisie itself, therefore, supplies the proletariat with its own elements of political and general education, in other words, it furnishes the proletariat with weapons for fighting the bourgeoisie.

Further, as we have already seen, entire sections of the ruling classes are, by the advance of industry, precipitated into the proletariat, or are at least threatened in their conditions of existence. These also supply the proletariat with fresh elements of enlightenment and progress.

Finally, in times when the class struggle nears the decisive hour, the process of dissolution going on within the ruling class, in fact within the whole range of old society, assumes such a violent, glaring character, that a small section of the ruling class cuts itself adrift, and joins the revolutionary class, the class that holds the future in its hands. Just as, therefore, at an earlier period, a section of the nobility went over to the bourgeoisie, so now a portion of the bourgeoisie goes over to the proletariat, and in particular, a portion of the bourgeois ideologists, who have raised themselves to the level of comprehending theoretically the historical movement as a whole.

Of all the classes that stand face to face with the bourgeoisie today, the proletariat alone is a really revolutionary class. The other classes decay and finally disappear in the face of Modern Industry; the proletariat is its special and essential product.

The lower middle class, the small manufacturer, the shopkeeper, the artisan, the peasant, all these fight against the bourgeoisie, to save from extinction their existence as fractions of the middle class. They are therefore not revolutionary, but conservative. Nay more, they are reactionary, for they try to roll back the wheel of history. If by chance they are revolutionary, they are so only in view of their impending transfer into the proletariat; they thus defend not their present, but their future interests, they desert their own standpoint to place themselves at that of the proletariat.

The 'dangerous class', the social scum, that passively rotting mass thrown off by the lowest layers of old society, may, here and there, be swept into the movement by a proletarian revolution; its conditions of life, however, prepare it far more for the part of a bribed tool of reactionary intrigue.

In the conditions of the proletariat, those of old society at large are already virtually swamped. The proletarian is without property; his relation to his wife and children has no longer anything in common with the bourgeois family relations; modern industrial labour, modern subjection to capital, the same in England as in France, in America as in Germany, has stripped him of every trace of national character. Law, morality, religion are to him so many bourgeois prejudices, behind which lurk in ambush just as many bourgeois interests.

All the preceding classes that got the upper hand, sought to fortify their already acquired status by subjecting society at large to their conditions of appropriation. The proletarians cannot become masters of the productive forces of society, except by abolishing their own previous mode of appropriation, and thereby also every other previous mode of appropriation. They have nothing of their own to secure and to fortify; their mission is to destroy all previous securities for, and insurances of, individual property.

All previous historical movements were movements of minorities, or in the interests of minorities. The proletarian movement is the self-conscious, independent movement of the immense majority, in the interests of the immense majority. The proletariat, the lowest stratum of our present society, cannot stir, cannot raise itself up, without the whole superincumbent strata of official society being sprung into the air.

Though not in substance, yet in form, the struggle of the proletariat with the bourgeoisie is at first a national struggle. The proletariat of each country must, of course, first of all settle matters with its own bourgeoisie.

In depicting the most general phases of the development of the proletariat, we traced the more or less veiled civil war, raging within existing society, up to the point where that war breaks out into open revolution, and where the violent overthrow of the bourgeoisie lays the foundation for the sway of the proletariat.

Hitherto, every form of society has been based, as we have already seen, on the antagonism of oppressing and oppressed classes. But in order to oppress a class, certain conditions must be assured to it under which it can, at least, continue its slavish existence. The serf, in the period of serfdom, raised himself to membership in the commune, just as the petty bourgeois, under the yoke of feudal absolutism, managed to develop into a bourgeois. The modern labourer, on the contrary, instead of rising with the progress of industry, sinks deeper and deeper below the conditions of existence of his own class. He becomes a pauper, and pauperism develops more rapidly than population and wealth. And here it becomes evident, that the bourgeoisie is unfit any longer to be the ruling class in society, and to impose its conditions of existence upon society as an overriding law. It is unfit to rule because it is incompetent to assure an existence to its slave within his slavery, because it cannot help letting him sink into such a state, that it has to feed him, instead of being fed by him. Society can no longer live under this bourgeoisie, in other words, its existence is no longer compatible with society.

The essential condition for the existence, and for the sway of the bourgeois class, is the formation and augmentation of capital; the condition for capital is wage-labour. Wage-labour rests exclusively on competition between the labourers. The advance of industry, whose involuntary promoter is the bourgeoisie, replaces the isolation of the labourers, due to competition, by their revolutionary combination, due to association. The development of Modern Industry, therefore, cuts from under its feet the very foundation on which the bourgeoisie produces and appropriates products. What the bourgeoisie, therefore, produces, above all, is its own grave-diggers. Its fall and the victory of the proletariat are equally inevitable. . . .

We have seen above, that the first step in the revolution by the working class is to raise the proletariat to the position of ruling class, to win the battle of democracy.

The proletariat will use its political supremacy to wrest, by degrees, all capital from the bourgeoisie, to centralize all instruments of production in the hands of the State, i.e., of the proletariat organized as the ruling class; and to increase the total of productive forces as rapidly as possible.

Of course, in the beginning this cannot be effected except by means of despotic inroads on the rights of property, and on the conditions of bourgeois production; by means of measures, therefore, which appear economically insufficient and untenable, but which, in the course of the movement, outstrip themselves, necessitate further inroads upon the old social order, and are unavoidable as a means of entirely revolutionizing the mode of production.

These measures will of course be different in different countries.

Nevertheless, in the most advanced countries, the following will be pretty generally applicable.

1. Abolition of property in land and application of all rents of land to public purposes.

2. A heavy progressive or graduated income tax.

3. Abolition of all right of inheritance.

4. Confiscation of the property of all emigrants and rebels.

5. Centralization of credit in the hands of the State, by means of a national bank with State capital and an exclusive monopoly.

6. Centralization of the means of communication and transport in the hands of the State.

7. Extension of factories and instruments of production owned by the State; the bringing into cultivation of wastelands, and the improvement of the soil generally in accordance with a common plan.

8. Equal liability of all to labour. Establishment of industrial armies, especially for agriculture.

9. Combination of agriculture with manufacturing industries; gradual abolition of the distinction between town and country, by a more equable distribution of the population over the country.

10. Free education for all children in public schools. Abolition of children's factory labour in its present form. Combination of education with industrial production, etc., etc.

When, in the course of development, class distinctions have disappeared, and all production has been concentrated in the hands of associated individuals, the public power will lose its political character. Political power, properly so called, is merely the organized power of one class for oppressing another. If the proletariat during its contest with the bourgeoisie is compelled, by the force of circumstances, to organize itself as a class, if, by means of a revolution, it makes itself the ruling class, and, as such, sweeps away by force the old conditions of production, then it will, along with these conditions, have swept away the conditions for the existence of class antagonisms and of classes generally, and will thereby have abolished its own supremacy as a class.

In place of the old bourgeois society, with its classes and class antagonisms, we shall have an association, in which the free development of each is the condition for the free development of all. . . .

28
Excerpts from *Capital*

Karl Marx

Commodities: Use-Value and Exchange-Value

The wealth of those societies in which the capitalist mode of production prevails presents itself as 'an immense accumulation of commodities', its unit being a single commodity. Our investigation must therefore begin with the analysis of a commodity.

A commodity is, in the first place, an object outside us, a thing that by its properties satisfies human wants of some sort or another. The nature of such wants, whether, for instance, they spring from the stomach or from fancy, makes no difference. Neither are we here concerned to know how the object satisfies these wants, whether directly as means of subsistence, or indirectly as means of production.

Every useful thing, as iron, paper, etc., may be looked at from the two points of view: of quality and quantity. It is an assemblage of many properties, and may therefore be of use in various ways. To discover the various uses of things is the work of history. So also is the establishment of socially recognized standards of measure for the quantities of these useful objects. The diversity of these measures has its origin partly in the diverse nature of the objects to be measured, partly in convention.

The utility of a thing makes it a use-value. But this utility is not a thing of air. Being limited by the physical properties of the commodity, it has no existence apart from that commodity. A commodity, such as iron, corn, or a diamond, is therefore, so far as it is a material thing, a use-value, something useful. This property of a commodity is independent of the amount of labour required to appropriate its useful qualities. When treating of use-value, we always assume we are dealing with definite quantities, such as dozens of watches, yards of linen, or tons of iron. The use-values of commodities furnish the material for a special study, that of the commercial knowledge of commodities. Use-values become a reality only by use or consumption; they also constitute the substance of all wealth, whatever may be the social form of that wealth. In the form of society we are about to consider, they are, in addition, the material depositories of exchange-value.

Exchange-value, at first sight, presents itself as a quantitative relation, as the proportion in which values in use of one sort are exchanged for those of another sort, a relation constantly changing with time and place. Hence exchange-value appears to be something accidental and purely relative, and consequently an intrinsic value, i.e. an exchange-value that is inseparably connected with, inherent in, commodities, seems a contradiction in terms. Let us consider the matter a little more closely.

A given commodity, e.g., a quarter of wheat is exchanged for x blacking, y silk, or z gold, etc.—in short, for other commodities in the most different proportions. Instead of one exchange-value, the wheat has, therefore, a great many. But since x blacking, y silk, or z gold, etc., each represent the exchange-value of one quarter of wheat, x blacking, y silk, z gold, etc., must, as exchange-values, be replaceable by each other, or equal to each other. Therefore, first: the valid exchange-values of a given commodity express something equal; secondly, exchange-value, generally, is only the mode of expression, the phenomenal form, of something contained in it, yet distinguishable from it.

Let us take two commodities, e.g., corn and iron. The proportions in which they are exchangeable, whatever those proportions may be, can always be represented by an equation in which a given quantity of corn is equated to some quantity of iron: e.g., 1 quarter corn = x cwt. iron. What does this equation tell us? It tells us that in two different things—in 1 quarter of corn and x cwt. of iron, there exists in equal quantities something common to both. The two things must therefore be equal to a third, which in itself is neither the one nor the other. Each of them, so far as it is exchange-value, must therefore be reducible to this third.

A simple geometrical illustration will make this clear. In order to calculate and compare the areas of rectilinear figures, we decompose them into triangles. But the area of the triangle itself is expressed by something totally different from its visible figure, namely, by half the product of the base into the altitude. In the same way the exchange-values of commodities must be capable of being expressed in terms of something common to them all, of which thing they represent a greater or less quantity.

This common 'something' cannot be either a geometrical, a chemical, or any other natural property of commodities. Such properties claim our attention only in so far as they affect the utility of those commodities, make them use-values. But the exchange of commodities is evidently an act characterized by a total abstraction from use-value. Then one use-value is just as good as another, provided only it be present in sufficient quantity. Or, as old Barbon says, 'one sort of wares is as good as another, if the values be equal. There is no difference or distinction in things of equal value. . . . A hundred pounds' worth of lead or iron is of as great value as one hundred pounds' worth of silver or gold.' As use-values, commodities are, above all, of different qualities, but as exchange-values they are merely different quantities, and consequently do not contain an atom of use-value.

If then we leave out of consideration the use-value of commodities, they have only one common property left, that of being products of labour. But even the product of labour itself has undergone a change in our hands. If we make abstraction from its use-value, we make abstraction at the same time from the material elements and shapes that make the product a use-value; we see in it no longer a table, a house, yarn, or any other useful thing. Its existence as a material thing is put out of sight. Neither can it any longer be regarded as the product of the labour of the joiner, the mason, the spinner, or of any other definite kind of productive labour. Along with the useful qualities of the products themselves, we put out of sight both the useful character of the various kinds of labour embodied in them, and the concrete forms of that labour; there is nothing left but what is common to them all; all are reduced to one and the same sort of labour, human labour in the abstract.

Let us now consider the residue of each of these products; it consists of the same unsubstantial reality in each, a mere congelation of homogeneous human labour, of labour power expended without regard to the mode of its expenditure. All that these things now tell us is that human labour power has been expended in their production, that human labour is embodied in them. When looked at as crystals of this social substance, common to them all, they are—Values.

We have seen that when commodities are exchanged, their exchange-value manifests itself as something totally independent of their use-value. But if we abstract from their use-value, there remains their Value as defined above. Therefore, the common substance that manifests itself in the exchange-value of commodities, whenever they are exchanged, is their value. The progress of our investigation will show that exchange-value is the only form in which the value of commodities can manifest itself or be expressed. For the present, however, we have to consider the nature of value independently of this, its form.

A use-value, or useful article, therefore, has value only because human labour in the abstract has been embodied or materialized in it. How, then, is the magnitude of this value to be measured? Plainly, by the quantity of the value-creating substance, the labour, contained in the article. The quantity of labour, however, is measured by its duration, and labour time in its turn finds its standard in weeks, days, and hours.

Some people might think that if the value of a commodity is determined by the quantity of labour spent on it, the more idle and unskilful the labourer, the more valuable would his commodity be, because more time would be required in its production. The labour, however, that forms the substance of value, is homogeneous human labour, expenditure of one uniform labour power. The total labour power of society, which is embodied in the sum total of the values of all commodities produced by that society, counts here as one homogeneous mass of human labour power, composed though it be of innumerable individual units. Each of these units is the same as any other, so far as it has the character of the average labour power of society, and takes effect as such; that is, so far as it requires for producing a commodity no more time than is needed on average, no more than is socially necessary. The labour time socially necessary is that required to produce an article under the normal conditions of production, and with the average degree of skill and intensity prevalent at the time. The introduction of power-looms into England probably reduced by one-half the labour required to weave a given quantity of yarn into cloth. The hand-loom weavers, as a matter of fact, continued to require the same time as before; but for all that, the product of one hour of their labour represented after the change only half an hour's social labour, and consequently fell to one-half its former value.

We see then that that which determines the magnitude of the value of any article is the amount of labour socially necessary, or the labour time socially necessary for its production. Each individual commodity, in this connection, is to be considered as an average sample of its class. Commodities, therefore, in which equal quantities of labour are embodied, or which can be produced in the same time, have the same value. The value of one commodity is to the value of any other, as the labour time necessary for the production of the one is to that necessary for the production of the other. 'As values, all commodities are only definite masses of congealed labour time.'

The value of a commodity would therefore remain constant, if the labour time required for its production also remained con-

stant. But the latter changes with every variation in the productiveness of labour. This productiveness is determined by various circumstances, among others, by the average amount of skill of the workmen, the state of science, and the degree of its practical application, the social organization of production, the extent and capabilities of the means of production, and by physical conditions. For example, the same amount of labour in favourable seasons is embodied in eight bushels of corn, and in unfavourable, only in four. The same labour extracts from rich mines more metal than from poor mines. Diamonds are of very rare occurrence on the earth's surface, and hence their discovery costs, on an average, a great deal of labour time. Consequently much labour is represented in a small compass. Jacob doubts whether gold has ever been paid for at its full value. This applies still more to diamonds. According to Eschwege, the total produce of the Brazilian diamond mines for the eighty years ending in 1823, had not realized the price of one-and-a-half years' average produce of the sugar and coffee plantations of the same country, although the diamonds cost much more labour, and therefore represented more value. With richer mines, the same quantity of labour would embody itself in more diamonds, and their value would fall. If we could succeed, at a small expenditure of labour, in converting carbon into diamonds, their value might fall below that of bricks. In general, the greater the productiveness of labour, the less is the labour time required for the production of an article, the less is the amount of labour crystallized in that article, and the less is its value; and vice versa, the less the productiveness of labour, the greater is the labour time required for the production of an article, and the greater is its value. The value of a commodity, therefore, varies directly as the quantity, and inversely as the productiveness, of the labour incorporated in it.

A thing can be a use-value, without having value. This is the case whenever its utility to man is not due to labour. Such are air, virgin soil, natural meadows, etc. A thing can be useful, and the product of human labour, without being a commodity. Whoever directly satisfies his wants with the produce of his own labour creates, indeed, use-values, but not commodities. In order to produce the latter, he must not only produce use-values, but use-values for others, social use-values. (And not only for others. The medieval peasant produced quit-rent-corn for his feudal lord and tithe-corn for his parson. But neither the quit-rent-corn nor the tithe-corn became commodities by reason of the fact that they had been produced for others. To become a commodity a product must be transferred to another, whom it will serve as a use-value, by means of an exchange.) Lastly, nothing can have value without being an object of utility. If the thing is useless, so is the labour contained in it; the labour does not count as labour, and therefore creates no value. . . .

The Rate of Surplus Value

. . . If we look at the means of production, in their relation to the creation of value, and to the variation in the quantity of value, apart from anything else, they appear simply as the material in which labour power, the value-creator, incorporates itself. Neither the nature, nor the value of this material is of any importance. The only requisite is that there be a sufficient supply to absorb the labour expended in the process of production. That supply once given, the material may rise or fall in value, or even be, as land and the sea, without any value in itself; but this will have no influence on the creation of value or on the variation in the quantity of value.

In the first place then we equate the constant capital to zero. The capital advanced is consequently reduced from c + v to v, and instead of the value of the product (c + v) + s we have now the value produced (v + s). Given the new value produced = £180, which sum consequently represents the whole labour expended during the process, then subtracting from it £90, the value of the variable capital, we have remaining £90, the amount of the surplus value. This sum of £90 or s expresses the absolute quantity of surplus value produced. The relative quantity produced, or the increase per cent of the vari-

able capital, is determined, it is plain, by the ratio of the surplus value to the variable capital, or is expressed by s/v. In our example this ratio is 90/90, which gives an increase of 100 per cent. This relative increase in the value of the variable capital, or the relative magnitude of the surplus value, I call, 'The rate of surplus value'.

We have seen that the labourer, during one portion of the labour process, produces only the value of his labour power, that is, the value of his means of subsistence. Now since his work forms part of a system, based on the social division of labour, he does not directly produce the actual necessaries which he himself consumes; he produces instead a particular commodity, yarn for example, whose value is equal to the value of those necessaries or of the money with which they can be bought. The portion of his day's labour devoted to this purpose will be greater or less, in proportion to the value of the necessaries that he daily requires on an average, or, what amounts to the same thing, in proportion to the labour time required on an average to produce them. If the value of those necessaries represent on an average the expenditure of six hours' labour, the workman must on an average work for six hours to produce that value. If instead of working for the capitalist, he worked independently on his own account, he would, other things being equal, still be obliged to labour for the same number of hours, in order to produce the value of his labour power, and thereby to gain the means of subsistence necessary for his conservation or continued reproduction. But as we have seen, during that portion of his day's labour in which he produces the value of his labour power, say three shillings, he produces only an equivalent for the value of his labour power already advanced by the capitalist; the new value created only replaces the variable capital advanced. It is owing to this fact, that the production of the new value of three shillings takes the semblance of a mere reproduction. That portion of the working-day, then, during which this reproduction takes place, I call 'necessary' labour time, and the labour expended during that time I call 'necessary' labour. Necessary, as regards the labourer, because independent of the particular social form of his labour; necessary, as regards capital, and the world of capitalists, because on the continued existence of the labourer depends their existence also.

During the second period of the labour process, that in which his labour is no longer necessary labour, the workman, it is true, labours, expends labour power; but his labour, being no longer necessary labour, he creates no value for himself. He creates surplus value which, for the capitalist, has all the charms of a creation out of nothing. This portion of the working-day, I name surplus labour time, and to the labour expended during that time, I give the name of surplus labour. It is every bit as important, for a correct understanding of surplus value, to conceive it as a mere congelation of surplus labour time, as nothing but materialized surplus labour, as it is, for a proper comprehension of value, to conceive it as a mere congelation of so many hours of labour, as nothing but materialized labour. The essential difference between the various economic forms of society, between, for instance, a society based on slave-labour, and one based on wage-labour, lies only in the mode in which this surplus labour is in each case extracted from the actual producer, the labourer.

Since, on the one hand, the values of the variable capital and of the labour power purchased by that capital are equal, and the value of this labour power determines the necessary portion of the working-day; and since, on the other hand, the surplus value is determined by the surplus portion of the working-day, it follows that surplus value bears the same ratio to variable capital, that surplus labour does to necessary labour, or in other words, the rate of surplus value

$$\frac{s}{v} = \frac{\text{surplus labour}}{\text{necessary labour}}.$$

Both ratios,

$$\frac{s}{v} \text{ and } \frac{\text{surplus labour}}{\text{necessary labour}},$$

express the same thing in different ways; in the one case by reference to materialized, incorporated labour, in the other by reference to living, fluent labour.

The rate of surplus value is therefore an exact expression for the degree of exploitation of labour power by capital, or of the labourer by the capitalist. . . .

Adapted from: Karl Marx, *Capital*, Volume I, pp. 71ff, 199ff. Copyright © 1986 by Lawrence and Wishart. Reprinted by permission of Lawrence and Wishart (London). ✦

29
Marx and the Engines of History

Steven Best

> *The first premise of all human history is, of course, the existence of living human individuals. Thus the first fact to be established is the physical organisation of these individuals and their consequent relation to the rest of nature. . . . The writing of history must always set out from these natural bases and their modification in the course of history through the action of men.*
>
> —Marx and Engels
> (1978: 149–150)

Karl Marx lived and wrote during what he understood to be the most momentous social transformation in the history of humanity—the emergence of capitalist modernity. Marx was one of the first social theorists to analyze systematically the capitalist mode of production and to see it as constituting a modern world radically different from all previous social forms. Marx noted that although capitalism produced a massive rupture in the fabric of history, knowledge of the origins and nature of the new social system transforming the entire globe was occluded. This was the result of the sheer novelty and complexity of the wage and market system, of the oppressiveness of its effects on human beings, and of an ideology that obscures underlying social relations, presenting the movement of commodities and the hegemony of exchange value as if governed by natural laws.

The underlying motivations of Marx's work were to understand thoroughly the nature of the capitalist mode of production, to analyze it as a radically new form of society, and to lay bare its fundamental mechanisms of operation. These analytic aims were subordinated to the political goals of exposing these operations as mechanisms of domination, of tearing off the veils that clouded the political vision of the working class, of organizing the working class into a unified international body, and of abolishing capitalism as a system based on exploitation, dehumanization, and class antagonism. In order to accomplish these tasks, Marx required immense historical knowledge, a historical method that treats all social and cultural phenomena as socially constituted, a social theory informed by this assumption, and a theory of history that grasps the basic outlines and mechanisms of historical change. Such modes of understanding allowed Marx to contextualize capitalism and understand its origins, trajectories, and seemingly impending demise.

Marx's critical outlook was developed by assimilating numerous theoretical and political influences. Most importantly, these included French utopian socialism, English political economy, and German idealism. Marx shared many political sentiments with the utopian socialists, but he condemned their lack of theoretical rigor and developed a "scientific socialism" (Engels) based on empirical analysis rather than moralizing rhetoric. Through a scientific account of human activity, Marx sought to grasp the dynamics of social and historical change, to uncover the constituting forces of the present, and to predict the probability of future events.

Although Marx uncritically embraced the positivist attitude that elevated scientific knowledge and method over all other forms of knowledge (1978: 155), he rejected the positivist search for ahistorial "laws" of development and its pretension to value neutrality. For Marx, the whole point of science was to help the working class overthrow forces of oppression. In *Capital*, Marx alternated passages of dense empirical analysis of capitalism with stinging attacks on its "vampire-like" thirst for the blood of living labor (see Kellner 1983). Marx's scientific attitude was informed by a strong moral sense, by a *"categorical imperative to overthrow all those conditions* in which man is an abased, enslaved, abandoned, contemptible being" (Marx 1978: 60). But Marx saw no contradiction between the "scientific" and moral-political character of his theory. Most theorists simply interpreted the world, but Marx maintained that the time had come to change it, by merging science and critique, theory and practice. Marx thus sought a theory of history and society that was both endowed "with the precision of natural science" (1978: 5) and also was "in its very essence critical and revolutionary" (1977: 103).

Marx believed that dialectics grants this revolutionary character to social and historical analysis.[1] Marx's version of science was radically different from what later emerged as "scientific Marxism," and the differences stemmed principally from Marx's more supple appropriation of Hegelian dialectics.[2] Against the ahistorical methods of Western philosophy, Hegel developed a dialectical vision of reality that treats all phenomena as historically and socially produced, and sees conflict and contradiction as the driving forces behind historical change. The dialectical method made it possible for Marx to overcome the reifying approach of positivist science that sees social reality as static and given. Marx's emphasis on the historical constitution of all things was evident in his critique of Feuerbach's materialism. According to Marx, Feuerbach grasped the reality of the sensuous empirical world, but failed to see that it was "not a thing given direct from all eternity, remaining ever the same, but the product of industry and of the state of society . . . an historical product" (1978: 170).

Hegel's dialectical method had revolutionary implications because, according to Marx, it helped to overcome fatalistic resignation to "the way things are," and shifted focus to how they have been constituted and can be changed. In Marx's hands, dialectical method revealed the changing forms of conflict and crisis that operate in society, undermine its stability, and create new social dynamics. Dialectics also enabled Marx to move beyond the positivist method of treating phenomena as external and separate from one another by grasping the movement of things in their interrelationship, as different aspects of the same structure or system, as "opposites" united in the same relation. This allowed Marx, for example, to see gross wealth and poverty as inseparable effects of the capitalist market.

Of course, Marx argued that Hegel, by emphasizing the causal primacy of consciousness over social activity and relationships, understood dialectics in a mystified, inverted manner; consequently, Marx redefined dialectics in a materialist context. For Marx, the contradictions that propel history forward are not, as for Hegel, logical contradictions among opposing ideas, but conflicting material forces rooted within a particular social system. Marx shared Hegel's view that human beings transform themselves and their societies through the activity of production, but Marx saw this activity as the work of human beings rather than "Spirit."[3] In his call for a "real history" of human beings in their changing forms of productive labor, Marx developed the "materialist interpretation of history" and was one of the first modern social theorists to interpret history as the product of human beings in their concrete, productive activity.

For Marx, the primary forces of history were not ideas, political machinations, or war, but rather production, commerce, and industry: "In the whole conception of history up to the present this real basis of history has either been totally neglected or else considered as a minor matter quite irrelevant to the course of history" (1978: 165). Marx's materialist standpoint placed him in opposition to the idealism of Dilthey, Collingwood, and others who understood historical explanation to consist of identifying and sympathetically reconstructing the thoughts and motives of past historical agents. Where humanist historians like Vico anticipated Marx in their analysis of history as a human product, and theorists such as Aristotle, Locke, Hobbes, Machiavelli, and St. Simon understood economics to be a central human activity, it was Marx who developed these ideas most forcefully and consistently. Against Carlyle and others who exalted the determinant role of great men in history, Marx, following Michelet and Vico, emphasized the crucial role of common people and the "masses" in shaping history.

On Marx's conception, dialectics is neither an immanent historical force, nor a totalizing worldview that subsumes all differences into an undifferentiated whole; rather, it is a supple empirical method, "a way of thinking that brings into focus the full range of changes and interactions that occur in the world" (Ollman 1993: 10). Theorists such as Lenin, Trotsky, Gramsci, and Lukács rightly emphasized dialectics as the heart of Marx's methodology, but dialectics must also be understood as a theoretical and political vision that projects future emancipatory possibilities based on the analysis of existing society and past history. Where dialectical *method* relates to analysis of the present and past, dialectical *vision* is future oriented and grounds the norm of human emancipation in actual historical possibilities disclosed by dialectical method, while seeking to overcome debilitating oppositions in social and personal life.

In order to carry out a materialist analysis of modern capitalism, Marx, beginning in 1844, immersed himself in the study of political economy. While he drew from Ricardo, Smith, Mill, and others, Marx developed a sharp critique of political economy and shifted its analytic and political perspective. He showed that political economy was not a science, but rather an ideology that analyzed rent, profit, and other categories apart from the exploitation of the working class. Where political economy operated from the hidden point of view of capital, Marx analyzed social and economic phenomena from the perspective of the working class and its struggles for autonomy from capitalist exploitation (see Cleaver 1979, 1992).

Marx was decisively influenced by the Enlightenment movement and was very much a "modernist" in his basic temperament. He personified the Enlightenment emphasis on critique and its demand for rational social reconstruction and universal values. Early in his life, he called for a "ruthless criticism of everything existing" and carried through sharp but fragmentary attacks on religion, philosophy, property, law, money, the state, and Hegel. It is no accident that Marx enti-

tled a later work, in the spirit of Kant, *Critique of Political Economy*. "Critique" for Marx, however, did not involve an analysis of autonomous forms of knowledge and their limits, but rather of the sociohistorical conditions underlying knowledge and the crisis tendencies that threaten the stability of capitalist society. Marx also embraced the modernist celebration of change and innovation as liberating forces (see Berman 1982). Far from advocating a return to simple communal life, Marx's historical vision was oriented toward the future. He emphasized the limitations of static, isolated social forms and praised the dynamic qualities of capitalism that overturned tradition and provincial boundaries to unleash new social forces and establish new universal human relations. Marx praised the "revolutionary" bourgeoisie for accomplishing "wonders far surpassing Egyptian pyramids, Roman aqueducts, and Gothic cathedrals" (1978: 476); for liberating the productive forces that "slumbered in the lap of social labour" (477); for creating new wants, international interdependency, and the urban environment; and for rescuing much of the population from the "idiocy of rural life" (477).

Despite its empirical and "scientific" character, Marx's theory belongs to the "philosophy of history" tradition. While rejecting the theological interpretation of history, Marx nevertheless retained the narrative codes of salvation within the secular context of progress. With Condorcet, Comte, and other Enlightenment thinkers, Marx developed a metanarrative that linked advances in science, technology, and rationality with advances in freedom and progress. Marx thus accepted the Enlightenment view that history, in however a tortured or indirect way, represents a progressive development toward a rational society and free individuality. But unlike apologists for the modern world, Marx was acutely aware of the negative side of modernity, and he condemned capitalism as a system of exploitation that thwarts the very possibilities for progress and emancipation that it calls into being. Moroever, unlike Habermas . . . , Marx did not accept the rationalist faith in the power of reason and lofty moral principles to dissolve social conflict and self-interest. Marx believed instead that those who abuse power can only be removed through force, and he derided all liberal attempts to reconcile antagonisms without changing their fundamental sources rooted in class domination. Marx was rationalist enough, however, to believe that the proletariat would break its capitalist chains once it attained a rational understanding of the material conditions of its oppression.

While Marx analyzed the emergence of a universal history, he saw this as the result of real historical developments, of an increasingly global form of capitalism, rather than as a manifest destiny or the autonomous march of reason. The idea of a universal history, of a common social goal and international form of association, was fundamental to Marx's vision of history and concept of human liberation. From the beginning to the end of his career, Marx was decisively influenced by the Hegelian-Romantic vision of a social and individual being no longer divided against itself, of a harmonious and unalienated mode of human existence that overcomes the forms of antagonism and fragmentation created by the historical process. Marx's vision of emancipation foresaw the possibility of a future communist society where the conflicts among human beings and between humanity and nature can be overcome, where the human species can join in a rational and democratic association that reconciles particular and general interests, where national differences are eliminated in an international social order, and where the contradiction between "human essence" and human existence is abolished so that human beings develop rather than mutilate themselves in their activity.

Following Hegel, Marx interpreted history as a process of differentiation, driven by conflicts and contradictions. In its historical development, an original unity, be it a concept or a communal clan, is sundered apart, alienated from itself, differentiated into various aspects, and eventually returns to itself in a climactic moment that signals the end of history, at least as hitherto known. For Marx, history involves the alienation of a subject—not Reason, but humanity—from its creative powers. But the movement of history allows for an eventual recuperation of these powers in a higher, more developed form. Marx's theory of history traced the historical process of domination and alienation, but it analyzed the tendencies whereby this same process ultimately can lead to human liberation.

Marx's historical vision, as I show below, is a materialist translation of Hegel's notion of a "concrete identity," of a differentiated unity that can become whole again after protracted alienation through historical movement.[4] Since Marx's unity, unlike Hegel's, is not guaranteed by history, but has to be produced out of tendencies and possibilities within the present, his emancipatory norm requires a political vision of how the working class can collectively transform present possibilities of freedom into a social reality and thereby win the emancipation of all humanity. Throughout his life, Marx sought a viable theory and practice that would empower workers all over the globe to seize the reins of history. Once this was accomplished, he believed, the movement of communism would bring the end of one history, the hitherto existing history of human alienation, and inaugurate the beginning of a new history of human freedom. This vision of a future communist society is an apocalyptic vision of a rupture in history as great as capitalism, yet which also builds on the achievements of the entire historical past.

Marx's dialectical method and vision of history is the focus of this chapter. Against all readings that essentialize Marx as a particular kind of theorist, such as a humanist or a positivist, or that claim he developed a crudely reductionist method, I present Marx as a supple and complex, but not always consistent, theorist of historical change and revolution. As Adamson (1985) forcefully demonstrated, we cannot speak of "*the* Marxist theory of history" since Marx developed various models and visions, and frequently changed his mind on fundamental issues. Although Marx advances a forceful, monoperspectival interpretation of history as determined by the dynamics of production and class struggle, he employs, within this context, various theoretical and political models to examine social reality from numerous standpoints. I undertake a "contextualist" reading of Marx, which maintains that he adopts different theoretical and political models in different contexts according to different analytical and political intentions and shifting historical conditions. This reading brings out the various tensions in Marx's work, such as have been resolved falsely one way or another by many of his interpreters and followers.

I begin with an analysis of Marx's concept of alienation and vision of human emancipation as it develops in his early and later texts. I show that Marx examines history from the standpoints of both continuity and discontinuity. Against some of Marx's critics, I argue that these models are complementary rather than contradictory, and consider their different political implications. I then turn to the argument, recently revived by analytic Marxists, that Marx is a technological determinist. I counter this thesis by showing that he employs a multicausal model of historical change which privileges forces or relations of production in different contexts. I then consider some of the key methodological assumptions and problems of Marx's work that relate to his use of "rational abstraction." Examining some of the critiques of Marx's analysis of precapitalist societies, I describe the tension between his continuity models— which treat all history as determined by economic, technological, and political dynamics, and so as amenable to a historical materialist analysis—and his discontinuity model, which argues for a fundamental rift between precapitalist and capitalist societies and calls into question the applicability of historical materialism to precapitalist modes of production. This chapter raises numerous issues and debates that are important for understanding the post-Marxist theories of Foucault and Habermas. As I argue throughout the book, Marx commits certain theoretical errors that Foucault and Habermas help to overcome, but he contributes a wealth of important insights and values that need to be retained and developed in our own historical context.

Models of Historical Continuity

Throughout all of his works, Marx advances a Hegelian vision of history as a continuous evolutionary process driven by the dynamic of "objectification." In their interaction with nature through productive activity, human beings concretize and embody their personality and creative powers in their objects. As they shape and change their world, they simultaneously shape and change themselves. The development of the individual follows the evolution of its social forms of interaction, which themselves are determined by the dynamics of production.

This evolutionary view emphasizes lines of continuity from tribal to communist society. Marx employs three different continuity models in different stages of his work: (1) the humanist model, which interprets history as both the alienation and realization of the "human essence"; (2) the productive forces model, which interprets history as the progressive augmentation of the productive forces, a movement governed by the contradiction between the forces and relations of production; and (3) the class struggle model, which interprets historical change as resulting from the struggles between contending classes.[5] While these are logically distinct models, Marx frequently combines them in his concrete historical analyses.

The humanist model is developed mainly in the early stage of Marx's work, but remnants of it turn up frequently in his later works. Following Hegel, Marx sees history as the progressive development of human freedom throughout various stages of history. But this is a double movement where freedom emerges only through the advance of alienation. For Hegel, alienation involves the separation of Reason from itself in the process of its objectification in history. Marx, in contrast, understands alienation as the separation of human producers from the "objective conditions of production," the communal context of their labor, and their own "species-being" and "human essence." These later two phrases derive from Feuerbach and designate sociality, historicity, and creative activity as fundamental attributes of a distinctly human, rather than "merely" animal, nature.

Like Hegel's Spirit, Marx's "human essence" unfolds in the process of historical development and is realized in a final stage of history. Marx views history as a continuous movement of a two-sided process: the humanization of nature and the naturalization of humanity. The humanization of nature is the process whereby human beings progressively enlarge the field of their objectification and gain increasing control over nature; the naturalization of humanity involves the evolution of the human being from a limited to a universal being and the consequent realization of its sensuous, natural powers in a free social context. Both aspects of the historical process result from the human interaction with nature through productive activity. As Marx says, "for the socialist man *the whole of what is called world history* is nothing more than the creation of man through human labor, and the development of nature for man" (1975: 357). Unlike Habermas, therefore . . . , Marx sees history strictly in terms of labor and production, excluding analysis of language and moral development as important dynamics of their own.

Marx grasps the totality of history not only as the alienation of the laboring subject from the process and products of production, but also as the "reintegration or return of man into himself" (1975 a: 347), a movement that culminates in communism. While presented as the "negation of the negation," communism is nonetheless defined as a *positive* movement, insofar as it appropriates the whole "wealth" of history, both human wealth (which Marx interprets in terms of human individuation and the formation of the senses) and technological-economic wealth (the development of the productive forces). The early Marx sees communism as "the *positive* supersession of *private property,* as *human self-estrangement,* and hence the true *appropriation of the human* essence through and for man; it is the complete restoration of man to himself as a *social,* i.e., human, being, a restoration which has become conscious and which takes place

within the entire wealth of previous periods of development" (84).

Usurping the place of Absolute Knowledge in Marx's materialist rewriting of the Hegelian narrative, communism is the practical movement that overcomes the conflicts, contradictions, and disunities produced in history. Communism reunites individuals with the material conditions of their existence, with nature, with one another, and with their own human essence: "it is the *genuine* resolution of the conflict between man and nature, and between man and man, the true resolution of the conflict between existence and being, between objectification and self-affirmation, between freedom and necessity, between individual and species. It is the solution to the riddle of history and knows itself to be the solution" (348). The riddle of history is that freedom is contained in alienation and cannot be attained without the entire process of social differentiation: " 'Liberation' is a historical and not a mental act, and it is brought about by historical conditions, the [development] of industry, commerce, [agri]culture, [and] the [conditions of intercourse]" (Marx and Engels 1978: 169). Marx believes the movement of history, the dynamic of differentiation/recuperation, leads toward the emergence of communism. The "very difficult and protracted process" of communism is "the goal of . . . historical movement" (Marx 1975: 365). While communism represents the next stage of history, it does not create itself; rather, Marx believes that communism requires a conscious and practical act of appropriation.

Thus, Marx's initial vision of history is thoroughly inspired by Hegel and Feuerbach. It deploys a metaphysical concept of a human essence whose inner nature is realized in the process of history. History is the single, totalizable story of the realization and universalization of human freedom. The self-actualization of humanity unfolds through a teleology. Like Hegel, Marx sees nature as completing itself through human freedom and self-awareness. "History itself is a *real* part of *natural history*—and of nature's becoming man" (1975: 355). The main difference is that Marx took nature to be primary and originary rather than as the objectification of a preexisting Spirit or Reason. Yet, in his vision of history—as determined by the logic of production and objectification, as constituted by a single "transsubjective" agent, as expressing the unfolding of its capacities, and as involving its emancipation through a conscious appropriation of the past—Marx adopts the standpoint of the "philosophy of the subject" that has been rejected by Foucault and (not altogether successfully) Habermas (see Benhabib 1986).[6]

The productive forces model first appears in *The German Ideology*. Just one year after completing the *Economic and Philosophic Manuscripts*, influenced by Engels' work on political economy, Marx attained a much more detailed and empirical understanding of the material forces behind historical change. He abandoned Feuerbach's terminology and much of his Hegelian baggage. The essentialist view of the *Economic and Philosophic Manuscripts* whereby a historical subject expresses its nature is relinquished in favor of a "pragmatological" view (Fleischer 1973) that stresses the active role of human beings in shaping their history. This view posits a dialectic between needs and productive activity, where the existence of needs requires production and production creates new needs.[7] In place of a nondifferentiated account of the "universal meaning" of history, Marx, with Engels, now divides history into a series of "modes of production"—tribal, ancient, feudal, capitalist, and communist—each of which represents a different form of social interaction with nature and creates different modes of life. Once again, we find a single, universal narrative of history, this time interpreted as the evolution of human activity through successive historical generations.

Despite a periodization scheme in which both capitalism and communism are represented as historical ruptures, Marx and Engels underline the fundamental continuity in history across successive modes of production. From this standpoint, continuity is understood not in terms of the realization of the human essence, but rather the cumulative development of the productive forces themselves: "at each stage [of history] there is found a material result: a sum of productive forces, a historically created relation of individuals to nature and to one another, which is handed down to each generation from its predecessor; a mass of productive forces, capital funds and conditions" (Marx and Engels 1978: 164). Each historical product is "the result of the activity of a whole succession of generations, each standing on the shoulders of the preceding one, developing its [i.e., the former's] industry and its intercourse, modifying its social system according to the changed needs [of the new system]" (170).

Marx and Engels find "the whole evolution of history" to be "a coherent series of forms of intercourse, the coherence of which consists in this: in the place of an earlier form of intercourse, which has become a fetter, a new one is put, corresponding to the more developed productive forces and, hence, to the advanced mode of the self-activity of individuals—a form that in its turn becomes a fetter and is then replaced by another" (Marx and Engels 1978: 194–195). For the first time, they make the claim that spawned technological determinist readings of their work: "all collisions in history have their origin . . . in the contradiction between the productive forces and the form of [social] intercourse" (196).

This and other statements made by Marx in subsequent works points to the following (seemingly universal) dynamic of historical change: the technical basis of a given society calls into being certain relations of production that serve optimally to promote the continued development of the productive forces. Relations of production "correspond to" forces when they further the growth of the productive forces, and they become a conservative "fetter" to this growth when a particular social class tries to retain its social power rather than promote technological development that threatens this power. At this stage there is a "contradiction" rather than a correspondence between the forces and relations of production; a new set of relations (and hence a new economic base and a new superstructure) will emerge in order to better promote technological advance. The relations of production are subordinate to forces of production insofar as their function merely is to promote technological development.[8] The contradiction between forces and relations is described as the fundamental "motor" of historical change. Thus, on this model, the development of the productive forces is the main impetus behind the ever-expanding division of labor and the process of social differentiation. Appearing first in the individual family, the division of labor, spurred on by technological advance, results in the formation of various social classes, of industrial, commercial, and agricultural forms of labor, as well as in divisions between town and country and mental and manual labor.

The third continuity model, the class struggle model, is anticipated both in *The Holy Family* and *The German Ideology*, but makes its first explicit appearance with the publication of *The Communist Manifesto*. It also turns up in the 1859 Preface to *A Contribution to the Critique of Political Economy*, and is the privileged model of *Capital*. On this perspective, the unity of all (written) history is interpreted from the standpoint of class struggle: "Freeman and slave, patrician and plebian, lord and serf, guild-master and journeyman, in a word, oppressor and oppressed, stood in constant opposition to one another, carried on an uninterrupted, now hidden, now open fight, a fight that each time ended, either in a revolutionary re-constitution of society at large, or in the common ruin of the contending classes" (Marx and Engels 1978: 473–474). Although capitalism is again represented as a break in history, it is also seen as "the product of a long course of development, of a series of revolutions in the modes of production and of exchange" (475). As a form of class society, capitalism stands in continuity with all past societies; it is "the last antagonistic form of the social process of production" and prepares to bring "the prehistory of human society" to a close (Marx 1978: 5). Communism inaugurates both the end of (alienated) history and the beginning of (nonalienated, free) history.

Thus, one can identify various continuity models that Marx develops in different stages of his thought. Rather than seeing these models as incompatible, or as discontinuous formulations divided by an "epistemological break" (Althusser 1979; Fleischer 1973; Adamson 1985), I suggest they stand as different perspectives on history, each articulating a different yet related aspect of continuity, and that Marx employs all of them together in his later work. To be sure, there are incompatible elements in these various models; the determinism of the anthropological and nomological models, for example, contradicts the emphasis on a humanly shaped history in the pragmatological model.

But there are also fundamental lines of coherence that link these models together in a multiperspectival vision of history. While after 1844 Marx abandoned the metaphysical concept of human essence, along with the anthropological model of history, the problematic of alienation is integral to later writings (e.g., the *Grundrisse, Capital*, and *Theories of Surplus Value*) where terms such as "alienation" and "objectification" still appear frequently (see Schaff 1970; Rosdolsky 1977). The humanist model is presupposed in both the productive forces and class struggle model insofar as the development of productive forces involves a progressive separation of labor from the process and products of production, and alienation is a motivating force of class struggle. There is a direct link, moreover, between the productive forces model, and the class struggle model since Marx sometimes interprets class struggle as the active political expression of the contradiction between the forces and relations of production. This contradiction "necessarily on each occasion burst[s] out in revolution" and the "collisions of various classes" (Marx and Engels 1978: 197). On the technological determinist model (see below), this involves a struggle between ascending and descending classes, between those classes that advance the development of the productive forces and those that impede it.

Underlying all three continuity models are the constant themes of the mutual transformation of human beings and nature through production; economics, technology, and class struggle as the decisive causal forces of social change; the evolution of individuals and society by means of the evolution of the productive forces and the division of labor; and the progressive advance of history toward communism and human emancipation. From the *Economic and Philosophic Manuscripts* to *Capital*, one finds the same Hegelian vision of a collective subject of history realizing its potentiality through a process of objectification whereby the estranged products of its labor can be regained. Although Marx interchanges human beings for Spirit, he retains the Hegelian motif of a Subject behind history that emerges through a process of externalization in its conscious objectifications. Marx's "Subject," however, is unified only in the abstract, in the name of the praxis of humanity; specified more concretely, the subject of world history is fragmented into warring classes. This specification, nevertheless, leaves intact the assimilation of different social groups and activities to the logic of production.

Moreover, Marx never abandons the metanarrative of progress and emancipation, whether phrased in terms of the formation of the five senses or the transition from "necessity to freedom." Marx's vision of emancipation as reconciliation of alienated divisions of life is most pronounced in his early text, *The Jewish Question*. Here, following Hegel, Marx represents capitalism as a structure where differentiation assumes the form of dualistic separation and mutual antagonism. Capitalism is organized around the division between state and civil society, where civil society is the economic sphere of private interests at war with one another and the state is the political sphere where individuals are integrated with one another in theory but not in practice.[9] For Marx, this social division leads to a fractured existence of the human individual itself since it is divided into a public and private being, into an abstract citizen and a concrete producer or worker.

Under these conditions, the social nature of the human being appears as something accidental or extraneous; it is degraded into a mere means for the realization of private, egoistic ends. To recover the true social nature and integrity of human beings, Marx

calls for the overthrow of private interests, the recuperation of species-being, and the return of the individual to itself as a coherent totality: "Only when real, individual man resumes the abstract citizen into himself and as an individual man has become a *species-being* in his empirical life, his individual work and his individual relationships, only when man has recognized and organized his *forces propres* as *social forces* so that social force is no longer separated from him in the form of *political force*, only then will human emancipation be completed" (Marx 1975: 234). A key opposition communism overcomes, therefore, is between society and the individual. Within the mediated unity of communism, as Marx envisages it, the communal integration of precapitalist societies exists, as does the individual element of capitalism, but the two elements are no longer in contradiction to one another; rather, communism creates the free, *social individual* whose rich inner being is dependent upon conditions of social equality where the freedom of each requires the freedom of all.

Discontinuity in History

We have just examined the various continuity models Marx employed. In addition to mapping the progressive development of the objective and subjective forces of history, Marx employs a vision of historical discontinuity to mark a rupture in history with the advent of capitalism and to project an emancipatory break with capitalism through the norm of a possible future communist society.

Marx's most sustained vision of historical discontinuity can be found in the long historical section of the *Grundrisse*, "Pre-capitalist Economic Formations." In this text, Marx tries to establish the historical originality of the capital–wage–labor relationship. His intention is not a theory of precapitalist modes of production, but rather a genealogy of capitalist forms and categories. Marx attempts to grasp the historical preconditions of capitalism, "the evolutionary history of both capital and wage-labour ... the historic origin of the bourgeois economy" (Marx 1965: 86). The relationship of labor to capital, where the worker finds the conditions of production external to him or her as capital and the capitalist finds the worker as a propertyless being, "presupposes a historic process which dissolves the different [precapitalist property] forms, in which the labourer is an owner and the owner labours" (97), with the result that the laborer owns nothing and the owners do not labor.

This genealogy has immediate political motivations and implications, for Marx is concerned to demystify the fetishized ideology of capitalism as an eternally present form of society and to underline it as a break from more organic types of society. Rather than seeing the "worker" as a universal category, as does bourgeois political economy, Marx insists that the worker is a specific historical creation. "The establishment of the individual as a worker . . . is itself a production of *history*" (1965: 68). The "worker" is precisely that abstract, laboring being who is divorced from the socionatural context of production, from both (1) the "objective conditions" of his production, and (2) its communal context. I shall briefly address each of these factors.

In his description of the various precapitalist societies, Marx argues that all are *relatively continuous modifications* of the basic tribal mode of production and its direct communal property form. He says, for instance, *"Where the fundamental relationship is the same* [in precapitalist societies], this [tribal property] form can realise itself in a variety of ways" (1965: 69, my emphasis). Thus, ancient society "is the product of a more dynamic historical life, of the fate and modification of the original tribes" (71), and "Slavery and serfdom are . . . simply further developments of property based on tribalism" (91).

Whatever their differences—which amount to a gradually evolving differentiation of the tribal form and hence emergent forms of private property—these historical mutations are always, until capitalism, *confined within the basic structural limits of tribal society.* The "original" definition of property, as Marx states throughout the *Formen,* articulates a symbiotic relation of the producing individual to the land and the community. *"Property—*and this applies to its Asiatic, Slavonic, ancient classical and Germanic forms—. . . originally signifies a relation of the working (producing) subject . . . to the conditions of his production or reproduction as his own" (1965: 95). In all precapitalist societies, producers are integrated with the materials of labor that constitute their objective conditions of production, and which they relate to as their property. "The individual is related to himself as a proprietor, as master of the conditions of his reality" (67) and these become his condition of "realisation," where the earth itself is his "natural laboratory" (67) and is understood as an extension of his very being. The purpose of production in these precapitalist societies is not the creation of exchange value, but of simple use value, of the maintenance of the individual, family, and the community as a whole. Each individual is related to the other, therefore, as a coproprietor, as a co-owner of common property.

Producers in these social formations are owners only insofar as they are members of the community that is the crucial mediating context of their relation to the land. Marx speaks, therefore, of the social "preconditions" of production, or the "communal character" of production, which is maintained throughout *all* precapitalist social formations: "Only in so far as the individual is a member—in the literal and figurative sense—of such a community, does he regard himself as an owner or possessor. In reality *appropriation* by means of the process of labour takes place under these *preconditions,* which are not the *product* of labour but appear as its natural or *divine* preconditions" (1965: 69). The fact that the "communal ties of blood, language, custom, etc." (68) are the preconditions of all appropriation explains Marx's remark that in precapitalist society labor is not the origin of property, rather, property is the origin of labor—property, that is, as a communal form and concept.[10]

Thus, in precapitalist societies producing individuals are tied to the land and immersed in the community. Individuals produce only insofar as they participate in the community, and communal property mediates all relations to the land. Community and land constitute a primordial bond in the unity of conditions of production in precapitalist society. Although Marx is concerned to grasp the specific differences of each precapitalist mode of production, the emphasis in the *Formen* is on *what they have in common:* the natural and communal character of production. Here, Marx wishes to underline their *continuity with one another* (as "precapitalist economic formations") and their *collective discontinuity from capitalism:* "What requires explanation is not the *unity* of living and active human beings with the natural, inorganic conditions of their metabolism with nature, and therefore their appropriation of nature . . . what we must explain is the *separation* of these inorganic conditions of human existence from their active existence, a separation which is only *fully completed* in the relationship between wage-labour and capital" (1965: 86–87).

While each new property form is a gradually emerging mode of alienation (in the most narrow sense of the separation of producers from the objective conditions of production), all property formations are confined within the structural limits of the tribal form and none represent the complete "dissolution" of the production–land–community triad that capitalism alone represents. While there are socially significant changes in the passage from one mode of production to another and an ever-growing division of labor and development of technology, the basic production–land–community triad and the "objective relation" of producers to the earth is preserved. It is only with capitalist society that this rupture occurs and we find, for the first time, "the total isolation of the mere free labourer" (1965: 82).

Capitalism is a radical negation of all precapitalist societies, of the basic tribal property form. It involves "the *dissolution*" (1965: 97) of the socionatural character of all prior forms of production, and fully alienates these individuals. It severs their relations to the land and community and renders them propertyless and divided; it destroys the organic "*attitude* to the land, to the earth as the property of the working individual"

(81), who now appears as a mere abstraction, the "worker." Capitalism overturns the simple priorities of production in use value and self-preservation in order to establish the hegemony of exchange value, production, and work for their own sake. Only in capitalist society do "the productive forces appear as a world for themselves, quite independent of and divorced from the [producing] individuals. . . . *Never,* in *any* earlier period, have the productive forces taken on a form so indifferent to the intercourse of individuals *as* individuals" (Marx and Engels 1978: 190, first two emphases mine).[11]

Capitalism shatters the inert ballast of tradition to generate modernity and its unique form of temporality, which is based on rapid and ceaseless change. All societies change and develop throughout history, but none as rapidly and drastically as capitalist societies, where crisis and instability are structural norms and constants. In Marx and Engels' famous words:

> The bourgeoisie cannot exist without constantly revolutionizing the instruments of production, and thereby the relations of production, and with them the whole relations of society. Conservation of the old modes of production in unaltered form, was, on the contrary, the first condition of existence for *all* earlier industrial classes. Constant revolutionizing of production, uninterrupted disturbance of all social conditions, everlasting uncertainty and agitation distinguish the bourgeois epoch from *all* earlier ones. All fixed, fast-frozen relations, with their train of ancient and venerable prejudices and opinions, are swept away, all newformed ones become antiquated before they can ossify. All that is solid melts into air, all that is holy is profaned, and man is at last compelled to face with sober senses, his real conditions of life, and his relations with his kind. (1978: 476, my emphases)

Thus, capitalism is not simply unique or specific, as one might say of any mode of production; it is radically different from all preceding modes of production. To employ Althusser's distinction—which is implicit in Marx—capitalism is the first society where the economic level of the mode of production is both dominant and determinant, rather than simply ("ultimately") determinant.[12] This perspective of discontinuity, which sees capitalism as a break from rather than a summation of history, is an independent one and should not be subsumed under a generalized continuity model. What we find are not two conflicting models of historical development, capitalism as summation of and break from all preceding history, but rather two different perspectives on the same historical transition.[13] Marx views *one and the same transition* to capitalism from *two different analytic levels:* a highly abstract level that seeks the lines of historical continuity at the level of the productive forces, and a more concrete and historical perspective that delves beneath this abstraction to see the radical changes that this development effects at the level of economic and social relations of production. These perspectives form two inseparable, complementary strands in the larger web of Marx's theory of history. . . .

Economic and Technological Determinism

In the social production of their life, men enter into definite relations that are indispensible and independent of their will, relations of production which correspond to a definite stage of development of their material productive forces. The sum total of these relations of production constitutes the economic structure of society, the real basis, on which rises a legal and political superstructure, and to which correspond definite forms of social consciousness. The mode of production of material life conditions the social, political and intellectual life process in general. It is not the consciousness of men that determines their being, but, on the contrary, their social being that determines their consciousness.

—Marx (1978: 4)

This passage from the Preface to *A Contribution to the Critique of Political Economy* is one of the most cited in Marx's work, but it is also one of the most misunderstood. As the main source of economic and technological deterministic misreadings, it is a bad place to begin understanding Marx. From reading this and other general statements of Marx's method, many interpreters have argued that Marx adheres to the following model of history: (1) all human history is a unified and coherent whole; (2) each mode of production, from tribal to communist society, succeeds the other through an invariable law of internal change; (3) this mechanism involves a progressively evolving state of productive forces bursting through a series of social fetters that thwart and "contradict" its motion; (4) history therefore unfolds with strict necessity and inexorably advances toward communist society.

According to this model, Marxism is a dogmatic, *a priori* system that deduces historical reality from application of a universal law of social constitution and change. From passages like this, theorists have drawn various absurd conclusions, such as that Marx denies human freedom and moral responsibility (Berlin 1957; Tucker 1961), or is committed to predictions about inevitable historical outcomes (Popper 1966). Such deterministic and scientistic interpretations of Marx's theory of history are caricatures of his actual analyses and political activities, although they have some textual support and Marx himself is partly responsible for these readings. In one oft-cited passage in *Capital*, for example, Marx refers to "the natural laws of capitalist production . . . working themselves out with iron necessity" (1977: 91). Similarly, Marx seems to hold a crude copy-theory of knowledge that denies human agency when he says "the ideal is nothing but the material world reflected in the mind of man, and translated into forms of thought" (102).

The problem with all reductionist and determinist readings of Marx's work is not that they lack a textual basis, but that they focus only on one aspect or passage of his work to the exclusion of others and ignore Marx's concrete political activities. In his *Theses on Feuerbach*, for example, Marx rejects a reflection theory of knowledge by praising idealism for grasping the active character of the mind. In *The Holy Family*, he and Engels explicitly repudiate the kind of Hegelian teleology found in the *Economic and Philosphic Manuscripts* and implied in other statements by Marx: "*History* does *nothing*, it possesses '*no* immense wealth,' it 'makes *no* battle.' It is *man*, real, living man who does all that, who possesses and fights; history is not, as it were, a person apart, using man as a means to achieve *its own* aims; history is *nothing but* the activity of man pursuing his aims" (Marx and Engels 1975: 110). Although Marx sees communism as the "goal of history," he is referring to a historically created potential that requires human intervention to be actualized. "Marx sharply rejects every school of thought which would subject history to some lawfulness or purposiveness . . . external and alien to the content of activities of concrete historical individuals" (Markus 1978: 54).

Such tensions in Marx's work can be resolved in a number of ways; the differences in interpretation of Marx, such as we find between Plekhanov and Lukács, result from the ambiguities and inconsistencies in his texts. There is therefore no "authentic" Marx, but a careful reading will avoid simple and dogmatic positions of any kind and bring out the tensions and changes in his work. The problem with relying on Marx's methodological reflections is that they often grossly oversimplify and misrepresent the complexity of his actual analyses.

Perhaps the most fundamental tension in Marx's work is the discrepancy between what he says in his theoretical summaries and what he does in his concrete studies. Here a key problem relates to the issue of whether or not Marx was a technological determinist, whether he privileged forces of production (technology, knowledge, work relations) over relations of production (social classes) as the fundamental causal dynamic of history. The crucial interpretative problems in the "Preface" concern the strength of the causal force behind the "determining" operations of the economic base, the meaning of the "correspondence" between forces and relations of production, and what elements constitute the economic base of society and its mode of production.[14] Deterministic readings of Marx in

large part emerge from different answers to these questions.

On the economic determinist reading, the base comprises both the forces and relations of production, both technology and economic classes, and it "determines" the superstructure in the strong sense of a one-way, mechanical causal force that prevents any reciprocal interaction between the base and superstructure. While many of Marx's critics still hold to this reading, orthodox Marxists such as Kautsky and Plekhanov rejected it and emphasized the reciprocal interaction between base and superstructure. Yet they and many others adopt a technological determinist reading of Marx.[15] Like economic determinism, the technological determinist reading holds that the base determines the superstructure, but it adds that the most important factor determining the base itself is technology. In other words, a more fundamental rung is added to the causal hierarchy of society: the growth of technology determines the nature of economic activity and relations, which in turn determine the superstructure of social life.[16]

On the technological determinist reading, Marx holds that the ultimate driving force in history is technological development and that class relations are to be explained according to their function in promoting or retarding this growth. This thesis need not argue for a one-way causal determination of forces over relations of production; it need only maintain that the productive forces ultimately determine the relations of production, that relations of production are ultimately to be explained by the development of the forces of production.[27] Thus, although "analytic Marxists" Cohen (1978) and Shaw (1978) criticize a nondialectical version of technological determinism that recognizes only one-way causality between forces and relations of production, and claim that Marx saw reciprocal influence on both sides, they remain technological determinists insofar as they functionally subordinate the relations to the forces of production and assert that the main role of social relations is to develop technology.[18] Cohen attempts to support his "primacy [of the productive forces] thesis" with the "developmental thesis" that human beings, fundamentally rational in nature and living in constant conditions of scarcity, seek to acquire ever greater control over nature and therefore strive constantly to develop the forces of production. The relations of production that best develop the forces of production become the ruling social classes and survive as long as they serve the role of advancing technological growth.

For all their analytic sophistication, the major flaw of Cohen and Shaw's interpretations is their failure to emphasize the distinctly political character of Marx's historical explanations and the complex political-economic dialectic he develops—a problem that stems from their false separation of productive forces and work relations (see below). They transform a revolutionary political vision intended for the working class into an academic theory of history designed for historians. It is precisely this functionalist subordination of the relations to the forces of production that prompts other theorists to decry determinism and to insist on the primacy of the relations of production. As early as 1933, theorists such as Sidney Hook had begun to argue against the technological determinist claims made by Kautsky and Plekhanov and to champion the primacy of the relations of production. This argument was most ambitiously developed by Hindess and Hirst (1975) who reject the primacy of the productive forces, however qualified or reciprocal in nature, as a "technicism," as a functionalist subordination of consciousness, politics, and class struggle to technology. For Hindess and Hirst, the primacy of the forces of production thesis "renders inexplicable any operation of the relations of production which has the effect of not [merely] distributing the conditions of production so as to reproduce the forces" (1977: 54).

Hindess and Hirst claim that for Marx, "it is the relations of production which are the crucial element in any concept of the economic level" (1975: 230). Unlike Cohen and Shaw, they privilege class struggle as the fundamental motor of history: "It is the forms of class struggle and their outcomes which determine the specific forms of the forces of production" (247). To support their reading, they point to quotes ignored by Cohen and Shaw where Marx defines class relations as "the specific economic form in which unpaid surplus-labor is pumped out of the direct producers," which suggests that the relations of production determine the forces of production.

The opposing claims of these theorists each provide only a partially correct and one-sided reading of Marx. The technological determinist reading rightly emphasizes that Marx grants fundamental importance to the role of technology in human life. For Marx, "Technology discloses man's mode of dealing with nature, the process of production by which he sustains his life, and thereby also lays bare the mode of formation of his social relations, and of the mental conceptions that flow from them" (quoted in Shaw 1978: 53). Marx does indeed claim that technology and the productive forces are key to explaining social change: "In acquiring new forces of production men change their mode of production; and in changing their mode of production, in changing the way of earning their living, they change all their social relations. The handmill gives you society with the feudal lord; the steam-mill, society with the industrial capitalist" (1963: 109). He also argues elsewhere that "The (economic) relations and consequently the social, moral, and political state of nations changes with the *change* in the material powers of production" (1972: 430). These emphases are conveniently glossed over in Hindess and Hirst's interpretation of Marx and they wrongly deny the forces of production any significant determining power in history.[19] But they correctly point to counteremphases on the role of class struggle in history as an independent causal force that cannot be adequately captured by technological determinism. Neither position grasps the tensions and ambiguities in Marx's analyses. The one-sidedness of the readings of Cohen and Shaw and Hindess and Hirst need to be rejected in favor of a more nuanced, contextualist approach. . . .

Visions of Reconciliation

Bifurcation is the origin of the need for philosophy.

—Hegel

Throughout this chapter I have tried to show that determinist readings of Marx's theory of history are one-sided and false. Although there are deterministic and teleological tendencies in Marx's work, these occur mainly in the abstract summaries or presentations of his method. The thrust of his concrete analyses, in contrast, points in nondeterminsitic and nonteleological directions. From his texts, it is clear that Marx does not posit a linear development of modes of production leading from tribal to communist society, does not see history as a seamless narrative of progress, does not believe in an immanent law of motion leading inevitably toward communism, and does not embrace an economic or technological determinist account of social change. Rather, he sees discontinuities between Western and non-Western social forms and, within Western history, between precapitalist and capitalist societies; he holds that human beings shape, and are shaped by, their social and natural environment; he claims that history is a human product; and he believes that the "unfolding" of the contradictions of capitalism guarantee nothing but what conscious political subjects can make of them.

I have also argued that the dominant view of Marx as a facile reductionist and totalizer is wrong. Although he treats all social practices as derivative of labor and is too economistic in his analysis of precapitalist societies, Marx is opposed to any universal method that attempts to substitute deduction of historical laws for concrete analysis of specific social situations. Within the framework of historical materialism, Marx adopts a rich, complex, and multicausal analysis of social change. Diachronically, he analyzes continuities and discontinuities; synchronically, he analyzes social change from the standpoints of economics, politics, technology, work relations, war, and other factors. As Daniel Little has argued, the methodology of *Capital* is "irreducibly pluralistic" in its "variety of different forms of analysis and descriptive matter" (1986: 20). These include economic, historical, political, and sociological arguments and modes of description, along with moral critiques of exploitation and alienation. "The variety displayed in these different elements in Marx's analysis in *Capital* shows that his treatment of capitalism does not take the form of a unified deductive system from which all relevant particulars can be deduced. Instead, Marx's account is a family of related explanatory arguments, bits of analysis, historical comments, and descriptive efforts loosely organized by a common perspective. No general theory akin to atomic theory permits Marx to unify all his material into a single deductive system" (18).

The fact that Marx adopts a pluralist, multicausal mode of analysis does not mean that he is an eclectic who vacuously believes everything determines everything else. As Althusser insisted (1979: 215), the logic of overdetermination Marx employs rejects both economistic monism and the "theoretical void" of epistemological pluralism, which asserts that all perspectives and explanatory frameworks are equally valid and which fails to specify ultimately determining causes in society. Marx believes that only a materialist analysis can represent real social dynamics, and yet within this framework he specifies numerous factors of determination as they interrelate within a "structure in dominance" (Althusser). Despite the different models, standpoints, and tensions in Marx's works, there is also a good deal of coherence and consistency. Marx always tries to account for change in terms of dynamic developments within a society that lead to internal contradictions, but he does not limit this to a simple contradiction between forces and relations of production. He consistently roots the basic factors of social change in the mode of production of social life, appealing to technology, economics, work relations, and political forces.

My argument has been that Marx adopts a contextualist approach that sees historical change as the result of a complex interaction of social phenomena, all of which must be analyzed in concrete empirical contexts, where no *a priori* rules determine the results beyond the general principle that it is the mode of production of a given society that determines its mode of life. The usual practice of distinguishing between an "early" and "late" Marx does not begin to do justice to the complexity of his different views of history, politics, culture, and ideology. A contextualist reading of this contextualist method allows us to look beyond surface contradictions in Marx's works and to see deeper continuities within a broad materialist framework. A contextualist approach does not try to absolve Marx of all inconsistencies or contradictions; rather, *as contextualist*, it examines each theoretical issue independently. When a complex and prolific writer like Marx analyzes a rapidly changing social world from different vantage points over a long period of time, contradictions and inconsistencies will certainly occur, but along many lines one also finds a great deal of continuity and coherence to Marx's work.

One such line of continuity and coherence is the Hegelian vision of history as a dialectic of alienation and freedom, differentiation and unification, loss and recuperation. On this vision, human emancipation, just like the freedom of Spirit, cannot be achieved in pure, abstract, and unmediated form; rather, freedom is a historical product that requires a process of differentiation and alienation. Against Rousseau, Marx does not believe that humanity is born free and then placed in chains. It is only when there is established a complex social division of labor, an advanced development of technology, a creation of universal forms of human association, and the evolution of individuals beyond "sheep-like or tribal consciousness" (Marx and Engels 1978: 158) into beings rich in abilities and needs that the historical preconditions of human freedom exist. But since differentiation unfolds as alienation, the process reaches a point where the divisions and antagonisms that dynamically drive history forward are no longer needed and become an impediment to further progress; emancipation can be attained only through the abolition of conflicts, contradictions, and oppositions.

For Marx, this stage in history is reached in nineteenth-century capitalist society. Marx praises capitalism for its powerful development of the productive forces, for establishing universal social relations, and for producing complex individuals, but he condemns it for organizing these dynamics around the imperatives of production for private profit and thereby blocking the historical movement of democracy, equality, and freedom. Only through the abolition of capitalism and the creation of communism can the historically accumulated powers of humanity be realized in conditions of freedom.

Through analysis of actual historical possibilities, Marx foresees the end of human need (as privation) and greed and envisages a transition from the realm of necessity to the realm of freedom. "Freedom . . . can only consist in socialized man, the associated producers, rationally regulating their interchange with Nature, bringing it under their common control, instead of being ruled by it as by the blind forces of Nature" (Marx 1978: 441). In Marx's vision, the task of communism is to overturn all forces of alienation in order to allow human beings to gain control over the conditions of their practical existence, to appropriate the objective and subjective wealth of history, and to overcome all debilitating oppositions. This requires the abolition of the capitalist state, private property, religion, money, and all other alienating forces that mediate the direct relationship among freely interacting human beings and between each individual and its own nature.

By abolishing all false mediations and oppositions, Marx believes that communism can resolve the most fundamental contradiction, that between (human) essence and existence, between potentiality and actuality, such that objectification (productive activity) is no longer alienation but self-actualization. By abolishing the division of labor in the form of the "fixation of social activity," communism is the movement of human beings developing their multifaceted abilities in various ways without being restricted to any one mode of activity. "Only at this stage [of history] does self-activity coincide with material life, which corresponds to the development of individuals into complete individuals" (Marx 1975: 192). The ultimate goal of communism is to return to the individual the most important possession he or she can have, the free time needed to develop one's personality and creative abilities.[20] Communism is defined therefore as a "fresh confirmation of *human* powers and a fresh enrichment of *human* nature" (358); it is designed to render it "impossible that anything should exist independently of individuals" as an alien power (Marx and Engels 1978: 193).

Human progress from now on is to be measured in terms of the degree of the all-around development of human individuals themselves; the social imperative shifts from development of objective to subjective forces. The social whole that Marx envisages is not an abstract or homogenous whole that erases all distinctions and levels individuality, but rather a concrete or mediated unity that allows for the genuine flourishing of differences in an unantagonistic way. Where precapitalist societies produced sociality without sufficient individuality, and capitalism produced individuality without sufficient sociality, Marx sees the goal of communism to be the overcoming of this opposition through the creation of the social individual, of free and creative individuals interacting harmoniously in solidarity with one another. To borrow Adorno's phrase, Marx's vision of history is informed by a "negative dialectics" that eschews oppressive homogeneity without abandoning the norm of unity and community. . . .

Notes

1. As first schematized by Engels, Marx's dialectics studies four kinds of relationships: identity/difference, interpenetration of opposites, quantity/quality, and contradiction. The first two relations focus on synchronic phenomena. Marx attempts to analyze various aspects of society, while understanding them as part of a single system. Within this system, seemingly "opposite" things (such as the capital/labor relation) are really contrasting aspects of the same relation. The last two relations focus on diachronic phenomena. As

discussed below, the impetus of historical change is contradictions within social orders. Gradual, quantitative accumulations of change eventually lead to a qualitative rupture and a new form of society. For a more complete analysis of dialectics, see Engels (1976), Lenin (1981), Ollman (1976, 1993), and Bologh (1979).

2. However "scientific" Marx's account of history, his analysis never relinqished strong ties to Hegelian dialectics. Later texts such as *Capital* and the *Grundrisse* are dialectic in their method and mode of exposition. For elaboration of this argument, see Ollman (1976) and Rosdolsky (1977).

3. "The act of reproduction itself changes not only the objective conditions—e.g. transforming village into town, the wilderness into agricultural clearings, etc.—but the producers change with it, by the emergence of new qualities, by transforming and developing themselves in production, forming new powers and new conceptions, new modes of intercourse, new needs, and new speech" (Marx 1965: 93). Thus, Marx believes that human subjects too are throughly historical in nature, that the human being itself is a historical product.

4. For Hegel, Spirit is originally an abstract and undifferentiated identity, an empty substance without any reality. To be actual and self-actualizing, it must undergo a process of externalization and differentiation in space and time, where it eventually becomes whole again, this time as a "concrete unity." Similarly, I am arguing, Marx recognizes that early human societies may be organically unified, but the human beings living within them cannot be free until a new unity, differentiated and "concrete," is historically produced.

5. My scheme differs in detail and substance from the valuable analyses of Rader (1979), Fleischer (1973), and Adamson (1985). Rader also identifies three different models of history in Marx—the "base/superstructure" model, the "dialectical" model, and the "organic" model—and emphasizes their logical continuity, but without seeing important points of discontinuity. Fleischer too distinguishes between three different historical models in Marx's work, which he identifies as "anthropological," "pragmatological," and "nomological." The anthropological model of the *Economic and Philosophic Manuscripts* is a form of metaphysical determinism that sees

history as the realization of the human essence. Immediately after developing this model, Fleischer claims, Marx abandons it in favor of the pragmatological model of *The German Ideology* and *Theses on Feuerubach*. These texts display a nonmetaphysical, empirical analysis of history as determined by the concrete practical activities of human beings. The nomological model is another form of determinism that sees history as the movement of objective processes and laws independent of human will.

Adamson adopts Fleischer's scheme, but adds a fourth model, found in the 1857 introduction to the *Grundrisse*, which breaks from the simple realism and evolutionism of *The German Ideology*. Unlike Fleischer, Adamson focuses on the discontinuities and logical incompatibilities between Marx's different models. In particular, Adamson stresses the conflict between the pragmatological focus on human freedom and the determinism of the nomological model. Both Fleischer and Adamson, however, occlude the continuities between the *Manuscripts* and *The German Ideology*. Just as the *Manuscripts* are not simply Hegelian and speculative, but show Marx's first attempts to incorporate empirical method and political economy into his work ("I have arrived at my conclusions through an entirely empirical analysis based on an exhaustive critical study of political economy" [Marx 1975: 281]), so *The German Ideology* has some residual speculative Hegelian and teleological aspects in the discussion of communism. As I discuss below, I use the *Grundrisse* to bring out a discontinuity model in Marx that sees ruptures rather than continuities in history. Neither Fleischer, Rader, nor Adamson identify such a model. Against Adamson and Fleischer, I find the nomological model to be more a rhetorical tendency in Marx than an analytic model in its own right.

6. As I will argue, against Benhabib, Marx breaks with the essentialism of this model after 1844 and shows that the "unitary" subject of history changes and is fragmented into competing classes. Still, because Marx reduces human activity to production, the general agent of history remains a continuous subject of production.

7. "The satisfaction of the first need (the action of satisfying, and the instrument of satisfaction which has been acquired) leads to new needs; and this production of new needs is the first historical act" (Marx and Engels 1978: 156). The productive forces model in

The German Ideology therefore suggests two different "motors" of history: the dialectic between needs and production and the dialectic between forces and relations of production. In Fleischer's terms, the former dynamic is the basis of the pragmatological view, while the latter became the basis of the nomological view. While these two versions of history are incompatible insofar as the former sees history as the outcome of free human practice and the later as the determined result of laws independent of human will, the causal dynamics as stated in *The German Ideology* are compatible insofar as the productive forces/relations dynamic is put into play by the existence of human needs, and together the forces/relations of production shape new needs historically.

8. In the words of Marx's orthodox followers, "a certain state of the productive forces *is the cause* of the given production relations" (Kautsky); relations of production are an "outgrowth of the system of technology" and the whole *"mental life of society is a function of the forces of production"* (Bukharin); changing *"in conformity with"* the productive forces (Stalin). Ultimately, "technical progress constitutes the basis of the entire development of humankind" (Kautsky). All quotes are cited in Larrain (1986: 45–46).

9. The important difference between Hegel and Marx on this point, of course, is that Hegel argued that the state, as the universal embodiment of Reason, worked to reconcile conflicting interests, whereas Marx saw it, on one major level, as the legal and political instrument of the bourgeoisie. For a detailed analysis of Marx's varying views on the state, see Miliband (1977).

10. "Hence the tribal community, the natural common body, appears not as the consequence, but as the precondition of the joint (temporary) appropriation and use of the soil" (Marx 1965: 68).

11. Marx also employs a discontinuity model to represent communist society. "The Communist revolution is the most radical rupture with traditional property relations; no wonder that its development involves the most radical rupture with traditional ideas" (Marx and Engels 1978: 489–490). Although communism builds from previous historical accomplishments, it is the first mode of production that abolishes antagonistic divisions between social classes, and in which human producers gain a conscious and practical

mastery over the material forces of social existence. "The bourgeois relations of production are the last antagonistic form of the social process of production" (Marx 1978: 5).

12. Althusser's distinction comes mainly from this key passage in *Capital:* "For our own times . . . material interests are preponderant, but not for the Middle Ages, dominated by Catholicism, nor for Athens and Rome, dominated by politics. . . . [Yet] [o]ne thing is clear: the Middle Ages could not live on Catholicism, nor could the ancient world live on politics. On the contrary, it is the manner in which they gained their livelihood which explains why on one case politics, in the other case Catholicism, played the chief part (1977: 176n.). Only in capitalism, Marx claims, is the producer separated from the means of production; in prepcapitalist forms of production, we find a nonseparation between producer and the means of production and the resulting necessity of noneconomic forms of sanctioning relations of exploitation that allow for the dominance of superstructural phenomena.

13. Anthony Giddens (1981) and Claude Lefort (1978) argue that Marx's continuity and discontinuity perspectives are contradictory and incompatible images of history. For a critique of their claims, see Best (1991).

14. Marx himself never rigorously defined the terms "forces and relations of production" and a great deal of controversy has ensued concerning what they actually mean, whether there is a valid distinction between them, how they relate to the term "mode of production," and even whether they can be defined at all. The problem is to find definitions that are not too narrow, and therefore are supple enough to include some of Marx's nuances, but that also are not too broad, and therefore conflate key distinctions that Marx wished to maintain, namely those between forces and relations of production, and base and superstructure.

The forces of production are the basic elements employed in the production process. Marx refers to them in various ways, as the "conditions," "instruments," or "means of production." In the *Grundrisse*, Marx distinguishes between objective and subjective dimensions of productive forces. The objective dimensions include raw materials and natural resources, tools and machines, and transportation and communication systems. The subjective conditions of production refer to

what Marx called "labour-power," or "the aggregate of those mental and physical capacities existing in a human being, which he exercises whenever he produces a use-value of any description" (Marx quoted in Shaw 1978: 15). The physical capacities of labor power involve strength and skill, and the mental capacities involve practical and scientific knowledge. On a too narrow definition of productive forces, important factors like science are left out, despite clear indications by Marx that it was a productive force: "But the *development of science* . . . is only one aspect, one form in which the *development of the human productive forces* i.e., of wealth, appears" (Marx quoted in Shaw 1978: 21). On a too broad definition (Rader 1979) law and morality are included, thus collapsing the distinction between base and superstructure. McMurtry (1978), Cohen (1978), and Shaw (1978) all define a force of production as anything that is directly, physically, and actually *used* in the process of production, rather than something that is necessary for production to occur (see Cohen [1978: 32ff.], McMurtry [1978: 55ff.], and Shaw [1978: 10ff.]). While government, law, or morality might be a necessary precondition of productive activity, they are not directly or physically employed in production as are tools, raw materials, or even scientific knowledge. Thus, the distinction between base and superstructure, while not rigid, can nevertheless be preserved. One important point of controversy concerns whether or not productive forces, include what Marx terms "modes of cooperation." I examine this below. . . .

15. Not all technological determinist interpretations of Marx are the same. The earlier orthodox readings (Kautsky, Plekhanov, Bukharin, Lenin, Stalin, and others) give a considerably more mechanistic and deterministic rendering of Marx than the neo-orthodox interpretations of analytic Marxists. The more narrow account tends to see the causal relationship between forces and relations as a one-way route with little reciprocal determination of relations on forces. Moreover, it sees history as moving through immanent laws of motion independent of and wholly determining human agency, such that the unfolding of the productive forces of history guarantee the transition from capitalism to socialism.

The crudest version of technological determinism, such as we can find in Marshall McLuhan and Jacques Ellul, sees technology as developing throughout history on its own dynamic in complete abstraction from social relations. Marx's analyses show that he did not understand technology as a self-generating process or as unfolding through some immanent rationality. For Marx, the material is social; the development of the productive forces occurs only within given social relations of production that play a crucial role in determining the development and nature of the productive forces. Social relations are built into Marx's definition of production: "All production is appropriation of nature on the part of an individual within and through a specific form of society" (Marx 1973: 87).

Marx never separated technological development from its economic and political context. He destroyed the fetishized concept of technology through a twofold contextualization: the invention, application, and development of modern technology was seen to be determined by capitalist accumulation imperatives, and these imperatives in turn were shaped by the struggles of the working class. For Marx, the existence of a given technical state of development, and the use to which technology is applied, is always conditioned by a given social context and the objectives of the class controlling the productive forces of society. "Crises," for example, do not result from a malfunction within a self-governing system, but rather are the result of the power of the working class to disrupt capitalist accumulation imperatives (see Cleaver 1979). Marx mediates between two antithetical arguments: (1) technology develops strictly on its own accord regardless of human goals or intentions, and (2) human beings have full and conscious control of technology and are self-determined in their thoughts and action. For Marx, the freedom of individuals to shape their world occurs within a pregiven history and context that conditions them; yet they are able to transform this context, altering it more or less to suit their purposes.

16. It is traditional to define the economic base as comprised of forces and relations of production. Cohen (1978) has challenged this view by arguing that Marx only meant to include relations of production within the base and that the forces of production belong outside of the base, as a sort of subfoundation of social life. The best account of the complexities in defining forces and relations of production is Shaw (1978). For an argument that there is no valid distinction between forces and rela-

tions of production see Althusser and Balibar (1970) and Leff (1969).

17. The relations of production, for example, define the nature of work (duration, intensity, means of extraction of surplus labor, etc.), the distribution of the products of labor, as well as the social division of labor. Relations of production can either promote the development of the forces of production (as the bourgeois revolution did by abolishing feudal restrictions on trade and production) or retard it (as workers can do by going on strike or as the state can do by passing proenvironmental legislation).

18. Shaw, for instance, states, "The relations of production must be understood on their own level, not as the 'effects' of the productive forces to which they correspond" (1978: 75). Cohen argues that the productive forces cannot *fully* explain the nature of the productive relations: "They might explain, for example, why the economy is self-based, without explaining the precise distribution of rights between lord and peasant" (1978: 163), which, presumably, would be specified through an account of relatively autonomous politico-legal relations and institutions. Shaw states, "Of course the productive force[s] 'depend' on the relations of production which utilise them because production cannot take place outside production relations, but this does not imply the productive relations determine the productive forces" (1978: 64). Rather, "The productive forces both articulate and provide the foundation for the introduction of new relations [of production]" (52). "The relations change only in response to the possibilities provided by man's improving productive abilities" (66). For Cohen, Marx's statement that the relations of production "correspond to" the forces of production means that the relations are "explained by" the forces (1978: 136ff.). Thus, however much the relations may condition the forces, they receive their character and function from the forces, and not vice versa. Cohen and Shaw therefore conceive the relations of production as an adaptive response to the forces of production.

19. As George Elliot observes, "In *Pre-Capitalist Modes of Production* productive forces were denied any effectivity whatsoever, dissolved as any independent variable and reduced to specifications of relations of production—from which, in any particular mode of production, could be 'deduced'" (1986: 90). Hindess and Hirst beg the question by failing

to block the argument by Cohen and Shaw that the efficacy of the relations of production is simply an assigned function of the forces of production. The technological determinist can grant the relations a dominant role in a given situation, while still insisting that this dominance itself was assigned by the productive forces. Indeed, in a later "auto-critique" of *Pre-Capitalist Modes of Production*, Hindess and Hirst themselves acknowledged the one-sidedness of their position and adopted a broader explanatory framework that granted more importance to the role of forces of production. They suggested the relation between forces and relations of production should be understood in terms of "conditions of existence" where each provides a context for the existence of the other and must be specified in terms of the other (1977: 50, 54, 72). Relations of production, for instance, cannot be specified without reference to "the determinate technical functions" necessary for their existence. There is an "interdependence of the technical and social divisions of labour" (72). Hence, they move toward the symmetrical thesis, although, quite curiously, they still privilege relations of production as a theoretical concept (5–6). This move is further supported by Hirst's later claim (1985: 15) that the proper response to the privileging of the forces of production is not to switch to the primacy of the relations of production.

20. Beyond the realm of necessity "begins that development of human energy which is an end in itself, the true realm of freedom, which, however, can blossom forth only with the realm of necessity as its basis. The shortening of the working day is its basic prequisite" (Marx 1978: 441). Marx's vision of a society organized around creature leisure, rather than arduous work, was an important emancipatory norm in the nineteenth-century context of radical thought, which was shaped by scarcity and problems of toil and want. As Bookchin notes, however, Marx's vision was not lost in twentieth-century socialism, which developed its own puritanical work ethic: "Instead of focusing their message on the emancipation of man from toil, socialists tended to depict socialism as a beehive of industrial activity, humming with work for all" (1986: 115).

References

Adamson, Walter (1985). *Marx and the Disillusionment of Marxism*. Berkeley: University of California Press.

Althusser, Louis (1979). *For Marx*. London: New Left Books.

Althusser, Louis, and Balibar, Etienne (1970). *Reading Capital*. London and New York: Verso.

Benhabib, Seyla (1986). *Critique, Norm, and Utopia: A Study in the Foundations of Critical Theory*. New York: Columbia University Press.

Berlin, Isaiah (1957). *Historical Inevitability*. Oxford, England: Oxford University Press.

Berman, Marshall (1982). *All That Is Solid Melts Into Air*. New York: Simon and Schuster.

Best, Steven (1991). "Chaos and Entropy: Metaphors in Postmodern Science and Social Theory." *Science as Culture*, #11: 188–226.

Bologh, Roslyn Wallach (1979). *Dialectical Phenomenology: Marx's Method*. Boston and London: Routledge and Kegan Paul.

Bookchin, Murray (1986). *Post-Scarcity Anarchism*. Montreal: Black Rose Books.

Cleaver, Harry (1979). *Reading Capital Politically*. Austin: University of Texas Press.

Cleaver, Harry (1992). "The Inversion of Class Perspective in Marxian Theory: From Valorisation to Self-Valorisation." In *Open Marxism*, Vol II, ed. Werner Bonefeld, Richard Gunn, and Kosmas Psychopedis, pp. 106–144. London: Pluto Press.

Cohen, G. A. (1978). *Karl Marx's Theory of History: A Defense*. Princeton, NJ: Princeton University Press.

Elliot, George (1986). "The Odyssey of Paul Hirst," *New Left Review*, 159: 81–105.

Engels, Frederick (1976). *Anti-Duhring*. New York: International Publishers.

Fleischer, Helmut (1973). *Marxism and History*. London: Allen Lane.

Giddens, Anthony (1981). *A Contemporary Critique of Historical Materialism*. Berkeley: University of California Press.

Hindess, Barry, and Hirst, Paul (1975). *Pre-Capitalist Modes of Production*. London: Routledge and Kegan Paul.

Hindess, Barry, and Hirst, Paul (1977). *Modes of Production and Social Formation: An Auto-Critique of Pre-Capitalist Modes of Production*. London: Macmillan.

Hirst, Paul (1985). *Marxism and Historical Writing*. London: Routledge and Kegan Paul.

Kellner, Douglas (1983). "Science and Method in Marx's Capital." *Radical Science Journal*, #13: 39–54.

Larrain, Jorge (1986). *A Reconstruction of Historical Materialism*. London: Allen and Unwin.

Leff, Gordon (1969). *History and Social Theory*. New York: Anchor.

Lefort, Claude (1978). "Marx: From One Vision of History to Another." *Social Research*, 45(4): 615–666.

Lenin, V. I. (1981). *Philosophical Notebooks*, Vol. 38. *Collected Works*. Moscow: Progress Publishers.

Little, Daniel (1986). *The Scientific Marx*. Minneapolis: University of Minnesota Press.

Markus, George (1978). *Marxism and Anthropology*. Assen, The Netherlands: Van Gorcium.

Marx, Karl (1963). *The Poverty of Philosophy*. New York: International Publishers.

Marx, Karl (1965). *Pre-Capitalist Economic Formations*. New York: International Publishers.

Marx, Karl (1972). *Theories of Surplus Value*, Vol. 3. London: Lawrence and Wishart.

Marx, Karl (1973). *Grundrisse*. New York: Vintage.

Marx, Karl (1975). *Early Writings*. New York: Vintage.

Marx, Karl (1977). *Capital*, Vol. I. New York: Vintage.

Marx, Karl (and Engels, Friedrich) (1978). *The Marx-Engels Reader*, ed. Robert Tucker, New York: Norton.

McMurtry, John (1978). *The Structure of Marx's World-View*. Princeton, NJ: Princeton University Press.

Miliband, Ralph (1977). *Marxism and Politics*. Oxford: Oxford University Press.

Ollman, Bertell (1976). *Alienation*. Cambridge, England: Cambridge University.

Ollman, Bertell (1993). *Dialectical Investigations*. London: Routledge.

Popper, Karl (1966). *The Open Society and Its Enemies*, 2 vols. Princeton, NJ: Princeton University Press.

Rader, Melvin (1979). *Marx's Interpretation of History*. New York: Oxford University Press.

Rosdolsky, R. (1977). *The Making of Marx's Capital*. London: Pluto.

Schaff, Adam (1970). *Marxism and the Human Individual*. New York: McGraw-Hill.

Shaw, William H. (1978). *Marx's Theory of History*. Stanford, CA: Stanford University Press.

Tucker, Robert (1961). *Philosophy and Myth in Karl Marx*. Cambridge, England: Cambridge University Press.

Adapted from: Steven Best, *The Politics of Historical Vision: Marx, Foucault, Habermas*, pp. 32–48, 52–56, 72–78, 80–82. Copyright © 1995. Reprinted by permission of The Guilford Press. ✦

30

Gone Fishing

Making Sense of Marx's Concept of Communism

William James Booth

Introduction

In a splendid essay entitled "On Being Conservative" Michael Oakeshott writes that certain activities are eminently attractive to those of a conservative disposition. Fishing is one such activity—not fishing in order to supply the immediate sustenance of life, nor fishing as a commercial venture intended to yield a profit. Rather, what Oakeshott is describing is the activity of a trout fisherman by a mountain stream. His casting of the fly into the passing waters is not compulsory, that is, he does not have to catch fish in order to survive. Nor is it directed to any other end, or purpose, for instance, the sale of his catch. It is the activity itself that is enjoyable, the display of skill or "perhaps merely passing the time."[1] In sum, fishing is neither something necessitous (survival) nor externally purposive (market oriented).

Let us now draw a few inferences from Oakeshott's account of the activity of fishing. The person engaged in such an activity is not, as such, a fisherman. A fisherman is one who earns a living by means of this activity: He cannot while away his hours at that mountain stream, because his dinner or his earnings depend upon success. Displays of skill in fishing will matter to him only insofar as they yield the desired consequences, a result external to the activity, for example, nutrition or a paycheck. Time, for him, is indeed money (productivity as yield over time) not something merely to be "passed." His associates in this activity will be cooperants in a production process, helpers in maximizing his yield. And lastly, his activity will be an in-

strument for him—a means of ensuring his continued survival. Insofar as he must maximize his catch (to feed his community, to make a greater profit, or to win a wage-bonus), he has to make himself an "expert" fisherman, a specialized practitioner of that one set of tasks, or allocate those tasks among his associates. He is, then, an expert, not an amateur, of the activity of fishing.

Another person, someone not a fisherman but merely fishing by the side of the stream, pursues this activity as time spent pleasurably. He passes his time at it and that time is not measured or determined by output. The underlying reason for the free, unbound quality of this time is that the activity that fills it is one neither compelled by natural necessity nor is it one bound to the production of surpluses. Freed from these external pressures, time can merely be passed, the activity savored for itself, not for what it may yield. One's fishing companions are presumably freely chosen friends, people who enjoy each other's company in a shared pursuit. They are not moments of a production process, cooperants in maximizing productivity. Finally, this person is an amateur of fishing; it is not his expertise (however skilled he may be), not something to which he must devote his whole life, but rather a chosen pastime.

In Oakeshott's analysis, the activity of fishing is evidence of a nonutilitarian disposition to enjoy the present as it is, a conservative attitude toward the relations between activity and the world. I have sought to unpack Oakeshott's account of fishing, that is, to show the features that such an activity must have. These are (1) that time can be "whiled away," that is, it is not subject to the compulsion of nature (essential needs) or of the market (productivity). Where time is determined by the latter constraints, output shapes the activity as an external end and transforms it from a pastime into disciplined labor. (2) Skill is valued for itself, not for what it can produce. This is another way of formulating the idea that the activity is not driven by a purpose external to itself. (3) As a corollary of the preceding point, the skill displayed must be that of the amateur, a chosen prowess and not a functionally defined role within a rationalized production process. (4) A group or community of such persons, of the amateurs of fishing, would be voluntary because the association, like the activity, would be one chosen for its intrinsic pleasure and not for its contribution to the meeting of an external end. This analysis goes well beyond Oakeshott's few paragraphs; nevertheless it draws on his central idea and it sets a framework (activity, time, community) for understanding another political philosopher who also wrote about fishing.

Karl Marx's *German Ideology* contains what is perhaps the single most celebrated description of communism: "In communist society, where nobody has one exclusive sphere of activity . . . society regulates production and thus makes it possible for me to do one thing today and another tomorrow, to hunt in the morning, fish in the afternoon, rear cattle in the evening, criticize after dinner, just as I have a mind, without ever becoming hunter, fisherman, shepherd or critic."[2] That this passage contains a tongue-in-cheek, polemical barb directed at Marx's erstwhile philosophical allies is certain; that it suggests important features of his vision of communist society is something that I shall argue for in this essay. The question before Marx's readers is how to interpret this exceedingly elliptical description of communism. Marx himself provides us some guidance: "We do not dogmatically anticipate the world, but only want to find the new world through criticism of the old one."[3] What this says is that the shape of the future can best be seen in the criticism, the exposure of the faults, of the present. In the paragraphs that follow, I wish to draw on the analysis of fishing presented in these opening pages, that is, on the intertwined themes of activity, time, and community in order to sketch central elements of Marx's critique of capitalism and to derive from that critique the sense of his portrait of communism. The traditional approach, what G. A. Cohen has called the Plain Marxist Argument, focuses its normative critique of capitalism on the phenomena of exploitation, domination of society by the bourgeoisie, and domination at the point of production. From that perspective, communist society is the corrective in that it is nonexploitative and classless. What I now wish to do is to cut into these issues from a different angle, to move from a reading of Marx that turns around questions of ownership, surplus extraction, and the rule of one class over society to one whose critical locus is to be found neither in issues of distribution (ownership and exploitation) nor in the rule of some over others but in the idea of domination by an autonomous economic process. The advantage of this reading of Marx over the Plain Argument account is that it allows us to grasp more precisely what Marx considered to be the *differentia specifica* of capitalism in relation to its antecedents and thereby to come to a new appreciation of his critique of capitalism as well as of his vision of communism. More important, perhaps, it sets the stage for the consideration of the profound radicalness of Marx's project in the history of political thought: the move away from the traditional question of justice between persons to the critique of political economy.

I. Being a Fisherman

To be a fisherman is different from going fishing. The latter is the result of choice among possible activities, hunting, rearing cattle, reading philosophy. The former is the consequence of a life determined. To go fishing or whatever just because "I have a mind" to do so is an activity that is the efflux of my will, that is, I set the purpose and make the choice. I am distinct from this activity that I have elected to pursue: It is chosen and therefore can be put aside. In brief, I am not subordinated to fishing; I elect to do it and I can reel in my line, walk away from it, and return to my philosophical books as I see fit.

Being a fisherman is something quite different. It suggests that in some way or other, my activity, a single activity, has come to be what I am simply. I am my function and that function is determined by nature or by an economic process. In precapitalist societies where human productive powers had not yet developed sufficiently to allow society to become the effective master of nature, that function was largely determined by nature and elementary need. Capitalist society, in which people have become perhaps as much as is possible the "sovereigns of nature," also "allocates" functional roles to its members. It is the source of that "allocation" that constitutes the perverse essence of capitalism, the key characteristics that distinguish it from earlier societies.

Under capitalism, according to Marx, the labor process is absorbed into the valorization process. The valorization process is expressed by the general formula, M-C-M', in which M' or surplus value is the self-renewing and unlimited purpose or goal of a circuit that includes both production and circulation. The whole of society's metabolic interaction with nature, that is, the labor process embracing equally the human, or subjective side, and the material instruments of that interaction is subsumed under a process the goal of which is to produce constantly expanding value. This process, that is, the *movement* of the various components of value through their transformation from labor-power and the materials and instruments of production into expanded surplus value is, according to Marx, an *autonomous* process, and its "dominant subject" is not the humans involved in the process but value itself.[4]

Capital, as self-valorizing value, comprises class, Marx writes.[5] The persons who occupy various and functionally different places along capital's circuit of metamorphoses have their behavior and their purposes determined by their particular functional positions. "Real political economy," he adds elsewhere must then treat the capitalist only "as personified capital, M-C-M, agent of production."[6] The capitalist's purpose is, consistent with his or her functional role in the valorization process, to maximize value, that is, to accumulate and not to consume. The capitalist, in sum, is "personified" capital, its mere "functionary." Workers, for their part, are personified labor-time or labor-power.[7] It is thus appropriate, Marx states, that in England workers are called "hands." Proletarian and capitalist are equally subsumed under the valorization process; both are its "slaves."

The functional positions allocated by the valorization process to the various "repre-

sentatives" along its circuit are duplicated, *mutatis mutandis*, in the smaller world of the factory, the "technological expression" of capital.[8] In the mechanized factory, a whole exists, a process, consisting of the movements of machines. The nature of each individual's work, the worker's physical location, and the work relationship with his or her associates are determined by the structure of the mechanized operations of the factory. The worker's activity is determined through the activity of the whole, of the "iron mechanism"; the worker loses independence and is "appropriated by the process." Similarly, the capitalist's activity of superintendence arises directly from the nature of capitalist factory production itself. Thus just as in the broader circuit of capital individuals are transformed into mere "bearers," "representatives," or "functionaries" of the phases of the valorization process, so too in the microcosm of the factory, activity is determined by the needs of the "iron" process of the mechanized atelier.

What happens in the broader circuit of capital (M-C-M') as well as in its reflection-in-miniature (the factory) is "deindividualization."[9] The persons involved become the bearers of the functional positions they occupy within the circuit of capital. Their activities are reduced to moments in capital's metamorphosis; moments that are determined by the self-recreating valorization process, that is, are not set by conscious human agency. The naturally imposed necessity of skill or physical prowess is overcome through cooperative, mechanized production; labor becomes the expenditure of homogeneous labor time, that is, contentless work subordinated to the creation of surplus value. In Marx's account, then, being a fisherman, a capitalist, or whatever is to be subsumed under an economic process. It is to be a member of a class, a functionally defined group of persons.

The (postcapitalist) world of those who hunt in the morning and fish in the afternoon is a classless society. Though in Marx's celebrated description, only a single individual is mentioned, we can infer the community's classlessness from the fact that neither the individual nor his or her activities are characterized as functionally related to a production process. The individual is not, as one in bourgeois society is, in a "situation of being assigned."[10] Rather, the individual does what "he has a mind to" and not what the "representative" of capital or labor power must do according to their roles in the metamorphosis of value. One's activities, hunting, philosophizing, and so forth are under the dominion neither of another person nor of a process and hence they are not bound down by some purpose or goal other than that set by the person. The result, then, of the abolition of classes (understood as the abolition of the allocation of functional roles by an economic process beyond human control) is, according to Marx, the individualization of humans in the sense of self-determination just outlined.

II. Whiling Away the Hours

Time is the "space" (*Raum*) of human development, the forum of one's "active existence."[11] A person's wealth, Marx adds, does not consist in the objects he or she accumulates, but rather in the time freely available to him or her. That is, wealth is not the sum of embodied past activity, of "dead labor" as Marx calls it, but time yet to be shaped, yet to be filled with hunting, philosophizing, or whatever. Now time can be either bound down or free. Time is bound down when its use is determined not by the agents' own purposes but by forces external to them. While humankind does not have technology sufficient to allow for the mastering of nature, nature is one such force. The cycle of the seasons imposes a labor-rhythm on agrarian communities independent of their wills. Time may also be determined by the class structure of society where the leisure of one segment of society, for example, the housemaid masters of Aristotle's *Politics*, Book I, is purchased at the expense of the time of the laboring population. Capitalist society, in which nature is less a constraint than in any preceding epoch and in which production is not intended to provide leisure and consumption goods for a few but rather aims at an ever increasing surplus for its own sake,

also binds time but in a radically different manner.

In his essay on *The Condition of the Working-Class in England*, Engels, describing the time pressure on the workers referred to them as being subject to the "despotic bell." Marx, in his 1861–1863 *Notebooks*, quoted that passage and put the phrase "despotic bell" in italics.[12] We may speculate that what struck Marx in the words "the despotic bell" was the notion of time (under capitalism) as a dominating, alien force rather than as the "space" for the development of human capacities.

Capital has "encroached" upon time; it has "usurped" the time of society, Marx writes. To understand what Marx means by this, it is important to recall that he considers capital to be not simply a bundle of property/appropriation relations, but a process, a "circulatory" movement of value. This movement is temporally measured and it is divided into the various phases of the reproduction and expansion of value. In brief, across the entire spectrum of its economic phenomena, from the most elementary, that is, the commodity as "congealed" labor time, to the most expansive, that is, the creation of a world market, capitalism more than any previous economic order is a process concerned with time.[13] This time, however, is subsumed under the requirements of capital for rapid reproduction (completion of its circuit and recommencement of its next cycle). In all the stages of its metamorphosis, capital seeks to compress time, to "close its pores." In other words, capital attempts to appropriate for its reproductive process all available time while also striving to reduce as far as possible the time necessary for the completion of its circuit. In this broadly formulated description, we can grasp the general import of Marx's reference to the "despotic bell" and we can also see the intimations of why Marx thought capitalism to be a liberating force.

For Marx, the consequence of this is that capitalism's greatest achievement, its historical "justification,"[14] the shortening of necessary labor time, does not in fact lead to a lessening of bound time for the producing population. Quite the contrary, the result of this unprecedented transformation and extension of society's productive powers is the simultaneous lengthening and intensification (closing the pores of production time) of the working day. This outcome does not depend, Marx argues, on the good or bad will of the capitalist; rather, it is determined by the laws of capitalism.

In sum, no previous epoch has seen such great time pressure on the population as is found under capitalism. Overwork, Marx claims, was not a significant problem in antiquity and, to the extent that laws dealt with additional labor, it was to try to compel more of it. It is, however, characteristic of capitalism that laws here are introduced to restrain the economic compulsion to excessive labor.[15] The concern for the reduction of necessary labor time (leaving aside the issue of the reduction of circulation time) is central in a process that seeks constantly to yield increasingly large surpluses (embodied surplus time); but since surplus is its purpose, not free time, the reduction of necessary labor does not alter the character of time for the living bearers of that process, except insofar as still more of their time is absorbed by the process.

We saw in the previous section that Marx observed how appropriate it was that in England laborers were called "hands," the living servants of machines, their activity subsumed under the systematic order and activity of those machines. Marx also commented on the common designation of workers as "full time" or "half time."[16] On the one hand, the worker is thereby shown to be mere personified labor time. On the other hand, time itself—full or half—is revealed as something determined by the valorization circuit of wealth. This, and not the horrors of child labor or overwork in early industrial Britain, is the principal locus of Marx's understanding and critique of capitalism's impact upon time. What capital has done is to provide human beings with that temporal "space" for their development, for the exercise of their free purposiveness, and it has, in the same moment, taken that time (liberated, as it were, from natural necessity) and subordinated it to a nondesigned and, in some ways, perversely purposeful process, M-C-M'.

The recovery of that time (now not from nature but from an economic order) is a part of what is being portrayed in the *German Ideology* passage concerning hunting and fishing. Not only can I *do* what "I have a mind to" (hence the overcoming of functional roles assigned by the circuit), but I can do it *when* I wish to (the overcoming of the circuit's appropriation of surplus or free time). Nor is there a need to rush: the fishing pole lying by my side is no longer fixed capital impatiently demanding valorization, but is rather something for me to use when I choose to. That I can so while away the hours has no other significance than this, that through the subordination of economic processes to the conscious human will time is brought under one's control and not that of an external purposiveness.

III. Fishermen All

Capital has made a world in its own image. It has, Marx argues, transformed human activity from a condition in which skill, physical prowess, age, and sex were the major determinants of one's labor into one in which an equal but contentless activity is in the service of capital generally and, within the factory (capital's portrait-in-miniature), in the service of the system of machines. We have observed, too, how capital has supplanted nature, human and inanimate both, as the force governing time and has subordinated time to its need for increased velocity of reproduction. What is more, capital determines the community, the association of persons, its creators who have also become its valets. It is this question, Marx's concept of the community under capital, that we shall now address. My concern here, then, will be less with the topic so central to Marx's early writings, that is, the illusory community of the state, than with his analysis of the community as it emerges from the mature critique of political economy.

III.A In the Market

What emerges in the capitalist market is the end of relations of personal dependence based on status and of the "natural bonds" of attachment of individuals to their community and their replacement by the interaction and exchanges of commodity owners. It is certain that, in Marx's view, the dissolution of the natural community and bound labor represented a genuine emancipation both of the individual worker and of society from the limits of a community that sought nothing higher than its own survival. Despite his many polemical references to wage-labor as "wage-slavery," Marx's analysis holds that there is a sharp difference between bound labor of all types and the labor power possessed as a commodity by the worker.

The existence of a pervasive labor market also presupposes what Marx calls capital's "original sin," that is, the expropriation of the producers, their separation from the means of production. This original act of expropriation leaves workers with only labor power to sell, and sell it the workers must since they no longer have the means to produce for themselves. However, the person whom one meets in the market, the owner of the means of production, does not stand before one as master over servant or lord over vassal but as a fellow owner of commodities, as an equal.

Marx's purpose in setting out capital's "original sin" is to make clear that the market did not appear *ex nihilo*, that its beginnings are coercive, and, lastly, that they are centered on a fundamental shift of ownership of the means of production away from the direct producers, that is, their expropriation, as well as the dissolution of the old system of personal bonds within the community. In short, Marx wants to take some of the bloom from the rose of the contract theory of the origins of the market and free enterprise. But what is important for our purposes is that from the debris of the now destroyed world of the precapitalist community, there emerges a new type, the one that we encounter in the market, the universe of commodity owners, buyers, and sellers, united by a money relation with each other: the nexus of "cash payment."

In this new world, this community under capital, individuals, according to Marx, appear to be and indeed are freed of ties of personal dependence and distinctions of blood. They exist, in the market expression of their community, in a condition of reciprocal isolation connected only by the need to exchange their commodities. They have been freed of any ties other than exchange and they therefore appear to be free. Marx's account of the genesis of this arrangement suggests force, not choice, as its foundation. But what of their present condition? Recall that the market is only one of the moments of the life cycle of capital, that time in which value realizes itself as money, which in turn reappears in the market, there to buy new labor-power and materials in order to start the circuit anew. The social relations of the market are not relations between individuals, Marx argues, but rather between proletarian and capitalist. They exist for one another as the "representatives" of their commodities, bearers of the metamorphoses of their wares.[17]

Thus the members of this community live in a "bewitched world," one where their relations appear as relations between things. The "social character," the communal nature, of their interchange appears as something independent of them, as a moment in the valorization process.[18] History and their respective functions in that process have assigned them different roles (though formally, in terms of ownership status, equal) in the market. Yet the fact that the market works through voluntary agreement and not direct coercion and that the market as a whole seems to be anarchical, that is, composed of the accidental "collisions" of individuals give it the appearance of the "very Eden of the innate rights of man." What I wish to look more closely at is the notion central to Marx's analysis, that the literal anarchy of the market is not freedom at all but merely a form of external rule, the "silent compulsion" of capital: "It is not individuals who are set free by free competition; it is, rather, capital which is set free."[19]

This argument of Marx's can be construed in two principal, and not necessarily consistent, ways. Here I shall do no more than to sketch them. (1) Buyers and sellers in the market are compelled to act as they do. Free will is not an adequate account of their interaction. They are compelled by the external purposive process, M-C-M', of which they are mere moments, functional bearers of phases or elements of the metabolism of capital. In this version, an all-embracing process is said to express and to be determined by the general, underlying laws of capital. Anarchy is mere appearance, the seeming surface of things. (2) The individual moments of circulation *are* the result of the "conscious will" of individuals. But the totality of the process, the result of their individual collisions, is an "objective" process, that is, something not under their control, an "alien social power" that generates, Marx concludes, their "objective dependency."[20] The idea here is that while wills and individual decisions are attributable to persons, the result of their interactions is a process that, viewed as a whole, takes on an independent existence. This is to be distinguished from the previous version in that the latter asserted an identity (and a causal relation) among the dominant, systemic purpose, accumulation or M-C-M', and the (determined) purpose of the individuals enmeshed in that process. For reasons that I have set out elsewhere, I am inclined to think that argument (1) above represents Marx's preferred position. What is important for the analysis of this article is that the community in one specific moment of the intercourse of its members, that of the market, is determined by the circuit of capital, however the latter is construed. Marx's fundamental point is that relations between individuals, the substance of their communal existence, are determined by the valorization process and not by the community itself. Those various relations are thus functionally and externally allocated by the movement of value through the phases of its life cycle.

III.B In the Factory

Beneath the "haze" of the world of circulation lies another sphere, a second form of the community under capital. This is the production process, the other major moment in value's circuit. The "interconnections of capital," its laws, that are barely visible in the world of the marketplace, that seemingly anarchical environment of competition, buying and selling, are more readily apparent in the production sphere, to which we shall now turn.

The "real subsumption" of labor to capital begins when workers and capitalists meet not only in the labor market but when the production process itself has come under the control of capital. The nature of labor is now altered: It becomes social, directly cooperative labor, that is, the factory. A second community, that of the factory, is thus formed. But this social form of production is not the "offspring of association."[21] What Marx means by this is that the character of their cooperation is not determined by the community, but rather by the needs of the M-C-M' circuit. It is thus a "fate," and not the result of choice. Their combination, the new productive community under capital, appears to them as an "alien" combination, as the "subjectivity" or will of capital.[22] Just as the origin of the free exchanges in the labor market is to be found in the coercive act of expropriation, so here the beginnings of the production community are located in a "will" external to that community, the "will" of a purposive process, the valorization of capital.

In the marketplace, individuals appear indeed as buyers and sellers, representatives of their commodities or capital, but also as juridical persons, as owners equal and free disposing over their commodities. In the production process, they lose even the semblance of autonomy from the capital circuit. Here they become "hands" and "full timers," accessories or servants of the process. This is not merely what has come to be known as domination at the point of production, the direct control of capitalist over worker or, in other words, the "barracks-like discipline" of the factory. More central for Marx, it is that the combination of labor, the community created by capital, stands over against the individual as an alien, controlling force. It is a community that abolishes the independence and individuality of its members.[23]

The association of the factory is not the association or community of its members, it is a "form of existence of capital," an objective association. Marx's analysis of the factory, that is, of the real subsumption of labor under capital, is not merely an account of what transpires within the walls of that institution. Rather, that commentary is one directed to a "form of existence of capital." Marx also uses the factory as a concretization of the entire capital relation in this sense: The subordination of living to objectified labor (man/machines = society/ M-C-M') that is the heart of capitalism, that is, the nature of its metabolism (the feeding on and replenishing itself from surplus labor), is in the factory rendered more plainly visible. Marx's account of the market and production moments of the community under capital (exchange and the factory system) is clearly *not* meant to suggest that they be judged against the measure of an arcadian, precapitalist community. The stagnant world of primitive communal ownership, the violence and degradation of the community of slaves and their masters, in general, all the forms of what Marx calls the "natural" community (ones not based on exchange) are inferior stages of humankind's development. Capitalism has broken down national boundaries and prejudices, created a universal community, and unleashed the powers of social labor. It has also subordinated the community that it has called into being to the demands of its autonomous valorization process. This community does not represent the wills of its members but rather the needs of the capital cycle.

In the passage from the *German Ideology* that has set the guiding thread for our discussion, only a single individual is mentioned. Moreover, all of his activities, fishing, hunting, and philosophizing are, given the circumstances in which he conducts them (i.e., not fishing for profit, where cooperation would be necessary or primitive food-hunting where cooperation is for different reasons also required), potentially solitary activities. If this person seeks the company of his fellow human beings it will not be because he is enmeshed in an economic cycle that demands cooperation of him, nor will it be the result of the underdevelopment of his productive powers, a condition that uses humans and their cooperation where machines do not yet exist that could take over a substantial part of the task. He will, we can imagine, associate freely with his fellows. Their combined (social) efforts will not be

something imposed on them from the outside; their community will be self-determined and not subject to the laws of the metabolism of capital.

There is clearly something Robinson Crusoe-like about this solitary fisherman/ hunter/philosopher and Marx himself provides a corrective in Volumes One and Three of *Capital*.[24] Transpose him, however, to a community of others like himself and the sense of Marx's image (moderated in his later writings) becomes at least somewhat more evident. Such a community would be the expression writ large of our fisherman/hunter/ philosopher's relation to his activity. Subordinated neither to nature nor to the dictates of the valorization process, this individual is not "assigned" a functional role in production; he fishes but is not a fisherman and he controls his time, rather than having it determined by capital's need for rapid reproduction. In sum, he does (as far as is possible) what he "has a mind to." So too would his community of the "freely associated" do as it has a mind to.

On one level, the idea of the community as a free association signifies, for Marx, that the cooperation of its members is not something wholly imposed on them from the outside. On a second and related level, it means that the community and its cooperation are not forces that abolish the individual, that is, rob the individual of his or her will (i.e., the community as a coercive, externally imposed power). From this element of Marx's critique, one can infer the outlines of his vision of a communist society. It is a "free association" in the sense that it sets its own ends and, presumably, the continued reduction of necessary labor time would be central among them.[25] It is also free inasmuch as its members are not "assigned" their cooperative situation, nor are they related to one another as bearers of functional moments in the production process. Both of these notions rest on the underlying idea that the *summum malum* of capitalism is domination by the valorization circuit, a circuit that is autonomous in relation to the will of the community that it controls.

Conclusion

The portrait of communist society set out in the passage from the *German Ideology* and the critique of capitalism that underpins it remained a centerpiece of Marx's project. The passage's youthful enthusiasm, especially evident in its implied claim that necessity could be overcome altogether, was in *Capital*, Volume Three, to be reined in by the recognition that material production, the "realm of necessity," would continue to be the foundation even of a postcapitalist society. Nevertheless, on those same pages of *Capital* in which the mature Marx moderated somewhat the wildly hopeful vision of his youth, the heart of that vision is still present: Material production is made as free as can be when "the associated producers govern the human metabolism with nature in a rational way, bringing it under their collective control instead of being dominated by it as a blind power. . . ."[26] This conscious control of the economy, the greatest achievable human autonomy in the productive interaction between human beings and nature, creates the foundation of the "true realm of freedom, the development of human powers as an end in itself. . . ." Here, as in the 1845 passage, the *summum malum* is the promise denied of autonomy, that is, the control over human affairs by forces external to their will, forces that provided humankind with the means to become the sovereign of nature. Communism cannot, in Marx's view, abolish the need for the continued interaction of human beings with nature, but it can deprive that process of its independent law-giving capacity by subordinating it to the community's conscious control.

This core of Marx's critique of capitalism is evident in one rather quiet passage from *Capital*, Volume One, in which he contrasts the legally limited working day to the "pompous catalogue of the 'inalienable rights of man.' "[27] To the reader steeped in the Plain Marxist Argument the importance that Marx here attaches to the limited working day must be perplexing, as also must be (for different reasons) his insistence in Volume Three that the shortening of the working day is a prerequisite of communism. The Ten Hours Act is not praised for its effects on income or asset endowments nor does it alter the fact of exploitation. Rather Marx lauds it as a "social barrier" to capital, that is, as an instance of the subordination of the economy to the purposes of the community rather than to the requirements of the valorization process. The "catalogue of the 'inalienable rights of man,' " Marx seems to suggest, has (to borrow the phrases of the *German Ideology*) freed people from the "violence of men" only to submit them to the "violence of things," that is, the autonomous economic process. In sum, the relation of master and servant, dominator and dominated, must be rethought and supplied with a new idiom. It is that idiom that Marx sought to provide.

The exegetical consequences of this analysis for the reading of Marx can be only briefly stated here. It suggests that the Plain Marxist Argument interpretation, with its emphasis on domination of persons over persons and on exploitation as the great evil of capitalism, is seriously misguided. Domination, class, and exploitation assume a sharply different form in a society (capitalist) in which the economy has become independent of, and legislative over, society. To put the matter rather too starkly, the reading presented in this article suggests that the principal issue for Marx is the relationship between the "blind power" of the autonomous economic process of capital and the community it governs, rather than the relationship between the bourgeoisie and the proletariat, both of which are governed in different ways by laws not of their own making.

Viewed in a broader compass, the interpretation set out here shows, on the one side, Marx's deep indebtedness to preliberal political economy, indeed to classical Greek conceptions of an embedded economy serving the leisure and cultivation of the virtue of citizens. On the other side, in its nonhierarchical, nonorganic concept of the free association of producers, Marxism draws on liberal ideas of the human community. Yet Marx's project seeks to move beyond the tradition of political philosophy, ancient and modern. That move is evident above all in Marx's silence about the central question of the tradition, that is, justice. Various efforts have been made to explain that silence: that Marx really had a theory of justice *malgré lui*, that Marx's historicism prevented him from using ideas of justice for critical purposes, or that his aspiration to a scientific critique led him to shun the normative propositions of his socialist ancestors. The argument of this essay suggests a different answer: Ideas of justice, the regulative norms of affairs among persons, have little to say to society in which the new master is not a person but an economic process become autonomous, a blind power ruling society. It is that understanding of capitalism, present in an inchoate form in Marx's early writings, that leads to the shift away from the question of justice and to the critique of political economy. And it is just that move that constitutes the most radical heart of Marx's challenge.

One of the principal moments of this challenge can be set out in a manner that neither requires of us that we accept the viability of Marx's counterfactual world of communism nor demands that we subscribe to the details of his analysis of capitalism. We might sketch this central point as follows: (1) liberalism grasps one form of unfreedom, coercion, or the arbitrary rule of one will over another, which was the dominant form in precapitalist societies; (2) contractarianism and the language of rights are the correctives to coercive unfreedom—power, private and public, is now made, by and large, to rest on a consensual, nonhierarchical foundation; (3) but the sources of unfreedom are not exhausted by the sea of coercion. There is another form, objective compulsion, the reduction of autonomy of persons not through the arbitrary wills of others but rather as a consequence of the independence of the process of production itself, in other words, of the fact that the economy is autonomous and, beyond the control of individuals who occupy its various stages, it comes to legislate over them. (4) The liberal concept of unfreedom as the state of being coerced is not adequate to an understanding of objective compulsion and, conversely, its idea of autonomy as exclusionary rights against others (that is, as a counter to coercion) is too limited—limitations evident in the coex-

istence of this autonomy with the most radical restrictions on the power of self-determination brought about by the "silent compulsion," the "cold-blooded inevitability" of economic laws.[28]

Like most painters of worlds to come, Marx was less concerned with the portrait itself than with the questions thereby raised about the present order of things. It is those questions, the center of his critique of liberalism, that remain of interest, however implausible (or impalatable) we may judge his vision of communism to have been and however flawed his arguments were in their details. It is the sense of that critique that I have sought to draw out in this essay.

Notes

1. Michael Oakeshott, "On Being Conservative," *Rationalism and Politics* (New York: Basic Books, 1962), 168–196.

2. Karl Marx and Frederick Engels, *The German Ideology*, in *Karl Marx and Frederick Engels Collected Works* (Vol. 5) (New York: International Publishers, 1976), 47. The *Collected Works* are cited hereafter as MECW plus the volume number. A brief discussion of the irony of this passage is to be found in Frank E. Manuel, "In Memoriam: Critique of the Gotha Program, 1875–1975," *Daedalus* (Fall 1975), 59–77. For an extended analysis of some of the issues raised in this essay, see chapter XI of G. A. Cohen, *Karl Marx's Theory of History: A Defense* (Princeton, NJ: Princeton University Press, 1978).

3. Marx, *Letters from the Deutsch-Franzoesische Jahrbuecher*, in MECW, 3, 142.

4. Marx, *Capital* (Vol. 2), trans. David Fernbach (New York: Vintage Books, 1981), 185–186; Marx, *Capital* (Vol. 1), trans. Ben Fowkes (New York: Vintage Books, 1977), 255. Cited hereafter, respectively, as C2 and C1. For a more detailed analysis of the method of Marx's political economy, see my "Explaining Capitalism: The Method of Marx's Political Economy." *Political Studies* (forthcoming).

5. Marx, C2, 185.

6. Marx, *Theories of Surplus Value* (Part 1), trans. Emile Burns (Moscow: Progress Publishers, 1963), 270.

7. Marx, *Zur Kritik der politischen Okonomie*, Manuscript 1861–1863, in *Karl Marx, Friedrich Engels Gesamtausgabe* II 3.6 (Berlin: Dietz

Verlag, 1982), 2024. These manuscripts are cited hereafter as MEGA plus the volume number.

8. Marx, MEGA II 3.6, 2058.

9. Marx, MEGA II 3.6, 2024.

10. Marx, *Grundrisse*, trans. Martin Nicolaus (New York: Vintage Books, 1974), 6.

11. Marx, MEGA II 3.6, 2026–2027.

12. Frederick Engels, *The Condition of the Working-Class in England*, MECW: 4, 467; Marx, MEGA II 3.6, 2023. In Engels's original the phrase is not in italics.

13. Marx, MEGA II 3.6, 174–175; Marx, *Grundrisse*, 615.

14. Marx, *Theories of Surplus Value* (Part 2), no translator cited (Moscow: Progress Publishers, 1968), 405. Cited hereafter as TSV2.

15. Marx, C1, 345; Marx, MEGA II 3.1, 203–204.

16. Marx, MEGA II 3.6, 2024.

17. Marx, MEGA II 3.1, 288; Marx, C1, 179.

18. Marx, *Grundrisse*, 157.

19. Marx, *Grundrisse*, 650; Marx, C1, 899.

20. Marx, *Grundrisse*, 164, 196–197.

21. Marx, *Grundrisse*, 158.

22. Marx, MEGA II 3.6, 2013; Marx, *Grundrisse*, 470.

23. Marx, C1: 638; Marx, *Grundrisse*, 700; Marx, MEGA II 3.1, 244–246.

24. Marx, C1: 171–172; Marx, *Capital* (Vol. 3), trans. David Fernbach (New York: Vintage Books, 1981), 958–959.

25. Marx, TSV2: 405; Marx, *Grundrisse*, 172–173.

26. Marx, C3: 958–959.

27. Marx, C1: 416.

28. Marx, C1: 899; Marx, "Moralising Criticism," MECW: 6, 336. See also G. A. Cohen, "The Structure of Proletarian Unfreedom." *Philosophy and Public Affairs* 12, no. 1 (1982): 3–33.

Reprinted from: William James Booth, "Gone Fishing: Making Sense of Marx's Concept of Communism." In *Political Theory*, Volume 17, Issue 2, pp. 205–222. Copyright © 1989. Reprinted by permission of Sage Publications, Inc. ✦

John Stuart Mill

If by the elusive term "liberalism" one means a philosophy based upon individual rights, a belief that reason can overcome prejudice, and a progressive view of history, then John Stuart Mill is perhaps liberalism's greatest spokesperson. While skeptical about political developments in his own day, Mill believed that a tolerant, democratic majority could be forged combining stability with individual freedom to think, to be heard, and to live a lifestyle of one's choosing. Mill struggled to develop this view against the Utilitarian philosophy instilled in him by his father, James. While John never abandoned the approach championed by his father and while he perhaps did not succeed completely in meshing his father's brand of utility with his own preferences he nevertheless gave vent to some of the strongest sentiments associated with the modern liberal state.

John Stuart Mill was born in London in 1806. His father, James, embarked on a great educational experiment with his son, providing him with early and rigorous intellectual training in the home. At three, John learned Greek; at six, Latin. All the while, he was treated to an intensive regimen of mathematics and logic. In 1823, John became a clerk with the East India Company and rose to a prominent position with the company. In 1831, he was introduced to Harriet Taylor, the wife of a wealthy merchant. Mill's platonic affair with Harriet is legendary. They had intense political conversations and Mill credits Harriet with inspiring much of his own thinking and writing. There continues to be debate in scholarly circles as to whether she penned any of Mill's work. Her husband died in 1849 and three years later Harriet and John married. She died in 1858. Thereafter, John wrote and served a term in Parliament from 1865–1868. He died in Avignon in 1873 after a brief illness.

John was early introduced to the doctrine associated with his father and his father's associate, Jeremy Bentham. Going under the name of Utilitarianism, the theory combined a straightforward view of human nature with a simple prescription for society. Humans, Bentham argued, are "governed by two sovereign masters: pleasure and pain." Each individual tries to maximize the total amount of pleasure while minimizing pain. By rationally ordering individual preferences, government could provide conditions for the achievement of the greatest happiness for the greatest number. According to the elder Mill, this order could be secured by a representative government, though the voting franchise would have to be limited to those who had demonstrated rationality in their own private pursuits. James reasoned this would limit the electorate to middle-class males.

John was a staunch supporter of his father's creed until about 1826, when he suffered a bout of severe depression. He attributed this condition to the failure in his education to attend to the emotive side of his personality. Turning to the works of poets like Wordsworth and Coleridge, he sought to correct this imbalance. He began as well to alter his view of human nature and politics by seeking to humanize utility theory and to broaden it. Perhaps not all pleasures were equally worthy of advance. Some are more conducive to the innate desire for self-improvement and society must support these efforts by guaranteeing individual expression. Only with such guarantees might society itself hope to benefit from the insights of the exceptional few.

In *System of Logic*, Mill explored the relation of the various sciences to each other. He advocated the study of human character (ethology, as he called it) as a scholarly enterprise which would stand somewhere between the solid principles of human psychology and emerging laws of sociology as gleaned by French scholars like August Comte. He wrote on economics as well, exploring socialistic proposals as perhaps necessary safeguards against the excesses of the free market. Finally, he was one of the first and most ardent exponents of feminism, surely a result of his association with Harriet Taylor.

On Liberty, The Subjection of Women, and *Utilitarianism*

Perhaps the work for which John Start Mill is best known in America is *On Liberty.* Published in 1859, it is an impassioned plea for social toleration of individual differences and free expression. Yet, it is still grounded in utilitarian language. According to Mill, the greatest threat to advanced civilizations like his own lay in the tyranny of the majority, expressed through political and social intolerance. Majority rule was a fine principle of self-government. But majorities had to be made to respect the beliefs and actions of a few if only because the majority stood to gain by the contributions of the occasional genius. The selection below from Chapter II reviews the reasons Mill advances for freedom of thought and expression.

The Subjection of Women often reads like contemporary feminist literature. In this work, which Mill completed in 1861—three years after Harriet Taylor's death—but not published until 1869, Mill describes the plight of women within a social order they do not control. He argues that women must be granted equal status with males in the family, in the workplace, and in the political arena. It should be clear from reading the excerpts below why *The Subjection of Women* continues to inspire feminist writers to the present day.

Two selections are included from Mill's 1863 work, *Utilitarianism.* In the first excerpt from Chapter 2, Mill reiterates the basic ideas of utility theory as conceptualized by his father and Jeremy Bentham but

goes further to distinguish between types of pleasures that individuals seek. Mill argues that society must respect "higher" pleasures even though not all members of society may be equally capable of partaking of them. In the second selection from Chapter 5, Mill presents an analysis of justice from the standpoint of utility theory. After a brief historic overview, Mill shows how utility theory captures the various intuitions about justice (involving ideas of right, nature, desert, equality, and the need for punishment) that have arisen in philosophic and popular treatments throughout time.

Commentaries

According to Bruce Baum, Mill maintains that people experience different degrees of freedom and unfreedom in proportion to their relative autonomy from or subjection to external forces. Autonomy is a necessary but not sufficient condition of freedom since even those with full capacity for planning their life goals may not be fully free due to external impediments. Thus, there is an important interplay between freedom and power. In the passage that follows, Baum takes up Mill's discussion of the interplay between freedom and power noting what he believes are the strengths of Mill's arguments as well as their weaknesses in our increasingly pluralistic cultural environment.

In her article, Mary Lyndon Shanley reviews propositions which some critics have advanced against Mill's feminism. While some critics believe Mill did not go far enough in advancing the cause of women, Shanley argues that such attacks fail to acknowledge the significant achievements of Mill's feminism, especially with regard to his call for inculcating genuine friendship between the sexes in marriage.

Web Sources

http://www.utm.edu/research/iep/m/milljs.htm
The Internet Encyclopedia of Philosophy. A guide to Mill's life and writings including *Utilitarianism* as well as his social and political writings.

http://websites.ntl.com/~julian.wates/JSMI_
Site/
The John Stuart Mill Institute. A think tank re-
volving around a brand of liberalism based on
the concepts of freedom and responsible democratic participation. Includes information
about Mill and essays on the continuing impact of his ideas.

http://socserv.socsci.mcmaster.ca/~econ/
ugcm/3ll3/mill/
John Stuart Mill. Includes links to full texts of
his original works plus commentaries.

http://cepa.newschool.edu/het/profiles/
mill.htm
History of Economic Thought Website. Extensive links to Mill's original works, essays, and
bibliographies.

Class Activities and Discussion Items

1. In the 1970s and 1980s, several universities around the country imposed
"speech codes" designed to limit the of-
fensiveness of speech on campus. These
were intended to avoid sexual harass-
ment and racial antagonism. Some
codes specified punitive action against
students or faculty if their speech led to
feelings of stigmatization or victimization among protected groups. In one
case, a graduate student in biopsychol-
ogy was disciplined for noting that certain theories posit biologically-based
differences between races and between
men and women. It was believed that
other students might take offense at the
possibly racist and sexist overtones of
this speech. Although the courts eventually threw out this code as being vague
and over-reaching (*Doe v. University of
Michigan,* 721F.Supp. 852, 1989), the
case is an example of the difficulties involved in keeping speech both civil and
free. Discuss Mill's solution to this dilemma and indicate whether you believe Mill would support a code of
speech on college campuses.

2. Critique Mill's utilitarian approach to
justice. Does his approach adequately
capture all the facets of justice we expect in a comprehensive theory?

3. The Supreme Court of the United
States has variously held that the utter-

ance of certain "fighting words" designed to "incite injury or breach of the
peace" is subject to punishment and in
other cases that ordinances designed to
preclude certain "offensive" words are
impermissible. Review key Supreme
Court cases listed below at http://
supct.law.cornell.edu/supct/ . Decipher
the Court's logic in each of the cases.
Which cases do you believe most easily
accord with John Stuart Mill's ideas on
free expression? Why?

Chaplinsky v. *New Hampshire* (1942)
Cohen v. *California* (1971)
Goodling v. *Wilson* (1972)
R.A.V. v. *St. Paul, Minnesota* (1992)

4. John Stuart Mill was an advocate of
women's rights not merely in theory but
in practice. For example, he advocated
women's suffrage while he was a member of the British Parliament. Research
the measures Mill advanced during his
days as a representative. What kind of
reaction did he encounter? How successful were his proposals?

5. Two major schools of feminism are equity feminists, who believe that in principle there are no major differences between the sexes that impact social and
political preferences, and difference
feminists, who believe there are major
differences in the life perspectives of
men and women that have consequences for public policy. Do some research on both types of feminist theory.
Based on your readings, with which
school do you believe Mill would find
the greatest compatibility?

Further Reading

Cowling, Maurice. 1990. *Mill and Liberalism.*
New York: Cambridge University Press. Classic look at Mill's impact on liberal political
thought.

Donner, Wendy. 1991. *The Liberal Self: John Stuart Mill's Moral and Political Philosophy.*
Ithaca, N.Y.: Cornell University Press. Mill,
Donner maintains, rejects the quantitative hedonism of Bentham's philosophy in favor of
an expanded qualitative version.

Dworkin, Gerald (ed.). 1997. *Mill's "On Liberty."*
New York: Routledge. Leading Mill scholars

offer essays on the continued relevance of Mill's work to contemporary struggles to protect individual rights without harming others.

Hamburger, Joseph. 1999. *John Stuart Mill on Liberty and Control*. Princeton, N.J. : Princeton University Press. Hamburger shows that Mill, far from being an advocate of a maximum degree of liberty, was an advocate of liberty *and* control—indeed, a degree of control ultimately incompatible with liberal ideals.

Jacobson, Daniel. 2000. "Mill on Liberty, Speech, and the Free Society." *Philosophy and Public Affairs* 29 (3): 276–309. Jacobson argues that the traditional interpretation of Mill's argument is mistaken, especially with regard to the role and content of the Harm Principle, and that this misreading distorts the fundamental purpose of *On Liberty* by undermining the essay's liberal ambitions.

Kahan, Alan S. 1992. *Aristocratic Liberalism: The Social and Political Thought of Jacob Burckhardt, John Stuart Mill, and Alexis de Tocqueville*. New York: Oxford University Press. An examination of economic aspects of the liberalism advanced by these thinkers.

Lyons, David (ed.). 1997. *Mill's "Utilitarianism."* New York: Rowman & Littlefield. Scholars offer fresh interpretations of Mill's ideas about happiness, moral obligation, justice, and rights.

O'Rourke, K.C. 2001. *John Stuart Mill and Freedom of Expression: The Genesis of a Theory*. New York: Routledge. An examination of Mill's contributions to intellectual freedom beyond speech.

Riley, Jonathan. 1998. *Routledge Philosophy Guidebook to Mill on Liberty*. New York: Routledge. This book focuses on situating Mill and his work in an historical context and assessing the philosopher's contribution to contemporary thought.

Zerilli, Linda M. G. 1994. *Signifying Woman: Culture and Chaos in Rousseau, Burke, and Mill*. Ithaca, N.Y.: Cornell University Press. Examines the ways in which theorists have portrayed women as elusive yet dangerous, by their nature fundamentally destructive to public life. ✦

31
Excerpts from *On Liberty*

John Stuart Mill

Chapter II: Of the Liberty of Thought and Discussion

The time, it is to be hoped, is gone by, when any defence would be necessary of the "liberty of the press" as one of the securities against corrupt or tyrannical government. No argument, we may suppose, can now be needed, against permitting a legislature or an executive, not identified in interest with the people, to prescribe opinions to them, and determine what doctrines or what arguments they shall be allowed to hear. This aspect of the question, besides, has been so often and so triumphantly enforced by preceding writers, that it needs not be specially insisted on in this place. Though the law of England, on the subject of the press, is as servile to this day as it was in the time of the Tudors, there is little danger of its being actually put in force against political discussion, except during some temporary panic, when fear of insurrection drives ministers and judges from their propriety;[1] and, speaking generally, it is not, in constitutional countries, to be apprehended, that the government, whether completely responsible to the people or not, will often attempt to control the expression of opinion, except when in doing so it makes itself the organ of the general intolerance of the public. Let us suppose, therefore, that the government is entirely at one with the people, and never thinks of exerting any power of coercion unless in agreement with what it conceives to be their voice. But I deny the right of the people to exercise such coercion, either by themselves or by their government. The power itself is illegitimate. The best government has no more title to it than the worst. It is as noxious, or more noxious, when exerted in accordance with public opinion, than when in opposition to it. If all mankind minus one were of one opinion, and only one person were of the contrary opinion, mankind would be no more justified in silencing that one person, than he, if he had the power, would be justified in silencing mankind. Were an opinion a personal possession of no value except to the owner; if to be obstructed in the enjoyment of it were simply a private injury, it would make some difference whether the injury was inflicted only on a few persons or on many. But the peculiar evil of silencing the expression of an opinion is, that it is robbing the human race; posterity as well as the existing generation; those who dissent from the opinion, still more than those who hold it. If the opinion is right, they are deprived of the opportunity of exchanging error for truth: if wrong, they lose, what is almost as great a benefit, the clearer perception and livelier impression of truth, produced by its collision with error.

It is necessary to consider separately these two hypotheses, each of which has a distinct branch of the argument corresponding to it. We can never be sure that the opinion we are endeavouring to stifle is a false opinion; and if we were sure, stifling it would be an evil still.

First: the opinion which it is attempted to suppress by authority may possibly be true. Those who desire to suppress it, of course deny its truth; but they are not infallible. They have no authority to decide the question for all mankind, and exclude every other person from the means of judging. To refuse a hearing to an opinion, because they are sure that it is false, is to assume that *their* certainty is the same thing as *absolute* certainty. All silencing of discussion is an assumption of infallibility. Its condemnation may be allowed to rest on this common argument, not the worse for being common.

Unfortunately for the good sense of mankind, the fact of their fallibility is far from carrying the weight in their practical judgment which is always allowed to it in theory; for while every one well knows himself to be fallible, few think it necessary to take any precautions against their own fallibility, or admit the supposition that any opinion, of which they feel very certain, may be one of the examples of the error to which they acknowledge themselves to be liable. Absolute princes, or others who are accustomed to unlimited deference, usually feel this complete confidence in their own opinions on nearly all subjects. People more happily situated, who sometimes hear their opinions disputed, and are not wholly unused to be set right when they are wrong, place the same unbounded reliance only on such of their opinions as are shared by all who surround them or to whom they habitually defer: for in proportion to a man's want of confidence in his own solitary judgment, does he usually repose, with implicit trust, on the infallibility of "the world" in general. And the world, to each individual, means the part of it with which he comes in contact; his party, his sect, his church, his class of society: the man may be called, by comparison, almost liberal and large-minded to whom it means anything so comprehensive as his own country or his own age. Nor is his faith in this collective authority at all shaken by his being aware that other ages, countries, sects, churches, classes, and parties have thought, and even now think, the exact reverse. He devolves upon his own world the responsibility of being in the right against the dissentient worlds of other people; and it never troubles him that mere accident has decided which of these numerous worlds is the object of his reliance, and that the same causes which make him a Churchman in London, would have made him a Buddhist or a Confucian in Pekin. Yet it is as evident in itself, as any amount of argument can make it, that ages are no more infallible than individuals; every age having held many opinions which subsequent ages have deemed not only false but absurd; and it is as certain that many opinions, now general, will be rejected by future ages, as it is that many, once general, are rejected by the present.

The objection likely to be made to this argument would probably take some such form as the following. There is no greater assumption of infallibility in forbidding the propagation of error, than in any other thing which is done by public authority on its own judgment and responsibility. Judgment is given to men that they may use it. Because it may be used erroneously, are men to be told that they ought not to use it at all? To prohibit what they think pernicious, is not claiming exemption from error, but fulfilling the duty incumbent on them, although fallible, of acting on their conscientious conviction. If we were never to act on our opinions, because those opinions may be wrong, we should leave all our interests uncared for, and all our duties unperformed. An objection which applies to all conduct can be no valid objection to any conduct in particular. It is the duty of governments, and of individuals, to form the truest opinions they can; to form them carefully, and never impose them upon others unless they are quite sure of being right. But when they are sure (such reasoners may say), it is not conscientiousness but cowardice to shrink from acting on their opinions, and allow doctrines which they honestly think dangerous to the welfare of mankind, either in this life or in another, to be scattered abroad without restraint, because other people, in less enlightened times, have persecuted opinions now believed to be true. Let us take care, it may be said, not to make the same mistake: but governments and nations have made mistakes in other things, which are not denied to be fit subjects for the exercise of authority: they have laid on bad taxes, made unjust wars. Ought we therefore to lay on no taxes, and, under whatever provocation, make no wars? Men and governments, must act to the best of their ability. There is no such thing as absolute certainty, but there is assurance sufficient for the purposes of human life. We may, and must, assume our opinion to be true for the guidance of our own conduct: and it is assuming no more when we forbid bad men to pervert society by the propagation of opinions which we regard as false and pernicious.

I answer, that it is assuming very much more. There is the greatest difference between presuming an opinion to be true, because, with every opportunity for contesting it, it has not been refuted, and assuming its truth for the purpose of not permitting its refutation. Complete liberty of contradicting and disproving our opinion is the very condition which justifies us in assuming its truth for purposes of action; and on no other terms can a being with human faculties have any rational assurance of being right.

When we consider either the history of opinion, or the ordinary conduct of human life, to what is it to be ascribed that the one and the other are no worse than they are? Not certainly to the inherent force of the human understanding; for, on any matter not self-evident, there are ninety-nine persons totally incapable of judging of it for one who is capable; and the capacity of the hundredth person is only comparative; for the majority of the eminent men of every past generation held many opinions now known to be erroneous, and did or approved numerous things which no one will now justify. Why is it, then, that there is on the whole a preponderance among mankind of rational opinions and rational conduct? If there really is this preponderance—which there must be unless human affairs are, and have always been, in an almost desperate state—it is owing to a quality of the human mind, the source of everything respectable in man either as an intellectual or as a moral being, namely, that his errors are corrigible. He is capable of rectifying his mistakes, by discussion and experience. Not by experience alone. There must be discussion, to show how experience is to be interpreted. Wrong opinions and practices gradually yield to fact and argument; but facts and arguments, to produce any effect on the mind, must be brought before it. Very few facts are able to tell their own story, without comments to bring out their meaning. The whole strength and value, then, of human judgment, depending on the one property, that it can be set right when it is wrong, reliance can be placed on it only when the means of setting it right are kept constantly at hand. In the case of any person whose judgment is really deserving of confidence, how has it become so? Because he has kept his mind open to criticism of his opinions and conduct. Because it has been his practice to listen to all that could be said against him; to profit by as much of it as was just, and expound to himself, and upon occasion to others, the fallacy of what was fallacious. Because he has felt, that the only way in which a human being can make some approach to knowing the whole of a subject, is by hearing what can be said about it by persons of every variety of opinion, and studying all modes in which it can be looked at by every character of mind. No wise man ever acquired his wisdom in any mode but this; nor is it in the nature of human intellect to become wise in any other manner. The steady habit of correcting and completing his own opinion by collating it with those of others, so far from causing doubt and hesitation in carrying it into practice, is the only stable foundation for a just reliance on it: for, being cognisant of all that can, at least obviously, be said against him, and having taken up his position against all gainsayers—knowing that he has sought for objections and difficulties, instead of avoiding them, and has shut out no light which can be thrown upon the subject from any quarter—he has a right to think his judgment better than that of any person, or any multitude, who have not gone through a similar process.

It is not too much to require that what the wisest of mankind, those who are best entitled to trust their own judgment, find necessary to warrant their relying on it, should be submitted to by that miscellaneous collection of a few wise and many foolish individuals, called the public. The most intolerant of churches, the Roman Catholic Church, even at the canonization of a saint, admits, and listens patiently to, a "devil's advocate." The holiest of men, it appears, cannot be admitted to posthumous honours, until all that the devil could say against him is known and weighed. If even the Newtonian philosophy were not permitted to be questioned, mankind could not feel as complete assurance of its truth as they now do. The beliefs which we have most warrant for have no safeguard to rest on, but a standing invitation to the whole world to prove them unfounded. If the challenge is not accepted, or is accepted and the attempt fails, we are far enough from certainty still; but we have done the best that the existing state of human reason admits of; we have neglected nothing that could give the truth a chance of reaching us: if the lists are kept open, we may hope that if there be a better truth, it will be found when the human mind is capable of receiving it; and in the meantime we may rely on having attained such approach to truth, as is possible in our own day. This is the amount of certainty attainable by a fallible being, and this the sole way of attaining it.

Strange it is, that men should admit the validity of the arguments for free discussion, but object to their being "pushed to an extreme"; not seeing that unless the reasons are good for an extreme case, they are not good for any case. Strange that they should imagine that they are not assuming infallibility, when they acknowledge that there should be free discussion on all subjects which can possibly be *doubtful*, but think that some particular principle or doctrine should be forbidden to be questioned because it is so *certain*, that is, because *they are certain* that it is certain. To call any proposition certain, while there is any one who would deny its certainty if permitted, but who is not permitted, is to assume that we ourselves, and those who agree with us, are the judges of certainty, and judges without hearing the other side.

In the present age—which has been described as "destitute of faith, but terrified at scepticism" —in which people feel sure, not so much that their opinions are true, as that they should not know what to do without them—the claims of an opinion to be protected from public attack are rested not so much on its truth, as on its importance to society. There are, it is alleged, certain beliefs so useful, not to say indispensable, to well-being that it is as much the duty of governments to uphold those beliefs, as to protect any other of the interests of society. In a case of such necessity, and so directly in the line of their duty, something less than infallibility may, it is maintained, warrant, and even bind, governments to act on their own opinion, confirmed by the general opinion of mankind. It is also often argued, and still oftener thought, that none but bad men would desire to weaken these salutary beliefs; and there can be nothing wrong, it is thought, in

restraining bad men, and prohibiting what only such men would wish to practise. This mode of thinking makes the justification of restraints on discussion not a question of the truth of doctrines, but of their usefulness; and flatters itself by that means to escape the responsibility of claiming to be an infallible judge of opinions. But those who thus satisfy themselves, do not perceive that the assumption of infallibility is merely shifted from one point to another. The usefulness of an opinion is itself matter of opinion: as disputable, as open to discussion, and requiring discussion as much, as the opinion itself. There is the same need of an infallible judge of opinions to decide an opinion to be noxious, as to decide it to be false, unless the opinion condemned has full opportunity of defending itself. And it will not do to say that the heretic may be allowed to maintain the utility or harmlessness of his opinion, though forbidden to maintain its truth. The truth of an opinion is part of its utility. If we would know whether or not it is desirable that a proposition should be believed, is it possible to exclude the consideration of whether or not it is true? In the opinion, not of bad men, but of the best men, no belief which is contrary to truth can be really useful: and can you prevent such men from urging that plea, when they are charged with culpability for denying some doctrine which they are told is useful, but which they believe to be false? Those who are on the side of received opinions never fail to take all possible advantage of this plea; you do not find *them* handling the question of utility as if it could be completely abstracted from that of truth: on the contrary, it is, above all, because their doctrine is the "truth," that the knowledge or the belief of it is held to be so indispensable. There can be no fair discussion of the question of usefulness when an argument so vital may be employed on one side, but not on the other. And in point of fact, when law or public feeling do not permit the truth of an opinion to be disputed, they are just as little tolerant of a denial of its usefulness. The utmost they allow is an extenuation of its absolute necessity, or of the positive guilt of rejecting it.

In order more fully to illustrate the mischief of denying a hearing to opinions because we, in our own judgment, have condemned them, it will be desirable to fix down the discussion to a concrete case; and I choose, by preference, the cases which are least favourable to me—in which the argument against freedom of opinion, both on the score of truth and on that of utility, is considered the strongest. Let the opinions impugned be the belief in a God and in a future state, or any of the commonly received doctrines of morality. To fight the battle on such ground gives a great advantage to an unfair antagonist; since he will be sure to say (and many who have no desire to be unfair will say it internally), Are these the doctrines which you do not deem sufficiently certain to be taken under the protection of law? Is the belief in a God one of the opinions to feel sure of which you hold to be assuming infallibility? But I must be permitted to observe, that it is not the feeling sure of a doctrine (be it what it may) which I call an assumption of infallibility. It is the undertaking to decide that question *for others*, without allowing them to hear what can be said on the contrary side. And I denounce and reprobate this pretension not the less, if put forth on the side of my most solemn convictions. However positive any one's persuasion may be, not only of the falsity but of the pernicious consequences—not only of the pernicious consequences, but (to adopt expressions which I altogether condemn) the immorality and impiety of an opinion; yet if, in pursuance of that private judgment, though backed by the public judgment of his country or his cotemporaries, he prevents the opinion from being heard in its defence, he assumes infallibility. And so far from the assumption being less objectionable or less dangerous because the opinion is called immoral or impious, this is the case of all others in which it is most fatal. These are exactly the occasions on which the men of one generation commit those dreadful mistakes which excite the astonishment and horror of posterity. It is among such that we find the instances memorable in history, when the arm of the law has been employed to root out the best men and the noblest doctrines; with deplorable success as to the men, though some of the doctrines have survived to be (as if in

mockery) invoked in defence of similar conduct towards those who dissent from *them*, or from their received interpretation.

Mankind can hardly be too often reminded, that there was once a man named Socrates, between whom and the legal authorities and public opinion of his time there took place a memorable collision. Born in an age and country abounding in individual greatness, this man has been handed down to us by those who best knew both him and the age, as the most virtuous man in it; while *we* know him as the head and prototype of all subsequent teachers of virtue, the source equally of the lofty inspiration of Plato and the judicious utilitarianism of Aristotle, *"i maëstri di color che sanno"* ["the masters of those who know"], the two headsprings of ethical as of all other philosophy. This acknowledged master of all the eminent thinkers who have since lived—whose fame, still growing after more than two thousand years, all but outweighs the whole remainder of the names which make his native city illustrious—was put to death by his countrymen, after a judicial conviction, for impiety and immorality. Impiety, in denying the gods recognised by the State; indeed his accuser asserted (see the "Apologia") that he believed in no gods at all. Immorality, in being, by his doctrines and instructions, a "corrupter of youth." Of these charges the tribunal, there is every ground for believing, honestly found him guilty, and condemned the man who probably of all then born had deserved best of mankind to be put to death as a criminal.

To pass from this to the only other instance of judicial iniquity, the mention of which, after the condemnation of Socrates, would not be an anti-climax: the event which took place on Calvary rather more than eighteen hundred years ago. The man who left on the memory of those who witnessed his life and conversation such an impression of his moral grandeur that eighteen subsequent centuries have done homage to him as the Almighty in person, was ignominiously put to death, as what? As a blasphemer. Men did not merely mistake their benefactor; they mistook him for the exact contrary of what he was, and treated him as that prodigy of impiety which they themselves are now held to be for their treatment of him. The feelings with which mankind now regard these lamentable transactions, especially the later of the two, render them extremely unjust in their judgment of the unhappy actors. These were, to all appearance, not bad men—not worse than men most commonly are, but rather the contrary; men who possessed in a full, or somewhat more than a full measure, the religious, moral and patriotic feelings of their time and people: the very kind of men who, in all times, our own included, have every chance of passing through life blameless and respected. The high-priest who rent his garments when the words were pronounced, which, according to all the ideas of his country, constituted the blackest guilt, was in all probability quite as sincere in his horror and indignation as the generality of respectable and pious men now are in the religious and moral sentiments they profess; and most of those who now shudder at his conduct, if they had lived in his time, and been born Jews, would have acted precisely as he did. Orthodox Christians who are tempted to think that those who stoned to death the first martyrs must have been worse men than they themselves are, ought to remember that one of those persecutors was Saint Paul. . . .

Let us now pass to the second division of the argument, and dismissing the supposition that any of the received opinions may be false, let us assume them to be true, and examine into the worth of the manner in which they are likely to be held, when their truth is not freely and openly canvassed. However unwillingly a person who has a strong opinion may admit the possibility that his opinion may be false, he ought to be moved by the consideration that however true it may be, if it is not fully, frequently, and fearlessly discussed, it will be held as a dead dogma, not a living truth.

There is a class of persons (happily not quite so numerous as formerly) who think it enough if a person assents undoubtingly to what they think true, though he has no knowledge whatever of the grounds of the opinion, and could not make a tenable defence of it against the most superficial objections. Such persons, if they can once get

their creed taught from authority, naturally think that no good, and some harm, comes of its being allowed to be questioned. Where their influence prevails, they make it nearly impossible for the received opinion to be rejected wisely and considerately, though it may still be rejected rashly and ignorantly; for to shut out discussion entirely is seldom possible, and when it once gets in, beliefs not grounded on conviction are apt to give way before the slightest semblance of an argument. Waiving, however, this possibility—assuming that the true opinion abides in the mind, but abides as a prejudice, a belief independent of, and proof against, argument—this is not the way in which truth ought to be held by a rational being. This is not knowing the truth. Truth, thus held, is but one superstition the more, accidentally clinging to the words which enunciate a truth.

If the intellect and judgment of mankind ought to be cultivated, a thing which Protestants at least do not deny, on what can these faculties be more appropriately exercised by any one, than on the things which concern him so much that it is considered necessary for him to hold opinions on them? If the cultivation of the understanding consists in one thing more than in another, it is surely in learning the grounds of one's own opinions. Whatever people believe, on subjects on which it is of the first importance to believe rightly, they ought to be able to defend against at least the common objections. But, some one may say, "Let them be *taught* the grounds of their opinions. It does not follow that opinions must be merely parroted because they are never heard controverted. Persons who learn geometry do not simply commit the theorems to memory, but understand and learn likewise the demonstrations; and it would be absurd to say that they remain ignorant of the grounds of geometrical truths, because they never hear any one deny, and attempt to disprove them." Undoubtedly: and such teaching suffices on a subject like mathematics, where there is nothing at all to be said on the wrong side of the question. The peculiarity of the evidence of mathematical truths is that all the argument is on one side. There are no objections, and no answers to objections. But on every subject on which difference of opinion is possible, the truth depends on a balance to be struck between two sets of conflicting reasons. Even in natural philosophy, there is always some other explanation possible of the same facts; some geocentric theory instead of heliocentric, some phlogiston instead of oxygen; and it has to be shown why that other theory cannot be the true one: and until this is shown, and until we know how it is shown, we do not understand the grounds of our opinion. But when we turn to subjects infinitely more complicated, to morals, religion, politics, social relations, and the business of life, three-fourths of the arguments for every disputed opinion consist in dispelling the appearances which favour some opinion different from it. The greatest orator, save one, of antiquity, has left it on record that he always studied his adversary's case with as great, if not with still greater, intensity than even his own. What Cicero practised as the means of forensic success requires to be imitated by all who study any subject in order to arrive at the truth. He who knows only his own side of the case, knows little of that. His reasons may be good, and no one may have been able to refute them. But if he is equally unable to refute the reasons on the opposite side; if he does not so much as know what they are, he has no ground for preferring either opinion. The rational position for him would be suspension of judgment, and unless he contents himself with that, he is either led by authority, or adopts, like the generality of the world, the side to which he feels most inclination. Nor is it enough that he should hear the arguments of adversaries from his own teachers, presented as they state them, and accompanied by what they offer as refutations. That is not the way to do justice to the arguments, or bring them into real contact with his own mind. He must be able to hear them from persons who actually believe them; who defend them in earnest, and do their very utmost for them. He must know them in their most plausible and persuasive form; he must feel the whole force of the difficulty which the true view of the subject has to encounter and dispose of; else he will never really possess himself of the portion of truth which meets and removes that difficulty. Ninety-nine in a hundred of what are called educated men are in this condition; even of those who can argue fluently for their opinions. Their conclusion may be true, but it might be false for anything they know: they have never thrown themselves into the mental position of those who think differently from them, and considered what such persons may have to say; and consequently they do not, in any proper sense of the word, know the doctrine which they themselves profess. They do not know those parts of it which explain and justify the remainder; the considerations which show that a fact which seemingly conflicts with another is reconcilable with it, or that, of two apparently strong reasons, one and not the other ought to be preferred. All that part of the truth which turns the scale, and decides the judgment of a completely informed mind, they are strangers to; nor is it ever really known, but to those who have attended equally and impartially to both sides, and endeavoured to see the reasons of both in the strongest light. So essential is this discipline to a real understanding of moral and human subjects, that if opponents of all important truths do not exist, it is indispensable to imagine them, and supply them with the strongest arguments which the most skilful devil's advocate can conjure up.

To abate the force of these considerations, an enemy of free discussion may be supposed to say, that there is no necessity for mankind in general to know and understand all that can be said against or for their opinions by philosophers and theologians. That it is not needful for common men to be able to expose all the misstatements or fallacies of an ingenious opponent. That it is enough if there is always somebody capable of answering them, so that nothing likely to mislead uninstructed persons remains unrefuted. That simple minds, having been taught the obvious grounds of the truths inculcated on them, may trust to authority for the rest, and being aware that they have neither knowledge nor talent to resolve every difficulty which can be raised, may repose in the assurance that all those which have been raised have been or can be answered, by those who are specially trained to the task.

Conceding to this view of the subject the utmost that can be claimed for it by those most easily satisfied with the amount of understanding of truth which ought to accompany the belief of it; even so, the argument for free discussion is no way weakened. For even this doctrine acknowledges that mankind ought to have a rational assurance that all objections have been satisfactorily answered; and how are they to be answered if that which requires to be answered is not spoken? or how can the answer be known to be satisfactory, if the objectors have no opportunity of showing that it is unsatisfactory? If not the public, at least the philosophers and theologians who are to resolve the difficulties, must make themselves familiar with those difficulties in their most puzzling form; and this cannot be accomplished unless they are freely stated, and placed in the most advantageous light which they admit of. The Catholic Church has its own way of dealing with this embarrassing problem. It makes a broad separation between those who can be permitted to receive its doctrines on conviction, and those who must accept them on trust. Neither, indeed, are allowed any choice as to what they will accept; but the clergy, such at least as can be fully confided in, may admissibly and meritoriously make themselves acquainted with the arguments of opponents, in order to answer them, and may, therefore, read heretical books; the laity, not unless by special permission, hard to be obtained. This discipline recognises a knowledge of the enemy's case as beneficial to the teachers, but finds means, consistent with this, of denying it to the rest of the world: thus giving to the *élite* more mental culture, though not more mental freedom, than it allows to the mass. By this device it succeeds in obtaining the kind of mental superiority which its purposes require; for though culture without freedom never made a large and liberal mind, it can make a clever *nisi prius* advocate of a cause. But in countries professing Protestantism, this resource is denied; since Protestants hold, at least in theory, that the responsibility for the choice of a religion must be borne by each for himself, and cannot be thrown off upon teachers. Besides, in the present state of the world, it is practically impossible that writings which are read by the instructed can be kept from the uninstructed. If the teachers of mankind are to be cognisant of all that they ought to know, everything must be free to be written and published without restraint.

If, however, the mischievous operation of the absence of free discussion, when the received opinions are true, were confined to leaving men ignorant of the grounds of those opinions, it might be thought that this, if an intellectual, is no moral evil, and does not affect the worth of the opinions, regarded in their influence on the character. The fact, however, is, that not only the grounds of the opinion are forgotten in the absence of discussion, but too often the meaning of the opinion itself. The words which convey it cease to suggest ideas, or suggest only a small portion of those they were originally employed to communicate. Instead of a vivid conception and a living belief there remain only a few phrases retained by rote; or, if any part, the shell and husk only of the meaning is retained, the finer essence being lost. The great chapter in human history which this fact occupies and fills, cannot be too earnestly studied and meditated on.

It is illustrated in the experience of almost all ethical doctrines and religious creeds. They are all full of meaning and vitality to those who originate them, and to the direct disciples of the originators. Their meaning continues to be felt in undiminished strength, and is perhaps brought out into even fuller consciousness, so long as the struggle lasts to give the doctrine or creed an ascendancy over other creeds. At last it either prevails, and becomes the general opinion, or its progress stops; it keeps possession of the ground it has gained, but ceases to spread further. When either of these results has become apparent, controversy on the subject flags, and gradually dies away. The doctrine has taken its place, if not as a received opinion, as one of the admitted sects or divisions of opinion: those who hold it have generally inherited, not adopted it; and conversion from one of these doctrines to another, being now an exceptional fact, occupies little place in the thoughts of their professors. Instead of being, as at first, constantly on the alert either to defend themselves against the world, or to bring the world over to them, they have subsided into acquiescence, and neither listen, when they can help it, to arguments against their creed, nor trouble dissentients (if there be such) with arguments in its favour. From this time may usually be dated the decline in the living power of the doctrine. We often hear the teachers of all creeds lamenting the difficulty of keeping up in the minds of believers a lively apprehension of the truth which they nominally recognise, so that it may penetrate the feelings, and acquire a real mastery over the conduct. No such difficulty is complained of while the creed is still fighting for its existence: even the weaker combatants then know and feel what they are fighting for, and the difference between it and other doctrines; and in that period of every creed's existence, not a few persons may be found, who have realized its fundamental principles in all the forms of thought, have weighed and considered them in all their important bearings, and have experienced the full effect on the character which belief in that creed ought to produce in a mind thoroughly imbued with it. But when it has come to be an hereditary creed, and to be received passively, not actively—when the mind is no longer compelled, in the same degree as at first, to exercise its vital powers on the questions which its belief presents to it, there is a progressive tendency to forget all of the belief except the formularies, or to give it a dull and torpid assent, as if accepting it on trust dispensed with the necessity of realizing it in consciousness, or testing it by personal experience, until it almost ceases to connect itself at all with the inner life of the human being. Then are seen the cases, so frequent in this age of the world as almost to form the majority, in which the creed remains as it were outside the mind, incrusting and petrifying it against all other influences addressed to the higher parts of our nature; manifesting its power by not suffering any fresh and living conviction to get in, but itself doing nothing for the mind or heart, except standing sentinel over them to keep them vacant. . . .

It still remains to speak of one of the principal causes which make diversity of opinion advantageous, and will continue to do so until mankind shall have entered a stage of intellectual advancement which at present seems at an incalculable distance. We have hitherto considered only two possibilities: that the received opinion may be false, and some other opinion, consequently, true; or that the received opinion being true, a conflict with the opposite error is essential to a clear apprehension and deep feeling of its truth. But there is a commoner case than either of these; when the conflicting doctrines, instead of being one true and the other false, share the truth between them; and the nonconforming opinion is needed to supply the remainder of the truth, of which the received doctrine embodies only a part. Popular opinions, on subjects not palpable to sense, are often true, but seldom or never the whole truth. They are a part of the truth; sometimes a greater, sometimes a smaller part, but exaggerated, distorted, and disjoined from the truths by which they ought to be accompanied and limited. Heretical opinions, on the other hand, are generally some of these suppressed and neglected truths, bursting the bonds which kept them down, and either seeking reconciliation with the truth contained in the common opinion, or fronting it as enemies, and setting themselves up, with similar exclusiveness, as the whole truth. The latter case is hitherto the most frequent, as, in the human mind, onesidedness has always been the rule, and many-sidedness the exception. Hence, even in revolutions of opinion, one part of the truth usually sets while another rises. Even progress, which ought to superadd, for the most part only substitutes, one partial and incomplete truth for another; improvement consisting chiefly in this, that the new fragment of truth is more wanted, more adapted to the needs of the time, than that which it displaces. Such being the partial character of prevailing opinions, even when resting on a true foundation, every opinion which embodies somewhat of the portion of truth which the common opinion omits, ought to be considered precious, with whatever amount of error and confusion that truth may be blended. No sober judge of human affairs will feel bound to be indignant because those who force on our notice truths which we should otherwise have overlooked, overlook some of those which we see. Rather, he will think that so long as popular truth is one-sided, it is more desirable than otherwise that unpopular truth should have one-sided asserters too; such being usually the most energetic, and the most likely to compel reluctant attention to the fragment of wisdom which they proclaim as if it were the whole.

Thus, in the eighteenth century, when nearly all the instructed, and all those of the uninstructed who were led by them, were lost in admiration of what is called civilisation, and of the marvels of modern science, literature, and philosophy, and while greatly overrating the amount of unlikeness between the men of modern and those of ancient times, indulged the belief that the whole of the difference was in their own favour, with what a salutary shock did the paradoxes of Rousseau explode like bombshells in the midst, dislocating the compact mass of one-sided opinion, and forcing its elements to recombine in a better form and with additional ingredients. Not that the current opinions were on the whole farther from the truth than Rousseau's were; on the contrary, they were nearer to it; they contained more of positive truth, and very much less of error. Nevertheless there lay in Rousseau's doctrine, and has floated down the stream of opinion along with it, a considerable amount of exactly those truths which the popular opinion wanted; and these are the deposit which was left behind when the flood subsided. The superior worth of simplicity of life, the enervating and demoralizing effect of the trammels and hypocrisies of artificial society, are ideas which have never been entirely absent from cultivated minds since Rousseau wrote; and they will in time produce their due effect, though at present needing to be asserted as much as ever, and to be asserted by deeds, for words, on this subject, have nearly exhausted their power.

In politics, again, it is almost a commonplace, that a party of order or stability, and a party of progress or reform, are both necessary elements of a healthy state of political life; until the one or the other shall have so enlarged its mental grasp as to be a party equally of order and of progress, knowing and distinguishing what is fit to be preserved from what ought to be swept away. Each of these modes of thinking derives its utility from the deficiencies of the other; but it is in a great measure the opposition of the other that keeps each within the limits of reason and sanity. Unless opinions favourable to democracy and to aristocracy, to property and to equality, to co-operation and to competition, to luxury and to abstinence, to sociality and individuality, to liberty and discipline, and all the other standing antagonisms of practical life, are expressed with equal freedom, and enforced and defended with equal talent and energy, there is no chance of both elements obtaining their due; one scale is sure to go up, and the other down. Truth, in the great practical concerns of life, is so much a question of the reconciling and combining of opposites, that very few have minds sufficiently capacious and impartial to make the adjustment with an approach to correctness, and it has to be made by the rough process of a struggle between combatants fighting under hostile banners. On any of the great open questions just enumerated, if either of the two opinions has a better claim than the other, not merely to be tolerated, but to be encouraged and countenanced, it is the one which happens at the particular time and place to be in a minority. That is the opinion which, for the time being, represents the neglected interests, the side of human well-being which is in danger of obtaining less than its share. I am aware that there is not, in this country, any intolerance of differences of opinion on most of these topics. They are adduced to show, by admitted and multiplied examples, the universality of the fact, that only through diversity of opinion is there, in the existing state of human intellect, a chance of fair play to all sides of the truth. When there are persons to be found who form an exception to the apparent unanimity of the world on any subject, even if the world is in the right, it is always probable that dissentients have something worth hearing to say for themselves, and that truth would lose something by their silence. . . .

I do not pretend that the most unlimited use of the freedom of enunciating all possible opinions would put an end to the evils of religious or philosophical sectarianism. Every truth which men of narrow capacity are in earnest about, is sure to be asserted, inculcated, and in many ways even acted on, as if no other truth existed in the world, or at all events none that could limit or qualify the first. I acknowledge that the tendency of all opinions to become sectarian is not cured by the freest discussion, but is often heightened and exacerbated thereby; the truth which ought to have been, but was not, seen, being rejected all the more violently because proclaimed by persons regarded as opponents. But it is not on the impassioned partisan, it is on the calmer and more disinterested bystander, that this collision of opinions works its salutary effect. Not the violent conflict between parts of the truth, but the quiet suppression of half of it, is the formidable evil; there is always hope when people are forced to listen to both sides; it is when they attend only to one that errors harden into prejudices, and truth itself ceases to have the effect of truth, by being exaggerated into falsehood. And since there are few mental attributes more rare than that judicial faculty which can sit in intelligent judgment between two sides of a question, of which only one is represented by an advocate before it, truth has no chance but in proportion as every side of it, every opinion which embodies any fraction of the truth, not only finds advocates, but is so advocated as to be listened to.

We have now recognised the necessity to the mental well-being of mankind (on which all their other well-being depends) of freedom of opinion, and freedom of the expression of opinion, on four distinct grounds; which we will now briefly recapitulate.

First, if any opinion is compelled to silence, that opinion may, for aught we can certainly know, be true. To deny this is to assume our own infallibility.

Secondly, though the silenced opinion be an error, it may, and very commonly does, contain a portion of truth; and since the general or prevailing opinion on any subject is rarely or never the whole truth, it is only by the collision of adverse opinions that the remainder of the truth has any chance of being supplied.

Thirdly, even if the received opinion be not only true, but the whole truth; unless it is suffered to be, and actually is, vigorously and earnestly contested, it will, by most of those who receive it, be held in the manner of a prejudice, with little comprehension or feeling of its rational grounds. And not only this, but, fourthly, the meaning of the doctrine itself will be in danger of being lost, or enfeebled, and deprived of its vital effect on the character and conduct; the dogma becoming a mere formal profession, inefficacious for good, but cumbering the ground, and preventing the growth of any real and heartfelt conviction, from reason or personal experience. . . .

Note

1. These words had scarcely been written, when, as if to give them an emphatic contradiction, occurred the Government Press Prosecutions of 1858. That ill-judged interference with the liberty of public discussion has not, however, induced me to alter a single word in the text, nor has it at all weakened my conviction that, moments of panic excepted, the era of pains and penalties for political discussion has, in our own country, passed away. For, in the first place, the prosecutions were not persisted in; and, in the second, they were never, properly speaking, political prosecutions. The offence charged was not that of criticizing institutions, or the acts or persons of rulers, but of circulating what was deemed an immoral doctrine, the lawfulness of Tyrannicide.

   If the arguments of the present chapter are of any validity, there ought to exist the fullest liberty of professing and discussing, as a matter of ethical conviction, any doctrine, however immoral it may be considered. It would, therefore, be irrelevant and out of place to examine here, whether the doctrine of Tyrannicide deserves that title. I shall content myself with saying that the subject has been at all times one of the open questions of morals; that the act of a private citizen in striking down a criminal, who, by raising himself above the law, has placed himself beyond the reach of legal punishment or control, has been accounted by whole nations, and by some of the best and wisest of men, not a crime, but an act of exalted virtue; and that, right or wrong, it is not of the nature of assassination, but of civil war. As such, I hold that the instigation to it, in a specific case, may be a proper subject of punishment, but only if an overt act has followed, and at least a probable connexion can be established between the act and the instigation. Even then, it is not a foreign government, but the very government assailed, which alone, in the exercise of self-defence, can legitimately punish attacks directed against its own existence.

Adapted from: John Stuart Mill, *Utilitarianism, Liberty, and Representative Government*, introduced by A. D. Lindsay, pp. 102–115, 126–134, 140–149. E. P. Dutton and Co., 1951. ✦

32
Excerpts from *The Subjection of Women*

John Stuart Mill

1

The object of this Essay is to explain as clearly as I am able grounds of an opinion which I have held from the very earliest period when I had formed any opinions at all on social political matters, and which, instead of being weakened or modified, has been constantly growing stronger by the progress reflection and the experience of life. That the principle which regulates the existing social relations between the two sexes—the legal subordination of one sex to the other—is wrong itself, and now one of the chief hindrances to human improvement; and that it ought to be replaced by a principle of perfect equality, admitting no power or privilege on the one side, nor disability on the other.

The very words necessary to express the task I have undertaken, show how arduous it is. But it would be a mistake to suppose that the difficulty of the case must lie in the insufficiency or obscurity of the grounds of reason on which my conviction rests. The difficulty is that which exists in all cases in which there is a mass of feeling to be contended against. So long as opinion is strongly rooted in the feelings, it gains rather than loses in stability by having a preponderating weight of argument against it. For if it were accepted as a result of argument, the refutation of the argument might shake the solidity of the conviction; but when it rests solely on feeling, the worse it fares in argumentative contest, the more persuaded adherents are

that their feeling must have some deeper ground, which the arguments do not reach; and while the feeling remains, it is always throwing up fresh intrenchments of argument to repair any breach made in the old. And there are so many causes tending to make the feelings connected with this subject the most intense and most deeply-rooted of those which gather round and protect old institutions and custom, that we need not wonder to find them as yet less undermined and loosened than any of the rest by the progress of the great modern spiritual and social transition; nor suppose that the barbarisms to which men cling longest must be less barbarisms than those which they earlier shake off. . . .

The generality of a practice is in some cases a strong presumption that it is, or at all events once was, conducive to laudable ends. This is the case, when the practice was first adopted, or afterwards kept up, as a means to such ends, and was grounded on experience of the mode in which they could be most effectually attained. If the authority of men over women, when first established, had been the result of a conscientious comparison between different modes of constituting the government of society; if, after trying various other modes of social organisation—the government of women over men, equality between the two, and such mixed and divided modes of government as might be invented—it had been decided, on the testimony of experience, that the mode in which women are wholly under the rule of men, having no share at all in public concerns, and each in private being under the legal obligation of obedience to the man with whom she has associated her destiny, was the arrangement most conducive to the happiness and well-being of both; its general adoption might then be fairly thought to be some evidence that, at the time when it was adopted, it was the best: though even then the considerations which recommended it may, like so many other primeval social facts of the greatest importance, have subsequently, in the course of ages, ceased to exist. But the state of the case is in every respect the reverse of this. In the first place, the opirion in favour of the present system, which entirely subordinates the weaker sex to the stronger, rests upon theory only; for there never has been trial made of any other: so that experience, in the sense in which it is vulgarly opposed to theory, cannot be pretended to have pronounced any verdict. And in the second place, the adoption of this system of inequality never was the result of deliberation, or forethought, or any social ideas, or any notion whatever of what conduced to the benefit of humanity or the good order of society. It arose simply from the fact that from the very earliest twilight of human society, every woman (owing to the value attached to her by men, combined with her inferiority in muscular strength) was found in a state of bondage to some man. Laws and systems of polity always begin by recognising the relations they find already existing between individuals. They convert what was a mere physical fact into a legal right, give it the sanction of society, and principally aim at the substitution of public and organised means of asserting and protecting these rights, instead of the irregular and lawless conflict of physical strength. Those who had already been compelled to obedience became in this manner legally bound to it. Slavery, from being a mere affair of force between the master and the slave, became regularised and a matter of compact among the masters, who, binding themselves to one another for common protection, guaranteed by their collective strength the private possessions of each, including his slaves. In early times, the great majority of the male sex were slaves, as well as the whole of the female. And many ages elapsed, some of them ages of high cultivation, before any thinker was bold enough to question the rightfulness, and the absolute social necessity, either of the one slavery or of the other. By degrees such thinkers did arise; and (the general progress of society assisting) the slavery of the male sex has, in all the countries of Christian Europe at least (though, in one of them, only within the last few years) been at length abolished, and that of the female sex has been gradually changed into a milder form of dependence. But this dependence, as it exists at present, is not an original institution, taking a fresh start from considerations of justice and social expediency—it is the primitive state of slavery lasting on, through successive mitigations and modifications occasioned by the same causes which have softened the general manners, and brought all human relations more under the control of justice and the influence of humanity. It has not lost the taint of its brutal origin. No presumption in its favour, therefore, can be drawn from the fact of its existence. The only such presumption which it could be supposed to have, must be grounded on its having lasted till now, when so many other things which came down from the same odious source have been done away with. And this, indeed, is what makes it strange to ordinary ears, to hear it asserted that the inequality of rights between men and women has no other source than the law of the strongest. . . .

The general opinion of men is supposed to be, that the natural vocation of a woman is that of a wife and mother. I say, is supposed to be, because, judging from acts—from the whole of the present constitution of society—one might infer that their opinion was the direct contrary. They might be supposed to think that the alleged natural vocation of women was of all things the most repugnant to their nature; insomuch that if they are free to do anything else—if any other means of living or occupation of their time and faculties, is open, which has any chance of appearing desirable to them—there will not be enough of them who will be willing to accept the condition said to be natural to them. If this is the real opinion of men in general, it would be well that it should be spoken out. I should like to hear somebody openly enunciating the doctrine (it is already implied in much that is written on the subject)—"It is necessary to society that women should marry and produce children. They will not do so unless they are compelled. Therefore it is necessary to compel them." The merits of the case would then be clearly defined. It would be exactly that of the slave-holders of South Carolina and Louisiana. "It is necessary that cotton and sugar should be grown. White men cannot produce them. Negroes will not, for any wages which we choose to give. *Ergo* they must be compelled." An illustration still closer to the point is that of impressment. Sailors must absolutely be had to defend the country. It often happens that they will not voluntarily enlist. Therefore there must be the power of forcing them. How often has this logic been used! and, but for one flaw in it, without doubt it would have been successful up to this day. But it is open to the retort—First pay the sailors the honest value of their labour. When you have made it as well worth their while to serve you, as to work for other employers, you will have no more difficulty than others have in obtaining their services. To this there is no logical answer except "I will not": and as people are now not only ashamed, but are not desirous, to rob the labourer of his hire, impressment is no longer advocated. Those who attempt to force women into marriage by closing all other doors against them, lay themselves open to a similar retort. If they mean what they say, their opinion must evidently be, that men do not render the married condition so desirable to women, as to induce them to accept it for its own recommendations. It is not a sign of one's thinking the boon one offers very attractive, when one allows only Hobson's choice, "that or none." And here, I believe, is the clue to the feelings of those men, who have a real antipathy to the equal freedom of women. I believe they are afraid, not lest women should be unwilling to marry, for I do not think that anyone in reality has that apprehension; but lest they should insist that marriage should be on equal conditions; lest all women of spirit and capacity should prefer doing almost anything else, not in their own eyes degrading, rather than marry, when marrying is giving themselves a master, and a master too of all their earthly possessions. And truly, if this consequence were necessarily incident to marriage, I think that the apprehension would be very well founded. I agree in thinking it probable that few women, capable of anything else, would, unless under an irresistible *entrainement*, rendering them for the time insensible to anything but itself, choose such a lot, when any other means were open to them of filling a conventionally honourable place in life: and if men are determined that the law of marriage shall be a law of despotism, they are quite right, in point of mere

policy, in leaving to women only Hobson's choice. But, in that case, all that has been done in the modern world to relax the chain on the minds of women, has been a mistake. They never should have been allowed to receive a literary education. Women who read, much more women who write, are, in the existing constitution of things, a contradiction and a disturbing element: and it was wrong to bring women up with any acquirements but those of an odalisque, or of a domestic servant.

2

It will be well to commence the detailed discussion of the subject by the particular branch of it to which the course of our observations has led us: the conditions which the laws of this and all other countries annex to the marriage contract. Marriage being the destination appointed by society for women, the prospect they are brought up to, and the object which it is intended should be sought by all of them, except those who are too little attractive to be chosen by any man as his companion; one might have supposed that everything would have been done to make this condition as eligible to them as possible, that they might have no cause to regret being denied the option of any other. Society, however, both in this, and, at first, in all other cases, has preferred to attain its object by foul rather than fair means: but this is the only case in which it has substantially persisted in them even to the present day. Originally women were taken by force, or regularly sold by their father to the husband. Until a late period in European history, the father had the power to dispose of his daughter in marriage at his own will and pleasure, without any regard to hers. The Church, indeed, was so far faithful to a better morality as to require a formal "yes" from the woman at the marriage ceremony; but there was nothing to show that the consent was other than compulsory; and it was practically impossible for the girl to refuse compliance if the father persevered, except perhaps when she might obtain the protection of religion by a determined resolution to take monastic vows. After marriage, the man had anciently (but this was anterior to Christianity) the power of life and death over his wife. She could invoke no law against him; he was her sole tribunal and law. For a long time he could repudiate her, but she had no corresponding power in regard to him. By the old laws of England, the husband was called the *lord* of the wife; he was literally regarded as her sovereign, inasmuch that the murder of a man by his wife was called treason (*petty* as distinguished from *high* treason), and was more cruelly avenged than was usually the case with high treason, for the penalty was burning to death. Because these various enormities have fallen into disuse (for most of them were never formally abolished, or not until they had long ceased to be practised) men suppose that all is now as it should be in regard to the marriage contract; and we are continually told that civilisation and Christianity have restored to the woman her just rights. Meanwhile the wife is the actual bond servant of her husband: no less so, as far as legal obligation goes, than slaves commonly so called. She vows a livelong obedience to him at the altar, and is held to it all through her life by law. Casuists may say that the obligation of obedience stops short of participation in crime, but it certainly extends to everything else. She can do no act whatever but by his permission, at least tacit. She can acquire no property but for him; the instant it becomes hers, even if by inheritance, it becomes *ipso facto* his. In this respect the wife's position under the common law of England is worse than that of slaves in the laws of many countries: by the Roman law, for example, a slave might have his peculium, which to a certain extent the law guaranteed to him for his exclusive use. The higher classes in this country have given an analogous advantage to their women, through special contracts setting aside the law, by conditions of pin-money, etc.: since parental feeling being stronger with fathers than the class feeling of their own sex, a father generally prefers his own daughter to a son-in-law who is a stranger to him. By means of settlements, the rich usually contrive to withdraw the whole or part of the inherited property of the wife from the absolute control of the husband: but they do not succeed in keeping it under her own control; the utmost they can do only prevents the husband from squandering it, at the same time debarring the rightful owner from its use. The property itself is out of the reach of both; and as to the income derived from it, the form of settlement most favourable to the wife (that called "to her separate use") only precludes the husband from receiving it instead of her: it must pass through her hands, but if he takes it from her by personal violence as soon as she receives it, he can neither be punished, nor compelled to restitution. This is the amount of the protection which, under the laws of this country, the most powerful nobleman can give to his own daughter as respects her husband. In the immense majority of cases there is no settlement: and the absorption of all rights, all property, as well as all freedom of action, is complete. The two are called "one person in law," for the purpose of inferring that whatever is hers is his, but the parallel inference is never drawn that whatever is his is hers; the maxim is not applied against the man, except to make him responsible to third parties for her acts, as a master is for the acts of his slaves or of his cattle. I am far from pretending that wives are in general no better treated than slaves; but no slave is a slave to the same lengths, and in so full a sense of the word, as a wife is. Hardly any slave, except one immediately attached to the master's person, is a slave at all hours and all minutes; in general he has, like a soldier, his fixed task, and when it is done, or when he is off duty, he disposes, within certain limits, of his own time, and has a family life into which the master rarely intrudes. "Uncle Tom" under his first master had his own life in his "cabin," almost as much as any man whose work takes him away from home, is able to have in his own family. But it cannot be so with the wife. Above all, a female slave has (in Christian countries) an admitted right, and is considered under a moral obligation, to refuse to her master the last familiarity. Not so the wife: however brutal a tyrant she may unfortunately be chained to—though she may know that he hates her, though it may be his daily pleasure to torture her, and though she may feel it impossible not to loathe him—he can claim from her and enforce the lowest degradation of a human being, that of being made the instrument of an animal function contrary to her inclinations. While she is held in this worst description of slavery as to her own person, what is her position in regard to the children in whom she and her master have a joint interest? They are by law *his* children. He alone has any legal rights over them. Not one act can she do towards or in relation to them, except by delegation from him. Even after he is dead she is not their legal guardian, unless he by will has made her so. He could even send them away from her, and deprive her of the means of seeing or corresponding with them, until this power was in some degree restricted by Serjeant Talfourd's Act. This is her legal state. And from this state she has no means of withdrawing herself. If she leaves her husband, she can take nothing with her, neither her children nor anything which is rightfully her own. If he chooses, he can compel her to return, by law, or by physical force; or he may content himself with seizing for his own use anything which she may earn, or which may be given to her by her relations. It is only legal separation by a decree of a court of justice, which entitles her to live apart, without being forced back into the custody of an exasperated jailer—or which empowers her to apply any earnings to her own use, without fear that a man whom perhaps she has not seen for twenty years will pounce upon her some day and carry all off. This legal separation, until lately, the courts of justice would only give at an expense which made it inaccessible to anyone out of the higher ranks. Even now it is only given in cases of desertion, or of the extreme of cruelty; and yet complaints are made every day that it is granted too easily. Surely, if a woman is denied any lot in life but that of being the personal body-servant of a despot, and is dependent for everything upon the chance of finding one who may be disposed to make a favourite of her instead of merely a drudge, it is a very cruel aggravation of her fate that she should be allowed to try this chance only once. The natural sequel and corollary from this state of things would be, that since her all in life depends upon obtaining a good master, she should be allowed to change again and again until she finds one. I am not saying that she ought to be allowed this privilege. That is a totally different consideration. The question of divorce, in the sense involving liberty of remarriage, is one into which it is foreign to my purpose to enter. All I now say is, that to those to whom nothing but servitude is allowed, the free choice of servitude is the only, though a most insufficient, alleviation. Its refusal completes the assimilation of the wife to the slave—and the slave under not the mildest form of slavery: for in some slave codes the slave could, under certain circumstances of ill usage, legally compel the master to sell him. But no amount of ill usage, without adultery superadded, will in England free a wife from her tormentor. . . .

3

On the other point which is involved in the just equality of women, their admissibility to all the functions and occupations hitherto retained as the monopoly of the stronger sex, I should anticipate no difficulty in convincing anyone who has gone with me on the subject of the equality of women in the family. I believe that their disabilities elsewhere are only clung to in order to maintain their subordination in domestic life; because the generality of the male sex cannot yet tolerate the idea of living with an equal. Were it not for that, I think that almost everyone, in the existing state of opinion in politics and political economy, would admit the injustice of excluding half the human race from the greater number of lucrative occupations, and from almost all high social functions; ordaining from their birth either that they are not, and cannot by any possibility become, fit for employments which are legally open to the stupidest and basest of the other sex, or else that however fit they may be, those employments shall be interdicted to them, in order to be preserved for the exclusive benefit of males. In the last two centuries, when (which was seldom the case) any reason beyond the mere existence of the fact was thought to be required to justify the disabilities of women, people seldom assigned as a reason their inferior mental capacity; which, in times when there was a real trial of personal faculties (from which all women were not excluded) in the struggles of public life, no one really believed in. The reason given in those days was not women's unfitness, but the interest of society, by which was meant the interest of men: just as the *raison d'état*, meaning the convenience of the government, and the support of existing authority, was deemed a sufficient explanation and excuse for the most flagitious crimes. In the present day, power holds a smoother language, and whomsoever it oppresses, always pretends to do so for their own good: accordingly, when anything is forbidden to women, it is thought necessary to say, and desirable to believe, that they are incapable of doing it, and that they depart from their real path of success and happiness when they aspire to it. But to make this reason plausible (I do not say valid), those by whom it is urged must be prepared to carry it to a much greater length than anyone ventures to do in the face of present experience. It is not sufficient to maintain that women on the average are less gifted then men on the average, with certain of the higher mental faculties, or that a smaller number of women than of men are fit for occupations and functions of the highest intellectual character. It is necessary to maintain that no women at all are fit for them, and that the most eminent women are inferior in mental faculties to the most mediocre of the men on whom those functions at present devolve. For if the performance of the function is decided either by competition, or by any mode of choice which secures regard to the public interest, there needs be no apprehension that any important employments will fall into the hands of women inferior to average men, or to the average of their male competitors. The only result would be that there would be fewer women than men in such employments; a result certain to happen in any case, if only from the preference always likely to be felt by the majority of women for the one vocation in which there is nobody to compete with them. Now, the most determined depreciator of women will not venture to deny, that when we add the experience of recent times to that of ages past, women, and not a few

merely, but many women, have proved themselves capable of everything, perhaps without a single exception, which is done by men, and of doing it successfully and creditably. The utmost that can be said is, that there are many things which none of them have succeeded in doing as well as they have been done by some men—many in which they have not reached the very highest rank. But there are extremely few, dependent only on mental faculties, in which they have not attained the rank next to the highest. Is not this enough, and much more than enough, to make it a tyranny to them, and a detriment to society, that they should not be allowed to compete with men for the exercise of these functions? Is it not a mere truism to say, that such functions are often filled by men far less fit for them than numbers of women, and who would be beaten by women in any fair field of competition? What difference does it make that there may be men somewhere, fully employed about other things, who may be still better qualified for the things in question than these women? Does not this take place in all competitions? Is there so great a superfluity of men fit for high duties, that society can afford to reject the service of any competent person? Are we so certain of always finding a man made to our hands for any duty or function of social importance which falls vacant, that we lose nothing by putting a ban upon one half of mankind, and refusing beforehand to make their faculties available, however distinguished they may be? And even if we could do without them, would it be consistent with justice to refuse to them their fair share of honour and distinction, or to deny to them the equal moral right of all human beings to choose their occupation (short of injury to others) according to their own preferences, at their own risk? Nor is the injustice confined to them: it is shared by those who are in a position to benefit by their services. To ordain that any kind of persons shall not be physicians, or shall not be advocates, or shall not be Members of Parliament, is to injure not them only, but all who employ physicians or advocates, or elect Members of Parliament, and who are deprived of the stimulating effect of greater competition on the exertions of the competitors, as well as re-stricted to a narrower range of individual choice.

It will perhaps be sufficient if I confine myself, in the details of my argument, to functions of a public nature: since, if I am successful as to those, it probably will be readily granted that women should be ad-missible to all other occupations to which it is at all material whether they are admitted or not. And here let me begin by marking out one function, broadly distinguished from all others, their right to which is entirely inde-pendent of any question which can be raised concerning their faculties. I mean the suf-frage, both parliamentary and municipal. The right to share in the choice of those who are to exercise a public trust, is altogether a distinct thing from that of competing for the trust itself. If no one could vote for a Member of Parliament who was not fit to be a candi-date, the government would be a narrow oli-garchy indeed. To have a voice in choosing those by whom one is to be governed, is a means of self-protection due to everyone, though he were to remain for ever excluded from the function of governing: and that women are considered fit to have such a choice, may be presumed from the fact, that the law already gives it to women in the most important of all cases to themselves: for the choice of the man who is to govern a woman to the end of life, is always supposed to be voluntarily made by herself. In the case of election to public trusts, it is the business of constitutional law to surround the right of suffrage with all needful securities and limi-tations; but whatever securities are suffi-cient in the case of the male sex, no others need be required in the case of women. Under whatever conditions, and within whatever limits, men are admitted to the suf-frage, there is not a shadow of justification for not admitting women under the same. The majority of the women of any class are not likely to differ in political opinion from the majority of the men of the same class, un-less the question be one in which the inter-ests of women, as such, are in some way in-volved; and if they are so, women require the suffrage, as their guarantee of just and equal consideration. This ought to be obvious even to those who coincide in no other of the doc-trines for which I contend. Even if every woman were a wife, and if every wife ought to be a slave, all the more would these slaves stand in need of legal protection: and we know what legal protection the slaves have, where the laws are made by their masters.

With regard to the fitness of women, not only to participate in elections, but them-selves to hold offices or practise professions involving important public responsibilities; I have already observed that this consider-ation is not essential to the practical ques-tion in dispute: since any woman, who suc-ceeds in an open profession, proves by that very fact that she is qualified for it. And in the case of public offices, if the political system of the country is such as to exclude unfit men, it will equally exclude unfit women: while if it is not, there is no additional evil in the fact that the unfit persons whom it ad-mits may be either women or men. As long therefore as it is acknowledged that even a few women may be fit for these duties, the laws which shut the door on those excep-tions cannot be justified by any opinion which can be held respecting the capacities of women in general. But, though this last consideration is not essential, it is far from being irrelevant. An unprejudiced view of it gives additional strength to the arguments against the disabilities of women, and rein-forces them by high considerations of practi-cal utility. . . .

Adapted from: John Stuart Mill and Harriet Taylor Mill, *Essays on Sex Equality*, Alice Ross, ed., pp. 125–126, 129–131, 155–161, 181–185. University of Chicago Press, 1970. ✦

33
Excerpts from
Utilitarianism

John Stuart Mill

Chapter 2: What Utilitarianism Is.

The creed which accepts as the foundation of morals, Utility, or the Greatest Happiness Principle, holds that actions are right in proportion as they tend to promote happiness, wrong as they tend to produce the reverse of happiness. By happiness is intended pleasure, and the absence of pain; by unhappiness, pain, and the privation of pleasure. To give a clear view of the moral standard set up by the theory, much more requires to be said; in particular, what things it includes in the ideas of pain and pleasure; and to what extent this is left an open question. But these supplementary explanations do not affect the theory of life on which this theory of morality is grounded—namely, that pleasure, and freedom from pain, are the only things desirable as ends; and that all desirable things (which are as numerous in the utilitarian as in any other scheme) are desirable either for the pleasure inherent in themselves, or as means to the promotion of pleasure and the prevention of pain.

Now, such a theory of life excites in many minds, and among them in some of the most estimable in feeling and purpose, inveterate dislike. To suppose that life has (as they express it) no higher end than pleasure—no better and nobler object of desire and pursuit—they designate as utterly mean and grovelling; as a doctrine worthy only of swine, to whom the followers of Epicurus were, at a very early period, contemptuously likened; and modern holders of the doctrine are occasionally made the subject of equally polite comparisons by its German, French, and English assailants.

When thus attacked, the Epicureans have always answered, that it is not they, but their accusers, who represent human nature in a degrading light; since the accusation supposes human beings to be capable of no pleasures except those of which swine are capable. If this supposition were true, the charge could not be gainsaid, but would then be no longer an imputation; for if the sources of pleasure were precisely the same to human beings and to swine, the rule of life which is good enough for the one would be good enough for the other. The comparison of the Epicurean life to that of beasts is felt as degrading, precisely because a beast's pleasures do not satisfy a human being's conceptions of happiness. Human beings have faculties more elevated than the animal appetites, and when once made conscious of them, do not regard anything as happiness which does not include their gratification. I do not, indeed, consider the Epicureans to have been by any means faultless in drawing out their scheme of consequences from the utilitarian principle. To do this in any sufficient manner, many Stoic, as well as Christian elements require to be included. But there is no known Epicurean theory of life which does not assign to the pleasures of the intellect, of the feelings and imagination, and of the moral sentiments, a much higher value as pleasures than to those of mere sensation. It must be admitted, however, that utilitarian writers in general have placed the superiority of mental over bodily pleasures chiefly in the greater permanency, safety, uncostliness, etc., of the former—that is, in their circumstantial advantages rather than in their intrinsic nature. And on all these points utilitarians have fully proved their case; but they might have taken the other, and, as it may be called, higher ground, with entire consistency. It is quite compatible with the principle of utility to recognise the fact, that some kinds of pleasure are more desirable and more valuable than others. It would be absurd that while, in estimating all other things, quality is considered as well as quantity, the estimation of pleasures should be supposed to depend on quantity alone.

If I am asked what I mean by difference of quality in pleasures, or what makes one pleasure more valuable than another, merely as a pleasure, except its being greater in amount, there is but one possible answer. Of two pleasures, if there be one to which all or almost all who have experience of both give a decided preference, irrespective of any feeling of moral obligation to prefer it, that is the more desirable pleasure. If one of the two is, by those who are competently acquainted with both, placed so far above the other that they prefer it, even though knowing it to be attended with a greater amount of discontent, and would not resign it for any quantity of the other pleasure which their nature is capable of, we are justified in ascribing to the preferred enjoyment a superiority in quality, so far outweighing quantity as to render it, in comparison, of small account.

Now it is an unquestionable fact that those who are equally acquainted with, and equally capable of appreciating and enjoying, both, do give a most marked preference to the manner of existence which employs their higher faculties. Few human creatures would consent to be changed into any of the lower animals, for a promise of the fullest allowance of a beast's pleasures; no intelligent human being would consent to be a fool, no instructed person would be an ignoramus, no person of feeling and conscience would be selfish and base, even though they should be persuaded that the fool, the dunce, or the rascal is better satisfied with his lot than they are with theirs. They would not resign what they possess more than he for the most complete satisfaction of all the desires which they have in common with him. If they ever fancy they would, it is only in cases of unhappiness so extreme, that to escape from it they would exchange their lot for almost any other, however undesirable in their own eyes. A being of higher faculties requires more to make him happy, is capable probably of more acute suffering, and certainly accessible to it at more points, than one of an inferior type; but in spite of these liabilities, he can never really wish to sink into what he feels to be a lower grade of existence. We may give what explanation we please of this unwillingness; we may attribute it to pride, a name which is given indiscriminately to some of the most and to some of the least es-

timable feelings of which mankind are capable: we may refer it to the love of liberty and personal independence, an appeal to which was with the Stoics one of the most effective means for the inculcation of it; to the love of power, or to the love of excitement, both of which do really enter into and contribute to it: but its most appropriate appellation is a sense of dignity, which all human beings possess in one form or other, and in some, though by no means in exact, proportion to their higher faculties, and which is so essential a part of the happiness of those in whom it is strong, that nothing which conflicts with it could be, otherwise than momentarily, an object of desire to them. Whoever supposes that this preference takes place at a sacrifice of happiness—that the superior being, in anything like equal circumstances, is not happier than the inferior—confounds the two very different ideas, of happiness, and content. It is indisputable that the being whose capacities of enjoyment are low, has the greatest chance of having them fully satisfied; and a highly endowed being will always feel that any happiness which he can look for, as the world is constituted, is imperfect. But he can learn to bear its imperfections, if they are at all bearable; and they will not make him envy the being who is indeed unconscious of the imperfections, but only because he feels not at all the good which those imperfections qualify. It is better to be a human being dissatisfied than a pig satisfied; better to be Socrates dissatisfied than a fool satisfied. And if the fool, or the pig, are a different opinion, it is because they only know their own side of the question. The other party to the comparison knows both sides.

It may be objected, that many who are capable of the higher pleasures, occasionally, under the influence of temptation, postpone them to the lower. But this is quite compatible with a full appreciation of the intrinsic superiority of the higher. Men often, from infirmity of character, make their election for the nearer good, though they know it to be the less valuable; and this no less when the choice is between two bodily pleasures, than when it is between bodily and mental. They pursue sensual indulgences to the injury of health, though perfectly aware that health is the greater good. It may be further objected, that many who begin with youthful enthusiasm for everything noble, as they advance in years sink into indolence and selfishness. But I do not believe that those who undergo this very common change, voluntarily choose the lower description of pleasures in preference to the higher. I believe that before they devote themselves exclusively to the one, they have already become incapable of the other. Capacity for the nobler feelings is in most natures a very tender plant, easily killed, not only by hostile influences, but by mere want of sustenance; and in the majority of young persons it speedily dies away if the occupations to which their position in life has devoted them, and the society into which it has thrown them, are not favourable to keeping that higher capacity in exercise. Men lose their high aspirations as they lose their intellectual tastes, because they have not time or opportunity for indulging them; and they addict themselves to inferior pleasures, not because they deliberately prefer them, but because they are either the only ones to which they have access, or the only ones which they are any longer capable of enjoying. It may be questioned whether any one who has remained equally susceptible to both classes of pleasures, ever knowingly and calmly preferred the lower; though many, in all ages, have broken down in an ineffectual attempt to combine both.

From this verdict of the only competent judges, I apprehend there can be no appeal. On a question which is the best worth having of two pleasures, or which of two modes of existence is the most grateful to the feelings, apart from its moral attributes and from its consequences, the judgment of those who are qualified by knowledge of both, or, if they differ, that of the majority among them, must be admitted as final. And there needs be the less hesitation to accept this judgment respecting the quality of pleasures, since there is no other tribunal to be referred to even on the question of quantity. What means are there of determining which is the acutest of two pains, or the intensest of two pleasurable sensations, except the general suffrage of those who are familiar with both?

Neither pains nor pleasures are homogeneous, and pain is always heterogeneous with pleasure. What is there to decide whether a particular pleasure is worth purchasing at the cost of a particular pain, except the feelings and judgment of the experienced? When, therefore, those feelings and judgment declare the pleasures derived from the higher faculties to be preferable in kind, apart from the question of intensity, to those of which the animal nature, disjoined from the higher faculties, is suspectible, they are entitled on this subject to the same regard.

I have dwelt on this point, as being a necessary part of a perfectly just conception of Utility or Happiness, considered as the directive rule of human conduct. But it is by no means an indispensable condition to the acceptance of the utilitarian standard; for that standard is not the agent's own greatest happiness, but the greatest amount of happiness altogether; and if it may possibly be doubted whether a noble character is always the happier for its nobleness, there can be no doubt that it makes other people happier, and that the world in general is immensely a gainer by it. Utilitarianism, therefore, could only attain its end by the general cultivation of nobleness of character, even if each individual were only benefited by the nobleness of others, and his own, so far as happiness is concerned, were a sheer deduction from the benefit. But the bare enunciation of such an absurdity as this last, renders refutation superfluous.

According to the Greatest Happiness Principle, as above explained, the ultimate end, with reference to and for the sake of which all other things are desirable (whether we are considering our own good or that of other people), is an existence exempt as far as possible from pain, and as rich as possible in enjoyments, both in point of quantity and quality; the test of quality, and the rule for measuring it against quantity, being the preference felt by those who in their opportunities of experience, to which must be added their habits of self-consciousness and self-observation, are best furnished with the means of comparison. This, being, according to the utilitarian opinion, the end of human action, is necessarily also the stan-

427 Mill ✦ Excerpts from Utilitarianism

dard of morality; which may accordingly be defined, the rules and precepts for human conduct, by the observance of which an existence such as has been described might be, to the greatest extent possible, secured to all mankind; and not to them only, but, so far as the nature of things admits, to the whole sentient creation.

Against this doctrine, however, arises another class of objectors, who say that happiness, in any form, cannot be the rational purpose of human life and action; because, in the first place, it is unattainable: and they contemptuously ask, what right hast thou to be happy? a question which Mr. Carlyle clenches by the addition, What right, a short time ago, hadst thou even to be? Next, they say, that men can do without happiness; that all noble human beings have felt this, and could not have become noble but by learning the lesson of Entsagen, or renunciation; which lesson, thoroughly learnt and submitted to, they affirm to be the beginning and necessary condition of all virtue.

The first of these objections would go to the root of the matter were it well founded; for if no happiness is to be had at all by human beings, the attainment of it cannot be the end of morality, or of any rational conduct. Though, even in that case, something might still be said for the utilitarian theory; since utility includes not solely the pursuit of happiness, but the prevention or mitigation of unhappiness; and if the former aim be chimerical, there will be all the greater scope and more imperative need for the latter, so long at least as mankind think fit to live, and do not take refuge in the simultaneous act of suicide recommended under certain conditions by Novalis. When, however, it is thus positively asserted to be impossible that human life should be happy, the assertion, if not something like a verbal quibble, is at least an exaggeration. If by happiness be meant a continuity of highly pleasurable excitement, it is evident enough that this is impossible. A state of exalted pleasure lasts only moments, or in some cases, and with some intermissions, hours or days, and is the occasional brilliant flash of enjoyment, not its permanent and steady flame. Of this the philosophers who have taught that happi-

ness is the end of life were as fully aware as those who taunt them. The happiness which they meant was not a life of rapture; but moments of such, in an existence made up of few and transitory pains, many and various pleasures, with a decided predominance of the active over the passive, and having as the foundation of the whole, not to expect more from life than it is capable of bestowing. A life thus composed, to those who have been fortunate enough to obtain it, has always appeared worthy of the name of happiness. And such an existence is even now the lot of many, during some considerable portion of their lives. The present wretched education, and wretched social arrangements, are the only real hindrance to its being attainable by almost all.

The objectors perhaps may doubt whether human beings, if taught to consider happiness as the end of life, would be satisfied with such a moderate share of it. But great numbers of mankind have been satisfied with much less. The main constituents of a satisfied life appear to be two, either of which by itself is often found sufficient for the purpose: tranquillity, and excitement. With much tranquillity, many find that they can be content with very little pleasure: with much excitement, many can reconcile themselves to a considerable quantity of pain. There is assuredly no inherent impossibility in enabling even the mass of mankind to unite both; since the two are so far from being incompatible that they are in natural alliance, the prolongation of either being a preparation for, and exciting a wish for, the other. It is only those in whom indolence amounts to a vice, that do not desire excitement after an interval of repose: it is only those in whom the need of excitement is a disease, that feel the tranquillity which follows excitement dull and insipid, instead of pleasurable in direct proportion to the excitement which preceded it. When people who are tolerably fortunate in their outward lot do not find in life sufficient enjoyment to make it valuable to them, the cause generally is, caring for nobody but themselves. To those who have neither public nor private affections, the excitements of life are much curtailed, and in any case dwindle in value as the time approaches when all selfish interests must be terminated by death: while those who leave after them objects of personal affection, and especially those who have also cultivated a fellow-feeling with the collective interests of mankind, retain as lively an interest in life on the eve of death as in the vigour of youth and health. Next to selfishness, the principal cause which makes life unsatisfactory is want of mental cultivation. A cultivated mind—I do not mean that of a philosopher, but any mind to which the fountains of knowledge have been opened, and which has been taught, in any tolerable degree, to exercise its faculties—finds sources of inexhaustible interest in all that surrounds it; in the objects of nature, the achievements of art, the imaginations of poetry, the incidents of history, the ways of mankind, past and present, and their prospects in the future. It is possible, indeed, to become indifferent to all this, and that too without having exhausted a thousandth part of it; but only when one has had from the beginning no moral or human interest in these things, and has sought in them only the gratification of curiosity.

Now there is absolutely no reason in the nature of things why an amount of mental culture sufficient to give an intelligent interest in these objects of contemplation, should not be the inheritance of every one born in a civilised country. As little is there an inherent necessity that any human being should be a selfish egotist, devoid of every feeling or care but those which centre in his own miserable individuality. Something far superior to this is sufficiently common even now, to give ample earnest of what the human species may be made. Genuine private affections and a sincere interest in the public good, are possible, though in unequal degrees, to every rightly brought up human being. In a world in which there is so much to interest, so much to enjoy, and so much also to correct and improve, every one who has this moderate amount of moral and intellectual requisites is capable of an existence which may be called enviable; and unless such a person, through bad laws, or subjection to the will of others, is denied the liberty to use the sources of happiness within his reach, he

will not fail to find this enviable existence, if he escape the positive evils of life, the great sources of physical and mental suffering—such as indigence, disease, and the unkindness, worthlessness, or premature loss of objects of affection. The main stress of the problem lies, therefore, in the contest with these calamities, from which it is a rare good fortune entirely to escape; which, as things now are, cannot be obviated, and often cannot be in any material degree mitigated. Yet no one whose opinion deserves a moment's consideration can doubt that most of the great positive evils of the world are in themselves removable, and will, if human affairs continue to improve, be in the end reduced within narrow limits. Poverty, in any sense implying suffering, may be completely extinguished by the wisdom of society, combined with the good sense and providence of individuals. Even that most intractable of enemies, disease, may be indefinitely reduced in dimensions by good physical and moral education, and proper control of noxious influences; while the progress of science holds out a promise for the future of still more direct conquests over this detestable foe. And every advance in that direction relieves us from some, not only of the chances which cut short our own lives, but, what concerns us still more, which deprive us of those in whom our happiness is wrapt up. As for vicissitudes of fortune, and other disappointments connected with worldly circumstances, these are principally the effect either of gross imprudence, of ill-regulated desires, or of bad or imperfect social institutions. All the grand sources, in short, of human suffering are in a great degree, many of them almost entirely, conquerable by human care and effort; and though their removal is grievously slow—though a long succession of generations will perish in the breach before the conquest is completed, and this world becomes all that, if will and knowledge were not wanting, it might easily be made—yet every mind sufficiently intelligent and generous to bear a part, however small and unconspicuous, in the endeavour, will draw a noble enjoyment from the contest itself, which he would not for any bribe in the form of selfish indulgence consent to be without.

And this leads to the true estimation of what is said by the objectors concerning the possibility, and the obligation, of learning to do without happiness. Unquestionably it is possible to do without happiness; it is done involuntarily by nineteen-twentieths of mankind, even in those parts of our present world which are least deep in barbarism; and it often has to be done voluntarily by the hero or the martyr, for the sake of something which he prizes more than his individual happiness. But this something, what is it, unless the happiness of others or some of the requisites of happiness? It is noble to be capable of resigning entirely one's own portion of happiness, or chances of it: but, after all, this self-sacrifice must be for some end; it is not its own end; and if we are told that its end is not happiness, but virtue, which is better than happiness, I ask, would the sacrifice be made if the hero or martyr did not believe that it would earn for others immunity from similar sacrifices? Would it be made if he thought that his renunciation of happiness for himself would produce no fruit for any of his fellow creatures, but to make their lot like his, and place them also in the condition of persons who have renounced happiness? All honour to those who can abnegate for themselves the personal enjoyment of life, when by such renunciation they contribute worthily to increase the amount of happiness in the world; but he who does it, or professes to do it, for any other purpose, is no more deserving of admiration than the ascetic mounted on his pillar. He may be an inspiriting proof of what men can do, but assuredly not an example of what they should.

Though it is only in a very imperfect state of the world's arrangements that any one can best serve the happiness of others by the absolute sacrifice of his own, yet so long as the world is in that imperfect state, I fully acknowledge that the readiness to make such a sacrifice is the highest virtue which can be found in man. I will add, that in this condition of the world, paradoxical as the assertion may be, the conscious ability to do without happiness gives the best prospect of realising such happiness as is attainable. For

nothing except that consciousness can raise a person above the chances of life, by making him feel that, let fate and fortune do their worst, they have not power to subdue him: which, once felt, frees him from excess of anxiety concerning the evils of life, and enables him, like many a Stoic in the worst times of the Roman Empire, to cultivate in tranquillity the sources of satisfaction accessible to him, without concerning himself about the uncertainty of their duration, any more than about their inevitable end.

Meanwhile, let utilitarians never cease to claim the morality of self devotion as a possession which belongs by as good a right to them, as either to the Stoic or to the Transcendentalist. The utilitarian morality does recognise in human beings the power of sacrificing their own greatest good for the good of others. It only refuses to admit that the sacrifice is itself a good. A sacrifice which does not increase, or tend to increase, the sum total of happiness, it considers as wasted. The only self-renunciation which it applauds, is devotion to the happiness, or to some of the means of happiness, of others; either of mankind collectively, or of individuals within the limits imposed by the collective interests of mankind.

Chapter 5: On the Connexion Between Justice and Utility.

. . . Having thus endeavoured to determine the distinctive elements which enter into the composition of the idea of justice, we are ready to enter on the inquiry, whether the feeling, which accompanies the idea, is attached to it by a special dispensation of nature, or whether it could have grown up, by any known laws, out of the idea itself; and in particular, whether it can have originated in considerations of general expediency.

I conceive that the sentiment itself does not arise from anything which would commonly, or correctly, be termed an idea of expediency; but that though the sentiment does not, whatever is moral in it does.

We have seen that the two essential ingredients in the sentiment of justice are, the desire to punish a person who has done harm, and the knowledge or belief that there is some definite individual or individuals to whom harm has been done.

Now it appears to me, that the desire to punish a person who has done harm to some individual is a spontaneous outgrowth from two sentiments, both in the highest degree natural, and which either are or resemble instincts; the impulse of self-defence, and the feeling of sympathy.

It is natural to resent, and to repel or retaliate, any harm done or attempted against ourselves, or against those with whom we sympathise. The origin of this sentiment it is not necessary here to discuss. Whether it be an instinct or a result of intelligence, it is, we know, common to all animal nature; for every animal tries to hurt those who have hurt, or who it thinks are about to hurt, itself or its young. Human beings, on this point, only differ from other animals in two particulars. First, in being capable of sympathising, not solely with their offspring, or, like some of the more noble animals, with some superior animal who is kind to them, but with all human, and even with all sentient, beings. Secondly, in having a more developed intelligence, which gives a wider range to the whole of their sentiments, whether self-regarding or sympathetic. By virtue of his superior intelligence, even apart from his superior range of sympathy, a human being is capable of apprehending a community of interest between himself and the human society of which he forms a part, such that any conduct which threatens the security of the society generally, is threatening to his own, and calls forth his instinct (if instinct it be) of self-defence. The same superiority of intelligence joined to the power of sympathising with human beings generally, enables him to attach himself to the collective idea of his tribe, his country, or mankind, in such a manner that any act hurtful to them, raises his instinct of sympathy, and urges him to resistance.

The sentiment of justice, in that one of its elements which consists of the desire to punish, is thus, I conceive, the natural feeling of retaliation or vengeance, rendered by intellect and sympathy applicable to those injuries, that is, to those hurts, which wound us through, or in common with, society at large. This sentiment, in itself, has nothing moral in it; what is moral is, the exclusive subordination of it to the social sympathies, so as to wait on and obey their call. For the natural feeling would make us resent indiscriminately whatever any one does that is disagreeable to us; but when moralised by the social feeling, it only acts in the directions conformable to the general good: just persons resenting a hurt to society, though not otherwise a hurt to themselves, and not resenting a hurt to themselves, however painful, unless it be of the kind which society has a common interest with them in the repression of.

It is no objection against this doctrine to say, that when we feel our sentiment of justice outraged, we are not thinking of society at large, or of any collective interest, but only of the individual case. It is common enough certainly, though the reverse of commendable, to feel resentment merely because we have suffered pain; but a person whose resentment is really a moral feeling, that is, who considers whether an act is blamable before he allows himself to resent it—such a person, though he may not say expressly to himself that he is standing up for the interest of society, certainly does feel that he is asserting a rule which is for the benefit of others as well as for his own. If he is not feeling this—if he is regarding the act solely as it affects him individually—he is not consciously just; he is not concerning himself about the justice of his actions. This is admitted even by anti-utilitarian moralists. When Kant (as before remarked) propounds as the fundamental principle of morals, "So act, that thy rule of conduct might be adopted as a law by all rational beings," he virtually acknowledges that the interest of mankind collectively, or at least of mankind indiscriminately, must be in the mind of the agent when conscientiously deciding on the morality of the act. Otherwise he uses words without a meaning: for, that a rule even of utter selfishness could not possibly be adopted by all rational beings—that there is any insuperable obstacle in the nature of things to its adoption—cannot be even plausibly maintained. To give any meaning to Kant's principle, the sense put upon it must be, that we ought to shape our conduct by a rule which all rational beings might adopt with benefit to their collective interest.

To recapitulate: the idea of justice supposes two things; a rule of conduct, and a sentiment which sanctions the rule. The first must be supposed common to all mankind, and intended for their good. The other (the sentiment) is a desire that punishment may be suffered by those who infringe the rule. There is involved, in addition, the conception of some definite person who suffers by the infringement; whose rights (to use the expression appropriated to the case) are violated by it. And the sentiment of justice appears to me to be, the animal desire to repel or retaliate a hurt or damage to oneself, or to those with whom one sympathises, widened so as to include all persons, by the human capacity of enlarged sympathy, and the human conception of intelligent self-interest. From the latter elements, the feeling derives its morality; from the former, its peculiar impressiveness, and energy of self-assertion.

I have, throughout, treated the idea of a right residing in the injured person, and violated by the injury, not as a separate element in the composition of the idea and sentiment, but as one of the forms in which the other two elements clothe themselves. These elements are a hurt to some assignable person or persons on the one hand, and a demand for punishment on the other. An examination of our own minds, I think, will show, that these two things include all that we mean when we speak of violation of a right. When we call anything a person's right, we mean that he has a valid claim on society to protect him in the possession of it, either by the force of law, or by that of education and opinion. If he has what we consider a sufficient claim, on whatever account, to have something guaranteed to him by society, we say that he has a right to it. If we desire to prove that anything does not belong to him by right, we think this done as soon as it is admitted that society ought not to take measures for securing it to him, but should leave him to chance, or to his own exertions. Thus, a person is said to have a right to what he can earn in fair professional competition; because society ought not to allow any other person to hinder him from endeavouring to earn in that manner as much as he can. But he has not a right to three hundred a-year, though he may happen to be earning it; because society is not called on to provide that he shall earn that sum. On the contrary, if he owns ten thousand pounds three per cent stock, he has a right to three hundred a-year; because society has come under an obligation to provide him with an income of that amount.

To have a right, then, is, I conceive, to have something which society ought to defend me in the possession of. If the objector goes on to ask, why it ought? I can give him no other reason than general utility. If that expression does not seem to convey a sufficient feeling of the strength of the obligation, nor to account for the peculiar energy of the feeling, it is because there goes to the composition of the sentiment, not a rational only, but also an animal element, the thirst for retaliation; and this thirst derives its intensity, as well as its moral justification, from the extraordinarily important and impressive kind of utility which is concerned. The interest involved is that of security, to every one's feelings the most vital of all interests. All other earthly benefits are needed by one person, not needed by another; and many of them can, if necessary, be cheerfully foregone, or replaced by something else; but security no human being can possibly do without; on it we depend for all our immunity from evil, and for the whole value of all and every good, beyond the passing moment; since nothing but the gratification of the instant could be of any worth to us, if we could be deprived of anything the next instant by whoever was momentarily stronger than ourselves. Now this most indispensable of all necessaries, after physical nutriment, cannot be had, unless the machinery for providing it is kept unintermittedly in active play. Our notion, therefore, of the claim we have on our fellow-creatures to join in making safe for us the very groundwork of our existence, gathers feelings around it so much more intense than those concerned in any of the more common cases of utility, that the difference in degree (as is often the case in psychology) becomes a real difference in kind. The claim assumes that character of absoluteness, that apparent infinity, and incommensurability with all other considerations, which constitute the distinction between the feeling of right and wrong and that of ordinary expediency and inexpediency. The feelings concerned are so powerful, and we count so positively on finding a responsive feeling in others (all being alike interested), that ought and should grow into must, and recognised indispensability becomes a moral necessity, analogous to physical, and often not inferior to it in binding force.

If the preceding analysis, or something resembling it, be not the correct account of the notion of justice; if justice be totally independent of utility, and be a standard per se, which the mind can recognise by simple introspection of itself; it is hard to understand why that internal oracle is so ambiguous, and why so many things appear either just or unjust, according to the light in which they are regarded.

We are continually informed that Utility is an uncertain standard, which every different person interprets differently, and that there is no safety but in the immutable, ineffaceable, and unmistakable dictates of justice, which carry their evidence in themselves, and are independent of the fluctuations of opinion. One would suppose from this that on questions of justice there could be no controversy; that if we take that for our rule, its application to any given case could leave us in as little doubt as a mathematical demonstration. So far is this from being the fact, that there is as much difference of opinion, and as much discussion, about what is just, as about what is useful to society. Not only have different nations and individuals different notions of justice, but in the mind of one and the same individual, justice is not some one rule, principle, or maxim, but many, which do not always coincide in their dictates, and in choosing between which, he is guided either by some extraneous standard, or by his own personal predilections.

For instance, there are some who say, that it is unjust to punish any one for the sake of example to others; that punishment is just, only when intended for the good of the sufferer himself. Others maintain the extreme reverse, contending that to punish persons who have attained years of discretion, for their own benefit, is despotism and injustice, since if the matter at issue is solely their own good, no one has a right to control their own judgment of it; but that they may justly be punished to prevent evil to others, this being the exercise of the legitimate right of self-defence. Mr. Owen, again, affirms that it is unjust to punish at all; for the criminal did not make his own character; his education, and the circumstances which surrounded him, have made him a criminal, and for these he is not responsible. All these opinions are extremely plausible; and so long as the question is argued as one of justice simply, without going down to the principles which lie under justice and are the source of its authority, I am unable to see how any of these reasoners can be refuted. For in truth every one of the three builds upon rules of justice confessedly true. The first appeals to the acknowledged injustice of singling out an individual, and making a sacrifice, without his consent, for other people's benefit. The second relies on the acknowledged justice of self-defence, and the admitted injustice of forcing one person to conform to another's notions of what constitutes his good. The Owenite invokes the admitted principle, that it is unjust to punish any one for what he cannot help. Each is triumphant so long as he is not compelled to take into consideration any other maxims of justice than the one he has selected; but as soon as their several maxims are brought face to face, each disputant seems to have exactly as much to say for himself as the others. No one of them can carry out his own notion of justice without trampling upon another equally binding. These are difficulties; they have always been felt to be such; and many devices have been invented to turn rather than to overcome them. As a refuge from the last of the three, men imagined what they called the freedom of the will; fancying that they could not justify punishing a man whose will is in a thoroughly hateful state, unless it be supposed to have come into that state through no influence of anterior circumstances. To escape from the other difficulties, a favourite contrivance has been the fiction of a contract, whereby at some unknown period all the members of society engaged to obey the laws, and consented to be punished for any disobedience to them, thereby giving to their legislators the right, which it is assumed they would not otherwise have had, of punishing them, either for their own good or for that of society. This happy thought was considered to get rid of the whole difficulty, and to legitimate the infliction of punishment, in virtue of another received maxim of justice, *Volenti non fit injuria;* that is not unjust which is done with the consent of the person who is supposed to be hurt by it. I need hardly remark, that even if the consent were not a mere fiction, this maxim is not superior in authority to the others which it is brought in to supersede. It is, on the contrary, an instructive specimen of the loose and irregular manner in which supposed principles of justice grow up. This particular one evidently came into use as a help to the coarse exigencies of courts of law, which are sometimes obliged to be content with very uncertain presumptions, on account of the greater evils which would often arise from any attempt on their part to cut finer. But even courts of law are not able to adhere consistently to the maxim, for they allow voluntary engagements to be set aside on the ground of fraud, and sometimes on that of mere mistake or misinformation.

Again, when the legitimacy of inflicting punishment is admitted, how many conflicting conceptions of justice come to light in discussing the proper apportionment of punishments to offences. No rule on the subject recommends itself so strongly to the primitive and spontaneous sentiment of justice, as the *lex talionis*, an eye for an eye and a tooth for a tooth. Though this principle of the Jewish and of the Mahometan law has been generally abandoned in Europe as a practical maxim, there is, I suspect, in most minds, a secret hankering after it; and when retribution accidentally falls on an offender in that precise shape, the general feeling of satisfaction evinced bears witness how natural is the sentiment to which this repayment in kind is acceptable. With many, the test of justice in penal infliction is that the punishment should be proportioned to the offence;

meaning that it should be exactly measured by the moral guilt of the culprit (whatever be their standard for measuring moral guilt): the consideration, what amount of punishment is necessary to deter from the offence, having nothing to do with the question of justice, in their estimation: while there are others to whom that consideration is all in all; who maintain that it is not just, at least for man, to inflict on a fellow creature, whatever may be his offences, any amount of suffering beyond the least that will suffice to prevent him from repeating, and others from imitating, his misconduct.

To take another example from a subject already once referred to. In a co-operative industrial association, is it just or not that talent or skill should give a title to superior remuneration? On the negative side of the question it is argued, that whoever does the best he can, deserves equally well, and ought not in justice to be put in a position of inferiority for no fault of his own; that superior abilities have already advantages more than enough, in the admiration they excite, the personal influence they command, and the internal sources of satisfaction attending them, without adding to these a superior share of the world's goods; and that society is bound in justice rather to make compensation to the less favoured, for this unmerited inequality of advantages, than to aggravate it. On the contrary side it is contended, that society receives more from the more efficient labourer; that his services being more useful, society owes him a larger return for them; that a greater share of the joint result is actually his work, and not to allow his claim to it is a kind of robbery; that if he is only to receive as much as others, he can only be justly required to produce as much, and to give a smaller amount of time and exertion, proportioned to his superior efficiency. Who shall decide between these appeals to conflicting principles of justice? Justice has in this case two sides to it, which it is impossible to bring into harmony, and the two disputants have chosen opposite sides; the one looks to what it is just that the individual should receive, the other to what it is just that the community should give. Each, from his own point of view, is unanswerable; and any choice between them, on grounds of justice, must be perfectly arbitrary. Social utility alone can decide the preference.

How many, again, and how irreconcilable, are the standards of justice to which reference is made in discussing the repartition of taxation. One opinion is, that payment to the State should be in numerical proportion to pecuniary means. Others think that justice dictates what they term graduated taxation; taking a higher percentage from those who have more to spare. In point of natural justice a strong case might be made for disregarding means altogether, and taking the same absolute sum (whenever it could be got) from every one: as the subscribers to a mess, or to a club, all pay the same sum for the same privileges, whether they can all equally afford it or not. Since the protection (it might be said) of law and government is afforded to, and is equally required by all, there is no injustice in making all buy it at the same price. It is reckoned justice, not injustice, that a dealer should charge to all customers the same price for the same article, not a price varying according to their means of payment. This doctrine, as applied to taxation, finds no advocates, because it conflicts so strongly with man's feelings of humanity and of social expediency; but the principle of justice which it invokes is as true and as binding as those which can be appealed to against it. Accordingly it exerts a tacit influence on the line of defence employed for other modes of assessing taxation. People feel obliged to argue that the State does more for the rich than for the poor, as a justification for its taking more from them: though this is in reality not true, for the rich would be far better able to protect themselves, in the absence of law or government, than the poor, and indeed would probably be successful in converting the poor into their slaves. Others, again, so far defer to the same conception of justice, as to maintain that all should pay an equal capitation tax for the protection of their persons (these being of equal value to all), and an unequal tax for the protection of their property, which is unequal. To this others reply, that the all of one man is as valuable to him as the all of an-

other. From these confusions there is no other mode of extrication than the utilitarian.

Is, then the difference between the just and the Expedient a merely imaginary distinction? Have mankind been under a delusion in thinking that justice is a more sacred thing than policy, and that the latter ought only to be listened to after the former has been satisfied? By no means. The exposition we have given of the nature and origin of the sentiment, recognises a real distinction; and no one of those who profess the most sublime contempt for the consequences of actions as an element in their morality, attaches more importance to the distinction than I do. While I dispute the pretensions of any theory which sets up an imaginary standard of justice not grounded on utility, I account the justice which is grounded on utility to be the chief part, and incomparably the most sacred and binding part, of all morality. Justice is a name for certain classes of moral rules, which concern the essentials of human well-being more nearly, and are therefore of more absolute obligation, than any other rules for the guidance of life; and the notion which we have found to be of the essence of the idea of justice, that of a right residing in an individual implies and testifies to this more binding obligation.

The moral rules which forbid mankind to hurt one another (in which we must never forget to include wrongful interference with each other's freedom) are more vital to human well-being than any maxims, however important, which only point out the best mode of managing some department of human affairs. They have also the peculiarity, that they are the main element in determining the whole of the social feelings of mankind. It is their observance which alone preserves peace among human beings: if obedience to them were not the rule, and disobedience the exception, every one would see in every one else an enemy, against whom he must be perpetually guarding himself. What is hardly less important, these are the precepts which mankind have the strongest and the most direct inducements for impressing upon one another. By merely giving to each other prudential instruction or exhortation, they may gain, or think they gain, nothing: in inculcating on each other the duty of positive beneficence they have an unmistakable interest, but far less in degree: a person may possibly not need the benefits of others; but he always needs that they should not do him hurt. Thus the moralities which protect every individual from being harmed by others, either directly or by being hindered in his freedom of pursuing his own good, are at once those which he himself has most at heart, and those which he has the strongest interest in publishing and enforcing by word and deed. It is by a person's observance of these that his fitness to exist as one of the fellowship of human beings is tested and decided; for on that depends his being a nuisance or not to those with whom he is in contact. Now it is these moralities primarily which compose the obligations of justice. The most marked cases of injustice, and those which give the tone to the feeling of repugnance which characterises the sentiment, are acts of wrongful aggression, or wrongful exercise of power over some one; the next are those which consist in wrongfully withholding from him something which is his due; in both cases, inflicting on him a positive hurt, either in the form of direct suffering, or of the privation of some good which he had reasonable ground, either of a physical or of a social kind, for counting upon.

The same powerful motives which command the observance of these primary moralities, enjoin the punishment of those who violate them; and as the impulses of self-defence, of defence of others, and of vengeance, are all called forth against such persons, retribution, or evil for evil, becomes closely connected with the sentiment of justice, and is universally included in the idea. Good for good is also one of the dictates of justice; and this, though its social utility is evident, and though it carries with it a natural human feeling, has not at first sight that obvious connection with hurt or injury, which, existing in the most elementary cases of just and unjust, is the source of the characteristic intensity of the sentiment. But the connection, though less obvious, is not less real. He who accepts benefits, and denies a return of them when needed, inflicts a real hurt, by disappointing one of the most natural and reasonable of expectations, and one which he must at least tacitly have encouraged, otherwise the benefits would seldom have been conferred. The important rank, among human evils and wrongs, of the disappointment of expectation, is shown in the fact that it constitutes the principal criminality of two such highly immoral acts as a breach of friendship and a breach of promise. Few hurts which human beings can sustain are greater, and none wound more, than when that on which they habitually and with full assurance relied, fails them in the hour of need; and few wrongs are greater than this mere withholding of good; none excite more resentment, either in the person suffering, or in a sympathising spectator. The principle, therefore, of giving to each what they deserve, that is, good for good as well as evil for evil, is not only included within the idea of justice as we have defined it, but is a proper object of that intensity of sentiment, which places the just, in human estimation, above the simply Expedient.

Most of the maxims of justice current in the world, and commonly appealed to in its transactions, are simply instrumental to carrying into effect the principles of justice which we have now spoken of. That a person is only responsible for what he has done voluntarily, or could voluntarily have avoided; that it is unjust to condemn any person unheard; that the punishment ought to be proportioned to the offence, and the like, are maxims intended to prevent the just principle of evil for evil from being perverted to the infliction of evil without that justification. The greater part of these common maxims have come into use from the practice of courts of justice, which have been naturally led to a more complete recognition and elaboration than was likely to suggest itself to others, of the rules necessary to enable them to fulfil their double function, of inflicting punishment when due, and of awarding to each person his right.

That first of judicial virtues, impartiality, is an obligation of justice, partly for the reason last mentioned; as being a necessary condition of the fulfilment of the other obligations of justice. But this is not the only source of the exalted rank, among human obligations, of those maxims of equality and impartiality, which, both in popular estimation and in that of the most enlightened, are included among the precepts of justice. In one point of view, they may be considered as corollaries from the principles already laid down. If it is a duty to do to each according to his deserts, returning good for good as well as repressing evil by evil, it necessarily follows that we should treat all equally well (when no higher duty forbids) who have deserved equally well of us, and that society should treat all equally well who have deserved equally well of it, that is, who have deserved equally well absolutely. This is the highest abstract standard of social and distributive justice; towards which all institutions, and the efforts of all virtuous citizens, should be made in the utmost possible degree to converge. But this great moral duty rests upon a still deeper foundation, being a direct emanation from the first principle of morals, and not a mere logical corollary from secondary or derivative doctrines. It is involved in the very meaning of Utility, or the Greatest Happiness Principle. That principle is a mere form of words without rational signification, unless one person's happiness, supposed equal in degree (with the proper allowance made for kind), is counted for exactly as much as another's. Those conditions being supplied, Bentham's dictum, "everybody to count for one, nobody for more than one," might be written under the principle of utility as an explanatory commentary.[1] The equal claim of everybody to happiness in the estimation of the moralist and the legislator, involves an equal claim to all the means of happiness, except in so far as the inevitable conditions of human life, and the general interest, in which that of every individual is included, set limits to the maxim; and those limits ought to be strictly construed. As every other maxim of justice, so this is by no means applied or held applicable universally; on the contrary, as I have already remarked, it bends to every person's ideas of social expediency. But in whatever case it is deemed applicable at all, it is held to be the dictate of justice. All persons are deemed to have a right to equality of treatment, except when some recognised social expediency requires the reverse. And hence all social inequalities which have ceased to be considered expedient, assume the character not of simple inexpediency, but of injustice, and appear so tyrannical, that people are apt to wonder how they ever could have been tolerated; forgetful that they themselves perhaps tolerate other inequalities under an equally mistaken notion of expediency, the correction of which would make that which they approve seem quite as monstrous as what they have at last learnt to condemn. The entire history of social improvement has been a series of transitions, by which one custom or institution after another, from being a supposed primary necessity of social existence, has passed into the rank of a universally stigmatised injustice and tyranny. So it has been with the distinctions of slaves and freemen, nobles and serfs, patricians and plebeians; and so it will be, and in part already is, with the aristocracies of colour, race, and sex.

Note

1. This implication, in the first principle of the utilitarian scheme, of perfect impartiality between persons, is regarded by Mr. Herbert Spencer (in his *Social Statics*) as a disproof of the pretensions of utility to be a sufficient guide to right; since (he says) the principle of utility presupposes the anterior principle, that everybody has an equal right to happiness. It may be more correctly described as supposing that equal amounts of happiness are equally desirable, whether felt by the same or by different persons. This, however, is not a pre-supposition; not a premise needful to support the principle of utility, but the very principle itself; for what is the principle of utility, if it be not that "happiness" and "desirable" are synonymous terms? If there is any anterior principle implied, it can be no other than this, that the truths of arithmetic are applicable to the valuation of happiness, as of all other measurable quantities.

   [Mr. Herbert Spencer, in a private communication on the subject of the preceding Note, objects to being considered an opponent of utilitarianism, and states that he regards happiness as the ultimate end of morality; but deems that end only partially attainable by empirical generalisations from the observed results of conduct, and completely attainable only by deducing, from the laws of life and the conditions of existence, what kinds of action necessarily tend to produce happiness, and what kinds to produce unhappiness. What the exception of the word "necessarily," I have no dissent to express from this doctrine; and (omitting that word) I am not aware that any modern advocate of utilitarianism is of a different opinion. Bentham, certainly, to whom in the *Social Statics* Mr. Spencer particularly referred, is, least of all writers, chargeable with unwillingness to deduce the effect of actions on happiness from the laws of human nature and the universal conditions of human life. The common charge against him is of relying too exclusively upon such deductions, and declining altogether to be bound by the generalisations from specific experience which Mr. Spencer thinks that utilitarians generally confine themselves to. My own opinion (and, as I collect, Mr. Spencer's) is, that in ethics, as in all other branches of scientific study, the consilience of the results of both these processes, each corroborating and verifying the other, is requisite to give to any general proposition the kind degree of evidence which constitutes scientific proof.]

Adapted from: John Stuart Mill, *Utilitarianism, Liberty, and Representative Government,* introduced by A. D. Lindsay, pp. 8–21, 62–79. E. P. Dutton and Co., 1951. ✦

34

J. S. Mill on Freedom and Power

Bruce Baum

In his *Autobiography* John Stuart Mill says that his essay *On Liberty* "is likely to survive longer than anything else that I have written . . . , because . . . [it is] a kind of philosophic text-book of a single truth . . . : the importance, to man and society, of a large variety in types of character, and of giving full freedom to human nature to expand itself in innumerable and conflicting directions."[1] That essay has had an enormous influence on subsequent thinking about individual freedom, but also a rather paradoxical one because many subsequent writers misleadingly have cast it as a classic statement of the "negative" view of freedom. R. H. Hutton stated in an 1859 review that "Mill's essay regards 'liberty' from first to last in its negative rather than its positive significance."[2] Likewise, J. C. Rees, one of Mill's most influential contemporary interpreters, says, "Mill is generally regarded . . . as a leading exponent of the negative idea of liberty—'liberty is just the absence of restraint'—which prevailed in England until the Idealists."[3]

According to the negative conception, the presence of freedom is marked, as Quentin Skinner says, "by the absence of some element of constraint that inhibits the agent concerned from being able to act independently in pursuit of his [or her] chosen ends."[4] Notably, this view implies that there is an *inverse relationship between freedom and power* such that freedom is diminished whenever, and insofar as, power is exercised.[5] Power is understood from this perspective as essentially restrictive or repressive in its effects.

Like freedom, then, it is conceived in negative terms.

At first glance, these appear to be accurate readings. Mill says, for example, that his subject in *On Liberty* is "Civil, or Social Liberty: the nature and limits of the power which can be legitimately exercised by society over the individual."[6] Similarly, he says in *The Subjection of Women*, "The love of power and the love of liberty are in eternal antagonism."[7] Yet a more careful reading reveals that Mill powerfully challenges the negative view of freedom as merely the absence of external constraints on people's efforts to satisfy their desires.[8] It also shows that he offers an important corrective to the view that freedom and power are inversely related. In sum, Mill's conception of freedom emphasizes the necessity of autonomy, a "variety of situations" and possibilities, and means and opportunities for self-development and self-government. By analyzing freedom in light of power struggles concerning working class and women's suffrage, women's rights more generally, socialism and the co-operative movement, British colonialism, public education, and religious diversity, he conceptualizes the freedom of individuals with respect to the political, economic, educational, gender, and family relationships situating them. He shows that freedom and power both have positive and negative aspects, thereby illuminating the complementarity of freedom and power.

Several recent interpreters have noted "positive" aspects of Mill's view of freedom, but none has directly addressed his rich view of the interplay of freedom and power.[9] I argue that Mill's conception of freedom is best understood, at base, in terms of the capacity of persons for self-determination and self-government. Mill consistently attends to ways in which the power of some persons *over* others limits the latter's freedom; yet he also highlights four ways in which the exercise of freedom is integrally related rather than opposed to the exercise of power. First, he maintains that having "power over our own character[s]" is a necessary condition of our being fully free.[10] This refers to our capacity for individuality or autonomy, the capacity reflectively to formulate and pursue

438

our own desires and purposes. Second, Mill maintains that freedom requires the presence of the material resources and opportunities that enable us to realize our aims and purposes. Third, Mill conceives of "mental freedom" and autonomy not in all-or-nothing terms, but rather as capacities that people develop to greater or lesser degrees, basically as "developmental powers."[11] In short, we are more or less autonomous and, thus, more or less free overall—all other things being equal—to the *degree* that we develop our capacity to pursue reflectively our more important purposes. At the same time, Mill argues that the extent to which individuals develop autonomy depends upon the extent to which the various power relationships situating them—i.e., educational, political, economic, gender, and family relations—cultivate their capacities for autonomy. Fourth, despite Mill's emphasis on the "sovereignty" of the individual in "self-regarding" matters (OL [*On Liberty*], 224), he does not conceive of individual freedom solely in terms of the actions of independent individuals. Freedom, in his view, also involves practices of democratic self-government that enable individuals to share in the collective decisionmaking with respect to key power relationships that govern their lives at home, at work, and as citizens. In Mill's view, then, freedom encompasses both of the two kinds of questions that Isaiah Berlin associates with "negative" and "positive" senses of freedom, respectively: "What am I free to do or be?" and "Who governs me?"[12]

There is, however, one aspect of the interplay between freedom and power that Mill fails to address adequately: the relationship between freedom, power, and culture. Mill presents a compelling account of practices of freedom that emphasize reflective choice, self-realization, and self-government. This view has wide resonance in modern societies—especially modern Western societies—where such practices are basic to the idea of a free person. Yet Mill underestimates the givenness of some religious and cultural identities and wrongly presents his notion of people as autonomous "choosers" as an essential feature of all practices of freedom. Consequently, he fails to appreciate that

freedom of action for some people is more a matter of pursuing their religious or cultural commitments rather than of *choosing* their religious or cultural identities.

I will begin by explaining how Mill distinguishes between "freedom" and "liberty." This distinction is important to his view of freedom. Then I will discuss his view of how freedom involves autonomy and how different degrees of autonomy entail different degrees of freedom. Next I will address his view of the interplay between freedom and power, paying special attention to his account of the interplay of freedom, power, and culture.

I. Freedom and Liberty

Mill never systematically articulates his conception of freedom. Therefore, to adequately grasp his view we need to look beyond the well known "principle of liberty" he articulates in *On Liberty* to clarify his analytically distinct notion of what it means for persons to be free.[13] As G. W. Smith points out, this requires that we consider Mill's account of "free will" in *A System of Logic* and *An Examination of Sir William Hamilton's Philosophy* to comprehend his underlying view of free agency.[14] It also requires us to reckon with his analysis of the freedom of individuals with respect to the political, economic, educational, gender, and family relationships situating them in such works as *Principles of Political Economy, Considerations on Representative Government*, and *The Subjection of Women*.

Mill's conception of freedom is often confused with his "principle of liberty." With the principle he prescribes a sphere of "self-regarding" choices and actions with respect to which the freedom of individuals ought not be restricted. That is, the liberty principle addresses the issue of when individual freedom should and should not be restricted.[15] By contrast, his *conception* of freedom is his view of what freedom means and entails. Mistaking the principle of liberty for Mill's conception of freedom gives rise to three misconceptions about his view of freedom. First, it conveys the false impression that Mill conceives of freedom in essentially negative terms, with the presence of freedom marked by the *absence* of constraints or restrictions on people's efforts to satisfy their existing desires, whatever these are. Second, it neglects important domains in which freedom, according to Mill, consists of sharing with others in practices of collective self-government rather than simply the choices and actions of independent individuals. Third, it suggests that Mill, like many other liberal theorists, conceives of freedom and power as inversely related rather than complementary but sometimes conflicting.

Mill employs the concepts "freedom" and "liberty" distinctly, in ways that correspond to the difference between his principle of liberty and his conception of freedom. Since he does not explicitly distinguish between them it would be wrong to overemphasize this distinction.[16] Still, he generally uses them in ways that capture the connotations stemming from their different histories, etymologies, and connotations.[17] Mill typically uses "liberty" and "individual liberty" to discuss more bounded practices of freedom. As Hanna Fenichel Pitkin notes, "Liberty implies an ongoing structure of controls, whether of external laws and regulations or the genteel self-control of the liberal gentleman. That, no doubt is part of its appeal to liberals and . . . one reason why John Stuart Mill wrote his essay 'On Liberty' rather than on freedom."[18] Mill is articulating what he calls "the principle of individual liberty," then, when he says in *On Liberty*, "The only freedom that deserves the name, is that of pursuing our own good in our own way, *so long as we do not attempt to deprive others of theirs, or impede their efforts to obtain it*" (OL, 293, 226, emphasis added). This freedom is rightfully bounded by our duties to others, including the respect we owe to the rights of others (OL, 293, 225–26). It refers to the freedom of action to which each mature individual is entitled *by right* (OL, 224). Therefore, Mill's "principle of liberty" cannot be redescribed as a "principle of freedom" without distorting his meaning.

Mill typically uses "freedom" more broadly to encompass a wider range of practices of individual self-determination and collective self-government.[19] He conveys the gist of his conception of freedom in a few remarks in *The Subjection of Women*. He conceives of the "freedom of action of the individual" as "the liberty of each to govern his own conduct by his own feelings of duty, and by such laws and social constraints as his conscience can subscribe to" (SW [*The Subjection of Women*], 336).[20] This involves not just the choices and actions of independent individuals, but also practices of democratic self-government that enable individuals to share in regulating their affairs within key power relationships that govern their lives. This emphasis on mutual self-government is a central feature of Mill's view of political freedom. Thus, he asks in *The Subjection*, "What citizen of a free country would listen to any offers of good and skillful administration, in return for the abdication of freedom?" (SW, 337).

Mill further clarifies his understanding of freedom when he identifies the most significant obstacles to freedom. He recognizes, of course, the significance of legal restraints (OL, 223, 276). But, as I will explain presently, he also identifies three other significant constraints: psychological constraints upon people's "mental freedom" and autonomy that limit their capacity to formulate desires and life plans of their own; a lack of material resources and opportunities for people to pursue their chosen occupations and ways of living; and the absence of opportunities for individuals to share in self-government with respect to household, workplace, and political institutions that govern their lives.

II. Freedom, Autonomy, and Individuality

The first aspect of Mill's view of the interplay of freedom and power concerns what he calls "the power of self-formation," or "power over our own character" (L [*System of Logic*], 842, 841). This notion is closely linked to the difference between his notion of the freedom of "pursuing our own good in our own way" and the empiricist and negative conception of freedom that has been dominant within the Anglo-American liberal tradition (OL, 226).[21] In the latter conception, the presence of freedom is construed merely in terms of the absence of external impediments on an agent's doing whatever she or he wants to do; the agent's existing desires are taken as given.[22] One implication of this view is that all laws by definition limit freedom because they either require or prohibit certain actions and thereby frustrate certain desires. Most proponents of this view—sometimes called "negative liberty"— acknowledge that some such constraints are desirable, though, since people must not be free to do anything they might want to do.

For Mill, by contrast, the presence of freedom is quite different from merely the absence of external impediments to satisfying our unreflective desires, or doing as we please. Mill's conception of freedom entails notions of self-development and self-mastery "according to which a free agent is someone who is capable of acknowledging responsibility for his desire as 'his own' because he, rather than others, has formed the character from which they spring."[23] Mill maintains that individual freedom is often restricted beyond the reach of the law by "the moral coercive of public opinion," a form of social power that can lead to a "social tyranny more formidable than many kinds of political oppression" (OL, 223, 220).[24] "Society can and does execute its own mandates," he says, through the powers of education and public opinion (OL, 220, 282). This kind of restraint is particularly insidious "since . . . it leaves fewer means of escape [than other restraints], penetrating much more deep, into the details of social life, and enslaving the soul itself" (OL, 220). It restricts people's freedom of action by stifling their mental freedom. Mill is concerned not just with the more obvious kinds of coercion or compulsion like "peer pressure" or public reproach, but also with a more thoroughgoing way that "society has now fairly got the better of individuality" (OL, 264). As he explains in *On Liberty*,

the danger which threatens human nature is not the excess, but the deficiency, of personal impulses and preferences. . . . Not only in what concerns others, but in what concerns themselves, the individual or the family do not ask themselves— what do I prefer? or what would suit my character and disposition? or, what would allow the best and highest in me to have fair play and enable it to grow and thrive? They ask themselves, what is suitable to my position? what is usually done by persons of my station and pecuniary circumstances?. . . I do not mean that they choose what is customary in preference to what suits their own inclination. It does not occur to them to have any inclination, except for what is customary. Thus the *mind itself is bowed to the yoke:* even in what people do for pleasure, conformity is the first thing thought of; they like in crowds; they exercise choice only among things commonly done: peculiarity of taste, eccentricity of conduct, are equally shunned with crimes: *until by dint of not following their own nature they have no nature to follow:* their human capacities are withered and starved: they become incapable of . . . any opinions or feelings of home growth, or properly their own. (OL, 264–5, emphasis added)

Mill regards the power of education and opinion to shape human character as everpresent and unavoidable features of society (OL, 282).[25] Therefore, the mere presence of such power is no cause for concern. Problems arise, though, when the powers of education and popular opinion operate to undermine people's capacities to formulate and pursue aims and purposes "properly their own." When this happens people are unfree with respect to their expressed desires and objectives. He makes this point emphatically in an 1850 letter to *The Leader* responding to a critic who misconstrued his warnings in *Principles of Political Economy* about the threat that "communistic" reforms pose to freedom. Mill explains that his concern is not that a communistic system would make people's lives "inane and monotonous" by freeing them from want and hunger. *This* freedom, he says, "is a good in every sense of the word."[26] His chief concern is the prospect of increased social tyranny. He says that the "yoke of conformity" would become more severe in cooperative communities if "people would be compelled to live as it pleased others, not as it pleased themselves." He adds, moreover, that this kind of "bondage" is already a problem in existing capitalist societies, even among the rich: "They do not cultivate and follow opinions, preferences, or tastes of their own, nor live otherwise than in the manner appointed by the world for persons of their class. Their lives are inane and monotonous because (in short) they are not free, because though they are able to live as pleases themselves, their minds are bent to an external yoke."[27] For Mill, then, people who lack the capacity to conceive of desires and life plans that are "properly their own" are not really self-determining, even when they have sufficient resources and opportunities "to live as pleases themselves." Such persons have some desires and inclinations, but these are not "of home growth, or properly their own" (OL, 264–65).[28]

Thus Mill's conception of freedom differs from the empiricist negative view because he insists that the issue of *why* people desire what they desire is indispensable for assessing the extent of their freedom.[29] For Mill, the freedom of "pursuing our own good in our own way" requires what he calls "mental freedom," and what is now commonly called *autonomy:* the capacity of persons reflectively to pursue beliefs, desires, and purposes that are "properly their own" (OL, 246, 265).

Mill articulates his view of free action most fully in *A System of Logic* where his chief concern is with the philosophical problem of "liberty and necessity." This has led some interpreters, notably J. C. Rees, to insist that this analysis has no bearing on his view of social and political freedom. Rees says, "No conclusions about the free-will problem entail any particular theory of civil or political liberty. Questions about human actions being determined by unalterable laws are not questions about legal or social restraints."[30] As evidence that Mill agrees, Rees cites Mill's comment that his subject in *On Liberty* is not "the so-called Liberty of the Will so unfortunately opposed to the misnamed doctrine of Philosophical Necessity; but Civil, or Social Liberty" (OL, 217). Yet while Mill's focus on societal restraints to freedom in *On Liberty* is distinct from the issue of whether it is possible to speak of human freedom at all in a causally determined world, this point is not decisive. In fact, the way that Mill addresses the question

of free will is crucial to his broader conception of freedom.[31]

Mill's view of "free will" is close to what is now called a compatibilist view: he holds that human actions are causally determined, but they *can* be free.[32] People's desires, he says, flow from their *characters* rather than being spontaneously chosen, and their characters are produced by their circumstances. He conceives of the connection between circumstances, on the one hand, and character and desires, on the other, however, as a contingent one that leaves room for freedom. Thus, he criticizes followers of social reformer Robert Owen as fatalists for maintaining that a person's "character is formed *for* him and not *by* him; therefore his wishing that it had been formed differently is of no use; he has no power to alter it" (L [*System of Logic*], 840, Mill's emphasis). This is a "grand error," according to Mill, since a person has, "to a certain extent, a power to alter his character" (L, 840). He explains that a person's character is formed "by his circumstances . . . , but his own desire to mould it in a particular way is one of those circumstances, and by no means the least influential." His character, then, may be "formed *by* him as one of the intermediate agents" (L, 840, Mill's emphasis). Mill accepts the Owenite claim that we cannot directly "will to be different from what we are." He insists, though, that each of us has potential power to shape our own character that is similar to the indirect power that others have to shape our character by shaping our circumstances: "We, when our habits are not too inveterate, can, by similarly willing the requisite means, make ourselves different. . . . We are exactly as capable of making our own character, *if we will*, as others are of making it for us" (L, 841, Mill's emphasis).[33]

This response to the free will problem is fraught with internal tensions. Mill says that our *will* or desire to change our character is a necessary ingredient to our doing so, but that even *this* desire "comes to us either from external causes, or not at all" (L, 840). He therefore provides an equivocal response to determinism. Nonetheless, the way that he resolves this problem enriches his conception of freedom and illuminates the way in which autonomy is relevant to the issue of free will. By emphasizing our potential power of self-formation he illuminates conditions of autonomous agency under which we can claim our desires and purposes as *our own* in the relevant sense that is compatible with determinism.[34]

Mill's account of "our feeling of moral freedom" is particularly instructive in this regard. He says,

> A person feels morally free who feels that his habits or his temptations are not his masters, but he theirs: who even in yielding to them knows that he could resist.... It is of course necessary, to tender our consciousness of freedom complete, that we should succeed in making our character all we have hitherto attempted to make it; for if we have wished and not attained, we have, to that extent the power over our own character, we are not free. Or at least, we must feel that our wish, if not our character, is strong enough to conquer our character when the two are brought into conflict.... And hence it is said with truth, that none but a person of confirmed virtue is completely free. (L, 841)

Mill's wording here is deceptive. He appears to conceive of freedom, as Smith says, "as, essentially, the exercise of virtue."[35] Such a moralized view is deeply problematic and illiberal since it entails that people achieve true freedom only when they act "rightly" or in accordance with their "best self." On such a view, people could be compelled to "choose rightly" in the name of freedom.[36] Mill is better understood, however, as insisting on autonomy rather than the exercise of virtue as a condition of being "completely free." His key claim in this regard is that we are fully free agents *only to the extent that* we are able to exercise "power over our own character[s]" (L, 841). Thus, when he says "that none but a person of confirmed virtue is completely free," his point is that only such persons manifestly wield sufficient "power over [their] own character[s]" to ensure that their desires and purposes are formed by them rather than *for* them. Persons "of confirmed virtue" tend to exhibit the strength of will or character necessary to

pursue their more considered aims and purposes even when this requires them to forego their more transient desires.[37] In his view, then, being "completely free" is *directly* related to autonomous agency and only *indirectly* to virtuous action. He does not construe freedom *as* the exercise of virtue.

Mill further refines his view of free action in *On Liberty*. He contends that people are fully free only to the extent that their desires and impulses reflect "their own individual character[s]"—i.e., to the extent that they achieve "individuality" (OL, 262). He says, "Where, not the person's own character, but the traditions and customs of other people are the rule of conduct, there is wanting one of the principle ingredients of human happiness" (261). Later he equates attaining individuality with "having character": "A person whose desires and impulses are his own—are the expression of his own nature, as it has been developed and modified by his own culture—is said to have character. One whose desires and impulses are not his own, has no character, no more than a steam engine has character" (OL, 264). In turn, he regards having character as a necessary condition of the freedom to pursue our own mode of life.

The gist of Mill's argument is that we can justifiably claim our desires and purposes as "properly our own" only insofar as we reflectively choose them in light of our own characters and circumstances. He clarifies his view of the kind of critical reflection required in the course of criticizing unreflective obedience to custom. He says,

> To conform to custom, merely as custom, does not educate or develop in [a person] any of the qualities which are the distinctive endowment of a human being. The human faculties of perception, judgment, discriminative feeling, mental activity, and even moral preference, are exercised only in making a choice. *He who does anything because it is the custom, makes no choice.* He who lets the world, or his own portion of it, choose his plan of life for him, has no need of any other faculty than the ape-like one of imitation. (OL, 262, emphasis added)

This does not mean that we can never freely choose to do what is customary or conventional. It does entail, though, that we freely follow customs or conventions only when we do so after a process of critical reflection through which we self-consciously affirm the customs or conventions as our own.

Although the contemporary terminology of autonomy and heteronomy is foreign to Mill, these concepts refer to precisely the sorts of distinctions that Mill makes.[38] According to Mill, we are more fully free, all other things being equal, to the extent that we choose our aims, purposes, and life plans autonomously—i.e., through critical reflection upon the norms and traditions we confront. Only such autonomous agents are fully self-determining in the sense of *pursuing their own good in their own way*. In contrast, those who unquestioningly follow custom and those to whom it "does not occur . . . to have any inclination, except for what is customary" are *other*-directed rather than self-determining, heteronomous rather than autonomous. Their conduct is governed or directed by desires and inclinations that, as John Gray says, they have internalized from their "social and cultural environment without ever subjecting them to critical evaluation."[39]

Thus, what distinguishes Mill's conception of freedom from moralized conceptions is that he construes "completely free" action in terms of a particular *mode of choosing* rather than in terms of a particular range of "right" choices.[40] He emphasizes the degree of autonomy, or power over their characters, that people exercise in the process of determining their own course of conduct. Mill insists, moreover, that "different persons . . . require different conditions for their spiritual development . . . ," and that "it is important to give the freest scope possible to uncustomary things" (OL, 270, 269). What is important, in his view, is the capacity of people to determine the courses of their own lives. By contrast, moralized conceptions of freedom focus on the *ends* chosen by agents as the distinguishing mark of whether or not their actions are truly free. People are truly free, in the latter view, when they choose ends that are "worth choosing."[41]

Still, these points do not completely clear Mill of the charge that his emphasis on au-

tonomy has moralistic and potentially repressive implications. As we have seen, Mill maintains that only people whose capacities for autonomy have been fully developed can be "completely free." At first glance, then, his view of freedom seems to open the door to paternalistic interference with the conduct of persons who are less than fully autonomous—e.g., due to "inveterate" habits or "infirmities of character"—without this being counted as a restriction of their freedom (L, 840; U, 212). That is, it seems to entail that certain people can be "forced to be free" since they are incapable of "completely free" action without external intervention. He appears to treat them like children who lack the maturity to take full responsibility for their own lives (OL, 226, 224).[42] As I will explain, though, Mill's way of addressing this issue is more subtle and less menacing than it first appears to be, although his view of "completely free" agency is not without limitations (see section V, below).

III. Degrees of Autonomy, Degrees of Freedom

Although Mill maintains that only people who have fully developed their capacities for autonomy can be "completely free" agents, he by no means regards them as the only persons capable of meaningful freedom. Rather than offering a simple dichotomy between the fully autonomous (or "completely free") and completely heteronomous agents, Mill recognizes varying *degrees of freedom* corresponding to different degrees of autonomy and heteronomy.[43] He insists that it is not only "persons of decided mental superiority who have a just claim to carry out their lives in their own way" (OL, 270). "If a person possesses any tolerable amount of common sense and experience," he says, "his own mode of laying out his existence is the best, not because it is the best in itself, but because it is his own mode" (OL, 270). Mill's understanding of the significance of autonomy for judgments about freedom and unfreedom can be aptly redescribed in terms of the distinction made by some contemporary philosophers of action between *anomic*, *autarchic*, and *autonomous* agents.[44] These concepts enable us to distinguish a variety of different constraints to freedom that are important for Mill.

First, there is the unfreedom of persons who are sufficiently autonomous to choose aims and purposes that are "properly their own," but who face significant external impediments to their freedom of action (e.g., Andrei Sahkarov or Nelson Mandela during their years in prison). Second, there is the unfreedom of those persons whose minds are "bowed to the yoke," and to whom "it does not occur . . . to have any inclination, except for what is customary" (OL, 264–65). As Gray says, such a person may be free with respect to a particular "action in so far as his [or her] doing that action is not prevented by the forcible or coercive intervention of another."[45] It would be misleading, though, to describe them as fully or even substantially free. The "freedom" of such persons is basically the limited freedom of those whom Stanley Benn calls "anomic" agents and Henry Frankfurt calls "wantons": they lack capacities of critical reflection and strength of will to such a degree that their desires and inclinations are their own only in a superficial sense.[46] This is not just a hypothetical problem. People sometimes find themselves in such oppressive and restrictive circumstances that they learn to accept or acquiesce to their oppression. Mill regards such persons as largely unfree since they cannot *pursue their own good* in a meaningful sense.

Finally, there is the freedom and unfreedom of those persons who lack full autonomy, but possess a "tolerable amount of common sense and experience" (OL, 270). Mill regards this situation as typical of most people. Their freedom corresponds to what Benn and Gray call the freedom of *autarchic* agents. As Gray explains, this notion refers to the freedom of a person who "while enjoying (over a wide range of actions) the negative freedom which covers the absence of both force and coercion, also exercises unimpaired all the normal capacities and powers of a rational chooser by reference to which as rational self-direction is defined."[47] Such persons possess in some pleasure the capacity to determine their "own mode" of life insofar as they can articulate reasons for their actions (OL, 270). They are not completely unreflective or impulsive like anomic (or heteronomous) persons; but they often fail to exercise the "second-order" capacity, characteristic of *autonomous* agents, to reflect critically upon their more immediate desires in light of their more considered aims and purposes.[48] Therefore, when people "exercise choice only among things commonly done" and "like in crowds" (OL, 265), they are neither completely free nor completely unfree. Moreover, this kind of conformist conduct may be even more common today than in Mill's time. People's characters and desires are now shaped by ever more sophisticated global communications media, while sources of immediate gratification and amusement have multiplied.

These distinctions are often difficult to make with respect to the conduct of actual persons. Nonetheless, they illuminate the subtlety of Mill's conception of freedom and they have a considerable heuristic value. Mill wisely rejects the false dichotomy of either regarding people as free *only* when they are fully autonomous or regarding people as fully free *even when* they are heteronomous. Instead, he maintains that people have different degrees of freedom and unfreedom, all other things being equal, in proportion to their relative autonomy or heteronomy. Rather than saying that only persons "of a better than ordinary mould" are capable of free action and that most others must be "forced to be free" through external intervention, his view is more subtle and compelling.[49] He insists that (virtually) all persons tend to develop the capacity for autonomous action to the extent their educations and life experiences cultivate their capacities for reasoning, judgment, deliberation, and self-control. Therefore, his conception of freedom does not open the door to paternalism in the name of freedom in any simple sense.[50]

Mill regards autonomy as a necessary but not a sufficient condition of freedom. He clearly recognizes that people may be fully autonomous and yet be largely unfree due to external impediments. At the same time, his account of free action has one further qualitative dimension that is significant for thinking about social and political aspects of freedom. While he rejects the view that freedom consists in exercising choice among things "worth doing," he highlights an important sense in which the *quality* of the choices and possibilities open to people is important for assessing their freedom. He construes freedom in terms of choices and opportunities that enable people to determine their own "plan of life" or "mode of existence" rather than as their ability to do whatever they desire. What is crucial, then, is not simply the number of choices open to us, but also the *significance* of the choices and possibilities for "pursuing our own good in our own way."[51] The extent of a person's freedom, then, depends more on her power to pursue more considered aims and purposes than on her capacity to satisfy "vague and transient desires" (OL, 261). Therefore, such things as freedom to express beliefs and opinions, freedom of religion and conscience, freedom to choose among different ways of life, opportunities to choose careers or modes of work, and opportunities to share in self-government with respect to spheres of power that govern our lives are particularly important for assessing the extent of our freedom.

IV. Freedom and Power

Mill recognizes that power is often exercised in ways that diminish freedom, both rightfully and wrongfully. Early in *On Liberty* he considers how the "liberty of action" of individuals may be limited by "physical force in the form of legal penalties," as well as by "the moral coercion of public opinion" (OL, 223). The more innovative part of his argument is his attention to four ways in which freedom is directly related to a positive aspect of power that he highlights in "Bentham": "the power of making our volitions effectual."[52] I have already discussed the most basic aspect of this relationship: "the power of self-formation," which is basically the capacity for autonomous action. Mill also emphasizes three other ways that freedom is directly related to the exercise of power: the necessity of material resources and opportunities for people effectively to pursue their aims and purposes; the neces-

sity of opportunities for people to share in practices of self-government with respect to the power relationships that govern their lives; and the role of what Mill calls "the powers of education" in cultivating or stifling people's capacities for freedom of thought and action.

Regarding the significance of material resources, Mill maintains that people require certain material resources—including educational opportunities, occupational choices, and a certain level of disposable income—to exercise meaningful freedom. He says, for example, that women to a greater extent than men are unable to enter marriages *freely* because existing laws and customs deny them the "power of gaining their own livelihood." Consequently, rather than marriage being "wholly a matter of choice" for women, it is "something approaching a matter of necessity; something, at least, which every woman is under strong artificial motives to desire."[53] He makes a similar point in the course of comparing the constraints to and prospects for freedom offered by various "communist" and socialist reform programs to those found in capitalist England. Concerning the existing system he says, "The generality of labourers in this and most other countries have as little choice of occupation or freedom of locomotion, are practically as dependent on fixed rules and on the will of others, as they could be on any system short of actual slavery."[54] Mill's view, in short, is that a sufficient level of material resources "to make our volitions effectual" is a necessary condition of the freedom of pursuing our own aims, purposes, and life plans.

With respect to practices of self-government, Mill extends the democratic tendencies of the liberal tradition. He addresses questions about freedom with respect to the various social and political power relationships in which people's choices and actions are embedded. These include political and economic institutions, gender relations, marital and family relations, educational institutions and practices, and spiritual and recreational activities. Accordingly, he conceives of the extent of people's freedom partly in terms of their opportunities to share in self-government with respect to key power relationships that govern their lives. Thus, political freedom is not the absence of state power or legal restraints, but rather a matter of each person being "under no other restraints than . . . [the] mandates of society which he has a share in imposing, and which it is open to him, if he thinks wrong, publicly to dissent from, and exert himself actively to get altered."[55] Similarly, he conceives economic freedom not just in terms of the economic activities of independent individuals, but also in terms of extending the "democratic spirit" into economic enterprises. He says that co-operative economic enterprises that give associated workers an equal voice in management would extend "the freedom and independence of the individual . . . [to] the industrial department" in modern societies.[56] His emphasis on mutual self-government as a component of freedom is also evident in his notion of marital partnerships in which men and women would share in governing "the affairs of [their] families" (SW, 290–92).

Mill also addresses the interplay between freedom and power with respect to how the various social relationships situating people shape their capacities for self-formation or autonomy. He sees the various social and political relationships situating people not only as the field of their possible choices and actions, but also as "powers of education" (OL, 282; U, 218). That is, they are *educative* relationships that shape people's characters and cognitive capacities.[57] In Mill's view, the *potential* for autonomous agency is a basic human attribute, but it must be developed. Accordingly, we achieve this potential only to the degree that the social and political relationships situating us call forth and exercise our faculties of reasoning, judgment, deliberation, and imagination, and encourage us to think for ourselves. People, in short, must be educated for freedom, and such education depends not just on quality schooling—"education" in the narrow sense—but also on mental cultivation (on balance at least) within all of their social and political relationships.

V. Freedom, Power, and Culture

Mill's understanding of rational autonomy as a condition of "completely free" agency betrays one significant limitation of his account of the relationship between freedom and power. His view of free action is culturally bounded rather than universal. He illuminates to some extent how the religious and cultural commitments of subjugated groups, such as women, often perpetuate their subjection; but his understanding of this problem is limited by his non-interpretive approach to social reality.[58] In particular, he fails adequately to grasp how religious and cultural traditions and identities are sources of meaning and value *as well as* media of power and domination. In turn, he does not address how the exercise of power and practices of freedom are themselves culturally shaped.

Mill displays both the strengths and limitations of his approach when he challenges the ideological power manifest when cultural traditions perpetuate oppression through repressive modes of education or socialization. In *The Subjection of Women* he is eloquent about how English women are educated for subordination. "All women," he says, "are brought up from the very earliest years in the belief that their ideal character is the very opposite to that of men; not self-will, . . . but submission, and yielding to the control of others" (SW, 211). Thus, he rejects the claim that women accept their subordinate status "voluntarily." He points out instead that many women "do not accept it" and, concerning those who apparently do accept it, he insists that men, preferring "not a forced slave but a willing one, . . . have therefore put everything in practice *to enslave their minds*," including "the whole force of education" (SW, 270–1, emphasis added). Thus, to the extent that women have learned this "morality of submission," their mental freedom has been stifled so that their freedom of action cannot be assessed simply in terms of whether or not they are unimpeded to pursue their unreflective desires (SW, 294; cf. OL, 290).

Mill rightly emphasizes that traditions are embedded within and expressive of relations of power, including the patriarchal power of men over women. Still, his analysis is limited because he gives short shrift to the symbolic or hermeneutical aspect of religious and cultural traditions and customs. He tends to regard religious and cultural identities and commitments as effects of power or signs of intellectual "immaturity" and "civilizational" backwardness. Thus, he underemphasizes their importance as sources of meaning and value.[59]

This means, in turn, that Mill also fails to grasp adequately how many "mature," rational agents—men as well as women—enact traditional religious or cultural norms and practices *as free agents*. This problem is evident in an important passage from *On Liberty* that I quoted earlier. Mill says, "To conform to custom, merely as custom, does not educate or develop in [a person] any of the qualities which are the distinctive endowment of a human being. . . . He who does anything because it is the custom, makes no choice" (OL, 262). Anyone who does something "because it is the custom" is not fully free in his view because she or he is acting upon premises "taken from reason" (OL, 251). The conduct of such persons is in effect directed by others rather than self-determined. Mill says, "Not the person's own character, but the traditions or customs of other people are the rule of conduct"; the person is permitting "the world, or his own portion of it, [to] choose his plan of life for him" (OL, 261–2).

For Mill, then, people can enact a custom or tradition as "completely free" agents only insofar as they reflectively choose their guiding religious and cultural commitments and values. Even when agents self-consciously act in accordance with a valued tradition or belief system, their conduct is not fully free if they have not reflectively chosen their fundamental beliefs and commitments in the first place. In this regard, Mill insists upon a rather radical view of critical reflection about received moral and religious beliefs as a necessary condition of being a "completely free" agent. He fleshes out this view in an 1868 letter concerning the proper role of parents in teaching their children about religion:

I do not think that there should be any *authoritative* teaching at all on such subjects. I think parents ought to point out to their children when the children begin to question them, or to make observations of their own, the various opinions on such subjects, & what the parents themselves think the most powerful reasons for & against. Then, if the parents show a strong feeling of the importance of truth & also of the difficulty of attaining it, it seems to me that young people's minds will be sufficiently prepared to regard popular opinion or the opinions of those about them with respectful tolerance, & may be safely left to form definite conclusions in the course of mature life. (Oct. 29, 1868, CW 16, 1469, Mill's emphasis)[60]

People can *freely choose* their religion and their religiously informed values, in his view, only when they are not brought up and instilled with the belief that any one religion is uniquely true or right.[61] This is a plausible account of being free with respect to our religious and cultural identities and commitments. At the same time, though, it brings to light the idealized and de-contextualized character of Mill's notion of "completely free" action. Taken to its logical conclusion, Mill's ideal entails that we are fully free only insofar as we are encouraged to choose reflectively our own beliefs and identities— that is, only insofar as we are not taught authoritatively any one set of religious and cultural commitments. This implies not only that all children should have a secular formal education (which includes the comparative study of religious and cultural traditions), but also that the informal education they receive from their parents or guardians be thoroughly non-sectarian.[62] It also entails that people are always more free, in an unequivocal sense, in proportion to the number of significant possible ways of life, philosophies, and religious and cultural identities that are made available to them. Thus, even the common practice of parents passing on their religion and culture to their children in some measure constrains the freedom of the latter.

Mill's standard of "completely free" agency hereby obscures the givenness—i.e., the unchosen character—of key aspects of *everyone's* social identities, fundamental commitments, and ideas of the good. Therefore, he poses a false dichotomy when he warns about cases in which "not the person's own character, but the traditions or customs of other people are the rule of conduct" (OL, 261). Our characters, beliefs, and values are inevitably shaped in some measure by the traditions and customs of the communities into which we are born. Consequently, people always act on the basis of desires, beliefs, and understandings that they appropriate from their social context.[63] Moreover, many (if not most) people choose numerous things—including important things—because they are their customs. Therefore, it is misleading to speak of people being "completely free" with respect to their aims, beliefs, values, characters, and social identities.

These points are especially salient when we consider people's freedom with respect to their religious beliefs, and identities. Many (if not most) people are authoritatively taught a particular religious identity as a matter of course. Their earliest encounters with religion commonly consist of being taught "their" religious identities in their families and/or communities as they learn their language, kinship, nationality, and other basic features of their social identities. People are rarely brought up with the understanding that there are a wide range of human religious and spiritual practices from among which they are free to choose their own path. We typically learn from our families, "*We* are Catholic (or Jewish, Muslim, Episcopalian, etc.)"—often through unspoken lessons, such as family or community participation in specific kinds of worship and rituals.[64] Thus, our religious identities are always partly formed by relationships of power and authority. Of course, we learn our religious (or non-religious) identities in varying ways depending upon other aspects of our social identities and social locations (e.g., our nationality, ethnicity, gender identity, "racial" identity, schooling, life experiences). Yet this does not undermine the givenness of most people's religious identities.[65] Religious faith typically rests on some received authority and certain "rock-bottom" beliefs and values that believers do not generally call into question.[66] Many believers question the meaning of their religious beliefs, but regard their religion itself as a basic part of their identities rather than an object of conscious choice.[67] Therefore, many people construe freedom with respect to religious beliefs or identities in terms of the capacity to practice religion as they see fit, rather than in terms of choosing fundamental religious commitments.[68]

In this light, Mill misleadingly construes freedom in an essentialist way—i.e., transhistorically—in terms of reflective choice, self-realization, and self-government such that any practice of freedom as freedom must include these elements. He maintains that "the peculiar character of the modern world . . . is, that human beings are no longer born to their place in life, . . . but are free to employ their faculties, and such favourable chances as offer, to achieve the lot which may appear to them most desirable" (SW, 272–73). This modern ethos has led people increasingly to construe freedom in terms of the freedom to choose—and also to share in choosing—how they wish to lead their lives. What Mill fails adequately to see is how the practices of freedom that he rightly regards as the logical expressions of the modern ethos of self-determination are rooted *in a particular historical and cultural constellation of social and political struggles and innovations*. For example, the Protestant Reformation and its aftershocks gave impetus to the development of new ideas and practices of religious freedom and freedom of conscience; the development of modern European nation-states and popular struggles for the extension of basic political rights and liberties produced a distinctively modern form of political freedom linked to representative government; modern capitalist development and class-based struggles against the emergent power of capitalists generated new and conflicting ideas and practices of "economic freedom"; and concepts and practices of sexual and reproductive freedom are also distinctly modern.[69] Most of these practices of freedom emphasize individual choice, self-realization, or self-government; yet religious freedom and freedom of conscience require no comparable presumptions of individual choice. The latter freedoms encompass the "free exercise" of religious creeds, regardless of whether they are inherited or freely chosen, as well as spiritual and philosophical quests in which some people consciously choose their fundamental spiritual and philosophical beliefs and commitments.

This brings us back to my earlier claim that different historical configurations of power and culture have produced different practices of freedom.[70] That is, different contexts generate divergent answers to basic questions concerning freedom. For example, Dorothy Lee explains that in traditional Navaho society in Arizona and New Mexico, learning to be free "involves learning to observe a large number of taboos and procedures, which are aspects of every act. . . . All this could be seen as inhibiting, or negative, or as interfering with the individual; but to the Navaho it is guidance in the acquisition of an essential skill—the freedom to act and to be."[71] This Navaho practice of freedom has striking affinities to other historical practices of freedom that involve similar modes of self-discipline, such as the ancient Greek view of freedom as "self-mastery," early Christian practices of "spiritual freedom," and the later Puritans' view of freedom as requiring "subjection . . . [to] the authority of Christ" and his worldly representatives in early colonial America.[72] One way to regard such practices of self-discipline is to start from the perspective of modern pluralistic societies, as Mill and Isaiah Berlin do, and then find them wanting as general conceptions of freedom.[73] Alternatively, we can acknowledge that such practices are forms of freedom while recognizing that, as Lee says, they are not general models of freedom for modern pluralistic societies, "but rather food for thought, the basis of new insights.[74] This approach offers a fresh perspective on modern practices of freedom that involve analogous unchosen commitments, and makes possible a respectful consideration of non-modern practices of freedom. Still, the close connection between freedom and subordination in some non-modern practices makes them suspect from a modern perspective—particularly to peo-

ple with liberal, democratic, feminist, and secular commitments. It is worth recalling here that Western practices of freedom have often combined freedom for some persons with the subordination of others. For instance, the political freedom of ancient Athenian male citizens and of propertied white men in the antebellum United States went hand-in-hand with slavery and the subordination of women. Furthermore, Mill himself insists that existing practices of economic freedom in modern capitalist societies conjoin considerable freedom and power for capitalists with unfreedom and subordination for the laboring classes.[75] Accordingly, one of the great merits of Mill's account of freedom and power is his insistence that democratic and critically reflective ways of organizing relations of power and authority, including the authority of received traditions, uniquely foster the equal freedom of all persons.[76]

In sum, to comprehend the interplay of freedom, power, and culture, we need a more pluralistic approach than Mill offers. Along with recognizing how modern practices of freedom emphasize autonomy, choice, and self-realization—at least in principle—we need to recognize that people in various contexts also exercise freedom in carrying out religious and cultural commitments that they have not reflectively chosen. At the same time, we must not jump to the false conclusion that any enactment of cultural or religious norms and rules is an expression of freedom regardless of the power dynamics under which it occurs.

Distinguishing free from unfree agency is not simply a matter of distinguishing conduct that emanates from conscience rather than from external authority. This distinction is untenable since people's fundamental religious and cultural beliefs and commitments are always partly constituted by *some* external authorities—e.g., parents, teachers, ministers, rabbis, or, in more pernicious cases, missionaries and colonial educators. Yet this crucial point can be elaborated in ways that leave us without any adequate conception of free agency. For instance, Stanley Fish argues that just as it makes no sense to speak of actions *free from all constraints* since people always act within back-ground conditions that make some actions possible while making others unavailable, "it follows, too, that there can be no continuum which differentiates institutions or structures as being more or less constrained, or more of less free."[77] As Mill points out, such situational "constraints" are not equally constraining (or freedom-generating) for all people. The effects of asymmetries of power, including relationships of oppression, leave differently situated people with different degrees of freedom. This is one of Mill's key insights in *The Subjection of Women:* while many women and men may do things *because* they are traditional or customary, this tendency is particularly burdensome to women. Pervasive patriarchal traditions and relationships sharply constrain their available choices and possibilities relative to those of men (SW, 272–82).[78] Women to a far greater extent than men find themselves in situations where they face extremely severe penalties for non-compliance with rules of conduct prescribed by their inherited religious and cultural traditions. This was true, for example, of the practice of self-immolation by widowed (usually upper caste) Hindu women in India, and it is true of practices of "female circumcision" in Sahelian Africa (particularly Sudan, Somalia, and Mali), some Arab countries, and parts of Asia.[79] Women in such circumstances often yield to prevailing norms and practices without freely consenting to them.[80]

Freedom, therefore, requires not just that the women and men are *agents* rather than passive objects of their social and political practices, but also that their conduct represents their own way of affirming a valued way of life in a meaningful sense. Mill rightly insists that to affirm freely an inherited religious or cultural identity, a person must be in a position to freely reject this identity or way of life without excessive cost to herself or himself (see OL, 290). Moreover, he rightly insists that people are unfree with respect to a received custom insofar as they reduce it to a "hereditary creed, . . . received passively, not actively" (OL, 248). Still, we need a more interpretive and pluralistic account than Mill offers of how the interplay of power and

culture shapes possibilities for free agency. Such an account must not prejudge *just* when agency should be regarded as free, but it can offer some guideposts. First, like Mill, we should be wary of regarding actions taken under notably constrained conditions as an exercise of freedom. Second, since people always start with some pre-given concepts and understandings, we ought to take seriously their own self-understandings— their own reasons for doing what they do and their conceptions of freedom. Third, insofar as people are never fully aware of all the social forces and power dynamics that shape them, their self-understandings will not tell the whole story of their freedom or unfreedom.

This last point has important implications. We need to acknowledge practices of freedom that do not conform to Mill's secular modernistic notion of reflective choice, but we also need to be aware of agents' unarticulated or barely articulated forms of resistance.[81] The latter will indicate cases in which people yield to religiously or culturally prescribed rules of conduct without freely enacting them. Further, prevailing ideas and self-understandings about freedom in *all* societies may be open to criticism. In this regard, Mill astutely criticizes many prevailing ideas about freedom in modern democratizing societies like his own.[82]

One important objection to this line of thought is that while conceptions of freedom such as Mill's originate in specific cultural contexts, they also "travel" *across* cultures.[83] Indeed, Mill's notion of freedom has traveled far. Yet two further points need to be appreciated to grasp the sense in which Mill's conception of freedom is culture-bound. First, the diffusion of concepts and practices across cultures takes place in part through asymmetrical relations of power—colonialism, capitalist globalization, and migrations—*between* them. This is not to say that transplanted conceptions and practices are necessarily "inauthentic" in new contexts. Nor is it to deny that they are often transformed en route. My point is that we need to take into account how the role of power in this process complicates the question of when concepts and practices are *freely* adopted.[84] Second, we need to address the losses as well as the gains entailed by such cultural traveling. Mill implies that when non-liberal cultures adopt (or are taught or forced to adopt) his conception of freedom, this change will be unequivocally progressive and emancipatory. He fails to consider what people with fundamental commitments to non-liberal ways of life might lose by adopting his view of conceptions of the good life as freely chosen and revisable. For instance, cultural assimilation of the Navaho people into the modern United States has undoubtedly brought them new practices of freedom, but it has also undermined older practices of freedom that, if Dorothy Lee is right, entailed distinctive modes of attunement among them and with their surroundings.

VI. Conclusions

Mill's developmental view of individuality and autonomy leads him to articulate an indispensable account of the interrelationship between freedom and power. Freedom, he maintains, consists of both the absence of burdensome constraints on people's possible actions and the capacity of persons for self-determination and self-government. While recognizing that the exercise of power often diminishes the freedom of individuals, he shows that there is no opposition between freedom and power *as such*. In his view, people are always embedded within power relationships that shape their capacities for free action and delimit their field of possibilities. Therefore, the real opposition is between forms of power that stifle people's autonomy and freedom of action and forms of power that support freedom. In this regard, Mill maintains that freedom must not be conceived solely in terms of what we are free to do or be (or not do or be) within the power relationships that govern our lives. It must also be assessed in terms of our opportunities to effectively share in self-government with respect to the various power relationships situating us. This requires more than merely formal opportunities for self-government since freedom entails individuals having "influence in the regulation of their af-

fairs." In the same breath, Mill's argument implies that individuals can be free in reflectively choosing *not to participate* in processes of collective self-government. Such choices are free, however, only when individuals have both developed capacities for self-government and available institutions and practices that would enable them, if they so chose, to share meaningfully in self-government. He construes freedom, then, as an "exercise-concept" rather than merely as an "opportunity-concept," to use Charles Taylor's terms. The presence of freedom requires that we actually exercise a directing influence over our lives.[85]

Mill recognizes potential tensions between individual liberty and democratic self-government, but he regards both as indispensable forms of freedom and neither one as more essential than the other.[86] Accordingly, he develops his principle of liberty—that a community can rightfully exercise power over the conduct of its individual members only to prevent "harm to others" (OL, 223)—as a means to reconcile democratization of the state, industrial relations, education, and marital relations with protection for individuals against tyrannical majorities.

Still, we need a more pluralistic view of freedom than Mill provides to grasp just how different contexts of power and culture constitute different possibilities for free agency. In particular, we need a view that accommodates how individuals can freely pursue fundamental commitments and beliefs that they have not reflectively chosen, as well as practices of freedom that emphasize reflective choice, self-realization, and self-government. Adopting this pluralistic view of freedom, however, should not lead us to overlook Mill's insight into the special significance of freedom of choice in modern societies. Even members of modern (and "modernizing") societies who are especially concerned with freely pursuing their fundamental religious or cultural commitments typically seek freedom of choice in other areas of their lives. Moreover, it is crucial to appreciate how Mill's notion of freedom of choice differs from the "freedom of choice" that is so widely celebrated in modern capitalist societies like the United States. The freedom of choice that matters, according to Mill, is *not* the limited freedom of choosing our favorite products in the marketplace. Rather, it is the freedom of "pursuing our own good in our own way"—the freedom of choosing our own "mode of existence" or "plan of life." It encompasses not only our field of possibilities as independent individuals, but also our opportunities for self-government.

Notes

1. John Stuart Mill, *Autobiography*, ed. Currin Shields (Indianapolis: Bobbs-Merrill, 1957), 162.

2. [R.H. Hutton], "Mill on Liberty" [1859], in Mill, *On Liberty*, ed. David Spitz (New York: W. W. Norton, 1975), 133. Hutton is identified as the author of this article by Alan Ryan. See Ryan, ed., *Mill* (New York: W. W. Norton, 1997).

3. John C. Rees, *John Stuart Mill's 'On Liberty'*, ed. G. L. Williams (Oxford: Clarendon Press, 1985), 175. This interpretation of Mill's conception of freedom is also defended by, among others, Isaiah Berlin, "John Stuart Mill and the Ends of Life," in Berlin, *Four Essays on Liberty* (Oxford: Oxford University press, 1969); David Spitz, "Freedom and Individuality: Mill's Liberty in Retrospect," in Mill, *On Liberty*, ed. Spitz; C. L. Ten, *Mill on Liberty* (Oxford: Oxford University Press, 1980); John Gray, *Mill on Liberty: A Defense* (London: Routledge & Kegan Paul, 1983); Fred R. Berger, *Happiness, Justice, and Freedom: The Moral and Political Philosophy of John Stuart Mill* (Berkeley: University of California Press, 1984); Jonathan Riley, *Liberal Utilitarianism: Social Choice Theory and J. S. Mill's Philosophy* (Cambridge: Cambridge University Press, 1988); and Wendy Donner, *The Liberal Self: John Stuart Mill's Moral Philosophy* (Ithaca: Cornell University Press, 1991).

4. Quentin Skinner, "The Idea of Negative Liberty: Philosophical and Historical Perspectives," in *Philosophy in History*, ed. Richard Rorty, J. B. Schneewind, and Quentin Skinner (Cambridge: Cambridge University Press, 1984), p. 194.

5. On this point, see Michel Foucault, "The Subject and Power," in Herbert Dreyfus and Paul Rabinow, *Michel Foucault: Beyond Structuralism and Hermeneutics*, with an afterword by and an interview with Michel Foucault, 2nd ed. (Chicago: University of Chicago Press, 1983), 221. For related critiques of "classical liberal" views, cf. Hannah Arendt, "What is Freedom?," in *Between Past and Future* (New York: Penguin, 1968); and John Dewey, "Liberty and Social Control," in Dewey, *Problems of Men* (New York: Philosophical Library, 1946). One contemporary liberal theorist who explicitly counterpoises freedom and power in the way that I am challenging is Giovanni Sartori, *The Theory of Democracy Revisited, Part Two: The Classic Issues* (Chatham, NJ: Chatham House Press, 1987).

6. Mill, *On Liberty*, in *Collected Works*, vol. 21, 337. Subsequent citations to this work will be to this edition and will be given in parentheses as follows: OL, 217.

7. Mill, *The Subjection of Women*, in *Collected Works*, vol. 21, 337. Subsequent citations to this work will be given in parentheses as follows: SW, 337.

8. On the place of this view of freedom in modern liberalism, see John Gray, *Liberalism* (Minneapolis: University of Minnesota Press, 1986).

9. On the "positive" aspects of Mill's view of freedom, see G. L. Williams, "Mill's Principle of Liberty," *Political Studies* 24 (June 1976): 132–40; G. W. Smith, "J. S. Mill on Freedom," in *Conceptions of Liberty in Political Philosophy*, ed. Zbigniew Pelczynski and John Gray (New York: St. Martin's Press, 1984); "Freedom and Virtue in Politics: Some Aspects of Character, Circumstances and Utility from Helvetius to J. S. Mill," *Utilitas* 1 (May 1989): 112–34; and "Social Liberty and Free Agency: Some Ambiguities in Mill's Conception of Freedom," in *J. S. Mill—'On Liberty': In Focus*, ed. John Gray and G. W. Smith (London: Routledge, 1991); Alan Ryan, "Property, Liberty, and On Liberty," in *Of Liberty*, ed. A. Phillips Griffiths (Cambridge: Cambridge University Press, 1983); Gregory Claeys, "Justice, Independence, and Industrial Democracy: The Development of John Stuart Mill's Views on Socialism," *Journal of Politics* 49 (February 1987): 122–47; and John Skorupski, *John Stuart Mill* (London: Routledge, 1989).

10. Mill, *A System of Logic, Collected Works*, vol. 8, 841. Subsequent citations to this work will be given in parentheses as follows: L, 841.

11. C. B. Macpherson, *Democratic Theory: Essays in Retrieval* (Oxford: Oxford University Press, 1973), 52–53.

12. Isaiah Berlin, "Two Concepts of Liberty," in Berlin, *Four Essays on Liberty*, 130.

13. See Smith, "J. S. Mill on Freedom," 183–84.

14. Smith, "J. S. Mill on Freedom," 182.

15. Smith, "J. S. Mill on Freedom," 182. The principle of liberty, sometimes called the "harm principle," entails that a community can rightfully exercise power over the conduct of its members only to prevent "harm to others" (OL, 223). Its purpose is to secure for individuals a large degree of freedom of thought and action by protecting them against social and political interference.

16. Smith, along with several other of Mill's interpreters, uses "freedom" and "liberty" interchangeably, and he says that Mill does the same. Cf. Smith, "J. S. Mill on Freedom"; cf. Berlin, "Two Concepts of Liberty"; Gray, *Mill on Liberty*; & Berger, *Happiness, Justice, and Freedom*.

17. Paul Ziff and Hanna Fenichel Pitkin explain that in English *freedom* has a broader range of usage than *liberty*, which has more formal and legal connotations. See Ziff, *Semantic Analysis* (Ithaca: Cornell University Press, 1960); and Pitkin, "Are Freedom and Liberty Twins?," *Political Theory* 16 (November 1988): 523-52. The different roots of the concepts correspond to different shades of meaning. Pitkin explains, for instance, that "the *frē*-family could characterize action as spontaneous, readily or gladly done, done of one's own accord, even zealously done. The 'liber-' family did not carry these meanings, despite its use for he capacity to choose between sin and goodness" (Pitkin, "Are Freedom and Liberty Twins?," 538).

18. Pitkin, "Are Freedom and Liberty Twins?," 543.

19. Thus, Mill uses "freedom" more frequently than "liberty" in works such as *Representative Government* and *The Subjection of Women* where he makes more far-ranging arguments about freedom; and he uses "liberty" much more frequently in *On Liberty*: "liberty" occurs 85 times in *On Liberty*, excluding the title and chapter titles, while "freedom" occurs only 46 times; in *The Subjection of Women*, he uses "freedom" 30 times and "liberty" only 10 times; and in *Representative Government* he uses "freedom" 38 times and "liberty" 27 times.

20. Although Mill typically uses masculine pronouns generically, referring to both women and men, he was an advocate of women's rights and even gave some attention to the problems of using sexist language—particularly to the misleading effects of "using the masculine *pronoun* where both sexes are equally concerned." See Mill, in *The Examiner*, 1 June 1834, *Collected Works*, vol. 23, 729, quoted in *Sexual Equality: Writings by John Stuart Mill, Harriet Taylor Mill, and Helen Taylor*, ed. Ann P. Robson and John M. Robson (Toronto: University of Toronto Press, 1994), xvii.

21. See Smith, "Social Liberty and Free Agency." Isaiah Berlin and Benjamin Gibbs have attributed to Mill a basically negative empiricist view of freedom. Berlin characterizes him as a defender of "the definition of negative liberty as the ability to do what one wishes" (Berlin, "Two Concepts of Liberty," 139). Cf. Benjamin Gibbs, *Freedom and Liberation* (London: Chatto and Windus, for Sussex University Press, 1976), 81.

22. Smith, "Social Liberty and Free Agency," 240–41; and Richard B. Friedman, "A New Exploration of Mill's Essay *On Liberty*," *Political Studies* 14 (October 1966): 281–302.

23. Smith, "J. S. Mill on Freedom," 211. For Mill, though, freedom does not *mean* self-development or self-realization as it does for some theorists of freedom. This is important because, as John Gray explains, people may freely choose to sacrifice chances for self-development for other goals (Gray, *Liberalism*, 58).

24. For related discussions, see Smith, "J. S. Mill on Freedom"; and "Social Liberty and Free Agency."

25. See Also Mill, *Utilitarianism, Collected Works*, vol. 10, 218.

26. Mill, "Constraints of Communism" (Aug. 3, 1850), *Collected Works*, vol. 25, 1179.

27. Mill, "Constraints of Communism," 1179, emphasis added.

28. As Berlin points out, conceiving of freedom as simply "the ability to do what one wishes" is problematic because it entails that freedom could be attained just as effectively by conditioning people to want less as by enabling them to satisfy their initial wants. See Berlin, "Introduction," in *Four Essays on Liberty*, xxxviii; and "Two Concepts of Liberty," 139–40.

29. Michael McPherson, "Mill's Moral Theory and the Problem of Preference Change," *Ethics* 92 (January 1982); and Smith, "Social Liberty and Free Agency."

30. Rees, *John Stuart Mill's 'On Liberty'*, 181.

31. G. W. Smith, "The Logic of J. S. Mill on Freedom," *Political Studies*, 28 (June 1980): 238–52; and Skorupski, *John Stuart Mill*.

32. Smith, "Social Liberty and Free Agency," 246. For a representative compatibilist view, see Phillippa Foot, "Free Will as Involving Determinism," in *Free Will and Determinism*, ed. Bernard Berofski (New York: Harper and Row, 1966).

33. Mill refers to this power as the power of "self-culture" or "self-education" in "Bentham" (*Collected Works*, vol. 10, 98). I examine Mill's view of power more fully in forthcoming work.

34. Cf. John Christman, "Constructing the Inner Citadel: Recent Work on Autonomy," *Ethics*, 99 (October 1988): 14.

35. Smith, "Freedom and Virtue in Politics," 116.

36. Smith, "Social Liberty and Free Agency," 244; and Berlin, "Two Concepts of Liberty," 134. Johann Gottlieb Fichte provides a striking example of the potential for authoritarian governance entailed in such notions. He says, "To compel men to adopt the right form of government, to impose Right upon them by force, is not only right, but the sacred duty of every man who has the insight and the power to do so" (Fichte, quoted in Berlin, "Two Concepts of Liberty," 151, n. 1).

37. According to Mill, actions can only be counted as *virtuous* when they spring from decisions made after deliberation ("Remarks on Bentham's Philosophy," *Collected Works*, vol. 10). Thus, he conceives of "the person of confirmed virtue" in *Utilitarianism* not just as someone who has "a confirmed will to do right," but also as a person who has the strength of character necessary to make and pursue reflective and deliberate choices (*Utilitarianism*, 238 and 237).

38. Gray, *Mill on Liberty*, 71. Mill uses the word autonomy only once in French, and in a way that connotes "independence" or "freedom from interference" rather than the current sense of the word in philosophy of action. In an 1871 letter to Emile Acollas, he says, "Quant à la partie philosophique, vous savez probablement par mon Essai sur la Liberté, dans quel sens et avec quelles limites j'entends notre principe commun, celui de l'autonomie de l'individu." ["As to the philosophical party, you probably know from my Essay on Liberty, in what sense and with what limits I understand our common principle, that of the autonomy of the individual."] See

Letter to Emile Acollas, September 20, 1871, *Collected Works*, vol. 17, 1831–32.

39. Gray, *Mill on Liberty*, 76.

40. Accordingly, his view of free action is related to but distinct from his view of the capacity for higher pleasures. Cf. Donner, *The Liberal Self*, ch. 6–8; and Smith, "Social Liberty and Free Agency."

41. Berlin, "Two Concepts of Liberty," 132–34.

42. Smith, "J. S. Mill on Freedom," 199; and "Social Liberty and Free Agency."

43. Skorupski, *John Stuart Mill*, 254.

44. Stanley I. Benn, "Freedom, Autonomy, and the Concept of a Person," *Proceedings of the Aristotelian Society* 76 (1975–76): 109–30; and Gray, *Mill on Liberty*.

45. Gray, *Mill on Liberty*, 74. Jon Elster identifies a closely related but distinct phenomena of "sour grapes." This is where persons who may have full *capacity* for autonomous agency restrictively adapt their preferences to "second-best" options in light of the constraints they face. See Elster, *Sour Grapes* (Cambridge: Cambridge University Press, 1983), ch. 3.

46. Frankfurt explains that "wantons" are motivated strictly by first-order desires—i.e., desires that do not reflect upon in light of more considered objectives. In contrast, persons with unimpaired capacities for rational action have the capacity to form second-order *volitions*—i.e., the capacity to *will what they want to will*. See Henry G. Frankfurt, "Freedom of the Will and the Concept of a Person," *The Journal of Philosophy* 68 (January 1971): 5–20.

47. Gray, *Mill on Liberty*, 74.

48. Gerald Dworkin explains that autonomy "is not merely an evaluative or reflective notion, but includes as well some ability both to alter one's preferences and to make them effective in one's actions and, indeed, to make them effective because one has reflected upon them and adopted them as one's own." See Gerald Dworkin, *The Theory and Practice of Autonomy* (Cambridge: Cambridge University Press, 1988), 17.

49. The first phrase is from Mill, "Utility of Religion," CW [*Collected Works*] 10, 411.

50. As Smith points out, though, Mill's view is more clearly paternalistic with regard to persons with "infirmities of character" or "inveterate" habits (*Utilitarianism*, 212; L, 840; and Smith, "Social Liberty and Free Agency," 247). Moreover, as I will explain later, Mill's view is strongly paternalistic with respect to

non-Western cultures. He justifies this stance with the ethnocentric claim that just as children need others to take care of them so do "states of society in which the race itself may be considered in its nonage" (OL, 224).

51. As Berlin says, the extent of a person's freedom depends not just on "how many doors are open," but also on "how open they are, [and] upon their relative importance" to his or her life (Berlin, "Introduction," xxxix–xl).

52. Mill, "Bentham," 96.

53. Mill, "Essay on Marriage and Divorce," in J. S. Mill and Harriet Taylor Mill, *Essays on Sex Equality*, ed. Alice Rossi (Chicago: University of Chicago Press, 1970), 77.

54. Mill, *Principles of Political Economy, Collected Works*, vols. 2 and 3, 209.

55. Mill, *Considerations on Representative Government, Collected Works*, vol. 19, 411, 432.

56. Mill, *Principles of Political Economy*, 763.

57. ' Mill, "Inaugural Address Delivered to the University of St. Andrews," *Collected Works*, vol. 21, 217.

58. See Skorupski, *John Stuart Mill*, 275–82.

59. He says in *Representative Government* that the "improvement" of human societies gradually leads people to abandon the "inveterate spirit of locality." "Experience proves," he says, "it is possible for one nationality to merge and be absorbed in another: and when it was originally an inferior or more backward portion of the human race the absorption is greatly to its advantage" (*Considerations on Representative Government*, 417, 549). On occasion he exhibits a more subtle appreciation for the meaning and significance of religious and cultural values and of the need to take account of agents' self-understandings (see esp. *Considerations on Representative Government*, 570; "Carlyle's French Revolution," *Collected Works*, vol. 20). Still, he never fully integrates these interpretive impulses into his approach to free action and social criticism. See Bhikhu Parekh, "Superior People: The narrowness of liberalism from Mill to Rawls," *The Times Literary Supplement* (February 25, 1994): 11–13; and Bruce Baum, "Feminism, Liberalism and Cultural Pluralism: J. S. Mill on Mormon Polygyny," *The Journal of Political Philosophy* 5 (September 1997): 230–53.

60. In the same letter he says, "I do not think it right either oneself to teach, or to allow any one else to teach one's children, authoritatively, what ever that one does not from the bottom of one's heart & by the clearest light of reason, believe to be true. . . . One assuredly has no right to incumber the reason & entangle the conscience of one's children" (Letter to Charles Friend, Oct. 29, 1869, *Collected Works*, vol. 16, 1468–9). Mill's standard of premises taken *from reason rather than from authority* refers to reasons that can be assessed on formal or logical grounds, independently of any appeal to received traditions or supernatural forces (OL, ch. 2; "Grote's History of Ancient Greece [I]," *Collected Works*, vol. 11, 290). His view is "radical" in the Enlightenment sense of seeking to bring all beliefs and practices progressively under the scrutiny of critical reasoning.

61. Mill develops this point further in "Dr. Whewell on Moral Philosophy," where he criticizes education within ecclesiastical institutions in which instructors must "vow adherence to a set of opinions made up and prescribed" as authoritative truths. He asks, "how can intellectual vigour be fostered by the teaching of those who, even as a matter of duty, would rather that their pupils were weak and orthodox, than strong with freedom of thought?" See Mill, "Dr. Whewell on Moral Philosophy," in Mill, *Dissertations and Discussions*, vol. 2 (New York: Haskell House Publishers, 1973; reprint of the 1859 edition), p. 168.

62. It is important to note here that Mill strongly supports the right of parents to determine the religious education of their children; he does so, however, despite his underlying notion of fully free action. In this regard, he clearly does not consider the goal of maximizing the freedom of children as the only value at stake, particularly social pluralism and parental freedom. Furthermore, Mill acknowledges that children must be taught authoritatively *some basic moral principles*, though not a sectarian view of the good life, as a basis for moral agency and critical thinking. This is reflected in his interest in a secular "religion of humanity." See, respectively, Mill, "On Religion and Guardianship" (1846), in Mill, *Prefaces to Liberty: Selected Writings of John Stuart Mill*, ed. Bernard Wishy (Boston: Beacon Press, 1959); "Secular Education" (1850), *Collected Works*, vol. 28, 4; and "The Utility of Religion," *Collected Works*, vol. 10).

63. Kwame Anthony Appiah, *In My Father's House: Africa in the Philosophy of Culture* (New York: Oxford University, 1993), 117. Cf. Ludwig Wittgenstein, *Lectures & Conversations on Aesthetics, Psychology and Religious Belief*, ed. Cyril Barrett (Berkeley: University

of California Press, n.d), 53–72. Some contexts of choice, of course, are more heterogeneous in this regard than others.

64. Consider the case of my 6-year-old friend Ben who has been learning his Jewish identity from his parents and from his Jewish Sunday school. Recently he asked me, "You're Jewish?" (His parents had just told him that I am, but I am actually a non-believer with an equivocal Jewish identity.) His mom was nearby and she signaled me to refrain from giving him the atheistic and equivocal response that I would have given him if I had answered him more *freely.* Therefore, I simply said, "Yes." This raises the following questions: Would Ben be *more free* in a straightforward way if I had introduced him at his impressionable age to such alternative possibilities as atheism and a non-religious (equivocally) Jewish identity? What does this mean for the intergenerational bonds that are partly constituted by parents passing on such religious and cultural identities? Cf. Will Kymlicka, *Multicultural Citizenship* (Oxford: Clarendon Press, 1996), 90; and James Nickel, "The Value of Cultural Belonging," *Dialogue,* 33 (Fall 1994): 639.

65. The same thing can be said of some aspects of our national, cultural, ethnic, and gender identities. These identities are arguably socially and politically constructed and, thus, learned, but this does not mean that we can simply put them on and take them off at will like a change of clothes.

66. See Ludwig Wittgenstein, *Culture and Value,* trans. Peter Winch (Chicago: The University of Chicago Press, 1980), 45e; and Talal Asad, *Genealogies of Religion: Discipline and Reasons of Power in Christianity and Islam* (Baltimore: The Johns Hopkins University Press, 1993).

67. This argument might appear to be controverted by the frequency of religious conversions. This would be so, however, only if we misleadingly suppose that all religious conversions are something people consciously choose upon reflection. See Talal Asad, "Comments on Conversion," in *Conversions to Modernities: The Globalization of Christianity,* ed. Peter van der Veer (New York: Routledge, 1996); and Baum, "Feminism, Liberalism, and Cultural Pluralism."

68. Michael Sandel has recently distinguished these two forms of religious freedom as "freedom of choice"—the freedom of choosing our own way of life or our own set of beliefs—and "freedom of conscience"—the freedom to practice our religion. See Michael Sandel, "Freedom of Conscience or Freedom of Choice?," in *Articles of Faith, Articles of Peace: The Religious Liberty Clauses and the American Public Philosophy,* ed. James Davison Hunter and Os Guinness (Washington, D.C.: Brookings, 1990).

69. On the first two examples, see John Plamenatz, "In What Sense Is Freedom a Western Idea?" *Current Law and Social Problems,* vol. 1 (Toronto: University of Toronto Press, 1960); and J. H. Hexter, "The Birth of Modern Freedom," *Times Literary Supplement* (January 21, 1983): 51–53.

70. Cf. Michel Foucault, *The Uses of Pleasure* (New York: Vintage Books, 1986); Serif Mardin, "Freedom in an Ottoman Perspective," in *State, Democracy, and the Military in Turkey in the 1980s,* ed. Metin Heper and Ahmet Evin (New York: W. de Gruyter, 1989), 23–25; and Orlando Patterson, *Freedom,* Volume 1: *Freedom in the Making of Western Culture* (Basic Books, 1991).

71. Dorothy Lee, *Freedom and Culture* (Prentice-Hall, 1959), 11.

72. Like the Hindu practice, these practices also existed within distinctly patriarchal cultures. For the ancient Greek practice of self-mastery, see Foucault, *The Uses of Pleasure,* 78–93; for early Christian "spiritual freedom," see Patterson, *Freedom,* ch. 10–15; and for the Puritan view, see John Winthrop, "A Little Speech on Liberty" (1645), in *Political Thought in America: An Anthology,* ed. Michael B. Levy (Chicago: The Dorsey Press, 1988), 13–14.

73. Mill, OL, 265–66; and Berlin, "Two Concepts of Liberty," 135ff. Mill promotes respect for "the religious feelings of the [Indian] people" (*Considerations on Representative Government,* 570; cf. OL, 240–41n). Yet his view of fully free action, *in league* with his historical evolutionism, undergirds his support of British colonial rule in India until the time when the Indian people "have become capable of improvement by free and equal discussion," independent of appeals to inherited traditions (OL, 224; *Considerations on Representative Government,* ch. 18).

74. Lee, *Freedom and Culture,* p. 14.

75. I develop this point more fully in "J. S. Mill's Conception of Economic Freedom," *History of Political Thought* (forthcoming). The broader historical intertwinement of freedom with slavery (and other forms of subor-

dination) is Orlando Patterson's central theme in *Freedom*.

76. He also contends that the kind of free action he promotes is uniquely conducive to full human flourishing (OL, ch. 3). This claim, however, is harder to substantiate as a universal truth about human beings than Mill suggests. See John Gray, "Postscript," in *Mill on Liberty: A Defense*, 2nd edition (London: Routledge, 1996); and Parekh, "Superior People."

77. Fish adds, "Rather than a continuum, what we have is . . . an array of structures of constraint, no one of which is more constraining than any other." See Stanley Fish, *Doing What Comes Naturally: Change, Rhetoric, and the Practice of Theory in Literary and Legal Studies* (Durham: Duke University Press, 1989), 459.

78. For a similar view, see Nancy Hirshmann, "Toward a Feminist Theory of Freedom," *Political Theory* 24 (February 1996): 57–63.

79. Regarding self-immolation in India, A. L. Basham explains that in medieval times the lot of widows was so hard that "it is not surprising that women often immolated themselves on their husbands' funeral pyres." Through self-immolation a widow would escape the hardships of widowhood and be recognized as "a virtuous woman" (*sati*). Despite legal prohibitions enacted in the nineteenth century, there have been some recent acts of self-immolation in India. See A. L. Basham, *The Wonder that Was India* (New York: Grove Press, 1959), 187; John Stratton Hawley, ed., *Sati, the Blessing and the Curse: The Burning of Wives in India* (New York: Oxford University Press, 1994): and Gayatri Chakravorty Spivak, "Can the Subaltern Speak?," in *Colonial Discourse and Postcolonial Theory: A Reader*, ed. Patrick Williams and Laura Christman (New York: Columbia University Press, 1994).

80. Nicole-Claude Mathieu, "When Yielding is Not Consenting: Material and Psychic Determinants of Women's Consciousness and Some of Their Interpretations in Ethnology" (Part 2), *Feminist Issues* 10 (Spring 1990): 81-82; and Spivak, "Can the Subaltern Speak?"

81. Peter Jones, "Bearing the Consequences of Belief," *The Journal of Political Philosophy* 2 (March 1994): 36; Michael Walzer, "Objectivity and Social Meaning," in *The Quality of Life*, ed. Martha Nussbaum and Amartya Sen (Oxford: Clarendon Press, 1994), 175, 173; and Spivak, "Can the Subaltern Speak?," 93.

82. For instance, he persuasively challenges the common view in capitalist democracies that, in Milton Friedman's words, "competitive capitalism [is] . . . a system of economic freedom." Cf. Milton Friedman, *Capitalism and Freedom* (Chicago: University of Chicago Press, 1962), 4; and Baum, "J. S. Mill's Conception of Economic Freedom."

83. I owe this point to an anonymous reviewer for *Polity*.

84. See Asad, *Genealogies of Religion*, chs. 5 and 7; James Clifford, "Traveling Cultures," in *Cultural Studies*, ed. Lawrence Grossberg, Cary Nelson, and Paula Treicher (New York and London: Routledge, 1992).

85. Charles Taylor, "What's Wrong With Negative Liberty?," in Taylor, *Philosophy and the Human Sciences: Philosophical Papers*, vol. 2 (Cambridge: Cambridge University Press, 1985), 214.

86. See Baum, "J. S. Mill's Conception of Economic Freedom."

35
Marital Slavery and Friendship

John Stuart Mill's *The Subjection of Women*

Mary Lyndon Shanley

John Stuart Mill's essay *The Subjection of Women* was one of the nineteenth century's strongest pleas for opening to women opportunities for suffrage, education, and employment. Some contemporary feminists, however, have denigrated the work, questioning the efficacy of merely striking down legal barriers against women as the way to establish equality between the sexes. These contemporary critics argue that Mill's failure to extend his critique of inequality to the division of labor in the household, and his confidence that most women would choose marriage as a "career," subverted his otherwise egalitarian impulses.[1]

I argue in this essay, however, that such critics have ignored an important aspect of Mill's feminism. *The Subjection of Women* was not solely about equal opportunity for women. It was also, and more fundamentally, about the corruption of male-female relationships and the hope of establishing friendship in marriage. Such friendship was desirable not only for emotional satisfaction, it was crucial if marriage were to become, as Mill desired, a "school of genuine moral sentiment."[2] The fundamental assertion of *The Subjection of Women* was not that equal opportunity would ensure the liberation of women, but that male-female equality, however achieved, was essential to marital friendship and to the progression of human society.

Mill's vision of marriage as a locus of sympathy and understanding between autonomous adults not only reforms our understanding of his feminism, but also draws attention to an often submerged or ignored aspect of liberal political thought. Liberal individualism is attacked by Marxists and neo-conservatives alike as wrongly encouraging the disintegration of affective bonds and replacing them with merely self-interested economic and contractual ties. Mill's essay, however, emphasizes the value of noninstrumental relationships in human life. His depictions of both corrupt and well-ordered marriage traces the relationship of family order to right political order. His vision of marriage as a locus of mutual sympathy and understanding between autonomous adults stands as an unrealized goal for those who believe that the liberation of women requires not only formal equality of opportunity but measures which will enable couples to live in genuine equality, mutuality, and reciprocity.

I. The Perversion of Marriage by the Master-Slave Relationship

Mill's reconstruction of marriage upon the basis of friendship was preceded by one of the most devastating critiques of male domination in marriage in the history of Western philosophy. In *The Subjection of Women* Mill repeatedly used the language of "master and slave" or "master and servant" to describe the relationship between husband and wife. In the first pages of the book, Mill called the dependence of women upon men "the primitive state of slavery lasting on" (1: 130). Later he said that despite the supposed advances of Christian civilization, "the wife is the actual bond-servant of her husband: no less so, as far as legal obligation goes, than slaves commonly so called" (2: 158). Still later he asserted that "there remain no legal slaves, except the mistress of every house" (4: 217). The theme of women's servitude was not confined to *The Subjection of Women*. In his speech on the Reform Bill of 1867, Mill talked of that "obscure feeling" which members of Parliament were "ashamed to express openly" that women had no right to care about anything except "how they may be the most useful and devoted servants of some man."[3] To Auguste Comte he wrote comparing women to "domestic slaves" and noted that women's capacities were spent "seeking happiness not in their own life, but exclusively in the favor and affection of the other sex, which is only given to them on the condition of their dependence."[4]

But what did Mill mean by denouncing the "slavery" of married women? How strongly did he wish to insist upon the analogy between married women and chattel slaves? I believe that he chose the image quite deliberately. For Mill, the position of married women resembled that of slaves in several ways: the social and economic system gave women little alternative except to marry; once married, the legal personality of the woman was subsumed in that of her husband; and the abuses of human dignity permitted by custom and law within marriage were egregious.

In Mill's eyes, women were in a double bind: they were not free within marriage, and they were not truly free not to marry.[5] What could an unmarried woman do? Even if she were of the middle or upper classes, she could not attend any of the English universities, and thus she was barred from a systematic higher education.[6] If somehow she acquired a professional education, the professional associations usually barred her from practicing her trade. "No sooner do women show themselves capable of competing with men in any career, than that career, if it be lucrative or honorable, is closed to them."[7] Mill's depiction of the plight of Elinor Garrett, sister of Millicent Garrett Fawcett, the suffrage leader, is telling:

A young lady, Miss Garrett, . . . studied the medical profession. Having duly qualified herself, she . . . knocked successively at all the doors through which, by law, access is obtained into the medical profession. Having found all other doors fast shut, she fortunately discovered one which had accidentally been left ajar. The Society of Apothecaries, it seems, had forgotten to shut out those who they never thought would attempt to come in, and through this narrow entrance this young lady found her way into the profession. But so objectionable did it appear to

this learned body that women should be the medical attendants even of women, that the narrow wicket through which Miss Garrett entered has been closed after her.[8]

Working-class women were even worse off. In the *Principles of Political Economy*, Mill argued that their low wages were due to the "prejudice" of society which "making almost every woman, socially speaking, an appendage of some man, enables men to take systematically the lion's share of whatever belongs to both." A second cause of low wages for women was the surplus of female labor for unskilled jobs. Law and custom ordained that a woman has "scarcely any means open to her of gaining a livelihood, except as a wife and mother."[9] Marriage was, as Mill put it, a "Hobson's choice" for women, "that or none" (1: 156).[10]

Worse than the social and economic pressure to marry, however, was women's status within marriage. Mill thoroughly understood the stipulations of the English common law which deprived a married woman of a legal personality independent of that of her husband. The doctrine of coverture or spousal unity, as it was called, was based on the Biblical notion that "a man [shall] leave his father and his mother, and shall cleave to his wife, and they shall be one flesh" (Genesis ii, 22–23). If "one flesh," then, as Blackstone put it, "by marriage, the husband and wife are one person in law." And that "person" was represented by the husband. Again Blackstone was most succinct: "The very being or legal existence of the woman is suspended during the marriage, or at least is incorporated and consolidated into that of the husband."[11] One of the most commonly felt injustices of the doctrine of spousal unity was the married woman's lack of ownership of her own earnings. As the matrimonial couple was "one person," the wife's earnings during marriage were owned and controlled by her husband.[12] During his term as a member of Parliament, Mill supported a Married Women's Property Bill, saying that its opponents were men who thought it impossible for "society to exist on a harmonious footing between two persons unless one of them has absolute power over the other," and insisting that England has moved beyond such a "savage state."[13] In *The Subjection of Women* Mill argued that the "wife's position under the common law of England [with respect to property] is worse than that of slaves in the laws of many countries: by the Roman law, for example, a slave might have his peculium, which to a certain extent the law guaranteed to him for his exclusive use" (2: 158–159). Similarly, Mill regarded the husband's exclusive guardianship over the married couple's children as a sign of the woman's dependence on her husband's will (2: 160). She was, in his eyes, denied any role in life except that of being "the personal body-servant of a despot" (2: 161).

The most egregious aspects of both common and statute law, however, were those which sanctioned domestic violence. During the Parliamentary debates on the Representation of the People Bill in 1867, Mill argued that women needed suffrage to enable them to lobby for legislation which would punish domestic assault:

> I should like to have a Return laid before this House of the number of women who are annually beaten to death, or trampled to death by their male protectors; and, in an opposite column, the amount of sentence passed. . . . I should also like to have, in a third column, the amount of property, the wrongful taking of which was . . . thought worthy of the same punishment. We should then have an arithmetical value set by a male legislature and male tribunals on the murder of a woman.[14]

But the two legal stipulations which to Mill most demonstrated "the assimilation of the wife to the slave" were her inability to refuse her master "the last familiarity" and her inability to obtain a legal separation from her husband unless he added desertion or extreme cruelty to his adultery (2: 160–161). Mill was appalled by the notion that no matter how brutal a tyrant a husband might be, and no matter how a woman might loathe him, "he can claim from her and enforce the lowest degradation of a human being," which was to be made the instrument of "an animal function contrary to her inclination" (2: 160). A man and wife being one body,

rape was by definition a crime which a married man could not commit against his own wife. By law a wife could not leave her husband on account of this offense without being guilty of desertion, nor could she prosecute him. The most vicious form of male domination of women according to Mill was rape within marriage; it was particularly vicious because it was legal. Mill thus talked not of individual masters and wives as aberrations, but of a legally sanctioned system of domestic slavery which shaped the character of marriage in his day.[15]

Mill's depiction of marriage departed radically from the majority of Victorian portrayals of home and hearth. John Ruskin's praise of the home in *Sesame and Lilies* reflected the feelings and aspirations of many: "This is the true nature of home—it is the place of Peace; the shelter, not only from all injury, but from all terror, doubt, and division. . . . It is a sacred place, a vestal temple, a temple of the hearth watched over by Household Gods."[16] Walter Houghton remarked that the title of Coventry Patmore's poem, *The Angel in the House*, captured "the essential character of Victorian love" and reflected "the exaltation of family life and feminine character" characteristic of the mid-nineteenth century.[17] James Fitzjames Stephen, who wrote that he disagreed with *The Subjection of Women* "from the first sentence to the last," found not only Mill's ideas but his very effort to discuss the dynamics of marriage highly distasteful. "There is something—I hardly know what to call it; indecent is too strong a word, but I may say unpleasant in the direction of indecorum—in prolonged and minute discussions about the relations between men and women, and the character of women as such."[18]

The Subjection of Women challenged much more than Victorian decorum, however; it was a radical challenge to one of the most fundamental and preciously held assumptions about marriage in the modern era, which is that it was a relationship grounded on the consent of the partners to join their lives. Mill argued to the contrary that the presumed consent of women to marry was not, in any real sense, a free promise, but one socially coerced by the lack of meaningful options. Further, the laws of marriage deprived a woman of many of the normal powers of autonomous adults, from controlling her earnings, to entering contracts, to defending her bodily autonomy by resisting unwanted sexual relations. Indeed, the whole notion of a woman "consenting" to the marriage "offer" of a man implied from the outset a hierarchical relationship. Such a one-way offer did not reflect the relationship which should exist between those who were truly equal, among beings who should be able to create together by free discussion and mutual agreement an association to govern their lives together.

In addition, Mill's view of marriage as slavery suggested a significantly more complicated and skeptical view of what constituted a "free choice" in society than did either his own earlier works or those of his liberal predecessors. Hobbes, for example, regarded men as acting "freely" even when moved by fear for their lives. Locke disagreed, but he in turn talked about the individual's free choice to remain a citizen of his father's country, as if emigration were a readily available option for all. In other of his works Mill himself seemed overly sanguine about the amount of real choice enjoyed, for example, by wage laborers in entering a trade. Yet Mill's analysis of marriage demonstrated the great complexity of establishing that any presumed agreement was the result of free volition, and the fatuousness of presuming that initial consent could create perpetual obligation. By implication, the legitimacy of many other relationships, including supposedly free wage and labor agreements and the political obligation of enfranchised and unenfranchised alike, was thrown into question. *The Subjection of Women* exposed the inherent fragility of traditional conceptualizations of free choice, autonomy, and self-determination so important to liberals, showing that economic and social structures were bound to limit and might coerce any person's choice of companions, employment, or citizenship.

Mill did not despair of the possibility that marriages based on true consent would be possible. He believed that some individuals even in his own day established such associations of reciprocity and mutual support. (He counted his own relationship with Harriet Taylor Mill as an example of a marriage between equals.)[19] But there were systemic impediments to marital equality. To create conditions conducive to a marriage of equals rather than one of master and slave, marriage law itself would have to be altered, women would have to be provided equal educational and employment opportunity, and both men and women would have to become capable of sustaining genuinely equal and reciprocal relationships within marriage. The last of these, in Mill's eyes, posed the greatest challenge.

II. The Fear of Equality

Establishing legal equality in marriage and equality of opportunity would require, said Mill, that men sacrifice those political, legal, and economic advantages they enjoyed "simply by being born male." Mill therefore supported such measures as women's suffrage, the Married Women's Property Bills, the Divorce Act of 1857, the repeal of the Contagious Diseases Acts, and the opening of higher education and the professions to women. Suffrage, Mill contended, would both develop women's faculties through participation in civic decisions and enable married women to protect themselves from male-imposed injustices such as lack of rights to child custody and to control of their income. Access to education and jobs would give women alternatives to marriage. It would also provide a woman whose marriage turned out badly some means of self-support if separated or divorced. The Divorce Act of 1857, which established England's first civil divorce courts, would enable women and men to escape from intolerable circumstances (although Mill rightly protested the sexual double standard ensconced in the Act).[20] And for those few women with an income of their own, a Married Women's Property Act would recognize their independent personalities and enable them to meet their husbands more nearly as equals.

However, Mill's analysis went further. He insisted that the subjection of women could not be ended by law alone, but only by law and the reformation of education, of opinion, of social inculcation, of habits, and finally of the conduct of family life itself. This was so because the root of much of men's resistance to women's emancipation was not simply their reluctance to give up their position of material advantage, but many men's fear of living with an equal. It was to retain marriage as "a law of despotism" that men shut all other occupations to women, Mill contended (1: 156). Men who "have a real antipathy to the equal freedom of women" were at bottom afraid "lest [women] should insist that marriage be on equal conditions" (1: 156). One of Mill's startling assertions in *The Subjection of Women* was that "[women's] disabilities [in law] are only clung to in order to maintain their subordination in domestic life: *because the generality of the male sex cannot yet tolerate the idea of living with an equal*" (3: 181; italics added). The public discrimination against women was a manifestation of a disorder rooted in family relationships. The progression of humankind could not take place until the dynamics of the master-slave relationship were eliminated from marriages and until the family was instead founded on spousal equality.

Mill did not offer any single explanation or account of the origin of men's fear of female equality. Elsewhere, he attributed the general human resistance to equality to the fear of the loss of privilege, and to apprehensions concerning the effect of leveling on political order.[21] But these passages on the fear of spousal equality bring to a twentieth-century mind the psychoanalytic works about human neuroses and the male fear of women caused by the infant boy's relationship to the seemingly all-powerful mother, source of both nurturance and love and of deprivation and punishment.[22] But it is impossible to push Mill's text far in this direction. His account of the fear of equality was not psychoanalytic. He did, however, undertake to depict the consequences of marital inequality both for the individual psyche and for social justice. The rhetorical purpose of *The Subjection of Women* was not only to convice men that their treatment of women in law was unjust, but also that their treatment of women in the home was self-defeating, even self-destructive.

Women were those most obviously affected by the denial of association with men on equal footing. Women's confinement to domestic concerns was a wrongful "forced repression" (1: 148). Mill shared Aristotle's view that participation in civic life was enriching and ennobling activity, but Mill saw that for a woman, no public-spirited dimension to her life was possible. There was no impetus to consider with others the principles which were to govern their common life, no incentive to conform to principles which defined their mutual activity for the common good, no possibility for the self-development which comes from citizen activity.[23] The cost to women was obvious; they were dull, or petty, or unprincipled (2: 168; 4: 238). The cost to men was less apparent but no less real; in seeking a reflection of themselves in the consciousness of these stunted women, men deceived, deluded, and limited themselves.

Mill was convinced that men were corrupted by their dominance over women. The most corrupting element of male domination of women was that men learned to 'worship their own will as such a grand thing that it is actually the law for another rational being" (2: 172). Such self-worship arises at a very tender age, and blots out a boy's natural understanding of himself and his relationship to others.

A boy may be "the most frivolous and empty or the most ignorant and stolid of mankind," but "by the mere fact of being born a male" he is encouraged to think that "he is by right the superior of all and every one of an entire half of the human race: including probably some whose real superiority he had daily or hourly occasion to feel" (4: 218). By contrast, women were taught "to live for others" and "to have no life but in their affections," and then further to confine their affections to "the men with whom they are connected, or to the children who constitute an additional indefeasible tie between them and a man" (1: 141). The result of this upbringing was that what women would tell men was not, could not be, wholly true; women's sensibilities were systematically warped by their subjection. Thus the reflections were not accurate and men were deprived of self-knowledge.[24]

The picture which emerged was strikingly similar to that which Hegel described in his passages on the relationship between master and slave in *The Phenomenology of Mind*.[25] The lord who sees himself solely as master, wrote Hegel, cannot obtain an independent self-consciousness. The master thinks he is autonomous, but in fact he relies totally upon his slaves, not only to fulfill his needs and desires, but also for his identity: "Without slaves, he is no master." The master could not acquire the fullest self-consciousness when the "other" in whom he viewed himself was in the reduced human condition of slavery: to be *merely* a master was to fall short of full self-consciousness, and to define himself in terms of the "thing" he owns. So for Mill, men who have propagated the belief that all men are superior to all women have fatally affected the dialectic involved in knowing oneself through the consciousness others have of one. The present relationship between the sexes produced in men that "self-worship" which "all privileged persons, and all privileged classes" have had. That distortion deceives men and other privileged groups as to both their character and their self-worth.[26]

No philosopher prior to Mill had developed such a sustained argument about the corrupting effects on men of their social superiority over and separation from women. Previous philosophers had argued either that the authority of men over women was natural (Aristotle, Grotius), or that while there was no natural dominance of men over women prior to the establishment of families, in any civil society such preeminence was necessary to settle the dispute over who should govern the household (Locke), or the result of women's consent in return for protection (Hobbes), or the consequence of the development of the sentiments of nurturance and love (Rousseau).[27] None had suggested that domestic arrangements might diminish a man's ability to contribute to public debates in the agora or to the rational governing of a democratic republic. Yet Mill was determined to show that the development of the species was held in check by that domestic slavery produced by the fear of equality, by spousal hierarchy, and by a lack of the reciprocity and mutuality of true friendship.

III. The Hope of Friendship

Mill's remedy for the evils generated by the fear of equality was his notion of marital friendship. The topic of the rather visionary fourth chapter of *The Subjection of Women* was friendship, "the ideal of marriage" (4: 233, 235). That ideal was, according to Mill, "a union of thoughts and inclinations" which created a "foundation of solid friendship" between husband and wife (4: 231, 233).

Mill's praise of marital friendship was almost lyrical, and struck resonances with Aristotle's, Cicero's, and Montaigne's similar exaltations of the pleasures as well as the moral enrichment of this form of human intimacy. Mill wrote:

When each of two persons, instead of being a nothing, is a something; when they are attached to one another, and are not too much unlike to begin with; the constant partaking of the same things, assisted by their sympathy, draws out the latent capacities of each for being interested in the things . . . by a real enriching of the two natures, each acquiring the tastes and capacities of the other in addition to its own [4: 233].

This expansion of human capacities did not, however, exhaust the benefits of friendship. Most importantly, friendship developed what Montaigne praised as the abolition of selfishness, the capacity to regard another human being as fully as worthy as oneself. Therefore friendship of the highest order could only exist between those equal in excellence.[28] And for precisely this reason, philosophers from Aristotle to Hegel had consistently argued that women could not be men's friends, for women lacked the moral capacity for the highest forms of friendship. Indeed, it was common to distinguish the marital bond from friendship not solely on the basis of sexual and procreative activity, but also because women could not be part of the school of moral virtue which was found in friendship at its best.

Mill therefore made a most significant break with the past in adopting the language of friendship in his discussion of marriage. For Mill, no less than for any of his predecessors, "the true virtue of human beings is the fitness to live together as equals." Such equality required that individuals "[claim] nothing for themselves but what they as freely concede to every one else," that they regard command of any kind as "an exceptional necessity," and that they prefer whenever possible "the society of those with whom leading and following can be alternate and reciprocal" (4: 174–175). This picture of reciprocity, of the shifting of leadership according to need, was a remarkable characterization of family life. Virtually all of Mill's liberal contemporaries accepted the notion of the natural and inevitable complementariness of male and female personalities and roles. Mill, however, as early as 1833 had expressed his belief that "the highest masculine and the highest feminine" characters were without any real distinction.[29] That view of the androgynous personality lent support to Mill's brief for equality within the family.

Mill repeatedly insisted that his society had no general experience of "the marriage relationship as it would exist between equals," and that such marriages would be impossible until men rid themselves of the fear of equality and the will to domination.[30] The liberation of women, in other words, required not just legal reform but a reeducation of the passions. Women were to be regarded as equals not only to fulfill the demand for individual rights and in order that they could survive in the public world of work, but also in order that women and men could form ethical relations of the highest order. Men and women alike had to "learn to cultivate their strongest sympathy with an equal in rights and in cultivation" (4: 236). Mill struggled, not always with total success, to talk about the quality of such association. For example, in *On Liberty*, Mill explicitly rejected von Humbolt's characterization of marriage as a contractual relationship which could be ended by "the declared will of either party to dissolve it." That kind of dissolution was appropriate when the benefits of partnership could be reduced to monetary terms. But marriage involved a person's expectations for the fulfillment of a "plan of life," and created "a new series of moral obligations . . . toward that person, which may possibly be overruled, but cannot be ignored."[31] Mill was convinced that difficult though it might be to shape the law to recognize the moral imperatives of such a relationship, there were ethical communities which transcended and were not reducible to their individual components.

At this juncture, however, the critical force of Mill's essay weakened, and a tension developed between his ideal and his prescriptions for his own society. For all his insight into the dynamics of domestic domination and subordination, the only specific means Mill in fact put forward for the fostering of this society of equals was providing equal opportunity to women in areas outside the family. Indeed, in *On Liberty* he wrote that "nothing more is needed for the complete removal of [the almost despotic power of husbands over wives] than that wives should have the same rights and should receive the same protection of law in the same manner, as all other persons."[32] In the same vein, Mill seemed to suggest that nothing more was needed for women to achieve equality than that "the present duties and protective bounties in favour of men should be recalled" (1: 154). Moreover, Mill did not attack the traditional assumption about men's and women's different responsibilities in an ongoing household, although he was usually careful to say that women "chose" their role or that it was the most "expedient" arrangement, not that it was theirs by "nature."

Mill by and large accepted the notion that once they marry, women should be solely responsible for the care of the household and children, men for providing the family income: "When the support of the family depends . . . on earnings, the common arrangement, by which the man earns the income and the wife superintends the domestic expenditure, seems to me in general the most suitable division of labour between the two persons" (2: 178). He did not regard it as "a desirable custom, that the wife should contribute by her labour to the income of the family" (2: 179). Mill indicated that women alone would care for any children of the marriage; repeatedly he called it the "care which . . . nobody else takes," the one vocation in which there is "nobody to compete with them," and the occupation which "cannot be fulfilled by others" (2: 178; 3: 183; 4: 241). Further, Mill seemed to shut the door on combining household duties and a public life: "like a man when he chooses a profession, so, when a woman marries, it may be in general understood that she makes a choice of the management of a household, and the bringing up of a family, as the first call upon her exertions . . . and that she renounces . . . all [other occupations] which are not consistent with the requirements of this" (1: 179).

Mill's acceptance of the traditional gender-based division of labor in the family has led some recent critics to fault Mill for supposing that legal equality of opportunity would solve the problem of women's subjection, even while leaving the sexual division of labor in the household intact. For example, Julia Annas, after praising Mill's theoretical arguments in support of equality, complains that Mill's suggestions for actual needed changes in sex roles are "timid and reformist at best. He assumes that most women will in fact want only to be wives and mothers."[33] Leslie Goldstein agrees that "the restraints which Mill believed should be imposed on married women constitute a major exception to his argument for equality of individual liberty between the sexes—an exception so enormous that it threatens to swallow up the entire argument."[34] But such arguments, while correctly identifying the limitations of antidiscrimination statutes as instruments for social change, incorrectly identify Mill's argument for equal opportunity as the conclusion of his discussion of male-female equality.[35] On the contrary, Mill's final prescription to end the subjection of women was not equal opportunity but spousal friendship; equal opportunity was a means whereby such friendship could be encouraged.

The theoretical force of Mill's condemnation of domestic hierarchy has not yet been sufficiently appreciated. Mill's commitment to equality in marriage was of a different theoretical order than his acceptance of a continued sexual division of labor. On the one hand, Mill's belief in the necessity of equality as a precondition to marital friendship was a profound theoretical tenet. It rested on the normative assumption that human relationships between equals were of a higher, more enriching order than those between unequals. Mill's belief that equality was more suitable to friendship than inequality was as unalterable as his conviction that democracy was a better system of government than despotism; the human spirit could not develop its fullest potential when living in absolute subordination to another human being or to government.[36] On the other hand, Mill's belief that friendship could be attained and sustained while women bore nearly exclusive responsibility for the home was a statement which might be modified or even abandoned if experience proved it to be wrong. In this sense it was like Mill's view that the question of whether socialism was preferable to capitalism could not be settled by verbal argument alone but must "work itself out on an experimental scale, by actual trial."[37] Mill believed that marital equality was a moral imperative; his view that such equality might exist where married men and women moved in different spheres of activity was a proposition subject to demonstration. Had Mill discovered that managing the household to the exclusion of most other activity created an impediment to the friendship of married women and men, *The Subjection of Women* suggests that he would have altered his view of practicable domestic arrangements, but not his commitment to the desirability of male-female friendship in marriage.

The most interesting shortcomings of Mill's analysis are thus not found in his belief in the efficacy of equal opportunity, but rather in his blindness to what other conditions might hinder or promote marital friendship. In his discussion of family life, for example, Mill seemed to forget his own warning that women could be imprisoned not only "by actual law" but also "by custom equivalent to law" (4: 241). Similarly, he overlooked his own cautionary observation that in any household "there will naturally be more potential voice on the side, whichever it is, that brings the means of support" (2: 170). And although he had brilliantly depicted the narrowness and petty concerns of contemporary women who were totally excluded from political participation, he implied that the mistresses of most households might content themselves simply with exercising the suffrage (were it to be granted), a view hardly consistent with his arguments in other works for maximizing the level of political discussion and participation whenever possible. More significantly, however, Mill ignored the potential barrier between husband and wife which such different adult life experiences might create, and the contribution of shared experience to building a common sensibility and strengthening the bonds of friendship.

Mill also never considered that men might take any role in the family other than providing the economic means of support. Perhaps Mill's greatest oversight in his paean of marital equality was his failure to entertain the possibilities that nurturing and caring for children might provide men with useful knowledge and experience, and that shared parenting would contribute to the friendship between spouses which he so ardently desired. Similarly, Mill had virtually nothing to say about the positive role which sex might play in marriage. The sharp language with which he condemned undesired sexual relations as the execution of "an animal function" was nowhere supplemented by an appreciation of the possible enhancement which sexuality might add to marital friendship. One of the striking features of Montaigne's lyrical praise of friendship was that it was devoid of sensuality, for Montaigne abhorred "the Grecian license," and he was adamant that women were incapable of the highest forms of friendship. Mill's notion of spousal friendship suggested the possibility of a friendship which partook of both a true union of minds and of a physical expression of the delight in one's companion, a friendship which involved all of the human faculties. It was an opportunity which (undoubtedly to the relief of those such as James Fitzjames Stephen) Mill himself was not disposed to use, but which was nonetheless implicit in his praise of spousal friendship.[38]

One cannot ask Mill or any other theorist to "jump over Rhodes" and address issues not put forward by conditions and concerns of his own society.[39] Nevertheless, even leaving aside an analysis of the oppression inherent in the class structure (an omission which would have to be rectified in a full analysis of liberation), time has made it clear that Mill's prescriptions alone will not destroy the master-slave relationship which he so detested. Women's aspirations for equality will not be met by insuring equal civic rights and equal access to jobs outside the home. To accomplish that end would require a transformation of economic and public structures which would allow wives and husbands to share those domestic tasks which Mill assigned exclusively to women. Some forms of publicly supported day-care, paternal as well as maternity leaves, flexible work schedules, extensive and rapid public transportation, health and retirement benefits for part-time employment are among commonly proposed measures which would make the choice of Mill's ideal of marriage between equals possible. In their absence it is as foolish to talk about couples choosing the traditional division of labor in marriage as it was in Mill's day to talk about women choosing marriage: both are Hobson's choices, there are no suitable alternatives save at enormous costs to the individuals involved.

Mill's feminist vision, however, transcends his own immediate prescriptions for reform. *The Subjection of Women* is not only one of liberalism's most incisive arguments for equal opportunity, but it embodies as well a belief in the importance of friendship for human development and progress. The recognition of individual rights is important in Mill's view because it provides part of the groundwork for more important human relationships of trust, mutuality and reciprocity. Mill's plea for an end to the subjection of women is not made, as critics such as Gertrude Himmelfarb assert, in the name of "the absolute primacy of the individual," but in the name of the need of both men and women for community. Mill's essay is valuable both for its devastating critique of the corruption of marital inequality, and for its argument, however incomplete, that one of the aims of a liberal polity should be to promote the conditions which will allow friendship, in marriage and elsewhere, to take root and flourish.

Notes

1. Contemporary authors who criticize Mill's analysis of equal opportunity for women as not far-reaching enough are Julia Annas, "Mill and the Subjection of Women," *Philosophy* 52 (1977), 179–194; Leslie F. Goldstein, "Marx and Mill on the Equality of Women," paper presented at the Midwest Political Science Association Convention, Chicago, April 1978; Richard Krouse, "Patriarchal Liberalism and Beyond: From John Stuart Mill to Harriet Taylor," unpublished manuscript, Williamstown, MA; Susan Moller Okin, *Women in Western Political Thought* (Princeton: Princeton University Press, 1979). From a different perspective, Gertrude Himmelfarb, *On Liberty and Liberalism: The Case of John Stuart Mill* (New York: Alfred Knopf, 1974) criticizes Mill's doctrine of equality as being too absolute and particularly takes issue with modern feminist applications of his theory.

2. J. S. Mill, *The Subjection of Women* (1869) in Alice Rossi, ed., *Essays on Sex Equality* (Chicago: University of Chicago Press, 1970), ch. 2, p. 173. All references to *The Subjection of Women* will be to this edition and will be given in the body of the text using chapter and page, i.e., (2: 173).

3. Hansard, *Parliamentary Debates*, series 3, v. 189 (May 20, 1867), p. 820.

4. Letter to August Comte, October, 1843, *The Collected Works of John Stuart Mill* (hereafter *C. W.*). v. XIII, *The Earlier Letters*, ed. Francis C. Mineka (Toronto: University of Toronto Press, 1963), p. 609, my translation.

5. Mill's analysis of women's choice of marriage as a state of life reminds one of Hobbes' discussion of some defeated soldier giving his consent to the rule of a conquering sovereign. Women, it is true, could decide which among several men to marry, while Hobbes' defeated yeoman had no choice of master. But what

could either do but join the only protective association available to each?

6. A brief account of the struggle to provide for women's higher education in England can be found in Ray Strachey, *The Cause* (London: G. Bell, 1928), pp. 124–165.

7. Hansard, v. 189 (May 20, 1867).

8. *Idem.* In the United States, one well-documented case in which a woman was prohibited from practicing law was Bradwell v. Illinois, 83 U.S. (16 Wall) 130 (1873).

9. *The Principles of Political Economy* (1848) in *C. W.*, II, p. 394 and III, pp. 765–766.

10. Tobias Hobson, a Cambridge carrier commemorated by Milton in two Epigraphs, would only hire out the horse nearest the door of his stable, even if a client wanted another. *Oxford Dictionary*, II, p. 369.

11. William Blackstone, *Commentaries on the Laws of England* 4 vols. (Oxford: Clarendon Press, 1765–1769), Book 1, ch. XV, p. 430. The consequences of the doctrine of spousal unity were various: a man could not make a contract with his wife since "to covenant with her would be to covenant with himself"; a wife could not sue without her husband's concurrence; a husband was bound to "provide his wife with necessaries . . . as much as himself"; a husband was responsible for certain criminal acts of his wife committed in his presence; and, as a husband was responsible for his wife's acts, he "might give his wife moderate correction . . . in the same moderation that (he is) allowed to correct his apprentices or children."

12. The rich found ways around the common law's insistence that the management and use of any income belonged to a woman's husband, by setting up trusts which were governed by the laws and courts of equity. A succinct explanation of the law of property as it affected married women in the nineteenth century is found in Erna Reiss, *Rights and Duties of Englishwomen* (Manchester, 1934), pp. 20–34.

13. Hansard, v. 192 (June 10, 1867), p. 1371. Several Married Women's Property Bills, which would have given married women possession of their earnings were presented in Parliament beginning in 1857, but none was successful until 1870.

14. Ibid., v. 189 (May 20, 1867), p. 826.

15. Mill's outrage at women's lack of recourse in the face of domestic violence is reminiscent of the protests in the United States during the

civil rights movement at token sentences pronounced by white juries against whites accused of assaulting Blacks in Southern states, and of Susan Brownmiller's argument in *Against Our Will: Men, Women and Rape*, that the desultory prosecution of rapists is itself a manifestation of violence against women.

16. John Ruskin, "Of Queen's Gardens," in *Works*, ed. E. T. Cook and A. D. C. Widderburn, 39 vols. (London: C. Allen, 1902–1912), XVIII, p. 122.

17. Walter E. Houghton, *The Victorian Frame of Mind* (New Haven: Yale University Press, 1957), p. 344.

18. James Fitzjames Stephen, *Liberty, Equality, Fraternity* (New York: Henry Holt, n. d.), p. 206.

19. On the relationship between John Stuart Mill and Harriet Taylor see F. A. Hayek, *John Stuart Mill and Harriet Taylor; their correspondence and subsequent marriage* (Chicago: University of Chicago Press, 1951); Michael St. John Packe, *The Life of John Stuart Mill* (New York: Macmillan, 1954); Alice Rossi, "Sentiment and Intellect," in *Essays on Sex Equality* (Chicago: University of Chicago Press, 1970); and Gertrude Himmelfarb pp. 187–238.

20. The Matrimonial Causes Act of 1857, as the divorce measure was known, allowed men to divorce their wives for adultery, but women had to establish that their husbands were guilty of either cruelty or desertion in addition to adultery in order to obtain a separation. Mill was reluctant to say what he thought the terms of divorce should be in a rightly ordered society (see note 31), but he was adamant that the double standard was wrong in policy and unjust in principle.

Mill also spoke out sharply against that sexual double standard in his testimony before the Commission studying the repeal of the Contagious Diseases Act, an act which allowed for the arrest and forced hospitalization of prostitutes with venereal disease, but made no provision for the arrest of their clients. "The Evidence of John Stuart Mill taken before the Royal Commission of 1870 on the Administration and Operation of the Contagious Diseases Acts of 1866 and 1869" (London, 1871).

21. For a discussion of Mill's views on equality generally, see Dennis Thompson, *John Stuart Mill and Representative Government* (Princeton: Princeton University Press, 1976), pp. 158–173.

22. See, for example, Dorothy Dinnerstein, *The Mermaid and the Minotaur: Sexual Arrangements and Human Malaise* (New York: Harper and Row, 1976); Nancy Chodorow, *The Reproduction of Mothering: Psychoanalysis and the Sociology of Gender* (Berkeley: University of California Press, 1978); and Philip Slater, *The Glory of Hera* (Boston: Beacon Press, 1971) and the references therein.

23. See also Mill's *Considerations on Representative Government* (1861) where he lambasted benevolent despotism because it encouraged "passivity" and "abdication of [one's] own energies," and his praise of the Athenian dicastry and ecclesia. *C. W.*, XIX, pp. 399–400, 411. During his speech on the Reform Bill of 1867, Mill argued that giving women the vote would provide "that stimulus to their faculties . . . which the suffrage seldom fails to produce." Hansard, v. 189 (May 20, 1867), 824.

24. Mill's insight was like that which Virginia Woolf used in *A Room of One's Own*. Woolf, trying to explain the source of men's anger at independent women, stated that such anger could not be "merely the cry of wounded vanity"; it had to be "a protest against some infringement of his power to believe in himself." Women have served throughout history as "looking glasses possessing the magic and delicious power of reflecting the figure of a man at twice its natural size." Mill also argued that in order to create such a mirror, men had distorted women by education and had warped the reflection which women showed to men. Virginia Woolf, *A Room of One's Own* (New York: Harcourt Brace and World, 1929), p. 35.

25. G. W. F. Hegel, *The Phenomenology of Mind*, trans. J. B. Baillie (New York: Harper and Row, 1969). This paragraph is indebted to the excellent study of the *Phenomenology* by Judith N. Shklar, *Freedom and Independence* (Cambridge: Cambridge University Press, 1976), from which the quote is taken, p. 61. Mill's analysis also calls to mind Simone de Beauvoir's discussion of "the Other" and its role in human consciousness: in *The Second Sex*, trans. H. M. Parshley (New York: Random House, Vintage Books, 1974), pp. xix ff.

26. Mill argued in addition that men's injustices to women created habits which encouraged them to act unjustly towards others. In *The Subjection of Women* Mill asserted that the habits of domination are acquired in and fostered by the family, which is often, as respects

its chief, "a school of wilfulness, overbearingness, unbounded self-indulgeance, and a double-dyed and idealized selfishness" (2: 165). Virtue, for Mill, was not simply action taken in accordance with a calculus of pleasure and pain, but was habitual behavior. In *Considerations on Representative Government*, he lamented the effects "fostered by the possession of power" by "a man, or a class of men" who "finding themselves worshipped by others . . . become worshipers of themselves." *C. W.*, XIX, p. 445.

27. For excellent studies of each of these authors' views on women (except for Grotius) see Okin. Grotius' views can be found in his *De Juri Belli ac Pacis Libri Tres* [*On the Law of War and Peace*] (1625), trans. Francis W. Kelsey (Oxford: Clarendon Press, 1925), Bk. II, ch. V, sec. i, p. 231.

28. Montaigne's essay, "Of Friendship" in *The Complete Works of Montaigne*, trans. Donald M. Frame (Stanford: Stanford University Press, 1948), pp. 135–144.

29. Letter to Thomas Carlyle, October 5, 1833, *C. W.*, XII, *Earlier Letters*, p. 184.

30. Letter to John Nichol, August 1869, *C. W.*, XVII, *The Later Letters*, ed. Francis C. Mineka and Dwight N. Lindley (Toronto: University of Toronto Press, 1972), p. 1834.

31. *C. W.*, XVIII, 300. Elsewhere Mill wrote, "My opinion on Divorce is that . . . nothing ought to be rested in, short of entire freedom on both sides to dissolve this like any other partnership." Letter to an unidentified correspondent, November 1855, *C. W.*, XIV, *Later Letters*, p. 500. But against this letter was the passage from *On Liberty*, and his letter to Henry Rusden of July 1870 in which he abjured making any final judgments about what a proper divorce law would be "until women have an equal voice in making it." He denied that he advocated that marriage should be dissoluble "at the will of either party," and stated that no well-grounded opinion could be put forward until women first achieved equality under the laws and in married life. *C. W.*, XVII, *Later Letters*, pp. 1750–1751.

32. *C. W.*, XVIII, p. 301.

33. Annas, 189.

34. Goldstein, p. 8. Susan Okin makes a similar point, stating that "Mill never questioned or objected to the maintenance of traditional sex roles within the family, but, expressly considered them to be suitable and desirable" (Okin, p. 237). Okin's reading of Mill is basically sound and sympathetic, but does not recognize the theoretical priority of Mill's commitment to marital equality and friendship.

35. Of recent writers on Mill, only Richard Krouse seems sensitive to the inherent tension in Mill's thought about women in the household. Mill's own "ideal of a reformed family life, based upon a full nonpatriarchal marriage bond," Krouse points out, requires "on the logic of his own analysis . . . [the] rejection of the traditional division of labor between the sexes" (Krouse, p. 39).

36. *Considerations on Representative Government*, *C. W.*, XIX, pp. 399–403.

37. *Chapters on Socialism* (1879), *C. W.*, V, p. 736.

38. Throughout his writings Mill displayed a tendency to dismiss or deprecate the erotic dimension of life. In his *Autobiography* he wrote approvingly that his father looked forward to an increase in freedom in relations between the sexes, freedom which would be devoid of any sensuality "either of a theoretical or of a practical kind." His own twenty-year friendship with Harriet Taylor before their marriage was "one of strong affection and confidential intimacy only." *Autobiography of John Stuart Mill* (New York: Columbia University Press, 1944), pp. 75, 161. In *The Principles of Political Economy* Mill remarked that in his own day "the animal instinct" occupied a "disproportionate preponderance in human life." *C. W.*, III, p. 766.

39. G. W. F Hegel, *The Philosophy of Right*, ed. T. M. Knox (London: Oxford University Press, 1952), p. 11, quoted in Krouse, p. 40.

Friedrich Nietzsche

The name Friedrich Nietzsche conjures in the mind a bold and dark vision of the human condition. This vision stems partly from his idiosyncratic manner of expression—short, choppy "aphorisms" punctuated by statements like "God is dead" and phrases like "will to power" which have the capacity to shock and bewilder the first-time reader. But largely this view is the inevitable legacy of a writer who forces us to view ourselves stripped of all illusion. If we find the vision frightening, it may be because he dares us to confront our innermost suspicions and insecurities with brutal honesty.

Nietzsche was born in Prussia in 1844. His father was a Lutheran pastor who died when Friedrich was quite young. His growing years were spent in a female-dominated household where he was surrounded by his mother, grandmother, sister, and two maiden aunts. He was apparently an excellent student, though not much liked by local children who found him odd and sickly. In 1864, he attended the University of Bonn where he studied philology and theology. A year later, he moved to Leipzig to study with Friedrich Ritschl, an influential classical scholar. It is during this period that he discovered the work of Arthur Schopenhauer, whose pessimistic philosophy of blind will he found alluring. He spent a year in required military service in 1867, and suffered a fall from a horse which caused him great pain and intensified the migraine headaches from which he suffered throughout his life. Upon discharge from the military he returned to Leipzig, where he befriended the German composer Richard Wagner, with whom he shared many discussions on art and culture until their falling-out over Wagner's zealous nationalism and racial prejudices.

In 1869, Nietzsche was awarded the position of associate professor at the University of Basel despite the fact that he had not completed his doctoral studies or the required thesis usually necessary for the position. No doubt his former teacher, Ritschl, had much to do with this appointment. Becoming a Swiss citizen at Basel, Nietzsche's lectures and early works focused on Greek culture, setting the stage for his later views on the rebirth of culture in Germany. In 1878, he gained a reputation as a social critic with the publication of *Human, All Too Human*. In 1879, Nietzsche retired from university teaching due to his health, but he continued writing significant philosophical works for the rest of his life.

Throughout the 1880s, Nietzsche published a spate of now-classic works, including *The Gay Science, Beyond Good and Evil, The Genealogy of Morals*, and *Thus Spoke Zarathustra*. In these works, Nietzsche argued that morality is merely a tool used by the weak to restrain the strong and that, eventually, a superman or over-man (*Übermensch*) will emerge—the kind of person who will not be afraid to break with conventional morality and pursue new horizons through intense self-criticism and personal challenge.

As his repeated bouts with illness and poverty gave way to madness, Nietzsche spent his last days in an asylum. He finally died of a stroke in 1900. Several works were published posthumously, including *The Will to Power*, a compilation of many scattered notes he left behind.

Among the many significant ideas Nietzsche advanced, the concept of a "will to power" is central. The term expresses the idea that all life, by its very presence, seeks to control its environment. This control can take various forms, from resource dominance among animal species, to self-confident assertions of mastery in more complex human interactions, such as intellectual argument or politics. Though this notion has been used to demonstrate his totalitarian tendencies, Nietzsche was more concerned with the will to power's artistic and philosophical aspects than with its political implications.

Nietzsche believed that Western civilization was in decline, largely because it had too long denied the elemental forces of human psychology and social life. Conventional morality, with such categories as sin, pity, and God, had submerged the will to power to an ethic of ascetic self-denial. At one time, moral viewpoints showed a capacity to elevate human horizons and to motivate noble action, but in modern times, morality has served only to perpetuate the control of the weak over the strong. This "slave morality" has outlived its usefulness and now stymies the opening of new intellectual and social horizons. With a fearless recognition that the old, illusory morality is now obsolete (i.e., that "God is dead"), civilization's only hope for regeneration lies in a re-evaluation of all values, the development of a new moral code by the "man of the future"—the *Übermensch*.

Perhaps Nietzsche's most obscure notion is that of eternal recurrence. As a proposed scientific doctrine, it refers to the perpetual recurrence of the same sequences of events—the same combinations of forces found in human life and history. Thus, we are destined to be reborn and live our lives again in future worlds. As a metaphor, however, eternal recurrence indicates one's eagerness to embrace life by willing its infinite repetition. The point Nietzsche makes with this concept is essentially the point of his whole philosophy: one must live a life of meaningful self-assertion and mastery, rather than a life of complacent mediocrity and servility.

Since his political views are seldom explicitly stated, Nietzsche is sometimes overlooked by political philosophers. Yet, his social criticism and penetrating psychology should force political theorists to reconsider their basic assumptions on a host of issues,

from the nature of human beings to the moral basis of the community. Nietzsche's influence has impacted philosophers from Heidegger and Sartre to Derrida and Foucault, as well as schools of thought from existentialism to post-modernism.

Beyond Good and Evil and *The Genealogy of Morals*

The selections reprinted here illustrate Nietzsche's unique manner of expression, his genealogical method, and his central philosophic concerns. First published in 1886, *Beyond Good and Evil* contains 296 wide-ranging aphorisms (brief discourses or truisms), arranged in nine major sections, and linked by the theme of morality. The central focus of the aphorisms included here is the nature of the will to power, especially as it relates to moral values. For example, aphorisms 257–260 and 263–264 suggest that one of the most important human characteristics is the drive to create new moral values—if we dare. Only through encouraging that creative energy can society overcome a corrupt civilization and achieve spiritual greatness.

The Genealogy of Morals, published in 1887, continues the discussion of morality—this time focusing on the question of its origins. In this work, Nietzsche explores the linguistic origins and philosophic implications of such concepts as "good," "bad," "guilt," and "bad conscience." He believes that modern values may be traced to a conflict between a master morality of the strong, creatively affirming what is good, and a slave morality of the weak, arising out of resentment and envy (*ressentiment*). The problem with Western civilization is that it has fallen victim to a pervasive sickness marked by philosophical illusion and ascetic self-denial—in short, a sickness brought about by the victory of slave morality.

Commentaries

The fact that Nietzsche's work continues to be controversial and inspire vast differences in interpretation is clear from the two commentaries reproduced here. One argues that Nietzsche's views are compatible with the political perspective and politics of postmodernism; the other denies that Nietzsche intended any political program at all. Careful attention to these commentaries at least gives one appreciation for the reasons Nietzsche's work continues to inflame political discourse.

To understand Nietzsche's moral perspective, it is useful to contrast his vision with the more traditional approach taken by theorists like Immanuel Kant. As Keith Ansell-Pearson demonstrates in an excerpt from his work, Nietzsche rejects the ahistorical conception of the self that for Kant (and modern liberalism) makes possible a universal (and universalizable) ethic. Nietzsche holds that genuinely autonomous individuals move beyond the homogenization of the "morality of custom" to create their own values and virtues in unique ways. Ansell-Pearson goes on to explore the problems and possibilities this holds for modern political thought: problems that include ambiguity of aims and uncertainty of community ties, and possibilities that include the kind of diversity and authenticity upon which feminist and postmodern authors build.

Ted Sadler takes issue with the "perspectival" approach many postmodern theorists claim to derive from Nietzsche's works. Indeed, Sadler claims that those theorists who believe Nietzsche divorced himself from the notions of truth and hierarchy and who ascribe to him support for a politics of diversity and plurality simply misconstrue what Nietzsche taught. According to Sadler, the type of authenticity and freedom about which Nietzsche spoke cannot be found in politics at all. It is available only in philosophy and only to those few capable of genuine philosophizing. If Sadler is correct, the pluralistic and democratizing implications drawn from Nietzsche by postmoderns and some feminists cannot be sustained on grounds Nietzsche would accept.

Web Sources

http://www.cwu.edu/~millerj/nietzsche/
Pirate Nietzsche Page. Links to a host of writings by and about Nietzsche.

http://www.knuten.liu.se/~bjoch509/philosophers/nie.html
Björn's Guide to Philosophy. Background on the philosopher's life and writings with links to articles and websites.

http://www.pitt.edu/~wbcurry/nietzsche.html
The Perspectives of Nietzsche. Short takes on Nietzsche's ideas on a host of subjects as well as links to on-line articles.

http://www.swan.ac.uk/german/fns/fns.htm
Nietzsche Society Homepage. Information about the society's journal and upcoming conferences around the world.

http://www.utm.edu/research/iep/n/nihilism.htm#
The Internet Encyclopedia of Philosophy: Friedrich Nietzsche and Nihilism. Discussion of Nihilism and Nietzsche's contribution to its development.

Class Activities and Discussion Items

1. Nietzsche drew inspiration for the transvaluation of values from cultural sources (e.g., the music of Wagner). Identify and discuss contemporary cultural sources that you believe serve the same function (e.g., "gangsta rap," etc.). Indicate how these sources transcend traditional societal notions of good and evil. Should these cultural products be viewed positively from the standpoint of individual growth? Should they be viewed positively from the standpoint of society?

2. Compare and contrast Nietzsche's idea of the "will to power" with Charles Darwin's concept of fitness. In what ways are the two concepts similar? In what ways are they different?

3. Some commentators believe that a culture of victimization has arisen in America in the past few decades in which disadvantaged individuals and groups blame their condition on the rest of society. Do you believe this is an example of Nietzsche's idea of *ressentiment* or are there legitimate reasons for these individuals to complain about ill-treatment by society? Sample the views of your classmates.

4. Nietzsche seems to glorify the individual who dares to be different and

unique. Do you believe a life lived in search of being different can be sustained? Do you know people who actively seek such uniqueness? Do you believe these individuals are achieving a sense of genuineness or are they simply searching for social acceptance? Do you believe it is possible to achieve authenticity as a member of a particular society?

5. Compare the views of Nietzsche with those of philosophic individualists like Henry David Thoreau. Each extols the virtues of individualism. How are their philosophies alike? How are they different? Whose views do you support, if either? Why?

Further Reading

Ansell-Pearson, Keith. 1994. *An Introduction to Nietzsche as Political Thinker: The Perfect Nihilist.* New York: Cambridge University Press. An exploration of the contributions of Nietzsche to postmodern political thought.

Appel, Fredrick. 1999. *Nietzsche Contra Democracy.* Ithaca, NY: Cornell University Press. A critique of contemporary analyses of Nietzsche that focusing on Nietzsche's distinction between higher and lower natures and what is noble and what is base.

Conway, Daniel W. 1997. *Nietzche's Dangerous Game: Philosophy in the Twilight of the Idols.* New York: Cambridge University Press. An examination of the latter part of Nietzsche's life. Nietzsche is seen to be aware of his own decadence and of his complicity with the very tendencies that he dissects and deplores.

Hollingdale, R. J. 2001. *Nietzsche: The Man and His Philosophy.* New York: Cambridge University Press. Highly respected examination of the life and contributions of Nietzsche.

Kaufmann, Walter A. 2000. *Basic Writings of Nietzsche (Modern Library Classics).* New York: Modern Library. Translations of three basic works: *The Birth of Tragedy, Beyond Good and Evil,* and *On the Genealogy of Morals.* Includes an additional 75 aphorisms drawn from Nietzsche's celebrated aphoristic works.

Magnus, Bernard and Kathleen Marie Higgins (eds.). 1996. *The Cambridge Companion to Nietzsche.* New York: Cambridge University Press. A compilation of viewpoints on the impact of Nietzsche in the modern age.

Owen, David. 1995. *Nietzsche, Politics and Modernity: A Critique of Liberal Reason.* Thousand Oaks, Calif.: Sage Publications. Nietzsche's impact on liberal political psychology is examined.

Parkes, Graham (ed.). 1991. *Nietzsche and Asian Thought.* Chicago: University of Chicago Press. A wide range of authors examine the meaning of Nietzsche from a distinctly Asian perspective.

Tanner, Michael. 1994. *Nietzsche.* New York: Oxford University Press. A slim but useful introduction to Nietzsche's life and the major themes present in his work.

Warren, M. 1988. *Nietzsche and Political Thought.* Cambridge, MA: MIT Press. The author attempts to identify Nietzsche's place in political theory as a "neo-aristocratic conservative." ✦

36

Excerpts from *Beyond Good and Evil*

Friedrich Nietzsche

Part One: On the Prejudices of Philosophers

9

"According to nature" you want to *live*? O you noble Stoics, what deceptive words these are! Imagine a being like nature, wasteful beyond measure, indifferent beyond measure, without purposes and consideration, without mercy and justice, fertile and desolate and uncertain at the same time; imagine indifference itself as a power—how *could* you live according to this indifference? Living—is that not precisely wanting to be other than this nature? Is not living—estimating, preferring, being unjust, being limited, wanting to be different? And supposing your imperative "live according to nature" meant at bottom as much as "live according to life"—how could you *not* do that? Why make a principle of what you yourselves are and must be?

In truth, the matter is altogether different: while you pretend rapturously to read the canon of your law in nature, you want something opposite, you strange actors and self-deceivers! Your pride wants to impose your morality, your ideal, on nature—even on nature—and incorporate them in her; you demand that she should be nature "according to the Stoa," and you would like all existence to exist only after your own image—as an immense eternal glorification and generalization of Stoicism. For all your love of truth, you have forced yourselves so long, so persis-

tently, so rigidly-hypnotically to see nature the wrong way, namely Stoically, that you are no longer able to see her differently. And some abysmal arrogance finally still inspires you with the insane hope that *because* you know how to tyrannize yourselves—Stoicism is self-tyranny—nature, too, lets herself be tyrannized: is not the Stoic—a *piece* of nature?

But this is an ancient, eternal story: what formerly happened with the Stoics still happens today, too, as soon as any philosophy begins to believe in itself. It always creates the world in its own image; it cannot do otherwise. Philosophy is this tyrannical drive itself, the most spiritual will to power, to the "creation of the world," to the *causa prima*. . . .

13

Physiologists should think before putting down the instinct of self-preservation as the cardinal instinct of an organic being. A living thing seeks above all to *discharge* its strength—life itself is *will to power*; self-preservation is only one of the indirect and most frequent *results*.

In short, here as everywhere else, let us beware of *superfluous* teleological principles—one of which is the instinct of self-preservation (we owe it to Spinoza's inconsistency).[1] Thus method, which must be essentially economy of principles, demands it. . . .

19

Philosophers are accustomed to speak of the will as if it were the best-known thing in the world; indeed, Schopenhauer has given us to understand that the will alone is really known to us, absolutely and completely known, without subtraction or addition. But again and again it seems to me that in this case, too, Schopenhauer only did what philosophers are in the habit of doing—he adopted a *popular prejudice* and exaggerated it. Willing seems to me to be above all something *complicated*, something that is a unit only as a word—and it is precisely in this one word that the popular prejudice lurks, which has defeated the always inadequate caution of philosophers. So let us for once be more cautious, let us be "unphilosophical": let us say that in all willing there is, first, a plurality of sensations, namely, the sensation of the state *"away from which,"* the sensation of the state *"towards which,"* the sensations of this *"from"* and *"towards"* themselves, and then also an accompanying muscular sensation, which, even without our putting into motion "arms and legs," begins its action by force of habit as soon as we "will" anything.

Therefore, just as sensations (and indeed many kinds of sensations) are to be recognized as ingredients of the will, so, secondly, should thinking also: in every act of the will there is a ruling thought—let us not imagine it possible to sever this thought from the "willing," as if any will would then remain over!

Third, the will is not only a complex of sensation and thinking, but it is above all an *affect,* and specifically the affect of the command. That which is termed "freedom of the will" is essentially the affect of superiority in relation to him who must obey: "I am free, 'he' must obey"—this consciousness is inherent in every will; and equally so the straining of the attention, the straight look that fixes itself exclusively on one aim, the unconditional evaluation that "this and nothing else is necessary now," the inward certainty that obedience will be rendered—and whatever else belongs to the position of the commander. A man who *wills* commands something within himself that renders obedience, or that he believes renders obedience.

But now let us notice what is strangest about the will—this manifold thing for which the people have only one word: inasmuch as in the given circumstances we are at the same time the commanding *and* the obeying parties, and as the obeying party we know the sensations of constraint, impulsion, pressure, resistance, and motion, which usually begin immediately after the act of will; inasmuch as, on the other hand, we are accustomed to disregard this duality, and to deceive ourselves about it by means of the synthetic concept "I," a whole series of erroneous conclusions, and consequently of false evaluations of the will itself, has become attached to the act of willing—to such a degree that he who wills believes sincerely that willing *suffices* for action. Since in the

great majority of cases there has been exercise of will only when the effect of the command—that is, obedience; that is, the action—was to be *expected,* the *appearance* has translated itself into the feeling, as if there were a *necessity of effect.* In short, he who wills believes with a fair amount of certainty that will and action are somehow one; he ascribes the success, the carrying out of the willing, to the will itself, and thereby enjoys an increase of the sensation of power which accompanies all success.

"Freedom of the will"—that is the expression for the complex state of delight of the person exercising volition, who commands and at the same time identifies himself with the executor of the order—who, as such, enjoys also the triumph over obstacles, but thinks within himself that it was really his will itself that overcame them. In this way the person exercising volition adds the feelings of delight of his successful executive instruments, the useful "under-wills" or under-souls—indeed, our body is but a social structure composed of many souls—to his feelings of delight as commander. *L'effet c'est moi:*[2] what happens here is what happens in every well-constructed and happy commonwealth; namely, the governing class identifies itself with the successes of the commonwealth. In all willing it is absolutely a question of commanding and obeying, on the basis, as already said, of a social structure composed of many "souls." Hence a philosopher should claim the right to include willing as such within the sphere of morals—morals being understood as the doctrine of the relations of supremacy under which the phenomenon of "life" comes to be. . . .

21

The *causa sui* is the best self-contradiction that has been conceived so far, it is a sort of rape and perversion of logic; but the extravagant pride of man has managed to entangle itself profoundly and frightfully with just this nonsense. The desire for "freedom of the will" in the superlative metaphysical sense, which still holds sway, unfortunately, in the minds of the half-educated; the desire to bear the entire and ultimate responsibility for one's actions oneself, and to absolve God, the world, ancestors, chance, and society involves nothing less than to be precisely this *causa sui* and, with more than Münchhausen's audacity, to pull oneself up into existence by the hair, out of the swamps of nothingness. Suppose someone were thus to see through the boorish simplicity of this celebrated concept of "free will" and put it out of his head altogether, I beg of him to carry his "enlightenment" a step further, and also put out of his head the contrary of this monstrous conception of "free will": I mean "unfree will," which amounts to a misuse of cause and effect. One should not wrongly reify "cause" and "effect," as the natural scientists do (and whoever, like them, now "naturalizes" in his thinking), according to the prevailing mechanical doltishness which makes the cause press and push until it "effects" its end; one should use "cause" and "effect" only as pure concepts, that is to say, as conventional fictions for the purpose of designation and communication—*not* for explanation. In the "in-itself" there is nothing of "causal connections," of "necessity," or of "psychological non-freedom"; there the effect does *not* follow the cause, there is no rule of "law." It is *we* alone who have devised cause, sequence, for-each-other, relativity, constraint, number, law, freedom, motive, and purpose; and when we project and mix this symbol world into things as if it existed "in itself," we act once more as we have always acted—*mythologically*. The "unfree will" is mythology; in real life it is only a matter of *strong* and *weak* wills.

It is almost always a symptom of what is lacking in himself when a thinker senses in every "causal connection" and "psychological necessity" something of constraint, need, compulsion to obey, pressure, and unfreedom; it is suspicious to have such feelings—the person betrays himself. And in general, if I have observed correctly, the "unfreedom of the will" is regarded as a problem from two entirely opposite standpoints, but always in a profoundly *personal* manner: some will not give up their "responsibility," their belief in *themselves*, the personal right to *their* merits at any price (the vain races belong to this class). Others, on the contrary, do not wish to be answerable

for anything, or blamed for anything, and owing to an inward self-contempt, seek to *lay the blame for themselves somewhere else.* The latter, when they write books, are in the habit today of taking the side of criminals; a sort of socialist pity is their most attractive disguise. And as a matter of fact, the fatalism of the weak-willed embellishes itself surprisingly when it can pose as *"la religion de la souffrance humaine"*;[3] that is *its* "good taste." . . .

23

All psychology so far has got stuck in moral prejudices and fears; it has not dared to descend into the depths. To understand it as morphology and *the doctrine of the development of the will to power,* as I do—nobody has yet come close to doing this even in thought—insofar as it is permissible to recognize in what has been written so far a symptom of what has so far been kept silent. The power of moral prejudices has penetrated deeply into the most spiritual world, which would seem to be the coldest and most devoid of presuppositions, and has obviously operated in an injurious, inhibiting, blinding, and distorting manner. A proper physio-psychology has to contend with unconscious resistance in the heart of the investigator, it has "the heart" against it: even a doctrine of the reciprocal dependence of the "good" and the "wicked" drives, causes (as refined immorality) distress and aversion in a still hale and hearty conscience—still more so, a doctrine of the derivation of all good impulses from wicked ones. If, however, a person should regard even the effects of hatred, envy, covetousness, and the lust to rule as conditions of life, as factors which, fundamentally and essentially, must be present in the general economy of life (and must, therefore, be further enhanced if life is to be further enhanced)—he will suffer from such a view of things as from seasickness. And yet even this hypothesis is far from being the strangest and most painful in this immense and almost new domain of dangerous insights; and there are in fact a hundred good reasons why everyone should keep away from it who—*can.*

On the other hand, if one has once drifted there with one's bark, well! all right! let us clench our teeth! let us open our eyes and keep our hand firm on the helm! We sail right *over* morality, we crush, we destroy perhaps the remains of our own morality by daring to make our voyage there—but what matter are *we!* Never yet did a *profounder* world of insight reveal itself to daring travelers and adventurers, and the psychologist who thus "makes a sacrifice"—it is *not* the *sacrifizio dell' intelletto,*[4] on the contrary!—will at least be entitled to demand in return that psychology shall be recognized again as the queen of the sciences, for whose service and preparation the other sciences exist. For psychology is now again the path to the fundamental problems. . . .

Part Six: We Scholars

211

I insist that people should finally stop confounding philosophical laborers, and scientific men generally, with philosophers; precisely at this point we should be strict about giving "each his due," and not far too much to those and far too little to these.

It may be necessary for the education of a genuine philosopher that he himself has also once stood on all these steps on which his servants, the scientific laborers of philosophy, remain standing—*have to* remain standing. Perhaps he himself must have been critic and skeptic and dogmatist and historian and also poet and collector and traveler and solver of riddles and moralist and seer and "free spirit" and almost everything in order to pass through the whole range of human values and value feelings and to be *able* to see with many different eyes and consciences, from a height and into every distance, from the depths into every height, from a nook into every expanse. But all these are merely preconditions of his task: this task itself demands something different—it demands that he *create values.*

Those philosophical laborers after the noble model of Kant and Hegel have to determine and press into formulas, whether in the realm of *logic* or *political* (moral) thought or *art,* some great data of valuations—that is,

former *positings* of values, creations of value which have become dominant and are for a time called "truths." It is for these investigators to make everything that has happened and been esteemed so far easy to look over, easy to think over, intelligible and manageable, to abbreviate everything long, even "time," and to *overcome* the entire past—an enormous and wonderful task in whose service every subtle pride, every tough will can certainly find satisfaction. *Genuine philosophers, however, are commanders and legislators:* they say, *"thus it shall* be!" They first determine the Whither and For What of man, and in so doing have at their disposal the preliminary labor of all philosophical laborers, all who have overcome the past. With a creative hand they reach for the future, and all that is and has been becomes a means for them, an instrument, a hammer. Their "knowing" is *creating,* their creating is a legislation, their will to truth is—*will to power.*

Are there such philosophers today? Have there been such philosophers yet? *Must* there not be such philosophers?

212

More and more it seems to me that the philosopher, being *of necessity* a man of tomorrow and the day after tomorrow, has always found himself, and *had* to find himself, in contradiction to his today: his enemy was ever the ideal of today. So far all these extraordinary furtherers of man whom one calls philosophers, though they themselves have rarely felt like friends of wisdom but rather like disagreeable fools and dangerous question marks, have found their task, their hard, unwanted, inescapable task, but eventually also the greatness of their task, in being the bad conscience of their time.

By applying the knife vivisectionally to the chest of the very *virtues of their time,* they betrayed what was their own secret: to know of a *new* greatness of man, of a new untrodden way to his enhancement. Every time they exposed how much hypocrisy, comfortableness, letting oneself go and letting oneself drop, how many lies lay hidden under the best honored type of their contemporary morality, how much virtue was *outlived.*

Every time they said: "We must get there, that way, where you today are least at home."

Facing a world of "modern ideas" that would banish everybody into a corner and "specialty," a philosopher—if today there could be philosophers—would be compelled to find the greatness of man, the concept of "greatness," precisely in his range and multiplicity, in his wholeness in manifoldness. He would even determine value and rank in accordance with how much and how many things one could bear and take upon himself, how *far* one could extend his responsibility.

Today the taste of the time and the virtue of the time weakens and thins down the will; nothing is as timely as weakness of the will. In the philosopher's ideal, therefore, precisely strength of the will, hardness, and the capacity for long-range decisions must belong to the concept of "greatness"—with as much justification as the opposite doctrine and the ideal of a dumb, renunciatory, humble, selfless humanity was suitable for an opposite age, one that suffered, like the sixteenth century, from its accumulated energy of will and from the most savage floods and tidal waves of selfishness.

In the age of Socrates, among men of fatigued instincts, among the conservatives of ancient Athens who let themselves go—"toward happiness," as they said; toward pleasure, as they acted—and who all the while still mouthed the ancient pompous words to which their lives no longer gave them any right, *irony* may have been required for greatness of soul, that Socratic sarcastic assurance of the old physician and plebeian who cut ruthlessly into his own flesh, as he did into the flesh and heart of the "noble," with a look that said clearly enough: "Don't dissemble in front of me! Here—we are equal."

Today, conversely, when only the herd animal receives and dispenses honors in Europe, when "equality of rights" could all too easily be changed into equality in violating rights—I mean, into a common war on all that is rare, strange, privileged, the higher man, the higher soul, the higher duty, the higher responsibility, and the abundance of creative power and masterfulness—today the concept of greatness entails being noble,

wanting to be by oneself, being able to be different, standing alone and having to live independently. And the philosopher will betray something of his own ideal when he posits: "He shall be greatest who can be loneliest, the most concealed, the most deviant, the human being beyond good and evil, the master of his virtues, he that is overrich in will. Precisely this shall be called *greatness:* being capable of being as manifold as whole, as ample as full." And to ask it once more: today—is greatness *possible?* . . .

Part Eight: Peoples and Fatherlands

241

We "good Europeans"—we, too, know hours when we permit ourselves some hearty fatherlandishness, a plop and relapse into old loves and narrownesses—I have just given a sample of that—hours of national agitations, patriotic palpitations, and various other sorts of archaizing sentimental inundations. More ponderous spirits than we are may require more time to get over what with us takes only hours and in a few hours has run its course: some require half a year, others half a life, depending on the speed and power of their digestion and metabolism. Indeed, I could imagine dull[5] and sluggish races who would require half a century even in our rapidly moving Europe to overcome such atavistic attacks of fatherlandishness and soil addiction and to return to reason, meaning "good Europeanism."

As I am digressing to this possibility, it so happens that I become an ear-witness of a conversation between two old "patriots": apparently both were hard of hearing and therefore spoke that much louder.

"*He* thinks and knows as much of philosophy as a peasant or a fraternity student," said one; "he is still innocent. But what does it matter today? This is the age of the masses: they grovel on their bellies before anything massive. In *politics*, too. A statesman who piles up for them another tower of Babel, a monster of empire and power, they call 'great'; what does it matter that we, more cautious and reserved, do not yet abandon the old faith that only a great thought can give a deed or cause greatness. Suppose a statesman put his people in a position requiring them to go in for 'great politics' from now on, though they were ill-disposed for that by nature and ill prepared as well, so that they would find it necessary to sacrifice their old and secure virtues for the sake of a novel and dubious mediocrity—suppose a statesman actually condemned his people to 'politicking' although so far they had had better things to do and think about, and deep down in their souls they had not got rid of a cautious disgust with the restlessness, emptiness, and noisy quarrelsomeness of peoples that really go in for politicking—suppose such a statesman goaded the slumbering passions and lusts of his people, turning their diffidence and delight in standing aside into a blot, their cosmopolitanism and secret infinity into a serious wrong, devaluating their most cordial inclinations, inverting their conscience, making their spirit narrow, their taste 'national'—what! a statesman who did all this, for whom his people would have to atone for all future time, if they have any future, such a statesman should be *great*?"

"Without a doubt!" the other patriot replied vehemently; "otherwise he would not have been *able* to do it. Perhaps it was insane to want such a thing? But perhaps everything great was merely insane when it started."

"An abuse of words!" his partner shouted back; "strong! strong! strong and insane! *Not* great!"

The old men had obviously become heated as they thus flung their truths into each other's faces; but I, in my happiness and beyond, considered how soon one stronger will become master over the strong; also that for the spiritual flattening[6] of a people there is a compensation, namely the deepening of another people.

242

Call that in which the distinction of the European is sought "civilization" or "humanization" or "progress," or call it simply—without praise or blame—using a political formula, Europe's *democratic* movement: behind all the moral and political foregrounds to which such formulas point, a tremendous *physiological* process is taking place and gaining momentum. The Europeans are becoming more similar to each other; they become more and more detached from the conditions under which races originate that are tied to some climate or class; they become increasingly independent of any *determinate* milieu that would like to inscribe itself for centuries in body and soul with the same demands. Thus an essentially supra-national and nomadic type of man is gradually coming up, a type that possesses, physiologically speaking, a maximum of the art and power of adaptation as its typical distinction.

The tempo of this process of the *"evolving European"* may be retarded by great relapses, but perhaps it will gain in vehemence and profundity and grow just on their account: the still raging storm and stress of "national feeling" belongs here, also that anarchism which is just now coming up. But this process will probably lead to results which would seem to be least expected by those who naïvely promote and praise it, the apostles of "modern ideas." The very same new conditions that will on the average lead to the leveling and mediocritization of man—to a useful, industrious, handy, multipurpose herd animal—are likely in the highest degree to give birth to exceptional human beings of the most dangerous and attractive quality.

To be sure, that power of adaptation which keeps trying out changing conditions and begins some new work with every generation, almost with every decade, does not make possible the *powerfulness* of the type, and the over-all impression of such future Europeans will probably be that of manifold garrulous workers who will be poor in will, extremely employable, and as much in need of a master and commander as of their daily bread. But while the democratization of Europe leads to the production of a type that is prepared for *slavery* in the subtlest sense, in single, exceptional cases the *strong* human being will have to turn out stronger and richer than perhaps ever before—thanks to the absence of prejudice from his training, thanks to the tremendous manifoldness of practice, art, and mask. I meant to say: the democratization of Europe is at the same time an involuntary arrangement for the cultivation of *tyrants*—taking that word in every sense, including the most spiritual. . . .

Part Nine: What Is Noble

257

Every enhancement of the type "man" has so far been the work of an aristocratic society—and it will be so again and again—a society that believes in the long ladder of an order of rank and differences in value between man and man, and that needs slavery in some sense or other. Without that *pathos of distance* which grows out of the ingrained difference between strata—when the ruling caste constantly looks afar and looks down upon subjects and instruments and just as constantly practices obedience and command, keeping down and keeping at a distance—that other, more mysterious pathos could not have grown up either—the craving for an ever new widening of distances within the soul itself, the development of ever higher, rarer, more remote, further-stretching, more comprehensive states—in brief, simply the enhancement of the type "man," the continual "self-overcoming of man," to use a moral formula in a supra-moral sense.

To be sure, one should not yield to humanitarian illusions about the origins of an aristocratic society (and thus of the presupposition of this enhancement of the type "man"): truth is hard. Let us admit to ourselves, without trying to be considerate, how every higher culture on earth so far has *begun.* Human beings whose nature was still natural, barbarians in every terrible sense of the word, men of prey who were still in possession of unbroken strength of will and lust for power, hurled themselves upon weaker, more civilized, more peaceful races, perhaps traders or cattle raisers, or upon mellow old cultures whose last vitality was even then flaring up in splendid fireworks of spirit and corruption. In the beginning, the noble caste was always the barbarian caste: their predominance did not lie mainly in physical strength but in strength of the soul—they were more *whole* human beings (which also means, at every level, "more whole beasts").

258

Corruption as the expression of a threatening anarchy among the instincts and of the fact that the foundation of the affects, which is called "life," has been shaken: corruption is something totally different depending on the organism in which it appears. When, for example, an aristocracy, like that of France at the beginning of the Revolution, throws away its privileges with a sublime disgust and sacrifices itself to an extravagance of its own moral feelings, that is corruption; it was really only the last act of that centuries-old corruption which had led them to surrender, step by step, their governmental prerogatives, demoting themselves to a mere *function* of the monarchy (finally even to a mere ornament and showpiece). The essential characteristic of a good and healthy aristocracy, however, is that it experiences itself *not* as a function (whether of the monarchy or the commonwealth) but as their *meaning* and highest justification—that it therefore accepts with a good conscience the sacrifice of untold human beings who, *for its sake,* must be reduced and lowered to incomplete human beings, to slaves, to instruments. Their fundamental faith simply has to be that society must *not* exist for society's sake but only as the foundation and scaffolding on which a choice type of being is able to raise itself to its higher task and to a higher state of *being*—comparable to those sun-seeking vines of Java—they are called *Sipo Matador*—that so long and so often enclasp an oak tree with their tendrils until eventually, high above it but supported by it, they can unfold their crowns in the open light and display their happiness.

259

Refraining mutually from injury, violence, and exploitation and placing one's will on a par with that of someone else—this may become, in a certain rough sense, good manners among individuals if the appropriate conditions are present (namely, if these men are actually similar in strength and value standards and belong together in *one* body). But as soon as this principle is extended, and possibly even accepted as the *fundamental principle of society*, it immediately proves to be what it really is—a will to the *denial* of life, a principle of disintegration and decay.

Here we must beware of superficiality and get to the bottom of the matter, resisting all sentimental weakness: life itself is *essentially* appropriation, injury, overpowering of what is alien and weaker; suppression, hardness, imposition of one's own forms, incorporation and at least, at its mildest, exploitation—but why should one always use those words in which a slanderous intent has been imprinted for ages?

Even the body within which individuals treat each other as equals, as suggested before—and this happens in every healthy aristocracy—if it is a living and not a dying body, has to do to other bodies what the individuals within it refrain from doing to each other: it will have to be an incarnate will to power, it will strive to grow, spread, seize, become predominant—not from any morality or immorality but because it is *living* and because life simply *is* will to power. But there is no point on which the ordinary consciousness of Europeans resists instruction as on this: everywhere people are now raving, even under scientific disguises, about coming conditions of society in which "the exploitative aspect" will be removed—which sounds to me as if they promised to invent a way of life that would dispense with all organic functions. "Exploitation" does not belong to a corrupt or imperfect and primitive society: it belongs to the *essence* of what lives, as a basic organic function; it is a consequence of the will to power, which is after all the will of life.

If this should be an innovation as a theory—as a reality it is the *primordial fact* of all history: people ought to be honest with themselves at least that far.

260

Wandering through the many subtler and coarser moralities which have so far been prevalent on earth, or still are prevalent, I found that certain features recurred regularly together and were closely associated—until I finally discovered two basic types and one basic difference.

There are *master morality* and *slave morality*—I add immediately that in all the higher and more mixed cultures there also appear attempts at mediation between these two moralities, and yet more often the interpenetration and mutual misunderstanding of both, and at times they occur directly alongside each other—even in the same human being, within a *single* soul. The moral discrimination of values has originated either among a ruling group whose consciousness of its difference from the ruled group was accompanied by delight—or among the ruled, the slaves and dependents of every degree.

In the first case, when the ruling group determines what is "good," the exalted, proud states of the soul are experienced as conferring distinction and determining the order of rank. The noble human being separates from himself those in whom the opposite of such exalted, proud states finds expression: he despises them. It should be noted immediately that in this first type of morality the opposition of "good" and "*bad*" means approximately the same as "noble" and "contemptible." (The opposition of "good" and "*evil*" has a different origin.) One feels contempt for the cowardly, the anxious, the petty, those intent on narrow utility; also for the suspicious with their unfree glances, those who humble themselves, the doglike people who allow themselves to be maltreated, the begging flatterers, above all the liars: it is part of the fundamental faith of all aristocrats that the common people lie. "We truthful ones"—thus the nobility of ancient Greece referred to itself.

It is obvious that moral designations were everywhere first applied to *human beings* and only later, derivatively, to actions. Therefore it is a gross mistake when historians of morality start from such questions as: why was the compassionate act praised? The noble type of man experiences *itself* as determining values; it does not need approval; it judges, "what is harmful to me is harmful in itself"; it knows itself to be that which first accords honor to things; it is *value-creating*. Everything it knows as part of itself it honors: such a morality is self-glorification. In the foreground there is the feeling of fullness, of power that seeks to overflow, the happiness of high tension, the consciousness of wealth that would give and bestow: the noble human being, too, helps the unfortunate, but not, or almost not, from pity, but prompted more by an urge begotten by excess of power. The noble human being honors himself as one who is powerful, also as one who has power over himself, who knows how to speak and be silent, who delights in being severe and hard with himself and respects all severity and hardness. "A hard heart Wotan put into my breast," says an old Scandinavian saga: a fitting poetic expression, seeing that it comes from the soul of a proud Viking. Such a type of man is actually proud of the fact that he is *not* made for pity, and the hero of the saga therefore adds as a warning: "If the heart is not hard in youth it will never harden." Noble and courageous human beings who think that way are furthest removed from that morality which finds the distinction of morality precisely in pity, or in acting for others, or in *désintéressement;* faith in oneself, pride in oneself, a fundamental hostility and irony against "selflessness" belong just as definitely to noble morality as does a slight disdain and caution regarding compassionate feelings and a "warm heart."

It is the powerful who *understand* how to honor; this is their art, their realm of invention. The profound reverence for age and tradition—all law rests on this double reverence—the faith and prejudice in favor of ancestors and disfavor of those yet to come are typical of the morality of the powerful; and when the men of "modern ideas," conversely, believe almost instinctively in "progress" and "the future" and more and more lack respect for age, this in itself would sufficiently betray the ignoble origin of these "ideas."

A morality of the ruling group, however, is most alien and embarrassing to the present taste in the severity of its principle that one has duties only to one's peers; that against beings of a lower rank, against everything alien, one may behave as one pleases or "as the heart desires," and in any case "beyond good and evil"—here pity and like feelings may find their place. The capacity for, and the duty of, long gratitude and long revenge—both only among one's peers—re-

finement in repaying, the sophisticated concept of friendship, a certain necessity for having enemies (as it were, as drainage ditches for the affects of envy, quarrelsomeness, exuberance—at bottom, in order to be capable of being good *friends*): all these are typical characteristics of noble morality which, as suggested, is not the morality of "modern ideas" and therefore is hard to empathize with today, also hard to dig up and uncover.

It is different with the second type of morality, *slave morality.* Suppose the violated, oppressed, suffering, unfree, who are uncertain of themselves and weary, moralize: what will their moral valuations have in common? Probably, a pessimistic suspicion about the whole condition of man will find expression, perhaps a condemnation of man along with his condition. The slave's eye is not favorable to the virtues of the powerful: he is skeptical and suspicious, *subtly* suspicious, of all the "good" that is honored there—he would like to persuade himself that even their happiness is not genuine. Conversely, those qualities are brought out and flooded with light which serve to ease existence for those who suffer: here pity, the complaisant and obliging hand, the warm heart, patience, industry, humility, and friendliness are honored—for here these are the most useful qualities and almost the only means for enduring the pressure of existence. Slave morality is essentially a morality of utility.

Here is the place for the origin of that famous opposition of "good" and "evil": into evil one's feelings project power and dangerousness, a certain terribleness, subtlety, and strength that does not permit contempt to develop. According to slave morality, those who are "evil" thus inspire fear; according to master morality it is precisely those who are "good" that inspire, and wish to inspire, fear, while the "bad" are felt to be contemptible.

The opposition reaches its climax when, as a logical consequence of slave morality, a touch of disdain is associated also with the "good" of this morality—this may be slight and benevolent—because the good human being has to be *undangerous* in the slaves' way of thinking: he is good-natured, easy to deceive, a little stupid perhaps, *un bon-*

homme.[7] Wherever slave morality becomes preponderant, language tends to bring the words "good" and "stupid" closer together.

One last fundamental difference: the longing for *freedom*, the instinct for happiness and the subtleties of the feeling of freedom belong just as necessarily to slave morality and morals as artful and enthusiastic reverence and devotion are the regular symptom of an aristocratic way of thinking and evaluating.

This makes plain why love *as passion*—which is our European specialty—simply must be of noble origin: as is well known, its invention must be credited to the Provençal knight-poets, those magnificent and inventive human beings of the *"gai saber"*[8] to whom Europe owes so many things and almost owes itself. . . .

263

There is an *instinct for rank* which, more than anything else, is a sign of a *high* rank; there is a delight in the nuances of reverence that allows us to infer noble origin and habits. The refinement, graciousness, and height of a soul is tested dangerously when something of the first rank passes by without being as yet protected by the shudders of authority against obtrusive efforts and ineptitudes—something that goes its way unmarked, undiscovered, tempting, perhaps capriciously concealed and disguised, like a living touchstone. Anyone to whose task and practice it belongs to search out souls will employ this very art in many forms in order to determine the ultimate value of a soul and the unalterable, innate order of rank to which it belongs: he will test it for its *instinct of reverence*.

Différence engendre haine:[9] the baseness of some people suddenly spurts up like dirty water when some holy vessel, some precious thing from a locked shrine, some book with the marks of a great destiny, is carried past; and on the other hand there is a reflex of silence, a hesitation of the eye, a cessation of all gestures that express how a soul *feels* the proximity of the most venerable. The way in which reverence for the *Bible* has on the whole been maintained so far in Europe is perhaps the best bit of discipline and refine-

ment of manners that Europe owes to Christianity: such books of profundity and ultimate significance require some external tyranny of authority for their protection in order to gain those millennia of *persistence* which are necessary to exhaust them and figure them out.

Much is gained once the feeling has finally been cultivated in the masses (among the shallow and in the high-speed intestines of every kind) that they are not to touch everything; that there are holy experiences before which they have to take off their shoes and keep away their unclean hands—this is almost their greatest advance toward humanity. Conversely, perhaps there is nothing about so-called educated people and believers in "modern ideas" that is as nauseous as their lack of modesty and the comfortable insolence of their eyes and hands with which they touch, lick, and finger everything; and it is possible that even among the common people, among the less educated, especially among peasants, one finds today more *relative* nobility of taste and tactful reverence than among the newspaper-reading *demimonde* of the spirit, the educated.

264

One cannot erase from the soul of a human being what his ancestors liked most to do and did most constantly: whether they were, for example, assiduous savers and appurtenances of a desk and cash box, modest and bourgeois in their desires, modest also in their virtues; or whether they lived accustomed to commanding from dawn to dusk, fond of rough amusements and also perhaps of even rougher duties and responsibilities; or whether, finally, at some point they sacrificed ancient prerogatives of birth and possessions in order to live entirely for their faith—their "god"—as men of an inexorable and delicate conscience which blushes at every compromise. It is simply not possible that a human being should *not* have the qualities and preferences of his parents and ancestors in his body, whatever appearances may suggest to the contrary. This is the problem of race.[10]

If one knows something about the parents, an inference about the child is permissible: any disgusting incontinence, any nook envy, a clumsy insistence that one is always right—these three things together have always constituted the characteristic type of the plebeian—that sort of thing must as surely be transferred to the child as corrupted blood; and with the aid of the best education one will at best *deceive* with regard to such a heredity.

And what else is the aim of education and "culture" today? In our very popularity-minded—that is, plebeian—age, "education" and "culture" *have* to be essentially the art of deceiving—about one's origins, the inherited plebs in one's body and soul. An educator who today preached truthfulness above all and constantly challenged his students, "be true! be natural! do not pretend!"—even such a virtuous and guileless ass would learn after a while to reach for that *furca* of Horace to *naturam expellere:* with what success? "Plebs" *usque recurret.*[11] . . .

Notes

1. Nietzsche admired Spinoza for, among other things, his critique of theology.
2. "*I* am the effect."
3. "The religion of human suffering."
4. Sacrifice of the intellect.
5. *Dumpf* has no perfect equivalent in English. It can mean hollow or muted when applied to a sound, heavy and musty applied to air, dull applied to wits, and is a cousin of the English words, dumb and damp. Goethe still used it with a positive connotation when he wrote poetry about inarticulate feelings; Nietzsche uses the word often—with a strongly negative, anti-romantic connotation.
6. *Verflachung* (becoming shallower) contrasted with *Vertiefung* (becoming more profound). The first people is, without a doubt, Ger-

many; the statesman, Bismarck; and the second people probably France. Of course, the points made are also meant to apply more generally, but this evaluation of Bismarck at the zenith of his success and power certainly shows an amazing independence of spirit, and without grasping the full weight of the final sentence one cannot begin to understand Nietzsche's conceptions of the will to power or of "beyond good and evil."

7. Literally "a good human being," the term is used for precisely the type described here.
8. "Gay science": in the early fourteenth century the term was used to designate the art of the troubadours, codified in *Leys d'amors.* Nietzsche subtitled his own *Fröhliche Wissenschaft* (1882), "*la gaya scienza.*" . . .
9. Difference engenders hatred.
10. Here, as elsewhere, Nietzsche gives expression to his Lamarckian belief in the heredity of acquired characteristics, shared by Samuel Butler and Bernard Shaw but anathema to Nazi racists and almost universally rejected by geneticists. His Lamarckism is not just an odd fact about Nietzsche but symptomatic of his conception of body and spirit: he ridiculed belief in "pure" spirit but believed just as little in any "pure" body; he claimed that neither could be understood without the other. . . .
11. Horace's *Epistles*, I.10, 24: "Try with a pitchfork to drive out nature, she always returns."

Adapted from: Friedrich Nietzsche, *Beyond Good and Evil: Prelude to the Philosophy of the Future*, translated by Walter Kaufmann, pp. 15–16, 21, 25–32, 133–139, 174–177, 201–208, 212–214. Copyright © 1966 by Random House, Inc. Reprinted by permission of Random House, Inc. ✦

37

Excerpts from *The Genealogy of Morals*

Friedrich Nietzsche

First Essay: "Good and Evil," "Good and Bad"

I

The English psychologists to whom we owe the only attempts that have thus far been made to write a genealogy of morals are no mean posers of riddles, but the riddles they pose are themselves, and being incarnate have one advantage over their books—they are interesting. What are these English psychologists really after? One finds them always, whether intentionally or not, engaged in the same task of pushing into the foreground the nasty part of the psyche, looking for the effective motive forces of human development in the very last place we would wish to have them found, e.g., in the inertia of habit, in forgetfulness, in the blind and fortuitous association of ideas: always in something that is purely passive, automatic, reflexive, molecular, and, moreover, profoundly stupid. What drives these psychologists forever in the same direction? A secret, malicious desire to belittle humanity, which they do not acknowledge even to themselves? A pessimistic distrust, the suspiciousness of the soured idealist? Some petty resentment of Christianity (and Plato) which does not rise above the threshold of consciousness? Or could it be a prurient taste for whatever is embarrassing, painfully paradoxical, dubious and absurd in existence? Or is it, perhaps, a kind of stew—a little meanness, a little bitterness, a bit of anti-Christianity, a touch of prurience and desire for condiments? . . . But, again, people tell me that these men are simply dull old frogs who hop and creep in and around man as in their own element—as though man were a bog. However, I am reluctant to listen to this, in fact I refuse to believe it; and if I may express a wish where I cannot express a conviction, I do wish wholeheartedly that things may be otherwise with these men—that these microscopic examiners of the soul may be really courageous, magnanimous, and proud animals, who know how to contain their emotions and have trained themselves to subordinate all wishful thinking to the truth—any truth, even a homespun, severe, ugly, obnoxious, unchristian, unmoral truth. For such truths do exist.

II

All honor to the beneficent spirits that may motivate these historians of ethics! One thing is certain, however, they have been quite deserted by the true spirit of history. They all, to a man, think unhistorically, as is the age-old custom among philosophers. The amateurishness of their procedure is made plain from the very beginning, when it is a question of explaining the provenance of the concept and judgment *good*. "Originally," they decree, "altruistic actions were praised and approved by their recipients, that is by those to whom they were useful. Later on, the origin of that praise having been forgotten, such actions were felt to be good simply because it was the habit to commend them." We notice at once that this first derivation has all the earmarks of the English psychologists' work. Here are the key ideas of utility, forgetfulness, habit, and, finally, error, seen as lying at the root of that value system which civilized man had hitherto regarded with pride as the prerogative of all men. This pride must now be humbled, these values devalued. Have the debunkers succeeded?

Now it is obvious to me, first of all, that their theory looks for the genesis of the concept *good* in the wrong place: the judgment *good* does not originate with those to whom the good has been done. Rather it was the "good" themselves, that is to say the noble, mighty, highly placed, and high-minded who

486

decreed themselves and their actions to be good, i.e., belonging to the highest rank, in contradistinction to all that was base, low-minded and plebeian. It was only this *pathos of distance* that authorized them to create values and name them—what was utility to them? The notion of utility seems singularly inept to account for such a quick jetting forth of supreme value judgments. Here we come face to face with the exact opposite of that lukewarmness which every scheming prudence, every utilitarian calculus presupposes—and not for a time only, for the rare, exceptional hour, but permanently. The origin of the opposites *good* and *bad* is to be found in the pathos of nobility and distance, representing the dominant temper of a higher, ruling class in relation to a lower, dependent one. (The lordly right of bestowing names is such that one would almost be justified in seeing the origin of language itself as an expression of the rulers' power. They say, "This *is* that or that"; they seal off each thing and action with a sound and thereby take symbolic possession of it.) Such an origin would suggest that there is no *a priori* necessity for associating the word *good* with altruistic deeds, as those moral psychologists are fond of claiming. In fact, it is only after aristocratic values have begun to decline that the egotism-altruism dichotomy takes possession of the human conscience; to use my own terms, it is the herd instinct that now asserts itself. Yet it takes quite a while for this instinct to assume such sway that it can reduce all moral valuations to that dichotomy—as is currently happening throughout Europe, where the prejudice equating the terms *moral, altruistic*, and *disinterested* has assumed the obsessive force of an *idée fixe*. . . .

VI

Granting that political supremacy always gives rise to notions of spiritual supremacy, it at first creates no difficulties (though difficulties might arise later) if the ruling caste is also the priestly caste and elects to characterize itself by a term which reminds us of its priestly function. In this context we encounter for the first time concepts of *pure* and *impure* opposing each other as signs of class, and here, too, *good* and *bad* as terms no lon-

ger referring to class, develop before long. The reader should be cautioned, however, against taking pure and impure in too large or profound or symbolic a sense: all the ideas of ancient man were understood in a sense much more crude, narrow, superficial and non-symbolic than we are able to imagine today. The pure man was originally one who washed himself, who refused to eat certain foods entailing skin diseases, who did not sleep with the unwashed plebeian women, who held blood in abomination—hardly more than that. At the same time, given the peculiar nature of a priestly aristocracy, it becomes clear why the value opposites would early turn inward and become dangerously exacerbated; and in fact the tension between such opposites has opened abysses between man and man, over which not even an Achilles of free thought would leap without a shudder. There is from the very start something unwholesome about such priestly aristocracies, about their way of life, which is turned away from action and swings between brooding and emotional explosions: a way of life which may be seen as responsible for the morbidity and neurasthenia of priests of all periods. Yet are we not right in maintaining that the cures which they have developed for their morbidities have proved a hundred times more dangerous than the ills themselves? Humanity is still suffering from the after-effects of those priestly cures. Think, for example, of certain forms of diet (abstinence from meat), fasting, sexual continence, escape "into the desert"; think further of the whole anti-sensual metaphysics of the priests, conducive to inertia and false refinement; of the self-hypnosis encouraged by the example of fakirs and Brahmans, where a glass knob and an *idée fixe* take the place of the god. And at last, supervening on all this, comes utter satiety, together with its radical remedy, nothingness—or God, for the desire for a mystical union with God is nothing other than the Buddhist's desire to sink himself in nirvana. Among the priests everything becomes more dangerous, not cures and specifics alone but also arrogance, vindictiveness, acumen, profligacy, love, the desire for power, disease. In all fairness it should be added, however, that only on this soil, the precarious soil of priestly existence, has man been able to develop into an interesting creature; that only here has the human mind grown both profound and evil; and it is in these two respects, after all, that man has proved his superiority over the rest of creation.

VII

By now the reader will have got some notion how readily the priestly system of valuations can branch off from the aristocratic and develop into its opposite. An occasion for such a division is furnished whenever the priest caste and the warrior caste jealously clash with one another and find themselves unable to come to terms. The chivalrous and aristocratic valuations presuppose a strong physique, blooming, even exuberant health, together with all the conditions that guarantee its preservation: combat, adventure, the chase, the dance, war games, etc. The value system of the priestly aristocracy is founded on different presuppositions. So much the worse for them when it becomes a question of war! As we all know, priests are the most evil enemies to have—why should this be so? Because they are the most impotent. It is their impotence which makes their hate so violent and sinister, so cerebral and poisonous. The greatest haters in history—but also the most intelligent haters—have been priests. Beside the brilliance of priestly vengeance all other brilliance fades. Human history would be a dull and stupid thing without the intelligence furnished by its impotents. Let us begin with the most striking example. Whatever else has been done to damage the powerful and great of this earth seems trivial compared with what the Jews have done, that priestly people who succeeded in avenging themselves on their enemies and oppressors by radically inverting all their values, that is, by an act of the most spiritual vengeance. This was a strategy entirely appropriate to a priestly people in whom vindictiveness had gone most deeply underground. It was the Jew who, with frightening consistency, dared to invent the aristocratic value equations good/noble/powerful/beautiful/happy/favored-of-the-gods and maintain, with the furious hatred of the underprivi-

leged and impotent, that "only the poor, the powerless, are good; only the suffering, sick, and ugly, truly blessed. But you noble and mighty ones of the earth will be, to all eternity, the evil, the cruel, the avaricious, the godless, and thus the cursed and damned!" . . . We know who has fallen heir to this Jewish inversion of values. . . . In reference to the grand and unspeakably disastrous initiative which the Jews have launched by this most radical of all declarations of war, I wish to repeat a statement I made in a different context (*Beyond Good and Evil*), to wit, that it was the Jews who started the slave revolt in morals; a revolt with two millennia of history behind it, which we have lost sight of today simply because it has triumphed so completely. . . .

Second Essay: "Guilt," "Bad Conscience," and Related Matters

XXII

By now the reader will have guessed what has really been happening behind all these façades. Man, with his need for self-torture, his sublimated cruelty resulting from the cooping up of his animal nature within a polity, invented bad conscience in order to hurt himself, after the blocking of the more natural outlet of his cruelty. Then this guilt-ridden man seized upon religion in order to exacerbate his self-torment to the utmost. The thought of being in God's debt became his new instrument of torture. He focused in God the last of the opposites he could find to his true and inveterate animal instincts, making these a sin against God (hostility, rebellion against the "Lord," the "Father," the "Creator"). He stretched himself upon the contradiction "God" and "Devil" as on a rack. He projected all his denials of self, nature, naturalness out of himself as affirmations, as true being, embodiment, reality, as God (the divine Judge and Executioner), as transcendence, as eternity, as endless torture, as hell, as the infinitude of guilt and punishment. In such psychological cruelty we see an insanity of the *will* that is without parallel: man's will to find himself guilty, and unredeemably so; his will to believe that he might be punished to all eternity without ever expunging his guilt; his will to poison the very foundation of things with the problem of guilt and punishment and thus to cut off once and for all his escape from this labyrinth of obsession; his will to erect an ideal (God's holiness) in order to assure himself of his own absolute unworthiness. What a mad, unhappy animal is man! What strange notions occur to him; what perversities, what paroxysms of nonsense, what bestialities of idea burst from him, the moment he is prevented ever so little from being a beast of action! . . . All this is exceedingly curious and interesting, but dyed with such a dark, somber, enervating sadness that one must resolutely tear away one's gaze. Here, no doubt, is sickness, the most terrible sickness that has wasted man thus far. And if one is still able to hear—but how few these days have ears to hear it!—in this night of torment and absurdity the cry *love* ring out, the cry of rapt longing, of redemption in love, he must turn away with a shudder of invincible horror. . . . Man harbors too much horror; the earth has been a lunatic asylum for too long. . . .

XXIV

It is clear that I am concluding this essay with three unanswered questions. It may occur to some reader to ask me, "Are you constructing an ideal or destroying one?" I would ask him, in turn, whether he ever reflected upon the price that had to be paid for the introduction of every new ideal on earth? On how much of reality, in each instance, had to be slandered and misconceived, how much of falsehood ennobled, how many consciences disturbed, how many gods sacrificed? For the raising of an altar requires the breaking of an altar: this is a law—let anyone who can prove me wrong. We moderns have a millennial heritage of conscience—vivisection and cruelty to the animals in our selves. This is our most ancient habit, our most consummate artistry perhaps, in any case our greatest refinement, our special fare. Man has looked for so long with an evil eye upon his natural inclinations that they have finally become inseparable from "bad conscience." A converse effort can be imagined, but who has the strength for it? It would consist of as-

sociating all the *unnatural* inclinations—the longing for what is unworldly, opposed to the senses, to instinct, to nature, to the animal in us, all the anti-biological and earth-calumniating ideals—with bad conscience. To whom, today, may such hopes and pretensions address themselves? The *good* men, in particular, would be on the other side; and of course all the comfortable, resigned, vain, moony, weary people. Does anything give greater offense and separate one more thoroughly from others than to betray something of the strictness and dignity with which one treats oneself? But how kind and accommodating the world becomes the moment we act like all the rest and let ourselves go! To accomplish that aim, different minds are needed than are likely to appear in this age of ours: minds strengthened by struggles and victories, for whom conquest, adventure, danger, even pain, have become second nature. Minds accustomed to the keen atmosphere of high altitudes, to wintry walks, to ice and mountains in every sense. Minds possessed of a sublime kind of malice, of that self-assured recklessness which is a sign of strong health. What is needed, in short, is just superb health. Is such health still possible today?

But at some future time, a time stronger than our effete, self-doubting present, the true Redeemer will come, whose surging creativity will not let him rest in any shelter or hiding place, whose solitude will be misinterpreted as a flight from reality, whereas it will in fact be a dwelling *on*, a dwelling *in* reality—so that when he comes forth into the light he may bring with him the redemption of that reality from the curse placed upon it by a lapsed ideal. This man of the future, who will deliver us both from a lapsed ideal and from all that this ideal has spawned—violent loathing, the will to extinction, nihilism—this great and decisive stroke of midday, who will make the will free once more and restore to the earth its aim, and to man his hope; this anti-Christ and anti-nihilist, conqueror of both God and Unbeing—*one day he must come. . . .*

Third Essay: What Do Ascetic Ideals Mean?

XIII

But let us return to our argument. The kind of inner split we have found in the ascetic, who pits "life against life," is nonsense, not only in psychological terms, but also physiologically speaking. Such a split can only be *apparent;* it must be a kind of provisional expression, a formula, an adaptation, a psychological misunderstanding of something for which terms have been lacking to designate its true nature. A mere stopgap to fill a hiatus in human understanding. Let me state what I consider to be the actual situation. The ascetic ideal arises from the protective and curative instinct of a life that is degenerating and yet fighting tooth and nail for its preservation. It points to a partial physiological blocking and exhaustion, against which the deepest vital instincts, still intact, are battling doggedly and resourcefully. The ascetic ideal is one of their weapons. The situation, then, is exactly the opposite from what the worshipers of that ideal believe it to be. Life employs asceticism in its desperate struggle against death; the ascetic ideal is a dodge for the preservation of life. The ubiquitousness and power of that ideal, especially wherever men have adopted civilized forms of life, should impress upon us one great, palpable fact: the persistent morbidity of civilized man, his biological struggle against death, or to put it more exactly, against *taedium vitae*, exhaustion, the longing for "the end." The ascetic priest is an incarnation of the wish to be different, to be elsewhere; he *is* that wish, raised to its highest power, its most passionate intensity. And it is precisely the intensity of his wishing that forges the fetter binding him to this earth. At the same time he becomes an instrument for bettering the human condition, since by this intensity he is enabled to maintain in life the vast flock of defeated, disgruntled sufferers and self-tormentors, whom he leads instinctively like a shepherd. In other words, the ascetic priest, seemingly life's enemy and great negator, is in truth one of the major conserving and affirmative forces. . . . But what about the sources of man's morbidity? For certainly man is sicker, less secure, less stable, less firmly anchored than any other animal; he is the *sick* animal. But has he not also been more daring, more defiant, more inventive than all the other animals together? man, the great experimenter on himself, eternally unsatisfied, vying with the gods, the beasts, and with nature for final supremacy; man, unconquered to this day, still unrealized, so agitated by his own teeming energy that his future digs like spurs into the flesh of every present moment. . . . How could such a brave and resourceful animal but be the most precarious, the most profoundly sick of all the sick beasts of the earth? There have been many times when man has clearly had enough; there have been whole epidemics of "fed-upness" (for example, around 1348, the time of the Dance of Death) but even this tedium, this weariness, this satiety breaks from him with such vehemence that at once it forges a new fetter to existence. As if by magic, his negations produce a wealth of tenderer affirmations. When this master of destruction, of self-destruction, wounds himself, it is that very wound that forces him to live.

XIV

The more regular morbidity becomes among the members of the human race, the more grateful we should be for the rare "windfalls"—men fortunate enough to combine a sound physical organization with intellectual authority. We should do our best to protect such men from the noxious air of the sickroom. It is the sick who are the greatest threat to the well; it is the weaklings, and not their own peers, who visit disaster upon the strong. But who, today, knows this, who acts on it? We try constantly to diminish man's fear of man; forgetting that it is the fear they inspire which forces the strong to be strong and, if need be, terrible. We should encourage that fear in every possible way, for it alone fosters a sound breed of men. The real danger lies in our loathing of man and our pity of him. If these two emotions should one day join forces, they would beget the most sinister thing ever witnessed on earth: man's *ultimate* will, his will to nothingness, nihilism. And indeed, preparations for that event are already well under way. One who smells not only with his nose but also with his eyes and ears will notice everywhere these days an air as of a lunatic asylum or sanatorium. (I am thinking of all the current cultural enterprises of man, of every kind of Europe now existing.) It is the diseased who imperil mankind, and not the "beasts of prey." It is the predestined failures and victims who undermine the social structure, who poison our faith in life and our fellow men. Is there anyone who has not encountered the veiled, shuttered gaze of the born misfit, that introverted gaze which saddens us and makes us imagine how such a man must speak to himself? "If only I could be someone else," the look seems to sigh, "but there's no hope of that. I am what I am; how could I get rid of myself? Nevertheless, I'm fed up." In the marshy soil of such self-contempt every poisonous plant will grow, yet all of it so paltry, so stealthy, so dishonest, so sickly-sweet! Here the worms of vindictiveness and *arrière-pensée* teem, the air stinks of secretiveness and pent-up emotion; here a perennial net of malicious conspiracy is woven— the conspiracy of the sufferers against the happy and successful; here victory is held in abomination. And what dissimulation, in order not to betray that this is hatred! What a display of grand attitudes and grandiose words! what an art of "honest calumny!" What noble eloquence flows from the lips of these ill-begotten creatures! What sugary, slimy, humble submissiveness swims in their eyes! What are they after, really? The ambition of these most abject invalids is to at least *mime* justice, love, wisdom, superiority. And how clever such an ambition makes them! For we cannot withhold a certain admiration for the counterfeiter's skill with which they imitate the coinage of virtue, even its golden ring. They have by now entirely monopolized virtue "We alone," they say, "are the good, the just, we alone the Men of Good Will." They walk among us as warnings and reprimands incarnate, as though to say that health, soundness, strength, and pride are vicious things for which we shall one day pay dearly; and how eager they are, at bottom, to be the ones to make us pay! How they long to

be the executioners! Among them are vindictive characters aplenty, disguised as judges, who carry the word *justice* in their mouths like a poisonous spittle and go always with pursed lips, ready to spit on all who do not look discontent, on all who go cheerfully about their business. Nor are there lacking among them those most unspeakably vain and loathsome frauds who are bent on parading as innocents, those moral masturbators who bring their stunted sensuality to the market swathed in rhymes and other swaddling clothes and labeled "one hundred per cent pure." Is there any place today where the sick do not wish to exhibit some form of superiority and to exercise their tyranny over the strong? Especially the sick females, who have unrivaled resources for dominating, oppressing, tyrannizing. The sick woman spares nothing dead or alive; she digs up the longest-buried things. (The Abyssinian Bogos say "Woman is a hyena.") One look into the background of every family, every institution, every commonwealth is enough to convince us that the battle of the sick against the well is raging on all sides; for the most part a quiet battle, conducted with small doses of poison, with pinpricks, the insidious long-suffering look, but quite often too with the loud pharisaical gesture simulating noble indignation. The indignant barking of these sick dogs can be heard even in the sacred halls of science. (I need only remind the reader once more of that Prussian apostle of vindictiveness, Eugen Dühring, who today makes the most indecent and offensive use of moralistic claptrap. He stands out, even among his own crew of anti-Semites, by the vehemence of his moralistic drivel.) What would these men, so tireless in their masquerades, so insatiable in their thirst for vengeance, require in order to see themselves as triumphant? Nothing less than to succeed in implanting their own misery, and all misery, in the consciences of the happy, so as to make the happy one day say to one another, "It is a disgrace to be happy! *There is too much misery in the world!*" But no greater and more disastrous misunderstanding could be imagined than for the strong and happy to begin doubting their right to happiness. Let us have done with such topsy-turviness, with such dreadful emasculation of feeling! Our first rule on this earth should be that the sick must not contaminate the healthy. But this requires that the healthy be isolated from the sick, be spared even the sight of the sick, lest they mistake that foreign sickness for their own. Or is it their task, perhaps, to be medical attendants and doctors? There could be no worse way for them to misjudge their role. The higher must not be made an instrument of the lower; the "pathos of distance" must to all eternity keep separate tasks separate. The right to exist of the full-toned bell is a thousand times greater than that of the cracked, miscast one: it alone heralds in the future of all mankind. What the healthy can and should do must never be demanded of the sick, or placed within their power; but how should the former be able to do what they alone can do, and at the same time act the part of physicians, comforters, saviors of the sick? . . . Then let us have fresh air, and at any rate get far away from all lunatic asylums and nursing homes of culture! And let us have good company, our own company! Or solitude, if need be. But let us get far away, at any rate, from the evil vapor of internal corruption and dry rot. In order, my friends, that we may, at least for a while yet, guard ourselves against the two worst plagues which perhaps lie in store for us more than anyone—unrelieved loathing of man and unrelieved pity of him!

Adapted from: Friedrich Nietzsche, *The Genealogy of Morals and Ecce Homo*, translated by Walter Kaufmann and R. J. Hollingdale. Copyright © 1967 by Random House, Inc. Reprinted by permission of Random House, Inc. ✦

38
Nietzsche on Autonomy and Morality

The Challenge to Political Theory

Keith Ansell-Pearson

Kant on Autonomy

For Kant every political theory must begin by paying homage to ethics.[1] In other words, politics is not based on power or on force but on the primacy of the autonomous individual. Kant's aim is to give philosophical expression to our common moral experience, to our sense of self as a free agent. The aim of a metaphysic of morals is to establish the grounds for a pure, *a priori* ethics in order to discover the supreme principle of morality, namely autonomy. Kant insists that 'the ground of obligation', that is, the nature of law and sovereignty, must be sought neither in the nature of man nor in the nature of the world, but rather 'solely *a priori* in the concepts of pure reason'.[2] Moral philosophy 'does not borrow in the slightest from acquaintance with man (in anthropology), but gives him laws *a priori* as a rational being'.[3]

Kant begins his inquiry into the supreme principle of morality by noting that the only good thing in the world which can be described as unconditionally good is a good will. A good will is one which wills nothing contingent and heteronomous but wills only its own rational nature. In determining the 'moral' value of action the emphasis is to be placed not on the consequences of one's actions, on what Nietzsche calls 'doing', but solely on the intentions behind one's actions.

The will must will nothing but its own will. The will is a kind of causality; the achievement of autonomy is characterized by the ability of the self to transcend its dual nature as a creature of instinct (heteronomy) and a creature of reason (autonomy) and achieve a level of rationality where it can freely prescribe to itself laws which are rational because they are valid for all rational beings. It is the universalization of one's laws which makes them 'moral'. Any doctrine which portrays the will as bound by a law which has its origin in some object or end other than the will itself is a doctrine, not of autonomy, but of heteronomy. A metaphysic of morals is thus designed to show that understood in these terms autonomy is a precondition of morality. Kant's argument, therefore, is that the law is moral because it is valid for all rational beings. He argues that we need an objective standard of human conduct, a principle which ensures that our actions conform to a universal law. Kant finds this objective standard or measure of value in the form of the categorical imperative which instructs us always to act in such a way that we can also will that the maxims of our actions can be made into universal laws (laws of nature).[4]

It is at this stage in his argument that Kant introduces what he calls 'the formula of autonomy'. This formula is derived from combining the idea of universal law with the idea of the end-in-itself. Your capacity to make the maxims of your action into universal laws is what distinguishes you as someone who can be regarded as an end-in-itself. From this formula of autonomy Kant derives the principle which is to supply his formalistic ethics with a content: one should always act in such a way as to treat humanity, whether in oneself or in others, as an end-in-itself and never merely as a means. Kant posits the idea of a kingdom of ends whose members form a community of self-legislating and rational beings considered as ends-in-themselves.[5]

Kant's attempt to ground a notion of autonomy in a metaphysic of morals establishes, in the words of Charles Taylor, 'a radical notion of freedom' in that the moral subject obeys only the dictates of its own will.[6] However, as Taylor has noted, the chief problem with Kant's metaphysic of morals is that it purchases moral autonomy at the price of vacuity. At the cost of excluding all historical and psychological determination, Kant delivers a conception of autonomy which is dualistic and moralistic and in which the social and historical grounds of human action are placed in a future kingdom of ends. As Nietzsche noted, Kant 'believed in morality, not because it is demonstrated in nature and history, but in spite of the fact that nature and history continually contradict it'.[7]

In terms of the concerns of political theory, Taylor has argued that because of the weaknesses of his conception of autonomy, Kant is forced to borrow from the utilitarian conception of nature which rests on an idea of nature as the pursuit of individual happiness. Because his conception of freedom of the will is so formal, and hence vacuous in the sense that its real ground of determination—the social and historical world—has been removed, Kant's metaphysic of morals is unable to generate a new substantive vision of the political in which the will would be actualized. Instead the goal of politics is reduced to the negative one of limiting the freedom of each so it can peacefully coexist with the freedom of all under universal laws. Taylor puts it well when he writes: 'Thus although Kant starts with a radically new conception of morality, his political theory is disappointingly familiar. It does not take us very far beyond utilitarianism, in that its main problem remains that of harmonizing individual wills'.[8] In order to criticize Kant in this fashion, Taylor draws on Hegel's argument that morality is defined so formally in Kant in terms of a set of abstract principles, without any reference to concrete social practices and customs (what Hegel calls 'ethical life'), that morality must forever remain condemned to an ethics of striving without any hope of realization in the actual historical world the self inhabits.[9] Such a conception of morality can only result in a divided self.

Kant's ethics attempt to philosophically ground that which Rousseau had already placed at the centre of political theory, the free and autonomous will.[10] Autonomy consists in the capacity of the will to will nothing other than its own will. As one commentator has noted, both Rousseau and Kant are insisting that when a person engages in reasoning about what to do they must generalize the particular situation they are in and consider what it would be right for anyone to do in similar circumstances to their own. Only when this is done is the individual capable of deducing what it ought to do in these circumstances.[11] Where Rousseau departs from the moral rigorism of Kant is in making an appeal to heteronomy (in the form of enlightened self-interest), while Kant strictly rules out self-interest as a basis for morality and establishes it solely on the motive of duty. However, both Rousseau and Kant conceive of autonomy in terms of a will acting in accordance with an objective and universalizable rule or law which the self freely imposes upon itself.[12] It is on this point of the universalizability of self legislation that we can locate the political import of Nietzsche's thinking on autonomy and his challenge to political theory. For Nietzsche the attempt to define morality by reference to laws which claim to possess universal validity and applicability represents a perfect example of the type of morality he defines as 'slave morality'. Unlike Kant, Nietzsche proposes a conception of autonomy in which the emphasis is placed, not on the morally pure intentions of an ahistorically conceived human agent, but on action as self-creation, on what he calls the impossibility of separating doer and deed. He offers a typology of master morality and slave morality in which the crucial distinction is between a morality of strength and courage which defines itself through self-affirmation, and a morality of weakness and pity which defines itself through negating everything which is other and different to itself. Slave morality is a morality of resentment which, in contrast to a noble morality that declares itself as 'good' and noble independent of altruistic concerns, only defines others as 'bad' after it has affirmed itself. The slave morality arrives at its self-identity by first denoting others as 'evil' and only after this act of negation does it define itself as 'good'.[13]

Nietzsche on Autonomy and Morality

Within the tradition of moral philosophy Nietzsche is frequently portrayed as an extreme individualist.[14] However, this is a highly misleading caricature of Nietzsche's moral and political thought which renders his relation to modernity unproblematic. Nietzsche criticizes modern politics for reducing individuals to a common herd morality by creating institutions which foster an ethic of collective mediocrity.

> . . . there is nothing more thoroughly harmful to freedom than liberal institutions. One knows, indeed, *what* they bring about: they undermine the will to power, they are the leveling of mountain and valley exalted to a moral principle, they make small, cowardly, and smug. . . . Liberalism: in plain words, *reduction to the herd animal*. . . . As long as they are still being fought for, these same institutions produce quite different effects; then they in fact promote freedom mightily. . . . For what is freedom? That one has the will to self-responsibility. That one preserves the distance which divides us. That one has become more indifferent to hardship, toil, privation, even to life. That one is ready to sacrifice men to one's cause, oneself not excepted. Freedom means that the manly instincts that delight in war and victory have gained mastery over the other instincts—for example, over the instinct for 'happiness'. . . . The free man is a *warrior*.[15]

In considering the nature of Nietzsche's alleged individualism it is important to appreciate that he does recognize that the capacity for self-legislation is a defining feature of the modern understanding of the self. In a section of *The Gay Science*, for example, entitled 'Herd Remorse', Nietzsche astutely notes:

> During the longest and most remote periods of the human past, the sting of conscience was not at all what it is now. Today one feels responsible only for one's will and actions, and one finds one's pride in oneself. All our teachers of law start from this sense of self and pleasure in the individual, as if this had always been the

fount of law. But during the longest period of the human past nothing was more terrible than to feel one stood by oneself. To be alone, to experience things by oneself, neither to obey or to rule, to be an individual—that was not a pleasure but a punishment: one was sentenced to 'individuality'. . . . To be a self and to esteem oneself according to one's weight and measure—that offended taste in those days. . . . There is no point on which we have learned to think and feel more differently.[16]

But although Nietzsche recognizes that self-legislation, the ability to impose a law upon oneself and to be judge and avenger of that law, is characteristic of the modern experience, he insists that this law can never be universalized. It is this argument which radically separates him from Rousseau and Kant and in which lies his fundamental challenge to political theory.[17] In order to appreciate this point fully it is necessary to examine his notion of sovereign individuality.

The overriding aim of the *Genealogy of Morals* is to show that what Kant and the modern liberal tradition of moral and political thought simply take for granted, the sovereign individual in possession of a free will and conscience, is in reality the product of a specific historical labour of culture or civilization. Thus, the *Genealogy* deals with a puzzle. Indeed, the puzzle it defines could be described as the most important puzzle of modern political thought. 'To breed an animal *with the right to make promises*—is not this the paradoxical task that nature has set itself in the case of man? is it not the real problem regarding man?'[18] In other words, the fundamental puzzle of political theory is the problem of breeding a *political animal*, that is, a sovereign individual who can make promises and thus be bound by obligations and to social contracts on account of its possession of a free will.

Nietzsche argues that originally everything in life—marriage, education, agriculture, war, sickness, speech and silence—had meaning and significance only within the domain of custom in which one observed society's prescriptions without thinking of oneself as an individual. Nietzsche refers to this period in mankind's history as the period of 'the morality of custom' which preceded world history and which has determined the fate and character of mankind.[19] For Nietzsche this constitutes the 'pre-moral' period in human evolution.[20] The 'moral' period denotes the evolution of the bad conscience under a Christian moral culture that posits a guilt-ridden human agent, a divided self, which is unable ever to emancipate the self from its internalization of the will to power, the turning of the will against itself, by actualizing its actions in the social and historical world.[21] The final period in the evolution of morality refers to the future of man as a promise, as a bridge between man and Overman, and which is characterized by a self that is able to will its own will as a will to power and emancipate itself from the spirit of resentment by embracing the radically contingent and finite nature of its existence. Nietzsche refers to this period as the extramoral and the supra-moral period.[22] His most detailed exposition of this evolution occurs in the second essay of the *Genealogy of Morals* where he outlines the historical story of how a sense of responsibility originated in mankind. As he points out, a memory of the will has to be cultivated so that between the original "I will" and the actual performance of the will in action a whole world of strange new circumstances can be interpreted without breaking the chain of this will. He writes:

> But how many things this presupposes! To ordain the future in advance in this way, man must first have learned to distinguish necessary events from chance ones, to think causally, to see and anticipate distant eventualities as if they belonged to the present, to decide with certainty what is the goal and what are the means to it, and in general be able to calculate and compute.[23]

Nietzsche's aim is to show that even the most seemingly natural capacities and attributes of the human self, such as free will and conscience, require an historical labour and a process of socialization for their existence.

For Nietzsche, therefore, the autonomous individual equipped with free will and conscience has to be viewed not as an ontologi-cal presupposition but as an historical creation. Political obligation is to be understood in terms of a prehistoric development that precedes conscious volition. The key passage in which he puts forward this conception of the historical achievement of autonomy is from the second essay in the *Genealogy*. It is a crucial passage in his work.

> The task of breeding an animal with the right to make promises evidently embraces and presupposes as a preparatory task that one first *makes* men to a certain degree necessary, uniform, like among like, regular, and consequently calculable. The tremendous labour of that which I have called 'morality of custom'—the labour performed by man upon himself during the greater part of the existence of the human race, his entire *prehistoric* labour, finds in this its meaning, its great justification, notwithstanding the severity, tyranny, stupidity, and idiocy involved in it: with the aid of the morality of custom and the social straitjacket, man was actually *made* calculable.

Nietzsche continues:

> If we place ourselves at the end of this tremendous process where the tree at last brings forth fruit, where society and the morality of custom at last reveal *what* they have simply been the means to: then we discover that the ripest fruit is the *sovereign individual*, like only to himself, liberated again from the morality of custom, the autonomous and supramoral individual (for "autonomous" and "moral" are mutually exclusive), in short the man who has his own independent, protracted will and the right to make promises.[24]

We see from this passage that what is taken by Kant as a precondition of morality, namely autonomy, is regarded by Nietzsche as a moment of individuation and difference, or in more explicitly aristocratic terms, 'distinction'. He speaks of the emancipated individual who is 'master of a *free* will', and which gives him mastery over himself, over nature, and over less fortunate creatures who have not succeeded in achieving sovereignty. The sovereign man is aware of his superiority over all those who lack the right to make promises and stand as their own guarantors . . . and of how this mastery over himself also necessarily gives him mastery over circumstances, over nature, and over all the more short-willed and unreliable creatures. The "free" man, the possessor of a protracted and unbreakable will, also possesses his *measure of value:* looking out upon others from himself, he honours or he despises; and just as he is bound to honour his peers, the strong and reliable (those with the *right* to make promises) . . . whose trust is a mark of distinction . . . he is bound to reserve a kick for the feeble windbags who promise without the right to do so.[25]

In contrast to Kant, Nietzsche describes the attainment of sovereign individuality not as 'moral' but rather as '*supra*-moral'.[26] This is because for Nietzsche genuine autonomy means that one is unique and incomparable. He argues that we should distrust those mendacious spirits who proudly pronounce their attainment of sovereign individuality to the world by declaring that everyone should behave as they do. Thus, *contra* Kant, Nietzsche insists that, 'a virtue has to be *our* invention, *our* most personal defence and necessity. . . . The profoundest laws of preservation and growth demand the reverse of Kant: that each one of us should devise *his own* virtue, *his own* categorical imperative'.[27] In achieving autonomy through self-discipline the aim is not to deny one's inclinations and instincts but rather to combine all of one's qualities into a controlled and coherent whole, to be beyond the opposition of 'good' and 'evil'.

> Love and hate, gratitude and revenge, good nature and anger, affirmative acts and negative acts, belong together. One is good on condition one also knows how to be evil; one is evil because otherwise one would not understand how to be good.[28]

Self-mastery is defined in terms of the ability to control one's pro and con. One must learn to grasp 'the *necessary* injustice in every For and Against, injustice is inseparable from life, life itself as conditioned by the sense of perspective and its injustice'.[29] In

contrast to Kant's emphasis on the link between autonomy and morality, where morality denotes the formal identity between individuals that has been created by the categorical imperative, in *Thus Spoke Zarathustra* Nietzsche suggests that the moment of individuation produced in the creation of the sovereign individual imposes on the self a terrible burden of solitude:

> Do you call yourself free? I want to hear your ruling idea, and not that you have escaped from a yoke. . . .
> Free from what? Zarathustra does not care about that! But your eye should clearly tell me: free *for* what?
> Can you furnish yourself with your own good and evil and hang up your own will above yourself as a law? Can you be judge of yourself and avenger of your law?
> It is terrible to be alone with the judge and avenger of one's own law. It is to be a star thrown forth into empty space and into the icy breath of solitude.[30]

Self-legislation for Nietzsche means that one bears the sole burden for one's self, that one creates one's own laws in terms of a will to self-responsibility. To universalize these laws in terms of their validity for all rational beings is described by Nietzsche as an extreme act of selfishness—and weakness, since the will does not have the courage to stand up on its own—on the part of Kant's categorical imperative.[31] The essence of what it means to become those who we are—new, unique, incomparable—is that one recognizes that this is a law which cannot be provided with universal legislation. But how does Nietzsche link this understanding of sovereign individuality—which, as we have seen, he arrives at from a critique of Kant—with a notion of politics?

Nietzsche, the Self and Political Theory

The question of Nietzsche's politics is a highly contentious one. In the wake of the historical identification of his thought with European fascism, it became the norm among admirers of his work to argue that he was primarily an antipolitical philosopher solely concerned with the fate of the isolated, existential individual.[32] Those commentators who have attempted to examine his politics have inevitably ended up by arguing for an inextricable link between his aristocratic radicalism and a fascist style of politics, a process which has led to a general denigration of his status as a political thinker.[33] I would suggest that the source of the problem, that of determining the nature of Nietzsche's politics, lies in the fact that nowhere in his writings does Nietzsche ever identify his conception of sovereign individuality with a modern political form. This constitutes a major lacuna and serves to explain why so many different and conflicting political readings of his work are possible. Instead, Nietzsche views the problem of politics in terms of overcoming European nihilism, of overcoming man. He assesses modern politics—what he calls the petty politics of nationalism and statism—in the light of this overriding concern.[34] In other words, Nietzsche is more preoccupied with questions of social and historical change than he is with constructing a model of the ideal society. He thus ends up by lambasting modern politics for preaching equality to the masses and by favouring an aristocratic elite of philosopher-legislators who are assigned the task of teaching the Overman (in contrast to the last man of liberal democracy and socialism). This point has important implications for how we are to understand the political import of Nietzsche's notion of sovereign individuality. It could be argued that there is no reason why an aristocratic emphasis on aesthetic distinction, on the inequality of creative greatness, could not exist within the framework of a democratic constitution established on the basis of equal political rights. For Nietzsche it is essentially a question of an order of rank, of conceiving society in such a way that the emphasis on formal legal equality does not result in a culture where creativity and individuality become stifled. There is, however, a further and perhaps more important aspect to this question concerning the political implications of Nietzsche's notion of sovereign individuality.

For Nietzsche the conception of autonomy found in Rousseau and Kant does not provide an account of genuine creative individuality; it offers little more than a rationalization of the morality of custom, what he calls the 'old morality' beyond which the modern individual is now compelled to live. He argues that the dangerous and uncanny point has been reached 'where the greater, more manifold, more comprehensive life transcends and lives beyond the old morality; the "individual" appears, obliged to give himself laws and to develop his own arts and artifices of self-preservation, self-enhancement, and self-redemption'.[35] It would be mistaken to infer from this that Nietzsche has in mind an individual who is able to live without social relationships. His image of the Overman is not that of Aristotle's God—or beast—capable of living without the *polis*. Rather, for Nietzsche the important question concerns the value-basis on which individuals emancipated from the morality of custom are to enter into social relationships with one another. Nietzsche's failure to provide us with an account of the ideal community might thus turn out to be a source, not of weakness, but of strength, as it means that he is able to raise the crucial question about how moral and political identities are formed between individuals and socially constructed. Are individuals to identify with one another, for example, on the basis of Rousseauian-inspired pity and Kantian-inspired rationality in which weakness is affirmed and strength negated, and in which the desire for a common identity results in the obliteration of otherness? Or are they to come together on the basis of Nietzschean-inspired courage in which difference is celebrated and otherness is affirmed?[36]

It is this question concerning the social construction of moral and political identities between individuals that Nietzsche raises which has been taken up by recent theorists, writing either under the inspiration of Foucault's critique of subjectivity or within feminism, in terms of an attempt to formulate a politics of difference. Thus, for example, inspired by Foucault's writings, the American political theorist William Connolly has recently advocated a Nietzschean perspective in order to interrogate the presumptions of the political discourse of modernity.[37] Nietzsche is significant, Connolly argues, because he aspires to call modernity into question without recourse either to nostalgia for a lost world or to a future utopia where history and politics have come to an end. In contrast to Rousseau, Hegel and Marx, it is Nietzsche, he argues, who allows otherness to be affirmed without incorporating it within some grand dialectical system of political thought. For at the heart of the political discourse of modernity is a belief in the subjugation of forms of otherness in the name of a higher, self-inclusive community.[38] We have constructed a series of oppositions—between man and woman, reason and desire, self and not-self—in which one aspect of the dualism is affirmed and the other negated as a form of otherness (madness, perversity, irrationality, sickness) which needs to be normalized and moralized so as to be brought under control. The discourse of modern political theory, established on the basis of oppositions, such as those between oppression and emancipation, rulers and ruled, presupposes the validity of the historical construction of the self as a juridical subject. However, Connolly argues, as Nietzsche shows us the subject is not simply the self which establishes its independence and self-transparency, but it is also the self that is required to respond to the demands of modernity by interiorizing a complex set of socially imposed standards and to regulate forms of otherness in itself and in society which deviate from established social norms.[39] Connolly's response to the moral and political dilemmas of postmodernity (or what he prefers to call late modernity) is to propose a politics of ambiguity in which difference and otherness, and the competing demands of individuality and community, are allowed to exist without being subjugated to a higher ethical reality in the name of justice and equality. This means that we need to grant recognition to, and provide space in political life for, those embodied and aesthetic aspects of subjectivity that have been either excluded or neglected in modern political thought in its emphasis upon the juridical and cognitive aspects of our subjectivity.[40]

A similar use of Nietzsche in constructing a politics of difference has recently been made by Rosalyn Diprose, who has argued that Nietzsche's thought, in its recognition that the site of otherness is both the condition of the subject's self identity and the threat to its coherence and stability, contains hitherto neglected openings by which women can explore possibilities for change beyond the impasse of equality.[41] Nietzsche is important for a radical political practice like feminism because he shows that the subject is a material construction which is dependent for its identity on the exclusion and negation of forms of otherness which are often judged to be socially inferior and which experience political marginalization. Thus, the subject needs to be understood as a corporeal entity that is socially constructed in relation to the other's difference. This notion of the subject in terms of an historical and social construction, resting on suppressed or unacknowledged relations of difference and on a denial of otherness, poses an important challenge to the notion of the subject found in liberal modernity in which the autonomy and rationality of the self are simply taken for granted and depoliticized. This insight is of tremendous importance to political theorists inspired by feminism since it can be shown that our identities as political and juridical subjects have been constructed on a negation of woman as a form of otherness. Nancy Fraser and Linda Nicholson have recently called for a postmodern feminism in terms of the type of non-universalism which lies behind Nietzsche's challenge to political theory. They propose a non-universalism which would replace unitary notions of 'woman' and 'feminine gender identity' with conceptions of social identity in which gender is treated as one relevant strand among others, such as class, race, ethnicity and sexual orientation, and which allows political space for the construction of plural and complex identities.[42]

These various readings show just how valuable Nietzsche's thinking on power, subjectivity and community can be for political theorists who are attempting to articulate a new *post-modern* conception of political theory. However, a post-modern reading of

Nietzsche should result neither in an underestimation of the tensions of modernity nor in any simple resolution of the various traditions which constitute the political discourse of modernity. . . .

For Nietzsche the important aspect of human agency is not the intentions behind an action but the doing of the action. This means that the self only exists through human action, that 'there is no "being" behind doing . . . "the doer" is merely a fiction added to the deed—the deed is everything'.[43] The notion of the human subject understood as a fixed and moral point of reference—where 'moral' refers to the human subject conceived as a person who acts in accordance with universalizable maxims, as opposed to engaging in the *creation* of new values him or herself—has been believed in more firmly than anything else, Nietzsche argues, because 'it makes possible to the majority of mortals, the weak and the oppressed of every kind, the sublime self-deception that interprets weakness as freedom, and their being thus-and-thus as a *merit*'.[44] He even goes so far as to suggest that the very idea of a social contract is a mere piece of sentimentalism on the part of the weak by which they attempt to convert the strong to the virtues of a society founded on the values of 'liberty', 'equality' and 'happiness'.[45] For Nietzsche the achievement of genuine autonomy is not to be conceived as a "moral" affair since there are no fixed or pre-established moral rules and conventions by which free, spontaneous, and creative human action can be judged. On the contrary, the essence of free human action lies in self-creation, for which one needs to be beyond good and evil. The importance of this notion of the subject in terms of the *creation* of the self is that it shows that self-identity is always a social construct determined by relations of difference. It thus opens up genuine possibilities for thinking about forms of political community in which otherness can be affirmed and difference celebrated.

The key insight which emerges from this inquiry into Nietzsche's political thought is that it is a mistake to view his conception of sovereign individuality as offering little more than an antipolitical conception of life or an aestheticization of politics. Such a reading fails to recognize that for Nietzsche the key question of political life in a condition of modernity concerns the value-basis on which social relationships are to be established and a common ethical and political identity created and constituted. In Nietzsche's construal of this problem of the competing demands of individuality and community, of identity and difference, we find an important but neglected challenge to political theory.

Notes

1. On this key point see Frank Thakurdas, *German Political Idealism* (New Jersey, Humanities Press, 1980), pp. 52–5. Compare Rousseau in *Emile*, translated by Barbara Foxley (London, Dent, 1974), p. 197. 'Society must be studied in the individual and the individual in society; those who wish to treat politics and morals separately will never understand either' (translation slightly modified).

2. I. Kant, *Groundwork for the Metaphysic of Morals*, trans. By H. J. Paton (New York, Harper and Row, 1964), p. 57.

3. Kant, *Groundwork*, p. 57.

4. Kant, *Groundwork*, pp. 69–71 and 88–91.

5. Kant, *Groundwork*, pp. 954–98–9 and 100–2.

6. Charles Taylor, *Hegel and Modern Society* (Cambridge, Cambridge University Press, 1979), p. 76.

7. F. Nietzsche, *Daybreak*, trans. by R. J. Hollingdale (Cambridge, Cambridge University Press, 1982), Preface, s. 3.

8. Taylor, *Hegel and Modern Society*, p. 78.

9. The contrast drawn here by Hegel is in terms of his well-known distinction between *Sittlichkeit* (the concrete ethical obligations of social life) and *Moralität* (the formal, abstract and universal principles of morality as defined by Kant); see Taylor, *Hegel and Modern Society*, pp. 83–4. See also Joachim Ritter, *Hegel and the French Revolution: Essays on 'The Philosophy of Right'*, translated by R.D. Winfield (Cambridge, MA, MIT Press, 1982), pp. 151–78. For an interpretation of Nietzsche's ethics as an ethics of practices (or virtues), not principles, see Robert C. Solomon, 'A more severe morality: Nietzsche's affirmative ethics', *Journal of the British Society for Phenomenology*, 16 (Oct. 1985), 250–68. Nietzsche rests the claims he makes for sovereign

individuality on the insight that a defining characteristic of modernity is that morality can no longer be justified or accounted for in terms of pre-given or ready-made customs and conventions. In contrast to Hegel's attempt to reconcile modern individualism with a renewed sense of ethical life. Nietzsche argues that it is necessary to first question the value-basis on which sovereign individuals are to enter into social relationships with one another and out of which they are to construct ethical identities.

10. See Rousseau, *The Social Contract*, Book 1, Ch. 8: 'The mere impulse of appetite is slavery, while obedience to a law we prescribe to ourselves is liberty'.

11. See John C. Hall, *Rousseau: an Introduction to his Political Philosophy* (London, Macmillan, 1972), p. 81.

12. For an illuminating discussion of Rousseau and Kant on self-legislation see F. M. Barnard, 'Will and political rationality in Rousseau', in A. Reeve and J. Lively (eds). *Modern Political Theory from Hobbes to Marx* (London, Routledge, 1989), pp. 129–49, especially pp. 136–7. See also Stephen Ellenburg, 'Rousseau and Kant: principles of political right', in R. A. Leigh (ed.), *Rousseau after Two Hundred Years* (Cambridge, Cambridge University Press, 1982).

13. See F. Nietzsche, *On the Genealogy of Morals*, translated by Walter Kaufmann and R. J. Hollingdale (New York, Random House, 1967), Essay I, s. 10, and *Beyond Good and Evil*, translated by Walter Kaufmann (New York, Random House, 1966), s. 260.

14. See, for example, J. P. Stern, *Nietzsche* (Glasgow, Collins, 1978), and Henry Kariel, 'Nietzsche's Preface to Constitutionalism', *Journal of Politics*, 25 (May 1963), 211–25.

15. F. Nietzsche, *Twilight of the Idols*, translated by R.J. Hollingdale (Harmondsworth, Penguin, 1968), p. 92; see Nietzsche, *The Will To Power*, s. 287: 'My philosophy aims at an ordering of rank, not an individualistic morality'.

16. Nietzsche, *The Gay Science*, s. 117.

17. Nietmen only: women are excluded from political life and the task of self-legislation. Despite his misogynistic remarks, Nietzsche's critique of universalism does have important implications for current feminist attempts to construct a politics of difference. For recent critical readings of Nietzsche's philosophy from a feminist position see Ofelia Schutte, *Beyond Nihilism: Nietzsche Without Masks* (Chicago, Chicago University Press, 1984), esp. Ch. 8; Ellen Kennedy, 'Women as Untermensch' and Kelly Oliver, 'Nietzsche's woman: the poststructural attempt to do away with women', *Radical Philosophy*, 48 (Spring 1988).

18. Nietzsche, *On the Genealogy of Morals*, Essay II, 1.

19. Nietzsche, *Daybreak*, ss. 9, 16 and 18.

20. Nietzsche, *Beyond Good and Evil*, s. 32.

21. Nietzsche, *On the Genealogy of Morals*, Essay II. s. 16.

22. Nietzsche, *Beyond Good and Evil*, s. 32.

23. Nietzsche, *On the Genealogy of Morals*, Essay II, s. 1.

24. Nietzsche, *On the Genealogy of Morals*, Essay II, s. 2.

25. Nietzsche, *On the Genealogy of Morals*, Essay II, 2. For a thoughtful consideration of whether attaining power over oneself necessarily entails exercising power *over others* in Nietzsche see James H. Read, 'Nietzsche: power as oppression', *Praxis International*, 9 (April–July 1989), 72–87. I am grateful to Liam O'Sullivan for bringing this essay to my attention.

26. The term used by Nietzsche is *'ubersittlich'*. He is thus referring to an individual who has transcended the standpoint of morality in the sense of 'customs' (*sitten*).

27. F. Nietzsche, *The Anti-Christ*, translated by R.H. Hollingdale (Harmondsworth, Penguin, 1968), s. 11.

28. Nietzsche, *The Will To Power*, s. 351.

29. F. Nietzsche. *Human, All Too Human*, Preface, s. 6.

30. F. Nietzsche, *Thus Spoke Zarathustra*, translated by R.J. Hollingdale (Harmondsworth, Penguin, 1969), p. 89.

31. Nietzsche, *The Gay Science*, s. 335.

32. The best example of this process of depoliticization in Nietzsche interpretation is Walter Kaufmann's classic study, originally published in 1950. *Nietzsche: Philosopher, Psychologist and Anti-Christ* (New Jersey, Princeton University Press, 4th edn, 1974).

33. One commentator sharply criticizes Kaufmann's study for encouraging a neglect of the political aspects of Nietzsche's teaching, but then goes on to speak of the 'embarrassingly political Nietzsche'; see Walter H. Sokel, 'The political uses and abuses of Nietzsche in Walter Kaufmann's image of Nietzsche', *Nietzsche-Studien*, 12 (1983), 436–42. See also

Werner Dannhauser's essay on Nietzsche in Leo Strauss and Joseph Cropsey (eds), *History of Political Philosophy* (Chicago, Chicago University Press, 3rd edn, 1987), pp. 829–51.

34. On Nietzsche's conception of a 'great politics' see *Ecce Homo*, translated by W. Kaufmann (New York, Random House, 1967), 'Why I Am a Destiny', s. 3, and the excellent biographical study by Peter Bergmann, *Nietzsche: 'The Last Antipolitical German'* (Bloomington, Indiana University Press, 1987).

35. Nietzsche, *Beyond Good and Evil*, s. 262. See also *Daybreak* 187, where Nietzsche speculates on a possible future lawgiving founded on the idea 'I submit only to the law which I myself have given, in great and small things'.

36. For a critical reading of Rousseau's moral and political philosophy in terms of its negation of otherness, see John Charvet, *The Social Problem in the Philosophy of Rousseau* (Cambridge, Cambridge University Press, 1974). See also the recent essay by M.E. Brint, 'Echoes of Narcisse', *Political Theory*, 16 (Nov. 1988), 617–35.

37. See William E. Connolly, *Political Theory and Modernity* (Oxford, Basil Blackwell, 1988). For an indication of the importance of Nietzsche for Foucault see L.D. Kritzman (ed.), *Michel Foucault: Politics, Philosophy, Culture, Interviews and Other Writings 1977–84* (London, Routledge, 1988). pp. 24, 31–4. 250–1 and 312.

38. Connolly, *Political Theory and Modernity*, p. 96.

39. Connolly, *Political Theory and Modernity*, p. 98. See also Connolly's earlier work, *Politics and Ambiguity*, (Madison, University of Wisconsin Press. 1987), and the debate between Connolly and Charles Taylor on Foucault and Otherness in *Political Theory*, 13 (Aug. 1985), 365–85.

40. For an excellent account of the nature of Foucault's challenge to political theory see Stephen K. White, 'Foucault's challenge to

critical theory', *American Political Science Review*, 80 (June 1986), 419–32.

41. Rosalyn Diprose, 'Nietzsche, ethics and sexual difference', *Radical Philosophy*, 52 (Summer 1989), 27–33. See also Iris Young, 'The ideal of community and the politics of difference', *Social Theory and Practice*, 12 (Spring 1986), 1–26. On p. 4 Young defines difference as 'the irreducible particularity of entities, which makes it impossible to reduce them to commonness or bring them into unity without remainder'.

42. Nancy Fraser and Linda Nicholson, 'Social criticism without philosophy: an encounter between feminism and post-modernism', *Theory, Culture and Society* 5 (June 1988), 373–94.

43. Nietzsche, *On the Genealogy of Morals*, Essay I, 13.

44. Nietzsche, *On the Genealogy of Morals*, Essay I, 13.

45. Nietzsche, *On the Genealogy of Morals*, Essay II, 17. For Nietzsche the social contract creates a social bond which rests on the exclusion of otherness. I disagree, therefore, with Ellen Kennedy's argument, 'Nietzsche: women as Untermensch', p. 191, that Nietzsche does not concern himself with what is perhaps the most fundamental problem of political philosophy, namely the question of the legitimacy of political power. The question of justification does concern Nietzsche but he refrains from replacing a pre-political notion of life in terms of 'force' with a discourse on 'right' (in the manner of Rousseau and Hegel) since he recognizes that such a discourse would only serve to conceal relations of power in which otherness is negated.

Adapted from: Keith Ansell-Pearson, "Nietzsche on Autonomy and Morality: the Challenge to Political Theory." In *Political Studies*, Volume 39, pp. 273–283, 285–286. Copyright © 1991 by Political Studies Association. Reprinted by permission of Blackwell Publishers. ✦

39
The Postmodernist Politicization of Nietzsche

Ted Sadler

> *There is perhaps nothing about the so-called cultured, the believers in 'modern ideas', that arouses so much disgust as their lack of shame, the self-satisfied insolence of eye and hand with which they touch, lick and fumble with everything; and it is possible that more relative nobility of taste and reverential tact is to be discovered today among the people, among the lower orders and especially among peasants, than among the newspaper-reading demimonde of the spirit, the cultured.*
>
> —(*Beyond Good and Evil*, no. 263)

Introduction

According to tradition (Diogenes Laertius, IX, 3) the Pre-Socratic philosopher Heraclitus of Ephesus was once found playing 'dice' with children in the Temple of Artemis. Upon being called to account, he is said to have replied that children's games were better than 'playing politics' with the rest of the Ephesian citizenry. Heraclitus was well known in antiquity for his solitude and disdain for the 'herd', attitudes fully shared by his nineteenth-century disciple Friedrich Nietzsche. For Nietzsche as for Heraclitus, politics is one of the most overestimated things in the world, mainly because it caters for the instincts of the common, unphilosophical natures who are always in the majority. Politics stands in opposition to the radically individualizing character of philosophy as expressed in Heraclitus' statement (Diels-Kranz: Fragment 246) 'I searched out myself'. Of course, the philosopher does not want anything so nonsensical as the abolition of politics: what he wants is to stand aside from this sphere. As Nietzsche puts it in Aphorism 438 of *Human, All Too Human*:

> If the purpose of all politics really is to make life endurable for as many as possible, then these as-many-as-possible are entitled to determine what they understand by an endurable life . . . there is little to be objected to, always presupposing that this narrow-mindedness does not go so far as to demand that *everything* should become politics in this sense, that everyone should live and work according to such a standard. For a few must first of all be allowed, now more than ever, to refrain from politics and step a little aside: they too are prompted to this by pleasure in self-determination; and there may also be a degree of pride attached to staying silent when too many, or even just many, are speaking. Then these few must be forgiven if they fail to take the happiness of the many, whether by the many one understands nations or social classes, so very seriously and are now and then guilty of an ironic posture; for their seriousness lies elsewhere, their happiness is something quite different.
>
> —(Nietzsche 1986: 161)

The kind of 'self-determination' sought in the political realm is rejected by Nietzsche as *philosophically* irrelevant because it is oriented to herd-autonomy, the autonomy of the herd-self. To this he opposes, in typical Heraclitean spirit, the autonomy of the solitary philosopher whose 'seriousness is located elsewhere'. Nietzsche maintains this attitude with complete consistency to the end of his career. In *Daybreak*, he speaks of the 'indecency' of politics (Nietzsche 1982: 120), while in *The Gay Science* he brands it as 'prostitution of the spirit' (Nietzsche 1974: 103). Again, in the 'Foreword' to *The Antichrist*, one of Nietzsche's last works, he counts, as one of the prime conditions for understanding him, that 'one must be accustomed to living on mountains—to seeing the wretched ephemeral chatter of politics and national egoism *beneath* one' (Nietzsche 1968: 114).

Such statements of Nietzsche do not by themselves preclude a political interpretation of his philosophy. It is possible to argue that Nietzsche really rejects only a certain kind of politics, or that there are 'political implications' of his thought which Nietzsche himself does not pursue. During the Third Reich in Germany, Nietzsche was used to support an authoritarian ideology of strength, a strategy which, at least superficially, by no means lacked textual support. From the opposite political pole, Georg Lukács, writing after the Second World War, attacked Nietzsche as an 'imperialist' and 'bourgeois' thinker (Lukács 1980: 309–99). For all their differences, Lukács and the Nazis concur in drawing authoritarian political consequences out of such prominent Nietzschean motifs as the 'will to-power' and the '*übermensch*'. More recently, however, an altogether different image of Nietzsche's 'politics' has emerged. Originating among French intellectuals who since the 1960s have been seeking an anti-authoritarian response to conventional politics (including Marxism), the 'postmodernist' tendency of Nietzsche interpretation finds quasi-anarchistic and pluralist values in his writings. Key figures from this school include Jacques Derrida, Michel Foucault and Gilles Deleuze, but its influence now extends far beyond France, having attained what is probably a dominant position in English-speaking countries. Typical of this tendency is Mark Warren's recent book *Nietzsche and Political Thought*, which sets out to show the relevance of Nietzsche for 'postmodern politics'. According to Warren, when appropriately purged of subjective 'political views', Nietzsche's philosophy implies 'a pluralistic society in which egalitarianism underwrites individuality' (Warren 1988: 157).

The aim of the following discussion is to refute the postmodernist attempt to install political values at the centre of Nietzsche's thought. Obviously, the whole range of postmodernist literature on Nietzsche cannot be reviewed here. By reference to just a few representative texts, I shall be content to indicate the essentials of the postmodernist position, particularly its emphasis on Nietzsche's 'perspectivism' and the pluralism which purportedly follows from this. I shall then indicate the counter-principle to the postmodernists' favoured motif of perspectivism: the principle of rank-order, which, it will be shown, presupposes the 'supra-perspectival' truth which the postmodernists deny. The position thus arrived at will then be further illustrated by a brief discussion of Nietzsche's views on freedom, obedience and the self. The outcome of the study will be a verification of the attitude expressed by Nietzsche in the quotations given at the outset, i.e. that philosophy and politics are worlds apart. It has always been tempting to find one's direction in philosophy by 'getting political', thinking that one is thereby becoming 'relevant'. For Nietzsche, this attitude is not at all the solution, but a large part of the problem.[1]

Perspective and Pluralism

No other aspect of Nietzsche's thought has received so much attention from his postmodernist commentators than has his so-called 'perspectivism'. The reason for this is easily understood. What the postmodernists want above all is a critique of authority, including a critique of dogmatic and politico-ideologically interested discourses. The collapse of any metaphysically guaranteed source of authority, which is what Nietzsche's perspectivism supposedly implies, is seen as holding out the promise of liberation from repressive 'closures' in discourse and practice. Thus Bergoffen describes Nietzsche's thought as 'inaugurating a higher history of humanity by constructing a philosophy of perspectivism where the concept of the interpretative centre replaces the convention of absolute centredness' (Bergoffen 1990: 68). Babich says that 'Nietzsche's multivalently heterogeneous perspectivalism anticipates the inherent ambivalence of the postmodern challenge to hierarchized discourse, specifically to the question of the authorial or traditional authority and the presumption of a final word' (Babich 1990: 259). Nehamas refers to Nietzsche's perspectivism as 'a refusal to grade people and views along a single scale' (Nehamas 1985: 68). For the postmodernists in general, liberation from 'singular' definitions of truth and 'the presumption of a final word' is not just an intellectual, but a politico-ideological accomplishment. Thus Warren can say that, although Nietzsche himself did not appreciate the 'progressive' implications of his fundamental perspectivist standpoint, and remained captive to a reactionary political ideology, this aspect can be deleted from his genuine philosophy, which will then stand forth as an 'implicit critique of domination' (Warren 1988: 11).

In its essentials, perspectivism is not a difficult idea to grasp. It is even, nowadays in western democratic societies and increasingly in the former territories of communism, very much a popular idea. The idea that everyone is entitled to their own 'point of view' and that there should be 'equal rights to all perspectives' is basic to modern political culture. A 'pluralist society' is seen as a natural development of ever-deepening democratization: in 'more advanced' countries the values of pluralism are expressed in law. Naturally there are many (the 'vanguard' of pluralism) who think that this process has not gone far enough and is not proceeding fast enough. But the general direction away from dogmatism towards an open political culture in incontrovertible and irreversible. The micro-structure of social life is just as important in this as are the over-arching political institutions. Definitions of social roles and value choices are more fluid than ever before: experimentation in life-style and morality have almost become the norm, while toleration of social deviance is at an all-time high. All this, considered as a world-historical development, is perspectivism in action, and certainly cannot be attributed to the writings of Friedrich Nietzsche. The importance of Nietzsche, as the postmodernists see him, lies in his philosophical legitimation of this development, and in his demand for its further radicalization. In the words of Warren, 'Nietzsche considers the dissolution

of the Christian-moral [read 'dogmatic'] world-view through recognition of the claims of experience to be the genuinely progressive aspect of European nihilism, opening the possibility of a practice-oriented culture' (Warren 1988: 42).

Pluralism at the level of culture and politics depends on pluralism at the level of truth. The deeper meaning of 'perspectivism' is that there is no such thing as One Truth but rather a multiplicity of mutually inconsistent 'truths' dependent on the particular conditions constituting different kinds of discourse. Metaphysics had assumed the possibility of a final, certain, and authoritative theory of ultimate reality. It is this assumption, so the postmodernists insist, that Nietzsche rejects by affirming the unavoidably anthropomorphic character of all knowledge. Kant had already recognized the subject-dependency of knowledge in the *Critique of Pure Reason*, but in Nietzsche's opinion Kant went astray in postulating universal structures of subjectivity, and thus reinstalled a form of dogmatism at the level of phenomena. Nietzsche's perspectivism, Warren and other postmodernists say, is a 'radicalization' of the Kantian critique of knowledge (Warren 1988: 122f). If there are unlimited possibilities for human subjectivity there are also unlimited perspectives on the world. These perspectives cannot be judged in terms of a fanciful adequacy relation to ultimate reality, for this would presuppose a non-anthropomorphic form of knowledge. All that can be said is that the various perspectives are useful or not useful in varying degrees for the purposes they serve, purposes which are themselves contextual and historically relative. Some perspectives, of course, have become hardened and fixed in the course of time, giving the impression that they are true in some absolute sense. However, what Nietzsche calls the 'genealogical' method will always reveal ('unmask') the hidden forces which underlie fictitious claims to universality. So, the postmodernists conclude, perspectivism is an invitation to experimentalism and pluralism in theory and practice.

The postmodernists see the 'political implications' of perspectivism as grounded in the connection between perspectives and 'interests': to adopt a particular perspective is the same as becoming involved in a certain constellation of interests. As Warren puts it, 'these involve interests in the material, social and cultural worlds as means to and conditions of power organized as subjectivity. Knowledge cannot be extricated from the interest the self has in increasing its "feeling of power" ' (Warren 1988: 90). If there are to be 'equal rights to all perspectives' there must also be 'equal rights to all interest-constellations', which is exactly what political pluralism is all about. Just as there is no metaphysically guaranteed theory of the world, so there is also no metaphysical or supra-perspectival source of authority for any particular structure of power or form of social existence. The struggle between perspectives is at bottom a struggle between opposed political forces, between the different interests of different social actors. This means, however, that the expression 'philosophy of perspectivism' is a misnomer. If no overarching standpoint is possible, whether in theory or in life, the concept of philosophy becomes obsolete. The philosopher gives way to the 'intellectual' or 'writer' who promotes a particular perspective and particular interests, conscious all the while that it is not an imaginary Truth he is serving but just himself and his own herd. In this sense perspectivism seems, at first sight paradoxically, to provide the intellectual with the good conscience for his own partisanship, for his own 'higher' dogmatism. Or is it the case, as suggested by Spivak, that 'if one is always bound by one's perspective, one can at least deliberately reverse perspectives as often as possible?' (Spivak 1974: 19). The purpose of wandering in and out of various perspectives is not entirely clear. It cannot be to get a better view of the 'whole', since every perspective itself defines the whole. And who is to say that any nebulous 'enrichment' of life thus attained is of greater value than a dogged uni-perspectival existence? In any case, whether one frequently 'reverses' perspectives or not, the main point of postmodernist perspectivism is that there is no absolute standard to which one is beholden. There is self-interest and there is group-interest, but the idea of a 'universal' interest goes the same way as the 'presumption of a final word'.

It is natural to ask how the perspectivists are aware of the existence of different perspectives. Does this knowledge originate from within a perspective, or is it supra-perspectival? If the former, then how does perspectivism differ from any other piece of advocacy? If the latter, is not perspectivism self-refuting? These are ticklish questions, which postmodernist perspectivism in general prefers to avoid. In fact, it avoids them in precisely the same way that our 'pluralist' society prefers to leave the meaning of 'pluralism' in decent obscurity, in order to handle practical difficulties 'as the occasion arises'. However, the problem of the One and the many, even when not explicitly posed, makes itself felt, and cannot be wished away by antipathy to a One which is taken as synonymous with terrible dogmatism. The difference between Nietzsche and the postmodernists emerges at precisely this point. Nietzsche does not doubt the necessity of the One, that is of truth in a philosophical sense. Contrary to the postmodernists, perspectivism is for Nietzsche a second-order and not a first-order principle: it is subordinate to a concept of philosophical truth which implies, not pluralism, but an order of rank.

Rank-Order and Supra-Perspectival Truth

Nietzsche writes in the 1886 'Preface' to *Human, All Too Human* that 'it is *the problem of the order of rank* of which we may say it is *our* problem, we free spirits' (Nietzsche 1986: 10). In *On the Genealogy of Morals* (1887) it is likewise stated that 'all the sciences have from now on to prepare the way for the future task of the philosophers: this task understood as the *problem of value*, the determination of the *order of rank among values*' (Nietzsche 1967a: 56). The task of clearly marking off what is 'aristocratic' from what is 'plebian' in the realm of the spirit first emerges in Nietzsche's writing when in *Human, All Too Human* (1878) he includes a section entitled 'Tokens of Higher and Lower Culture'. It remains an abiding concern thereafter. Of course, Nietzsche understands that talk of 'rank-order' is unwelcome in a democratic and egalitarian age. He realizes that there will be an almost irresistible tendency among 'men of modern ideas' to suppress this fundamental theme from his philosophy and thus to distort the real meaning of 'free-spirit':

> In all the countries of Europe and likewise in America there exists at present something that misuses this name, a very narrow, enclosed, chained up species of spirits who desire practically the opposite of that which informs our aims and instincts. . . . They belong, in short and regrettably, among the *levellers*, these falsely named 'free-spirits'—eloquent and tirelessly scribbling slaves of the democratic taste and its 'modern ideas', men without solitude one and all, without their own solitude, good clumsy fellows who, while they cannot be denied courage and moral respectability, are unfree and ludicrously superficial, above all in their fundamental inclination to see in the forms of existing society the cause of practically *all* human failure and misery: which is to stand the truth happily on its head . . . their two most oft-recited doctrines and ditties are 'equality of rights' and 'sympathy for all that suffers'.

—(Nietzsche 1973: 53–4)

Contemporary postmodernist commentators cannot be unaware that rank-order is a prominent motif in Nietzsche's writings. However, because it is somewhat of an embarrassment for the all-important message of pluralism, they adopt one or other of two strategies (or a combination thereof) to deal with it. Either, like Warren, they consign it to Nietzsche's allegedly reactionary 'political views' and deny any organic connection with his basic philosophical standpoint. Or, like Nehamas, they try to subordinate the principle of rank order to perspectivism, whereupon it becomes legitimate to speak of 'noble' and 'plebian' perspectives. Nietzsche obviously does not speak in a very pluralist spirit when comparing his own philosophy with other outlooks, but this, according to Nehamas, only reflects his right to a forth-

right and creative defence of his own perspective (Nehamas 1985: 59). While Warren sees rank-order as a foreign body in Nietzsche's thought, Nehamas reduces it in glib fashion to an ordering of subjective preferences. Both strategies are artificial and untrue to Nietzsche, because, as will now be shown, rank-order is a fundamental principle of Nietzsche's thought without which his perspectivism cannot be comprehended at all.

In the statement from *On the Genealogy of Morals* quoted at the beginning of this section Nietzsche speaks of the 'order of rank among values'. Two questions immediately arise. First, what are 'values'? Second, in respect of what are values to be ranked? For Nietzsche, values do not exist just as abstract ideals but as concrete practices, specific modes of living and acting. Throughout his works, Nietzsche ranks in the sense that he 'evaluates' values, for example the values of religion, politics, money-making, family life, honour-seeking, sensual pleasure, scholarship, science, and so on. One does not need to read very far in Nietzsche to realize that all these latter are accorded a low, or at least relatively low, rank. As to what is ranked highly, Nietzsche praises such virtues of the 'aristocracy' as strength, courage, trust, gratitude, lack of sentimentality, capacity for solitude, etc. What *measure* of rank, then, yields a rank-*order* of this kind? To understand Nietzsche's answer one must keep firmly in mind his basic opposition between the 'herd' and the 'individual': 'First question concerning order of rank: how solitary or how herd-bound (*herdenhaft*) one is' (Nietzsche 1967a: 472). All values which are rooted in the herd-nature of man are ranked low, while values are ranked high in the degree to which they express real independence from the herd. Now it may appear at first sight that this approach to ranking affirms a kind of pluralism and individualism not unwelcome to Nietzsche's postmodernist interpreters. Nothing, however, could be more wrong. For the kinds of individualism and independence so extolled by Nietzsche are attainable only through a relation to something universal. This universal value, this ultimate principle of rank-order, is truth.[2]

If this latter claim is correct, there must be a meaning to 'truth' in Nietzsche which is different from 'perspectival truth'. It has long been recognized that Nietzsche does indeed (and very regularly) use the word 'truth' (*Wahrheit*) and its cognates in ways which suggest a non-perspectival meaning. It has long been acknowledged that Nietzsche's philosophy as a whole strongly suggests the need for a conception of *absolute* non-perspectival truth.[3] But certain prejudices of the western metaphysical tradition have impeded the understanding of what Nietzsche thereby intends. The most important of these prejudices is the assumption that 'truth' can refer only to something doctrinal-theoretical, or at least to something linguistic. Once this assumption is made, one immediately runs up against Nietzsche's insistence on the perspectival character of all theory and all language, so that his apparently non-perspectival use of 'truth' has to be explained away as ironic. However, Nietzsche breaks with the said assumption. He breaks from the idea that truth is something which is stated, that truth consists in acts of signification. Although truth in the supra-perspectival sense is indeed inseparable from thought, Nietzsche denies that thought is inseparable from language.

Since the thesis that I have just stated runs contrary to accepted (particularly postmodernist) opinion on Nietzsche, let me quote a pertinent passage from *The Gay Science*:

This is the essence of phenomenalism and perspectivism as *I* understand them: owing to the nature of *animal consciousness*, the world of which we become conscious is only a surface-and-sign-world, a world that is made commoner and meaner; whatever becomes conscious *becomes* by the same token shallow, thin, relatively stupid, general, sign, herd-signal; all becoming conscious involves a great and thorough corruption, falsification, reduction to superficialities, and generalization.

—(Nietzsche 1974: 299–300)

The difficulty of reconciling this passage with a postmodernist understanding of perspectivism is at once apparent, because

how could one thereby explain the pejorative tones in which the 'surface-and-sign-world' (the world of perspectives) is described? It seems that perspective-creating consciousness produces some kind of 'corruption' and 'falsification', but what exactly is corrupted and falsified here? A clue is given in a passage a little earlier in the same aphorism:

My idea is, as you see, that consciousness does not really belong to man's individual existence but rather to his social or herd nature; that, as follows from this, it has developed subtlety only insofar as this is required by social or herd-utility. . . . Our thoughts themselves are continually governed by the character of consciousness—by the genius of the species that commands it—and translated back into the perspective of the herd. Fundamentally, all our actions are altogether incomparable, personal, unique, and infinitely individual; there is no doubt of that. But as soon as we translate them into consciousness *they no longer seem to be.*

The herd nature of man: every reader of Nietzsche knows that he detests nothing more than this. If thoughts are translated by consciousness into herd-perspectives, then a great deal, on Nietzsche's reckoning, must be 'lost in translation'.

Is it possible to 'think' without having one's 'thoughts' translated by 'consciousness' into 'herd perspectives'? Can the animal nature of man be overcome to this extent? For Nietzsche, the answer in both cases is yes. To begin with, some familiarity with what is prior to consciousness must be presupposed if Nietzsche is to speak of a process of 'falsification' and 'corruption'. And more generally, Nietzsche's whole concern to break from the 'herd' and affirm 'individual existence' would otherwise be senseless. To be sure, Nietzsche realizes that every time he opens his mouth to speak or puts pen to paper, he becomes enmeshed in some perspective or other. On the other hand, he is also quite emphatic that the significance of his own utterances is not given along with the publicly available words or signs in which he expresses himself. This is the reason that Nietzsche knows he will not be understood by those (the vast majority) who do not share his basic experiences. The average human being, and therefore Nietzsche's average reader, is inattentive and unalert to what is prior to consciousness, is fundamentally dominated by his herd nature and the perspectives which go along with it, by words, concepts and conventions. And as long as one tries to understand Nietzsche merely through his words or his 'perspective' one is doomed to failure:

> We no longer have a sufficiently high estimate of ourselves when we communicate. Our true experiences are not garrulous. They could not communicate themselves if they wanted to: they lack words. We have already grown beyond whatever we have words for. In all talking there lies a grain of contempt. Speech, it seems, was devised only for the average, medium, communicable. The speaker has already *vulgarized* himself by speaking.

—(Nietzsche 1968: 82–3)[4]

Those whose existence is not bound to words and perspectives are called by Nietzsche 'philosophers' and 'free-spirits'. This is not to deny that philosophers too employ speech and find herd perspectives indispensable for life. But it is to affirm that philosophers are able in some degree to transcend their animal natures, to look beyond the sphere of utility and herd-interests to experience the ground, or perhaps the abyss, of Being itself. Not, to repeat, in order to 'know' anything or to construct a 'theory' about anything, but simply to be who they are, humans and not just animals;

> We must be raised up—and who are they, who raise us up? They are those true *human beings, those who are no longer animal, the philosophers, artists, and saints.*

—(Nietzsche 1983: 159)

'Rank-order', therefore, does not refer at all to a hierarchy of perspectives but to the degree in which perspectival existence and perspectival thinking is overcome. The reason that perspectivism is none the less important for Nietzsche is that he wishes to deny the equation of 'truth' in the philosophical sense with any kind of doctrine or theory of the world: just on account of the perspectival (relative) character of all doctrines and theories, philosophical (absolute) truth cannot be theoretical-doctrinal. Despite the 'radical' posturing of Nietzsche's postmodernist commentators, they do not understand the genuine radicalism of his thought. Obsessed by the bogey of a 'singular truth', they wish to free up theory, doctrine, knowledge, 'writing', etc. from the normative constraint of a 'final perspective'. They take perspectivism to be Nietzsche's conclusion whereas in reality it is only a premise. They fail to see that Nietzsche is not just a critic of some narrow concept of rationality which would subject discourse to an authoritarian 'closure', but goes beyond this to reject the assimilation of discourse and truth. Nietzsche of course does not oppose a pluralism of discourses and perspectives: he regards this as desirable in so far as the relative character of these latter are thereby exposed. But pluralism is not an end in itself. On the contrary, those who remain within the sphere of pluralism and perspectivism are for Nietzsche precisely the non-philosophers, precisely those who live outside the truth, and who pursue, just like animals do, their perspectivally conditioned 'interests'.

Writers like Nehamas, who see Nietzsche's perspectivism as primary, very naturally conclude that Nietzsche refuses 'to grade people and views along a single scale'. But the opposite is true. Nietzsche takes the utterly uncompromising attitude that there is only one standard which counts: the degree to which a given individual is a philosopher. Everything else is secondary, relevant only to the second-order realm of perspectival living:

> The great majority of people does not consider it contemptible to believe this or that and to live accordingly, without first having given themselves an account of the final and most certain reasons pro and con, and without even troubling themselves about such reasons afterward: the most gifted men and the noblest women still belong to this 'great majority'. But what is goodheartedness,

refinement, or genius to me, when the person who has these virtues tolerates slack feelings in his faith and judgements and when he does not account the desire for certainty as his inmost craving and deepest distress—as that which separates the higher human beings from the lower.

—(Nietzsche 1974: 76)

It does not follow, just because philosophy is an *absolute* value, that everything else is to be denigrated and declared as worthless. Other values have their place, but they are *relative*. For Nietzsche, what is perverse and 'contemptible' among human beings is the adherence to relative values as if they were absolute, something which is ultimately identical with the denial of absolute value as such and the celebration of complete relativity. There is no essential difference, in Nietzsche's view, between the person whose 'absolute' value is something like 'family life' or 'the nation', and the person who, like the 'last men' portrayed in *Thus Spoke Zarathustra*, confesses himself a nihilist. The point is that relative values retain their integrity only to the extent that they exist in a proper relation to an absolute value. Herein is the key to Nietzsche's attitude to politics. What Nietzsche objects to in politics is its absolutization as a value, to the lack of appreciation of the relativity of all political values *vis-à-vis* philosophy and truth. This tendency to an absolutization of politics, he considers, is particularly strong in democratic-socialist movements, because driven by a moral faith in the absolute value of 'equal rights'. But although historical circumstances dictate that Nietzsche gives a particularly sustained critique of democratic egalitarianism, it is clear that any other political value (e.g. the nation-state) is equally objectionable to him if it is absolutized.

Freedom, Obedience and the Self

The advocates of politics and pluralism have the word 'freedom' constantly on their lips. Nietzsche would have little argument with the proposition that to be genuinely human is the same thing as to be 'free'. However, what Nietzsche understands by 'free-dom', and what the pluralists, perspectivists and postmodernists understand by this, are very different things. The essence of this difference is that, for Nietzsche, freedom is attainable exclusively through philosophy, that is exclusively through overcoming all perspectival orientations to the world. Like Kant, Nietzsche believes that freedom is possible only through *obedience* to a universal value, but for him it is the intellectual conscience which binds one to the supreme value of truth.[5] The vulgar conception of freedom, which is the one held by Nietzsche's postmodernist critics, is not positive but negative: it is freedom *from* authority and *from* obedience of every kind. Once again, Mark Warren provides an exemplary illustration of the postmodernist approach. According to Warren,

> Nietzsche's philosophy is in many ways an extended answer to a pivotal question: How can humans be subjects of actions, historically effective and free individuals, in a world in which subjectivity is unsupported by transcendent phenomena or metaphysical essences?

—(Warren 1988: 7)

Warren believes that Nietzsche's thought is directed to a 'crisis of human agency' and tells 'a political story about the relation between oppression, culture, and the constitution of subjects' (Warren 1988: 17–18). The question of *for what* human beings should be 'historically effective' and 'free' admits of no general answer on this account, because it depends in every case on perspectively constituted interests. Gilles Deleuze takes a similar view in a chapter entitled 'Nomad thought', where he suggests that Nietzsche 'announces the advent of a new kind of politics', the politics of the 'nomad' who wants to 'evade the codes of settled people', particularly the codes of 'the despotic and bureaucratic organization of the party or state apparatus' (Deleuze 1977: 149). Especially through the influence of Foucault and Derrida, Nietzsche's 'genealogical' method is seen by postmodernists as a tool of 'deconstruction', able to unmask hidden 'strategies of power' which 'repress subjectivity'.

These views have very little to do with Nietzsche's thought. In reality, Nietzsche has no interest whatsoever in the quasi-anarchistic autonomy intended by the postmodernists because this latter is based on a negative conception of freedom characteristic of 'slave morality':

> the longing for freedom, the instinct for the happiness and the refinements of the feeling of freedom, belong just as necessarily to slave morality and morals as the art of reverence and devotion and the enthusiasm for them are the regular symptom of an aristocratic mode of thinking and valuating.

—(Nietzsche 1973: 178)

The vulgar idea of freedom is negative because it is reactive. It proceeds from experienced repression, exclusion, or wounded dignity, and turns on the sources of these, wanting 'liberation'. It is accompanied by the mistrust also characteristic of the slave, the mistrust which always suspects ulterior motives where 'values' are spoken of or commands issued.[6] If it wants anything in particular (which it often does not) this will be something thoroughly perspectival, variable, changing from one moment to the next. The postmodernists, with their anarchistic proclivities, pride themselves on an ideal of freedom which goes beyond the rather staid ambitions of law-abiding democrats and socialists. For Nietzsche, however, anarchism is just a more hysterical manifestation of the *ressentiment* mentality which governs all those who believe in a political idea of (negative) freedom:

> they (the anarchists) are in fact at one with them all in their total and instinctive hostility towards every form of society other than that of the *autonomous* herd (to the point of repudiating even the concepts 'master' and 'servant'); at one in their tenacious opposition to every special claim, every special right and privilege, at one in their mistrust of punitive justice.

—(Nietzsche 1973: 107)

On Nietzsche's thinking, liberation into herd-autonomy does not amount to any kind of liberation worth mentioning. This does not make him a political 'reactionary', as Warren concludes. It indicates only that his 'seriousness lies elsewhere'. The democrats and anarchists can be left to themselves in the political arena, and need be opposed only when their pseudo-ideals threaten to usurp the authority of philosophy. It is not the case, as the postmodernists believe, that Nietzsche is especially relevant to the marginalized or disfranchised elements of society, whose interests are legitimized by the slogan 'equal rights to all perspectives'. His thought is relevant to everyone, provided only that it is responded to in a philosophical manner. A response of this kind, however, is impossible on the basis of a reactive conception of freedom.

Nietzsche's own philosophical conception of freedom is non-reactive and positive. It is non-reactive because philosophers simply do not feel repressed, excluded, or wounded in their dignity, even in the most unfortunate circumstances. This is what Nietzsche expresses with his idea of the 'eternal return': the philosopher 'affirms life' to the ultimate degree, to the point of wanting the repetition of his own life, right down to the most minute details, an infinite number of times (Nietzsche 1974: 273–4). The philosopher can do this only to the extent that he has detached himself from all perspectives and their attendant interests, for after all, who cannot imagine their interests accommodated more happily, if only to the slightest degree, by a different course of events to the one actually lived through? Furthermore, the freedom of the philosopher is positive because, in his orientation to supra-perspectival and disinterested truth, he is responding to a positive command:

> But there is no doubt that a 'thou shalt' still speaks to us too, that we too still obey a stern law set over us—and this is the last moral law which can make itself audible even to us, which even we know how to *live*, in this if in anything we too are *men of conscience* . . . it is only as men of *this* conscience that we still feel ourselves related to the German integrity and piety of millennia, even if as its most questionable and final descendants, we

immoralists, we godless men of today, indeed in a certain sense as its heirs, as the executors of its innermost will.

—(Nietzsche 1982: 4)

Nothing is more antithetical to postmodernist sentiment than the idea of obedience, because it is automatically associated with 'repression' and runs counter to the negative, reactive conception of freedom. However, everything depends on what is obeyed. There is a species of obedience based on fear and weakness, where one obeys because of one's real or imagined perspectival interest. Although political radicals ostensibly revolt against obedience of this kind, they frequently fall into it themselves, through the conformism euphemistically called 'solidarity': the trendiness and jargon-ridden nature of postmodernist writing is a case in point. But philosophical obedience, as Nietzsche knew, is based on, and at the same time engenders, strength and self-command. This is what Nietzsche means by self-overcoming: command over one's herd-self, obedience to the absolute command to become who one authentically is.[7]

The postmodernists believe that for Nietzsche there is no such thing as the 'self', more precisely that he sees the 'self' as constituted through variable perspectives and not as a stable entity. What they thereby fail to notice is the difference between the 'herd-self', which is indeed perspectivally constituted, and the supraperspectival 'philosophical-self', which is always oriented to one thing alone, to truth. Nietzsche is well known for his 'fundamental hostility and irony for self-lessness': for him, the self should want above all itself (Nietzsche 1973: 177). This 'itself', however, is not a herd-self, but something universal, something which is attainable only *in* truth and *as* truth. Thus Nietzsche can comment, in the 'Preface' to the second edition of *Human, All Too Human*:

Shall my experience—the history of an illness and recovery was what eventuated—have been my personal experience alone? And only *my* 'human, all too human'? Today, I would like to believe the reverse; again and again I feel sure my travel books were not written solely for myself, as sometimes seems to be the case.

—(Nietzsche 1986: 213)

In other words, Nietzsche's books were not written for his own 'perspectival-self', for the perspectively constituted 'empirical' self. They were written for the self which exists deep down, underneath all social determinations, for the self which is attainable only to the 'subterranean man' who tunnels and burrows beneath all perspectival reality (Nietzsche 1982: 1). The postmodernists are blind to this latter self, which explains why they are also blind to the very prominent motif of solitude in Nietzsche. As observed above, Nietzsche sees the 'falsely-named free spirits' of his own time as 'men without solitude one and all, without their own solitude'. Our contemporary postmodernists are no different. In their desire to politicize everything in sight, in their garrulousness and exaltation of 'writing', in their preference for idolatry and hero-worship over reverence, they betray a fear of solitude and lack of self-confidence which is the hallmark of what Nietzsche calls *ressentiment*. Again in Nietzsche's words, they 'are unfree and ludicrously superficial, above all in their fundamental inclination to see in the forms of existing society the cause of practically *all* human failure and misery, which is to stand the truth happily on its head'. The real cause of human failure, as Nietzsche recognized, is not 'society', but the underlying perversity of human nature, the perversity through which demands of the true self are sacrificed for the ephemeral interests of the herd-self. In truth, the overcoming of human failure begins with the examination of oneself, something which cannot be undertaken within the raucous arena of 'postmodernist ideas'.

Notes

1. A good start in the critique of the 'postmodernist Nietzsche' has been made by Robert Solomon in his article 'Nietzsche, postmodernism, and resentment: a genealogical hypothesis', in Koelb (1990: 267–93). The present chapter fully concurs with Solomon's views that 'perspectivism was never itself the

key to Nietzsche's outlook or method' (270) and that postmodernism has its origins in resentment, as 'an expression of disappointment, a retreat, a purely negative thesis' (282). However, Solomon's study fails to situate Nietzsche's perspectivism with respect to his notion of supra-perspectival truth, and thus does not provide a real alternative to the postmodernist position. Correspondingly, he fails to give sufficient attention to Nietzsche's crucial opposition between the 'individual' and the 'herd'.

2. To be noted is the statement from *Ecce Homo*, that 'Zarathustra is more truthful (*wahrhaftiger*) than any other thinker. His doctrine, and his alone, posits truthfulness (*Wahrhaftigkeit*) as the highest virtue' (Nietzsche 1967a: 328).

3. See e.g. the section 'Nietzsche's passionate longing for unlimited Truth' in Jaspers (1965). Other major studies which do not fall into 'perspectivist' errors are those of Heidegger (1979–87), Löwith (1987) and Fink (1960).

4. Note the statement from *On the Genealogy of Morals*: 'Whoever thinks in *words* thinks as an orator and not as a thinker' (Nietzsche 1967a: 110).

5. The fact that Nietzsche, after his early period, maintains an almost exclusively hostile attitude to Kant, should not obscure their common commitment to absolute value and indeed to 'duty' (see the quotation from *Daybreak* in the text below). An illuminating recent discussion of the relation between the two philosophers is Simon (1989).

6. Postmodernism, particularly in connection with its campaigns of deconstruction, fosters an attitude of mistrust and suspicion towards all established values and theories. Nietzsche himself says that the philosopher 'has today a duty to be mistrustful, to squint wickedly up out of every abyss of suspicion' (Nietzsche 1973: 47), but on the other hand, he also regards mistrust as a basic feature of 'slave morality' (e.g. Nietzsche 1973: 176). The difference lies in the *motives* of mistrustfulness: the slave or 'common' type is anxious lest his practical herd-interest is adversely effected; the philosopher's 'interest', however, is 'incomprehensible and impractical' (Nietzsche 1974: 78). Postmodernism's neglect of this distinction is conspicuous.

7. Aphorism 270 of *The Gay Science* consists of the single question and answer '*What does your conscience say?*—"You shall become who you are" ' (Nietzsche 1974: 219).

Bibliography

Allison, D. B. (ed.) (1977) *The New Nietzsche*, Cambridge, Mass.: MIT Press.

Babich, B. E. (1990) 'Post-Nietzschean postmodernism', in C. Koelb (ed.) *Nietzsche as Postmodernist*, Albany, NY: State University of New York Press.

Bergoffen, D. B. (1990) 'Perspectivism without nihilism', in C. Koelb (ed.) *Nietzsche as Postmodernist*, Albany, NY: State University of New York Press.

Deleuze, G. (1977) 'Nomad thought', in D. B. Allison (ed.) *The New Nietzsche*, Cambridge, Mass.: MIT Press.

Fink, E. (1960) *Nietzsches Philosophie*, Stuttgart: Kohlhammer.

Heidegger, M. (1979–87) *Nietzsche* (4 vols), trans. D. F. Krell, J. Stambaugh and F. Capuzzi, New York: Harper & Row.

Jaspers, K. (1965) *Nietzsche: An Introduction to the Understanding of his Philosophical Activity*, trans. C. F. Wallraff and F. J. Schmitz, South Bend, Ind.: Gateway.

Koelb, C. (ed.) (1990) *Nietzsche as Postmodernist*, Albany, NY: State University of New York Press.

Löwith, K. (1987) *Nietzsches Philosophie der ewigen Wiederkehr des Gleichen*, in K. Löwith, *Sämtliche Schriften* 6, Stuttgart: J. B. Metzlersche Verlag.

Lukács, G. (1980) *The Destruction of Reason*, London: Merlin.

Nehamas, A. (1985) *Nietzsche: Life as Literature*, Cambridge, Mass.: Harvard University Press.

Nietzsche, F. (1967a) *On the Genealogy of Morals and Ecce Homo*, trans. W. Kaufmann and R. J. Hollingdale, New York: Vintage.

—— (1967b) *The Will to Power*, trans. W. Kaufmann, New York: Vintage.

—— (1968) *Twilight of the Idols and The Anti-Christ*, trans. R. J. Hollingdale, Harmondsworth: Penguin.

—— (1973) *Beyond Good and Evil*, trans. R. J. Hollingdale, Harmondsworth: Penguin.

—— (1974) *The Gay Science*, trans. W. Kaufmann, New York: Vintage.

—— (1982) *Daybreak*, trans. R. J. Hollingdale, Cambridge: Cambridge University Press.

—— (1983) *Untimely Meditations*, trans. R. J. Hollingdale, Cambridge: Cambridge University Press.

—— (1986) *Human, All Too Human*, trans. R. J. Hollingdale, Cambridge: Cambridge University Press.

Simon, J. (1989) 'Die Krise des Wahrheitsbegriffs als Krise der Metaphysik', *Nietzsche-Studien* 18.

Spivak, G. C. (1974) 'Translator's preface', to J. Derrida, *Of Grammatology*, Baltimore, Md. and London: Johns Hopkins University Press.

Warren, M. (1988) *Nietzsche and Political Thought*, Cambridge, Mass.: MIT Press.

Simone de Beauvoir

The legacy of Simone de Beauvoir is a somewhat contradictory one. Trained to be a teacher of philosophy, she downplayed her philosophical talents and stressed her literary ones. Author of the most influential feminist work of the 20th century, she repeatedly distanced herself from feminism until the late 1960s—indeed, some feminists both in France and the United States returned the favor, criticizing her thought as "masculinist." Despite her advocacy of intellectual and moral independence for women, de Beauvoir's life and name have long been inextricably linked with that of her colleague and lover, Jean-Paul Sartre.

Born in 1908 into a Parisian middle-class family, de Beauvoir attended Catholic schools for her elementary and secondary education. In an era when women had only recently been permitted to train in and teach certain subjects, she entered the Sorbonne in 1925 to obtain her *license* and a teaching diploma so that she could teach in secondary schools. After completing her studies in 1929, she sat for the *agrégation* in philosophy, a competitive examination that was the basis for awarding teaching positions in the *lycées*. Despite her less-than-premier training, de Beauvoir finished second only to Sartre on the examination. She then taught philosophy in various schools around France until 1943, when she embarked on a literary career. After the war, she and Sartre founded and edited *Les Temps Modernes*, an influential literary and political journal.

Her 1954 novel *Les Mandarins* (*The Mandarins*) won the Prix Goncourt, and in 1958 de Beauvoir published the first part of her multi-volume memoir. In addition to her literary works, she also published two works of philosophical importance—*The Ethics of Ambiguity* (1948), in which she advanced an existentialist ethic, and *The Second Sex* (1949), in which she sought to explain women's subordinate position in society. Her lifelong companion and kindred spirit, Sartre, died in 1980 after a prolonged illness. Simone de Beauvoir herself passed away in 1986, and was buried in Paris alongside Sartre.

All too often, de Beauvoir's philosophical work has been regarded as little more than an extension of Sartre's existentialism. In many ways, Sartre's views on freedom and responsibility, and the opposition between self and other, do provide the context for her work in *The Ethics of Ambiguity* and *The Second Sex*. More recent studies of de Beauvoir's thought, however, have emphasized her independent contributions to both existentialist philosophy and feminism. For example, new evidence from de Beauvoir's diaries indicates that she preceded Sartre in formulating the philosophical problem of the Other.[1] Further, careful readings of her work underscore the importance her thought gives to the ways in which the thought and action of individuals are shaped by historical and cultural circumstances as well as by other people. The social constructivism so central to her position can be aptly summarized in this most famous aphorism from *The Second Sex*: "One is not born, but rather becomes, a woman."[2]

The Second Sex

The selections reprinted from de Beauvoir's classic work highlight both the problem of women's subordination and her proposed remedies for it. Handicapped by legal and social inequality, women are also constrained by the concept of "the eternal feminine"—a term for the cultural interpretations of and expectations for women's lives. Rather than being able to live as free, autonomous, and transcendent beings, women are condemned to live life as immanent, relative beings—as the Other.

After describing the nature of the problem faced by women, de Beauvoir's question is how can women obtain genuine liberty, fulfillment, and equal status? Her ultimate response is that women can achieve transcendence only when they have become independent. For de Beauvoir, an independent woman must certainly be one who works outside the home, but should be one living the life of an artist or intellectual. She should strive to be free of both marriage and maternity, for these situations do not permit women to freely pursue the gratifications of both love and career. Additionally, one should note that de Beauvoir acknowledges that women are most likely to achieve this independence under the social and economic equality created by an authentic socialism.

Commentaries

Karen Vintges explores the philosophical background of de Beauvoir's argument in *The Second Sex*. In her view, de Beauvoir adapted existentialist categories (e.g., self/other, as well as being-in-itself/being-for-itself) to suit the purposes of her investigation into women's situation. These "engendered" categories helped de Beauvoir analyze women's condition from the standpoint of immanence and then describe how women could become authentic subjects. Where the myths of femininity and the social division of labor have rendered women Other, de Beauvoir's own spin on existentialist philosophy held out the possibility that women could achieve independence and selfhood.

The essay by Margaret A. Simons discusses the extent to which de Beauvoir's work laid a foundation for contemporary feminism. For example, de Beauvoir saw legal reforms (of the sort promoted by liberal feminists) as simply insufficient to achieve lasting change in the status of women. Somewhat critical of both Marxist and psychoanalytic explanations for women's condition, de Beauvoir nonetheless drew on the history of class struggles and the psychology of oppression to employ the concept of the Other to full effect. For Simons, because of

her existentialism and her social constructionism, Simone de Beauvoir is rightly seen as a significant precursor of radical feminism.

Notes

1. Margaret A. Simons, *Beauvoir and the Second Sex: Feminism, Race, and the Origins of Existentialism* (Lanham, MD: Rowman & Littlefield, 1999), xvii.
2. Simone de Beauvoir, *The Second Sex* (New York: Vintage, 1989), 267.

Web Sources

http://kirjasto.sci.fi/beauvoir.htm
Simone de Beauvoir. Brief biographical profile.

http://www.marxists.org/reference/subject/ philosophy/works/fr/2ndsex.htm
Philosophy Archive @ Marxists.org. An English translation of portions of *The Second Sex.*

http://www.bu.edu/wcp/Papers/Gend/ GendSimo.htm
Is The Second Sex *Beauvoir's Application of Sartrean Existentialism?* Essay discussing existentialism and *The Second Sex.*

Class Activities and Discussion Items

1. How did de Beauvoir both describe and explain the situation or condition of women? Are her descriptions and explanations accurate? Why or why not?
2. For de Beauvoir, how might the condition of women be improved or transformed? Is such a strategy likely to be effective? Why or why not?
3. Compare and contrast the conceptions of human nature and politics held by de Beauvoir and other theorists. Which theorist has the most adequate conception of human nature? Why?

Further Reading

Bair, Deirdre. 1990. *Simone de Beauvoir: A Biography.* New York: Summit. A major biographical profile of de Beauvoir.

Evans, Ruth. 1998. *Simone de Beauvoir's* The Second Sex: *New Interdisciplinary Essays.* New York: St. Martin's. Important essays that examine de Beauvoir's life and work, both as novelist and as philosopher.

Moi, Toril. 1994. *Simone de Beauvoir: The Making of an Intellectual Woman.* Cambridge: Blackwell. Challenging essays highlighting de Beauvoir's contributions to modern thought.

Simons, Margaret A. 1999. *Beauvoir and the Second Sex: Feminism, Race, and the Origins of* *Existentialism.* Lanham, MD: Rowman & Littlefield. A significant collection of interviews with and essays about Simone de Beauvoir by a premier scholar. ✦

40

Excerpts from *The Second Sex*

Simone de Beauvoir

Introduction

For a long time I have hesitated to write a book on woman. The subject is irritating, especially to women; and it is not new. Enough ink has been spilled in the quarreling over feminism, now practically over, and perhaps we should say no more about it. It is still talked about, however, for the voluminous nonsense uttered during the last century seems to have done little to illuminate the problem. After all, is there a problem? And if so, what is it? Are there women, really? Most assuredly the theory of the eternal feminine still has its adherents who will whisper in your ear: "Even in Russia women still are *women*"; and other erudite persons—sometimes the very same—say with a sigh: "Woman is losing her way, woman is lost." One wonders if women still exist, if they will always exist, whether or not it is desirable that they should, what place they occupy in this world, what their place should be. "What has become of women?" was asked recently in an ephemeral magazine.[1]

But first we must ask: what is a woman? "*Tota mulier in utero,*" says one, "woman is a womb." But in speaking of certain women, connoisseurs declare that they are not women, although they are equipped with a uterus like the rest. All agree in recognizing the fact that females exist in the human species; today as always they make up about one half of humanity. And yet we are told that femininity is in danger; we are exhorted to be women, remain women, become women. It would appear, then, that every female human being is not necessarily a woman; to be so considered she must share in that mys-terious and threatened reality known as femininity. Is this attribute something secreted by the ovaries? Or is it a Platonic essence, a product of the philosophic imagination? Is a rustling petticoat enough to bring it down to earth? Although some women try zealously to incarnate this essence, it is hardly patentable. It is frequently described in vague and dazzling terms that seem to have been borrowed from the vocabulary of the seers, and indeed in the times of St. Thomas it was considered an essence as certainly defined as the somniferous virtue of the poppy.

But conceptualism has lost ground. The biological and social sciences no longer admit the existence of unchangeably fixed entities that determine given characteristics, such as those ascribed to woman, the Jew, or the Negro. Science regards any characteristic as a reaction dependent in part upon a *situation*. If today femininity no longer exists, then it never existed. But does the word *woman,* then, have no specific content? This is stoutly affirmed by those who hold to the philosophy of the enlightenment, of rationalism, of nominalism; women, to them, are merely the human beings arbitrarily designated by the word *woman.* Many American women particularly are prepared to think that there is no longer any place for woman as such; if a backward individual still takes herself for a woman, her friends advise her to be psychoanalyzed and thus get rid of this obsession. In regard to a work, *Modern Woman: The Lost Sex,* which in other respects has its irritating features, Dorothy Parker has written: "I cannot be just to books which treat of woman as woman.... My idea is that all of us, men as well as women, should be regarded as human beings." But nominalism is a rather inadequate doctrine, and the antifemininists have had no trouble in showing that women simply *are not* men. Surely woman is, like man, a human being; but such a declaration is abstract. The fact is that every concrete human being is always a singular, separate individual. To decline to accept such notions as the eternal feminine, the black soul, the Jewish character, is not to deny that Jews, Negroes, women exist today—this denial does not represent a liberation for those concerned, but rather a flight from reality. Some years ago a well-known woman writer refused to permit her portrait to appear in a series of photographs especially devoted to women writers; she wished to be counted among the men. But in order to gain this privilege she made use of her husband's influence! Women who assert that they are men lay claim none the less to masculine consideration and respect. I recall also a young Trotskyite standing on a platform at a boisterous meeting and getting ready to use her fists, in spite of her evident fragility. She was denying her feminine weakness; but it was for love of a militant male whose equal she wished to be. The attitude of defiance of many American women proves that they are haunted by a sense of their femininity. In truth, to go for a walk with one's eyes open is enough to demonstrate that humanity is divided into two classes of individuals whose clothes, faces, bodies, smiles, gaits, interests, and occupations are manifestly different. Perhaps these differences are superficial, perhaps they are destined to disappear. What is certain is that right now they do most obviously exist.

If her functioning as a female is not enough to define woman, if we decline also to explain her through "the eternal feminine," and if nevertheless we admit, provisionally, that women do exist, then we must face the question: what is a woman?

To state the question is, to me, to suggest, at once, a preliminary answer. The fact that I ask it is in itself significant. A man would never get the notion of writing a book on the peculiar situation of the human male.[2] But if I wish to define myself, I must first of all say: "I am a woman"; on this truth must be based all further discussion. A man never begins by presenting himself as an individual of a certain sex; it goes without saying that he is a man. The terms *masculine* and *feminine* are used symmetrically only as a matter of form, as on legal papers. In actuality the relation of the two sexes is not quite like that of two electrical poles, for man represents both the positive and the neutral, as is indicated by the common use of *man* to designate human beings in general; whereas woman represents only the negative, defined by limiting criteria, without reciprocity. In the midst of an abstract discussion it is vexing to hear a man say: "You think thus and so because you are a woman"; but I know that my only defense is to reply: "I think thus and so because it is true," thereby removing my subjective self from the argument. It would be out of the question to reply: "And you think the contrary because you are a man," for it is understood that the fact of being a man is no peculiarity. A man is in the right in being a man; it is the woman who is in the wrong. It amounts to this: just as for the ancients there was an absolute vertical with reference to which the oblique was defined, so there is an absolute human type, the masculine. Woman has ovaries, a uterus; these peculiarities imprison her in her subjectivity, circumscribe her within the limits of her own nature. It is often said that she thinks with her glands. Man superbly ignores the fact that his anatomy also includes glands, such as the testicles, and that they secrete hormones. He thinks of his body as a direct and normal connection with the world, which he believes he apprehends objectively, whereas he regards the body of woman as a hindrance, a prison, weighed down by everything peculiar to it. "The female is a female by virtue of a certain *lack* of qualities," said Aristotle; "we should regard the female nature as afflicted with a natural defectiveness." And St. Thomas for his part pronounced woman to be an "imperfect man," an "incidental" being. This is symbolized in Genesis where Eve is depicted as made from what Bossuet called "a supernumerary bone" of Adam.

Thus humanity is male and man defines woman not in herself but as relative to him; she is not regarded as an autonomous being. Michelet writes: "Woman, the relative being. . . ." And Benda is most positive in his *Rapport d'Uriel:* "The body of man makes sense in itself quite apart from that of woman, whereas the latter seems wanting in significance by itself. . . . Man can think of himself without woman. She cannot think of herself without man." And she is simply what man decrees; thus she is called "the sex," by which is meant that she appears essentially to the male as a sexual being. For him she is sex—absolute sex, no less. She is defined and differentiated with reference to man and not he with reference to her; she is the incidental, the inessential as opposed to the essential. He is the Subject, he is the Absolute—she is the Other.[3]

The category of the *Other* is as primordial as consciousness itself. In the most primitive societies, in the most ancient mythologies, one finds the expression of a duality—that of the Self and the Other. This duality was not originally attached to the division of the sexes; it was not dependent upon any empirical facts. It is revealed in such works as that of Granet on Chinese thought and those of Dumézil on the East Indies and Rome. The feminine element was at first no more involved in such pairs as Varuna-Mitra, Uranus-Zeus, Sun-Moon, and Day-Night than it was in the contrasts between Good and Evil, lucky and unlucky auspices, right and left, God and Lucifer. Otherness is a fundamental category of human thought.

Thus it is that no group ever sets itself up as the One without at once setting up the Other over against itself. If three travelers chance to occupy the same compartment, that is enough to make vaguely hostile "others" out of all the rest of the passengers on the train. In small-town eyes all persons not belonging to the village are "strangers" and suspect; to the native of a country all who inhabit other countries are "foreigners"; Jews are "different" for the anti-Semite, Negroes are "inferior" for American racists, aborigines are "natives" for colonists, proletarians are the "lower class" for the privileged.

Lévi-Strauss, at the end of a profound work on the various forms of primitive societies, reaches the following conclusion: "Passage from the state of Nature to the state of Culture is marked by man's ability to view biological relations as a series of contrasts; duality, alternation, opposition, and symmetry, whether under definite or vague forms, constitute not so much phenomena to be explained as fundamental and immediately given data of social reality."[4] These phenomena would be incomprehensible if in fact human society were simply a *Mitsein* or fellowship based on solidarity and friendliness. Things become clear, on the contrary, if, following Hegel, we find in consciousness itself a fundamental hostility toward every other consciousness; the subject can be posed only in being opposed—he sets himself up as the essential, as opposed to the other, the inessential, the object.

But the other consciousness, the other ego, sets up a reciprocal claim. The native traveling abroad is shocked to find himself in turn regarded as a "stranger" by the natives of neighboring countries. As a matter of fact, wars, festivals, trading, treaties, and contests among tribes, nations, and classes tend to deprive the concept *Other* of its absolute sense and to make manifest its relativity; willy-nilly, individuals and groups are forced to realize the reciprocity of their relations. How is it, then, that this reciprocity has not been recognized between the sexes, that one of the contrasting terms is set up as the sole essential, denying any relativity in regard to its correlative and defining the latter as pure otherness? Why is it that women do not dispute male sovereignty? No subject will readily volunteer to become the object, the inessential; it is not the Other who, in defining himself as the Other, establishes the One. The Other is posed as such by the One in defining himself as the One. But if the Other is not to regain the status of being the One, he must be submissive enough to accept this alien point of view. Whence comes this submission in the case of woman?

There are, to be sure, other cases in which a certain category has been able to dominate another completely for a time. Very often this privilege depends upon inequality of numbers—the majority imposes its rule upon the minority or persecutes it. But women are not a minority, like the American Negroes or the Jews; there are as many women as men on earth. Again, the two groups concerned have often been originally independent; they may have been formerly unaware of each other's existence, or perhaps they recognized each other's autonomy. But a historical event has resulted in the subjugation of the weaker by the stronger. The scattering of the Jews, the introduction of slavery into America, the conquests of imperialism are examples in point. In these cases the oppressed retained at least the memory of former days; they possessed in common a past, a tradition, sometimes a religion or a culture.

The parallel drawn by Bebel between women and the proletariat is valid in that neither ever formed a minority or a separate collective unit of mankind. And instead of a single historical event it is in both cases a historical development that explains their status as a class and accounts for the membership of *particular individuals* in that class. But proletarians have not always existed, whereas there have always been women. They are women in virtue of their anatomy and physiology. Throughout history they have always been subordinated to men,[5] and hence their dependency is not the result of a historical event or a social change—it was not something that *occurred*. The reason why otherness in this case seems to be an absolute is in part that it lacks the contingent or incidental nature of historical facts. A condition brought about at a certain time can be abolished at some other time, as the Negroes of Haiti and others have proved; but it might seem that a natural condition is beyond the possibility of change. In truth, however, the nature of things is no more immutably given, once for all, than is historical reality. If woman seems to be the inessential which never becomes the essential, it is because she herself fails to bring about this change. Proletarians say "We"; Negroes also. Regarding themselves as subjects, they transform the bourgeois, the whites, into "others." But women do not say "We," except at some congress of feminists or similar formal demonstration; men say "women," and women use the same word in referring to themselves. They do not authentically assume a subjective attitude. The proletarians have accomplished the revolution in Russia, the Negroes in Haiti, the Indo-Chinese are battling for it in Indo-China; but the women's effort has never been anything more than a symbolic agitation. They have gained only what men have been willing to grant; they have taken nothing, they have only received.[6]

The reason for this is that women lack concrete means for organizing themselves into a unit which can stand face to face with the correlative unit. They have no past, no history, no religion of their own; and they have no such solidarity of work and interest as that of the proletariat. They are not even promiscuously herded together in the way that creates community feeling among the American Negroes, the ghetto Jews, the workers of Saint-Denis, or the factory hands of Renault. They live dispersed among the males, attached through residence, housework, economic condition, and social standing to certain men—fathers or husbands—more firmly than they are to other women. If they belong to the bourgeoisie, they feel solidarity with men of that class, not with proletarian women; if they are white, their allegiance is to white men, not to Negro women. The proletariat can propose to massacre the ruling class, and a sufficiently fanatical Jew or Negro might dream of getting sole possession of the atomic bomb and making humanity wholly Jewish or black; but woman cannot even dream of exterminating the males. The bond that unites her to her oppressors is not comparable to any other. The division of the sexes is a biological fact, not an event in human history. Male and female stand opposed within a primordial *Mitsein*, and woman has not broken it. The couple is a fundamental unity with its two halves riveted together, and the cleavage of society along the line of sex is impossible. Here is to be found the basic trait of woman: she is the Other in a totality of which the two components are necessary to one another.

One could suppose that this reciprocity might have facilitated the liberation of woman. When Hercules sat at the feet of Omphale and helped with her spinning, his desire for her held him captive; but why did she fail to gain a lasting power? To revenge herself on Jason, Medea killed their children; and this grim legend would seem to suggest that she might have obtained a formidable influence over him through his love for his offspring. In *Lysistrata* Aristophanes gaily depicts a band of women who joined forces to gain social ends through the sexual needs of their men; but this is only a play. In the legend of the Sabine women, the latter soon abandoned their plan of remaining sterile to punish their ravishers. In truth woman has not been socially emancipated through man's need—sexual desire and the desire for offspring—which makes the male dependent for satisfaction upon the female.

Master and slave, also, are united by a reciprocal need, in this case economic, which does not liberate the slave. In the relation of master to slave the master does not make a point of the need that he has for the other; he has in his grasp the power of satisfying this need through his own action; whereas the slave, in his dependent condition, his hope and fear, is quite conscious of the need he has for his master. Even if the need is at bottom equally urgent for both, it always works in favor of the oppressor and against the oppressed. That is why the liberation of the working class, for example, has been slow.

Now, woman has always been man's dependent, if not his slave; the two sexes have never shared the world in equality. And even today woman is heavily handicapped, though her situation is beginning to change. Almost nowhere is her legal status the same as man's,[7] and frequently it is much to her disadvantage. Even when her rights are legally recognized in the abstract, long-standing custom prevents their full expression in the mores. In the economic sphere men and women can almost be said to make up two castes; other things being equal, the former hold the better jobs, get higher wages, and have more opportunity for success than their new competitors. In industry and politics men have a great many more positions and they monopolize the most important posts. In addition to all this, they enjoy a traditional prestige that the education of children tends in every way to support, for the present enshrines the past—and in the past all history has been made by men. At the present time, when women are beginning to take part in the affairs of the world, it is still a world that belongs to men—they have no doubt of it at all and women have scarcely any. To decline to be the Other, to refuse to be a party to the deal—this would be for women to renounce all the advantages conferred upon them by their alliance with the superior caste. Man-the-sovereign will provide woman-the-liege with material protection and will undertake the moral justification of her existence; thus she can evade at once both economic risk and the metaphysical

risk of a liberty in which ends and aims must be contrived without assistance. Indeed, along with the ethical urge of each individual to affirm his subjective existence, there is also the temptation to forgo liberty and become a thing. This is an inauspicious road, for he who takes it—passive, lost, ruined—becomes henceforth the creature of another's will, frustrated in his transcendence and deprived of every value. But it is an easy road; on it one avoids the strain involved in undertaking an authentic existence. When man makes of woman the *Other*, he may, then, expect her to manifest deep-seated tendencies toward complicity. Thus, woman may fail to lay claim to the status of subject because she lacks definite resources, because she feels the necessary bond that ties her to man regardless of reciprocity, and because she is often very well pleased with her role as the *Other*.

But it will be asked at once: how did all this begin? It is easy to see that the duality of the sexes, like any duality, gives rise to conflict. And doubtless the winner will assume the status of absolute. But why should man have won from the start? It seems possible that women could have won the victory; or that the outcome of the conflict might never have been decided. How is it that this world has always belonged to the men and that things have begun to change only recently? Is this change a good thing? Will it bring about an equal sharing of the world between men and women?

These questions are not new, and they have often been answered. But the very fact that woman *is the Other* tends to cast suspicion upon all the justifications that men have ever been able to provide for it. These have all too evidently been dictated by men's interest. A little-known feminist of the seventeenth century, Poulain de la Barre, put it this way: "All that has been written about women by men should be suspect, for the men are at once judge and party to the lawsuit." Everywhere, at all times, the males have displayed their satisfaction in feeling that they are the lords of creation. "Blessed be God . . . that He did not make me a woman," say the Jews in their morning prayers, while their wives pray on a note of resignation: "Blessed be the Lord, who created me according to His will." The first among the blessings for which Plato thanked the gods was that he had been created free, not enslaved; the second, a man, not a woman. But the males could not enjoy this privilege fully unless they believed it to be founded on the absolute and the eternal; they sought to make the fact of their supremacy into a right. "Being men, those who have made and compiled the laws have favored their own sex, and jurists have elevated these laws into principles," to quote Poulain de la Barre once more.

Legislators, priests, philosophers, writers, and scientists have striven to show that the subordinate position of woman is willed in heaven and advantageous on earth. The religions invented by men reflect this wish for domination. In the legends of Eve and Pandora men have taken up arms against women. They have made use of philosophy and theology, as the quotations from Aristotle and St. Thomas have shown. Since ancient times satirists and moralists have delighted in showing up the weaknesses of women. We are familiar with the savage indictments hurled against women throughout French literature. Montherlant, for example, follows the tradition of Jean de Meung, though with less gusto. This hostility may at times be well founded, often it is gratuitous; but in truth it more or less successfully conceals a desire for self-justification. As Montaigne says, "It is easier to accuse one sex than to excuse the other." Sometimes what is going on is clear enough. For instance, the Roman law limiting the rights of woman cited "the imbecility, the instability of the sex" just when the weakening of family ties seemed to threaten the interests of male heirs. And in the effort to keep the married woman under guardianship, appeal was made in the sixteenth century to the authority of St. Augustine, who declared that "woman is a creature neither decisive nor constant," at a time when the single woman was thought capable of managing her property. Montaigne understood clearly how arbitrary and unjust was woman's appointed lot: "Women are not in the wrong when they decline to accept the rules laid down for them, since the men make these rules without consulting them. No wonder intrigue and strife abound." But he did not go so far as to champion their cause.

It was only later, in the eighteenth century, that genuinely democratic men began to view the matter objectively. Diderot, among others, strove to show that woman is, like man, a human being. Later John Stuart Mill came fervently to her defense. But these philosophers displayed unusual impartiality. In the nineteenth century the feminist quarrel became again a quarrel of partisans. One of the consequences of the industrial revolution was the entrance of women into productive labor, and it was just here that the claims of the feminists emerged from the realm of theory and acquired an economic basis, while their opponents became the more aggressive. Although landed property lost power to some extent, the bourgeoisie clung to the old morality that found the guarantee of private property in the solidity of the family. Woman was ordered back into the home the more harshly as her emancipation became a real menace. Even within the working class the men endeavored to restrain woman's liberation, because they began to see the women as dangerous competitors—the more so because they were accustomed to work for lower wages.[8]

In proving woman's inferiority, the antifeminists then began to draw not only upon religion, philosophy, and theology, as before, but also upon science—biology, experimental psychology, etc. At most they were willing to grant "equality in difference" to the *other* sex. That profitable formula is most significant; it is precisely like the "equal but separate" formula of the Jim Crow laws aimed at the North American Negroes. As is well known, this so-called equalitarian segregation has resulted only in the most extreme discrimination. The similarity just noted is in no way due to chance, for whether it is a race, a caste, a class, or a sex that is reduced to a position of inferiority, the methods of justification are the same. "The eternal feminine" corresponds to "the black soul" and to "the Jewish character." True, the Jewish problem is on the whole very different from the other two—to the anti-Semite the Jew is not so much an inferior as he is an enemy for whom there is to be granted no place on earth, for whom annihilation is the fate desired. But there are deep similarities between the situation of woman and that of the Negro. Both are being emancipated today from a like paternalism, and the former master class wishes to "keep them in their place"—that is, the place chosen for them. In both cases the former masters lavish more or less sincere eulogies, either on the virtues of "the good Negro" with his dormant, childish, merry soul—the submissive Negro—or on the merits of the woman who is "truly feminine"—that is, frivolous, infantile, irresponsible—the submissive woman. In both cases the dominant class bases its argument on a state of affairs that it has itself created. As George Bernard Shaw puts it, in substance, "The American white relegates the black to the rank of shoeshine boy; and he concludes from this that the black is good for nothing but shining shoes." This vicious circle is met with in all analogous circumstances; when an individual (or a group of individuals) is kept in a situation of inferiority, the fact is that he *is* inferior. But the significance of the verb *to be* must be rightly understood here; it is in bad faith to give it a static value when it really has the dynamic Hegelian sense of "to have become." Yes, women on the whole *are* today inferior to men; that is, their situation affords them fewer possibilities. The question is: should that state of affairs continue?

Many men hope that it will continue; not all have given up the battle. The conservative bourgeoisie still see in the emancipation of women a menace to their morality and their interests. Some men dread feminine competition. Recently a male student wrote in the *Hebdo-Latin:* "Every woman student who goes into medicine or law robs us of a job." He never questioned his rights in this world. And economic interests are not the only ones concerned. One of the benefits that oppression confers upon the oppressors is that the most humble among them is made to *feel* superior; thus, a "poor white" in the South can console himself with the thought that he is not a "dirty nigger"—and the more prosperous whites cleverly exploit this pride.

Similarly, the most mediocre of males feels himself a demigod as compared with women. It was much easier for M. de Montherlant to think himself a hero when he faced women (and women chosen for his purpose) than when he was obliged to act the man among men—something many women have done better than he, for that matter. And in September 1948, in one of his articles in the *Figaro littéraire,* Claude Mauriac—whose great originality is admired by all—could[9] write regarding woman: "*We* listen on a tone [*sic!*] of polite indifference . . . to the most brilliant among them, well knowing that her wit reflects more or less luminously ideas that come from *us.*" Evidently the speaker referred to is not reflecting the ideas of Mauriac himself, for no one knows of his having any. It may be that she reflects ideas originating with men, but then, even among men there are those who have been known to appropriate ideas not their own; and one can well ask whether Claude Mauriac might not find more interesting a conversation reflecting Descartes, Marx, or Gide rather than himself. What is really remarkable is that by using the questionable *we* he identifies himself with St. Paul, Hegel, Lenin, and Nietzsche, and from the lofty eminence of their grandeur looks down disdainfully upon the bevy of women who make bold to converse with him on a footing of equality. In truth, I know of more than one woman who would refuse to suffer with patience Mauriac's "tone of polite indifference."

I have lingered on this example because the masculine attitude is here displayed with disarming ingenuousness. But men profit in many more subtle ways from the otherness, the alterity of woman. Here is miraculous balm for those afflicted with an inferiority complex, and indeed no one is more arrogant toward women, more aggressive or scornful, than the man who is anxious about his virility. Those who are not fear-ridden in the presence of their fellow men are much more disposed to recognize a fellow creature in woman; but even to these the myth of Woman, the Other, is precious for many reasons.[10] They cannot be blamed for not cheerfully relinquishing all the benefits they derive from the myth, for they realize what they would lose in relinquishing woman as they fancy her to be, while they fail to realize what they have to gain from the woman of tomorrow. Refusal to pose oneself as the Subject, unique and absolute, requires great self-denial. Furthermore, the vast majority of men make no such claim explicitly. They do not *postulate* woman as inferior, for today they are too thoroughly imbued with the ideal of democracy not to recognize all human beings as equals.

In the bosom of the family, woman seems in the eyes of childhood and youth to be clothed in the same social dignity as the adult males. Later on, the young man, desiring and loving, experiences the resistance, the independence of the woman desired and loved; in marriage, he respects woman as wife and mother, and in the concrete events of conjugal life she stands there before him as a free being. He can therefore feel that social subordination as between the sexes no longer exists and that on the whole, in spite of differences, woman is an equal. As, however, he observes some points of inferiority—the most important being unfitness for the professions—he attributes these to natural causes. When he is in a co-operative and benevolent relation with woman, his theme is the principle of abstract equality, and he does not base his attitude upon such inequality as may exist. But when he is in conflict with her, the situation is reversed: his theme will be the existing inequality, and he will even take it as justification for denying abstract equality.[11]

So it is that many men will affirm as if in good faith that women *are* the equals of man and that they have nothing to clamor for, while *at the same time* they will say that women can never be the equals of man and that their demands are in vain. It is, in point of fact, a difficult matter for man to realize the extreme importance of social discriminations which seem outwardly insignificant but which produce in woman moral and intellectual effects so profound that they appear to spring from her original nature.[12] The most sympathetic of men never fully comprehend woman's concrete situation. And there is no reason to put much trust in the men when they rush to the defense of

privileges whose full extent they can hardly measure. We shall not, then, permit ourselves to be intimidated by the number and violence of the attacks launched against women, nor to be entrapped by the self-seeking eulogies bestowed on the "true woman," nor to profit by the enthusiasm for woman's destiny manifested by men who would not for the world have any part of it.

We should consider the arguments of the feminists with no less suspicion, however, for very often their controversial aim deprives them of all real value. If the "woman question" seems trivial, it is because masculine arrogance has made of it a "quarrel"; and when quarreling one no longer reasons well. People have tirelessly sought to prove that woman is superior, inferior, or equal to man. Some say that, having been created after Adam, she is evidently a secondary being; others say on the contrary that Adam was only a rough draft and that God succeeded in producing the human being in perfection when He created Eve. Woman's brain is smaller; yes, but it is relatively larger. Christ was made a man; yes, but perhaps for his greater humility. Each argument at once suggests its opposite, and both are often fallacious. If we are to gain understanding, we must get out of these ruts; we must discard the vague notions of superiority, inferiority, equality which have hitherto corrupted every discussion of the subject and start afresh.

Very well, but just how shall we pose the question? And, to begin with, who are we to propound it at all? Man is at once judge and party to the case; but so is woman. What we need is an angel—neither man nor woman—but where shall we find one? Still, the angel would be poorly qualified to speak, for an angel is ignorant of all the basic facts involved in the problem. With a hermaphrodite we should be no better off, for here the situation is most peculiar; the hermaphrodite is not really the combination of a whole man and a whole woman, but consists of parts of each and thus is neither. It looks to me as if there are, after all, certain women who are best qualified to elucidate the situation of woman. Let us not be misled by the sophism that because Epimenides was a

Cretan he was necessarily a liar; it is not a mysterious essence that compels men and women to act in good or in bad faith, it is their situation that inclines them more or less toward the search for truth. Many of today's women, fortunate in the restoration of all the privileges pertaining to the estate of the human being, can afford the luxury of impartiality—we even recognize its necessity. We are no longer like our partisan elders; by and large we have won the game. In recent debates on the status of women the United Nations has persistently maintained that the equality of the sexes is now becoming a reality, and already some of us have never had to sense in our femininity an inconvenience or an obstacle. Many problems appear to us to be more pressing than those which concern us in particular, and this detachment even allows us to hope that our attitude will be objective. Still, we know the feminine world more intimately than do the men because we have our roots in it, we grasp more immediately than do men what it means to a human being to be feminine; and we are more concerned with such knowledge. I have said that there are more pressing problems, but this does not prevent us from seeing some importance in asking how the fact of being women will affect our lives. What opportunities precisely have been given us and what withheld? What fate awaits our younger sisters, and what directions should they take? It is significant that books by women on women are in general animated in our day less by a wish to demand our rights than by an effort toward clarity and understanding. As we emerge from an era of excessive controversy, this book is offered as one attempt among others to confirm that statement.

But it is doubtless impossible to approach any human problem with a mind free from bias. The way in which questions are put, the points of view assumed, presuppose a relativity of interest; all characteristics imply values, and every objective description, so called, implies an ethical background. Rather than attempt to conceal principles more or less definitely implied, it is better to state them openly at the beginning. This will make it unnecessary to specify on every page

in just what sense one uses such words as *superior, inferior, better, worse, progress, reaction,* and the like. If we survey some of the works on woman, we note that one of the points of view most frequently adopted is that of the public good, the general interest; and one always means by this the benefit of society as one wishes it to be maintained or established. For our part, we hold that the only public good is that which assures the private good of the citizens; we shall pass judgment on institutions according to their effectiveness in giving concrete opportunities to individuals. But we do not confuse the idea of private interest with that of happiness, although that is another common point of view. Are not women of the harem more happy than women voters? Is not the housekeeper happier than the working-woman? It is not too clear just what the word *happy* really means and still less what true values it may mask. There is no possibility of measuring the happiness of others, and it is always easy to describe as happy the situation in which one wishes to place them.

In particular those who are condemned to stagnation are often pronounced happy on the pretext that happiness consists in being at rest. This notion we reject, for our perspective is that of existentialist ethics. Every subject plays his part as such specifically through exploits or projects that serve as a mode of transcendence, he achieves liberty only through a continual reaching out toward other liberties. There is no justification for present existence other than its expansion into an indefinitely open future. Every time transcendence falls back into immanence, stagnation, there is a degradation of existence into the *"en-soi"*—the brutish life of subjection to given conditions—and of liberty into constraint and contingence. This downfall represents a moral fault if the subject consents to it; if it is inflicted upon him, it spells frustration and oppression. In both cases it is an absolute evil. Every individual concerned to justify his existence feels that his existence involves an undefined need to transcend himself, to engage in freely chosen projects.

Now, what peculiarly signalizes the situation of woman is that she—a free and autonomous being like all human creatures—nevertheless finds herself living in a world where men compel her to assume the status of the Other. They propose to stabilize her as object and to doom her to immanence since her transcendence is to be overshadowed and forever transcended by another ego (*conscience*) which is essential and sovereign. The drama of woman lies in this conflict between the fundamental aspirations of every subject (ego)—who always regards the self as the essential—and the compulsions of a situation in which she is the inessential. How can a human being in woman's situation attain fulfillment? What roads are open to her? Which are blocked? How can independence be recovered in a state of dependency? What circumstances limit woman's liberty and how can they be overcome? These are the fundamental questions on which I would fain throw some light. This means that I am interested in the fortunes of the individual as defined not in terms of happiness but in terms of liberty.

Quite evidently this problem would be without significance if we were to believe that woman's destiny is inevitably determined by physiological, psychological, or economic forces. Hence I shall discuss first of all the light in which woman is viewed by biology, psychoanalysis, and historical materialism. Next I shall try to show exactly how the concept of the "truly feminine" has been fashioned—why woman has been defined as the Other—and what have been the consequences from man's point of view. Then from woman's point of view I shall describe the world in which women must live; and thus we shall be able to envisage the difficulties in their way as, endeavoring to make their escape from the sphere hitherto assigned them, they aspire to full membership in the human race. . . .

Chapter XXV
The Independent Woman

According to French law, obedience is no longer included among the duties of a wife, and each woman citizen has the right to vote; but these civil liberties remain theoretical as long as they are unaccompanied by eco-nomic freedom. A woman supported by a man—wife or courtesan—is not emancipated from the male because she has a ballot in her hand; if custom imposes less constraint upon her than formerly, the negative freedom implied has not profoundly modified her situation; she remains bound in her condition of vassalage. It is through gainful employment that woman has traversed most of the distance that separated her from the male; and nothing else can guarantee her liberty in practice. Once she ceases to be a parasite, the system based on her dependence crumbles; between her and the universe there is no longer any need for a masculine mediator.

The curse that is upon woman as vassal consists, as we have seen, in the fact that she is not permitted to do anything; so she persists in the vain pursuit of her true being through narcissism, love, or religion. When she is productive, active, she regains her transcendence; in her projects she concretely affirms her status as subject; in connection with the aims she pursues, with the money and the rights she takes possession of, she makes trial of and senses her responsibility. Many women are aware of these advantages, even among those in very modest positions. I heard a charwoman declare, while scrubbing the stone floor of a hotel lobby: "I never asked anybody for anything; I succeeded all by myself." She was as proud of her self-sufficiency as a Rockefeller. It is not to be supposed, however, that the mere combination of the right to vote and a job constitutes a complete emancipation: working, today, is not liberty. Only in a socialist world would woman by the one attain the other. The majority of workers are exploited today. On the other hand, the social structure has not been much modified by the changes in woman's condition; this world, always belonging to men, still retains the form they have given it.

We must not lose sight of those facts which make the question of woman's labor a complex one. An important and thoughtful woman recently made a study of the women in the Renault factories; she states that they would prefer to stay in the home rather than work in the factory. There is no doubt that they get economic independence only as members of a class which is economically oppressed; and, on the other hand, their jobs at the factory do not relieve them of housekeeping burdens.[13] If they had been asked to choose between forty hours of work a week in the factory and forty hours of work a week in the home, they would doubtless have furnished quite different answers. And perhaps they would cheerfully accept both jobs, if as factory workers they were to be integrated in a world that would be theirs, in the development of which they would joyfully and proudly share. At the present time, peasants apart,[14] the majority of women do not escape from the traditional feminine world; they get from neither society nor their husbands the assistance they would need to become in concrete fact the equals of the men. Only those women who have a political faith, who take militant action in the unions, who have confidence in their future, can give ethical meaning to thankless daily labor. But lacking leisure, inheriting a traditional submissiveness, women are naturally just beginning to develop a political and social sense. And not getting in exchange for their work the moral and social benefits they might rightfully count on, they naturally submit to its constraints without enthusiasm.

It is quite understandable, also, that the milliner's apprentice, the shopgirl, the secretary, will not care to renounce the advantages of masculine support. I have already pointed out that the existence of a privileged caste, which she can join by merely surrendering her body, is an almost irresistible temptation to the young woman; she is fated for gallantry by the fact that her wages are minimal while the standard of living expected of her by society is very high. If she is content to get along on her wages, she is only a pariah: ill lodged, ill dressed, she will be denied all amusement and even love. Virtuous people preach asceticism to her, and, indeed, her dietary regime is often as austere as that of a Carmelite. Unfortunately, not everyone can take God as a lover: she has to please men if she is to succeed in her life as a woman. She will therefore accept assistance, and this is what her employer cynically counts on in giving her starvation wages.

This aid will sometimes allow her to improve her situation and achieve a real independence; in other cases, however, she will give up her work and become a kept woman. She often retains both sources of income and each serves more or less as an escape from the other; but she is really in double servitude: to job and to protector. For the married woman her wages represent only pin money as a rule; for the girl who "makes something on the side" it is the masculine contribution that seems extra; but neither of them gains complete independence through her own efforts.

There are, however, a fairly large number of privileged women who find in their professions a means of economic and social autonomy. These come to mind when one considers woman's possibilities and her future. This is the reason why it is especially interesting to make a close study of their situation, even though they constitute as yet only a minority; they continue to be a subject of debate between feminists and antifeminists. The latter assert that the emancipated women of today succeed in doing nothing of importance in the world and that furthermore they have difficulty in achieving their own inner equilibrium. The former exaggerate the results obtained by professional women and are blind to their inner confusion. There is no good reason, as a matter of fact, to say they are on the wrong road; and still it is certain that they are not tranquilly installed in their new realm: as yet they are only halfway there. The woman who is economically emancipated from man is not for all that in a moral, social, and psychological situation identical with that of man. The way she carries on her profession and her devotion to it depend on the context supplied by the total pattern of her life. For when she begins her adult life she does not have behind her the same past as does a boy; she is not viewed by society in the same way; the universe presents itself to her in a different perspective. The fact of being a woman today poses peculiar problems for an independent human individual.

The advantage man enjoys, which makes itself felt from his childhood, is that his vocation as a human being in no way runs counter to his destiny as a male. Through the identification of phallus and transcendence, it turns out that his social and spiritual successes endow him with a virile prestige. He is not divided. Whereas it is required of woman that in order to realize her femininity she must make herself object and prey, which is to say that she must renounce her claims as sovereign subject. It is this conflict that especially marks the situation of the emancipated woman. She refuses to confine herself to her role as female, because she will not accept mutilation; but it would also be a mutilation to repudiate her sex. Man is a human being with sexuality; woman is a complete individual, equal to the male, only if she too is a human being with sexuality. To renounce her femininity is to renounce a part of her humanity. Misogynists have often reproached intellectual women for "neglecting themselves"; but they have also preached this doctrine to them: if you wish to be our equals, stop using make-up and nail-polish.

This piece of advice is nonsensical. Precisely because the concept of femininity is artificially shaped by custom and fashion, it is imposed upon each woman from without; she can be transformed gradually so that her canons of propriety approach those adopted by the males: at the seashore—and often elsewhere—trousers have become feminine.[15] That changes nothing fundamental in the matter: the individual is still not free to do as she pleases in shaping the concept of femininity. The woman who does not conform devaluates herself sexually and hence socially, since sexual values are an integral feature of society. One does not acquire virile attributes by rejecting feminine attributes; even the transvestite fails to make a man of herself—she is a travesty. As we have seen, homosexuality constitutes a specific attitude: neutrality is impossible. There is no negative attitude that does not imply a positive counterpart. The adolescent girl often thinks that she can simply scorn convention; but even there she is engaged in public agitation; she is creating a new situation entailing consequences she must assume. When one fails to adhere to an accepted code, one becomes an insurgent. A woman who dresses in an outlandish manner lies when she affirms with an air of simplicity that she dresses to suit herself, nothing more. She knows perfectly well that to suit herself is to be outlandish. . . .

We have seen that it is possible to avoid the temptations of sadism and masochism when the two partners recognize each other as equals; if both the man and the woman have a little modesty and some generosity, ideas of victory and defeat are abolished: the act of love becomes a free exchange. But, paradoxically, it is much more difficult for the woman than for the man to recognize an individual of the other sex as an equal. Precisely because the male caste has superiority of status, there are a great many individual women whom a man can hold in affectionate esteem: it is an easy matter to love a woman. In the first place, a woman can introduce her lover into a world that is different from his own and that he enjoys exploring in her company; she fascinates and amuses him, at least for a time. For another thing, on account of her restricted and subordinate situation, all her qualities seem like high achievements, conquests, whereas her mistakes are excusable; Stendhal admires Mme de Rênal and Mme de Chasteller in spite of their detestable prejudices. If a woman has false ideas, if she is not very intelligent, clear-sighted, or courageous, a man does not hold her responsible: she is the victim, he thinks—and often with reason—of her situation. He dreams of what she might have been, of what she perhaps will be: she can be credited with any possibilities, because she *is* nothing in particular. This vacancy is what makes the lover weary of her quickly; but it is the source of the mystery, the charm, that seduces him and makes him inclined to feel an easy affection in the first place.

It is much less easy for a woman to feel affectionate friendship for a man, for he *is* what he has made himself, irrevocably. He must be loved as he is, not with reference to his promise and his uncertain possibilities; he is responsible for his behavior and ideas; for him there are no excuses. Fellowship with him is impossible unless she approves his acts, his aims, his opinions. Julien can love a legitimist, as we have seen; a Lamiel could not cherish a man whose ideas she despised. Even though prepared to compromise, woman will hardly be able to take an attitude of indulgence. For man opens to her no verdant paradise of childhood. She meets him in this world which is their world in common: he comes bearing the gift of himself only. Self-enclosed, definite, decided, he is not conducive to daydreaming; when he speaks, one must listen. He takes himself seriously: if he is not interesting, he bores her, his presence weighs heavily on her. Only very young men can be endued with facile marvels; one can seek mystery and promise in them, find excuses for them, take them lightly: which is one reason why mature women find them most seductive. The difficulty is that, for their part, they usually prefer young women. The woman of thirty is thrown back on adult males. And doubtless she will encounter among them some who will not discourage her esteem and friendship; but she will be lucky if they make no show of arrogance in the matter. When she contemplates an affair or an adventure involving her heart as well as her body, the problem is to find a man whom she can regard as an equal without his considering himself superior.

I will be told that in general women make no such fuss; they seize the occasion without asking themselves too many questions, and they manage somehow with their pride and their sensuality. True enough. But it is also true that they bury in their secret hearts many disappointments, humiliations, regrets, resentments, not commonly matched in men. From a more or less unsatisfactory affair a man is almost sure of obtaining at least the benefit of sex pleasure; a woman can very well obtain no benefit at all. Even when indifferent, she lends herself politely to the embrace at the decisive moment, sometimes only to find her lover impotent and herself compromised in a ridiculous mockery. If all goes well except that she fails to attain satisfaction, then she feels "used," "worked." If she finds full enjoyment, she will want to prolong the affair. She is rarely quite sincere when she claims to envisage no more than an isolated adventure undertaken merely for pleasure, because her pleasure,

far from bringing deliverance, binds her to the man; separation wounds her even when supposedly a friendly parting. It is much more unusual to hear a woman speak amicably of a former lover than a man of his past mistresses.

The peculiar nature of her eroticism and the difficulties that beset a life of freedom urge woman toward monogamy. Liaison or marriage, however, can be reconciled with a career much less easily for her than for man. Sometimes her lover or husband asks her to renounce it: she hesitates, like Colette's Vagabonde, who ardently desires the warm presence of a man at her side but dreads the fetters of marriage. If she yields, she is once more a vassal; if she refuses, she condemns herself to a withering solitude. Today a man is usually willing to have his companion continue her work; the novels of Colette Yver, showing young women driven to sacrifice their professions for the sake of peace and the family, are rather outdated; living together is an enrichment for two free beings, and each finds security for his or her own independence in the occupation of the mate. The self-supporting wife emancipates her husband from the conjugal slavery that was the price of hers. If the man is scrupulously well-intentioned, such lovers and married couples attain in undemanding generosity a condition of perfect equality.[16] It may even be the man that acts as devoted servant; thus, for George Eliot, Lewes created the favorable atmosphere that the wife usually creates around the husband-overlord. But for the most part it is still the woman who bears the cost of domestic harmony.

To a man it seems natural that it should be the wife who does the housework and assumes alone the care and bringing up of the children. The independent woman herself considers that in marrying she has assumed duties from which her personal life does not exempt her. She does not want to feel that her husband is deprived of advantages he would have obtained if he had married a "true woman"; she wants to be presentable, a good housekeeper, a devoted mother, such as wives traditionally are. This is a task that easily becomes overwhelming. She assumes it through regard for her partner and out of fidelity to herself also, for she intends, as we have already seen, to be in no way unfaithful to her destiny as woman. She will be a double for her husband and at the same time she will be herself; she will assume his cares and participate in his successes as much as she will be concerned with her own fate—and sometimes even more. Reared in an atmosphere of respect for male superiority, she may still feel that it is for man to occupy the first place; sometimes she fears that in claiming it she would ruin her home; between the desire to assert herself and the desire for self-effacement she is torn and divided.

There is, however, an advantage that woman can gain from her very inferiority. Since she is from the start less favored by fortune than man, she does not feel that she is to blame *a priori* for what befalls him; it is not her duty to make amends for social injustice, and she is not asked to do so. A man of good will owes it to himself to treat women with consideration, since he is more favored by fate than they are; he will let himself be bound by scruples, by pity, and so runs the risk of becoming the prey of clinging, vampirish women from the very fact of their disarmed condition. The woman who achieves virile independence has the great privilege of carrying on her sexual life with individuals who are themselves autonomous and effective in action, who—as a rule—will not play a parasitic role in her life, who will not enchain her through their weakness and the exigency of their needs. But in truth the woman is rare who can create a free relation with her partner; she herself usually forges the chains with which he has no wish to load her: she takes toward him the attitude of the *amoureuse*, the woman in love.

Through twenty years of waiting, dreaming, hoping, the young girl has cherished the myth of the liberating savior-hero, and hence the independence she has won through work is not enough to abolish her desire for a glorious abdication. She would have had to be raised exactly[17] like a boy to be able easily to overcome her adolescent narcissism; but as it is, she continues into adult life this cult of the ego toward which her whole youth has tended. She uses her professional successes as merits for the enrichment of her image; she feels the need for a witness from on high to reveal and consecrate her worth. Even if she is a severe judge of the men she evaluates in daily life, she none the less reveres Man, and if she encounters him, she is ready to fall on her knees.

To be justified by a god is easier than to justify herself by her own efforts; the world encourages her to believe it possible for salvation to be *given*, and she prefers to believe it. Sometimes she gives up her independence entirely and becomes no more than an *amoureuse;* more often she essays a compromise; but idolatrous love, the love that means abdication, is devastating; it occupies every thought, every moment, it is obsessing, tyrannical. If she meets with professional disappointments, the woman passionately seeks refuge in her love; then her frustrations are expressed in scenes and demands at her lover's expense. But her amatory troubles have by no means the effect of redoubling her professional zeal; she is, on the contrary, more likely to be impatient with a mode of life that keeps her from the royal road of a great love. A woman who worked ten years ago on a political magazine run by women told me that in the office they seldom talked about politics but incessantly about love: this one complained that she was loved only for her body to the neglect of her splendid intelligence; that one moaned that only her mind was appreciated, to the neglect of her physical charms. Here again, for woman to love as man does—that is to say, in liberty, without putting her very *being* in question—she must believe herself his equal and be so in concrete fact; she must engage in her enterprises with the same decisiveness. But this is still uncommon, as we shall see.

There is one feminine function that it is actually almost impossible to perform in complete liberty. It is maternity. In England and America and some other countries a woman can at least decline maternity at will, thanks to contraceptive techniques. We have seen that in France she is often driven to painful and costly abortion; or she frequently finds herself responsible for an unwanted child that can ruin her professional life. If this is a heavy charge, it is because, inversely, custom does not allow a woman to procreate when she pleases. The unwed mother is a scandal to the community, and illegitimate birth is a stain on the child; only rarely is it possible to become a mother without accepting the chains of marriage or losing caste. If the idea of artificial insemination interests many women, it is not because they wish to avoid intercourse with a male; it is because they hope that freedom of maternity is going to be accepted by society at last. It must be said in addition that in spite of convenient day nurseries and kindergartens, having a child is enough to paralyze a woman's activity entirely; she can go on working only if she abandons it to relatives, friends, or servants. She is forced to choose between sterility, which is often felt as a painful frustration, and burdens hardly compatible with a career.

Thus the independent woman of today is torn between her professional interests and the problems of her sexual life; it is difficult for her to strike a balance between the two; if she does, it is at the price of concessions, sacrifices, acrobatics, which require her to be in a constant state of tension. Here, rather than in physiological data, must be sought the reason for the nervousness and the frailty often observed in her. It is difficult to determine to what extent woman's physical constitution handicaps her. Inquiry is often made, for example, about the obstacle presented by menstruation. Women who have made a reputation through their publications or other activities seem to attach little importance to it. Is this because, as a matter of fact, they owe their success to their relatively slight monthly indisposition? One may ask whether it is not because, on the contrary, their choice of an active and ambitious life has been responsible for this advantage; the interest woman takes in her maladies tends to aggravate them. Women in sports and other active careers suffer less from them than others, because they take little notice of them. There are certainly organic factors also, and I have seen the most energetic women spend twenty-four hours in bed each month, a prey to pitiless tortures; but this difficulty never prevented their enterprises from succeeding.

I am convinced that the greater part of the discomforts and maladies that overburden women are due to psychic causes, as gynecologists, indeed, have told me. Women are constantly harassed to the limit of their strength because of the moral tension I have referred to, because of all the tasks they assume, because of the contradictions among which they struggle. This does not mean that their ills are imaginary: they are as real and destructive as the situation to which they give expression. But the situation does not depend on the body; the reverse is true. Thus woman's health will not affect her work unfavorably when the woman worker comes to have the place she should; on the contrary, work will improve her physical condition by preventing her from being ceaselessly preoccupied with it.

* * *

These facts must not be lost sight of when we judge the professional accomplishments of woman and, on that basis, make bold to speculate on her future. She undertakes a career in a mentally harassing situation and while still under the personal burdens implied traditionally by her femininity. Nor are the objective circumstances more favorable to her. It is always difficult to be a newcomer, trying to break a path through a society that is hostile, or at least mistrustful. In *Black Boy* Richard Wright has shown how the ambitions of a young American Negro are blocked from the start and what a struggle he had merely in raising himself to the level where problems began to be posed for the whites. Negroes coming to France from Africa also find difficulties—with themselves as well as around them—similar to those confronting women.

Woman first finds herself in a position of inferiority during her period of apprenticeship, a point already made with reference to the young girl, but which must now be dealt with more precisely. During her studies and in the first decisive years of her career, woman rarely uses her opportunities with simple directness, and thus she will often be handicapped later by a bad start. The conflicts I have spoken of do, in fact, reach their greatest intensity between the ages of eighteen and thirty, precisely the time when the professional future is at stake. Whether the woman lives with her family or is married, her family will rarely show the same respect for her work as for a man's; they will impose duties and tasks on her and infringe on her liberty. She herself is still profoundly affected by her bringing up, respectful of values affirmed by her elders, haunted by her dreams of childhood and adolescence; she finds difficulty in reconciling the heritage of her past with the interests of her future. Sometimes she abjures her femininity, she hesitates between chastity, homosexuality, and an aggressive virago attitude; she dresses badly or wears male attire; and in this case she wastes much time in defiance, play-acting, angry fuming. More often she wants to emphasize her feminine qualities: she is coquettish, she goes out, she flirts, she falls in love, oscillating between masochism and aggressiveness. She questions, agitates, scatters herself in every way. These outside activities alone are enough to prevent complete absorption in her enterprise; the less she profits by it, the more tempted she is to give it up.

What is extremely demoralizing for the woman who aims at self-sufficiency is the existence of other women of like social status, having at the start the same situation and the same opportunities, who live as parasites. A man may feel resentment toward the privileged, but he has solidarity with his class; on the whole, those who begin with equal chances reach about the same level in life. Whereas women of like situation may, through man's mediation, come to have very different fortunes. A comfortably married or supported friend is a temptation in the way of one who is intending to make her own success; she feels she is arbitrarily condemning herself to take the most difficult roads; at each obstacle she wonders whether it might not be better to take a different route. "When I think that I have to get everything by my own brain!" said one little poverty-stricken student to me, as if stunned by the thought. Man obeys an imperious necessity; woman must constantly reaffirm her intention. She goes forward not with her eyes fixed straight ahead on a goal, but with her glance wandering around her in every direction; and her gait is also timid and uncertain. The more she seems to be getting ahead on her own hook—as I have already pointed out—the more her other chances fade; in becoming a bluestocking, a woman of brains, she will make herself unattractive to men in general, or she will humiliate her husband or lover by being too outstanding a success. So she not only applies herself the more to making a show of elegance and frivolity, but also restrains her aspiration. The hope of being one day delivered from taking care of herself, and the fear of having to lose that hope if she assumes this care for a time, combine to prevent her from unreservedly applying herself to her studies and her career.

In so far as a woman wishes to be a woman, her independent status gives rise to an inferiority complex; on the other hand, her femininity makes her doubtful of her professional future. This is a point of great importance. We have seen that girls of fourteen declared to an investigator: "Boys are better than girls; they are better workers." The young girl is convinced that she has limited capacities. Because parents and teachers concede that the girls' level is lower than that of the boys, the pupils readily concede it also; and as a matter of fact, in spite of equal curricula, the girls' academic accomplishment in French secondary schools is much lower. Apart from some exceptions, all the members of a girls' class in philosophy, for example, stand clearly below a boys' class. A great majority of the girl pupils do not intend to continue their studies, and work very superficially; the others lack the stimulus of emulation. In fairly easy examinations their incompetence will not be too evident, but in a serious competitive test the girl student will become aware of her weaknesses. She will attribute them not to the mediocrity of her training, but to the unjust curse of her femininity; by resigning herself to this inequality, she enhances it; she is persuaded that her chances of success can lie only in her patience and application; she resolves to be as economical as possible of her time and strength—surely a very bad plan.

The utilitarian attitude is especially disastrous in studies and professions that call for a modicum of invention and originality, and some lucky little finds. Discussions, extracurricular reading, a walk with the mind freely wandering, can be much more profitable, even for translating a Greek text, than the dull compilation of involved points of syntax. Overwhelmed by respect for authorities and the weight of erudition, her view restricted by pedantic blinders, the over-conscientious student deadens her critical sense and her very intelligence. Her methodical eagerness causes tension and weariness of spirit. In the classes, for example, where students prepare for the Sèvres competitive examinations, a suffocating atmosphere reigns that discourages all individualities with any semblance of life. The candidate has no wish but to escape from her self-created prison; once she closes her books, her mind is on quite different subjects. Unknown to her are those fertile moments when study and diversion fuse, when the adventures of the mind assume living warmth. Disheartened by the thankless nature of her tasks, she feels more and more inept at doing them well. I recall a girl student, preparing for teachers' examinations, who said in reference to a competition in philosophy open to men and women: "Boys can succeed in one or two years; for us it takes at least four years." Another, told to read a book on Kant, an author on the reading list, protested: "That book is too difficult; it is a book for men students!" She seemed to think women could go through the competition at a reduced rate. To take that attitude was to be beaten in advance and, in effect, to concede to the men all chances of winning.

In consequence of this defeatism, woman is easily reconciled to a moderate success; she does not dare to aim too high. Entering upon her profession with superficial preparation, she soon sets limits to her ambitions. It often seems to her meritorious enough if she earns her own living; she could have entrusted her lot, like many others, to a man. To continue in her wish for independence requires an effort in which she takes pride, but which exhausts her. It seems to her that she has done enough when she has chosen to do something. "That in itself is not too bad for a woman," she thinks. A woman practicing an unusual profession once said: "If I were a man, I should feel obliged to climb to the top; but I am the only woman in France to occupy such a position: that's enough for me." There is prudence in this modesty. Woman is afraid that in attempting to go farther she will break her back.

It must be said that the independent woman is justifiably disturbed by the idea that people do not have confidence in her. As a general rule, the superior caste is hostile to newcomers from the inferior caste: whites will not consult a Negro physician, nor males a woman doctor; but individuals of the inferior caste, imbued with a sense of their specific inferiority and often full of resentment toward one of their kind who has risen above their usual lot, will also prefer to turn to the masters. Most women, in particular, steeped in adoration for man, eagerly seek him out in the person of the doctor, the lawyer, the office manager, and so on. Neither men nor women like to be under a woman's orders. Her superiors, even if they esteem her highly, will always be somewhat condescending; to be a woman, if not a defect, is at least a peculiarity. Woman must constantly win the confidence that is not at first accorded her: at the start she is suspect, she has to prove herself. If she has worth she will pass the tests, so they say. But worth is not a given essence; it is the outcome of a successful development. To feel the weight of an unfavorable prejudice against one is only on very rare occasions a help in overcoming it. The initial inferiority complex ordinarily leads to a defense reaction in the form of an exaggerated affectation of authority.

Most women doctors, for example, have too much or too little of the air of authority. If they act naturally, they fail to take control, for their life as a whole disposes them rather to seduce than to command; the patient who likes to be dominated will be disappointed by plain advice simply given. Aware of this fact, the woman doctor assumes a grave accent, a peremptory tone; but then she lacks the bluff good nature that is the charm of the medical man who is sure of himself.

Man is accustomed to asserting himself; his clients believe in his competence; he can act naturally: he infallibly makes an impression. Woman does not inspire the same feeling of security; she affects a lofty air, she drops it, she makes too much of it. In business, in administrative work, she is precise, fussy, quick to show aggressiveness. As in her studies, she lacks ease, dash, audacity. In the effort to achieve she gets tense. Her activity is a succession of challenges and self-affirmations. This is the great defect that lack of assurance engenders: the subject cannot forget himself. He does not aim gallantly toward some goal: he seeks rather to make good in prescribed ways. In boldly setting out toward ends, one risks disappointments; but one also obtains unhoped-for results; caution condemns to mediocrity.

We rarely encounter in the independent woman a taste for adventure and for experience for its own sake, or a disinterested curiosity; she seeks "to have a career" as other women build a nest of happiness; she remains dominated, surrounded, by the male universe, she lacks the audacity to break through its ceiling, she does not passionately lose herself in her projects. She still regards her life as an immanent enterprise: her aim is not at an objective but, through the objective, at her subjective success. This is a very conspicuous attitude, for example, among American women; they like having a job and proving to themselves that they are capable of handling it properly; but they are not passionately concerned with the *content* of their tasks. Woman similarly has a tendency to attach too much importance to minor setbacks and modest successes; she is turn by turn discouraged or puffed up with vanity. When a success has been anticipated, one takes it calmly; but it becomes an intoxicating triumph when one has been doubtful of obtaining it. This is the excuse when women become addled with importance and plume themselves ostentatiously over their least accomplishments. They are forever looking back to see how far they have come, and that interrupts their progress. By this procedure they can have honorable careers, but not accomplish great things. It must be added that many men are also unable to build any but mediocre careers. It is only in comparison with the best of them that woman—save for

very rare exceptions—seems to us to be trailing behind. The reasons I have given are sufficient explanation, and in no way mortgage the future. What woman essentially lacks today for doing great things is forgetfulness of herself; but to forget oneself it is first of all necessary to be firmly assured that now and for the future one has found oneself. Newly come into the world of men, poorly seconded by them, woman is still too busily occupied to search for herself.

There is one category of women to whom these remarks do not apply because their careers, far from hindering the affirmation of their femininity, reinforce it. These are women who seek through artistic expression to transcend their given characteristics; they are the actresses, dancers, and singers. For these centuries they have been almost the only women to maintain a concrete independence in the midst of society, and at the present time they still occupy a privileged place in it. Formerly actresses were anathema to the Church, and the very excessiveness of that severity has always authorized a great freedom of behavior on their part. They often skirt the sphere of gallantry and, like courtesans, they spend a great deal of their time in the company of men; but making their own living and finding the meaning of their lives in their work, they escape the yoke of men. Their great advantage is that their professional successes—like those of men—contribute to their sexual valuation; in their self-realization, their validation of themselves as human beings, they find self-fulfillment as women: they are not torn between contradictory aspirations. On the contrary, they find in their occupations a justification of their narcissism; dress, beauty care, charm, form a part of their professional duties. It is a great satisfaction for a woman in love with her own image to *do* something in simply exhibiting what she *is;* and this exhibition at the same time demands enough study and artifice to appear to be, as Georgette Leblanc said, a substitute for action. A great actress will aim higher yet: she will go beyond the given by the way she expresses it; she will be truly an artist, a creator, who gives meaning to her life by lending meaning to the world.

These are rare advantages, but they also hide traps: instead of integrating her narcissistic self-indulgence and her sexual liberty with her artistic life, the actress very often sinks into self-worship or into gallantry; I have already referred to those pseudo-artists who seek in the movies or in the theater only to make a name for themselves that represents capital to exploit in men's arms. The conveniences of masculine support are very tempting in comparison with the risks of a career and with the discipline implied by all real work. Desire for a feminine destiny—husband, home, children—and the enchantment of love are not always easy to reconcile with the will to succeed. But, above all, the admiration she feels for her ego in many cases limits the achievement of an actress; she has such illusions regarding the value of her mere presence that serious work seems useless. She is concerned above all to put herself in the public eye and sacrifices the character she is interpreting to this theatrical quackery. She also lacks the generous-mindedness to forget herself, and this deprives her of the possibility of going beyond herself; rare indeed are the Rachels, the Duses, who avoid this reef and make their persons the instruments of their art instead of seeing in art a servant of their egos. In her private life, moreover, the bad actress will exaggerate all the narcissistic defects: she will reveal herself as vain, petulant, theatric; she will consider all the world a stage.

. . . Once again: in order to explain her limitations it is woman's situation that must be invoked and not a mysterious essence; thus the future remains largely open. Writers on the subject have vied with one another in maintaining that women do not have "creative genius"; this is the thesis defended by Mme Marthe Borély, an erstwhile notorious antifeminist; but one would say that she sought to make her books a living proof of feminine illogicality and silliness, so self-contradictory are they. Furthermore, the concept of a creative "instinct" must be discarded, like that of the "eternal feminine," from the old panel of entities. Certain misogynists assert, a little more concretely, that woman, being neurotic, could not create anything worth while; but they are often the same men that pronounce genius a neurosis. In any case, the example of Proust shows clearly enough that psychophysiological disequilibrium signifies neither lack of power nor mediocrity.

As for the argument drawn from history, we have just been considering what to think of that; the historical fact cannot be considered as establishing an eternal truth; it can only indicate a situation that is historical in nature precisely because it is undergoing change. How could women ever have had genius when they were denied all possibility of accomplishing a work of genius—or just a work? The old Europe formerly poured out its contempt upon the American barbarians who boasted neither artists nor writers. "Let us come into existence before being asked to justify our existence," replied Jefferson, in effect. The Negroes make the same reply to the racists who reproach them for never having produced a Whitman or a Melville. No more can the French proletariat offer any name to compare with those of Racine or Mallarmé.

The free woman is just being born; when she has won possession of herself perhaps Rimbaud's prophecy will be fulfilled: "There shall be poets! When woman's unmeasured bondage shall be broken, when she shall live for and through herself, man—hitherto detestable—having let her go, she, too, will be poet! Woman will find the unknown! Will her ideational worlds be different from ours? She will come upon strange, unfathomable, repellent, delightful things; we shall take them, we shall comprehend them."[18] It is not sure that her "ideational worlds" will be different from those of men, since it will be through attaining the same situation as theirs that she will find emancipation; to say in what degree she will remain different, in what degree these differences will retain their importance—this would be to hazard bold predictions indeed. What is certain is that hitherto woman's possibilities have been suppressed and lost to humanity, and that it is high time she be permitted to take her chances in her own interest and in the interest of all.

Notes

1. *Franchise,* dead today.

2. The Kinsey Report [Alfred C. Kinsey and others: *Sexual Behavior in the Human Male* (W. B. Saunders Co., 1948)] is no exception, for it is limited to describing the sexual characteristics of American men, which is quite a different matter.

3. E. Lévinas expresses this idea most explicitly in his essay *Temps et l'Autre.* "Is there not a case in which otherness, alterity [*altérité*], unquestionably marks the nature of a being, as its essence, an instance of otherness not consisting purely and simply in the opposition of two species of the same genus? I think that the feminine represents the contrary in its absolute sense, this contrariness being in no wise affected by any relation between it and its correlative and thus remaining absolutely other. Sex is not a certain specific difference . . . no more is the sexual difference a mere contradiction. . . . Nor does this difference lie in the duality of two complementary terms, for two complementary terms imply a pre-existing whole. . . . Otherness reaches its full flowering in the feminine, a term of the same rank as consciousness but of opposite meaning."

   I suppose that Lévinas does not forget that woman, too, is aware of her own consciousness, or ego. But it is striking that he deliberately takes a man's point of view, disregarding the reciprocity of subject and object. When he writes that woman is mystery, he implies that she is mystery for man. Thus his description, which is intended to be objective, is in fact an assertion of masculine privilege.

4. See C. Lévi-Strauss: *Les Structures élémentaires de la parenté.* My thanks are due to C. Lévi-Strauss for his kindness in furnishing me with the proofs of his work, which, among others, I have used liberally in Part II.

5. With rare exceptions, perhaps, like certain matriarchal rulers, queens, and the like.—Tr.

6. See Part II, ch. viii.

7. At the moment an "equal rights" amendment to the Constitution of the United States is before Congress.—Tr.

8. See Part II, pp. 115–17.

9. Or at least he thought he could.

10. A significant article on this theme by Michel Carrouges appeared in No. 292 of the *Cahiers du Sud.* He writes indignantly: "Would that there were no woman-myth at all but only a cohort of cooks, matrons, prostitutes, and bluestockings serving functions of pleasure or usefulness!" That is to say, in his view woman has no existence in and for herself; he thinks only of her *function* in the male world. Her reason for existence lies in man. But then, in fact, her poetic "function" as a myth might be more valued than any other. The real problem is precisely to find out why woman should be defined with relation to man.

11. For example, a man will say that he considers his wife in no wise degraded because she has no gainful occupation. The profession of housewife is just as lofty, and so on. But when the first quarrel comes, he will exclaim: "Why, you couldn't make your living without me!"

12. The specific purpose of Book II of this study is to describe this process.

13. I have indicated in Book I, p. 135, how heavy these are for women who work outside.

14. We have examined their situation in Book I, pp. 109, 134.

15. If that is the word.—Tr.

16. It would appear that the life of Clara and Robert Schumann attained a success of this kind for a time.

17. That is to say, not only by the same methods but in the same climate, which is impossible today, in spite of all the efforts of educators.

18. In a letter to Pierre Demeney, May 15, 1871.

Adapted from: Simone de Beauvoir, *The Second Sex,* H. M. Parshley, ed. and trans., pp. xix–xxxv, 679–683, 692–704, 714–715. Copyright © 1952. Reprinted by permission of Alfred A. Knopf, Inc. ✦

41
The Second Sex and Philosophy

Karen Vintges

In her voluminous study, *Le deuxième sexe* (1949), Beauvoir explored the historic situation of women and concluded they have been prevented from taking active control of their own lives. Woman has been unfree throughout history; she was subjected to man who, partly with woman's consent, made her merely an extension of himself. Men and women have never shared an equal relationship, and it would be advantageous to all if this situation were to change.

The Second Sex evoked intense criticism. As soon as it appeared, it was dismissed as one-sided and tendentious. Beauvoir herself was labeled a man-hater, frigid, or nymphomaniacal, depending on the critic, and this negative response continued for years to come. Although in the late 1960s, part of the emerging women's movement embraced Beauvoir, other sections reviled her. *The Second Sex* had been superceded by the new, "real" feminism that advocated radical change for women, and Beauvoir's book was said to contain a *male* view of women. Moreover, it was labeled a careless or meaningless work, unsystematic in structure, and overtaken by the facts.

However, in spite of enormous sales figures, this book appears to be at the same time one of the most criticized *and* one of the least read works in feminism. Feminists have it on their shelves because it simply has to be there, but few have actually read it. This is why I will dwell fairly extensively on the contents.

First, I want to go into the background to the philosophical concepts used in *The Second Sex*. A global summary of the contents themselves will follow, then I will discuss the

work's genre and structure. Beauvoir wrote it in a very short period of time[1] which, she said, was only possible because the book followed a logical structure. "Of all my books," she said, "this was the easiest to write, especially in the beginning. The material seemed to organize itself in a natural series of analytical frameworks" (Bair, 1990: 371). We shall take a closer look here at its structure.

Today's feminist theoreticians tend to consider the book a superceded sociological study. New research has brought to light a wealth of empirical facts about women's lives that would have been inconceivable in Beauvoir's day. The research shows that the reality of those lives was often far more variegated than Beauvoir's study suggests. For example, cultural anthropologist Judith Okely has come up with counterexamples for a number of Beauvoir's claims with regard to non-Western cultures.[2] However, it could well be that *The Second Sex* should not be evaluated on the correctness of single facts because the work has a different aim. Before making a final judgment on its actual content . . . we will have to determine the work's structure and genre. The chapter ends with an examination of the critique of contemporary feminists who claim *The Second Sex* contains a male view of women. Beauvoir's so-called rationalism is the main focus of the attack: she is said to reject the body in favor of consciousness, and to perceive as negative the female body in particular. We will evaluate the criticism that she embraced masculine thinking and, with *The Second Sex*, produced a "masculine" book.

The Philosophical Concepts of *The Second Sex*

In *The Second Sex*, Beauvoir made extensive use of the philosophical concepts of Sartre's main work *L'être et le néant* (1943; *Being and Nothingness*). Before examining Beauvoir's actual text, we will look at this conceptual framework. In *Being and Nothingness*, Sartre distinguished two kinds of being: being-in-itself (*être en-soi*) and being-for-itself (*être pour-soi*); the first refers to the existence of material things, the second to the existence of consciousness. Sartre's primary goal was to articulate consciousness as opposed to the being of material things. He characterized consciousness as non-being. In itself, it is no-thing, or rather nothing(ness) (*néant*), for consciousness is always aimed at something other than itself; it is always a consciousness *of* something. That is why Sartre said it is not what it is, and is what it is not.[3] In order to exist, consciousness is doomed to transcend itself and reach out for a thing (*en-soi*), or it ceases to be consciousness and coincides with the being of things. Being no-thing, consciousness disengages itself from the things of which it is conscious, or as Sartre has it, it "negates." As it always has to focus on something other than itself, consciousness has to be pure emptiness. As soon as there is any question of content, then there is already an *inauthentic* human way of being. The counterpart of the *pour-soi*'s total emptiness is the *en-soi*'s absolute fullness or opaqueness (*opacité*). It is this that has to be given meaning through the *pour-soi*. But as such, it is completely meaningless or "contingent," a state that evokes disgust in the main character, Roquentin, in Sartre's novel *Nausea* (1938).

Sartre thus distinguishes radically between the *pour-soi* and the *en-soi*, i.e., the world of beings. If these have an immanent existence, by definition the *pour-soi* transcends: it reaches out continually and never coincides with itself. The fact that human consciousness is no thing means that a human being is not a permanent essence, but continually creates itself through intentional activity. The existence of a human being thus precedes every essence. As a consequence, Sartre argued, the human being is fundamentally free. Freedom and non-being are the characteristics of human existence.

But the human being also has a desire to *be*. If he gives in to that desire, and constructs an "I" from which he can experience and determine himself, he declines into an *être-en-soi*. If he lives as such, he fails to live a true and authentic human existence, but lives inauthentically or in "bad faith." Moreover, his desire to *be* is not fulfilled this way. The status of non-being is experienced by consciousness as a lack of being (a *manque d'être*); it wants to be a being *as* consciousness. Sartre called this man's *désir d'être*. This fullness of being as consciousness could only be achieved through a being-for-others: only through the observation of an other would it be possible for the *pour-soi* to exist simultaneously as entity and as nothingness. After all, consciousness could only be observed and reflected as such in the eyes of an other, resulting in the desired status of being an *en-soi* as *pour-soi*.

However, the problem is that in view of its *néant* nature (its existence in the form of a negation of being), every consciousness can only observe the other as a being—in other words, as an object and not as a "nothingness," as an *en-soi* instead of a *pour-soi*. I try in vain to meet the other as consciousness. My look petrifies him into a thing in the world: "everything happens as if I wished to get hold of a man who runs away and leaves only his coat in my hands. It is the coat, it is the outer shell which I possess." Sartre called the other "a reality which is on principle beyond my reach" and "a sphere of existence from which I am on principle excluded" (see BN, 1943: 393). Thus, our consciousness is radically separated from that of others. Our fellow man is always an object; we can never meet him as subject.

One result is that the "*désir d'être*" can never be fulfilled. The other can only exist as a being in relation to my consciousness; for me he loses his subjectivity and can thus no longer affirm me as consciousness. Second, this means the self can only ever exist through a negation of the other. We have already seen that consciousness as such is selfless because it consists only of intentionality, i.e., a focus on something else. (If this were not the case, consciousness would be a finite entity and thus identical to the being of things.) This implies that an experience of selfness can only become apparent in a focus on another consciousness. But as we have seen, the focus is always a negation. The self can thus only become manifest as negation of the other; I am not the other. Schuetz coined a term for this notion—"internal negation"—which indicates the negation is not of an external, spacial nature, but is constituent to the existence of the self and the other

(Schuetz, 1948: 187). Arntz (1960) summarizes as follows:

> This is not about "John is not Peter." This would mean John and Peter manifest themselves to a third party who then places a negation between both. Such a negation would be an external negation. Sartre is concerned with an internal negation in which I position myself as not the other in the same way as when I focus on an *en-soi*. (Arntz: 144)

Contact between myself and the other cannot come about based on a selfness of both, but it is as such the constitution of the other as other, and of the self as not the other. It is not the case that I am there first and subsequently try to make the other into an object, but rather that making the other into an object is the basis of my existence. According to Sartre, in this process the other now loses not only his subjectivity for me, but also for himself. Under my look, the other knows he is a being; he feels that I give him a "being." We know this when we examine feelings evoked when other people look at us. We feel as though we have acquired an exterior; in other words, we feel we have become objects. Now, there are two possibilities here: either we accept our being an object for the other and thus subjugate ourselves to him (in which case we are no longer a free subject), or we make the other the object, the Other. The contact between people can only take the form of a subject-object relationship, and is continually concerned with who is the subject and who is the object within that contact. Thus, conflict is the basis of human relations. Sartre's statement, *"l'enfer, c'est les Autres"* (Hc: 609), is well known, and we now understand *why* the other is hell for me: under the gaze of the other, I can stultify into an object if I do not succeed in making him the object.

The notion of enmity and conflict between consciousnesses, which Sartre propounded, concurs with Hegel's ideas, but deviates from them inasmuch as Hegel argues that in a specific phase of history, enmity can be overcome if everyone recognizes himself in universal humanity. This is impossible for Sartre because of the internal negation mechanism which, by definition, causes a Self-Other structure in human contact, and separates us from each other irrevocably.

In *The Second Sex*, Beauvoir "gendered" this Self-Other structure. She argued that women in history have been made the Other and that men have appropriated the position of Self, or subject. Men wanted recognition of themselves as consciousness—which is a problem because pure matter cannot provide it. Woman appeared eminently suited to the role, an entity that was both corporal and at the same time gifted with a kind of consciousness. This is how man made woman the Other. She was made into the one who, through her kinship with the corporal, allowed him to experience continually his superiority as transcending subject; who through her corporality offered him the opportunity of losing himself in "being," and thus occasionally relinquishing the painful status of subject; who had just enough consciousness to observe and reflect him as superior subject. Thus, the myth of femininity is no more than a projection and a product of man. The experiences and way of life imposed upon woman in the name of femininity serve only *man's* needs.

Woman has only developed in the position of Other allotted to her by man. She formed no threat as alternating freedom. In her turn, she could never exist as a free human being and affirm herself the way the slave is able to in the (Hegelian) master-slave relationship. . . . Although this position was imposed upon her—in her introduction, Beauvoir speaks of an "oppression"—she often resigned herself to it through her (human) tendency to bad faith. "Half victims, half accomplices, just like everyone else" is the quotation Beauvoir used to introduce the second book of *Le deuxième sexe*,[4] and she borrowed it from Sartre. In history, woman never raised herself up as subject, turning man into the Other; her position was that of the absolute Other.

It will now be clear that, in *The Second Sex*, Beauvoir developed the norm that insists women must/can become subjects. Women should have the chance to realize their *pour-soi* potential so that men and women can be equal human beings in relation to each other. *The Second Sex* is a passionate call to women to shake off the status of the Other and to accept as equal human beings the freedom of existence *whenever they have the chance to do so.*

The Text

The Second Sex runs to about a thousand pages and is divided into two "books," each composed of a number of sections which are, in their turn, organized into chapters. The first book, entitled *Facts and Myths,* comprises an introduction and sections on "Destiny," "History," and "Myths." The second book, *Woman's Life Today,* contains the sections "The Formative Years," "Situation," "Justifications," and "Towards Liberation." The compact introduction, which could actually stand alone as a pamphlet, covers some twenty pages and explains the theoretical framework in a nutshell. Here, Beauvoir advanced the theory of the Other applied in *The Second Sex.* Following Hegel's philosophy, she said, we discover in human consciousness a fundamental enmity toward every other consciousness. The subject constitutes itself in the Self-Other opposition. It positions itself as the subject, the essential, opposite the Other as inessential, as the object. The Self-Other structure is found at all levels and places in human life, Beauvoir argued, and it is therefore not surprising that we also find it at the gender level. Man has appropriated the role of Self and made woman the absolute Other: thus, woman has been made into an *"être relatif,"* i.e., into a being that only exists in relation to man, and that is definitively subjugated to his sovereignty.

In the first section, "Destiny" (about seventy pages), Beauvoir argued that biological, psychoanalytical, and Marxist approaches all fall short as explanation for the historic supremacy of the male sex. Biology does not even explain the existence of two sexes (reproduction could be organized just as well in an alternative manner), let alone the hierarchy between the two. Biological facts are always embedded in social and cultural contexts and in themselves have no significance. It is culture ("second nature") that determines whether muscle power has an impor-

tant role to play and whether pregnancy is an impeding factor for women. The merit of psychoanalysis lies in the fact that it has understood everything centers on human allocation of significance to the body. But it also fails to explain male dominance: "For Freud himself admits that the prestige of the penis is explained by the sovereignty of the father, and, as we have seen, he confesses that he is ignorant regarding the origin of male supremacy" (TSS: I, 81). Nor do economic factors explain why it is the woman and not the man who has become the slave.

In the following section, "History" (around a hundred pages), Beauvoir revealed the true facts behind the oppression of woman. Because woman has the greater physical reproductive function, a division of roles emerged: men appropriated the production sphere, i.e., the active conquest of nature, often risking their lives in the process; women remained limited to the reproductive sphere and the home, or rather to the repetition of life. The human race happens to allocate a different value to both roles. As human beings differ from animals in their ability to transcend life—a difference whose keenest expression is a human's conscious risk of life which makes clear he does not coincide with it—action is valued more highly than the mere repetition of life. This is how man was able to appropriate the role of subject and place woman in the position of the Other.

Beauvoir further described history as a succession of deeds of male supremacy over women. Even when a woman occupied a position of power, she occupied it only with male permission. So she always remained imprisoned in the immanent sphere, in spite of apparent indications to the contrary. Beauvoir examined the history of the family, law, and private property, whose emergence meant the definitive dethroning of woman: man denies her every right to her own possessions. Then it is the turn of literate women: their marginal role, the resistance they evoked, their attempts to live by their pens. Beauvoir also treated the history of women's industrial labor, contraceptive practices, and the women's suffrage movement. Finally, Beauvoir described the then-contemporary position of women and concluded it was still not equal to that of men.

In her third section, "Myths" (close to 160 pages), she provided an inventory of the representations of woman and femininity that man has created. To fulfill her function as the absolute Other, woman had to be invested with special traits. A whole range of apparently contradictory characteristics were attributed to woman, such as idol and handmaiden, healer and witch, madonna and whore. This contradiction is caused by the fact that, as the Other, she represents everything man is not. Everything man desires and fears, loves and hates, is projected onto woman. If she exemplifies evil because she forms the negation of the masculine, she also embodies good, because she is essential to man's existence.

As absolute Other, woman especially represents the corporal and nature. Thus, all ambivalent feelings evoked in man by nature have been projected onto woman: his fear of death, his need for life. For example, we find this reflected in the disgust for menstruation as "unclean," evil power, and in the importance of virginity (nature that has to be conquered); the exaltation of female beauty and the distaste for old and ugly women; the idolization of the mother alongside the hate (the mother-in-law and stepmother myths). Subsequently, Beauvoir explored the exceptional way these myths are presented in authors such as Montherlant, D. H. Lawrence, Claudel, Breton, and Stendhal—woman only emerges as a full human being in the work of the last writer. The myth of the real woman and the Eternal Feminine also plays an important role in everyday life. If the myth is contradicted by the behavior of flesh-and-blood women, then the accusing finger is pointed not at the myth, but at the women concerned: their behavior is considered unfeminine.

The myth of woman continues to live in men's hearts, but it could disappear one day: "the more women assert themselves as human beings, the more the marvellous quality of the Other will die out in them" (TSS I: 174). Undoubtedly, this will also be advantageous for men. What could be more wonderful than relating to a real human being, a person, rather than to an abstract cliché? The absolute nature of the position of woman as Other presupposes that she also has to be an Other to herself: the "real woman" was also the absolute Other subjectively. What did this subjective world look like? This is the question Beauvoir asks as she takes us into the second book of *The Second Sex*.

In this second book, *Woman's Life Today*, which opens with the famous line, "*On ne nait pas femme, on le devient*" (One is not born, but rather becomes, a woman), Beauvoir sketched the subjective world of woman from earliest youth to old age.

The first section, "The Formative Years" (consisting of around 150 pages), examines the raising of girls that imposes on them the identity of the absolute Other. All children attempt to combat the first separation from the mother by courting her approval. Seduction, seeking admiration, and seeking approbation—all are strategies used by both boys and girls in their first three to four years. Subsequently, a distinction is made in the raising of male and female children: boys are taught to avoid this behavior, whereas it is reinforced in girls. The boy is encouraged to realize himself in concrete projects. The girl is continually reinforced in tendencies to make herself into an object. There is a fundamental contrast between girls' autonomous existence and the role that is demanded from them, while for boys these matters are extensions of each other. As the girl does not focus her expressive abilities on the world, she becomes internalized: a whole inner world develops whereby romantic dreams and fantasies take on paramount importance. She becomes alienated from her body, acquires a narcissistic attitude and an inner insecurity. But a girl is also often more developed physically than a boy, and is more receptive to impressions, such as natural beauty. (In the world of flora and fauna she is a human creature, while in society she has to "relinquish" herself.)

Finally, at around fifteen years of age, she gives in to reality: she assumes her subordination and focuses on achieving marriage. The capture of a husband becomes an increasingly urgent task. It is therefore difficult for a girl to focus her interest totally on education, sports, learning a trade. Her attempts to realize her individual autonomy are only half supported by her environment. The girl is often afraid that if she puts too much energy into this or that enterprise, she will fail in her destiny as a woman.

Nor is she allowed to assert herself actively in a sexual way; she has to remain chaste. The man is the one who *takes;* the woman *gives* herself. Well used to her role as object, the woman only discovers her autonomy in pleasure after some time—if at all. She has to fight for it and overcome her passivity in order to achieve a relationship based on mutuality. This mutuality is possible if each partner both desires the other's body and recognizes the other's freedom, something that requires mutual generosity of body and soul. Only then can both—in their own way—know a reciprocal pleasure. The dimension of otherness may continue to exist, but it loses its hostile character.

The woman can also make a lesbian choice. The biological explanation that a lesbian has a disturbed hormonal balance, and the psychoanalytical approach to homosexuality as an incomplete development are inadequate. "The chief misunderstanding underlying this line of interpretation is that it is natural for the female human being to make herself a feminine woman," whereas such a woman is in fact an artificial product made by society "as formerly eunuchs were made" (TSS II: 428). The lesbian woman has found a way to avoid subordination to the fetters of femininity. She can establish herself as active subject and reject the role of the Other, or she can assume this role, but she can then find herself again by seeking her equivalent.

The second section, "Situation" (in the region of two hundred pages), opens with a treatise on traditional marriage. Socially speaking, the man is perceived as an autonomous and complete individual. His existence is justified by the work he does in the community's service. He can choose marriage or remain single—the choice is his. To him, marriage is a way of life, not a destiny. In contrast, the unmarried state reduces woman to the status of pariah. Marriage is her only source of income and the only social

justification of her existence. In marriage, the woman becomes the man's *other half*, with the man as legal and economic head of the family. Marriage and love are difficult to reconcile because love can never be an obligation: "marriage is obscene in principle in so far as it transforms into rights and duties those mutual relations which should be founded on a spontaneous urge" (TSS II: 463). Eroticism is a movement toward the other; herein lies its essential nature. But spouses lose the function of other for each other: they become one self. No exchange is possible any longer, no gift, no conquest. Traditional marriage locks up woman in immanence. Her reward consists of her having avoided the feeling of loneliness. "Man is but mildly interested in his immediate surroundings because he can find self-expression in projects" (TSS II: 468–69). In contrast, a woman's home is the center of her universe.

Her household work is not an activity that wrests her from immanence. It is a Sisyphean task, an eternal fight against evil: dust, dirt, stains. It is a sad fate to be constantly focused on the repression of evil instead of on a *positive* goal. The housewife often becomes furious, fanatical, vengeful, or nervous. She only appreciates her husband's activities if they fit in with the framework she has built. Husband and children are always wanting to exceed the boundaries of the home. The woman tries to prevent them doing so: she is dependent on them; they justify her existence. However respected she may be, she remains subordinate, a second-rate figure, a parasite.

Marriage for the woman is a final destination, not a stop on the way; there is no other future for her. The limitations of her situation soon become clear to her. She transforms her disappointment into a maniacal need for her husband's proximity. Often older, he also has the advantage of professional training. As worker and citizen, his thinking is aimed at activity. He has developed a feeling for facts and a critical sense and thus usually acquires the role of mentor and guide. He likes to feel superior and so exaggerates woman's inabilities. Even if the woman recognizes male prestige, her husband's gloss soon fades. Sometimes, she will accept her subordination, but she also often rebels openly, attempts in her turn to tyrannize him, and to humiliate his manhood. But she still wants to "hold onto" her man—her social and moral security, her own home, the status of married woman, and a more or less successful surrogate for love and happiness are all at stake. Sophie Tolstoy, Belle van Zuylen, Madame Proudhon—there are countless examples of fiery and lively women who were suffocated by marriage. It is true that marriage also restricts the man, but it almost always destroys the woman. The traditional form of marriage is changing. The woman today has occupations outside the home and often has a profession that earns her money. But as long as the man remains economically responsible for the couple, equality is no more than an illusion. As long as he alone realizes himself in work or actions, and marriage for his spouse remains the primary "career," then their situation will continue unequal. The birth of a child usually obliges a woman to give up her job or education; it remains very difficult to combine motherhood with work.

For about a century, motherhood has been a choice and not a biological fate. But contraception is still difficult to obtain in many countries. Abortion tends to evoke a sanctimonious attitude. In France, it is widely practiced but remains a crime. Society, which is so active on behalf of the fetus, ceases to be interested in the child once it is born. Mental and physical abuse of children occurs on a massive scale but is punished lightly. Those for and those against abortion agree that attempts at elimination have failed completely. An illegal abortion is often life-threatening for a woman with no money. But it is also a trauma for the better-off woman who can at least afford better treatment; even if she wants the abortion, she still experiences it as a sacrifice of her womanhood.

Pregnancy and motherhood are experienced in very different ways, depending on how they come about—in resistance, acceptance, satisfaction, or enthusiasm. Pregnancy for a woman is both an enrichment and a mutilation. The embryo is both part of her and a parasite that exploits her. The subject-object opposition is abolished in the future mother. She forms a duality with the child. But ultimately it proves an illusion. The mother does not control her future child—it proves a separate being. This explains the contradictory fantasies and notions of a pregnant woman. Even if she is happy with the child, her body can still resist, e.g., through excessive nausea. Pregnancy and labor are tolerated most easily by women who do not allow themselves to become absorbed by their bodies.

When the child is born, the mother's reaction is determined by a whole range of socioeconomic and emotional factors. She seeks in the child what men are continually seeking in women: an other who is simultaneously nature and consciousness, who is prey and doppelgänger. The great danger to children in our culture is that the mother, to whom they are entrusted completely, is almost always a frustrated woman. Through her children she attempts to compensate for her frustrations: she kneads the children into a model or makes herself their slave. The children develop feelings of guilt that often last a lifetime. The majority of women tend to impose their own lot onto their daughters. It is a criminal paradox to refuse women all kinds of opportunities for self-realization and then entrust to them the most delicate and serious task there is: the forming of a human being.

The marital relationship, housekeeping, and motherhood form a whole in which all the factors are mutually influential. But real harmony is still hard to achieve because the various functions allocated to women are difficult to conform. Women's magazines give advice on how to reconcile sexual attractiveness with motherhood and thrift. The woman is caught up in contradictions, and attempts to compensate through a "social life." The wife "shows off" herself, her home, her children, and her husband. Visits and parties thus often become a chore rather than a pleasure. Friendships between women have a totally different character than relationships between men. Women search for affirmation from each other. Their relationships are not built on individuality, but on sameness, which introduces an element of hostility. Because a woman's husband has lost his prestige in her eyes, she often gives other men the roles of guide and mentor (e.g., priests or doctors) and of lover.

But adultery, friendships, and social intercourse in married life are no more than diversions. They are illusionary escapes: none enables the woman to take control of her own destiny. The existence of the "fallen" woman makes possible the exaltation of the "respectable" woman. The prostitute is a scapegoat and is treated as a pariah. Basic prostitution is a tough profession in which the woman is oppressed both sexually and economically. Hetaerae, courtesans, Hollywood movie stars—all have a certain independence. Yet, when it comes down to it, they are all still dependent on the man. They lose their means of earning a living when he no longer finds them desirable.

The menopause is often a relief for working women, but it is a radical transformation for women who have focused totally on their femininity. They often experience a personal crisis, feel misunderstood, rekindle feelings of regret and sorrow. They sometimes attempt to salvage something of their failed lives in a sudden surge of energy. They fall in love with one young man after another, seek salvation in God or religious sects, spiritism, prophets, and charlatans. If the woman comes to terms with her aging, then her situation changes. She now becomes a sexless creature: an elderly woman. Released from her obligations, she finally discovers her freedom but often no longer knows what to do with it.

Woman's situation often leads her to a fanatic belief in the heroes and laws of the male world. The man knows that he can construct other institutions, another morality, and other laws. Women, on the other hand, are far more energetic than men when it comes to tackling misery and misfortune. There is a whole area of human experience that the man purposely chooses to ignore because he cannot *think* it. This is why women believe men know nothing of life, and for this reason they reject male logic.

In the section "Justifications" (in the region of fifty pages), Beauvoir looks at a trio of attitudes used by women in their attempt to turn their prison into a glorious heaven: the narcissistic, the infatuated, and the mystical. The narcissist tries to be *en-soi-pour-soi*. She devotes herself to herself in an attempt at independence. But she cannot maintain the illusion. No real relationship can exist between an individual and his double, because that double does not exist. The narcissistic woman suffers a radical defeat, which often ends in loneliness and paranoia. The woman who surrenders completely to love and makes her loved one her whole life also attempts to transcend her situation by accepting it absolutely. Self-effacement and "serving" her lover in all ways are supposed to make her happy. But the man she worships like a god is not a god, and that is where the trouble starts. This love religion often ends in catastrophe: the man leaves the woman who has imprisoned him in this way. The mystical woman offers herself to God in total surrender. This is not straightforward "sexual sublimation." Like the woman who idolizes her lover, the mystical woman seeks a sovereign glance full of attention and love for her, i.e., the apotheosis of her narcissism. A mystical glow, love, and narcissism can be integrated in an active and independent life. But as such, these attempts at individual salvation are doomed to failure; in human society, freedom is only achieved through acting positively.

In the fourth and final section, "Towards Liberation," (also comprising around fifty pages), Beauvoir states that having the right to vote and a profession is not sufficient to liberate women. The world still carries the stamp men have placed upon it. Privileged women who have found economic and social independence through a profession still do not feel at home in their new situation. A woman who deviates from current norms devalues herself sexually and as a result also socially because society has integrated sexual values. The woman knows she will always be judged on her appearance. She feels obliged to maintain a fairly complicated elegance. But she encounters real problems in sexual areas. Sometimes she compensates for her active existence with a masochistic love affair. She has to behave passively on the sexual market and be a so-called object. Fortunately, there are increasingly more men who are beginning to accept her equality. But motherhood remains difficult to combine with a profession and career.

The independent woman is also still torn between the interests of her job and her sexual vocation. It takes a lot of effort to find her balance, and she dares not aim too high in her work. Very few women in art and literature have had the boldness needed to create major works. As long as women have to struggle to become free human beings, there will be few creative women; until now women's abilities have been suppressed and have been lost to humanity.

Today, the new woman is still nowhere—not in Russia, not in France or America. But humanity is a historic becoming: the free woman is on the brink of being born. Men and women all win if woman can realize her full human potential. There will then be a mutuality that will allow the human couple to find its true form.

The Second Sex's Genre

The Second Sex has often been weighed against scientific norms and found wanting. According to cultural anthropologist Margaret Mead, "theoretically, the book violates every canon of science and disinterested scholarship in its partisan selectivity" (Mead, 1953: 31). Bair quotes historian Mary Beard's dismissal of the book as "utter nonsense" and "folly" (Bair, 1990: 392). Anne Whitmarsh also labeled *The Second Sex* bad science. Beauvoir is said to have attempted to carry out a sociological analysis, but only succeeded in piling up numerous literary examples (Whitmarsh, 1981: 149). This criticism assumes Beauvoir's pretensions were of a scientific nature. But is that really true?

Methodological remarks in *The Second Sex* are rare. In the introduction, Beauvoir stated her intention was to leave behind all earlier debates on the position of woman and to start all over again. She believed that, as a woman, she knew the world of women intimately and could therefore elucidate the problem. She went on to say, "But it is doubtless impossible to approach any human problem with a mind free from bias" (TSS I: 28). Beauvoir then raised the question of her own "ethical background" and stated that her position is based on existentialist principles. Subsequently, she discussed the specificity of woman's situation, i.e., her position as the Other, a position which, in Beauvoir's view, cannot be explained through either psychological, physiological, or economic factors alone, as scientific disciplines attempt to do. Instead we should investigate the *total* situation of woman: "We shall study woman in an existential perspective with due regard to her total situation" (TSS I: 83). This approach can be traced back to an affinity with a phenomenological perspective in philosophical anthropology, which approaches humans as situated beings. Beauvoir shares this approach, which is influenced by Heidegger and others, with Merleau-Ponty, Lévinas, and Sartre. The point of departure of the phenomenological perspective is that humans are always involved in the world, and so can only be understood within the total, very complex context of that world. However, this also implies that humans are seen as beings who continually give meaning to their situation. Thus, humans are objective subjectivity and subjective objectivity. According to this approach, the person should be understood within his or her situation; therefore, this situation itself has to be charted in an unbiased manner.

The point of departure here is that reality can be perceived directly if we are open to what the phenomena themselves tell us. Feelings, intuitive understanding, but also critical researches—all are ingredients of this basic approach. This epistemology derives from the thinking of philosopher Edmund Husserl. His aim was the refutation of Descartes' dualistic epistemology, which had introduced a strict distinction between thinking and being, and thus also between knowing subject and known object. Husserl only accepted the world of the phenomenon (*phainomenon* = "that which shows itself"). He argued that objects only exist as objects for a subject. He thus abolished the subject-object dichotomy. Husserl believed that phenomena could be described accurately and without bias, thus revealing their truth. For Husserl, explanatory, scientific theories were of secondary importance; according to him, *Aufklärung* (elucidation) rather than *Erklärung* (explanation) was required. Scientific approaches alone were inadequate, and as such had denied man access to phenomena and hidden reality from view. Philosophical phenomenology reinterprets the sciences by integrating them into a phenomenological total view.

Beauvoir narrated how Sartre turned pale with emotion when he first came across these ideas. "Aron pointed to his glass: 'You see, my dear fellow, if you are a phenomenologist, you can talk about this cocktail and make philosophy out of it.' " That was exactly what Sartre had had in mind for years: "to describe objects just as he saw and touched them and extract philosophy from the process" (PoL: 135). On the way home from the cafe, Sartre immediately bought Lévinas's book on Husserl, paging through it as he walked to see if Husserl had already formulated his ideas. Beauvoir concluded her account with the observation that, fortunately, this was not the case on a number of essential points (see PoL: 136).

In 1933, Sartre left for Berlin to make a serious study of both Husserl's and Heidegger's work. In that same period, Beauvoir immersed herself in the works of these German philosophers because, she said, she wanted to be able to follow the way Sartre's thinking evolved. Therefore, it is not surprising that from then on we also find traces of this philosophy in her work and that her thinking showed a clear affinity with phenomenology. Looking back on her discussions with Sartre during this period, Beauvoir recalled, "There was a phrase which we borrowed from phenomenology and much abused during these arguments: 'self-evident truth.' Emotions and all other 'psychological entities' had only a probable existence; whereas the *Erlebnis* (experience) contained its own self-evident truth (*sa propre évidence*)" (PoL: 2.58).

In her review of Merleau-Ponty's *Phénoménologie de la perception* (1945) Beauvoir expressed explicit approval of the "*élucidation phénoménologique*" method. She called the abolition of the subject-object dichotomy one of phenomenology's greatest achievements: "it is impossible to define an object by cutting it from the subject through and for which it is object; and the subject manifests itself only through the object with which it is involved" (TM, 1945: 363). Thus, our own judgments again acquire the relevance they are due. Through education and morality, the child unlearns the ability to take itself seriously as a presence in the world. Phenomenology restores the importance of subjectivity by denying a distinction between objectivity and subjectivity. It gives back to the adult the childlike audacity that allows him to say, "I am here," and to take seriously again his own judgments; an audacity that has to be recaptured from the sciences. The sciences present us with a universe full of "petrified" objects and teach us to perceive ourselves as subject to universal and anonymous laws.

Thus, Beauvoir also criticized scientific explanations of the world and wanted a return to direct observation of the world. Initially, she considered philosophy by definition superior to the sciences.

> The thing that attracted me about philosophy was that it went straight to essentials. I had never liked fiddling detail; I perceived the general significance of things rather than their singularities, and I preferred understanding to seeing; I had always wanted to know everything; philosophy would allow me to appease this desire, for it aimed at total reality; philosophy went right to the heart of truth and revealed to me, instead of an illusory whirlwind of facts or empirical laws, an order, a reason, a necessity in everything. The sciences, literature, and all the other disciplines seemed to me to be very poor relations of philosophy. (MDD: 158)

However, in *The Second Sex* her approach is more refined; she certainly applied scientific theory here. For example, she incorporated theories of Lévi-Strauss. In a footnote, she thanked him for allowing her to see the proofs of his *The Elementary Structures of Kinship* (see *Le deuxième sexe* I: 16–17). Lévi-Strauss's thesis on exogamy is the point of departure for Beauvoir's chapter on history. She also made use of Lacanian psychoanalysis when she referred to the mirror stage in the earliest development of the child as basis for her own socialization theory (see TSS II: 297). In general, in *The Second Sex* she applied the perceptions of sciences, such as biology, psychoanalysis, and historical materialism, but criticized them when they pretend to offer the whole explanation for the historically suppressed position of woman.

In her review of Lévi-Strauss's *The Structures*, Beauvoir stated that his theories can be placed in a broader philosophical framework—something Lévi-Strauss himself never ventured to do: "Lévi-Strauss never allowed himself to enter the domain of philosophy. He adhered strictly to scientific objectivity, but his thinking is clearly linked to the grand humanist tradition" (TM, 1949: 949).

So there is a question of division of tasks between the sciences and philosophy; philosophy places the results of the sciences in a broader framework. Beauvoir's view in *The Second Sex* is in line with Husserl's on this point. Her point of departure is also the necessity of a broad, direct approach, as opposed to the reductionism of the sciences.

Based on the foregoing, the structure of *The Second Sex* now becomes comprehensible. In this work, Beauvoir wanted to chart the whole situation of woman. She believed she knew that situation thoroughly, and in the introduction she stated that women are best suited to illuminating the situation of women: "we know the feminine world more intimately than do the men because we have our roots in it, we grasp more immediately than do men what it means to a human being to be feminine" (TSS I: 27). We should now see this against the backdrop of phenomenological epistemology, in which the immediate experience is decisive. It also gives us insight into how Beauvoir could claim she was beginning "all over again"; the phenomena could be observed and described directly. We also understand now that, in contrast to the sciences, she wanted to examine the *total* experience and circumstances, i.e., situation, of woman, this being the reason why *The Second Sex* became such a lengthy work, exploring such a broad set of aspects of women's lives.

As now becomes clear, far from being a clumsy eclectic work, *The Second Sex* is structured systematically as a philosophical phenomenological enterprise. Beauvoir was criticized by Whitmarsh for merely "piling up examples," but this is totally in line with the methodology of philosophical phenomenology; in this approach examples are not used as empirical evidence but rather as a means to show something, to pass on a specific insight. The Dutch phenomenologist Theo de Boer argues, "It is important that in a philosophical argument examples are chosen with the aim of transferring the spark of insight to the reader. Thus, the philosophical argument does not have the form of a deductive proof or an empiric theory" (de Boer, 1989: 181). My conclusion is that *The Second Sex* cannot be weighed against scientific norms alone but should be evaluated on its own merits, that is, as a philosophical work. When we come to examine the actual importance of *The Second Sex*, we will take its philosophical character into consideration. It may well be that some of the facts have been superceded, but this does not apply to the philosophical proposition of the work as such. . . .

The Second Sex in Translation

We have now seen that *The Second Sex*'s structure and conceptual framework rank it within the philosophical genre. In the original French text, Beauvoir made free use of philosophical concepts. This shows she perceived the work as philosophical and intended it to be included in this tradition, a tradition that by definition was critical of common-sensical ordinary language and used its own jargonese. But *Le deuxième sexe* is rarely read in the French. Interest in Beauvoir is almost nonexistent in France (with the exception of Michèle Le Doeuff),[5] and Anglo-Saxon readers are unlikely to use the French version.[6]

This makes it all the more regrettable that, in English (and Dutch) translations, the philosophical concepts have either been suppressed completely or even wrongly translated, detracting greatly from the work's philosophical vigor. Simons (1983) has shown this for the English translation—she discovered that translator Parshley translated *pour-soi* (for-itself) as the opposite, i.e., as "in-itself." "*La réalité humaine*" becomes "the real nature of man," a term that also means the contrary of what Beauvoir intended, as she herself told Simons: "It is a serious mistake to speak of 'human nature' instead of 'human reality' (*Dasein*-KV), which is a Heideggerian term. I was infused with Heidegger's philosophy and when I speak about human reality, that is, about man's presence in the world, I'm not speaking about human nature, it's completely different" (Simons, 1983: 20). The translation "nature of man" is incorrect, she goes on to explain, "since the base of existentialism is precisely that there is no human nature, and thus no 'feminine nature' " (Simons, 1983: 18).[7]

Masculine Thinking?

The systematic philosophical nature of *The Second Sex* tends to go unrecognized—partly through the translations in which it is read. If *The Second Sex* is examined from a philosophical standpoint at all, usually only the Sartrean notions it contains are considered. Because Beauvoir applied these concepts, she is accused of unleashing male thinking on (the subject of) woman. Male values are said to dominate in her work because she is believed to place consciousness above the body, thinking above feeling, activity over passivity, and transcendence above nature (see e.g., Greene, 1980: 205; Leighton, 1975: 213; Moi, 1994: 153; Seigfried, 1984: 441). Margaret Walters believes Beauvoir's own life and her view of human history comprise a devaluation of the feminine. In her attempts to escape stereotyping, Beauvoir has lost something (see Walters, 1977: 377, 359). Mary Evans suggests Beauvoir took her own prolonged student existence as a measure: the values in *The Second Sex* are those of a childless, hard-working bachelor (see Evans, 1985: 56–57, xi). With *The Second Sex*, Beauvoir is said to have joined the ranks of our culture's long tradition of mysogyny (see Lilar, 1970: 9 et passim).[8] All these critics place the blame on Sartre's conceptual

framework. Beauvoir's use of the Sartrean distinction between transcendence and immanence, and her adoption of his hierarchical relationship between both, are said to reproduce the Western rationalistic image of humanity and thus, through the underevaluation of the body, embrace a masculine thinking.

Now, in my view, this kind of strict genderlabeling of a certain philosophic thinking forms a problem in itself. The label is grafted onto socially prevalent definitions of masculinity and femininity: masculinity as consciousness and rationalism, femininity as body and nature. When, based on this, Sartre's philosophy is labeled masculine, the stereotypes that are so liberally available in our culture are only reproduced, and what still has to be proven is in fact presupposed. Besides this problem, the criticism of the book's content is also off the mark. . . . Beauvoir did not simply copy Sartre's thinking. Her own ethical theory represents a wholly Beauvoirian version of existential philosophy's body of ideas, in which connection with fellow human beings, bodily contact, and emotion have a major place and, in contrast to Sartre's thinking, transcendence does not occupy the foreground.

However, Beauvoir's thinking was not deemed masculine on the above-mentioned general bases alone. Another, more specific reasoning was put forward by Genevieve Lloyd: Sartre's conceptual framework was said to be characterized by a rejection of the female body; in this sense then, *The Second Sex* was also believed to have a masculine content. According to Lloyd (1984), transcendence in Sartre signifies nothing less than an abhorrence of the *female* body. Thus, the masculine perspective was said to have made a definitive mark on the concept. We will examine this criticism more closely here. Is Sartre's existential philosophical framework sexist, and in *The Second Sex* does Beauvoir adopt and apply it to the subject of woman in an identical manner? Let us first look more closely at Sartre's reasoning in *Being and Nothingness*.

The first woman we meet in this work is the so-called "frigid woman." She serves to illustrate Sartre's argument that the unconscious does not exist. According to his argument, the frigid woman consciously ignores the pleasure that she, as her husband testifies (?!), actually experiences in the sexual act.[9] The frigid woman is presented to us as an example of bad faith: by assuming the attitude of frigidity, she falls back on a fixed identity and thus places herself on the side of the *en-soi*. The second woman we meet is similarly reproached. She has "accepted" a man's invitation to go out with him. So she knows what the man is after, but elects to ignore this for the time being, thus postponing her decision on whether or not to accept his advances. Sartre apparently hates this: according to him, the woman is shirking her responsibilities. In both cases, he cites woman as an illustration of bad faith, implying that she can, in principle, act as free subject, but, in practice, functions as object. So although woman potentially has a consciousness, in *Being and Nothingness* we see her continually in the role of an *être-en-soi*.

In the final section, which discusses the sexes explicitly, it becomes clear this is no coincidence.[10] Sartre talks here of the threat to the *pour-soi* from the "slimy," which is said to be a "moist and feminine sucking," a "sickly-sweet, feminine revenge." All "holes" threaten the *pour-soi*. These are an *"appel d'être"*; they seduce the subject into becoming flesh and thus fill the hole. And Sartre continues,

> The obscenity of the feminine sex is that of everything which "gapes open." . . . In herself woman appeals to a strange flesh which is to transform her into a fullness of being by penetration and dissolution. Conversely woman senses her condition as an appeal precisely because she is "in the form of a hole." . . . Beyond any doubt her sex is a mouth and a voracious mouth which devours the penis. (BN: 609, 614)

How should we think about these sexist passages in *Being and Nothingness?* Do they mean Sartre's conceptual framework is essentially infected by masculine thinking, as Lloyd argues, and does *The Second Sex* suffer from the same malady? Kaufmann McCall (1979) and Le Doeuff (1979) also addressed this question. Both distinguish gender-specific and gender-neutral sections in Sartre's

work, and subsequently conclude Beauvoir took on board the latter only. Dorothy Kaufmann McCall introduces a distinction between Sartre's philosophical and "personal" contributions:

> When Sartre evokes the feminine in *Being and Nothingness*, his language bears more resemblance to the language of his obsessions in the novels than it does to the language of his philosophical discourse. . . . Sartre's descriptions of "the slimy" and "holes" in *Being and Nothingness* do not derive logically from his analysis of the *en-soi* and the *pour-soi*. They are not inherent in either his ontology or in existentialist thought in general; they are rooted in Sartre's particular sensibility. Obsessed with his horror of the vital in all its manifestations, Sartre the writer takes over from Sartre the philosopher, using words as magical means to impose those obsessions on his reader. (Kaufmann McCall, 1979: 214)

So Kaufmann McCall distinguishes the philosopher Sartre and the writer Sartre as the objective and subjective Sartre respectively. However, she forgets this distinction is one of philosophy's continually recurrent problems—what basis can we use for such a distinction? Kaufmann McCall builds her argument on a premise that in fact forms a problem in itself. Sartre's sexual metaphors are probably not so much projections of his personal *Ängste*, but, according to Michèle Le Doeuff (1979: 52), more an indispensable part of his metaphysics of authenticity. Her view is that the sexual metaphors are not a coincidental appendage, but an essential tailpiece for Sartre's theoretic system. Woman fulfills the role of unceasingly drawing the *pour-soi* into the *en-soi*, so that the *pour-soi* is forced continually to transcend anew. According to Le Doeuff, Sartre needs woman to complete the circle and lend his theory the status of philosophical system.

Now, in my view, this is not the case. The fact that transcendence has to be striven for again and again is explained by Sartre through the constant tendency to bad faith present in every human being, which emerges from his *désir d'être*. The task of transcendence is completed only on death.

So Sartre does not need woman to let transcendence start again and again. Moreover, by considering the sexual metaphors as a tailpiece, Le Doeuff herself introduces a distinction between those metaphors and the so-called real theory. Hazel Barnes also makes a distinction between Sartre's "objectionable images" and his theoretical system: these images only cast a shadow over his work and do not form its substance (see Barnes, 1990: 346).

The distinction between imagery and theory, however, is in itself problematic, as I suggested above. Wouldn't this be an ideal way to explain away the less agreeable elements in any philosophical work, by characterizing them as literary or metaphorical nonessentials that do not belong to the actual core of the body of philosophical ideas? The sexual metaphors in Sartre's theory articulate the characteristics of transcendence and immanence in gender-specific terms. So no other conclusion would appear justified than that Sartre's conceptual framework in *Being and Nothingness* includes a masculine thinking. If, to him, transcendence, consciousness, *pour-soi*, and being human are equivalents, then by making transcendence and the female body opposites, the female body is brought into line with immanence, nature, matter, *en-soi*. It would seem then that transcendence is the preserve of people with a male body, and woman emerges as the opposite of transcendence and consciousness.

The question now is in which form Sartre's conceptual framework appears in *The Second Sex*. Is it applied in its original form, and does Beauvoir also see the female body as the enemy par excellence of transcendence? We have already seen that *The Second Sex*'s central proposition is that man has made woman the Other. Beauvoir argues that an existentialist point of departure can make clear how this happened.

> The female, to a greater extent than the male, is the prey of the species; and the human race has always sought to escape its specific destiny. The support of life became for man an activity and a project through the invention of the tool; but in maternity woman remained closely bound to her body, like an animal. It is be-

cause humanity calls itself in question in the matter of living—that is to say, values the reasons for living above mere life— that, confronting woman, man assumes mastery. (TSS I: 97)

How should we take this? Does Beauvoir also consider women's anatomy as their destiny? Can their subordinate position in history be traced back to their body? There are passages in *The Second Sex* that would suggest this. In the chapter on history, Beauvoir states literally that the historic position of women as Other originates in their anatomy. In this sense, she talks about the biological advantage of men. We can also find passages in which she speaks very negatively about female bodily functions, including those describing menstruation, pregnancy, and labor as extremely painful and disagreeable experiences for women (see e.g., TSS I: 61–62; II: 512–13).

In addition, however, in *The Second Sex* we also find an emphasis on the fact that the body is not a thing, but an always "experienced" reality. Beauvoir states explicitly, "it is not the body-object described by biologists that actually exists, but the body as lived in by the subject" (TSS I: 69), and "It is not merely as a body, but rather as a body subject to taboos, to laws, that the subject is conscious of himself and attains fulfilment—it is with reference to certain values that he evaluates himself. And, once again, it is not upon physiology that values can be based; rather, the facts of biology take on values that the existent bestows upon them" (pp. 68–69). So according to Beauvoir, the body always has a signifying component. Referring to the insights of Heidegger, Sartre, and Merleau-Ponty, she states that the body is not a thing, but a "situation" (see p. 66). By doing so, she approaches the body explicitly from the phenomenological perspective discussed above: the perception of the human being as objective subjectivity and subjective objectivity. For her, one can never be a mere body; there is always a dimension of meaning.[11] Thus, in *The Second Sex* reductionist biological perceptions of woman are subject to permanent criticism.

Here follow a number of Beauvoir's own comments on this subject:

[Woman is only a female] to the extent that she feels herself as such. (p. 69)

Woman is determined not by her hormones or by mysterious instincts, but by the manner in which her body and her relation to the world are modified through the action of others than herself. (II: 734)

. . . if body and sexuality are concrete expressions of existence, it is with reference to this that their significance can be discovered. (I: 77)

It is not nature that defines woman; it is she who defines herself by dealing with nature on her own account in her emotional life. (p. 69)

Experience, understanding, meaning, feeling—for Beauvoir the body is always linked to the human experience of it. It is never a separate entity, and woman's historic role as the Other can, therefore, never be determined by pure biology. The biological facts

are insufficient for setting up a hierarchy of the sexes; they fail to explain why woman is the other; they do not condemn her to remain in this subordinate role for ever. (p. 65)

Thus we must view the facts of biology in the light of an ontological, economic, social, and psychological context. (p. 69)

As we have seen, the two essential traits that characterize woman, biologically speaking, are the following: her grasp upon the world is less extended than man's, and she is more closely enslaved to the species. But these facts take on quite different values according to the economic and social context. In human history grasp upon the world has never been defined by the naked body. (p. 84)

As for the burdens of maternity, they assume widely varying importance according to the customs of the country: they are crushing if the woman is obliged to undergo frequent pregnancies and if she is compelled to nurse and raise the children without assistance; but if she procreates voluntarily and if society comes to her aid during pregnancy, and is concerned with child welfare, the burdens of maternity are light and can be easily offset by suitable adjustments in working conditions. (pp. 84–85).

If we examine more closely Beauvoir's own explanation for woman's historical position as the Other, then we find she indicates a combination of factors. Human beings find transcendence important; woman, through her greater role in procreation, is more subject to biology. That is why men have been able to appropriate transcendence and postulate woman as its opposite. So the oppression of women is a historical contingent result of a number of factors. Men have grasped women's biology to relegate women to a specific role—the Other. In history, the biology of woman has been assimilated into a process of specific cultural meaning, and as such has caused the development of the asymmetrical relationship between the sexes. Thus, biology certainly has its place in the explanation of woman's oppression, but it is not a unique place, because stating that biology has been used is not the same as stating it is an ultimate cause. Beauvoir's historic explanatory model perceives biology as a factor, but it is not infected by biologism.

There is no essence in woman, or in her body, that by definition places her on the side of *en-soi;* in principle, woman can also realize herself as subject, as self. Beauvoir claims woman has become the absolute Other through a historic contingent process, but states this is in no way an inevitable consequence of bodily functions. Woman has been the historic (contingent) Other but in no way the inevitable (necessary) Other. Through the central role of this thesis of woman as historic Other in *The Second Sex*, it is clear that whenever Beauvoir talks about the female body, she has the situated body in mind, i.e., the body embedded in and shaped by sociocultural practices and meanings. Beauvoir stated literally, "the situation does not depend on the body; the reverse is true" (II: 706). The phenomenological-anthropological approach of *The Second Sex*, i.e., the approach of woman as a situated human being, made it impossible for Beauvoir to share Sartre's rejection of the female body as such. In *The Second Sex*, Beauvoir removed the female body from Sartre's dualistic ontology and ranked it at a sociocultural level. Thus, Beauvoir has disaggregated Sartre's series of equivalents—nature/female body/

immanence/*en-soi*, breaking down his antagonism between the female body and transcendence.

In her introduction to *The Second Sex*, she quoted the following passage from "Mister"—the intended irony is missing from the English translation—Lévinas's *Le Temps et l'Autre:* "Otherness reaches its full flowering in the feminine, a term of the same rank as consciousness but of opposite meaning" (TSS I: 16, note 1). She continued as follows: "I suppose that Lévinas does not forget that woman, too, is aware of her own consciousness, or ego. But it is striking that he deliberately takes a man's point of view, disregarding the reciprocity of subject and object. . . . Thus his description, which is intended to be objective, is in fact an assertion of masculine privilege" (ibid).

What Beauvoir actually did here was to reformulate Sartre's theory in a nutshell. Sartre had also defined the traits of transcendence in gender-specific terms (a transcendence of the female body). He also implied woman was diametrically opposed to transcendence. In *The Second Sex*, Beauvoir eliminated this gender-specific connotation by introducing her thesis of woman as historic Other. In doing so, she transformed the very core of Sartre's conceptual framework. *The Second Sex* opposes the traditional situation of woman, not the female body. Beauvoir's negative evaluation of female bodily functions is targeted against the experience of motherhood, labor, and pregnancy, which is inherent to a specific objective situation where women have no active control over their own bodies and lives. My conclusion is that criticisms of Beauvoir that claim she is in opposition to the female body as such ignore the main thesis in *The Second Sex*, which we can characterize as the thesis of woman as the historic Other.

Beauvoir opposed a specific cultural embedding and organization of the female body, which made it impossible for women to develop and experience themselves and their bodies as active subjects. If women could live as active subjects, also in their reproductive role, they would also experience pregnancy, labor, and motherhood actively, and real love between mothers and children and between men and women would then be possible. Beauvoir herself noted, "It was said that I refused to grant any value to the maternal instinct and to love. This was not so. I simply asked that women should experience them truthfully and freely, whereas they often use them as excuses and take refuge in them, only to find themselves imprisoned in that refuge when those emotions have dried up in their hearts" (FoC: 201). . . .

Notes

1. To be precise, she wrote it between October 1946 and June 1949, with interruptions for a four-month stay in the United States and the writing of *L'amérique au jour le jour* which took her five months.

2. Judith Okely refutes Beauvoir's claim that women are always equated with nature. Indians in the Bolivian highlands equate the married couple with "culture" and all unmarried people with "nature." "The opposition nature-culture is not simply linked to a gendered opposition" (Okely, 1986: 82). Beauvoir's notion of a universal menstruation taboo has also been proved untenable by cultural anthropological research (see pp. 84–85).

3. The *pour-soi* exists "*à titre d'être qui n'est pas ce qu'il est et qui est ce qu'il n'est pas*" (EN: 177).

4. This quotation is omitted from the English translation.

5. This is confirmed by Françoise Collin, editor-in-chief of the Franco-Belgian feminist journal *Cahiers du Griff* (Collin, personal communication).

6. I was told this by the American philosopher and Beauvoir-specialist Margaret Simons.

7. Parshely also cut the text by about 10 percent. He scrapped from the "Myths" section Beauvoir's examination of the work of a number of writers and also skipped a number of passages from "History."

8. Alice Schwarzer notes that, in the first French collective feminist publication, which appeared in 1970 under the title *Libération des femmes année zero*, the editors could not come up with anything better to write about than a demolition job on Beauvoir (see Schwarzer, 1986: 14–15).

9. "*. . . fréquemment, en effet, le mari révèle . . . que sa femme a donné des signes objectifs de plaisir et ce sont ces signes que la femme, interogée s'applique farouchement à nier*" (EN: 90).

10. Le Doeuff (1979) and Collins and Pierce (1976) have already gone into the following passages from *Being and Nothingness* at length.
11. This is also clear from the structure of *The Second Sex*, book II, dealing with the "lived experience" of woman as absolute Other.

Abbreviations

Quotations and references are drawn where possible from current English editions of Beauvoir's work. Translations have been revised only where necessary. This is apparent when reference is made to the French original.

BN	*Being and Nothingness*
EN	*L'être et le niant*
FoC	*Force of Circumstance*
Hc	*Huis clos*
MDD	*Memoirs of a Dutiful Daughter*
PoL	*The Prime of Life*
TM	*Les temps modernes*
TSS	*The Second Sex*

References

Arntz, J. Th. C. (1960). *De liefde in de ontologie van Sartre*. Nijmegen.

Barnes, Hazel (1990). "Sartre and Sexism." *Philosophy and Literature* 14, 340–47.

Bair, Deirdre (1990). *Simone de Beauvoir: A Biography*. New York: Summit.

Collins, M., and C. Pierce (1976). "Holes and Slime: Sexism in Sartre's Psychoanalysis" (pp. 112–27). In C. Gould and M. Wartofsky, eds., *Women and Philosophy: Toward a Theory of Liberation*. New York: Putnam.

Boer, Theo de (1989). *Van Brentano tot Levinas*. Meppel: Boom.

Evans, Mary (1985). *Simone de Beauvoir: A Feminist Mandarin*. London: Tavistock.

Greene, Naomi (1980). "Sartre, Sexuality and the Second Sex." *Philosophy and Literature* (Fall), 199–211.

Kaufmann McCall, Dorothy (1979). "Simone de Beauvoir, The Second Sex, and Jean-Paul Sartre." *Signs: Journal of Women in Culture and Society* 5, 2, 109–23.

Le Doeuff, Michele (1979). "Simone de Beauvoir and Existentialism." *Ideology and Consciousness* 6 (Autumn), 47–57.

Leighton, Jean (1975). *Simone de Beauvoir on Woman*. Rutherford: Fairleigh Dickinson University Press.

Lilar, Suzanne (1970). *Le malentendu du deuxieme sexe*. Paris: Presses Universitaires de France.

Lloyd, Genevieve (1984). *The Man of Reason*. London: Methuen.

Mead, Margaret (1953). "A SR Panel Takes Aim at 'The Second Sex.'" *Saturday Review of Literature* 211 February.

Moi, Toril (1994). "She Came to Stay." *Paragraph*, vol. 8, 110–20.

Sartre, Jean-Paul (1943). *L'être et le néant, essai d'ontologie phénoménologique*. Paris: Gallimard.

Schuetz, Alfred (1948). "Sartre's Theory of the Alter Ego." *Philosophy and Phenomenological Research* 9, 2, 181–99.

Seigfried, Charlene Haddock (1984). "Gender-specific Values." *Philosophical Forum* 115 (Summer), 415–42.

Simons, Margaret (1983). "The Silencing of Simone de Beauvoir. Guess What's Missing from 'The Second Sex.'" *Women's Studies International Forum* 6, 5, 559–64.

Walters, Margaret (1977). "The Rights and Wrongs of Women: Mary Wollstonecraft, Harriet Martineau, Simone de Beauvoir" (pp. 304–78). In J. Mitchell and A. Oakley, eds., *The Rights and Wrongs of Women*. Middlesex: Penguin.

Whitmarsh, Anne (1981). *Simone de Beauvoir and the Limits of Commitment*. Cambridge: Cambridge University Press.

42

The Second Sex

From Marxism to Radical Feminism

Margaret A. Simons

Despite the acknowledgment by radical feminist theorists of the women's liberation movement in the 1960s that Simone de Beauvoir provided a model for their theorizing,[1] *The Second Sex* (1949) has yet to find a secure place in the history of political philosophy.[2] The feminist philosopher Alison Jaggar, for example, whose pioneering work defined the categories of feminist political philosophy (i.e., liberal, socialist, and radical feminism), does not include a discussion of *The Second Sex* in her definitive text, *Feminist Politics and Human Nature*, despite her recognition of the "historical significance" of *The Second Sex* as "a forerunner of the contemporary women's liberation movement" (Jaggar 1983, 10).

Jaggar omits "religious and existentialist conceptions of women's liberation" (including Beauvoir's) because they fall "outside the mainstream of contemporary feminist theorizing" and she finds them "implausible" from her socialist feminist perspective (Jaggar 1983, 10). But I shall argue in this paper that far from being outside the mainstream of feminist philosophy, Beauvoir provides the very foundation for radical feminism in *The Second Sex*, where the historical importance of radical feminism to both socialist and radical black theorizing of racial oppression is apparent.

Demonstrating the foundational relationship of *The Second Sex* to radical feminism addresses one of Jaggar's fundamental criticisms of radical feminism: that it lacks a "comprehensive theoretical framework" and in particular any psychological explanation of male behavior. Ignoring Beauvoir's work

in *The Second Sex*, Jaggar traces the roots of radical feminism to a "contradictory heritage" in "the basically liberal civil rights movement and in the Marxist-inspired left" (Jaggar 1983, 10–11). Liberal feminism and socialist feminism, in contrast, have strong foundations in the philosophies of Mill and Marx, respectively. But a recovery of Beauvoir's philosophy in *The Second Sex* can both reveal the philosophical foundation for radical feminism, and challenge the conception of the civil rights movement as "basically liberal," since Beauvoir drew upon the challenge to Marxist reductionism in radical black theorizing of racial oppression in formulating her theory. Her work thus challenges the definition of the feminist "mainstream" by affirming the interconnections of different forms of oppression while challenging the reductionism of identity politics.

In the discussion that follows I draw upon the definition of radical feminism provided by the feminist historian, Alice Echols (1989), author of *Daring To Be Bad: Radical Feminism in America, 1967–1975*, the first comprehensive historical study of the radical feminist movement. Echols, unlike Jaggar, makes a helpful distinction between radical feminism and "cultural feminism," the movement that followed it in the 1970s. Jaggar charges radical feminism with falling back on biological determinism for an explanation of men's behavior, defining women's oppression under patriarchy as seamless and absolute with women as absolute victims, and focusing on the construction of a womanculture as the sole political strategy. But Echols differentiates these "cultural feminist" positions from earlier radical feminism, which was "a political movement dedicated to eliminating the sex-class system." According to Echols, radical feminists were both "typically social constructionists who wanted to render gender irrelevant," and at least "implicitly" "anticapitalists" who "believed that feminism entailed an expansion of the left analysis." Cultural feminists, in contrast, "conceived of feminism as an antidote to the left," "dismissed economic class struggle as 'male' and, therefore, irrelevant to women," and sought to establish a womanculture where " 'male values' would be exorcized and 'female values' nurtured" (Echols 1989, 6, 7, 5).

In Echols's view Jaggar's analysis of radical feminism reflects a misreading of the movement common to socialists: "Most leftist and socialist-feminists mistakenly characterized radical feminism as apolitical. To them radical feminism involved changing the 'cultural super-structure' and developing alternative life-styles, rather than effecting serious economic and political change. . . . So when radical feminism began to give way to cultural feminism, socialist feminists simply did not notice" (Echols 1989, 7). Echols can provide convincing evidence for the existence of a radical feminist movement that was social-constructionist and leftist in its critique of racism and economic class oppression. But her focus on American movement history prevents her from identifying Beauvoir's contribution to radical feminism in writing *The Second Sex* in France some twenty years earlier. To do that, it is most useful to adopt a methodology more akin to Jaggar's own philosophical analysis.

Echols's history of the movement reminds us that radical feminism was born out of dissatisfaction with both liberal feminism and socialism, and inspired by the transformation of the liberal civil rights struggle into the radical black power movement, a development that Jaggar does not acknowledge. In obvious parallels with radical black criticisms of the civil rights movement, radical feminists criticized liberal feminists for pursuing "formal equality within a racist, class stratified system, and for refusing to acknowledge that women's equality in the public domain was related to their subordination in the family" (Echols 1989, 3). Much like the radical black theorists who defended the specificity of the African-American experience against Marxist reductionism, radical feminists also differed from socialists "who attributed women's oppression to capitalism, whose primary loyalty was to the left, and who longed for the imprimatur of the 'invisible audience' of male leftists." For radical feminists "male supremacy was not a mere epiphenomenon" (Echols 1989, 3).

In *The Second Sex* Beauvoir rejects liberalism and its legalistic model of society as a public sphere governed by a social contract, and accepts instead a Marxist model of history as shaped by material factors and class struggle. Beauvoir recognized in 1949 the importance of the hard-fought battle for legal equality but saw it as insufficient. "Abstract rights . . . have never sufficed to assure woman a concrete hold on the world" (*DS* 1:223). Women have yet to attain "the union of abstract rights and concrete opportunities" without which "freedom is only a mystification" (*DS* 1:222). Even with many legal rights won, "the institutions and the values of patriarchal civilization have largely survived" (*DS* 1:223). Liberal individualism is no solution: "The success of a few privileged women can neither compensate for nor excuse the systematic degradation on the collective level" (*DS* 1:222). The analysis of the causes of women's oppression would have to go much deeper.

In an important theoretical step toward radical feminism—one paralleled by the radical African-American writer Richard Wright, whose work Beauvoir read and published in the 1940s—Beauvoir begins with a Marxist historical-materialist analysis of oppression and class struggle. In *The Second Sex* she argues that economic and technological developments provided the conditions for a women's liberation struggle. The industrial revolution "transformed women's lot in the nineteenth century and . . . opened a new era for her" by enabling her "to escape from the home and take a new part in production in the factory," thus "winning again an economic importance lost to her since the prehistoric era" (*DS* 1:191). Developments in technology made this possible by "annulling the difference in physical strength between male and female workers in a large number of cases" (*DS* 1:191).

New methods of birth control "permitted the dissociation of two formerly inseparable functions: the sexual function and the reproductive function" (*DS* 1:199). Reproductive technology will provide the material conditions for further gains by women: "By artificial insemination the evolution will be achieved which will permit humanity to master the reproductive function. . . . [Woman] can reduce the number of her pregnancies, and integrate them rationally into her life instead of being a slave to them. . . . It is by the convergence of these two factors: participation in production and emancipation from the slavery of reproduction that the evolution of woman's condition is to be explained" (*DS* 1:203).

When economic developments in advanced capitalist societies freed bourgeois women from dependence on their families, the material conditions were laid for the collective struggle by women, across economic classes, for their liberation. Beauvoir's feminism is activist: the only recourse for women is the collective struggle for their own liberation. "Freedom remains abstract and empty in woman, and can be authentically assumed only in revolt. . . . There is no other issue for woman than to work for her liberation. This liberation can only be collective, and it demands before all else that the economic evolution of the feminine condition be achieved" (*DS* 2:455).

An analogy with racism was important to both 1960s radical feminists and Beauvoir, as is evident in this passage:

Whether it's a question of a race, of a caste, of a class, of a sex reduced to an inferior condition, the processes of justification are the same: "the eternal feminine" is the homologue of "the black soul" and "the Jewish character." . . . [T]here are profound analogies between the situation of women and that of Blacks: both are emancipating themselves from a same paternalism and the formerly master caste wants to keep them in "their place," that is to say in the place the master caste has chosen for them. (*DS* 1:24)

Beauvoir's analysis of the underlying paternalism common to justifications of both sexism and racism bears striking resemblance to an essay by Alva Myrdal, "A Parallel to the Negro Problem," included as an appendix to the classic text on American racism *An American Dilemma: The Negro Problem and Modern Democracy* (Myrdal, Sterner, and Rose 1944), a book Beauvoir consulted while writing *The Second Sex*.

For Beauvoir ethnocentrism seems to encompass sexism historically in the experience of alterity. Women were not the original, or the only Other: "[Woman] has not represented the sole incarnation of the Other for [man], and she has not always kept the same importance in the course of history" (*DS* 1:234). Drawing on the structuralism of Lévi-Strauss, Beauvoir argues that: "The category of the *Other* is as original as consciousness itself. In the most primitive societies, in the most ancient mythologies, one finds the expression of a duality—that of the Same and the Other. This duality was not originally attached to the division of the sexes. . . . Jews are 'others' for the antisemite, Blacks for the American racists, indigenous peoples for the colonialists, the proletariat for the class of owners" (*DS* 1:16).

According to Jaggar, the defining feature of radical feminist theory, which set it apart from liberal and Marxist theories "was a conviction that the oppression of women was fundamental: that is to say, it was causally and conceptually irreducible to the oppression of any other group" (Jaggar 12). Echols agrees that radical feminists "expanded the left analysis" of oppression and "argued that women constituted a sex class, that relations between women and men needed to be recast in political terms, and that gender rather than class was the primary contradiction" (Echols 6, 3). Beauvoir's support for this fundamental claim is evident in the following passage from *The Second Sex*, where she acknowledges Marxist insights into the historically changing role of technology and economic factors in shaping women's lives, but criticizes Marxism for failing to recognize the irreducible nature of women's oppression: "Engels does not recognize the singular character of this oppression. He tried to reduce the opposition of the sexes to a class conflict. . . . It's true that the division of work by sex and the oppression that results from it evokes the class division on certain points. But one must not confuse them. . . . The situation of the woman is different, singularly due to the community of life and interests that renders her in solidarity with the man, and by the complicity which he meets in her" (*DS* 1:101). For Beauvoir, "the bond that attaches [woman] to her oppressors is comparable to no other" (*DS* 1:19).

To expand Marxism to include an analysis of gender oppression, and to argue on one level for the primacy of gender contradiction, as later radical feminists would, Beauvoir returns to the philosophical roots of Marxism in Hegel's distinction between immanence and transcendence and his analysis of the master/slave relation. Turning Hegel against himself, Beauvoir argues that his description of the relationship of men, whose warfare and inventions create values that transcend the mere repetition of Life, and women, whom biology destines to immanence, to the passive and dependent reproduction of Life, is more reflective of the absolute opposition of the master/slave relationship than any relationship between men: "Certain passages of the dialectic by which Hegel defines the relation of the master to the slave would better apply to the relation of the man to the woman. . . . Between the male and she there has never been combat. Hegel's definition applies singularly to her" (*DS* 1:112).

Beauvoir described the relationship between men and women as a "caste" relationship defined by struggle: "All oppression creates a state of war; this is no exception" (*DS* 2:561). "[W]oman has always been, if not the slave of man, at least his vassal" (*DS* 1:20). In the past,

> the woman confined to immanence tried to keep the man in this prison as well. . . . She denied his truth and his values. . . . Today, the combat takes on another face. Instead of wanting to enclose man in a dungeon, woman is trying to escape from it herself. She no longer attempts to drag him into the regions of immanence but to emerge into the light of transcendence. . . . It is no longer a question of a war between individuals each enclosed in their sphere. A caste with demands mounts an assault and it is held in check by the privileged caste. (*DS* 2:561–62)

For Beauvoir, a historical analysis is necessary to understand the differences between women and other oppressed groups, and explain why women's liberation has been so long in coming:

> [Women] have no past, no history, no religion of their own; and they have no such solidarity of work and interest as that of the proletariat. They are not even promiscuously herded together in the way that creates community feeling among the American Blacks, the ghetto Jews, the workers of Saint-Denis, or the factory hands at Renault. They live dispersed among the males, attached through residence, housework, economic condition, and social standing to certain men—fathers or husbands—more firmly than they are to other women. (*DS* 1:19)

This situation elicits woman's moral complicity with her oppression, a willingness to accept dependence as a way of fleeing the responsibility of freedom facing any existent. Women are not simply victims in Beauvoir's analysis, as Jaggar charges of radical feminism. Beauvoir argues, in anticipation of the later radical feminist "pro-woman line" (Echols 91–92), that women find both material and ontological advantages from their dependence on men.

But unlike many radical feminists, Beauvoir also holds women morally responsible for complicity with their own oppression once an alternative is presented to them:

> To decline to be the Other, to refuse complicity with the man, would be for women to renounce all the advantages conferred upon them by their alliance with the superior caste. Man-the-sovereign will provide woman-the-liege with material protection and will undertake the justification of her existence; thus she can evade at once both economic risk and the metaphysical risk of a freedom which must invent its ends without aid. . . . The man who makes woman an Other will then meet profound complicities in her. Thus, woman may fail to claim herself as subject because she lacks the concrete means to do it, because she feels the necessary bond that ties her to man regardless of reciprocity, and because she is often well pleased with her role as *Other.* (*DS* 1:21)

The complexity of Beauvoir's analysis of gender difference and women's oppression is evident in her critiques of Marxism and psychoanalysis. Both theories attempt, unsuccessfully, to apply a model derived from men's experience to women. Beauvoir's version of existential phenomenology provides her with the ontological and methodological grounds for reclaiming the specificity of women's experience while avoiding the essentialism of identity politics. Her criticism of the Marxist analysis of woman's situation is both existentialist and feminist. She charges Marxist economic reductionism with denying the reality of woman's lived experience.

Engels's attempt to reduce woman's situation, including her reproductive role, to economic production is "not tenable." Sexuality and maternity are dramas in the lives of individual women that defy integration into society and control by the State. "One cannot without bad faith consider woman uniquely as a worker. Her reproductive function is as important as her productive capacity, as much in the social economy as in individual life. . . . Engels evaded the problem; he limited himself to declaring that the socialist community will abolish the family: it is an abstract solution indeed" (*DS* 1:102).

The practice in the Soviet Union reveals the limits of such a reductionist theory, which fails to recognize the patriarchal power of the State as oppressive to women. "Suppressing the family is not necessarily to emancipate the woman: the example of Sparta and the Nazi regime prove that by being directly bound to the State she can be no less oppressed by the males" (*DS* 1:102). In the interest of rebuilding its population, the Soviet Union was trying to once again "enclose her in situations where maternity is for her the only outlet. . . . These are exactly the old patriarchal constraints that the USSR is resuscitating today. . . . This example shows well that it is impossible to consider the woman uniquely as a productive force" (*DS* 1:103).

For Beauvoir a true socialist revolution must affirm, not deny individualism, and thus acknowledge gender difference in individual experience and the uniqueness of women's situation. "For a democratic socialism where class will be abolished but not individuals, the question of individual destiny will keep all of its importance: sexual differentiation will keep all its importance. The

sexual relation which unites the woman to the man is not the same as that which he sustains with her; the link which bonds her to the child is irreducible to every other. She was not created only by the bronze tool, the machine will not suffice to abolish her. Demanding for her all the rights, all the chances of the human being in general does not signify that one must blind oneself to her singular situation. And to become acquainted with it one must go beyond historical materialism that sees in man and woman only economic entities" (*DS* 1:103).

So Marxism, by imposing a male theoretical model of economic production on women's experience, falsifies the experiences of individual women and fails to provide the grounds for challenging patriarchal oppression of women by a male-dominated socialist state. Beauvoir's rejection of the mystification of gender difference by antifeminists and cultural feminists thus does not entail the denial of gender differences in the lives of individual women.

Beauvoir argues that psychoanalysis as well as Marxism reduces women's experience to that of men, thus silencing women. Her argument against essentialist reductionism reflects an existentialist ontology that links her with the new left's "politics of experience" and 1960s radical feminism. It also differentiates her position from that of cultural feminism, and in its combination of cultural critique and celebration of spontaneity and the transgressing of boundaries, aligns her with post-modernism.[3]

Beauvoir criticizes Freud's psychoanalytic theory for attempting to impose a male model onto female experience: "Freud concerned himself little with the destiny of the woman; it is clear that he modelled it on the description of the masculine destiny of which he limited himself to modifying several traits" (*DS* 1:78). Freud "admitted that woman's sexuality is as evolved as man's; but he scarcely studied it in itself. He wrote: 'The libido is in a constant and regular fashion essentially male, whether it appears in a man or a woman.' He refused to pose the feminine libido in its originality" (*DS* 1:79).

By relying on a reductive male model of female sexuality, Beauvoir argues, Freud was unable to explain either penis envy or the Electra complex, primary features of his psychology of woman. Freud "supposed that the woman felt herself to be a mutilated man. But the idea of mutilation implies a comparison and a valorization . . . it cannot be born from a simple anatomical confrontation. . . . Freud took [this valorization] for granted when it was necessary to account for it" (*DS* 1:81).

An adequate explanation of both penis envy and the Electra complex, in which Freud accounts for women's heterosexuality, would require that one leave the confines of the psychoanalytic model and examine the larger social, historical, and ontological dimensions of individual life and woman's oppression: "Psychoanalysis can only find its truth in the historical context" (*DS* 1:90). "The fact that feminine desire focussed on a sovereign being [as it does in the Electra complex] gives it an original character; but [feminine libido] is not constitutive of its object, it submits to it. The sovereignty of the father is a fact of the social order, and Freud fails to account for it" (*DS* 1:82).

Thus for Beauvoir a primary feature of the development of female heterosexuality and the transference of a girl's attraction from her mother to her father, is the father's sovereignty, that is, the social context of woman's oppression. Here we see Beauvoir extending social constructivism to sexuality. Her alternative description of the female libido further undermines the assumption of normative female heterosexuality by postulating an original resistance and repulsion toward men. Psychoanalysts who have approached the female libido only from the male libido, "seem to have ignored the fundamental ambivalence of the attraction that the male exerts on the female. . . . It is the indissoluble synthesis of attraction and of repulsion that characterizes it." Psychoanalysis has failed to acknowledge gender difference in female sexuality: "The idea of a 'passive libido' disconcerts because one has defined the libido on the basis of the male as drive, energy; but neither could one conceive *a priori* that a light could be at once yellow and blue; it's necessary to have the intuition of green" (*DS* 1:91). Beauvoir's social constructivist analy-

sis of sexual difference, and her challenge, albeit limited, to normative female heterosexuality anticipates the later radical feminist critiques of "compulsory heterosexuality."

But in arguing for gender difference, Beauvoir avoids essentialist claims. She lays the groundwork for an appreciation of differences among women in arguing against the reductionism of Freudian psychoanalytic theory: "One must not take sexuality as an irreducible given. . . . Work, war, play, art define manners of being in the world which do not allow themselves to be reduced to any other" (*DS* 1:86–87). Sexuality is one manner among others of ontologically discovering the world. Thus Beauvoir, unlike the radical feminists described by Echols, rejects the a priori primacy of sexual difference. An individual women establishes a unity among her activities as she chooses herself through her work, play, struggles, and sexuality.

Beauvoir criticizes psychoanalytic theory for reducing women to passive objects in the world and for denying women the possibility of authentic choices. "We will situate woman in a world of values and we will give to her actions a dimension of freedom. We think that she has to choose between the affirmation of her transcendence and her alienation as an object; she is not the plaything of contradictory drives; she invents solutions between which exist an ethical hierarchy" (*DS* 1:92). In describing a subject's failure to effect a transference or a sublimation (and surely the most obvious example here is in the "failure" of a woman to become a heterosexual), a psychoanalyst, Beauvoir argues, "does not suppose that they perhaps refused it and that perhaps they had good reasons for doing so; one does not want to consider that their conduct could have been motivated by ends freely posed" (*DS* 1:93).

Freedom is a central theme of *The Second Sex*. If "one is not born a woman" (*DS* 2:13), then with the reality of social intervention comes the possibility of individual action, as Butler argues (Butler 1986). Beauvoir is celebrating woman's freedom, the expansion of her choices, not confinement in a role, whether defined by Freud, or by implication here, essentialist identity politics. In her critique of psychoanalytic theory Beauvoir rejects as inauthentic the pursuit of Being, of a substantive self, which was to become prominent in cultural feminism.

> In the psychoanalytic sense "to identify oneself" with the mother or the father is to *alienate oneself* in a model; it is to prefer an alien image to the spontaneous movement of her own existence, to play at being. One shows us woman solicited by two modes of alienation; it is indeed evident that playing at being a man will be a source of failure for her. But playing at being a woman is also a trap. To be a woman would be to be an object, the *Other*; and the Other remains subject in the heart of its abdication. The real problem for woman is refusing these flights in order to accomplish herself as transcendence. (*DS* 1:92–93)

Beauvoir's description of the contemporary struggle as one in which women claim the values of "transcendence" and refuse the limits of "immanence" differentiates her from the cultural feminist position Echols describes as seeking a womanculture where " 'male values' would be exorcized and 'female values' nurtured" (Echols 5). For Beauvoir, women's "demand is not to be exalted in their femininity; they want transcendence to prevail over immanence for themselves as for all of humanity" (*DS* 1:222).

> In truth women have never opposed female values to male values. It is men desirous of maintaining the masculine prerogatives who have invented this division. They have claimed to create a feminine domain—realm of life and immanence—only in order to enclose woman there. It is beyond all sexual specification that the existent seeks her justification in the movement of her transcendence. . . . What [women] are demanding today is to be recognized as existents as men are and not to subjugate existence to life, man to his animality. (*DS* 1:113)

But Beauvoir's theory of gender difference is complex. She rejects both the mystification of gender difference and the abstract, gender-free nominalism of liberal modernity as well.

Some feminist critics, such as Iris Young (1990) have charged *The Second Sex* with typifying a nineteenth-century "humanist feminism" that, leaving gender largely unexamined, calls on women to assume men's public roles. Beauvoir does reject the mystification of gender difference typical of both nineteenth-century antifeminists, who argued that women's intellectual and physical inferiority and sensitive natures warranted their exclusion from public life and confinement to the private sphere, and their contemporaries, the "domestic feminists," who argued that women should have access to both education and the vote in order to improve and extend the influence of their special moral sense. But Beauvoir does not deny there are differences.

In the introduction to *The Second Sex*, Beauvoir differentiates her position from modernism, from "the philosophy of the enlightenment, of rationalism, of nominalism; women, to them, are merely the human beings arbitrarily designated by the word *woman.* . . . But nominalism is a rather inadequate doctrine. . . . Surely woman is, like man, a human being; but such a declaration is abstract. The fact is that every concrete human being is always singularly situated. To decline to accept such notions as the eternal feminine, the black soul, the Jewish character, is not to deny that Jews, Blacks, women exist today—this denial does not represent a liberation for those concerned, but rather a flight from reality. It is clear that no woman can claim without bad faith to situate herself beyond her sex" (*DS* 1:12–13).

Beauvoir is a social constructionist who sees women's liberation as requiring the dismantling of the male cultural construct of woman as Other. She certainly wants women to gain access to the public sphere, to escape the confines of women's traditional role of wife and mother, to emerge as an individual. But the public sphere will be transformed in the process: "The future can only lead to a more and more profound assimilation of the woman into the *formerly* masculine society" (*DS* 1:216; my emphasis). She describes how philosophy, for example, has been distorted by men who have taken their own unique perspective as absolute. Her alternative is not to argue for the possibility of an absolute perspective without differences, that is, a return to the nominalism of modernity, but to both critique the male claim to objectivity and to begin constructing a knowledge based on a phenomenological description of women's experience. Hence the title of the second volume "Lived Experience," where Beauvoir tries to move outside the context of men's constructions of woman as Other, which are primarily useful in understanding not women but the men themselves, into women's ways of knowing their own experience.

Beauvoir does not demand access to a gender-free objectivity of modernity, but rather challenges the objective/subjective dualism itself and provides a phenomenological description of how men's perspectives shape their views of women, and reality. Laying the groundwork for women's studies in her feminist cultural critique, Beauvoir argues that men, in defining knowledge from their own point of view, have mistaken that perspective as absolute: "[Man] seizes his body as a direct and normal connection with the world, which he believes he apprehends in its objectivity, whereas he regards the body of woman as an obstacle, a prison, weighed down by what specifies it" (*DS* 1:14). "She is defined and differentiated with reference to man and not he with reference to her; she is the inessential as opposed to the essential. He is the Subject, he is the Absolute—she is the Other" (*DS* 1:15).

According to Beauvoir, Lévinas exemplifies this masculinist view in his essay *Le Temps et l'Autre* where he writes that: " 'Otherness reaches its full flowering in the feminine, a term of the same rank as consciousness but of opposite meaning.' I suppose that Lévinas does not forget that woman is also consciousness for herself. But it is striking that he deliberately takes a man's point of view, disregarding the reciprocity of subject and object. . . . Thus his description, which is intended to be objective, is in fact an assertion of masculine privilege" (*DS* 1:15). Beauvoir would have men, as well as women, claim the subjectivity of their situated consciousnesses, rather than lay claim to false objectivity.

Beauvoir's psychological explanation of men's behavior is derived from her close reading of myths and male-authored texts with which she began her research for *The Second Sex*. Her analyses of the images of women in the works of Montherlant, D. H. Lawrence, Claudel, Breton, and Stendhal provided the model for Millett's cultural critique in *Sexual Politics*. Psychologically, men's oppression of women is, in Beauvoir's existential analysis, an inauthentic attempt to evade the demands of authentic human relationships and the ambiguous realities of human existence. For men who would define themselves as pure spirit, women represent an odious link to the absurd contingency of a man's own life: his birth, embodiment, and death. "In all civilizations and in our own day, [woman] inspires horror in man: it is horror of his own carnal contingence which he projects onto her" (*DS* 1:242).

Woman as Other also seems a privileged prey of men desirous of the confirmation of self found in relationships with others, and yet fearful of the dangers in relationships with their peers. "[Woman] opposes to him neither the enemy silence of nature, nor the hard exigencies of a reciprocal recognition; by a unique privilege she is a consciousness and yet it seems possible to possess her in her flesh. Thanks to her, there is a means of escaping the implacable dialectic of master and slave which has its source in the reciprocity of freedoms" (*DS* 1:233).

Authentic human relationships, on the contrary, must be constantly created. Beauvoir's vision does not offer a comforting if static social order, but a future of ceaseless struggle in morally challenging relationships. According to Beauvoir, the master/slave dialectic can be surmounted, but only by

the free recognition of each individual in the other, each posing at once himself and the other as object and as subject in a reciprocal movement. But friendship, generosity, which realize concretely this recognition of freedoms, are not easy virtues. They are assuredly the highest accomplishment of man, the means by which he finds himself in his truth. But this truth is that of a struggle forever opening up, forever abolished; it demands that man surmount himself at each instant. One could say also in another language that man attains an authentic moral attitude when he renounces *being* in order to assume his existence. (*DS* 1:232)

"One is not born, but rather becomes a woman." This familiar quotation (eloquently translated by Parshley) which opens volume 2 of *The Second Sex*, indicates Beauvoir's social constructionism, a position Echols sees as key in differentiating radical feminism from the biological determinism of cultural feminism. In fact Jaggar unknowingly points toward Beauvoir as a theoretical source for the social constructivism of radical feminism in recognizing Monique Wittig as one of the few radical feminists to reject biological determinism; Jaggar cites Wittig's influential 1979 essay "One is not born a woman"—clear reference to Beauvoir.

Judith Butler has argued that Beauvoir's concept of the body as situation "suggests an alternative to the gender polarization of masculine disembodiment and feminine enslavement to the body" (Butler 1986, 45). For Beauvoir, Butler writes, "any effort to ascertain the 'natural' body before its entrance into culture is definitionally impossible, not only because the observer who seeks this phenomenon is him/herself entrenched in a specific cultural language, but because the body is as well. The body is, in effect, never a natural phenomenon" (Butler 46). Butler draws our attention to the conclusion of the biology chapter in *The Second Sex*, where Beauvoir writes: "it is not merely as a body, but rather as a body subject to taboos, to laws, that the subject takes consciousness of himself and accomplishes itself. . . . It is not physiology that can found values; rather, the biological givens assume those that the existent confers upon them" (*DS* 1:75).

If Beauvoir's view, Butler argues, is that the body exists as a locus of cultural interpretations, "then Simone de Beauvoir's theory seems implicitly to ask whether sex was not gender all along," a view radicalized in the work of Monique Wittig and Foucault who both "challenge the notion of natural sex and

expose the political uses of biological discriminations in establishing a compulsory binary gender system" (Butler 47). Butler, it should be noted, claims that Foucault, a student of Merleau-Ponty, was not influenced by Beauvoir. But an indirect influence is not unlikely given Merleau-Ponty's long association with Beauvoir.

Beauvoir "suggests," according to Butler, "that a binary gender system has no ontological necessity" (Butler 47). In fact, Beauvoir argues explicitly against the ontological necessity of sexual dimorphism earlier in the biology chapter. Beauvoir argues there against Hegel that "it is in exercising sexual activity that men define the sexes and their relations as they create the sense and the value of all the functions that they accomplish: but [sexual activity] is not necessarily implied in the nature of the human body" (*DS* 1:39). "The perpetuation of the species appears as the correlative of individual limitation. One can thus consider the phenomenon of reproduction as ontologically founded. But we must stop there. The perpetuation of the species does not entail sexual differentiation. If [sexual differentiation] is assumed by existents in such a manner that in return it enters into the concrete definition of existence, so be it. It nonetheless remains that a consciousness without a body and an immortal man are rigorously inconceivable, while one can imagine a society reproducing itself by parthenogenesis or composed of hermaphrodites" (*DS* 1:40).

Butler's analysis provides an alternative reading of existentialist concepts of freedom and choice found in radical feminism, which Jaggar discredits as liberal and idealist (as in one "choosing a sex role" from a transsocial standpoint). For Butler:

In making the body into an interpretive modality, Beauvoir has extended the doctrines of embodiment and prereflective choice that characterized Sartre's work. . . . Simone de Beauvoir, much earlier on and with greater consequence [than Sartre himself], sought to exorcise Sartre's doctrine of its Cartesian ghost. She gives Sartrean choice an embodied form and places it in a world thick with tradition. To "choose" a gender in this context is not to move in upon gender from a disembodied locale, but to reinterpret the cultural history which the body already wears. The body becomes a choice, a mode of enacting and reenacting received gender norms which surface as so many styles of the flesh. (Butler, 48)

Beauvoir's rejection of the mystification of gender difference evident in her ontology is based, in part, on her analysis of the historical deployment of an ideology of difference in women's oppression. She concludes from her historical analysis in *The Second Sex* that: "Those epoques that regard woman as the *Other* are those that refuse most bitterly to integrate her into society as a human being. Today she is becoming a fellow *other* only in losing her mystical aura. Antifeminists are always playing on this equivocation. They gladly agree to exalt woman as *Other* in order to constitute her alterity as absolute, irreducible, and to refuse her access to the human *Mitsein* [being-with]" (*DS* 1:120). Beauvoir's intent, here as elsewhere, is not to deny gender difference as women experience it concretely, but to demystify it.

In the nineteenth century, glorification of woman's difference was common to both antifeminists such as Comte and Balzac, as well as utopian socialists such as the Saint-Simonians, who, in a foreshadowing of the goddess worship of contemporary cultural feminism, awaited the advent of the female messiah. But neither, according to Beauvoir, served well the interests of women's liberation: "The doctrines that call for the advent of the woman as flesh, life, immanence, as the Other, are masculine ideologies that in no way express feminine demands" (*DS* 1:217).

Beauvoir's analysis of the historical relationship of socialism and goddess worship provides an interesting context for reading the critiques of cultural feminism in both Jaggar and Echols. Some utopian socialists of the nineteenth century such as Saint-Simon, Fourier, and Cabet called for an end to all slavery and for the ideal of the "free woman." But later followers of Saint-Simon, "exalted woman in the name of her femininity, which is the surest means of her disservice." Enfantin "awaited the coming of a

better world from the woman messiah, and the Companions of the Woman embarqued for the Orient in search of the female savior." But for all the glorification of the feminine, with few exceptions, "women held only a secondary place in the Saint-Simonien movement" (*DS* 1:189). The socialist Flora Tristan, we learn later, also "believed in the redemption of the people by the woman, but she interested herself in the emancipation of the working class rather than in that of her own sex" (*DS* 1:190). Thus socialism, which Jaggar argued could provide the only clear alternative to goddess worship and cultural feminism, is, ironically, itself a historically problematic root of both.

Beauvoir's historical analysis reveals other limitations of socialism for feminists, problems still apparent in contemporary socialism. There was Fourier, for example, "who confused the enfranchisement of women with the rehabilitation of the flesh. . . . He considered woman not in her person but in her amorous function" (*DS* 1:189). But the most serious problem for socialist feminism stems from the reductive Marxist analysis that conceives of women's liberation as contained within the proletariat revolution instead of, as Beauvoir argues, requiring women's own collective struggle as a separate development.

In arguing for the importance of recognizing gender difference in experience, Beauvoir does not maintain that the relationship between men and women has been historically unchanging. Her analysis of women's oppression is not a simple analogy, neither trivializing other forms of oppression nor asserting that gender is always the primary contradiction. Class differences figure prominently in Beauvoir's analysis of how the historically different situations of bourgeois and proletariat women have undermined feminist solidarity and activism. For example, in her analysis of the bourgeois French Revolution, Beauvoir argues that neither working-class women, "who experienced, as women, the most independence," nor bourgeois women were able to make many gains: "The women of the bourgeoisie were too integrated into the family to know any concrete solidarity among themselves;

they did not constitute a separate caste able to impose their demands: economically, their existence was parasitic. Thus the women who, despite their sex, would have been able to participate in the events were prevented from doing so by their class, while those of the activist class were condemned as women to remain at a distance" (*DS* 1:184). No analysis that ignores class differences can understand the history of women's oppression and the problems of feminist activism.

Beauvoir criticized the so-called independent French feminist movement at the turn of the twentieth century for reflecting bourgeois interests. But the "revolutionary feminism" of the same era, which "took up the Saint-Simonien and Marxist tradition," also contributed to the internal divisions that were the source of the "weakness of feminism." "Women lacked solidarity as sex; they were first linked to their class; the interests of the bourgeois women and those of the proletariat women did not intersect.... Louise Michel pronounced herself against feminism because this movement only served to divert forces which ought to be in their entirety employed in the class struggle; women's lot will find itself well ordered by the abolition of capital." "Since it is from the emancipation of workers in general that women await their freedom, they only attach themselves in a secondary manner to their own cause" (*DS* 1:205).

Beauvoir reserves her highest praise for the Woman's Social and Political Union established in Britain by the Pankhursts around 1903. Progressive without putting women's issues second, it was "allied with the laborist party," and "undertook a resolutely militant action." "It is the first time in history that one sees women try an effort as women: that is what gives a particular interest to the adventure of the 'suffragettes' in Britain and America." In a detailed account, deleted by Parshley from the English edition, Beauvoir pays tribute to their inventiveness: "During fifteen years they led a campaign of political pressure which recalls on certain sides the attitude of a Gandhi: refusing violence, they invented more or less ingenious substitutes" (*DS* 1:208).

Identifying with an earlier feminist movement, drawing on insights of radical African-American theorists of racial oppression, Beauvoir, in *The Second Sex*, laid the theoretical foundations for a radical feminist movement of the future and defined a feminist political philosophy of lasting importance.

Notes

1. See Kate Millett's discussion of Beauvoir, for example, in Forster and Sutton (1989), 21–23. See also Echols (1989) who writes that "[Ti-Grace] Atkinson had read Simone de Beauvoir's *The Second Sex* in 1962, and, like so many other women who helped spark the second wave of feminism, she was profoundly affected by it." Echols elaborates in a footnote: "For instance, Roxanne Dunbar of Cell 16 cited *The Second Sex* as the book that 'changed our lives.' Shulamith Firestone dedicated her book The Dialectic of Sex to de Beauvoir. And Katie Sarachild called the book 'crucial to the development of the W[omen's] L[iberation] M[ovement]'" (Echols 1989, 167, 337 n. 155).

2. Mistranslations of philosophical terms and unindicated deletions in the English translation by H. M. Parshley are barriers to the philosophical analysis of *The Second Sex*. For a critical discussion of these problems, see Margaret A. Simons (1983). Passages from the Simons article are included without quotation marks or citation in the introduction to the most recent edition of *The Second Sex* (Bair 1989, xxii).

3. In fact Linda Singer has argued in a groundbreaking 1985 article that Beauvoir's "gynocentric" feminism is an "unacknowledged source" of the postmodern discourse "of 'difference' of deconstruction." According to Singer, by "taking the insights of existentialism seriously with respect to its denial of a supervening perspective and its affirmation of the situational character of discourse, Beauvoir begins the project of writing the other side, of giving voice to the discourse of otherness" (Singer 1990, 324–25).

References

Bair, Deirdre. 1989. Introduction to *The Second Sex*, by Simone de Beauvoir, translated by H. M. Parshley, xiii–xxiii. New York: Vintage Books.

Beauvoir, Simone de. 1949. *Le Deuxième Sexe.* 2 vols. Paris: Gallimard; cited in text as *DS*; all quotations are my translation unless otherwise indicated.

Butler, Judith. 1986. "Sex and Gender in Simone de Beauvoir's *Second Sex.*" In *Simone de Beauvoir: Witness to a Century.* Special issue of *Yale French Studies* 72:35–49.

Echols, Alice. 1989. *Daring To Be Bad: Radical Feminism in America, 1967–1975.* Minneapolis: University of Minnesota Press.

Forster, Penny, and Imogen Sutton, eds. 1989. "Kate Millett." In *Daughters of de Beauvoir,* 17–31. London: Women's Press.

Jaggar, Alison. 1983. *Feminist Politics and Human Nature.* Totowa, N.J.: Rowman and Allanheld.

Myrdal, Gunnar, Richard Sterner, and Arnold Rose. 1944. *An American Dilemma: The Negro Problem and Modern Democracy.* New York: Harper.

Simons, Margaret A. 1983. "The Silencing of Simone de Beauvoir: Guess What's Missing From *The Second Sex.*" *Women's Studies International Forum* 6, no. 6:559–64.

Singer, Linda. 1990. "Interpretation and Retrieval: Rereading Beauvoir." In *Hypatia Reborn: Essays in Feminist Philosophy,* edited by Azizah al-Hibri and Margaret A. Simons, 323–35. Bloomington: Indiana University Press.

Young, Iris. 1990. "Humanism, Gynocentrism and Feminist Politics." In *Hypatia Reborn: Essays in Feminist Philosophy,* edited by Azizah al-Hibri and Margaret A. Simons, 231–48. Bloomington: Indiana University Press.

Hannah Arendt

In the 1950s, a number of intellectuals believed that scholarly efforts to develop a comprehensive philosophy of political life had come to an end. The political and economic ideologies that once stirred popular passions and generated mass movements were similarly a thing of the past. The triumph of liberal democracy after two world wars, and the increasing sophistication of the social sciences, had ushered in an era in which contentious debates about political ends had given way to technical disagreements about administrative means.

However, for Hannah Arendt and other thinkers, the postwar world—indeed, the modern world of the 19th and 20th centuries—was not entirely worthy of celebration. The apparent death of political theory marked as well the end of politics as a meaningful activity. The end of ideology meant the success of bureaucratic rationality, the same unthinking processes that produced the totalitarian horrors characteristic of Nazism and Stalinism. Modernity had supplanted politics with administration and replaced action with technique.

Arendt's writings thus have an anti-modernist character. She tends to lament the well-known evils of the modern age—totalitarian assaults on freedom; bureaucratic administration; politics affected by lying, violence, or absolute morality; and the end of the grand tradition of political theory. Although she discusses topics that now seem commonplace to us, her analyses of them often surprise us with unique approaches and sharp observations.

Born in Hanover, Germany, in 1906, Hannah Arendt made analyzing the meaning of modernity and politics her life's work. A student of both Martin Heidegger and Karl Jaspers, she became active in the Jewish opposition to the Nazis and fled Germany in 1933. Living in France until 1941, she fled to the United States where she entered a circle of New York intellectuals and writers. Arendt became famous with the publication of *The Origins of Totalitarianism* in 1951. Other noteworthy books soon followed. She held several college and university teaching posts and wrote many significant essays on philosophy, culture, and the American political scene. Hannah Arendt died in 1975. Her last theoretical work, *The Life of the Mind*, was published posthumously in 1978.

As a phenomenologist, Arendt saw her project as one of getting us "to think what we are doing." In other words, her goal was to isolate the essence of our political experience in the modern world. As Arendt worked to create a sort of political ontology, she first had to wrestle with the discontinuities and sense of loss brought by modernity. One of the most important aspects of the past, which modernity had lost, was an understanding of the proper meaning of political action. Venerating the public life of the ancient Greek *polis*, Arendt believed that authentic politics could occur only through public deliberation over common purposes, not through blind partisan conflict or routine administration. Political action (rightly understood) reveals the best aspects of human beings; it involves people making decisions as a community of equals. While the institutions of representative democracy brought advances such as civil liberties, they did not bring true freedom. Authentic freedom can come only from the noble words and great deeds of people engaged in political action. Arendt's stress on the will to act as essential to freedom and politics, and her preference for extensive democratic participation, gave her more than a few admirers among the activists in the 1960s. She, in turn, gave them support and encouragement until their movement took an intolerant and violent turn.

The Human Condition

Arendt's classic work, *The Human Condition* (1958), is a study of the relationship between thinking and doing, between contemplation and action, between the *vita contemplativa* and the *vita activa*. For Arendt, the modern age has reversed the traditional priority given to contemplation over action; moreover, it has blurred the boundaries between three fundamental human activities: labor, work, and action. For Arendt, action (the speech and deeds of people in public affairs) represents a more authentically human realm than either labor (toiling for survival) or work (making artifacts). Western civilization has long since deprived "action" of its original political meaning, and, merging it with the concepts of labor and work, has made the *vita activa* synonymous with being busy. Thus, despite her glorification of politics as the quintessential realm of action, Arendt closes the book with the suggestion that the *vita contemplativa* may well be the most desirable life, after all.

Commentaries

For Lisa Jane Disch, Arendt's contribution lies in the development of a new language of politics and power. This language draws from the standpoint of the pariah—a marginalized, even persecuted critic of society. In this selection, Disch explores the meanings of several key concepts in that lexicon. Plurality, natality, the public realm, and commonality are all terms vital to understanding Arendt's writings on politics. At the center of her political theory, though, is an alternative conception of power. To understand power correctly, one should locate the core of its meaning in the act of "promise-making," since promising both constitutes selves (makes us who we are) and establishes relationships with others. According to Disch, and ultimately for Arendt, our practices of making promises show that it is possible to bring about a newer form of politics.

Mary G. Dietz reminds us that Arendt's political theory has been subject to differing interpretations by feminists. Some have found Arendt useful for developing a feminist political theory, while others have regarded her as not very helpful at all. Still, Arendt's thought is noteworthy for her view that the modern world has placed too much emphasis on the categories of labor and work, with too little attention paid to the realm of action. Taking Arendt seriously means that we should regard politics as an arena marked by a plurality of voices and by the creation of new things and relationships ("natality"). Despite her use of masculine language and her lack of concern for the sexual division of labor, Arendt's thought can still provide the basis for a feminist politics.

Web Sources

http://memory.loc.gov/ammem/arendthtml/special.html
The Role of Experience in Hannah Arendt's Political Thought. Three intriguing essays on Arendt's life and thought.

http://memory.loc.gov/ammem/arendthtml/arendthome.html
The Hannah Arendt Papers. From the Manuscript Division of the Library of Congress.

http://www.us-israel.org/jsource/biography/arendt.html
Jewish Virtual Library. A biographical profile.

Class Activities and Discussion Items

1. Explain Arendt's understanding of the concepts of labor, work, and action. Do these concepts actually capture the essence of human experience?

2. Describe Arendt's political ideals, particularly as they relate to the concept of action. Do you believe that these ideals have any relevance for contemporary political life? Why or why not?

3. Compare and contrast the analysis of the modern condition presented by Arendt and other theorists. What fundamental flaws can be found in modern society, according to each of these theorists? What suggested remedy to the problems of modernity does each theorist offer?

Further Reading

Canovan, Margaret. 1994. *Hannah Arendt: A Reinterpretation of Her Political Thought.* Cambridge: Cambridge University Press. An excellent overview of Arendt's views.

Honig, Bonnie (ed.). 1995. *Feminist Interpretations of Hannah Arendt.* University Park, PA: Pennsylvania State University Press. Superb collection of essays examining Arendt's views and their implications for understanding agency, identity, and feminism.

May, Larry, and Jerome Kohn (eds.). 1996. *Hannah Arendt: Twenty Years Later.* Cambridge, MA: MIT Press. Useful essays on Arendt's political and ethical theory, with an extensive bibliography of writings about Arendt.

McGowan, John. 1998. *Hannah Arendt: An Introduction.* Minneapolis: University of Minnesota Press. A good exposition of Arendt's views on politics—especially such concepts as totalitarianism, action, and evil.

Young-Bruehl, Elisabeth. 1982. *Hannah Arendt: For Love of the World.* New Haven, CT: Yale University Press. The premier biography of Arendt. ✦

43

Excerpts from *The Human Condition*

Hannah Arendt

1: *Vita Activa* and the Human Condition

With the term *vita activa*, I propose to designate three fundamental human activities: labor, work, and action. They are fundamental because each corresponds to one of the basic conditions under which life on earth has been given to man.

Labor is the activity which corresponds to the biological process of the human body, whose spontaneous growth, metabolism, and eventual decay are bound to the vital necessities produced and fed into the life process by labor. The human condition of labor is life itself.

Work is the activity which corresponds to the unnaturalness of human existence, which is not imbedded in, and whose mortality is not compensated by, the species' ever-recurring life cycle. Work provides an "artificial" world of things, distinctly different from all natural surroundings. Within its borders each individual life is housed, while this world itself is meant to outlast and transcend them all. The human condition of work is worldliness.

Action, the only activity that goes on directly between men without the intermediary of things or matter, corresponds to the human condition of plurality, to the fact that men, not Man, live on the earth and inhabit the world. While all aspects of the human condition are somehow related to politics, this plurality is specifically *the* condition—not only the *conditio sine qua non*, but the *conditio per quam*—of all political life. Thus the language of the Romans, perhaps the most political people we have known, used the words "to live" and "to be among men" (*inter homines esse*) or "to die" and "to cease to be among men" (*inter homines esse desinere*) as synonyms. But in its most elementary form, the human condition of action is implicit even in Genesis ("Male and female created He *them*"), if we understand that this story of man's creation is distinguished in principle from the one according to which God originally created Man (*adam*), "him" and not "them," so that the multitude of human beings becomes the result of multiplication.[1] Action would be an unnecessary luxury, a capricious interference with general laws of behavior, if men were endlessly reproducible repetitions of the same model, whose nature or essence was the same for all and as predictable as the nature or essence of any other thing. Plurality is the condition of human action because we are all the same, that is, human, in such a way that nobody is ever the same as anyone else who ever lived, lives, or will live.

All three activities and their corresponding conditions are intimately connected with the most general condition of human existence: birth and death, natality and mortality. Labor assures not only individual survival, but the life of the species. Work and its product, the human artifact, bestow a measure of permanence and durability upon the futility of mortal life and the fleeting character of human time. Action, in so far as it engages in founding and preserving political bodies, creates the condition for remembrance, that is, for history. Labor and work, as well as action, are also rooted in natality in so far as they have the task to provide and preserve the world for, to foresee and reckon with, the constant influx of newcomers who are born into the world as strangers. However, of the three, action has the closest connection with the human condition of natality; the new beginning inherent in birth can make itself felt in the world only because the newcomer possesses the capacity of beginning something anew, that is, of acting. In this sense of initiative, an element of action, and therefore of natality, is inherent in all human activities. Moreover, since action is the political activity par excellence, natality, and not mortality, may be the central category of political, as distinguished from metaphysical, thought.

The human condition comprehends more than the conditions under which life has been given to man. Men are conditioned beings because everything they come in contact with turns immediately into a condition of their existence. The world in which the *vita activa* spends itself consists of things produced by human activities; but the things that owe their existence exclusively to men nevertheless constantly condition their human makers. In addition to the conditions under which life is given to man on earth, and partly out of them, men constantly create their own, self-made conditions, which, their human origin and their variability notwithstanding, possess the same conditioning power as natural things. Whatever touches or enters into a sustained relationship with human life immediately assumes the character of a condition of human existence. This is why men, no matter what they do, are always conditioned beings. Whatever enters the human world of its own accord or is drawn into it by human effort becomes part of the human condition. The impact of the world's reality upon human existence is felt and received as a conditioning force. The objectivity of the world—its object- or thing-character—and the human condition supplement each other; because human existence is conditioned existence, it would be impossible without things, and things would be a heap of unrelated articles, a non-world, if they were not the conditioners of human existence.

To avoid misunderstanding: the human condition is not the same as human nature, and the sum total of human activities and capabilities which correspond to the human condition does not constitute anything like human nature. For neither those we discuss here nor those we leave out, like thought and reason, and not even the most meticulous enumeration of them all, constitute essential characteristics of human existence in the sense that without them this existence would no longer be human. The most radical change in the human condition we can imagine would be an emigration of men from the earth to some other planet. Such an event, no longer totally impossible, would imply that man would have to live under man-made conditions, radically different from those the earth offers him. Neither labor nor work nor action nor, indeed, thought as we know it would then make sense any longer. Yet even these hypothetical wanderers from the earth would still be human; but the only statement we could make regarding their "nature" is that they still are conditioned beings, even though their condition is now self-made to a considerable extent.

The problem of human nature, the Augustinian *quaestio mihi factus sum* ("a question have I become for myself"), seems unanswerable in both its individual psychological sense and its general philosophical sense. It is highly unlikely that we, who can know, determine, and define the natural essences of all things surrounding us, which we are not, should ever be able to do the same for ourselves—this would be like jumping over our own shadows. Moreover, nothing entitles us to assume that man has a nature or essence in the same sense as other things. In other words, if we have a nature or essence, then surely only a god could know and define it, and the first prerequisite would be that he be able to speak about a "who" as though it were a "what."[2] The perplexity is that the modes of human cognition applicable to things with "natural" qualities, including ourselves to the limited extent that we are specimens of the most highly developed species of organic life, fail us when we raise the question: And *who* are we? This is why attempts to define human nature almost invariably end with some construction of a deity, that is, with the god of the philosophers, who, since Plato, has revealed himself upon closer inspection to be a kind of Platonic idea of man. Of course, to demask such philosophic concepts of the divine as conceptualizations of human capabilities and qualities is not a demonstration of, not even an argument for, the non-existence of God; but the fact that attempts to define the nature of man lead so easily into an idea which definitely strikes us as "superhuman" and therefore is identified with the divine may cast suspicion upon the very concept of "human nature."

On the other hand, the conditions of human existence—life itself, natality and mortality, worldliness, plurality, and the earth—can never "explain" what we are or answer the question of who we are for the simple reason that they never condition us absolutely. This has always been the opinion of philosophy, in distinction from the sciences—anthropology, psychology, biology, etc.—which also concern themselves with man. But today we may almost say that we have demonstrated even scientifically that, though we live now, and probably always will, under the earth's conditions, we are not mere earth-bound creatures. Modern natural science owes its great triumphs to having looked upon and treated earth-bound nature from a truly universal viewpoint, that is, from an Archimedean standpoint taken, wilfully and explicitly, outside the earth.

2: The Term *Vita Activa*

The term *vita activa* is loaded and overloaded with tradition. It is as old as (but not older than) our tradition of political thought. And this tradition, far from comprehending and conceptualizing all the political experiences of Western mankind, grew out of a specific historical constellation: the trial of Socrates and the conflict between the philosopher and the *polis*. It eliminated many experiences of an earlier past that were irrelevant to its immediate political purposes and proceeded until its end, in the work of Karl Marx, in a highly selective manner. The term itself, in medieval philosophy the standard translation of the Aristotelian *bios politikos*, already occurs in Augustine, where, as *vita negotiosa* or *actuosa*, it still reflects its original meaning: a life devoted to public-political matters.[3]

Aristotle distinguished three ways of life (*bioi*) which men might choose in freedom, that is, in full independence of the necessities of life and the relationships they originated. This prerequisite of freedom ruled out all ways of life chiefly devoted to keeping one's self alive—not only labor, which was the way of life of the slave, who was coerced by the necessity to stay alive and by the rule of his master, but also the working life of the

free craftsman and the acquisitive life of the merchant. In short, it excluded everybody who involuntarily or voluntarily, for his whole life or temporarily, had lost the free disposition of his movements and activities.[4] The remaining three ways of life have in common that they were concerned with the "beautiful," that is, with things neither necessary nor merely useful: the life of enjoying bodily pleasures in which the beautiful, as it is given, is consumed; the life devoted to the matters of the *polis*, in which excellence produces beautiful deeds; and the life of the philosopher devoted to inquiry into, and contemplation of, things eternal, whose everlasting beauty can neither be brought about through the producing interference of man nor be changed through his consumption of them.[5]

The chief difference between the Aristotelian and the later medieval use of the term is that the *bios politikos* denoted explicitly only the realm of human affairs, stressing the action, *praxis*, needed to establish and sustain it. Neither labor nor work was considered to possess sufficient dignity to constitute a *bios* at all, an autonomous and authentically human way of life; since they served and produced what was necessary and useful, they could not be free, independent of human needs and wants.[6] That the political way of life escaped this verdict is due to the Greek understanding of *polis* life, which to them denoted a very special and freely chosen form of political organization and by no means just any form of action necessary to keep men together in an orderly fashion. Not that the Greeks or Aristotle were ignorant of the fact that human life always demands some form of political organization and that ruling over subjects might constitute a distinct way of life; but the despot's way of life, because it was "merely" a necessity, could not be considered free and had no relationship with the *bios politikos*.[7]

With the disappearance of the ancient city-state—Augustine seems to have been the last to know at least what it once meant to be a citizen—the term *vita activa* lost its specifically political meaning and denoted all kinds of active engagement in the things of this world. To be sure, it does not follow that work and labor had risen in the hierarchy of human activities and were now equal in dignity with a life devoted to politics.[8] It was, rather, the other way round: action was now also reckoned among the necessities of earthly life, so that contemplation (the *bios theōrētikos*, translated into the *vita contemplativa*) was left as the only truly free way of life.[9]

However, the enormous superiority of contemplation over activity of any kind, action not excluded, is not Christian in origin. We find it in Plato's political philosophy, where the whole utopian reorganization of *polis* life is not only directed by the superior insight of the philosopher but has no aim other than to make possible the philosopher's way of life. Aristotle's very articulation of the different ways of life, in whose order the life of pleasure plays a minor role, is clearly guided by the ideal of contemplation (*theōria*). To the ancient freedom from the necessities of life and from compulsion by others, the philosophers added freedom and surcease from political activity (*skholē*),[10] so that the later Christian claim to be free from entanglement in worldly affairs, from all the business of this world, was preceded by and originated in the philosophic *apolitia* of late antiquity. What had been demanded only by the few was now considered to be a right of all.

The term *vita activa*, comprehending all human activities and defined from the viewpoint of the absolute quiet of contemplation, therefore corresponds more closely to the Greek *askholia* ("unquiet"), with which Aristotle designated all activity, than to the Greek *bios politikos*. As early as Aristotle the distinction between quiet and unquiet, between an almost breathless abstention from external physical movement and activity of every kind, is more decisive than the distinction between the political and the theoretical way of life, because it can eventually be found within each of the three ways of life. It is like the distinction between war and peace: just as war takes place for the sake of peace, thus every kind of activity, even the processes of mere thought, must culminate in the absolute quiet of contemplation.[11] Every movement, the movements of body and soul as well as of speech and reasoning, must cease before truth. Truth, be it the ancient truth of Being or the Christian truth of the living God, can reveal itself only in complete human stillness.[12]

Traditionally and up to the beginning of the modern age, the term *vita activa* never lost its negative connotation of "un-quiet," *nec-otium, a-skholia*. As such it remained intimately related to the even more fundamental Greek distinction between things that are by themselves whatever they are and things which owe their existence to man, between things that are *physei* and things that are *nomō*. The primacy of contemplation over activity rests on the conviction that no work of human hands can equal in beauty and truth the physical *kosmos*, which swings in itself in changeless eternity without any interference or assistance from outside, from man or god. This eternity discloses itself to mortal eyes only when all human movements and activities are at perfect rest. Compared with this attitude of quiet, all distinctions and articulations within the *vita activa* disappear. Seen from the viewpoint of contemplation, it does not matter what disturbs the necessary quiet, as long as it is disturbed.

Traditionally, therefore, the term *vita activa* receives its meaning from the *vita contemplativa*; its very restricted dignity is bestowed upon it because it serves the needs and wants of contemplation in a living body.[13] Christianity, with its belief in a hereafter whose joys announce themselves in the delights of contemplation,[14] conferred a religious sanction upon the abasement of the *vita activa* to its derivative, secondary position; but the determination of the order itself coincided with the very discovery of contemplation (*theōria*) as a human faculty, distinctly different from thought and reasoning, which occurred in the Socratic school and from then on has ruled metaphysical and political thought throughout our tradition.[15] It seems unnecessary to my present purpose to discuss the reasons for this tradition. Obviously they are deeper than the historical occasion which gave rise to the conflict between the *polis* and the philosopher and thereby, almost incidentally, also led to the discovery of contemplation as the philosopher's way of life. They must lie in an altogether different aspect of the human condition, whose diversity is not exhausted in the various articulations of the *vita activa* and, we may suspect, would not be exhausted even if thought and the movement of reasoning were included in it.

If, therefore, the use of the term *vita activa*, as I propose it here, is in manifest contradiction to the tradition, it is because I doubt not the validity of the experience underlying the distinction but rather the hierarchical order inherent in it from its inception. This does not mean that I wish to contest or even to discuss, for that matter, the traditional concept of truth as revelation and therefore something essentially given to man, or that I prefer the modern age's pragmatic assertion that man can know only what he makes himself. My contention is simply that the enormous weight of contemplation in the traditional hierarchy has blurred the distinctions and articulations within the *vita activa* itself and that, appearances notwithstanding, this condition has not been changed essentially by the modern break with the tradition and the eventual reversal of its hierarchical order in Marx and Nietzsche. It lies in the very nature of the famous "turning upside down" of philosophic systems or currently accepted values, that is, in the nature of the operation itself, that the conceptual framework is left more or less intact.

The modern reversal shares with the traditional hierarchy the assumption that the same central human preoccupation must prevail in all activities of men, since without one comprehensive principle no order could be established. This assumption is not a matter of course, and my use of the term *vita activa* presupposes that the concern underlying all its activities is not the same as and is neither superior or inferior to the central concern of the *vita contemplativa*. . . .

41: The Reversal of Contemplation and Action

Perhaps the most momentous of the spiritual consequences of the discoveries of the modern age and, at the same time, the only one that could not have been avoided, since it followed closely upon the discovery of the Archimedean point and the concomitant rise of Cartesian doubt, has been the reversal of the hierarchical order between the *vita contemplativa* and the *vita activa*.

In order to understand how compelling the motives for this reversal were, it is first of all necessary to rid ourselves of the current prejudice which ascribes the development of modern science, because of its applicability, to a pragmatic desire to improve conditions and better human life on earth. It is a matter of historical record that modern technology has its origins not in the evolution of those tools man had always devised for the twofold purpose of easing his labors and erecting the human artifice, but exclusively in an altogether non-practical search for useless knowledge. Thus, the watch, one of the first modern instruments, was not invented for purposes of practical life, but exclusively for the highly "theoretical" purpose of conducting certain experiments with nature. This invention, to be sure, once its practical usefulness became apparent, changed the whole rhythm and the very physiognomy of human life; but from the standpoint of the inventors, this was a mere incident. If we had to rely only on men's so-called practical instincts, there would never have been any technology to speak of, and although today the already existing technical inventions carry a certain momentum which will probably generate improvements up to a certain point, it is not likely that our technically conditioned world could survive, let alone develop further, if we ever succeeded in convincing ourselves that man is primarily a practical being.

However that may be, the fundamental experience behind the reversal of contemplation and action was precisely that man's thirst for knowledge could be assuaged only after he had put his trust into the ingenuity of his hands. The point was not that truth and knowledge were no longer important, but that they could be won only by "action" and not by contemplation. It was an instrument, the telescope, a work of man's hands, which finally forced nature, or rather the universe, to yield its secrets. The reasons for trusting *doing* and for distrusting *contemplation* or *observation* became even more cogent after the results of the first active inquiries. After being and appearance had parted company and truth was no longer supposed to appear, to reveal and disclose itself to the mental eye of a beholder, there arose a veritable necessity to hunt for truth behind deceptive appearances. Nothing indeed could be less trustworthy for acquiring knowledge and approaching truth than passive observation or mere contemplation. In order to be certain one had to *make sure*, and in order to know one had to do. Certainty of knowledge could be reached only under a twofold condition: first, that knowledge concerned only what one had done himself—so that its ideal became mathematical knowledge, where we deal only with self-made entities of the mind—and second, that knowledge was of such a nature that it could be tested only through more doing.

Since then, scientific and philosophic truth have parted company; scientific truth not only need not be eternal, it need not even be comprehensible or adequate to human reason. It took many generations of scientists before the human mind grew bold enough to fully face this implication of modernity. If nature and the universe are products of a divine maker, and if the human mind is incapable of understanding what man has not made himself, then man cannot possibly expect to learn anything about nature that he can understand. He may be able, through ingenuity, to find out and even to imitate the devices of natural processes, but that does not mean these devices will ever make sense to him—they do not have to be intelligible. As a matter of fact, no supposedly suprarational divine revelation and no supposedly abstruse philosophic truth has ever offended human reason so glaringly as certain results of modern science. One can indeed say with Whitehead: "Heaven knows what seeming nonsense may not to-morrow be demonstrated truth."[16]

Actually, the change that took place in the seventeenth century was more radical than what a simple reversal of the established traditional order between contemplation and doing is apt to indicate. The reversal, strictly speaking, concerned only the relationship between thinking and doing, whereas contemplation, in the original sense of beholding the truth, was altogether eliminated. For thought and contemplation are not the same. Traditionally, thought was conceived as the most direct and important way to lead to the contemplation of truth. Since Plato, and probably since Socrates, thinking was understood as the inner dialogue in which one speaks with himself (*eme emautō*, to recall the idiom current in Plato's dialogues); and although this dialogue lacks all outward manifestation and even requires a more or less complete cessation of all other activities, it constitutes in itself a highly active state. Its outward inactivity is clearly separated from the passivity, the complete stillness, in which truth is finally revealed to man. If medieval scholasticism looked upon philosophy as the handmaiden of theology, it could very well have appealed to Plato and Aristotle themselves; both, albeit in a very different context, considered this dialogical thought process to be the way to prepare the soul and lead the mind to a beholding of truth beyond thought and beyond speech—a truth that is *arrhēton*, incapable of being communicated through words, as Plato put it,[17] or beyond speech, as in Aristotle.[18]

The reversal of the modern age consisted then not in raising doing to the rank of contemplating as the highest state of which human beings are capable, as though henceforth doing was the ultimate meaning for the sake of which contemplation was to be performed, just as, up to that time, all activities of the *vita activa* had been judged and justified to the extent that they made the *vita contemplativa* possible. The reversal concerned only thinking, which from then on was the handmaiden of doing as it had been the *ancilla theologiae*, the handmaiden of contemplating divine truth in medieval philosophy and the handmaiden of contemplating the truth of Being in ancient philosophy. Contemplation itself became altogether meaningless.

The radicality of this reversal is somehow obscured by another kind of reversal, with which it is frequently identified and which, since Plato, has dominated the history of

Western thought. Whoever reads the Cave allegory in Plato's *Republic* in the light of Greek history will soon be aware that the *periagōgē*, the turning-about that Plato demands of the philosopher, actually amounts to a reversal of the Homeric world order. Not life after death, as in the Homeric Hades, but ordinary life on earth, is located in a "cave," in an underworld; the soul is not the shadow of the body, but the body the shadow of the soul; and the senseless, ghostlike motion ascribed by Homer to the lifeless existence of the soul after death in Hades is now ascribed to the senseless doings of men who do not leave the cave of human existence to behold the eternal ideas visible in the sky.[19]

In this context, I am concerned only with the fact that the Platonic tradition of philosophical as well as political thought started with a reversal, and that this original reversal determined to a large extent the thought patterns into which Western philosophy almost automatically fell wherever it was not animated by a great and original philosophical impetus. Academic philosophy, as a matter of fact, has ever since been dominated by the neverending reversals of idealism and materialism, of transcendentalism and immanentism, of realism and nominalism, of hedonism and asceticism, and so on. What matters here is the reversibility of all these systems, that they can be turned "upside down" or "downside up" at any moment in history without requiring for such reversal either historical events or changes in the structural elements involved. The concepts themselves remain the same no matter where they are placed in the various systematic orders. Once Plato had succeeded in making these structural elements and concepts reversible, reversals within the course of intellectual history no longer needed more than purely intellectual experience, an experience within the framework of conceptual thinking itself. These reversals already began with the philosophical schools in late antiquity and have remained part of the Western tradition. It is still the same tradition, the same intellectual game with paired antitheses that rules, to an extent, the famous modern reversals of spiritual hierarchies, such as Marx's turning Hegelian dialectic upside down or Nietzsche's revaluation of the sensual and natural as against the supersensual and supernatural.

The reversal we deal with here, the spiritual consequence of Galileo's discoveries, although it has frequently been interpreted in terms of the traditional reversals and hence as integral to the Western history of ideas, is of an altogether different nature. The conviction that objective truth is not given to man but that he can know only what he makes himself is not the result of skepticism but of a demonstrable discovery, and therefore does not lead to resignation but either to redoubled activity or to despair. The world loss of modern philosophy, whose introspection discovered consciousness as the inner sense with which one senses his senses and found it to be the only guaranty of reality, is different not only in degree from the age-old suspicion of the philosophers toward the world and toward the others with whom they shared the world; the philosopher no longer turns from the world of deceptive perishability to another world of eternal truth, but turns away from both and withdraws into himself. What he discovers in the region of the inner self is, again, not an image whose permanence can be beheld and contemplated, but, on the contrary, the constant movement of sensual perceptions and the no less constantly moving activity of the mind. Since the seventeenth century, philosophy has produced the best and least disputed results when it has investigated, through a supreme effort of self-inspection, the processes of the senses and of the mind. In this aspect, most of modern philosophy is indeed theory of cognition and psychology, and in the few instances where the potentialities of the Cartesian method of introspection were fully realized by men like Pascal, Kierkegaard, and Nietzsche, one is tempted to say that philosophers have experimented with their own selves no less radically and perhaps even more fearlessly than the scientists experimented with nature.

Much as we may admire the courage and respect the extraordinary ingenuity of philosophers throughout the modern age, it can hardly be denied that their influence and importance decreased as never before. It was not in the Middle Ages but in modern thinking that philosophy came to play second and even third fiddle. After Descartes based his own philosophy upon the discoveries of Galileo, philosophy has seemed condemned to be always one step behind the scientists and their ever more amazing discoveries, whose principles it has strived arduously to discover *ex post facto* and to fit into some overall interpretation of the nature of human knowledge. As such, however, philosophy was not needed by the scientists, who—up to our time, at least—believed that they had no use for a handmaiden, let alone one who would "carry the torch in front of her gracious lady" (Kant). The philosophers became either epistemologists, worrying about an over-all theory of science which the scientists did not need, or they became, indeed, what Hegel wanted them to be, the organs of the *Zeitgeist*, the mouthpieces in which the general mood of the time was expressed with conceptual clarity. In both instances, whether they looked upon nature or upon history, they tried to understand and come to terms with what happened without them. Obviously, philosophy suffered more from modernity than any other field of human endeavor; and it is difficult to say whether it suffered more from the almost automatic rise of activity to an altogether unexpected and unprecedented dignity or from the loss of traditional truth, that is, of the concept of truth underlying our whole tradition. . . .

45: The Victory of the *Animal Laborans*

The victory of the *animal laborans* would never have been complete had not the process of secularization, the modern loss of faith inevitably arising from Cartesian doubt, deprived individual life of its immortality, or at least of the certainty of immortality. Individual life again became mortal, as mortal as it had been in antiquity, and the world was even less stable, less permanent, and hence less to be relied upon than it had been during the Christian era. Modern man, when he lost the certainty of a world to come, was thrown back upon himself and not upon this world; far from believing that

the world might be potentially immortal, he was not even sure that it was real. And in so far as he was to assume that it was real in the uncritical and apparently unbothered optimism of a steadily progressing science, he had removed himself from the earth to a much more distant point than any Christian otherworldliness had ever removed him. Whatever the word "secular" is meant to signify in current usage, historically it cannot possibly be equated with worldliness; modern man at any rate did not gain this world when he lost the other world, and he did not gain life, strictly speaking, either; he was thrust back upon it, thrown into the closed inwardness of introspection, where the highest he could experience were the empty processes of reckoning of the mind, its play with itself. The only contents left were appetites and desires, the senseless urges of his body which he mistook for passion and which he deemed to be "unreasonable" because he found he could not "reason," that is, not reckon with them. The only thing that could now be potentially immortal, as immortal as the body politic in antiquity and as individual life during the Middle Ages, was life itself, that is, the possibly everlasting life process of the species mankind.

We saw before that in the rise of society it was ultimately the life of the species which asserted itself. Theoretically, the turning point from the earlier modern age's insistence on the "egoistic" life of the individual to its later emphasis on "social" life and "socialized man" (Marx) came when Marx transformed the cruder notion of classical economy—that all men, in so far as they act at all, act for reasons of self-interest—into forces of interest which inform, move, and direct the classes of society, and through their conflicts direct society as a whole. Socialized mankind is that state of society where only one interest rules, and the subject of this interest is either classes or mankind, but neither man nor men. The point is that now even the last trace of action in what men were doing, the motive implied in self-interest, disappeared. What was left was a "natural force," the force of the life process itself, to which all men and all human activities were equally submitted ("the thought process itself is a natural process")[20] and whose only aim, if it had an aim at all, was survival of the animal species man. None of the higher capacities of man was any longer necessary to connect individual life with the life of the species; individual life became part of the life process, and to labor, to assure the continuity of one's own life and the life of his family, was all that was needed. What was not needed, not necessitated by life's metabolism with nature, was either superfluous or could be justified only in terms of a peculiarity of human as distinguished from other animal life—so that Milton was considered to have written his *Paradise Lost* for the same reasons and out of similar urges that compel the silkworm to produce silk.

If we compare the modern world with that of the past, the loss of human experience involved in this development is extraordinarily striking. It is not only and not even primarily contemplation which has become an entirely meaningless experience. Thought itself, when it became "reckoning with consequences," became a function of the brain, with the result that electronic instruments are found to fulfil these functions much better than we ever could. Action was soon and still is almost exclusively understood in terms of making and fabricating, only that making, because of its worldliness and inherent indifference to life, was now regarded as but another form of laboring, a more complicated but not a more mysterious function of the life process.

Meanwhile, we have proved ingenious enough to find ways to ease the toil and trouble of living to the point where an elimination of laboring from the range of human activities can no longer be regarded as utopian. For even now, laboring is too lofty, too ambitious a word for what we are doing, or think we are doing, in the world we have come to live in. The last stage of the laboring society, the society of jobholders, demands of its members a sheer automatic functioning, as though individual life had actually been submerged in the over-all life process of the species and the only active decision still required of the individual were to let go, so to speak, to abandon his individuality, the still individually sensed pain and trouble of living, and acquiesce in a dazed, "tranquilized," functional type of behavior. The trouble with modern theories of behaviorism is not that they are wrong but that they could become true, that they actually are the best possible conceptualization of certain obvious trends in modern society. It is quite conceivable that the modern age—which began with such an unprecedented and promising outburst of human activity—may end in the deadliest, most sterile passivity history has ever known.

But there are other more serious danger signs that man may be willing and, indeed, is on the point of developing into that animal species from which, since Darwin, he imagines he has come. If, in concluding, we return once more to the discovery of the Archimedean point and apply it, as Kafka warned us not to do, to man himself and to what he is doing on this earth, it at once becomes manifest that all his activities, watched from a sufficiently removed vantage point in the universe, would appear not as activities of any kind but as processes, so that, as a scientist recently put it, modern motorization would appear like a process of biological mutation in which human bodies gradually begin to be covered by shells of steel. For the watcher from the universe, this mutation would be no more or less mysterious than the mutation which now goes on before our eyes in those small living organisms which we fought with antibiotics and which mysteriously have developed new strains to resist us. How deep-rooted this usage of the Archimedean point against ourselves is can be seen in the very metaphors which dominate scientific thought today. The reason why scientists can tell us about the "life" in the atom—where apparently every particle is "free" to behave as it wants and the laws ruling these movements are the same statistical laws which, according to the social scientists, rule human behavior and make the multitude behave as it must, no matter how "free" the individual particle may appear to be in its choices—the reason, in other words, why the behavior of the infinitely small particle is not only similar in pattern to the planetary system as it appears to us but resembles the life and behavior patterns in human society is, of course, that we look and live in this society as though we were as far removed from our own human existence as we are from the infinitely small and the immensely large which, even if they could be perceived by the finest instruments, are too far away from us to be experienced.

Needless to say, this does not mean that modern man has lost his capacities or is on the point of losing them. No matter what sociology, psychology, and anthropology will tell us about the "social animal," men persist in making, fabricating, and building, although these faculties are more and more restricted to the abilities of the artist, so that the concomitant experiences of worldliness escape more and more the range of ordinary human experience.[21]

Similarly, the capacity for action, at least in the sense of the releasing of processes, is still with us, although it has become the exclusive prerogative of the scientists, who have enlarged the realm of human affairs to the point of extinguishing the time-honored protective dividing line between nature and the human world. In view of such achievements, performed for centuries in the unseen quiet of the laboratories, it seems only proper that their deeds should eventually have turned out to have greater news value, to be of greater political significance, than the administrative and diplomatic doings of most so-called statesmen. It certainly is not without irony that those whom public opinion has persistently held to be the least practical and the least political members of society should have turned out to be the only ones left who still know how to act and how to act in concert. For their early organizations, which they founded in the seventeenth century for the conquest of nature and in which they developed their own moral standards and their own code of honor, have not only survived all vicissitudes of the modern age, but they have become one of the most potent power-generating groups in all history. But the action of the scientists, since it acts into nature from the standpoint of the universe and not into the web of human relationships, lacks the revelatory character of action as well as the ability to produce stories and become historical, which together

form the very source from which meaningfulness springs into and illuminates human existence. In this existentially most important aspect, action, too, has become an experience for the privileged few, and these few who still know what it means to act may well be even fewer than the artists, their experience even rarer than the genuine experience of and love for the world.

Thought, finally—which we, following the premodern as well as the modern tradition, omitted from our reconsideration of the *vita activa*—is still possible, and no doubt actual, wherever men live under the conditions of political freedom. Unfortunately, and contrary to what is currently assumed about the proverbial ivory-tower independence of thinkers, no other human capacity is so vulnerable, and it is in fact far easier to act under conditions of tyranny than it is to think. As a living experience, thought has always been assumed, perhaps wrongly, to be known only to the few. It may not be presumptuous to believe that these few have not become fewer in our time. This maybe irrelevant, or of restricted relevance, for the future of the world; it is not irrelevant for the future of man. For if no other test but the experience of being active, no other measure but the extent of sheer activity were to be applied to the various activities within the *vita activa*, it might well be that thinking as such would surpass them all. Whoever has any experience in this matter will know how right Cato was when he said: *Numquam se plus agere quam nihil cum ageret, numquam minus solum esse quam cum solus esset*— "Never is he more active than when he does nothing, never is he less alone than when he is by himself."

Notes

1. In the analysis of postclassical political thought, it is often quite illuminating to find out which of the two biblical versions of the creation story is cited. Thus it is highly characteristic of the difference between the teaching of Jesus of Nazareth and of Paul that Jesus, discussing the relationship between man and wife, refers to Genesis 1:27: "Have ye not read, that he which made *them* at the beginning made them male and female" (Matt.

19:4), whereas Paul on a similar occasion insists that the woman was created "of the man" and hence "for the man," even though he then somewhat attenuates the dependence: "neither is the man without the woman, neither the woman without the man" (I Cor. 11:8–12). The difference indicates much more than a different attitude to the role of woman. For Jesus, faith was closely related to action (cf. § 33 below); for Paul, faith was primarily related to salvation. Especially interesting in this respect is Augustine (*De civitate Dei* xii. 21), who not only ignores Genesis 1:27 altogether but sees the difference between man and animal in that man was created *unum ac singulum*, whereas all animals were ordered "to come into being several at once" (*plura simul iussit exsistere*). To Augustine, the creation story offers a welcome opportunity to stress the species character of animal life as distinguished from the singularity of human existence.

2. Augustine, who is usually credited with having been the first to raise the so-called anthropological question in philosophy, knew this quite well. He distinguishes between the questions of "Who am I?" and "What am I?" the first being directed by man at himself ("And I directed myself at myself and said to me: You, who are you? And I answered: A man"—*tu, quis es?* [*Confessiones* x. 6]) and the second being addressed to God ("What then am I, my God? What is my nature?"— *Quid ergo sum, Deus meus? Quae natura sum?* [x. 17]). For in the "great mystery," the *grande profundum*, which man is (iv. 14), there is "something of man [*aliquid hominis*] which the spirit of man which is in him itself knoweth not. But Thou, Lord, who has made him [*fecisti eum*] knowest everything of him [*eius omnia*]" (x. 5). Thus, the most familiar of these phrases which I quoted in the text, the *quaestio mihi factus sum*, is a question raised in the presence of God, "in whose eyes I have become a question for myself" (x. 33). In brief, the answer to the question "Who am I?" is simply: "You are a man—whatever that may be"; and the answer to the question "What am I?" can be given only by God who made man. The question about the nature of man is no less a theological question than the question about the nature of God; both can be settled only within the framework of a divinely revealed answer.

3. See Augustine *De civitate Dei* xix. 2, 19.

4. William L. Westermann ("Between Slavery and Freedom," *American Historical Review*,

Vol. L [1945]) holds that the "statement of Aristotle... that craftsmen live in a condition of limited slavery meant that the artisan, when he made a work contract, disposed of two of the four elements of his free status [viz., of freedom of economic activity and right of unrestricted movement], but by his own volition and for a temporary period"; evidence quoted by Westermann shows that freedom was then understood to consist of "status, personal inviolability, freedom of economic activity, right of unrestricted movement," and slavery consequently "was the lack of these four attributes." Aristotle, in his enumeration of "ways of life" in the *Nicomachean Ethics* (i. 5) and the *Eudemian Ethics* (1215a35 ff.), does not even mention a craftsman's way of life; to him it is obvious that a *banausos* is not free (cf. *Politics* 1337b5). He mentions, however, "the life of money-making" and rejects it because it too is "undertaken under compulsion" (*Nic. Eth.* 1096a5). That the criterion is freedom is stressed in the *Eudemian Ethics:* he enumerates only those lives that are chosen *ep' exousian*.

5. For the opposition of the beautiful to the necessary and the useful see *Politics* 1333a30 ff., 1332b32.

6. For the opposition of the free to the necessary and the useful see *ibid.* 1332b2.

7. See *ibid.* 1277b8 for the distinction between despotic rule and politics. For the argument that the life of the despot is not equal to the life of a free man because the former is concerned with "necessary things," see *ibid.* 1325a24.

8. On the widespread opinion that the modern estimate of labor is Christian in origin, see below, § 44.

9. See Aquinas *Summa theologica* ii. 2. 179, esp. art. 2, where the *vita activa* arises out of the *necessitas vitae praesentis*, and *Expositio in Psalmos* 45.3, where the body politic is assigned the task of finding all that is necessary for life: *in civitate oportet invenire omnia necessaria ad vitam.*

10. The Greek word *skholē*, like the Latin *otium*, means primarily freedom from political activity and not simply leisure time, although both words are also used to indicate freedom from labor and life's necessities. In any event, they always indicate a condition free from worries and cares. An excellent description of the everyday life of an ordinary Athenian citizen, who enjoys full freedom from labor and work, can be found in Fustel de Coulanges,

The Ancient City (Anchor ed. 1956), pp. 334–36; it will convince everybody how time-consuming political activity was under the conditions of the city-state. One can easily guess how full of worry this ordinary political life was if one remembers that Athenian law did not permit remaining neutral and punished those who did not want to take sides in factional strife with loss of citizenship.

11. See Aristotle *Politics* 1333a30–33. Aquinas defines contemplation as *quies ab exterioribus motibus* (*Summa theologica* ii. 2. 179. 1).

12. Aquinas stresses the stillness of the soul and recommends the *vita activa* because it exhausts and therefore "quietens interior passions" and prepares for contemplation (*Summa theologica* ii. 2. 182. 3).

13. Aquinas is quite explicit on the connection between the *vita activa* and the wants and needs of the human body which men and animals have in common (*Summa theologica* ii. 2. 182. 1).

14. Augustine speaks of the "burden" (*sarcina*) of active life imposed by the duty of charity, which would be unbearable without the "sweetness" (*suavitas*) and the "delight of truth" given in contemplation (*De civitate Dei* xix. 19).

15. The time-honored resentment of the philosopher against the human condition of having a body is not identical with the ancient contempt for the necessities of life; to be subject to necessity was only one aspect of bodily existence, and the body, once freed of this necessity, was capable of that pure appearance the Greeks called beauty. The philosophers since Plato added to the resentment of being forced by bodily wants the resentment of movement of any kind. It is because the philosopher lives in complete quiet that it is only his body which, according to Plato, inhabits the city. Here lies also the origin of the early reproach of busy-bodiness (*polypragmosyne*) leveled against those who spent their lives in politics.

16. *Science and the Modern World*, p. 116.

17. In the *Seventh Letter* 341C: *rhēton gar oudamōs estin hōs alla mathēmata* ("for it is never to be expressed by words like other things we learn").

18. See esp. *Nicomachean Ethics* 1142a25 ff. and 1143a36 ff. The current English translation distorts the meaning because it renders *logos* as "reason" or "argument."

19. It is particularly Plato's use of the words *eidolon* and *skia* in the story of the Cave which makes the whole account read like a reversal of and a reply to Homer; for these are the key words in Homer's description of Hades in the *Odyssey*.

20. In a letter Marx wrote to Kugelmann in July, 1868.

21. This inherent worldliness of the artist is of course not changed if a "non-objective art" replaces the representation of things; to mistake this "non-objectivity" for subjectivity, where the artist feels called upon to "express himself," his subjective feelings, is the mark of charlatans, not of artists. The artist, whether painter or sculptor or poet or musician, produces worldly objects, and his reification has nothing in common with the highly questionable and, at any rate, wholly unartistic practice of expression. Expressionist art, but not abstract art, is a contradiction in terms.

Adapted from: Hannah Arendt, *The Human Condition,* pp. 7–17, 289–294, 320–325. Copyright © 1958. Reprinted by permission of the University of Chicago Press. ✦

44
The Critique of Power as Leverage

Lisa Jane Disch

If the mark of a rich and complex work of political theory is to inspire multiple interpretations, then *The Human Condition* must be counted either a great work or a hopelessly ambiguous one. Of the many books considered classics in contemporary political thought, this one may be unique for being better loved by poets than by scholars. W. H. Auden wrote that it is a book "which gives me the impression of having been especially written for me . . . [in that] it seems to answer precisely those questions which I have been putting to myself."[1] Martin Jay counters that "despite the obvious breadth of her knowledge and the unquestionable ingenuity of her mind, the political thought of Hannah Arendt is . . . [b]uilt on a foundation of arbitrary definitions and questionable, if highly imaginative, interpretations of history and previous political thought."[2] It is also unique as a study of action by a philosopher who, though she was herself no political actor "except by accident and by necessity," set out explicitly to understand politics from an activist's perspective and created a language to give it voice.[3] In fact, this vocabulary did inspire students who participated in the Free Speech Movement and Freedom Summer[4] In this chapter I lay out the terms of Arendt's political lexicon, which, I argue, establishes a vocabulary for a conception of political power that anticipates debates in contemporary feminist and democratic theory.

If this seems an implausible project, that is because Arendt's relationship to both democracy and feminism is contested. Where Jürgen Habermas credits her with writing a critique of Western political thought "which articulates the historical experiences and the normative perspectives of what we today call participatory democracy,"[5] Sheldon Wolin accuses Arendt of having a deep antagonism toward democratic equality. Wolin is relentless in his criticism of her vision, which he describes as "a politics of actors rather than citizens, agonistic rather than participatory, encouraging qualities that would enable men to stand out rather than to take part of."[6] On the other hand, Nancy Hartsock argues that Arendt participates in an alternative tradition of "women on power" because she alters "the concept of heroic action . . . shifting it away from an individual competition for dominance and toward action in connection with others with whom one shares a common life and common concerns."[7] An early essay by Hanna Pitkin appears to close Arendt's work to both feminist and democratic readings, as she pronounces that Arendt's inability to escape the confines of the classic ideal of Homeric heroism "undermine[s] her own effort to save public, political life."[8] More recently, Seyla Benhabib has argued that there are both "agonal" and "associative" dimensions to Arendt's work, the former corresponding to the exclusive realm of the *polis*, "a competitive space in which one competes for recognition, precedence and acclaim," and the latter to no particular place or time but, rather, to collective action "coordinated through speech and persuasion" wherever and whenever it occurs.[9]

I think that the debate over the question of Arendt's disposition toward the masculinized, elitist politics of the Homeric age has obscured one of the most exciting aspects of her work: Arendt's critique of the Archimedean norm. This norm consists in conceiving of power as leverage and assuming that abstract impartiality is requisite to knowledge. Arendt counters leverage with "acting in concert," which is a model of solidarity premised not on a common identity or essential sameness but on a limited, principled commitment to respond to a particular problem. She counters abstract impartiality by specifying the political and intellectual position of the pariah. Pariahs are those who are forcibly excluded from power by their persecution as a people and who learn as a consequence a special humanity and solidarity not just with their own but with other perse-cuted peoples.[10] One of the most innovative aspects of Arendt's political theory is her at-tempt, over the course of her work, to define the vantage point of the pariah without ei-ther reproducing the norm of Archimedean impartiality or lapsing into an uncritical par-tisanship.[11] Arendt's pariahs are poets, nov-elists, and essayists who would have nothing to write about if they were not embedded in the web of human experience but whose very commitment to the act of *writing* means that they are not fully at home anywhere in the world. They are marginals in the sense of ex-isting on the fringes of a plurality of inter-secting worlds, neither at the "absolute mar-gin" of the Archimedean vantage point nor at the center of a particular tribe.[12]

In *The Human Condition*, Arendt takes up the position of the pariah, or self-con-sciously marginal critic, by claiming to write in "manifest contradiction to the tradition" of Western political theory (HC, 17). From the start, Arendt positions herself as a critic who works within a tradition while attempt-ing to renegotiate its fundamental assump-tions. She considers the first and most im-portant of these to be the belief—that she takes to originate with Plato and to deter-mine the course of the tradition thereafter—that the ideal *polis* "has no aim other than to make possible the philosopher's way of life" (14). To this end, philosophers have at-tempted to discipline the noisy inconsisten-cies of politics by turning "action into a mode of making" (229). The success of this project "is easily attested by the whole termi-nology of political theory and political thought, which indeed makes it almost im-possible to discuss these matters without using the category of means and ends and thinking in terms of instrumentality" (229). This argument locates Arendt in a tradition of critics of modernity that includes thinkers on the left—from Marx, to Weber, to the Frankfurt school—and the right—from Nietzsche, to Heidegger, to Allan Bloom—who have chronicled and protested the rise of instrumental rationality.

What makes Arendt's position in this tra-dition interesting is that her work is not easy to locate on the left-right ideological contin-uum. She is most often recognized for argu-ing that action is in danger of disappearing from the modern age because of the rise of the social, which she describes as the infil-tration of the public realm, an arena that should be reserved for human excellence in speech and action, by the routine tasks asso-ciated with "housekeeping," or the satisfac-tion of human needs (28). Although this ar-gument allies Arendt with the right by affirming a traditional separation of eco-nomics and politics, there is a second aspect of her critique of modernity that is less fre-quently remarked upon. Arendt argues that action is endangered not only by the bu-reaucratization of public life but also by the very language of politics and political philos-ophy. Language is crucial to the possibility of action because the public realm exists only by virtue of the "presence of others who see what we see and hear what we hear" (50). Ac-cording to Arendt, deeds and the various in-terpretations they inspire in those who wit-ness them constitute the "reality" of politics. Absent a language that admits of meaningful distinctions between instrumental behavior and principled conduct, *there can be no ac-tion at all.* This claim that the language of the Western tradition is inadequate for princi-pled action makes Arendt a pariah to that tradition. Her project in *The Human Condi-tion* is to introduce a new lexicon of political theory that provides for the possibility of act-ing on principle.[13]

Despite Arendt's claim to write "in mani-fest contradiction" against the fundamental assumptions of Western political theory, her most important works seem at once to break new ground and retreat from it (HC, 17). Arendt's groundbreaking acts are her cri-tique of Archimedean posturing in philoso-phy and her creation of a new lexicon of poli-tics that begins with the terms *plurality, natality,* and *publicity.*[14] Her retreat is the distinction she draws between the "public" and the "social," which echoes classic dualisms. These two aspects of her theory are internally inconsistent. Arendt's claim that there is a crisis of freedom in the mod-ern world that is due to the erosion of the boundaries that protect the private and pub-lic realms from the pressures of necessity and her narration of this crisis of modernity as a story about the "rise of the social" are nothing short of an Archimedean pronouncement (HC, 38). But it is precisely such pronouncements and such narratives against which she directs her critique of political philosophy. Thus, the position Arendt takes as a theorist in the Western political tradition who writes against its fundamental assumptions is more radical than the one she takes up as a public intellectual in contemporary debates about the putative crisis of modernity.

No doubt, these inconsistencies are one reason Arendt's work has generated a multiplicity of incompatible readings. I do not aim to reconcile the tensions in Arendt's work or to resolve the confusions her writing has generated. But I will argue that many scholars have read and evaluated her work in light of the very norms and assumptions she calls into question, thereby playing out on its terrain the drama of assimilation that protects established ideas against the challenges of pariahs.[15] I propose to do with her work what she did with the writings of Lessing, Kafka, and others whom she deemed pariahs: to read it through the frame of its most radical insights.

Political theorists who are in search of models of democratic politics adequate to challenges raised by contemporary feminism and other critical theories are mistaken to rule Arendt's work out of consideration. Her work anticipates two distinct but mutually implicating problems in contemporary democratic theory. The first is the problem of solidarity or the "unified public," and the second is that of public judgment.

As Iris Young has argued, contemporary theorists of participatory democracy have tended to make collective action contingent on the achievement of a "unified public that in practice tends to exclude or silence some groups."[16] Even when democrats explicitly acknowledge differences among citizens and recognize the inevitability of conflict, the ideal of the unified public can be smuggled into a theory in two ways. This can happen as a result of cultural imperialism, which is the failure by a dominant group to recognize that it is just one social group among others

and that its values and practices are no less particular than those of the various groups it constructs as different. The ideal of the unified public can also insinuate itself into a conception of democracy through what Nancy Fraser calls the "socio-cultural means of interpretation and communication."[17] These might be summed up as the authoritative "voice" through which groups constitute themselves in public and articulate demands for resources and other forms of recognition. The ideal of the unified public emerges whenever a community advances a narrow conception of voice, whether it be defined juridically, as an argument to which any reasonable person would have to assent, or romantically, as the shared intuitions and experiences of a particular alienated group. I argue in this chapter that Arendt's new lexicon of politics offers a conception of solidarity that is not unifying because it appeals to neither a common identity nor a reductionist conception of rationality but, instead, is enacted by means of promising.

The second point at which Arendt's work intersects with contemporary democratic theory is the problem of public judgment. If Benjamin Barber is correct in claiming that democratic politics calls for "public action and thus for reasonable public choice, in the presence of conflict and in the absence of private or independent grounds for judgment," then its possibility depends on there being some way to justify public principles and goals that neither reintroduces an abstract imperative nor plays on parochial prejudice.[18] Like many contemporary theorists, Arendt argued that rationalist moral imperatives and prejudices, however different they may be in theory, have a similar political effect in that both impose a certainty on politics that forecloses debate and relieves citizens of their responsibility to make decisions.[19] . . .

In this chapter I lay out Arendt's critique of one aspect of the Archimedean norm, its construction of power as leverage. I argue that the vision of politics she recommends is neither elitist nor stereotypically male. After explicating Arendt's vocabulary in such a way as to highlight its possible connections to contemporary democratic and feminist theory, in the concluding section I identify the ways in which Arendt reproduces aspects of Western political thought that are antagonistic to both of these.

Criticizing Political Philosophy as Archimedean Thinking

Archimedean thinking is characterized by a claim to a vantage point outside of time and place that is, by virtue of its disinterested impartiality, uniquely and exclusively qualified to arbitrate worldly conflicts of interest. This vantage point purports to be detached and disembodied, that is, it ignores particular characteristics such as skin color, gender, and sexual or ethnic identity. In contemporary critical theories, the Archimedean point is frequently invoked as an exemplar of the myth of perfect objectivity, the claim to a position from which to observe and to judge "reality" without participating in it or having an impact on it.[20] It is taken to be a classic example of the legitimation of unlimited power by a claim to knowledge that purports to be disconnected from political interests.

Although Arendt is a critic of the Archimedean norm, she describes it somewhat differently. She argues that, far from concealing the knowledge/power relationship, Archimedes quite explicitly sought the position at which knowledge and power intersect. What Archimedes wanted was to move the earth, and what he proposed was a theory of leverage, recognizing that "our power over things grows in proportion to our distance from them."[21] Thus, the Archimedean point is not *beyond* power but, rather, a position from which to exercise a certain kind of power made possible by the claim to a certain kind of knowledge. In contrast to Michel Foucault and to critical theories influenced by his work, Arendt does not claim that truth is always complicit in power relations; rather, she makes a more limited claim only against the Archimedean norm.[22] She argues that its model of objective detachment assimilates *both* knowledge and power to a mechanical model of leverage that, when applied to the realm of human affairs, becomes an exhortation to force. Furthermore, the problem she identifies with the Archimedean model of

knowledge is not even that it claims to be impartial but that its version of impartiality takes the thinker too far out of the world. Arendt writes that although "we must always remove ourselves . . . from the object we wish to study . . . the withdrawal needed for cognitive acts is much more limited than what Archimedes . . . had in mind." As she sees it, the problem with the Archimedean vantage point is that it makes *abstraction* a requisite of impartiality and thereby makes possible the exercise of power absent "any attention to human interests."[23] Arendt's claim differs from those of radical critics of humanism in two respects. Not only does she hold open the possibility for ways of knowing that do not involve the subjugation of the self and of others, but she even suggests that it might be possible to have some version of impartiality that would not be detached from "human interests."

Though her critique of knowledge is carefully qualified, Arendt's argument against the tradition of Western political philosophy is quite sweeping. She argues that political philosophers of the tradition are to be faulted for reproducing the knowledge/power relation that is prescribed by the Archimedean norm.[24] The heart of her criticism is that Plato, and those political philosophers who followed him, have written about politics as if from an Archimedean vantage point that assumes not just that the life of the mind is preferable to that of action but also that the latter has to be constrained for the sake of the former. It is this second assumption, that "every kind of activity, even the processes of mere thought, must culminate in the absolute quiet of contemplation," to which Arendt objects because it has produced a tradition of political philosophy that is inimical to action (HC, 15). The problem is that all political philosophers are Archimedean thinkers who have conceived of politics in terms of "the concept of rule," which Arendt defines as "the notion that men can lawfully and politically live together only when some are entitled to command and the others forced to obey" (222). Arendt rejects this conception of politics by introducing a distinction between rulership and leadership.

Rulership and leadership can be distinguished on the basis of their different constructions of the relationship between knowledge and action. Rulership, Arendt claims, "opens a gulf" between two modes of action that the Greeks prior to Plato considered interconnected (222). These two modes are "the *beginning* made by a single person and the *achievement* in which many join by 'bearing' and 'finishing' the enterprise, by seeing it through" (189; emphasis added). Plato not only separates these modes of action but also casts them hierarchically and in opposition to each other, defining beginning as a function of knowledge and achievement as a function of execution without thought. Thus, rulers exert the power of their expertise over subjects whose task it is to execute commands. If the two modes—beginning and achievement—are understood to be interconnected aspects of action, then there can be no vanguard but the tasks of leaders and followers must be interdependent. The leader, who begins or "set[s] something into motion," is dependent for its achievement on the help of others who "join the enterprise of their own accord, with their own motives and aims," (177, 222). In turn, those who participate in achieving the action depend upon the leader "for an occasion to act themselves "(189). Although Arendt recognizes a distinction between leaders and participants, both are simultaneously knowers and doers; consequently, the relationship between the two is one of collaboration rather than command.

Leaders depend on the spontaneous participation of a plurality of others who are actors in their own right and who, as such, can neither predict nor control the course of events they set into motion. Philosophers have attempted to substitute vanguard rule for leadership "in the hope that the realm of human affairs may escape the haphazardness and moral irresponsibility inherent in a plurality of agents" (220). Consequently, "he who acts never quite knows what he is doing [and so] . . . becomes 'guilty' of consequences he never intended or even foresaw" (233). The advantage of vanguard rule is that it introduces a "division between those who know and do not act and those who act and know

do not know," thereby assigning full responsibility to the ruler in exchange for absolute sovereignty over the subjects (223). This separation of knowledge from action is the definitive character of sovereignty.

Arendt describes leadership in a letter to Karl Jaspers. She writes that the "most remarkable thing" about the student protests against the Viet Nam War at the University of Chicago was that "there were no leaders before, but then leaders emerged. Primarily responsible for the exemplary order was a very gifted, twenty-year old Jewish girl who led the proceedings and had absolute authority" (C [*Correspondence*], 641). In contrast to rulers, leaders emerge in the very performance of an action. Their authority rests not on credentials, prior expertise, or an "office," but on the things they do and say at the scene.

Arendt's critique of rulership, then, is a critique of the Archimedean norm. This norm has two aspects, both of which carry perverse consequences for politics. It prescribes a model of power as control over others. This power is legitimated, in turn, by a model of knowledge as that which is prior to the "human interests" of a particular time and place. She counters this norm with a model of collaborative power and situated knowledge.

The New Political Lexicon

Arendt effects her departure from the philosopher's view of politics with a metaphor: that freedom and power are not individual prerogatives but, rather, conditional on "the human ability not just to act but to act in concert" (OV [*On Violence*], 44). She takes the premise from which philosophers have tried to escape, that politics begins with "a plurality of agents" in relation to each other, and transforms it from an "intrinsic 'weakness' " of the human condition to a source of uniquely human power (HC, 234). In opposition to philosophers' claim that freedom is impossible if one must depend on the collaboration of others who are knowers and actors in their own right, Arendt claims that solitary sovereignty is not possible for human beings; human freedom depends, instead, on collective action. To unfold the implications of "acting in concert" as a critique of Archimedean thinking and an alternative to it, it is necessary to first lay out Arendt's new lexicon of politics, beginning with the terms *natality* and *plurality*.

The first and most important word in Arendt's lexicon is "plurality," which she calls "*the* condition—not only the *conditio sine qua non*, but the *conditio per quam*—of all political life" (HC, 7). Plurality is a rich term, with several intertwining meanings. Most simply, it names human multiplicity. It signifies that "men, not Man, live on the earth and inhabit the world" (7). It also names diversity, which she describes paradoxically as *sameness* in *difference*. By this she does not mean that deep down we are all the same in spite of apparent differences, but that "we are all the same, that is, human, in such a way that nobody is ever the same as anyone else who ever lived, lives, or will live" (8). This second aspect of plurality means that the possibility of community is never simply given or essential to human beings but must, rather, be built by speech and action. Finally, plurality names the fact of human interconnection, the "web of human relationships which exists wherever men live together" (184). This web is actualized in speech, the faculty by which human beings communicate what is distinct about themselves and acknowledge others as equals (178). Plurality is *the* condition of political life because if it were destroyed or suppressed, "the world, which can form only in the interspaces between men in all their variety, would vanish altogether" (MDT [*Men in Dark Times*], 31).

Next to plurality, the most important word in Arendt's lexicon is "natality," "the capacity of beginning something anew, that is, of acting" (HC, 9). Natality is not literally synonymous with birth; rather, it is a "second birth" in which we begin "something new on our own initiative" (176–177). She writes, "Politically speaking, the decisive trait of the human condition is not that men are mortal, but that they are being born; birth, rather than death, is the decisive factor in all political organization which must ever stand ready to receive new beginners into a communal pattern which is more per-

manent than each of them."[25] To think of natality in terms of biological birth is to lose what makes it distinctive for Arendt, which is that natality is neither the inevitable outcome of a biological process nor the equally inevitable consequence of social conditioning. She calls natality "a second birth" in which "With word and deed we insert ourselves into the human world" (HC, 176). Where the first birth is the involuntary outcome of biological and technological processes, this second birth is the outcome of the education we receive after we are born. The task of education is not just socialization, but individuation, to inspire "beginners" with the spirit "of undertaking something new, something unforeseen by us" (BPF [*Between Past and Future*], 196). Education culminates in natality—the enactment of something new.

Although it seems more straightforward than the concept of plurality, natality is also a concept in which many themes intersect. One of these might be termed the dilemma of entrance. Emancipated Jews in Europe prior to the Holocaust who were confronted with the task of integration into Christian society faced three possible courses of action. These were to accept the terms of that world as it was and assimilate to it (the course of the *parvenu*), to establish enclaves of Jewish culture even at the cost of material deprivation (the course of the pariah), or to attempt to enter society and change it to acknowledge Jews *as Jews*. The last one, the course of the conscious pariah, is an entrance in the spirit of natality because it means refusing both separatism and assimilation. It may be "stimulated by the presence of others whose company we may wish to join, but . . . never conditioned by them" (HC, 177). Thus, it is original in two distinct senses, as a spontaneous public performance, and as an act of judgment. Dagmar Barnouw brings out this second aspect, describing it as an act of "choosing the company with whom one wants to spend one's life (of the mind)."[26] Natality is an act of individuation that is achieved, paradoxically, by a declaration of connection to those whom one respects enough to want to be joined in friendship with. It is, then, far more complex than it appears, encapsulating themes from Arendt's post-war writings on Jewish identity and anticipating her last writings on judgment.

A deep respect for individuality inheres in the terms natality and plurality that is distinct from competitive individualism. Arendt celebrates initiative but defines it against the grain of the image of the lone hero who succeeds against the odds of the mediocrity that surrounds him. Where the lone hero story sets up an opposition between individualism and community, Arendt transforms both sides of this dichotomy. She argues that individuality, although of course at odds with conformity, depends on being recognized by people one respects and recognizes in turn. This tension Arendt maintains between individuality and community is one of the distinctive aspects of her political theory. She affirms that every person is unique but cautions that this individuality only manifests itself in acting in concert with others.

There is a third concept that is so critical to Arendt's political vision that it is surprising that she does not make it a distinct term in her lexicon. This concept is "publicity," which means everything that "can be seen and heard by everybody" and the "common world" that is both the artifice created by human hands and the "affairs which go on among those who inhabit the man-made world together."[27] The distinctively political connotation of publicity is openness, which exists wherever a question, problem, or event is submitted to argumentation. Publicity depends on natality, which initiates the process of discussion, and on plurality, which gives it a space in which to occur. This space, the public realm, exists by: "the simultaneous presence of innumerable perspectives and aspects in which the common world presents itself and for which no common measurement or denominator can ever be devised. For though the common world is the common meeting ground of all, those who are present have different locations in it, and the location of one can no more coincide with the location of another than the location of two objects." Public realms exist wherever those who gather to discuss an event or a problem "see and hear from a dif-

ferent position" (HC, 57). Their multiple locations guarantee that they will not be fused together, as in the collective will of a totalitarian regime, but arrayed around an open space.[28]

Arendt calls this space variously the "interspace" (MDT, 31), "inbetween" or "*inter-est*, which lies between people and therefore can relate and bind them together" (HC, 182). She writes, "This 'between' can be a common ground and it can be a common purpose; it always fulfills the double function of binding men together *and* separating them in an articulate way" (R ["A Reply"], 81). With her insistence on commonality and articulate separation, Arendt makes an observation that bears on the conflict between proponents of "unitary" democracy who envision political community grounded in an essential sympathy, and proponents of "adversary" democracy, who argue that given a diversity of identities and interests, abstract procedure is the best protection against tyranny.[29] Although these two seem quite different in that the former is premised on unity and cooperation and the latter on competition, Arendt's work suggests that they are alike in leaving individuals' points of connection and points of difference unstated and unarticulated. Where attention to differences jeopardizes unitary democracy, which depends on the myth of a common consciousness that is so deeply felt that it would not be contested and may not even need to be stated, the effort to achieve commonality is simply irrelevant in a liberal democratic society, which is adversarial precisely because it is assumed that contestation is *all* there is and no common interest can come of it. Consequently, the integrity of liberal democracy turns on a tacit consensus with respect to the procedures that guarantee the interests and rights of individuals in the abstract. With Arendt, contemporary critical theorists have argued that both unitary identity politics and adversarial liberalism tend toward homogeneity, the former by virtue of assuming that "we" all are particular in the same way (i.e., as blacks, as sisters), and the latter by virtue of abstract categories that purport to be neutral but in fact represent a particular perspective.[30]

Arendt's suggestion of the possibility of a common interest that accomplishes the contradictory task of uniting individuals and separating them in an "articulate way" departs in important ways from both liberal and communitarian understandings of interest. In contrast to the interests of interest group pluralism, Arendt's interests are not private bargaining chips, defined with reference to individual goals and traded competitively on the political "market." In contrast to the communitarian ideal, the *"inter-est"* is not a common cause that in some way expresses the authentic beings of its disparate participants and harmonizes their wills. That she calls it an "in-between" suggests that it is a commonality; at the same time, however, her insistence on argumentation suggests that commonality does not mean concord. As she puts it, the public realm is an "area in which there are many voices and where the announcement of what each 'deems truth' both links and separates men, establishing in fact those distances between men which together comprise the world" (MDT, 30). Arendt defines *"inter-est"* with characteristic perversity. It is not a commonality that unites individuals, such as a competitively achieved bargain or revealed common essence, but one that "links and separates" them: the "between" that sustains Arendtian solidarity is *distance*.

Arendt's description of the public space as an area that is created when people exchange the "announcement of what each 'deems truth,'" suggests that there is a relationship between *"inter-est"* and principle. This relationship is not deterministic, where the common interest would simply follow from shared principles. Rather, the *"inter-est"* is a matter of principle that lies "in-between" in the sense that it affects citizens' relationships with each other sufficiently to move them to argument and possibly to collective action. It can be defined only as they debate the terms of those relationships and as they learn, over the course of an action, what is compelling enough to sustain a collective commitment.

It is crucial to Arendt's conception of action that *"inter-est,"* which is the catalyst to action, not be defined as a determining force, which would put it at odds with natality. Consequently, she is careful to differentiate principles from motives and intents. Motives and goals are "determining factors" that necessarily reduce action to behavior; in order to conceive of action in terms of natality, as that activity in which freedom is "primarily experienced," there must be a political language for action that can call it to account without deducing it either from a predetermined motive or a projected goal. Arendt's answer to this problem is the "principle" that neither determines nor calculates an action, but "inspire[s], as it were, from without." Because they are not internal to individuals' wills, principles are distinct from motives; they are also "much too general to prescribe particular goals, although every particular aim can be judged in the light of its principle once the act has been started" (BPF, 151–152). As is typical of Arendt, her remarks at this crucial point in her thought are brief and beguiling; she seems at once to invoke and to resist the conventional understanding of principles.

For example, her list of principles includes some customary examples—honor, glory, virtue, distinction, excellence—together, surprisingly, with "fear or distrust or hatred." While the first five of these are typically timeless and abstract ideals, the last three are emotional responses that can be principled depending on the context in which they are expressed. Even more contradictory than her list of principles is her discussion of their characteristics. She seems to make timelessness a feature of principles when she asserts that they differ from goals in that they "can be repeated time and time again" and from motives in that their "validity . . . is universal . . . not bound to any particular person or to any particular group." But she retreats from this position when she introduces a second set of distinctions among "the judgment of the intellect which *precedes* action . . . the command of the will which *initiates* it, [and] the *inspiring* principle [that] becomes fully manifest only in the performing act itself" (emphasis added; BPF, 152). Here she differentiates principles from concepts and from imperatives, both of which can be stated in words and apprehended intellectually. Principles have to be enacted. As such, they are embedded in history and their meaning, though not their validity, is tied to the particular stories they inspire. Finally, principles seem to be neither concrete nor abstract; they are not concrete because they can never be fully realized but are subject to "inexhaustible" repetition, and they are not abstract because they have to be seen and heard by everybody.

Although it eludes definition in terms of the usual oppositions between universality and particularity, reason and emotion, and ideal and actuality, this conception of principle makes perfect sense in light of publicity. Principles do not motivate action, they cannot be used to pass judgment on it, nor can they be achieved by it. But they are uniquely public in that it is in action that they come to light. The speeches that people make in the attempt to cast a problem, event, or question as an "*inter-est*" and the actions they make in response to it reveal their principles. This is not to say that principles can be stated by a declaration of purpose or list of accomplishments; this suggests that they can be fully determined and so confuses them with motives and goals. Although a person can be said to "have" motives and goals, a principle cannot be possessed by or attributed to anyone. Principles are revealed indirectly by what we say and do, not defined by what we say about them or claim to do in their name. Principles are the intangible "in-between" that sustains Arendtian solidarity.

Principled solidarity is Arendt's proposed alternative to liberal and communitarian understandings of common good. This alternative is a politics defined neither by an all-encompassing common identity nor by a putatively natural characteristic such as rational self-interest; rather, it is defined by a question or problem that admits of principled disagreement. As she puts it, "The reality of the public realm relies on the simultaneous presence of innumerable perspectives and aspects in which the common world presents itself" (HC, 57). In other words Arendt's concept of publicity redefines solidarity by shifting the locus of the possible common purpose that inspires collective action from the "inner selves" of political ac-

tors to an "articulated" common interest in the world.[31] This would be a duplicitous move if Arendt simply instantiated a putative "common world" in place of "common sense." Although Arendt maintains that there is a common world "out there" separate from individuals' perceptions of it, she argues that in itself this world is no more than a "meeting ground" that in no way determines or produces a common interest. On the contrary, Arendt writes that "Without being talked about by men and without housing them, the world would not be a human artifice but a heap of unrelated things to which each isolated individual was at liberty to add one more object" (HC 204). The "common world," then, is not present *in itself* in the public realm; instead, it only appears refracted through the perspectives and aspects that "throw light" on an event (MDT, viii). Consequently, the bases for common interests are no more "out there" to be seen than they are "given" by a common identity or consciousness.

Arendt's answer to the problem of collective self-determination in a plural society is this conception of public spaces that exist around common interests that are relative to a particular situation. But the terms of this situation are not given in advance, and neither are its members designated in advance. Rather, it is by means of disagreeing about the meaning of an event or problem that people talk themselves into a common situation. What they have in common is not something inside them. Instead, commonality is potentially "in" a situation, depending on how that situation is defined. This potential is realized if, in exchanging the "innumerable perspectives and aspects" in which the situation appears to each of them, people manage to articulate these aspects into an interpretation that renders it a problem compelling enough to inspire their cooperative action. Even among those who decide to make common cause, commonality is not discovered by recognizing how "we" are all alike; rather, it is constructed by learning how each of us sees differently. The articulation of a public space involves committing to an action while acknowledging the possibility of ongoing differences among the participants and providing for the possibility of continuing public criticism.[32]

I have argued so far that Arendt's understanding of democracy differs from both the liberal pluralist conception of adversarial interest group competition and the unitary ideal that identity politics often presupposes. A further distinction can be made between Arendt's "plurality" and the radical pluralism that purportedly describes the "postmodern condition." Lyotard characterizes postmodern society as a discontinuous aggregate of incommensurable language games. Using terms that call Arendt's "web" of plurality to mind, he describes a social "fabric formed by the intersection of at least two (and in reality an indeterminate number of) language games, obeying different rules."[33] There is a crucial difference between Arendt and Lyotard, however. Where Lyotard takes "plurality" to denote the presence of incommensurable differences, Arendt claims not the *incommensurability* of differences but their *irreducibility* "to a common measurement or denominator." This distinction is important because irreducibility holds out the possibility of intersubjective dialogue and mutual understanding. At the same time, however, the fact of plurality suggests the likelihood that such dialogue will generate not one all-encompassing public but various publics with various *inter-ests*; in turn, the articulation of *inter-est* within them will involve dispute and conflict.[34]

Arendt's new lexicon of politics addresses the problem of the unitary public by redefining solidarity from something that is grounded in abstract rationality or common identity to something that is articulated by means of public speech and action. This redefinition of solidarity opens the way for Arendt to propose a new understanding of collective action, one that draws its energy not from unanimity but from plurality. This is what she is getting at with the metaphor "acting in concert." The possibility for acting in concert exists *in potential* wherever people who are otherwise different meet in a common situation and manage to articulate its various aspects into an interpretation that renders it a problem that is compelling

enough to inspire their collective action. By the articulation of a common problem, they open a space "in-between" and constitute themselves as a public. The question is, Just what is the process of articulation by which publics are constituted?

It is significant that there is no theoretical account of the processes of collective speech and action in *The Human Condition*. Absent such an account, as Jürgen Habermas has argued, Arendt has no way to differentiate between an ideologically forced consensus and a publicly achieved democratic agreement.[35] The closest Arendt herself comes to such an account is in an unpublished essay, written in 1954, in which she presents Socratic dialogue as a model of public discourse.[36] In her discussion of the dialogues of the "historical" Socrates, Arendt confirms what is only implicit in *The Human Condition*—that articulating a common interest does not mean resolving all difference and dissent into an all-encompassing communal consensus but means, on the contrary, coming to understand just how different we may be apart from our concern with the specific matter at hand.[37]

Arendt sees in the Socratic dialogue a shift of solidarity from the self to the world that is similar to that which she effects with publicity. According to this model, the possibility for commonality is not in the essential identities of the persons in conversation but in the fact that they exist in the same world. But, even though the sameness of that world is a given, the commonality is not. This distinction between sameness and commonality follows from plurality: that any situation is constituted by a plurality of perspectives means that people can be in a "same" situation without having a common experience. For sameness to take on the quality of a common-ness about which one feels deeply enough to take action in concert, there must be an exchange of perspectives so that each friend comes to understand "More than his friend as a person, [but] . . . how and in which specific articulateness the common world appears to the other who as a person is forever unequal or different."[38] This exchange takes place in the Socratic dialogue, which neither begins from a common consciousness nor proceeds by means of empathic identification. It starts instead from the assumption that "the world opens up differently to every man, according to his position in it; and that the 'sameness' of the world, its common-ness . . . or 'objectivity' (as we would say from the subjective viewpoint of modern philosophy) resides in the fact that the same world opens up to all and that despite all differences between men and their positions in the world—and consequently their *doxai* (opinions)—'both you and I are human'." What Arendt is describing in this somewhat unwieldy sentence is a process of articulation that begins from plurality, the recognition of equal humanity in light of differences. The condition that makes this articulation possible is friendship, which equalizes the discussants, not economically but politically, by enabling them to "become equal partners in a common world."[39] It is friendship that makes possible the articulation of common interests.

The kind of friendship Arendt has in mind is not intimacy, but public friendship, mediated by individuals' partnership in a common world. It is the common world, and the distance it imposes between friends, that makes room for plurality in the relationship.[40] Intimate friendship values sameness, which is confirmed in personal conversations that proceed by the intuitive recognition of another's point of view with a minimum of explanation. By contrast, in public conversation, the claim to immediate understanding is suspect, because it shuts down communication. Where intimate exchanges begin in mutual recognition, public dialogue might be described as beginning in what Mikhail Bakhtin calls "mutual non-understanding," proceeding in the mode of translation.[41] Conversation in the mode of translation is the process that makes it possible to understand the "specific articulateness" in which the world appears to the plurality of individuals located in it.

There is an example of public friendship in Arendt's exchange with Gershom Scholem over *Eichmann in Jerusalem.* The comment she writes to Gershom Scholem about their strongly worded and deeply felt differences of opinion over that work illustrates just how much she prizes debate and difference as an aspect of public friendship and how important she took that kind of exchange to be in political life. Urging Scholem to publish his criticisms of her work and her response not in the third person but in their original form as a personal exchange of letters, she tells him that "The value of this controversy consists in its epistolary character, namely in the fact that it is informed by personal friendship" (JP [*The Jew as Pariah*], 251).

Although suggestive, the model of the Socratic dialogue is inadequate to the task of specifying the means by which to articulate a common *inter-est*. First, it prescribes face-to-face, one-on-one communication that is not transferrable to politics. Second, Arendt's stipulations about the "historical" Socrates notwithstanding, his rhetorical skill is a kind of power that it would be disingenuous to deny if he is to be a model of democratic citizenship.[42] Possibly Arendt never developed this line of argument for publication because she recognized its inadequacy. In any case, her failure to specify the communicative practices by which democratic communities can be articulated is an important shortfall in her account of the public space.

So far, I have explicated three words that I take to be the most important terms in Arendt's political vocabulary: plurality, natality, and publicity. I have argued that these terms anticipate contemporary critical theorists' attempts to provide a nonfoundationalist account of democratic community. That is, a community grounded neither in common identity nor in universally valid moral principles. Arendt attempts to account for the possibility of solidarity and collective action without either invoking an underlying common identity or appealing to transcendent reason. I think Arendt's account is distinctive for the tension in her concept of plurality, which affirms that the starting place of political theory is simultaneously the irreducible differentiation of human beings and their inextricable connectedness across those differences. Arendt argues for a democratic public space constituted by common interests, but at the same time she maintains that commonality is not the *ground* of politics but is revealed in public speeches and actions. I have also noted that in *The Human Condition* Arendt breaks off this train of thought without completing it because she fails to specify the institutions and practices in which individuals can be bound together and separated "in an articulate way." I turn now to examine Arendt's critique of the Western political tradition in greater detail.

Promise-Making—An Alternative Conception of Power

When Arendt looks at Western political philosophy through the lens of her new lexicon, the results are startling. She finds that "Our political tradition is almost unanimous in holding that freedom begins where men have left the realm of public life inhabited by the many, and that it is not experienced in association with others but in intercourse with one's self" (BPF, 157). If the tradition is any example, then "political philosophy" is an oxymoron. It "tends to derive the political side of human life from the necessity which compels the human animal to live together with others, rather than from the human capacity to act," regards plurality as an "unfortunate" weakness, and aims to "enable the philosopher at least to live undisturbed by it."[43] Philosophy is irreconcilably at odds with politics because solitude, not plurality, is for the philosopher a "way of life and a condition of work" (OT [*The Origins of Totalitarianism*], 476). The effort to escape plurality is evidenced in philosophers' attempts to "replace acting with making [which] is manifest in the whole body of argument against 'democracy' [and] which, the more consistently and better reasoned it is, will turn into an argument against the essentials of politics" (HC, 220).

This orientation toward solitude and contemplation gives philosophers a distorted understanding of power and freedom. She claims that they mistake strength—"the fallacy of the strong man who is powerful because he is alone"—for power (190), and sovereignty—"the ideal of uncompromising self-sufficiency and mastership"—for freedom (234). Where valuing strength identifies power with leverage, valuing sovereignty

identifies freedom with free will. The philosophical view is ultimately self-defeating because, as Arendt remarks, "If it were true that sovereignty and freedom are the same, then indeed no man could be free, because sovereignty, the ideal of uncompromising self-sufficiency and mastership, is contradictory to the very condition of plurality" (234). This preoccupation with sovereignty in the Western political tradition might be deemed a kind of "philosophical onanism"—the wish that politics were something one could do with oneself and power and freedom could be enjoyed without interference by others.

It is tempting to read Arendt's critique of this traditional confusion of power with mastery in terms of contemporary feminist theory. There is an intimation of that work in her references to the "fallacy of the strong man who is powerful because he is alone" and to historical "examples of the impotence of the strong and superior man who does not know how to enlist the help, the co-acting of his fellow men" (188–189). These references bear some similarity to feminists' claim that the purportedly abstract ideal of the rational individual is not neutral but male and that its autonomy is an illusion sustained by some form of dominance.[44] But Arendt's is not a "feminist" critique of power, at least not in the sense of an argument in which gender is a central category and for which discerning sexism is a principal hermeneutic objective.

Arendt explains the traditional misconceptions about freedom and power in terms of the fact that the men responsible for them were *philosophers*, not that they were privileged as *men*. The problem with the philosophical perspective is that it identifies freedom exclusively with contemplation and reduces all worldly activity with necessity, thereby blurring "the distinctions and articulations within the *vita activa* itself" (17). It is because they disregard the differences among the tasks of politics and those of labor and work that they mistake power, which Arendt calls a "potentiality in being together," for a physical property that can be "possessed like strength or applied like force" (201). Arendt reconfigures this traditional conception of power to be conditional on plurality.

Although Adrienne Rich judged it to be irredeemably misogynist in 1976, it is precisely Arendt's silence about gender, ironic as it may seem, that makes a partial connection to contemporary feminist work. Specifically, her reconfiguration of power intersects with efforts to reposition gender in feminist theory and politics. This is a response to the charge that the unquestioned primacy of gender directed feminist theory toward analyses of women's difference from and oppression by men at the expense of recognizing differences of race, class, and ethnicity among women. In turn, it focused the movement on the needs of white middle-class professional women, which is probably the only social group that could perceive gender to be a sole or exclusive obstacle to its life chances.[45] In this context, the task of feminism is not to define "feminine" models of power but to define and practice democracy in what Iris Young calls a "heterogeneous public."[46] It would be rash to attempt to recover Arendt as a feminist in spite of herself, given that she quite explicitly distanced herself from the movement; nonetheless, I agree with Maria Markus that given Arendt's treatment of themes such as plurality, her work has received less attention from feminist theorists than it merits.[47]

Public power is Arendt's counter to the Archimedean ideal of power as leverage. But in contrast to the civic public, which Young has criticized for its aspiration to "transcend particularities of interest and affiliation to seek a common good," Arendt begins from the assumption that if power is public, then it can be held only on the condition of plurality, *the* condition of public space.[48] If power, like the public space, is contingent on plurality, then it depends on being connected to and distinct from others in an articulate way. Power cannot be exercised as leverage over others; it exists only *in relationships with* them. It is "generated when people gather together and 'act in concert,' [and] disappears the moment they depart" (HC, 244). Consequently, it "is always, as we would say, a power potential and not an unchangeable, measurable, and reliable entity like force or

strength" (200). Where leverage is calculable, power *in relationship* is uncertain; it rests "upon the unreliable and only temporary agreement of many wills and intentions" and so shifts with the ebb and flow of those alliances (201). Unlike articulated solidarity, this power is not founded on a pre-political ground like truth, faith, shared identity, or even force. Rather, it is constituted by a "mutual promise" to act on a specific response to an interpreted situation (HC, 245).[49]

Promise-making is the alternative Arendt proposes to the Archimedean fiction of power as sovereignty or leverage. Unlike the fiction of mastery, which is an attempt to escape the web of plurality and to deny "the impossibility of foretelling the consequences of an act within a community of equals where everybody has the same capacity to act," promise-making acknowledges those limits and attempts to work within them. She calls promising "the only alternative to a mastery which relies on domination of one's self and rule over others," because promising brings into being a sovereignty that is necessarily shared (because you cannot make a promise to yourself) and limited by "an agreed purpose." Promising creates "isolated islands of certainty in an ocean of uncertainty" by defining an action to which the promisers agree to be bound. Mutual promise serves to mitigate the uncertainty of acting under the conditions of natality and plurality while protecting those conditions. It is because a promise is only a partial abrogation of both natality and plurality that it focuses individuals on a *limited* common purpose. That this purpose be a precisely specified short-term goal is crucial to the legitimacy of a promise, because the "basic unreliability" of human beings conditioned by natality puts it beyond their capacity to commit to anything absolutely. Human beings "never can guarantee today who they will be tomorrow" and so cannot bind themselves exclusively to a purpose that supercedes all others in perpetuity (HC, 244–245).

This stipulation that promising temporarily unite actors around a specific "agreed purpose" may seem at odds with Arendt's insistence that action not be reduced to its motives or goals. This critique of political instrumentalism is central to her critique of modernity as an era that has eroded the distinction between action, which is meaningful, and work, which is merely useful. That utility had increasingly become a political imperative she took to be a consequence of the rise of the social, with its constriction of public space and denigration of human ideals. Although it seems inconsistent, her insistence that action be meaningful (rather than determined by utility) and that it be limited by a specific purpose is not a contradiction but an insight that follows from her analysis of totalitarianism.

One difference between politics and totalitarianism is that where the former is organized by the articulation of common interests, the latter is unified by propaganda that plays on mass sentiment. The goal of a mass movement is not power, but strength. Power which comes to be in the "interspaces" when human beings are joined together *and* distinguished from one another by their participation in speech and action, respects the condition of plurality. By contrast, strength is accomplished by fusion: "Masses are not held together by a consciousness of common interest and they lack that specific class *articulateness* which is expressed in *determined, limited, and obtainable goals*" (OT, 311; emphasis added). What Arendt rejects here is the way in which mass movements conflate meaningful action with the pretense to world-historical significance. Where a mass movement demands that its followers be unconditionally loyal to unspecified goals such as world conquest, the "concrete content" of a political program is the condition on which its participants lend their support and the standard against which they evaluate its success (OT, 324). There is something more to this action's "concrete content" than its goals: its principles. As I have argued, the principles of action are concrete in the sense that they cannot just be held intellectually but must be enacted. But the concreteness of enactment is distinct from instrumentality in that principles, in contrast to goals, can be neither implemented nor exhausted.

How well does Arendt's promise-making counter the traditional model of sover-eignty? As Hanna Pitkin has argued, there is nothing revolutionary about promises; on the contrary, promising is fundamental to the concept of liberty as understood by the tradition of social contract theory against which Arendt claims to be in "manifest contradiction."[50] Where Pitkin might say there is nothing unique about promises, Michel Foucault would argue that there is nothing liberating about them. Foucault claims that promises "efface the domination intrinsic to power" by establishing what seems to be reciprocity of obligation between sovereign and subjects. Contrary to the claim to set the parameters of legitimate power by the device of mutual entailment, Foucault argues that the discourse of right "puts in motion relations that are not relations of sovereignty but of domination." Such domination is not enforced overtly as leverage, "that solid and global kind of domination that one person exercises over others, or one group over another"; rather, it is insinuated into putatively cooperative relations through the norm of integrity that is taken to be a condition of intersubjective agreement.[51] In the very ideal of concerted action in accord with a "mutual promise," it would seem that Arendt has not offered a democratic alternative to coercion; instead, she has reiterated what Peter Digeser calls the "fourth face of power" that produces "the responsible subject and the practice of promising, [and] is conveyed only by acting upon specific intentions and goals."[52]

There are some important differences, however, between promising as Arendt describes it and promising in the modern social contract tradition to which both Pitkin and Foucault refer. In that tradition, a promise is understood as a contract that is binding because it occurs in a context where obligatory acts are already stabilized either by an explicit prior agreement (as in the Hobbesian contract with the sovereign) or by common recognition of the practice of giving one's word (as in Rawls's original position). Typically, then, a promise is a private contract whose reliability is secured either by the guarantee that the sovereign will enforce it or (in the more nearly just society) by the confidence that people can be trusted to keep their word. Arendt's innovation is to attempt to define promising as a public act, not in the ordinary sense of something that can be concluded "in" public, but in the sense of a capacity that is conditional on natality. The uniqueness of promising, as animated by natality, is that it need not rely on a previously secured context of relations but brings new publics into being. Drawing attention to its innovative aspect, Bonnie Honig calls Arendt's promises "performative utterances" whose purpose "is to bring something into being that did not exist before."[53] The performative quality of promising gives it the capacity to authorize political power without reference to anything outside the practice of promising itself.[54] Thus, promising does not serve to fix the boundaries of individuals but opens up new possibilities by means of new connections. It is oriented to action, not exchange.

Against Honig's claim, it could be argued that far from bringing something new into being, promises originate in and express individuals' authentic, prepolitical identities. This would mean that Arendt does not reconfigure the autonomous individual subject of Enlightenment political thought but reinstates it. Once again, however, it is deceptively easy to assimilate Arendt's work to the conventions she resists; although she seems to work with it, her account of promising goes against the grain. Arendt argues that it is not the *self* that makes the promise, but the *promise* that makes the self: "Without being bound to the fulfillment of promises, we would never be able to keep our identities; we would be condemned to wander helplessly and without direction in the darkness of each man's lonely heart, caught in its contradictions and equivocalities—a darkness which only the light shed over the public realm through the presence of others, who confirm the identity between the one who promises and the one who fulfills, can dispel" (HC, 237).

Arendt locates the moral force of promises not in the integrity of a putatively inner self but in the presence of those who witness the promise. She argues, in effect, that the self exists as a reliable entity only in public.[55] The inner self known through introspection is no more than "an ever-moving stream" of fragmentary perceptions.[56] The return to companionship is a relief to solitary thinkers because "it makes them 'whole' again, saves them from the dialogue of thought in which one remains always equivocal, restores the identity which makes them speak with the single voice of one unexchangeable person" (OT, 476). Despite the fact that we commonly speak of making promises "to ourselves," Arendt's denial of the "inner self" renders this claim nonsensical. She insists that the "moral code ... inferred from the faculties of forgiving and making promises, rests on experiences which nobody could ever have with himself, which, on the contrary, are entirely based on the presence of others."[57] Contrary to subject-centered understandings of promises, Arendt suggests that the belief that promises are proof of character and integrity has always been fundamentally misconceived. The moral force of a promise derives not from a continuity internal to the self who utters it but from that which is conferred by the presence of others before whom it is performed; it is not subjectivity but intersubjectivity that makes promises morally binding.

Arendt's discussion of promises is unusual, then, in that far from confirming the fiction of an "inner self," she shifts the locus of the moral force of commitment from that self to the world. As in the redefinition of sovereignty, this shift depends on conceiving of promises in performative terms. That is, it depends on the understanding that promises do not originate in subjectivity but rather bring new agency into being by constituting new relationships. Even understood in its capacity to enact new relationships, promising is still double-sided in that relationships engender new expectations, the aspect of power that Foucault identifies with discipline.

Second, promising does not establish a sovereign power with leverage "over" subjects. If power is collaborative, if it "springs up between men when they act together and vanishes the moment they disperse," then there can be no fulcrum external to the web of plurality from which to exercise control "over" it (HC, 200). Obviously, no one can be in public in a web of relations with others and at the same time be at a vantage point outside the public realm. This means that leverage—power exercised *over* others—could not pass itself off as legitimate in Arendt's public space.

Most important, promising does not confirm the fiction of sovereignty in Hobbes's sense of a total, all-encompassing, and perpetual power—or even in the sense of Rousseau's general will. In the first place, the power that promising authorizes can be neither all-encompassing nor perpetual because the selves who constitute it are multiple and shifting. Arendtian solidarity is a partial consensus, limited to the particular locality defined by a specific problem. In addition, this local consensus is partial with respect to each individual who enters into agreement with the others; that is, there is no expectation that they identify themselves exclusively in terms of any one particular locality and, hence, no expectation that they will be permanently allied and perfectly in harmony with each other. . . .

Notes

1. W. H. Auden, "Thinking What We Are Doing," *The Griffin* 7 (September 1958): 4.

2. Martin Jay and Leon Botstein, "Hannah Arendt: Opposing Views," *Partisan Review* 45 (1978): 361.

3. Paul Ricoeur, "Action, Story, and History," *Salmagundi* 60 (1983): 63.

4. Jay and Botstein, "Hannah Arendt," 349. During a personal conversation in 1988 Richard Bernstein told me of Arendt's influence on the northern activists who participated in Freedom Summer. James Miller uses Arendt's vocabulary to describe the New Left's experimentation with participatory democracy in *Democracy Is in the Streets* (New York: Simon & Schuster, 1987).

5. Jürgen Habermas, "Notes and Commentary: On the German-Jewish Heritage," *Telos* 44 (1980): 128.

6. Sheldon S. Wolin, "Hannah Arendt: Democracy and the Political," *Salmagundi* 60 (1983) 7.

7. Nancy Hartsock, *Money, Sex, and Power* (Boston: Northeastern University Press, 1984), 217.

8. Hanna Fenichel Pitkin, "Justice: On Relating Private and Public," *Political Theory* 9 (1981): 338.

9. Seyla Benhabib, *Situating the Self* (New York: Routledge, 1992), 93.

10. Jennifer Ring has also called attention to the importance of the pariah to appreciating the differences between Arendt's conception of political action and the agonistic model of the polis, arguing that the pariah is "more quietly central in Arendt's work than the blustering Greek man of action." "The Pariah as Hero: Hannah Arendt's Political Actor," *Political Theory* 19 (1991): 441.

11. Thirty years ago, many readers missed the subtleties of Arendt's arguments that look so innovative in the present context. For example, Daniel Bell interpreted Arendt's refusal of Jewish partisanship in her analysis of the Eichmann controversy as Archimedean arrogance. He charged that she had "cut all ties" to her Jewish identity and found in her reports "the unmoved quality of the Stoic, transcending tribe and nation, seeking only the single standard of universal order." "Alphabet of Justice," *Partisan Review* 30 (Fall 1963): 418. Summing up the polemical readings of many of her contemporaries, Jeffrey Isaac observes that Arendt "was accused of virtual treason against her people, for effacing the line between the guilt of the Nazis and the innocence of the Jews, for having more sympathy with Eichmann than with the six million he had helped to murder." See "At the Margins: Jewish Identity and Politics in the Thought of Hannah Arendt," *Tikkun* 5 (1990): 89.

12. I borrow this phrase from Kristina Rollin, who proposed it in a seminar at the Center for Advanced Feminist Studies, University of Minnesota, 1993.

13. See Gerard P. Heather and Matthew Stolz, "Hannah Arendt and Critical Theory," *The Journal of Politics* 41 (1979): 18.

14. Other scholars have remarked on the significance of Arendt's vocabulary. Sheldon Wolin writes that The Human Condition "brought something new into the world. It introduced a distinctive language and with it a new political sensibility which invested politics with a high seriousness and dignity that transcended the dreary and trivial categories of academic political science." In "Hannah Arendt and the Ordinance of Time," *Social Research* 44 (1977): 92. Similarly, Heather and Stolz argue that "*The Human Condition* should remind us of the *Leviathan*, for both are great exercises in the arts of political naming," "Hannah Arendt and Critical Theory," 18.

15. A striking exception to this is Margaret Canovan's recent study. Reading Arendt's work with an eye for the complexity of her thought and a sensibility for her unconventionally poetic "voice," Canovan concludes unequivocally that Arendt's work is rightfully mentioned "in the same breath" as that by Hobbes, Locke, and the rest. Arendt's work, Canovan argues, stands the very test of greatness that she herself proposed: "in the course of her own response to the experiences of her time, Arendt also 'augmented' the world by one word: the word 'plurality'." *Hannah Arendt: A Reinterpretation of Her Political Thought* (New York: Cambridge University Press, 1992), 281.

16. Iris Young, *Justice and the Politics of Difference* (Princeton: Princeton University Press, 1990), 5.

17. Nancy Fraser, "Toward a Discourse Ethic of Solidarity," *Praxis International* 5 (1986): 425. According to Fraser, these include "the officially recognized vocabulary in which one can press claims; the idioms available for interpreting and communicating one's needs; the established narrative conventions available for constructing the individual and collective histories which are constitutive of social identities; the paradigms of argumentation accepted as authoritative in adjudicating conflicting claims; the ways in which various discourses constitute their respective subject matters as specific sorts of objects; the repertory of available rhetorical devices; the bodily and gestural dimensions of speech which are associated in a given society with authority and conviction."

18. Benjamin R. Barber, *Strong Democracy: Participatory Politics for a New Age* (Berkeley: University of California Press, 1984), 120.

19. Jeffrey C. Isaac criticizes Arendt for the extremism of her position on judgment, arguing that her suspicion of "the claims of any theory purporting to speak with epistemic authority about the world of opinion" rules out all possibility of a critical social science. *Arendt, Camus, and Modern Rebellion* (New Haven: Yale University Press, 1992), 238. If democratic political transformation cannot occur without the systematic critical analysis of social inequality that such a science aims to provide, then the work of Arendt and others who make judgment so central to their theories is more visionary than pragmatic.

20. This vision of impartiality corresponds to what Thomas Nagel calls "overobjectification," which he deems the mistake of seeking "a single complete objective account of reality." *The View from Nowhere* (New York: Oxford University Press, 1986), 162.

21. Hannah Arendt, "The Archimedean Point," reprint of a lecture for the University of Michigan College of Engineers, 1968, Library of Congress, MSS Box 61, 6.

22. See, for example, the interview "Truth and Power," where Foucault appears to identify all truth claims with the Archimedean ideal of disembodied objectivity. He claims that "truth isn't the reward of free spirits, the child of protracted solitude, nor the privilege of those who have succeeded in liberating themselves. Truth is a thing of this world: it is produced only by virtue of multiple forms of constraint." Michel Foucault, *Power/Knowledge*, ed. Colin Gordon, trans. Colin Gordon, Leo Marshall, John Mepham, and Kate Soper (New York: Pantheon, 1980), 131. Maybe Foucault recommends the genealogy of "subjugated knowledges" as a way out of the knowledge/power conundrum, but the extensive debates on this question are beyond the scope of this book.

23. Arendt, "Archimedean Point," 6, 25.

24. As Bhikhu Parekh and Margaret Canovan have noted, Arendt's monolithic construction of "the" tradition is somewhat mitigated by the distinction she makes between "political 'philosophers' and political 'writers' who 'write out of political experiences and for the sake of politics'." Canovan, *Hannah Arendt*, 202, citing an unpublished essay by Hannah Arendt, "From Machiavelli to Marx," 1965 Library of Congress, MSS Box 39 023453. Parekh, *Hannah Arendt and the Search for a New Political Philosophy* (Atlantic Highlands: Humanities Press, 1981), 2. Nonetheless, in *The Human Condition* she appears to identify the tradition primarily with Plato, as if no subsequent thinkers offered a meaningful alternative to that theoretical framework. However contestable this vision of the tradition may be, it is not my purpose to entertain that debate. It has already been argued effectively and by many scholars that the Western political tradition is not reducible to a single plot but contains multiple stories that can be both oppressive and liberating.

25. Hannah Arendt, "Philosophy and Politics: The Problem of Action and Thought after the French Revolution," 1954, 15a, Library of Congress, MSS Box 76.

26. Dagmar Barnouw, *Visible Spaces: Hannah Arendt and the German-Jewish Experience* (Baltimore: Johns Hopkins University Press, 1990), 19.

27. HC, 50, 52. Parekh has also noted the peculiarity of Arendt's presentation of publicity, writing that "although the concept of public space is crucial to her ontology, she neither clearly defines it nor articulates its structure," *Hannah Arendt*, 92.

28. Canovan has charted the connections between the main themes of *The Human Condition*, *The Origins of Totalitarianism*, and Arendt's unpublished writings on the totalitarian elements in Marx. Her investigation of these unpublished writings shows that arguments from the various studies of totalitarianism influence the later work in two ways. Plurality and the public space are, as it is commonly understood, a kind of antidote to totalitarian rule. In addition, however, Canovan argues that the story Arendt tells about modernity in *The Human Condition* is determined by the parallel she saw between totalitarian terror and what she took to be the modern rise to prominence of the activities of labor and consumption, together with the values associated with them. Canovan suggests that some of the polemicism of the later work follows from predispositions Arendt carries into it from the earlier study. See *Hannah Arendt*, chaps. 3 and 4.

29. Jane Mansbridge lays out these two categories and compares their conceptions of interest in *Beyond Adversary Democracy* (Chicago: University of Chicago Press, 1980).

30. There is a vast body of scholarship criticizing the tendency toward false universality in both the essentialism of identity politics and the abstraction of liberalism. Some especially cogent examples of these arguments include Susan Moller Okin, *Women in Western Political Thought* (Princeton: Princeton University Press, 1979), and *Justice, Gender, and the Family* (New York: Basic Books, 1989); Young, *Justice;* Carole Pateman, *The Disorder of Women* (Stanford: Stanford University Press, 1989).

31. Political theorists Ernesto Laclau and Chantal Mouffe employ the term *articulation* to explain the way in which an hegemonic order constitutes a position of dominance and to account for the possibility of democratic opposition that is not grounded in a unitary class, ethnic, or gender identity. As Arendt does, these theorists pose articulation as an alternative to the fragmentation of pluralist liberalism on one hand and to totalizing or essentialist conceptions of community on the other. It displaces both the concept of a plurality of competing interests given prior to and represented through politics and the belief in an underlying essential unity that is expressed in communitarian politics. In contrast, articulation is "the result of political construction and struggle." Its starting point is plurality, and its task is to build connections around various democratic demands by means of a contest in which none of the contestants is privileged by its structural position. *Hegemony and Socialist Strategy* (New York: Verso, 1985), 65.

32. Ron Feldman's account of Arendt's preference for the *Yishuv* (the Jewish community in Palestine prior to statehood) over the establishment of the majority Jewish state of Israel suggests that it is precisely this conception of an articulated public space that accounts for her position on Israel. Arendt viewed the *Yishuv*, with its construction of a specifically Jewish cultural homeland, as sufficient to the articulation of a public space and opposed the move to establishing Israel as a traditionally sovereign state on the basis of religious identity. "For Arendt, the Jewish homeland is a political space, a human world created by conscious human effort where a Jewish culture can come into being; this the *Yishuv* achieved, without political sovereignty and without being a majority in Palestine. Precisely because a Jewish community had been built where people could appear to each other, where there was an audience for works of literature and art, Jewish cultural genius no longer needed to either abandon its Jewish roots in favor of 'universal' European culture or else be relegated to the category of folklore." Ron H. Feldman, "Introduction," JP, 36.

33. Jean-François Lyotard, *The Postmodern Condition: A Report on Knowledge*, trans. Geoff Bennington and Brian Massumi (Minneapolis: University of Minnesota Press, 1984), 40.

34. There is no small controversy regarding what Arendt's elusive concept of "public space" refers to. Margaret Canovan, for example, equates it with the "common set of worldly institutions" by which all citizens of a particular community are joined together (*Hannah Arendt*, 226). The problem with equating the public with common institutions is that it begins to elide the discontinuity in Arendt's work between government and politics. As

Canovan herself notes, the public spaces Arendt cites as exemplary of politics were opened by demonstrations like the civil rights movement and anti-war protests (183). Such actions were certainly not coterminous with the institutions of liberal government and society but protests against them. As Jeffrey C. Isaac has recently argued, far from envisioning a single, all-encompassing public "that might replace the institutions of representative government, Arendt envisions the pluralization of political space." In "Oases in the Desert: Hannah Arendt on Democratic Politics," *American Political Science Review* 88 (1994): 160.

35. Jürgen Habermas, "Hannah Arendt's Communications Concept of Power," *Social Research* 44 (1977): 3–24.

36. Arendt apparently revised one section of this essay—"Philosophy and Politics"—for publication, even though she never published it. It was published posthumously in *Social Research* 57 (1990): 73–103.

37. LM: 1, 168. It could be objected that Arendt exaggerates the publicity of the Socratic dialogue. It is neither plural, as Plato frequently depicts Socrates' interlocutors as morally and intellectually unworthy of him, nor open, as Socrates knows in advance what he wants to accomplish by it. Arendt's portrait of Socrates rests on a belief that she stipulates but does not defend, that "there exists a sharp dividing line between what is authentically Socratic and the philosophy taught by Plato," 168. The historical, "authentic" Socrates, Arendt argues, was genuinely uncertain, believed he had nothing to teach, engaged in questioning for its own sake, and believed everyone was worth talking to.

38. Arendt, "Philosophy and Politics," 83–84. This reference and subsequent references in this section are to the posthumous version of the text.

39. Ibid., 80, 83.

40. Fred Dallmayr suggests that this peculiar close-distant quality is common to both public and intimate friendship when he writes, "In cultivating a friendship, I believe, we also become susceptible to a certain uniqueness or unfamiliarity which we do not wish to invade or transgress—a belief congruent with a Heideggerian passage which depicts man basically as a 'creature of distance,' or rather as a creature whose farness emerges precisely under conditions of nearness or close proximity." Whether it is only a quality of public friendship or of both public and intimate friendship, Dallmayr's words are a beautiful rendering of the connection between Arendtian plurality and friendship. See *Polis and Praxis* (Cambridge: MIT Press, 1984), 10.

41. Bakhtin introduces the idea of conversation in the mode of translation in the analogy he draws between novels and conversations. Bakhtin argues that the distinctive character of a novel is that it is a form of narrative that can (though it need not) accommodate multiple speakers, languages, and ideological perspectives. He calls this its "Galilean perception of language." M. M. Bakhtin, *The Dialogic Imagination* (Austin: University of Texas Press, 1981), 366. In contrast to the story of a novel told from the Archimedean position of an omniscient narrator, the story of a Galilean novel is dialogic: it is told from multiple perspectives and in multiple languages. Bakhtin suggests that a Galilean novel exemplifies for its readers the dynamics of a good conversation: its "dialogues . . . push to the limit the mutual nonunderstanding represented by people who *speak in different languages,*" 356. If conversations are, indeed, Galilean and "multiple" with respect to language, then communication in a conversational mode cannot be a matter of unmediated understanding but must proceed instead in the mode of translation. See also Donna Haraway, "Situated Knowledges: The Science Question in Feminism and the Privilege of Partial Perspective," *Feminist Studies* 14 (1988): 589–590.

42. For a provocative discussion of this question and defense of Socrates, see Gregory Vlastos, *Socrates: Ironist and Moral Philosopher* (Ithaca: Cornell University Press, 1991).

43. Hannah Arendt, "Concern with Politics in Recent European Philosophical Thought," undated, Library of Congress, MSS Box 63 02348.

44. Jane Flax, for example, has argued that the gender socialization of privileged males inclines them to mistake strength for power, and that it is a projection of their separation anxiety to mistake freedom for sovereignty. See "Political Philosophy and the Patriarchal Unconscious: A Psychoanalytic Perspective on Epistemology and Metaphysics," in *Discovering Reality*, ed. Sandra Harding and Merrill B. Hintikka (Boston: D. Reidel, 1983), 245–281.

45. The relevant literature here is too numerous to list, but it includes bell hooks, *From Margin to Center* (Boston: South End Press, 1984), Nancy Fraser and Linda Nicholson, "Femi-

nism without Foundations," in *Feminism/Postmodernism*, ed. Linda Nicholson (New York: Routledge, 1990), and Donna Haraway, "A Manifesto for Cyborgs: Science, Technology, and Socialist Feminism in the 1980s," *Socialist Review* 80 (1985): 82.

46. Young, *Justice*, esp. chap. 6.

47. Maria Markus attributes the reluctance to engage with Arendt's work to a "disturbing tendency in contemporary feminist theory . . . [to be] prepared to re-think, re-evaluate, re-interpret, or even simply learn from different theoretical propositions produced by males," but to dismiss as male-identified those women thinkers who neither identified with feminism nor employed gender as an analytic category. "The 'Anti-Feminism' of Hannah Arendt," *Thesis Eleven* 17 (1987): 76.

48. Young, *Justice*, 97.

49. Steven Lukes is simply off the mark when, basing his argument solely on the abbreviated account in Arendt's *On Violence*, he claims that she conceives of power as an " 'ability,' not a relationship." Missing altogether what I have called Arendt's critique of power as leverage, the centrality of plurality to an Arendtian "public," and her attempt to define a uniquely activist conception of power, Lukes deems her work to be a conceptualization of " 'influence' but not of 'power.' " In *Power: A Radical View* (London: Macmillan, 1974), 31.

50. Pitkin, "Justice," 337.

51. Foucault, *Power/Knowledge*, 95–96. Dana Villa argues that both Foucault and Arendt are critics of sovereignty, claiming that they "present complementary narratives about the closure of the space for action in the modern age." Both see this closure as a consequence of the normalization of this space by mechanisms of social power that discipline bodies, thereby precluding the enactment of natality. See "Beyond Good and Evil: Arendt, Nietzsche, and the Aestheticization of Political Action," *Political Theory* 20 (1992): 274–308.

52. Peter Digeser, "The Fourth Face of Power," *The Journal of Politics* 54 (1992): 984.

53. Bonnie Honig, "Declarations of Independence: Arendt and Derrida on the Problem of Founding a Republic," *American Political Science Review* 85 (1991): 101.

54. Honig notes that Arendt's account of promises is incomplete in that she addresses neither "the question of the legitimacy of the practice" nor that "of its own techniques of self-legitimation," ibid., 103. This is consistent with my claim that Arendt's account of publicity is partial because she gives no account of the processes by which to distinguish common interests from forced consensus. I suggest here, however, that Arendt rules out some of the techniques of self-legitimation that usually accompany promise-making by her unconventional account of the self.

55. Bonnie Honig makes a similar argument in a poststructuralist idiom, claiming that "Arendt's actors do not act because of what they already are, their actions do not express a prior, stable identity; they presuppose an unstable, multiple self that seeks its, at best, episodic self-realization in action and in the identity that is its reward." Bonnie Honig, "Toward an Agonistic Feminism: Hannah Arendt and the Politics of Identity," in *Feminists Theorize the Political*, ed. Judith Butler and Joan W. Scott (New York: Routledge, 1992), 220.

56. Ibid., 282.

57. HC, 238. I found this to be especially true for me when I was in graduate school, and it is demonstrated to me over again in my work now with graduate students. The commitment to write a dissertation is an unusually difficult one to make precisely because in the beginning it is a promise that you have no choice but to make largely to yourself. It is unusual because at that stage neither you, nor your advisors, nor even your best friends know what you are doing, no matter how engaged they are in your project. It is only as you progress in an academic career that you establish a public space for your work by virtue of the way it is received and the expectations it generates, not just among those who sympathize with it but also among those who question it. Beginning the dissertation is so difficult because of what Arendt calls the "unbearable isolation" of being without "the most elementary form of human creativity," which is the trust that your work will have a place in the world (OT, 475).

References

Arendt, Hannah. *Between Past and Future*. Enlarged ed. New York: Penguin, 1977.

——. *The Human Condition*. Chicago: University of Chicago Press, 1958.

——. *The Jew as Pariah: Jewish Identity and Politics in the Modern Age*. Ed. Ron H. Feldman. New York: Random House, 1978.

——. *Men in Dark Times*. New York: Harcourt Brace Jovanovich,

1968.

——. *The Origins of Totalitarianism.* New York: 1 vol. New York: Harcourt Brace Jovanovich, 1979.

——. *On Violence.* New York: Harcourt Brace Jovanovich, 1969.

——. "A Reply [to Eric Voegelin's Review of *The Origins of Totalitarianism*]," *Review of Politics* 15 (1953): 76–84.

—— and Karl Jaspers. *Correspondence: 1926–1969.* Ed. Lotte Kohler and Hans Saner. Trans. Robert Kimber and Rita Kimber. New York: Harcourt Brace Jovanovich, 1992.

45
Hannah Arendt and Feminist Politics

Mary G. Dietz

Hannah Arendt, perhaps the most influential female political philosopher of the twentieth century, continuously championed the *bios politikos*—the realm of citizenship—as the domain of human freedom. In her major work, *The Human Condition*, Arendt appropriated the Aristotelian distinction between "mere life" and "the good life" in order to characterize the crisis of the contemporary age in the West. What we are witnessing, she argued, is the eclipse of the public realm of participatory politics and the emergence of an atomized society bent on sheer survival. Arendt's political vision was decisively Hellenic: the classical Greek *polis* of male citizens was her model of the public; Pericles, the Athenian statesman, was her exemplary citizen-hero; and the quest for freedom as glory was her political ideal.

A political theory so indebted to a culture of masculinity and hero worship was bound to meet with resistance in the feminist writings of the 1970s and 1980s, as feminists began to pursue a woman-centered theory of knowledge, and debunk the patriarchal assumptions of "male-stream" Western political thought. Thus Arendt was not spared the critical, anticanonical gaze of feminist theory. For Adrienne Rich and Mary O'Brien, *The Human Condition* was simply another attempt to discredit "women's work," to deny the value of reproductive labor, and to reassert the superiority of masculinity. Pulling few punches, Rich argued that Arendt's work "embodies the tragedy of a female mind nourished on male ideologies"; and O'Brien called Arendt "a woman who accepts the normality and even the necessity of male supremacy."[1] For both Rich and O'Brien, Arendt's sins were not simply those of omission. By elevating politics and "the common world of men," they contended, she reinforced the legitimacy of "paterfamilias on his way to the freedom of the political realm," and denied the truly liberatory potential of the female realm of reproduction and mothering.[2]

Other scholars, however, drew some distinctively feminist dimensions from Arendt's political thought. In *Money, Sex, and Power*, Nancy Hartsock noted the significance of Arendt's concept of power as collective action, and her appreciation of "natality" or beginning anew, as promising elements for a feminist theory "grounded at the epistemological level of reproduction."[3] Hanna Pitkin observed that *The Human Condition* is located within "a framework of solicitude for the body of our Earth, the Mother of all living creatures"; so Arendt could hardly be described as hostile in principle to women's concerns.[4] More recently, Terry Winant found in Arendt's work, "the missing element in recent attempts to address the problem of grounding the feminist standpoint."[5]

These differing feminist interpretations of Arendt's political theory serve as the organizational framework of this essay. With the critical attacks of Rich and O'Brien in mind, I argue that *The Human Condition* does, in fact, exhibit a gender blindness that renders it a far less powerful account of politics and human freedom than it otherwise might have been had Arendt been attentive to women's place in the human condition. Unlike Rich and O'Brien, however, I am not ready to dismiss *The Human Condition* as hopelessly "male-stream"; nor do I think "the necessity of male supremacy" follows from Arendt's theoretical presuppositions. This essay also contends, then—in line with Hartsock and others—that Arendt's work has much to offer feminist thought, especially in its attempts to articulate a vision of politics and political life. Unlike Hartsock, however, I argue that an "Arendtian feminism" must continue to maintain an analytical distinction between political life on the one hand, and reproduction on the other, and also recognize the problematical nature of a feminist politics grounded in reproductive processes. Before proceeding to these arguments, it is necessary to outline in brief Arendt's understanding of the *vita activa*—labor, work, and action—which is the core of her theory in *The Human Condition* and the subject of so much feminist debate.

Labor, Work, and Action

Arendt begins *The Human Condition* by distinguishing among three "general human capacities which grow out of the human condition and are permanent, that is, which cannot be irretrievably lost so long as the human condition itself is not changed."[6] The three capacities and their "corresponding conditions" are labor and life, work and worldliness, and action and plurality; together they constitute the *vita activa*.[7] Arendt envisions labor, work, and action not as empirical or sociological generalizations about what people actually do, but rather as existential categories intended to distinguish the *vita activa* and reveal what it means to be human and "in the presence of other human beings" in the world.[8] These "existentials," however, do more than disclose that human beings cultivate, fabricate, and organize the world. In an expressly normative way, Arendt wants to judge the human condition, and to get us, in turn, "to think what we are doing" when we articulate and live out the conditions of our existence in particular ways.[9] Underlying *The Human Condition* is the notion that human history has been a story of continuously shifting "reversals" within the *vita activa* itself. In different historical moments from the classical to the contemporary age, labor, work, and action have been accorded higher or lower status within the hierarchy. Arendt argues that some moments of human experience—namely those in which "action" has been understood as the most meaningful human activity—are more glorious and free than those in which either "the labor of our body or the work of our hands" is elevated within the *vita activa*.[10] Hence her reverence for the age of Socrates and the public realm

of the Greek *polis*, and her dismay over the ensuing events within Western culture and political thought (including liberalism and Marxism), as citizen-politics is increasingly lost and the world of action is displaced by the primacy of labor and work. The critique of the modern world that *The Human Condition* advances rests on the claim that we are now witnessing an unprecedented era in which the process-driven activity of labor dominates our understanding of human achievement. As a result, we live in and celebrate a world of automatically functioning jobholders, having lost all sense of what constitutes true freedom and collective public life.

When Arendt calls "life" the condition of labor, "worldliness" the condition of work, and "plurality" the condition of action, she means to associate a corresponding set of characteristics with each. Labor (*animal laborans*) corresponds to the biological process of the human body and hence to the process of growth and decay in nature itself. Necessity defines labor, insofar as laboring is concentrated exclusively on life and the demands of its maintenance. Labor takes place primarily in the private realm, the realm of the household, family, and intimate relations. The objects of labor—the most natural and ephemeral of tangible things—are the most consumed and, therefore, the least worldly. They are the products of the cyclical, biological, life process itself, "where no beginning and no end exist and where all natural things swing in changeless, deathless, repetition."[11] *Animal laborans* is also distinguished by a particular mentality or mode of thinking-in-the-world. It cannot conceive of the possibility of breaking free or beginning anew; "sheer inevitability" and privatization dominate it. Hence, Arendt refers to the "essential worldly futility" of the life process and the activity of *animal laborans*.[12]

In contrast to labor, work (*homo faber*) is the activity that corresponds to the "unnaturalness" of human existence. If "life" and the private realm locate the activity of *animal laborans*, then "the world" locates *homo faber*. Work is, literally, the working up of the world, the production of things-in-the-world. If *animal laborans* is caught up in nature and in the cyclical movement of the body's life processes, then *homo faber* is, as Arendt puts it, "free to produce and free to destroy."[13] The fabrication process, with its definite beginning and predictable end, governs *homo faber* activity. Repetition, the hallmark of labor, may or may not characterize work; at least it is not inherent in the activity itself. The objects of this activity, unlike those of labor, are relatively durable, permanent endproducts. They are not consumed, but rather used or enjoyed. The "fabrications" of *homo faber* have the function of "stabilizing" human life and they bear testimony to human productivity.[14]

Insofar as they are all *homo faber*, human beings think in terms of gaining mastery over nature, and approach the world itself as a controllable object, the "measure of man." This tendency to objectify things and persons in the world is a foreboding of, in Arendt's words, "a growing meaninglessness, where every end is transformed into a means," and even those things not constructed by human hands lose their value and are treated as instruments at the behest of the "lord and master of all things."[15] The corresponding mentality of *homo faber*, then, is a rational-instrumental attitude concerned with the usefulness of things and with the "sheer worldly existence" made possible through human artifice. Understood as an existential "type," *homo faber* is that aspect of human beingness that places its confidence in the belief that "every issue can be solved and every human motivation reduced to the principle of utility."[16]

What Arendt calls "action" stands in sharp contrast with, but is not unrelated to the activities of labor and work. In order to act, human beings must first have satisfied the demands of life, have a private realm for solitude, and also have a stable world within which they can achieve "solidity" and "retrieve their sameness . . . their identity."[17] At the same time, human beings possess extraordinary capabilities that neither labor nor work encompass. They can disclose themselves in speech and deed, and undertake new beginnings, thereby denying the bonds of nature and moving beyond the means–end confines of *homo faber*.[18] Without action to bring new beginnings (natality) into the play of the world, Arendt writes, there is nothing new under the sun; without speech, there is no memorialization, no remembrance.[19] Unlike either labor or work, action bears no corresponding singular Latin synonym, perhaps because Arendt means for it to capture an aspect of human life that is essentially collective, rather than solitary or distinguished by the "separateness" of persons. This collective condition, where speech and action materialize, Arendt calls "the human condition of plurality."[20]

Plurality is perhaps the key concept in Arendt's understanding of action. She uses it to explore the situation humans achieve when they "gather together and act in concert," thus finding themselves enmeshed within a "web of relationships."[21] In general terms, plurality is the simultaneous realization of shared equality and distinctive, individual differences. Arendt calls it "the basic condition of both action and speech."[22] Without equality, individuals would not be able to comprehend each other or communicate, and without distinctiveness, they would have no need or reason to communicate, no impetus to interject themselves as *unique* selves into the shared world. Plurality, then, is the common condition in which human beings reveal their "unique distinctiveness." Arendt presents this in terms of a paradox: "Plurality is the condition of human action because we are all the same, that is, human, in such a way that nobody is ever the same as anyone else who ever lived, lives, or will live."[23] Thus, plurality promotes the notion of a politics of shared differences.

Because Arendt introduces plurality as a political and not a metaphysical concept, she also locates this common condition in a discernible space which she calls "the public" or "the space of appearances."[24] The public exists in stark contrast to the private realm; it is where the revelation of individuality amidst collectivity takes place. The barest existence of a public realm "bestowed upon politics a dignity," Arendt writes, "that even today has not altogether disappeared."[25]

Arendt's concept of plurality as the basic condition of action and speech allows her to reconceptualize politics and power in significant ways. Put simply, politics at its most dignified is the realization of human plurality—the activity that simply *is* the sharing of the world and exemplary of the human capacity for "beginning anew" through mutual speech and deed.[26] Power, which Arendt understands as "acting together," maintains the space of appearances; as long as it persists, the public realm is preserved.[27] Politics is the activity that renders us something more than just the *animal laborans*, subject to the cyclicality of human biological processes, or the *homo faber*, artificer of the world. When Arendt characterizes action as the only activity entirely dependent on "being together" and "the existence of other people," she intends to posit the existential difference between politics on the one hand, and labor and work on the other. She also wants to use action as a way of getting us to consider yet one other dispositional capacity we possess—something she variously calls common sense, judging insight, or "representative thinking."[28] Representative thinking can be distinguished from both the process logic of *animal laborans* and the instrumentalism of *homo faber* insofar as it is guided by a respect for persons as distinctive agents, as "speakers of words and doers of deeds." In order to flourish, the public realm requires this way of thinking; it proceeds from the notion that we can put ourselves in the place of others, in a manner that is open, communicative, and aware of individual differences, opinions, and concerns.

Without question, Arendt understands politics as existentially superior to both labor and work. Thus she has often been interpreted as devaluing the latter, or worse, as having contempt for the lives of the poor and working classes—in her own words, "the vast majority of humankind."[29] Here it is worth repeating that Arendt presents labor, work, and action *not* as constructs of class or social relations, but rather as properties of the human condition which are within the range of every human being. Likewise, our "world alienation" is not a matter of rising masses or threatened aristocracies, but has to do with the fact that, as *humans*, we are rapidly losing our collective capacity for exercising power through shared word and deed, and succumbing ever more steadily to an existence governed by the instrumental calculations of *homo faber* and the process mentality of *animal laborans*. Freedom is fast disappearing in the face of the sheer survivalism and automatic functioning that is the condition of the modern world.

Women and the Human Condition

The feminist critic who approaches *The Human Condition* for the first time is likely to conclude that Arendt's *magnum opus*, with its generic male terms of reference, its homage to the canon of Western political thought, and its silences about women, reads like another contribution to a long line of political works in the tradition. Inconceivable as it may sound to contemporary feminists, Arendt mentions women only twice (aside from a few footnotes) in her lengthy discussion of the classical conception of labor and work, public and private. She observes, without comment, that in the sphere of the Greek household, men and women performed different tasks, and she acknowledges, briefly, that women and slaves "belonged to the same category and were hidden away" because their lives were devoted to bodily functions.[30] Her scholarly development of a conceptual history of labor and work is remarkably silent on the sexual division of labor in the family and on the way in which gender informed traditional understandings of labor and work in both classical and modern thought. Also missing from *The Human Condition* is any sustained discussion of women's systematic exclusion from the public realm throughout occidental history. Not only does Arendt seem to be trading in abstract, ahistorical categories; she also seems to have little awareness of the gender assumptions that underlie and complicate them.

Nevertheless, the feminist critic is well advised to give *The Human Condition* a second look. For, not unlike many other supposedly "male-stream" texts in political thought, Arendt's work is an enriching, not simply a frustrating, site for feminist criticism. Partly this is because of its scope and complexity;

as the various feminist accounts mentioned earlier reveal, *The Human Condition* admits of no definitive interpretive conclusions. Moreover, Arendt herself offers some promising directions for feminist speculation concerning labor, work, and action. In this sense, although a feminist analysis never emerges in *The Human Condition*, the materials for one are always threatening to break out. What these materials are, and how they might enrich a feminist political theory despite Arendt's neglect of women and gender, is what I explore below. What I want to argue is that, from one possible feminist perspective, *The Human Condition* is *both* flawed and illuminating.

Although Arendt has been accused of romanticizing the public realm and ignoring the brutality and patriarchalism that attends politics, she is, in fact, not wholly inattentive to the historically grounded relationships that have structured the activities she posits as fundamental to the human condition.[31] From the beginning, she argues, some have sought ways to ease the burden of life by forcibly assigning to others the toil of *animal laborans*. Those who have been regularly reduced to the status of "worldless specimens of the species mankind," have made it possible for others to transcend "the toil and trouble of life" by standing on the backs of those they subordinate.[32] In the modern age, this subordination is most vividly revealed within the working class. The activity of *homo faber* has lost its worldly character and is now performed by a mass of workers who are bent upon sheer survival and reduced to little more than servants of mechanized processes. (Work of this kind brings *homo faber* ever closer to *animal laborans*.) Arendt is also aware that the freedom of the "man of action"—the speaker of words and doer of deeds in the public realm—is made possible because of others who labor, fabricate, and produce. The man of action, as citizen, thus "remains in dependence upon his fellow men."[33] She does not press the sociological analysis of labor, work, and action along the lines of master and slave, elite and mass, privileged and oppressed, nearly as far as she could. But she is not completely unconcerned with the coercive and oppressive aspects of human experience that have allowed the privileged alone to enjoy the benefits of action in the public realm.

Likewise, Arendt cannot be accused of completely overlooking the manifestations of patriarchal power within the historical development of the public and private realm. Although she literally renders the discussion as footnotes, she provides in small print some illuminating insights into various dimensions of our patriarchal history. She tells us, for instance, that the terms *dominus* and *paterfamilias* were synonymous throughout "the whole of occidental antiquity."[34] The realm of the ancient household was, literally, a miniature *patria*—a sphere of absolute, uncontested rule exercised by the father over women, children, and slaves. Only in the public realm did the *paterfamilias* shed his status as ruler, and become one among equals, simultaneously ruling and ruled. Only he was able to move between public and private as both citizen among citizens, and ruler over those not fit for admission to the public realm.

In her subtext discussion of the Greek distinction between labor and work (*ponos* and *ergon*), Arendt notes that Hesiod considered labor an evil that came out of Pandora's box. Work, however, was the gift of Eris, the goddess of good strife.[35] Earlier she also tells us that, for Aristotle, "the life of woman" is called *ponetikos*—that is, women's lives are "laborious, driven by necessity, and devoted, by nature, to bodily functions."[36] Following the poet and the philosopher, our patriarchal history begins by counting painful labor (*ponon alginoenta*) as "the first of the evils plaguing man," and by assigning to women and slaves the inevitable and ineliminable task of carrying out this labor, according to their respectively less rational and irrational natures.[37] These are the tasks that, for the Greeks, occupied and defined the private realm and were forced into hiding within the interior (*megaron*) of the house. Here Arendt observes that the Greek *megaron* and the Latin *atrium* have a strong connotation of darkness and blackness.[38] Thus the realm of women and slaves is, for the ancients, a realm of necessity, painful labor, and blackness. In its toil and trouble, the private realm symbolizes the denial of freedom and equality, and the deprivation of being heard and seen by others. In its material reality, it makes possible the Greek male's escape from the "first evil" into the life of the public.

As Arendt implies, then, for the realm of freedom and politics to exist and take on meaning, it needed an "other"—a realm of necessity and privacy against which it could define and assert itself.[39] That this realm of the other and the human practices that distinguish it came to be conceptualized in terms of the female and made the domain of women's lives is something feminist theorists have brought to light in powerful detail. In *The Human Condition*, Arendt presents even more evidence for this argument, but it is evidence she does not utilize in her own theorizing of the human condition. Indeed, despite numerous instances in which she comes close to something like a nascent "gender insight" in her analysis of the public and private realm, and the activity of labor and work, Arendt never fully develops this insight or incorporates it systematically into her theory of the human condition.

Nowhere, perhaps, is Arendt's failure to develop her evidence about gender more striking than in her discussion of the character and conditions of *animal laborans*. It is the most illuminating example of how the materials for a feminist analysis are present in *The Human Condition*, but in the end are left unplumbed by Arendt herself. Consider again some of the characteristics that distinguish the life of *animal laborans*, as Arendt presents them: enslavement by necessity and the burden of biological life, a primary concern with reproduction, absorption with the production of life and its regeneration, and a focus on the body, nature, and natural life processes. Labor assures "not only individual survival, but the life of the species," and, finally, there is the elemental happiness that is tied to laboring, to the predictable repetition of the cycle of life and from just "being alive."[40] As Arendt writes:

> The blessing or joy of labor is the human way to experience the sheer bliss of being alive which we share with all living creatures, and it is even the only way men, too, can remain and swing contentedly in

nature's prescribed cycle . . . with the same happy and purposeless regularity with which day and night and life and death follow each other.[41]

The reference to "men" in this last passage sounds especially odd because the laboring Arendt has captured so vividly is more readily recognizable for the feminist reader as that associated with women's traditional activities as childbearers, preservers, and caretakers within the household and family.[42] Yet the activity of "world-protection, world-preservation, world-repair" that Arendt encompasses in her category "labor" is not acknowledged in *The Human Condition* as indicative of women's practices and activities.[43] But surely being "submerged in the over-all life process of the species," and identified with nature has been *women's* lot; being tied to biological processes has been women's destiny; facing the "essential worldly futility" of the lifecycle, within the darkness of the private realm, has been women's challenge. The cyclical, endlessly repetitive processes of household labor—cleaning, washing, mending, cooking, feeding, sweeping, rocking, tending—have been time-honored female ministrations, and also conceived of and justified as appropriate to women. Since the Greeks, the cyclical, biological processes of reproduction and labor have been associated with the female, and replicated in a multitude of historical institutions and practices. It is indeed curious that Arendt never makes this central feature of the human condition an integral part of her political analysis. Let us speculate nonetheless: what if *The Human Condition* had explored the category *animal laborans* as a social construction of "femaleness"? What else might we learn? A number of lessons emerge.

First, an Arendtian analysis enlightened by gender reveals that the "permanent capacities" of labor, work, and action are neither antiseptic analytical categories, nor "generic" human activities but rather social practices that have been arranged according to socially constituted and deeply entrenched sex differences. From Aristotle on, women have been systematically constructed as *animal laborans*, and deemed neither capable nor worthy of location with in the "space of appearances" that is action. Moreover, even when they are in the guise of *homo faber*—in the workplace of the "artificer"—women have carried out the routinized tasks of stoop labor on assembly lines, and as cleaners, cooks, and clericals. The mechanisms of institutionalized sexism have assigned to women unpaid, devalued, monotonous work, both within the private realm and within the world outside. Nominally *homo faber*, they are really *animal laborans*, transported from life into worldliness. It seems, then, that the fundamental existentials Arendt designates have actually been lived out as either male or female *identities. Animal laborans*, the "reproducer," has been structured and experienced as if it were natural to the female, and *homo faber*, the "fabricator," has been constructed as if it were natural to the male. Once we see this, we can no longer understand the *vita activa* as a neutral stage on which male and female players appear in modes of laboring, working, or acting. These activities have, from the start, been "cordoned off" according to sex, and women have been consistently relegated—both materially and symbolically— to the lowest dimension of the *vita activa*, to the life or world of labor.

Second, and following from the above, an Arendtian analysis informed by gender allows us to see that the disappearance of the public world, and the loss of freedom, has been a reality for only one small part of humanity. Just as "citizen" is an identity until recently granted to (some) men alone, so the "lost treasure" of political freedom, as Arendt calls it, has in fact been the historical possession of only (some) men. The feminist reader who shares Arendt's regret over the disappearance of freedom in the modern world is also aware that the treasure was never women's to lose.[44] The most emancipatory aspect of human experience as Arendt presents it—the collective determination of human community through shared speech and deliberation in the public sphere—is not a central aspect of female experience. Thus the human condition must be assessed not only for what it has lost, but for what it has done—for how it has systemati-

cally subordinated a portion of the human race, and refused them, on Arendt's telling, the most meaningful experience of human freedom.

Finally, an Arendtian analysis informed by gender, and the recognition of women's exclusion from the public, amplifies our conception of the relationship between public and private, and of freedom itself. Even if we were to recover the public realm Arendt so vividly imagines, no society could count itself free so long as women were refused admittance to the space of appearances or confined to gendered institutions within the private realm. But the admission of women into the public raises other questions, not the least of which is "who will tend to the private?" Or, as a graduate student I know puts it wryly, "Every citizen needs a wife."[45] Thus, if we are to have a truly emancipated *human* condition, we must inquire after both the arrangements that constitute the public, and the conditions of the realm of necessity, without which the public world of citizens cannot flourish. Susan Okin acknowledges this when she writes:

> Only when men participate equally in what have been principally women's realms of meeting the daily material and psychological needs of those close to them, and when women participate equally in what have been principally men's realms of larger scale production, government, and intellectual and creative life, will members of both sexes develop a more complete *human* personality than has hitherto been possible.[46]

Notice that this formulation does not require the abandonment of a conception of public and private, or a refusal of the distinction between labor, work, and action. But it does require us, in both theory and practice, to disconnect gender from these conceptions and reconceptualize them accordingly, as genderless realms and genderless activities. By "genderless" I do not mean "androcentric," but rather relations and realms unfettered by roles assigned according to perceived "natural" differences between the sexes. As Hanna Pitkin writes: "Women should be as free as men to act publicly; men should be as free as women to nurture. . . . A life confined entirely to personal and household concerns seems . . . stunted and impoverished, and so does a life so public or abstracted that it has lost all touch with the practical, everyday activities that sustain it."[47]

Arendt's failure to recognize, much less develop, the issues that surround the constitution of women as *animal laborans* is readily apparent. Her failure to integrate these issues into *The Human Condition* is particularly serious given her belief that we must "think what we are doing," lest we lose forever our understanding of those "higher and more meaningful activities" for the sake of which "our release from the bonds of necessity deserves to be won."[48] Had she recognized that "thinking what we are doing" entails not just a reconsideration of the *vita activa*, but also an account of how gender is implicated in the *vita activa* itself, *The Human Condition* would have been a far more emancipatory project. For all her attentiveness to the relationship between public and private, however, Arendt's gender blindness prevents her from seeing these realms as domains that have historically enforced women's subordination. For all her concern for freedom, she seems not to consider the exclusion of women from the public world at all informative of her analysis of the alienation of the contemporary age. In these respects, the androcentrism of Arendt's political theory diminishes her account of the very human condition she wishes us to comprehend.

Feminist Theory and the Public Realm

To the extent that *The Human Condition* fails to acknowledge the problem of women's subordination and (in bell hooks' terms) "the sexism perpetuated by institutions and social structures," it does not contribute to what we might call the "world-disclosing" aspect of a feminist theory.[49] It does not help us understand the ways in which the symbolic construction of gender has organized existing social practices and legitimized relations of domination.

Nevertheless, despite its inattention to issues related to sex and gender, *The Human Condition* has much to offer a feminist political theory. Accordingly, in the final section, I want to turn the tables and argue that Arendt's understanding of action and plurality as meaningful experiences of human freedom is something feminist theory should heed. In this respect, *The Human Condition* provides an orienting role for political self-understanding, and it encourages us to reconsider the way we think about the relationship between human practices and human identities.

Part of Arendt's critique of contemporary society involves her argument that politics as public life, as a space of appearances where citizens engage one another, deliberate, and debate, has nearly disappeared. As her emphasis on plurality indicates, Arendt means more by "participation in the space of appearances" than casting a ballot every four years or engaging in interest group activities. Indeed, the fact that we need to clarify the difference between voting and the active, public self-revelation of equals and peers as citizens is proof to Arendt that we have ceased to think of ourselves as, potentially, something more than just reproducers, producers, laborers, role-players, or fragile psyches. As the *vita activa* steadily becomes the province of *animal laborans*, so too, it seems, do our self-understandings. Our conceptualizations of who we are and what we are capable of doing are driven by the imperatives of "the last stage of laboring society"; hence we are less and less capable of imagining ourselves as mutually engaged citizens, or of thinking in terms of a political "we" rather than just an isolated "me." Our access to an understanding of politics as a public happiness has diminished; "mere" life overrules other considerations, the body supercedes the body politic, and the sheer survival of the individual as a "self" predominates over sensitivity to human plurality.

Athough it is not easy to say precisely what Arendt means by the notion that we have come to think what we are doing as *animal laborans*, she surely is getting at something more than just a cliché about the "me generation." Perhaps her argument is best summed up in terms of her own concepts: the modern age operates under the assumption that life, and not the world, is the highest good; the *immortality* of life—the possibility of achieving glory through speech and deed as public-spirited citizens—is a fading ideal. We are turned inward, and thrown back upon ourselves and our endlessly analyzed psyches. We are obsessed with society, wealth, and entertainment, but at a loss to comprehend the human condition as a being-in-the-presence-of-others in the *political* world. Remarking on the modern age, Arendt writes (in gendered language): "none of the higher capacities of man was any longer necessary to connect individual life with the life of the species; individual life became part of the life process, and to labor, to assure the continuity of one's own life and the life of the family, was all that was needed."[50]

Arendt intends for this indictment to cover philosophers of the modern age as well as ordinary agents. She numbers Marx, Kierkegaard, Nietzsche, and Bergson among those for whom political freedom and the worldliness of action have lost their meaning, or at least been radically transfigured. Hence the ultimate point of reference in their writings is not politics, action or plurality, but rather "life and life's fertility."[51] At least in the case of Kierkegaard and Nietzsche, the alternately agitated or aesthetic "I" replaces the politically engaged "we."

In the late twentieth century, a similar reluctance to theorize in political terms, by grounding the identity of human agents in the condition of plurality and in the capacity for speech and deed, seems to characterize certain forms of feminist theory. Nowhere perhaps is the temptation to theorize in the terms of *animal laborans*—with heightened attention to nature, reproduction, birth, the body, and the rhythmic processes of life itself—more prevalent than among those feminists who are concerned to argue that a privileged epistemological perspective emerges from specifically female practices and a generalizable women's condition. Consider, as examples, Mary O'Brien's emphasis on birth and reproduction as a starting point for a feminist theory of material relations, Nancy Hartsock's attention to the body's "de-sires, needs, and mortality" as a primary element in feminist epistemology, Adrienne Rich's concentration on "housework, childcare, and the repair of daily life" as the distinctive feature of women's community, Sara Ruddick's claim that daily nurturance and maternal work give women special insights into peace, and Julia Kristeva's case for the subversive potential of gestation, childbirth, and motherhood.[52] Although these theories are variously materialist, maternalist, and poststructuralist, they have in common an emancipatory vision that defends the moral (or subversive) possibilities of women's role as reproducer, nurturer, and preserver of vulnerable human life. O'Brien, for one, envisions a feminist theory "which celebrates once more the unity of cyclical time with historical time in the conscious and rational reproduction of the species. It will be a theory of the celebration of life in life rather than death in life."[53] Within this presumably celebratory vision an Arendtian might notice a tribute to *animal laborans*.

The temptation to theorize from the standpoint of women's bodies, and with an emphasis on reproduction, childbirth and mothering, bears a compelling logic. Women have been construed in terms of bodily processes and the so-called imperative of nature, and feminist theory, in its "world-disclosing" or critical aspects, confronts these putatively natural attributes and demystifies them. Feminist theory has revealed that, in O'Brien's words, "the private realm is where the new action is," insofar as the unmasking of structures of female subordination is concerned.[54] However, in the process of unmasking the manifold faces of power, many feminist theorists have, in effect, elevated the activities of *animal laborans* as the central features of women's identity and feminist politics. Guided by a reading of *The Human Condition* and Arendt's categories of the *vita activa*, we might consider why this feminist maneuver poses problems for a feminist theory of politics.

Unavoidably, when feminist theorists locate emancipatory or interventionist possibilities in "female reproductive consciousness" or within traditional female activities, they grant some warrant to the very patriarchal arrangements that have historically structured the *vita activa*. Of course, feminists appropriate these arrangements for purposes of emancipatory consciousness, but the subordination of women to *animal laborans* remains intact nonetheless. Accordingly, these feminist arguments—despite their transvaluation of women's work and bodily processes—legitimize a minimalist conception of women without considering a more expansive set of possibilities about what it means to be "in the presence of other human beings in the world." The celebration of *animal laborans* plays to a reduced, uniform conception of women's range of capabilities and their human identity within the *vita activa*. As Arendt's discussion of labor, work, and action invites us to see, however, being human involves more than just what Kristeva (appreciatively) calls "cycles, gestation, [and] the eternal recurrence of a biological rhythm which conforms to that of nature."[55] If female subjectivity has been traditionally linked to this latter form of temporality, then the goal of a feminist political theory should be to disengage female subjectivity from the straitjacket rather than to reinforce so restrictive a view of existential possibility and human potentiality.

Moreover, for an Arendtian, this disengagement from a theory of subjectivity rooted in *animal laborans* must be undertaken with a specifically political goal in mind. Whatever else we might wish to make of women as reproducers, mothers, or "celebratory of life in life," we should not confuse gender identification—or theories of subjectivity—with *political* emancipation. A feminist theory of political emancipation needs more than a focus on reproduction, birth, and childcare to sustain it. For, as much as we need to be reminded of the centrality of these experiences in the human condition, they do not and cannot serve as the focal point of a liberatory political theory. This is not only because, historically, reproduction, birth, and childcare have been practices as conducive to political oppression as to liberation. In addition, and perhaps more importantly, the language of birth and reproduc-

tion—constrained by its emphasis on a singular female physiology (or orientation) and the uniformity of women—simply does not provide feminism with the linguistic or conceptual context necessary for a theory of politics and political action. A theory of emancipatory politics must pay attention to diversity, solidarity, action-coordination, conflict, plurality, and the political equality (not the sameness) of women as citizens. None of these conceptual categories are forthcoming in theories grounded on singularity, physiology, necessity, uniformity, subjectivity, and the identity of women as reproducers.

Here, I think is where *The Human Condition* has the most to offer a feminist political theory. By articulating a conception of politics and political equality as collective action and the mutual engagement of peers in a public realm Arendt has us focus on what it means to be "speakers of words and doers of deeds" whose particular and distinctive identities deserve revelation in the public space of citizen politics. As a result, we shift our focus on human practices away from sheer biological, bodily processes on the one hand, and economic productivity on the other, and toward the constitution of public, political life. In this sense, Arendt forces theory to become expressly political, because she directs us toward the *public* aspect of human life and toward the human activity that determines all other human relations and arrangements in demonstrable ways. Moreover, she argues that the only polity that truly advances the freedom and plurality human beings are capable of experiencing, not to mention the conditions of existence they value and defend, is the polity that exhibits widespread participation in the public realm. To return to the notion of plurality, freedom is advanced when politics unfolds as the communicative interaction of diverse equals acting together as citizens.

Few feminist theorists have confronted the question of what constitutes a feminist politics in any systematic fashion, and fewer still have attempted to outline the contours of a feminist public realm.[56] In part, perhaps, this is because feminist theory has long had an ambivalence about matters public and political, and theoretical difficulties in distinguishing "politics" from "the patriarchal state." What has been historically constituted as the province of masculinity is often ceded to the male-stream, as feminists turn their attention toward the private domain of women's lives, thereby perpetuating the binary oppositions of "private woman, public man." As Arendt's existential analysis of the *vita activa* suggests, however, there is nothing intrinsically or essentially masculine about the public realm, just as there is nothing intrinsically or essentially feminine about laboring in the realm of necessity. The point is not to accept these gendered realms as fixed and immutable, but rather to undermine the gendering of public and private and move on to a more visionary and liberating conception of human practices, including those that constitute politics.

For feminists, Arendt's conception of plurality as politics may provide a promising place to begin. Plurality reinforces the notion of what Iris Young calls a "politics of difference," and emphasizes the heterogeneity of citizens. The unity Arendt imagines in the public realm is not mere uniformity, but rather a kind of solidarity engendered by the engagement of diversely constituted, unique individuals. Although Arendt did not pursue the concrete manifestations of plurality in any depth, she laid the groundwork for a political theory of action and difference, and a conception of civic "publics" as spaces where plurality can manifest itself. Without question, a feminist turn to plurality and politics would require the abandonment of some of the epistemological longings that underlie some current feminist theories—particularly the quest for univocality, certainty, and a fixed "standpoint" on reality. A feminist theory of politics as plurality needs to acknowledge multivocality, conflict, and the constantly shifting and ambiguous nature of politics itself. Given their appreciation of "otherness," however, and a growing attention to cultural diversity and heterogeneity, feminist theorists are also particularly well-situated for the task of developing our understanding of politics as plurality. Feminist theory also provides a powerful critique of the masculine virtue of "glory" that plays such an important role in Arendt's vision of action in the public realm. A feminist ethic of care, for example, might encourage us to imagine other dimensions of freedom, beyond glory, as vital to the public realm.

Equally significantly, Arendt's conception of politics places emphasis on a human capacity that has been central to much feminist theorizing—speech or "voice." Her case for political equality is informed by two basic insights concerning the human condition: that it is within the range of all human beings to insert themselves into the public realm through speech; and that the communicative interaction in which shared speakers engage as self-determining agents and representative thinkers is the essence of freedom. These insights raise other interesting questions for feminists that Arendt herself did not pursue, among them: what constitutes an ethic of communicative interaction among citizens? How can the diversity of speech and speakers be maintained and allowed to flourish? Do women bring a "different voice" or a "female consciousness" into the public realm? If so, how have these been manifested in practical, historical experience?[57] What should a feminist politics make of this voice and consciousness, if they indeed exist? All of these questions invite feminist attention, and encourage us to theorize both about who women are as citizens and about citizenship itself as a non-gendered activity.

I have argued that Arendt's concepts of action and plurality provide an orienting role for a feminist theory of politics. Implicit in my argument is also an acceptance of the general distinctions she draws between labor, work, and action as general and permanent human capacities. In accepting the general framework of Arendt's theory, however, I do not mean to suggest that the distinctions she draws between these three modes of the *vita activa* are completely unproblematic. Nor are they exhaustive. Maternalist theorists, for instance, could rightly argue that mothering is as vital and perennial a human activity as labor, work, and action, and rightly insist that it does not fit easily under the parameters Arendt establishes for the *vita activa*. But neither are

Arendt's analytical categories marked by the "artificiality" and "literal thoughtlessness" that O'Brien attributes to them. In some respects, of course, all analytical constructions are "artificial"; the issue is whether or not the theorist makes them a convincing and illuminating source for political reflection, as I think Arendt does.

In closing, then, I want briefly to reassert my case for *The Human Condition* as a source of political reflection, and with the hope of deflecting some possible responses to my appropriation of Arendt for a feminist theory of politics. Perhaps the most predictable response to this case for Arendt is that her theory not only privileges male "logocentric" reason but also continues in a tradition of disparaging the female body—or a "politics of the body"—and women's work. Rich comes close to the latter when she alludes to the "contempt and indifference" for the efforts of "women in labor" that typify theories like Arendt's.[58] But Rich misunderstands Arendt's characterization of labor. Nowhere does Arendt suggest that labor is a contemptible or insignificant activity. Her refusal to romanticize it should not be taken as offhand dismissal. To the contrary, Arendt writes that, "From the viewpoint of the life of the species, all activities indeed find their common denominator in laboring," and she says that the "blessing of life as a whole" is inherent in labor.[59] What Rich rightly wants to have philosophers acknowledge is not, however, in Arendt's view, the highest expression of human *freedom*. That comes only with collective action in the public realm. In fact, the glorification of *animal laborans* that Rich, like O'Brien, comes very close to exhibiting is precisely what Arendt thinks characterizes alienation and the loss of our capacity to think coherently about freedom in the contemporary world.

As for a "politics of the body," there is nothing in Arendt's discussion of plurality that posits "reason" over "passion" or condemns the literal body (or issues concerning life or the social control of the body) to the sphere of the private realm. In fact, Arendt's account of politics in the public realm brings courage, the spontaneity of passion, and "appearance" to the foreground, as crucial elements in the revelation of self that is part of collective speech and action. What she rejects, then, is not the presence of the body or a bodily politics but rather a political theory that locates the identity of persons only in a collective, singular, physiology—or in practices tied to the rhythmic cycles of nature. Arendt realizes human beings are ineliminably bound to nature, but we are also able to act in ways that at least temporarily defy the unremitting play of natural forces. Our bodies, in other words, are not merely the vessels of generative forces; they are also, along with our voices, integral to our appearance in the public world. This is one thing Arendt's discussion of plurality and individuals attempts to have us recognize. It is the *distinction* between the processes of reproduction on the one hand, where the body is conceived in a singularly narrow way, and action on the other, the collective power of embodied persons made political, that Arendt wants to preserve. Thus, Nancy Hartsock's attempt to return Arendt's theory of power to the body at "the epistemological level of reproduction" misses a fundamental point. In Arendt's theory, a "bodily politics" exists and exhibits itself in the life of action within the public realm. To ground politics in reproduction, as Hartsock wants to do, and thereby make *animal laborans* the source of power, is apples and oranges—Arendt's theory simply cannot be transformed this way and remain coherent.[60]

Finally, the problem of "reason." Although Arendt obviously considers thinking and rational argumentation essential to the interaction of citizens in the public realm, she distinguishes between the communicative rationality indicative of plurality, and the instrumental rationality of *homo faber*, who thinks in terms of ends and means. In short, Arendt is rightly aware that there are many different forms of reason, some of which are appropriate to the realm of politics and not antithetical to the recognition of otherness, some of which are not. Representative thinking, the mentality that distinguishes action in the public realm, is a good example of a form of reason that defies characterization in terms that would have us drive a wedge between reason and passion. It encompasses and incorporates both. Those who would dismiss her conception of public life as "too rational" or lacking in passion misapprehend the complexity of rationality in general and Arendt's "communications theory" of power more specifically.[61] We need only remember Tiananmen Square, a perfect example of the boundless and unpredictable "space of appearances" as Arendt envisions it, to understand that her vision of public life admits of passion and spontaneity as well as rational discourse, and the drama of visual, bodily appearances as well as *"logos"* and reason.

My defense of *The Human Condition* as a possible starting place for a feminist theory of politics is not an endorsement of Arendt's theory *tout court*. As I hope I have shown, a feminist analysis reveals much about the inadequacies of Arendt's major work as a commentary on both the classical and the contemporary age. Still, feminism—at least in its academic guise—needs a calling back to politics. In this respect, *The Human Condition* gives feminist thought ground on which to stand and develop an action-coordinating theory of political emancipation. Because she articulates such a powerful defense of public, participatory citizenship and of empowerment as speech and action in plurality, Arendt provides feminist thinkers with a way to proceed toward politics. For a movement such as feminism, which has so vividly illuminated the inequalities and injustices of existing gender relations, but has not yet advanced a transformative vision of politics, *The Human Condition* offers a place to begin anew, as we try to imagine better political worlds.

Notes

1. Adrienne Rich, *On Lies, Secrets, and Silence: Selected Prose 1966–1978* (New York: W. W. Norton, 1979), p. 212; and Mary O'Brien, *The Politics of Reproduction* (London: Routledge and Kegan Paul, 1981), pp. 99–100.

2. O'Brien, *Politics of Reproduction*, p. 101.

3. Nancy Hartsock, *Money, Sex, and Power* (Boston: Northeastern University Press, 1985), p. 259.

4. Hanna Fenichel Pitkin, "Justice: On Relating Private and Public," *Political Theory*, 9, 1981, pp. 303–26.

5. Terry Winant, "The Feminist Standpoint: A Matter of Language," *Hypatia*, 2, 1987, p. 124.

6. Hannah Arendt, *The Human Condition* (Chicago: University of Chicago Press, 1958), p. 6.

7. Ibid., p. 7.

8. Ibid., p. 22.

9. Ibid., p. 5.

10. Arendt takes the phrase in quotes from Locke, and uses it to set off her discussion of labor and work as the human activities elevated in both liberal and Marxist thought.

11. Arendt, *Human Condition*, p. 96.

12. Ibid., p. 131. For a helpful clarification of the relationship between labor, work, and action and the mentalities Arendt associates with them, see Pitkin, "Justice."

13. Arendt, *Human Condition*, p. 144. Or, as she also puts it, *homo faber*, the creator of human artifice, is also a "destroyer of nature" (p. 139).

14. Ibid., pp. 136–7.

15. Ibid., p. 157.

16. Ibid., p. 305.

17. Ibid., p. 137.

18. Ibid., p. 190.

19. Ibid., p. 204.

20. Ibid., p. 7.

21. Ibid., p. 244.

22. Ibid., p. 175. The spontaneous political uprising of the Chinese people in Tiananmen Square was one of the most dramatic examples of what Arendt means by "action" and "plurality." What arose there was a community of equals, "where everybody has the same capacity to act . . . and the impossibility of remaining unique masters of what they do, of knowing its consequences and relying upon the future" (p. 244). Arendt calls this the "price paid for plurality"—for the joy of inhabiting together with others a world whose reality is guaranteed for each by the presence of all. Hence her emphasis on the "unpredictability" and the "boundlessness" of action, as well as its inherent glory and irreducible collectivity.

23. Ibid., p. 8.

24. Ibid., pp. 52, 204.

25. Ibid., p. 205.

26. Ibid., p. 9.

27. Ibid., p. 204.

28. Arendt develops the dimensions of this mentality more fully in her essay, "The Crisis in Culture," in her *Between Past and Future* (New York: Viking Press, 1961), pp. 220–4. In contemporary terminology, the capacity to judge is communicative, not rational-instrumental.

29. Arendt is well aware that, throughout history, vast numbers of people have been prevented from realizing their existentially highest human activities. See *Human Condition*, p. 199.

30. Ibid., p. 72.

31. See O'Brien, *Politics of Reproduction*, pp. 103–7.

32. Arendt, *Human Condition*, pp. 118–19.

33. Ibid., p. 144.

34. Ibid., p. 28.

35. Ibid., p. 83.

36. Ibid., p. 72.

37. Ibid., p. 48.

38. Ibid., p. 71.

39. Arendt notes that the private "was like the other, the dark and hidden side of the public realm." Ibid., p. 64.

40. Ibid., pp. 8, 88, 111, 119.

41. Ibid., p. 106.

42. By putting this point in this way I do not mean to imply that the activity of labor has been everywhere the same for all women or that we can understand women's laboring in some universal, transhistorical fashion. For my purposes, what is significant is that Arendt leaves out of her discussion any acknowledgement that it is *women* who have in fact been assigned this activity she describes as the "lowest" in the human condition.

43. The phrase in quotes is from Rich, *On Lies, Secrets, and Silence*, p. 205. As far as I can tell, she was the first to make this prescient observation about Arendt's *animal laborans.*

44. I am not suggesting that women have never participated in political life, only that, historically, they have not been accorded formal recognition as the equals and peers of men as citizens in the public realm. For a stimulating account of the ways in which women in the United States have found ways of participating in public life despite the denial of political equality, see Sara Evans, *Born for Liberty: A History of Women in America* (New York: Free Press, 1989).

45. Thanks to Ron Steiner.

46. See p. 195 above.

47. Hanna Fenichel Pitkin, "Food and Freedom in *The Founder*," *Political Theory*, 12, 1984, p. 481.

48. Arendt, *Human Condition*, p. 5.

49. bell hooks, *Feminist Theory from Margin to Center* (Boston: South End Press, 1984), p. 43. For a lucid discussion of the difference between "world-disclosing" and "action-coordinating" theories, see Stephen White, "Poststructuralism and Political Reflection," *Political Theory*, 16, 1988, pp. 186–208.

50. Arendt, *Human Condition*, p. 321.

51. Ibid., p. 313.

52. See O'Brien, *Politics of Reproduction*; Hartsock, *Money, Sex and Power*; Rich, *On Lies, Secrets, and Silence*; Sara Ruddick, *Maternal Thinking: Toward a Politics of Peace* (Boston: Beacon Press, 1989); and Ann Rosalind Jones, "Julia Kristeva on Femininity: The Limits of a Semiotic Politics," *Feminist Review*, 18, 1984, pp. 56–73.

53. O'Brien, *Politics of Reproduction*, p. 209.

54. Ibid., p. 208.

55. Julia Kristeva, "Women's Time," in *Feminist Theory: A Critique of Ideology*, ed. Nannerl O. Keohane, Michelle Z. Rosaldo, and Barbara C. Gelpi (Chicago: University of Chicago Press, 1981), pp. 31–54.

56. One exception is Iris Marion Young, whose work has expressly addressed the nature of a feminist politics and civic public. See "Impartiality and the Civic Public: Some Implications of Feminist Critiques of Moral and Political Theory," in *Feminism as Critique*, ed. Seyla Benhabib and Drucilla Cornell (Cambridge: Polity; Minneapolis: University of Minnesota Press, 1987), pp. 56–76; "The Ideal of Community and the Politics of Difference," *Social Theory and Practice*, 12, 1986, pp. 1–26; and "Polity and Group Difference: A Critique of the Ideal of Universal Citizenship," *Ethics*, 99, 1989, pp. 250–74. Also see Nancy Fraser, "Toward a Discourse Ethic of Solidarity," *Praxis International*, 5, 1986, pp. 42–59.

57. On the significance of a "female consciousness" in politics, see Temma Kaplan, "Female Consciousness and Collective Action: The Case of Barcelona, 1910–1915," in *Feminist Theory*, ed. Keohane et al., pp. 55–76.

58. Rich, *On Lies, Secrets and Silence*, p. 206.

59. Arendt, *Human Condition*, pp. 107–8.

60. Hartsock, *Money, Sex, and Power*, pp. 258–9.

61. For a cogent critique of how some feminists misapprehend rationality and reason, see

Mary Hawkesworth, "Knowers, Knowing, and Known: Feminist Theory and Claims of Truth," *Signs: Journal of Women in Culture and Society,* 14, 1989, pp. 533–57.

John Rawls

How do we know when a contemporary work in political theory has achieved the status of a classic? One answer must surely be, when nearly every contemporary theorist has felt compelled to read and comment upon it. Upon its publication in 1971, *A Theory of Justice* quickly became such a work and by the mid-1970s, a veritable Rawls industry had developed among theorists in political science, philosophy, sociology, and the law. Liberals hailed the book as a solution to the tensions between liberty and equality, conservatives viewed it as a brief for activist government, and radicals saw it as an ideological expression of the liberal welfare state. No matter one's perspective, though, *A Theory of Justice* was never seen as an uninspiring volume of academic philosophy. Indeed, *A Theory of Justice* has sometimes been credited with reviving Anglo-American political philosophy and renewing concern with such concepts as justice, liberty, and equality.

Rawls was born in Baltimore in 1921. He started his education in a preparatory school in Connecticut and pursued an undergraduate degree in philosophy at Princeton. Upon his graduation in 1943, he enlisted in the army and saw action in the Pacific theater for the remainder of World War II. He returned to Princeton in 1949, where he first developed the idea for a treatise on justice while he completed the work for his doctoral degree. With his Ph.D. in hand by 1950, he spent time at Oxford and then began a career of teaching philosophy at Cornell University, the Massachusetts Institute of Technology, and since the mid-1960s, Harvard University. In the 1990s, Rawls published his second book, *Political Liberalism*, and a few collections of his published and unpublished essays. The National Endowment for the Humanities honored Rawls with the National Humanities Medal in 1999.

A Theory of Justice

A rather simple thought experiment forms the premise of the book. Imagine that a group of rational people, knowing nothing about their own positions in society or their eventual fates, meet to discuss what principles of justice should govern their community. Under these conditions, in this hypothetical "original position," Rawls believes that rational agents would agree upon two principles that not only have everyone's consent, but also fit with our intuitions about the nature of social justice. Acceptance of these principles would mean that the just society is one in which "primary social goods" (e.g., political liberties, economic opportunities, offices, and self-esteem) are distributed in ways that provide individuals with equal respect, equal liberty, and equal opportunity. In the selections that follow, Rawls offers a preliminary discussion of the central concepts employed by his theory of "justice as fairness"—the basic structure, the original position, the principle of liberty, and the difference principle.

Political Liberalism

After the extensive discussion surrounding *A Theory of Justice*, the expectations for Rawls's second book were quite high. Most scholars believed that it would answer the serious questions about his views that were raised by communitarians, radicals, and feminists. However, in *Political Liberalism* (1993), Rawls shifted his focus from debating principles of justice to discussing how society handles major disagreements about justice and morality. In clarifying his idea of the original position, for example, Rawls essentially argues that the scholars who understood his previous work as offering a "metaphysical" conception of justice were mistaken. The theory of justice should instead be understood as a "political" conception, one deeply rooted in the culture of a liberal society—a culture that sees comprehensive doctrines as threats to both social peace and individual liberty.

Commentaries

In their book on Rawls, Chandran Kukathas and Philip Pettit begin by presenting a "brisk exposition" of the argument in *A Theory of Justice*. This overview, excerpted below, examines the assumptions underlying the selection of the principles of justice in the original position. It also discusses the relationship between the two principles and the concept of the basic structure—those institutions necessary for a constitutional democracy, and thereby, a just social and economic order.

In their essay, Elizabeth Frazer and Nicola Lacey examine the theory of justice from a feminist standpoint. Although Rawls tries to address a number of his critics in *Political Liberalism*, he does so only by papering over key distinctions. For example, Frazer and Lacey suggest that Rawls is generally unable to reconcile two contrary voices in his work—a universal one (the philosophical voice) and a particularistic one (the voice of a liberal democratic citizen). They also assert that while he tries to maintain the distinction between public and the private, he is not able to do so consistently. In short, the efforts made by Rawls to modify his original theory of justice have not been successful in meeting the challenges posed by feminism. Further, those same efforts have made it difficult for Rawls to adequately address issues of political power and opposition.

Web Sources

http://chronicle.com/free/v47/i45/ 45b00701.htm
The Enduring Significance of John Rawls. A readable overview and assessment of the Rawlsian corpus.

http://www.baylor.edu/~Lynette_Sweidel/ Rawls.html

Life and Work of John Rawls. Links to a number of essays and short pieces.

Class Activities and Discussion Items

1. Explain the following Rawlsian concepts: the original position, the veil of ignorance, maximin decision making, and the rational autonomy of moral persons. Imagine yourself as an agent in an original position, charged with developing rational and just principles for distributing a basic good—course grades, for example.

2. Compare and contrast the conceptions of human nature and politics held by Rawls and other theorists. Which theorist has the most adequate conception of human nature? Why?

3. State and evaluate Rawls's theory of the hypothetical social contract. Does his contract theory suffer from the defects of earlier ones? Why or why not?

4. Do the principles of justice really fit our moral intuitions? In what sense are they liberal? How might they be applied to contemporary policy issues?

Further Reading

Daniels, Norman (ed.). 1975. *Reading Rawls.* Oxford: Basil Blackwell. An early collection of essays responding to *A Theory of Justice.*

Okin, Susan Moller. 1989. *Justice, Gender, and the Family.* New York: Basic Books. A feminist discussion of theories of justice, with special attention paid to Rawls.

Ryan, Alan. 1985. "John Rawls." In *The Return of Grand Theory in the Human Sciences* (Quentin Skinner, ed.), pp. 101–119. Cambridge: Cambridge University Press. An excellent, brief introduction to the theory and the controversy.

Sandel, M. 1982. *Liberalism and the Limits of Justice.* Cambridge, Mass.: Harvard University Press. One significant effort to respond to and offer an alternative to Rawls.

Wolff, Robert Paul. 1977. *Understanding Rawls: A Reconstruction and Critique of "A Theory of Justice."* Princeton, NJ: Princeton University Press. An early and cogent critique of Rawls's first work. ✦

46

Excerpts from *A Theory of Justice*

John Rawls

Chapter I
Justice as Fairness

In this introductory chapter I sketch some of the main ideas of the theory of justice I wish to develop. The exposition is informal and intended to prepare the way for the more detailed arguments that follow. Unavoidably there is some overlap between this and later discussions. I begin by describing the role of justice in social cooperation and with a brief account of the primary subject of justice, the basic structure of society. I then present the main idea of justice as fairness, a theory of justice that generalizes and carries to a higher level of abstraction the traditional conception of the social contract. The compact of society is replaced by an initial situation that incorporates certain procedural constraints on arguments designed to lead to an original agreement on principles of justice. I also take up, for purposes of clarification and contrast, the classical utilitarian and intuitionist conceptions of justice and consider some of the differences between these views and justice as fairness. My guiding aim is to work out a theory of justice that is a viable alternative to these doctrines which have long dominated our philosophical tradition.

1. The Role of Justice

Justice is the first virtue of social institutions, as truth is of systems of thought. A theory however elegant and economical must be rejected or revised if it is untrue; likewise laws and institutions no matter how efficient and well-arranged must be reformed or abol-

ished if they are unjust. Each person possesses an inviolability founded on justice that even the welfare of society as a whole cannot override. For this reason justice denies that the loss of freedom for some is made right by a greater good shared by others. It does not allow that the sacrifices imposed on a few are outweighed by the larger sum of advantages enjoyed by many. Therefore in a just society the liberties of equal citizenship are taken as settled; the rights secured by justice are not subject to political bargaining or to the calculus of social interests. The only thing that permits us to acquiesce in an erroneous theory is the lack of a better one; analogously, an injustice is tolerable only when it is necessary to avoid an even greater injustice. Being first virtues of human activities, truth and justice are uncompromising.

These propositions seem to express our intuitive conviction of the primacy of justice. No doubt they are expressed too strongly. In any event I wish to inquire whether these contentions or others similar to them are sound, and if so how they can be accounted for. To this end it is necessary to work out a theory of justice in the light of which these assertions can be interpreted and assessed. I shall begin by considering the role of the principles of justice. Let us assume, to fix ideas, that a society is a more or less self-sufficient association of persons who in their relations to one another recognize certain rules of conduct as binding and who for the most part act in accordance with them. Suppose further that these rules specify a system of cooperation designed to advance the good of those taking part in it. Then, although a society is a cooperative venture for mutual advantage, it is typically marked by a conflict as well as by an identity of interests. There is an identity of interests since social cooperation makes possible a better life for all than any would have if each were to live solely by his own efforts. There is a conflict of interests since persons are not indifferent as to how the greater benefits produced by their collaboration are distributed, for in order to pursue their ends they each prefer a larger to a lesser share. A set of principles is required for choosing among the various social arrangements which determine this division of advantages and for underwriting an agreement on the proper distributive shares. These principles are the principles of social justice: they provide a way of assigning rights and duties in the basic institutions of society and they define the appropriate distribution of the benefits and burdens of social cooperation.

Now let us say that a society is well-ordered when it is not only designed to advance the good of its members but when it is also effectively regulated by a public conception of justice. That is, it is a society in which (1) everyone accepts and knows that the others accept the same principles of justice, and (2) the basic social institutions generally satisfy and are generally known to satisfy these principles. In this case while men may put forth excessive demands on one another, they nevertheless acknowledge a common point of view from which their claims may be adjudicated. If men's inclination to self-interest makes their vigilance against one another necessary, their public sense of justice makes their secure association together possible. Among individuals with disparate aims and purposes a shared conception of justice establishes the bonds of civic friendship; the general desire for justice limits the pursuit of other ends. One may think of a public conception of justice as constituting the fundamental charter of a well-ordered human association.

Existing societies are of course seldom well-ordered in this sense, for what is just and unjust is usually in dispute. Men disagree about which principles should define the basic terms of their association. Yet we may still say, despite this disagreement, that they each have a conception of justice. That is, they understand the need for, and they are prepared to affirm, a characteristic set of principles for assigning basic rights and duties and for determining what they take to be the proper distribution of the benefits and burdens of social cooperation. Thus it seems natural to think of the concept of justice as distinct from the various conceptions of justice and as being specified by the role which these different sets of principles, these different conceptions, have in common. Those who hold different conceptions of justice can, then, still agree that institutions are just when no arbitrary distinctions are made between persons in the assigning of basic rights and duties and when the rules determine a proper balance between competing claims to the advantages of social life. Men can agree to this description of just institutions since the notions of an arbitrary distinction and of a proper balance, which are included in the concept of justice, are left open for each to interpret according to the principles of justice that he accepts. These principles single out which similarities and differences among persons are relevant in determining rights and duties and they specify which division of advantages is appropriate. Clearly this distinction between the concept and the various conceptions of justice settles no important questions. It simply helps to identify the role of the principles of social justice.

Some measure of agreement in conceptions of justice is, however, not the only prerequisite for a viable human community. There are other fundamental social problems, in particular those of coordination, efficiency, and stability. Thus the plans of individuals need to be fitted together so that their activities are compatible with one another and they can all be carried through without anyone's legitimate expectations being severely disappointed. Moreover, the execution of these plans should lead to the achievement of social ends in ways that are efficient and consistent with justice. And finally, the scheme of social cooperation must be stable: it must be more or less regularly complied with and its basic rules willingly acted upon; and when infractions occur, stabilizing forces should exist that prevent further violations and tend to restore the arrangement. Now it is evident that these three problems are connected with that of justice. In the absence of a certain measure of agreement on what is just and unjust, it is clearly more difficult for individuals to coordinate their plans efficiently in order to insure that mutually beneficial arrangements are maintained. Distrust and resentment corrode the ties of civility, and suspicion and hostility tempt men to act in ways they would otherwise avoid. So while the distinctive role of conceptions of justice is to specify basic rights and duties and to determine the appropriate distributive shares, the way in which a conception does this is bound to affect the problems of efficiency, coordination, and stability. We cannot, in general, assess a conception of justice by its distributive role alone, however useful this role may be in identifying the concept of justice. We must take into account its wider connections; for even though justice has a certain priority, being the most important virtue of institutions, it is still true that, other things equal, one conception of justice is preferable to another when its broader consequences are more desirable.

2. The Subject of Justice

Many different kinds of things are said to be just and unjust: not only laws, institutions, and social systems, but also particular actions of many kinds, including decisions, judgments, and imputations. We also call the attitudes and dispositions of persons, and persons themselves, just and unjust. Our topic, however, is that of social justice. For us the primary subject of justice is the basic structure of society, or more exactly, the way in which the major social institutions distribute fundamental rights and duties and determine the division of advantages from social cooperation. By major institutions I understand the political constitution and the principal economic and social arrangements. Thus the legal protection of freedom of thought and liberty of conscience, competitive markets, private property in the means of production, and the monogamous family are examples of major social institutions. Taken together as one scheme, the major institutions define men's rights and duties and influence their life-prospects, what they can expect to be and how well they can hope to do. The basic structure is the primary subject of justice because its effects are so profound and present from the start. The intuitive notion here is that this structure contains various social positions and that men born into different positions have different expectations of life determined, in part, by the political system as well as by eco-

nomic and social circumstances. In this way the institutions of society favor certain starting places over others. These are especially deep inequalities. Not only are they pervasive, but they affect men's initial chances in life; yet they cannot possibly be justified by an appeal to the notions of merit or desert. It is these inequalities, presumably inevitable in the basic structure of any society, to which the principles of social justice must in the first instance apply. These principles, then, regulate the choice of a political constitution and the main elements of the economic and social system. The justice of a social scheme depends essentially on how fundamental rights and duties are assigned and on the economic opportunities and social conditions in the various sectors of society.

The scope of our inquiry is limited in two ways. First of all, I am concerned with a special case of the problem of justice. I shall not consider the justice of institutions and social practices generally, nor except in passing the justice of the law of nations and of relations between states (§ 58). Therefore, if one supposes that the concept of justice applies whenever there is an allotment of something rationally regarded as advantageous or disadvantageous, then we are interested in only one instance of its application. There is no reason to suppose ahead of time that the principles satisfactory for the basic structure hold for all cases. These principles may not work for the rules and practices of private associations or for those of less comprehensive social groups. They may be irrelevant for the various informal conventions and customs of everyday life; they may not elucidate the justice, or perhaps better, the fairness of voluntary cooperative arrangements or procedures for making contractual agreements. The conditions for the law of nations may require different principles arrived at in a somewhat different way. I shall be satisfied if it is possible to formulate a reasonable conception of justice for the basic structure of society conceived for the time being as a closed system isolated from other societies. The significance of this special case is obvious and needs no explanation. It is natural to conjecture that once we have a sound theory for this case, the remaining problems of justice will prove more tractable in the light of it. With suitable modifications such a theory should provide the key for some of these other questions.

The other limitation on our discussion is that for the most part I examine the principles of justice that would regulate a well-ordered society. Everyone is presumed to act justly and to do his part in upholding just institutions. Though justice may be, as Hume remarked, the cautious, jealous virtue, we can still ask what a perfectly just society would be like. Thus I consider primarily what I call strict compliance as opposed to partial compliance theory (§§ 25, 39). The latter studies the principles that govern how we are to deal with injustice. It comprises such topics as the theory of punishment, the doctrine of just war, and the justification of the various ways of opposing unjust regimes, ranging from civil disobedience and militant resistance to revolution and rebellion. Also included here are questions of compensatory justice and of weighing one form of institutional injustice against another. Obviously the problems of partial compliance theory are the pressing and urgent matters. These are the things that we are faced with in everyday life. The reason for beginning with ideal theory is that it provides, I believe, the only basis for the systematic grasp of these more pressing problems. The discussion of civil disobedience, for example, depends upon it (§§ 55–59). At least, I shall assume that a deeper understanding can be gained in no other way, and that the nature and aims of a perfectly just society is the fundamental part of the theory of justice.

Now admittedly the concept of the basic structure is somewhat vague. It is not always clear which institutions or features thereof should be included. But it would be premature to worry about this matter here. I shall proceed by discussing principles which do apply to what is certainly a part of the basic structure as intuitively understood; I shall then try to extend the application of these principles so that they cover what would appear to be the main elements of this structure. Perhaps these principles will turn out to be perfectly general, although this is unlikely. It is sufficient that they apply to the most important cases of social justice. The point to keep in mind is that a conception of justice for the basic structure is worth having for its own sake. It should not be dismissed because its principles are not everywhere satisfactory.

A conception of social justice, then, is to be regarded as providing in the first instance a standard whereby the distributive aspects of the basic structure of society are to be assessed. This standard, however, is not to be confused with the principles defining the other virtues, for the basic structure, and social arrangements generally, may be efficient or inefficient, liberal or illiberal, and many other things, as well as just or unjust. A complete conception defining principles for all the virtues of the basic structure, together with their respective weights when they conflict, is more than a conception of justice; it is a social ideal. The principles of justice are but a part, although perhaps the most important part, of such a conception. A social ideal in turn is connected with a conception of society, a vision of the way in which the aims and purposes of social cooperation are to be understood. The various conceptions of justice are the outgrowth of different notions of society against the background of opposing views of the natural necessities and opportunities of human life. Fully to understand a conception of justice we must make explicit the conception of social cooperation from which it derives. But in doing this we should not lose sight of the special role of the principles of justice or of the primary subject to which they apply.

In these preliminary remarks I have distinguished the concept of justice as meaning a proper balance between competing claims from a conception of justice as a set of related principles for identifying the relevant considerations which determine this balance. I have also characterized justice as but one part of a social ideal, although the theory I shall propose no doubt extends its everyday sense. This theory is not offered as a description of ordinary meanings but as an account of certain distributive principles for the basic structure of society. I assume that any reasonably complete ethical theory must include principles for this fundamental prob-

624 Part II ♦ *The 19th Century and Beyond*

lem and that these principles, whatever they are, constitute its doctrine of justice. The concept of justice I take to be defined, then, by the role of its principles in assigning rights and duties and in defining the appropriate division of social advantages. A conception of justice is an interpretation of this role.

Now this approach may not seem to tally with tradition. I believe, though, that it does. The more specific sense that Aristotle gives to justice, and from which the most familiar formulations derive, is that of refraining from *pleonexia*, that is, from gaining some advantage for oneself by seizing what belongs to another, his property, his reward, his office, and the like, or by denying a person that which is due to him, the fulfillment of a promise, the repayment of a debt, the showing of proper respect, and so on. It is evident that this definition is framed to apply to actions, and persons are thought to be just insofar as they have, as one of the permanent elements of their character, a steady and effective desire to act justly. Aristotle's definition clearly presupposes, however, an account of what properly belongs to a person and of what is due to him. Now such entitlements are, I believe, very often derived from social institutions and the legitimate expectations to which they give rise. There is no reason to think that Aristotle would disagree with this, and certainly he has a conception of social justice to account for these claims. The definition I adopt is designed to apply directly to the most important case, the justice of the basic structure. There is no conflict with the traditional notion.

3. The Main Idea of the Theory of Justice

My aim is to present a conception of justice which generalizes and carries to a higher level of abstraction the familiar theory of the social contract as found, say, in Locke, Rousseau, and Kant. In order to do this we are not to think of the original contract as one to enter a particular society or to set up a particular form of government. Rather, the guiding idea is that the principles of justice for the basic structure of society are the object of the original agreement. They are the principles that free and rational persons concerned to further their own interests would accept in an initial position of equality as defining the fundamental terms of their association. These principles are to regulate all further agreements; they specify the kinds of social cooperation that can be entered into and the forms of government that can be established. This way of regarding the principles of justice I shall call justice as fairness.

Thus we are to imagine that those who engage in social cooperation choose together, in one joint act, the principles which are to assign basic rights and duties and to determine the division of social benefits. Men are to decide in advance how they are to regulate their claims against one another and what is to be the foundation charter of their society. Just as each person must decide by rational reflection what constitutes his good, that is, the system of ends which it is rational for him to pursue, so a group of persons must decide once and for all what is to count among them as just and unjust. The choice which rational men would make in this hypothetical situation of equal liberty, assuming for the present that this choice problem has a solution, determines the principles of justice.

In justice as fairness the original position of equality corresponds to the state of nature in the traditional theory of the social contract. This original position is not, of course, thought of as an actual historical state of affairs, much less as a primitive condition of culture. It is understood as a purely hypothetical situation characterized so as to lead to a certain conception of justice. Among the essential features of this situation is that no one knows his place in society, his class position or social status, nor does any one know his fortune in the distribution of natural assets and abilities, his intelligence, strength, and the like. I shall even assume that the parties do not know their conceptions of the good or their special psychological propensities. The principles of justice are chosen behind a veil of ignorance. This ensures that no one is advantaged or disadvantaged in the choice of principles by the outcome of natural chance or the contingency of social circumstances. Since all are similarly situated and no one is able to design principles to favor his particular condition, the principles of justice are the result of a fair agreement or bargain. For given the circumstances of the original position, the symmetry of everyone's relations to each other, this initial situation is fair between individuals as moral persons, that is, as rational beings with their own ends and capable, I shall assume, of a sense of justice. The original position is, one might say, the appropriate initial status quo, and thus the fundamental agreements reached in it are fair. This explains the propriety of the name "justice as fairness": it conveys the idea that the principles of justice are agreed to in an initial situation that is fair. The name does not mean that the concepts of justice and fairness are the same, any more than the phrase "poetry as metaphor" means that the concepts of poetry and metaphor are the same.

Justice as fairness begins, as I have said, with one of the most general of all choices which persons might make together, namely, with the choice of the first principles of a conception of justice which is to regulate all subsequent criticism and reform of institutions. Then, having chosen a conception of justice, we can suppose that they are to choose a constitution and a legislature to enact laws, and so on, all in accordance with the principles of justice initially agreed upon. Our social situation is just if it is such that by this sequence of hypothetical agreements we would have contracted into the general system of rules which defines it. Moreover, assuming that the original position does determine a set of principles (that is, that a particular conception of justice would be chosen), it will then be true that whenever social institutions satisfy these principles those engaged in them can say to one another that they are cooperating on terms to which they would agree if they were free and equal persons whose relations with respect to one another were fair. They could all view their arrangements as meeting the stipulations which they would acknowledge in an initial situation that embodies widely accepted and reasonable constraints on the choice of principles. The general recognition of this fact would provide the basis for a pub-

lic acceptance of the corresponding principles of justice. No society can, of course, be a scheme of cooperation which men enter voluntarily in a literal sense; each person finds himself placed at birth in some particular position in some particular society, and the nature of this position materially affects his life prospects. Yet a society satisfying the principles of justice as fairness comes as close as a society can to being a voluntary scheme, for it meets the principles which free and equal persons would assent to under circumstances that are fair. In this sense its members are autonomous and the obligations they recognize self-imposed.

One feature of justice as fairness is to think of the parties in the initial situation as rational and mutually disinterested. This does not mean that the parties are egoists, that is, individuals with only certain kinds of interests, say in wealth, prestige, and domination. But they are conceived as not taking an interest in one another's interests. They are to presume that even their spiritual aims may be opposed, in the way that the aims of those of different religions may be opposed. Moreover, the concept of rationality must be interpreted as far as possible in the narrow sense, standard in economic theory, of taking the most effective means to given ends. I shall modify this concept to some extent, as explained later (§ 25), but one must try to avoid introducing into it any controversial ethical elements. The initial situation must be characterized by stipulations that are widely accepted.

In working out the conception of justice as fairness one main task clearly is to determine which principles of justice would be chosen in the original position. To do this we must describe this situation in some detail and formulate with care the problem of choice which it presents. . . . It may be observed, however, that once the principles of justice are thought of as arising from an original agreement in a situation of equality, it is an open question whether the principle of utility would be acknowledged. Offhand it hardly seems likely that persons who view themselves as equals, entitled to press their claims upon one another, would agree to a principle which may require lesser life prospects for some simply for the sake of a greater sum of advantages enjoyed by others. Since each desires to protect his interests, his capacity to advance his conception of the good, no one has a reason to acquiesce in an enduring loss for himself in order to bring about a greater net balance of satisfaction. In the absence of strong and lasting benevolent impulses, a rational man would not accept a basic structure merely because it maximized the algebraic sum of advantages irrespective of its permanent effects on his own basic rights and interests. Thus it seems that the principle of utility is incompatible with the conception of social cooperation among equals for mutual advantage. It appears to be inconsistent with the idea of reciprocity implicit in the notion of a well-ordered society. Or, at any rate, so I shall argue.

I shall maintain instead that the persons in the initial situation would choose two rather different principles: the first requires equality in the assignment of basic rights and duties, while the second holds that social and economic inequalities, for example inequalities of wealth and authority, are just only if they result in compensating benefits for everyone, and in particular for the least advantaged members of society. These principles rule out justifying institutions on the grounds that the hardships of some are offset by a greater good in the aggregate. It may be expedient but it is not just that some should have less in order that others may prosper. But there is no injustice in the greater benefits earned by a few provided that the situation of persons not so fortunate is thereby improved. The intuitive idea is that since everyone's well-being depends upon a scheme of cooperation without which no one could have a satisfactory life, the division of advantages should be such as to draw forth the willing cooperation of everyone taking part in it, including those less well situated. Yet this can be expected only if reasonable terms are proposed. The two principles mentioned seem to be a fair agreement on the basis of which those better endowed, or more fortunate in their social position, neither of which we can be said to deserve, could expect the willing cooperation of others when some workable scheme

is a necessary condition of the welfare of all. Once we decide to look for a conception of justice that nullifies the accidents of natural endowment and the contingencies of social circumstance as counters in quest for political and economic advantage, we are led to these principles. They express the result of leaving aside those aspects of the social world that seem arbitrary from a moral point of view.

The problem of the choice of principles, however, is extremely difficult. I do not expect the answer I shall suggest to be convincing to everyone. It is, therefore, worth noting from the outset that justice as fairness, like other contract views, consists of two parts: (1) an interpretation of the initial situation and of the problem of choice posed there, and (2) a set of principles which, it is argued, would be agreed to. One may accept the first part of the theory (or some variant thereof), but not the other, and conversely. The concept of the initial contractual situation may seem reasonable although the particular principles proposed are rejected. To be sure, I want to maintain that the most appropriate conception of this situation does lead to principles of justice contrary to utilitarianism and perfectionism, and therefore that the contract doctrine provides an alternative to these views. Still, one may dispute this contention even though one grants that the contractarian method is a useful way of studying ethical theories and of setting forth their underlying assumptions.

Justice as fairness is an example of what I have called a contract theory. Now there may be an objection to the term "contract" and related expressions, but I think it will serve reasonably well. Many words have misleading connotations which at first are likely to confuse. The terms "utility" and "utilitarianism" are surely no exception. They too have unfortunate suggestions which hostile critics have been willing to exploit; yet they are clear enough for those prepared to study utilitarian doctrine. The same should be true of the term "contract" applied to moral theories. As I have mentioned, to understand it one has to keep in mind that it implies a certain level of abstraction. In particular, the content of the relevant agreement is not to enter a given society or to adopt a given form of government, but to accept certain moral principles. Moreover, the undertakings referred to are purely hypothetical: a contract view holds that certain principles would be accepted in a well-defined initial situation.

The merit of the contract terminology is that it conveys the idea that principles of justice may be conceived as principles that would be chosen by rational persons, and that in this way conceptions of justice may be explained and justified. The theory of justice is a part, perhaps the most significant part, of the theory of rational choice. Furthermore, principles of justice deal with conflicting claims upon the advantages won by social cooperation; they apply to the relations among several persons or groups. The word "contract" suggests this plurality as well as the condition that the appropriate division of advantages must be in accordance with principles acceptable to all parties. The condition of publicity for principles of justice is also connoted by the contract phraseology. Thus, if these principles are the outcome of an agreement, citizens have a knowledge of the principles that others follow. It is characteristic of contract theories to stress the public nature of political principles. Finally there is the long tradition of the contract doctrine. Expressing the tie with this line of thought helps to define ideas and accords with natural piety. There are then several advantages in the use of the term "contract." With due precautions taken, it should not be misleading.

A final remark. Justice as fairness is not a complete contract theory. For it is clear that the contractarian idea can be extended to the choice of more or less an entire ethical system, that is, to a system including principles for all the virtues and not only for justice. Now for the most part I shall consider only principles of justice and others closely related to them; I make no attempt to discuss the virtues in a systematic way. Obviously if justice as fairness succeeds reasonably well, a next step would be to study the more general view suggested by the name "rightness as fairness." But even this wider theory fails to embrace all moral relationships, since it would seem to include only our relations with other persons and to leave out of account how we are to conduct ourselves toward animals and the rest of nature. I do not contend that the contract notion offers a way to approach these questions which are certainly of the first importance; and I shall have to put them aside. We must recognize the limited scope of justice as fairness and of the general type of view that it exemplifies. How far its conclusions must be revised once these other matters are understood cannot be decided in advance.

4. The Original Position and Justification

I have said that the original position is the appropriate initial status quo which insures that the fundamental agreements reached in it are fair. This fact yields the name "justice as fairness." It is clear, then, that I want to say that one conception of justice is more reasonable than another, or justifiable with respect to it, if rational persons in the initial situation would choose its principles over those of the other for the role of justice. Conceptions of justice are to be ranked by their acceptability to persons so circumstanced. Understood in this way the question of justification is settled by working out a problem of deliberation: we have to ascertain which principles it would be rational to adopt given the contractual situation. This connects the theory of justice with the theory of rational choice.

If this view of the problem of justification is to succeed, we must, of course, describe in some detail the nature of this choice problem. A problem of rational decision has a definite answer only if we know the beliefs and interests of the parties, their relations with respect to one another, the alternatives between which they are to choose, the procedure whereby they make up their minds, and so on. As the circumstances are presented in different ways, correspondingly different principles are accepted. The concept of the original position, as I shall refer to it, is that of the most philosophically favored interpretation of this initial choice situation for the purposes of a theory of justice.

But how are we to decide what is the most favored interpretation? I assume, for one thing, that there is a broad measure of agreement that principles of justice should be chosen under certain conditions. To justify a particular description of the initial situation one shows that it incorporates these commonly shared presumptions. One argues from widely accepted but weak premises to more specific conclusions. Each of the presumptions should by itself be natural and plausible; some of them may seem innocuous or even trivial. The aim of the contract approach is to establish that taken together they impose significant bounds on acceptable principles of justice. The ideal outcome would be that these conditions determine a unique set of principles; but I shall be satisfied if they suffice to rank the main traditional conceptions of social justice.

One should not be misled, then, by the somewhat unusual conditions which characterize the original position. The idea here is simply to make vivid to ourselves the restrictions that it seems reasonable to impose on arguments for principles of justice, and therefore on these principles themselves. Thus it seems reasonable and generally acceptable that no one should be advantaged or disadvantaged by natural fortune or social circumstances in the choice of principles. It also seems widely agreed that it should be impossible to tailor principles to the circumstances of one's own case. We should insure further that particular inclinations and aspirations, and persons' conceptions of their good do not affect the principles adopted. The aim is to rule out those principles that it would be rational to propose for acceptance, however little the chance of success, only if one knew certain things that are irrelevant from the standpoint of justice. For example, if a man knew that he was wealthy, he might find it rational to advance the principle that various taxes for welfare measures be counted unjust; if he knew that he was poor, he would most likely propose the contrary principle. To represent the desired restrictions one imagines a situation in which everyone is deprived of this sort of information. One excludes the knowledge of those contingencies which sets men at odds and allows them to be guided by their prejudices. In this manner the veil of ignorance is arrived at in a natural way. This concept should cause no difficulty if we keep in mind the constraints on arguments that it is meant to express. At any time we can enter the original position, so to speak, simply by following a certain procedure, namely, by arguing for principles of justice in accordance with these restrictions.

It seems reasonable to suppose that the parties in the original position are equal. That is, all have the same rights in the procedure for choosing principles; each can make proposals, submit reasons for their acceptance, and so on. Obviously the purpose of these conditions is to represent equality between human beings as moral persons, as creatures having a conception of their good and capable of a sense of justice. The basis of equality is taken to be similarity in these two respects. Systems of ends are not ranked in value; and each man is presumed to have the requisite ability to understand and to act upon whatever principles are adopted. Together with the veil of ignorance, these conditions define the principles of justice as those which rational persons concerned to advance their interests would consent to as equals when none are known to be advantaged or disadvantaged by social and natural contingencies.

There is, however, another side to justifying a particular description of the original position. This is to see if the principles which would be chosen match our considered convictions of justice or extend them in an acceptable way. We can note whether applying these principles would lead us to make the same judgments about the basic structure of society which we now make intuitively and in which we have the greatest confidence; or whether, in cases where our present judgments are in doubt and given with hesitation, these principles offer a resolution which we can affirm on reflection. There are questions which we feel sure must be answered in a certain way. For example, we are confident that religious intolerance and racial discrimination are unjust. We think that we have examined these things with care and have reached what we believe is an impartial judgment not likely to be distorted by an excessive attention to our own interests. These convictions are provisional fixed points which we presume any conception of justice must fit. But we have much less assurance as to what is the correct distribution of wealth and authority. Here we may be looking for a way to remove our doubts. We can check an interpretation of the initial situation, then, by the capacity of its principles to accommodate our firmest convictions and to provide guidance where guidance is needed.

In searching for the most favored description of this situation we work from both ends. We begin by describing it so that it represents generally shared and preferably weak conditions. We then see if these conditions are strong enough to yield a significant set of principles. If not, we look for further premises equally reasonable. But if so, and these principles match our considered convictions of justice, then so far well and good. But presumably there will be discrepancies. In this case we have a choice. We can either modify the account of the initial situation or we can revise our existing judgments, for even the judgments we take provisionally as fixed points are liable to revision. By going back and forth, sometimes altering the conditions of the contractual circumstances, at others withdrawing our judgments and conforming them to principle, I assume that eventually we shall find a description of the initial situation that both expresses reasonable conditions and yields principles which match our considered judgments duly pruned and adjusted. This state of affairs I refer to as reflective equilibrium. It is an equilibrium because at last our principles and judgments coincide; and it is reflective since we know to what principles our judgments conform and the premises of their derivation. At the moment everything is in order. But this equilibrium is not necessarily stable. It is liable to be upset by further examination of the conditions which should be imposed on the contractual situation and by particular cases which may lead us to revise our judgments. Yet for the time being we have done what we can to render coherent and to justify our convictions of social justice. We have reached a conception of the original position.

I shall not, of course, actually work through this process. Still, we may think of

the interpretation of the original position that I shall present as the result of such a hypothetical course of reflection. It represents the attempt to accommodate within one scheme both reasonable philosophical conditions on principles as well as our considered judgments of justice. In arriving at the favored interpretation of the initial situation there is no point at which an appeal is made to self-evidence in the traditional sense either of general conceptions or particular convictions. I do not claim for the principles of justice proposed that they are necessary truths or derivable from such truths. A conception of justice cannot be deduced from self-evident premises or conditions on principles; instead, its justification is a matter of the mutual support of many considerations, of everything fitting together into one coherent view.

A final comment. We shall want to say that certain principles of justice are justified because they would be agreed to in an initial situation of equality. I have emphasized that this original position is purely hypothetical. It is natural to ask why, if this agreement is never actually entered into, we should take any interest in these principles, moral or otherwise. The answer is that the conditions embodied in the description of the original position are ones that we do in fact accept. Or if we do not, then perhaps we can be persuaded to do so by philosophical reflection. Each aspect of the contractual situation can be given supporting grounds. Thus what we shall do is to collect together into one conception a number of conditions on principles that we are ready upon due consideration to recognize as reasonable. These constraints express what we are prepared to regard as limits on fair terms of social cooperation. One way to look at the idea of the original position, therefore, is to see it as an expository device which sums up the meaning of these conditions and helps us to extract their consequences. On the other hand, this conception is also an intuitive notion that suggests its own elaboration, so that led on by it we are drawn to define more clearly the standpoint from which we can best interpret moral relationships. We need a conception that enables us to envision our objective from afar: the intuitive notion of the original position is to do this for us. . . .

Chapter II
The Principles of Justice

11. Two Principles of Justice

I shall now state in a provisional form the two principles of justice that I believe would be chosen in the original position. In this section I wish to make only the most general comments, and therefore the first formulation of these principles is tentative. As we go on I shall run through several formulations and approximate step by step the final statement to be given much later. I believe that doing this allows the exposition to proceed in a natural way.

The first statement of the two principles reads as follows.

First: each person is to have an equal right to the most extensive basic liberty compatible with a similar liberty for others.

Second: social and economic inequalities are to be arranged so that they are both (a) reasonably expected to be to everyone's advantage, and (b) attached to positions and offices open to all.

There are two ambiguous phrases in the second principle, namely "everyone's advantage" and "open to all." Determining their sense more exactly will lead to a second formulation of the principle in § 13. The final version of the two principles is given in § 46; § 39 considers the rendering of the first principle.

By way of general comment, these principles primarily apply, as I have said, to the basic structure of society. They are to govern the assignment of rights and duties and to regulate the distribution of social and economic advantages. As their formulation suggests, these principles presuppose that the social structure can be divided into two more or less distinct parts, the first principle applying to the one, the second to the other. They distinguish between those aspects of the social system that define and secure the equal liberties of citizenship and those that specify and establish social and economic inequalities. The basic liberties of citizens are, roughly speaking, political liberty (the right to vote and to be eligible for public office) together with freedom of speech and assembly; liberty of conscience and freedom of thought; freedom of the person along with the right to hold (personal) property; and freedom from arbitrary arrest and seizure as defined by the concept of the rule of law. These liberties are all required to be equal by the first principle, since citizens of a just society are to have the same basic rights.

The second principle applies, in the first approximation, to the distribution of income and wealth and to the design of organizations that make use of differences in authority and responsibility, or chains of command. While the distribution of wealth and income need not be equal, it must be to everyone's advantage, and at the same time, positions of authority and offices of command must be accessible to all. One applies the second principle by holding positions open, and then, subject to this constraint, arranges social and economic inequalities so that everyone benefits.

These principles are to be arranged in a serial order with the first principle prior to the second. This ordering means that a departure from the institutions of equal liberty required by the first principle cannot be justified by, or compensated for, by greater social and economic advantages. The distribution of wealth and income, and the hierarchies of authority, must be consistent with both the liberties of equal citizenship and equality of opportunity.

It is clear that these principles are rather specific in their content, and their acceptance rests on certain assumptions that I must eventually try to explain and justify. A theory of justice depends upon a theory of society in ways that will become evident as we proceed. For the present, it should be observed that the two principles (and this holds for all formulations) are a special case of a more general conception of justice that can be expressed as follows.

All social values—liberty and opportunity, income and wealth, and the bases of self-respect—are to be distributed equally unless an unequal distribution of any, or all, of these values is to everyone's advantage.

Injustice, then, is simply inequalities that are not to the benefit of all. Of course, this conception is extremely vague and requires interpretation.

As a first step, suppose that the basic structure of society distributes certain primary goods, that is, things that every rational man is presumed to want. These goods normally have a use whatever a person's rational plan of life. For simplicity, assume that the chief primary goods at the disposition of society are rights and liberties, powers and opportunities, income and wealth. (Later on in Part Three the primary good of self-respect has a central place.) These are the social primary goods. Other primary goods such as health and vigor, intelligence and imagination, are natural goods; although their possession is influenced by the basic structure, they are not so directly under its control. Imagine, then, a hypothetical initial arrangement in which all the social primary goods are equally distributed: everyone has similar rights and duties, and income and wealth are evenly shared. This state of affairs provides a benchmark for judging improvements. If certain inequalities of wealth and organizational powers would make everyone better off than in this hypothetical starting situation, then they accord with the general conception.

Now it is possible, at least theoretically, that by giving up some of their fundamental liberties men are sufficiently compensated by the resulting social and economic gains. The general conception of justice imposes no restrictions on what sort of inequalities are permissible; it only requires that everyone's position be improved. We need not suppose anything so drastic as consenting to a condition of slavery. Imagine instead that men forego certain political rights when the economic returns are significant and their capacity to influence the course of policy by the exercise of these rights would be marginal in any case. It is this kind of exchange which the two principles as stated rule out; being arranged in serial order they do not permit exchanges between basic liberties and economic and social gains. The serial or-

dering of principles expresses an underlying preference among primary social goods. When this preference is rational so likewise is the choice of these principles in this order.

In developing justice as fairness I shall, for the most part, leave aside the general conception of justice and examine instead the special case of the two principles in serial order. The advantage of this procedure is that from the first the matter of priorities is recognized and an effort made to find principles to deal with it. One is led to attend throughout to the conditions under which the acknowledgment of the absolute weight of liberty with respect to social and economic advantages, as defined by the lexical order of the two principles, would be reasonable. Offhand, this ranking appears extreme and too special a case to be of much interest; but there is more justification for it than would appear at first sight. Or at any rate, so I shall maintain (§ 82). Furthermore, the distinction between fundamental rights and liberties and economic and social benefits marks a difference among primary social goods that one should try to exploit. It suggests an important division in the social system. Of course, the distinctions drawn and the ordering proposed are bound to be at best only approximations. There are surely circumstances in which they fail. But it is essential to depict clearly the main lines of a reasonable conception of justice; and under many conditions anyway, the two principles in serial order may serve well enough. When necessary we can fall back on the more general conception.

The fact that the two principles apply to institutions has certain consequences. Several points illustrate this. First of all, the rights and liberties referred to by these principles are those which are defined by the public rules of the basic structure. Whether men are free is determined by the rights and duties established by the major institutions of society. Liberty is a certain pattern of social forms. The first principle simply requires that certain sorts of rules, those defining basic liberties, apply to everyone equally and that they allow the most extensive liberty compatible with a like liberty for all. The only reason for circumscribing the rights defining liberty and making men's freedom less extensive than it might otherwise be is that these equal rights as institutionally defined would interfere with one another.

Another thing to bear in mind is that when principles mention persons, or require that everyone gain from an inequality, the reference is to representative persons holding the various social positions, or offices, or whatever, established by the basic structure. Thus in applying the second principle I assume that it is possible to assign an expectation of well-being to representative individuals holding these positions. This expectation indicates their life prospects as viewed from their social station. In general, the expectations of representative persons depend upon the distribution of rights and duties throughout the basic structure. When this changes, expectations change. I assume, then, that expectations are connected: by raising the prospects of the representative man in one position we presumably increase or decrease the prospects of representative men in other positions. Since it applies to institutional forms, the second principle (or rather the first part of it) refers to the expectations of representative individuals. As I shall discuss below, neither principle applies to distributions of particular goods to particular individuals who may be identified by their proper names. The situation where someone is considering how to allocate certain commodities to needy persons who are known to him is not within the scope of the principles. They are meant to regulate basic institutional arrangements. We must not assume that there is much similarity from the standpoint of justice between an administrative allotment of goods to specific persons and the appropriate design of society. Our common sense intuitions for the former may be a poor guide to the latter.

Now the second principle insists that each person benefit from permissible inequalities in the basic structure. This means that it must be reasonable for each relevant representative man defined by this structure, when he views it as a going concern, to prefer his prospects with the inequality to his prospects without it. One is not allowed to justify differences in income or organizational powers on the ground that the disadvantages of those in one position are outweighed by the greater advantages of those in another. Much less can infringements of liberty be counterbalanced in this way. Applied to the basic structure, the principle of utility would have us maximize the sum of expectations of representative men (weighted by the number of persons they represent, on the classical view); and this would permit us to compensate for the losses of some by the gains of others. Instead, the two principles require that everyone benefit from economic and social inequalities. It is obvious, however, that there are indefinitely many ways in which all may be advantaged when the initial arrangement of equality is taken as a benchmark. How then are we to choose among these possibilities? The principles must be specified so that they yield a determinate conclusion. . . .

Adapted from: John Rawls, *A Theory of Justice*, pp. 3–22, 60–65. Copyright © 1971, 1999 by the President and Fellows of Harvard College. Reprinted by permission of The Belknap Press of Harvard University Press: Cambridge, MA. ✦

47
Excerpts from *Political Liberalism*

John Rawls

Fundamental Ideas

Political liberalism, the title of these lectures, has a familiar ring. Yet I mean by it something quite different, I think, from what the reader is likely to suppose. Perhaps I should, then, begin with a definition of political liberalism and explain why I call it "political." But no definition would be useful at the outset. Instead I begin with a first fundamental question about political justice in a democratic society, namely what is the most appropriate conception of justice for specifying the fair terms of social cooperation between citizens regarded as free and equal, and as fully cooperating members of society over a complete life, from one generation to the next?

We join this first fundamental question with a second, that of toleration understood in a general way. The political culture of a democratic society is always marked by a diversity of opposing and irreconcilable religious, philosophical, and moral doctrines. Some of these are perfectly reasonable, and this diversity among reasonable doctrines political liberalism sees as the inevitable long-run result of the powers of human reason at work within the background of enduring free institutions. Thus, the second question is what are the grounds of toleration so understood and given the fact of reasonable pluralism as the inevitable outcome of free institutions? Combining both questions we have: how is it possible for there to exist over time a just and stable society of free and equal citizens, who remain profoundly divided by reasonable religious, philosophical, and moral doctrines?

The most intractable struggles, political liberalism assumes, are confessedly for the sake of the highest things: for religion, for philosophical views of the world, and for different moral conceptions of the good. We should find it remarkable that, so deeply opposed in these ways, just cooperation among free and equal citizens is possible at all. In fact, historical experience suggests that it rarely is. If the problem addressed is all too familiar, political liberalism proposes, I believe, a somewhat unfamiliar resolution of it. To state this resolution we need a certain family of ideas. In this lecture I set out the more central of these and offer a definition at the end (§8).

§1. Addressing Two Fundamental Questions

1. Focusing on the first fundamental question, the course of democratic thought over the past two centuries or so makes plain that there is at present no agreement on the way the basic institutions of a constitutional democracy should be arranged if they are to satisfy the fair terms of cooperation between citizens regarded as free and equal. This is shown in the deeply contested ideas about how the values of liberty and equality are best expressed in the basic rights and liberties of citizens so as to answer to the claims of both liberty and equality. We may think of this disagreement as a conflict within the tradition of democratic thought itself, between the tradition associated with Locke, which gives greater weight to what Constant called "the liberties of the moderns," freedom of thought and conscience, certain basic rights of the person and of property, and the rule of law, and the tradition associated with Rousseau, which gives greater weight to what Constant called "the liberties of the ancients," the equal political liberties and the values of public life.[1] This familiar and stylized contrast may serve to fix ideas.

As a way to answer our first question, justice as fairness[2] tries to adjudicate between these contending traditions, first, by proposing two principles of justice to serve as

633

guidelines for how basic institutions are to realize the values of liberty and equality; and second, by specifying a point of view from which these principles can be seen as more appropriate than other familiar principles of justice to the idea of democratic citizens viewed as free and equal persons. What must be shown is that a certain arrangement of basic political and social institutions is more appropriate to realizing the values of liberty and equality when citizens are so conceived. The two principles of justice (noted above) are as follows:[3]

a. Each person has an equal claim to a fully adequate scheme of equal basic rights and liberties, which scheme is compatible with the same scheme for all; and in this scheme the equal political liberties, and only those liberties, are to be guaranteed their fair value.

b. Social and economic inequalities are to satisfy two conditions: first, they are to be attached to positions and offices open to all under conditions of fair equality of opportunity; and second, they are to be to the greatest benefit of the least advantaged members of society.

Each of these principles regulates institutions in a particular domain not only in regard to basic rights, liberties, and opportunities but also in regard to the claims of equality; while the second part of the second principle underwrites the worth of these institutional guarantees.[4] The two principles together, with the first given priority over the second, regulate the basic institutions that realize these values.

2. Much exposition would be needed to clarify the meaning and application of these principles. Since in these lectures such matters are not our concern, I make only a few comments. First, I view these principles as exemplifying the content of a liberal political conception of justice. The content of such a conception is given by three main features: first, a specification of certain basic rights, liberties and opportunities (of a kind familiar from constitutional democratic regimes); second, an assignment of special priority to those rights, liberties, and opportunities, es-

pecially with respect to claims of the general good and of perfectionist values; and third, measures assuring to all citizens adequate all-purpose means to make effective use of their liberties and opportunities. These elements can be understood in different ways, so that there are many variant liberalisms.

Further, the two principles express an egalitarian form of liberalism in virtue of three elements. These are a) the guarantee of the fair value of the political liberties, so that these are not purely formal; b) fair (and again not purely formal) equality of opportunity; and finally c) the so-called difference principle, which says that the social and economic inequalities attached to offices and positions are to be adjusted so that, whatever the level of those inequalities, whether great or small, they are to the greatest benefit of the least advantaged members of society.[5] All these elements are still in place, as they were in *Theory*; and so is the basis of the argument for them. Hence I presuppose throughout these lectures the same egalitarian conception of justice as before; and though I mention revisions from time to time, none of them affect this feature of it.[6] Our topic, however, is political liberalism and its component ideas, so that much of our discussion concerns liberal conceptions more generally, allowing for all variants, as for example when we consider the idea of public reason (in VI).

Finally, as one might expect, important aspects of the principles are left out in the brief statement as given. In particular, the first principle covering the equal basic rights and liberties may easily be preceded by a lexically prior principle requiring that citizens' basic needs be met, at least insofar as their being met is necessary for citizens to understand and to be able fruitfully to exercise those rights and liberties. Certainly any such principle must be assumed in applying the first principle.[7] But I do not pursue these and other matters here.

3. I return instead to our first question and ask: How might political philosophy find a shared basis for settling such a fundamental question as that of the most appropriate family of institutions to secure democratic liberty and equality? Perhaps the most that

can be done is to narrow the range of disagreement. Yet even firmly held convictions gradually change: religious toleration is now accepted, and arguments for persecution are no longer openly professed; similarly, slavery, which caused our Civil War, is rejected as inherently unjust, and however much the aftermath of slavery may persist in social policies and unavowed attitudes, no one is willing to defend it. We collect such settled convictions as the belief in religious toleration and the rejection of slavery and try to organize the basic ideas and principles implicit in these convictions into a coherent political conception of justice. These convictions are provisional fixed points that it seems any reasonable conception must account for. We start, then, by looking to the public culture itself as the shared fund of implicitly recognized basic ideas and principles. We hope to formulate these ideas and principles clearly enough to be combined into a political conception of justice congenial to our most firmly held convictions. We express this by saying that a political conception of justice, to be acceptable, must accord with our considered convictions, at all levels of generality, on due reflection, or in what I have called elsewhere "reflective equilibrium."[8]

The public political culture may be of two minds at a very deep level. Indeed, this must be so with such an enduring controversy as that concerning the most appropriate understanding of liberty and equality. This suggests that if we are to succeed in finding a basis for public agreement, we must find a way of organizing familiar ideas and principles into a conception of political justice that expresses those ideas and principles in a somewhat different way than before. Justice as fairness tries to do this by using a fundamental organizing idea within which all ideas and principles can be systematically connected and related. This organizing idea is that of society as a fair system of social cooperation between free and equal persons viewed as fully cooperating members of society over a complete life. It lays a basis for answering the first fundamental question and is taken up below in §3.

4. Now suppose justice as fairness were to achieve its aims and a publicly acceptable political conception were found. Then this conception provides a publicly recognized point of view from which all citizens can examine before one another whether their political and social institutions are just. It enables them to do this by citing what are publicly recognized among them as valid and sufficient reasons singled out by that conception itself. Society's main institutions and how they fit together into one system of social cooperation can be assessed in the same way by each citizen, whatever that citizen's social position or more particular interests.

The aim of justice as fairness, then, is practical: it presents itself as a conception of justice that may be shared by citizens as a basis of a reasoned, informed, and willing political agreement. It expresses their shared and public political reason. But to attain such a shared reason, the conception of justice should be, as far as possible, independent of the opposing and conflicting philosophical and religious doctrines that citizens affirm. In formulating such a conception, political liberalism applies the principle of toleration to philosophy itself. The religious doctrines that in previous centuries were the professed basis of society have gradually given way to principles of constitutional government that all citizens, whatever their religious view, can endorse. Comprehensive philosophical and moral doctrines likewise cannot be endorsed by citizens generally, and they also no longer can, if they ever could, serve as the professed basis of society.

Thus, political liberalism looks for a political conception of justice that we hope can gain the support of an overlapping consensus of reasonable religious, philosophical, and moral doctrines in a society regulated by it.[9] Gaining this support of reasonable doctrines lays the basis for answering our second fundamental question as to how citizens, who remain deeply divided on religious, philosophical, and moral doctrines, can still maintain a just and stable democratic society. To this end, it is normally desirable that the comprehensive philosophical and moral views we are wont to use in debating fundamental political issues should give way in public life. Public

636 Part II ✦ *The 19th Century and Beyond*

reason—citizens' reasoning in the public forum about constitutional essentials and basic questions of justice—is now best guided by apolitical conception the principles and values of which all citizens can endorse (VI). That political conception is to be, so to speak, political and not metaphysical.[10]

Political liberalism, then, aims for a political conception of justice as a freestanding view. It offers no specific metaphysical or epistemological doctrine beyond what is implied by the political conception itself. As an account of political values, a freestanding political conception does not deny there being other values that apply, say, to the personal, the familial, and the associational; nor does it say that political values are separate from, or discontinuous with, other values. One aim, as I have said, is to specify the political domain and its conception of justice in such a way that its institutions can gain the support of an overlapping consensus. In this case, citizens themselves, within the exercise of their liberty of thought and conscience, and looking to their comprehensive doctrines, view the political conception as derived from, or congruent with, or at least not in conflict with, their other values.

§ 2. The Idea of a Political Conception of Justice

1. To this point I have used the idea of a political conception of justice without explaining its meaning. From what I have said, one can perhaps gather what I mean by it and why political liberalism uses that idea. Yet we need an explicit statement thus: a political conception of justice has three characteristic features, each of which is exemplified by justice as fairness. I assume some but not much acquaintance with that view.

The first concerns the subject of a political conception. While such a conception is, of course, a moral conception,[11] it is a moral conception worked out for a specific kind of subject, namely, for political, social, and economic institutions. In particular, it applies to what I shall call the "basic structure" of society, which for our present purposes I take to be a modern constitutional democracy. (I use "constitutional democracy" and "democratic regime," and similar phrases inter-

changeably unless otherwise stated.) By the basic structure I mean a society's main political, social, and economic institutions, and how they fit together into one unified system of social cooperation from one generation to the next.[12] The initial focus, then, of a political conception of justice is the framework of basic institutions and the principles, standards, and precepts that apply to it, as well as how those norms are to be expressed in the character and attitudes of the members of society who realize its ideals.

Moreover, I assume that the basic structure is that of a closed society: that is, we are to regard it as self-contained and as having no relations with other societies. Its members enter it only by birth and leave it only by death. This allows us to speak of them as born into a society where they will lead a complete life. That a society is closed is a considerable abstraction, justified only because it enables us to focus on certain main questions free from distracting details. At some point a political conception of justice must address the just relations between peoples, or the law of peoples, as I shall say. In these lectures I do not discuss how a law of peoples might be worked out, starting from justice as fairness as applied first to closed societies.[13]

2. The second feature concerns the mode of presentation: a political conception of justice is presented as a freestanding view. While we want a political conception to have a justification by reference to one or more comprehensive doctrines, it is neither presented as, nor as derived from, such a doctrine applied to the basic structure of society, as if this structure were simply another subject to which that doctrine applied. It is important to stress this point: it means that we must distinguish between how a political conception is presented and its being part of, or as derivable within, a comprehensive doctrine. I assume all citizens to affirm a comprehensive doctrine to which the political conception they accept is in some way related. But a distinguishing feature of a political conception is that it is presented as freestanding and expounded apart from, or without reference to, any such wider background. To use a current phrase, the political

conception is a module, an essential constituent part, that fits into and can be supported by various reasonable comprehensive doctrines that endure in the society regulated by it. This means that it can be presented without saying, or knowing, or hazarding a conjecture about, what such doctrines it may belong to, or be supported by.

In this respect a political conception of justice differs from many moral doctrines, for these are widely regarded as general and comprehensive views. Utilitarianism is a familiar example: the principle of utility, however understood, is usually said to hold for all kinds of subjects ranging from the conduct of individuals and personal relations to the organization of society as a whole as well as to the law of peoples.[14] By contrast, a political conception tries to elaborate a reasonable conception for the basic structure alone and involves, so far as possible, no wider commitment to any other doctrine.

This contrast will be clearer if we observe that the distinction between a political conception of justice and other moral conceptions is a matter of scope: that is, the range of subjects to which a conception applies and the content a wider range requires. A moral conception is general if it applies to a wide range of subjects, and in the limit to all subjects universally. It is comprehensive when it includes conceptions of what is of value in human life, and ideals of personal character, as well as ideals of friendship and of familial and associational relationships, and much else that is to inform our conduct, and in the limit to our life as a whole. A conception is fully comprehensive if it covers all recognized values and virtues within one rather precisely articulated system; whereas a conception is only partially comprehensive when it comprises a number of, but by no means all, nonpolitical values and virtues and is rather loosely articulated. Many religious and philosophical doctrines aspire to be both general and comprehensive.

3. The third feature of a political conception of justice is that its content is expressed in terms of certain fundamental ideas seen as implicit in the public political culture of a democratic society. This public culture comprises the political institutions of a constitutional regime and the public traditions of their interpretation (including those of the judiciary), as well as historic texts and documents that are common knowledge. Comprehensive doctrines of all kinds—religious, philosophical, and moral—belong to what we may call the "background culture" of civil society. This is the culture of the social, not of the political. It is the culture of daily life, of its many associations: churches and universities, learned and scientific societies, and clubs and teams, to mention a few. In a democratic society there is a tradition of democratic thought, the content of which is at least familiar and intelligible to the educated common sense of citizens generally. Society's main institutions, and their accepted forms of interpretation, are seen as a fund of implicitly shared ideas and principles.

Thus, justice as fairness starts from within a certain political tradition and takes as its fundamental idea[15] that of society as a fair system of cooperation over time, from one generation to the next (§3). This central organizing idea is developed together with two companion fundamental ideas: one is the idea of citizens (those engaged in cooperation) as free and equal persons (§§3.3 and 5); the other is the idea of a well-ordered society as a society effectively regulated by a political conception of justice (§6).[16] We suppose also that these ideas can be elaborated into a political conception of justice that can gain the support of an overlapping consensus (IV). Such a consensus consists of all the reasonable opposing religious, philosophical, and moral doctrines likely to persist over generations and to gain a sizable body of adherents in a more or less just constitutional regime, a regime in which the criterion of justice is that political conception itself.[17] Whether justice as fairness (or some similar view) can gain the support of an overlapping consensus so defined is a speculative question. One can reach an educated conjecture only by working it out and exhibiting the way it might be supported.

§ 3. The Idea of Society as a Fair System of Cooperation

1. As I have indicated, the fundamental organizing idea of justice as fairness, within

which the other basic ideas are systematically connected, is that of society as a fair system of cooperation over time, from one generation to the next. We start the exposition with this idea, which we take to be implicit in the public culture of a democratic society. In their political thought, and in the discussion of political questions, citizens do not view the social order as a fixed natural order, or as an institutional hierarchy justified by religious or aristocratic values.

Here it is important to stress that from other points of view, for example, from the point of view of personal morality, or from the point of view of members of an association, or of one's religious or philosophical doctrine, various aspects of the world and one's relation to it may be regarded in a different way. These other points of view are not, in general, to be introduced into political discussion of constitutional essentials and basic questions of justice.

2. We can make the idea of social cooperation more specific by noting three of its elements:

a. Cooperation is distinct from merely socially coordinated activity, for example, from activity coordinated by orders issued by some central authority. Cooperation is guided by publicly recognized rules and procedures that those cooperating accept and regard as properly regulating their conduct.

b. Cooperation involves the idea of fair terms of cooperation: these are terms that each participant may reasonably accept, provided that everyone else likewise accepts them. Fair terms of cooperation specify an idea of reciprocity: all who are engaged in cooperation and who do their part as the rules and procedure require, are to benefit in an appropriate way as assessed by a suitable benchmark of comparison. A conception of political justice characterizes the fair terms of cooperation. Since the primary subject of justice is the basic structure of society, these fair terms are expressed by principles that specify basic rights and duties within its main institutions and regulate the arrange-

ments of background justice over time, so that the benefits produced by everyone's efforts are fairly distributed and shared from one generation to the next.

c. The idea of social cooperation requires an idea of each participant's rational advantage, or good. This idea of good specifies what those who are engaged in cooperation, whether individuals, families, or associations, or even the governments of peoples, are trying to achieve, when the scheme is viewed from their own standpoint.

Several points about the idea of reciprocity introduced in (b) above call for comment. One is that the idea of reciprocity lies between the idea of impartiality, which is altruistic (being moved by the general good), and the idea of mutual advantage understood as everyone's being advantaged with respect to each person's present or expected future situation as things are.[18] As understood in justice as fairness, reciprocity is a relation between citizens expressed by principles of justice that regulate a social world in which everyone benefits judged with respect to an appropriate benchmark of equality defined with respect to that world. This brings out the further point that reciprocity is a relation between citizens in a well-ordered society (§6) expressed by its public political conception of justice. Hence the two principles of justice with the difference principle (§1.1), with its implicit reference to equal division as a benchmark, formulate an idea of reciprocity between citizens.

Finally, it is clear from these observations that the idea of reciprocity is not the idea of mutual advantage. Suppose that we transpose people from a society in which property, in good part as a result of fortune and luck, is very unequal into a well-ordered society regulated by the two principles of justice. There is no guarantee that all will gain by the change if they judge matters by their previous attitudes. Those owning large properties may have lost greatly and historically they have resisted such changes. No reasonable conception of justice could pass the test of mutual advantage thus interpreted. This is not, however, to the point. The aim is to specify an idea of reciprocity between free and equal citizens in a well-ordered society. The so-called strains of commitment are strains that arise in such a society between its requirements of justice and citizens' legitimate interests its just institutions allow. Important among these strains are those between the political conception of justice and permissible comprehensive doctrines. These strains do not arise from a desire to preserve the benefits of previous injustice. Strains such as these belong to the process of transition but questions connected with this are covered by nonideal theory and not by the principles of justice for a well-ordered society.[19]

3. Now consider the fundamental idea of the person.[20] There are, of course, many aspects of human nature that can be singled out as especially significant, depending on our point of view. This is witnessed by such expressions as "homo politicus" and "homo oeconomicus," "homo ludens" and "homo faber." Since our account of justice as fairness begins with the idea that society is to be conceived as a fair system of cooperation over time between generations, we adopt a conception of the person to go with this idea. Beginning with the ancient world, the concept of the person has been understood, in both philosophy and law, as the concept of someone who can take part in, or who can play a role in, social life, and hence exercise and respect its various rights and duties. Thus, we say that a person is someone who can be a citizen, that is, a normal and fully cooperating member of society over a complete life. We add the phrase "over a complete life" because society is viewed not only as closed (§2.1) but as a more or less complete and self-sufficient scheme of cooperation, making room within itself for all the necessities and activities of life, from birth until death. A society is also conceived as existing in perpetuity: it produces and reproduces itself and its institutions and culture over generations and there is no time at which it is expected to wind up its affairs.

Since we start within the tradition of democratic thought, we also think of citizens as free and equal persons. The basic idea is that in virtue of their two moral powers (a capacity for a sense of justice and for a conception of the good) and the powers of reason (of judgment, thought, and inference connected with these powers), persons are free. Their having these powers to the requisite minimum degree to be fully cooperating members of society makes persons equal.[21]

To elaborate: since persons can be full participants in a fair system of social cooperation, we ascribe to them the two moral powers connected with the elements in the idea of social cooperation noted above: namely, a capacity for a sense of justice and a capacity for a conception of the good. A sense of justice is the capacity to understand, to apply, and to act from the public conception of justice which characterizes the fair terms of social cooperation. Given the nature of the political conception as specifying a public basis of justification, a sense of justice also expresses a willingness, if not the desire, to act in relation to others on terms that they also can publicly endorse (II:1). The capacity for a conception of the good is the capacity to form, to revise, and rationally to pursue a conception of one's rational advantage or good.

In addition to having these two moral powers, persons also have at any given time a determinate conception of the good that they try to achieve. Such a conception must not be understood narrowly but rather as including a conception of what is valuable in human life. Thus, a conception of the good normally consists of a more or less determinate scheme of final ends, that is, ends we want to realize for their own sake, as well as attachments to other persons and loyalties to various groups and associations. These attachments and loyalties give rise to devotions and affections, and so the flourishing of the persons and associations who are the objects of these sentiments is also part of our conception of the good. We also connect with such a conception a view of our relation to the world—religious, philosophical, and moral—by reference to which the value and significance of our ends and attachments are understood. Finally, persons' conceptions of the good are not fixed but form and develop as they mature, and may change more or less radically over the course of life.

4. Since we begin from the idea of society as a fair system of cooperation, we assume that persons as citizens have all the capacities that enable them to be cooperating members of society. This is done to achieve a clear and uncluttered view of what, for us, is the fundamental question of political justice: namely, what is the most appropriate conception of justice for specifying the terms of social cooperation between citizens regarded as free and equal, and as normal and fully cooperating members of society over a complete life?

By taking this as the fundamental question we do not mean to say, of course, that no one ever suffers from illness and accident; such misfortunes are to be expected in the ordinary course of life, and provision for these contingencies must be made. But given our aim, I put aside for the time being these temporary disabilities and also permanent disabilities or mental disorders so severe as to prevent people from being cooperating members of society in the usual sense. Thus, while we begin with an idea of the person implicit in the public political culture, we idealize and simplify this idea in various ways in order to focus first on the main question.

Other questions we can discuss later, and how we answer them may require us to revise answers already reached. This back-and-forth procedure is to be expected. We may think of these other questions as problems of extension. Thus, there is the problem of extending justice as fairness to cover our duties to future generations, under which falls the problem of just savings.[22] Another problem is how to extend justice as fairness to cover the law of peoples, that is, the concepts and principles that apply to international law and the relations between political societies.[23] Moreover, since we have assumed (as noted above) that persons are normal and fully cooperating members of society over a complete life, and so have the requisite capacities for assuming that role, there is the question of what is owed to those who fail to meet this condition, either temporarily (from illness and accident) or permanently, all of which covers a variety of cases.[24] Finally, there is the problem of what is owed to animals and the rest of nature.

While we would like eventually to answer all these questions, I very much doubt whether that is possible within the scope of justice as fairness as a political conception. I think it yields reasonable answers to the first two problems of extension: to future generations and to the law of peoples, and to part of the third, to the problem of providing for what we may call normal health care. With regard to the problems on which justice as fairness may fail, there are several possibilities. One is that the idea of political justice does not cover everything, nor should we expect it to. Or the problem may indeed be one of political justice but justice as fairness is not correct in this case, however well it may do for other cases. How deep a fault this is must wait until the case itself can be examined. Perhaps we simply lack the ingenuity to see how the extension may proceed. In any case, we should not expect justice as fairness, or any account of justice, to cover all cases of right and wrong. Political justice needs always to be complemented by other virtues.

In these lectures I leave aside these problems of extension and focus on what above I called the fundamental question of political justice. I do this because the fault of *Theory* these lectures address . . . lies in its answer to that fundamental question. And that this question is indeed fundamental is shown by the fact that it has been the focus of the liberal critique of aristocracy in the seventeenth and eighteenth centuries, of the socialist critique of liberal constitutional democracy in the nineteenth and twentieth centuries, and of the conflict between liberalism and conservatism at the present time over the claims of private property and the legitimacy (as opposed to the effectiveness) of the social policies associated with what has come to be called the "welfare state." It is this question that fixes the initial boundaries of our discussion. . . .

§ 5. The Political Conception of the Person

1. I remarked earlier that the idea of the original position and the description of the parties may tempt us to think that a metaphysical doctrine of the person is presupposed. While I said that this interpretation is

mistaken, it is not enough simply to disavow reliance on metaphysical doctrines, for despite one's intent they may still be involved. To rebut claims of this nature requires discussing them in detail and showing that they have no foothold. I cannot do that here.[25]

I can, however, sketch an account of a political conception of the person drawn on in setting up the original position (§3.3). To understand what is meant by describing a conception of the person as political, consider how citizens are represented in that position as free persons. The representation of their freedom seems to be one source of the idea that a metaphysical doctrine is presupposed. Now citizens are conceived as thinking of themselves as free in three respects, so I survey each of these and indicate the way in which the conception of the person is political.

2. First, citizens are free in that they conceive of themselves and of one another as having the moral power to have a conception of the good. This is not to say that, as part of their political conception, they view themselves as inevitably tied to the pursuit of the particular conception of the good that they affirm at any given time. Rather, as citizens, they are seen as capable of revising and changing this conception on reasonable and rational grounds, and they may do this if they so desire. As free persons, citizens claim the right to view their persons as independent from and not identified with any particular such conception with its scheme of final ends. Given their moral power to form, revise, and rationally pursue a conception of the good, their public identity as free persons is not affected by changes over time in their determinate conception of it.

For example, when citizens convert from one religion to another, or no longer affirm an established religious faith, they do not cease to be, for questions of political justice, the same persons they were before. There is no loss of what we may call their public, or institutional, identity, or their identity as a matter of basic law. In general, they still have the same basic rights and duties, they own the same property and can make the same claims as before, except insofar as these claims were connected with their previous religious affiliation. We can imagine a society (history offers many examples) in which basic rights and recognized claims depend on religious affiliation and social class. Such a society has a different political conception of the person. It lacks a conception of equal citizenship, for this conception goes with that of a democratic society of free and equal citizens.

There is a second sense of identity specified by reference to citizens' deeper aims and commitments. Let's call it their noninstitutional or moral identity.[26] Citizens usually have both political and nonpolitical aims and commitments. They affirm the values of political justice and want to see them embodied in political institutions and social policies. They also work for the other values in nonpublic life and for the ends of the associations to which they belong. These two aspects of their moral identity citizens must adjust and reconcile. It can happen that in their personal affairs, or in the internal life of associations, citizens may regard their final ends and attachments very differently from the way the political conception supposes. They may have, and often do have at any given time, affections, devotions, and loyalties that they believe they would not, indeed could and should not, stand apart from and evaluate objectively. They may regard it as simply unthinkable to view themselves apart from certain religious, philosophical, and moral convictions, or from certain enduring attachments and loyalties.

These two kinds of commitments and attachments—political and nonpolitical—specify moral identity and give shape to a person's way of life, what one sees oneself as doing and trying to accomplish in the social world. If we suddenly lost them, we would be disoriented and unable to carry on. In fact, there would be, we might think, no point in carrying on.[27] But our conceptions of the good may and often do change over time, usually slowly but sometimes rather suddenly. When these changes are sudden, we are likely to say that we are no longer the same person. We know what this means: we refer to a profound and pervasive shift, or reversal, in our final ends and commitments; we refer to our different moral (which includes our religious) identity. On the road to Damascus Saul of Tarsus became Paul the Apostle. Yet such a conversion implies no change in our public or institutional identity, nor in our personal identity as this concept is understood by some writers in the philosophy of mind.[28] Moreover, in a well-ordered society supported by an overlapping consensus, citizens' (more general) political values and commitments, as part of their noninstitutional or moral identity, are roughly the same.

3. A second respect in which citizens view themselves as free is that they regard themselves as self-authenticating sources of valid claims. That is, they regard themselves as being entitled to make claims on their institutions so as to advance their conceptions of the good (provided these conceptions fall within the range permitted by the public conception of justice). These claims citizens regard as having weight of their own apart from being derived from duties and obligations specified by a political conception of justice, for example, from duties and obligations owed to society. Claims that citizens regard as founded on duties and obligations based on their conception of the good and the moral doctrine they affirm in their own life are also, for our purposes here, to be counted as self-authenticating. Doing this is reasonable in a political conception of justice for a constitutional democracy, for provided the conceptions of the good and the moral doctrines citizens affirm are compatible with the public conception of justice, these duties and obligations are self-authenticating from a political point of view.

When we describe the way in which citizens regard themselves as free, we describe how citizens think of themselves in a democratic society when questions of political justice arise. That this aspect belongs to a particular political conception is clear from the contrast with a different political conception in which people are not viewed as self-authenticating sources of valid claims. Rather, their claims have no weight except insofar as they can be derived from the duties and obligations owed to society, or from their ascribed roles in a social hierarchy justified by religious or aristocratic values.

To take an extreme case, slaves are human beings who are not counted as sources of claims, not even claims based on social duties or obligations, for slaves are not counted as capable of having duties or obligations. Laws that prohibit the maltreatment of slaves are not based on claims made by slaves, but on claims originating from slaveholders, or from the general interests of society (which do not include the interests of slaves). Slaves are, so to speak, socially dead: they are not recognized as persons at all.[29] This contrast with slavery makes clear why conceiving of citizens as free persons in virtue of their moral powers and their having a conception of the good goes with a particular political conception of justice.

4. The third respect in which citizens are viewed as free is that they are viewed as capable of taking responsibility for their ends and this affects how their various claims are assessed.[30] Very roughly, given just background institutions and given for each person a fair index of primary goods (as required by the principles of justice), citizens are thought to be capable of adjusting their aims and aspirations in the light of what they can reasonably expect to provide for. Moreover, they are viewed as capable of restricting their claims in matters of justice to the kinds of things the principles of justice allow.

Citizens are to recognize, then, that the weight of their claims is not given by the strength and psychological intensity of their wants and desires (as opposed to their needs as citizens), even when their wants and desires are rational from their point of view. The procedure is as before: we start with the basic idea of society as a fair system of cooperation. When this idea is developed into a conception of political justice, it implies that, viewing citizens as persons who can engage in social cooperation over a complete life, they can also take responsibility for their ends: that is, they can adjust their ends so that those ends can be pursued by the means they can reasonably expect to acquire in return for what they can reasonably expect to contribute. The idea of responsibility for ends is implicit in the public political culture and discernible in its practices. A political conception of the person articulates this idea and fits it into the idea of society as a fair system of cooperation.

5. To sum up, I recapitulate three main points of this and the preceding two sections:

First, in §3 persons were regarded as free and equal persons in virtue of their possessing to the requisite degree the two powers of moral personality, namely, the capacity for a sense of justice and the capacity for a conception of the good. These powers we associated with the two main elements of the idea of cooperation, the idea of the fair terms of cooperation, and the idea of each participant's rational advantage, or good.

Second, in this section (§5), we surveyed three respects in which persons are regarded as free, and have noted that in the public political culture of a constitutional democratic regime citizens conceive of themselves as free in these ways.

Third, since the question of which conception of political justice is most appropriate for realizing in basic institutions the values of liberty and equality has long been deeply controversial within the very tradition in which citizens are regarded as free and equal, the aim of justice as fairness is to resolve this question by starting from the idea of society as a fair system of cooperation in which the fair terms of cooperation are agreed upon by citizens so conceived. In §4, we saw why this approach, once the basic structure of society is taken as the primary subject of justice, leads to the idea of the original position as a device of representation.

§ 6. The Idea of a Well-Ordered Society

1. I have said that in justice as fairness the fundamental idea of society as a fair system of cooperation over generations is developed in conjunction with two companion ideas: the idea of citizens as free and equal persons, and the idea of a well-ordered society as a society effectively regulated by a public political conception of justice. Having discussed the first companion idea, I now discuss the second.

To say that a society is well-ordered conveys three things: first (and implied by the idea of a publicly recognized conception of justice), it is a society in which everyone accepts, and knows that everyone else accepts, the very same principles of justice; and second (implied by the idea of the effective regulation of such a conception), its basic structure—that is, its main political and social institutions and how they fit together as one system of cooperation—is publicly known, or with good reason believed, to satisfy these principles. And third, its citizens have a normally effective sense of justice and so they generally comply with society's basic institutions, which they regard as just. In such a society the publicly recognized conception of justice establishes a shared point of view from which citizens' claims on society can be adjudicated.

This is a highly idealized concept. Yet any conception of justice that cannot well order a constitutional democracy is inadequate as a democratic conception. This might happen because of the familiar reason that its content renders it self-defeating when it is publicly recognized. It might also happen because, adopting a distinction from Cohen, a democratic society is marked by the fact of reasonable pluralism.[31] Thus, a conception of justice may fail because it cannot gain the support of reasonable citizens who affirm reasonable comprehensive doctrines; or as I shall often say, it cannot gain the support of a reasonable overlapping consensus. Being able to do this is necessary for an adequate political conception of justice.

2. The reason for this is that the political culture of a democratic society is characterized (I assume) by three general facts understood as follows.

The first is that the diversity of reasonable comprehensive religious, philosophical, and moral doctrines found in modern democratic societies is not a mere historical condition that may soon pass away; it is a permanent feature of the public culture of democracy. Under the political and social conditions secured by the basic rights and liberties of free institutions, a diversity of conflicting and irreconcilable—and what's more, reasonable—comprehensive doctrines will come about and persist if such diversity does not already obtain.

This fact of reasonable pluralism must be distinguished from the fact of pluralism as such. It is the fact that free institutions tend to generate not simply a variety of doctrines and views, as one might expect from peoples' various interests and their tendency to focus on narrow points of view. Rather, it is the fact that among the views that develop are a diversity of reasonable comprehensive doctrines. These are the doctrines that reasonable citizens affirm and that political liberalism must address. They are not simply the upshot of self- and class interests, or of peoples' understandable tendency to view the political world from a limited standpoint. Instead, they are in part the work of free practical reason within the framework of free institutions. Thus, although historical doctrines are not, of course, the work of free reason alone, the fact of reasonable pluralism is not an unfortunate condition of human life. In framing the political conception so that it can, at the second stage, gain the support of reasonable comprehensive doctrines, we are not so much adjusting that conception to brute forces of the world but to the inevitable outcome of free human reason.[32]

A second and related general fact is that a continuing shared understanding on one comprehensive religious, philosophical, or moral doctrine can be maintained only by the oppressive use of state power. If we think of political society as a community united in affirming one and the same comprehensive doctrine, then the oppressive use of state power is necessary for political community. In the society of the Middle Ages, more or less united in affirming the Catholic faith, the Inquisition was not an accident; its suppression of heresy was needed to preserve that shared religious belief. The same holds, I believe, for any reasonable comprehensive philosophical and moral doctrine, whether religious or nonreligious. A society united on a reasonable form of utilitarianism, or on the reasonable liberalisms of Kant or Mill, would likewise require the sanctions of state power to remain so.[33] Call this "the fact of oppression."[34]

Finally, a third general fact is that an enduring and secure democratic regime, one not divided into contending doctrinal confessions and hostile social classes, must be willingly and freely supported by at least a substantial majority of its politically active citizens. Together with the first general fact, this means that to serve as a public basis of justification for a constitutional regime a political conception of justice must be one that can be endorsed by widely different and opposing though reasonable comprehensive doctrines.[35]

3. Since there is no reasonable religious, philosophical, or moral doctrine affirmed by all citizens, the conception of justice affirmed in a well-ordered democratic society must be a conception limited to what I shall call "the domain of the political" and its values. The idea of a well-ordered democratic society must be framed accordingly. I assume, then, that citizens' overall views have two parts: one part can be seen to be, or to coincide with, the publicly recognized political conception of justice; the other part is a (fully or partially) comprehensive doctrine to which the political conception is in some manner related. How it may be related I note later in IV:8. The point to stress here is that, as I have said, citizens individually decide for themselves in what way the public political conception all affirm is related to their own more comprehensive views.

With this understood, I note briefly how a well-ordered democratic society meets a necessary (but certainly not sufficient) condition of realism and stability. Such a society can be well-ordered by a political conception of justice so long as, first, citizens who affirm reasonable but opposing comprehensive doctrines belong to an overlapping consensus: that is, they generally endorse that conception of justice as giving the content of their political judgments on basic institutions; and second, unreasonable comprehensive doctrines (these, we assume, always exist) do not gain enough currency to undermine society's essential justice. These conditions do not impose the unrealistic—indeed, the utopian—requirement that all citizens affirm the same comprehensive doctrine, but only, as in political liberalism, the same public conception of justice.

4. The idea of an overlapping consensus is easily misunderstood given the idea of consensus used in everyday politics. Its meaning for us arises thus: we suppose a constitutional democratic regime to be reasonably just and workable, and worth defending. Yet given the fact of reasonable pluralism, how can we frame our defense of it so that it can win sufficiently wide support to achieve stability?

To this end, we do not look to the comprehensive doctrines that in fact exist and then draw up a political conception that strikes some kind of balance of forces between them. To illustrate: in specifying a list of primary goods,[36] say, we can proceed in two ways. One is to look at the various comprehensive doctrines actually found in society and specify an index of such goods so as to be near to those doctrines' center of gravity, so to speak; that is, so as to find a kind of average of what those who affirmed those views would need by way of institutional claims and protections and all-purpose means. Doing this might seem the best way to insure that the index provides the basic elements necessary to advance the conceptions of the good associated with existing doctrines and thus improve the likelihood of securing an overlapping consensus.

This is not how justice as fairness proceeds; to do so would make it political in the wrong way. Rather, it elaborates a political conception as a freestanding view (§1.4) working from the fundamental idea of society as a fair system of cooperation and its companion ideas. The hope is that this idea, with its index of primary goods arrived at from within, can be the focus of a reasonable overlapping consensus. We leave aside comprehensive doctrines that now exist, or that have existed, or that might exist. The thought is not that primary goods are fair to comprehensive conceptions of the good associated with such doctrines, by striking a fair balance among them, but rather fair to free and equal citizens as those persons who have those conceptions.

The problem, then, is how to frame a conception of justice for a constitutional regime such that those who support, or who might be brought to support, that kind of regime might also endorse the political conception provided it did not conflict too sharply with their comprehensive views. This leads to the idea of a political conception of justice as a freestanding view starting from the fundamental ideas of a democratic society and presupposing no particular wider doctrine. We put no doctrinal obstacles to its winning allegiance to itself, so that it can be supported by a reasonable and enduring overlapping consensus. . . .

Notes

1. See "Liberty of the Ancients Compared with that of the Moderns," (1819), in Benjamin Constant, *Political Writings*, translated and edited by Biancamaria Fontana (Cambridge: Cambridge University Press, 1988). The discussion in the introduction of the difference between the problem of political philosophy in the ancient and modern worlds illustrates the significance of Constant's distinction.

2. The conception of justice presented in *Theory*.

3. The statement of these principles differs from that given in *Theory* and follows the statement in "The Basic Liberties and Their Priority," *Tanner Lectures on Human Values*, vol. III (Salt Lake City: University of Utah Press, 1982), p. 5. The reasons for these changes are discussed on pp. 46–55 of that lecture. They are important for the revisions in the account of the basic liberties found in *Theory* and were made to try to answer the forceful objections raised by H. L. A. Hart in his critical review in the *University of Chicago Law Review* 40 (Spring 1973):535–55. In this volume, see VIII, pp. 291, 331–34, respectively.

4. The worth of these guarantees is specified by reference to an index of primary goods. How this is done is mentioned in II:5 and discussed more fully in V:3–4.

5. There are a number of questions that arise concerning the intended interpretation of the difference principle. For example, the least advantaged members of society are given by description and not by a rigid designator (to use Saul Kripke's term in *Naming and Necessity* [Cambridge, Mass.: Harvard University Press, 1972]). Further, the principle does not require continual economic growth over generations to maximize upward indefinitely the expectations of the least advantaged. It is compatible with Mill's idea of a society in a just stationary state where (real) capital accu-

mulation is zero. What the principle does require is that however great inequalities are, and however willing people are to work so as to earn their greater return, existing inequalities are to be adjusted to contribute in the most effective way to the benefit of the least advantaged. These brief remarks are hardly clear; they simply indicate the complexities that are not our concern in these lectures.

6. I make this comment since some have thought that my working out the ideas of political liberalism meant giving up the egalitarian conception of *Theory*. I am not aware of any revisions that imply such a change and think the surmise has no basis.

7. For the statement of such a principle, as well as an instructive fuller statement in four parts of the two principles, with important revisions, see Rodney Peffer's *Marxism, Morality, and Social Justice* (Princeton: Princeton University Press, 1990), p. 14. I should agree with most of Peffer's statement, but not with his 3(b), which appears to require a socialist form of economic organization. The difficulty here is not with socialism as such; but I should not include its being required in the first principles of political justice. These principles I see (as I did in *Theory*) as setting out fundamental values in terms of which, depending on the tradition and circumstances of the society in question, one can consider whether socialism in some form is justified.

8. See *Theory*, pp. 20f, 48–51, and 120f. One feature of reflective equilibrium is that it includes our considered convictions at all levels of generality; no one level, say that of abstract principle or that of particular judgments in particular cases, is viewed as foundational. They all may have an initial credibility. There is also an important distinction between narrow and wide reflective equilibrium, which is implicit in the distinction between the first and second kind of reflective equilibrium on pp. 49–50 (though the terms are not used). The terms narrow and wide were used first in §1 of "Independence of Moral Theory," *Proceedings of the American Philosophical Association* 49 (1974).

9. The idea of an overlapping consensus is defined in §2.3 and discussed further in §6.3–4.

10. The context here serves to define the phrase: "political not metaphysical."

11. In saying that a conception is moral, I mean, among other things, that its content is given by certain ideals, principles and standards; and that these norms articulate certain values, in this case political values.

12. See *Theory*, §2 and the index, and also "The Basic Structure as Subject," in *Political Liberalism*, pp. 257–88.

13. See my "Law of Peoples" (an Oxford Amnesty Lecture), to be published with the other Amnesty Lectures by Basic Books, 1993.

14. See "Basic Structure as Subject," p. 260f.

15. I comment that I use "ideas" as the more general term and as covering both concepts and conceptions. This pair is distinguished as they were in *Theory*, pp. 5f. Roughly, the concept is the meaning of a term, while a particular conception includes as well the principles required to apply it. To illustrate: the concept of justice, applied to an institution, means, say, that the institution makes no arbitrary distinctions between persons in assigning basic rights and duties, and that its rules establish a proper balance between competing claims. Whereas a conception includes, besides this, principles and criteria for deciding which distinctions are arbitrary and when a balance between competing claims is proper. People can agree on the meaning of the concept of justice and still be at odds, since they affirm different principles and standards for deciding those matters. To develop a concept of justice into a conception of it is to elaborate these requisite principles and standards. Thus, to give another example, in §3.3 I consider the concept of the person in law and in political philosophy, while in §5 I set out the further necessary elements of a conception of the person as a democratic citizen. This distinction between concept and conception I took from H. L. A. Hart's *The Concept of Law* (Oxford: Clarendon Press, 1961), pp. 155–59.

16. Two other fundamental ideas are those of the basic structure, discussed in §2.1; and of the original position, discussed in §4. These are not seen as ideas familiar to educated common sense but rather as ideas introduced for the purpose of presenting justice as fairness in a unified and prespicuous way.

17. The idea of an overlapping consensus, or perhaps better the term, was introduced in *Theory*, pp. 387f., as a way to weaken the conditions for the reasonableness of civil disobedience in a nearly just democratic society. Here and later in these lectures I use it in a different sense and in a far wider context.

18. This thought is expressed by Allan Gibbard in his review of Brian Barry's *Theories of Justice* (Berkely: University of California Press, 1989).

Barry thinks justice as fairness hovers uneasily between impartiality and mutual advantage, where Gibbard thinks it perches between on reciprocity. I think Gibbard is right about this. See his "Constructing Justice," *Philosophy and Public Affairs* 20 (Summer 1991):266f.

19. Allen Buchanan has an instructive discussion of these points in his *Marx and Justice* (Totowa, NJ.: Rowman and Littlefield, 1982), pp. 145–49.

20. It should be emphasized that a conception of the person, as I understand it here, is a normative conception, whether legal, political, or moral, or indeed also philosophical or religious, depending on the overall view to which it belongs. In the present case the conception of the person is a moral conception, one that begins from our everyday conception of persons as the basic units of thought, deliberation, and responsibility, and adapted to a political conception of justice and not to a comprehensive doctrine. It is in effect a political conception of the person, and given the aims of justice as fairness, a conception suitable for the basis of democratic citizenship. As a normative conception, it is to be distinguished from an account of human nature given by natural science and social theory and it has a different role in justice as fairness. On this last, see II:8.

21. See *Theory*, §77, where this basis of equality is discussed.

22. The account in *Theory*, §44, is defective. A better approach is one based on an idea given to me by Thomas Nagel and Derek Parfit, I believe in February of 1972. The same idea was proposed independently later by Jane English in her "Justice Between Generations," *Philosophical Studies* 31 (1977):98. This better account is indicated in "The Basic Structure as Subject." ... See VII:6 and n. 12. I simply missed this better solution, which leaves the motivation assumption unchanged.

23. See *Theory*, §58.

24. See V:3.5 and the writings of Norman Daniels there referred to.

25. Part of the difficulty is that there is no accepted understanding of what a metaphysical doctrine is. One might say, as Paul Hoffman has suggested to me, that to develop a political conception of justice without presupposing, or explicitly using, a particular metaphysical doctrine, for example, some particular metaphysical conception of the person, is already to presuppose a metaphysical thesis: namely, that no metaphysical doctrine is required for this purpose. One might also say that our ordinary conception of persons as the basic units of deliberation and responsibility presupposes, or in some way involves, certain metaphysical theses about the nature of persons as moral or political agents. Following the precept of avoidance, I should not want to deny these claims. What should be said is the following. If we look at the presentation of justice as fairness and note how it is set up, and note the ideas and conceptions it uses, no particular metaphysical doctrine about the nature of persons, distinctive and opposed to other metaphysical doctrines, appears among its premises, or seems required by its argument. If metaphysical presuppositions are involved, perhaps they are so general that they would not distinguish between the metaphysical views—Cartesian, Leibnizian, or Kantian; realist, idealist, or materialist—with which philosophy has traditionally been concerned. In this case they would not appear to be relevant for the structure and content of a political conception of justice one way or the other. I am grateful to Daniel Brudney and Paul Hoffman for discussion of these matters.

26. I am indebted to Erin Kelly for the distinction between the two kinds of aims that characterize people's moral identity as described in this and the next paragraph.

27. This role of commitments is often emphasized by Bernard Williams, for example, in "Persons, Character and Morality," in *Moral Luck* (Cambridge: Cambridge University Press, 1981), pp. 10–14.

28. Though I may have used the term *identity* in the text, it would, I think, cause less misunderstanding to use the phrase "our conception of ourselves," or "the kind of person we want to be." Doing so would distinguish the question with important moral elements from the question of the sameness, or identity, of a substance, continuant, or thing, through different changes in time and space. In saying this I assume that an answer to the problem of personal identity tries to specify the various criteria (for example, psychological criteria of memories and physical continuity of body, or some part thereof) in accordance with which two different psychological states or actions, say, which occur at two different times may be said to be states or actions of the same person who endures over time; and it also tries to specify how this enduring person is to be conceived, whether as a Cartesian or a Leibnizian substance, or a

Kantian transcendental ego, or as a continuant of some kind, for example, bodily or physical. See the collection of essays edited by John Perry, *Personal Identity* (Berkeley: University of California Press, 1975), especially Perry's introduction, pp. 1–30; and Sydney Shoemaker's essay in *Personal Identity* (Oxford: Basil Blackwell, 1984), both of which consider a number of views. Sometimes in discussions of this problem, continuity of fundamental aims is largely ignored, for example in views like H. P. Grice's (in Perry's collection), which emphasizes continuity of memory. However, once the continuity of these aims is counted as also basic, as in Derek Parfit's *Reasons and Persons* (Oxford: Clarendon Press, 1984), pt. III, there is no sharp distinction between the problem of a person's nonpublic or moral identity and the problem of their personal identity. The latter problem raises profound questions on which past and current philosophical views widely differ and surely will continue to differ. For this reason it is important to try to develop a political conception of justice that avoids this problem as far as possible. Even so, to refer to the example in the text, all agree, I assume, that for the purposes of public life, Saul of Tarsus and St. Paul the Apostle are the same person. Conversion is irrelevant to our public, or institutional, identity.

29. For the idea of social death, see Orlando Patterson's *Slavery and Social Death* (Cambridge, Mass.: Harvard University Press, 1982), esp. pp. 5–9, 38–45, 337.

30. See further V:3–4, esp. 3.6.

31. I am grateful to Joshua Cohen for instructive discussion on this point; and also for insisting on the importance of the distinction between reasonable pluralism and pluralism as such, as specified in the paragraphs immediately below in §6.2, and later in II:3. These matters he discusses in illuminating detail in "Moral Pluralism and Political Consensus," in *The Idea of Democracy*, edited by David Copp, Jean Hampton, and John Roemer (Cambridge: Cambridge University Press, 1993).

32. In II:2–3 there is an account of the burdens of judgment and a discussion of a reasonable comprehensive doctrine that gives rather minimal necessary conditions for such a doctrine, though conditions suitable for the purposes of political liberalism. It is not suggested that all reasonable doctrines so defined are equally reasonable for other purposes or from other points of view. Plainly citizens will have different opinions about these further matters.

33. This statement may seem paradoxical. If one objects that, consistent with Kant's or Mill's doctrine, the sanctions of state power cannot be used, I quite agree. But this does not contradict the text, which says that a society in which every one affirms a reasonable liberal doctrine if by hypothesis it should exist, cannot long endure. With unreasonable doctrines, and with religions that emphasize the idea of institutional authority, we may think the text correct; and we may mistakenly think there are exceptions for other comprehensive views. The point of the text is: there are no exceptions. I owe this observation to comments of Cass Sanstein.

34. I borrow this name from Sanford Shieh.

35. For completeness I add as a fourth general fact a fact we have used all along in speaking of the public culture. This is the fact that the political culture of a democratic society, which has worked reasonably well over a considerable period of time, normally contains, at least implicitly, certain fundamental intuitive ideas from which it is possible to work up a political conception of justice suitable for a constitutional regime. This fact is important when we specify the general features of a political conception of justice and elaborate justice as fairness as such a view.

36. The idea of primary goods is introduced in II:5.3 and discussed in some detail in V:3–4.

Adapted from: John Rawls, *Political Liberalism*, pp. 3–40. Copyright © 1993. Reprinted by permission of Columbia University Press. ✦

48
A Theory of Justice

Chandran Kukathas
Philip Pettit

The task Rawls has set himself is that of establishing what moral principles should govern the basic structure of a just society. We have seen how he thinks the problem should be approached: by asking, not simply what principles are desirable and feasible, but what principles would we choose from an impartial standpoint, concerned as we are to establish arrangements which are both desirable and feasible? We turn now to examine the answer Rawls offers.

That answer, we might note at the outset, is that we would choose to be governed by two principles of justice, the first guaranteeing fundamental individual liberties (of speech, association and worship, among others), and the second ensuring that social and economic inequalities are arranged to offer the greatest possible benefit to the worst-off in society, while upholding fair equality of opportunity. These are the principles that would be chosen by the parties to the hypothetical contract agreed to in the original position (OP).

In this chapter we try to flesh out this answer, giving an overview of the three parts of *A Theory of Justice*. First we consider how the answer was reached, looking at the strategy of choice Rawls thinks would be adopted in the OP and at the general reasons for the final choice of principles. This involves a close examination of the arguments of Part One of *A Theory of Justice*. That done, we shall turn to Rawls's concerns in Part Two, in which he considers the application of his theory of justice to a range of questions about actual social institutions and prac-

tices. We conclude with an analysis of the arguments in the final part of the book, in which Rawls presents a sustained defence of the feasibility of his conception of justice. When these tasks are completed we should be in a better position to offer, in the next chapter, a more general assessment of the character of Rawls's argument.

Selecting a Strategy of Choice

Confronted with the task of choosing principles of justice, the parties in the OP face a particular problem. Given the limitless number of possible principles, how should they go about deciding which principles are appropriate? Rawls makes two moves to render their task more manageable. The first is to stipulate a set of options which includes a list of 'traditional conceptions of justice' as well as his preferred principles; 'the parties are presented with this list and required to agree unanimously that one conception is the best among those enumerated' (122). The second is to argue for a particular strategy which he thinks the parties should adopt for making the choice among these options under the conditions of uncertainty that prevail in the OP. It is this second move that has drawn most critical attention, and it is our primary concern in this section. But we should be clear about the nature of the first move, for it reveals a good deal about Rawls's theory.

The list of eligible conceptions of justice is divided into five categories (conveniently tabulated on p. 124 of *A Theory of Justice*). The first contains Rawls's preferred conception: the principles of justice as fairness. The other four contain classical teleological conceptions (such as utilitarianism); 'mixed' conceptions, which combine principles protecting liberty with, for example, variants of utilitarianism; intuitionistic conceptions (which require us, typically, to balance a list of prima facie principles 'as appropriate'); and egoistic conceptions (such as the principle that everyone is to serve my interests).

Although Rawls opines that the 'merits of these traditional theories surely suffice to justify the effort to rank them' (124), it is hard to see much worth in any of the egoistic conceptions; indeed they seem scarcely describable as principles at all. Rawls does in due course indicate that egoistic conceptions are not to be considered as alternatives by the parties in the OP, since the 'formal constraints of the concept of right' preclude their admission as conceptions of justice. What is not so clearly indicated, but we shall come to see, is that several of the other alternatives appear to be ruled out too, before the parties face the problem of selecting the right conception.

It must be said that the list Rawls presents is a very restricted one. It omits, for example, any form of libertarianism, principles requiring distribution according to need, and desert-based conceptions of justice, to name just three other options. Admittedly, libertarianism does receive some philosophically significant treatment in Rawls's discussion of 'the system of natural liberty' (65–72); equally, desert-based conceptions of justice are later discussed and rejected (103–4; 310–15); and it could be argued that something like 'basic need' is integrated into the two principles of justice Rawls finally defends. (See also Rawls 1975 for his arguments against more radical notions of distribution according to need.) Nevertheless, Rawls's *contractarian* method appears to rule out many conceptions of justice before rational deliberation within the social contract begins. But we leave this point aside for the moment to focus on the OP and the reasoning that goes on within it.

So, how would the parties in the OP decide which (set of) principles of justice to choose? Or should we say, for what reasons would they choose the two principles of 'justice as fairness'? In order to uncover their reasonings, Rawls says, it is 'a useful heuristic device' to regard the two principles 'as the maximin solution to the problem of social justice' (152). The two principles would be chosen if the parties in the OP adopted the maximin strategy of choice under uncertainty.

The maximin strategy tells us to rank alternatives by their worst possible outcomes, adopting the alternative whose worst outcome is superior to the worst outcome of any other. This is clearly a strategy which would prove attractive to someone with a conservative or pessimistic outlook. The OP, Rawls says, has been so described as to make it 'rational for the parties to adopt the conservative attitude expressed by this rule' (153). In effect, the parties choose principles for the design of a society as if their places in it were to be determined by their worst enemies. This is not, of course, to say that the parties in fact assume that their position is to be decided by a malevolent opponent, since they may not, according to Rawls, reason from false premises. But adopting maximin would be analogous to adopting such an assumption (153). . . .

The Two Principles of Justice

From the range of conceptions of justice availabe to them, the parties in the OP choose the two principles which comprise 'justice as fairness'. The final formulation of this conception is presented on p. 302 of *A Theory of Justice*, and we reproduce it below.

> *First principle.* Each person is to have an equal right to the most extensive total system of equal basic liberties compatible with a similar system of liberty for all.
>
> *Second principle.* Social and economic inequalities are to be arranged so that they are both:
> (a) to the greatest benefit of the least advantaged, consistent with the just savings principle, and
> (b) attached to offices and positions open to all under conditions of fair equality of opportunity.

The principles are presented in 'lexical order', which means that they come in order of priority. In fact, Rawls stipulates two 'priority rules' to make clear the respective importance of the various elements in the two principles.

The first priority rule establishes the 'priority of liberty', allowing liberty to be restricted only for the sake of liberty. The first principle must be satisfied before the second is invoked. Only considerations of liberty are allowed to qualify liberty; thus 'a less extensive liberty must strengthen the total system of liberty shared by all', and 'a less equal liberty must be acceptable to those with the lesser liberty' (303).

The second priority rule establishes the priority of justice over efficiency and welfare. This means, firstly, that the second principle as a whole takes precedence over the 'principle of efficiency', and the idea of 'maximizing the sum of advantages' in society. Secondly, within the second principle, (b), the principle of fair equality of opportunity takes priority over (a), the principle of greatest benefit to the least advantaged (known as the *difference* principle). This means that 'an inequality of opportunity must enhance the opportunities (*sic*) of those with the lesser opportunity' (*sic*), and that, given the requirement of inter-generational justice that a certain level of savings for the future be maintained, 'an excessive rate of saving must on balance mitigate the burden of those bearing this hardship' (303).

The general conception of justice embodied by the two principles, as they are governed by the priority rules, may be expressed in a sentence.

> All social primary goods—liberty and opportunity, income and wealth, and the bases of self-respect—are to be distributed equally unless an unequal distribution of any or all of these goods is to the advantage of the least favoured. (303)

Why would this conception of justice be chosen? Rawls offers two sorts of reasons. First, it is the conception that would survive a critical comparative examination in the OP: utilitarian, egoistic, perfectionist and other conceptions would be rejected, and 'justice as fairness' would remain. Second, justice as fairness has certain 'positive advantages'. Let us examine these sets of reasons in turn.

Justice as fairness would be chosen in the OP, Rawls maintains, because the maximin strategy would lead to its being ranked higher than any of the available alternatives. This conclusion enjoys a certain plausibility. The difference principle in particular looks to the welfare of the worst-off group and ensures that that group fares as well as possible without endangering liberty. And the lexical priority of the principle of liberty ensures

that individuals in the worst position in society cannot be deprived of important liberties. Justice as fairness is thus bound to keep the lowest position within the system higher than the corresponding position in the system organized by any alternative.

Utilitarianism, for example, leaves open the possibility that maximization of utility will lead some people to fare very badly. If slavery were required to maximize average or total utility, utilitarianism would, *in principle*, allow it. So utilitarianism would probably have to be excluded by the maximining members of the OP.

But there is a second set of reasons why the two principles would be chosen in the OP. Justice as fairness possesses several positive advantages, according to Rawls. There are three considerations he discusses in some detail. All of these, in our terms, are considerations which suggest that the two principles are the only really feasible proposal.

First, the principles of justice as fairness are principles that, given the general facts of moral psychology, the parties in the OP can rely on one another to adhere to once adopted. There will be no consequences they cannot accept. Thus there is no risk that they will be asked to accept a lesser liberty for the sake of a greater good for others. We might wonder whether an agreement involving such a risk could be assumed in good faith (176; but see Kukathas 1989). People who agree to justice as fairness will be able to make the agreement in good faith because they will be able to keep to it and know they will be able to keep to it. Compacts which involve utilitarian principles do not enjoy this advantage, since utilitarianism may require us to do or condone things we would find ourselves psychologically incapable of accepting. 'Compacts of this sort exceed the capacity of human nature' (176).

Secondly, justice as fairness would be preferred because it is a conception that generates its own support and so would be stable. The system it supports is one in which everyone's good is affirmed: each person's liberties are secured, and yet the difference principle ensures that everyone is benefited by social cooperation. 'Therefore we can explain the acceptance of the social system and the principles it satisfies by the psychological law that persons tend to love, cherish, and support whatever affirms their own good. Since everyone's good is affirmed, all acquire inclinations to uphold the scheme' (177). This is not so with utilitarianism, for example, which requires a greater identification with the interests of others and, hence, a greater willingness to accept sacrifices for their good. The facts of human moral psychology make this difficult to achieve; justice as fairness is a more stable conception insofar as it does not depend upon such psychological achievements.

Thirdly, a conception of justice, Rawls says, 'should publicly express men's respect for one another'; in this way 'they ensure a sense of their own value' (179). The two principles of justice as fairness do just this, for 'when society follows these principles, everyone's good is included in a scheme of mutual benefit and this public affirmation in institutions of each man's endeavours supports men's self-esteem' (179). The support given to people's self-respect in turn increases the effectiveness of social cooperation. This provides strong reason for choosing these principles. Again, utilitarianism, by contrast, cannot guarantee a person's self-respect; indeed, in Rawls's view, the principle of utility puts it in jeopardy.

These, then, are the detailed reasons Rawls offers as to why the two principles would be adopted. But Rawls also presents the case for them in what he thinks is a more intuitively appealing way (150-2). We conclude our discussion of the principles with a summary of this line of argument.

Take as a starting point the requirement that all primary goods be distributed equally. This would be agreed to by any person selected arbitrarily insofar as he has no way of winning any special advantages for himself—nor any grounds for accepting disadvantages. It is unreasonable for him to expect more than an equal share, and irrational to agree to less. Parties looking to establish principles of justice would therefore be well disposed towards principles upholding equal liberty and opportunity for all,

while guaranteeing an equal distribution of wealth.

But suppose the parties ask: why should this be final? Why not permit some inequalities if these would make everyone better off—for example by eliciting more productive efforts? The thought will lead them to consider moderating the initially attractive egalitarian view. 'In order to make the principle regulating inequalities more determinate', Rawls suggests, 'one looks at the system from the standpoint of the least advantaged representative man. Inequalities are permissible when they maximize, or at least contribute to, the long-term expectations of the least fortunate group in society' (151).

The final step in this intuitive presentation of the contractarian argument is to consider where the parties will hold firm to the initial egalitarian view, and where they will break with it. Rawls suggests that they will draw the line at allowing less than equal basic liberties for the sake of any other good. Thus they will be led towards the conception represented by the lexically ordered two principles of justice.

Just Institutions

Having identified the two principles of justice as the outcome of rational choice under controlled conditions, Rawls is confident that he has derived a conception of justice which is clearly attractive. But that conception is still an abstract notion. More needs to be said to indicate what are the substantive implications of adopting these principles. This is necessary not only to see the practical point of the principles, but also to make clear precisely what they mean. Otherwise, such notions as liberty, opportunity, fairness, and 'least advantaged', which are used to describe the two principles, will remain vague and ambiguous.

In Part Two of his book Rawls attempts to 'illustrate the content of the principles of justice' (195) by describing a basic structure which satisfies them. His intention is to show that 'the principles of justice, which so far have been discussed in abstraction from institutional forms, define a workable political conception, and are a reasonable approximation to and extension of our considered judgments' (195).

The institutions Rawls goes on to describe are those of a constitutional democracy. And although he insists that the arrangements he proposes are not the only ones that could be just, it becomes quite clear that the principles he defends can only be understood as the principles of a liberal democratic society.

In fleshing out his principles in the account of the basic structure of the just society Rawls tries to show how certain basic institutions or practices flow from them. This leads him to offer an account of the just political constitution and just economic arrangements, and to address the question of the nature of the obligation of people in the imperfect world, outside the OP, to comply with the laws of an imperfectly just society. To make clear the link between the principles of justice chosen in the OP and just institutions, Rawls asks us to imagine a four-stage sequence of events. At the first stage, in the OP, principles are chosen. When this is done, the parties in the OP move on to meet in a constitutional convention where they decide upon the justice of political forms and choose a constitution: this is the second stage, in which the basic rights and liberties are made clear. Now it is possible to legislate—to make laws affecting the economic and social structure of society. This is the third stage, when the justice of laws and economic and social policies are considered. When this is complete it remains only for us to consider, in the fourth stage, the application of the rules by judges and other officials.

The four-stage sequence is intended to make clear that the institutions of justice as fairness are just because it can be shown that they would be chosen by society's members suitably constrained by their ignorance of their own parochial interests and attachments. In the first stage, under the veil of ignorance, they would choose the two principles. In the second stage, with the principles of justice no longer in contention, the parties at the constitutional convention are given knowledge of the general facts of their own society—of its economic resources and political culture—so they would choose the political constitution that 'satisfies the principles of justice and is best calculated to lead to just and efficient legislation' (197). And in the third stage, with the political constitution no longer in doubt, and their information more complete, they would choose the welfarist economic and social policies Rawls recommends. In the last stage we view our particular situation with complete access to the facts, the veil of ignorance having been gradually removed altogether in the sequential descent from the world of the OP to our own, and we are able to consider the application of rules with a full understanding of the (just) basic structure of our society.

What, then, are the substantive political and economic arrangements of Rawls's just society?

A just political constitution is one which upholds the first principle of justice—the principle of liberty. This, for Rawls, means that it must be one which conceives of the state as an association of equal citizens (212). The state, under such a constitution, 'does not concern itself with philosophical and religious doctrine but regulates individuals' pursuit of their moral and spiritual interests in accordance with principles to which they themselves would agree in an initial situation of equality' (212). This means that the government has 'neither the right nor the duty to do what it or a majority . . . wants to do in questions of morals and religion' (212).

While the government may on occasion limit liberty, it may do so only when the common interest in public order and security is at stake, for only on such occasions does 'the government [act] on a principle that would be chosen in the original position' (212–13). Liberty can be restricted only for the sake of liberty. This means that liberty of conscience cannot ever be denied. And when the constitution itself is secure, it means that there is no reason to deny freedom even to the intolerant (219).

The constitution, for Rawls, is to be understood as 'a just procedure satisfying the requirements of equal liberty, . . . framed so that of all the just arrangements which are feasible, it is more likely than any other to result in a just and effective system of legislation' (221). The principle of equal liberty requires that citizens be allowed the opportunity to participate in the political processes of what is best described as a constitutional democracy. But liberty also requires checks on the powers of legislatures. And these Rawls thinks can be supplied by the 'traditional devices of constitutionalism': bicameral legislature, separation of powers mixed with checks and balances, and a bill of rights with judicial review (224). Moreover, liberty requires the rule of law; otherwise the uncertainty of the boundaries of our liberty will make its exercise risky and less secure (239).

A just political constitution is thus one which limits the powers of government, while according it the authority to make and enforce the law. The principle of liberty requires that there be checks upon that authority. Yet it is the same principle from which we derive the government's authority to impose sanctions upon those who break the law, since an ineffective government cannot act to preserve important liberties (240–2).

A just economic order is one which upholds the second principle of justice. A state governed by a just political constitution would thus try to uphold the second of Rawls's two principles through appropriate legislation. Although Rawls does go into the question of justice in political economy, he does not really tackle the question of which economic system is to be preferred, insisting that both capitalist and socialist institutions are *in principle* compatible with the second principle. 'While the notion that a market economy is in some sense the best scheme has been most carefully investigated by so-called bourgeois economists, this connection is a historical contingency in that, theoretically at least, a socialist regime can avail itself of the advantages of this system' (271).

So in his discussion of the economic arrangements of a just society Rawls concentrates on the question of how equal opportunity and the difference principle are to be upheld. He concludes that fair, as opposed to formal, equality of opportunity requires that the government, in addition to 'maintaining the usual kinds of social overhead capital', tries to ensure equal chances of education

and culture through subsidized or public schooling, tries to ensure equality of opportunity in economic activities by policing the conduct of firms, and preventing monopolies, and generally guarantees a social minimum income (275).

Economic justice in fact requires four branches of government: an *allocation* branch to 'keep the price system workably competitive and to prevent the formation of unreasonable market power' (276); a *stabilization* branch to maintain full employment and so, with the allocative branch, to help maintain the efficiency of the market economy; a *transfer* branch responsible for dealing with the provision of a social minimum; and a *distribution* branch to 'preserve an approximate justice in distributive shares by means of taxation and the necessary adjustments in the rights of property' (277). Although Rawls does not put it in these terms, it looks as if economic justice is given institutional expression by the organs of a welfare state.

There is one other important constraint. Justice does not permit one generation to take advantage of its descendants by simply consuming its wealth. A just savings principle is a corollary of the difference principle, requiring one generation to save for the welfare of future generations. Interpreted through the contract doctrine, however, there is an upper bound on how much a generation can be asked to save for future people (298).

Thus far, the political and economic institutions of a just society. The question now is, why should we comply with the laws of a society which, at best, is able only to offer an approximation to the ideal? In the real world, justice is realized imperfectly—if at all.

Rawls's answer to this question is of crucial importance in his account of how his principles of justice might find institutional expression, because it explains how his theory of justice bears on the real world. His answer is that the 'injustice of a law is not, in general, a sufficient reason for not adhering to it any more than the legal validity of legislation (as defined by the existing constitution) is a sufficient reason for going along with it' (350–1). By this he makes clear that what the parties in the OP do when they choose principles of justice is not simply agree to abide by rules which adhere to these principles; they make a more open-ended commitment to enter into a juridical state of affairs. In the OP they ask the question, 'what is a just society', and the principles they arrive at define 'a perfectly just society, given favourable conditions' (351). But they do not agree to abide by social rules only if society is perfectly just, since such a society can never be. They agree to find, and abide by just constitutional arrangements, recognizing that the constitution is a 'just but imperfect procedure framed as far as the circumstances permit to insure a just outcome', and that 'there is no feasible political process which guarantees that the laws enacted in accordance with it will be just' (353).

The contract doctrine, indeed, does not offer us the option of selecting the ideal basic structure; in the OP the parties are confronted with a limited set of feasible procedures of justice. In the end, Rawls says, it is agreed that 'consenting to one of these procedures is surely preferable to no agreement at all' (354). And, under certain conditions, 'the parties agree to put up with unjust laws' (355)—while working for their improvement. We have, Rawls says, 'a natural duty of civility not to invoke the faults of social arrangements as a too ready excuse for not complying with them' (355).

Now in all this Rawls is not insisting that we must obey the law, come what may. While under ideal conditions we can assume that full compliance with the law will be the case, under non-ideal conditions we can assume only partial compliance. Since there will be injustices perpetrated by both citizens and the law, there will be questions of punishment, compensatory justice, and civil disobedience, for example, which cannot arise under ideal theory. Partial compliance theory, according to Rawls, must deal with such questions not just by invoking the principles uncovered by ideal theory and commanding obedience; it must deal with the problem of injustice.

Taking the issue of civil disobedience as an example, Rawls argues that while the natural duty of justice requires us to comply with the laws of an imperfectly just society, the perpetual violation of the principle of liberty and the exhaustion of legal means of seeking redress may justify civil disobedience and, in the more extreme circumstances of repression, rebellion. Then we say that 'if justified civil disobedience seems to threaten civic discord, the responsibility falls not upon those who protest but upon those whose abuse of authority and power justifies such opposition' (390–1).

In all of this there is, of course, a large measure of indeterminacy. In his account of the institutions of justice as fairness, he does not supply any more than a general account of the form social practices might take. But this is all that can reasonably be expected, and it is all that he aims to provide (201). His hope is that by defining the 'range of justice . . . in accordance with our considered convictions' he will single out 'with greater sharpness the graver wrongs a society should avoid' (201).

Goodness, Stability and the Sense of Justice

Having established that his two principles of justice are desirable principles to govern the basic structure, and having explained how they might be embodied in the political, legal and economic institutions of the real world, Rawls turns to his concluding defence of justice as fairness. His concern now is to show that his conception of justice would be acceptable to us because it would make for a stable society based on moral principles which uphold our most cherished values. He wants to show that his theory is 'rooted in human thought and feeling, and tied in with our ends' (391). Part Three of *A Theory of Justice* is an attempt to show how the theory gains support when it is examined in the light of a fuller consideration of the nature of *goodness*, and when its *stability* as a moral conception is made clear. Rawls wants to show that his just society is also a good society: justice and goodness are congruent.

To see how Rawls tries to do this, we need to note a distinction he makes between deontological and teleological moral theories. A deontological theory asserts that what is right does not depend on, but is independent of, what is good. So, for example, that we should keep our promises is not determined by the good consequences, if there are any, of doing so; right conduct requires us to keep promises, and this injunction is in no way dependent on the goodness of keeping promises. Promise-keeping is good because it is right; it is not right because it is good or produces good results. Teleological theories maintain that what is right depends upon what is good. If promise-keeping is right, it can only be because it leads to good. Utilitarianism is an example of a teleological theory.

Rawls's theory is deontological because it maintains that respecting the two principles is right independently of whether it produces good. It holds that 'something is good only if it fits into ways of life consistent with the principles of right already on hand' (396). The right is prior to the good. Yet Rawls also wants to show that the right is consistent or congruent with the good: that he is not simply dreaming up abstract principles which conflict with what we regard as good. And that is what the third part of his book attempts to do, offering an argument for the feasibility of his conception of justice which supports the three feasibility considerations mentioned earlier.

In this part of the book Rawls does two things. First, he argues that the parties who select the two principles of justice can be represented as doing so in order to further a weak and uncontentious conception of what is good for them—a 'thin theory of the good'. Acting with 'deliberative rationality', they assume that their good is that which they would choose if they had full knowledge of the effects of their choices, and they conclude that any good life requires a supply of 'primary goods'. The 'Aristotelian Principle', which suggests that, 'other things equal, human beings enjoy the exercise of their realized capacities . . . and this enjoyment increases the more the capacity is realized' (426), helps to specify what the primary goods are. The persons in the OP can be seen as choosing the two principles of justice in order to promote their share of such primary goods. So Rawls thinks his conception of jus-

tice is one which is consistent with a concern for the good. A society which is just in his terms is also, in this sense, a good society.

The second thing Rawls does, in Part Three of his book, is to try to show that the just society, as he conceives of it, will be stable and consistent with the good of its members. Why will it be stable? A stable society is one governed by a stable conception of justice. 'One conception of justice is more stable than another if the sense of justice that it tends to generate is stronger and more likely to override disruptive inclinations and if the institutions it allows foster weaker impulses to act unjustly' (454). Justice as fairness is a conception which will generate a strong sense of justice. This is so primarily because of the laws of human psychology which suggest that, if a society's institutions are just, and publicly known to be just, a person will acquire 'the corresponding sense of justice as he recognizes that he and those for whom he cares are the beneficiaries of these arrangements' (490–1). The two principles of justice as fairness Rawls believes are just and of benefit to citizens and those they care about; and furthermore they will be publicly known to be so in any society where they are introduced. Thus they will strengthen the sense of justice and bring stability.

But is the just society as Rawls conceives of it—the society governed by the two principles—going to be really consistent with the good of its members? Rawls thinks so. And he tries to explain why in his account of 'the good of the sense of justice'. In the penultimate section of *A Theory of Justice* Rawls turns to the question of whether the disposition to take up and be guided by the sense of justice accords with the individual's good. Since a sense of justice is understood to be an effective desire to apply and act from the principles of justice, what has to be established is that it is rational for those in a well-ordered society to affirm their sense of justice as regulative of their plan of life. This does not mean justifying being just to an egoist, showing how acting justly would best advance private ends. 'Rather, we are concerned with the goodness of the settled desire to take up the standpoint of justice'

(568). Is having this inclination consistent with a persons's good?

Rawls provides three main grounds for the claim that, yes, taking up the standpoint of justice promotes a person's own good. The first ground is that the principles of justice are public and would serve to tie people together, supplementing the bonds of affection and fellow-feeling with 'institutional forms' (571). We could not abandon our sense of justice then without hurting the community—and so, our friends and associates. Granted the laws of our moral psychology (498), this is something we would want to avoid.

Secondly, given that such a society is itself a good in which we would wish to share, preserving our sense of justice would be important. This follows from the fact that participating in the life of a well-ordered society—a society ordered publicly by principles like the two principles of justice—is a great good. Because society is a 'social union of social unions', it 'realizes to a pre-eminent degree the various forms of human activity' (571). Moreover, our nature and our potentialities are such that 'we depend upon the co-operative endeavours of others not only for the means of well-being but to bring to fruition our latent powers' (571). Yet to share fully in such a life, we must 'acknowledge the principles of its regulative conception, and this means that we must affirm our sentiment of justice' (571).

Finally, the inclination to take up the standpoint of justice in a well-ordered society would be consistent with our good because 'acting justly is something we want to do as free and equal rational beings' (572). Indeed, Rawls suggests that the 'desire to act justly and the desire to express our nature as free moral persons turn out to specify what is practically speaking the same desire' (572).

This final claim puts forward a consideration which lies at the heart of Rawls's moral philosophy, and which helps us make sense of his endeavour. What is in our good, he assumes, cannot go against our nature. But how, he asks, can anyone demand that we live by principles of right which require us to subordinate the pursuit of the good to the commands of justice? The answer is that only by doing so can we be true to our nature and be free.

[T]he desire to express our nature as a free and equal rational being can be fulfilled only by acting on the principles of right and justice as having first priority. This is a consequence of the condition of finality: since these principles are regulative, the desire to act upon them is satisfied only to the extent that it is likewise regulative with respect to other desires. It is acting from this precedence that expresses our freedom from contingency and happenstance. (574)

To be true to our nature, we cannot let justice take a back seat; justice must regulate our other desires, and not be overridden by them. 'Therefore in order to realize our nature we have no alternative but to plan to preserve our sense of justice as governing our other aims' (574). And this sentiment, Rawls insists, 'cannot be fulfilled if it is compromised and balanced against other ends as but one desire among the rest' (574). Many of our aims can often be fulfilled even if they are subordinated to others as circumstances dictate. Not so with our sense of justice. Acting wrongly will thus always arouse feelings of guilt and shame. Such emotions reveal 'the defeat of our regulative moral sentiments' (574–5).

This argument makes it clear that the most important consideration for Rawls is that of whether a conception of justice is one which we, as human beings with an equal capacity for freedom, can live by. A conception of justice which denied our nature would not be a feasible conception for us—and it would not long survive. Such a conception would not command our allegiance. This, ultimately, is the basis of Rawls's rejection of utilitarianism. It is an infeasible moral conception because it misrepresents our nature, viewing us as creatures concerned primarily with desire-satisfaction, and failing to see how important freedom and equality are. Rawls's line of argument in the third part of his book illustrates how large a part considerations of feasibility play in his theory.

Summary

In this chapter we have offered a brisk exposition of the three parts of *A Theory of Jus-*

tice. In the first part Rawls puts his case for the two principles of justice, and the associated priority rules, that he defends. This is the contractarian argument that parties in the original position would find it rational—specifically, would find it rational in maximin terms—to prefer the two principles to the rather limited list of alternatives that Rawls considers. In the second part Rawls looks at what the two principles would be likely to mean in the detailed arrangement of social affairs. He plots their impact on constitutional choice, on legislation about economic and social matters and on the behaviour of citizens which the courts have to arbitrate, in particular on the behaviour of citizens who judge that certain laws offend against those principles. In the third part of the book Rawls provides an unexpected, further line of defence for the two principles. Respecting the principles is supposed to be fight independently of any good that it produces. But in any case, Rawls argues, the two principles connect appropriately with the production of the good. They are principles which the contractors can be represented as choosing out of a concern for primary, uncontentious goods. And they are principles which ought to generate a stable society, being consistent with the good of the members of the society.

References

Kukathas, Chandran 1989, 'Welfare, Contract, and the Language of Charity', *Philosophical Quarterly*, 39, 75–80.

Rawls, John 1971, *A Theory of Justice*, Oxford: Oxford University Press.

Rawls, John 1975, 'Fairness to Goodness', *Philosophical Review*, 84, 536–54.

49
Politics and the Public in Rawls' *Political Liberalism*

Elizabeth Frazer
Nicola Lacey[1]

In this paper we discuss John Rawls' conceptions of the 'political' and the 'public', as elaborated in *Political Liberalism*.[2] We consider Rawls' conception of the political to be unsatisfactory in a number of ways. If this is right, it is significant for Rawls because the definition of his theory as political is central to his defence against critics who accuse him of metaphysical abstraction and universalism. More importantly, it is significant for contemporary debate in political theory, much of which continues to take Rawls' work as its point of departure.

In *Political Liberalism* Rawls emphasizes above all else, as he has in other writings since the publication of *A Theory of Justice*,[3] that 'justice as fairness' is a *political* theory—it is not intended to be a comprehensive doctrine covering questions to do with justice in all aspects of our being. He has made this point in response to a number of criticisms, some of which he considers to be based on misreadings of *A Theory of Justice*.[4] But it is also a response to his own view that the conception of the 'well ordered society' advanced in that work was unsatisfactory.[5] He now makes it clear that the well ordered society will normally be characterized by a plurality of reasonable yet incompatible comprehensive doctrines held by its members; and that members of such a society would endorse justice as fairness, as a political, but not as a comprehensive, doctrine.[6] This emphasis evidently means that a great deal rests on the characterization of 'the political'. The task for members of this well ordered society characterized by 'reasonable pluralism' is to find a proper justification for their political coercion of one another and, in particular, of members who espouse unreasonable comprehensive doctrines.[7]

Rawls' conception of the 'political', as deployed in both *A Theory of Justice* and his later writings, has been subject to criticism from a number of perspectives. Perhaps the most significant source has been feminist political and social theory. The feminist challenge to conventional distinctions between public and private, political and personal, if it succeeds, has profound implications both for the conduct of practical politics and for political theory and political science.[8]

Whilst Rawls responds in some detail in *Political Liberalism*, explicitly or implicitly, to a wide range of criticisms of his theory, his dismissal of the so-called public/private critique verges on the peremptory.[9] This is striking for two reasons. First, one of its main exponents, Susan Moller Okin, is in other respects a firm defender of Rawls' principles.[10] Her reasoning constitutes a very constructive internal critique of *A Theory of Justice*, and one whose lucid and eminently sensible arguments one might have expected Rawls to take up in any substantial clarification of his theory. Okin suggests that liberal theorists can take on board the full implications of the public/private critique without threatening the fundamentals of their position.[11] Yet, as we shall see, Rawls' treatment of the family and the conception of the political in *Political Liberalism* leaves the important issues raised by Okin unaddressed. His explicit reluctance to address them suggests that he may be unwilling to entertain such modifications as are necessitated.[12] We shall argue that this is because, contrary to Okin's optimistic assessment, the public/private critique mounts a fundamental challenge to the coherence of Rawls' and other liberal conceptions of justice.

It is not only a feminist critique which suggests difficulties with Rawls' treatment and deployment of the public/non-public divide. They are suggested also by analyses of the political and economic conditions of the post-industrial world generated by political science, political economy and sociology. One of the most important themes in contemporary political science is the claim that, in order to understand how political relations work, we must extend our horizons beyond the institutions conventionally associated with the state. Our vision must comprehend the operation of a large number of 'public', 'quasi-public' and indeed 'private' bodies. In other words, in terms of post-industrial social governance the power of the state is no longer (if it ever was) exclusive.

This insight, which has obvious and radical implications for the conceptions of the public and the political, has been incompletely digested by political theorists, and Rawls is no exception. We shall argue that Rawls' now explicitly constructionist method implies that, in the elaboration of public reason, a detailed understanding of how a wide variety of actual institutions work will be of the first importance.[13] Yet his elaboration of the political entails a narrow focus on state government and the enforcement of laws.[14]

This consideration of the scope of the concept of the political flows into consideration of the relationship between political philosophy, political theory, and political and other social science. It raises the question of methods of political theorists and philosophers. What are we to make of Rawls' developed view that political theory must be an interpretive enterprise—interpretive of the values and ideals immanent in social institutions and ways of life and, presumably, reflective discussions of these? In this context, we shall argue that there is an uneasy relationship between two voices in Rawls' text. First, his disavowal of universalism and metaphysical abstraction has produced an insistent location of his analysis in modern democratic states,[15] a frequent adversion to the relationship between justice as fairness and 'you and me',[16] and the awareness that philosophical principles have to be realized in concrete social institutions. That is, the text is produced by a practical, interpretive, sociological voice. Second, an analytic, purely philosophical voice which denies that the practicalities of social institutions are relevant is also powerful.[17] Our argument is that the untenable boundary of 'the political' and the mapping of this onto the public v. non-public distinction is symptomatic of an unresolved conflict between these two voices. Our answer would be the production and practice of a self-consciously theoretical voice: but this is undoubtedly at odds with some cherished characteristics of political philosophical method.

Universalism to Particularism?

A common criticism levelled at Rawls' previous work is that the conception of the well ordered society, and the concomitant assumption that 'justice as fairness' could be relied upon to command universal assent, is sociologically unconvincing and normatively dubious. Rawls and other liberal philosophers have been accused of universalism in two senses. First, they hold that members of all societies can be assumed to be equally open or subject to a core conception of rationality which transcends cultural specificities. This we might call inter-societal universalism. Second, they assume that all members of any society could be expected to assent to these rationally based values and principles—in other words, intra-societal universalism, or the assumption of intra-societal homogeneity.

Critics argue that this invalidly attributes a culturally specific form of reasoning to all cultures and social groups; and that other forms of reasoning should be incorporated in or accounted for in political philosophy. Furthermore, it is pointed out that there are values which are at odds with liberal values. We cannot assume that these would be overridden by rational thought, or that liberal values will trump others.

Rawls' analysis, especially the adjustment of the conception of the well ordered society, now goes some way to meeting such objections. It is quite clear that he does not assume, indeed he denies, intra-societal homogeneity; and he makes it clear that his is a theory of justice for a liberal democratic society—one which is characterized by the fact of pluralism and rooted in, rather than generating, a particular set of values. He also denies that his method or his substantive analysis is universalist as such.[18] 'Rawlsian constructivism' avoids the assumption that a theoretical schema is applicable beyond the domain in which it was built. If, as he argues elsewhere, social contract doctrine is nevertheless universal in its reach[19] this is because the structure of the international order is in relevant respects similar to the structure of the social situation at the point when political society is ordered.[20]

Yet Rawls is also at pains to defend a certain kind of abstraction, and to deny that he deploys abstract concepts and principles with universalist pretensions (while acknowledging that abstractness invites misunderstanding).[21] He argues that where there are deep and genuine conflicts of value and principle (political or otherwise) we must 'ascend' to a higher level of analysis in order to see the conflict.[22] But we start by examining actually existing public cultures, which we take to be a shared fund of implicitly recognized basic ideas and principles.[23] An aim of the project of constructing a public political culture would be to identify, organize and, presumably, seek to resolve such philosophical dilemmas (for instance, the clash between freedom and equality) as may already be present.[24]

Rawls is open to challenge here from the empirically minded reader. What are the grounds of his evidence—what method has been used in studying the 'implicitly recognized basic ideas and principles'? Is it acceptable for this project to be undertaken from the philosopher's armchair, or the academic seminar room? As soon as claims to particularity of this kind are made it is incumbent upon the claimant to produce some evidence. At some points Rawls seems to do just that: he discusses Lincoln's correspondence on abolition, for example,[25] and in an extended discussion of different versions of parliamentary and constitutional democracy launches what looks like a straightforward defence of the US system.[26]

Yet in a constant reversion to the purely philosophical, non-particular and non-empirical voice Rawls denies this kind of interpretation—explaining that such discussions are merely illustrative of the kinds of arguments which justice as fairness might help to develop and endorse.[27] These remarks imply that justice as fairness is wholly *pre*-empirical. *Political Liberalism*'s appeal to the capacities for rationality and a sense of justice as invariant bases for the construction of principles of political justice must also be read as a retreat to abstract and universalistic conceptual argument. But given Rawls' commitment to particularism and socially grounded interpretivism, would it not be better to go the whole way and accept (as Dworkin arguably comes close to doing in his more recent work) that political theory can be, in effect, no more (or less) than an immanent critique of particular (liberal) cultural practices and systems?[28]

The Analytic Categories of Political Liberalism

Before proceeding to a detailed discussion of Rawls' conception of the political, it will be useful to raise some questions about the salient features of the analytic framework which now informs his work.

The Political Conception of the Person

The avowed particularism of Rawls' analysis flows into his insistence that the conception of the person deployed and developed is a *political* conception—not a 'metaphysical' one. The question here is whether this distinction does the work Rawls requires. He argues that the political conception is indifferent as between realism, idealism and materialism, for example, or between Descartes, Leibniz and Kant.[29] It does, however, make substantive assumptions about the nature of citizenship. Persons are simply conceptualized as having a capacity for a sense of justice, and a capacity for having a conception of the good. As citizens, persons are regarded as free and equal, and as having capacities for cooperation and reciprocity.[30]

Beginning with the sociological fact of pluralism, we are asked to imagine the following. What would representatives of different social groups institute in the way of a basic structure for society if they did not know whether the groups they represented had majority or minority tastes and commitments to comprehensive doctrines, but did know that those they represent have a capacity for a commitment to some good or comprehensive doctrine, and a capacity for a sense of justice? The resulting structure consists of the relations between the political constitution, a system of property, economic organization, and families and associations.[31] The parties to the contract exercise *rationality* within the constraint of the *reasonable*. The 'reasonable' is not derived from or generated by rationality; the reasonable is public, as rationality is not.[32]

Rawls does address the issue of why the deliberations of the parties to such a hypothetical contract would have any legitimacy for the citizens of a real polity, emphasizing how the reasonable, the practicable and the rational come together. The overlapping consensus does not require a coincidence of value, but it may be the only workable alternative to violence; and citizens, that is, real citizens, like 'you and I, here and now',[33] can appreciate that a refusal to take certain matters off the agenda perpetuates deep social divisions, while political institutions incorporating Rawlsian principles encourage co-operation.[34]

Yet the line which Rawls draws here between political and metaphysical does not actually get him off the relevant hook. It raises questions of social theory which he consistently attempts to keep at arm's length, but which are not avoided merely by sidestepping the questions of realism, idealism and materialism that worry philosophers. For example, one specific implication of his conception of the person is that human subjectivity is reflexive. If our subjectivity can develop only in relation to our social context—others, our bodies, social institutions such as families, companies, associations—the actual shape of these contexts forms a relevant part of the hypothetical agreement. Thus it seems inappropriate that their relevance or lack of it should be determined merely by a set of assumptions which are themselves outwith the bounds of critical theoretical appraisal.

What is more, theories like psychoanalysis offer particular conceptualizations and explanations of reflexivity and rationality which substantially alter the way we think about human beings in relation to each other and themselves. That is, the nature of the *political* subject is substantially altered according to our underlying theory of the subject. On a theory of personhood which took sexual difference to be an essential feature (as does much psychoanalytic theory) the idea of what constituted the 'fair terms for social co-operation' might look very different.[35]

The Rational and the Reasonable

As we have seen Rawls now insists that rationality is exercised in the context of the 'reasonable'. In his original conception the principles of justice as fairness are seen as setting the fair terms on which stable social *co-operation* between equal citizens can proceed. In an important sense, justice as fairness is presented as the formal solution to a co-ordination problem under conditions of rational choice. In shifting the focus from the rational to the reasonable, the vision is modified in the sense that it becomes one in which the idea of *reciprocity* becomes a key *value* as well as a *means* of solving the game.

What counts as reasonable is not derivable, for Rawls, from the rational.[36] While the atomistic individual can engage in rational inference, the reasonable individual is an individual in a social context—for to be reasonable means desiring a working social world in which reciprocity is possible.[37] It is because of this that Rawls can say unambiguously that there is no such thing as private reason—that the reasonable, as such, is social or public.[38] Yet whilst the emphasis on the reasonable also brings with it the possibility of incorporating the affective and emotive within the vision of political practice, this possibility is not by any means realized in *Political Liberalism*. Both the affective dimensions of human life and the embodied nature of human subjectivity remain outside the spotlight of Rawls' analysis.

Individualism and the Value of Autonomy

Rawls argues that full political autonomy is achieved by citizens (that is, human subjects in their role of citizen, or in their citizenship aspect). It is realized by the political principles of justice and the basic rights and liberties which are safeguarded in the kind of basic political and social structure he conceptualizes—a structure in which citizens share in collective self-determination.[39] However, while political autonomy is affirmed, the 'weight of ethical autonomy' is left to be decided by citizens severally in light of their comprehensive doctrines.[40]

This means that Rawls can envisage and accept a situation like the following. As citizens, all individuals have their autonomy affirmed and legally and politically guaranteed. However, certain individuals from non-autonomy valuing cultures (from certain religions for example) may never *exercise* their legal and political autonomy because their comprehensive doctrines emphasize other values (examples might include traditional notions of domesticity or hierarchical relationships).

Whilst Rawls' account of political autonomy often emphasizes the importance of the context in which autonomous decisions can be made and autonomous lives lived, he follows through the implications of this insight incompletely.[41] A commitment to freedom or autonomy conceived *positively* is indicated by his emphasis on context, by his recognition of the importance of political representatives' roles in creating the material circumstances in which autonomous lives can be led, and by his commitment to the difference principle. Yet at other points he seems still to be operating with a more classically liberal, *negative* conception of freedom.[42] This is suggested both by the limited scope of the difference principle's conception of fair equality of opportunity and by its subordination to the principle of liberty. The subordination of the fair equality principle is underlined in *Political Liberalism* by the definition of the difference principle as *not* a 'constitutional essential'. Although it is a feature of the 'public conception of justice' it is not a principle on which, according to Rawls, judges may draw in constitutional cases, absent explicit legislative endorsement.[43]

Furthermore, Rawls' commitment to ontological individualism severely constrains

the extent to which his critical principles are likely to recognize and hence bite against structural aspects of injustice based on factors such as class, ethnicity or gender (the aspects of injustice that might be effectively addressed by a robust equality principle). This tendency to leave social structural disadvantage unaddressed is confirmed by the political and non-political, public and non-public distinctions. For they denote as non-public or nonpolitical many practices, forms of association like the family and others, and various kinds of cultural production, which are significant in maintaining these disadvantages.

The Political

Rawls offers a number of glosses on the conception of the political—mainly by way of contrastive and comparative terms. Apart from these, it is clear that he conceives of the political as a 'domain'[44] and as demarcated from a number of other domains by boundaries. As we have seen the integrity of this boundary is important in Rawls' defence of his liberalism from charges of abstraction and universal pretensions. The domain of the political is constructed, in the rational process (within the constraints of the reasonable) of adoption of principles to regulate the basic structure.[45] It is part of a particular conception of politics (notably, modern and democratic) that this should be so.[46]

Thus, the political is contrasted with the 'ethical' and the 'moral': the liberal commitment to the political value of equality, or freedom, does not entail any particular ethical or moral values (although of course it may be incompatible with some such values). Rawls also associates these with particular kinds of reasoning.[47] He distinguishes political from 'philosophical' and 'psychological' reasoning.[48] Elsewhere, 'political' is contrasted with the 'personal', the 'familial', the 'domestic', the 'associational' and the 'communal'.[49] Here it is kinds of social institutions that are at issue, as well as the sorts of values that might be associated with or realized in these institutions. Rawls also distinguishes political institutions from 'social' and 'economic' institutions. Finally, the political is contrasted with the 'constitutional'.[50]

Rawls is concerned to establish that his theory of justice—the ordered principles of maximum liberty in a framework of the liberty of all, the redistributive part of the difference principle, and that of fair equality of opportunity—applies only to the realm of the political. Here it can be legislated for, whereas in our personal lives in families and associations (including, presumably, commercial associations—one wonders about private educational institutions) such legislation could not apply. Similarly, the fact of plurality—the empirical remoteness of the possibility of value consensus in ethical and moral beliefs and commitments, or in religious beliefs and practices—means that the conception of justice as fairness cannot be a comprehensive doctrine. Rawls says more than once that a single shared comprehensive doctrine could and can be maintained only by the oppressive use of state power. Such use would, of course, be at variance with liberal democracy.[51]

The Public

Rawls is at pains to make it clear in *Political Liberalism* that he does not intend the contrast term to the 'public' to be the 'private'; instead it is the non-public. 'The public' for Rawls seems to be normatively related to 'the political'. Everything that is political should be public; and public reason is exercised in the domain of the political, by citizens, for the good of the public.[52] Nonpolitical institutions and relations—the economic, social, domestic and associational for example—are also non-public in this strong sense.[53]

Basic Structure

The concept 'basic structure' refers to certain major institutions—the family, economic and political institutions—in relation to one another.[54] The particular relations are precisely what is determined in the process of political construction. In Rawls' view the basic structure must safeguard the primary goods—the basic rights and liberties of speech, association, etc.; individuals' freedom and movements and choice of occupation against a background of diverse opportunities, the rights to partake of powers of office and positions of political responsibility; a level of income and wealth constrained by the framework of the difference principle; and the social bases of self-respect. These last are glossed, in a circular argument, as furnished by all of the above—'the structure and content of just institutions together with features of the public political culture, such as the public recognition and acceptance of the principles of justice'.[55]

This means that certain comprehensive doctrines (such as the doctrine that slavery is a proper social relation, and that societies may or should institute slavery in their basic structure) are coercively ruled out. As Rawls puts it, one point of political liberalism is to get certain things off the political agenda, once and for all.[56]

The Scope of the Political

Having set out the analytic framework of *Political Liberalism* we now question whether Rawls' delineation of 'the political' will either deliver the social justice that the difference principle seems to demand or maintain his liberal schema intact.

The first issue to address is the exact status of the institutions which make up the basic structure. If we take the political v. non-political distinction one way we can read Rawls' theory as follows: *within* such institutions as the family, and associations like churches, clubs and businesses, but *not* within political institutions of government (Rawls does not mention political institutions like parties—an omission we find significant in a political philosopher) we may cherish our own beliefs about inequality and hierarchy. We may be sceptical about the value of autonomy, embrace particularist ethical reasoning and judgement, and engage in all kinds of anti-social practices. However, from the point of view of the polity we are attributed with autonomy. Furthermore the polity safeguards our right of exit from such institutions—as far as *it* is concerned we are free and equal citizens.

But this does not quite work, for Rawls makes it perfectly clear that the state *can* in certain circumstances intervene within non-political institutions—to redistribute wealth and income through taxation, for example.[57] That is, he does not treat these institutions as black boxes whose affairs are beyond the scope of the political theory of justice, or beyond the scope of coercive intervention and regulation. So the question arises, what criteria are to be applied to determine when intervention and regulation is, and when it is not, warranted.

Certainly Rawls' denial that he relies on a conventional public v. private distinction removes one obvious pitfall. He is presumably not prepared to say—as liberals frequently have said—that the public is the sphere of regulation while the private (whether this refers to sexual, familial or economic relations, or all three) is beyond regulation or intervention. That is, his use of the term 'non-public' leaves open the possibility that certain aspects of the non-public can and might be regulated. But which? It is unclear what Rawls' answer is going to be; and it is notable that he does not address these crucial cases.

Rawls does have a quite clear formal criterion: intervention is permissible to maintain the basic structure, within the constraint that the integrity of reasonable comprehensive doctrines must be maintained. However, the substantive implications of this criterion are extremely vague. If intervention were appropriate wherever indicated by breaches of the public conception of justice, widespread intervention would be legitimated. But this would be to fall back on justice as fairness as a comprehensive doctrine. What then determines which aspects of human institutions and relations are beyond the scope of legal and coercive intervention?

In certain kinds of liberal ideology sexuality has often been thought to be one such set of practices. Yet most liberal states do legislate about sexuality, and the phenomenon of distinctively sexual violence means that states will have to continue to do so. Similarly, the relationship between sexual and other forms of power (meaning, in this context, the ability to get other people to do things that they might not otherwise have done) means that neither regulatory systems nor—even more importantly—*political activism and critique* can ignore sexual practices.

Again, it might be thought that beyond the removal of formal and legal barriers to occupational choice the state cannot legislate for a particular pattern in the sexual division of labour, whether in the world of paid work (conventional economic markets) or in the 'domestic sphere'.

Yet for at least three reasons this is insufficient to put such questions beyond the ambit of the political. First, the states with which Rawls is concerned have consistently taken up a normative view on what constitutes and what is permissible within marriage. Rawls expresses no criticism of this. Second, it is often impossible to draw any meaningful distinction between legislating and declining to legislate (for example, passing the Married Women's Property Act, or recognizing the act of rape within marriage, or decategorizing illegitimacy). Similarly, states must enforce certain contracts and decline to enforce others. This cannot help but be normative for all participants in an institution, whether they go to law to have contracts enforced or not. Finally, as we shall argue below, what is properly regarded as *political* activism and critique extends beyond the activities of the state.

If Rawls is committed to the idea that economic inequalities are such significant barriers to citizenship, to the social basis of self-respect and the enjoyment of basic rights and freedoms, and prepared to impose redistributive mechanisms, it is unclear on what grounds he can decline to take the view that racial and sexual divisions of labour are proper objects of remedial policy (for the same ends) in the same way.

Rawls does say that we must 'recognize the limits of the political and practicable: we must stay within the limits of justice as fairness . . . and we must respect the constraints of simplicity and availability of information to which any practicable political conception (as opposed to a comprehensive moral doctrine) is subject'.[58] At this point Rawls is considering the extent to which we can compensate people for disabilities, or incapacitating tastes (for unobtainable luxuries, for example).

Whatever the problems here it seems that intervention to prevent, say, the concentration of people from certain ethnic groups in dirty jobs is possible (we have the necessary information), is not less simple than redistributing wealth and income (that is not to say that it is simple), and would not violate the constraints of justice as fairness as a political conception. It might, of course, violate people's sense of privacy and freedom in their choice of occupation; but so do taxation and welfare institutions.[59] And if Rawls finds such intervention in labour markets acceptable, in order to maintain the basic structure, then it is incumbent upon him to explain why similar intervention would not be acceptable within families.

Rawls does not discuss the state's reach into families in order, say, to prevent parents neglecting or otherwise mistreating children. But he does set out the implications of political liberalism for the education of children. They should know about their constitutional and civic rights, and should be prepared to become fully cooperating and self supporting members of society; and they should be encouraged in the political virtues.[60] He adds the caveat that 'we try to answer the question of children's education entirely within the political conception. Society's concern with their education lies in their role as future citizens . . .'.[61]

This again raises the issue of the scope of politics. An alternative way of reading Rawls is to say: institutions like the education system, associations, families, are not black boxes—what goes on inside them is politically relevant. Further, people do not have to exit before their rights can be safeguarded—rather they enjoy political rights inside these institutions. However, not everything that goes on inside them can be regulated. And it is true that some of the things that go on inside them that cannot be regulated are nevertheless in Cohen's word 'fateful'.[62] Not all that is fateful—not all that is going to determine our well-being, our exercise of our citizenship rights and capacities—can be said to be within the scope of political coercion.

However, here the unsatisfactory limitations of Rawls' conception of politics and power become apparent. Not all political action is coercive—demonstrating, campaigning, making personal small changes, are also political. Equally, legislative and coercive measures—the passing of laws, their implementation and enforcement—rely on the use of influence rather than force. You cannot, within a liberal democracy, send the troops into Parliament to force MPs to pass a bill, nor is direct coercion either attractive or feasible as a means of enforcing civil obedience. Hence, legislative reforms rely, typically, on discursive processes of definition and redefinition, on manoeuvres, bargaining, the exploitation of formal and informal procedures. They also rely, importantly, on emotion, developed identities and affective ties, and psychic responses.

Such factors have generally been marginalized in accounts which focus on a narrow conception of means-end rationality. As we have seen, Rawls now deploys an expanded and socially based conception of the reasonable, which is distinct from the rational. Notably, however, he still explicitly excludes 'affect' and 'emotion' from the public and political domain.[63] His conception of the political rules out any extension in the scope of political action, whether by the state, individuals, or groups to incorporate processes of social construction, Neither does he acknowledge that the key processes in citizens' 'proper exercise of coercive political power over one another' are the kinds of processes that will change people's associational, domestic and personal relations (those fateful relations which cannot be legislated about).

His own central principle that all have the equal rights of citizens within the sphere of (for example) domestic reason makes it impossible for him consistently to maintain a line between public and private.[64] For, if that sphere is outwith the scope of the public conception of justice and of the political, it is not clear what this guarantee amounts to. Indeed the very idea of the status of 'citizen *as such*'[65] presupposes an account of the conditions under which equal membership of such a status is possible.[66] It is precisely this idea which feminist arguments about the spillage of 'non-public' disadvantage into the 'public' world renders deeply problematic.

Rawls has no response to this fundamental question in *Political Liberalism*, and appears to be content with the mere assertion that the feminist critique can be met.[67] When combined with the limited scope and subordinate status of the difference principle, this suggests that the capacity of 'political liberalism' to effect significant changes over time in patterns of structural disadvantage such as that associated with gender is likely to be highly circumscribed.

One possible answer to this limitation is, however, sketched in Lecture VI. In developing the idea of public reason and its proper scope, Rawls is concerned to elaborate the role of comprehensive doctrines within and without political life. As we have seen, it is a central tenet of his position that comprehensive moral or religious doctrines are outwith the sphere of the political. They are simply a feature of the 'reasonable pluralism' in spite of which the overlapping consensus around a public conception of justice allows a society to live peacefully. Nonetheless, in a telling discussion of the history of the abolitionist and civil rights movements in the USA, Rawls suggests that under certain circumstances it may be appropriate to appeal to (oppositional, reasonable) comprehensive doctrines in public political debate.[68] This appears to be so where the reasonable aspiration in doing so is that one may further a more complete realization of the ideal of public reason.

Yet the boundaries of this striking concession are remarkably vague. Would it legitimize the propulsion of feminist ideas onto the public agenda of a society marked by oppressive gender division, or of socialist argument onto that of a class society? Rawls' account lacks the kinds of conceptual tools—notably developed notions of oppression, exploitation, power—which might allow him to elaborate a clearer and more sophisticated account of when the appeal to comprehensive doctrines is an appropriate counter in public political debate.

Pursuing this thought a little further, it is interesting to note that, although the concept of power is now quite an important counter in Rawls' construction of his theory, it is remarkably under-elaborated. He constructs power in terms of what might be called the 'sovereignty' conception: typically as the capacity to get someone to do something which they might otherwise not have done. Hence the broader notion of power as inhering in discourses and practices finds no place in Rawls' scheme. Such a notion is a crucial supplement to the sovereignty conception if political theory is to build on the insights and findings of political science and sociology. The sovereignty conception of power is inadequate to address the sociological facts of, say, gender subordination. For such subordination is sustained not only by the actions of power-holders but also by influential discourses and regimes of knowledge which are not within the control of identifiable agents or groups, but which rather present the inescapable context within (and against) which individuals live and act.[69]

More surprisingly, Rawls' account of what is distinctive about *political* power—that its coercive force cannot be evaded by any citizen of the polity—suggests a scope for political power far wider than that which Rawls envisages.[70] For example, in a society in which gender, class or racial oppression are so endemic that they can plausibly be argued to be part of social *structure* (no small number of actual societies) this conception of political power would include the power which men have over women, which the ruling have over the working classes, which the dominant have over the suppressed racial or ethnic groups. Indeed, it seems precisely to express the broader conception of power described in the last paragraph.

Thus a number of the moves made by Rawls to accommodate criticisms of his original theory obstruct his attempts to answer the very question which is central for liberal political philosophers: the delineation of the proper limits of the political. Could the notion of structural disadvantage be the clue to how Rawls might mark the line between when comprehensive doctrines can and cannot be appealed to in public debate? We would argue that political action—whether this is appropriately through state intervention or campaigning and critique has to be determined in particular contexts—is legitimate wherever political power, in the broad sense outlined above, has been used to perpetrate or perpetuate structural oppression which is inconsistent with the full exercise of citizenship in a genuinely democratic society.[71] This possibility is unlikely to be attractive to Rawls, given both its very radical implications and the fact that, as we have already observed, his theory lacks in other important respects the developed conceptual framework which would allow such an argument to be elaborated. But the logic of his own argument pulls him in precisely this direction.

Conclusion

We have tried to show that Rawls' political domain cannot be as clearly bounded as he wishes. His primary motive in establishing this boundary is to defend 'justice as fairness' from charges of unwarranted pretensions to universalism and generality, and of metaphysical rather than concrete status. He also wants to elaborate a distinctive and normative conception of the political to order processes of government and safeguard the integrity of nonpolitical institutions. His commitment to a form of interpretivism, and a degree of particularism, commit him to an analysis of how political power actually operates and interacts with other kinds of power (social, economic, sexual etc.) in real societies. But his sociological analysis can be faulted, empirically and theoretically; and he frequently denies that the political philosopher is committed to this sociological task in any case. This ambivalence between the sociological and the philosophical voices means that Rawls fails to articulate the real, sociological contours of political power and authority in contemporary post-industrial societies.

Political Liberalism constitutes a challenge to its critics to take up the enterprise of refining the conceptual framework within which political theory, in productive dialogue with social theory and political science, can develop a more adequate analysis of some of the pressing injustices of the contemporary world. This entails the development of a theoretical voice with which to ar-

ticulate adequate concepts of power and oppression. To delineate a conception of the public which neither depoliticizes genuine instances of oppression (*whether or not they can be remedied by the state*) nor dispenses entirely with an appropriate commitment to autonomy and privacy remains among the most pressing tasks of contemporary political theory.

Notes

1. We are indebted to G. A. Cohen for a discussion which prompted us to write this paper, and for helpful comments on the first draft. We are also grateful to referees of *Political Studies* for useful criticisms.

2. John Rawls, *Political Liberalism* (New York, Columbia University Press, 1993).

3. John Rawls, *A Theory of Justice* (Oxford, Oxford University Press, 1971).

4. See e.g. Rawls, *Political Liberalism*, p. xxix.

5. Rawls, *Political Liberalism*, pp. xvii, xxx.

6. Rawls, *Political Liberalism*, e.g. p. 10.

7. Rawls, *Political Liberalism*, pp. xvii, 136–7, 214.

8. See for example: Jean Bethke Elshtain, *Public Man, Private Woman: Women in Social and Political Thought* (Princeton NJ, Princeton University Press, 1981); Alison M. Jaggar, *Feminist Politics and Human Nature* (Brighton, Harvester, 1983); Susan Moller Okin, *Justice, Gender and the Family* (New York, Basic, 1989); Frances Olsen, 'The family and the market', *Harvard Law Review*, 96 (1983), 1497–1578; Carole Pateman, 'Feminist critiques of the public/private dichotomy', and 'Sublimation and reification: Locke Wolin and the liberal democratic conception of the political', in *The Disorder of Women* (Oxford, Polity, 1989), pp. 118–40, 90–117.

9. Rawls does not do feminist critics the honour of referencing their work in his footnotes, although it seems clear that works such as the following have come to his attention: Susan Moller Okin, *Justice, Gender and the Family* (New York, Basic, 1989); 'John Rawls: justice as fairness—for whom?', in Mary Lyndon Shanley and Carole Pateman (eds), *Feminist Interpretations and Political Theory* (Oxford, Polity, 1989), pp. 181–98; Carole Pateman, 'Feminist critiques of the public/private dichotomy', and 'The fraternal social contract', in *The Disorder of Women*, pp. 118–40, 33–57.

10. Okin, *Justice, Gender and the Family*, pp. 101–9.

11. In addition to *Justice, Gender and the Family* see 'Humanist liberalism', in Nancy Rosenblum (ed.), *Liberalism and the Moral Life* (Cambridge MA, Harvard University Press, 1989), pp. 39–53.

12. Rawls explains his position in a note within Lecture VI: 'The public v. non-public distinction is not the distinction between public and private. This latter I ignore: there is no such thing as private reason'. Rawls, *Political Liberalism*, p. 220 n7. Unfortunately the sense here is not entirely clear: it could be either the public-private distinction, or the private, which he proposes to ignore. It is, however, difficult to imagine how the relevance of either to the construction of a liberal theory of justice could be dismissed, as it were, by fiat.

13. See, for example, Rawls, *Political Liberalism*, pp. 266–7 for such attention to detail.

14. See Rawls, *Political Liberalism*, p. 136 for one such clear definition.

15. e.g. Rawls, *Political Liberalism*, p. 300.

16. e.g. Rawls, *Political Liberalism*, p. 28. In 'The law of peoples', in Stephen Shute and Susan Hurley (eds), *On Human Rights: The Oxford Amnesty Lectures 1993* (New York, Basic, 1993), pp. 41–82, Rawls speaks of 'you and me, here and now'.

17. For example, Rawls, *Political Liberalism*, p. 327.

18. Rawls, *Political Liberalism*, Lecture II (see also 'Kantian constructivism in moral theory', *Journal of Philosophy*, 77 (1980) 515–72); Rawls, 'The law of peoples'.

19. Rawls, 'The law of peoples', pp. 44–7.

20. Rawls, 'The law of peoples', p. 47.

21. Rawls, *Political Liberalism*, p.27.

22. Rawls, *Political Liberalism*, pp. 43–6.

23. Rawls, *Political Liberalism*, p. 8.

24. Rawls, *Political Liberalism*, p. 9.

25. Rawls, *Political Liberalism*, pp. 44–5.

26. Rawls, *Political Liberalism*, pp. 231–40.

27. Rawls, *Political Liberalism*, p. 240.

28. Ronald Dworkin, *A Matter of Principle* (Oxford, Clarendon, 1985); also see *Life's Dominion* (London, Harper Collins, 1993) for illustration of how such analysis may be applied to substantive ethical and political issues.

29. Rawls, *Political Liberalism*, p. 29 n.

30. Rawls, *Political Liberalism*, pp. 4, 18, 20.

31. Rawls, *Political Liberalism*, p. 258.

32. Rawls, *Political Liberalism*, pp. 52–3.

33. Rawls, 'The law of peoples', pp. 53 and 54.

34. *Political Liberalism*, pp. 158–62.

35. *Political Liberalism*, p. 78; for an excellent analysis of psychoanalytic dimensions of Rawls' theory of justice, see Anne Barron, 'The illusions of the "I": citizenship and the politics of identity' in Alan Norrie (ed.), *Closure and Critique: New Directions in Legal Theory* (Edinburgh, Edinburgh University Press, 1993), pp. 80–100.

36. Rawls, *Political Liberalism*, p. 53.

37. Rawls, *Political Liberalism*, p. 50.

38. Rawls, *Political Liberalism*, pp. 220 n7, 53.

39. Rawls, *Political Liberalism*, p. 77.

40. Rawls, *Political Liberalism*, p. 78.

41. Rawls, *Political Liberalism*, p. 228.

42. See Isaiah Berlin, *Four Essays on Liberty* (Oxford, Oxford University Press, 1989); Joseph Raz, *The Morality of Freedom* (Oxford, Clarendon, 1986); Elizabeth Frazer and Nicola Lacey, *The Politics of Community: a Feminist Critique of the Liberal-Communitarian Debate* (Hemel Hempstead, Harvester Wheatsheaf, 1993), pp. 60–1.

43. Rawls, *Political Liberalism*, pp. 228–30, 237.

44. Rawls, *Political Liberalism*, p. xv.

45. Rawls, *Political Liberalism*, p. xx.

46. Rawls, *Political Liberalism*, p. xxi.

47. Rawls, *Political Liberalism*, pp. xv, xix, 77, 78–81.

48. Rawls, *Political Liberalism*, p. 86f.

49. Rawls, *Political Liberalism*, pp. 10, 40–3, 220f.

50. e.g. Rawls, *Political Liberalism*, p. 230.

51. Rawls, *Political Liberalism*, p. 37.

52. See e.g. Rawls, *Political Liberalism*, pp. 68, 213.

53. Presumably some non-political relations are public in the sense of 'on show' or visible to the public's gaze; but they are not citizenship relations.

54. Rawls, *Political Liberalism*, p. 258.

55. Rawls, *Political Liberalism*, p. 181.

56. e.g. Rawls, *Political Liberalism*, p. 151.

57. e.g. Rawls, *Political Liberalism*, p. 184.

58. Rawls, *Political Liberalism*, p. 182.

59. On tensions within the difference principle see further G. A. Cohen, *The Tanner Lectures on Human Values* (Salt Lake City, University of Utah Press, 1992).

60. Rawls, *Political Liberalism*, p. 199.

61. Rawls, *Political Liberalism*, p. 200.

62. G. A. Cohen proposed this formulation in discussion.
63. See Rawls, *Political Liberalism*, p. 137.
64. See Rawls, *Political Liberalism*, p. 220.
65. See Rawls, *Political Liberalism*, p. 213.
66. A thin account is given on p. 280.
67. Rawls, *Political Liberalism*, p. xxix.
68. Rawls, *Political Liberalism*, pp. 247–8, 250ff.
69. See Michel Foucault, *Power/Knowledge: Selected Writings and Interviews* (Brighton, Harvester, 1980); Frazer and Lacey, *Politics of Community*, ch. I, pp. 31–6, ch. 6, pp. 193–8; also Carol Smart, *Feminism and the Power of Law* (London, Routledge, 1989), ch. 1.
70. Rawls, *Political Liberalism*, pp. 68, 216, 222.
71. See Frazer and Lacey, *Politics of Community*, ch. 6; for an important contribution to the development of the necessary conceptual framework, see Iris Marion Young, *Justice and the Politics of Difference* (Princeton NJ, Princeton University Press, 1990).

Reprinted from: Elizabeth Frazer and Nicola Lacey, "Politics and the Public in Rawls' *Political Liberalism*." In *Political Studies* Volume 43, pp. 233–247. Copyright © 1995 by Political Studies Association. Reprinted by permission of Blackwell Publishers. ✦

About the Editors

Joseph Losco is professor and current chairman of the political science department at Ball State University in Muncie, Indiana. He has published in the fields of political theory, bioethics, and public policy. Among his publications are *Human Nature and Politics* (with Albert Somit, 1995) and *Higher Education in Transition: The Challenges of the New Millennium* (with Brian Fife, 2000). He is a member of the Executive Council of the Association for Politics and the Life Sciences and on the Biopolitics Research Committee of the International Political Science Association.

Leonard Williams is professor of political science at Manchester College in North Manchester, Indiana. He has published in the fields of political theory, political communication, and electoral politics. Among his publications are *American Liberalism and Ideological Change* (1997), essays in *Women and Elective Office* (1998) and *The Year of the Woman* (1994), as well as articles in *New Political Science* and *The Social Science Journal*. He has served as president of the Indiana Academy of the Social Sciences and the Indiana Political Science Association. ✦

About the Contributors

Keith Ansell-Pearson is a professor of government at Queen Mary and Westfield College, University of London.

Richard Ashcraft is a professor of political science at the University of California at Los Angeles.

Bruce Baum is a professor of political science at Macalaster College in St. Paul, Minnesota.

Deborah Baumgold is a professor of political science at the University of Oregon in Eugene, Oregon.

Steven Best is a professor of philosophy at the University of Texas at El Paso.

William James Booth is a professor of political science at Vanderbilt University in Nashville, Tennessee.

James Conniff is a professor of political science at San Diego State University in California.

Mary G. Dietz is a professor of political science at the University of Minnesota in Minneapolis.

Lisa Jane Disch is a professor of political science at the University of Minnesota in Minneapolis.

Susan Ferguson is a professor of sociology at Grinnell College in Grinnell, Iowa.

Elizabeth Frazer is a professor of politics at New College, Oxford, England.

Bruce Frohnen is a professor of legal history and constitutional law at the Ave Maria School of Law in Ann Arbor, Michigan. Prior to this appointment, he was a visiting scholar at the Johns Hopkins school of advanced international studies.

Anne Harper holds a doctorate in political science from the University of Michigan in Ann Arbor and is currently employed in the private sector.

Chandran Kukathas is a professor in the school of politics at the University of New South Wales at the Defense Force Academy in Sydney, Australia.

Nicola Lacey is a professor in the Law Department of the London School of Economics and Political Science in London, England.

John Leonard received his Ph.D. in political theory from the University of California at Berkeley.

Harvey C. Mansfield, Jr. is the William R. Kenan, Jr. professor of government at Harvard University.

Philip Pettit is a professor of social and political theory in the research school of social sciences at the Australian National University in Canberra, Australia, and holds a joint appointment with the department of philosophy at Columbia University in New York.

Patrick Riley is a professor of political science at the University of Wisconsin in Madison, Wisconsin.

Ted Sadler is a professor of philosophy at the University of Sydney in Australia.

Virginia Sapiro is a professor of political science at the University of Wisconsin at Madison.

Gordon J. Schochet is a professor of political science at Rutgers University.

Mary Lyndon Shanley is a professor of political science at Vassar College in Poughkeepsie, New York.

Margaret A. Simons is a professor of philosophical studies and co-director of the Society for Phenomenology and Existential Philosophy at Southern Illinois University at Edwardsville.

Charles Taylor is professor emeritus in the department of philosophy at McGill University in Montreal, Quebec, Canada.

Karen Vintges is a professor of social and political philosophy at the University of Amsterdam in the Netherlands.

Mary B. Walsh received her Ph.D. from Loyola University in Chicago, Illinois and has taught at a number of universities.

Penny Weiss is a professor of political science and history at Purdue University in West Lafayette, Indiana.

Kenneth Westphal is a professor of philosophy in the school of economics and social studies at the University of East Anglia in Norwich, England. ✦